Lecture Notes in Computer Science　　10417

Commenced Publication in 1973
Founding and Former Series Editors:
Gerhard Goos, Juris Hartmanis, and Jan van Leeuwen

Advanced Research in Computing and Software Science

Subline of Lecture Notes in Computer Science

More information about this series at http://www.springer.com/series/7407

Francisco F. Rivera · Tomás F. Pena
José C. Cabaleiro (Eds.)

Euro-Par 2017:
Parallel Processing

23rd International Conference
on Parallel and Distributed Computing
Santiago de Compostela, Spain, August 28 – September 1, 2017
Proceedings

 Springer

Editors
Francisco F. Rivera [iD]
University of Santiago de Compostela
Santiago de Compostela
Spain

José C. Cabaleiro [iD]
University of Santiago de Compostela
Santiago de Compostela
Spain

Tomás F. Pena [iD]
University of Santiago de Compostela
Santiago de Compostela
Spain

ISSN 0302-9743   ISSN 1611-3349 (electronic)
Lecture Notes in Computer Science
ISBN 978-3-319-64202-4   ISBN 978-3-319-64203-1 (eBook)
DOI 10.1007/978-3-319-64203-1

Library of Congress Control Number: 2017947501

LNCS Sublibrary: SL1 – Theoretical Computer Science and General Issues

Printed on acid-free paper

This Springer imprint is published by Springer Nature
The registered company is Springer International Publishing AG
The registered company address is: Gewerbestrasse 11, 6330 Cham, Switzerland

Preface

This volume contains the papers presented at Euro-Par 2017: the 23rd International Conference on Parallel and Distributed Computing, held from 28 August to 1 September 2017 in Santiago de Compostela (Spain).

Euro-Par is a prestigious annual series of international conferences dedicated to parallel and distributed computing. The topics covered by the conference include aspects related to both software and hardware technologies and, in particular, applications in different hardware platforms, ranging from small embedded systems to cloud computing and supercomputers. The specific topics on which the conference focuses have been renewed along the years extending the state of the art in the field. Nowadays, the challenges of building exascale performance computing systems and their programming are among the main motivations in the parallel and distributed computing community. This challenge opens opportunities to deal with issues related to health, climate, security, and many more. Various topics are deeply impacted by this scenario like energy optimization, scalability, heterogeneous computing, fault-tolerance, etc.

The main audience of Euro-Par are researchers in academic institutions, public and private laboratories, and industrial organizations. Euro-Par's main objective is to be the primary choice of such professionals for the presentation of new results in the field.

Previous Euro-Par conferences took place in Stockholm, Lyon, Passau, Southampton, Toulouse, Munich, Manchester, Paderborn, Klagenfurt, Pisa, Lisbon, Dresden, Rennes, Las Palmas, Delft, Ischia, Bordeaux, Rhodes, Aachen, Porto, Vienna, and Grenoble. This year Euro-Par 2017 was the 23rd conference and was organized in Santiago de Compostela, Spain, by the IT Research Centre of the University of Santiago de Compostela, called CiTIUS – Centro de Investigación en Tecnoloxías da Información. The topics were organized into 12 tracks, namely: Support Tools and Environments; Performance and Power Modelling, Prediction and Evaluation; Scheduling and Load Balancing; High-Performance Architectures and Compilers; Parallel and Distributed Data Management and Analytics; Cluster and Cloud Computing; Distributed Systems and Algorithms; Parallel and Distributed Programming, Interfaces, and Languages; Multicore and Manycore Parallelism; Theory and Algorithms for Parallel Computation and Networking; Parallel Numerical Methods and Applications; and Accelerator Computing. In all, 176 papers were submitted from 39 countries from all continents. Finally, only 50 papers were accepted in a selection meeting in which all the global or local chairs, as well as three members of the Steering Committee, participated. A selective rate of acceptance of 28.4% resulted: 691 reviews were performed by 317 experts; 151 papers received four reviews, 19 papers were reviewed by three experts, and 6 papers by five. The huge work of bringing many innovative ideas by the Scientific Committee made that the evaluation and selection processes proceed smoothly.

Apart from the parallel sessions to present the accepted papers, we were pleased to present two keynotes talks of well-recognized colleagues, namely, David Padua "High-Level Abstractions and Automatic Optimization Techniques for the Programming of Irregular Algorithms," and Jürgen Döllner "Software Analytics – Effectively Managing Complex Software Systems," as well as an invited paper by Ian Foster et al. entitled "Computing Just What You Need: Online Data Analysis and Reduction at Extreme Scales." The program was complemented by two days of dedicated workshops and tutorials on specialized topics. The huge task of managing them was efficiently conducted by Dr. Dora B. Heras. The selected papers will be published in separated proceedings volumes after the conference.

The Euro-Par conference in Santiago de Compostela would not have been possible without the support of many individuals and organizations. We owe special thanks to the authors of all the submitted papers, the members of the topic committees, in particular the global and local chairs, as well as the reviewers for their contributions to the success of the conference. We would also like to express our gratitude to the members of the Organizing Committee and the local staff who helped us. Moreover, we are indebted to the members of the Euro-Par Steering Committee, especially Christian Lengauer, Luc Bougé, and Fernando Silva, for their trust, guidance, and support. Finally, a number of institutional and industrial sponsors contributed to the organization of the conference. Their names appear on the Euro-Par 2017 website.

It was a pleasure and an honour to organize and host Euro-Par 2017 in Santiago de Compostela.

August 2017

Francisco F. Rivera
Tomás F. Pena
José C. Cabaleiro

Organization

Steering Committee

Full Members

Christian Lengauer (Chair)	University of Passau, Germany
Luc Bougé (Vice-Chair)	ENS Rennes, France
Emmanuel Jeannot	LaBRI-Inria, Bordeaux, France
Christos Kaklamanis	Computer Technology Institute, Patras, Greece
Paul Kelly	Imperial College, London, UK
Thomas Ludwig	University of Hamburg, Germany
Emilio Luque	University Autonoma of Barcelona, Spain
Tomàs Margalef	University Autonoma of Barcelona, Spain
Wolfgang Nagel	Dresden University of Technology, Germany
Rizos Sakellariou	University of Manchester, UK
Fernando Silva	University of Porto, Portugal
Henk Sips	Delft University of Technology, The Netherlands
Domenico Talia	University of Calabria, Italy
Jesper Larsson Träff	TU Vienna, Austria
Denis Trystram	Grenoble Institute of Technology, France
Felix Wolf	TU Darmstadt, Germany

Honorary Members

Ron Perrott	Oxford e-Research Centre, UK
Karl Dieter Reinartz	University of Erlangen-Nürnberg, Germany

Observers

Marco Aldinucci	University of Turin, Italy
Francisco F. Rivera	University of Santiago de Compostela, Spain

Euro-Par 2017 Organization

Chair

Francisco F. Rivera

Co-chairs

Tomás F. Pena
José C. Cabaleiro
Dora B. Heras

Proceedings

Tomás F. Pena
José C. Cabaleiro

Workshops

Dora B. Heras
Luc Bougé

Local Organization

Elisardo Antelo
Francisco Argüello
Antonio G. Loureiro
Juan C. Pichel
Natalia Seoane
David L. Vilariño

Web and Publicity

Tomás F. Pena

Program Committee

Topic 1: Support Tools and Environments

Chair

Matthias Müller   RWTH Aachen University, Germany

Local Chair

Andrés Gómez   CESGA, Spain

Members

Martin Schulz   LLNL, Livermore, USA
Olivier Richard   LIG/Inria, France
João M.P. Cardoso   University of Porto, Portugal
Tomàs Margalef   Universitat Autònoma de Barcelona, Spain
Michael Gerndt   Technische Universität München, Germany

Topic 2: Performance and Power Modelling, Prediction, and Evaluation

Chair

Petr Tůma   Charles University, Czech Republic

Local Chair

Basilio Fraguela   University of A Coruña, Spain

Members

Ana Lucia Varbanescu   University of Amsterdam, The Netherlands
Denis Barthou   Inria, France
Lizy Kurian John   University of Texas, USA
Marc González Tallada   Universitat Politècnica de Catalunya, Spain
Andreas Knüpfer   T.U. Dresden, Germany
Diwakar Krishnamurthy   University of Calgary, Canada

Topic 3: Scheduling and Load Balancing

Chair

Florina Ciorba   University of Basel, Switzerland

Local Chair

Ester Garzón   University of Almería, Spain

Members

José Luis Bosque Orero   University of Cantabria, Spain
Radu Prodan   University of Innsbruck, Austria
José Gracia   High-Performance Computing Center Stuttgart,
                                       Germany
Ioana Banicescu   Mississippi State University, USA
Julius Zilinskas   Vilnius University, Lithuania
Bora Uçar   CNRS and LIP ENS Lyon, France

Topic 4: High-Performance Architectures and Compilers

Chair

Christophe Dubach   University of Edinburgh, UK

Local Chair

Juan Touriño   University of A Coruña, Spain

Members

Aaron Smith   Microsoft Research, USA
Louis-Nöel Pouchet   Colorado State University, USA
Laura Pozzi   University of Lugano, Switzerland
Jerónimo Castrillón   TU Dresden, Germany
Thomas Fahringer   University of Innsbruck, Austria
Chris Adeniyi-Jones   ARM, UK

Topic 5: Parallel and Distributed Data Management and Analytics

Chair

Bruno Raffin   Inria, France

Local Chair

David E. Singh   Carlos III University of Madrid, Spain

Members

Julian Kunkel   German Climate Computing Center, Germany
Lars Nagel   Johannes Gutenberg University of Mainz, Germany
Toni Cortés   Barcelona Supercomputing Center, Spain
Matthieu Dorier   Argonne National Laboratory, USA
Wolfgang Frings   Jülich Supercomputing Centre, Germany

Topic 6: Cluster and Cloud Computing

Chair

Alfredo Goldman   University of São Paulo, Brazil

Local Chair

Patricia González   University of A Coruña, Spain

Members

Laura Ricci   University of Pisa, Italy
Luiz Bittencourt   University of Campinas, Brazil
Ian Foster   Argonne National Laboratory, USA
Frèderic Desprez   Inria, France
Ivona Brandic   Technische Universität Wien, Austria
Giorgio Lucarelli   Inria, France
Rizos Sakellariou   University of Manchester, UK
Ramón Doallo   University of A Coruña, Spain

Topic 7: Distributed Systems and Algorithms

Chair

Luís Veiga   INESC-ID, Portugal

Local Chair

Rafael Asenjo   University of Málaga, Spain

Members

Sonia Ben Mokhtar	LIRIS CNRS, France
Óscar Plata González	University of Málaga, Spain
Gheorghe Almasi	IBM, USA
Rui Oliveira	Universidade do Minho, Portugal
Javier Navaridas Palma	The University of Manchester, UK
Fabio Kon	University of São Paulo, Brazil

Topic 8: Parallel and Distributed Programming, Interfaces, Languages

Chair

María Jesús Garzarán	University of Illinois, USA

Local Chair

Vicente Blanco	University of La Laguna, Spain

Members

Mª Ángeles González Navarro	University of Málaga, Spain
Evelyn Duesterwald	T. J. Watson Research Center, IBM, USA
Didem Unat	Koç Universitesi, Turkey
Francisco Almeida	University of La Laguna, Spain
Georges da Costa	Irit, France
Marco Danelutto	University of Pisa, Italy
Mary Hall	University of Utah, USA

Topic 9: Multicore and Manycore Parallelism

Chair

Hans Vandierendonck	Queen's University, UK

Local Chair

Juan Carlos Pichel	University of Santiago de Compostela, Spain

Members

Bingsheng He	National University of Singapore, Singapore
Paul Harvey	Queen's University Belfast, UK
Michele Weiland	EPCC at University of Edinburgh, UK
Yiannis Nikolakopoulos	TU Chalmers, Sweden
Polyvios Pratikakis	FORTH, Greece
Martin Burtscher	Texas State University, USA

Georgios Goumas	National Technical University of Athens, Greece
Rutger Hofman	Vrije Universiteit Amsterdam, The Netherlands
Vania Marangozova-Martin	Grenoble University, France

Topic 10: Theory and Algorithms for Parallel Computation and Networking

Chair

Geppino Pucci	University of Padua, Italy

Local Chair

Pedro Ribeiro	University of Porto, Portugal

Members

Kieran T. Herley	University College Cork, Ireland
Christos Zaroliagis	University of Patras, Greece
Mauro Bianco	Swiss National Supercomputing Centre, Switzerland
Henning Meyerhenke	Karlsruher Institut für Technologie, Germany
Michele Scquizzato	University of Houston, USA

Topic 11: Parallel Numerical Methods and Applications

Chair

Maya Neytcheva	Uppsala University, Sweden

Local Chair

María Martín	University of A Coruña, Spain

Members

Yvan Notay	Université Libre de Bruxelles, Belgium
Peter Arbenz	ETH Zürich, Switzerland
Enrique S. Quintana	Jaime I University, Spain
Fred Wubs	University of Groningen, The Netherlands
Osni Marques	Lawrence Berkeley National Laboratory, USA

Topic 12: Accelerator Computing

Chair

Bertil Schmidt	Johannes Gutenberg University of Mainz, Germany

Local Chair

Arturo González	University of Valladolid, Spain

Members

Tobias Grosser	ETH Zürich, Switzerland
Josef Weidendorfer	Technische Universität München, Germany
Rob Van Nieuwpoort	Netherlands eScience Center, The Netherlands
Seyong Lee	Oak Ridge National Laboratory, USA
Jorge González-Domínguez	University of A Coruña, Spain
Deming Chen	University of Illinois, USA

Euro-Par 2017 Reviewers

Euro-Par is grateful to all the reviewers for their willingness and effort in providing good feedback to authors and topic committees. All external reviewers are listed and hereby thanked.

Abuín, José M.
Acosta, Alejandro
Aliaga, José Ignacio
Alonso, Pedro
Alonso-Monsalve, Saul
Amannejad, Yasaman
Amor, Margarita
Ananthanarayanan, Ganesh
Andión, José M.
Andrade, Diego
Anzt, Hartwig
Aparício, David
Aral, Atakan
Arantes, Luciana
Argüello, Francisco
Arif, Mahwish
Arlandini, Claudio
Atalar, Aras
Azimi, Sahar
Baars, Sven
Baiardi, Fabrizio
Bamha, Mostafa
Barros Lourenço, Ricardo
Belviranli, Mehmet
Benedict, Shajulin
Benson, Austin
Bleuse, Raphaël
Boisvert, Sébastien
Boito, Francieli Zanon

Bonifaci, Vincenzo
Braghetto, Kelly Rosa
Brown, Jed
Brunie, Hugo
Buenabad-Chávez, Jorge
Calotoiu, Alexandru
Carlini, Emanuele
Caron, Eddy
Cała, Jacek
Cesar, Eduardo
Chard, Kyle
Chard, Ryan
Chau, Vincent
Chen, Lizhong
Cheng, Xuntao
Cheptsov, Alexey
Chowdhury, Anamika
Chowdhury, Mosharaf
Chuvelev, Michael
Coimbra, Miguel E.
Cojean, Terry
Collange, Sylvain
Comprés Ureña, Isaías
Coplin, Jared
Coppola, Massimo
Cordeiro, Daniel
Costa, Fabio
Dai, Dong
De Maio, Vincenzo
De Sande, Francisco

Dichev, Kiril
Dolgov, Sergey
Dorostkar, Ali
Dreher, Matthieu
Dufossé, Fanny
Durillo, Juan J.
Elafrou, Athena
Eleliemy, Ahmed
Erpen De Bona, Luis Carlos
Espinosa, Toni
Expósito, Roberto R.
Farsarakis, Emmanouil
Fernández, Javier
Flegar, Goran
Flehmig, Martin
Foerster, Klaus-Tycho
Frangoudis, Pantelis
Fujita, Hajime
Gabriel, Edgar
Galante, Guilherme
García Blas, Javier
Garcia, Islene
Genez, Thiago
Georgakoudis, Giorgis
Ghimire, Amrita
Giannoula, Christina
Giménez, Domingo
Glantz, Roland
Gonçalves, Rui

Gorman, Gerard
Grelck, Clemens
Greve, Fabiola
Grimley Evans, Edmund
Gschwandtner, Philipp
Guidi, Barbara
Gulur, Nagendra
Gupta, Abhishek
Gupta, Amit
Hager, Georg
Haine, Christopher
Hashemian Harandi,
    Raoufehsadat
Hernández, Francisco
Herold, Christian
Herrera, Juan F.R.
Hijma, Pieter
Hirsch, Alex
Horký, Vojtěch
Huchant, Pierre
Huedo, Eduardo
Hugo, Andra-Ecaterina
Hundt, Christian
Hupp, Daniel
Hünich, Denis
Igumenov, Aleksandr
Ilic, Aleksandar
Iliev, Hristo
Ilsche, Thomas
Iosup, Alexandru
Jaiganesh, Jayadharini
Janetschek, Matthias
Jorba, Josep
Kalbasi, Amir
Kamienski, Carlos
Kanellou, Eleni
Karakostas, Vasileios
Katsogridakis, Pavlos
Kavoussanakis,
    Konstantinos
Kecskemeti, Gabor
Kimovski, Dragi
Klinkenberg, Jannis
Kotselidis, Christos
Kruliš, Martin
Kumaraswamy, Madhura
Küstner, Tilman

Lachaize, Renaud
Lago, Daniel
Lan, Haidong
Lančinskas, Algirdas
Latham, Robert
Lebeane, Michael
Lee, Wooseok
Letsios, Dimitrios
Lirkov, Ivan
Liu, Yongchao
Liu, Zhengchun
Llanos, Diego
Llopis Sanmillán, Pablo
Lobeiras Blanco, Jacobo
Lopez Redondo, Juani
Lorenzo del Castillo,
    Juan Ángel
Lujic, Ivan
Lulli, Alessandro
Luque, Emilio
Lèbre, Adrien
Madduri, Ravi
Madeira, Edmundo
Magni, Alberto
Maia, Francisco
Maleki, Saeed
Mandli, Kyle
Mantas Ruiz, J. Miguel
Marathe, Yashwant
Marinescu, María Cristina
Mathà, Roland
Mercier, Michael
Meyer, Marcel
Michelogiannakis, George
Mijaković, Robert
Milenkovic, Aleksandar
Miranda, Alberto
Mohammed, Ali
Mommessin, Clement
Moreno-Vozmediano,
    Rafael
Moti, Nafiseh
Mounié, Grégory
Moure, Juan Carlos
Mouriño Gallego,
    José Carlos
Mukherjee, Joydeep

Mulder, Thomas
Mäsker, Markus
Nachtmann, Mathias
Nadjaran Toosi, Adel
Nagarajan, Arthi
Nasre, Rupesh
Netto, Marco
Nickolay, Sam
Niethammer, Christoph
Nou, Ramon
Nussbaum, Lucas
O'Neil, Molly
Oeste, Sebastian
Ortega, Gloria
Padrón, Emilio
Pai, Sreepathi
Palka, Michal
Panda, Reena
Papadopoulou, Nikela
Papagiannis, Anastasios
Papakonstantinou,
    Nikolaos
Pardo, Xoán C.
Parsons, Mark
Pascual, Fanny
Pascual, Jose A.
Passarella, Andrea
Paul, Johns
Pérez, Borja
Pérez Diéguez, Adrián
Pérez, Christian
Petcu, Dana
Phan, Tien-Dat
Pietri, Ilia
Pilla, Laércio L.
Polato, Ivanilton
Poquet, Millian
Prieto-Matias, Manuel
Prokosch, Thomas
Protze, Joachim
Prountzos, Dimitrios
Pruyne, Jim
Queralt, Anna
Reid, Fiona
Rexachs, Dolores
Reyes, Ruymán
Richard, Jerome

Rico, Juan Antonio
Riedel, Morris
Ristov, Sasko
Rocki, Kamil
Rodríguez Gutiez,
  Eduardo
Rodríguez Martínez,
  Diego
Rodríguez, Gabriel
Ropars, Thomas
Ryoo, Jee Ho
Santana, Eduardo
Saurabh, Nishant
Schoene, Robert
Schuchart, Joseph
Schulz, Christian
Sclocco, Alessio
Sedaghati, Naser
Senger, Hermes
Seoane, Natalia
Shamakina, Anastasia
Shontz, Suzanne
Siakavaras, Dimitrios
Sikora, Anna

Silla, Federico
Silva, Miguel
Silva, Pedro Paulo
Singh, Shikhar
Sinnen, Oliver
Siqueira, Rodrigo
Sitchinava, Nodari
Skluzacek, Tyler
Solsona, Francesc
Song, Shuang
Srivastav, Abhinav
Srivastava, Srishti
Stafford, Esteban
Starikovicius, Vadimas
Strout, Michelle
Stylianopoulos,
  Charalampos
Symeonidou, Christi
Tchoua, Roselyne
Terboven, Christian
Termier, Alexandre
Tomás, Andrés
Tonellotto, Nicola
Torquati, Massimo

Toss, Julio
Tschueter, Ronny
Tzovas, Charilaos
van der Plas, P
van Werkhoven, Ben
Vázquez, Álvaro
Verdi, Fabio
Walulya, Ivan
Wang, Feiyi
Wang, Jiajun
Weber, Matthias
Wellein, Gerhard
Werner, Matthias
Winkler, Frank
Wozniak, Justin
Yang, Chih-Chieh
Yang, Dai
Zafari, Afshin
Zangerl, Peter
Zhani, Mohamed Faten
Zhou, Huan
Zois, Georgios

Euro-Par 2017 Invited Talks

High Level Abstractions and Automatic Optimization Techniques for the Programming of Irregular Algorithms

David Padua, University of Illinois at Urbana-Champaign, USA

High-performing irregular algorithms are typically implemented using simple operations and conventional control structures. In addition, due to today's compilers inability to manipulate these implementations, program tuning must usually be done by hand. Better notations and automatic optimization would help improve programmer productivity, portability, and maintainability. This talk will review high level notation proposals for the description of irregular algorithms, as well as compiler and autotuning techniques for the optimization of these algorithms. A short discussion of open research problems and necessary conditions for adoption of these more advanced notations and strategies will conclude the presentation.

Software Analytics – Effectively Managing Complex Software Systems

Jürgen Döllner, Hasso-Plattner-Institute for IT Systems Engineering, Germany

Digital transformation and industry 4.0 are among the key terms that reference a fundamental change in almost all branches of industry and society: Information technologies become essential building blocks of systems, applications, and processes. Access to and analytics for big data, along with machine learning, become key and competitive factors for transforming businesses in the next decade.

In this talk, we focus on and reflect how methods and techniques of big data analytics can be adapted and applied to the context of software engineering and IT industry. Here, the so called "software crisis" yet persists regardless of the manifold progress in programming concepts, languages, software modelling, software development methodologies, etc. Software analytics aims at boosting effectiveness of software development by providing new means of transparency within their corresponding ecosystems.

Euro-Par 2017 Topics Overview

Topic 1: Support Tools and Environments

Matthias Müller, Andrés Gómez, Martin Schulz, Olivier Richard,
João M. P. Cardoso, Tomàs Margalef, Michael Gerndt

Hardware and software of high performance computing (HPC) platforms are evolving every day. This evolution is very fast and is contributing to a very complex ecosystem. Applications must cope with large systems, with thousands of cores (even with millions in the largest HPC environments), several levels of memory hierarchy, hardware accelerators, heterogeneity, etc. Even more, it is becoming of paramount importance to extract the best performance with a strong control of the power consumption. Thus, HPC designers and programmers must have the tools to manage this complex scenario.

The Euro-Par Support Tools and Environments is a privileged forum to show new techniques and tools that allow all the stakeholders in the development and execution of HPC applications to manage the complexity involved, focusing on main challenges regarding programmability, resilience, performance and energy efficiency, monitoring, correctness, etc.

This track received 10 papers. After a reviewing process involving all the track TPC members and 21 external reviews, overall resulting in at least 4 reviews per paper, we decided to accept 3 of the submitted papers.

We acknowledge here the work of the reviewers who provided important feedback to the authors and helped us to select the best papers. Finally, we thank all authors who submitted papers. They really make this conference a key world event for presenting new Support Tools and Environments.

Topic 2: Performance and Power Modelling, Prediction, and Evaluation

Petr Tůma, Basilio Fraguela, Ana Lucia Varbanescu, Denis Barthou,
Lizy Kurian John, Marc González Tallada, Andreas Knüpfer, Diwakar Krishnamurthy

In recent years, a range of novel methods and tools have been developed for the evaluation, design, and modelling of parallel and distributed systems and applications. At the same time, the term 'performance' has broadened to also include scalability and energy efficiency, and touching reliability and robustness in addition to the classic resource-oriented notions. The aim of the 'performance' topic is to gather researchers working on different aspects of performance modelling, evaluation, and prediction, be it for systems or for applications running on the whole range of parallel and distributed systems (multi-core and heterogeneous architectures, HPC systems, grid and cloud contexts etc.)

This year, the track proved very popular, receiving a large number of submissions. Out of them, six papers were selected for presentation following a rigorous review process in which each manuscript received four independent reviews, either from the committee members or their subreviewers. We would like to thank all the authors who submitted papers to this topic as well as the external reviewers, for their contribution to the success of the conference.

Topic 3: Scheduling and Load Balancing

Florina M. Ciorba, Ester Garzón, José Luis Bosque Orero, Radu Prodan, José Gracia, Ioana Banicescu, Julius Zilinskas, Bora Uçar

New computer systems offer an opportunity to improve the performance and the energy consumption of the applications by the exploitation of several parallelism levels. Heterogeneity and complexity are the main characteristics of modern computer architectures. Thereby, the optimal exploitation of modern computing platforms becomes a challenge. The scheduling and load balancing techniques are relevant topics for the optimal exploitation of modern computers in terms of performance, energy consumption, cost of using resources, and so on.

This topic covered all aspects related to scheduling and load balancing on parallel and distributed systems, ranging from theoretical foundations for modelling and designing efficient and robust strategies, to experimental studies, applications, and practical tools and solutions. The main interest was focussed on modern multi/many-core processors, distributed/cloud platforms and data centres. The proposals to improve the performance were centred on the simulation of dynamic load balancing; scheduling based on genetic algorithms, approximations, and pinning; resource co-allocation; communications optimization; and graph partitioning.

A total of seventeen full-length submissions were received in this track, each of which received at least four reviews, from the eight program committee members and/or from the thirty-five additional sub-reviewers. Following the thorough discussion of the reviews, seven submissions have been accepted (42% acceptance rate), including one that was nominated as distinguished paper.

The chair and local chair sincerely thank all the authors for their submissions, the Euro-Par 2017 Organizing Committee for all their valuable help, and the reviewers and sub-reviewers for their excellent review work. Each has contributed to making this topic and Euro-Par an excellent forum to discuss Scheduling and Load Balancing challenges.

Topic 4: High Performance Architectures and Compilers

Christophe Dubach, Juan Touriño, Chris Adeniyi-Jones, Jerónimo Castrillón, Thomas Fahringer, Louis-Nöel Pouchet, Laura Pozzi, Aaron Smith

This topic deals with architecture design, languages, and compilation for parallel high performance systems. The areas of interest range from microprocessors to large-scale parallel machines (including multi-/many-core, possibly heterogeneous, architectures);

from general-purpose to specialized hardware platforms (e.g., graphic coprocessors, low-power embedded systems); and from architecture design to compiler technology and language design.

On the compilation side, topics of interest include programmer productivity issues, concurrent and/or sequential language aspects, vectorization, program analysis, program transformation, automatic discovery and/or management of parallelism at all levels, autotuning and feedback directed compilation, and the interaction between the compiler and the system at large. On the architecture side, the scope spans system architectures, processor micro-architecture, memory hierarchy, and multi-threading, architectural support for parallelism, and the impact of emerging hardware technologies.

The track received 13 submissions, all of which received, in a first stage, at least 3 reviews. In a second stage, all the papers and reviews were thoroughly discussed by all PC members. As a result, three papers were finally accepted for the conference (23% acceptance rate) covering both architecture and compiler topics.

Topic 5: Parallel and Distributed Data Management and Analytics

Bruno Raffin, David E. Singh, Julian Kunkel, Lars Nagel, Toni Cortés, Matthieu Dorier, Wolfgang Frings

Many areas of science, industry, and commerce are producing extreme-scale data that must be processed —stored, managed, analysed— in order to extract useful knowledge. This topic seeks papers in all aspects of distributed and parallel data management and data analysis. For example, HPC in situ data analytics, cloud and grid data-intensive processing, parallel storage systems, and scalable data processing workflows are all in the scope of this topic. More in detail, aspects in which this conference topic is interested are:

- Parallel, replicated, and highly-available distributed databases
- Cloud and HPC storage architectures and systems
- Scientific data analytics (Big Data or HPC based approaches)
- Middleware for processing large-scale data
- Programming models for parallel and distributed data analytics
- Workflow management for data analytics
- Coupling HPC simulations with in situ data analysis
- Parallel data visualization
- Distributed and parallel transaction, query processing and information retrieval
- Internet-scale data-intensive applications
- Sensor network data management
- Data-intensive clouds and grids
- Parallel data streaming and data stream mining
- New storage hierarchies in distributed data systems
- Parallel and distributed knowledge discovery and data mining

Thirteen full-length papers were submitted to this topic, and each paper received four reviews. After discussion with the reviewers and track chairs, two papers were selected for publication, one related to distributed database design, the second one to workload partitioning and scheduling algorithms for Apache Spark.

Topic 6: Cluster and Cloud Computing

Alfredo Goldman, Patricia González, Laura Ricci, Luiz Bittencourt, Ian Foster, Frèderic Desprez, Ivona Brandic, Giorgio Lucarelli, Rizos Sakellariou, Ramón Doallo

Cloud Computing is not a concept anymore, but a reality with many providers around the world. The use of massive storage and computing resources accessible remotely in a seamless way has become essential for many applications in various areas, including High Performance Computing. While significant progresses have been achieved in the past decade, the complete adoption of the Utility Computing paradigm is still facing important challenges. There are still unsolved challenges related to performance, reliability and energy efficiency of the infrastructures that should be addressed by research. Moreover, up to this time fundamental capabilities and services are required to achieve the goals of user-friendliness, security, privacy and service guarantees in such environments. Finally, there are important trends as going from large centralized infrastructures to smaller ones massively distributed at the edge of the network, and also to execute more efficiently High Performance Computing applications on Clouds.

Topic 6 sought papers covering many aspects of Cluster and Cloud Computing dealing with infrastructure layer challenges, such as performance/energy optimizations, and security enhancements, as well as cloud-enabled applications, workflow management and High Performance Computing on Clouds. This year, 26 papers have been submitted to Topic 6. There were authors from 18 different countries from all the continents. Four expert reviewers analysed each submission. Overall, more than 70 specialists were involved into the reviewing process. Finally, despite the high quality of the submitted papers, only 7 papers were accepted for publication.

We would like to thank all the authors for their submissions, the PC members and the reviewers for providing us with constructive and informative reviews, and the Euro-Par 2017 Organizing committee for all the help that allows us to smoothly take over the whole process.

Topic 7: Distributed Systems and Algorithms

Luís Veiga, Rafael Asenjo, Gheorghe Almasi, Sonia Ben Mokhtar, Fabio Kon, Javier Navaridas, Rui Oliveira, Oscar Plata

Parallel computing today is increasingly related to and dependent on developments and challenges of distributed systems. Problems including load balancing, asynchrony, failures, malicious and selfish behaviour, long latencies, network partitions, disconnected operations, distributed computing models and concurrent data structures, and heterogeneity are representative of typical distributed issues that often appear along the design of parallel applications.

This track of Euro-Par provides a forum for both theoretical and practical research, of interest to both academia and industry, on distributed computing, distributed algorithms, distributed systems, distributed data structures, and parallel processing on distributed systems, in particular in relation to efficient high performance computing. This year, 8 complete papers have been submitted to this track. After a bidding phase, each paper has been evaluated by 4 or 5 reviewers with high expertise. Overall, 14 experts have been involved into the review process. Finally, from this set of high quality submitted papers, only three papers have been selected for publications.

The PC chairs, Luís Veiga (INESC-ID/IST, University of Lisbon, Portugal) and Rafael Asenjo (Universidad de Málaga, Spain), are very grateful to all the authors, and all researchers that have participated to the review process and permitted to select three high-quality papers.

Topic 8: Parallel and Distributed Programming, Interfaces, Languages

María Jesús Garzarán, Vicente Blanco, Didem Unat, Angeles Navarro, Mary Hall, Evelyn Duesterwald, Marco Danelutto, Francisco Almeida, George Da Costa

Parallel and distributed applications require adequate programming abstractions and models, efficient design tools, parallelization techniques and practices. This topic was open for the submission of new results and practical experience in this domain: efficient and effective parallel languages, interfaces, libraries and frameworks, as well as solid practical and experimental validation.

It provides a forum for research on high-performance, correct, portable, and scalable parallel programs via adequate parallel and distributed programming model, interface and language support. Contributions that assess programming abstractions, models and methods of usability, performance prediction, scalability, self-adaptations, rapid prototyping and fault-tolerance, as is needed, for instance, in dynamic heterogeneous parallel and distributed infrastructures, were accepted.

All twelve papers on this topic received four reviews that were further discussed among all nine PC members. As a result, four strong papers were accepted for the conference, covering important topics. One of them was proposed for the best paper award.

Topic 9: Multicore and Manycore Parallelism

Hans Vandierendonck, Juan Carlos Pichel, Bingsheng He, Paul Harvey, Michele Weiland, Yiannis Nikolakopoulos, Polyvios Pratikakis, Martin Burtscher, Georgios Goumas, Rutger Hofman, Vania Marangozova-Martin

Over the last ten years the trend in processor design has been towards an ever-increasing number of cores. The complexity of emerging many- and multi-core architectures makes it increasingly hard to program these devices efficiently. Efficient algorithms must scale to large degrees of parallelism, use optimized data formats, minimize runtime system overhead and must use efficient synchronization mechanisms. Moreover, it is important to tune algorithms to the specific organization and dimensions of the target processor. The breadth of approaches that are investigated to achieve high-performance on multi- and many-core processors is a reflection of the complexity of these processors and the difficulty of designing algorithms that match the architecture of the processor.

This topic presents novel research contributions on a wide range of performance optimization techniques that are indispensable to programming multi- and many-cores, including efficient sparse matrix formats, optimization of linear algebra operations through batching, optimization of the fast multipole method on Intel many-cores, parallelization of remeshing algorithms, parallelization of model checking algorithms, thread-level speculation using transactional memories, non-blocking algorithms for radix trees, and concurrency-optimal search trees.

Eight papers out of 26 submissions were selected for publication in this track. All papers received at least 3 reviews.

We thank the authors who submitted papers, the PC members and referees who rigorously reviewed the submissions and provided constructive and informative feedback. We also thank the organizing committee for creating a smooth process and we look forward to an exciting edition of Euro-Par.

Topic 10: Theory and Algorithms for Parallel Computation and Networking

Geppino Pucci, Pedro Ribeiro, Mauro Bianco, Kieran T. Herley, Henning Meyerhenke, Michele Scquizzato, and Christos Zaroliagis

Parallel computing is everywhere, on smartphones, laptops; at online shopping sites, universities, computing centres; behind the search engines. Efficiency and productivity at these scales and contexts are only possible by scalable parallel algorithms using efficient communication schemes, routing and networks. Theoretical tools enabling scalability, modelling and understanding parallel algorithms, and data structures for exploiting parallelism are more important than ever. Topic 10 solicits high quality, original papers on the general topic of theory and algorithms for parallel computation including communication and network algorithms.

Topic 10 received 10 submissions, all of which received 4 reviews, either from the 7 PC members or from their subreviewers. The papers and their reviews were discussed extensively, and 2 submissions were eventually accepted.

Topic 11: Parallel Numerical Methods and Applications

Maya Neytcheva, María Martín, Yvan Notay, Peter Arbenz, Enrique S. Quintana, Fred Wubs, Osni Marques

The demand for high performance computations is driven by the need for large-scale computer simulations in nearly all activity areas - science and engineering, finance, life sciences etc. In turn, high performance computing goes hand in hand with the necessity to develop highly scalable numerical methods and algorithms that are able to efficiently exploit modern computer architectures and to fully utilize their computing power. The scalability of these algorithms and methods and their suitability to efficiently utilize the available high performance, but in general heterogeneous, computer resources, is a key point to improve the performance of the target applications and enable fast and reliable computer simulations.

This conference topic aims at presenting and discussing recent developments in parallel numerical algorithms and their implementation on current parallel architectures, including many-core and hybrid architectures.

This year the topic received 9 contributions. Each submission was reviewed by at least four reviewers. Overall, 27 experts have been involved into the review process. Finally, three papers were accepted for presentation. We thank all authors for their valuable contributions, as well as the Program Committee members and the external reviewers for investing their time, sharing their expertise and keeping the high scientific level of the Euro-Par conference.

Topic 12: Accelerator Computing

Bertil Schmidt, Arturo González, Tobias Grosser, Josef Weidendorfer, Rob Van Nieuwpoort, Seyong Lee, Jorge González-Domínguez, Deming Chen

The need for high-performance computing is constantly growing in all kind of scenarios, from high-end scientific applications, to consumer electronics software. Hardware manufactures are involved in a race to develop specialized hardware to cover these critical demands.

Currently, hardware accelerators of various kinds offer a potential for achieving massive performance in applications that can leverage their high degree of parallelism and customization. Examples include graphics processors (GPUs), manycore co-processors, as well as more customizable devices, such as FPGA-based systems or streaming data-flow architectures.

The research challenge for this topic is to explore new directions for actually realizing this potential. Significant advances in all areas related to accelerators are considered, with special focus in architectures, algorithms, languages, compilers, libraries, runtime systems, coordination of accelerators and CPU, debugging and profiling tools, and application-related contributions that provide new insights into fundamental problems or solution approaches in this domain.

The program committee of this topic was formed by seven members of different backgrounds and specializations in the accelerators field, with the collaboration of several other subreviewers. We received 13 contributions from researchers in many different countries. After the review process and the general PC meeting, two high-quality papers were selected for presentation in Euro-Par 2017 at Santiago de Compostela. They are focused on important hot-topics: exploiting the GPUs potential on sparse linear algebra, and the question of load balancing for performance or energy.

The committee members want to thank all the authors that submitted their work to this track, the reviewers for their timely and constructive comments, and the organization committee for the efforts to easy our task, and to provide a nice conference environment in Santiago de Compostela for a high-quality discussion of research results in this interesting topic.

Contents

Scheduling and Load Balancing

High Performance Architectures and Compilers

Parallel and Distributed Data Management and Analytics

Cluster and Cloud Computing

Distributed Systems and Algorithms

Parallel and Distributed Programming, Interfaces, and Languages

Multicore and Manycore Parallelism

Theory and Algorithms for Parallel Computation and Networking

Parallel Numerical Methods and Applications

Accelerator Computing

Invited Paper

Computing Just What You Need: Online Data Analysis and Reduction at Extreme Scales

Ian Foster[1,2]([✉]), Mark Ainsworth[3], Bryce Allen[2], Julie Bessac[1],
Franck Cappello[1], Jong Youl Choi[4], Emil Constantinescu[1], Philip E. Davis[5],
Sheng Di[1], Wendy Di[1], Hanqi Guo[1], Scott Klasky[3], Kerstin Kleese Van Dam[6],
Tahsin Kurc[7], Qing Liu[8], Abid Malik[6], Kshitij Mehta[4], Klaus Mueller[7],
Todd Munson[1,2], George Ostouchov[4], Manish Parashar[5], Tom Peterka[1],
Line Pouchard[6], Dingwen Tao[1], Ozan Tugluk[3], Stefan Wild[1], Matthew Wolf[3],
Justin M. Wozniak[1], Wei Xu[6], and Shinjae Yoo[6]

[1] Argonne National Laboratory, Lemont, IL, USA
foster@anl.gov
[2] University of Chicago, Chicago, IL, USA
[3] Brown University, Providence, RI, USA
[4] Oak Ridge National Laboratory, Oak Ridge, TN, USA
[5] Rutgers University, New Brunswick, NJ, USA
[6] Brookhaven National Laboratory, Brookhaven, NY, USA
[7] Stony Brook University, Stony Brook, NY, USA
[8] New Jersey Institute of Technology, Newark, NJ, USA

Abstract. A growing disparity between supercomputer computation speeds and I/O rates makes it increasingly infeasible for applications to save all results for offline analysis. Instead, applications must analyze and reduce data online so as to output only those results needed to answer target scientific question(s). This change in focus complicates application and experiment design and introduces algorithmic, implementation, and programming model challenges that are unfamiliar to many scientists and that have major implications for the design of various elements of supercomputer systems. We review these challenges and describe methods and tools that we are developing to enable experimental exploration of algorithmic, software, and system design alternatives.

1 Introduction

Technology trends are creating a crisis in high performance computing. Computer speeds are increasing much faster than are storage technology capacities and I/O rates. For example, the Mira supercomputer installed at Argonne National Laboratory in 2012 has a peak compute rate of 10 petaflop/s (10^{16} op/s) and disk write rate of 500 GB/s (5×10^{11} bytes/s). By 2024, computers are projected to compute at 10^{18} ops/sec but write to disk only at 10^{12} bytes/sec: a compute-to-output ratio 50 times worse. Figure 1 provides another perspective on this trend. We can no longer output every piece of information that we might ever possibly *want*. Instead, we need to output just the information that

© Springer International Publishing AG 2017
F.F. Rivera et al. (Eds.): Euro-Par 2017, LNCS 10417, pp. 3–19, 2017.
DOI: 10.1007/978-3-319-64203-1_1

we *need* to answer some question(s). This new goal requires new thinking about the design and implementation of both applications and system software.

In both purely computational and coupled experimental–computational studies, these growing disparities between computational speeds and I/O rates demand new application structures that link previously disjoint activities: experiment, simulation, data analysis, data reduction. Yet while many algorithms and tools exist to treat separate pieces of such problems, these capabilities are often inoperable or inaccessible to the research scientist. Scientists need new tools for coupling components and new methods for co-optimizing the resulting workflows. These tasks introduce algorithmic, implementation, and programming model challenges that are unfamiliar to many scientists and

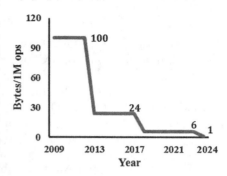

Fig. 1. Total filesystem throughput of leadership class facilities vs. total floating point operations per second [25,32, 40]. I/O throughput scales more slowly than computational speed.

that have major implications for the design of various elements of high performance systems.

The emerging exascale landscape offers many opportunities to address these problems. Additional storage features such as non-volatile random access memory (NVRAM) will provide powerful caching and aggregation capabilities. A variety of operating systems, runtime, scheduling, and fault tolerance features may become available to applications and middleware developers. Advanced workflow systems, I/O frameworks, and data reduction techniques can be integrated to construct efficient data processing pipelines. These features will be adopted by a range of exascale-ready applications, so there is a unique window of opportunity to develop solutions that are widely applicable, reusable, and beneficial.

The Co-design center for Online Data Analysis and Reduction (CODAR) engages scientists at three national laboratories and five partner universities, to address these challenges. Working closely with applications teams, CODAR is undertaking a co-design process that targets both common data analysis and reduction methods (e.g., feature and outlier detection, and compression) and methods specific to particular data types and domains (e.g., particle and structured finite-element methods). Our goal is to understand and guide trade-offs in the development of computer systems, applications, and software frameworks, given constraints relating to application development costs and fidelity, performance portability, scalability, and power efficiency, and to answer these questions:

Q1: What are the best data analysis and reduction algorithms for different application classes, in terms of speed, accuracy, and resource needs? How can we implement those algorithms for scalability and performance portability?

Q2: What are the tradeoffs in data analysis accuracy, resource needs, and overall performance between online reduction and offline analysis vs. online analysis? How do these tradeoffs vary with hardware and software choices?

Q3: How do we effectively orchestrate online data analysis and reduction to reduce associated overheads? How can hardware and software help?

2   Related Work and Context

We are not the first to observe that both the growing disparity between compute and I/O rates and the need for near-real-time feedback requires online data analysis and reduction. Much work has been performed on "in-situ" and "in-transit" analysis methods [4, 9], motivated by a desire to conserve I/O bandwidth, storage, and/or power; increase accuracy of data analysis results; and/or make optimal use of parallel platforms [31], among other factors [2]. The need to reduce output data volumes has also spurred various science teams to create custom online data analysis and reduction techniques [16, 22, 26, 27, 34, 36] and also stimulated work on general-purpose methods [8, 10, 21].

Such work reveals complex relationships between application design, data analysis and reduction methods, programming models, system software, hardware, and other elements of extreme-scale systems, particularly given constraints such as applicability, fidelity, performance portability, and power efficiency.

The community is far from completely understanding the many co-design issues posed by online data analysis and reduction. For the broader community to leverage and expand the knowledge gained by early adopters, they will require an effective, usable and sustainable software infrastructure that allows scientists to use the *best techniques* to extract the *right information* that can then be pushed through the straw to the parallel file system. It is in this context that we established the CODAR co-design project.

3   Example Applications

We use examples from climate, fusion, and materials science to motivate the need for online data analysis and reduction.

3.1   Climate Science

Climate scientists want to run large ensembles of high-fidelity 1 km × 1 km simulations on exascale systems, with each instance simulating 15 years of climate in 24 h of computing time. They estimate that outputting the full model state for each ensemble member once per simulated day would generate 260 TB every 16 s across the ensemble, approximately 16× what can be written to the parallel file system at the expected peak output rate of 1 TB/sec. (Currently, climate models achieve much lower I/O rates, due to their relatively small model grids.) Furthermore, even following data reduction to 1 TB/sec, such runs would output 85 PB per day, posing major storage and offline data analysis challenges.

While 85 PB is a lot of data to output in a day's computing, this quantity represents just a small subset of the total data to be produced by the ensemble. Outputting state just once per simulated day represents a highly lossy reduction, given that the climate model time step may be just 100 simulated seconds, and indeed some analyses may require access to the full state at higher frequency. For example, feature detection (e.g., tracking cyclones, detecting areas of extreme heat) may require access to model state once per simulated five minutes, a rate $24 \times 12 = 288$ times greater. Clearly, climate models need new online data analysis and reduction methods that can both preserve more information than once-per-day snapshots and produce considerably less data.

3.2   Fusion Science

Fusion scientists are developing a high-fidelity whole device model for magnetically confined fusion plasmas, for use in planning experiments on the ITER facility and simulating future experimental fusion devices [6]. The X-point included Gyrokinetics Code (XGC) [24], one potential component of a whole device model, models the plasma edge. A single XGC simulation can produce hundreds of petabytes of data describing particle positions and the state of the field within which the particles move.

We use this example to illustrate the need for application-aware data reduction methods. To reduce this data to manageable sizes, ultimately allowing 100 PB to be reduced to 100 TB, a 1000:1 reduction, fusion scientists and CODAR participants collaborated to devise a multistep data reduction process. The first step was to simply decrease output frequency. However, this approach cannot be taken beyond physically relevant time

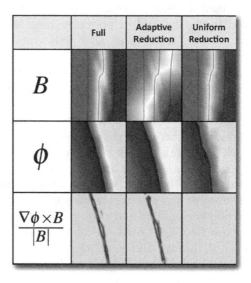

Fig. 2. XGC fusion simulation results near the plasma edge illustrates the need for fidelity preserving data reduction. The full data for the magnetic field $||B||$ and the scalar potential ϕ both show close approximation to the full solution. However, in the case of the derived fluid velocity $\frac{\nabla \phi \times B}{||B||}$, the adaptive method retains the four major features from the full data; the uniform method does not.

scales; important information would be lost by decreasing the frequency further. The second step was to use application knowledge to further reduce the data without losing essential information. The XGC particles are assumed to follow a Maxwellian distribution. Therefore, we fitted a distribution to the data and saved the parameters for the distribution and the particles falling outside that distribution (the "outliers"). For the field data, adaptive data reduction methods were used to preserve features (see Fig. 2). Finally, generic compression methods were applied to achieve further data reduction. The reduced data was then output and used for offline data analysis.

3.3 Materials Science

Materials scientists regularly run billion-atom atomistic simulations with femtosecond time steps on leadership-class machines [33,37]. In order to understand phenomena such as the structural properties of lignin-based macromolecules, information essential for improving biofuel production, measurable vibrational responses that arise at the tens of femtoseconds must be studied, requiring per-time step data access. Yet folding and bonding properties arise only on the scale of seconds. Saving the full state to simultaneously study both quantities would generate exabytes on exascale computers. Intelligent, statistically valid spatial and temporal data analyses and/or reductions that can be applied online are needed to achieve accurate scientific characterizations with reduced data.

3.4 Real-Time Decisions and Data Assimilation

Increasing use of supercomputers for near-real-time decision making is another factor motivating new thinking about application and system software design [1]. For example, both experimental fusion energy experiments and next-generation light sources are moving to a new frontier where data must be processed rapidly to enable near-real-time decisions.

In light source science, high-fidelity simulation models are used to fit parameters that describe sample structure [11]. Coupling emerging high-frame-rate, high-resolution detectors with high-performance computing and networks allows these models to be calibrated by streaming data from the experiment hall. Future experiments may also be guided by active learning methods that prioritize observations that reduce error and uncertainty in the model. Due to the growth in detector and simulation capabilities, it is no longer feasible to input experimental data, perform some computation (e.g., simulation of the experiment's future trajectory), and store results for later analysis. Data must be transmitted and assimilated immediately to maximize the quality of the simulated model, process significant events, and/or permit rapid feedback to the experiment.

International experimental fusion energy experiments are moving to a new frontier where data needs to be processed as soon as possible to make near-real-time decisions. Data sizes, rates, and durations are increasing faster than Moore's Law, and new software technologies are needed to cope with their ability to do their science quickly and accurately. One critical challenges is to understand which data need to be processed immediately (in near real rime), and we need the ability to express this during the data generation, and to compose a workflow that can help scientist get the best out of their data with a given amount of work.

4   A High-Performance Co-design Architecture

Some science teams have already developed application-specific online data analysis and/or reduction methods on petascale systems, methods they now need to scale for exascale. Others face the prospect of having to integrate such methods from scratch as part of their preparation for exascale. In both cases, we want to make it easy for them to integrate a variety of scalable online data analysis and reduction methods into their existing infrastructure, so that they can easily experiment with co-design alternatives and achieve performance portability.

4.1   The Need for Modular Implementations

A first key to achieving this goal of easy co-design, we argue, is to modularize implementations so that analysis and reduction methods, resource allocations, and coupling methods can be varied with little or no changes to an application. In this way we facilitate experimentation with design alternatives and investigation of co-design and performance portability questions.

The key to modular integration of applications with online data analysis and reduction methods is access to both the application data of interest and metadata describing that data's structure. Once this access is enabled, it becomes straightforward to access and exchange the data to be analyzed and/or reduced. Our team has much experience in instrumenting applications to provide and use such information, particularly in the context of the Adaptable IO System (ADIOS) [17,43], the Swift [3,42] system, and in earlier work [12,44]. In many cases, this instrumentation involves adding simple procedure calls, for example via the ADIOS application program interface (API) [28], to the application to indicate the data structures in question. A runtime system can then extract the specified data and pass it to specified data analysis and reduction services. Only the runtime implementation, not the application, needs to be modified to explore alternative implementation strategies, such as processing on the same or different nodes, using NVRAM, varying clock speeds for power efficiency, or varying the number of data analysis nodes.

The characteristics of data in extreme scale simulations will be highly dynamic with respect to volume and relative importance. For example, the detection of a rare event in a simulation could trigger analysis of additional complexity, or even require a different analysis routine to be loaded and executed. Thus, the runtime must be highly reconfigurable. It must enable the user to programmatically branch into new analysis pipelines or rebalance resources among components. This will require a novel integration of high-level directives and hints with low-level I/O reconfiguration features to allow the overall workflow to adapt to conditions that emerge during execution.

4.2   CODAR System Components

These considerations lead us to identify three major classes of CODAR co-designed technologies. Figure 3 shows how they fit together.

First, the **CODAR Data API** allows applications to specify the data to be analyzed and/or reduced, and its structure. We leverage the ADIOS API [23], which has been integrated into more than thirty science applications [17, 30, 38, 43]. One co-design question will be how to extend this API so that applications can convey actionable information for exascale optimizations relating to performance and power efficiency.

Second, **CODAR Data Services** provide scalable implementations of data analysis and reduction methods, plus ancillary monitoring methods, all packaged to permit their use by any application. The data reduction methods will provide effective reduction of the simulation outputs, both the application state and the results of online data analyses applied to that state, while retaining simulation fidelity. Data monitoring is needed to verify that a particular data reduction method is retaining the necessary information and to provide feedback when the data reduction is either too aggressive or not aggressive enough (see Fig. 2). These services will include a mix of those developed by us and those imported from other sources. We are developing only a modest number of such implementations ourselves, but our methods and co-design knowledge will be broadly applicable. Anyone will be able to add generic or application-specific data services. An important co-design question here concerns the methods and support required for efficient execution of a broad range of such services.

Third, the **CODAR Runtime** provides methods for the deployment, configuration, execution, and computational monitoring of applications and associated data analysis and reduction pipelines on exascale platforms. Given a specified set of data analysis, reduction, and monitoring services, it will enable their efficient composition and configuration; their deployment to appropriate nodes and cores; efficient communication among them; computational monitoring of both individual services and the complete computation; and adaptation of service configurations and parameters.

We intend that these three co-designed technologies allow application teams to instantiate versions of the Fig. 3 pipeline to address their specific science

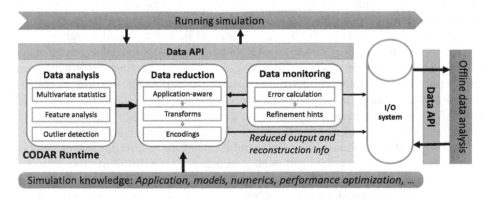

Fig. 3. Prototypical data analysis and reduction pipeline, showing how a simulation communicates to our services through an API that conveys data and their structure.

goals. Lessons learned from experiments with diverse applications, methods, and platforms will in turn feed back to ECP application projects, software projects, vendors, and other stakeholders.

5   CODAR Data Services

We show in Fig. 3 a prototypical application pipeline in which an online data analysis service consumes simulation data and produces extracted information that is communicated back to the simulation and/or sent to a data reduction service for further processing prior to storage on a parallel file system. A monitoring service can also be engaged to evaluate the quality of the data reduction results. More generally, data analysis methods may extract information from several states—for example, a sliding window of time—and use results from previous data analyses. We review some of the analysis, reduction, and monitoring methods that we are studying in the CODAR project.

5.1   Analysis Services

Our initial catalog of data analysis methods concentrates on multidimensional statistical and image analysis and outlier detection and extraction. We develop this set based on application requirements and their relevance to important co-design questions, such as the following. When should a data analysis be performed online versus offline? How frequently can data analyses be performed online, given a specified computational budget? How can data analyses make use of increased CPU on-node concurrency? When do we use burst buffers to stage and extend memory for online data analysis? How do we take advantage of deep memory hierarchies for tracking changes over time?

Multidimensional Statistical Analysis. Application scientists frequently find it useful to extract multidimensional statistics and geometrical characteristics from simulations, since these analyses reflect properties on a larger scale than do point-wise and time-instant measurements, and carry information about structures, aggregated quantities, and statistical measurements.

We plan to build on our stochastic flow map [15], which provides understanding of uncertain transport behavior. This map has been successfully applied to climate [15,35] and weather [14] applications. We are further developing our data analysis methods to model multivariate and multiscale features in statistical ensembles using the concepts of specific mutual information between variables [5] and information flows based on association rules [29]. These methods all have a wide range of applications including climate and combustion.

As an example, climate model ensembles produce a distribution of velocities, instead of a single velocity at each grid point. These distributions allow climate scientists to quantify the uncertainty in convergent and divergent transport behaviors and in derived features such as eddies, flow segmentation, and large-scale teleconnections. Tracking these features via stochastic flow maps enables scientists to understand their evolution and advance their scientific mission.

Outlier Detection and Extraction. Outliers and rare events are the needles that application scientists frequently seek in the massive haystack of exascale data. We are developing semi-supervised machine learning techniques that incorporate existing prior knowledge (such as a Bayes classifier) within an unsupervised learning algorithm to select the most relevant targets for later inspection and addition to a corpus of information. We are integrating the iForest [20] unsupervised machine learning algorithm to project data into a subspace where outliers deviate sharply from the remaining data, and applying kernel-based signatures to detect outliers [18–20]. This combination is particularly effective in the case of complex data with extremely high dimensionality [19, 20].

5.2 Reduction Services

As illustrated in Sect. 3, the communication, analysis and storage of data from exascale simulations will only be possible through aggressive data reduction capable of shrinking datasets by one or more orders of magnitude. Such data reduction level is not feasible with lossless data reduction (e.g., lossless compression) that only typically achieve reduction factors of 2 (initial size/reduced size) on scientific data. Only lossy data reduction has the potential to reach reduction factors of orders of magnitude.

As shown in Fig. 3, online data reduction services consume both simulation outputs and the results from online data analyses and prepare data to be written to a file system. A crude but commonly used data reduction technique is to save data only periodically (e.g., every n-th time step) and use linear interpolation to approximate the missing values for offline data analysis. This technique can achieve arbitrary reduction ratios, but it lacks control over the errors. While we support this technique, our data reduction goal is to preserve the essential information in the reduced output while satisfying resource constraints on I/O bandwidth. Thus, we need reduction methods that provide control over errors.

The consumer big data domain is in advance of science in the systematic use of lossy data reduction. Most photos taken on a smartphone are stored in lossy compressed form, as are audio and video files. The projection made by CISCO about the Internet traffic is striking: in 2025, 80% of the Internet traffic will be video streaming; which means that more than 80% of the data transiting on the Internet will be lossy compressed. Microsoft has already deployed FPGAs into its data centers to accelerate JPEG compression (among other operations). An important distinction between the scientific and consumer big data domains is the specificity of the data reduction techniques. The consumer big data domain relies on generic lossy compressors (e.g., JPEG for images, MP3 for audio and MPEG4 for video). Many scientific applications at extreme scale already need aggressive data reduction. Spatial sampling and decimation in time are used to reduce data but these techniques also reduce significantly the quality of the data analytics performed on the sampled or decimated datasets. Advanced lossy compression techniques provide a solution to this problem by allowing the user to better control the data reduction error. However, the adoption of lossy data reduction techniques in the scientific domain is still limited because of the lack of comprehensive understanding of the errors introduced by lossy data reduction.

Although lossy data reduction is critical to evolve many scientific domains to the next step, the technology of scientific data reduction and the understanding on how to use it are still in their infancy. The first evidence is the lack of results in this domain: over the 26 years of the prestigious IEEE Data Compression Conferences, only 12 papers identify an aspect of scientific data in their title (floating-point data, data from simulation, numerical data, scientific data). The second evidence is the poor data lossy reduction performance on some datasets. Beyond the research on data reduction techniques, scientists also need to understand how to use lossy data reduction. The classic features of compressors (integer data compression, floating-point data compression, fast compression and decompression, error bounds for lossy compressors) do not characterize data reduction algorithms specifically with respect to their integration into a high-performance computing and data analytics workflow.

The CODAR co-design project is addressing these two gaps by collecting data reduction need from exascale application, investigating and developing new lossy data reduction algorithms, collecting error assessment needs from applications and developing a tool, called Z-checker, to assess comprehensively the error introduced by lossy data reduction.

One approach to lossy scientific data reduction is for application and system developers to design application-specific lossy data reduction technique. This approach is used, for example, at the Large Hadron Collider, where experiments use specialized hardware and software to extract only "interesting" events from TB/s data streams. An alternative approach is to design and use generic lossy compressors for scientific data. Several teams have worked and are still working on this problem. The difficulty here is to develop lossy compressors that provide excellent data reduction performance for a large variety of scientific applications: regular mesh, irregular mesh, particle simulation, instrument, etc.

Appropriately chosen reduction methods can improve the information content of output data. For example, the FLASH hydrodynamics simulation code [13] is widely used to perform extremely large simulations. Conventionally, data are not output every time step, the remaining data are discarded. An alternative curve-fitting technique exploits the fact that hydrodynamic flows are mostly smooth and thus can be greatly reduced by lossy compressors that nevertheless provide error bounds. Our SZ compressor [8], for example, can achieve 100:1 reduction for the BLAST2 hydrodynamics data [7].

Currently, the two leading lossy compressors for scientific data are SZ [8,39] and ZFP [41]. They are error-bounded lossy compressors, meaning that they respect user-specified error constraints. Each uses a completely different compression strategy. One is based on a prediction method and the other one is transform based. One is better than the other, depending on the application and the dataset. Research in this domain aims to reach compression factors of 10 for hard to compress datasets and >100 for easy to compress ones. These two lossy compressors as well as other generic lossy compressors for scientific data work well for smooth datasets. They are less effective when the datasets are very irregular and presents large variations. One important aspect of the CODAR project is to understand what compression algorithm (or sequence of algorithms) to use according to the characteristics of the datasets. We return to this question in the next section.

5.3   Monitoring Services

Scientific and consumer big data are distinguished by their quite different quality requirements for reduced datasets. JPEG, MP3 and MPEG4 are not only generic but universal: all users have the same perception of images and sound. Thus, compression quality criteria can be defined that meet the needs of a large population of users. In science, on the other hand, each combination of application and data may involve different quality requirements. One open question is the relevant set of quality criteria for scientific datasets. As illustrated in Fig. 2, blindly applying a reduction method can result in a failure to capture features that are essential for subsequent analysis. Users have already expressed needs to assess spectral alteration, correlation alteration, the statistical properties of the compression error, the alteration of first and second order derivatives, and more. As the domain of lossy data reduction for scientific datasets grows, the community will learn what metrics are relevant and needed.

Another open question is how to express quality requirements, in particular when there are many such requirements with interdependencies. Perhaps the most important open question is the comprehensive assessment of the error introduced by lossy data reduction. The classic lossy compressor assessment metrics, PSNR (peak signal to noise ratio) and its extension, the rate distortion diagram, are not enough to represent the potential impact of the error on scientific datasets and the analyses that may be performed on them. Users may also be interested in other distortions (spectral, derivative, distribution) and other characterization of the error (autocorrelation, distribution).

To address these concerns, we are developing data monitoring services for estimating data reduction errors and providing (1) feedback to the reduction methods so that their tolerances can be adjusted and (2) reduction error maps for the application scientist. These maps can be imported into offline data analysis routines or visualized to observe the evolution of reduction errors.

Our first step is a simple monitoring service, Z-checker, that applies an extensible set of metrics to assess both initial dataset properties and the alterations introduced by lossy data reduction. The Z-checker is designed to permit the integration of a wide range of analysis modules, in C, C++, Fortran, and R. An initial set allow its use to characterize critical properties (such as entropy, distribution, power spectrum, principle component analysis, auto-correlation) of any dataset to improve compression strategies, detect the compression quality (compression ratio, bit-rate), and provide global distortion analysis comparing the original data with the decompressed data (peak signal-to-noise ratio, normalized mean square error, rate-distortion, rate-compression error, spectral, distribution, derivatives) and statistical analysis of the compression error (maximum/minimum/average error, autocorrelation, distribution of errors). Our initial Z-checker runs offline; it will evolve into an online application that can be configured to run multiple user-specified analyses concurrently, either for the purpose of online steering of data reduction or to produce assessment reports that can be used to evaluate reduction performance under different settings.

As we gain experience with online use of Z-checker, important questions to be answered include the following. How frequently should we estimate the reduction error? What data analysis methods and metrics should we use for this estimation? How quickly can we provide the refinement hints so that the information provided is actionable? How effective are the refinement hints at influencing the reduction error?

6   The CODAR Runtime

The CODAR Runtime provides methods for controlling the placement and configuration of CODAR Data Services for purposes of co-design exploration and performance optimization. The initial focus is on simple manual configuration of service delivery choices; in later stages of the project, we will also provide for automated configuration, once co-design strategies are better understood. Figure 4 shows the initial set of components.

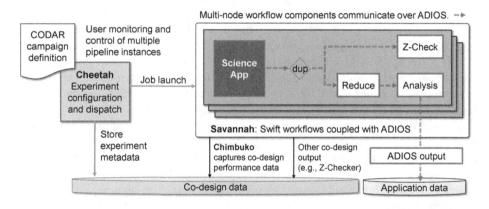

Fig. 4. The CODAR co-design system, showing in particular the Cheetah experiment management component and the Savannah runtime.

The **Cheetah** experiment management framework defines a set of conventions and re-usable scripts for conducting parameter sweep experiments on different science applications. Such experiments are intended to be run on supercomputers, particularly on existing machines, but may also be run on local workstations for debugging. An 'application' may be a single science code or, more typically, one or more science codes plus a set of online analysis and reduction codes that are coupled with the science codes and each other. The goal of such parameter sweep experiments is to determine the best set of parameters to use to run the application as efficiently as possible on different target machines. This 'best' set of parameters usually varies over different machines.

The **Savannah** in situ runtime serves three purposes. It provides a tested deployment framework for any application (or software technology) project to use online data analysis and reduction; provides the infrastructure needed to create a testing framework (Cheetah) to evaluate reduction and analysis functions for performance on a variety of levels (application and platform); and provides a reference approach for teams that have specialized needs that exceed the infrastructure design constraints

Savannah is not intended to be the only possible way of deploying CODAR-developed or vetted analytics and reduction functions; multiple cooperating ecosystems are needed to make the total system thrive. However, Savannah offers a convenient and straight-forward approach, making it easier for applications to focus on the science, rather than the details of advanced scheduler settings, RDMA network transfers, and other technical details that tend to interfere with the deployment of online techniques.

Finally, the **Chimbuko** performance data capture suite captures, analyzes and visualizes performance metrics for complex scientific workflows and relates these metrics to the context of their execution on extreme-scale machines to enable empirical performance studies. Because capturing performance metrics can quickly escalate in volume and provenance can be highly verbose, Chimbuko interfaces with (lossy) data compression modules specialized for high-velocity performance data.

To quantify co-design tradeoffs involved in online data analysis and reduction for a particular application, an ensemble of executions would be run using Cheetah and Savannah, each involving an application X plus an analysis A and a reduction R (e.g., from Z-checker) with different specifications of the information that needs to be saved when (e.g., different data reduction mechanisms and parameters) and what work is to be placed where (e.g., different numbers of nodes allocated to X, A, and R; X, A, and R allocated to the same or different nodes; and different mechanisms used to transfer data between components). Chimbuko would capture the performance information for each member of the ensemble and enable analysis across the ensemble to answer co-design questions.

7   Conclusion

We have presented the rationale, technical approach, and some initial results for the new Co-design center for Online Data Analysis and Reduction (CODAR). This project is motivated by the growing disparity between compute and I/O speeds on high-performance computers, and the consequent need to perform data analyses and reductions increasingly online, while an application is running, rather than offline. Such new computational structures in turn lead to new co-design questions, such as which analysis and reduction methods to use in different contexts, how to construct such application–analysis–reduction computations, and how to map and configure different components. CODAR is developing new methods that will allow the principled investigation of such questions.

Acknowledgments. This research was supported in part by the Exascale Computing Project (17-SC-20-SC) of the U.S. Department of Energy (DOE), and by DOE's Advanced Scientific Research Office (ASCR) under contract DE-AC02-06CH11357.

References

1. Future Online Analysis Platform Workshop, April 2017. https://press3.mcs.anl.gov/futureplatform/about
2. Ahrens, J.: Increasing scientific data insights about exascale class simulations under power and storage constraints. IEEE Comput. Graph. Appl. **35**(2), 8–11 (2015)
3. Armstrong, T.G., Wozniak, J.M., Wilde, M., Foster, I.T.: Compiler techniques for massively scalable implicit task parallelism. In: International Conference for High Performance Computing, Networking, Storage and Analysis, SC 2014 (2014)
4. Bauer, A.C., Abbasi, H., Ahrens, J., et al.: In situ methods, infrastructures, and applications on high performance computing platforms. Comput. Graph. Forum **35**(3), 577–597 (2016)
5. Biswas, A., Dutta, S., Shen, H.W., Woodring, J.: An information-aware framework for exploring multivariate data sets. IEEE Trans. Vis. Comput. Graph. **19**(12), 2683–2692 (2013)
6. Bonoli, P., McInnes, L.C.: Report of the workshop on integrated simulations for magnetic fusion energy sciences (2015). https://www.burningplasma.org/resources/ref/Workshops2015/IS/ISFusionWorkshopReport.11.12.2015.pdf
7. Colella, P., Woodward, P.R.: The piecewise parabolic method (PPM) for gas-dynamical simulations. J. Comput. Phys. **54**(1), 174–201 (1984)
8. Di, S., Cappello, F.: Fast error-bounded lossy HPC data compression with SZ. In: IEEE International Parallel and Distributed Processing Symposium, pp. 730–739 (2016)
9. Dorier, M., Dreher, M., Peterka, T., Wozniak, J.M., Antoniu, G., Raffin, B.: Lessons learned from building in situ coupling frameworks. In: 1st Workshop on In Situ Infrastructures for Enabling Extreme-Scale Analysis and Visualization, pp. 19–24. ACM (2015)
10. Dreher, M., Raffin, B.: A flexible framework for asynchronous in situ and in transit analytics for scientific simulations. In: 14th International Symposium on Cluster, Cloud and Grid Computing, pp. 277–286. IEEE (2014)
11. Foster, I., Ananthakrishnan, R., Blaiszik, B., Chard, K., Osborn, R., Tuecke, S., Wilde, M., Wozniak, J.: Networking materials data: accelerating discovery at an experimental facility. In: Big Data and High Performance Computing, pp. 117–132. IOS Press (2015)
12. Foster, I., Kohr Jr., D.R., Krishnaiyer, R., Choudhary, A.: Double standards: bringing task parallelism to HPF via the message passing interface. In: ACM/IEEE Conference on Supercomputing, pp. 36–36 (1996)
13. Fryxell, B., Olson, K., Ricker, P., Timmes, F., et al.: FLASH: an adaptive mesh hydrodynamics code for modeling astrophysical thermonuclear flashes. Astrophys. J. Suppl. Ser. **131**(1), 273 (2000)

14. Guo, H., He, W., Peterka, T., Shen, H.W., Collis, S., Helmus, J.: Finite-time Lyan-punov exponents and Lagrangian coherent structures in uncertain unsteady flows. IEEE Trans. Vis. Comput. Graph. **22**(6), 1672–1682 (2016)
15. Guo, H., He, W., Seo, S., Shen, H.W., Peterka, T.: Extreme-scale stochastic particle tracing for uncertain unsteady flow analysis. Mathematics and Computer Science Division, Argonne National Laboratory (2016, preprint). http://www.mcs.anl.gov/papers/P6000-0416.pdf
16. Habib, S., Pope, A., Finkel, H., Frontiere, N., Heitmann, K., Daniel, D., Fasel, P., Morozov, V., Zagaris, G., Peterka, T., et al.: HACC: simulating sky surveys on state-of-the-art supercomputing architectures. New Astron. **42**, 49–65 (2016)
17. Herbein, S., Matheny, M., Wezowicz, M., Krogel, J., Logan, J., Kim, J., Klasky, S., Taufer, M.: Performance impact of I/O on QMCPack simulations at the petas-cale and beyond. In: 16th International Conference on Computational Science and Engineering, pp. 92–99. IEEE (2013)
18. Huang, H., Qin, H., Yoo, S., Yu, D.: Local anomaly descriptor: a robust unsu-pervised algorithm for anomaly detection based on diffusion space. In: 21st ACM International Conference on Information and Knowledge Management, pp. 405–414 (2012). http://doi.acm.org/10.1145/2396761.2396815
19. Huang, H., Qin, H., Yoo, S., Yu, D.: A new anomaly detection algorithm based on quantum mechanics. In: 12th IEEE International Conference on Data Mining, pp. 900–905 (2012). http://dx.doi.org/10.1109/ICDM.2012.127
20. Huang, H., Qin, H., Yoo, S., Yu, D.: Physics-based anomaly detection defined on manifold space. ACM Trans. Knowl. Discov. Data **9**(2), 14:1–14:39 (2014). http://doi.acm.org/10.1145/2641574
21. Iverson, J., Kamath, C., Karypis, G.: Fast and effective lossy compression algo-rithms for scientific datasets. In: Kaklamanis, C., Papatheodorou, T., Spirakis, P.G. (eds.) Euro-Par 2012. LNCS, vol. 7484, pp. 843–856. Springer, Heidelberg (2012). doi:10.1007/978-3-642-32820-6_83
22. Jenkins, J., et al.: ALACRITY: analytics-driven lossless data compression for rapid in-situ indexing, storing, and querying. In: Hameurlain, A., Küng, J., Wagner, R., Liddle, S.W., Schewe, K.-D., Zhou, X. (eds.) Transactions on Large-Scale Data- and Knowledge-Centered Systems X. LNCS, vol. 8220, pp. 95–114. Springer, Heidelberg (2013). doi:10.1007/978-3-642-41221-9_4
23. Koziol, Q., Podhorszki, N., Klasky, S., Liu, Q., Tian, Y., Parashar, M., Schwan, K., Wolf, M., Lakshminarasimhan, S.: ADIOS. In: High Performance Parallel I/O, pp. 203–213. Chapman and Hall/CRC (2014)
24. Ku, S., Chang, C., Adams, M., Cummings, J., Hinton, F., Keyes, D., Klasky, S., Lee, W., Lin, Z., Parker, S., et al.: Gyrokinetic particle simulation of neoclassical transport in the pedestal/scrape-off region of a Tokamak plasma. J. Phys: Conf. Ser. **46**(1), 87 (2006)
25. Kumaran, K.: Introduction to Mira. https://www.alcf.anl.gov/files/bgq-perfengr.pdf
26. Lakshminarasimhan, S., Jenkins, J., Arkatkar, I., Gong, Z., Kolla, H., et al.: ISABELA-QA: query-driven analytics with ISABELA-compressed extreme-scale scientific data. In: International Conference for High Performance Computing, Net-working, Storage and Analysis, SC 2011, pp. 1–11. ACM (2011). http://doi.acm.org/10.1145/2063384.2063425
27. Lakshminarasimhan, S., Shah, N., Ethier, S., Ku, S.H., Chang, C.S., Klasky, S., Latham, R., Ross, R., Samatova, N.F.: ISABELA for effective in situ compression of scientific data. Concurr. Comput.: Pract. Exp. **25**(4), 524–540 (2013)

28. Liu, Q., Logan, J., Tian, Y., Abbasi, H., Podhorszki, N., Choi, J.Y., Klasky, S., et al.: Hello ADIOS: the challenges and lessons of developing leadership class I/O frameworks. Concurr. Comput.: Pract. Exp. **26**(7), 1453–1473 (2014). http://dx.doi.org/10.1002/cpe.3125

29. Liu, X., Shen, H.: Association analysis for visual exploration of multivariate scientific data sets. IEEE Trans. Vis. Comput. Graph. **22**(1), 955–964 (2016). http://dx.doi.org/10.1109/TVCG.2015.2467431

30. Liu, Z., Wang, B., Wang, T., Tian, Y., Xu, C., Wang, Y., Yu, W., Cruz, C.A., Zhou, S., Clune, T., et al.: Profiling and improving I/O performance of a large-scale climate scientific application. In: 22nd IEEE International Conference on Computer Communication and Networks, pp. 1–7 (2013)

31. Malakar, P., Vishwanath, V., Munson, T., Knight, C., Hereld, M., Leyffer, S., Papka, M.E.: Optimal scheduling of in-situ analysis for large-scale scientific simulations. In: ACM International Conference for High Performance Computing, Networking, Storage and Analysis, SC 2015 (2015)

32. Nowell, L.: Science at extreme scale: architectural challenges and opportunities (2014). http://www.mcs.anl.gov/~hereld/doecgf2014/slides/ScienceAt ExtremeScale_DOECGF_Nowell_140424v2.pdf

33. Perilla, J.R., Goh, B.C., Cassidy, C.K., Liu, B., Bernardi, R.C., Rudack, T., Yu, H., Wu, Z., Schulten, K.: Molecular dynamics simulations of large macromolecular complexes. Curr. Opin. Struct. Biol. **31**, 64–74 (2015)

34. Peterka, T., Kwan, J., Pope, A., Finkel, H., Heitmann, K., Habib, S., Wang, J., Zagaris, G.: Meshing the universe: integrating analysis in cosmological simulations. In: Ultrascale Visualization Workshop, SC 2012, pp. 186–195. IEEE (2012)

35. Peterka, T., Ross, R., Nouanesengsey, B., Lee, T.Y., Shen, H.W., Kendall, W., Huang, J.: A study of parallel particle tracing for steady-state and time-varying flow fields. In: IEEE International Parallel and Distributed Processing Symposium, pp. 580–591 (2011)

36. Schendel, E.R., Jin, Y., Shah, N., Chen, J., Chang, C.S., Ku, S.H., Ethier, S., Klasky, S., Latham, R., Ross, R., Samatova, N.F.: ISOBAR preconditioner for effective and high-throughput lossless data compression. In: 28th International Conference on Data Engineering, pp. 138–149, April 2012

37. Shekhar, A., Nomura, K.I., Kalia, R.K., Nakano, A., Vashishta, P.: Nanobubble collapse on a silica surface in water: billion-atom reactive molecular dynamics simulations. Phys. Rev. Lett. **111**(18), 184503 (2013)

38. Slawinska, M., Clark, M., Wolf, M., Bode, T., Zou, H., Laguna, P., Logan, J., Kinsey, M., Klasky, S.: A Maya use case: adaptable scientific workflows with ADIOS for general relativistic astrophysics. In: ACM Conference on Extreme Science and Engineering Discovery Environment: Gateway to Discovery, p. 54 (2013)

39. Tao, D., Di, S., Chen, Z., Cappello, F.: Significantly improving lossy compression for scientific data sets based on multidimensional prediction and error-controlled quantization. In: IEEE International Parallel and Distributed Processing Symposium (2017)

40. Thibodeau, P.: Coming by 2023, an exascale supercomputer in the U.S. IEEE Spectrum. http://spectrum.ieee.org/computing/hardware/when-will-we-have-an-exascale-supercomputer

41. Windstorm, P.: Fixed-rate compressed floating-point arrays. IEEE Trans. Vis. Comput. Graph. **20**(12), 2674–2683 (2014)

42. Wozniak, J.M., Armstrong, T.G., Wilde, M., Katz, D.S., Lusk, E., Foster, I.T.: Swift/T: Scalable data flow programming for distributed-memory task-parallel applications. In: 13th IEEE/ACM International Symposium on Cluster, Cloud and Grid Computing, pp. 95–102 (2013)
43. Wu, L., Wu, K., Sim, A., Churchill, M., Choi, J.Y., Stathopoulos, A., Chang, C., Klasky, S.: Towards real-time detection and tracking of blob-filaments in fusion plasma big data. IEEE Trans. Big Data **2**(3), 262–275 (2016)
44. Zhao, Y., Wilde, M., Foster, I.: Virtual data language: a typed workflow notation for diversely structured scientific data. In: Taylor, I., Deelman, E., Gannon, D., Shields, M. (eds.) Workflows for e-Science, pp. 258–278. Springer, London (2007). doi:10.1007/978-1-84628-757-2_17

Support Tools and Environments

Scaling Energy Adaptive Applications for Sustainable Profitability

Fabien Hermenier[1,2(✉)], Giuliani Giovanni[3], Andre Milani[3], and Sophie Demassey[4]

[1] Université Côte d'Azur, CNRS, I3S, Paris, France
`fabien.hermenier@unice.fr`
[2] Nutanix Inc., San Jose, USA
`fabien.hermenier@nutanix.com`
[3] Hewlett Packard Enterprise, Milano, Italy
`{giuliani,andrea.milani}@hpe.com`
[4] Centre for Applied Mathematics – MINES ParisTech, PSL, Paris, France
`sophie.demassey@mines-paristech.fr`

Abstract. Energy efficiency in data centres is addressed through workload management usually to reduce the operational costs and as a byproduct, the environmental footprint. This includes to minimise total power consumption or to minimise the power issued from non-renewable energy sources. Hence, the performance requirements of the client's applications are either totally overlooked or strictly enforced.

To encourage profitable sustainability in data centres, we consider the total financial gain as a trade-off between energy efficiency and client satisfaction. We propose Carver to orchestrate energy-adaptive applications, according to performance and environmental preferences and given forecasts of the renewable energy production. We validated Carver by simulating a testbed powered by the grid and a photovoltaic array and running the Web service HP LIFE.

1 Introduction

Energy efficiency in data centre is a major topic over the last decade. The earliest approaches focused on spatial optimisation using workload consolidation. The use of renewable energies led to temporal optimisation where the workload is shifted to periods of green and cheap energy [1, 6, 7, 9, 10]. In parallel, applications moved from monolithic to elastic then to *energy-adaptive* [4, 8, 12] designs to align their performance with explicit energy concerns. Finally, smart city energy authorities pressure data centre managers to reduce their environmental footprint, conflicting with the data center client's performance expectations. While clients and energy authorities have competing objectives, they both interact with the data centre through financial agreements and their associated penalties. Energy-adaptive applications should then be scaled according to economic concerns when looking either for service or sustainability or both.

© Springer International Publishing AG 2017
F.F. Rivera et al. (Eds.): Euro-Par 2017, LNCS 10417, pp. 23–35, 2017.
DOI: 10.1007/978-3-319-64203-1_2

In this paper, we present Carver, a tool to reach profitable sustainability for data centre managers inside a smart city. Carver orchestrates energy-adaptive applications on a 24-h horizon, based on performance level, the variable availability of renewable energies, and the variable price of multiple power sources. It adjusts the application's working modes to minimise a financial cost combining the power cost and penalties for not complying with the client's performance and the smart city authority's expectations in terms of renewable energy use.

We validated Carver benefits by simulating a real testbed powered by the grid and a photovoltaic array and running the application HP LIFE. Carver reduced running costs by 34.71% compared to the current scenario, which runs the applications at peak performance. In practice, it reduced incomes by 2.17% to increase the use of renewables by 3.48%. Carver also reduced running costs by 52.40% compared to a scenario that maximises the usage of renewable energies, by decreasing the use of renewables by 1.61% to increase incomes by 52.35%.

The rest of this paper is organised as follows: Sect. 2 presents Carver's architecture. Section 3 details the implementation. Section 4 evaluates our prototype. Section 5 describes related works and Sect. 6 presents our conclusions.

2   CARVER Overview

Carver orchestrates energy-adaptive applications for profitable sustainability. At regular intervals, it analyses the forecasts of the energy providers powering the data centre, the application's characteristics and the smart city authority's expectations in terms of sustainable development, to compute an economically viable way to run the applications. In this section, we introduce Carver's architecture and detail the supported application's characteristics. We finally present Carver's general behaviour.

2.1   Architecture

Carver is a Web service written in Java. It interacts with energy providers, a smart city authority, and energy-adaptive applications using Rest APIs.

The energy providers characterise the power sources that are connected to the data centre. This includes commercial energy providers, through power distribution grids, but also a local production using a photovoltaic array for example. Each energy provider comes up with forecasts on a typical two-day horizon of the variable energy pricing and availability, as well as the proportion that comes from renewable sources. Pure renewable sources such as photovoltaic arrays display a constant 100% proportion while the power grid usually exhibits a variable ratio over time. Forecasting issues are outside the scope of this paper. We consider that the data supplier possesses its own algorithms or existing ones [14].

The smart city authority draws up agreements to regulate the energy used by consumers inside a smart city. An agreement declares a sustainable objective to reach and the financial penalties to pay in case of failure. By default, Carver supports agreements stating a minimal percentage of renewable energy to consume. It is however extensible enough to support other kinds of energy-related agreements.

The energy-adaptive applications form the auto-scalable workload of the data centre. Each application can run under different *working modes* that vary in performance and power consumption. Carver interacts with the applications through an *Energy Adaptive Software Controller* (EASC) connected to each of them. This controller enables developers to make their application adaptive to variable energy availability and sets out the application's characteristics in a textual description [4].

2.2   The EASC Description Script

A script describes the scalability characteristics of an application and its service-level objectives.

The Service Level Objective (SLO) is a business objective to reach over a validity period, and a pricing model. Carver currently supports *cumulative* and *instant* performance models. Cumulative models mainly concern batch-oriented applications that must achieve a given amount of work within a given time frame. Instant models concern interactive applications, such as a Web service that fulfills a given amount of requests per second that vary over the day.

The pricing model defines the base price the client pays when the objective is achieved, as well as a list of *modifiers*, i.e. financial penalties refund to the client depending on the gap between the actual and target performance levels. Each price modifier specifies a threshold and a flat or linear penalty. When the objective is not reached, the penalty to apply is given by the modifier with the largest threshold that is below or equal to the performance achieved. A flat penalty value is subtracted once from the base price, while a linear value is expressed as a price per performance unit.

The Working modes correspond to the possible deployments of the application (*e.g.* by a variable number of running replicas). It is described by a performance level, a power consumption, and a shell command to use to start the reconfiguration. When the application switches to a new working mode, it may temporary undergo a performance loss that depends on the previous working mode. A matrix indicates these transition costs. We assume that establishing the working modes it is done manually during a training phase, or using automated methods [3].

2.3   General Workflow

Carver schedules the application execution on a time frame spanning from 24 to 48 h. The time frame is discretised into time slots of 15 min and its duration is computed to include the complete validity period of each contract established between the data centre business service, the smart city authority and the application owners. Each contract starts at midnight and imposes a validity period of 24 h. Accordingly, the time frame covers the ongoing day only when Carver is called at midnight; otherwise it covers the period from the present time to the end of the following day.

By default, Carver is called every 15 min. This means that future decisions can be revised with regards to the refinement of the forecasts made by the energy providers. Carver first computes the time frame duration, then requests the forecasts from the energy providers, the smart city authority objective, and the EASC descriptions. Using this data, Carver computes, for each time slot of the time frame, the most suitable working mode for each application in order to maximise the data centre's profits. Once the computation is done, it informs each EASC of the schedule to follow.

3   Implementation

We refer to the optimisation problem computed by Carver as the EASC Allocation Problem (EascAP). The basic EascAP with only one power source, two modes per application, no smart city objectives, no instant performance goals, and no transition costs is already NP-hard in the strong sense as it contains Bin Packing as a special case because of the limited amount of power available at each time slot. As a consequence, no simple algorithm exists to solve real instances of the EascAP. The situation naturally becomes even more complicated when the instances exhibit all of the problem facets and heterogeneous components.

Carver relies on constraint programming to solve EascAP, using the Choco solver[1]. Constraint programming (CP) is a declarative paradigm to solve combinatorial decision problems. [13] We choose CP over alternative declarative approaches, such as mathematical or logic programming, because it tends to be more efficient on allocation and scheduling problems, and even more so with composite aspects: its higher-level modelling language enables the direct encoding of a wide variety of constraints and prevents the aggregated model from becoming intractable because of its size.

Applications and SLO. The execution of an application $a \in A$ is defined by its working mode $m \in M_a$ during each time slot $t \in T$. This is modelled as a sequence of decision variables $\mathtt{mode}_a = (\mathtt{mode}_{at})_{t \in T}$, each having an initial domain M_a. Each variable-value assignment $\mathtt{mode}_{at} = m$ is associated with the amount of work done by application a in mode m, possibly lowered by the transition cost incurred by a mode switch at time t, i.e. when $\mathtt{mode}_{a(t-1)} = m' \neq m$. Let $W_a(m', m)$ denote the resulting value. The total instant and cumulative performance penalty costs over the time frame T can be respectively computed as $\mathtt{icost}_a = \sum_{t \in T} K_I(W_a(\mathtt{mode}_{a(t-1)}, \mathtt{mode}_{at}))$ and $\mathtt{ccost}_a = K_C(\sum_{t \in T} W_a(\mathtt{mode}_{a(t-1)}, \mathtt{mode}_{at}))$ where K_I and K_C describe any penalty functions associated with the non-achievement of the instant and cumulative performance goals.

---

[1] http://choco-solver.org.

The two later relations could be encoded as such in a CP model. However, we obtain a deeper inference if they are grouped into one *multicost-regular* constraint [11]. This constraint captures the dependence of the mode transitions on the penalty values. This constraint is specified with a weighted finite automaton, over the variable sequence $mode_a$ and two numerical variables $perf_a$ and $icost_a$, and enforces that: (1) sequence $mode_a$ has no forbidden mode switches if any exist, (2) $perf_a$ is the cumulative performance of application a over time frame T, i.e. $perf_a = \sum_{t \in T} W_a(mode_{a(t-1)}, mode_{at})$, and (3) $icost_a$ is the total instant penalty cost of application a.

The instant penalty function K_I is directly modelled by this constraint, within the pre-computed automaton weights. Since the cumulative penalty cost depends on the entire sequence, function K_C must be modelled with an extra constraint relating the cumulative performance to the penalty cost variable:

$$ccost_a = K_C(perf_a) \tag{1}$$

Without any assumption on the nature of the function K_C, we model Eq. (1) with the *element* constraint after calculating the penalty costs associated with every possible value of $perf_a$.

Power Sources and Consumption. The data centre is powered with a dedicated set of power sources S. Each source $s \in S$ is available in a limited amount at each period $t \in T$. We introduce a variable $psrc_{st}$ stating the power usage and a constant k_{st} stating the unit energy price of source s at time t. Equation (2) models the total energy cost $pcost$ of the data centre over one day:

$$pcost = \sum_{t \in T} \sum_{s \in S} psrc_{st} \times k_{st} \tag{2}$$

The power consumption of application $a \in A$ during time slot t is modelled as a variable $papp_{at}$ and its value only depends on the current working mode $mode_{at}$. This relation is modelled using an *element* constraint. Finally, Eq. (3) link the power consumed by the applications to the power provided by the sources at each time slot:

$$\forall t \in T, \sum_{a \in A} papp_{at} = \sum_{s \in S} psrc_{st} \tag{3}$$

Smart City Objective. The smart city authority controls the minimum rate of renewable energy consumed by the data centre. According to the energy forecasts, i.e. the percentage r_{st} of green power provided by any source s at time t, the total ratio is a variable $rpart$ computed as:

$$rpart = \frac{\sum_{t \in T} \sum_{s \in S} psrc_{st} \times r_{st}}{\sum_{t \in T} \sum_{s \in S} psrc_{st}} \tag{4}$$

The penalty cost is again modelled by an *element* constraint, whatever the applied penalty function K_R:

$$rcost = K_R(rpart) \tag{5}$$

Economic Profit. The daily net benefits for the data centre are given as the base revenue for running the applications minus the energy cost and the penalties incurred for violating the application performance goals and the smart city objective. The optimisation criterion is then to minimise the sum of the expenses:

$$\min \sum_a (\text{ccost} + \text{icost}) + \text{pcost} + \text{rcost} \qquad (6)$$

4 Evaluation

The goal of Carver is to minimise the total running costs of a data centre inside a smart city so that its sustainability-oriented investments are viable. To evaluate its practical benefits in as realistic an environment as possible, we used a simulator to replay a 4-day trial inside a company data centre powered by the grid and a photovoltaic array set from 16 to 20 January 2015. We replayed the environment and the production workload with different solar profiles and compared the running cost obtained by Carver with the scaling used in production, and another one focusing on maximising the use of renewable energy.

4.1 Environment Setup

The simulated environment reproduces the testbed of the HP Innovation Lab in Milan. The testbed is composed of 20 Moonshot cartridges[2] that have a power consumption in the range of 20 Watt-peaks each. Such a size in terms of node stay representative in the context of a private cloud. Indeed Cano *et al.* [2] studied more than 2,000 private cloud installations. They observed their size vary between 3 and 40 servers, with an average of 6.18 nodes per cluster.

The testbed is powered by the grid and a photovoltaic array. The grid provides energy at a price of 0.16 €/kWh. The photovoltaic array produces 1 kWatt peak. Because the trial represents a negligible period compared to the array's lifespan, we ignore the investment cost for the photovoltaic array and assume an energy production cost of zero. The solar irradiation and the percentage of renewable energy in the grid vary on a daily basis. The supply of dual energy is simulated using 4 characteristic pre-defined profiles for each source, extracted from a 7-month history using the methodology in [15].

The testbed runs the HP LIFE project, a highly available Web-based e-learning platform spread over the globe. The platform is composed of 3 energy-adaptive applications whose characteristics are summarised in Table 1. The *Website* application has 6 working modes and uses from 10 to 17 cartridges. The unused ones are turned off to save power. The 10 cartridges that are always running host the database replicas and the load balancers to ensure high availability. This results in high consumption in the lowest working mode relative to its low performance. The *E-learning* and *G-learning* applications are responsible for indexing the content of the *Website* application. Each uses 1 cartridge,

---

[2] http://www8.hp.com/us/en/products/servers/moonshot/.

Table 1. HP LIFE project characteristics. The *Website* application is the 3-tier Web service that delivers static and dynamic contents. The *E-learning* and *G-learning* applications are responsible for indexing *Website* content.

Application	Performance	Power (W)	Working modes	Cartridges
Website	1050–3250 Req/s	360–550	6	10–17
G-learning	0–565 kPages/h	6–33	3	1
E-learning	0–60 kPages/h	6–33	3	1

has 3 working modes, and a number of concurrent crawlers that increases with the working mode performance. The applications are deployed statically on the cartridges without any virtualisation layer or co-location. The trial workload is based on the scenarios used by the operation team of the HP LIFE project. For the *Website*, we analysed the production traces to identify the day on which the highest request rate was observed. This load was multiplied by a correction factor to cope with the higher computing power of the Moonshots compared to the production cluster. The workload for *E-learning* and *G-learning* consists in crawling 200,000 then 300,000 pages.

The *Website* SLO requires the first working mode that can absorb the average hourly load, and uses a piecewise linear penalty function with a penalty of up to 2 € when the request rate is below the expectations by at least 800 requests per second. Inside the simulator, we consider that the request rate is constant per time slot, and equal to its SLO. Accordingly, the simulated behaviour slightly exaggerates the power consumption. This simplification does not impact the evaluation as the simulated conditions are constant for the whole experiment.

The SLOs for the *G-learning* and the *E-learning* require to crawl all of the *Website* pages, their penalty functions being linear with the number of missing indexations. For *G-learning* and *E-learning*, they equal 0.2 € and 0.01 € per 1000 missing indexations, respectively. For each time slot, these applications always run at peak performance within the limits of their working mode. Inside the simulator we then assume a constant power consumption and performance.

Finally, we stated that the smart city authority's objective requires that the data centre use at least 65% of renewable energy every day, with a penalty of 100 € per missing percent point. These values were chosen to evaluate Carver in situations where it is not always possible to attain the expected threshold, and with a penalty high enough to evaluate Carver trade-off decisions.

We evaluated the simulator accuracy in [15] and reported the amount of renewable energy used in reality and in the simulator deviated by less than a percent point. We ran the evaluation on a MacBook Pro with 3.1 GHz Intel Core i7 and 16 GB RAM and gave Carver 15 s to compute the best solution possible. As Carver is called every 15 min by default, it is possible to increase the time limit. However, we observed that usually Carver reaches a local optimum in less than 15 s.

We compared Carver with two representative scenarios named `perf` and `green` that were also executed using the simulator to avoid any comparison bias. `perf` mimics the scaling used in production. The working mode used for the Website is the one that ensures the SLO while using the least power. The *G-learning* and *E-learning* applications are launched at 00:00 and 03:00, respectively; a common time for background jobs. Each runs at peak performance until it reaches its SLO. In the `green` scenario, the applications are scaled to use as much renewable energy as possible. For this scenario, we ran Carver with a heuristic that selects the most efficient working mode when the photovoltaic array produces enough energy to power the entire testbed, and the least efficient working mode otherwise. Furthermore, each time a solution is computed, Carver must compute a new solution that provides a better renewable energy percentage.

4.2   Results

The resulting power profiles for the three scenarios are depicted in Figs. 1a to c. We observe that the profiles vary with the scenario despite identical workloads. This confirms that the applications were scaled differently depending the photovoltaic array production.

Figure 2 depicts the achieved daily renewable energy percentage per scenario. We first observe that the percentages vary depending on the day and the scenario with a maximum margin of 3.5 percentage points. This shows that `perf` provides a respectable value even when the renewable energy availability is ignored. First, this is because the servers have low power consumption and because the photovoltaic array can supply the entire testbed at peak period. Second, the Website, which is the biggest energy consumer, delivers pages upon request from daytime workers. Its workload, so its power consumption, is thus naturally aligned with the solar irradiation. Finally, its flexibility in terms of energy proportionality is limited, as its lowest working mode uses only 34.5% less energy than the most efficient one, and yet is 67.7% less efficient.

We also observe that Carver improves the daily percentage by 3.48% on average compared to `perf`, while `green` exhibits a 1.61% increase with regards to Carver. Figure 1a to c explain this increase. Indeed, the power profiles of Carver and `green` indicate that the two indexing applications were deferred to periods with maximum renewable energy, while the Website was scaled down during the evenings of 18 to 20 January to cope with the low share of renewables. Finally, the extra gain obtained in `green` is justified by its aggressive scale down of the Website to its minimal working mode each time that energy was not provided by the photovoltaic array. In terms of energy consumption, `perf` was the highest energy consumer, while `green` was the lowest one. `Carver` consumed 5.21% less than `perf` and 6.01% more than `green`.

Figure 3 shows the daily incomes. This income equals the cost of running the HP LIFE project (estimated at 1 euro per user per year by the HP LIFE managers), reduced by the penalties the data centre must pay to the application owner when the SLO is not reached. As expected, `perf` provides the maximum

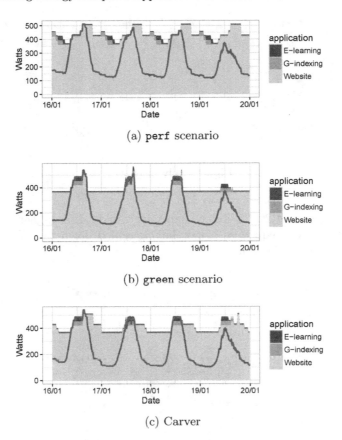

(a) **perf** scenario

(b) **green** scenario

(c) Carver

Fig. 1. Power profiles depending on the running scenario. The line indicates the share of renewable energy used.

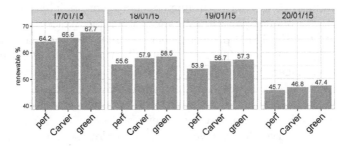

Fig. 2. Daily usage of renewable energy. The expected threshold is 65%.

incomes as the applications are scaled manually and statically to ensure the SLOs. **Green** provides the lowest income. This is explained by its unique objective of maximising the renewable percentage, without any consideration of the SLOs. We finally observe that **Carver** establishes a trade-off with these two baselines.

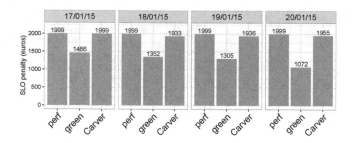

Fig. 3. Daily incomes

It provides an income 2.17% lower than `perf` but 52.48% higher than `green`. This exhibits the consequences of not having scaled down the Website during the evenings of 18 to 20 January.

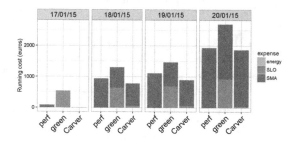

Fig. 4. Data centre running costs

Figure 4 summarises the daily running cost per scenario. This cost is the sum of the energy to be paid for and any financial penalties paid to the smart city authority and to the HP LIFE project owner. We first observe that energy does not play a significant role here. This is explained by the pricing model. For a data centre business manager, it is important to be sure that it is always economically viable to host a client's application even when the SLO is not achieved, to avoid bankruptcy. The incomes must then always cover energy expenses or the payment of human resources. For example, Amazon refunds its clients a maximum of 30% of their bill[3]. We observe that Carver provides the lowest daily running costs. This shows that Carver found a valuable compromise between prioritising the HP LIFE application or the smart city authority. Compared to `perf`, Carver reduced incomes by 2.17% to increase renewable energy use by 3.48% and the resulting running costs by 34.71%. Contrary to `green`, Carver did not over-commit on the smart city objective. It traded 1.61% of renewable energy to increase the incomes by 52.48% and the resulting running costs by 52.35%.

---

[3] https://aws.amazon.com/fr/ec2/sla/.

It is worth noting that the running costs of Carver and **perf** are close on the first and the last days. The difference on the first day is justified by the high solar irradiation as stated earlier. The difference on the last day is explained by the lack of flexibility in terms energy consumption for the Website application coupled with the low solar irradiation. Indeed, the objective was unrealistic and the high power consumption of the Website, even in its lowest working mode, precludes paying a small SLO penalty to avoid paying a high one to the smart city authority. In addition to validating the benefits of Carver, this evaluation also confirms the important of employing energy-adaptive applications with high variable working modes.

5 Related Works

Initial solutions to address energy efficiency focused on minimising the number of online servers, the power consumption, and gas emissions. With the democratisation of renewable energies, solutions have evolved to integrate their intermittent nature. Accordingly, the community integrated a temporal dimension going as far as to leave the spatial dimension to the underlying resource manager.

Li *et al.* [9] propose a scheduler for batch and service jobs that dynamically adjusts the number of online servers to maximise the usage of a purely renewable power source. Contrary to Carver, SLOs are not explicitly considered and the proposed scheduler presumes non-elastic jobs.

Goiri *et al.* propose with GreenSlot [5] and Greenswitch [6] a job scheduler that reduces the grid's electricity cost when the grid is up and reduces the performance degradation otherwise. The proposed scheduler is devoted to a modified version of Hadoop, called GreenHadoop [7] that supports deferrable and non-deferrable jobs, and the performance degradation denotes the amount of the workload to process. Lui *et al.* [10] consider the cooling costs along with the energy cost and the renewable share. The SLO represents a certain response time for interactive applications, or a completion time for the batch jobs. However, the proposed scheduler forces SLO satisfaction. Similarly to these works, Carver supports deferrable and non-deferrable applications through cumulative and instant SLOs while the penalty model is flexible enough to support their notion of performance degradation, but also instantaneous performance metrics. Carver does not integrate a cooling model, but does include the flexibility offered by constraint programming, and the economic objective provides the required entry points to integrate this concern. Most importantly, Carver offers the benefits of elastic applications, while its economic objective helps identify which of the clients or smart city authority is likely to minimise the total running costs.

Recently, Wang *et al.* [16] proposed a game-based, cloud-pricing framework to maximise the cloud profit regarding energy costs. Carver also addresses profit maximisation but at a lower level. While these authors centre on computing a pricing model that guides clients to profitable periods, Carver focuses on scaling applications with regards to their pricing model and trade-off possibilities.

In terms of energy-adaptive applications, Oliviera and Ledoux [12] proposed applications that revise their design with regards to their current performance expectations and an energy regulation imposed by the underlying resource manager that focuses on maximising data centre revenue. Similarly, Carver supports variadic application architectures with the notion of working modes and trading possibilities to minimise running costs. However, Carver differs through its integration of the temporal dimension of the problem to integrate intermittent power sources. This makes it possible to study the energy dispatch over time, support cumulative performance models, and take care of transition costs. Hasan *et al.* [8] provides green awareness in interactive cloud applications. Their controllers increase revenues through better response times, and decrease renewable and non-renewable energy use. Carver also scales interactive applications. Thanks to an explicit manipulation of the temporal dimension, it also supports non-interactive applications and join the business and the energy-awareness dimensions using an economical model to reach a sustainable profitability.

6 Conclusion

Energy efficiency in data centres is addressed through workload management to reduce the environmental footprint or operational costs. Recent approaches take also into account the intermittent nature and lower prices of renewable energy sources and aim to limit the *brown* energy input by shaving or shifting the load. In doing so, they often overlook the performance requirements of the client's applications, even though the economic return of a data centre depends on these two factors. Our approach is driven by a broader view: (1) data centre managers are encouraged to adopt environmental measures, if these measures translate in terms of financial gain; and (2) financial gain results from a trade-off between energy consumption and client satisfaction.

We proposed Carver, a tool to orchestrate on a 24-h horizon, energy-adaptive applications according to their performance level, the variable availability of renewable energies, and the variable price of multiple power sources. Carver adjusts the application's working modes in order to minimise a global financial cost combining the power cost and penalties for not complying with the client service level objectives and the smart city authority's requirements in terms of renewable energy use. Carver currently supports performance models for batch- and service-oriented applications, and flexible penalty functions that go beyond standard piecewise linear models.

We validated Carver by simulating a 4-day execution of a testbed powered by the grid and a photovoltaic array. The simulator mimicked the production workload of the e-learning application HP LIFE. Carver provided the best incomes for the data centre provider by balancing the SLOs the smart-city authority penalties with regards to the workload and the availability of renewable energies.

References

1. Aksanli, B., Venkatesh, J., Zhang, L., Rosing, T.: Utilizing green energy prediction to schedule mixed batch and service jobs in data centers. SIGOPS OSR **45**(3), 53–57 (2012)
2. Cano, I., Aiyar, S., Krishnamurthy, A.: Characterizing private clouds: a large-scale empirical analysis of enterprise clusters. In: Proceedings of the Seventh ACM Symposium on Cloud Computing, SoCC 2016. ACM, New York (2016). http://doi.acm.org/10.1145/2987550.2987584
3. Colmant, M., Kurpicz, M., Felber, P., Huertas, L., Rouvoy, R., Sobe, A.: Process-level power estimation in VM-based systems. In: Proceeding of the Tenth EuroSys. ACM (2015)
4. Dupont, C., Sheikhalishahi, M., Facca, F.M., Hermenier, F.: An energy aware framework for virtual machine placement in cloud federated data centres. In: 8th IEEE/ACM International Conference on Utility and Cloud Computing, December 2015
5. Goiri, I.N., Katsak, W., Le, K., Nguyen, T.D., Bianchini, R.: Parasol and GreenSwitch: managing datacenters powered by renewable energy. In: SIGARCH Computer Architecture News, vol. 41, no. 1, March 2013
6. Goiri, I.N., Le, K., Haque, M.E., Beauchea, R., Nguyen, T.D., Guitart, J., Torres, J., Bianchini, R.: Greenslot: scheduling energy consumption in green datacenters. In: Proceedings of International Conference for High Performance Computing, Networking, Storage and Analysis. ACM (2011)
7. Goiri, I.N., Le, K., Nguyen, T.D., Guitart, J., Torres, J., Bianchini, R.: Green-Hadoop: leveraging green energy in data-processing frameworks. In: Proceeding of the 7th ACM Eurosys. ACM (2012)
8. Hasan, M.S., de Oliveira, F.A., Ledoux, T., Pazat, J.L.: Enabling green energy awareness in interactive cloud application. In: 2016 IEEE International Conference on Cloud Computing Technology and Science (CloudCom), pp. 414–422, December 2016
9. Li, Y., Orgerie, A.C., Menaud, J.M.: Opportunistic scheduling in clouds partially powered by green energy. In: IEEE International Conference on GreenCom (2015)
10. Liu, Z., Chen, Y., Bash, C., Wierman, A., Gmach, D., Wang, Z., Marwah, M., Hyser, C.: Renewable and cooling aware workload management for sustainable data centers. In: Proceeding of the 12th ACM SIGMETRICS. ACM (2012)
11. Menana, J., Demassey, S.: Sequencing and counting with the multicost-regular constraint. In: Hoeve, W.-J., Hooker, J.N. (eds.) CPAIOR 2009. LNCS, vol. 5547, pp. 178–192. Springer, Heidelberg (2009). doi:10.1007/978-3-642-01929-6_14
12. de Oliveira Jr., F.A., Ledoux, T.: Self-management of cloud applications and infrastructure for energy optimization. SIGOPS OSR **46**(2), 10 (2012)
13. Rossi, F., van Beek, P., Walsh, T. (eds.): Handbook of Constraint Programming, Foundations of Artificial Intelligence, vol. 2. Elsevier, Amsterdam (2006)
14. Sharma, N., Sharma, P., Irwin, D., Shenoy, P.: Predicting solar generation from weather forecasts using machine learning. In: IEEE International Conference on Smart Grid Communications, October 2011
15. The DC4Cities Consortium: D6.3 - Report on the experimentation phase 2. Evaluation report on the second trial cycle (2015). http://www.dc4cities.eu/
16. Wang, C., Nasiriani, N., Kesidis, G., Urgaonkar, B., Wang, Q., Chen, L.Y., Gupta, A., Birke, R.: Recouping energy costs from cloud tenants: tenant demand response aware pricing design. In: Proceedings of the 6th International Conference on Future Energy Systems. ACM (2015)

Off-Road Performance Modeling – How to Deal with Segmented Data

M. Kashif Ilyas$^{(\boxtimes)}$, Alexandru Calotoiu, and Felix Wolf

Technische Universität Darmstadt, 64289 Darmstadt, Germany
cashif.pk@gmail.com, {calotoiu,wolf}@cs.tu-darmstadt.de

Abstract. Besides correctness, scalability is one of the top priorities of parallel programmers. With manual analytical performance modeling often being too laborious, developers increasingly resort to empirical performance modeling as a viable alternative, which learns performance models from a limited amount of performance measurements. Although powerful automatic techniques exist for this purpose, they usually struggle with the situation where performance data representing two or more different phenomena are conflated into a single performance model. This not only generates an inaccurate model for the given data, but can also either fail to point out existing scalability issues or create the appearance of such issues when none are present. In this paper, we present an algorithm to detect segmentation in a sequence of performance measurements and estimate the point where the behavior changes. Our method correctly identified segmentation in more than 80% of 5.2 million synthetic tests and confirmed expected segmentation in three application case studies.

Keywords: Parallel computing · Performance tools · Performance modeling

1 Introduction

The increasing number of processors in our computing hardware poses new challenges to developers. Increasing software parallelism challenges traditional ways of writing and debugging programs. Badly designed parallel programs may fail to reach the expected performance when run on a larger number of processors. Therefore, finding and removing scalability bugs is key to the achievement of sustainable parallel performance. The term scalability bug refers to those parts of a program whose scaling behavior is unintentionally poor, i.e., which perform worse than expected when using a larger number of processors [2]. As scalability bugs do not become manifest unless the program is actually run at larger scales, it is very difficult for developers to discover them. Often, they are found when the software is already deployed and changes are more expensive.

One approach capable of finding such bugs early and easily is empirical performance modeling: a performance model of a program is built from measurements of relevant performance metrics. We can do this even for individual regions

© Springer International Publishing AG 2017
F.F. Rivera et al. (Eds.): Euro-Par 2017, LNCS 10417, pp. 36–48, 2017.
DOI: 10.1007/978-3-319-64203-1_3

of the code, henceforth called kernels. Typically, we run the program on different numbers of processors p and measure the metric m of interest for each run, creating for each kernel data points of the form (p, m). These data points are then analyzed using regression and turned into a mathematical performance model of the kernel. Empirical models are not necessarily as accurate as analytical models but are good enough to show the scaling trend of the kernel. Problematic kernels can then be examined by the developer in more detail. The whole process can be automated to obtain empirical models for all possible kernels of a program, hence avoiding the risk of overlooking any critical kernel, at least for the given input set.

Extra-P [2] is an automatic tool that implements the above approach. It generates empirical models for each kernel (i.e., call path) of a program in a human-readable form. Extra-P also extrapolates performance to a chosen target scale such that it can be compared with developer expectations. While Extra-P's workflow is quite effective in finding scalability bugs, it fails if the input data represents two or more distinct behaviors of a program. Extra-P assumes that the performance of a kernel can be characterized by a single function, however, some kernels do not follow a single trend in every situation. There are many practical scenarios where programs change their behavior. For example, modern MPI implementations switch from one algorithm to another, depending on the message size, the number of processes, or the network topology [9]. Overlooking such segmentation not only results in the creation of inaccurate models but also poses the risk of ignoring potential scalability bugs or confusing the user with false positives.

In this paper, we introduce a novel method to detect such segmentation before generating empirical models. Driven by the requirements of performance modeling in HPC, where trial runs can be quite expensive, a particular challenge our method addresses is the low number of data points. Specifically, we propose

- an algorithm to find segmentation in data with as few as six points, and
- a method to estimate the change point.

Our approach (i) correctly identified segmentation in more than 80% of more than five million randomly generated datasets and (ii) confirmed expected segmented behavior in three realistic use cases, including a climate code, a simple matrix multiplication benchmark, and several MPI collective operations.

In the next section, we review the existing workflow of Extra-P and explain how it struggles with segmented data. In Sect. 3, we explain our approach with the help of an example. We demonstrate its effectiveness in Sect. 4. In Sect. 5, we compare it to related work and argue why it fits our purpose best. We conclude the paper in Sect. 6, where we also discuss future work.

2   Performance Modeling with Extra-P

As our work is intended to improve Extra-P, we briefly review how it generates models from performance data.

Extra-P exploits the observation that performance models of most practical programs can be expressed as n terms involving logarithms and powers of the model parameter p, which is usually the number of processors but can also be something different like the input size. Hence, performance models can be represented in the *performance model normal form* (PMNF):

$$f(p) = \sum_{k=1}^{n} c_k \cdot p^{i_k} \cdot log_2^{j_k}(p)$$

As identification of scalability bugs rather than prediction accuracy is the primary objective of Extra-P, the sets I and J from which i_k and j_k are selected, do not need to be arbitrarily large to obtain reasonably accurate models. The authors suggest $n = 2$, $I = \{\frac{0}{2}, \frac{1}{2}, \frac{2}{2}, \frac{3}{2}, \frac{4}{2}, \frac{5}{2}, \frac{6}{2}\}$ and $J = \{0, 1, 2\}$ as default. The generation algorithm starts with a set of simple (i.e., short) candidate models and chooses the winner using K-fold validation. The size of the candidates is gradually increased until either the maximum of n is reached or signs of overfitting appear.

This approach works as long as all the performance measurements represent a single behavior. However, if a certain kernel exhibits segmented behavior, i.e., its performance trend changes after a certain point, the resulting model will be inaccurate. To clarify our point, we consider an example of segmented data and the corresponding model generated by Extra-P, which are shown in Fig. 1. The data was generated using the functions $f_1(p) = p^2$ for $p \in \{1, 2, ..., 5\}$ and $f_2(p) = 30 + p$ for $p \in \{6, 7, ..., 10\}$.

With these data as input, Extra-P generates the model $f(p) = 1.65 + 3.97 \cdot log_2^2(p)$. This is misleading because the actual functions are quadratic and linear, but not logarithmic. At $p = 1024$, the prediction error of the model is almost 62%.

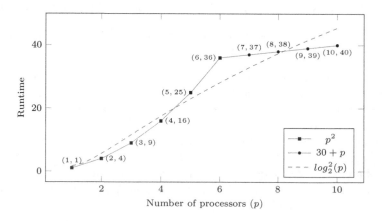

Fig. 1. Data points from two different functions (solid lines) and the model generated by Extra-P (dashed line).

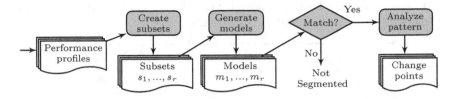

Fig. 2. Steps involved in segematation detection and change-point identification.

3 Approach

Our algorithm is designed to help Extra-P detect segmentation in the data before models are generated. Its input is a set of performance measurements, while the output indicates whether the given measurements show segmented behavior or not. If the data turns out to be segmented, the algorithm tries to identify the change point. With this information, Extra-P can generate separate models for each segment and/or request new measurements if any segment is too small for model generation. Figure 2 highlights the different steps of our algorithm. Below, we discuss each step in detail and apply it to the example from Sect. 2.

3.1 Detecting Segmentation

Our algorithm rests on the observation that models generated from *homogeneous* subsets of the input data set (i.e., subsets representing a single behavior), will differ from models created from *heterogeneous* subsets (i.e., subsets representing multiple behaviors). In this work we focus on subsets defined by consecutive data points corresponding to subintervals of the input parameter.

As an example, we try to divide the segmented data from Fig. 1 into subsets representing five consecutive values of the model parameter p. We use a sliding window of five measurement points to create subsets which results in a total of six subsets, each containing five points. The first subset s_1 contains the first five points $\{1, 4, 9, 16, 25\}$, the second subset s_2 contains the five points starting from second point $\{4, 9, 16, 25, 36\}$, and so on. All these subsets are listed in Table 1. Note that the subsets s_1, s_2, and s_6 are homogeneous, as they exhibit a single behavior while the subsets s_3, s_4, and s_5 are heterogeneous, mixing points from the two behaviors. Then, we create models $m_1, \ldots, m_r$ for each of the subsets $s_1, \ldots, s_r$, respectively. The number of subsets r depends on the number of input data points and on the number of values each subset is allowed to contain. Ideally, each subset should contain five data points, as recommended in the original research work by Calotoiu et al. [2]. Below, we introduce two model properties that can be used to decide whether a subset is segmented or not.

Absolute nRSS. We define a generalized error value for each model, which is a normalized form of the common RSS. Residual Sum of Squares (RSS) is a measure of the discrepancy between the data and an estimation model and is

Table 1. Subsets created for the data from Fig. 1, their respective models, and their nRSS values. Heterogeneous subsets are highlighted.

Subset	Model	nRSS	ϵ
$s_1 = \{1, 4, 9, 16, 25\}$	p^2	≈ 0	$-$
$s_2 = \{4, 9, 16, 25, 36\}$	p^2	≈ 0	≈ 1
$s_3 = \{9, 16, 25, 36, 37\}$	$-49.41 + 33.45 \cdot \sqrt{p}$	0.18	$5 \cdot 10^{18}$
$s_4 = \{16, 25, 36, 37, 38\}$	$-28.53 + 23.17 \cdot log_2(p)$	0.19	1.05
$s_5 = \{25, 36, 37, 38, 39\}$	$-6.19 + 14.83 \cdot log_2(p)$	0.16	0.84
$s_6 = \{36, 37, 38, 39, 40\}$	$30 + p$	≈ 0	≈ 0

used to measure the goodness of a model. The normalized residual sum of squares (nRSS) is calculated by dividing the square root of the RSS by the mean of the points used to generate the models:

$$nRSS = \frac{\sqrt{RSS}}{\bar{y}}$$

Calculating the nRSS for each subset yields r error terms $e_1, \ldots, e_r$. For our example data from Fig. 1, we get six models and their corresponding nRSS values, which are shown in Table 1. The nRSS of the heterogeneous subsets is much higher than the one of the homogeneous subsets because a well-fitting model cannot be found for such diverse data. We identify a subset s_i as potentially heterogeneous if its nRSS $e_i > 0.1$ and homogeneous otherwise. We classify a data set as segmented if the maximum absolute value of the nRSS across all subsets exceeds a threshold of $\theta = 0.5$, an empirically determined value reflecting our experiences after analyzing more than five million synthetic data sets. In most cases, using $\theta = 0.5$ correctly identifies segmented behavior if it exists, while producing only few false positives (i.e., non-segmented behavior falsely identified as segmented).

Relative nRSS. The secondary indicator is the relative nRSS, which is the ratio of the nRSS values of two consecutive subsets. It is applied only when $0.1 \leq nRSS \leq 0.5$. The relative nRSS ϵ can be mathematically expressed as $\epsilon_i = e_{i+1}/(e_i + \eta)$. η is a minimal non-zero value added to avoid division by zero. This criterion has the advantage that it rules out false positives that occur when noise lifts all errors above the threshold. It also covers those scenarios where the absolute nRSS values are smaller than the threshold but the heterogeneous subsets still show a much higher nRSS than the homogeneous ones. We found that $\epsilon > 4$ provides a good additional criterion to determine segmentation when $0.1 \leq nRSS \leq 0.5$.

In our example from Table 1, it is clear that the heterogeneous subsets s_3, s_4 and s_5 have much higher absolute nRSS values than the homogeneous ones, but the maximum resides still below the threshold. However, because $\epsilon_3 >> 4$ we still conclude correctly that the data is segmented.

Fig. 3. Selection of points for the subsets $s3$, $s4$ and $s5$. Squares and circles represent data points from different behaviors, the sixth point is common to both behaviors.

3.2   Identifying the Change Point

Identifying the change point goes beyond a binary decision whether the data is segmented or not. If a change point can be detected, then a separate model for each behavior, divided by the change point, can be determined, provided enough data points are available. To accomplish this, we tag each subset with a zero if its nRSS classifies it as homogeneous and with a one otherwise. For the data from Table 1, we obtain the pattern 001110.

For the sake of simplicity, we assume that there is a single change point in the data, but the same method can be extended to multiple change points via recursion. Since we create subsets containing five points and we assume that only two different behaviors are present in the data, at most four subsets can be heterogeneous (one point representing the first behavior combined with four points representing the second one, then two combined with three, and so forth). If the two behaviors share a common data point such as in the example, only three such subsets will exist. Therefore, each sequence of values corresponding to the series of subsets will contain either three or four ones, preceded and followed by an arbitrary number of zeros.

The location of the change point can therefore be deduced by examining only the pattern of ones. Practically, we select the subset corresponding to the second one in the pattern. If a common data point for both behaviors exists and therefore the pattern contains three ones, then the change point will be the third data point of that subset. If no common data point for both behaviors exists, then the change point will be between the third and the fourth data point of that subset. In the example, the relevant subsets are $s3$, $s4$, and $s5$, thus the change point is $p = 6$, as shown in Fig. 3. In most cases, we do not see a single change point, but two points between which the change happens.

4   Evaluation

To ensure our method correctly distinguishes segmented from non-segmented behavior, we first applied it to millions of synthetic data sets. After that, we tested it with application data known to be segmented, which we correctly identified as such without producing false positives.

4.1   Synthetic Data

We ran our algorithm on data from two categories of randomly generated functions:

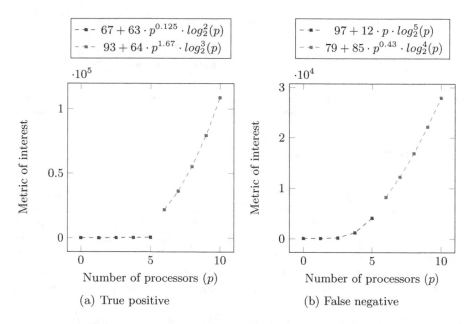

Fig. 4. Two examples from synthetic data set used for evaluation of the algorithm. Both functions were generated with random coefficients and exponents and a 5% of noise was added. In first case, the segmentation was correctly detected while the second case is a false negative because algorithm failed to detect segmentation.

- Functions guaranteed to be within the search space, with randomly generated coefficients and exponents chosen at random from those present in the search space. These functions can be exactly matched by the algorithm and errors will only appear due to noise or segmentation.
- Functions not guaranteed to be within the search space, with randomly generated exponents and coefficients. These functions are unlikely be matched exactly and likely to have larger overall errors, therefore making the detection of segmented behavior harder.

For each category, we generated tests using data from one function, which should not be marked as segmented, and from two different functions, which should be marked as segmented. A failure in the first case is a false positive, while a failure in the second case is a false negative. Additionally, to observe the accuracy of our algorithms under production conditions, we applied different levels of noise ranging from 0% to 15%. For a noise level of x%, we added a randomly selected percentage of noise between −x and x to the original value. For each noise level, Fig. 5a presents the percentages where the algorithm correctly identified the data as segmented or not segmented. The algorithm was always provided with ten data points, either all from one function or equally divided among two different functions. Figure 4a shows an example where randomly

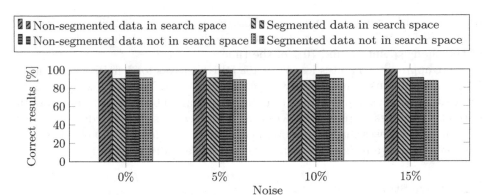

(a) Fraction of correct results for different noise levels.

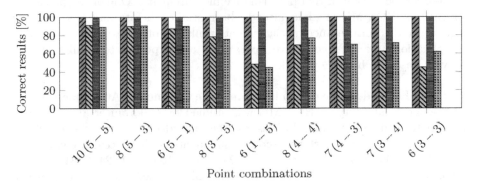

(b) Fraction of correct results for different point combinations with 5% noise. The x-axis shows the total number of points used. The numbers in brackets represent the split of points between the different behaviors.

Fig. 5. Fractions of correctly classified data sets (i.e., neither falsely positive nor falsely negative) for different levels of noise. Each bar was created by analyzing 100,000 synthetic data sets.

generated data was correctly detected as segmented while Fig. 4b represents a case of false negative.

Apart from different noise levels, we also tested the accuracy of our algorithm for different numbers and combinations of measurement points. We used a maximum of ten and a minimum of six points and tried various combinations of contributions from each function. In general, our algorithm works best when there are ten or more data points with at least five data points from each function. If there are less than five data points from either of the functions, the percentage of true positives decreases. Figure 5b shows the fractions of point combination where data was correctly identified as segmented or not segmented.

For functions within the search space, the algorithm correctly found the location of the change point in about 90% of the cases. However, the percentage decreases with increasing noise. In those cases where the functions were not guaranteed to be in the search space, the algorithm correctly found the location of the change point around 70% of the time.

Our approach generates less than 1% false positives for a noise level of upto 5%, sparing the user unnecessary confusion and work. With as few as six data points, or one measurement more than usually required by Extra-P, our approach correctly identifies more than 50% of the occurrences of segmented data, and this percentage increases sharply if more measurements are made available. The user can therefore obtain significant gains at very little additional cost.

4.2   Case Studies

In this section, we present three cases studies where we correctly identify expected segmentation in real performance measurements. One of the presented applications, HOMME [4], had already been studied before and has a known segmentation in performance measurements while the other two, namely matrix multiplication and MPI collective operations, are expected to exhibit such a behavior based on how they work.

HOMME. This code is the dynamical core of the Community Atmosphere Model (CAM). The scalability of HOMME was studied by Calotoiu et al. [2] and in addition to identifying scalability issues, they found certain kernels to exhibit segmentation. We used performance measurements with processor counts $p \in$ {600, 1176, 2400, 4056, 7776, 11616, 13824, 14406, 15000, 16224, 23814, 31974, 43350, 54150} which were taken on the IBM Blue Gene/Q system Juqueen in Jülich according to developer recommendations.

Our algorithm identified 25 out of 664 kernels as segmented and estimated the change point each time to lie between $15,000$ and $16,224$. The execution time of one such kernel, laplace_sphere_wk, was previously characterized as $f(p) = 27.7 + 2.23 \cdot 10^{-7} \cdot p^2$ using the non-segmented algorithm. Using the segmented approach, we came up with the following segmented model:

$$f_{seg}(p) = \begin{cases} 49.36 & p \leq 15,000 \\ 20.8 + 2.3 \cdot 10^{-7} \cdot p^2 & p \geq 16,224 \end{cases}$$

Figure 6a shows the measured execution times and both segmented and non-segmented models for this kernel. The reason for this segmentation is a ceiling term in the code, causing those kernels to be called only once when using 15,000 processors or less, hence resulting in constant time. However, beyond 15,000 processors, the kernels are called quadratically, causing quadratic models to appear. This case study illustrates the advantage of our algorithm, which can detect such segmentation automatically without any user intervention.

Matrix Multiplication. A practical scenario of abrupt change in behavior is the effect of cache spilling. The runtime of a memory-bound program heavily depends on the time required to fetch data from the memory. If the data is small enough to

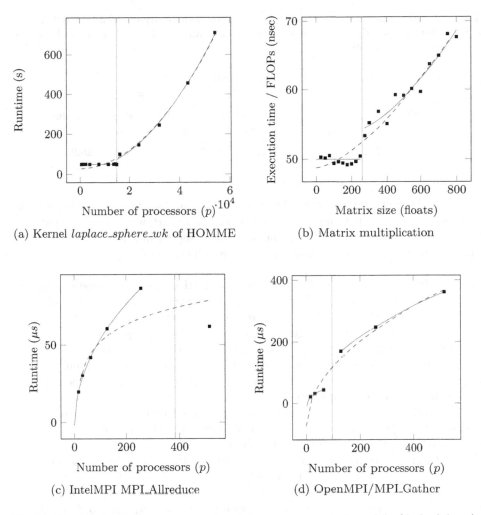

Fig. 6. Graphs showing measurement points, non-segmented models (dashed lines) and segmented models (solid lines). Estimated locations of change points are shown by vertical lines.

fit in the cache, the runtime stays very small. However, as soon as the amount of data exceeds the size of the cache and memory access time becomes the limiting factor, the runtime changes abruptly and follows a completely different pattern.

We used a sequential naive matrix multiplication to observe this effect and see whether our algorithm can correctly identify the change. We ran our program with increasing matrix sizes and measured the runtime for each matrix size on an Intel Core i5 processor with 2 cores, one 256 kB L2 cache per core, and a 3 MB shared L3 cache. We then divided the runtime by the number of FLOPs to measure the influence of the memory-access time. As the matrix reached a size large enough to not fit in the L2 cache, we saw a sudden drop in the performance

Table 2. MPI collective operations which exhibit segmentation. While the left model is listed for all operations, the right model is listed only for those where we had enough data points to create one.

Library	Collective operation	Segmented models	
		Left	Right
IntelMPI	`MPI_Gather`	$4.80 + 0.06 \cdot p \cdot log_2(p)$	Not enough points
	`MPI_Allreduce`	$-1.71 + 5.50 \cdot \sqrt{p}$	Not enough points
OpenMPI	`MPI_Gather`	$-23.3 + 11.17 \cdot log_2(p)$	$-23.11 + 16.95 \cdot \sqrt{p}$

(Fig. 6b). We not only detected the segmentation of data but also identified the change point between a matrix size of 244 kB and 295 kB, which roughly matches the size of the L2 cache. Overall, the segmented model much better reflects the memory hierarchy than the more inaccurate unified model.

MPI Collective Operations. The performance of MPI collective operations highly depends on the network topology, the number of processes, and the size of messages. Some algorithms perform very well on short messages but fail to perform the same way on larger messages while others behave the opposite way [10]. To maximize performance in every situation, modern MPI libraries offer a wide variety of algorithms for each collective operation and switch between them according to the environment [5,9]. Of course, switching between algorithms leads to segmented performance behavior.

To study this, we measured the runtimes of selected MPI collective operations from Open MPI and Intel MPI for different numbers of processes $p \in \{16, 32, 64, 128, 256, 512\}$ on the Lichtenberg Cluster of TU Darmstadt. We found that MPI_Allreduce and MPI_Gather from Intel MPI change their behavior after 256 and 128 processes, respectively. With Open MPI, such behavior was only noticed for MPI_Gather after 64 processes, as shown in Table 2. The change point was in agreement with the threshold found in the code base of Open MPI, at which the default decision function switches the gather algorithm from linear to binomial. The performance measurements and both the segmented and the non-segmented models are shown in Fig. 6c and d. Despite restricting the segmentation analysis to only six data points in this case study, our algorithm provides valuable feedback on the performance variability of these collectives. By looking at the results of the analysis, the user can know which extra measurement points he needs to provide to improve model accuracy. It is also evident from Fig. 6 that the non-segmented models predicted by Extra-P would result in misleading predictions at higher scales.

5   Related Work

The change point estimation problem has been discussed in the literature since 1966. Several algorithms have been suggested and used by researchers since then and are being further improved to this day. Auger and Lawrance [1] suggested an algorithm in 1989 to find segmented neighborhoods in the data collected by the experiments of molecular biology. The algorithm runs in $O(kn^2)$ time, where k is the maximum number of change points. The algorithm was later improved by Jackson et al. [6] to decrease the time complexity to $O(n^2)$. In 2012, Killick et al. [7] proposed a variation of the same algorithm that runs in linear time in the best case, but incurs quadratic cost in the worst case. All the above mentioned methods are collectively called *optimal partitioning* methods and give the exact location of the change point. However, these algorithms are too slow and need much more points than we have in our experiments.

Another popular method and the most similar one to ours was suggested by Scott and Knott [8] in 1944 and is known as *binary segmentation*. It is a recursive algorithm that finds the change points by first finding a point and then recursively dividing and reapplying the method to each segment. It continues to do so until no more change points can be found. To tackle multiple change points, our method could be used in a similar way, but in general too few data points are provided to justify its recursive application. The main difference, however, is that our change-point identification scheme is much simpler and faster.

Chang et al. [3] used fuzzy c-partitioning as a way to find change points in data. They argue that finding change points is similar to arranging data in clusters and hence fuzzy logic can be applied. Similarly, Zhang et al. [11] used the sparse group lasso (SGL) method to estimate change points. In SGL, two penalty terms of the fitting function make sure to find the best fit for the data. Both of the methods, however, require much more data points than our method to give any reasonable answers. It is important to mention that all of those methods are generic and do not take advantage of the small search space resulting from the performance model normal form like our method does and hence, are much slower, more complicated, and need more data points than our method does.

6 Conclusion

The results of our synthetic data tests as well as the case studies confirm that the proposed algorithm can be used as an effective way to find segmentation in performance data when creating empirical performance models. The suggested algorithm does not require any extra effort on the user's side, is very simple to implement, and can work very well on as few as six points. The algorithm has correctly identified segmented behavior, and did not signal such behavior when none was present in more than 80% of 5.2 million test cases. Hence, it is capable of finding segmentation in the majority of cases, where it would go unnoticed otherwise and leave the user with inaccurate models. We plan to integrate our approach into the next release of Extra-P.

Acknowledgements. This work was supported in part by the German Research Foundation (DFG) through the Priority Programme 1648 *Software for Exascale Computing* (SPPEXA) and the Programme *Performance Engineering for Scientific Software*. Additional support was provided by the German Federal Ministry of Education and Research (BMBF) under Grant No. 01IH16008, and by the US Department of Energy under Grant No. DE-SC0015524. Finally, we would like to thank the University Computing Center (Hochschulrechenzentrum) of TU Darmstadt for providing us with access to the Lichtenberg Cluster.

References

1. Auger, I., Lawrance, C.: Algorithms for the optimal identification of segment neighborhoods. Bull. Math. Biol. **51**(1), 39–54 (1989)
2. Calotoiu, A., Hoefler, T., Poke, M., Wolf, F.: Using automated performance modeling to find scalability bugs in complex codes. In: Proceedings of the International Conference on High Performance Computing, Networking, Storage and Analysis, SC 2013, November 2013
3. Chang, S., Lu, K., Yang, M.: Fuzzy change-point algorithms for regression models. IEEE Trans. Fuzzy Syst. **23**, 2343–2357 (2015)
4. Dennis, J.M., Edwards, J., Evans, K.J., Guba, O., Lauritzen, P.H., Mirin, A.A., St-Cyr, A., Taylor, M.A., Worley, P.H.: CAM-SE: a scalable spectral element dynamical core for the community atmosphere model. Int. J. High Perform. Comput. Appl. **26**, 74–89 (2012)
5. Fagg, G.E., Pjesivac-grbovic, J., Bosilca, G., Dongarra, J.J., Jeannot, E.: Flexible collective communication tuning architecture applied to OpenMPI. In: 2006 Euro PVM/MPI (2006)
6. Jackson, B., Sargle, J.D., Barnes, D., Arabhi, S., Alt, A., Gioumousis, P., Gwin, E., Sangtrakulcharoen, P., Tan, L., Tsai, T.T.: An algorithm for optimal partitioning of data on an interval. Sig. Process. Lett. **12**(2), 105–108 (2005)
7. Killick, R., Fearnhead, P., Eckley, I.: Optimal detection of change points with a linear computational cost. J. Am. Stat. Assoc. **107**, 1590–1598 (2012)
8. Scott, A., Knott, M.: A cluster analysis method for grouping means in the analysis of variance. Biometrics **30**, 507–512 (1974)
9. Steve, H.: *Intel*® MPI library collective optimization on the Intel Xeon Phi coprocessor using environment variable collective operation control (2015). https:// software.intel.com/en-us/articles/intel-mpi-library-collective-optimization-on-int el-xeon-phi
10. Thakur, R., Gropp, W.D.: Improving the performance of collective operations in MPICH. In: Dongarra, J., Laforenza, D., Orlando, S. (eds.) EuroPVM/MPI 2003. LNCS, vol. 2840, pp. 257–267. Springer, Heidelberg (2003). doi:10.1007/978-3-540-39924-7_38
11. Zhang, B., Geng, J., Lai, L.: Change-point estimation in high dimensional linear regression models via sparse group LASSO. In: 53rd Annual Allerton Conference on Communication, Control, and Computing (Allerton), pp. 815–821 (2015)

Online Dynamic Monitoring of MPI Communications

George Bosilca[1], Clément Foyer[2(✉)], Emmanuel Jeannot[2(✉)],
Guillaume Mercier[2,3], and Guillaume Papauré[4]

[1] Innovative Computing Laboratory, University of Tennessee, Knoxville,
Knoxville , USA
bosilca@icl.utk.edu
[2] Inria, LaBRI, CNRS Univ. Bordeaux , Talence, France
{clement.foyer,emmanuel.jeannot}@inria.fr
[3] Bordeaux INP, Talence, France
guillaume.mercier@bordeaux-inp.fr
[4] Echirolles, France
guillaume.papaure@atos.net

Abstract. As the complexity and diversity of computer hardware and
the elaborateness of network technologies have made the implementation of portable and efficient algorithms more challenging, the need to
understand application communication patterns has become increasingly
relevant. This paper presents details of the design and evaluation of a
communication-monitoring infrastructure developed in the Open MPI
software stack that can expose a dynamically configurable level of detail
concerning application communication patterns.

Keywords: MPI · Monitoring · Communication pattern · Process
placement

1 Introduction

With the expected increase of applications concurrency and input data size, one
of the most important challenges to be addressed in the forthcoming years is
data transfer and locality (i.e., how to improve data accesses and transfers in
the application). Among the various aspects of locality, one issue stems from the
memory and the network. Indeed, the transfer time of data exchanges between
processes of an application depends on both the affinity of the processes and
their location. A thorough analysis of the application's behavior and of the target
underlying execution platform combined with clever algorithms and strategies
have the potential to dramatically improve the application communication time,
making it more efficient and robust in the midst of changing network conditions
(e.g., contention).

The general consensus is that the performance of many existing applications
could benefit from improved data locality [9].

© Springer International Publishing AG 2017
F.F. Rivera et al. (Eds.): Euro-Par 2017, LNCS 10417, pp. 49–62, 2017.
DOI: 10.1007/978-3-319-64203-1_4

Hence, to compute an optimal – or at least an efficient – process placement we need to understand the underlying hardware characteristics (including memory hierarchies and network topology) and how the application processes are exchanging messages. The two inputs of the decision algorithm are therefore the machine topology and the application communication pattern. The machine topology information can be gathered through existing tools or be provided by a management system. Among these tools Netloc/Hwloc [4] provides a (nearly) portable way to abstract the underlying topology as a graph interconnecting the various computing resources. Moreover, the batch scheduler and system tools can provide the list of resources available to the running jobs and their interconnections.

To address the second point and understand the data exchanges between processes, precise information about the application communication patterns is needed. Existing tools are either addressing the issue at a high level and thus failing to provide accurate details, or they are intrusive and deeply embedded in the communication library. To confront these issues, we designed a light and flexible monitoring interface for MPI applications with the following features. First, the need to monitor more than simply two-sided communications interactions in which the source and destination of the message are explicitly invoking an API for each message is becoming prevalent. As such, our monitoring support is capable of extracting information about all types of data transfers: two-sided, one-sided (or remote memory access), and I/O. In the scope of this paper, we will focus our analysis on one- and two-sided communications.

We recorded the number of messages, the sum of message sizes, and the distribution of the sizes between each pair of processes. We also recorded how these messages have been generated by direct user calls via the two-sided API or automatically generated as a result of collective algorithms, a process related to one-sided messages. Second, we provided mechanisms for the MPI applications themselves to access this monitoring information through the MPI tool information interface. This allowed the monitoring—which may involve recording only specific parts of the code or recording only during particular time periods—to be dynamically enabled or disabled, and it gave the ability to introspect the application behavior. Last, the output of this monitoring provides different matrices describing this information for each pair of processes. Such data is available both online (i.e., during the application execution) and off-line (i.e., for the post-mortem analysis and optimization of a subsequent run).

We conducted experiments to assess the overhead of this monitoring infrastructure and to demonstrate its effectiveness as compared with other solutions from the literature.

In Sect. 2 of this paper we present the related work; in Sect. 3, the required background; in Sect. 4, the design; in Sect. 5, the implementation; in Sect. 6, the result; and in Sect. 7, the conclusion.

2 Related Work

Monitoring an MPI application can be achieved in many ways but in general relies on intercepting the MPI API calls and delivering aggregated information. We present here some examples of such tools.

PMPI is a customizable profiling layer that allows tools to intercept MPI calls. Therefore, when a communication routine is called, keeping track of the processes involved and the amount of data exchanged is possible. This approach has drawbacks, however. First, managing MPI datatypes is awkward and requires a conversion at each call. Also, PMPI cannot comprehend some of the most critical data movements, because an MPI collective is eventually implemented by point-to-point communications, and yet the participants in the underlying data exchange pattern cannot be guessed without knowledge of the collective algorithm implementation. A reduce operation is, for instance, often implemented with an asymmetric tree of point-to-point sends/receives in which every process has a different role (i.e., root, intermediary, and leaves). Known examples of stand-alone libraries using PMPI are DUMPI [10] and mpiP [15].

Another tool for analyzing and monitoring MPI programs is Score-P [13]. It is based on different but partially redundant analyzers that have been gathered within a single tool to allow both online and offline analysis.

Score-P relies on MPI wrappers and call-path profiles for online monitoring. Nevertheless, the application monitoring support offered by these tools is kept outside of the library, which means access to the implementation details and the communication pattern of collective operations once decomposed is limited.

PERUSE [12] takes a different approach, in that it allows the application to register callbacks that will be raised at critical moments in the point-to-point request lifetime. This method provides an opportunity to gather information on state-changes inside the MPI library and gain detailed insight on what type of data (i.e., point-to-point or collectives) is exchanged between processes, as well as how and when. This technique has been used in [5,12].

Tools that provide monitoring that is both light and precise (e.g., showing collective communication decomposition) do not exist.

3 Background

The OPEN MPI Project [8] is a comprehensive implementation of the MPI 3.1 standard [7] that was started in 2003 and takes ideas from four earlier institutionally based MPI implementations. OPEN MPI is developed and maintained by a consortium of academic, laboratory, and industry partners and is distributed under a modified BSD open-source license. It supports a wide variety of CPU and network architectures used in HPC systems. It is also the base for a number of commercial MPI offerings from vendors, including Mellanox, Cisco, Fujitsu, Bull, and IBM. The OPEN MPI software is built on the Modular Component Architecture (MCA) [1], which allows for compile or runtime selection of the components used by the MPI library. This modularity enables experiments with new designs, algorithms, and ideas to be explored while fully maintaining functionality and performance. In the context of this study, we take advantage of this functionality to seamlessly interpose our profiling components along with the highly optimized components provided by the stock OPEN MPI version.

MPI Tool Information Interface has been added in the MPI-3 standard [7]. This interface allows the application to configure internal parameters of the MPI library and get access to internal information from the MPI library. In our context, this interface will offer a convenient and flexible way to access the monitored data stored by the implementation and control of the monitoring phases.

Process placement is an optimization strategy that takes into account the affinity of processes (represented by a communication matrix) and the machine topology to decrease the communication costs of an application [9]. Various algorithms to compute such a process placement exist, one being TreeMatch [11] (designed by a subset of the authors of this article). We can distinguish between static process placement, which is computed from traces of previous runs, and dynamic placement computed during the application execution (see the experiments in Sect. 6).

4   Design

Monitoring generates the application communication pattern matrix. The order of the matrix is the number of processes, and each (i, j) entry gives the amount of communication between process i and process j. Monitoring outputs several values and, hence, several matrices: the number of bytes and the number of messages exchanged. Moreover, it distinguishes between point-to-point communications and collective or internal protocol communications.

It is also able to keep track of collective operations after their transition to point-to-point communications. Therefore, monitoring requires interception of the communication inside the MPI library itself instead of relinking weak symbols to a third-party dynamic one, which allows this component to be used in parallel with other profiling tools (e.g., PMPI).

For scalability reasons, we can automatically gather the monitoring data into one file instead of dumping one file per rank.

In summary, we plan to cover a wide spectrum of needs while employing different levels of complexity for various levels of precision. Our design provides an API for each application to enable, disable, or access its own monitoring information. Otherwise, an application can be monitored without any modification of its source code by activating the monitoring components at launch time; results are retrieved when the application completes.

We also supply a set of mechanisms to combine monitored data into communication matrices. They can be used either at the end of the application (when MPI_Finalize is called) or post-mortem. For each pair of processes, a histogram of geometrically increasing message sizes is available.

5 Implementation

The precision required for the results prompted us to implement the solution within the OPEN MPI stack[1]. The component described in this article was developed in a branch of OPEN MPI (available at [14]) and now is available in the development version of OPEN MPI, and on all stable versions after 3.0. Because we were planning to intercept all types of communications—two-sided, one-sided, and collectives—we exposed a minimalistic common API for the profiling as an independent engine and then linked all the MCA components doing the profiling with this engine. Due to the flexibility of the MCA infrastructure, the active components can be configured at runtime either via `mpirun` arguments or via the API (implemented with the MPI Tool Information Interface). All implementation details are available at [3].

To cover the wide range of operations provided by MPI, we added four components to the sofware stack: one in the collective communication layer (COLL), one in the one-sided layer (remote memory accesses, OSC), one in the point-to-point management layer (PML), and one common layer capable of orchestrating the information gathered by the other layers and record data. When activated at launch time (through the `mpiexec` option `--mca pml_monitoring_enable x`), this enable all monitoring components, as indicated by the comma-separated value of x.

The design of OPEN MPI allows for easy distinctions between different types of communication tags, and x allows the user to include or exclude tags related to collective communications or to other internal coordination (these are called internal tags as opposed to external tags, which are available to the user via the MPI API).

Specifically, the PML layer sees communications after collectives have been decomposed into point-to-point operations. COLL and OSC both work at a higher level to be able to record operations that do not go through the PML layer (e.g. when dedicated drivers are used). Therefore, as opposed to the MPI standard profiling interface (`PMPI`) method where the MPI calls are intercepted, we monitored the actual point-to-point calls that are issued by OPEN MPI, which yields much more precise information. For instance, we can infer the underlying topologies and algorithms behind the collective algorithms (e.g. the tree topology used for aggregating values in an `MPI_Reduce` call). However, this comes at the cost of a possible redundant recording of data for collective operations when the data-path goes through the COLL and the PML components[2].

For an application to enable, disable or access its own monitoring, we implemented a set of callback functions using the MPI Tool Information Interface. The functions make knowing the amount of data exchanged between a pair of processes possible at any time and in any part of the applications code. An example of such code is given in Fig. 1. The call to `MPI_T_pvar_get_index` provides

---

[1] A proof-of-concept version of this monitoring has been implemented in MPICH.

[2] Nevertheless, a precise monitoring is still possible with the use of the monitoring API.

the index (e.g., the key) of the performance variable. This variable is allocated and attached to the communicator with a call to MPI_T_pvar_handle_alloc. This starts a monitoring phase that resets the internal monitoring state. Then, an MPI_T session is started with the MPI_T_pvar_start call. When necessary, the monitored values are retrieved with MPI_T_pvar_read. Last, a call to MPI_Allreduce allows each processes to get the maximum of each value.

Furthermore, the final summary dumped at the end of the application gives us a detailed output of the data exchanged between processes for each point-to-point, one-sided, and collective operation. The user is then able to refine the results.

Internally, these components use an internal process identifier (ids) and a single associative array employed to translate sender and receiver ids into their MPI_COMM_WORLD counterparts. Our mechanism is, therefore, oblivious to communicator splitting, merging, or duplication. When a message is sent, the sender updates three arrays: the number of messages, the size (in bytes) sent to the specific receiver, and the message size distribution. Moreover, to distinguish between external and internal tags, one-sided emitted and received messages, and collective operations, we maintain five versions of the first two arrays. Also, the histogram of message sizes distribution is kept for each pair of ids, and goes from 0 byte messages to messages of more than 2^{64} bytes. Therefore, the memory overhead of this component is at maximum 10 arrays of N 64 bits elements, in addition to the N arrays of 66 elements of 64 bits for the histograms, with N being the number of MPI processes. These arrays are lazily allocated, so they exist for a remote process only if communications occur with it.

In addition to the amount of data and the number of messages exchanged between processes, we keep track of the type of collective operations issued on each communicator: one-to-all operations (e.g., MPI_Scatter), all-to-one operations (e.g., MPI_Gather) and all-to-all operations (e.g., MPI_Alltoall). For the first two types of operations, the root process records the total amount of data sent and received respectively and the count of operations of each kind. For all-to-all operations, each process records the total amount of data sent and the count of operations. All these pieces of data can be flushed into files either at the end of the application or when requested through the API.

6   Results

We conducted out the experiments on an Infiniband cluster (HCA: Mellanox Technologies MT26428 (ConnectX IB QDR)). Each node features two INTEL XEON NEHALEM X5550 CPUs with 4 cores (2.66 GHz) per each CPU.

6.1   Overhead Measurement

One of the main issues of monitoring is the potential impact on the application time-to-solution. As our monitoring can be dynamically enabled and disabled, we can compute the upper bound of the overhead by measuring the impact with

```
MPI_T_pvar_handle count_handle;
int count_pvar_idx;
const char count_pvar_name[] = "pml_monitoring_messages_count";
size_t *counts;
int count; /*size of the array*/

/* Retrieve the proper pvar index */
MPI_T_pvar_get_index(count_pvar_name, MPI_T_PVAR_CLASS_SIZE,
                     &count_pvar_idx);

/* Allocating a new PVAR in a session will reset the counters and set count */
MPI_T_pvar_handle_alloc(session, count_pvar_idx, MPI_COMM_WORLD,
                        &count_handle, &count);

counts = (size_t*)malloc(count * sizeof(size_t));

/* start monitoring session */
MPI_T_pvar_start(session, count_handle);

/* Begin communications */
/* [...] */
/* End communications */

/*
   Retrieve the number of messages sent to each
   peer in MPI_COMM_WORLD
*/

/* get the monitored values */
MPI_T_pvar_read(session, count_handle, counts);

/*
   Global reduce so everyone knows the maximum
   messages sent to each rank
*/
MPI_Allreduce(MPI_IN_PLACE, counts, count, MPI_UNSIGNED_LONG,
              MPI_MAX, MPI_COMM_WORLD);

/* Operations on counts */
/* [...] */

free(counts);

MPI_T_pvar_stop(session, count_handle);

MPI_T_pvar_handle_free(session, &count_handle);
```

Fig. 1. Monitoring code snippet.

the monitoring enabled on the entire application. We wrote a micro benchmark that computes the overhead induced by our component for various kinds of MPI functions and measured this overhead for both shared- and distributed-memory cases. The number of processes varies from 2 to 24, and the amount of data ranges from 0 up to 1 MB. Figure 2 displays the results as heatmaps (the median of a thousand measures). Blue nuances correspond to low overhead, and yellow colors to higher overhead. As expected, the overhead was more visible on a shared memory setting, where the cost of the monitoring is more significant compared with the decreasing cost of data transfers. Also, as the overhead is related to the number of messages and not to their content, the overhead decreases as the size of the messages increased. Overall, the median overhead is 4.4% and 2.4% respectively for the shared- and distributed-memory cases, which proves that our monitoring is cost effective.

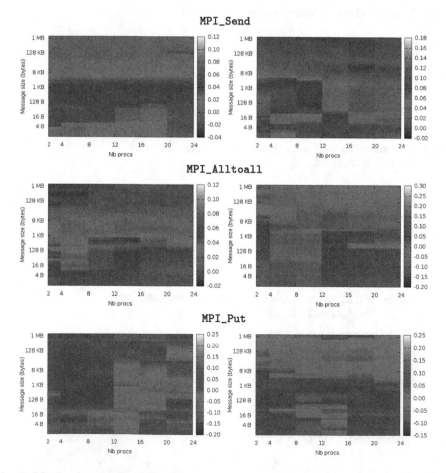

Fig. 2. Monitoring overhead for MPI_Send, MPI_Alltoall and MPI_Put operations. Left: distributed memory, right: shared memory. (Color figure online)

To measure the impact on applications, we used some of the NAS parallel benchmarks—namely BT, CG and LU. These tests have the highest number of MPI calls, and so we chose them to maximize the potential impact of the monitoring on the application. Table 1 shows the results, which are an average of 20 runs. Shaded rows mean that the measures display a statistically significant difference (using the Student's t-Test on the measures) between a monitored run and non-monitored one. Overall, we see that the overhead is consistently below 1% and on average around 0.35%. Interestingly, for the LU kernel, the overhead seems lightly correlated with the message rate, meaning the larger the communication activity, the higher the overhead. For the CG kernel, however, the timings are so small that it is hard to see any influence of this factor beyond measurements noise.

We have also tested the *Minighost* mini-application [2] that computes a stencil in various dimensions to evaluate the overhead. An interesting feature of this

Table 1. Overhead for the BT, CG and LU NAS kernels

Kernel	Class	NP	Monitoring time	Non mon. time	#msg/proc	Overhead	#msg/sec
bt	A	16	6.449	6.443	2436.25	0.09%	6044.35
bt	A	64	1.609	1.604	4853.81	0.31%	193066.5
bt	B	16	27.1285	27.1275	2436.25	0.0%	1436.87
bt	B	64	6.807	6.8005	4853.81	0.1%	45635.96
bt	C	16	114.6285	114.5925	2436.25	0.03%	340.06
bt	C	64	27.23	27.2045	4853.81	0.09%	11408.15
cg	A	16	0.1375	0.1365	1526.25	0.73%	177600.0
cg	A	32	0.103	0.1	2158.66	3.0%	670650.49
cg	A	64	0.087	0.0835	2133.09	4.19%	1569172.41
cg	B	8	11.613	11.622	7487.87	-0.08%	5158.27
cg	B	16	6.7095	6.7675	7241.25	0.03%	17115.0
cg	B	32	3.8015	3.796	10243.66	0.14%	86228.33
cg	B	64	2.5065	2.495	10120.59	0.46%	258415.32
cg	C	32	9.539	9.565	10243.66	-0.27%	34363.87
cg	C	64	6.023	6.0215	10120.59	0.02%	107540.76
lu	A	8	8.5815	8.563	19793.38	0.22%	18452.14
lu	A	16	4.2185	4.2025	23753.44	0.38%	90092.45
lu	A	32	2.233	2.2205	25736.47	0.56%	368816.39
lu	A	64	1.219	1.202	27719.36	1.41%	1455323.22
lu	B	8	35.2885	35.2465	31715.88	0.12%	7190.08
lu	B	16	18.309	18.291	38060.44	0.1%	33260.53
lu	B	32	9.976	9.949	41235.72	0.27%	132271.75
lu	B	64	4.8795	4.839	44410.86	0.84%	582497.18
lu	C	16	72.656	72.5845	60650.44	0.1%	13356.19
lu	C	32	38.3815	38.376	65708.22	0.01%	54783.24
lu	C	64	20.095	20.056	70765.86	0.19%	225380.19

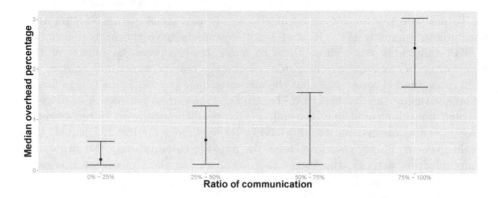

Fig. 3. Minighost application overhead as a function of the communication percentage of the total execution time.

mini-application is that it outputs the percentage of time spent to perform communication. In Fig. 3, we depict the overhead depending on this communication ratio. We ran 114 different executions of the MiniGhost application and split those runs into four range categories depending on the percentage of time spent in communications (0%–25%, 25%–50%, 50%–75% and 75%–100%). A point represents the median overhead (in percent) and the error bars represent the first and third quantile. We see that the median overhead is increasing with the percentage of communication. Indeed, the more time you spend in communication the more visible the overhead for monitoring these communications. However, the overhead accounts for only a small percentage.

6.2   MPI Collective Operations Optimization

In these experiments we have executed an `MPI_Reduce` collective call on 32 and 64 ranks (on 4 and 8 nodes respectively), with a buffer that ranged from 1.10^6 to 2.10^8 integers and a rank of 0 acting as the root. We took advantage of the OPEN MPI infrastructure to block the dynamic selection of the collective algorithm and instead forced the reduce operation to use a binary tree algorithm. Because we monitored the collective communications after they have been broken down into point-to-point communications, we were able to identify details of the collective algorithm implementation and expose the underlying binary tree algorithm (see Fig. 4b). This provided a much more detailed understanding of the underlying communication pattern compared with existing tools, where the use of a higher-level monitoring tool (e.g., PMPI) completely hides the collective algorithm communications. With this pattern, we used the TreeMatch algorithm to compute a new process placement and compared it with the placement obtained using a high-level monitoring method (that does not see the tree and hence is equivalent to the round-robin placement). Results are shown in Fig. 4a. We see that the optimized placement is much more efficient than the

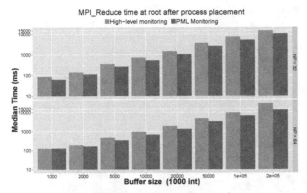

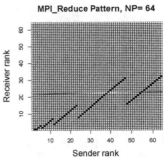

(a) MPI_Reduce (MPI_MAX) walltime (x and y log-scale) for 32 and 64 ranks and various buffer sizes. Process placement based on our PML monitoring vs. high-level monitoring (RR placement)

(b) Communication pattern as seen by our monitoring tool (once the collective communication is decomposed into point-to-point communications).

Fig. 4. MPI_Reduce optimization.

one based on high-level monitoring. For instance with 64 ranks and a buffer of 5.10^6 integers the walltime is 338 ms vs. 470 ms (39% faster).

6.3   Use Case: Fault Tolerance with Online Monitoring

In addition to the usage scenarios mentioned above, the proposed dynamic monitoring tool has been demonstrated in our recent work. In [6] we used the dynamic monitoring feature to compute the communication matrix during the execution of an MPI application. The goal was to perform elastic computations in case of node failures or when new nodes are available. The runtime system migrated MPI processes when the number of computing resources changed. To this end, the authors used the TreeMatch [11] algorithm to recompute the process mapping onto the available resources. The algorithm decides how to move processes based on the applications gathered communication matrix: the more two processes communicate, the closer they are remapped onto the physical resources. Gathering the communication matrix was performed online using the callback routines of the monitoring: such a result would not have been possible without the tool proposed in this paper.

6.4   Static Process Placement of Applications

We tested the TreeMatch algorithm for performing static placement to show that the monitoring provides relevant information allowing execution optimization. To do so, we first monitored the application using the proposed monitoring tool of this paper. Second, we built the communication matrix (here using the number of messages) and then applied the TreeMatch algorithm on this matrix and

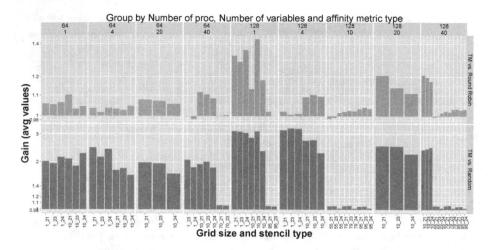

Fig. 5. Average gain of TreeMatch placement vs. Round Robin and random placements for various MiniGhost runs.

the topology of the target architecture. Finally, we re-executed the application using the newly computed mapping. Different settings (kind of stencil, the stencil dimension, number of variables per stencil point, and number of processes) are shown in Fig. 5. We see that the gain is up to 40% when compared with round-robin placement (the standard MPI placement) and 300% against random placement. The decrease of performance is never greater than 2%.

7   Conclusion

Parallel applications tend to use a growing number of computational resources connected via complex communication schemes that naturally diverge from the underlying network topology. Optimizing the performance of applications requires any mismatch between the application communication pattern and the network topology to be identified, and this demands a precise mapping of all data exchanges between the application processes.

In this paper we proposed a new monitoring framework to consistently track all types of data exchanges in MPI applications. We implemented the tool as a set of modular components in OPEN MPI that allow fast and flexible low-level monitoring (with collective operation decomposed to their point-to-point expression) of all types of communications supported by the MPI-3 standard (including one-sided communications and I/O). We also provided an API based on the MPI Tool Information Interface standard for applications to monitor their state dynamically, with a focus on only the critical portions of the code. The basic use of this tool does not require any change in the application nor any special compilation flag. The data gathered can be provided at different granularities, either as communication matrices or as histograms of message sizes. Another significant feature of this tool is that it leaves the PMPI interface available for other usages, allowing additional monitoring of the application using more traditional tools.

Microbenchmarks show that the overhead is minimal for intra-node communications (over shared memory) and barely noticeable for large messages or distributed memory. After being applied to real applications, the overhead remain hardly visible (at most, a few percentage points). Having such a precise and flexible monitoring tool opens the door to dynamic process placement strategies and could lead to highly efficient process placement strategies. Experiments show that this tool enables large gain for dynamic or static cases. The fact that the monitoring records the communication after collective decomposition into point-to-points allows optimizations that were not otherwise possible.

Acknowledgments. This work is partially funded under the ITEA3 COLOC project #13024, and by the USA NSF grant #1339820. The PlaFRIM experimental testbed is being developed with support from Inria, LaBRI, IMB, and other entities: Conseil Régional d'Aquitaine, FeDER, Université de Bordeaux, and CNRS.

References

1. Barrett, B., Squyres, J.M., Lumsdaine, A., Graham, R.L., Bosilca, G.: Analysis of the component architecture overhead in open MPI. In: Martino, B., Kranzlmüller, D., Dongarra, J. (eds.) EuroPVM/MPI 2005. LNCS, vol. 3666, pp. 175 182. Springer, Heidelberg (2005). doi:10.1007/11557265_25
2. Barrett, R.F., Vaughan, C.T., Heroux, M.A.: MiniGhost: a miniapp for exploring boundary exchange strategies using stencil computations in scientific parallel computing. Sandia National Laboratories, Technical report SAND2011-5294832 (2011)
3. Bosilca, G., Foyer, C., Jeannot, E., Mercier, G., Papauré, G.: Online dynamic monitoring of MPI communications: scientific user and developper guide. Research Report RR-9038, Inria Bordeaux Sud-Ouest, March 2017. https://hal.inria.fr/hal-01485243
4. Broquedis, F., Clet-Ortega, J., Moreaud, S., Furmento, N., Goglin, B., Mercier, G., Thibault, S., Namyst, R.: hwloc: a generic framework for managing hardware affinities in HPC applications. In: 2010 18th Euromicro International Conference on Parallel, Distributed and Network-Based Processing (PDP), pp. 180–186. IEEE (2010)
5. Brown, K.A., Domke, J., Matsuoka, S.: Tracing data movements within MPI collectives. In: Proceedings of the 21st European MPI Users' Group Meeting, EuroMPI/ASIA 2014, pp. 117:117–117:118. ACM, New York (2014). http://doi.acm.org/10.1145/2642769.2642789
6. Cores, I., Gonzalez, P., Jeannot, E., Martín, M., Rodriguez, G.: An application-level solution for the dynamic reconfiguration of MPI applications. In: 12th International Meeting on High Performance Computing for Computational Science (VECPAR 2016), Porto, Portugal, June 2016 (to appear)
7. Forum, M.P.I.: MPI: A Message-Passing Interface Standard. http://www.mpi-forum.org/

8. Gabriel, E., et al.: Open MPI: goals, concept, and design of a next generation MPI implementation. In: Kranzlmüller, D., Kacsuk, P., Dongarra, J. (eds.) EuroPVM/MPI 2004. LNCS, vol. 3241, pp. 97–104. Springer, Heidelberg (2004). doi:10.1007/978-3-540-30218-6_19

9. Hoefler, T., Jeannot, E., Mercier, G.: An overview of topology mapping algorithms and techniques in high-performance computing. In: High-Performance Computing on Complex Environments, pp. 73–94 (2014)

10. Janssen, C.L., Adalsteinsson, H., Cranford, S., Kenny, J.P., Pinar, A., Evensky, D.A., Mayo, J.: A simulator for large-scale parallel computer architectures. In: Technology Integration Advancements in Distributed Systems and Computing, p. 179 (2012)

11. Jeannot, E., Mercier, G., Tessier, F.: Process placement in multicore clusters: algorithmic issues and practical techniques. IEEE Trans. Parallel Distrib. Syst. **25**(4), 993–1002 (2014)

12. Keller, R., Bosilca, G., Fagg, G., Resch, M., Dongarra, J.J.: Implementation and usage of the PERUSE-interface in open MPI. In: Mohr, B., Träff, J.L., Worringen, J., Dongarra, J. (eds.) EuroPVM/MPI 2006. LNCS, vol. 4192, pp. 347–355. Springer, Heidelberg (2006). doi:10.1007/11846802_48

13. Knüpfer, A., et al.: Score-P: a joint performance measurement run-time infrastructure for Periscope, Scalasca, TAU, and Vampir. In: Brunst, H., Müller, M., Nagel, W., Resch, M. (eds.) Tools for High Performance Computing 2011, pp. 79–91. Springer, Heidelberg (2012). doi:10.1007/978-3-642-31476-6_7

14. Open MPI development repository. https://github.com/open-mpi/ompi

15. Vetter, J.S., McCracken, M.O.: Statistical scalability analysis of communication operations in distributed applications. In: ACM SIGPLAN Notices, vol. 36, pp. 123–132. ACM (2001)

Performance and Power Modeling, Prediction and Evaluation

Micro-benchmarking MPI Neighborhood Collective Operations

Felix Donatus Lübbe[(✉)]

Research Group for Parallel Computing, TU Wien, Vienna, Austria
luebbe@par.tuwien.ac.at

Abstract. In this article, performance expectations for MPI neighborhood collective operations are formulated as *self-consistent performance guidelines*. A microbenchmark and an experimental methodology are presented to assess these guidelines. Measurement results from a large, InfiniBand-based cluster, the Vienna Scientific Cluster (VSC), as well as from a small commodity cluster computer are shown and discussed to illustrate the methodology and to gain first insights into the performance of current MPI implementations. Results show that the examined libraries seem to be sensitive to the order in which topological neighbors are specified, and that in some cases Cartesian topologies can be outperformed by simulating them with distributed graph topologies.

Keywords: MPI · Process topology · Neighborhood collectives · Performance guidelines · Benchmarking

1 Problem Statement

Neighborhood collective operations have been introduced to the MPI standard in version 3.0 [5]. Not only could they simplify the code of, for example, multidimensional stencil computations, but also offer a performance benefit over naive handwritten exchange algorithms using `MPI_Send` and `MPI_Recv`.

So far no microbenchmarks are available to assess the performance of MPI neighborhood collectives on virtual topologies. Intel MPI Benchmarks 2017[1], OSU Micro-Benchmarks 5.3.2[2] and SKaMPI 5.0.4[3] [6] do not offer such functionality at all. While NBCBench 1.1[4] [2] can measure LibNBC's nonblocking neighborhood Alltoall(v) algorithms, it has not been extended and used to measure the corresponding MPI operations. Further, the used neighborhood is built using the deprecated operation `MPI_Graph_create`. The only parameter available for topology construction is the number of neighbors per process. The structure of the neighborhood can not be varied further.

---

[1] https://software.intel.com/en-us/articles/intel-mpi-benchmarks, last checked 2017-05-26.

[2] http://mvapich.cse.ohio-state.edu/benchmarks/, last checked 2017-05-26.

[3] http://liinwww.ira.uka.de/~skampi/, last checked 2017-05-26.

[4] http://htor.inf.ethz.ch/research/nbcoll/perf/, last checked 2017-05-26.

© Springer International Publishing AG 2017
F.F. Rivera et al. (Eds.): Euro-Par 2017, LNCS 10417, pp. 65–78, 2017.
DOI: 10.1007/978-3-319-64203-1_5

In [9] a microbenchmark has been used to compare the durations of a new family of sparse collective operations, which work on isomorphic neighborhoods, to those of the corresponding MPI neighborhood collectives. However, while the MPI operations served as a baseline to explicate performance expectations for the new operations, no expectations for the MPI functions have been formulated and assessed there.

In this article, performance expectations for MPI neighborhood collective operations, as well as for the topology creation functions `MPI_Cart_create`, `MPI_Dist_graph_create` and `MPI_Dist_graph_create_adjacent` are motivated and semiformalized using the concept of self-consistent performance guidelines [7]. A microbenchmark based on the one used in [9] is described in detail, which is able to semiautomatically assess these guidelines and generate plots of violations, partly using the concepts presented in [4]. Setup and results of first measurements on two different cluster computers, as well as the assessment of a subset of the presented guidelines are shown to illustrate the methodology and to gain first insights into the performance of current MPI libraries.

Section 2 describes performance guidelines for neighborhood collectives and topology creation functions. In Sect. 3 the benchmark is introduced. Section 4 details the experimental setup of the measurements carried out. The results of the experiments are shown and analyzed in Sect. 5. Section 6 concludes the article.

2   Performance Guidelines for Neighborhood Collectives

Self-consistent performance guidelines are a means to express performance expectations for MPI in a semiformal way by relating the durations of different (combinations of) MPI operations which yield the same effect. Since the MPI standard does not impose any performance requirements, the guidelines are argued for on the basis of self-evident user expectations, which are represented by a set of metarules in [7].

A guideline of the form $a \preceq b$ means that operation a shall not be slower than operation b, given all common parameters of both operations are equal [7]. Accordingly, $a \approx b$ means a and b shall perform similar. The relation is required to hold in the average case for many runs, while isolated counterexamples possibly due to lazy initialization or disturbing factors during the measurement are not considered a violation. If $a \preceq b$ is violated, performance would increase if the user replaced a with b in the violating scenario.

In this section, the following performance guidelines will be motivated:

$$\text{Cart\_create} \preceq \text{Dist\_graph\_create\_adjacent}_{\text{Cart}} \quad \text{(GL1)}$$

$$\text{Dist\_graph\_create\_adjacent} \preceq \text{Dist\_graph\_create} \quad \text{(GL2)}$$

$$\text{X\_create}_{\text{reorder=0}} \preceq \text{X\_create}_{\text{reorder=1}} \quad \text{(GL3)}$$

$$\text{Neigh\_allgather(v)} \preceq \text{Neigh\_alltoall(v)} \quad \text{(GL4)}$$

$$\texttt{Neigh\_allgather} \preceq \texttt{Neigh\_allgatherv} \tag{GL5}$$

$$\texttt{Neigh\_alltoall} \preceq \texttt{Neigh\_alltoallv}$$
$$\preceq \texttt{Neigh\_alltoallw} \tag{GL6}$$

$$\texttt{Allgather(v)}_{\text{full}} \preceq \texttt{Neigh\_allgather(v)}_{\text{full}} \tag{GL7}$$

$$\texttt{Alltoall(v/w)}_{\text{full}} \preceq \texttt{Neigh\_alltoall(v/w)}_{\text{full}} \tag{GL8}$$

$$\texttt{Neigh\_x}_{\text{Cart}} \preceq \texttt{Neigh\_x}_{\text{Graph\_adj(Cart)}} \tag{GL9}$$

$$\texttt{Neigh\_x}_{\text{Graph\_adj}} \approx \texttt{Neigh\_x}_{\text{Graph}} \tag{GL10}$$

$$\texttt{Neigh\_x}_{\text{rank list ordering 1}} \approx \texttt{Neigh\_x}_{\text{rank list ordering 2}} \tag{GL11}$$

$$\texttt{Neigh\_x}_{\text{reorder=1}} \preceq \texttt{Neigh\_x}_{\text{reorder=0}} \tag{GL12}$$

GL1 states that if a Cartesian-shaped topology is constructed, the specialized `MPI_Cart_create` should not be slower than `MPI_Dist_graph_create_adjacent`, which can construct topologies of arbitrary shape (cf. metarule 3).

A `DISTGRAPH` topology can be created either by `MPI_Dist_graph_create` or by `MPI_Dist_graph_create_adjacent`. While in a call to `MPI_Dist_graph_create` every process may specify an arbitrary set of edges of the topology graph, `MPI_Dist_graph_create_adjacent` imposes the precondition that every process passes exactly its incident edges. Because of this additional requirement, `MPI_Dist_graph_create_adjacent` shall not be slower (GL2, cf. metarule 2).

GL3 asserts that allowing a topology constructor to change the mapping of rank numbers to actual processes by setting the reorder flag to 1 should not speed up the actual creation, since reordering would be beneficial for subsequent communication operations on the topology and disabling it is, from a performance point of view, only reasonable to save extra cost during communicator creation.

`MPI_Neighbor_allgather` could be mimicked by `MPI_Neighbor_alltoall`, if the send buffer is copied locally n times, and should therefore not be slower. The same is true for the respective vector variants (GL4). `MPI_Neighbor_allgatherv` and `MPI_Neighbor_alltoallv/-w` can mimic their regular counterparts, which should therefore not be slower (GL5, GL6, cf. metarule 3).

The neighborhood collectives can be used to simulate the global collectives `MPI_Allgather(v)` and `MPI_Alltoall(v/w)`, if a fully connected graph topology is created. While neighborhood collectives support any topology, global collectives always follow a complete graph and because of this specialization should not be slower (GL7, 8, cf. metarule 3).

If a Cartesian-shaped topology is created using one of the distributed graph constructors, neighborhood collectives should not get faster compared to the semantically stricter Cartesian topology created by `MPI_Cart_create` (GL9, cf. metarule 2). However, their performance for any `DISTGRAPH` topology should be independent of the constructor, because `DISTGRAPH` constructors produce semantically equivalent topologies (GL10).

GL11 states that neighborhood collectives should perform similar on isomorphic topologies, independent of the ordering of the list of ranks passed to the topology constructor to define edges. If this was not respected by an MPI library, the user would be tempted to find the "sweet" ordering herself, possibly breaking performance portability between libraries. If the implementations of the neighborhood collectives of a specific library had such sweet orderings, the topology constructor should reorder its input lists accordingly.

Allowing the ranks to be reordered during communicator creation shall not slow down any neighborhood collective since the whole point with reordering is optimizing communication performance (GL12).

3   The Benchmark

The microbenchmark used for the experiments comprises a kernel executing the actual measurements and a framework of scripts responsible for control flow, input generation and output analysis. It makes use of findings from [3,4,9].

The main goal of the benchmark is to help identify performance problems of MPI implementations in specific environments. Although some decision metrics are defined to enable automatically finding violations of performance guidelines, the quantification of a violation is of less interest than the fact that a violation has been found. While the question for the severeness of a certain violation might uncover sensational answers, it will not help much solving it, except maybe to set priorities for which one to tackle first. In fact, investigating its cause by, for example, looking into algorithms and parameters of the MPI implementation is the step meant to follow the use of the benchmark.

3.1   Kernel

The kernel implements *measurement setups* for different MPI operations, following the form of Algorithm 1. All input parameters are read from a CSV input file with each line describing one experiment. Apart from the parameters specific to the topology and explained below, an experiment description includes the communication operation to use, the MPI datatype, the message length, the number of consecutive repetitions n_{rep} and a 64-bit integer w which is decremented down to 0 in a loop written in inline assembler to accurately simulate local computation of specific CPU time when measuring the overlap of nonblocking operations.

The synchronization is implemented as a handwritten dissemination barrier like in [9] to improve comparability between different MPI implementations, which might use different algorithms for their MPI_Barrier. MPI_Wtime is used to retrieve wall clock time with high resolution. The maximum duration of all parallel processes is output as the result time $\Delta t[i]$ of each single repetition i.

Currently, four different types of neighborhoods are supported, three of which can be described using a similar mask of relative coordinates for each process and a mapping of process ranks to a virtual Cartesian grid of variable dimensionality: The *Cartesian* neighborhood just uses the MPI_Cart_create topology constructor, giving the simplest form of a multidimensional isomorphic neighborhood by only including the two immediate neighbors along each dimension

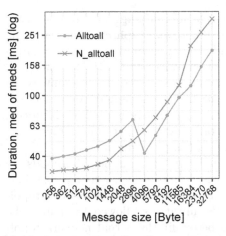

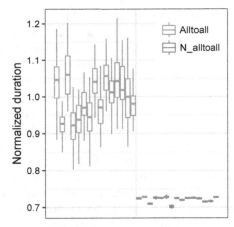

(a) Absolute durations for all message sizes, accumulated over all runs.

(b) Box plot of durations in individual runs for message size 2896 B, normalized to median of medians of `Alltoall`. Boxes mark quartiles, whiskers the total range of durations.

Fig. 1. Results comparing `Alltoall` to `Neigh_alltoall`, campaign full-rand-jupiter, 35×16 processes, Full neighborhood with `RAND` ordering and `reorder` = 0, outliers removed.

Algorithm 1. Measurement procedure in the kernel

---

  for all experiment descriptions in input file **do**
    Create topology communicator
    for $i = 0$ to $n_{\mathrm{rep}} - 1$ **do**
      Barrier synchronization
      $t_0 \leftarrow$ `Wtime`
      `MPI_(I)Neighbor_X`
      Simulate work: Count from w down to 0
      (`MPI_Wait`)
      $\Delta t[i] \leftarrow$ `Wtime` $- t_0$
      Barrier synchronization
    end for
    Free topology communicator
    `MPI_Reduce`($\Delta t[]$, length i, maximum, to rank 0)
    Output $\Delta t[]$ at rank 0
  end for

---

in the Cartesian grid. The *Moore* neighborhood of radius r, on the other hand, includes all ranks in the grid within a hypercube with edges of length $2r + 1$ around the process. The *von Neumann* neighborhood of radius r is a subset of the Moore neighborhood, including only those ranks with relative coordinates c with a Manhattan distance $\leq r$ from the process, i.e. $\sum_{i=1}^{n_{\mathrm{dim}}} |c_i| \leq r$.

The communicators for Moore and von Neumann neighborhoods are constructed using `MPI_Dist_graph_create` or `MPI_Dist_graph_create_adjacent`. The relative coordinates are computed and then translated to a list of source- and destination ranks respectively using an intermediate Cartesian communicator and `MPI_Cart_rank`. The list of source ranks is coordinatewise inverse to the list of destination ranks. `MPI_Dist_graph_create_adjacent` constructs the topology using both lists. In case `MPI_Dist_graph_create` is used, each process only passes its destination list, leaving the ordering of any internal processwise source list within the communicator to the MPI implementation.

Input parameters for Cartesian, Moore and von Neumann neighborhoods are the number of dimensions n_{dim}, the number of finite dimensions n_{fin}, i.e. how many of the dimensions are nontoroidal, and the `reorder` flag of the MPI topology constructor specifying whether the MPI library is allowed to change the mapping of rank numbers to processes to better fit the actual network topology and accelerate communication. This flag does not affect the intermediate Cartesian communicator used to construct Moore and von Neumann neighborhoods, whose `reorder` flag is always set to 0.

Further parameters for Moore and von Neumann neighborhoods include the radius r and the ordering of the list of relative coordinates before translation to rank numbers. Possible orderings are first- and last-coordinate-major (FMAJ, LMAJ) and randomized (RAND). FMAJ (LMAJ) means coordinatewise sorted in ascending order with first (last) coordinate changing last. RAND means the list is permuted using a different random seed for each process.

The dimensions of the Cartesian grid in case of Cartesian, Moore and von Neumann neighborhoods are calculated using the `TUW_Dims_create` function implementing the algorithm described in [8], as the result of `MPI_Dims_create` has proven to break portability between MPI libraries in the past.

The fourth neighborhood type, the *Full* neighborhood, connects all processes in a complete graph, i.e. every process is neighbor of all other processes. Like with Moore and von Neumann neighborhoods, it can be selected whether `MPI_Dist_-graph_create` or `MPI_Dist_graph_create_adjacent` is used as the constructor. Input parameters further include the reordering flag and the ordering of the sources- and destinations list. `LINEAR` ordering means all rank numbers starting from the process itself are enumerated incrementally (sources) and decrementally (destinations) modulo the total number of processes. `RAND` ordering means both sources and destinations array are randomized independently and with a different random seed for each process. If `MPI_Dist_graph_create` is used, only the destinations array is passed.

3.2   Framework Scripts

Control flow of a measurement campaign is programmed in bash scripts, which offer an immediate way to automatize calling programs and manage input- and output files. The work flow to run a measurement campaign is semiautomatized by encapsulating five user-invoked steps: (1) building the kernel, (2) creating input files and job scripts, (3) submitting the job scripts to the scheduling system, (4) archiving the results, (5) analyzing results for performance guideline violations and drawing plots of detected violations.

The files to configure a measurement campaign include a *campaign configuration* file, in which a list of process deployments is specified, e.g. $[2 \times 8, 4 \times 8]$ for 2 and 4 nodes with 8 processes each. The number of distinct calls to the kernel, n_{run}, is set, as well as a maximum run time, after which the scheduler will kill the job. A separate *environment configuration* is referenced, containing all machine specific settings like paths and the syntax of the mpirun command.

The input to the kernel, i.e. the actual experiments carried out, is generated in step (2) using a Python script, which makes modelling all kinds of relations between different input parameters easy, e.g. "for all n_{dim} create experiments with $n_{\mathrm{fin}} \in \{0, 1, \ldots, n_{\mathrm{dim}}\}$". For each run of the kernel, a separate input file is created with a different random permutation of the same set of experiments to mitigate systematic bias by disturbing factors.

Processing results and assessing the guidelines is done in an R script in step (5). Some assessment configuration needs to be set up by the user: all parameters of the campaign must be subdivided into a *guideline parameter*, a *varied parameter* and *grouping parameters*. The guideline parameter contains the levels to be compared within a guideline – if Neigh_allgather and Neigh_alltoall are to be compared, the guideline parameter would be the *measurement setup*. A list of guidelines of the form $a \preceq b$, with a, b being levels of the selected guideline parameter, must be provided. The varied parameter will be on the x axis of subsequently generated plots and could, for example, be the message size. All remaining parameters, e.g., neighborhood type, n_{dim}, n_{fin}, ..., are considered grouping parameters, with every combination of their levels implying a unique group. For each group containing at least one violation, plots will be generated. The script must be rerun for every different guideline parameter.

The script will first calculate the median $m_l^r := \mathrm{med}(\mathrm{dropOutliers}(\Delta t_l^r[0], \ldots, \Delta t_l^r[n_{\mathrm{rep}} - 1]))$ of the n_{rep} single durations of each run r and each combination of parameter levels l after filtering outliers. This results in n_{run} medians $m_l^0, \ldots, m_l^{n_{\mathrm{run}}-1}$ for each combination of parameter levels l. Outliers are values outside of $[q_1 - 1.5(q_3 - q_1), q_3 + 1.5(q_3 - q_1)]$, with quartiles q_1, q_3, like suggested by Tukey [1, Subsect. 3.2.4].

For each guideline $a \preceq b$ and each unique combination of the grouping parameters and the varied parameter, the n_{run} medians for a and b are selected. The Wilcoxon rank sum test is then carried out to test whether the medians of a are shifted to the right of b [1,4, Subsect. 7.4.6]. Further, the *violation ratio* $v := \frac{\mathrm{med}(m_a^0, \ldots, m_a^{n_{\mathrm{run}}-1})}{\mathrm{med}(m_b^0, \ldots, m_b^{n_{\mathrm{run}}-1})}$ is computed to quantify the difference between a and b. $a \preceq b$ is considered violated for the selected parameter levels, if $v \geq v_{\mathrm{thres}}$ and the test returns a p-value $\leq p_{\mathrm{thres}}$. $p_{\mathrm{thres}}, v_{\mathrm{thres}}$ are set by the user. The threshold for v filters very small violations considered significant by the statistical test.

For each violation, an *overview plot* of the affected group is created, which shows the medians of the medians of the result times for both parameter levels a, b in absolute numbers on a log scale, with the varied parameter, e.g. the message size, on the x axis. Further, for each violation, a *focus plot* is generated, which shows the distributions of the raw results within the individual runs as box plots, normalized to the median of the medians of the durations of a. Figures 1a and 2a give examples for overview plots, Figs. 1b and 2b for focus plots.

4   Experimental Setup

Five measurement campaigns on two different cluster computers have been carried out to assess a subset of the formulated guidelines (see Table 2). In the *nbhcoll* campaigns, neighborhood collective operations have been executed on Cartesian topologies, as well as on von Neumann and Moore neighborhoods of radius 1, which could all be used in real-world applications performing stencil computations [9]. In the *full* campaigns, a complete graph is used as topology, making the neighborhood collectives behave like their global collective counterparts, which have been measured here as well. Campaigns *full-rand-jupiter* and *full-tuned-jupiter* have been set up and executed because of findings from *full-jupiter*; see Sect. 5 for details.

The von Neumann neighborhood of radius 1 exactly resembles a Cartesian topology; the subsequently used notation `Cart` $\preceq$ `Vneum` refers to GL9. GL11 is tested by comparing neighbor list orderings `FMAJ` and `LMAJ` (nbhcoll) or `LINEAR` (full) to `RAND`. The term `reorder=1` $\preceq$ `reorder=0` refers to GL12.

Table 2 lists all parameters of the executed experiments together with the parameter levels used in the respective campaigns. For example, in campaign nbhcoll-jupiter, the two operations `Neigh_allgather` and `Neigh_alltoall` have each been measured with 15 different message sizes, on three different topologies, with four different numbers of dimensions, two different values for the number of finite dimensions, three different orderings of the list of neighbors in case of von Neumann and Moore neighborhoods (Cartesian topologies do not have an ordering), and both possible values for the reorder flag during communicator creation. This makes a total of 3360 unique combinations of parameter levels, which are experimentally measured $n_{rep} = 50$ times in each of $n_{run} = 30$ runs. If, for example, the guideline `Neigh_allgather` $\preceq$ `Neigh_alltoall` is evaluated, i.e. the *measurement setup* is chosen as the guideline parameter, the statistical test is executed for the $\frac{3360}{2} = 1680$ unique combinations of the remaining parameter levels. Since the varied parameter is the message size, results are presented in $\frac{1680}{15} = 112$ groups.

The first system, Jupiter, has 36 nodes with two AMD Opteron 6134 8-core processors at 2.3 GHz and 32 GB memory each, connected via a Mellanox MT4036 InfiniBand QDR crossbar switch. The second system is VSC3 at the Vienna Scientific Cluster, consisting of 2020 nodes with two Intel Xeon E5-2650v2 8-core processors at 2.6 GHz and 64 GB memory each. The nodes are connected by an InfiniBand QDR-80 fat tree architecture. On Jupiter, both nodes and network links involved in the measurements were dedicated to the benchmark. On VSC3, only the nodes were dedicated, while network switches were possibly shared with other jobs. The benchmark has been compiled and run using gcc 4.4.7 and Open MPI 2.0.1 on Jupiter and gcc 5.3.0 and Intel MPI 2017.1 on VSC3.

The dimensions of the virtual Cartesian grid of processes for the different process deployments and number of dimensions in the nbhcoll campaigns are listed in Table 1.

Table 1. Dimensions array returned by `TUW_Dims_create` for different n_{dim} and n_{procs}.

n_{dim}	Process deployment		
	10×16	20×16	35×16
2	$\{16, 10\}$	$\{20, 16\}$	$\{28, 20\}$
3	$\{8, 5, 4\}$	$\{8, 8, 5\}$	$\{10, 8, 7\}$
4	$\{5, 4, 4, 2\}$	$\{5, 4, 4, 4\}$	$\{7, 5, 4, 4\}$

5 Results

Table 3 lists the numbers of violations of different guidelines for the nbhcoll campaigns on Jupiter and VSC3. Each cell contains two rows: first, the total numbers of violations and tests, second the numbers of groups containing at least one violation as well as the total number of groups. In a group, all parameters are similar except the message length (varied parameter) and the respective guideline parameter. The threshold values for the assessment are set to $p_{\mathrm{thres}} = 0.001$ and $v_{\mathrm{thres}} = 1.03$. Different thresholds have been tried, but for higher p-values and lower violation ratios, violations were often not clearly visible in the plots.

In the nbhcoll campaigns, the guideline `Neigh_allgather` $\preceq$ `Neigh_alltoall` was only violated for the smaller numbers of processes. On Jupiter, violations occurred for $n_{\mathrm{dim}} \in \{2, 4\}$ and $n_{\mathrm{fin}} = 0$, on all three neighborhoods, for all orderings of the neighborhood coordinates, with ratios up to 1.049. The two violations on VSC3 occurred with a fourdimensional Moore neighborhood, $n_{\mathrm{fin}} = 4$, LMAJ ordering, `reorder` $\in \{0, 1\}$ and a message size of 4 KB. Their exceptionally high ratio of about 13.8 each stems from a peculiar effect observed on VSC3 for different measurements: the relative dispersion of many runs is in the same order of magnitude like the violation ratio, with the quartiles of many runs spanning from the median of medians of the `Neigh_allgather` times to the median of medians of the `Neigh_alltoall` times. Usually, dispersion was much lower, like in the figures from Jupiter in this article. Unfortunately, due to time restrictions, this effect could not be investigated further for this article. The measurements should be rerun with a different node allocation to eliminate a possible interdependency between node allocation, virtual topology and communication algorithm. Note that temporary network effects can already be excluded as a cause due to the randomization of experiments.

Table 2. Measurement campaigns referenced in this article.

	nbhcoll-jupiter	nbhcoll-vsc3	full-jupiter	full-rand-jupiter	full-tuned-jupiter
n_{run}	30	15	15	15	15
n_{rep}	50	50	50	50	50
Measurement setups	Neigh_allgather Neigh_alltoall	Neigh_allgather Neigh_alltoall	Neigh_allgather Neigh_alltoall Allgather Alltoall	Neigh_alltoall Alltoall	Neigh_alltoall Alltoall
Message sizes	256 B, 362 B, 512 B, . . . , 32 KiB (factor $\sqrt{2}$ between sizes)				
Neighborhoods	Cartesian v.Neum.* Moore* *$r = 1$, using Dist_graph_create_adjacent	Cartesian v.Neum.* Moore*	Full using Dist_graph_create_ adjacent	Full using Dist_graph_create_ adjacent	Full using Dist_graph_create_ adjacent
n_{dim}	1, 2, 3, 4	1, 2, 3, 4	—	—	—
n_{fin}	0, n_{dim}	0, n_{dim}	—	—	—
Order of adj.list (Moore, v.Neum., Full)	FMAJ LMAJ RAND	FMAJ LMAJ RAND	LINEAR only Neigh_*: RAND	RAND	LINEAR RAND
Reorder	0, 1	0, 1	0, 1	0	0
Open MPI MCA Parameters	default	—	default	default	coll_tuned_use_dynamic_ rules=true, coll_tuned_alltoall_ intermediate_msg=256

On Jupiter, the guideline Cart $\preceq$ Vneum has been violated only with four-dimensional neighborhoods, while the violation ratio did not exceed 1.045. On VSC3, most violations happened for $n_{dim} = 4$ as well, including the most severe ones with ratios up to 1.222. For 35×16, violations occurred only with $n_{dim} = 4$, for 20×16 with $n_{dim} \in \{3, 4\}$, and for 10×16 even with $n_{dim} \in \{2, 3, 4\}$.

The guideline FMAJ $\preceq$ RAND was violated only by Moore neighborhoods with $n_{dim} \in \{2, 3, 4\}$ on Jupiter, with a ratio of up to 1.147. LMAJ $\preceq$ RAND was violated by both Moore and von Neumann neighborhoods, but only for $n_{dim} = 4, n_{fin} = 0$ and 10×16 processes. Moore neighborhoods yielded a ratio of up to 1.206. On VSC3, violations of both guidelines occurred for all values of the grouping parameters. The biggest ratio observed in all experiments, 141.9, occurred for FMAJ $\preceq$ RAND, Neigh_alltoall, a Moore neighborhood with $n_{dim} = 2, n_{fin} = 2$, independent of reordering and for a message size of 11585 B. This enormous ratio was due to the same effect on VSC3 mentioned above. However, most of the other reported violations did not suffer from this effect.

The only guideline violated in campaign full-jupiter was LINEAR $\preceq$ RAND and most violations were quite clear. Top ratios increased with number of processes from 1.083 (10×16) to 1.828 (35×16). While for 10×16 processes, only the smaller message sizes up to 1448 B were affected, for 30×16 processes violations occurred in the whole spectrum of the message sizes used.

In the full-jupiter campaign, to save time, the global collectives were only executed on topologies with LINEAR ordering because ordering was assumed to make no difference for them. Since the architecture of the benchmark only allows for the levels of one parameter being compared to each other, with all other parameters being the same, comparing neighborhood collectives with RAND orderings to global collectives was not possible in this campaign. However, the fact that the guideline LINEAR $\preceq$ RAND was violated so often together with the observation of Alltoall and Neigh_alltoall performing similar with LINEAR ordering for small message sizes lead to the assumption that Alltoall $\preceq$ Neigh_alltoall could be violated on full RAND topologies. Therefore, campaign full-rand-jupiter was set up and executed, and indeed showed the expected violations for small message sizes (cf. Fig. 1).

A closer look into Open MPI revealed that the algorithm for Alltoall is changed by default at a message size of 3000 B. The so called *MCA parameters* allow to change such thresholds at runtime. In the campaign full-tuned-jupiter, the violations could be healed by setting the threshold message size to 256 B (cf. Fig. 2). In the case of LINEAR ordering, Alltoall now was considerably faster than Neigh_alltoall as well.

In the three campaigns nbhcoll-jupiter, nbhcoll-vsc3 and full-jupiter, the reorder=1 $\preceq$ reorder=0 guideline was never violated and the reordering flag did not seem to have an effect on violations of the other guidelines (cf. Tables 3 and 4). Subsequent experiments just creating the topologies used in the campaigns with reordering enabled and checking for a change in process-to-rank mapping in the new communicator confirmed this conjecture. Campaigns full-rand-jupiter and full-tuned-jupiter have therefore been set up with reordering disabled in general.

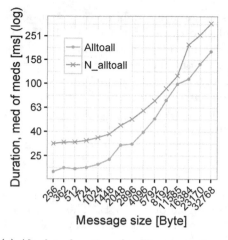
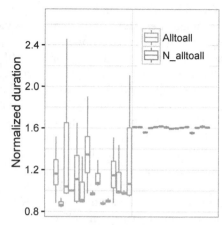

(a) Absolute durations for all message sizes, accumulated over all runs.

(b) Box plot of durations in individual runs for message size 2896 B, normalized to median of medians of `Alltoall`. Boxes mark quartiles, whiskers the total range of durations.

Fig. 2. Results comparing `Alltoall` to `Neigh_alltoall`, campaign full-tuned-jupiter, 35×16 processes, Full neighborhood with `RAND` ordering and `reorder` $= 0$, outliers removed.

Table 3. Number of guideline violations in experiments with different neighborhoods of radius 1 on Jupiter and VSC3. Format: $n_{\text{vioTests}}/n_{\text{tests}}$ ($n_{\text{vioGroups}}/n_{\text{groups}}$).

	nbhcoll-jupiter			nbhcoll-vsc3		
	10×16	20×16	35×16	10×16	20×16	35×16
Neigh_allgather $\preceq$ Neigh_alltoall	15/1680 (15/112)	1/1680 (1/112)	0/1680 (0/112)	2/1680 (2/112)	0/1680 (0/112)	0/1680 (0/112)
Cart $\preceq$ Vneum	19/480 (8/32)	2/480 (2/32)	1/480 (1/32)	117/480 (20/32)	36/480 (13/32)	9/480 (7/32)
FMAJ $\preceq$ RAND	81/960 (16/64)	118/960 (20/64)	104/960 (14/64)	87/960 (36/64)	276/960 (36/64)	25/960 (13/64)
LMAJ $\preceq$ RAND	27/960 (7/64)	0/960 (0/64)	0/960 (0/64)	198/960 (33/64)	208/960 (35/64)	14/960 (13/64)
reorder=1 $\preceq$ reorder=0	0/1680 (0/112)	0/1680 (0/112)	0/1680 (0/112)	0/1680 (0/112)	0/1680 (0/112)	0/1680 (0/112)

Table 4. Number of guideline violations in campaign full-jupiter. Format: $n_{\text{vioTests}}/n_{\text{tests}}$ $(n_{\text{vioGroups}}/n_{\text{groups}})$.

	Full-jupiter		
	10×16	20×16	35×16
Allgather $\preceq$ Neigh_allgather	0/30 (0/2)	0/30 (0/2)	0/30 (0/2)
Alltoall $\preceq$ Neigh_alltoall	0/30 (0/2)	0/30 (0/2)	0/30 (0/2)
Neigh_allgather $\preceq$ Neigh_alltoall	0/60 (0/4)	0/60 (0/4)	0/60 (0/4)
LINEAR $\preceq$ RAND	22/60 (4/4)	30/60 (4/4)	50/60 (4/4)
reorder=1 $\preceq$ reorder=0	0/90 (0/6)	0/90 (0/6)	0/90 (0/6)

6   Conclusion and Outlook

Performance guidelines help to express expectations for neighborhood collectives in a formal way, to enable computers to automatically check them on a large number of measurements. Results show that current MPI implementations probably have room for improvement of their performance, although admittedly, not every violation can easily be attributed to the MPI implementation in the complex environment of a cluster computer without further investigation. Still, especially the cases where simulating a Cartesian with a similar DISTGRAPH topology increases performance are surprising, since algorithms could benefit from the fixed structure of Cartesian topologies. This, together with the violations of GL11, suggests that the examined MPI implementations are sensitive to the ordering of neighbors.

In the future it would be interesting to execute similar campaigns on further cluster computers, especially such with a network topology resembling a Cartesian grid. Measuring with bigger neighborhoods could be interesting as well, although the question arises whether there are problems from the real world which would be affected by the results. Of course, the remaining guidelines formulated, but not evaluated in this article should be tested – especially those dealing with different methods of communicator creation. Since some MPI implementations nowadays promise true asynchronous progress, guidelines for nonblocking neighborhood collectives should be formulated and assessed as well.

Acknowledgments. This work was supported by the Austrian Science Fund (FWF): P25530. The author would like to thank Alexandra Carpen-Amarie, Sascha Hunold, Jesper Larsson Träff and Thomas Worsch for helpful discussions concerning this article, as well as the anonymous reviewers for their valuable feedback.

References

1. Hedderich, J., Sachs, L.: Angewandte Statistik, 15th edn. Springer Spektrum, Heidelberg (2016)
2. Hoefler, T., Lumsdaine, A., Rehm, W.: Implementation and performance analysis of non-blocking collective operations for MPI. In: Proceedings of 2007 International Conference on High Performance Computing, Networking, Storage and Analysis, SC 2007. IEEE Computer Society/ACM, November 2007
3. Hunold, S., Carpen-Amarie, A.: Reproducible MPI benchmarking is still not as easy as you think. IEEE Trans. Parallel Distrib. Syst. **27**(12), 3617–3630 (2016). http://dx.doi.org/10.1109/TPDS.2016.2539167
4. Hunold, S., Carpen-Amarie, A., Lübbe, F.D., Träff, J.L.: Automatic verification of self-consistent MPI performance guidelines. In: Dutot, P.-F., Trystram, D. (eds.) Euro-Par 2016. LNCS, vol. 9833, pp. 433–446. Springer, Cham (2016). doi:10.1007/978-3-319-43659-3_32
5. MPI Forum: MPI: a message-passing interface standard, version 3.0, September 2012
6. Reussner, R.H., Sanders, P., Träff, J.L.: SKaMPI: a comprehensive benchmark for public benchmarking of MPI. Sci. Program. **10**(1), 55–65 (2002). http://content.iospress.com/articles/scientific-programming/spr00094
7. Träff, J.L., Gropp, W.D., Thakur, R.: Self-consistent MPI performance guidelines. IEEE Trans. Parallel Distrib. Syst. **21**(5), 698–709 (2010). http://dx.doi.org/10.1109/TPDS.2009.120
8. Träff, J.L., Lübbe, F.D.: Specification guideline violations by MPI_Dims_create. In: Proceedings of 22nd European MPI Users' Group Meeting, EuroMPI 2015, 21–23 September 2015, Bordeaux, France, pp. 19:1–19:2 (2015). http://doi.acm.org/10.1145/2802658.2802677
9. Träff, J.L., Lübbe, F.D., Rougier, A., Hunold, S.: Isomorphic, sparse MPI-like collective communication operations for parallel stencil computations. In: Proceedings of 22nd European MPI Users' Group Meeting, EuroMPI 2015, 21–23 September 2015, Bordeaux, France, pp. 10:1–10:10 (2015). http://doi.acm.org/10.1145/2802658.2802663

Performance Characterization of De Novo Genome Assembly on Leading Parallel Systems

Marquita Ellis[1,2(✉)], Evangelos Georganas[1,2,5], Rob Egan[3], Steven Hofmeyr[2], Aydın Buluç[1,2], Brandon Cook[4], Leonid Oliker[2], and Katherine Yelick[1,2]

[1] EECS Department, University of California, Berkeley, USA
mme@eecs.berkeley.edu
[2] Computational Research Division, Lawrence Berkeley National Laboratory, Berkeley, USA
[3] Joint Genome Institute, Lawrence Berkeley National Laboratory, Berkeley, USA
[4] National Energy Research Scientific Computing Center, Berkeley, USA
[5] Parallel Computing Lab, Intel Corp., Santa Clara, USA

Abstract. De novo genome assembly is one of the most important and challenging computational problems in modern genomics; further, it shares algorithms and communication patterns important to other graph analytic and irregular applications. Unlike simulations, it has no floating point arithmetic and is dominated by small memory transactions within and between computing nodes. In this work, we focus on the highly scalable HipMer assembler and identify the dominant algorithms and communication patterns, also using microbenchmarks to capture the workload. We evaluate HipMer on a variety of platforms from the latest HPC systems to ethernet clusters. HipMer performs well on all single node systems, including the Xeon Phi manycore architecture. Given large enough problems, it also demonstrates excellent scaling across nodes in an HPC system, but requires a high speed network with low overhead and high injection rates. Our results shed light on the architectural features that are most important for achieving good parallel efficiency on this and related problems.

1 Introduction

De novo genome assembly is essential to understanding the genomic structure of plants, animals and microbial communities and has applications in health, the environment, and energy. It involves constructing long genomic sequences from short, overlapping and possibly erroneous DNA fragments produced by modern sequencers. Due to the continued exponential increase in the size (multi-terabyte) and complexity of the sequence datasets, massive parallelism is required to overcome the huge memory and computational requirements, but efficient parallelization is challenging. The genome assembly computation, not unlike other graph analytic and irregular applications, involves graphs and hash tables and is dominated by irregular memory access patterns and fine-grained synchronization. Many assemblers therefore target shared memory hardware, where assembly problems are limited in size and may run for days or even weeks.

© Springer International Publishing AG 2017
F.F. Rivera et al. (Eds.): Euro-Par 2017, LNCS 10417, pp. 79–91, 2017.
DOI: 10.1007/978-3-319-64203-1_6

In this study we present the first cross-architectural analysis of HipMer [8], an extreme scale distributed memory genome assembler. HipMer produces biologically equivalent results to a serial assembler called Meraculous [3], which has been exhaustively studied for quality and found to excel relative to other assemblers in most metrics [6]. Our HipMer performance evaluation includes a broad range of platforms, ranging from a supercomputer with Intel Xeon Phi processors and a custom HPC network to off-the-shelf Ethernet clusters. HipMer stresses the communication fabric of these systems using communication patterns that are increasingly important for irregular applications. These include all-to-all exchanges, fine-grained lookups, and global atomic operations. Our work presents a detailed analysis of these communication patterns and points to requirements for future architectural designs for scalability on this important class of codes.

2   The Parallel HipMer Assembly Pipeline

In this section we describe the basic algorithms used in the pipeline, our parallelization strategy, and the consequent communication patterns. Although we focus on HipMer, the algorithms are relevant to all *de novo* assembly pipelines that are based on de Bruijn graphs [14]. We describe four major stages of Hipmer (see Fig. 1-Left), *k-mer analysis, contig generation, read-to-contig alignment* and *scaffolding*, as well as *gap closing*, which is part of the scaffolding stage. Other stages implemented in HipMer assist these main computations and are included in the experimental results. The input to the pipeline is a set of *reads*, which are short, erroneous sequence fragments of 100–250 letters sampled at random from a genome. The sampling is redundant at a depth of coverage d, so on average each position (base) in the genome is covered by d reads. This redundancy is used to filter out errors in the first stage (k-mer analysis). The k-mer analysis can work with relatively high error rates in the data (2.5%, $k = 40+$); the user may also choose to decrease k when given data with higher error rates. Sequencers produce reads in pairs with a known distance between them, a fact which is exploited later in the pipeline (scaffolding) to improve the assembly.

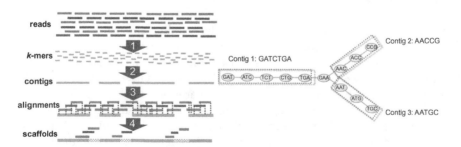

Fig. 1. Left: the HipMer de novo assembly pipeline. Right: a de Bruijn graph of k-mers with $k = 3$.

2.1 k-mer Analysis

In this step, the input reads are processed to exclude errors. Each processor reads a portion of the reads and chops them into k-*mers*, which are formed by a sliding window of length k. A deterministic function is used to map each k-mer to a target processor, assigning all the occurrences of a particular k-mer to the same processor, thus eliminating the need for a global hash table. The k-mers are communicated among the processors using **irregular all-to-all communication**, which is performed when each processor fills up out of its outgoing buffers and is repeated until all k-mers have been redistributed. A total of $\Theta(\frac{Gd}{L}(L-k+1))$ k-mers need to be communicated, where G is the genome size (number of characters in the output) and L is the read length (number of characters in the input). Next, all the k-mers are counted, and those that appear fewer times than a threshold are discarded as erroneous. This filtering is enabled by the redundancy d in the read data set: k-mers that appear close to d times are likely error-free, whereas k-mers that appear infrequently are likely erroneous. k-mer counting is challenging for large datasets because an error in just a single base creates k erroneous k-mers, and it is not uncommon to have over 80% of all distinct k-mers erroneous; as a result the memory footprint increases substantially. We address this problem [10] through the use of Bloom filters, which results in irregular all-to-all communication. Also, highly complex plant genomes, such as wheat, are extremely repetitive and it is not uncommon to see some k-mers occurring millions of times. Such high frequency k-mers create a significant load imbalance problem, since the processors assigned to high-frequency k-mers require significantly more memory and processing times. We deal with these "heavy hitters" using a streaming algorithm, described further in [8] that does not require any

Table 1. Major communication operations in the HipMer pipeline. G is the genome size, L is the read length L, d is the coverage, a is the average number of contigs that each read aligns onto (with $a < L - k + 1$), and γ is the fraction of reads that are not assembled into contigs.

Stage	Communication pattern	Volume of data
k-mer analysis	All-to-all exchange	$\Theta(Gd \cdot (L - k + 1)/L)$
Contig generation	All-to-all exchange	$\Theta(G)$
	Irregular lookups	$\Theta(G)$
	Global atomics	$\Theta(G)$
Sequence alignment	All-to-all exchange	$\Theta(G)$
	Irregular lookups	$\Theta(Gd \cdot a)$
Scaffolding	All-to-all exchange	$\Theta(G)$
	Irregular lookups	$\Theta(G)$
	Global atomics	$\Theta(dG/L \cdot e^{-d})$
Gap closing	All-to-all exchange	$\Theta(\gamma Gd/L)$
	Irregular lookups	$\Theta(\gamma Gd/L)$

additional communication since it is merged into the initialization of the Bloom filters. Additionally, for each k-mer, the *extensions* are recorded: these are the two left and right neighboring bases in the original reads. If multiple extensions occur, the most likely one is used; if there is no obvious agreement then none is recorded. The result of k-mer analysis is a set of k-mers and their extensions that with high probability include no errors. This set contains $\Theta(G)$ k-mers, and is a compressed representation of the original read dataset because multiple occurrences of a k-mer have been collapsed to a single instance.

2.2 Contig Generation

The k-mers are assembled into longer sequences called *contigs*, which are error-free (with high probability) sequences that are typically longer than the original reads. In HipMer, Contig generation utilizes a de Bruijn graph, which is a special graph that represents overlaps in sequences. The k-mers are the vertices in the graph and two k-mers are connected by an edge if they overlap by $k-1$ consecutive bases and have corresponding extensions that are compatible (see Fig. 1-Right for a de Bruijn graph example with $k=3$).

A hash table is used to store a compact representation of the graph: A vertex (k-mer) is a key in the hash table and the incident vertices are stored implicitly as a two-letter code [ACGT][ACGT] that indicates the unique bases that immediately precede and follow the k-mer in the read dataset. By combining the key and the two-letter code, the neighboring vertices in the graph can be identified. These graphs can require terabytes of memory for storing large genomes (e.g. pine or wheat [4]), and traditionally have required specialized, very large shared-memory machines. We overcome this limitation by employing the global address space of Unified Parallel C [11] (UPC) in order to transparently store the hash table in distributed memory, thereby utilizing the memory of many individual machines in a unified address space.

During the parallel hash table construction, the input k-mers are hashed and sent to the proper (potentially remote) bucket of the hash table by leveraging the one-sided communication capabilities of UPC. We avoid fine-grained communication and excessive locking on the hash table buckets with a dynamic aggregation algorithm [10]. This algorithm dynamically aggregates the k-mers in batches before they are sent to the appropriate processors. The pattern here is similar to k-mer analysis but is done asynchronously, where a single processor will send an aggregation of remote hash table inserts without waiting for other processors. Unlike k-mer analysis, the total number of k-mers that have to be communicated is $\Theta(G)$, since multiple occurrences of k-mers have been collapsed during the k-mer analysis stage and this condensed k-mer set has size proportional to the genome size.

The resulting de Bruijn subgraph is traversed in parallel to identify the connected components, which are linear chains of k-mers, since we have excluded all the vertices that do not have unique neighbors in both directions. Traditional parallelization strategies of the traversal would not scale to large concurrencies due to the size and shape of this high diameter graph (extremely long chains).

First, the de Bruijn subgraph is sparse (e.g. for human the de Bruijn graph would be a $3 \cdot 10^9 \times 3 \cdot 10^9$ adjacency matrix with 2–8 eight non-zeros per row). Second, the de Bruijn graph has also extremely high diameter (the connected components in theory can have size up to the length of chromosomes, which is order tens of millions of bases). In our specialized parallel traversal algorithm [10], a processor P_i chooses a random k-mer as seed and initializes with it a new subcontig. Then P_i attempts to extend the subcontig towards both of its endpoints by performing **lookups** for the neighboring vertices in the distributed hash table. The extending process continues until no more new edges can be found, or there are forks in the graph (e.g. the vertex GAA in Fig. 1-Right represents a fork). The access pattern in the distributed hash table consists of **irregular, fine-grained lookup** operations. If two processors work on the same connected component (i.e. both selected seed k-mers from the same contig), race conditions are avoided via a lightweight synchronization scheme [10] based on **remote atomics** and we have proved that our synchronization scheme scales to massive concurrencies (thousands of compute nodes). The parallel traversal is terminated when all the connected components in the de Bruijn graph are explored. Since the size of the de Bruijn graph is proportional to the genome size, the traversal involves accessing $\Theta(G)$ vertices via atomics and irregular lookup operations.

2.3   Read-to-Contig Sequence Alignment

For the alignment phase, we do not use alternative aligners, because, unlike other aligners, HipMer's parallel alignment scales to extreme concurrencies. It also outputs all possible alignments, rather than a pruned subset, as input to the scaffolding phase. HipMer's alignment phase [9] maps the original reads onto the contigs to provide information about the relative ordering and orientation of the contigs, which is used in the final step of the assembly pipeline. First, each processor stores a distinct subset of the contigs in the global address space so that any other processor can access them. Then, substrings of length k, called *seeds*, are extracted in parallel from the contigs and stored in the seed index, which is a distributed hash table. Although seeds are conceptually the same as k-mers, the value of k may be different than in earlier phases, and have a somewhat different purpose. Each hash table entry has a seed as the key and a pointer to the corresponding source contig as the value. There are $\Theta(G)$ seeds in total, because the contigs constitute a fragmented version of the genome. The seed index is constructed via an irregular **all-to-all communication** step similar to the hash table construction in the contig generation phase. The seed index is then used to align reads onto contigs. Each read of length L contains $L - k + 1$ seeds of length k. For each seed s in a read, a **fine-grained lookup** in the global seed index produces a set of candidate contigs that contain s. Although an exhaustive lookup of all possible seeds would require a total of $\Theta(\frac{Gd}{L}(L - k + 1))$ lookups, in practice we perform $\Theta(\frac{Gd}{L} \cdot a)$ lookups where $a < L - k + 1$, through the use of optimizations that identify properties in the contigs during the seed index construction [9]. Finally, after locating a candidate contig that has a matching seed with the read under consideration, the Smith-Waterman algorithm [17] is executed in order to perform local sequence alignment between the contig and the read. The output of this stage is a set of reads-to-contig alignments.

2.4   Scaffolding and Gap Closing

The scaffolding step aims to "stitch" together contigs into sequences called *scaffolds* by assessing the paired-end information from the reads and the reads-to-contigs alignments. Figure 2(a) shows three pairs of reads that map onto the same pair of contigs i and j, creating a link that connects contigs i and j. A graph of contigs can be created by generating links for all the contigs that are supported by pairs of reads (see Fig. 2(b)). The contig graph is stored in a distributed hash table, which requires **irregular all-to-all communication** for construction. The graph of contigs (and consequently the number of links among them) is orders of magnitude smaller that the k-mer de Bruijn graph because the connected components in the k-mer graph are contracted to single vertices in the contig-graph. According to the Lander-Waterman statistics [5], the expected number of contigs is $\Theta(dG/L \cdot e^{-d})$. A parallel traversal of the contig graph is then performed to identify and remove "bubbles", which are localized structures involving divergent paths. This requires **irregular lookups** and **global atomics**. A final traversal is done by selecting start vertices in order of decreasing contig length (this heuristic tries to first stitch together "long" contigs) and therefore it is inherently serial. At smaller scales, this will not have much of an impact since the contig graph is relatively small compared to the k-mer graph. At larger scales, the serial component will become the bottleneck. It is likely that there will be gaps between the contigs within a scaffold (see Fig. 2(b)). An attempt is made to close these gaps using the read-to-contig alignments, which are processed in parallel and projected into the gaps. A distributed hash table is used to localize the unassembled reads onto the appropriate gaps. Construction of the table uses an **irregular all-to-all communication** pattern, but accessing the information in the table requires **irregular lookups**. Assuming that a fraction γ of the genome is not assembled into contigs, this communication step involves $\Theta(\gamma Gd/L)$ reads. Finally, the gaps are divided into subsets and each set is processed by a separate thread, in a parallel phase. The localized reads are used to attempt to close the gaps via a mini-assembly algorithm (an algorithm that performs only k-mer analysis and contig generation on a strict subset of the reads). The outcome of this step is a set of scaffolds (possibly with some remaining gaps), constituting the result of the HipMer assembly pipeline. For simplicity, we do not go into further detail on HipMer's algorithms for diploid assembly.

2.5   Summary of Communication Patterns

Table 1 summarizes the main communication patterns along with the corresponding volume of communication for each stage. These communications patterns govern the efficiency of the parallel pipeline at large scale, where most of the stages are communication bound. The different communication patterns

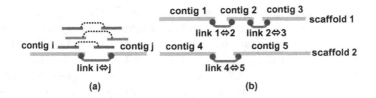

Fig. 2. (a) A link between contigs i and j that is supported by three read pairs. (b) Two scaffolds formed by traversing a graph of contigs.

have, however, vastly different overheads. For example, the all-to-all communication exchange is typically bounded by the bisection bandwidth of the system, assuming that the partial messages are large enough and there is enough concurrency to saturate the available bandwidth. Conversely, fine-grained, irregular lookups and global atomics are typically latency-bound. Although conventional wisdom would suggest that these sorts of communication patterns are prohibitive for distributed memory systems, we have shown that HipMer can strong scale effectively [7], because there are fewer communication operations on the critical path as concurrency increases.

3 Experimental Results and Analysis

Our experiments are conducted on 5 computing platforms, including the Cori II Cray XC40 and Edison Cray XC30 supercomputers at NERSC, the Cray XK7 MPP at the Oak Ridge National Lab (CPU only), the Genepool heterogenous Mellanox InfiniBand NERSC cluster, and an Ethernet Cluster consisting of 3 SunFire x4600 servers networked via 1 Gb shared switch as well as 10 Gb fiber optic patch. Architectural details are presented in Table 2.

For the experimental evaluation, we used 2 datasets. The first dataset, referred to as *chr14*, consists of 36.5 million paired-end reads from the fragment

Table 2. Evaluated platforms. *128 byte Get message latency in microseconds. †Using the optimal number of cores per node. ‡Measured over approx. 2K cores or maximum (128 for ethernet cluster). §MB/s with 8 K message sizes. $^{\alpha}$CPU nodes only

Processor	Cori II Cray XC40	Edison Cray XC30	Titan Cray XK7$^{\alpha}$	Genepool	Ethernet cluster
	Intel Xeon-Phi (Knights Landing)	Intel Xeon (Ivy Bridge)	AMD Opteron 16-Core	Intel Xeon (Haswell)	AMD Opteron 8376 HE
Freq (GHz)	1.4	2.4	2.2	2.3	2.3
Cores/node	68	24	16	32	32
Intranode LAT$^{\dagger *}$	3.3	0.8	1.1	2.7	0.6
BW/node $^{\dagger \ddagger \S}$	57.3	436.2	99.2	113.0	1.2
Memory (GB)	96	64	32	256	512
Network and topology	Aries Dragonfly	Aries Dragonfly	Gemini 3D Torus	Infiniband Mellanox	Ethernet 1 Gb and 10 Gb

library of human chromosome 14, also used in the GAGE [15] evaluation. The reads are 101 bp (base pair) in length and the fragment library has mean insert size 155 bp. This relatively small dataset will be used to investigate the single node performance and scalability at small scales. The second dataset, referred as *human*, is a member of the CEU HapMap population (identifier NA12878) sequenced by the Broad Institute. The genome contains 3.2 Gbp assembled from 2.9 billion reads, which are 101 bp in length, from a paired-end insert library with mean insert size 395 bp. This dataset which is two orders of magnitude bigger than *chr14* will be used for the evaluation of the pipeline at larger scales, although it is still relatively small compared to the genome size of some plants and microbial communities.

3.1   Single-Node Performance Analysis

First, we examine the on-node scalability of HipMer on Cori II (our largest multicore node with 68 cores). HipMer attains perfect single node scaling (see Fig. 3) between 1 and 68 threads (1 thread per core) on the *chr14* dataset (37,609.7 s on a single thread and 556.5 s on 68 threads, yielding a 67.6× speedup). If we enable hyper-threading and use 2 threads per core on 64 cores, we observe a reduction in the execution time by 19%. If we further use 4 threads per core we observe an additional 3% reduction in the execution time. These results suggest that hyper-threading can help on a single node. However, our benchmarking revealed that the increased concurrency due to hyper-threading on a single node affects severely the efficiency of the off-node communication operations. Therefore we configure all the experiments in this paper with 1 thread per core (no hyper-threading).

Figure 4 displays the total runtime per stage on the *chr14* dataset for one and two nodes of each machine utilizing all cores. For now, we consider only the performance bars that correspond to the single node experiments. Examining single node total runtimes, shows that the ratio between the slowest (Titan, AMD

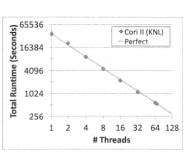

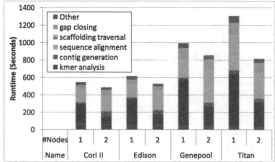

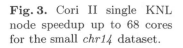

Fig. 3. Cori II single KNL node speedup up to 68 cores for the small *chr14* dataset.

Fig. 4. Cross-architecture single-node and two-node performance by stages.

Opteron) and fastest (Cori II, Intel KNL) systems is a factor of 2.4×. Across architectures, each stage of the pipeline takes similar portion of the respective total execution time. The most time consuming part is k-mer analysis, followed by the sequence alignment stage, confirming our analysis in Sect. 2.

These results also highlight the idiosyncrasies of the genome assembly workload; it does not include any arithmetic computations, instead it heavily relies on irregular memory accesses and string and integer operations. As such, the modern trends in multicore processor design with wider vectors accommodating higher arithmetic throughput do not result in substantial performance improvements (e.g. the single node Cori II execution is only slightly faster than the single node Edison experiment). Efficient vectorization of the key string computations can increase performance, but the major improvements on a single node come from the increased concurrency/parallelism and the ability of the memory subsystem to facilitate concurrent irregular memory accesses. At the same time, the simpler core design in conjunction with the decreased clock frequency results in worse *single core* performance for Knights Landing compared to the other processors.

3.2   Scalability from Single Node to Multiple Nodes

Having examined HipMer's single node performance, we now examine how it scales to multiple nodes, again using the *chr14* dataset - one small enough for single nodes. Figure 4 shows the performance difference by stage as we scale from 1 to 2 nodes. For all machines, we observe speedups well under 2×. The speedup is between 1.12× and 1.18× for Cori II, Edison, and Genepool. Titan has the highest speedup at 1.6×; however note, in absolute runtime, its single node performance is 2.1× slower than Edison's (for example), and due to its relatively limited on-node memory and parallelism (see Table 2), it has the most to benefit from additional node resources. Its relative internode latency is also a significant factor, as we will discuss momentarily. The Ethernet Cluster, ran for 810 s on a single node and with either a 1 Gb or a 10 Gb interconnect, actually has a 18.2× and 10.6× slowdown respectively (not shown due to scale).

This behavior is justified via a detailed analysis of each stage. The k-mer analysis step typically is computation bound because its communication involves efficient collective all-to-all exchanges with large messages (see Table 1) which effectively utilizes the available bandwidth. For example, on 2 Cori II nodes, 6% of the k-mer analysis time is spent in communication, and we observe almost linear scaling of the k-mer analysis step. On the other hand, the sequence alignment step does not speedup and in some cases actually slows down. The communication pattern necessitated in the alignment stage consists of irregular, fine-grained lookups implemented with *get* operations. Such operations are latency bound and their efficiency depends on the underlying machine/network. Consequently, we expect the alignment phase to be communication bound. For example, the *get* latency for small messages on a fully occupied Edison node is 0.75 μs, while the average latency for two nodes is 2.39 μs (measured via microbenchmarks). We refer to "average" latency in the latter case because, under such a setting, half the *get* operations are expected to result in on-node communication and the remaining in off-node communication. Note, the number of lookups on the critical path can be calculated from the number of reads assigned to each processor. Even though the number of threads is increased by a factor of two and the number of irregular lookups on the critical path is decreased by a factor of two, each of those operations is 3.2× more expensive, eventually yielding larger overall communication time in the alignment step. However, on Titan the respective *get* latencies for small messages are 1.10 μs for a single node and 1.79 μs for 2 nodes. As a result we expect a speedup in the alignment phase, which is confirmed in Fig. 4. The same scaling argument holds for the remaining parallel algorithms that rely on fine-grained irregular lookups and atomics (see Table 1). For a description of the microbenchmarks used, see [7]; we were not able to include our microbenchmarking data for all machines due to space limitations.

Figure 5 shows the strong scaling results for all machines on the *chr14* dataset. Efficiency (the y axis) is calculated as $T_1/(T_p \cdot p)$ where T_1 is the total runtime on a single node, p is the number of nodes (x axis), and T_p is the total runtime on p nodes. From 1 to 2 nodes, Cori II, Edison, and Genepool's efficiencies decrease down to 55–60%. This behavior is explained in the previous paragraph. As we scale from 2 to 8 nodes, the respective parallel efficiencies drop at most by 26%. At this range of node counts most of the irregular accesses in the parallel algorithms are off-node and as such the efficiency levels should remain the same as we strong scale. This is the regime where we can observe good strong scaling. Titan has the smallest parallel efficiency decrease between 1 and 2 nodes (20%), but it is still the most significant decrease in its series (which continues to decrease roughly by 10% as the number of nodes doubles). While its relative efficiency is higher than other machines, its absolute runtime is much worse, and improves significantly with more memory and compute cores (hence, higher speedups, as discussed in the previous section). The Ethernet Cluster drops in efficiency by 95% or more from 1 to 2 nodes; because the Ethernet cluster has only 3 nodes, we do not present further data. These trends show that parallelizing the computation across some minimum number of nodes is necessary to overcome the overhead incurred by internode communication. This minimum number is dependent on the network and node characteristics. Beyond this minimum number, the application can scale efficiently to large number of nodes. We emphasize here that for realistically large datasets, one might have to use multiple nodes to acquire the necessary aggregate memory. In such scenarios the baseline performance is of that of multiple nodes and as such the strong scaling efficiency is even better as we will see in the next subsection.

Another interesting feature in the data presented in Fig. 5, is the cross-over in efficiency between Edison and Cori II at 64 nodes. Between 1 and 32 nodes, the two machines maintain relatively close levels of efficiency (≤4% difference). At 64 nodes onwards, Edison maintains a higher level of efficiency by roughly 10%. The key factors here are the higher core count of the Cori II nodes (64 versus 24 on Edison nodes) and the relatively small size of the dataset. At 64 nodes, the workload is parallelized over 4 K cores on Cori II, while Edison has

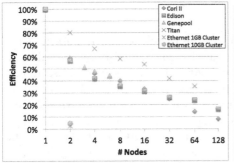
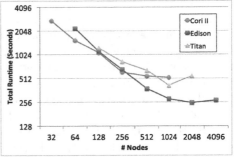

Fig. 5. Strong scaling efficiency for the small *chr14* dataset

Fig. 6. Execution time for the *human* dataset

1.5 K cores at that same node count. Because the data set is relatively small, at the concurrency of 4 K cores, Cori II lacks sufficient work per thread that can be efficiently parallelized, especially during the scaffolding and gapclosing phases.

3.3   Large Scale Experimental Results

Finally, we present results from running HipMer at scale on the *human* dataset. In Fig. 6, we show the total runtime of the pipeline (y axis) over the number of nodes (x axis) for Cori II, Edison, and Titan. Not shown are the Ethernet Cluster results, which ran for 22.56 h on a single node and on two nodes took approximately 280 h and 161 h on the 1 Gb and 10 Gb interconnects respectively a 12.4× and 7.1× slowdown. Genepool results are also not shown since sufficiently many nodes for this data set were not reservable.

The first thing to observe is the different node count that constitutes the baseline for each machine. Since the memory requirement of the *human* dataset, and the communication data structures for its effective distribution are quite large, we need at least 32, 64, and 128 nodes on Cori II, Edison, and Titan, respectively, to obtain the minimum required aggregate memory (approximately 4TB, see Table 2). On Cori II we scale up to 512 nodes (32,768 cores) with 47% strong scaling efficiency, on Edison up to 1,024 nodes (24,576 cores) with 49% efficiency and on Titan up to 1024 nodes (16,384 cores) with 37% efficiency. After these levels of parallelism, the parallel efficiency drops substantially because the work per thread is not sufficient. Other factors influencing the pipeline's scalability is the serial traversal in the scaffolding step and the initial I/O overhead to load the input data. As the scale increases, the percentage of the total runtime spent in the serial scaffolding traversal also increases. For example, on Cori II at 512 nodes 29% of the total execution time is spent in the serial part of the scaffolding while the corresponding serial component takes only 4% of the overall execution time at 32 nodes.

4   Related Work

Our performance study in this paper captures the workload of other assemblers, and here we described the most closely related ones that also use distributed memory parallelism. Ray [2] is an end-to-end parallel *de novo* genome assembler that utilizes MPI and exhibits strong scaling up to a modest number of nodes. It produces both contigs and scaffolds directly from raw sequencing reads. One drawback of Ray is the lack of parallel I/O support for reading and writing files. ABySS [16] was the first *de novo* assembler written in MPI that also exhibits strong scaling. Unfortunately, only the first assembly step of contig generation is fully parallelized with MPI, and the subsequent scaffolding steps must be performed on a single shared memory node. Spaler [1] is a contig generating assembler based on Spark and GraphX. Results from Spaler have been given for our smaller data set, *chr14*, and it shows good scaling. PASHA [12] is another partly MPI based de Bruijn graph assembler, though not all steps are fully parallelized as its algorithm, like ABySS, requires a large-memory single node for the last scaffolding stages. SWAP 2 [13] is a parallelized MPI based de Bruijn assembler that has been shown to assemble contigs efficiently for the human genome, however it does not provide parallel scaffolding modules.

5   Conclusion

This work presents a cross-architectural evaluation of large-scale genome assembly, a first study of its kind. The algorithms described in Sect. 2, are relevant for all *de novo* assembly pipelines based on de Bruijn graphs [14], and is characterized by a workload dominated by fine-grained irregular memory accesses, with no floating point arithmetic. Nonetheless, as shown in Sect. 3, HipMer attains both excellent single node and distributed multinode scalability. We identified the key computation and communication patterns, and associated architecture and network characteristics, for achieving such effective scalability; namely all-to-all exchanges (bisection bandwidth bounded), fine-grained irregular lookups and global atomics (latency bounded). Further, we find the key to on-node scalability for this type of workload is the available concurrency *coupled* with the memory subsystems' performance. We expect that these insights will help impact future implementations of irregularly structured parallel methods and the underlying architectural designs targeting these classes of computations.

Acknowledgments. All authors at Lawrence Berkeley National Laboratory (LBNL) were supported by Department of Energy (DOE) Offices of Advanced Scientific Computing Research (ASCR) and Biological and Environmental Research (BER), both under contract number DE-AC02-05CH11231. This includes funding to BER's Joint Genome Institute, the ASCR-funded Exascale Computing Project, and the ASCR Mathematics and Computer Science Research Programs. This word used resources of ASCR's National Energy Research Scientific Computing Center (NERSC) under the same LBNL contract and ASCR's Oak Ridge Leadership Facility (OLCF) under Contract No. DE-AC05-00OR22725.

References

1. Abu-Doleh, A., Catalyurek, U.V.: Spaler: Spark and GraphX based de novo genome assembler. In: 2015 IEEE International Conference on Big Data (Big Data), October 2015
2. Boisvert, S., Laviolette, F., Corbeil, J.: Ray: simultaneous assembly of reads from a mix of high-throughput sequencing technologies. J. Comput. Biol. **17**(11), 1519–1533 (2010)
3. Chapman, J.A., Ho, I., Sunkara, S., Luo, S., Schroth, G.P., Rokhsar, D.S.: Meraculous: de novo genome assembly with short paired-end reads. PLoS ONE **6**(8), e23501 (2011)
4. Chapman, J.A., Mascher, M., Buluç, A., Barry, K., Georganas, E., Session, A., Strnadova, V., Jenkins, J., Sehgal, S., Oliker, L., Schmutz, J., Yelick, K.A., Scholz, U., Waugh, R., Poland, J.A., Muehlbauer, G.J., Stein, N., Rokhsar, D.S.: A whole-genome shotgun approach for assembling and anchoring the hexaploid bread wheat genome. Genome Biol. **16**, 26 (2015)
5. Deonier, R.C., Tavaré, S., Waterman, M.: Computational Genome Analysis: An Introduction. Springer Science & Business Media, New York (2005). doi:10.1007/0-387-28807-4
6. Earl, D., Bradnam, K., St John, J., Darling, A., et al.: Assemblathon 1: a competitive assessment of de novo short read assembly methods. Genome Res. **21**(12), 2224–2241 (2011)
7. Georganas, E.: Scalable parallel algorithms for genome analysis. Ph.D. thesis, EECS Department, University of California, Berkeley (2016)
8. Georganas, E., Buluç, A., Chapman, J., Hofmeyr, S., Aluru, C., Egan, R., Oliker, L., Rokhsar, D., Yelick, K.: HipMer: an extreme-scale de novo genome assembler. In: International Conference for High Performance Computing, Networking, Storage and Analysis (SC 2015) (2015)
9. Georganas, E., Buluç, A., Chapman, J., Oliker, L., Rokhsar, D., Yelick, K.: merAligner: a fully parallel sequence aligner. In: Proceedings of the IPDPS (2015)
10. Georganas, E., Buluç, A., Chapman, J., Oliker, L., Rokhsar, D., Yelick, K.: Parallel de Bruijn graph construction and traversal for de novo genome assembly. In: Proceedings of the International Conference for High Performance Computing, Networking, Storage and Analysis (SC 2014) (2014)
11. Husbands, P., Iancu, C., Yelick, K.: A performance analysis of the Berkeley UPC compiler. In: Proceedings of International Conference on Supercomputing, ICS 2003, pp. 63–73. ACM, New York (2003)
12. Liu, Y., Schmidt, B., Maskell, D.L.: Parallelized short read assembly of large genomes using de Bruijn graphs. BMC Bioinform. **12**(1), 354 (2011)
13. Meng, J., Seo, S., Balaji, P., Wei, Y., Wang, B., Feng, S.: Swap-assembler 2: optimization of de novo genome assembler at extreme scale. In: 45th International Conference on Parallel Processing (ICPP), pp. 195–204. IEEE (2016)
14. Miller, J.R., Koren, S., Sutton, G.: Assembly algorithms for next-generation sequencing data. Genomics **95**(6), 315–327 (2010)
15. Salzberg, S.L., Phillippy, A.M., Zimin, A., Puiu, D., et al.: GAGE: a critical evaluation of genome assemblies and assembly algorithms. Genome Res. **22**(3), 557–567 (2012)
16. Simpson, J.T., Wong, K., et al.: ABySS: a parallel assembler for short read sequence data. Genome Res. **19**(6), 1117–1123 (2009)
17. Smith, T.F., Waterman, M.S.: Identification of common molecular subsequences. J. Mol. Biol. **147**(1), 195–197 (1981)

NVIDIA Jetson Platform Characterization

Hassan Halawa, Hazem A. Abdelhafez[(✉)], Andrew Boktor, and Matei Ripeanu

The University of British Columbia, Vancouver, Canada
{hhalawa,hazem,boktor,matei}@ece.ubc.ca

Abstract. This study characterizes the NVIDIA Jetson TK1 and TX1 Platforms, both built on a NVIDIA Tegra System on Chip and combining a quad-core ARM CPU and an NVIDIA GPU. Their heterogeneous nature, as well as their wide operating frequency range, make it hard for application developers to reason about performance and determine which optimizations are worth pursuing. This paper attempts to inform developers' choices by characterizing the platforms' performance using Roofline models obtained through an empirical measurement-based approach as well as through a case study of a heterogeneous application (matrix multiplication). Our results highlight a difference of more than an order of magnitude in compute performance between the CPU and GPU on both platforms. Given that the CPU and GPU share the same memory bus, their Roofline models' *balance points* are also more than an order of magnitude apart. We also explore the impact of frequency scaling: build CPU and GPU Roofline profiles and characterize both platforms' balance point variation, power consumption, and performance per watt as frequency is scaled.

The characterization we provide can be used in two main ways. First, given an application, it can inform the choice and number of processing elements to use (i.e., CPU/GPU and number of cores) as well as the optimizations likely to lead to high performance gains. Secondly, this characterization indicates that developers can use frequency scaling to tune the Jetson Platform to suit the requirements of their applications. Third, given a required power/performance budget, application developers can identify the appropriate parameters to use to tune the Jetson platforms to their specific workload requirements. We expect that this optimization approach can lead to overall gains in performance and/or power efficiency without requiring application changes.

1 Introduction

Optimizing software based on the underlying platform is non-trivial. This is due to complex interactions between the application code, the compiler, and the underlying architecture. Typically it is difficult to reason about the achievable application performance and decide on the best potential optimizations to apply. The problem becomes much harder for heterogeneous systems consisting of multiple processing elements of different types each with unique properties that make them suitable for different kinds of computing patterns and optimizations.

© Springer International Publishing AG 2017
F.F. Rivera et al. (Eds.): Euro-Par 2017, LNCS 10417, pp. 92–105, 2017.
DOI: 10.1007/978-3-319-64203-1_7

Thus, figuring out how best to distribute work over the different processing elements, what the best optimizations are, and how to manage the communication overhead due to data transfer between the processors, represent key challenges for the development of efficient heterogeneous applications.

NVIDIA introduced their own embedded heterogeneous systems in the form of the Jetson TK1 (in 2014) and, recently, the TX1 (in 2015) Platforms. Two characteristics make those systems stand out compared to most commodity heterogeneous architectures. First, their integrated nature: the various computing elements share the same memory bus; and second the wide range (one order of magnitude) of frequency scaling. These characteristics, as well as their low power consumption, makes them a great choice for today's embedded applications and outline a possible future path for tomorrow's high-performance platforms. However, their performance characteristics are still not well understood and optimizing applications to make full use of their heterogeneous capabilities is non-trivial.

One method to characterize the performance of a platform is through a bound-and-bottleneck analysis. Such an analysis aims to provide simple and insightful performance bounds on applications. An example of such an approach is the *Roofline model* [10] which ties together peak computation capability (e.g., floating-point compute rate) and the memory bandwidth of a platform with the observed application performance. The Roofline model provides a visual guideline which can help explain the observed application performance, relate it to the peak performance obtainable, help determine whether an application is compute- or memory-bound, and guide the reasoning of which/whether further investment in performance optimization is worthwhile (Sect. 5).

This paper presents a performance characterization of the NVIDIA Jetson TK1 and TX1 based on the Roofline model. We use an empirical measurement-based approach[1] (Sect. 2) with the aim of achieving a more reliable characterization as opposed to merely relying on back-of-the-envelope calculations based on theoretical peak performance. Moreover, due to the complexity of the underlying hardware, the theoretical peak may not even be achievable in practice (e.g., due to power caps, as we demonstrate using our empirical Roofline profiles). Additionally, given the wide operating frequency range offered, we investigate and characterize the impact of frequency scaling on floating-point performance, power consumption, balance point, and performance per watt (Sect. 3). Finally we present our experience with tuning a matrix multiplication kernel, a crucial component of many scientific and HPC applications, for both platforms. Our aim is to provide application developers with the necessary data to allow them to tune the Jetson Platforms to suit the requirements of their applications. Such an optimization approach could lead to increases in performance and/or energy efficiency without requiring any application changes as we discuss in Sect. 6.

---

[1] Our benchmarks are available online at: https://bitbucket.org/nsl_europar17/benchmarks.

Table 1. Jetson TK1 and TX1 platform specifications as reported by the running OS and collected from relevant documentation such as [4,5]

	TK1 platform	TX1 platform
CPU	4+1-core 32-bit ARM Cortex-A15	4+4-core 64-bit ARM Cortex-A57
Architecture	ARMv7-A	ARMv8-A
L1/L2 cache	32 KB/512 KB	32 KB/2 MB
Main core frequency range	204 MHz → 2.3205 GHz	102 MHz → 1.734 GHz
Power-saving core frequency range	51 MHz → 1.092 GHz	N/A
Peak theoretical FLOPS	74.26 GFLOPS	55.48 GFLOPS
GPU	Kepler (192 CUDA Cores)	Maxwell (256 CUDA Cores)
L2 Cache	128 KB	256 KB
Frequency range	72 MHz → 852 MHz	76.8 MHz → 998.4 MHz
Peak theoretical FLOPS	327 GFLOP/s	511 GFLOP/s
DRAM	2 GB DDR3L RAM (933 MHz, 2 Channels)	4 GB LPDDR4 RAM (1.6 GHz, 2 Channels)
Data bus width	64 bit	64 bit
Peak theoretical bandwidth	14.93 GB/s	25.6 GB/s

2 Methodology

Table 1 presents in detail the TK1 and TX1 specifications. To construct the empirical Roofline profiles we developed two approaches: the first, similar to that proposed in [7], relies on hardware counters (available for the CPUs only), while the second obtains the same level of information for the GPUs by using microbenchmarking techniques similar to those used by Wong et al. [11]. We rely on an empirical measurement-based approach as opposed to one just based on peak performance calculations for two main reasons. First, the presented empirical results arguably provide a more realistic, and reliable characterization. Secondly, the theoretical peaks may not even be achievable in practice due to various complexities in the underlying hardware and power caps. We demonstrate this disparity between the two approaches as part of our evaluation in Sect. 3.

2.1 CPU Micro-Benchmarks

The ARM Cortex A15 and A57 both support various types of floating-point operations including fused multiply-add (FMA) and SIMD operations. Typical scalar floating-point operations are handled by the ARM core's Vector Floating-Point (VFP) unit whereas vector floating-point operations (SIMD) are handled by the ARM core's NEON 128 bit SIMD engine. The VFP and NEON units share the same floating-point registers.

We designed a micro-benchmark in assembly that can operate with a user-defined variable operational intensity (i.e., a variable ratio between floating-point and memory operations). This micro-benchmark mixes SIMD double-word store instructions (using an unrolled loop of store instructions operating on 2 single-precision floating-point operands) as well as SIMD floating-point operations (using the NEON SIMD unit to compute an FMA of 4 single-precision floating-point operands). By varying the ratio between the store instructions and the SIMD floating-point instructions, we vary the operational intensity of the micro-benchmark to generate the Roofline profiles.

The Cortex-A15 and Cortex-A57 include a Performance Monitor Unit (PMU) that provides access to six hardware counters. We used the counters to estimate: the number of Floating-Point Instructions, the number of Vector (SIMD) Instructions, and the number of Loads and Stores. We then used this to derive the rate of Floating-Point Operations (FLOPS) as well as the memory bandwidth.

2.2 GPU Micro-Benchmarks

To obtain the Roofline profile for the GPU, where no hardware counters are available, we developed a benchmark with variable compute intensity (from 0.125 FLOPs/Byte to 1024 FLOPs/Byte). The benchmark loads 3 values from memory, performs a variable number of FMA operations on them, then stores the results. We disassembled the binary and verified that the benchmark contains exactly the intended number of memory and FMA operations.

We built two additional benchmarks: a memory bandwidth benchmark and a *FLOPS* benchmark. The memory bandwidth benchmark performs a vector add operation and is completely memory-bound. We use this benchmark to compute the memory bandwidth for the GPU and compare it to a similar benchmark on the CPU since memory is shared. The *FLOPS* benchmark is a high compute intensity benchmark, performing around a hundred thousand FMA instructions for each 4 float values loaded from memory. We use it to estimate the maximum achievable FLOPS. The results of those two benchmarks validate our variable intensity benchmark which approaches those asymptotes but does not cross them.

2.3 Other Methodology Notes

Scaling. The Jetson platforms offer a wide range of configuration options that include: the number of operational CPU cores, the CPU cores' operating frequency, as well as the number of application threads to execute. Each configuration point changes the performance characteristics in terms of single-precision floating-point performance, memory bandwidth, and power consumption.

Power Consumption. We use a Watts Up? PRO Power Meter [2] connected via USB to the Jetson development boards. This allows us to collect power consumption statistics (at 1 Hz) during our benchmarks. As a baseline for the subsequent power consumption measurements, we measured the idle power consumption with the default dynamic frequency scaling and power-saving profiles. The idle power draw was ≈3.1 W for TK1 and ≈3.8 W for TX1.

3 Platform Characterization

3.1 CPU Characterization

Roofline Profiles. Figure 1 shows the theoretical peak as well as the measured Roofline profiles for both platforms (at peak frequency and with the number of application threads equal to the number of cores). For the TK1, the maximum single-precision FLOPS rate achieved was 73.02 GFLOPS. This represents ≈98.3% of the theoretical peak and defines the upper limit for a compute-bound application. The maximum observed memory bandwidth was 13.72 GByte/Sec which represents ≈91.9% of the theoretical peak and defines the upper bound for memory-bound applications. The intersection of the two bounds defines the *balance point* (i.e., the point where an application spends the same amount of time fetching data from memory and computing on it) at 5.32 FLOPS/Byte. For the TX1, the maximum FLOPS rate achieved was 54.31 GFLOPS (≈97.8% of the theoretical peak), the maximum observed memory bandwidth was 20.2 GB/s (≈78.9% of the theoretical peak), and the balance point is at 2.68 FLOPS/Byte.

Figure 1 highlights that, on the one hand, the measured peak TX1 FLOPS rate is lower than that of the TK1 (by ≈25.6%). This can be attributed to its lower maximum frequency while using the same 128-bit wide SIMD engine. On the other hand, the measured peak TX1 memory bandwidth is higher than that for the TK1 (by ≈47.2%). This difference is caused by the higher DRAM frequency for the TX1 (1.6 GHz) compared to the TK1 (933 MHz) given that both utilize dual channel DRAM with the same 64-bit wide data bus. These differences cause the balance point to shift from 5.32 FLOPS/Byte for the TK1 to 2.68 FLOPS/Byte for the TX1. Thus, the TX1 CPU is more suitable for memory-bound applications (given its higher memory bandwidth and lower balance point).

The Impact of Frequency Scaling on Power Consumption and Roofline Profiles. We investigated the performance characteristics of both platforms for all CPU frequency scaling configurations. Due to space constraints we present only a subset of the results for the TK1 (Fig. 2). There are two important observations: firstly, frequency scaling has a larger impact on the FLOPS rate achieved than on memory bandwidth, and, secondly, the platform has a large dynamic power range (3.2x from 3.4 W to 10.8W). Using the power-saving core (labelled **0c** in the figure) increases the power range to 3.6x. It can also be observed that the power-saving core does not offer a good power/performance trade-off: when running the TK1's power-saving core at 204 MHz compared to all 4 high-performance cores at the same frequency, a power-saving of ≈11.7% is achieved but at the cost of a ≈78.4% decrease in performance.

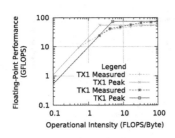

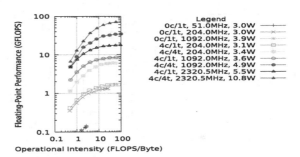

Fig. 1. CPU Roofline profiles: theoretical peak and measured CPU performance for the TK1 (blue) and TX1 (red). (Color figure online)

Fig. 2. TK1 Roofline profiles for the power-saving core (labelled **0c**) and *all* normal cores (labelled **4c**). We also vary the number of threads (labels **1t** vs. **4t**). Each line label includes measured power consumption.

The Impact of Frequency Scaling on the Balance Point. For each frequency, we compute the balance point. Surprisingly, in Fig. 3, we observe that the TK1 can be configured to cover a wider range of balance points, a potentially useful feature when attempting to match hardware capabilities to the application demand as we discuss in Sect. 6.

The Impact of Frequency Scaling on Power-Normalized Computational Rate (FLOPS/Watt). Figure 4 examines the power consumption (left y-axis) and performance per watt (right y-axis) for all possible CPU frequencies for a compute intensive application. It can be seen that the TK1 typically consumes less power across the entire frequency range compared to the TX1. This, in addition to its higher floating-point performance, results in a higher energy efficiency (performance per watt) across the entire frequency range.

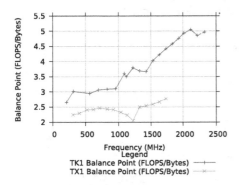

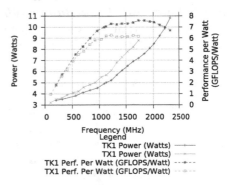

Fig. 3. The impact of frequency scaling on the balance point (4 cores, 4 threads) for TK1 (blue) and TX1 (red). (Color figure online)

Fig. 4. Power and performance per Watt while scaling CPU frequency (4 cores, 4 threads) for TK1 (blue) and TX1 (red). (Color figure online)

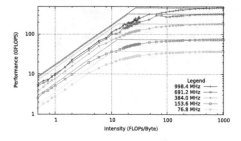

Fig. 5. TX1 Maxwell GPU Roofline: theoretical (solid line) and achieved (dots). (Color figure online)

Fig. 6. GPU power and performance per watt for a compute-bound benchmark.

3.2 GPU Characterization

Roofline Profiles. Figure 5 shows the Roofline profiles constructed for the TX1 GPU (TK1 profiles are similar, not shown here to conserve space). We find that, in some cases, the theoretical peak is unattainable even with highly tuned benchmarks. We therefore use our benchmarks to estimate the Roofline bounds (solid lines in the figures). The Kepler GPU on the TK1 is able to achieve up to 218 GFLOP/s while the Maxwell GPU on the TX1 achieves 465 GFLOP/s. The memory bandwidth is at 12 GB/s and 17.3 GB/s respectively (similar to the CPU results). For better readability, we only show a subset of the frequencies.

The Impact of Frequency Scaling: Power-Normalized Computational Rate (FLOPS/Watt). NVIDIA focused on power efficiency when designing the TX1's Maxwell GPU. Our results confirm this: TX1 provides 3x higher performance per watt compared to TK1 (Fig. 6). Note the impressive 6x (TK1) and 20x (TX1) higher FLOPS/Watt for GPUs compared to CPUs.

The Impact of Frequency Scaling on the GPU Balance Point, Peak FLOPS Rate, and Peak Bandwidth. We observe similar behaviors on both platforms in Fig. 7: at low GPU frequencies, both memory and compute bandwidth increase linearly as the frequency is scaled. The memory bandwidth at

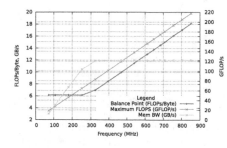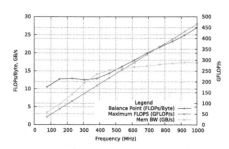

Fig. 7. The impact of frequency scaling on the TK1 (left) and TX1 (right) balance point (left y-axis), peak bandwidth (left y-axis), and peak FLOPS rate (right y-axis). Note the different scales on the y-axes.

low frequencies is bottlenecked by the ability of the processor to issue instructions fast enough to saturate the memory bus. After $\approx$300–400 MHz, the peak FLOPS rate continues to increase linearly with frequency, however, the memory bandwidth stops increasing linearly and becomes constant. As such, the balance point is constant for the lower frequencies while for higher frequencies the balance point increases linearly as the frequency is scaled.

It is worth noting that the platforms offer a different range for the balance point: on the TK1, the GPU balance point ranges between 6 and 18 FLOPs/Byte while on the TX1 it ranges from 11 to 27. This is largely due to the superior performance of the Maxwell architecture. In contrast with the CPU results, the TK1's Kepler GPU can be better tuned for applications with lower intensity while the TX1's Maxwell GPU can be better tuned for applications with higher intensity. However, due to the TX1's higher memory bandwidth and higher compute rate we find that its GPU provides equal or better performance regardless of the application's arithmetic intensity. In other words, the TX1's GPU provides better performance than that on the TK1 for all intensities, despite the fact that it is operating sub-optimally at the lower ones.

4   Case Study: Matrix Multiplication

To study the effect of frequency scaling on performance/energy beyond microbenchmarks, we developed a tuned matrix multiplication kernel that can be run on the CPU only, the GPU only, or be partitioned on the heterogeneous platform. We chose matrix multiplication as it is an operation that is essential in many scientific and HPC applications.

Our CPU implementation is based on the OpenBLAS matrix multiplication single precision subroutine (SGEMM). For OpenBLAS, we enable optimization flags for the ARMV8 architecture to support the advanced features present in the processor. This enables the use of NEON SIMD instructions for performing vector floating point operations. The library also implements matrix tiling (blocking) optimized for the multi-level caches of each processor and loop unrolling. For the NVIDIA GPUs we use the cuBLAS [6] library, a BLAS implementation optimized for NVIDIA GPUs. Our developed heterogeneous matrix multiplication kernel can partition the matrices between the CPU and the GPU to take advantage of the optimizations by OpenBLAS and cuBLAS.

Collecting Results: In each run we measure the performance in terms of FLOPS and power consumed. The number of floating point operations in a matrix multiplication routine is independent of the underlying hardware or the processor used. Assuming square matrices of size $n \times n$, then matrix multiplication generates $2 \times n^3$ FLOPS. We measure the running time which we then use to obtain the computation rate (GFLOPS).

Configurations: We used different matrix sizes to cover the fit-in-cache and non-fit in cache cases, this shows the effect of matrix tiling (blocking) on performance. In the heterogeneous case, for space limitations, we selected the lowest and highest frequencies for each of the CPU and GPU. Moreover, we fixed the matrix size to 4096 and limited the *cpuColumns* to be a value out of (16, 128, 512) columns. From our experience, increasing the *cpuColumns* to more than 512 degrades the performance as the computation is heavily unbalanced between the CPU and the GPU.

CPU/GPU Only Experiments: Figures 8 and 9 present the energy efficiency (GFLOPS/Watt) while scaling frequency. The figures show a sample of the results that covers fit-in-cache (matrix sizes 32 and 64) and non-fit in cache (matrix sizes 128, 512 and 4096) cases. We note that efficiency saturates (or even decreases) above 1428 MHz for the CPU and 691 MHz for the GPU: scaling up frequency, while improving runtime, leads to higher power consumption and thus lower energy efficiency.

Heterogeneous (CPU and GPU): The CUDA toolkit v8.0, deployed on the TX1, offers multiple software-level mechanisms to use the shared global physical memory between the CPU and the GPU such as the Unified Memory Architecture (UMA). Using UMA allows us to allocate and initialize the matrix on the shared memory with no need for explicit memory transfers. At first glance, one would think that with UMA and shared memory, an efficient heterogeneous matrix multiplication can be easily implemented. However, NVIDIA's documentation [1, J2.2] states that for GPUs with compute capability less than 6.x (the TX1's is 5.3), it is not possible for the CPU and GPU to access (read or write) a memory location allocated using UMA simultaneously.[2]

After evaluating the alternatives, we settled on the following solution: to compute $A \times B = C$, we split matrices B and C by columns. We specify the number of columns that the CPU will process as *cpuColumns* and the rest is processed on the GPU. The allocation is performed using UMA to avoid copying

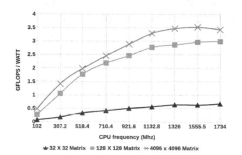

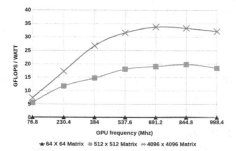

Fig. 8. CPU power efficiency values for different matrix sizes

Fig. 9. GPU power efficiency for different matrix sizes

---

[2] We tried several alternative techniques such as using *mprotect()* which changes memory access permissions on a specific memory range. The NVIDIA driver locks the memory accessed by the GPU kernels until they complete. Therefore, it is not possible to have a shared matrix object accessed at the same time by the CPU and GPU even when we use UMA, even if all accesses are read-only.

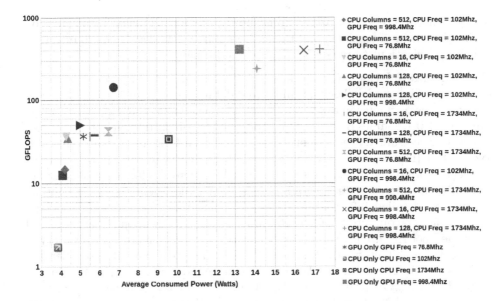

Fig. 10. Run-time configurations effect on performance and power consumption

the results back from the GPU. With this approach, we eliminated any write conflict between the GPU and the CPU on the shared memory, at the cost of wasting memory by duplicating matrix A (imposed by the limited compute capability).

Figure 10, plots a chart that highlights the value of the configurable frequency scaling of the TX1. The figure highlights the multiple criteria that can be used to select a configuration (CPU/GPU frequencies, cpuColumns values). For example, in situations where capping power is the limiting factor one can determine the best frequency configuration that meets the power cap. Alternatively, in situations where meeting a runtime constraint is important, one can select the most energy efficient configuration that meets the imposed runtime deadline. It is worth noting that that the observed operational space varies over a wide range along the performance and power dimensions (over one order of magnitude on performance and 4x on power).

5   Related Work

The Roofline Model [10], is a visual model that makes it easier to reason about bounds to attainable performance. It combines the operational intensity (FLOPS per Byte), floating-point performance (FLOPS) and memory bandwidth (Bytes per Second) together into a two-dimensional plot that outlines the performance bounds of the platform (defined by a Roofline *profile* which acts as an envelope). Moreover, such a bound-and-bottleneck characterization approach provides insights into the primary factors affecting the performance of individual applications based on their *position* on the plot with respect to the Roofline profile (e.g., whether they are compute-bound or memory-bound depending on their operational intensities) and thus allows application developers to prioritize which optimizations to pursue to improve performance.

Roofline Model Uses. Ofenbeck et al. [7] take a practical approach to applying the Roofline model. They use measured data based on benchmarks to reason about the performance in a way similar to the methodology we employ to generate our CPU Roofline. However, this study focuses on an Intel architecture with access to fine-grained event counters through the Performance Monitoring Unit. Wong et al. [11] use a carefully crafted set of benchmarks to discover the microarchitecture of GPUs. Their approach is to craft microbenchmarks that amplify the different microarchitecture parameters and make them visible at runtime to uncover detailed information about GPU internals. We use similar benchmark design to compute the GPU Roofline. Lo et al. [3] developed the Empirical Roofline Tool and use it to empirically construct Roofline models for a variety of accelerated architectures (including multicore, manycore, and GPU-accelerated architectures). The toolkit makes use of instrumented microbenchmarks implemented in MPI, OpenMP, and CUDA. Our methodology is similar to that used in the Empirical Roofline Tool to construct the GPU Roofline, however, we rely on hardware performance counters to generate the CPU Roofline.

NVIDIA Jetson Platform Characterization. Although there are many applications that use the unique capabilities of the studied platforms (particularly TK1 such as [8,9]), to the best of our knowledge, we are the first to carry out a complete characterization. In [8], the authors employ an application: a distributed MPI-based neural network simulation, to compare a distributed embedded platform (based on several interconnected TK1s) with a server platform (based on an Intel quad-core dual socket system). The authors show that the distributed embedded platform's instantaneous power consumption is 14.4x lower despite the server platform being 3.3x faster (in terms of execution time). Another study [9] evaluates the TK1 in an HPC context as a cloud offload unit for a discrete Tesla K40 GPU. The study shows that such a cluster approach offers superior power efficiency compared to using a separate discreet GPU, while offering substantially better performance than using the TK1 by itself.

6   Summary and Discussion

We characterized the performance of the NVIDIA Jetson TK1 and TX1 Platforms by presenting Roofline profiles for both the CPU and the GPU on each platform. When comparing the CPU vs. GPU performance, our Roofline profiles showed a difference of more than an order of magnitude on compute performance suggesting that the GPU on the Jetson Platforms is preferable for compute intensive applications. Since the CPU and GPU share the same memory bandwidth, the balance points are also more than an order of magnitude apart. Additionally, we explored the impact of frequency scaling on floating-point performance, balance point, power consumption, and efficiency (GFLOPS/watt).

The data provided by this study offers application developers a starting point when tuning the platforms to their applications' requirements (by choosing the optimal operational frequency on the CPU/GPU) and indicates that net gains in performance and/or power efficiency without any modifications to the applications can be obtained.

We discuss below the key implications of our observations for application developers and device manufacturers.

6.1 Implications for Application Developers

Modular Application Design and the Division of Work. The asymmetric nature of the CPU and GPU can be harnessed by application developers during runtime for optimum performance and energy efficient computing. Highly parallelizable portions of the application are more suited for deployment on the GPU with its larger number of SIMD units while the less parallelizable parts (or those requiring a more complex processor pipeline) can be executed on the CPU. As such, developers should design their applications in a modular way so as to allow for the efficient distribution of work across the available asymmetric cores.

A Free Lunch? Reducing Power Consumption without Performance Degradation. If an application's computational intensity is below the platform's balance point, then the application could potentially be able to save energy without sacrificing performance by scaling the frequency down until the balance point is equal to its required intensity. This works only down to the point where the system becomes bottle-necked on the memory bandwidth. Beyond this point, further reduction of frequency will result in performance degradation.

Tuning the Platform, an Alternative Method to Optimize Application Performance. Typically application developers apply various optimizations to their code in order to try to attain the maximum performance possible on the target platform. We propose that application developers can alternatively tune the platform to the operational intensity of the developed application in order to achieve optimum compute performance and/or power-saving. One way to do this is for application developers to statically determine the appropriate frequency scaling for their applications and then set the CPU/GPU to this frequency at runtime. Our analysis suggests that application developers can tune the Jetson Platforms to the applications' requirements to achieve net gains in application performance and/or energy efficiency without the need to modify the application itself.

Full System Power. In addition to the other benefits provided by the shared memory architecture on the Jetson platform, we find that the emphasis on low full system power has important implications. The platform was designed for embedded applications, thus, emphasis was placed on optimizing its idle power as well as the power consumed by supporting components. At idle, we find that both platforms consume less than 3W. This is negligible when compared to traditional machines that host a CPU and/or a GPU. As a result, under load, close to all of the power consumed goes to the active components (CPU, GPU and DRAM), and makes the full system's power efficiency much better compared to other platforms.

6.2 Implications for Device Manufacturers

Simplify Application Development. In order to increase the adoption of heterogeneous compute platforms, device manufacturers should focus on simplifying the application development process as well as the tools available to developers. The promise of such platforms is higher performance and better energy efficiency but, in our experience, this potential is not currently attainable without significant effort by application developers.

This is currently a major drawback of the NVIDIA Jetson platform. In order to provide implementations optimized for the CPU and the GPU, application developers need to rewrite their applications specifically for each processor. For the CPU, almost any general purpose programming language can be utilized but typically a low-level programming language such as C or Assembly is used to extract the maximum performance possible. While for the GPU, CUDA must be used in order to make full use of the features and libraries provided by NVIDIA. There is little reuse of application code between optimized CPU and GPU implementations with this development approach. The significant development effort and costs involved represent a high barrier to entry.

Better Dynamic Frequency Scaling. In theory, manufacturers could potentially instrument the hardware to dynamically estimate the running application's arithmetic intensity. Based on the computed intensity, the device can apply dynamic frequency scaling to reduce the consumed power even under 100% utilization. A good guess for the frequency that would work best can be based on trying to match the hardware balance point with the application's intensity. Following such an approach could potentially lead to reduced power consumption as well as increased performance per watt without any changes to the running applications.

Memory Bandwidth at Lower Frequencies. Based on our findings, the memory bandwidth becomes a performance bottleneck at lower operating frequencies. Device manufacturers can try to avoid this bottleneck by designing the hardware to support the full memory bandwidth even at the lowest frequencies. This would allow a wider range of achievable balance points and, in turn, lead to larger power-savings for applications with low computational intensity.

References

1. NVIDIA   CUDA   toolkit   v8.0:   https://docs.nvidia.com/cuda/cuda-c-programming-guide/index.html#um-unified-memory-programming-hd. Accessed 16 Feb 2017

2. Watts-up: https://www.wattsupmeters.com/. Accessed 23 Aug 2016
3. Lo, Y.J., Williams, S., Van Straalen, B., Ligocki, T.J., Cordery, M.J., Wright, N.J., Hall, M.W., Oliker, L.: Roofline model toolkit: a practical tool for architectural and program analysis. In: Jarvis, S.A., Wright, S.A., Hammond, S.D. (eds.) PMBS 2014. LNCS, vol. 8966, pp. 129–148. Springer, Cham (2015). doi:10.1007/978-3-319-17248-4_7
4. NVIDIA: Technical brief NVIDIA Jetson TK1 development kit: bringing GPU-accelerated computing to embedded systems. Technical report, April 2014
5. NVIDIA: Tegra X1: NVIDIA's new mobile superchip. Technical report, January 2015
6. NVIDIA: CUBLAS library. Technical report, September 2016
7. Ofenbeck, G., et al.: Applying the Roofline model. In: ISPASS 2014, pp. 76–85, March 2014
8. Paolucci, P.S., et al.: Power, energy and speed of embedded and server multi-cores applied to distributed simulation of spiking neural networks: ARM in NVIDIA Tegra vs Intel Xeon quad-cores. CoRR abs/1505.03015 (2015)
9. Ukidave, Y., et al.: Performance of the NVIDIA Jetson TK1 in HPC. In: 2015 IEEE International Conference on Cluster Computing (CLUSTER), pp. 533–534, September 2015
10. Williams, S., et al.: Roofline: an insightful visual performance model for multicore architectures. Commun. ACM 52(4), 65–76 (2009)
11. Wong, H., et al.: Demystifying GPU microarchitecture through microbenchmarking. In: ISPASS 2010, pp. 235–246. IEEE (2010)

Following the Blind Seer – Creating Better Performance Models Using Less Information

Patrick Reisert, Alexandru Calotoiu, Sergei Shudler$^{(\boxtimes)}$, and Felix Wolf

Technische Universität Darmstadt, 64289 Darmstadt, Germany
kpreisert@gmail.com, {calotoiu,shudler,wolf}@cs.tu-darmstadt.de

Abstract. Offering insights into the behavior of applications at higher scale, performance models are useful for finding performance bugs and tuning the system. Extra-P, a tool for automated performance modeling, uses statistical methods to automatically generate, from a small number of performance measurements, models that can be used to predict performance where no measurements are available. However, the current version requires the manual pre-configuration of a search space, which might turn out to be unsuitable for the problem at hand. Furthermore, noise in the data often leads to models that indicate a worse behavior than there actually is. In this paper, we propose a new model-generation algorithm that solves both of the above problems: The search space is built and automatically refined on demand, and a scale-independent error metric tells both when to stop the refinement process and whether a model reflects faithfully enough the behavior the data exhibits. This makes Extra-P easier to use, while also allowing it to produce more accurate results. Using data from previous case studies, we show that the mean relative prediction error decreases from 46% to 13%.

Keywords: Parallel computing · Performance tools · Performance modeling

1 Introduction

As the computing world moves towards more and more parallelism and high-performance computing (HPC) systems become ever larger, the complexity of performance analysis is compounded. Understanding the performance of parallel programs at larger scale and getting correct insights requires prohibitive resources. Developers and users must benchmark their applications at the full extent of available parallelism to obtain the insights they desire. It requires both expensive computing time and manpower. Performance modeling offers a way to alleviate this problem by providing users with models (i.e., analytical expressions) of the application behavior. With these models users are able to predict application behavior at higher scale. One example of a performance model, which can also help uncover scalability bottlenecks, is the expression of execution time as a function of the number of processors.

© Springer International Publishing AG 2017
F.F. Rivera et al. (Eds.): Euro-Par 2017, LNCS 10417, pp. 106–118, 2017.
DOI: 10.1007/978-3-319-64203-1_8

We distinguish between analytical and empirical performance modeling. Analytical performance models are constructed by experts that infer the laws that govern application behavior as a function of a pre-selected parameter (e.g., the number of processors). Not only is this a laborious process that requires intuition and small-scale tests, but it might also require experts to apply this process to every individual module of the application. Empirical performance modeling, on the other hand, infers models automatically from a relatively small number of measurements. It offers a practical way for common users to find scalability bugs and bottlenecks [5], predict performance [11,16], compare algorithmic alternatives [20], and understand the effects of resource contention [17].

Extra-P [1] is a tool to create such empirical performance models, primarily scaling models, with one or more model parameters [4,5]. However, in its current version it relies on a manually defined search space, requiring users either to provide a large enough space to accommodate a wider range of models or to have an initial guess as to how a model would look like. Both options have their drawbacks since the former means increased computation costs, and the latter means increased expertise on the user's part. In addition, *false positives* (i.e., models that indicate a worse behavior than there really is) can sometimes occur due to artifacts in performance measurements. Although such artifacts can usually be identified manually, actually doing it would substantially prolong the performance modeling process. In this work, we make the following contributions to address the aforementioned shortcomings:

- Automatic search-space configuration—in our new iterative model-generation approach, we configure the search space on demand and iteratively raise the accuracy of the model until no meaningful improvement can be made. In this way, we increase both the tool's ease of use and its range of application without sacrificing accuracy.
- Significant reduction of false positives—by using a heuristic to increase Extra-P's resilience to noise in the measurements, we are able to save users from wasting valuable time trying to analyze problems that do not really exist.

The remainder of the paper is organized as follows. In Sect. 2, we provide the background on automatic performance modeling and the current technique for model generation. Section 3 continues with a detailed description of the new, iterative refinement approach, followed by an evaluation in Sect. 4. Finally, we review related work in Sect. 5, before drawing our conclusion in Sect. 6.

2   Empirical Performance Modeling with Extra-P

In this section, we briefly introduce Extra-P and the way it generates empirical performance models.

2.1   The Performance Model Normal Form

A key concept underlying Extra-P is the *performance model normal form* (PMNF). The PMNF models the effect of a single parameter (predictor) x on a response variable of interest $f(x)$, typically a performance metric such as execution time or a performance counter. It is specified as follows:

$$f(x) = c_0 + \sum_{k=1}^{n} c_k \cdot x^{i_k} \cdot \log_2^{j_k}(x)$$

The PMNF allows building a function search space, which we then traverse to find the member function that comes closest to representing the set of measurements. This assumes that the true function is contained in this search space. A possible assignment of all i_k and j_k in a PMNF expression is called a *model hypothesis*. The sets $I, J \subset \mathbb{Q}$ from which the exponents i_k and j_k are chosen and the number of terms n define the discrete model search space. Our experience suggests that neither I and J nor n have to be particularly large to achieve a good fit, but although a common default set of about 40 terms can be sufficient, for some applications the search space needs to be tuned manually with the help of domain experts and application developers. Having chosen the sets, we then automatically determine the coefficients of all hypotheses using regression and choose the hypothesis with the smallest error such that we get the most likely model function.

For the above process to yield good results, the true function that is being modeled should not be qualitatively different from what the normal form can express. Discontinuities, piece-wise defined functions, and other behaviors that cannot be modeled by the normal form will lead to sub-optimal results. There are, however, many practical scenarios where programs change their behavior. For example, modern MPI implementations switch from one algorithm to another, depending on the message size, the number of processes, or the network topology. Whether an application fits within the cache or not also affects performance in a discontinuous manner. Ilyas et al. [10] introduce a novel method in Extra-P to detect such segmentation before generating empirical models. Specifically, the authors developed heuristics to successfully find segmentation in data with as few as six points, and a method to estimate the change point. In this way we can continue to use the PMNF on the level of individual segments.

2.2 Model Generation

Extra-P requires a set of performance profiles as input, representing runs where one or more parameters are varied. These profiles can be obtained using existing performance measurement tools. Here, we use the performance measurement system Score-P [14], which collects several performance metrics, including execution time and various hardware and software counters, broken down by call path and process. Other data sources from other performance measurement tools are equally possible and simply require some form of input format conversion.

Based on the profiles, we compute one model for each combination of target metric and call path, enabling a very fine-grained scalability analysis even of very complex applications.

Past experience has shown that as few as five different measurements for one parameter are enough for successful model generation, allowing the automatic discovery of scalability bottlenecks at very low cost.

3 Approach

We now introduce our novel modeling algorithm, starting with some key ideas and then presenting the algorithm as a whole. We focus here on the case of single-parameter modeling. Calotoiu et al. [4] have shown that finding multi-parameter models can be reduced to combining the best single-parameter models in different ways and selecting the combination which fits the measurements best. Therefore our approach can be used as a drop-in replacement in the multi-parameter scenario while maintaining all the benefits shown in this paper.

3.1 The SMAPE Metric

A key component of our new approach is the *symmetric mean absolute percentage error* (SMAPE) metric [12]. Previously, Extra-P used the *residual sum of squares* (RSS) to compare the quality of generated models and model hypotheses. Given N experiments with measurements $y_i (1 \le i \le N)$ for the parameter values x_i, the RSS of a model $f(x_i)$ is calculated as $\sum_{i=1}^{N}(y_i - f(x_i))^2$. One disadvantage of the RSS is that its value depends on the scale of the data that are being modeled. Smaller input values will lead to a smaller RSS, and the squaring of the residuals amplifies this problem. Furthermore, the RSS does not have a well defined range, so its value cannot be interpreted easily.

SMAPE is a scale-independent, relative error metric that overcomes the shortcomings of the RSS. It originates from time series forecasting and is defined as:

$$\frac{1}{N} \cdot \sum_{i=1}^{N} \frac{|y_i - f(x_i)|}{(|y_i| + |f(x_i)|)/2} \cdot 100\%.$$

Taken apart, it is the mean of a ratio, expressed as a percentage. The SMAPE value is always in a range of 0% to 200%, where 0% means no error at all. This makes it a helpful error metric that can be easily interpreted by a user and compared across models with different scales. In contrast to the slightly simpler MAPE metric, SMAPE does not break down when any y_i is 0.

However, we still use the RSS to decide which of two model hypotheses better fits the data, simply because we use regression to fit the hypothesis to the data, which relies on the least squares method and thus optimizes the RSS metric. We have observed that in most cases[1] both metrics agree as far as the relative order is concerned, so if one hypothesis has a better RSS than another, it usually has a better SMAPE value as well.

---

[1] This is not generally true, which also makes the *unimodality* results presented in Sect. 3.2 not hold for SMAPE, even though the plots shown there usually show the same patterns when generated from SMAPE instead of the RSS.

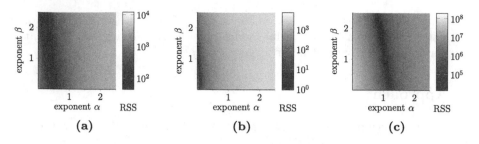

Fig. 1. Error of fitted simplified PMNF models for measurements from three different kernels, sampled with a resolution of $\frac{1}{40}$ for both α and β. (Color figure online)

3.2   Revisiting the PMNF

Over time, we have accumulated experiences of common use cases and what type of analyses and configurations yield the most insightful results [5,11,16,20]. Based on these experiences, we propose to simplify the PMNF itself so that not only it fits the common use cases better, but also increases resilience to noise.

Given the cost of gathering measurements, users commonly provide less than 10 different data points per parameter. We have discovered that allowing more than one term in addition to c_0 almost always leads to modeling insufficiently understood behavior unless there are significantly more data points available, especially if the data is affected by noise. Therefore, we suggest to use the following *simplified PMNF*:

$$f(x) = c_0 + c_1 \cdot x^\alpha \cdot \log_2^\beta(x)$$

Since optimal values for c_0 and c_1 are determined by regression whenever α and β have been fixed, the remaining challenge is to select the best exponents α and β, where $\alpha = 0$ and/or $\beta = 0$ is allowed. Following the observed behavior of real applications [5,11,16,20], we can restrict $\alpha < 6$ and $\beta < 3$.

To gain insights into the space spanned by α and β, we created heatmap plots, where each point represents the RSS of an optimal (fitted) model hypothesis with exponents α and β. A representative selection of such plots is presented in Fig. 1. From these plots we can see that the hypotheses with minimal error run along a line, which starts on the horizontal axis ($\beta = 0$) and goes upwards and to the left, approaching the vertical axis ($\alpha = 0$). In some cases (usually for data that require a purely logarithmic model, as in Fig. 1b), the line first slightly bends to the right before finally turning to the left. Thus, the function that assigns the error of the best hypothesis to a choice of α and β has the following properties:

- It is unimodal (i.e., it has a single minimum, and the function value decreases as you approach that minimum from either side) over α for any choice of β.
- It is unimodal over β for $\alpha = 0$.
- It is generally *not* unimodal over β for $\alpha > 0$.

This, together with the fact that the variation along the line of minimal error is very small, is the reason for the choice of four one dimensional *slices* of this two dimensional space, along which we will search for a minimum. We define these slices as $\beta = 0, \beta = 1, \beta = 2$ and $\alpha = 0$.

Along each of these slices we can now search for appropriate values of α (for the slices where β is fixed) or β (where α is fixed), respectively. When we say *appropriate*, we do not necessarily mean *optimal*, as we want to find exponents that are representable by (preferably simple) fractions. We consider a fraction[2] to be simpler than another whenever it has a smaller denominator than the other.[3] We have developed an algorithm to find such exponents, which we shall introduce in the following section.

3.3   Iterative Refinement

Our algorithm is based on the idea that we can start with integer exponents (i.e., fractions with denominator 1) and then iteratively refine the search space by increasing the denominators while approximating the true minimum. Search space refinement has previously been proposed by Shudler et al. [16] who suggested repeated halving of an initial interval, which resulted in denominators that are always powers of two. However, a computational kernel simulating a three dimensional process, for example, can actually require an exponent of $\frac{n}{3}$ to model its complexity.

For the sake of presentation, let us now first look only at the slice $\beta = 0$, where no logarithmic term is involved and the algorithm tries to find an appropriate value for α. We shall later expand on how the algorithm deals with multiple slices. First, all hypotheses with integer exponents $\alpha = 0, \ldots, 5$ are computed and compared. The exponent leading to the best model is stored, and its successor and predecessor are used as initial upper and lower bounds, respectively. After this initialization, the actual iterative refinement process, presented in Fig. 2, starts. It constitutes a variant of the golden section search [15], but uses the *mediant* instead of the golden section to determine new candidate exponents, for reasons explained below. The mediant of two fractions $\frac{n_1}{d_1}$ and $\frac{n_2}{d_2}$ is defined as $\frac{n_1 + n_2}{d_1 + d_2}$ and has the property that it always lies in between the two original fractions [8]. For example, the mediant of $\frac{1}{2}$ and 1 (represented as $\frac{1}{1}$) is $\frac{2}{3}$.

In every iteration, two new hypotheses are computed from the two mediants in between the currently best hypothesis and each of the two bounds, and their errors are compared to the best hypothesis. If the left mediant has the smallest error, we cut off the right part of the search space by using the left mediant for the new best hypothesis. If the right mediant is the winner, we do the same on the other side. If none of the mediants has a smaller error, then the best hypothesis remains the same and we use the two mediants as new upper and lower bounds.

If we kept computing mediants in this way, we would obtain a sequence of fractions with ever increasing denominators, ever more accurately approximating the true minimum. This sequence is a path in the *Stern-Brocot tree*, an infinite

---

[2] We are only concerned with *fully reduced* (also called *irreducible*) fractions here.
[3] This is in line with a simplicity metric presented by Guthery [8, p. 163].

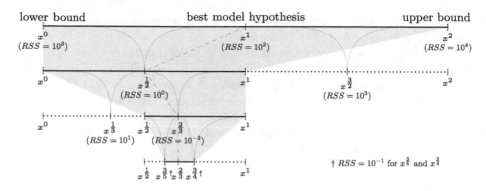

Fig. 2. Example showing three iterations of our refinement algorithm. In the first iteration, the search space is cut on the right side, because the left mediant has the smallest error; in the second iteration, it is cut on the left side; in the third iteration, it is cut on both sides, because no mediant has a smaller error. Orange curved lines indicate the calculation of the mediant. (Color figure online)

binary tree that enumerates all positive rational numbers [8]. Hence, when we arrive at a fraction $\frac{n_i}{d_i}$ in our algorithm, no fraction in between with a denominator less than d_i was missed, because such a fraction would have appeared earlier along the path in the tree.

However, we want to stop after a small number of iterations (usually 1 to 3) to keep the exponents readable and more intuitive. In order to decide when to stop, we can draw on the benefits of the SMAPE metric, as it allows our algorithm to make decisions based on the relative improvement of its value. Thus, the SMAPE improvement will serve as a termination criterion in our algorithm. Moreover, we have observed that most models which have a SMAPE value that is not at least twice as good (where smaller is better) as that of the constant model do not justify the choice of a non-constant model. After manual inspection of the underlying data, in the vast majority of cases the data appears roughly constant, with small deviations in both directions that can be explained by noise. Since any model will fit the data better than the constant model in such a case (because the constant model cannot bend in any way), we penalize the choice of the non-constant model to reduce false positives. We can now outline the full algorithm:

Step 1. For each slice, find and remember the best integer exponent.

Step 2. Refine each slice according to the previously described method. All slices execute one iteration of the algorithm before the next iteration is started. In each iteration, the best model hypothesis among all slices is considered as a candidate for the globally best hypothesis. To be accepted it needs to provide an improvement over the previously accepted best hypothesis that is large enough to justify a finer grained exponent. We use SMAPE to measure this improvement and define an *acceptance threshold* of 1.5 (i.e., an improvement of at least 50%)

per iteration. The search terminates when in a single iteration no slice improves its SMAPE value by at least a factor of 2 (we call this the *termination threshold*).

Step 3. After the iterative refinement has terminated, the winner hypothesis from the previous step is compared to the constant model and accepted only if the SMAPE value has improved by at least a factor of 2 (the *non-constancy threshold*), otherwise, as discussed earlier, it is rejected in favor of the simpler constant model.

4   Evaluation

We have evaluated our algorithm in two different ways. First, to gauge the accuracy of the algorithm, we evaluated it on synthetic data with known underlying functions. We compared the results with the output of the original algorithm, for which the following default search space was used, matching the one suggested in the latest publication by Calotoiu et al. [4]: $n = 2$, $I = \{\frac{0}{4}, \frac{1}{4}, \ldots, \frac{12}{4}\}$, and $J = \{0, 1, 2\}$. Second, to understand how helpful the new algorithm is in practice and the improvements it offers, we evaluated it on measured data collected in previous case studies. The latter results, however, are more difficult to interpret because the ground truth (i.e., the true underlying functions, which the modeling ideally should recover) is with few exceptions practically inaccessible.

4.1   Synthetic Data

Figure 3 presents evaluation results based on randomly generated synthetic data. Because we have found most real models to be constant or very simple—the common case that our method is primarily designed for and that matches the asymptotic complexities of many known algorithms—we defined different classes of functions based on the following classification of terms:

– Common: x, x^2, x^3, $\log_2(x)$
– Rare: $x^{\frac{i}{2}}$ for $i \in \{1, 3, 5\}$, $x^{\frac{i}{3}}$ for $i \in \{1, 2, 4, 5, 7, 8\}$, $\log_2^2(x)$
– Exotic: $x^{\frac{i}{4}}$ for $i \in \{1, 3, \ldots, 11\}$, $x^{\frac{i}{5}}$ for $i \in \{1, \ldots, 14\} \setminus \{5, 10\}$, $\log_2^{\frac{1}{2}}(x)$, $\log_2^{\frac{3}{2}}(x)$

A function classified as *rare* may contain terms classified as *common*, but it must contain at least one *rare* term. Likewise, *exotic* functions might contain terms from the other classes, but must contain at least one of the *exotic* terms, which are terms that we have not observed so far in real applications but we assume that they could occur.

For each of the seven distinct cases shown in Fig. 3, we generated 1000 random functions and evaluated them for each of four different sets of x values that are representative for Extra-P's use cases ($\{2, 4, 8, 16, 32\}$, $\{8, 16, 32, 64, 128\}$, $\{32, 64, 128, 256, 512\}$, and $\{128, 256, 512, 1024, 2048\}$). To each function value we added $\pm 2\%$ of noise, drawn from a uniform distribution, before using the values as input for the modeling algorithms.

114   P. Reisert et al.

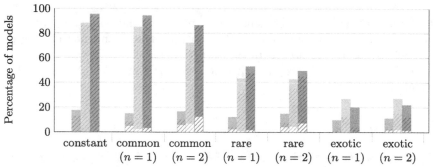

Fig. 3. Comparison of the original and our new algorithm using values of randomly generated functions with ±2% of noise as input. The functions are built according to the PMNF with $n = 1$ or $n = 2$, and their coefficients c_0, c_1 and c_2 are calculated by sampling $a \in [-2, 3]$ uniformly and then computing 10^a. (Color figure online)

We then checked whether (1) the resulting model's exponents were matching exactly the expected lead order exponents of the input function and/or (2) the model's prediction for an x value that is four times as large as the largest value used for modeling is within the ±2% noise level of the actual function value. For functions with two additive non-constant terms, we define the lead order term to be the one that contributes to the function more than the other when evaluated at an x value that is four times as large as the largest one used for modeling.

For constant, common, and rare functions, our algorithm shows improvements upon the original one with respect to both the amount of exactly matched exponents as well as the number of accurate predictions, even when that algorithm is restricted to model only a single term. While the results for the exotic functions are less favorable, the old algorithm is not able to produce significantly better results with either $n = 1$ or $n = 2$, and we still have to find such functions in practice.

4.2   Case Studies

We used measurements from previous case studies to evaluate our new algorithm on measured data. The measurements include a variety of call paths (i.e., kernels) and different metrics, such as runtime, number of function calls, memory footprint, and network traffic. Whereas the evaluation using synthetic data gives us confidence that the method works in principle, the evaluation with real applications shows its practical benefit.

The results of the comparison, which are presented in Table 1, show that when the last (i.e., largest) measured data point is excluded from the data used to calculate the model, the model produced by our new algorithm allows for a better

Table 1. Comparison of the original and our improved algorithm, using data from previous case studies, showing the quality of predictions of the last data point when that point is not used for modeling.

Benchmark	Number of points	Model count	Model predictions (percentage of all models)			Mean relative prediction error [%]	
			Better	Same	Worse	Before	Now
Sweep3D [5]	7	96	26.04	56.25	17.71	17.26	6.31
HOMME [5]	9	670	18.81	68.51	12.69	3.69	3.03
MILC [5]	9	1496	30.95	56.48	12.57	36.71	14.53
UG4 [20]	5	2026	52.62	38.01	9.38	68.30	15.58
MPI collect. [16]	7–8	26	65.38	7.69	26.92	52.53	15.89
BLAST [4]	5	103	31.07	41.75	27.18	34.92	10.38
Kripke [4]	5	36	36.11	38.89	25.00	33.05	8.32
Total	5–9	4453	39.12	49.11	11.77	45.71	12.97

prediction of the last point in 19%–65% of the cases, which corresponds to 53%–85% of those models that changed in each benchmark. Although some predictions do get worse, the mean relative prediction error, which we computed using the SMAPE formula (but this time averaging over the last data point of all models instead of all data points of a single model), decreases across all applications, in all but one case even significantly. We use this metric here for reasons similar to those discussed in Sect. 3.1: We need a scale-independent error metric because the scale of the data varies heavily among the different benchmarks and modeled performance metrics.

Not shown in the table is the number of models that are constant, which has considerably increased in every single case study (from 44% to 76% overall). Because the synthetic evaluation has shown that our new algorithm is able to recognize constant functions more reliably, this indicates that the previous algorithm might have modeled noise or tried to fit a PMNF function to inaccurate measurements.

5   Related Work

In recent years, performance modeling of HPC applications has become a very active field of study [3,4,6,7,13,17,19]. Previous work explored regression-based approaches for predicting program scalability [2,7]. In one case [2], Barnes et al. used linear regression to fit the measured execution time to a second-order polynomial. In a different study [7], the authors used Active Learning to improve regression-based models they produced from measured data. Active Learning is a group of machine learning techniques in which the learner can decide to query the information source, at some additional cost, to label a datapoint that is otherwise hard to label. It means that to improve the initial performance model the technique would decide in which configuration it should run the next experiment so that the result produces the best improvement in the model with minimal cost. Active Learning complements our methodology by starting with a small set of measurements and deciding which experiments to run next. In contrast to regression-based techniques, our methodology produces simplified PMNF models that are based on combinations of logarithmic and linear terms one often finds in common algorithms. It provides the user with more insights into the behavior of the modeled applications.

A number of previous studies [3,9] relied on semi-analytical modeling to produce performance models. However, unlike semi-analytical approaches, empirical performance modeling focuses on a common user, who might not have the necessary expertise to construct the initial model. The refinement algorithm advances this concept even further by relieving the user from the burden of providing the terms for the model search space.

Aspen [18] and Palm [19] are both top-down analytical modeling approaches. The former offers a domain-specific language and the latter source-code annotations. While both of these approaches produce accurate models, they are not empirical and therefore can miss potential bottlenecks and scalability limitations.

Meswani et al. [13] present a different modeling approach that focuses only on hybrid CPU-GPU systems. Another approach which focuses only on shared memory machines is ESTIMA [6]. It measures the number of stalled cycles on a small number of cores and estimates the slowdown on a higher number of cores. Although both approaches predict future scalability of applications, they do not offer the same degree of flexibility as Extra-P does.

6   Conclusion

In this paper, we propose a novel algorithm for empirical performance modeling as part of the Extra-P tool. In contrast to previous work, we remove the need for a predefined search space and also significantly reduce the number of false positives by being more resilient to noisy measurements of constant behavior. Yet most of the models generated with our algorithm are able to make predictions that are equally or even more accurate than before, which we demonstrate with experiments using both synthetic and real data. Thus, our work opens the way for a performance modeling workflow that is more automated than ever and equips developers with a tool that helps them efficiently find scalability bugs in large applications.

Acknowledgements. This work was supported in part by the German Research Foundation (DFG) through the Priority Programme 1648 *Software for Exascale Computing* (SPPEXA) and the Programme *Performance Engineering for Scientific Software*. Additional support was provided by the German Federal Ministry of Education and Research (BMBF) under Grant No. 01IH16008, and by the US Department of Energy under Grant No. DE-SC0015524. Finally, we would like to thank the University Computing Center (Hochschulrechenzentrum) of TU Darmstadt for providing us with access to the Lichtenberg Cluster.

References

1. Extra-P - automated performance-modeling tool. www.scalasca.org/software/extra-p
2. Barnes, B.J., Rountree, B., Lowenthal, D.K., Reeves, J., de Supinski, B., Schulz, M.: A regression-based approach to scalability prediction. In: Proceedings of the International Conference on Supercomputing (ICS), pp. 368–377. ACM (2008)
3. Bauer, G., Gottlieb, S., Hoefler, T.: Performance modeling and comparative analysis of the MILC lattice QCD application Su3_Rmd. In: Proceedings of the 2012 12th IEEE/ACM International Symposium on Cluster, Cloud and Grid Computing (CCGRID), pp. 652–659. IEEE Computer Society (2012)
4. Calotoiu, A., Beckingsale, D., Earl, C.W., Hoefler, T., Karlin, I., Schulz, M., Wolf, F.: Fast multi-parameter performance modeling. In: Proceedings of the 2016 IEEE International Conference on Cluster Computing (CLUSTER), pp. 1–10. IEEE Computer Society (2016)
5. Calotoiu, A., Hoefler, T., Poke, M., Wolf, F.: Using automated performance modeling to find scalability bugs in complex codes. In: Proceedings of the 2013 ACM/IEEE Conference on Supercomputing (SC), pp. 45:1–45:12. ACM (2013)
6. Chatzopoulos, G., Dragojević, A., Guerraoui, R.: ESTIMA: extrapolating scalability of in-memory applications. In: Proceedings of the ACM SIGPLAN Symposium on Principles and Practice of Parallel Programming (PPoPP), pp. 27:1–27:11. ACM (2016)
7. Duplyakin, D., Brown, J., Ricci, R.: Active learning in performance analysis. In: Proceedings of the 2016 IEEE International Conference on Cluster Computing (CLUSTER), pp. 182–191. IEEE Computer Society (2016)
8. Guthery, S.B.: A Motif of Mathematics. Docent Press, Boston (2011)
9. Hoefler, T., Gropp, W., Thakur, R., Träff, J.L.: Toward performance models of MPI implementations for understanding application scaling issues. In: Keller, R., Gabriel, E., Resch, M., Dongarra, J. (eds.) EuroMPI 2010. LNCS, vol. 6305, pp. 21–30. Springer, Heidelberg (2010). doi:10.1007/978-3-642-15646-5_3
10. Ilyas, K., Calotoiu, A., Wolf, F.: Off-road performance modeling - how to deal with segmented data. In: Rivera, F.F., et al. (eds.) Euro-Par 2017. LNCS, vol. 10417, pp. 36–48. Springer, Cham (2017)
11. Iwainsky, C., Shudler, S., Calotoiu, A., Strube, A., Knobloch, M., Bischof, C., Wolf, F.: How many threads will be too many? On the scalability of OpenMP implementations. In: Träff, J.L., Hunold, S., Versaci, F. (eds.) Euro-Par 2015. LNCS, vol. 9233, pp. 451–463. Springer, Heidelberg (2015). doi:10.1007/978-3-662-48096-0_35
12. Kreinovich, V., Nguyen, H.T., Ouncharoen, R.: How to estimate forecasting quality: a system-motivated derivation of symmetric mean absolute percentage error (SMAPE) and other similar characteristics. Technical report, Paper 865, University of Texas at El Paso (2014)
13. Meswani, M.R., Carrington, L., Unat, D., Snavely, A., Baden, S., Poole, S.: Modeling and predicting performance of high performance computing applications on hardware accelerators. Int. J. High Perform. Comput. Appl. **27**(2), 89–108 (2013)
14. an Mey, D., et al.: Score-P: a unified performance measurement system for petascale applications. In: Bischof, C., Hegering, H.G., Nagel, W., Wittum, G. (eds.) Competence in High Performance Computing 2010, pp. 85–97. Springer, Heidelberg (2011). doi:10.1007/978-3-642-24025-6_8
15. Press, W.H., Teukolsky, S.A., Vetterling, W.T., Flannery, B.P.: Numerical Recipes: The Art of Scientific Computing, 3rd edn. Cambridge University Press, Cambridge (2007)

16. Shudler, S., Calotoiu, A., Hoefler, T., Strube, A., Wolf, F.: Exascaling your library: will your implementation meet your expectations? In: Proceedings of the International Conference on Supercomputing (ICS), pp. 165–175. ACM (2015)
17. Shudler, S., Calotoiu, A., Hoefler, T., Wolf, F.: Isoefficiency in practice: configuring and understanding the performance of task-based applications. In: Proceedings of the ACM SIGPLAN Symposium on Principles and Practice of Parallel Programming (PPoPP), pp. 1–13. ACM (2017)
18. Spafford, K.L., Vetter, J.S.: Aspen: a domain specific language for performance modeling. In: Proceedings of the 2012 ACM/IEEE Conference on Supercomputing (SC), pp. 84:1–84:11. IEEE Computer Society Press (2012)
19. Tallent, N.R., Hoisie, A.: Palm: easing the burden of analytical performance modeling. In: Proceedings of the 28th ACM International Conference on Supercomputing (ICS), pp. 221–230. ACM (2014)
20. Vogel, A., Calotoiu, A., Strube, A., Reiter, S., Nägel, A., Wolf, F., Wittum, G.: 10,000 performance models per minute – scalability of the UG4 simulation framework. In: Träff, J.L., Hunold, S., Versaci, F. (eds.) Euro-Par 2015. LNCS, vol. 9233, pp. 519–531. Springer, Heidelberg (2015). doi:10.1007/978-3-662-48096-0_40

An Accurate Simulator of Cache-Line Conflicts to Exploit the Underlying Cache Performance

Yukinori Sato$^{(\boxtimes)}$ and Toshio Endo

Tokyo Institute of Technology, Tokyo 152-8550, Japan
yukinori@el.gsic.titech.ac.jp, endo@is.titech.ac.jp

Abstract. This paper describes a cache-line conflict profiling method that advances the state of the art performance tuning workflow by accurately highlighting the sources of conflicts. The basic idea behind this is the use of cache simulators as a diagnosis tool for cache-line conflicts. We also propose a mechanism that enables to identify where line conflict misses are incurred and the reasons why the conflicts occur. We evaluate our conflict simulator using some of the benchmark codes used in the HPC field. From the results, we confirm that our simulator can accurately model the cache behaviors that cause line conflicts and reveal the sources of them during the execution. Finally, we demonstrate that optimizations assisted by our mechanism contribute to improving performance for both of serial and parallel executions.

Keywords: Accurate cache simulation · Conflict miss detection · Performance tuning · Array padding

1 Introduction

Recently, compiler technologies have made significant progress in automatic vectorization and thread-level parallel execution techniques. However, further source code refactoring for performance tuning is often required to obtain performance close to the versions manually optimized by expert programmers [15]. Primary sources that cause this inefficiency are derived from memory subsystems composed of caches. To increase effective memory bandwidth, or to reduce the latency for a memory access, we need to make good use of cache memories. However, current compilers are often oblivious to cache-conscious optimizations needed to fully utilize the locality in the application. As shown later in this paper, executable binary generated by a compiler does not always fit well to the underlying cache memories. Mostly this is caused by cache-line conflict misses, which often degrade performance significantly.

In this paper, we strive to eliminate performance degradation or performance variability due to line conflict misses. Modern CPU systems typically have highly associative cache structures to avoid conflict misses as much as possible. One example seen in Intel Sandy Bridge CPU is that the L3 cache is organized as a 20-way associative cache. Even in the lower L1 and L2 caches, their associativity

© Springer International Publishing AG 2017
F.F. Rivera et al. (Eds.): Euro-Par 2017, LNCS 10417, pp. 119–133, 2017.
DOI: 10.1007/978-3-319-64203-1_9

is 8-way. However, in some of applications that intensively access a particular set in the associative cache, the number of elements mapped onto the same set can easily exceed the degree of associativity [5] and cause conflict misses. Since this often impacts on performance seriously, we should avoid it by refactoring the source code.

The actual behavior of cache memories within a real system is normally invisible from software. Hence, we provide a way to diagnose avoidable cache misses and a simple workflow to get rid of them. To diagnose cache behaviors, we propose a cache-line conflict simulator called **C2Sim** and attempt to mimic the occurrence of cache-line conflicts by concurrent dual cache simulations. For accurate line conflict detection, we simulate fully-associative (FA) caches as a subsidiary simulation of the underlying set-associative (SA) caches. Furthermore, to assist a performance tuning workflow, we provide a mechanism that reveals the sources of cache-line conflicts and attempts to ease the actual code modification process.

The primary contributions of this paper are as follows:

- We develop C2Sim for identifying cache-line conflict misses effectively. We show that C2Sim provides practically accurate detection of conflicts based on its advanced cache modeling.
- We present a mechanism that can monitor the actual locations of code where line conflict misses are incurred and the reasons why the conflicts occur.
- We show that cache-line conflict misses can be avoided by padding to the appropriate arrays suggested through our mechanism, and such optimizations also contribute to scalable performance improvements on parallel executions.

2   Modeling Cache Structures in Modern CPUs

Driven by semiconductor technology scaling, capacity and associativity of cache memories is continuously increasing. On the other hand, the complexity of algorithms and applications is increasing year by year, which often makes their memory access patterns complicated. Under these situations, cache memories are desired to be useful in all the situations. However, there are no universal cache structures that can exploit locality of references for everything. This is why the underlying cache performance is sensitive to memory access patterns derived from application-specific characteristics and the underlying hierarchical caches and memories.

Therefore, we need to perform source code refactoring to improve cache performance. However, it is hard for skilled programmers to estimate application-specific cache behaviors and apply these to the performance tuning. One of the solutions for this situation is to build a simulator of modern x86_64 CPU caches for performance tuning. Formulating the cache model as a simulator, we can monitor time-varying behaviors of cache memories, which are normally invisible from software. By analyzing sequences of particular events during the simulation, we can detect how the cache miss occurs and whether it could be avoidable or not.

In this paper, we focus on simulating occurrences of cache-line conflicts and a reasoning mechanism upon it for assisting cache performance tuning. Situations where massive amount of requests to a particular set of a cache causes conflict misses are also called cache thrashing. Since it results in serious performance degradation, it should be avoided as much as possible. While cache thrashing is considered to be obvious only in caches that have low associativity, we reveal that it occurs even in current high associative cache structures. Especially, it is seen in typical scientific computing applications that calculate large multi-dimensional arrays.

Here, we investigate how such conflicts normally invisible from application programmers are detected precisely from actual execution. Collins and Tullsen attempted to identify line conflict misses by storing the history of replaced cache lines using an FIFO for every set of caches [4]. In their method, when the miss to a cache set matches a previously evicted tag stored in the FIFO, then it is identified as a line conflict miss. However, as we show later in this paper, this sometimes leads false detections due to the sensitivity to the number of entries of the FIFO. Since this approach fundamentally includes under- or overestimation of conflicts, this is impossible to detect conflicts precisely. To resolve this issue, we propose a detection scheme based on comparison to FA (fully associative) cache behavior.

3   Cache-Line Conflict Simulator

3.1   FA Cache Based Conflict Detection

We propose a cache-line conflict simulator called **C2Sim**. The key idea for accurate line conflict detection is to conduct FA cache simulation as side simulation to the baseline cache simulation for the target configuration. We also provide a mechanism that identifies where and why line conflict misses occurs.

A cache-line conflict occurs when the number of accessed data elements mapping to the same set exceeds the degree of associativity. In this situation, the original cache line to be accessed was replaced before it is requested again. Such a cache line conflict miss consequently appears only in SA (set-associative) or direct-mapped structures where the number of cache lines within a set is limited. Here, we define a conflict miss as a miss that could be avoided in the FA cache with the same capacity. Since for FA cache there are no limits of associativity, its behavior is a theoretical upper bound for optimization that completely avoids cache-line conflicts. From this definition, when an access to the FA cache hits whereas that for the SA cache misses, it is classified as a conflict miss. When an access both for the FA cache and the SA cache simultaneously misses, it is classified as a capacity miss. Based on these, we implement an FA cache simulator and compare its behavior with the SA cache simulator having the same capacity so that we can detect conflict misses.

It is believed that simulating actual FA caches that maintains true LRU order incurs much overhead compared with a typical SA cache simulation because FA

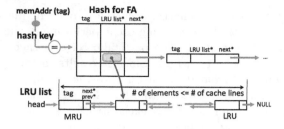

Fig. 1. An efficient FA cache simulation method.

cache needs tag comparison across all entries[1]. To reduce this overhead, we develop an efficient algorithm for FA cache simulation as illustrated in Fig. 1. Instead of using an O(N) or a non-linear algorithm for keeping a true LRU order, we use a hash and a list structure for it. Here, we can directly map a tag to the corresponding entry of the hash with an O(1) lookup unless the entry is heavily shared by other tags (hash collision). If the tag cannot be found in the first entry of the hash, we search the following list structure. After the corresponding tag is found, we have a pointer to the LRU list. This list is implemented using a doubly linked list and maintains a true LRU order. The maximum length of this list corresponds to the number of cache lines and is decided by the capacity of the cache.

3.2   Reasoning Around Line Conflicts

A straightforward conflict detection mechanism discussed above is still insufficient to assist a performance tuning workflow done by programmers. Because the said mechanism only returns how many conflicts appear in the execution, programmers need to read source code carefully and find out where and why the conflicts occur. To improve the productivity of this process, we present a new interface that maps simulation results as clues for performance tuning. We also provide a new mechanism that reveals the locations where and why line-conflict misses occur.

In order to keep track of these, we propose LT-WET (Last Time Who EvicT): a data structure that records key events at instruction level granularity. Figure 2 illustrates how we monitor cache-line conflicts using the LT-WET structure. The key idea here is to store which memory reference instruction triggers a cache-line eviction, and to resolve the reason when a conflict miss for the same set is detected in future. The details are as follows: First, when a cache miss occurs in the SA cache, we store the tag of evicted line to the EvictedTag field and cache miss instruction's address to the Originator field respectively as shown in Fig. 2(a). At the same time, when the memory access is identified as a conflict miss, we search the tag corresponding to the current memory reference instruction from the EvictedTag field. We then identify the miss originator that had

---

[1] Here, we focus only on true LRU replacement policy for both of FA and SA caches.

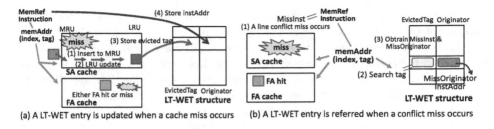

Fig. 2. How to find out where and why the conflict occurs.

caused the last eviction to the current miss as shown in Fig. 2(b). Here, the LT-WET structure is implemented using a hash structure similar to the one used in FA cache simulation to reduce the time for searching tags.

The conflict miss instruction coupled with its originator indicates where and why the conflict miss occurs. The instructions that cause conflict miss can easily be traced back to the source code through debug information that compilers embed inside application binaries.

We also perform memory object relative profiling, which correlates every memory reference to the objects in memory layout appearing in the actual execution. To obtain accessed memory regions, we monitor the ranges (min, max) of accessed memory addresses for all memory reference instructions. Then, each memory region is mapped to a symbol found inside the program. We extract static symbols such as global variables and constants by analyzing the executable-and-linkable (ELF) code. To obtain the symbols of memory regions allocated at runtime, we monitor the memory map at '/proc/pid/maps' for stack regions and hook functions for memory allocators such as malloc. Finally, these memory access related information are consolidated and outputted as results of memory object relative profiling.

3.3   Advanced Cache Modeling for Accurate Simulation

To prevent false conflict detections due to cache modeling inaccuracy, we develop the following advanced simulation mechanisms to C2Sim: a virtual to physical address translation, and a slice mapping mechanism for an L3 cache.

The first mechanism, virtual to physical address translation, enables C2Sim to model Physically Indexed Physically Tagged (PIPT) caches for L2 and L3, and a Virtually Indexed Physically Tagged (VIPT) cache for L1. Here, when the total capacity per associativities is greater than the page size, the mapping for physical address affects cache indexing. This is seen in the typical L2 and L3 caches when using a default 4 KB page. To reflect the actual physical addresses in our simulation, we monitor the mapping table located at '/proc/pid/pagemap' provided by Linux OS when a new page is accessed and record them in a hash table.

The second one, a slice mapping algorithm for L3 cache, is needed to model L3 caches accurately. An L3 cache in modern Intel CPUs is known to be divided into pieces, usually referred to as slices [6]. The number of slices matches the number of physical cores, and each slice contains 2048 sets, which are equal to 2.5 MB in 20 way set associative configurations. Dividing an L3 cache into slices will spread the traffic almost evenly across the slices and prevent conflicts inside an L3 cache. Therefore, knowing the details of the slice selection algorithm is crucial for building accurate cache simulators. In [6], the authors recover the slice selection algorithm used in modern Intel CPUs based on the Prime+Probe side channel technique. In this paper, following the hash function in [6] (for 8 core CPUs in Table 2), we model the slice selection and mapping mechanism.

As far as we know, C2Sim is the first cache simulator that implements physical address translation and L3 slice mapping algorithm. In Sect. 4, we will validate the accuracy of C2Sim by comparing its cache miss ratio with the one obtained using hardware performance counters in the actual CPUs.

4 Evaluation

4.1 Methodology

In this section, we evaluate our cache-line conflict simulator, C2Sim, using a typical x86_64 Linux server running CentOS 6.7 with two of Intel Xeon E5-2680 CPUs. We implement C2Sim on the top of Pin tool set [9]. For the baseline cache simulation, we set up the same configuration as the underlying CPU, that is L1 = 32 KB 8way, L2 = 256 KB 8way and L3 = 20 MB 20way. Here, we model three level data caches with true LRU replacement where L3 is managed with inclusion policy and L2 is with non-inclusive policy. In the current implementation, C2Sim does not model a shared L3 cache and coherence protocols among different cores, and it just simulates cache behaviors without any delays for cache coherence and communication among other levels.

We use the following benchmarks in HPC field: PolyBench/C 4.2, 3D-FDTD and Himeno benchmark. The PolyBench is a benchmark suite composed of 30 numerical computation kernels in various application domains such as linear algebra computations, image processing, physics simulation, dynamic programming, statistics [3]. Here, we set the data type to double and use LARGE dataset. 3D-FDTD is a benchmark code that evaluates three-dimensional finite-difference time-domain method which is widely used in high-frequency electromagnetic field analysis for the design of electrical devices [10]. Himeno benchmark is composed of a kernel code used in incompressible fluid analysis [2], and one of well-known memory bottleneck applications. We generate executable binary code of these target applications using GNU gcc 4.4.7 with '-O3 -g' option, and first examine cache behaviors for single thread execution. To examine effectiveness for parallel code, we generate multithreaded code with '-fopenmp' option and evaluate their effects for scalability.

In this evaluation, we apply the concept of sampling based cache simulation technique [12] to C2Sim in order to reduce the overheads of on-line cache simulation. Here, we set 100M instructions for the warm-up phase and 500M instructions for the evaluation phase after skipping 4G clock cycles for the first forward phase. We also note that we turn off the hardware prefetch implemented in the CPU when we examine the cache statistics using our simulator. While the hardware prefetch affects cache behaviors and in most cases results in performance improvements, it sometimes obscures fundamentals of cache conflicts. This is why we turn off the hardware prefetch for evaluating cache behaviors.

4.2   Verification of Our Simulator

Next, we validate accuracy of C2Sim by comparing the cache miss ratio with that from Performance Monitoring Unit (PMU) implemented in the underlying CPU[2]. We note that these cache miss ratios are observed during whole the execution. Here, we use PolyBench suite for this evaluation and measure cache miss ratios during whole the execution. We exclude the programs whose native execution time is less than 0.8 s (gemver, gesummv, atax, bicg, mvt, durbin, trisolv, deriche, jacobi-1d) since a short measurement interval tends to be unsound for sampling simulation.

Table 1. Evaluating our cache simulator with statistics obtained from PMU.

	Native time [s]	C2Sim overheads	PMU			C2Sim			Maximum abs. error
			L1 miss	L2 miss	L3 miss	L1 miss	L2 miss	L3 miss	
floyd-warshall	122.62	27.45	6.24%	50.00%	100.00%	6.25%	50.06%	99.98%	0.06%
correlation	3.98	209.87	66.97%	52.00%	0.00%	66.45%	51.63%	0.02%	0.52%
3mm	5.20	138.85	38.24%	11.00%	1.00%	37.51%	11.12%	0.26%	0.74%
gemm	2.04	81.20	3.15%	100.00%	1.00%	3.13%	100.00%	0.17%	0.83%
ludcmp	39.08	73.50	31.39%	37.00%	22.00%	32.59%	38.28%	20.53%	1.47%
2mm	4.04	150.58	38.06%	12.00%	1.00%	36.27%	11.50%	0.31%	1.79%
covariance	4.00	116.09	67.01%	53.00%	0.00%	66.42%	51.18%	0.02%	1.82%
trmm	1.13	330.67	60.00%	7.00%	2.00%	61.06%	7.62%	0.08%	1.92%
lu	39.55	72.75	29.29%	37.00%	23.00%	29.63%	38.84%	20.97%	2.03%
cholesky	37.55	55.56	25.44%	13.00%	80.00%	25.07%	13.19%	83.20%	3.20%
gramschmidt	3.84	140.91	57.05%	13.00%	1.00%	57.16%	17.20%	0.05%	4.20%
heat-3d	21.08	20.89	9.99%	100.00%	46.00%	6.37%	99.84%	50.66%	4.66%
jacobi-2d	11.29	30.49	3.69%	48.00%	93.00%	8.35%	50.00%	100.00%	7.00%
nussinov	9.36	80.03	34.47%	12.00%	19.00%	34.21%	12.24%	26.34%	7.34%
symm	2.14	110.14	33.96%	29.00%	3.00%	33.36%	21.46%	1.65%	7.54%
fdtd-2d	11.60	26.51	7.91%	85.00%	66.00%	7.73%	87.23%	75.13%	9.13%
syrk	1.16	274.93	23.96%	23.00%	2.00%	23.71%	13.19%	0.26%	9.81%
syr2k	2.29	225.06	33.77%	23.00%	4.00%	33.48%	12.48%	1.61%	10.52%
doitgen	0.92	87.75	33.95%	3.00%	14.00%	34.23%	2.71%	2.80%	11.20%
adi	21.23	37.10	16.77%	43.00%	81.00%	17.03%	30.56%	79.75%	12.44%
seidel-2d	34.98	10.57	8.35%	48.00%	93.00%	3.75%	33.37%	100.00%	14.63%

Table 1 shows the time for native execution of the program and the simulation overheads (slowdown factor) calculated by measuring the time needed for cache

---

[2] Here, we measure L2/L3 cache miss ratio by Intel PCM, and L1 miss ratio by LIKWID using counters such as L1D_REPLACEMENT and MEM_UOPS_RETIRED.

simulation for the same program. While the simulation overheads have a wide range of variation, the average overhead is 109. To compare the other simulators, we calculate MIPS (Million Instructions Per Second) rates for simulating these programs. The resultant average MIPS rate is 40.06. This is several orders of magnitude faster than typical microarchitectural simulators and the state of the art cache simulators [17].

The result in Table 1 also shows the accuracy of cache modeling on our C2Sim compared with the statistics obtained from PMU. Here, we calculate the average maximum absolute errors of all programs and use it as a criterion for accuracy. The maximum absolute error of each program is obtained by picking up the maximum one among three cache levels after calculating absolute errors between PMU and C2Sim for each cache level. From the results, we find the maximum absolute errors of half of these programs are less than 5%. For all of the programs, the observed maximum absolute error is less than 15%. In average, it is 5.37%. These results indicate that C2Sim is accurate and practical enough to model the performance of hierarchical caches implemented in modern CPUs.

Table 2. Effects of physical address translation and L3 slice mapping.

	VA	PA	VA + slice	PA + slice	PA + slice sampling
Avg. max abs error	48.76%	40.73%	9.33%	5.18%	5.37%

Table 2 shows the accuracy of simulation compared with that of the real machine. Here, VA represents simulations only using virtual addresses; PA represents ones with physical address translation. 'PA + slice (sampling)' indicates typical C2Sim configuration. All of the maximum absolute errors are average of 21 PolyBench programs listed above. From these results, we observe that the L3 slice mapping is an important factor for accurate simulation. It contributes to reducing the average maximum absolute error to 5.37%. It is also observed that even if we enable sampling simulation, the error just increases slightly (0.19%). We also observe that the simulation speed becomes 1.6 times faster if we enable sampling. Therefore, we can understand that coupling these three techniques (PA + slice and sampling) contributes to building an accurate and light-weight cache simulator. These results indicate that our simulator is accurately model the performance of hierarchical caches implemented in modern CPUs.

4.3   Accuracy for Line Conflict Detection

Next, we show the advantages of C2Sim over the existing conflict detection mechanism. Here, we compare the FIFO-based method in [4,17] with C2Sim, where the number of FIFO entries is set to the twice the number of associativities as seen in these papers. Table 3 shows the ratios of line conflicts to the total misses detected in each level. We calculate absolute errors among them and

Table 3. Detected line conflicts in the FIFO-based mechanism and C2Sim.

	FIFO-based			C2Sim			Maximum abs. error
	L1conflict	L2conflict	L3conflict	L1conflict	L2conflict	L3conflict	
gemm	0.00%	0.00%	0.00%	0.00%	0.00%	0.00%	0.00%
covariance	0.00%	88.04%	0.00%	0.00%	88.04%	0.00%	0.00%
correlation	0.00%	88.03%	0.00%	0.00%	88.01%	0.00%	0.02%
doitgen	87.62%	98.90%	0.00%	87.68%	98.90%	0.00%	0.06%
symm	10.12%	37.14%	0.73%	10.04%	37.30%	0.73%	0.16%
2mm	0.29%	0.41%	0.00%	0.00%	0.42%	0.00%	0.29%
gramschmidt	0.00%	84.19%	0.00%	0.00%	84.57%	0.00%	0.38%
syr2k	9.84%	0.26%	2.02%	0.53%	0.27%	2.02%	9.31%
nussinov	21.23%	0.05%	24.78%	0.45%	0.02%	5.89%	20.78%
lu	2.51%	71.45%	21.42%	1.76%	71.58%	0.07%	21.35%
ludcmp	2.51%	71.04%	21.38%	1.74%	71.12%	0.02%	21.36%
3mm	23.17%	0.00%	0.00%	0.00%	0.00%	0.00%	23.17%
trmm	25.75%	2.25%	0.00%	0.62%	2.01%	0.00%	25.13%
syrk	45.08%	0.00%	0.00%	0.06%	0.00%	0.00%	45.02%
floyd-warshall	49.98%	0.00%	0.11%	0.00%	0.08%	0.03%	49.98%
heat-3d	0.00%	47.02%	50.69%	0.00%	0.00%	0.00%	50.69%
fdtd-2d	12.51%	0.00%	73.26%	0.00%	0.00%	5.36%	67.90%
adi	11.91%	6.20%	81.34%	1.09%	6.21%	0.99%	80.35%
cholesky	0.01%	0.12%	87.47%	0.00%	0.51%	0.24%	87.23%
seidel-2d	66.63%	0.00%	95.90%	0.00%	0.00%	0.00%	95.90%
jacobi-2d	50.00%	0.00%	100.00%	0.00%	0.00%	0.00%	100.00%

represent the maximum one across all three level as Maximum abs. error. All the elements are sorted by the field of Maximum abs. error.

From the results, we observe that the FIFO-based mechanism approximates C2Sim's FA-based behaviors in 7 programs (gemm, covariance, correlation, symm, doitgen, 2mm, gramschmidt) with less than 1% absolute errors. However, the rest of them contains a lot of false judgments, where the FIFO-based classifies a miss to a conflict but actually it should be classified to a capacity miss (not to conflict). Since the cache miss behavior of FA caches is a theoretical lower bound that excludes any possible conflict misses, C2Sim can detect the accurate number of cache-line conflicts by combining it with the underlying SA caches.

On the other hand, the FIFO-based method is a kind of approximation of such an FA cache behavior. These judgments cause the difference of 33.3% in average of the maximum absolute errors. The evaluation done by Collins and Tullsen in [4] also showed that their FIFO-based method could identify 88% of conflict misses on the direct-mapped or the 2-way associative cache. From our preliminary evaluation, we observed that the number of FIFO entries is sensitive to the detection accuracy especially for configurations with highly associative caches. Hence, there are no way to completely exclude false judgments in the FIFO-based method. On the contrary, C2Sim accurately models the behavior of cache conflicts based on their definition, and it is robust for highly associative cache structures (such as 20 ways) in modern CPUs.

Considering the actual use cases against performance tuning, the false judgments should be avoided as much as possible to correctly provide the opportunity for cache optimization. For instance, the FIFO-based method correctly reveals the conflicts in covariance while it completely fails in jacobi-2d. If the programmers who perform cache optimization use the wrong target information created by the FIFO-based method, they will never achieve the performance gain from any memory layout optimizations related to line conflicts. On the other hand, our C2Sim can productively reach the precise targets in the performance tuning workflow.

4.4   Reasoning Around Line Conflicts for Performance Tuning

To examine where and why the conflicts occur and to apply these for an actual performance tuning workflow, we pick up three programs (doitgen from PolyBench, 3D-FDTD, Himeno). Figure 3(a) summarizes their cache conflicts detected by C2Sim. Here, we observe conflicts in L1 cache for these programs. For doitgen, we observe conflicts in L2 cache.

	Conflicts [%]		
	L1	L2	L3
doitgen	87.68%	98.44%	0.00%
3D-FDTD [1]	37.45%	0.00%	0.00%
Himeno [2]	92.94%	0.00%	1.76%

[1] FDTD: 128x128x64, timestep=50,
    # of mediums (prescribed by array 'id')=10
[2] Himeno Benchmark: OpenMP, C_Dynamic, size=S

(a) Detected cache-line conflicts by C2Sim

```
Memory object-relative view:
malloc[#3]  total=336299057  conflictMissPC= 4008a2
       --> malloc[#3]  cnt= 308503621, 17620466, 0, originPC= 4008a2
       --> malloc[#1]  cnt= 9951731, 107283, 0, originPC= 400898
       --> malloc[#2]  cnt= 0, 115952, 0, originPC= 400888  4008c8
       --> Stack(7fff72dde2c4, 4)  cnt= 0, 4, 0, originPC= 4008ee
malloc[#1]  total=10603920  conflictMissPC= 400898  4008ce
       --> malloc[#3]  cnt= 10603920, 0, 0, originPC= 4008a2
malloc[#2]  total=115953  conflictMissPC= 400888  4008c8
       --> malloc[#3]  cnt= 0, 115953, 0, originPC= 4008a2
==============================================================
Reason classification view:
                 sum        inter-array   intra-array    scalar    unknown
#conflict   347018930:       20894839     326124087        4         0
Ratio                          6.02%        93.98%       0.00%     0.00%
```

(b) A snapshot of observed sources of conflicts (doitgen)

Fig. 3. The detected conflicts and their sources.

To investigate the sources of conflicts further, we analyze the data recorded in the LT-WET structure. Figure 3(b) shows the observed sources of line conflicts during the execution of doitgen. Here, we represent the sources in the following two manners: memory object-relative view and reason classification view. In the memory object-relative view, we track the appearances of conflicts using symbols that represent the memory objects. Here, we see that the malloc[#3] (the thirdly invoked malloc in this execution) causes 336M conflicts at the instruction 0x4008a2. In the following four lines, four of its miss originators are represented with the number of L1, L2, L3 conflicts and their miss originate PCs. Here, we observe that the most significant miss originator is malloc[#3], the same object as the one that causes the miss, and then find the primary reason is intra-array conflict. Similarly, we find the other three originators are caused by inter-array conflict. In the reason classification view, we collect the total number of intra- and inter-array conflicts for the program execution. From these results, we find that the intra-array conflicts within malloc[#3] are dominant in doitgen.

These information assists us in making strategies for avoiding the unnecessary conflict misses and improving the potential performance of caches. Table 4(a) shows the actual strategies formulated in this paper. While padding is a traditional technique and some existing papers build analytical models to decide the amount of padding [5], the locations to be padded are heuristically determined by hands of expert programmers. Therefore, we propose a workflow that inserts padding to the appropriate arrays suggested through our source analysis mechanism.

Table 4. Cache tuning conducted for doitgen, 3D-FDTD, Himeno.

(a) Strategies for avoiding cache-line conflicts

	Tuning strategy
Opt.1	Intra-array padding insertion
Opt.2	Use of hugetlbfs (2MB page)
Opt.3	Inter-array padding insertion

(b) Cache optimizations in doitgen

	Speedup
Original	1.00
Opt.1	1.19
Opt.1+Opt.2	1.21
Opt.2	1.02

(c) Cache optimizations in 3D-FDTD

	Speedup
Original	1.00
Opt.3	1.32

(d) Scalability for parallel threads and sensitivity to HW prefetch in Himeno

	HW PF	Speedup [**]
1 thread	off	1.62
	on	1.75
16 threads	off	1.50
	on	1.70

[**] **Opt.3** is performed

Table 4(b) shows cache optimizations performed for doitgen and their resultant performance gains. Since the intra-array conflicts within malloc[#3] is the dominant source of conflicts, we insert an extra space within the first dimension of the corresponding 2D array 'C4' in the program. Here, we set 8 elements (64 Bytes) as the amount of intra-array padding to insert an extra space equivalent to one cache-line size. After this optimization (Opt.1), we observe 1.19 times speedup from its original code.

Next, we check whether the conflicts are resolved using C2Sim. The results show that conflicts in L2 still remain although these in L1 are completely eliminated. Here, this phenomenon is derived from the page size used for evaluation. When we use a default 4KB page, the lower 12 bits of memory addresses becomes offsets within the page. Also, for the L1 cache indexing, the lower 12 bits are used. Therefore, all of L1 indexing can be done within a page. However, the L2 and the L3 cache need to use the upper parts of these 12 bits for their indexing, and these are affected by physical address mapping. Since typical linux systems randomize its address space layout through ASLR, the upper parts of the indexes are fragmented. These random index generation makes the effect of intra-array padding diminished. To avoid this, we set 2MB pages through hugetlbfs and control the cache indexing for L2 and L3. After this optimization (Opt.1 + Opt.2), the conflicts within L2 cache are eliminated, and this results in a further speedup.

Here, we note that we cannot achieve such performance improvement if we just adopt hugetlb without intra-array padding (Opt.2).

Then, we shift to the cache optimization for 3D-FDTD. From the result of conflict source analysis using C2Sim, we observe that the conflicts found in L1 are dominated by inter-array conflicts across 7 arrays. Based on this, we insert extra spaces to these arrays. To distribute positions of sets in the L1 cache, we arrange the amount of the padding as $interPad += LineSize \times \lfloor N_{\#sets}/N_{\#arrays} \rfloor$. This means that $M \times 64 \times 9$ bytes padding is inserted at the beginning of Mth array, where $N_{\#sets} = 64, N_{\#arrays} = 7$. From this intra-array padding (Opt.3), we can achieve 1.32 times speedup as shown in Table 4(c).

Next, we examine scalability for multithread executions. Table 4(d) shows the speedup obtained from the original code using an OpenMP version of Himeno. First, we analyze cache miss behaviors for serial and 16-thread execution using C2Sim and observe that both of them are dominated by L1 inter-array conflicts across 7 major arrays[3]. Then, we insert inter-padding by displacing the starting position of each array 64×9 bytes from the adjacent arrays similar to the case of 3D-FDTD. Additionally, to validate feasibility in the actual use cases, we compare the speedup with the configuration that enables the hardware prefetch. From the results, we observe that the performance gain due to the padding is kept even if the number of threads is increased to 16. It is also observed that additional speedup can be obtained when we turn on the HW prefetch. Here, we observe that 1.75x speedup in 1 thread and 1.70x speedup in 16 threads can be achieved compared with their baseline before the padding. From these, we can understand that the optimal padding decision assisted by C2Sim contributes to scalable performance improvement for multithread programs.

We note that the workflow consisting of three strategies (Opt.1 to Opt.3) presented in this Section could be performed automatically by feeding back the dominant source of conflicts to the code generation or runtime parts implemented as a software stack composed of compilers and memory management systems. As a future work, we plan to enhance our C2Sim for a basis of fully automated tuning system.

5   Related Works

C2Sim is a simulation-driven model for detecting cache-line misses to exploit the underlying cache performance. The core part of C2Sim is similar to the algorithm used in cachegrind [1,11], which models SA caches, aligned and unaligned memory accesses and true LRU replacement policy on the top of a dynamic binary translator. In addition to the model found in cachegrind, we implement mechanisms for identifying cache-line conflicts and model more detailed cache structures such as three level caches, physical address translation, and a slice mapping mechanism.

---

[3] The 16-thread execution might underestimates conflicts in a shared L3 cache because we assume 16 independent L3 caches in the current C2Sim implementation.

CMP\$im [7] is a cache simulator implemented using the Pin tool set like ours. While it models details of cache structures across a multi-core CPU, it does not provide any mechanisms to reveal line conflict misses in their original form. On the other hand, C2Sim provides a concurrent dual cache simulation mechanism to accurately identify cache-line conflicts and their sources.

The authors of [19] implement a comprehensive cache simulator that provides cache performance data needed for code optimization. They focus on reuse distance and define conflict miss as follows: If the reuse distance of an access is smaller than the number of cache lines, the resulted miss is regarded as a conflict miss. However, their definition based on reuse distance is a kind of approximation like the FIFO-based method [4,17]. The judgments for conflicts depend on their threshold distance and this leads errors for the detection.

A profiler called DProf presented in [13] uses CPU performance counters to categorize types of cache misses. They attempt to identify line conflict misses (associativity miss in that paper) by finding repeated cycles of the same address in a single associativity set. However, it is not clear how accurate they classify the type of miss using information from hardware performance counters. On the other hand, our C2Sim models line-conflict misses based on theoretical upper bound using FA cache and detect them accurately.

Seshadri et al. proposed a special hardware mechanism called Evicted-Address Filter (EAF) to mitigate cache-line conflicts [18]. They classify line conflict into cache pollution and cache thrashing and attempt to record them on EAF. While their approach can prevent line conflicts to some extent by adjusting cache insertion policy, theirs are hardware-based approach and require modification of hardware.

To the best of our knowledge, this paper is the first one that presents cache-line conflict detection within actual programs using software-based advanced cache simulation techniques. The essential part of this is to reveal detail cache behavior normally invisible from software. Therefore, our simulator is capable of evaluating the impact of different cache organization and strategies like prefetching and replacement policy in addition to cache conflicts focused on this paper.

Padding is a traditional performance optimization technique to avoid cache line conflict misses [5,16]. For inserting pads appropriately, we need to investigate where the extra spaces should be inserted and how much space is good for performance. While some existing papers build analytical models to decide the amount of padding [5,8,14], the locations to be padded are heuristically determined by hands of expert programmers. On the other hand, our C2Sim provides practically accurate sources of conflict and their locations. We believe this dramatically eases the actual performance tuning workflow.

6   Conclusions

In this paper, we have presented a method that reveals cache-line conflicts during the actual execution. Here, we developed a cache-line conflict simulator called C2Sim. C2Sim is capable to simultaneously simulate both ideal fully associative caches and realistic baseline caches derived from existing architectures. We also proposed a mechanism that enables users to identify where and why line conflict miss occurs. We have shown that cache-line conflict misses can be avoided by padding the appropriate arrays as suggested by our C2Sim analysis. We also showed that these clues manifest themselves in improved execution performance in both serial and parallel executions.

C2Sim is available at https://github.com/YukinoriSato/ExanaPkg as a part of Exana tool kit. We encourage researchers and developers to download it as a basis for productive performance tuning.

Acknowledgments. This work was supported by CREST, Japan Science and Technology Agency.

References

1. Cachegrind. http://valgrind.org/docs/manual/cg-manual.html
2. Himeno benchmark. http://accc.riken.jp/en/supercom/himenobmt/
3. PolyBench. https://sourceforge.net/projects/polybench/
4. Collins, J.D., Tullsen, D.M.: Runtime identification of cache conflict misses: the adaptive miss buffer. ACM Trans. Comput. Syst. **19**(4), 413–439 (2001)
5. Hong, C., et al.: Effective padding of multidimensional arrays to avoid cache conflict misses. In: Proceedings of the 37th ACM Conference on Programming Language Design and Implementation, PLDI 2016, pp. 129–144 (2016)
6. Irazoqui, G., Eisenbarth, T., Sunar, B.: Systematic reverse engineering of cache slice selection in Intel processors. In: 2015 Euromicro Conference on Digital System Design (DSD), pp. 629–636, August 2015
7. Jaleel, A., Cohn, R., Luk, C.-K., Jacob, B.: CMP$im: a pin-based on-the-fly multi-core cache simulator. In: Proceedings of the Fourth Annual Workshop on Modeling, Benchmarking and Simulation (MOBS 2008) (2008)
8. Li, Z.: Simultaneous minimization of capacity and conflict misses. J. Comput. Sci. Technol. **22**(4), 497–504 (2007)
9. Luk, C.-K., et al.: Pin: building customized program analysis tools with dynamic instrumentation. In: Proceedings of the 2005 ACM SIGPLAN Conference on Programming Language Design and Implementation, pp. 190–200 (2005)
10. Minami, T., Hibino, M., Hiraishi, T., Iwashita, T., Nakashima, H.: Automatic parameter tuning of three-dimensional tiled FDTD kernel. In: Daydé, M., Marques, O., Nakajima, K. (eds.) VECPAR 2014. LNCS, vol. 8969, pp. 284–297. Springer, Cham (2015). doi:10.1007/978-3-319-17353-5_24
11. Nethercote, N., Seward, J.: Valgrind: a framework for heavyweight dynamic binary instrumentation. In: Proceedings of the 28th ACM Conference on Programming Language Design and Implementation, PLDI 2007, pp. 89–100 (2007)
12. Nikoleris, N., Eklov, D., Hagersten, E.: Extending statistical cache models to support detailed pipeline simulators. In: 2014 IEEE International Symposium on Performance Analysis of Systems and Software, pp. 86–95, March 2014
13. Pesterev, A., Zeldovich, N., Morris, R.T.: Locating cache performance bottlenecks using data profiling. In: Proceedings of the 5th European Conference on Computer Systems, EuroSys 2010, pp. 335–348 (2010)

14. Rivera, G., Tseng, C.-W.: Tiling optimizations for 3D scientific computations. In: Proceedings of the 2000 ACM/IEEE Conference on Supercomputing, SC 2000 (2000)
15. Satish, N., et al.: Can traditional programming bridge the Ninja performance gap for parallel computing applications? Commun. ACM **58**(5), 77–86 (2015)
16. Sato, S., Sato, Y., Endo, T.: Investigating potential performance benefits of memory layout optimization based on roofline model. In: Proceedings of the 2nd International Workshop on Software Engineering for Parallel Systems, SEPS 2015, pp. 50–56 (2015)
17. Sato, Y., Sato, S., Endo, T.: Exana: an execution-driven application analysis tool for assisting productive performance tuning. In: Proceedings of the 2nd International Workshop on Software Engineering for Parallel Systems, SEPS 2015, pp. 1–10 (2015)
18. Seshadri, V., et al.: The evicted-address filter: a unified mechanism to address both cache pollution and thrashing. In: 21st International Conference on Parallel Architectures and Compilation Techniques (PACT), pp. 355–366 (2012)
19. Tao, J., Karl, W.: Detailed cache simulation for detecting bottleneck, miss reason and optimization potentialities. In: Proceedings of the 1st International Conference on Performance Evaluation Methodolgies and Tools, VALUETOOLS 2006 (2006)

Shutdown Policies with Power Capping for Large Scale Computing Systems

Anne Benoit[1], Laurent Lefèvre[1(✉)], Anne-Cécile Orgerie[2], and Issam Raïs[1]

[1] Univ. Lyon, Inria, CNRS, ENS de Lyon, Univ. Claude-Bernard Lyon 1, LIP,
Lyon, France
{Anne.Benoit,laurent.lefevre}@ens-lyon.fr, issam.rais@inria.fr
[2] CNRS, IRISA, Rennes, France
anne-cecile.orgerie@irisa.fr

Abstract. Large scale distributed systems are expected to consume huge amounts of energy. To solve this issue, shutdown policies constitute an appealing approach able to dynamically adapt the resource set to the actual workload. However, multiple constraints have to be taken into account for such policies to be applied on real infrastructures, in particular the time and energy cost of shutting down and waking up nodes, and power capping to avoid disruption of the system. In this paper, we propose models translating these various constraints into different shutdown policies that can be combined. Our models are validated through simulations on real workload traces and power measurements on real testbeds.

Keywords: Large scale distributed systems · Energy models · Shutdown policies · Simulations

1 Introduction

Reducing the energy consumption of large scale distributed systems (high performance computing centers, networks, datacenters) is a mandatory step to address, in order to build a sustainable digital society. Since more than a decade, several technological solutions have been made available by system designers to help reducing power, like shutdown and slowdown approaches. The first and most explored solution consists in shutting down and waking up some resources depending on platform usage. In this paper, the question on how resource providers and managers can be helped to validate their constraints while reducing the energy consumption using only the shutdown and wake-up of large amount of resources is addressed.

Resource providers and managers can be human who are responsible of the administration of large supercomputers, but they can also be software components that deal with resources (schedulers, resource management frameworks, etc.). Nowadays, hardware components of a datacenter or supercomputer (servers, network switches, data storage, etc.) are not yet energy proportional.

© Springer International Publishing AG 2017
F.F. Rivera et al. (Eds.): Euro-Par 2017, LNCS 10417, pp. 134–146, 2017.
DOI: 10.1007/978-3-319-64203-1_10

In fact, the static part (i.e., the part that does not vary with workload) of the energy consumed for example by computing units, represents a high part of the overall energy consumed by the node. Therefore, shutting unused nodes or routers, that are idle and not expected to be used in a predicted duration, could lead to non negligible energy savings. This paper focuses on shutting down and waking up any kind of resources like servers, network devices, memory banks, cores, etc. For clarity's sake, here, the proposed models and validations focus on servers (called *nodes*).

Off-the-shelf software eco-systems are nowadays integrating (mainly basic) shutdown policies. Data center resource managers propose techniques or hooks to configure such capabilities. For example, Slurm [16], an open-source cluster management system, introduces a *SuspendTime*[1] that represents the minimum idle time after which it allows the node to be switched off. Then, the resource manager is responsible for deciding when to switch on and off servers. It takes decisions either based on pre-determined policy [16], on workload predictions [8], on queuing models [5] or on control theory approach [15].

Overall, shutdown seems to be an interesting leverage to save energy (referred to as *OnOff leverage*). But this technique cannot be applied at large scale if no constraint is respected on the target system. This is especially true if the resource providers take into account several types of constraints, such as the cost of shutdown and wake-up (in time and energy), or power-capping constraints imposed to the whole system. In particular, shutting down too many nodes could cause the power consumption to be under the minimum power capping decided with the electricity provider. Likewise, if too many nodes are waked up, and if providers take into account the energy consumed during shutdown and wake-up sequences (which is far from being free), limits fixed by the electricity provider can be greatly exceeded. If providers do not take into account such constraints, they can put into danger machines composing the studied computing facility.

In this paper, we propose several models of shutdown that can be used under actual and future supercomputer constraints, and that takes into account the impact of shutting down and waking up nodes (time, power and energy) and the Idle and Off states observed after such actions as they impact the power usage. Our formalization allows for a mono or combined usage of models in order to help resource managers and providers respect several constraints at the same time. Several shutdown models that can be handled by resource providers and that deal with infrastructure constraints are explored:

- The *basic models* allow comparisons with several related works where shutting down and waking up nodes can either be free and immediate, or not allowed.
- The *sequence-aware models* account for the cost of shutting down or waking up nodes, in terms of time or energy.
- The *power-capping models* aim at respecting power capping requirements.

The models are used as follows: knowing that there is an idle interval of length T_{gap} on a given node, the model decides whether the node should be shut down, given the enforced constraints.

---

[1] http://slurm.schedmd.com/power_save.html.

The paper is organized as follows. Section 2 presents the modeling of the various shutdown (OnOff) policies for basic models, sequence-aware models, and finally models dealing with power-capping. It also deals with the usage and combination of these models. The experimental setup is described in Sect. 3 and experimental results are analyzed in Sect. 4. Section 5 presents related work on shutdown techniques for large scale systems. Section 6 concludes and presents future work.

2 Modeling Shutdown Policies

This section presents our characterization of the impact of shutting down and waking up a node in terms of time and power consumption. It also introduces models acting on the OnOff leverage.

2.1 Model Inputs

To monitor nodes' wake-up and shutdown sequences, an external power monitoring allowing us to trace power consumption of nodes is used. It has a rate of one power value per second. The sequences have been monitored to detect when every event happened. For the wake-up sequence, unfortunately, no information could be extracted between BIOS (Basic Input Output System) bootstrap and GRUB (Grand Unified Bootloader) loading. The first monitorable event in this sequence is the Kernel launch; this is displayed on Fig. 1, which shows how the power evolves with time during a monitored boot sequence on a node. The time where kernel starts has been recovered with the *dmesg* tool (which is a logging of what happened during the launch of the kernel). The INIT monitoring is made by modifying the runlevel scripts.

These monitored profiles are modeled by a sequence for each node. For node i, $Seq_i = \{(t_0; AvrgP_0), \ldots, (t_n; AvrgP_n)\}$ is the set of timestamps and average power consumption measurements of a wake-up (or Off→On sequence) or shutdown (or On→Off sequence), where t_0 and t_n represent the starting and ending time respectively of sequence Seq on node i. The length of the sequence is therefore $t_n - t_0$, and at time-step t_k ($1 \leq k \leq n$), $AvrgP_k$ is the average power consumption of node i.

2.2 Model Definitions

Basic Models. Two basic models are used by most papers in the literature: either the nodes are never shut down (No-OnOff model), or there is no cost (time, energy, power) to wake up or shutdown a node (LB-ZeroCost-OnOff model: *Lower-Bound Zero-Cost OnOff Model*), making it very simple to shutdown a node (but very far from reality). In this context, the node consumes nothing when executing an On→Off or Off→On sequence. Thus, there is no cost nor time spent to switch state, and no power peak observed during the sequence. In this context, no influence could be derived from waking up or shutting down nodes. This LB-ZeroCost-OnOff model therefore provides a theoretical upper bound on the gains that can be achieved by shutting down nodes.

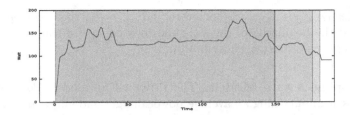

Fig. 1. Monitored boot sequence of a node running Linux: BIOS-MBR-GRUB period in red; Kernel in green; INIT in gray. (Color figure online)

Sequence-Aware Models. The sequence-aware models make sure that the sequence observed on a node or set of nodes during On→Off or Off→On sequences fits in time or are beneficial in energy. Therefore, information for every node composing the studied case needs to be recorded, in particular a record of the Off→On and On→Off sequences.

Time Constrained. The first model, SEQ-AW-T (*Sequence-Aware-Time*), checks whether there is enough time to perform an On→Off sequence followed by an Off→On sequence on a node, given the available time when the node is idle. Let T_{gap} be the size of the "gap", i.e., the interval of idle time of the node. Then, SEQ-AW-T will allow the addition of sequences in this time slot if and only if $T_{\text{OnOff}} + T_{\text{OffOn}} \leq T_{\text{gap}}$, where T_{OnOff} (resp. T_{OffOn}) is the time spent by the node during an On→Off (resp. Off→On) sequence.

Energy Constrained. The SEQ-AW-E model (*Sequence-Aware-Energy*) further refines SEQ-AW-T by checking whether changing the state of the node is beneficial in terms of energy. The minimum time T_s of the gap is now further constrained by the energy savings:

$$T_s = \max\left(T_{\text{OnOff}} + T_{\text{OffOn}}, \frac{E_{\text{OnOff}} + E_{\text{OffOn}} - P_{\text{off}}(T_{\text{OnOff}} + T_{\text{OffOn}})}{P_{\text{idle}} - P_{\text{off}}}\right),$$

where:

- P_{idle} is the power consumption when the node is in the Idle state (unused, but powered on);
- P_{off} is the power consumption when the node is switched off (typically not null and lower than P_{idle});
- E_{OnOff} is the energy consumed during the On→Off sequence;
- E_{OffOn} is the energy consumed during the Off→On sequence.

The first term states, as for SEQ-AW-T, that at least a time $T_{\text{OnOff}} + T_{\text{OffOn}}$ is needed to shutdown the node (and to wake it up) during the idle interval. The second term ensures that there will be gains in energy: the energy saved by running at P_{off} rather than P_{idle} is $T_s(P_{\text{idle}} - P_{\text{off}})$ during the interval, but the additional energy due to the On→Off and Off→On sequences is $E_{\text{OnOff}} +$

$E_{\text{OffOn}} - P_{\text{off}}(T_{\text{OnOff}} + T_{\text{OffOn}})$. Therefore, if $T_{\text{gap}} > T_s$, then it is beneficial to shutdown (at the beginning of the gap) and to wake up (at the end of the gap) the node, in terms of energy consumption.

Power-Capping-Aware Models. The POWER-CAP model (*Power-Capping-Aware*) aims at maintaining an average power budget and guaranteeing minimal or maximal electrical power consumption. Indeed, shutting down and waking up components could lead to hard power-capping disruptions. Such actions energetically stress the node, whether it is in an upper or lower way. Here, information about the power capping that should be respected is provided.

A minimum power capping (PC_Min) represents a constraint set by the electrical provider, and is defined by providing a lower bound on power. A maximum power capping (PC_Max) represents power limit fixed by the electrical provider, and it is defined by an upper limit on power. These minimum and maximum power capping values may be a function of the time, i.e., the requirements may change in time.

We introduce the function $PowerSum(X, t)$, which returns the sum of the power consumed by nodes in set X at time-step t. We denote by ALL the set of all nodes. Nodes in X can be shut down or waked up only if $PowerSum(ALL, t) \geq PC\_Min$ and $PowerSum(ALL) \leq PC\_Max$ at all time during the sequence.

2.3 Model Usages

Several models have been derived, assuming that local knowledge about the node reservations is available, i.e., the current state of each node: *On* (*Working* or *Idle*) or *Off*. At current time-step T_c, a model aims at deciding whether this node can be shut down and then waked up, while respecting the constraints of the system. If the node is neither in a *Working* or *Off* state, it is in an *Idle* interval of length T_{gap}. Therefore, an entity giving advice on changing the state of a node (or set of nodes) is provided, making sure that the overall system responds to the described constraints.

3   Experimental Setup

To instantiate our models in various configurations, we developed a simulator capable of replaying a real datacenter trace, with real node and job calibrations (time, power, energy). Grid'5000 [1], a large-scale and versatile testbed for experiment-driven research in all areas of computer science, was used as a testbed. Grid'5000 deploys clusters linked with dedicated high performance networks in several cities in France (Lille, Nancy, Sophia, Lyon, Nantes, Rennes, Grenoble). On the Lyon site, the energy consumption of every node from all available clusters (Orion, Taurus, Sagittaire) is monitored through a dedicated wattmeter, exposing one power measurement per second with a 0.125 W accuracy. Therefore, detailed traces concerning the energy consumption of jobs at any time step are available. An average power consumption of each job was obtained.

Thanks to these traces, realistic replays of jobs with their corresponding energy consumption is performed. Taurus nodes were monitored to calibrate in time, energy and power the Off→On and On→Off sequences, as explained in Sect. 2 (see Table 1).

Table 1. Calibration nodes' characteristics and energy parameters for On→Off and Off→On sequences (average on 50 experimental measurements).

Taurus	Features	Parameters	Values
Server model	Dell PowerEdge R720	E_{OffOn} (Joules)	23,683
CPU model	Intel Xeon E5-2630	T_{OffOn} (seconds)	182
Number of CPU	2	E_{OnOff} (Joules)	1,655
Cores per CPU	6	T_{OnOff} (seconds)	15
Memory (GB)	32	P_{idle} (Watts)	91
Storage (GB)	2 × 300 (HDD)	P_{off} (Watts)	8
T_s (seconds)	286.29		

For our evaluation, two real workload traces of the Grid'5000 Lyon site were extracted. Traces only contain nodes that received jobs during the chosen period to avoid doping of the energy saving results with nodes that will potentially always be shutdown. The first one runs from October 24, 2016 at 7 pm to November 1, 2016 at 8 am, thus representing approximately one week of resource utilization on this site. During this period, the number of used nodes is 76. The second one runs from October 29, 2016 at 7 pm to December 1, 2016 at 3 am, thus representing approximately one month of resource utilization. The number of used nodes is 69. Nodes are considered homogeneous concerning the P_{idle}, P_{off} characteristics, Off→On and On→Off sequences. This study is focused on shutting down nodes, scheduled jobs are considered fixed. Moreover, we only add sequences if possible, thus not impacting nor overlaying scheduled jobs. For the week trace, there are 1,768 jobs with an average power consumption of 167.5 Watts and an average job size of 13,776.96 s (approximately four hours). For the month trace, there are 5,505 jobs with an average power consumption of 166.5 Watts and an average job size of 14,203.42 s (approximately four hours). Yet, these traces exhibit high workload variations as shown on Figs. 2 and 3, where the upper curve corresponds to the NO-ONOFF model.

4   Experimental Validation

This section presents the simulation results for the proposed setup as proposed in Sect. 3. All graphs represent a trace replay of the application of one or multiple combined models of Sect. 2. Table 2 presents the energy consumption in Joules of all models in the figures included in this section. This section presents results of the simulator on the extracted traces with calibration of Taurus nodes while applying previously defined models. The first trace, which spreads over one week, will be used to extensively study behavior of models. The second trace, over one month, will validate observations and model tendencies at a larger scale.

For the experiments involving POWER-CAP, SEQ-AW-T is always combined with this model to ensure that the node is in the *On* state when a scheduled job starts. Shutting down a node is allowed only when it can be waked up before the end of the idle time interval, to ensure that no job is delayed.

Table 2. Trace replay's energy consumption (in Joules), number of added double sequences (On→Off and Off→On), and percentage of energy saved compared to NO-ONOFF replay.

Model	Total energy consumed	# (On→Off and Off→On)	% Saved
Grid'5000 trace, 1 week			
NO-ONOFF	6,083,698,688	0	0.0
LB-ZEROCOST-ONOFF	3,983,408,384	1794	34.52
SEQ-AW-T	4,015,736,064	964	33.99
SEQ-AW-E	4,015,201,024	844	34.00
POWER-CAP 2000 min	4,401,067,520	855	27.65
POWER-CAP 4000 min	4,593,668,096	761	24.49
POWER-CAP 6000 min	5,059,857,408	617	16.82
Grid'5000 trace, 1 month			
NO-ONOFF	22,866,315,264	0	0.0
LB-ZEROCOST-ONOFF	12,935,132,160	5,559	43.43
SEQ-AW-T	13,038,270,464	3,819	42.9804
SEQ-AW-E	13,037,558,784	3,605	42.9835
POWER-CAP 4000 min	17,864,194,048	2,376	21.87

4.1   Sequence-Aware Models: Seq-Aw-T and Seq-Aw-E

Figures 2 and 3 show results of the different models, namely NO-ONOFF, SEQ-AW-T, SEQ-AW-E, and LB-ZEROCOST-ONOFF on, respectively, one week and one month traces. Between the two sequence-aware models, minor differences can be witnessed on the complete replay. For example on Fig. 2, for October 31 at 4:40 am, SEQ-AW-T allows more Off→On sequences to be scheduled. Both of these models lead to major energy savings, respectively 34.00% and 39.9% of energy savings on the one week trace compared to NO-ONOFF, as shown in Table 2. In comparison with the NO-ONOFF trace replay, major power peaks are witnessed because of the application of these models. For instance, in the one week trace, for October 31 at 12:00 pm, after a peak of work around 12,000 W, a very low peak is witnessed under 1,000 W. Such a behavior could be witnessed in an amplified way on Fig. 3 for instance around November 12, November 3, and

November 21. Such behaviors could lead to abrupt thermal changes and thus to hot and cool spots, so to possible deterioration of the nodes.

LB-ZEROCOST-ONOFF, the model with immediate On→Off with zero cost is also presented for comparison. There is no significant difference in energy consumption observed when the cost of On→Off and Off→On sections are accurately described. However, the number of On→Off that are effectively triggered is significantly lower, implying that LB-ZEROCOST-ONOFF allows the addition of sequences when T_{gap} is smaller that $T_{\mathrm{OnOff}} + T_{\mathrm{OffOn}}$.

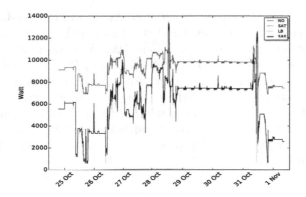

Fig. 2. Replay for a week of Grid'5000 trace with NO-ONOFF (NO) and with SEQ-AW-T (SAT), SEQ-AW-E (SAE), LB-ZEROCOST-ONOFF (LB) models.

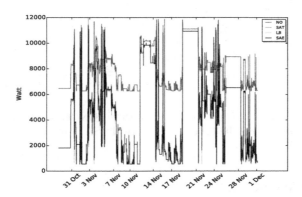

Fig. 3. Replay for a month of Grid'5000 trace with NO-ONOFF (NO) and with SEQ-AW-T (SAT), SEQ-AW-E (SAE), LB-ZEROCOST-ONOFF (LB) models.

4.2   Power-Capping Model

Next, a focus on the POWER-CAP model is made. A maximum and a minimum power cap is set throughout the simulation. Modulation of the minimum power cap to see how it acts with the trace replay is then simulated. Recall that since only the OnOff leverage is evaluated, scheduled jobs are fixed. Therefore, maximum power cap does not vary because it highly depends on jobs and also because the difference between P_{idle} and P_{off} is more important than the difference between the peaks witnessed during the Off→On or On→Off sequences and P_{idle}.

Figure 4 shows results of NO-ONOFF, SEQ-AW-T and POWER-CAP with various PC_Min scenarios (2000, 4000 and 6000) during the one week trace. Even with the highest minimum power cap, here 6,000 W, important energy savings (around 16.82 % compared to NO-ONOFF) are made. The stratified power usage for every respected power cap was expected. In fact, a lower power cap permits more sequences to be scheduled and thus, more energy savings. The lowest cap constraint (2,000 W) shows that a minimum power capping could be always respected and would still have a close to minimum consumption. Finally, Fig. 5 shows results for larger scale replay (one month) on NO-ONOFF, SEQ-AW-T and POWER-CAP with 4,000 as PC_Min, and leads to the same conclusions.

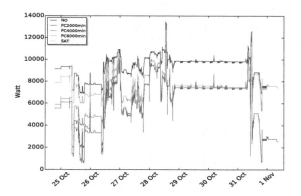

Fig. 4. Replay for a week of Grid'5000 trace with NO-ONOFF (NO) and with POWER-CAP (with $PC\_Min = 2000, 4000, 6000$), SEQ-AW-T (SAT) models.

5   Related Work

Pioneering work on studying the energy-related impacts of shutdown techniques started in 2001 [2, 11]. These early efforts did not consider any transition cost for switching between *Idle* and *Off* states, but they nonetheless showed the potential impact of such techniques. Yet, aggressive shutdown policies are not always the best solution to save energy [9].

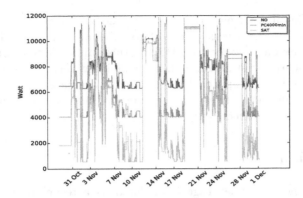

Fig. 5. Replay for a month of Grid'5000 trace with No-OnOff (NO) and with Power-Cap (with $PC\_Min = 4000$), Seq-Aw-T (SAT) models.

Demaine et al. examine the power minimization problem where the objective is to minimize the total transition costs plus the total time spent in the active state [3]. They develop a $(1+2\alpha)$-approximation algorithm, with α the transition cost. However, the parameters considered for this transition cost highly vary across the literature. Gandhi et al. take into account the energy cost of waking up servers (no shutting down cost as it is estimated to be negligible in comparison with the waking-up cost) [5]. This energy cost is assumed to be equal to the transition time multiplied by the power consumption while in the *Idle* state. Lin et al. take into account the energy used for the transition, the delay in migrating connections or data, the increased wear-and-tear on the servers, and the risk associated with server toggling [7]. We go one step beyond and carefully assess the cost of shutting down or waking up a node, in terms of time, power and energy.

Moreover, supporting shutdown and wake-up of large amount of resources can be risky as it impacts the whole infrastructure of supercomputers, such as the cooling system [18]. Shutdown techniques can also be used for limiting the dark silicon effect, i.e., the under-utilization of the device integration capacity due to power and temperature effects [4]. This issue has lead to the introduction of user-specified, dynamic, hardware-enforced processor power bounds, as for the Intel's Sandy Bridge family of processors for instance [13]. At a data center level, it translates into power budgeting, where the total power budget is partitioned among the cooling and computing units, and where the cooling power has to be sufficient to extract the heat of the computing power. Given the computing power budget, Zhan and Reda propose an optimal computing budgeting technique based on knapsack-solving algorithms to determine the power caps for the individual servers [17].

Shutdown policies are often combined with consolidation algorithms that gather the load on a restricted number of servers to favor the shutdown of the others. Employing either reactive or proactive scheduling options [6,10], consolidation algorithms increase the energy gains brought by shutdown techniques at a cost of a trade-off with performance [14]. The rich diversity in power management techniques and levers can lead to substantial issues if they are not coordinated at the data center level [12]. In this paper, shutdown policies (i.e., when to shutdown) are studied, without combining them to scheduling algorithms and consolidation approaches in order to evaluate the impacts of such policies without interfering with the workload of real platforms and with the users' expected performance.

6   Conclusion

In this paper, the OnOff leverage is explored as a technique to save energy on large scale computing systems. While it is often assumed that nodes can change state at no cost, realistic scenarios are explored where several constraints (time and energy of changing the state of a node, global power capping on the platform) may prevent us from shutting down a node at a given time. This paper presents a formal definition of such models, targeting various scenarios on selected architectures.

A possible application of these models, either alone or combined, is provided through a set of simulations on real workload traces, showing the gain in energy that can be achieved, given the constraints on the platform, and providing clear guidelines about when a node can change state. Overall, the gain of the non-realistic model, where nodes are instantaneously shutdown during an idle period, is very small over the sequence-aware model, that shutdowns a node only if there is time to wake it up again before the next computation (SEQ-AW-T), and accounts for the power consumption during the Off→On and On→Off sequences (SEQ-AW-E). On top of previous models, power-capping constraints (POWER-CAP) could be enforced, thus reducing the number of added On-Off sequences, and hence leading to losses in energy, but fully respecting the imposed constraints.

We plan to further add several models by considering for example a cooling-aware model that accounts for the system temperature in order to avoid abrupt thermal changes (and thus hot and cool spots), provoked by changing the state of a large number of nodes. We also plan to deeply analyze combinations of shutdown models in order to jointly take into account more realistic constraints imposed to supercomputers.

Acknowledgements. This work is integrated and supported by the ELCI project, a French FSN ("Fond pour la Société Numérique") project that associates academic and industrial partners to design and provide software environment for high performance computing. Experiments presented in this paper were carried out using the Grid'5000 testbed, supported by a scientific interest group hosted by Inria and including CNRS, RENATER and several Universities as well as other organizations (see https://www.grid5000.fr).

References

1. Bolze, R., et al.: Grid'5000: a large scale and highly reconfigurable experimental Grid testbed. Int. J. High Perform. Comput. Appl. **20**(4), 481–494 (2006). https://hal.inria.fr/hal-00684943
2. Chase, J.S., Anderson, D.C., Thakar, P.N., Vahdat, A.M., Doyle, R.P.: Managing energy and server resources in hosting centers. In: ACM Symposium on Operating Systems Principles (SOSP), pp. 103–116 (2001)
3. Demaine, E.D., Ghodsi, M., Hajiaghayi, M.T., Sayedi-Roshkhar, A.S., Zadimoghaddam, M.: Scheduling to minimize gaps and power consumption. In: ACM Symposium on Parallel Algorithms and Architectures (SPAA), pp. 46–54 (2007)
4. Esmaeilzadeh, H., Blem, E., St. Amant, R., Sankaralingam, K., Burger, D.: Power limitations and dark silicon challenge the future of multicore. ACM Trans. Comput. Syst. (TOCS) **30**(3), 11:1–11:27 (2012)
5. Gandhi, A., Gupta, V., Harchol-Balter, M., Kozuch, M.A.: Optimality analysis of energy-performance trade-off for server farm management. Perform. Eval. **67**(11), 1155–1171 (2010)
6. Gmach, D., Rolia, J., Cherkasova, L., Kemper, A.: Resource pool management: reactive versus proactive or let's be friends. Comput. Netw. **53**(17), 2905–2922 (2009)
7. Lin, M., Wierman, A., Andrew, L.L.H., Thereska, E.: Dynamic right-sizing for power-proportional data centers. IEEE/ACM Trans. Netw. (TON) **21**(5), 1378–1391 (2013)
8. Orgerie, A.C., Lefèvre, L.: ERIDIS: energy-efficient reservation infrastructure for large-scale distributed systems. Parallel Process. Lett. **21**(02), 133–154 (2011)
9. Orgerie, A.C., Lefèvre, L., Gelas, J.P.: Save watts in your grid: green strategies for energy-aware framework in large scale distributed systems. In: IEEE International Conference on Parallel and Distributed Systems (ICPADS), pp. 171–178 (2008)
10. Pernici, B., et al.: Setting energy efficiency goals in data centers: the GAMES approach. In: Huusko, J., de Meer, H., Klingert, S., Somov, A. (eds.) E2DC 2012. LNCS, vol. 7396, pp. 1–12. Springer, Heidelberg (2012). doi:10.1007/978-3-642-33645-4_1
11. Pinheiro, E., Bianchini, R., Carrera, E.V., Heath, T.: Load balancing and unbalancing for power and performance in cluster-based systems. In: Workshop on Compilers and Operating Systems for Low Power, pp. 182–195 (2001)
12. Raghavendra, R., Ranganathan, P., Talwar, V., Wang, Z., Zhu, X.: No "power" struggles: coordinated multi-level power management for the data center. In: ACM International Conference on Architectural Support for Programming Languages and Operating Systems (ASPLOS), pp. 48–59 (2008)
13. Rountree, B., Ahn, D.H., de Supinski, B.R., Lowenthal, D.K., Schulz, M.: Beyond DVFS: a first look at performance under a hardware-enforced power bound. In: IEEE International Parallel and Distributed Processing Symposium Workshops PhD Forum (IPDPSW), pp. 947–953, May 2012
14. Srikantaiah, S., Kansal, A., Zhao, F.: Energy aware consolidation for cloud computing. In: USENIX Conference on Power Aware Computing and Systems (HotPower), pp. 1–5 (2008)
15. Urgaonkar, R., Kozat, U.C., Igarashi, K., Neely, M.J.: Dynamic resource allocation and power management in virtualized data centers. In: IEEE Network Operations and Management Symposium (NOMS), pp. 479–486, April 2010

16. Yoo, A.B., Jette, M.A., Grondona, M.: SLURM: simple linux utility for resource management. In: Feitelson, D., Rudolph, L., Schwiegelshohn, U. (eds.) JSSPP 2003. LNCS, vol. 2862, pp. 44–60. Springer, Heidelberg (2003). doi:10.1007/10968987_3
17. Zhan, X., Reda, S.: Techniques for energy-efficient power budgeting in data centers. In: ACM/EDAC/IEEE Design Automation Conference (DAC), pp. 1–7, May 2013
18. Zhang, W., Wen, Y., Wong, Y.W., Toh, K.C., Chen, C.H.: Towards joint optimization over ICT and cooling systems in data centre: a survey. IEEE Commun. Surv. Tutor. **18**(3), 1596–1616 (2016)

Scheduling and Load Balancing

Partitioning Strategy Selection for In-Memory Graph Pattern Matching on Multiprocessor Systems

Alexander Krause$^{(\boxtimes)}$, Thomas Kissinger$^{(\boxtimes)}$, Dirk Habich$^{(\boxtimes)}$, Hannes Voigt, and Wolfgang Lehner

Database Systems Group, Technische Universität Dresden, Dresden, Germany
{alexander.krause,Thomas.Kissinger,dirk.habich,hannes.voigt,
wolfgang.lehner}@tu-dresden.de

Abstract. Pattern matching on large graphs is the foundation for a variety of application domains. The continuously increasing size of the underlying graphs requires highly parallel in-memory graph processing engines that need to consider non-uniform memory access (NUMA) and concurrency issues to scale up on modern multiprocessor systems. To tackle these aspects, a fine-grained graph partitioning becomes increasingly important. Hence, we present a classification of graph partitioning strategies and evaluate representative algorithms on medium and large-scale NUMA systems in this paper. As a scalable pattern matching processing infrastructure, we leverage a data-oriented architecture that preserves data locality and minimizes concurrency-related bottlenecks on NUMA systems. Our in-depth evaluation reveals that the optimal partitioning strategy depends on a variety of factors and consequently, we derive a set of indicators for selecting the optimal partitioning strategy suitable for a given graph and workload.

1 Introduction

Recognizing comprehensive patterns on large graph-structured data is a prerequisite for a variety of application domains such as fraud detection [11], biomolecular engineering [8], scientific computing [13], or social network analytics [9]. Due to the ever-growing size and complexity of the patterns and underlying graphs, *pattern matching* algorithms need to leverage an increasing amount of available compute resources in parallel to deliver results with an acceptable latency. Since modern hardware systems feature main memory capacities of several terabytes, state-of-the-art graph processing systems (e.g., Ligra [12], Galois [7] or, Green-Marl [4]) tend to store and process graphs entirely in main memory, which significantly improves scalability, because hardware threads are not limited by disk accesses anymore. To reach such high memory capacities and to provide enough bandwidth for the compute cores, modern servers contain an increasing number of memory domains resulting in a *non-uniform memory access (NUMA)*. For instance, on a multiprocessor system each processor maintains at least one

© Springer International Publishing AG 2017
F.F. Rivera et al. (Eds.): Euro-Par 2017, LNCS 10417, pp. 149–163, 2017.
DOI: 10.1007/978-3-319-64203-1_11

separate memory domain that is accessible for other processors via a communication network. However, efficient data processing on those systems faces several issues such as the increased latency and the decreased bandwidth when accessing remote memory domains. To further scale up on those NUMA systems, pattern matching on graphs needs to carefully consider these issues as well as the limited scalability of synchronization primitives such as atomic instructions [18].

To scale up *pattern matching* on those NUMA systems, we employ a fine-grained *data-oriented architecture (DORA)* in this paper, which turned out to exhibit a superior scalability behavior on large-scale NUMA systems as shown by Pandis et al. [10] and Kissinger et al. [6]. This architecture is characterized by implicitly partitioning data into small partitions that are pinned to a NUMA node to preserve a local memory access. In contrast to the bulk synchronous parallel (BSP) processing model [15], which is often used for graph processing, the data partitions are processed by local worker threads that communicate asynchronously via a high-throughput message passing layer. Hence, the overall performance of the *pattern matching* mainly depends on the graph partitioning.

In this paper, we systematically evaluate the influence of different graph partitioning strategies on the performance of *pattern matching* using a data-oriented architecture. Therefore, we introduce a novel classification of graph partitioning strategies and evaluate performance aspects of representative partitioning algorithms for each class. Our exhaustive evaluation on medium (4 sockets) and large-scale (64 sockets) NUMA systems reveals that the selection of the appropriate partitioning strategy depends on a multitude of factors such as graph characteristics, query pattern, the number of partitions, and worker threads. Thus, we argue that there is no one-size-fits-all strategy for partitioning graphs within a NUMA system and identify key features that shall guide partitioning strategy selection process.

Contributions. Our contributions are summarized as follows:

(1) We present a graph pattern matching processing model that is based on a fine-grained *data-oriented architecture* that is designed to operate on large scale-up NUMA systems (Sect. 2).
(2) We provide a classification of graph partitioning strategies that arranges the individual strategies based on a *partitioning criterion* and a *balancing criterion*. Moreover, we describe instances of the respective classes that we consider for our evaluations (Sect. 3).
(3) We exhaustively evaluate our identified partitioning strategies for different graphs and patterns on a medium and large-scale NUMA system and reason about the results. Our investigations show that the optimal partition strategy depends on a variety of factors (Sect. 4).
(4) Based on our evaluations, we derive a set of indicators that should be considered in the process of selecting the optimal partitioning strategy for pattern matching on graphs (Sect. 4.3).

Finally, we will give an overview of the related work (Sect. 5) and conclude the paper (Sect. 6).

2   Graph Pattern Matching on NUMA Systems

Within this paper, we focus on *edge-labeled multigraphs* as a general and widely employed graph data model [8, 9, 11]. An edge-labeled multigraph $G(V, E, \rho, \Sigma, \lambda)$ consists of a set of vertices V, a set of edges E, an incidence function $\rho : E \to V \times V$, and a labeling function $\lambda : E \to \Sigma$ that assigns a label to each edge. Hence, edge-labeled multigraphs allow any number of labeled edges between a pair of vertices. A prominent example for edge-labeled multigraphs is RDF [3].

Pattern matching is a declarative topology-based querying mechanism where the query is given as a graph-shaped pattern and the result is a set of matching subgraphs [14]. For instance, the *query pattern* depicted on the left hand side of Fig. 1 searches for all vertices that have two outgoing edges resulting in three matching subgraphs for the given underlying graph. A well-studied mechanism for expressing such query patterns are *conjunctive queries (CQ)* [17], which decompose the pattern into a set of *edge predicates* each consisting of a pair of vertices and an edge label. Assuming a wildcard label, the exemplary query pattern is decomposed into the conjunctive query $\{(V_1, *, V_2), (V_1, *, V_3)\}$.

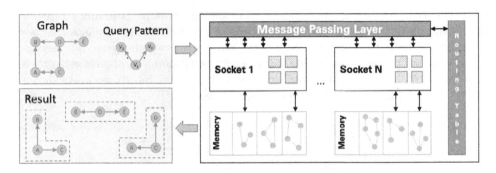

Fig. 1. Scalable graph pattern matching based on a data-oriented architecture [6, 10].

To scale up graph pattern matching on large multiprocessor systems, we employ an approach that is based on a *data-oriented architecture (DORA)* [10], which is known for its superior scalability on NUMA systems [6]. As illustrated on the right hand side of Fig. 1, the graph is implicitly split into a set of disjoint partitions. Each partition is placed in the local memory of a specific processor that runs *workers* on its local hardware threads. These workers are limited to operate exclusively on local graph partitions and leverage a high-throughput message passing layer for the inevitable communication. Only one worker is allowed to access a partition at a time to avoid costly fine-grained lockings of the data structures. Consequently, the number of workers is limited to the available local hardware threads and the number of local partitions can be chosen arbitrarily. An integral part of the message passing layer is the *routing table*, which keeps track of the partitioning and thus, maps the *partitioning criteria* (cf., Sect. 3) to the corresponding partition using a hash table. The overall goal of this architecture is (1) to restrict the access of threads to data structures in the local main memory, (2) to reduce the necessity of locks or atomic instructions, and (3) to hide remote memory latency using the high-throughput message passing layer.

To actually process *conjunctive queries* on such a data-oriented architecture, the *edge predicates* – CQs are consisting of – are evaluated one after another. Every time an edge predicate matches within a partition, a new message is generated by the worker thread to evaluate the successive edge predicate unless the predicate was the last one of the CQ. These messages are either sent to a single partition (unicast) or to all partitions (broadcast) depending on the edge predicate and partitioning criterion. Due to the topology-driven nature of pattern matching and the comprehensive structure of graphs, the appropriate selection of a *partitioning strategy* for a specific combination of query pattern and underlying graph is crucial for such an architecture as we will show throughout this paper.

3   Graph Partitioning Strategies

In this section, we provide a classification of known graph partitioning strategies and detail on our heuristic implementations of the individual strategies that we consider for further evaluation. We restrict our considerations to one representative algorithm per partitioning strategy, where partitioning strategies generate a disjoint set of graph partitions and leave redundancy for future work. As shown in Fig. 2, our classification spans two dimensions:

		Balancing Criterion		
		Edges (E)	Vertices (V)	Components (C)
Partition Criterion Granularity	Edges (E)	E/E Strategy RR	E/V not possible	E/C not possible
	Vertices (V)	V/E Strategy BE/DS	V/V Strategy RRV	V/C not possible
	Components (C)	C/E unknown	C/V Strategy k-Way	C/C unknown

Fig. 2. Classification of graph partitioning strategies and representative algorithms.

(1) The *partitioning criterion* that denominates the basic unit of the graph a partitioning strategy is operating on.
(2) The *balancing criterion* describing the unit of the graph that is balanced to achieve an equal utilization of the parallel compute resources.

For both dimensions those units are either fine-grained *edges (E)*, *vertices (V)*, or coarse-grained *components (C)* naming a connected set of vertices. Hence, a *partitioning strategy* is a combination of a *partitioning criterion* and a *balancing criterion*. Partitioning a graph at a specific granularity implies that more coarse-grained balancing criteria are not applicable (i.e., E/V, E/C, and V/C strategy).

To the best of our knowledge, there are no known viable representatives for the C/E and C/C strategy. In the following, we detail on the feasible strategies and describe our heuristic implementations that we use for our evaluation:

E/E Strategy. This partitioning strategy works on the most fine-grained level. We implemented this strategy using the *round-robin (RR)* algorithm, which evenly distributes edges to partitions in a lightweight fashion. This strategy is likely to distribute many or all outgoing edges of one vertex to multiple partitions. This decomposition leads to the necessity of broadcasts for the evaluation of all *edge predicates*.

V/V Strategy. This strategy partitions a graph by its vertices and balances the amount of vertices per partition. Hence, our *round-robin vertices (RRV)* algorithm is a specific implementation of this strategy and distributes every vertex and all of its outgoing edges to the partitions using the lightweight round-robin method. The advantage with regard to our pattern matching processing model (cf., Sect. 2) is that all outgoing edges of a vertex belong to a single partition being listed in the routing table. Thus, each *edge predicate* with a known source vertex can be routed to a single partition (unicast).

V/E Strategy. Similar to the *RRV* strategy, the graph is partitioned by its vertices. However, this partitioning strategy balances the number of edges. We consider two specific algorithms as implementation of this strategy: *balanced edges (BE)* and *distributed skew (DS)*. Both algorithms sort the vertices by the number of outgoing edges in a descending order. The BE algorithm iterates over this sorted list and assigns each vertex and all of its outgoing edges to the currently smallest partition to greedily balance the edges across the partitions. Thus, all outgoing edges of a vertex belong to the same partition, which once again results in a unicast for *edge predicates* with a known source vertex. The DS algorithm is a state-of-the-art approximation for handling skewed data in distributed joins [2] and extends the BE algorithm. To relieve highly connected vertices, DS equally distributes the edges of vertices that have significantly more outgoing edges compared to the average vertex across all partitions. Nevertheless, *edge predicates* aiming at those source vertices require a broadcast to all partitions. Because most real world graphs exhibit a non-uniform edge per vertex distribution, all vertex-oriented partitioning strategies (RRV, BE and DS) lead to different partitioning results.

C/V Strategy. The goal of a component-oriented strategy is to preserve locality by storing strongly connected vertices within the same partition. We leverage the well-known state-of-the-art *multilevel k-Way* algorithm as representative, which tries to balance the vertices among the partitions. In this paper, we use the k-Way implementation from the METIS library 5.1 [5]. Similar to the vertex-oriented strategies, we store all outgoing edges of a vertex in the same partition to avoid broadcasts during the pattern matching process.

4   Experimental Evaluation

To investigate the influence of the *partitioning strategies* (c.f, Sect. 3) on the *pattern matching* performance, we conducted an exhaustive evaluation on a medium and large-scale multiprocessor system. We use four test data graphs, each representing an individual application domain, that are generated with the graph benchmark framework gMark [1]. Additionally, we defined two *conjunctive queries* as depicted in Fig. 3: (1) the *V* query shapes a V with five vertices and four edges and (2) the *Quad* query is a rectangle, which consists of four vertices and four edges. For both queries, four *edge predicate* evaluations are necessary. Based on the query semantics, the evaluation of the edge predicates happens as follows:

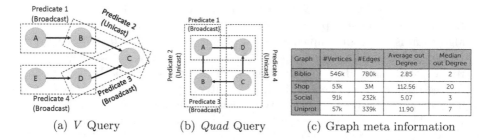

(a) *V* Query   (b) *Quad* Query   (c) Graph meta information

Fig. 3. Query patterns and test graphs for the medium-scale system.

V Query. The first edge predicate evaluation is broadcasted to all partitions, because only the edge label is known and not the source vertex. The intermediate result is a set of end vertices, which are used as source vertices for the second request. Depending on the partitioning strategy, the second edge request is evaluated using either unicast or broadcast messages (cf., Sect. 3). The intermediate result is a set of destination vertices, which are destination vertices for the third edge predicate. Hence, the third request needs to be broadcasted to all partitions, because the source vertex is unknown. The same applies for the fourth edge predicate evaluation.

Quad Query. The edge predicate evaluation of the *Quad* query is similar to the one of the *V* query with the difference that the evaluation of the fourth edge predicate depends on the partitioning strategy. Thus, this predicate can mostly be evaluated without the need of a broadcast.

As the edge predicate evaluation of our two queries suggests, pattern matching is a combination of unicasts and broadcasts within a partitioned environment. On the one hand, broadcasts distribute the evaluation of edge predicates to all partitions favoring edge-balanced partitions for an efficient execution. On the other hand, unicast messages assign edge predicate evaluations to single partitions, which – in contrast – favors vertex-balanced partitions.

For all of our experiments, we loaded the graph-under-test into main memory, partitioned it, and evenly distributed the partitions across the sockets and executed both pattern queries for all partitioning strategies and all possible *system configurations (SCs).* In our case a system configuration denominates a combination of the active workers and the total number of partitions. We repeated each experiment 20 times and calculated the average over all runs.

4.1 Evaluation on a Medium-Scale Multiprocessor System

Our medium-scale multiprocessor system consists of 4 sockets each equipped with an Intel Xeon CPU E7-4830 – resulting in 32 physical cores and 64 hardware threads – and 128 GB of main memory. Because of the possible size of intermediate results during the pattern matching process, it is advisable to have sufficient main memory, even if the stored graphs size is rather small, compared to the total amount of memory. For this system, we use the graphs with the characteristics listed in Fig. 3(c).

Partitioning Results. Figure 4 shows an overview of partitioning results for the different strategies and our test graphs. Since we have 64 hardware threads, we split the graphs into 64 partitions. The plots show the distribution of vertices and edges over the 64 partitions using box plots. From these plots and our experiments with a varying number of partitions, we can derive the following observations:

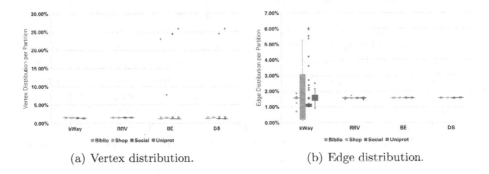

(a) Vertex distribution.   (b) Edge distribution.

Fig. 4. Partitioning results for 64 partitions.

(1) The partitioning and balancing criteria of the respective strategies are fulfilled independently of the graphs. For instance, our *round-robin vertices (RRV)* algorithm partitions the graphs by vertices and ideally balances the vertices among the 64 partitions, i.e., the vertices are evenly distributed over the partitions as depicted in Fig. 4(a). The same applies for *balanced edges (BE)* and *distributed skew (DS)*, which perfectly balance the edges among the partitions, as shown in Fig. 4(b).
(2) Depending on the strategy, balancing is done either by vertices or edges. This can lead to an imbalance on the non-balancing criterion depending on the underlying graph. For instance, *BE* and *DS* balance the partitions on edges.

However, there are few partitions with a much higher number of vertices than the others (illustrated as single dots in Fig. 4(a)). These outliers depend on the graph data. For *DS* outlier partitions exist for Uniprot and Social, but not for Biblio and Shop. The same effect is observable for *RRV*, however the imbalance on the edges over the partitions is not as remarkable.

(3) The k-Way algorithm partitions graphs by components and balances the vertices. On the one hand, this leads to an even distribution of the vertices over the partitions for our test graphs as shown in Fig. 4(a). This potentially leads to an imbalanced number of edges per partition and this imbalance is very different for the four test graphs, as visible in Fig. 4(b).

(4) The E/E strategy performs worst. The round-robin distribution of the edges among all partitions leads to the necessity of broadcasts during all edge predicate evaluations, which massively inhibits the system. Therefore, we omit the E/E results henceforward.

To summarize, each partitioning strategy is able to successfully maintain its respective balancing criterion while partitioning the graph into the considered number of partitions. However, the quality of the result is different for each case. Depending on the graph, there are partitions that vary greatly from the majority.

Number of Partitions and Workers. If we compare the partitioning results of Fig. 4 for the Biblio graph, we find that the V/V strategy (RRV) achieves the best partitioning result in terms of balanced partitions for both vertices and edges. Generally, such partitioning is very beneficial for our pattern matching.

In the first set of experiments, we use that setting to investigate the influence of the system configuration on the pattern matching performance for the *V* query. Thus, we varied the number of active workers between 8 and 64 and used 8 to 256 partitions. The heat map from Fig. 5 shows the slowdown factors compared to the optimal configuration. The optimal configuration uses 32 partitions and 32 workers. Generally, the pattern matching scales well for physical hardware threads, which is indicated by the coloring trend from orange to green

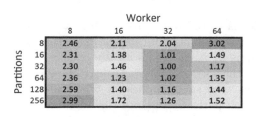

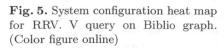

	Worker			
Partitions	8	16	32	64
8	2.46	2.11	2.04	3.02
16	2.31	1.38	1.01	1.49
32	2.30	1.46	1.00	1.17
64	2.36	1.23	1.02	1.35
128	2.59	1.40	1.16	1.44
256	2.99	1.72	1.26	1.52

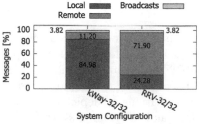

Fig. 5. System configuration heat map for RRV. V query on Biblio graph. (Color figure online)

Fig. 6. Messages per partitioning algorithm. V query on Biblio graph.

between the columns for 8 and 32 workers. In this case, 64 workers are not beneficial, because the V query employs two broadcasting requests at the end and the hyper-threads do not provide as much performance as their physical siblings.

Partitioning Strategies. After examining the query performance for a single graph partitioning strategy, we conducted the same experiments with the remaining strategies to show the influence of the different partitioning strategies in detail. The resulting heat maps are depicted in Fig. 7. From these heat maps, we derive the following three facts:

(1) The V/E strategy, represented by the *BE* and *DS* algorithms, performs comparatively bad. This happens because the query massively hits the vertex outlier partition, which can be seen in Fig. 4(a). Hence, this partition becomes a bottleneck for the second edge predicate of the V query.
(2) The k-Way partitioning results in a better query performance and utilizes the whole system with its optimal system configuration being 64 partitions by 64 workers. The advantage of k-Way is the partitioning and balancing of components. For the Biblio graph this results in even distribution of vertices and an almost even distribution of edges among the partitions. Furthermore, connected vertices are partitioned together, which is not necessarily the case for RRV as illustrated in Fig. 6. For the k-Way partitioning, the system creates mostly socket local messages and only a few remote messages, whereas the V/V strategy results in many remote messages as connected vertices are distributed among partitions on remote sockets.

From these results, we can conclude that the C/V partitioning strategy results in partition population that allows the system to scale up to its full potential.

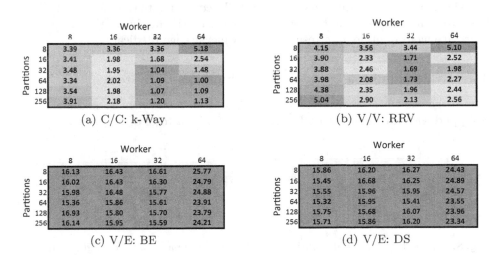

(a) C/C: k-Way   (b) V/V: RRV

(c) V/E: BE   (d) V/E: DS

Fig. 7. System configuration heat map. V query on Biblio graph. Color shadings relative to the global optimum (k-Way 64/64). (Color figure online)

Varying Graphs. After thoroughly examining the influences of different partitioning strategies on one graph, we conducted the same experiments for all other graphs from Fig. 3(c). Figure 8 presents the best system configurations per partitioning strategy and highlights the overall optimum. We showed that the C/C strategy performs best for the V query on the Biblio graph by utilizing the whole system and therefore should be used as the best strategy. However, when querying the Shop graph with a k-Way partitioning, the query performance drops by a factor of 2.3 while employing 32/32 as its optimal system configuration. The slowdown can be explained by the massive imbalance of edges within the partitions of k-Way as shown in Fig. 4(b). The other strategies show well balanced edges per partition, therefore all of them result in equal query performance. The same holds for the Social graph. The Uniprot graph is special in terms of the intermediate results, which are shown in Fig. 11. Compared to the Biblio graph, the V query produces a huge number of broadcasts for the Uniprot graph in the third edge predicate (c.f. Fig. 3(a)), which inhibits the system from scaling well, and therefore yields better performance for less workers. We conclude that the behavior of the query is strongly tied to the underlying graph.

Varying Queries. The previous paragraph concluded our test series for the V query. Now we want to show the performance implications of all considered influence factors for a second query type, namely the $Quad$ query from Fig. 3(b). The results for all system configurations, graphs and partitioning strategies are shown in the heat maps of Figs. 9 and 10. The optimal configurations are now always tied to 32 Workers with a varying number of partitions. We see the same run time behavior as for the V query, except for the V/E strategy. The $Quad$ query does not hit the vertex outlier partitions (c.f. Fig. 4(a)), which enables the BE and DS partitionings to compete with RRV and k-Way. The Shop and Social graphs show an equal slowdown for C/V, compared to the other strategies. However, the Uniprot graph now scales well with the hardware threads, since there are more intermediate results in the Unicast edge predicate.

4.2   Evaluation on a Large-Scale Multiprocessor System

Our large multiprocessor system is an SGI UV 3000 with 64 sockets each equipped with an Intel Xeon CPU E5-4655 v3 and a total of 8 TB main mem-

Strategy	Biblio		Shop		Social		Uniprot	
	SC	ms	SC	ms	SC	ms	SC	Ms
V/V: RRV	32/32	65	**32/32**	11790	**32/32**	665	8/8	884
V/E: BE	32/128	838	32/32	12387	16/16	666	**8/8**	878
V/E: DS	8/16	849	32/32	11964	32/32	673	8/8	890
C/V: k-Way	**64/64**	48	32/32	27376	32/32	864	8/8	885

Fig. 8. Optimal system configurations per graph and partitioning strategy for the V query.

Strategy	Biblio		Shop		Social		Uniprot	
	SC	ms	SC	ms	SC	ms	SC	Ms
V/V: RRV	32/32	2663	**32/64**	5773	32/32	102	32/32	22
V/E: BE	32/32	2617	32/64	5850	16/16	132	**32/32**	21
V/E: DS	32/32	2682	32/64	5982	**32/32**	94	32/32	22
C/V: k-Way	**32/32**	2254	64/128	15217	32/64	304	32/32	24

Fig. 9. Optimal system configurations per graph and partitioning strategy for the Quad query.

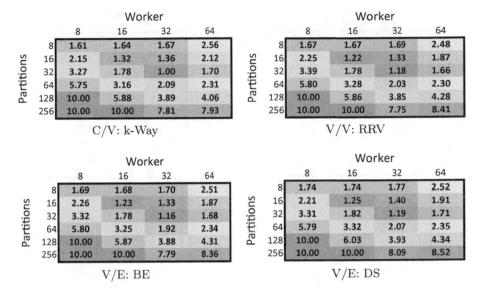

Fig. 10. System configuration heat maps. Quad query on Biblio graph.

Messages per Edge Request	Biblio	Uniprot
1	299,488	971
2	117	970
3	267	294,932
4	837	10.320

Unicast	Broadcast	Final result

Fig. 11. Intermediate results for each edge predicate of the *V* query

ory. We conducted the same experiments as for Sect. 4.1 and used gMark to scale up all graphs from Fig. 3(c) by a factor of 10 while preserving all other graph properties. All in all, we found that the entirety of our experiments on the large-scale system confirmed our observations from the medium-scale system. Figure 12 illustrates the heat maps for the *Quad* query on the *Social* graph for the SGI system. As for the medium-scale system, we see that using the hyperthreads is also not feasible on the SGI system. However, utilizing all physical cores leads to optimal performance in many cases, which underlines that our processing scales well with the employed hardware. In contrast to the medium-scale system, we see more variations in the heat maps, which is explained by the bigger number of sockets and the increasing influence of the NUMA effect on query performance.

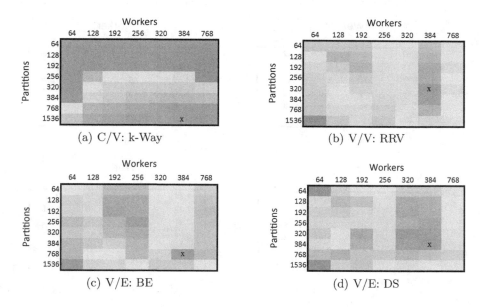

Fig. 12. System configuration heat maps. Quad query on Social graph.

4.3 Lessons Learned

Employing an optimal partitioning strategy is crucial for query performance. To find out the best strategy for a given query, we found that weighing the amount of broadcasts against unicasts, which result from the query pattern, is important.

Dominant Unicasts. It is desirable to partition the graph using a strategy which balances both edges and vertices. We argue that employing the C/V strategy is beneficial, even if there is a minor edge imbalance, since the unicast part of the query will benefit from the locality property of adjacent graph partitions. However, if the edge imbalance exceeds a certain limit, we suggest switching to the V/V strategy.

Dominant Broadcasts. Each partitioning strategy performs well. However it is desirable to achieve a balanced amount of edges between the partitions. As edges represent the amount of data records per partition, balancing them results in a more evenly distributed work in the system. All of the evaluated partition strategies have proven to be viable for graph pattern matching on a data-oriented architecture, except for the E/E strategy because of its broadcast-only nature.

The challenge is to adequately estimate the influences of broadcasts and unicasts due to their dependency on the underlying graph. Our experiments showed, that the optimal system configuration varies among the different workloads. As a rule of thumb, we found that it is beneficial to not use hyper threads in most cases and directly map the number of graph partitions to the number of workers.

5   Related Work

Many graph systems like Ligra [12] or Galois [7] often only state that the data will be partitioned but omit the reasoning behind the selected graph partitioning. We have shown that using one specific partitioning scheme for all graphs or workloads is not the optimal solution and may result in huge slowdown factors, compared to the possibly best system configuration.

Verma et al. [16] examine different graph partitioning strategies of existing systems and suggest which strategy is to be used for specific analytical algorithms. In contrast to the authors, we generally categorize graph partitioning strategies based on their partitioning and balancing criterion. Also, we don't evaluate specific algorithms but whole graph partitioning categories with respect to their influence on the query performance.

Graph processing on NUMA systems is considered by a broad community. There are many studies on optimizing the data partitioning for a Breadth First Search (BFS) on a NUMA machine as Yasui et al. show in [18]. We have shown that it is not always the best practice to always utilize the maximum number of available cores, depending on the executed query.

Running BFS is furthermore considered by the authors of Polymer [19], who argue that using an edge-balanced partitioning is the best way to go. However, this is only true if the edges are directly addressed instead of the vertices. We found that, for our architecture, direct addressing of vertices is more important. Thus we argue that the partitioning scheme is also dependent on the processing system. However, we also found that having an evenly distributed workload, i.e. the employment of a suitable partitioning, is crucial for optimal performance.

6   Conclusions and Future Work

In this paper, we could show a plethora of dependencies for graph partitioning and processing on NUMA systems. We could show for the variety of our tested domains and the employed graph partitioning strategies, that there is no one-size-fits-all strategy in terms of a good combination of a system configuration and partitioning algorithms out of the box. As outlined in Sect. 3, we see a need to examine the effects of optimization measures such as vertex or edge replication.

Acknowledgments. This work is partly funded within the Collaborative Research Center SFB 912 (HAEC).

References

1. Bagan, G., Bonifati, A., Ciucanu, R., Fletcher, G.H.L., Advokaat, N.: Generating flexible workloads for graph databases. PVLDB **9**(13), 1447–1460 (2016). http://www.vldb.org/pvldb/vol9/p1457-bagan.pdf

2. Cheng, L., Kotoulas, S., Ward, T.E., Theodoropoulos, G.: Efficiently handling skew in outer joins on distributed systems. In: 14th IEEE/ACM International Symposium on Cluster, Cloud and Grid Computing, CCGrid 2014, Chicago, IL, USA, 26–29 May 2014, pp. 295–304 (2014)
3. Decker, S., Melnik, S., van Harmelen, F., Fensel, D., Klein, M.C.A., Broekstra, J., Erdmann, M., Horrocks, I.: The semantic web: the roles of XML and RDF. IEEE Internet Comput. **4**(5), 63–74 (2000)
4. Hong, S., Chafi, H., Sedlar, E., Olukotun, K.: Green-Marl: a DSL for easy and efficient graph analysis. In: Proceedings of the 17th International Conference on Architectural Support for Programming Languages and Operating Systems, ASP-LOS 2012, London, UK, 3–7 March 2012, pp. 349–362 (2012)
5. Karypis, G., Kumar, V.: MeTis: unstructured graph partitioning and sparse matrix ordering system, version 5.1 (2013). http://www.cs.umn.edu/~metis
6. Kissinger, T., Kiefer, T., Schlegel, B., Habich, D., Molka, D., Lehner, W.: ERIS: a NUMA-aware in-memory storage engine for analytical workload. In: International Workshop on Accelerating Data Management Systems Using Modern Processor and Storage Architectures - ADMS 2014, Hangzhou, China, 1 September 2014, pp. 74–85 (2014). http://www.adms-conf.org/2014/adms14_kissinger.pdf
7. Nguyen, D., Lenharth, A., Pingali, K.: A lightweight infrastructure for graph analytics. In: ACM SIGOPS 24th Symposium on Operating Systems Principles, SOSP 2013, Farmington, PA, USA, 3–6 November 2013, pp. 456–471 (2013)
8. Ogata, H., Fujibuchi, W., Goto, S., Kanehisa, M.: A heuristic graph comparison algorithm and its application to detect functionally related enzyme clusters. Nucleic Acids Res. **28**(20), 4021–4028 (2000)
9. Otte, E., Rousseau, R.: Social network analysis: a powerful strategy, also for the information sciences. J. Inf. Sci. **28**(6), 441–453 (2002)
10. Pandis, I., Johnson, R., Hardavellas, N., Ailamaki, A.: Data-oriented transaction execution. PVLDB **3**(1), 928–939 (2010). http://www.comp.nus.edu.sg/ vldb2010/proceedings/files/papers/R83.pdf
11. Pandit, S., Chau, D.H., Wang, S., Faloutsos, C.: Netprobe: a fast and scalable system for fraud detection in online auction networks. In: Proceedings of the 16th International Conference on World Wide Web, WWW 2007, Banff, Alberta, Canada, 8–12 May 2007, pp. 201–210 (2007)
12. Shun, J., Blelloch, G.E.: Ligra: a lightweight graph processing framework for shared memory. In: ACM SIGPLAN Symposium on Principles and Practice of Parallel Programming, PPoPP 2013, Shenzhen, China, 23–27 February 2013, pp. 135–146 (2013)
13. Tas, M.K., Kaya, K., Saule, E.: Greed is good: optimistic algorithms for bipartite-graph partial coloring on multicore architectures. CoRR abs/1701.02628 (2017). http://arxiv.org/abs/1701.02628
14. Tran, T., Wang, H., Rudolph, S., Cimiano, P.: Top-k exploration of query candidates for efficient keyword search on graph-shaped (RDF) data. In: Proceedings of the 25th International Conference on Data Engineering, ICDE 2009, Shanghai, China, 29 March–2 April 2009, pp. 405–416 (2009)
15. Valiant, L.G.: A bridging model for parallel computation. Commun. ACM **33**(8), 103–111 (1990)
16. Verma, S., Leslie, L.M., Shin, Y., Gupta, I.: An experimental comparison of partitioning strategies in distributed graph processing. Proc. VLDB Endow. **10**(5), 493–504 (2017)
17. Wood, P.T.: Query languages for graph databases. SIGMOD Rec. **41**(1), 50–60 (2012)

18. Yasui, Y., Fujisawa, K., Goh, E.L., Baron, J., Sugiura, A., Uchiyama, T.: NUMA-aware scalable graph traversal on SGI UV systems. In: Proceedings of the ACM Workshop on High Performance Graph Processing, HPGP@HPDC 2016, Kyoto, Japan, 31 May 2016, pp. 19–26 (2016)
19. Zhang, K., Chen, R., Chen, H.: NUMA-aware graph-structured analytics. In: Proceedings of the 20th ACM SIGPLAN Symposium on Principles and Practice of Parallel Programming, PPoPP 2015, San Francisco, CA, USA, 7–11 February 2015, pp. 183–193 (2015)

Efficient Dynamic Pinning of Parallelized Applications by Reinforcement Learning with Applications

Georgios C. Chasparis[1]($\boxtimes$), Michael Rossbory[1], and Vladimir Janjic[2]

[1] Software Competence Center Hagenberg GmbH,
Softwarepark 21, 4232 Hagenberg, Austria
{georgios.chasparis,michael.rossbory}@scch.at
[2] School of Computer Science, University of St Andrews, Scotland, UK
vj32@st-andrews.ac.uk

Abstract. This paper describes a dynamic framework for mapping the threads of parallel applications to the computation cores of parallel systems. We propose a feedback-based mechanism where the performance of each thread is collected and used to drive the *reinforcement-learning* policy of assigning affinities of threads to CPU cores. The proposed framework is flexible enough to address different optimization criteria, such as maximum processing speed and minimum speed variance among threads. We evaluate the framework on the Ant Colony optimization parallel benchmark from the heuristic optimization application domain, and demonstrate that we can achieve an improvement of 12% in the execution time compared to the default operating system scheduling/mapping of threads under varying availability of resources (e.g. when multiple applications are running on the same system).

1 Introduction

Resource allocation is an indispensable part of the design of any engineering system that consumes resources, such as electricity power in home energy management [1], access bandwidth and battery life in wireless communications [10], computing bandwidth under certain QoS requirements [2] and computing bandwidth and memory in parallelized applications [4]. In this paper, we are focusing on the problem of allocating CPU cores to the tasks/threads of a parallel application (sometimes referred to as *mapping*). When resource allocation is performed online and the number, arrival and departure times of the tasks are not known a priori, the role of a *resource manager* is to guarantee the *efficient* operation (according to some criteria) of all tasks by appropriately allocating resources to them. This requires formulation of a centralized optimization problem (e.g., mixed-integer linear programming formulations [2]). However, it is usually difficult to formulate the problem precisely, and the methods to solve the resulting optimization problem are typically computationally very expensive. Additionally, most of the currently used allocation strategies [5,11,15] encounter issues

© Springer International Publishing AG 2017
F.F. Rivera et al. (Eds.): Euro-Par 2017, LNCS 10417, pp. 164–176, 2017.
DOI: 10.1007/978-3-319-64203-1_12

when dealing with *dynamic* environments (e.g., varying availability of resources), such as information complexity involved in retrieving the exact affinity relations during runtime and slow response to irregular application behaviour (e.g. degradation of performance due to presence of other applications). Such environments are suitable for *learning-based* optimization techniques, where the mapping/scheduling policy is updated based on performance measurements from the running threads. Through such learning-based scheme, we can (i) *reduce information complexity* when dealing with a large number of possible thread/memory bindings, since only performance measurements need to be collected during runtime; and, (ii) *adapt to uncertain/irregular application behavior.*

In our previous work [8], we have proposed a novel dynamic, *reinforcement-learning* based scheme for optimal allocation of parallel applications' threads to a set of available CPU cores. In this scheme, each thread responds to its current performance independently of other threads, requiring minimal information exchange. Furthermore, it exhibits robustness and is able to adapt to possible irregularities in the behavior of a thread (such as sudden drop of performance) or to possible changes in the availability of resources. In this paper, we extend the work presented there in two main directions:

- we introduce a new type of reinforcement-learning dynamics that allows faster adjustment towards better allocations;
- we evaluate the reinforcement-learning scheme on a real-world application (Ant Colony Optimization), demonstrating the reduction in application completion time of 12% compared to the default Linux Operating System scheduler.

These results are very encouraging, taking into account that our mechanisms does not require any input from the user.

The paper is organized as follows. Section 2 describes the overall framework and objective. Section 3 presents a reinforcement-learning algorithm for dynamic placement of threads. Section 4 presents experiments of the proposed algorithm in a Linux platform and comparison tests with the operating system's performance. Finally, Sect. 5 presents concluding remarks.

2   Problem Formulation and Objective

A substantial body of work has demonstrated the importance of the appropriate thread-to-core bindings in achieving a good performance of parallel applications. For example, Klug et al. [11] describe a tool that checks the performance of each of the available thread-to-core bindings and searches for an optimal placement. Unfortunately, this employs *exhaustive search*, which is usually prohibitively expensive. Broquedis et al. [5] combine the problem of thread scheduling with scheduling hints related to thread-memory affinity issues. These hints are able to accommodate load distribution given information for the application structure and the hardware topology. Scheduling itself is hierarchical, with *work stealing* [3] being used within neighboring cores to maintain data locality, while at

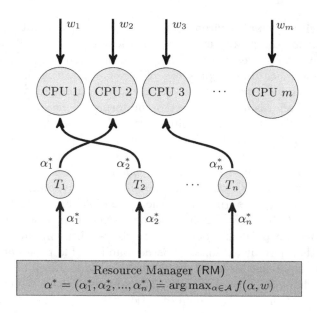

Fig. 1. Schematic of *static* resource allocation framework.

the memory-node level, the thread scheduler deals with larger groups of threads. A similar scheduling policy is also implemented by [14].

In this paper, we are interested in the problem of dynamic pinning of a set of threads $\mathcal{I} = \{1, 2, \ldots, n\}$ that comprise a parallel application to the set of (not necessarily homogeneous) CPU cores $\mathcal{J} = \{1, 2, \ldots, m\}$. We denote the *assignment* of a thread i to an available CPU by $\alpha_i \in \mathcal{A}_i \doteq \mathcal{J}$, i.e., α_i denotes the id of the CPU to which this thread has been assigned. Let also $\alpha = \{\alpha_i | i \in \mathcal{I}\}$ denote the *assignment profile*, which takes values on the Cartesian product $\mathcal{A} \doteq \mathcal{A}_1 \times \ldots \times \mathcal{A}_n$. The *resource manager* (RM) periodically checks the performance of each thread and makes decisions about their pinning to CPUs so that a (user-specified) objective is maximized. Throughout the paper, we will assume that:

(i) The internal properties and details of the threads are not known to the resource manager. Instead, the resource manager may only have access to measurements related to their performance (e.g., their processing speed).

(ii) Threads may not be suspended and their execution cannot be postponed. Instead, the goal of the resource manager is to assign the *currently* available resources to the *currently* running threads.

(iii) Each thread may only be assigned to a single CPU core.

2.1 Static Optimization and Issues

Let $v_i = v_i(\alpha, w)$ denote the processing speed of thread i, which depends on both the overall assignment α, as well as external parameters aggregated within

w. The parameters w summarize, for example, the impact of other applications running on the same platform or other irregularities of the applications. The centralized objective for optimization is of the form

$$\max_{\alpha \in \mathcal{A}} f(\alpha, w). \tag{1}$$

In this paper, we will consider two different objectives, in order to show the flexibility of the proposed resource allocation scheme to address different optimization criteria. The considered objectives are the following:

(O1) $f(\alpha, w) \doteq \sum_{i=1}^{n} v_i/n$, corresponds to the *average processing speed of all threads*;
(O2) $f(\alpha, w) \doteq \sum_{i=1}^{n} [v_i - \gamma(v_i - \sum_{\ell=1}^{n} v_\ell/n)^2]/n$, for some $\gamma > 0$, corresponds to the *average processing speed minus a penalty that is proportional to the speed variance among threads*.

In the objective (O1), the goal is to minimize the average processing speed over all threads, and in the objective (O2) the goal is to achieve an optimal combination of processing speed and speed variance among threads.

Any solution to (1) corresponds to an *efficient assignment*. Figure 1 presents a schematic of a *static* resource allocation framework, where the centralized objective (1) is solved by the RM upfront, and then the optimal assignment (or mapping) is communicated to threads.

However, there are two significant issues when posing an optimization problem in the form of (1). In particular,

1. the function $v_i(\alpha, w)$ is *unknown* and it may only be approximated through measurements of the *processing speed*, denoted $\tilde{v}_i$;
2. the external influence w is *unknown* and may vary with time, thus the optimal assignment may not be fixed with time.

2.2 Measurement- or Learning-Based Optimization

We wish to target the objective (1) through a *measurement-based* (or *learning-based*) optimization approach. In such approach, the RM reacts to the approximation of the function $f(\alpha, w)$ that is obtained by measuring the processing speed of threads. Measurements are taken at time instances $k = 1, 2, \ldots$, and the approximation of function f at the time instance k is denoted by $\tilde{f}(k)$. For example, in the case of objective (O1), $\tilde{f}(k) \doteq \sum_{i=1}^{n} \tilde{v}_i(k)/n$. Given the approximation $\tilde{f}(k)$ and the current assignment of threads to cores, $\alpha(k)$, the RM selects the next assignment $\alpha(k+1)$ so that the measured objective approaches the true optimum of the unknown function $f(\alpha, w)$. In other words, the RM employs an update rule of the form:

$$\{(\tilde{v}_i(1), \alpha_i(1)), \ldots, (\tilde{v}_i(k), \alpha_i(k))\}_i \mapsto \{\alpha_i(k+1)\}_i \tag{2}$$

according to which prior pairs of measurements and assignments for each thread i are mapped into a new assignment $\alpha_i(k+1)$ that will be employed during the next evaluation interval.

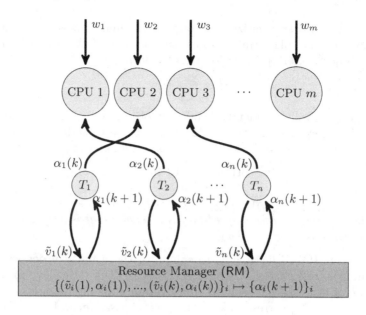

Fig. 2. Schematic of *dynamic* resource allocation framework.

The overall framework is illustrated in Fig. 2, describing the flow of information and steps executed. In particular, at any given time instance $k = 1, 2, \ldots$, each thread i communicates to the RM its current processing speed $\tilde{v}_i(k)$. Then the RM updates the assignment, $\alpha_i(k+1)$, and communicates it to i.

2.3   Objective

The goal of our work is to utilize a distributed learning framework for *dynamic* (*adaptive*) pinning of threads to cores. Each thread constitutes an independent decision maker. It selects the CPU core to which it is pinned independently of others, using its own preference criterion. The job of the RM is to collect performance information and send it to the threads so that they can make the placement decisions. Our goal is to design a preference criterion and a selection rule for each thread so that maximizing the thread's own *criterion* ensures certain overall performance for the parallel application. Furthermore, the selection criterion of each thread should be adaptive and robust to possible resource variations. In the next section, we present such a (distributed) learning scheme.

3   Reinforcement Learning (RL)

The question that naturally emerges is *how should threads choose CPU cores based only on their available measurements, so that eventually an efficient assignment is established for all threads.* We achieve this by using a learning framework, *perturbed learning automata*, that is based on the reinforcement learning algorithm introduced by the authors in [6,7]. It belongs to the general class of *learning automata* [13]. The basic idea behind reinforcement learning is rather simple. Each *agent* i (in this case, a thread), keeps track of a strategy vector that holds its estimates over the best choice (in this case, the CPU core). We denote this strategy by $\sigma_i = [\sigma_{ij}]_{j \in \mathcal{A}_i} \in \Delta(|\mathcal{A}_i|)$, where $\Delta(m)$ denotes the *probability simplex* of size m, i.e., the set of probability vectors in $\mathbb{R}^m$. To provide an example, consider the case of 3 available CPU cores, i.e., $\mathcal{A}_i \equiv \mathcal{J} = \{1,2,3\}$. In this case, the strategy $\sigma_i \in \Delta(3)$ of thread i may take the following form:

$$\sigma_i = \begin{pmatrix} 0.2 \\ 0.5 \\ 0.3 \end{pmatrix},$$

which denotes that there is 20% probability of assigning the thread i to the CPU core 1, 50% probability of assigning the thread i to the CPU core 2 and 30% probability of assigning the thread i to the core 3. We will denote the assignment selection by $\alpha_i = \text{rand}_{\sigma_i}[\mathcal{A}_i]$.

Note that if σ_i is a unit vector e_j, with 0 in all places except for the j-th, and 1 in the j-th place, then the thread i will be mapped to the core j with probability one. Such a strategy is usually called *pure strategy*.

3.1 Strategy Update

According to the *perturbed reinforcement learning* [6,7], the probability that a thread i selects action j at time $k = 1, 2, \ldots$ is:

$$\sigma_{ij}(k) = (1 - \lambda)x_{ij}(k) - \frac{\lambda}{|\mathcal{A}_i|} \qquad (3)$$

where $\lambda > 0$ corresponds to a perturbation term (or *mutation*) and $x_i = [x_{ij}]_j$ corresponds to the *nominal strategy* of thread i. The nominal strategy is updated according to the following recursion formula:

$$x_i(k+1) = \begin{cases} x_i(k) + \epsilon \cdot u_i(\alpha(k)) \cdot [e_{\alpha_i(k)} - x_i(k)], & u_i(\alpha(k)) > \bar{u}_i(k) \\ x_i(k), & u_i(\alpha(k)) \leq \bar{u}_i(k), \end{cases} \qquad (4)$$

for some constant step size $\epsilon > 0$, where $\bar{u}_i(k)$ denotes the running-average performance at time k and $u_i(\alpha(k))$ is the *utility* of thread i at time k, defined as $u_i(\alpha(k)) = \tilde{f}(k)$. In other words, each thread is assigned a performance index that coincides with the overall objective function (*identical interest*). In words, according to (4), if the performance of thread i at time k, when placed on core $\alpha_i(k)$, is higher than the average performance, i.e., $u_i(\alpha(k)) > \bar{u}_i(k)$, then at time $k + 1$ we increase the probability of that thread being placed on the same core and proportionally to the thread utilisation. So the better the thread performs, the more likely it is to be assigned to the same core. Otherwise, if the performance of the thread is the same or worse than the average, we do not change preference for its placement (the second case in (4)). In comparison to our previous work [6,7], here we use the constant step size $\epsilon > 0$ (instead of a decreasing step-size sequence). This increases the adaptivity and robustness of the algorithm to possible changes in the environment. This is because a constant step size provides a fast transition of the nominal strategy from one pure strategy to another. Compared to [8], here we use a different reinforcement direction. In the Eq. (4), the strategy vector is only adjusted when a performance is higher than the running-average performance $\bar{u}_i$, which provides a faster adjustment towards better assignments. The perturbation term λ provides the possibility for the nominal strategy to escape (suboptimal) pure strategy profiles. Setting $\lambda > 0$ is essential for providing an adaptive response of the algorithm to changes in the environment.

The convergence properties of this class of dynamics can be derived following the exact same reasoning used for the learning dynamics presented in [8]. In fact, it can be shown that the dynamics approach asymptotically a set of allocations that includes the solutions of the centralized optimization (1). Such a set may in fact include sub-optimal allocations; however, as we shall see in the forthcoming evaluation section, they are still notably better that the allocations provided by the default operating system scheduler.

As a final notice, the algorithm is augmented with a *reset* strategy when a thread becomes inactive (e.g., due to termination), in which case the assignment profile is reset based on a round-robin initialization strategy.

3.2   Discussion

The reinforcement-learning algorithm of Eq. (4) provides a performance-based optimization. No a-priori knowledge of the type of the application or the underlying hardware is necessary. Furthermore, its memory complexity is minimal, since at any update instance of the resource manager, only the strategy vectors of each one of the threads needs to be kept in memory, whose size is linear to the number of the CPU cores. Furthermore, for each thread, the dynamics exhibit linear complexity to the number of CPU cores.

4   Experiments

In this section, we present an experimental study of the proposed reinforcement learning scheme for dynamic pinning of threads of parallel applications. The experiments were conducted on $20 \times$ Intel©Xeon©CPU E5-2650 v3 2.30 GHz running Linux Kernel 64bit 3.13.0-43-generic. The machine divides the physical cores into two NUMA nodes (Node 1: CPUs 0–9, Node 2: CPUs 10–19). As an example application, we consider a parallel implementation of the Ant Colony Optimization heuristic for solving NP-complete optimization problems. The proposed reinforcement learning dynamics is implemented in scenarios under which the availability of resources may vary with time. We compare the overall performance of the algorithm, with respect to the completion time of the application.

4.1   Ant Colony Optimization (ACO)

Ant Colony Optimization (ACO) [9] is an optimization algorithm used for solving NP-hard combinatorial optimization problems. The metaheuristics, given in Algorithm 1, consist of a number of iterations. In each iteration, each individual agent (*ant*) independently finds a solution to a given problem. The solution is biased by a pheromone trail (t), which is stronger along previously successful routes. After all ants have computed their solution, the best solution is chosen and, if needed, the pheromone trail is updated according to the quality of the new best solution. After that, the next iteration starts. The metaheuristics are applied to a specific problem by providing the objective function, evaluate the solution and update the pheromone trail.

Data: Ants - a set of ants
p - a set of problem parameters
t - pheromone trail
Result: *best_result*
initialization;
for $i = 0$ *to* $i < num\_iter$ **do**
  foreach $a \in Ants$ **do**
    | $a = $ find_one_solution(p,t);
  end
  best=choose_best_solution(Ants);
  $t = $ update_pheromone_trail(best, t);
end

Algorithm 1. Pseudocode of metaheuristics in ACO.

In this paper, we apply ACO to the Single Machine Total Weighted Tardiness Problem (SMTWTP). We are given n jobs. Each job, i, is characterised by its processing time, p_i (p in the code below), deadline, d_i (d in the code below), and weight, w_i (w in the code below). The goal is to find the schedule of jobs that minimizes the total weighted *tardiness*, defined as $\sum w_i \cdot \max\{0, C_i - d_i\}$ where C_i is the completion time of the job, i. The pheromone trail is defined as a matrix τ, where $\tau[i, j]$ is a real number between 0 and 1 that represents preference of putting job i at the j-th place in the schedule. The pseudocode for a function to find one solution is given in Algorithm 2. It iterates over the positions in the schedule. For each position, first an auxiliary function ϵ is applied for each job to compute the probability of that job being assigned to that position. This probability is then further tuned to take into account the pheromone trail τ. Then, according to some probability, one of the two actions are taken - either the job with the highest probability or a random job (according to the calculated probabilities). The latter is done to add a degree of randomisation to the solutions, in order to escape possible local maxima.

Data: p - a set of problem parameters
τ - initial pheromone trail
Result: schedule
for $k = 0$ *to* num_jobs **do**
    foreach *unscheduled job* i **do**
        // probability of selecting job i as the k-th in the schedule
        $\text{prob}[i] = \epsilon(i,p)^\beta \cdot \tau[k,i]$;
    end
    $q = \text{rand}()$;
    if $q < Q$ **then**
        job = select the job with the highest probability, according to prob;
    else
        job = select a random job, according to probabilities in prob;
    end
    schedule$[k]$ = job;
end

Algorithm 2. Pseudocode for find_one_solution function for SMTWTP instance of ACO.

4.2 Parallelization and Experimental Setup

The ACO metaheuristics can be parallelized by dividing ants into groups and computing the find_one_solution function in Algorithm 1 for groups of ants in parallel. We consider a uniform division of ants to threads (*task farm* parallel pattern). Parallelization is performed using the `pthreads` parallel library.

Throughout the execution, and with a fixed period of 0.2 s, the RM collects measurements of the total instructions per sec (using the PAPI profiling library [12]) for each of the threads separately. Taking into account these measurements, the update rule of Eq. (4) under (O2) is executed by the RM. Pinning of the threads to the available CPUs is achieved with the `sched.h` library (in particular, the `pthread_setaffinity_np` function). In the following, we evaluate the completion time of the test application under the reinforcement-learning scheme, compared to the time achieved under the Linux Operating System (OS) default scheduling mechanism. We compare them for different values of $\gamma \geq 0$ in order to investigate the influence of more balanced speeds to the overall running time.

In all the forthcoming experiments, the RM is executed by the master thread which is always running on CPU 0. Furthermore, in all experiments, only the first one of the two NUMA nodes are utilized, since our intention is to investigate the benefit of efficient placement of thread to cores without taking into account effects of non-uniform memory layout on the execution speed.

4.3 Experiment 1: ACO Under Uniform CPU Availability

In the first experiment, we consider the ACO application consisting of 20 threads and utilizing 7 CPU cores. Table 1 shows the completion times under the OS and reinforcement-learning (RL) for different values of $\gamma > 0$, with $\epsilon = 0.01$ and $\lambda = 0.03$ in formulas (3) and (4). We select a step size and perturbation that are not so small in order to allow a rather fast adaptation (via $\epsilon > 0$) and a rather often experimentation (via $\lambda > 0$).

Table 1. Statistical results regarding the completion time (in sec) of OS and RL under Experiment 1.

Run #	OS	$\epsilon = 0, \lambda = 0$	$\epsilon = 0.01, \lambda = 0.03$		
		RL ($\gamma = 0$)	RL ($\gamma = 0$)	RL ($\gamma = 0.02$)	RL ($\gamma = 0.04$)
1	138.39	139.41	142.08	142.69	141.69
2	138.57	137.60	143.28	141.69	141.27
3	138.80	138.39	142.87	142.10	140.92
4	138.38	137.97	144.08	143.47	142.71
5	138.78	138.40	143.28	142.65	141.28
Aver.	**138.58**	**138.35**	**143.12**	**142.52**	**141.57**
s.d.	**0.20**	**0.67**	**0.73**	**0.68**	**0.69**

We observe that the RL scheduler can almost match the completion time by the OS scheduler. The RL scheduler with $\gamma = 0.04$ gives just about 2.12% worse completion time, compared to the OS scheduler. This difference can be attributed to the necessary adaptation and experimentation incorporated into the scheduler. To see this, note that when the scheduler sticks with the initial round-robin static initialization of the assignments, i.e., when $\epsilon = \lambda = 0$, then the completion time matches very accurately the time achieved by the OS scheduler (Table 1). Such experimentation is absolutely necessary for the dynamic scheduler to be able to react to variations in the availability of resources, as it will become obvious in the following experiments.

Another interesting observation comes from the fact that as γ increases, the overall completion time of the application decreases. In other words, when penalizing high speed variance among threads, the overall completion time decreases. Such conclusion may not necessarily be generalized beyond this experimental setup of identical threads and uniform resource availability; however, it indicates a potential benefit that needs to be further investigated.

4.4 Experiment 2: ACO Under Non-uniform CPU Availability

In the second experiment, the execution speed of the CPU cores is not uniform. To achieve this variation, we have another (*exogenous*) application running on some of the available CPU cores. In particular, this exogenous application places equal work-load to the first three CPU cores. The exogenous application already runs when the ACO starts running. Figure 3 shows the running average processing speed under OS and RL, which is further supported by the statistical data of

Table 2. The RL achieves a significant speed improvement that results in about 12% reduction in completion time.

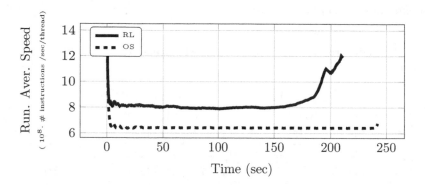

Fig. 3. Running average execution speed for OS and RL ($\gamma = 0.04$) under Experiment 2.

4.5 Experiment 3: ACO Under Time-Varying CPU Availability

This is an identical experiment to Experiment 2, except for the fact that the exogenous application starts running 30 s after ACO starts running. This form of test examines the ability of RL to respond after a significant variation in the availability of some of the CPU cores. Figure 4 illustrates the evolution of the running-average processing speed under OS and RL for this experiment.

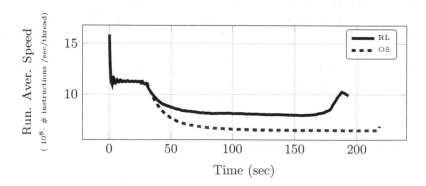

Fig. 4. Running average execution speed for OS and RL ($\gamma = 0.04$) under Experiment 3.

It is evident in Fig. 4 that the RL dynamic scheduler is able to better react to variations in the availability of resources, and achieves a shorter completion time by about 10%. This is also supported by the statistical data of Table 2.

Table 2. Statistical results of the completion time (in sec) under OS and RL in Experiments 2 and 3, respectively.

Run #	Experiment 2		Experiment 3	
	OS	RL ($\gamma = 0.04$)	OS	RL ($\gamma = 0.04$)
1	241.30	207.33	218.48	193.30
2	239.10	201.92	218.70	196.45
3	240.90	220.11	218.88	201.92
4	241.11	221.54	219.27	195.88
5	241.51	210.09	218.52	193.41
Aver.	**241.06**	**212.20**	**218.77**	**196.19**
s.d.	**0.99**	**8.42**	**0.33**	**3.50**

5   Conclusions and Future Work

We proposed a measurement-based reinforcement learning scheme for addressing the problem of efficient dynamic pinning of threads of a parallel application to the processing units. According to this scheme, a centralized objective is decomposed into thread-based objectives, where each thread is assigned its own utility function. A resource manager updates a strategy for each of the threads corresponding to its beliefs over the most beneficial CPU placement for this thread. Updates are based on a reinforcement learning rule, where prior actions are reinforced proportionally to the resulting utility. Besides its reduced computational complexity, the proposed scheme is adaptive and robust to possible changes in the environment. We further demonstrated that in the ACO metaheuristics algorithm, the proposed scheduler may reduce the completion time up to 12% under varying resource availability. This is a significant result, as the reinforcement-learning based scheduler does not require any input from the user, nor it requires any information from the application itself, therefore it can be readily plugged in instead of the default operating system scheduler. In future, we plan to investigate the effect of non-uniform memory layout to our scheduler and to adapt the scheduling policies for these kind of systems.

Acknowledgments. This work has been partially supported by the European Union grant EU H2020-ICT-2014-1 project RePhrase (No. 644235).

References

1. De Angelis, F., Boaro, M., Fuselli, D., Squartini, S., Piazza, F., Wei, Q.: Optimal home energy management under dynamic electrical and thermal constraints. IEEE Trans. Ind. Inform. **9**(3), 1518–1527 (2013). doi:10.1109/TII.2012.2230637. ISSN 1551-3203
2. Bini, E., Buttazzo, G.C., Eker, J., Schorr, S., Guerra, R., Fohler, G., Årzén, K.E., Vanessa, R., Scordino, C.: Resource management on multicore systems: the ACTORS approach. IEEE Micro **31**(3), 72–81 (2011)

3. Blumofe, R., Leiserson, C.: Scheduling multithreaded computations by work stealing. In: Proceedings of SFCS 1994, pp. 356–368 (1994)
4. Brecht, T.: On the importance of parallel application placement in NUMA multiprocessors. In: Proceedings of the Symposium on Experiences with Distributed and Multiprocessor Systems (SEDMS IV), San Deigo, CA, pp. 1–18, July 1993
5. Broquedis, F., Furmento, N., Goglin, B., Wacrenier, P.A., Namyst, R.: Forest-GOMP: an efficient OpenMP environment for NUMA architectures. Int. J. Parallel Program. **38**, 418–439 (2010)
6. Chasparis, G.C., Shamma, J.S., Rantzer, A.: Nonconvergence to saddle boundary points under perturbed reinforcement learning. Int. J. Game Theory **44**(3), 667–699 (2015)
7. Chasparis, G., Shamma, J.: Distributed dynamic reinforcement of efficient outcomes in multiagent coordination and network formation. Dyn. Games Appl. **2**(1), 18–50 (2012)
8. Chasparis, G.C., Rossbory, M.: Efficient Dynamic Pinning of Parallelized Applications by Distributed Reinforcement Learning. arXiv:1606.08156 [cs], June 2016
9. Dorigo, M., Stützle, T.: Ant Colony Optimization. Bradford Company, Scituate (2004)
10. Inaltekin, H., Wicker, S.: A one-shot random access game for wireless networks. In: International Conference on Wireless Networks, Communications and Mobile Computing (2005)
11. Klug, T., Ott, M., Weidendorfer, J., Trinitis, C.: autopin - automated optimization of thread-to-core pinning on multicore systems. In: Stenstrom, P. (ed.) Transactions on High-Performance Embedded Architectures and Compilers III. LNCS, vol. 6590, pp. 219–235. Springer, Berlin Heidelberg (2011). doi:10.1007/978-3-642-19448-1_12
12. Mucci, P.J., Browne, S., Deane, C., Ho, G.: PAPI: A portable interface to hardware performance counters. In: Proceedings of the Department of Defense HPCMP Users Group Conference, pp. 7–10 (1999)
13. Narendra, K., Thathachar, M.: Learning Automata: An introduction. Prentice-Hall, Upper Saddle River (1989)
14. Olivier, S., Porterfield, A., Wheeler, K.: Scheduling task parallelism on multi-socket multicore systems. In: ROSS 2011, Tuscon, Arizona, USA, pp. 49–56 (2011)
15. Thibault, S., Namyst, R., Wacrenier, P.-A.: Building portable thread schedulers for hierarchical multiprocessors: the bubblesched framework. In: Kermarrec, A.-M., Bougé, L., Priol, T. (eds.) Euro-Par 2007. LNCS, vol. 4641, pp. 42–51. Springer, Heidelberg (2007). doi:10.1007/978-3-540-74466-5_6

Accelerating by Idling: How Speculative Delays Improve Performance of Message-Oriented Systems

Aleksandar Prokopec[(⊠)]

Oracle Labs, Zurich, Switzerland
aleksandar.prokopec@gmail.com

Abstract. We propose a technique called *speculative lagging*, which improves performance by dynamically adding periods of idle execution into the message-oriented system. The speculation is guided by a statistical model, which predicts context switches that benefit from delays. We analytically derive the expected speedup, which, for a fixed confidence, allows identifying lagging opportunities in $O(1)$ time, without a performance overhead. We describe the corresponding speculation algorithm and use it to extend an existing scheduler. Comparison with other actor frameworks on standard benchmarks shows improvements of up to $2.1\times$.

1 Introduction

Consider a system with concurrent processes that communicate by exchanging messages. We call these processes *actors*. When a message arrives, it is placed on the message queue of the corresponding actor, and we say that it is *available*. The system is tasked with assigning CPUs to any number of actors with available messages. An actor cooperatively yields the CPU back to the system after emptying its message queue. Assigning and yielding is called *context switching* – this is *the period of time required to switch the CPU between two actors*.

The main question in this paper is the following: can the overall performance of a message-based system be improved by slowing down individual actors with periods of idle execution? Generally, adding extra execution cycles to a program slows it down, so the first reaction is to say no. Counter-intuitively, this paper shows that selectively adding periods of idle execution improves performance. The essential idea is that it can be less costly to wait for another message, than it is to undergo a context switch when there are no messages. The key difficulty addressed in the paper is to quickly detect (at runtime) that a program benefits from delays, apply those delays selectively to some actors, and do so without compromising the performance of programs that do not benefit from delays.

This paper brings forth the following contributions:

- A probabilistic model of *speculative lagging*, a new runtime technique that increases program performance by $O((1+\delta-P)^{-1})$, where P is the probability that a relative delay δ is beneficial for a given program (Sect. 2), along with a decision criteria for applying speculative lagging (Sect. 2.2).

© Springer International Publishing AG 2017
F.F. Rivera et al. (Eds.): Euro-Par 2017, LNCS 10417, pp. 177–191, 2017.
DOI: 10.1007/978-3-319-64203-1_13

- A sampling strategy that, for some fixed confidence α, when speculation is beneficial, is expected to correctly decide in $O(1)$ time, and when delays are not beneficial, concludes this in $O(\varphi^{-1})$ time, where φ is the allowed performance overhead from sampling (Sects. 2.1 and 2.3).
- An algorithm and an implementation of speculative lagging (Sect. 3).
- An evaluation on standard actor benchmarks [12], where we identify specific benchmarks on which speculative lagging achieves up to 2.1× speedups, without any noticeable performance overhead otherwise (Sect. 4).

2   A Model of Speculative Lagging

In this section, we construct a model of speculative lagging. The speculation is based on the bet that a context switch is expensive, and that another message will arrive between the start and the end of the context switch. We investigate how each actor determines the minimal number of messages to receive before making a speculation decision, how it decides whether to speculate or not, and how to minimize the time until making the decision.

2.1   Determining the Sample Size

To decide whether speculation is beneficial, an actor must have a sample – a set of delayed context switches. We start by estimating the necessary sample size.

Definition 1. *Consider an actor that, upon processing a message at some time t, waits for a fixed duration of time d before returning control to the scheduler. A speculation hit is the event in which at least one other message arrives in the time interval $\langle t, t + d\rangle$. A speculation miss is the event in which no message arrives in the interval $\langle t, t + d\rangle$.*

Definition 2 (Delay sampling). *Consider a sampling strategy in which an actor, before context switching, waits some fixed time d with a probability φ, and counts speculation hits. We call this process speculation hit sampling.*

Theorem 1 (Speculation hit estimate). *Consider a speculation hit sampling process that estimates the probability P of a speculation hit, which is independent between speculation hits. Let n be the sample size, and h_i a random variable, equal to 1 if there was a speculation hit in the i-th sampling iteration, and 0 otherwise. The sampled probability $\hat{p} = \overline{p} = \frac{1}{n}\Sigma_i h_i$ is a consistent estimate for P.*

An estimate $\hat{p}$ is consistent for the value P if $\hat{p} \to P$ when $n \to \infty$. We assumed that the probability P is independent between speculation hits, a method which is called *simple random sampling* [5]. It was shown in the related work [5] that $\hat{p}$ is in this case a consistent estimate for P.

Theorem 2 (Sample size). *Consider a speculation hit sampling process that estimates the speculation hit probability P with $\overline{p} = \frac{1}{n}\Sigma_i h_i$. Let α be the probability that a **normally distributed value** is within the $\pm z_{1-\alpha/2}$ range (α uniquely defines $z_{1-\alpha/2}$). The minimum sample size is at least $\frac{z_{1-\alpha/2}^2}{4 \cdot e^2}$, for the probability α that the estimated probability P is approximately within the range $\langle 0.1, 0.9\rangle$.*

Proof. We are sampling speculation hits with replacement, so the number of observed speculation hits follows the binomial distribution. It was shown that in this case, the confidence interval e can be approximated with $z_{1-\alpha/2}$ · $\sqrt{\hat{p}(1-\hat{p})/n}$, where n is the sample size [5]. The term $\hat{p}(1-\hat{p})$ is maximized for $\hat{p} = 0.5$, which allows deriving the worst case n from e. $\qquad\square$

The result in Theorem 2 allows us to calculate the minimum number of samples required for deciding, with a specific confidence α, the interval of the possible values of the speculation probability P. As we show later, this allows deciding whether speculation improves program performance or not.

2.2   Estimating Speculation Benefits

Theorem 2 shows how to pick the sample size, but does not mention the delay time d. The probability P, and the estimated speculation hit probability $\hat{p}$, both depend on the chosen delay d. In this section, we investigate how to find the optimal value for the delay d. We first show that d is not unbounded – an actor only needs to search through a finite interval to find the optimal value d.

Definition 3. *The* setup cost c_s *is the time between the point when the scheduler assigns an actor to a processor, and the point when the actor starts processing the first pending message. The* teardown cost c_t *is the time between the point when the actor finishes processing the last pending message, and the point when the actor returns control to the scheduler. We define the* context-switch cost c *as the sum* $c_s + c_t$ *of the setup and teardown cost.*

Definition 4. *An actor* speculates with a delay d *if, after processing the last available message, it spends an additional time d waiting for the arrival of another message. The* speculation efficiency $\Psi_{spec} = T_{spec}/T_{base}$ *is the ratio between the total actor execution time with speculation T_{spec} and the time without speculation T_{base}, and its inverse value $S_{spec} = \Psi_{spec}^{-1}$ is the* speculation speedup.

Lemma 1 (Delay bound). *Consider an actor that speculates with a delay d. Let there always exist at least one inactive actor with an available message. Then for every $d > c$, the program execution time is not optimal.*

Proof. Assume that there is some time $d_0 > c$ for which the execution is optimal. Consider a specific actor R that, at some point in the execution schedule E_0, speculates with d_0. By assumption, when R starts speculating, there exists another actor Q with an available message. Consider now an alternative execution schedule E_1 in which the actor R does not speculate, but instead releases the processor. The scheduler can then assign the processor time to another actor Q, after a context switch with duration c. The execution schedule E_1 is at least $d_0 - c$ faster than E_0. By contradiction, E_0 is not optimal. $\qquad\square$

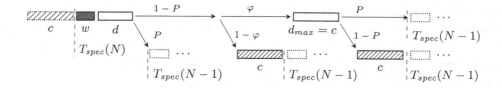

Fig. 1. Probability tree for the running time with speculative lagging

Lemma 1 states that there exists an upper bound on the benefits from speculatively delaying the context switch. Consequently, the sampling plan needs to focus only on the values of d in the interval $\langle 0, c \rangle$. We now investigate how to choose d from this interval to maximize the benefits.

Lemma 2 (Speculative running time). *Consider an actor that speculates with a delay d, and with probability $\varphi \ll 1$, prior to context switching, samples speculation hits. The time required to receive and process N messages is then $T_{spec}(N) = [(1 - P) \cdot c + w + d] \cdot N$, where P is the speculation hit probability for the delay d, c is the context switch time, and w is the time to process a message.*

Proof. Consider the execution of an actor in Fig. 1, which has one message available at the beginning, and still has to process N messages. The time required to process these messages is $T_{spec}(N)$. The actor spends w time to process the first message, and d time speculating for the next message. During the time d, another message arrives with probability P, which brings the actor into a state with one available message, where the remaining execution time is recursively $T_{spec}(N-1)$. Alternatively, with a probability $1 - P$, another message does not arrive during the time d. In this case, the actor may decide to return control to the scheduler with a probability $1 - \varphi$ (i.e. not to sample speculation hits) and spend c time in a context switch. Alternatively, with a probability φ, the actor spends additional $d_{max} = c$ units of time sampling speculation hits. When the sampling ends, another message will appear with probability that is at least P, bringing the actor into the state with an available message – the remaining execution time is here $T_{spec}(N-1)$. Alternatively, with probability $1 - P$, no message arrives, and the actor spends c time in a context switch.

Putting this together, we get the following execution time recurrence:

$$T_{spec}(N) = w + d + \Big((1-P) \cdot \varphi + (1-P) \cdot (1-\varphi) + (1-P)^2 \cdot \varphi \Big) \cdot c + T_{spec}(N-1)$$

This recurrence has the following closed-form solution:

$$T_{spec}(N) = (w + d + (1 - P) \cdot (1 + \varphi - \varphi \cdot P) \cdot c) \cdot N \qquad (1)$$

Under the assumption that sampling is done infrequently, that is, $\varphi \ll 1$, the term $1 + \varphi - \varphi \cdot P$ becomes 1, and the claim follows. $\square$

Theorem 3 (Speculation efficiency and speedup). *Let c be the context switch duration, w the time required to process a message, and $\overline{p}$ be the sampled speculation hit rate. Define $\delta = d/c \in \langle 0, 1 \rangle$ and $\eta = w/c$ as ratios between the delay, the work and context switch time. Then, the expected efficiency of speculative lagging is $\overline{\Psi}_{spec} = 1 + \frac{\delta - \overline{p}}{1 + \eta}$, and the expected speedup $\overline{S}_{spec} > \frac{1 + \eta}{1 + \eta + \delta - \overline{p}}$.*

Proof. The expected efficiency is defined as $E[\Psi_{spec}] = E[T_{spec}(N)/T_{base}(N)]$, where $T_{base}(N)$ is the time required to process N messages without speculation, and $T_{spec}(N)$ is the same time with speculation.

Without speculation, in the worst case, an actor always processes only a single message before returning control to the scheduler. The time without speculation is then $T_{base}(N) = (c + w) \cdot N$. By Lemma 2, expected time with speculation is $T_{spec}(N) = [(1 - P) \cdot c + w + d] \cdot N$. Since $T_{base}(N)$ does not depend on random variables, linearity of expectation gives us:

$$\overline{\Psi}_{spec} = E[\Psi_{spec}] = \frac{N \cdot [(1 - E[P]) \cdot c + w + d]}{N \cdot (c + w)} \tag{2}$$

Using $E[P] = \overline{p}$ from Theorem 1, this further simplifies to:

$$\overline{\Psi}_{spec} = 1 + \frac{\delta - \overline{p}}{1 + \eta} \tag{3}$$

By expressing the inverse Ψ_{spec}^{-1} of Ψ_{spec} with its Taylor series, it can be shown that $\overline{S}_{spec} = E[S_{spec}] = E[\Psi_{spec}^{-1}] > E[\Psi_{spec}]^{-1}$, as noted previously [9]. □

The result from Theorem 3 provides a way to decide whether speculative lagging improves performance. This is captured with the following corollary.

Corollary 1 (Speculation decision). *An actor that speculates with a relative delay $\delta = d/c \in \langle 0, 1 \rangle$ improves program performance when $\delta \leq \overline{p}$.*

Proof. Program performance is expected to improve when the expected speedup $\overline{S}_{spec} > 1$. Using the result from Theorem 3, we have:

$$\overline{S}_{spec} > \frac{1 + \eta}{1 + \eta + \delta - \overline{p}} \geq 1 \tag{4}$$

We can rewrite the second inequality as $1 + \eta \geq 1 + \eta + \delta - \overline{p}$, and the result follows irrespective of the work ratio η. □

The previous corollary states the necessary conditions to apply delays. Let's assume that we have a set of $(\delta_i, \overline{p}_i)$ pairs, and we need to pick the δ_i that maximizes speedup. The next corollary shows how to do this.

Corollary 2 (Speculation choice). *Given a set of $(\delta_i, \overline{p}_i)$ pairs, where δ_i is the speculated delay and $\overline{p}_i$ is the respective sampled speculation hit probability, speedup is maximal for the relative delay δ_i that has the minimum $\delta_i - \overline{p}_i$.*

Proof. Expression for $\overline{S}_{spec}$ from Theorem 3 is monotonic with respect to $\overline{p}$ and δ, and is maximized when $\overline{p} - \delta$ is minimized, irrespective of η. □

2.3 Better Time-to-Speculation with an Adaptive Sampling Rate

We can use the Theorem 2 to estimate the sample size n. For example, for a $\alpha = 95\%$ confidence that speculation hit probability P lies within $e = 15\%$ of the true value, we need $n = 43$. Our analysis implicitly assumed that the sampling frequency φ is so low that it can be ignored. As an example, for $\varphi = 1\%$, execution overhead less than 1%, but the expected number of context switches that an actor must undergo before deciding on speculation is $N = n \cdot \varphi^{-1}$, which is 4300 for the confidence $\alpha = 95\%$ and the interval $e = 15\%$, assumed previously. This value is impractical for applications in which the actor lifetime is short.

To reduce the time until a speculation decision, we note that increasing the sampling frequency φ causes a slowdown only if speculation hits are unlikely. If speculation helps, it is likely that a message arrives during sampling. In what follows, we substantiate this intuition with an upper bound on the allowed sampling rate φ. We then compute an upper bound on the expected number of messages $\overline{N}$ that must be received before deciding on δ, when φ gets dynamically adapted.

Lemma 3 (Sampling rate bound). *Consider an actor that speculates with a relative delay $\delta = d/c$, and, before a context switch, samples speculation hits with the rate φ. Sampling does not decrease performance as long as $\varphi \leq \frac{P-\delta}{(1-P)^2}$.*

Proof. We are investigating the upper bound for φ, so the previous assumption that $\varphi \ll 1$ no longer holds, and we cannot use the result from Theorem 3. Instead, we rely on (1) from Lemma 2. We require that the speculative running time is less than equal than the baseline:

$$w + d + c \cdot (1 - P) \cdot (1 + \varphi - \varphi \cdot P) \leq w + c \tag{5}$$

By simplifying and substituting $\delta = d/c$, we get the desired bound on φ. $\qquad \square$

We could (prematurely) conclude that a newly created actor must set the sampling rate φ to the bound from Lemma 3. However, a new actor does not know the speculation hit probability P. At the end of each sampling iteration i, the actor only has an imprecise estimate p_i of P, which, as shown in Theorem 2, is only adequately accurate with the desired sample size $n \geq i$.

We now show that, somewhat surprisingly, the actor can indeed use its current estimate p_i as a proxy for P to increase the sampling rate φ, and reduce the expected number of messages $\overline{N}$ needed to reach the sample size n, without compromising performance. The bound on $\overline{N}$ will be proportional with the speculation miss probability $1 - P$, confirming the initial intuition.

Theorem 4 (Adaptive sampling). *Consider a newly created actor that starts with an initial sampling frequency φ_0, and then changes the sampling frequency to $\varphi = max(\varphi_0, min(1, \frac{p_i}{(1-p_i)^2}))$ after every sampling iteration i. The expected number of messages $\overline{N}$ that an actor will receive before gathering the sample of size n is bounded by $\overline{N} \leq 1 + \varphi_0^{-1} \cdot (1 + (2 + \varphi_0)^{-1}) \cdot (1 - P) \cdot O(n) + O(n)$. Expected speedup $\overline{S}$ between speculation and baseline is bounded by $\overline{S} \geq 1 - (1 + \varphi_0^{-1})^{-1}$.*

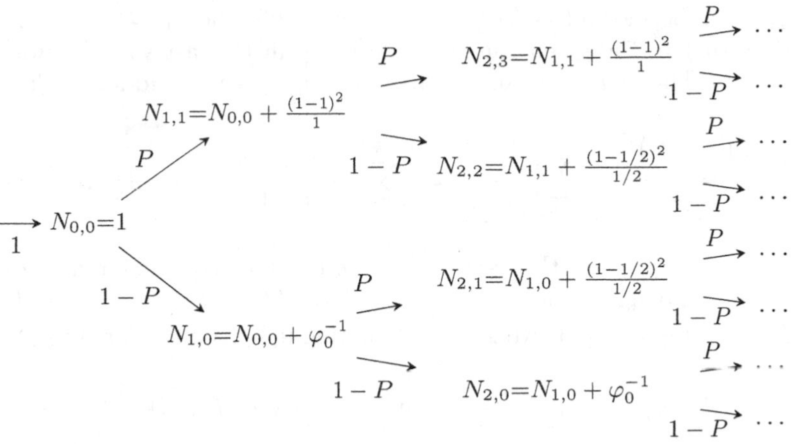

Fig. 2. Probability tree and message counts in adaptive sampling

Proof. After each sampling event, the sampling probability φ is modified using the expression $\frac{P-\delta}{(1-P)^2}$ from Lemma 3, where δ is 0 because the newly created actor does not speculate yet, and P is replaced with the current value $\bar{p}$.

The probability tree in Fig. 2 shows a series of sampling events, and the number of messages received $N_{i,j}$, which are needed to reach the respective sampling iteration i and state j. $N_{0,0}$ is 1, since a newly created actor can immediately sample once – the sampling cost is amortized by the actor creation costs. Sampling can result in a speculation hit with a probability P, or a speculation miss with $1-P$, where P is the true speculation hit probability. The expected number of messages between two sampling iterations is φ^{-1}, so we have:

$$N_{i,j} = N_{i-1,j\div 2} + min\left(\varphi_0^{-1}, \frac{(1-\overline{p_i})^2}{\overline{p_i}}\right) \tag{6}$$

Our task is compute the expected number of messages after n sampling iterations, in other words, to produce a sum of the messages received at the depth n in the tree, weighted by the respective probabilities. This is given with the expression $\overline{N} = \Sigma_j P_{n,j} \cdot N_{n,j}$, where $P_{n,j}$ is the probability of the outcome j after n sampling iterations. We now compute the upper bound for $\overline{N}$ by grouping the execution paths according to the number of speculation hits k, and choosing the longest path in each such group k. The execution is longest when the initial k sampling iterations are speculation misses, followed by $n-k$ speculation hits.

$$\overline{N} \le 1 + \sum_{k=0}^{n} \binom{n}{k} P^{n-k}(1-P)^k \left(k \cdot f \cdot \varphi_0^{-1} + \sum_{i=k\cdot f+1}^{n} \frac{\left(1-\frac{i-k}{i}\right)^2}{\frac{i-k}{i}}\right) \tag{7}$$

Note that in the *min* in (6), the second term does not outweigh φ_0^{-1} at $i = k+1$, but only after a few additional iterations. For this reason, we include the factor

f in (7). It can be shown that the upper bound holds when $f = 1 + (2 + \varphi_0^{-1})^{-1}$. Next, note that in the given range, the fraction in the last sum is always less than $i/(i-k)$. Therefore, we can use the following upper bound for the last sum:

$$\sum_{i=k+1}^{n} \frac{\left(1 - \frac{i-k}{i}\right)^2}{\frac{i-k}{i}} \leq \sum_{i=k+1}^{n} \frac{i}{i-k} = \sum_{j=0}^{n-k-1} \frac{j+k+1}{j+1} \leq (k+1) \cdot H_n + n \quad (8)$$

Above, $H_n = \sum_{i=1}^{n} i^{-1}$ is the n-th harmonic number. By combining this with (7), and by applying the identities $\sum_{k=0}^{n} \binom{n}{k} P^{n-k}(1-P)^k k = n(1-P)$ and $\sum_{k=0}^{n} \binom{n}{k} P^{n-k}(1-P)^k = 1$, we get the following upper bound for $\overline{N}$:

$$\overline{N} \leq 1 + \varphi_0^{-1} \cdot (1 + \frac{1}{2 + \varphi_0^{-1}}) \cdot n \cdot (1-P) + n \cdot H_n \cdot (1-P) + n \quad (9)$$

The bound in (9) is too conservative – in particular, the term $n \cdot H_n$ never exceeds $n \cdot \varphi_0^{-1}$ (in the worst case, the sampling frequency stays φ_0), so we can replace it with $n \cdot min(\varphi_0^{-1}, H_n)$. This proves the first part. To prove the second part, we find a lower bound for $\overline{N}$ – we consider the path in the probability tree that starts with $n - k$ hits (which set φ to 1), followed by k misses:

$$\overline{N} \geq 1 + \sum_{k=0}^{n} \binom{n}{k} P^{n-k}(1-P)^k \left((n-k)\cdot 1 + \sum_{i=n-k+1}^{n} min(\varphi_0^{-1}, \frac{(1 - \frac{n-k}{i})^2}{\frac{n-k}{i}})\right) \quad (10)$$

The term $n - k$ becomes $n \cdot P$ under the outer sum. The second term (the inner sum) consists of two parts, depending on which part under the min dominates. The part with φ_0 is alone greater than $k\varphi_0^{-1}$ when $P \to 0$. From this, it can be shown that $\overline{N}$ is lower bound by $n \cdot P + \varphi_0^{-1} \cdot n \cdot (1-P)$. When work tends to 0, the speedup $\overline{S} = \overline{T}_{base}/\overline{T}_{sampling}$ becomes the ratio between the time spent in context switching without sampling and the time spent with sampling. Note that sampling spends $n \cdot c$ extra time, but only in the $1 - P$ cases that do not end in a speculation hit. By substituting the lower bound into the speedup:

$$\overline{S} \geq \frac{\overline{N} \cdot c}{\overline{N} \cdot c + n \cdot c \cdot (1-P)} \geq 1 - \frac{1-P}{1 + \varphi_0^{-1} \cdot (1-P)} \quad (11)$$

The last expression in (11) is minimal when $P = 0$, and the claim follows.   □

We interpret the Theorem 4 as follows. First, when $P \to 1$, the term with the initial frequency φ_0 disappears, and the expected number of messages $\overline{N}$ depends only on the sample size n. From (9) and (10), for $P = 0.9$, $n = 43$ and $\varphi_0 = 0.01$, the expected number of messages $\overline{N}$ is between 468 and 497, an 8× improvement. Second, when $P \to 0$, the sampling overhead depends only on the initial sampling frequency φ_0. If we pick an unreasonably high value $\varphi_0 \to 1$ for the initial sampling frequency, the performance degrades by at most 50% – this is the case when we always sample after receiving a message, without benefiting from speculation hits, and effectively paying the context switch cost twice.

3   Algorithm and Implementation

We can summarize the results from Sect. 2 as follows. When the speculation hit probability P is greater than the relative delay δ, where $\delta = d/c$ is the ratio between the absolute delay $d \in \langle 0, c \rangle$ and the context switch time c, an actor must speculatively delay its context switches by the duration d. For a confidence level α, an actor must gather a sample of speculation hits of size $n = z_{1-\alpha/2}^2/(4e^2)$, where e is the confidence interval for the sampled speculation hit probability p. These n values are sampled with some probability φ, which is a small value φ_0 initially, but can be set to $\varphi = (\overline{p}_i - \delta)/(1 - \overline{p}_i)^2$ after every sampling iteration.

```
 1 global φ = φ0                         18 if random(0.0, 1.0) < φ:
 2 global L = 32                         19   spins = 0, i = 0
 3 global counts = [1..L]                20   while spins < C:
 4 global d_best = 0                     21     spins += 1
 5 global sample_count = 0               22     if spins%(C/L) == 0:
 6                                       23       has_more = poll()
 7 has_more = poll()                     24     i += 1
 8 while has_more:                       25     if has_more:
 9   has_more = false                    26       counts[j ∈ i..L] += 1
10   if drain():                        27       spins = C
11     spins = d_best                   28   sample_count += 1
12     while spins > 0:                 29   φ = max(φ0, calc_p())
13       spins -= 1                     30 if sample_count == n:
14       if spins%(C/L) == 0:          31   sample_count = 0
15         has_more = poll()           32   k = argmin(counts[i]-C/L*i)
16       if has_more:                  33   d_best = C/L*k
17         spins = 0                   34   counts[i ∈ 1..L] = 0
```

Fig. 3. Pseudocode for speculative lagging

The algorithm in Fig. 3 collects a set of sampled probabilities $\overline{p}_i$ for equidistant delays $d_i \in \langle 0, c \rangle$. An actor runs the algorithm immediately before each context switch. The algorithm maintains the current best delay d_best, initially zero, and the array counts of speculation hit counts for each d_i. It first checks for messages with poll in line 7, and handles them by calling drain in line 10. The drain method returns false only when the scheduler externally disallows further execution – in this case, the actor must immediately yield. Otherwise, the actor spins for d_best time units, and calls poll on the message queue every C / L time units, where L is the total number of delays d_i, and C is the context switch time. If the actor finds that the message is available, it calls drain again and this process is repeated. After the loop in line 8 ends, the actor samples the delays, with the probability φ, by finding the first delay d_i after which a method is available, and updates the speculation hit counts accordingly in line 26. The actor adapts the sampling frequency φ in line 29. Upon reaching the sample size

n, the actor sets `d_best` to the d_i with the largest value $p_i - d_i$ in line 33, and then resets the speculation hit counts in line 34.

We implemented our algorithm in the Reactors framework [2,19], as a modification of the pluggable scheduling system in Reactors [18]. Context switch in this framework consists of finding a worker thread, creating a task object, interacting with the work queue, and setting up actor-local state on the worker. The largest deviation from the analysis in Sect. 2 is that the number of messages a reactor can process is upper bound, and kept around 50 – this already amortizes the context switch times, but ensures fair scheduling (i.e. a bound on latency).

4   Evaluation

In this section, we (1) show the running times of the benchmarks from the Savina actor suite [12], using three different processor models. We identify a subset of benchmarks on which speculative lagging improves performance, and use them to estimate the context switch time c. We then (2) study the performance of these benchmarks for a different number of actors in the system. Finally, to validate that speculative lagging does not degrade performance when it is not beneficial, we (3) identify a subset of benchmarks for which speculative lagging is

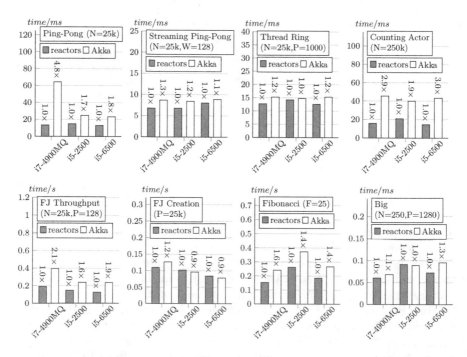

Fig. 4. Running time comparison between Reactors and Akka on the Savina benchmark suite (lower better; N – number of messages, P – number of actors, W – streaming window size, F – computed Fibonacci number)

potentially harmful, and compare the running time for different initial sampling frequencies φ_0. We use standard performance evaluation techniques [10].

We emphasize that we only expect to see a performance improvement on specific benchmarks, in which a majority of actors normally spend a lot of time context switching compared to doing useful work. On other benchmarks, where the actors' mailboxes are saturated and the context switches are rare compared to the amount of useful work, it is unreasonable to expect a speedup – here, eliminating the context switch is unnoticeable by definition. However, we require that the addition of our speculation algorithm *does not degrade performance on any benchmark* – in the worst case, the performance must stay the same.

In Fig. 4, we compare the running time between Reactors with speculative lagging and the Akka framework [1] on the Savina benchmark suite, using three different processors, quad-core 2.8 GHz i7-4900MQ with hyperthreading, quad-core 3.2 GHz i7-6500, and quad-core 3.3 GHz i5-2500. We distinguish between benchmarks for which speculative lagging is beneficial, namely, *Ping-Pong*, *Thread Ring* and *Fork-Join Throughput*, and the remaining benchmarks on which lagging does not improve performance. We note that Reactors is 2–3× faster on the *Counting Actor* benchmark due to primitive type specialization optimization [7], which is only used in that particular benchmark.

In the first row of Fig. 5, we compare the running times for different values of the estimated context switch time C. Here, C is expressed as the number of spins in the algorithm from Fig. 3. In *Ping-Pong*, two actors repetitively exchange N messages, where N is shown on the x-axis. For $C = 128$, the running time is slightly below the Akka version, and converges after C reaches 512. In *Thread Ring*, a total of $P = 4$ actors form a ring, and send a message N/P times around, and C also converges after 512. In both these benchmarks, the running time is additionally improved by keeping an actor-local 1-element message *miniqueue*, which the actor can steal a message from to avoid context switching. The miniqueue optimization has no effect on *FJ Throughput*, where a single producer sends messages to $P = 128$ consumer actors in a roundabout manner. Here, speculative delays cause messages to pile up at non-active actors, which decreases the overall number of context switches, and improves performance by up to 10× for $C > 1024$ (note the logarithmic y-axis).

In the second row in Fig. 5, we analyze the performance of *FJ Throughput* by keeping the total number of delivered messages fixed at 3.2 million, and changing the number of consumers from 1 to 256. The speculation benefits are less pronounced when there are 2 to 8 consumers, which coincides with the number of hardware threads in i7-4900MQ – when each consumer is assigned to a CPU core, speculative delays are just long enough to let the producer run a full cycle, but messages cannot pile up. The situation is reversed on *Thread Ring*, where performance is improved only when ring size is 8 or less. Since there is a single message passed around, speculative delays only help when each actor can be pinned to a CPU. For $P > 8$, Akka is noticeably faster when miniqueues are disabled in Reactors, since Akka's scheduler runs the next actor directly.

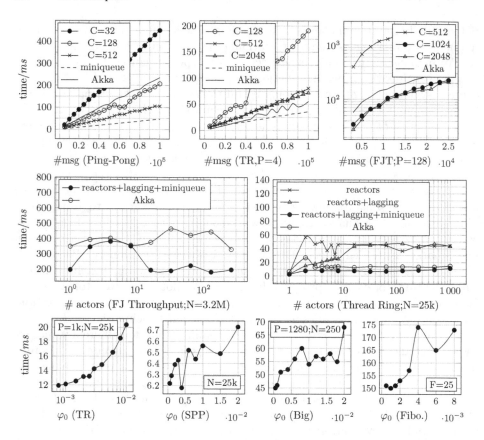

Fig. 5. First row – impact of estimated context switch time C (i7-4900MQ); Second row – impact of parallelism level P (i7-4900MQ; $C = 2048$); Third row – impact of initial frequency φ_0 (i7-4900MQ; $C = 2048$; note that smallest φ_0 is 0.1%)

In *Thread Ring* (when $P \gg 8$), *Big* and *Fibonacci*, each actor receives only very few messages in total, so speculative delays can only slow down the program. We vary initial sampling frequency φ_0 in the third row of Fig. 5, and find that the optimal value is $\varphi_0 \leq 0.2\%$ (**we note that we used $\varphi_0 = 0.2\%$ and $C = 2048$ for the benchmarks in Fig. 4**). For comparison, actors in *Streaming Ping-Pong* (SPP) always have a large number of messages waiting in the mailbox, so that benchmark is insensitive to the sampling frequency.

5   Related Work

Speculation is in practice frequently used to improve execution performance. Many compiler optimizations speculate on program sections that execute less frequently [8], and optimistic concurrency control is based on the bet that synchronization can be omitted [13]. CPUs speculatively execute instructions out of order, and speculatively eliding locks improves performance in some cases [15]. In the context of cluster computing, delaying the start of a job can improve throughput [21]. To cope with straggler jobs, some cluster runtimes speculatively execute them in parallel [3].

In the context of concurrent computing, existing related work can be separated into two groups. The first group consists of various spin lock techniques, and was studied extensively [16]. When acquiring a spin lock, a process repetitively polls the availability of a critical section until another process releases the spin lock. Spin locks were used in a variety of applications, from general-purpose locking [6] to concurrent data structures [4]. Spin locks are similar to speculative lagging, proposed in this work, but differ in several crucial ways. First, in speculative lagging, the release of a computing resource is preceded by spinning, whereas with spin locks, a process spins prior to acquiring a lock. Second, after acquiring a spin lock, a process may attempt to acquire other locks, potentially entering a deadlock. In speculative lagging, the wait time is bound, and cannot lead to a deadlock. Third, spin locks are exposed as a programming primitive, while speculative lagging is performed transparently by a scheduler.

The second group deals with speculatively applying optimizations to concurrent programs. Optimistic concurrency techniques [13] speculate that it is more efficient to run a computation without synchronization, and pay the price only occasionally, compared to always synchronizing concurrent processes. Optimistic concurrency is used in databases and in software transactional memory [11]. Techniques for eliding locks in multithreaded programs were proposed in the past both as microarchitectural solutions [20] and as compiler techniques [15]. Some lock implementations speculatively assume that there are no concurrently executing modifications, and validate memory reads by only reading the lock state [17], which is cheaper compared to writes. Just-in-time compilation techniques make statistical assumption about the program behaviour, and deoptimize the program to a slower variant if an assumption is broken [8]. Common to all of these techniques is the idea of *speculation* – running a simpler, cheaper version of the execution, and potentially reverting to the more costly implementation if it turns out that the assumption is invalidated.

Speculation is often applied blindly, but was in some cases guided by a statistical model. For example, a statistical model was used in the past to predict which threads are more likely to acquire a lock next [14].

We are unaware of prior work on speculatively delaying context switches in actors and other message-based systems, and believe that this is the first contribution in this area.

6   Conclusion

We proposed a new technique for scheduling message-based programs, called *speculative lagging*. The speculation is based on the bet that waiting for another message is less costly than context-switching to another process. To correctly detect speculation opportunities at runtime, we proposed a statistical sampling model that predicts whether delaying a context switch is beneficial. The sampling is adaptive – when it believes that lagging helps, the algorithm increases the sampling rate, hence reaching the conclusion faster. We showed the bounds for the expected speedup, and derived their proofs. When applied to an existing actor system, our speculative lagging algorithm improves performance on benchmarks that spend considerable time in context switches. We experimentally identified the standard benchmarks in which speculative lagging improves performance, and we showed that performance is otherwise not degraded.

Our conclusion is that speculative lagging improves program performance by reducing the amount of context switching. The sampling overhead of detecting speculation opportunities at runtime can be made arbitrarily small with the correct choice of initial parameters. We found that the initial sampling frequency $\varphi_0 = 0.2\%$ and the maximum spin count $C = 2048$ work well, but these numbers may need to be tuned on a per-system basis. Thus, speculation lagging *does not degrade* the performance of programs that cannot benefit from context switches, and it improves the overall throughput otherwise.

References

1. Akka documentation (2017). http://akka.io/docs/
2. Reactors.IO website (2017). http://reactors.io/
3. Ananthanarayanan, G., Hung, M.C.C., Ren, X., Stoica, I., Wierman, A., Yu, M.: GRASS: trimming stragglers in approximation analytics. In: NSDI 2014 (2014)
4. Bronson, N.G., Casper, J., Chafi, H., Olukotun, K.: A practical concurrent binary search tree. In: PPoPP 2010. ACM, New York (2010)
5. Cochran, W.: Sampling Techniques. Wiley, Hoboken (1977)
6. Dice, D.: Biased locking in HotSpot (2006). https://blogs.oracle.com/dave/biased-locking-in-hotspot
7. Dragos, I., Odersky, M.: Compiling generics through user-directed type specialization. In: ICOOOLPS 2009 (2009)
8. Duboscq, G., Würthinger, T., Stadler, L., Wimmer, C., Simon, D., Mössenböck, H.: An intermediate representation for speculative optimizations in a dynamic compiler. In: VMIL 2013 (2013)
9. Fleiss, J.L.: The Teacher's corner: a note on the expectation of the reciprocal of a random variable (1966)
10. Georges, A., Buytaert, D., Eeckhout, L.: Statistically rigorous Java performance evaluation. SIGPLAN Not. (2007)
11. Herlihy, M., Moss, J.E.B.: Transactional memory: architectural support for lock-free data structures. SIGARCH Comput. Archit. News **21**(2), 289–300 (1993)
12. Imam, S.M., Sarkar, V.: Savina - an actor benchmark suite: enabling empirical evaluation of actor libraries. In: AGERE! 2014 (2014)
13. Kung, H.T., Robinson, J.T.: On optimistic methods for concurrency control. ACM Trans. Database Syst. (1981)
14. Lucia, B., Devietti, J., Bergan, T., Ceze, L., Grossman, D.: Lock prediction. In: Proceedings of the 2nd USENIX Workshop on Hot Topics in Parallelism (2010)
15. Martínez, J.F., Torrellas, J.: Speculative synchronization: applying thread-level speculation to explicitly parallel applications. SIGOPS Oper. Syst. Rev. (2002)

16. Mellor-Crummey, J.M., Scott, M.L.: Algorithms for scalable synchronization on shared-memory multiprocessors. ACM Trans. Comput. Syst. **9**(1), 21–65 (1991)

17. Nakaike, T., Michael, M.M.: Lock elision for read-only critical sections in Java. In: Proceedings of the 31st ACM SIGPLAN Conference on Programming Language Design and Implementation, PLDI 2010. ACM, New York (2010)

18. Prokopec, A.: Pluggable scheduling for the Reactor programming model. In: AGERE 2016 (2016)

19. Prokopec, A., Odersky, M.: Isolates, channels, and event streams for composable distributed programming. In: Onward! 2015 (2015)

20. Rajwar, R., Goodman, J.R.: Speculative lock elision: enabling highly concurrent multithreaded execution. In: Proceedings of 34th ACM/IEEE International Symposium on Microarchitecture, MICRO 34. IEEE Computer Society, Washington, D.C. (2001)

21. Zaharia, M., Borthakur, D., Sen Sarma, J., Elmeleegy, K., Shenker, S., Stoica, I.: Delay scheduling: a simple technique for achieving locality and fairness in cluster scheduling. In: EuroSys 2010 (2010)

Using Simulation to Evaluate and Tune the Performance of Dynamic Load Balancing of an Over-Decomposed Geophysics Application

Rafael Keller Tesser[1]([✉]), Lucas Mello Schnorr[1], Arnaud Legrand[2],
Fabrice Dupros[3], and Philippe Olivier Alexandre Navaux[1]

[1] Informatics Institute, Federal University of Rio Grande do Sul, Porto Alegre, Brazil
`{rktesser,schnorr,navaux}@inf.ufrgs.br`
[2] Univ. Grenoble Alpes, CNRS, Inria, Grenoble INP, LIG, 38000 Grenoble, France
`arnaud.legrand@imag.fr`
[3] BRGM, Orléans, France
`f.dupros@brgm.fr`

Abstract. Finite difference methods are commonplace in scientific computing. Despite their apparent regularity, they often exhibit load imbalance that damages their efficiency. We characterize the spatial and temporal load imbalance of Ondes3D, a seismic wave propagation simulator. We reveal that this imbalance originates from the nature of the input data and from low-level CPU optimizations. Such dynamic imbalance should therefore be quite common and is intractable by any static approach or classical code reorganization. An effective solution, with few code modifications, combines domain over-decomposition and dynamic load balancing (e.g., with AMPI), migrating data and computation at the granularity of an MPI rank. It generally requires a careful tuning of the over-decomposition level, the load balancing heuristic and frequency. These choices are quite dependent on application and platform characteristics. In this paper, we propose a methodology that leverages the capabilities of the SimGrid framework to conduct such study at low experimental cost. It combines emulation, simulation, and application modeling that requires minimal code modification and yet manages to capture both spatial and temporal load imbalance, faithfully predicting its overall performance. We compare simulation and real executions results and show how our strategy can be used to determine the best load balancing configuration for a given application/hardware configuration.

Keywords: Load balancing and over-decomposition · Performance prediction · Simulation · Geophysics FDM application

1 Introduction

The Ondes3D seismic wave propagation simulator [7], developed by computational science researchers at the French Geological and Mining Research Bureau

© Springer International Publishing AG 2017
F.F. Rivera et al. (Eds.): Euro-Par 2017, LNCS 10417, pp. 192–205, 2017.
DOI: 10.1007/978-3-319-64203-1_14

(BRGM), is a typical iterative application tailored for homogeneous HPC platforms. Unfortunately like many other similar applications, Ondes3D suffers from scalability issues [6] due to the difficulty of evenly distributing the computational load among processes. One of the contributions of this article is to demonstrate that, despite the regularity of the finite difference method kernels it relies on, Ondes3D presents both non-trivial spatial and temporal load imbalance.

The performance of Ondes3D could be improved by partially rewriting it [13] to run on modern heterogeneous HPC platforms. The undesired side-effect is that computational science researchers, the people who actually understand the physics behind the code, often become incapable to contribute anymore. An alternative way to improve performance with less intrusive modifications is to rely on domain over-decomposition and runtimes that support dynamic process migration, as implemented by Charm++ [11]. In the specific case of legacy iterative MPI applications, one may employ Adaptive MPI (AMPI) [10], which is a full-fledged MPI implementation built over the Charm++ runtime and benefits from its load balancing infrastructure. AMPI encapsulates each MPI rank in a task that can be dynamically migrated when necessary. The migration phase is triggered when the `MPI_Migrate` operation is called. The load balancer decides the new task mapping based on previously collected load measurements.

Such porting has already been applied to Ondes3D in a previous work [12], enabling spatial load imbalance to be dynamically mitigated. However, anticipating performance gains when using such adaptive HPC runtimes is usually difficult. Finding the best configuration for AMPI involves conducting real experiments at scale to identify the best (a) over-decomposition level, (b) load balancing heuristic, (c) load balancing frequency, and (d) number of resources to request. Such parameter tuning is platform-specific, and time-consuming.

In this paper, we propose a simulation-based methodology to evaluate the potential performance benefits brought by adaptive MPI runtimes to legacy codes. This methodology accelerates the evaluation of over-decomposition coupled with dynamic load balancing with almost no modification of the target application. Our approach relies on the SMPI emulation and trace replay mechanisms of SimGrid [5] to simulate the computation/communication behavior of the application and to mimic the behavior of the load balancing heuristics. Our methodology is faithful in terms of total makespan, as well as from the load balancing perspective. The application has to be executed only once to obtain a fine-grain trace that can be replayed multiple times to evaluate the best parameter configuration for a given HPC platform. Since the replay is fast (usually less than a minute on a laptop), it enables a quick inspection of many load balancing parameters. Although our validation is conducted only with Ondes3D and two earthquake scenarios (Chuetsu-Oki and Ligurian), we believe that it has nothing specific to it. Our strategy could be applied to any iterative MPI application.

Section 2 presents a detailed analysis of the spatial and temporal load imbalances in Ondes3D. Section 3 details our evaluation workflow and its validation procedure. In Sect. 4, we compare our method against real executions, and confirm the usefulness of our simulation for load balancing parameter tuning.

Section 5 presents related work on simulation-based tools, justifying our choices. Section 6 concludes the paper, listing major contributions and future work. More details on experiments, analysis, and simulation workflow can be found in an extended version at https://hal.inria.fr/hal-01391401.

2 Ondes3D: A Typical Imbalanced MPI Code

Ondes3D is a simulator to conduct seismic hazard assessment at regional scale. It approximates the differential equations governing the elastodynamics of rock medium using finite-differences methods (FDM). The 3D domain is statically partitioned in cuboids, as depicted in Fig. 1. Each iteration (see Fig. 2a) corresponds to a given time step and consists in calling three macro kernels (Intermediates, Stress, and Velocity) that apply a series of micro kernels (example in Fig. 2b) to the whole domain. Message passing consists in asynchronous neighborhood communications intertwined with the three macro kernels. There is no global barrier, each process evolves asynchronously up to some extent.

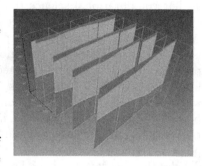

Fig. 1. 3D rock medium, with a 4×4 domain decomposition; each process calculates a cuboid.

```
for (ts = 0; ts < N; ts++){
  Intermediates();

  Stress();
  //Intertwined Asynchronous
  //Neighborhood Communication

  Velocity();
  //Intertwined Asynchronous
  //Neighborhood Communication

}
```

```
static inline double CPML4 (double vp, double dump,
    double alpha, double kappa, double phidum, double dx,
    double dt, double x1, double x2, double x3, double x4) {
  double a, b;
  b = exp(-(vp * dump / kappa + alpha) * dt);
  a = 0.0;
  if (abs(vp * dump) > 0.000001)
    a = vp * dump * (b - 1.0) / (kappa * (vp * dump + kappa *
    alpha));
  return b * phidum + a *
    ((9. / 8.) * (x2 - x1) / dx - (1. / 24.) * (x4 - x3) /dx);
}
```

(a) The main loop with three kernels: Intermediates, Stress and Velocity; no global synchronization.

(b) The CPML4 kernel, called nine times for each cell i, j, k in the Intermediates kernel when processing a subdomain. Variables x1, x2, x3, and x4 represent the rock medium states (e.g., speed) that evolves along iterations.

Fig. 2. The Ondes3D application: (a) the three macro kernels of the main loop, with intertwined neighborhood communications; (b) and the CPML4 micro kernel.

Ondes3D suffers from load imbalance that limits its scalability despite its regularity (cuboids have the same geometry; code is always the same). Extra-computation dealing with boundary conditions has been previously identified [6] as the main source of spatial imbalance. In Sect. 2.1, we report another source of spatial imbalance caused by the heterogeneous rock substrate. Temporal imbalances had been overlooked due to the regular shape of the code. In Sect. 2.1, we show that temporal imbalance is stronger than the spatial one. Evidences of its origin are related to low level optimizations taking place inside the CPU.

We have used a Mw6.3 earthquake workload [2] identified as Ligurian. Code compilation uses GCC 6.1.1 with −03 and PAPI [14] instrumentation. While we report results only for this setup, we have observed the issues with other workloads, CPUs (Xeon X3440, X5650, E5-2630, and i7 4600M), and compilers.

2.1 Identifying New Sources of Load Imbalance

Spatial Imbalance Due to Heterogeneous Rock Medium.
Figure 3 depicts a 16 × 16 domain decomposition where each cell in the cartesian grid represents one of the 256 processes, each in charge of a cuboid subdomain. The color in the heatmap indicates the total computational load per process during the first iteration, before the main earthquake event that originates in the (13, 5) subdomain coordinate. Processes on the borders demonstrate a much higher computational load (red color) than those located inside the physical domain. Another, much more subtle, source of spatial imbalance (blue shades), depends mostly on the rock multi-layer configuration of the input (six layers for this scenario). Although minor, such effect exists and solely depends on the substrate geometry.

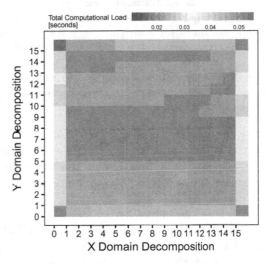

Fig. 3. Spatial imbalance for the first iteration represented by a color gradient for each rank in a 16 × 16 grid (256 processes). (Color figure online)

Temporal Imbalance Due to Low-Level CPU Optimizations. The Ondes3D code does not exhibit any structure (convergence loops, refinements, thresholds) that could lead to an evolution of computation load along simulation iterations. There are conditional branches (see Fig. 2b), but they are related solely to absorbing boundary conditions. Yet, as illustrated in Fig. 4a, one can observe a variability in computational costs along iterations that is even higher than the spatial variability incurred by the absorbing conditions. This figure details the behavior of all 64 processes (each box in the 8 × 8 grid), showing

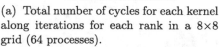

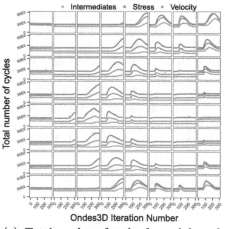

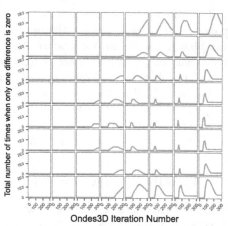

(a) Total number of cycles for each kernel along iterations for each rank in a 8×8 grid (64 processes).

(b) How much the differences evaluate to contrasting values in the CPML4 kernel along iterations, for each of the 64 ranks.

Fig. 4. Load imbalances for the Ligurian workload: (a) spatial load imbalance; (b) temporal load imbalance for three kernels; and (c) CPML4 substrate values evaluating to distinct values.

(in the vertical axis of each box) the total number of cycles (PAPI_TOT_CYC) per macro kernel as a function of the iteration (horizontal axis). The number of cycles seems to follow the earthquake shock progression, standing out around the eightieth iteration.

We take the CPML4 kernel (see Fig. 2b) to explain the origin of this dynamic computational cost. CPML4 represents well all the 24 small inlined kernels. It is called by the Intermediates macro kernel that iterates over the cuboid sub-domain with three nested loops. For each subdomain's cell, the CPML4 kernel is called nine times with different parameters, resulting in many calls for each process and time step. The values dx and dt are constants, while variables x1, x2, x3, and x4 represent how the rock medium state unfolds along the iterations.

Let us consider the x1, x2, x3, and x4 arguments of the CPML4 kernel (Fig. 2b). They are used in the return statement, considered by the FPU for arithmetic evaluation. We instrumented the CPML4 kernel to count how many times per time step and per process these differences are equal to zero (let us name these numbers $n_{2,1}^0$ for x2-x1 and $n_{4,3}^0$ for x4-x3). The difference $|n_{2,1}^0 - n_{4,3}^0|$ (Fig. 4b) perfectly correlates with the computational load change (Fig. 4a) and with the growth of the branch miss-prediction counters. Intuitively, this value measures how often only one of the two differences is zero. This hypothesis has been confirmed with a manual instrumentation of the CPML4 kernel, recording its duration for each call (in cycles) along with the result of the two differences (x2-x1 and x4-x3). The observed duration increase originates from the combination of both a speed-up of multiplications by zero and of branch miss-predictions in the FPU incurred by the irregular sequence of zeros and non-zeros. All other small inlined kernels share the same structure of CPML4. It is thus the aggregated contribution of all these small additional cycles that generates the temporal load variation.

2.2 Need for Dynamic Load Balancing: The AMPI Approach

Modeling and predicting the Ondes3D load imbalance is hard, as it strongly depends on the initial and evolving conditions of the earthquake simulations. Even if we could rewrite Ondes3D to allow uneven domain decomposition, some periodic data/computation re-balancing would still be required to cope with temporal load imbalance. We thus employ a simpler approach by mixing load balancing at runtime with over-decomposition, using Charm++'s Adaptive MPI [10] (AMPI). This framework enables over-decomposition, i.e., dividing the problem domain in more tasks than the number of available cores. Each task becomes a user-level thread suitable for migration. Load balancing heuristics, sensitive to load variations from the near past, can periodically redistribute load.

Porting from MPI to AMPI requires three application changes. First, there should be no global or static variables, to avoid data sharing among tasks. Second, Pack-and-Unpack functions are necessary to make data migrations possible. And third, the application must call MPI_Migrate to indicate when the application has no active communications or open files, and is ready for load balancing.

2.3 Costly Tuning of Load Balancing Parameters in Real Platforms

Many parameters influence the effectiveness of the load balancing. Some **load balancing heuristics** are more scalable than others (e.g., centralized *vs* distributed). The **level of over-decomposition** defines the granularity for the load balancer. As over-decomposition increases, we also increase the communication cost. At some point, such cost exceeds the benefit of load balancing. Likewise, **the number of processors** is a critical parameter in the overall performance. Finally, fine-tuning the **frequency of load balancing** is essential to obtain good performance since frequent calls might become overhead, hiding any load balancing benefits. Moreover, since calling MPI_Migrate incurs a global barrier, it may also destroy any natural compensation of load imbalance throughout iterations afforded by asynchronous neighborhood communications.

Using real executions to evaluate the load balancing benefits present several difficulties. The optimal configuration often depends on application and platform characteristics. Running the same earthquake simulation many times at scale on a production system solely to determine such parameters is both resource and time consuming. To overcome this, we propose a lightweight simulation workflow to avoid the burden of real executions. Performance gains are evaluated with few code changes (even before AMPI porting), and the application needs to be executed only once. Such approach saves development and evaluation time.

3   Simulated Adaptive MPI (SAMPI)

Our workflow relies on SimGrid's SMPI, which offers two key features we have built upon. First, SMPI's flexibility allows to study MPI applications either in *emulation mode* or through *trace-replay*. In emulation, unmodified MPI applications are sequentially executed on top of the simulator, in a controlled way. In trace replay, the events of an MPI application are replayed on top of the simulator, in a small fraction of the time it takes to finish a normal run at full scale. Second, SMPI builds on the hybrid flow-level network models of SimGrid [4] that allow to faithfully model network contention, which is essential in our context.

SMPI has been modified to simulate AMPI in three ways. (1) The API is extended with the non-standard `MPI_Migrate` function both in the emulation mode (to generate an event in the trace) and in the trace replay. When replaying with load-balancing, this function calls the `MPI_Barrier` function, the load balancing heuristic to define a new mapping, and simulates all task migrations. (2) We have manually extracted and slightly adapted two centralized load balancers (LB) by hand: **GreedyLB** and **RefineLB**. We removed internal references to the original Charm++ implementation, making sure that the heuristic remains intact. A few trace replay routines also had to be modified to collect the load data that is fed to these heuristics. (3) The migration payload is estimated by trapping `malloc` function calls in emulation, which is prone to migration cost understimation. We rely on SimGrid's contention-aware network models when sending the data of the migrated task from its original location to its destination.

Tracing one workload requires to run the code for real, hence it takes 3–5 h with SMPI's emulation on a laptop. Then, while exploring parameters, it can be replayed many times with SAMPI and an LB configuration (frequency, heuristic). Each configuration simulation takes only a few minutes on a laptop.

4   Experimental Results and Evaluation

Several issues should be solved to correctly validate the accuracy of predictions obtained in simulation. Solely comparing the (predicted) makespan of simulations with the one of real-life executions on a few examples is insufficient to be fully trusted. Yet, comparing detailed execution traces (e.g., with Gantt charts) of an application as complex as Ondes3D is simply impossible. Other adhoc intermediate and aggregated representations are thus needed. In our context, iterations and load imbalance are of primary importance. Therefore, we decided to track the resource usage per processor and per iteration and to study its evolution both temporally and spatially. We use this performance metric, to compare reality and simulation both qualitatively and quantitatively.

Real measurements have been collected in 16 nodes of the Parapluie cluster (part of Grid'5000 [3]). Each node has two 12-core 1.7 GHz AMD Opteron 6164 HE processors, interconnected through a 20 G Infiniband 4x QDR network.

We tested two very different earthquake scenarios in Ondes3D. The first one is the Mw6.6 Niigata *Chuetsu-Oki* (2007) from Japan [1]. Running the full simulation (6000 time steps) takes an unreasonable amount of time, mainly because many runs are needed to obtain statistically significant results. We limited this simulation to the first 500 time steps to keep a reasonable experimental time. We also reduced the number of cells to $300 \times 300 \times 150$. The second simulated scenario is the same used in Sect. 2, with $500 \times 350 \times 130$ cells.

4.1 Validation: Comparing SAMPI (Simulation) Against AMPI

In our validation experiments, we fix the domain decomposition to 64 tasks (always mapped to 16 processes) and call MPI_Migrate every 20 time steps. From our experience, this configuration is relatively good and allows to focus our evaluation on sound scenarios. The comparison of SAMPI with AMPI for situations without load balancer, with GreedyLB and with RefineLB, is depicted for the two workloads: Chuetsu-Oki in Fig. 5, and Ligurian in Fig. 6.

Per-Process Computational Load Analysis. The heatmaps in Figs. 5a (Chuetsu-Oki) and 6a (Ligurian) show the computational load (as a color gradient) for each core (in the vertical axis) along the Ondes3D iterations. A reddish color represents higher computational load, while blue represents idleness. Each heatmap corresponds to an execution, either real (AMPI in the top row) or simulated (SAMPI in the bottom), with a given load balancer (no load balancing on the left column, Greedy in the center, and Refine on the right). The real and simulated load distribution are very similar, showing the ability of our workflow to capture the complex behavior of AMPI in simulation.

Figure 5a shows that for Chuetsu-Oki, the case without load balancing leads to many underutilized resources (white and bluish regions). Both LB seem to significantly improve this situation by making processes 2 to 13 receive more load. GreedyLB achieves a much better load balancing than RefineLB (being more conservative) and this is visible in simulation as well as in real execution traces. The load structure for the Ligurian workload is quite different (see Fig. 6a). There seems to exist an alternating load irregularity in processes whose ranks belong to the center of the domain decomposition (those with white and bluish colors without load balancing). The Greedy and Refine load balancers are again effective to redistribute the load. We observe a much more even computational load across processes but not as good as for the Chuetsu-Oki workload.

The heatmap views are based on one run for each case. Any new execution (either real or in simulation from a new trace) leads to slightly different outcomes. Thus, focusing on the load of a given core at a given time-step is not really meaningful. From such view, it seems that GreedyLB is the best choice from the load balancing perspective, but communication (both from the application and load balancer) should also be taken into account. In the following, we provide makespan analyses using the average load as a function of the execution time.

Average Load and Makespan Comparison Analysis. The plots in Figs. 5b (Chuetsu-Oki) and 6b (Ligurian) depict the evolution of the average load for each core. This metric (in vertical axis) is drawn as a function of time (horizontal) for both SAMPI (blue) and AMPI (red). The points along the lines indicate the

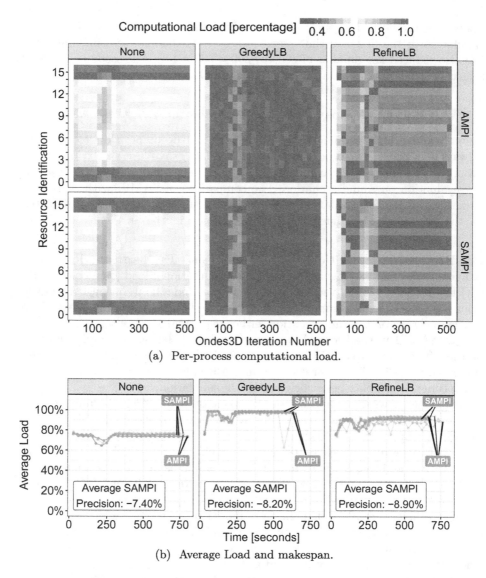

(a) Per-process computational load.

(b) Average Load and makespan.

Fig. 5. Comparison of SAMPI (simulation) against AMPI (reality) for the Chuetsu-Oki workload; the top row shows six heatmaps (no LB, Greedy, and Refine) illustrating the computation load (color gradient) for each iteration and all 16 processes; the bottom row shows the average aggregated load along time, with the makespan of multiple runs. (Color figure online)

moments when the metric is computed (when `MPI_Migrate` starts, at the end of the LB interval); lines show the trend. Horizontal facetting indicates the metric without load balancing, with GreedyLB and with RefineLB.

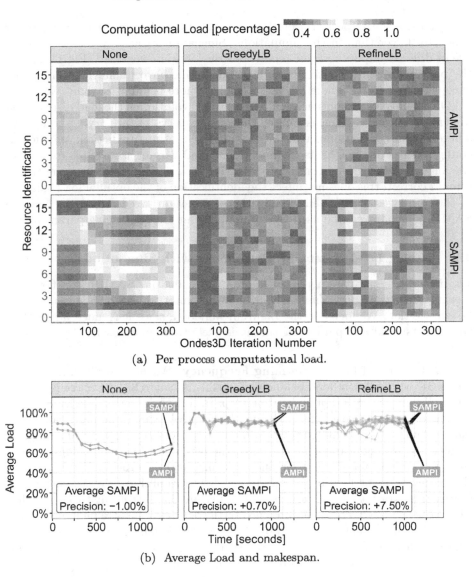

(a) Per process computational load.

(b) Average Load and makespan.

Fig. 6. Comparison of SAMPI against AMPI for the Ligurian workload. (Color figure online)

For the Chuetsu-Oki workload (Fig. 5b), GreedyLB performs better than RefineLB, both in simulation as in real life. One could expect GreedyLB to be worse instead, due to the larger amount of migrations. It seems however that, in this case, the default overload tolerance of 1.05 used by RefineLB is too high. Regarding the comparison of SAMPI against the real AMPI, we see that SAMPI is slightly too optimistic across several runs. That being said, such inaccuracy would not affect our choice of load balancer. There is a significant variability in real executions (perfect isolation is tough to achieve on a cluster), being generally larger than in the simulations. Simulation variability comes from the use of different inputs to trace replay. For the Ligurian workload (Fig. 6b), as on the previous scenario, both simulation and real life have similar load unfolding, except for RefineLB, where SAMPI is slightly more pessimistic than real life.

Our simulation mimics in a realistic way the evolution of the load distribution of real executions, which is one of the main aspects we are trying to obtain. There remains some minor inaccuracies in absolute time prediction: ≈9% for all configurations of the Chuetsu-Oki workload, and varying from ≈1% to ≈8% in the Ligurian. We are currently investigating their origin. Yet, since the trends remain correct, this does not affect the identification of the optimal load balancer in the two investigated scenarios. In the next section, we demonstrate how the SAMPI simulator can be used to explore different load balancing parameters.

4.2   Tuning Load-Balancing Parameters with Simulation

We investigate the parameter space of AMPI using our SAMPI workflow. We measure four configurations for load balancing interval; and five levels of over-decomposition. We focus on the Ligurian workload, since it is much larger than the Chuetsu-Oki and parameter tuning is likely to be more useful.

The Influence of Load Balancing Frequency. We measure the makespan of Ondes3D with different load balancing intervals. A call to MPI_Migrate is present for each task at the end of every time step. During the simulation with SAMPI, we control and enforce a different load balancing frequency by actually calling the barrier and the load balancing, for example, only every 10, 20, 30 or 40 iterations. Intuitively, the more frequent the calls, the better the load balancing but also the more important the barrier and data migration overhead. Figure 7 shows the influence of the load balancing frequency (horizontal axis) on the makespan (vertical axis) of a 16 × 4 task configuration. In this setting, it turns out that LB frequency has no or little influence in the performance attained when using GreedyLB or RefineLB. Even though GreedyLB balances the load carelessly whereas RefineLB is much more conservative, the communication performance of the system is sufficiently good to hide the migration costs.

The Influence of Decomposition Level. Another important performance affecting parameter is the over-decomposition level. The influence of over-decomposition on the makespan of Ondes3D, when calling MPI_Migrate every 20 time steps, is depicted in Fig. 7 (right plot). The average makespan (vertical axis) is shown as a function of five over-decomposition configurations (horizontal). In the absence of load balancing (None), over-decomposing is, as expected, generally deterring since this creates extra-communication between tasks. Yet having more and smaller tasks allows for a better redistribution of the load. The RefineLB sweet spot is reached with a 16 × 8 decomposition (≈13% gain over the original version). However, for GreedyLB the decomposition level should be

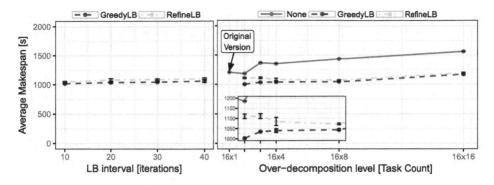

Fig. 7. Simulated makespan predictions for the Ligurian earthquake simulation with (left) four load balancing intervals (in number of iterations) and (right) with six over-decomposition levels (1, 2, 3, 4, 8, and 16) on 16 cores.

as small as possible (which leads to ≈19% gain over the original version), which is again explained by the fact that its careless migrations scale very badly. In the end, the 16 × 2 GreedyLB configuration is slightly better than the 16 × 4 RefineLB configuration but exhibits quite different load balancing behaviors.

From a series of similar simple studies using SAMPI, it appears that, for this application, RefineLB executed every 20 time steps with an over-decomposition level of 8 provides, in general, a decent performance and gracefully handles a larger number of nodes. This parameter combination has been tested a real execution of the Chuetsu-Oki simulation on a 12-node cluster (288 cores) at BRGM. We obtained an ≈36% faster execution than the original unbalanced execution. Further tuning can be done at low cost using SAMPI to guide the analyst toward a better configuration.

5 Related Work

The SAMPI workflow we propose mostly depends on two factors. First, a faithful model of modern HPC networks and MPI implementations are essential since communications play a crucial role in the load balancing trade-offs. Second, the ability to run simulations both in trace-replay and emulation modes is helpful to select the approach most suited to the resources at hand. There is a plethora of simulation tools to study MPI applications [5] and at least four of them support both modes and could thus have been modified: BigSim [17], SST/Macro [15], xSim [8], and SimGrid [5] (through SMPI). BigSim is part of Charm++, thus supporting the AMPI applications simulation, such as our Ondes3D code. Although linked to Charm++, BigSim is uncapable to change the load balancing parameters during trace replay and this would require major code modifications. SST-Macro allows both trace replay through the DUMPI module and emulation through skeletonization. Although SST-macro is flexible with many network models, including flow-based ones, its emulation support still seems unsufficiently mature to run an application as complex as Ondes3D. Finally, xSim mostly focuses on extreme-scale executions and its validity remains questionable at small scale [9]. Furthermore, the source code of xSim is currently unavailable.

For this work, we therefore chose to rely on the free software SimGrid, whose SMPI interface allows both emulation and trace replay of MPI applications. SMPI leverages SimGrid's thoroughly validated flow communication models [16], while also accounting for specific characteristics of MPI implementations [5]. Hence, SMPI allows us to collect accurate execution traces from emulation, and its replay mechanism allows us to quickly simulate one execution many times.

6   Conclusion

We propose a simulation based approach for the performance evaluation and tuning of dynamic load balancing applied to iterative MPI applications. Our approach allows the estimation of performance gains from load balancing at low cost, both in terms of time and of resource requirements. Although we apply it to a geophysics application (Ondes3D), its structure is very typical among legacy MPI applications. Therefore, we believe the usefulness of our approach is not limited to Ondes3D. Our contributions are three-fold: (a) An in-depth analysis of the spatial and temporal load balancing issues found in Ondes3D. The latter demonstrates how dynamic load imbalance can arise even when there is no indication of temporal variability in the code. (b) A validated simulator called SAMPI that simulates over-decomposition and AMPI load balancing. This simulator is integrated in the open-source SimGrid framework, and allows the fast and faithful exploration of different load balancing scenarios from a single execution trace. (c) A sensibility analysis showing both the importance of activating a load balancer ($\approx$20–30% gains), and the rather low influence of specific load balancing parameters in the Ondes3D makespan.

As future work, we plan to build on other Ondes3D characteristics to understand how spatial aggregation and trace extrapolation can be used together to further accelerate the simulations.

Acknowledgements. We thank CAPES/Cofecub 764-13, FAPERGS/Inria ExaSE, FAPERGS Green-Cloud, CNPq 447311/2014-0, CNRS/LICIA Intl. Lab, the EU H2020 Programme and from MCTI/RNP-Brazil under the HPC4E Project, grant 689772. Some experiments were carried out at the Grid'5000 platform (https://www.grid5000. fr), with support from Inria, CNRS, RENATER and several other organizations.

References

1. Aochi, H., Ducellier, A., Dupros, F., Delatre, M., Ulrich, T., Martin, F., Yoshimi, M.: Finite difference simulations of seismic wave propagation for the 2007 mw 6.6 Niigata-ken Chuetsu-Oki earthquake: Validity of models and reliable input ground motion in the near-field. Pure Appl. Geophys. **170**(1–2), 43–64 (2013)

2. Aochi, H., Ducellier, A., Dupros, F., Terrier, M., Lambert, J.: Investigation of historical earthquake by seismic wave propagation simulation: source parameters of the 1887 M6.3 Ligurian, north-western Italy, earthquake. In: 8ème colloque AFPS, Vers une maitrise durable du risque sismique. p. 6, September 2011

3. Balouek, D., et al.: Adding virtualization capabilities to the Grid'5000 testbed. In: Ivanov, I.I., Sinderen, M., Leymann, F., Shan, T. (eds.) CLOSER 2012. CCIS, vol. 367, pp. 3–20. Springer, Cham (2013). doi:10.1007/978-3-319-04519-1_1

4. Bédaride, P., et al.: Toward better simulation of MPI applications on Ethernet/TCP networks. In: Jarvis, S.A., Wright, S.A., Hammond, S.D. (eds.) PMBS 2013. LNCS, vol. 8551, pp. 158–181. Springer, Cham (2013). doi:10.1007/978-3-319-10214-6_8

5. Casanova, H., Giersch, A., Legrand, A., Quinson, M., Suter, F.: Versatile, scalable, and accurate simulation of distributed applications and platforms. Parallel Distrib. Comput. **74**(10), 2899–2917 (2014)

6. Dupros, F., Do, H.T., Aochi, H.: On scalability issues of the elastodynamics equations on multicore platforms. In: International Conference on Computer Science, Procedia Computer Science, p. 9. Elsevier, Barcelone, June 2013

7. Dupros, F., Martin, F.D., Foerster, E., Komatitsch, D., Roman, J.: High-performance finite-element simulations of seismic wave propagation in three-dimensional nonlinear inelastic geological media. Parallel Comput. **36**(5–6), 308–325 (2010)

8. Engelmann, C.: Scaling to a million cores and beyond: using light-weight simulation to understand the challenges ahead on the road to exascale. Future Gener. Comput. Syst. **30**, 59–65 (2014)

9. Engelmann, C., Naughton, T.: A network contention model for the extreme-scale simulator. In: Press, A. (ed.) 34th IASTED International Conference on Modelling, Identification and Control (MIC) (2015)

10. Huang, C., Lawlor, O., Kalé, L.V.: Adaptive MPI. In: Rauchwerger, L. (ed.) LCPC 2003. LNCS, vol. 2958, pp. 306–322. Springer, Heidelberg (2004). doi:10.1007/978-3-540-24644-2_20

11. Kalé, L., Krishnan, S.: CHARM++: a portable concurrent object oriented system based on C++. In: Proceedings of OOPSLA 1993, pp. 91–108. ACM Press (1993)

12. Keller Tesser, R., Lima Pilla, L., Dupros, F., Navaux, P., Mehaut, J.F., Mendes, C.: Improving the performance of seismic wave simulations with dynamic load balancing. In: International Conference Parallel, Distributed and Network-Based Processing (2014)

13. Martinez, V., Michéa, D., Dupros, F., Aumage, O., Thibault, S., Aochi, H., Navaux, P.O.A.: Towards seismic wave modeling on heterogeneous many-core architectures using task-based runtime system. In: SBAC-PAD. IEEE Computer Society (2015)

14. Mucci, P.J., Browne, S., Deane, C., Ho, G.: PAPI: a portable interface to hardware performance counters. In: Proceedings of the Department of Defense HPCMP Users Group Conference, pp. 7–10 (1999)

15. Rodrigues, A.F., Hemmert, K.S., Barrett, B.W., Kersey, C., Oldfield, R., Weston, M., Risen, R., Cook, J., Rosenfeld, P., CooperBalls, E., et al.: The structural simulation toolkit. ACM SIGMETRICS Perform. Eval. Rev. **38**(4), 37–42 (2011)

16. Velho, P., Schnorr, L.M., Casanova, H., Legrand, A.: On the validity of flow-level TCP network models for grid and cloud simulations. ACM Trans. Model. Comput. Simul. **23**(4), 23:1–23:26 (2013)

17. Zheng, G., Kakulapati, G., Kale, L.: Bigsim: a parallel simulator for performance prediction of extremely large parallel machines. In: Parallel and Distributed Processing Symposium, Proceedings, 18th International, p. 78, April 2004

Optimizing Egalitarian Performance in the Side-Effects Model of Colocation for Data Center Resource Management

Fanny Pascual[1] and Krzysztof Rzadca[2(✉)]

[1] Sorbonne Universités, UPMC, LIP6, CNRS, UMR 7606, Paris, France
fanny.pascual@lip6.fr
[2] Institute of Informatics, University of Warsaw, Warsaw, Poland
krz@mimuw.edu.pl

Abstract. In data centers, up to dozens of tasks are colocated on a single physical machine. Machines are used more efficiently, but tasks' performance deteriorates, as colocated tasks compete for shared resources. As tasks are heterogeneous, the resulting performance dependencies are complex. In our previous work [18] we proposed a new combinatorial optimization model that uses two parameters of a task—its size and its type—to characterize how a task influences the performance of other tasks allocated to the same machine.

In this paper, we study the egalitarian optimization goal: maximizing the worst-off performance. This problem generalizes the classic makespan minimization on multiple processors ($P||C_{max}$). We prove that polynomially-solvable variants of $P||C_{max}$ are NP-hard and hard to approximate when the number of types is not constant. For a constant number of types, we propose a PTAS, a fast approximation algorithm, and a series of heuristics. We simulate the algorithms on instances derived from a trace of one of Google clusters. Algorithms aware of jobs' types lead to better performance compared to algorithms solving $P||C_{max}$.

The notion of type enables us to model degeneration of performance caused by colocation using standard combinatorial optimization methods. Types add a layer of additional complexity. However, our results—approximation algorithms and good average-case performance—show that types can be handled efficiently.

Keywords: Cloud computing · Scheduling · Heterogeneity · Co-tenancy · Complexity

1 Introduction

The back-bone of cloud computing, the modern data center redefines how industry and academia use computers. Resource management in data centers significantly differs from scheduling jobs on a typical HPC supercomputer. First, the workload is much more varied [22]: data centers act as a physical infrastructure

© Springer International Publishing AG 2017
F.F. Rivera et al. (Eds.): Euro-Par 2017, LNCS 10417, pp. 206–219, 2017.
DOI: 10.1007/978-3-319-64203-1_15

providing virtual machines, or higher-level services, such as memory-cached databases or network-intensive servers; in contrast, there are relatively few HPC-like computationally-intensive batch jobs (later, we will use a generic term *task* for all these categories). Consequently, a task usually does not saturate the resources of a single node [12]. Tasks' loads vastly differ: in a published trace [22], tasks' average CPU loads span more than 4 orders of magnitude. In contrast to HPC scheduling in which jobs rarely share a node, heterogeneity in both the type and the amount of needed resources makes it reasonable to allocate multiple tasks to the same physical machine.

Tasks colocated on a machine compete for shared hardware. Despite significant advances in both OS-level fairness and VM hypervisors, virtualization is not transparent: multiple studies show [12–14, 21, 27] that the performance of colocated tasks drops. Suspects include difficulties in sharing the CPU cache or the memory bandwidth. The resource manager should thus colocate tasks that are compatible, i.e., that use different kinds of resources—hence, it should optimize tasks' performance. This, however, requires a performance model.

Our side-effects model [18] bridges the gap between colocation in datacenters and the theoretical scheduling, bulk of which has been developed for non-shared machines.

Rather than trying to predict tasks' performance from OS-level metrics, we abstract by characterizing a task by two characteristics: *type* (e.g.: a database, or a computationally-intensive job) and *load* relative to other tasks of the same type (e.g.: number of requests per second). The total load of a machine is a vector: its i-th dimension is the sum of loads of tasks of the i-th type located on this machine. Each type additionally defines a performance function mapping this vector of loads to a type-relevant performance metric. As datacenters execute multiple instances of tasks such function can be inferred by a monitoring module [13, 21, 27] matching task's reported performance (such as the 95th percentile response time) with observed or reported loads.

In this paper, we consider optimization of the worst-off performance (analogous to makespan in classic multiprocessor scheduling problem, $P||C_{\max}$ [8]). We use a linear performance function: on each machine, the influence a type t' has on type t performance is a product of the load of type t' and a coefficient $\alpha_{t',t}$. The coefficient $\alpha_{t',t}$ describes how compatible t' load is with t performance (the coefficient is similar to interference/affinity metrics proposed in [13, 21]). Low values ($0 \leq \alpha_{t',t} < 1$) correspond with compatible types (e.g.: colocating a memory-intensive and a CPU-intensive task): it is preferable to colocate a task t with tasks of the other type t', rather than with other tasks of its own type t. High values ($\alpha_{t'',t} > 1$) denote types competing for resources.

The contribution of this paper is as follows. (1) We prove that the notion of type adds complexity, as makespan minimization with unit tasks $P|p_i = 1|C_{\max}$ (a polynomially solvable variant of $P||C_{\max}$) becomes NP-hard and hard to approximate when the number of types T is not constant (Sect. 3). We then show how to cope with that added complexity. We propose (2) a PTAS for a constant T and a constant α (Sect. 4.1); and (3) a fast greedy approximation algorithm (Sect. 4.2). (4) We also propose natural greedy heuristics (Sect. 5) (in the accompanying technical report [19] we show they are approximations for $T = 2$). (5) We also test our algorithm by simulation on a trace derived from one of Google clusters (Sect. 6).

2   Side-Effects of Colocating Tasks: A Model

We study a min-max (egalitarian) performance criteria for our side-effects performance model (introduced in [18], where we studied a utilitarian objective, min-sum). We consider a system that allocates n tasks $J = \{1, \ldots, n\}$ to m identical machines $\mathcal{M} = \{M_1, \ldots, M_m\}$. Each task i has a known size $p_i \in \mathbb{N}$ (i.e., clairvoyance, a common assumption in scheduling; the sizes can be estimated by previous instances or users' estimates). The size corresponds to the load the task imposes on a machine: the request rate for a web server; or the cpu load for a cpu-intensive computation. We take other assumptions standard in scheduling theory: all tasks are known (off-line) and ready to be scheduled (released at time 0). We take these assumptions to derive results on the basic model before tackling more complex ones. We denote by $p_{\max} = \max p_i$ the largest task and by W the total load, $W = \sum p_i$. We assume that the tasks are indexed by non-increasing sizes: $p_1 \geq p_2 \geq \cdots \geq p_n$.

A *partition* (an *allocation*) is an assignment of each of the n tasks to one of the m machines. A partition separates the tasks into at most m subsets: each subset corresponds to the tasks allocated on the same machine. Given a partition P, we denote by $M_{P,i} \in \mathcal{M}$ the machine on which task i is allocated. Due to the similarities with $P||C_{max}$, we sometimes use the term "schedule" (and the symbol σ) for an allocation (and even the term of length for the size of a task). In this case, only the allocation is meaningful (not the order of the tasks on the machines).

The main contribution of this paper lies in analyzing side-effects of colocating tasks. The impact of task i on the performance of another task j is a function of task's size p_i and *task's type* t_i. Types generalize tasks' impact on the performance and may have different granularities: for instance, "a webserver" and "a database"; or "a read-intensive MySQL database"; or, as in [13], "an instance of Blast". We assume that the type t_i is known (which again corresponds to the clairvoyance assumption in classic scheduling; typically a data center runs many instances of the same task, so task's type can be derived from the past). Let $\mathcal{T} = \{1, \ldots, T\}$ be a set of T different types of tasks. Each task i has type $t_i \in \mathcal{T}$. For each type $t \in \mathcal{T}$, we denote by $J^{(t)}$ the tasks which are of type t; and by $p_i^{(t)}$ the size of the i-th largest task of type t (ties are broken arbitrarily).

We express performance of a task i by a cost function c_i: to simplify presentation of our results, we prefer to express our problems as minimization of costs, rather than maximization of performance (for a single type, our cost is synonymous with the makespan). Note that the cost is unrelated to monetary cost (the amount of money that a job pays to the machine)—we do not consider monetary costs in this paper. Task's i cost c_i depends on to the *total load* of tasks j colocated on the same machine $M_{P,i}$, but different types have different impacts: $c_i = \sum_j$ on machine $_{M_{P,i}} p_j \cdot \alpha_{t_j, t_i}$, the cost function also takes into account the task i itself, as well as other tasks of the same type. A coefficient $\alpha_{t,t'} \in \mathbb{R}_{\geq 0}$ defined for each pair of types $(t, t') \in \mathscr{T}^2$, measures the impact of the tasks of type t on the cost of the tasks of type t' (allocated on the same machine). If $\alpha_{t,t'} = 0$ then a task of type t has no impact on the cost of a task of type t'; the higher the $\alpha_{t,t'}$, the larger the impact. Coefficients are not necessarily symmetric, i.e., it is possible that $\alpha_{t,t'} \neq \alpha_{t',t}$. The coefficients $\alpha_{t,t'}$ can be estimated by monitoring tasks' performance in function of their colocation and their sizes (a data center runs many instances of similar services [13,21,27]). We consider the linear cost function as it generalizes, by adding coefficients $\alpha_{t,t'}$, the fundamental scheduling problem $P||C_{\max}$ [8] (if $\forall (t, t') \in \mathscr{T}^2 : \alpha_{t,t'} = 1$, our problem reduces to $P||C_{\max}$). Assuming linearity is a common approach when constructing models in operational research or statistics (e.g. linear regressions). Likewise, in selfish load balancing games [15], it is assumed that the cost of each task is the total load of the machine (but their model does not consider types). We assume that the impact the type has on itself is *normalized* with regards to tasks' sizes, i.e., $\alpha_{t,t} = 1$ (although some of our results, notably the PTAS, do not need this assumption).

We denote by MSE (MINMAXCOST WITH SIDE EFFECTS) the problem of finding a partition P^* minimizing the maximum cost $C(P) = \max_i c_i$, with c_i defined by the linear cost function. The partition P^* minimizes the worst performance a task experiences in the system, thus corresponds to the egalitarian fairness.

3   Complexity and Hardness of MSE for T Not Fixed

MSE is NP-hard as it generalizes an NP-hard problem $P||C_{\max}$ when there is only one type. Our main result is that a polynomially-solvable variant of mupltiprocessor scheduling ($P|p_i = 1|C_{\max}$) becomes NP-hard when tasks are of different types. Thus types add another level of complexity onto an already NP-complete $P||C_{\max}$.

Proposition 1. *The decision version of MSE is NP-complete, even if all the tasks have unit size, and even if $m = 2$.*

Proof. (Sketch) Reduction from PARTITION [7]. Given a set $S = \{a_i\}$ of n positive integers summing to $2B$, we build an instance of MSE with n tasks, each of size 1 and each of a different type. For a task i, we set its coefficients $\forall j : \alpha_{i,j} = a_i$. Partition of S into two sets each with sum B exists if and only if there exists an allocation P with maximal cost B: cost of each task j allocated to a machine k is equal to $c_j = \sum_{i:M_{P,i}=k} \alpha_{i,j} = \sum_{i \in S_k} a_i$.

Proposition 2. *MSE is strongly NP-hard, even if all tasks have unit size. Moreover, there is no polynomial time r-approximate algorithm for MSE, for any number $r > 1$, unless $P = NP$.*

Proof. Let $r > 1$. We show that if there is a r-approximate algorithm for MSE, the algorithm solves NP-complete PARTITION INTO CLIQUES, PIC [7]. In PIC, given a graph $G = (V, E)$ and a positive integer $K \leq |V|$, can the vertices of G be partitioned into $k \leq K$ disjoint sets $V_1, V_2, \ldots, V_k$ such that, for $1 \leq i \leq k$, the subgraph induced by V_i is a complete graph? We assume that V are labeled from 1 to $|V|$.

Given an instance of PIC, we create K instances of MSE. Let $i \in \{1, \ldots, K\}$. The i-th instance of MSE is as follows: the number of machines is $m = i$; there are $n = |V|$ tasks, each of a different type (types are labeled from 1 to $|V|$). All the tasks are of size 1. For each type i, $\alpha_{i,i} = 1$. For each pair of types $(i, j), i \neq j$: $\alpha_{i,j} = 0$ if $\{i, j\} \in E$ and $\alpha_{i,j} = r$ if $\{i, j\} \notin E$.

We claim that a solution of a MSE instance costs either 1 or at least $r + 1$. We also claim that the answer for the instance of PIC is "yes" if and only if the optimal cost of one of these MSE instances is 1. Therefore, an r-approximate algorithm for MSE will find a solution of cost 1 if it exists (when there is a solution of cost 1, an r-approximate algorithm has to return a solution of cost at most r, which is thus necessarily the optimal solution since all the other solutions have a cost of at least $r + 1$). Since $K \leq |V|$, if we assume that our r-approximate algorithm runs in polynomial time, then by using it K times we can solve in polynomial time PIC, which is an NP-complete problem. This leads to a contradiction, unless $P = NP$.

We show that the cost of a solution of each of the MSE instances is either 1, or at least $r + 1$. If, on all the machines, for each pair (i, j) of tasks on the same machine we have $\alpha_{i,j} = 0$, then the maximum cost of a task is 1 (its own size, 1, times $\alpha_{i,i} = 1$). Otherwise, there is a machine with two tasks of types i and j with $\alpha_{i,j} = r$. The maximum cost is thus at least the cost of task i, which is at least $1 \times \alpha_{i,i} + 1 \times \alpha_{i,j} = 1 + r$.

We show that the solution for the instance of PIC is "yes" if and only if there is a solution of cost 1 for (at least) one of the $|V|$ instances of MSE. Assume first that there is a solution for PIC: the vertices of G can be partitioned into $k \leq K$ disjoint sets $V_1, V_2, \ldots, V_k$ such that, for $1 \leq i \leq k$, the subgraph induced by V_i is a complete graph. We take the k-th MSE instance. For each $i \in \{1, \ldots, k\}$, we assign to machine M_i the tasks corresponding to the vertices of V_i. Since all the tasks on the same machine correspond to a clique in G, their coefficients $\alpha_{i,j}$ are all 0 ($i \neq j$). The only cost of a task i is its own size times $\alpha_{i,i}$, that is 1. Thus, the cost of the optimal solution of the k-th instance of MSE is 1.

Likewise, assume that there is a solution of cost 1 for (at least) one of the $|V|$ instances of MSE (wlog, for the k-th instance). Then there is a "yes" solution for PARTITION INTO CLIQUES: since the maximum cost for the instance of MSE is 1, it means that all the values $\alpha_{i,j}$ between tasks on the same machines are 0 (for $i \neq j$) and thus that corresponding vertices form a clique in G.

4   Approximation for Fixed Number of Types

The inapproximability proof of the previous section means that we can develop constant-factor approximations only for MSE with a constant number of types

---

Algorithm 1. A PTAS for MSE with constant T and α

---

1 $J' = \emptyset$;
2 **for** $j \in J, p_j \geq C/(\gamma k)$ **do** // *round down long tasks*
3 $\quad$ $p_{j'} = p_j - (p_j \mod C/(\gamma k)^2)$;
4 $\quad$ $J' = J' \cup \{j'\}$;
5 **for** $t \in T$ **do** // *glue short tasks to containers*
6 $\quad$ $W_s^{(t)} = \sum_{j \in J^{(t)}, p_j < C/(\gamma k)} p_j$; // *load of small tasks of type t* ;
7 $\quad$ **while** $W_s^{(t)} > 0$ **do**
8 $\quad\quad$ $p_{j''} = \min(C/(\gamma k), W_s^{(t)})$;
9 $\quad\quad$ $J' = J' \cup \{j''\}$; // *j'' is a new container* ;
10 $\quad\quad$ $W_s^{(t)} = W_s^{(t)} - p_{j''}$;
11 **for** $t \in T$ **do** remove from J' m containers of type t ;
12 $\sigma'^* =$ partition of J' by solving (by dynamic programming)
$$OPT(n_1'^{(1)}, \ldots, n_{(\gamma k)^2}'^{(1)}, \ldots, n_1'^{(T)}, \ldots, n_{(\gamma k)^2}'^{(T)}) =$$
$$1 + \min_{s_1^{(1)}, \ldots, s_{(\gamma k)^2}^{(T)} \in \mathscr{C}} OPT(n_1'^{(1)} - s_1^{(1)}, \ldots, n_{(\gamma k)^2}'^{(T)} - s_{(\gamma k)^2}^{(T)});$$
13 **if** σ'^* requires more than m machines **then** return $\emptyset$;
14 $\sigma = \sigma'^*$;
15 **for** $k=1$ **to** m **do** // *add removed containers*
16 $\quad$ **for** $k=1$ **to** T **do** $\sigma[k] = \sigma[k] \cup \{C/(\gamma k)\}$;
17 **for** $k=1$ **to** m **do** // *replace containers by small tasks*
18 $\quad$ **for** $t \in T$ **do**
19 $\quad\quad$ $i =$ number of type t containers in $\sigma[k]$;
20 $\quad\quad$ replace i containers by tasks of total load W, $iC/(\gamma k) \leq W \leq (i+1)C/(\gamma k)$;
21 replace in σ rounded long tasks with original long tasks ;

(and constant coefficients). We show in this section two approximation algorithms. First, a PTAS running in time $O(n^{T(\gamma k)^2})$, and thus mostly of theoretical interest. Then we introduce a fast greedy approximation algorithm.

4.1 A PTAS

Our PTAS (Algorithm 1) has a similar structure to the PTAS for $P||C_{\max}$[9]: the two main differences are the treatment of short tasks (which we pack into containers, and not simply greedy schedule) and the sizing of long tasks. Our PTAS works even if $\alpha_{i,i} \neq 1$, and $\alpha_{i,j} \neq \alpha_{j,i}$. The algorithm uses parameters: C, the requested maximum cost; k, an integer; and $\gamma = T\alpha_{\max}\left(2 + 1/(\min \alpha_{i,i})\right)$ (we assume that T and $\alpha_{i,j}$ are constants). Given C, the algorithm either returns a schedule of cost at most $C(1 + 1/k)$, or proves that a schedule of cost at most C does not exist.

The algorithm starts by constructing an instance I' which will form a lower bound for C of the original instance I. The algorithm partitions tasks into two sets: long tasks of size at least $C/(\gamma k)$; and short tasks. Long tasks are rounded down to the nearest multiple of $C/(\gamma k)^2$. Short tasks of a single type are "glued" into *container tasks* of sizes $C/(\gamma k)$, except the last container task which might be shorter (of size $W_s^{(t)} \mod (C/(\gamma k))$, where $W_s^{(t)}$ is the load of short tasks of type t, $W_s^{(t)} = \sum_{j \in J^{(t)}, p_j < C/(\gamma k)} p_j$). Then, the algorithm reduces the load in container tasks by removing m containers (the shortest one and $m - 1$ others) of each type. (Note that if the total load of short tasks of type t is smaller than $mC/(\gamma k)$, there are less than m containers, and they are all removed in this step; later, when reconstructing schedule, the algorithm adds the same number of containers that were removed. We omit this detail from Algorithm 1 to make the code more readable). The resulting instance I' has at most as many tasks and at most as high overall load as the original instance I (the number of tasks and the load does not change only if all the tasks are long and their sizes are multiples of $C/(\gamma k)^2$).

The algorithm then schedules the lower-bound instance I' using dynamic programming. For a given configuration $n_1'^{(1)}, \ldots, n_{(\gamma k)^2}'^{(1)}, \ldots, n_1'^{(T)}, \ldots, n_{(\gamma k)^2}'^{(T)}$, where $n_i'^{(t)}$ is the number of tasks in I' of type t and size $iC/(\gamma k)^2$, OPT denotes the minimal number of machines needed to schedule the configuration with cost smaller than C. To find OPT, the dynamic programming approach checks all possible configurations $\mathscr{C}$ of task sizes for a single machine $s_1^{(1)}, \ldots, s_{(\gamma k)^2}^{(T)}$ (where $s_i^{(t)}$ denotes the number of tasks) that result in cost smaller than C, i.e.: $s_1^{(1)}, \ldots, s_{(\gamma k)^2}^{(T)} \in \mathscr{C} \Leftrightarrow \forall t$ such that $\sum_i s_i^{(t)} > 0 : \sum_{t'} \sum_{i=1}^{(\gamma k)^2} \alpha_{t',t} s_i^{(t')} iC/(\gamma k)^2 \leq C$. If OPT is larger than m, the algorithm ends. Otherwise, the returned schedule σ'^* forms a scaffold to build a schedule σ for the original instance I. First, the algorithm adds a container for each type on each machine (this container was removed before the dynamic programming). Then, the algorithm replaces containers by actual short tasks. Assume that σ'^* scheduled $i-1$ containers of type t on machine m; the previous step added at most one container. The algorithm replaces i containers of a total load $iC/(\gamma k)$ by scheduling unscheduled short tasks of type t with a total load of at least $iC/(\gamma k)$ and at most $(i+1)C/(\gamma k)$ (which is always possible as a short task is shorter than $C/(\gamma k)$). Finally, the algorithm replaces long tasks that were rounded down by the original long tasks.

Proposition 3. *The PTAS returns a solution to* MSE *if and only if there is a solution of* MSE *of cost at most C. Moreover, if such a solution of cost C exists, the cost of the solution returned by the PTAS is at most $C(1 + 1/k)$.*

Proofs omitted due to space constraints are in the accompanying technical report [19].

Proposition 4. *The PTAS runs in time $\mathscr{O}(n^{T(\gamma k)^2})$.*

4.2 A Greedy List-Scheduling Approximation

FILLGREEDY is a greedy $\frac{2Tm}{m-T}$-approximate algorithm for MSE with constant number of types. FILLGREEDY groups tasks by *clusters*. All the tasks of the same type are in the same cluster. Two tasks of type i and j are in the same cluster iff their types are compatible ($\alpha_{i,j} \leq 1$ and $\alpha_{j,i} \leq 1$). While minimizing the number of clusters is NP-hard (by an immediate reduction from PARTITION INTO CLIQUES), any heuristics can be used, as the approximation ratio does not depend on the number of clusters.

Clusters are processed one by one. Each cluster is allocated to at least one, dedicated machine. (We assume that m, the number of machines, is smaller than or equal to the number of clusters K; $K \leq T$, and in a data center T should be much smaller than m). The algorithm puts tasks from a cluster on a machine until machine load reaches $L_{max} = \max\{2L, L + p_{max}\}$ (where $L = (\sum p_i)/(m - T)$ is the average load), then opens the next machine. In practice, rather than fixing the maximum machine load to L_{max}, we do a dichotomic search over $[1, L_{max}]$ to find the smallest possible threshold leading to a feasible schedule. The complexity of FILLGREEDY with dichotomic search is $\mathcal{O}(T^2 n \log(L_{max}))$.

Proposition 5. *Algorithm* FILLGREEDY *is a $\frac{2Tm}{m-T}$-approximate algorithm for* MSE.

Proof. We first show that the allocation is feasible, i.e. the algorithm uses at most m machines. Let m_{used} be the number of machines to which at least one task is allocated. Among these m_{used} machines, at most K have load smaller than L. Indeed, for each cluster the algorithm allocates tasks to a machine beyond L (as $L_{max} \geq L + p_{max}$), unless there are no remaining tasks. Thus, for each cluster, only the load of the last opened machine can be smaller than L. Thus, the load allocated on these m_{used} machines is at least $(m_{used} - K)L = (m_{used} - K)\frac{W}{m-T}$. Since the total load is W, we have $(m_{used} - K)\frac{W}{m-T} \leq W$. Thus $\frac{m_{used}-K}{m-T} \leq 1$, and so $m_{used} - K \leq m - T$. Since $K \leq T$, we have $m_{used} \leq m$. Thus, the allocation returned by FILLGREEDY is feasible.

We now show that the cost is $\frac{2Km}{m-T}$-approximate. We consider an instance I of MSE. Let $\mathcal{O}$ be an optimal solution of I for MSE, and let OPT be the maximum cost of a task in $\mathcal{O}$. Since, for each type i, $\alpha_{i,i} = 1$, we have $OPT \geq p_{max}$. Let $L_{max}(\mathcal{O})$ be the maximum load of a machine in $\mathcal{O}$. Let us consider that this load is achieved on machine i. We have $L_{max}(\mathcal{O}) \geq \frac{W}{m}$ (by the surface argument). Since there are at most T types on machine i, there is at least one type which has a load of at least $\frac{L_{max}(\mathcal{O})}{T}$ on machine i. The cost of a task of this type on machine i is thus at least $\frac{L_{max}(\mathcal{O})}{T}$, and therefore $OPT \geq \frac{L_{max}(\mathcal{O})}{T} \geq \frac{W}{Tm}$.

Let $\mathcal{S}$ be the solution returned by FILLGREEDY for instance I. Let $C(\mathcal{S})$ be the maximum cost of a task in $\mathcal{S}$. Let $L_{max}(\mathcal{S})$ be the maximum load of a machine in $\mathcal{S}$. Since two tasks i and j are scheduled on the same machine only if they belong to the same cluster, i.e. only if $\alpha_{t_i,t_j} \leq 1$, the cost of each task is at most equal to $L_{max}(\mathcal{S})$, and thus $C(\mathcal{S}) \leq L_{max}(\mathcal{S})$. Moreover, by construction, we have $L_{max}(\mathcal{S}) \leq \max\{2L, L + p_{max}\}$. We consider the two following cases:

- case 1: $\max\{L, p_{max}\} = p_{max}$. In this case, $C(\mathcal{S}) \leq L_{max} \leq L + p_{max} = \frac{W}{m-T} + p_{max} = \left(\frac{Tm}{m-T}\right)\frac{W}{Tm} + p_{max}$. Since $OPT \geq p_{max}$ and $OPT \geq \frac{W}{Tm}$, we have $C(\mathcal{S}) \leq (\frac{Tm}{m-T} + 1)OPT < \frac{2Tm}{m-T}OPT$.
- case 2: $\max\{L, p_{max}\} = L$. In this case, $C(\mathcal{S}) \leq L_{max} \leq 2L = \frac{2W}{m-T} \leq 2\left(\frac{Tm}{m-T}\right)\frac{W}{Tm} \leq \frac{2Tm}{m-T}OPT$ because $OPT \geq \frac{W}{Tm}$.

5   Heuristics

We propose a few other algorithms for MSE. These algorithms are fast approximations when $T = 2$ (see [19]). They all use as a subprocedure an algorithm $\mathscr{A}$ for $P||C_{\max}$, such as LPT (used in our experiments). $\mathscr{A}$ uses task's size p_i as task's length.

SCHEDMIXED uses $\mathscr{A}$ on all tasks and all machines. Let σ be the schedule constructed by $\mathscr{A}$ on m machines with tasks J. SCHEDMIXED($\mathscr{A}$) returns the partition P of the tasks equal to allocation in σ (tasks on M_i in P are the tasks on M_i in σ).

SCHEDJUXTAPOSE uses $\mathscr{A}$ on all machines for each type separately and then joins the schedules. Let σ_t be the schedule obtained by applying $\mathscr{A}$ on tasks $J^{(t)}$ of type t on m machines. SCHEDJUXTAPOSE merges schedules reversing the order of machines for every other type, i.e.: tasks on machine M_i are tasks allocated to M_i in σ_{2k+1} and to M_{m-i+1} in σ_{2k} (when $\mathscr{A} = LPT$ and with a small number of tasks, the machines with smallest indices have the highest load).

BESTSCHEDULE($\mathscr{A}$) returns the partition with the lowest cost among the results of SCHEDJUXTAPOSE($\mathscr{A}$) and SCHEDMIXED($\mathscr{A}$).

GREEDYDEDICATED($\mathscr{B}$) separates types into K clusters (as in Sect. 4.2). Clusters do not share machines. The algorithm runs a subprocedure $\mathscr{B}$ (SCHEDMIXED, SCHEDJUXTAPOSE or BESTSCHEDULE) to put tasks of k-th cluster onto m_k machines. GREEDYDEDICATED returns the allocation with the minimal cost over all possibilities of assigning $[m_k]$ to clusters (by exhaustive search over $[m_k] : \sum_{k \in K} m_k = m$).

Let $C_{\mathscr{A}}$ be the complexity of Algorithm $\mathscr{A}$. Algorithm SCHEDMIXED is in $O(C_{\mathscr{A}})$; SCHEDJUXTAPOSE and BESTSCHEDULE are in $O(TC_{\mathscr{A}})$; GREEDYDEDICATED is in $O(Km^K C_{\mathscr{A}})$.

6   Experiments

We used the Google Cluster Trace [22], the standard dataset for datacenter/cloud resource management research, as an input data. The trace is certainly not ideal for our needs as it shows the usage of raw resources (CPU, memory, network, disk), and not the load of applications. However, to our best knowledge, there are no publicly-available traces describing loads and performance of applications. Due to space constraints we describe the details of conversion in the accompanying technical report [19].

We generate a random sample of 10 000 task records. Each task record corresponds to a task in our model. To generate loads and types, we use data on the (normalized) mean CPU utilization and the assigned memory. Task's type is determined by the ratio of the CPU to the memory usage. We generate the coefficients α in four different ways: *compatible*: smaller than 1; *incompatible*: between 1 and 2; *clashing*: at least 2; *mixed*: 2 incompatible clusters. There are $T \in \{2, 3, 4\}$ types. Instances have two sizes: in *small* ones, the there are $n \in \{10, 20, 50\}$ tasks and $m \in \{2, 3, 5, 10\}$ machines; In *large* ones, there are

$n \in \{200, 500, 1\,000\}$ tasks and $m \in \{20, 50, 100\}$ machines. For each combination we generate 30 instances; after discarding some unfeasible combinations (e.g., mixed, $T = 2$), we have 6 390 instances.

We tested the following algorithms: FILLGREEDY (*fill* in plots); SCHED-MIXED (*mix*); SCHEDJUXTAPOSE (*jux*); BESTSCHEDULE (*best*); GREEDYDED-ICATED with either SCHEDJUXTAPOSE ($d - jux$), SCHEDMIXED ($d - mix$) or BESTSCHEDULE ($d - best$). We omit some algorithms on some instances if they are clearly sub-optimal: GREEDYDEDICATED on compatible instances; and SCHEDJUXTAPOSE on all but compatible instances. On incompatible and clashing instances, all variants of GREEDYDEDICATED result in the same allocation—we denote the algorithm by *ded* in this case.

We compared the maximum cost returned by the algorithms to the lower bound and computed the relative performance. We used the following lower bounds. (1) $p_{\max}$, the maximum size of the task (as we assume $\alpha_{t,t} = 1$, the cost on the machine on which the longest task is allocated is at least $p_{\max}$). (2) For incompatible and clashing instances, the average load of a machine, W/m. (3) For compatible instances, a solution of a LP that optimizes the fraction of type t's load to be allocated to machine k. (4) For mixed instances, the same LP solved for each cluster on m machines (this lower bound assumes that there are mK machines available).

Figure 1 presents the normalized cost (scores on clashing and incompatible instances are exactly the same). We had two kinds of problems with the lower bound (details in [19]), both resulting in underestimation of the optimal solution and thus overestimation of the cost of our algorithms. First, the LP solver we used (python-scipy) often failed on large compatible instances: on 6% of $T = 3$ and 70% of $T = 4$ instances. Second, the LP lower bound underestimates the optimal cost of mixed instances. In such problematic instances, $p_{\max}$ was often used, which resulted in a lower bound that might significantly underestimate the cost of the optimum. To reduce the effect of such outliers, we discuss medians, rather than means, in the sequel.

Overall, all algorithms have similar performance and the performance is close to the lower bound except in mixed instances. On average, GREEDYDEDICATED, SCHEDMIXED and SCHEDJUX produce schedules with lower costs than FILL GREEDY (note that SCHEDMIXED and SCHEDJUX are used directly for compatible instances, and as sub-procedures for GREEDYDEDICATED for the mixed instances); and BESTSCHEDULE optimizes even further. All the results below are statistically-significant (two sided paired t-test, p-values smaller than 0.0001).

Incompatible coefficients isolate the difference between FILL GREEDY, GREEDYDEDICATED, and SCHEDMIXED (as all clusters have a single type, neither FILL GREEDY nor GREEDYDEDICATED allocate different types onto a single machine). Results clearly show that sharing machines (SCHEDMIXED) leads to higher costs. GREEDYDEDICATED produces allocations with the lowest cost: its median costs are 1.02 for large instances and from 1.12 for small instances.

Compatible coefficients isolate the difference between FILL GREEDY, SCHED-MIXED and SCHEDJUX. On the average, SCHEDMIXED produces schedules with

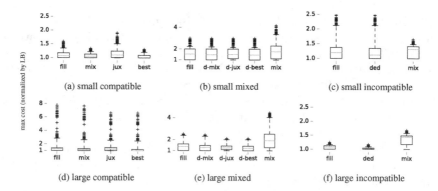

Fig. 1. The maximum cost of the solutions returned by various heuristics normalized by the lower bound. All instances. In boxplots the middle line represents the median, the box spans between the 25th and the 75th percentile, the whiskers span between the 5th and the 95th percentile, and the asterisks show all the remaining points (outliers).

a lower cost than SCHEDJUX (medians are 1.06 for small instances and 1.18 for large). However, BESTSCHEDULE, choosing for each instance the best out of SCHEDMIXED and SCHEDJUX has even lower costs (1.01 for both small and large), demonstrating the need to occasionally use SCHEDJUX.

Finally, mixed coefficients test both aspects; however, the scores of all algorithms are higher due to an imprecise lower bound. GREEDYDEDICATED using BESTSCHEDULE dominates other algorithms with medians 1.46 for small instances and 1.22 for large ones. While the numerical values are higher, we still clearly see the advantage of using type-aware algorithms, as SCHEDMIXED (used without GREEDYDEDICATED) has a significantly higher median score (1.77 for small instances, 1.91 for large).

Due to space constraints, we do not present results in function of the number of tasks or the number of types. However, we have not found any strong dependencies between these variables and the results of our algorithm (apart from slightly—up to 1.18—higher medians for 500 and 1000-task instances for compatible coefficients, caused by the LP problems discussed above).

Our results clearly show that using $P||C_{\max}$ algorithms without regarding types (SCHEDMIXED) is dominated by approaches considering types: using dedicated machines for $\alpha > 1$ or, in some $\alpha < 1$ instances, merging schedules of different types.

7   Related Work

We introduced the side-effects performance model [18], where we studied a utilitarian (min-sum) objective. We proved that the problem is NP-hard, and we showed a dominance property (for each type, there is an order of the machines such that the tasks are assigned by decreasing sizes to the machines). This allows us to give an exact polynomial time algorithm when there is a single type. For the general case, we proposed two algorithms, which are exponential in one data of the problem (number of types, and either the number of machines or the number of admissible sizes of the tasks).

Alternative Models of Data Center Resource Management. A recent survey is [20]. Many colocation performance models are too complex for combinatorial results [11,16,17]. Schedulers rely on heuristic approaches with no formal performance guarantees [3,4,10,26]. In *bin-packing* approaches (e.g.,[23,25]), tasks are modeled as items to be packed into bins (machines) of known capacity [5]. To model heterogeneity, bin packing is extended to vector packing: item's size is a vector with dimensions corresponding to requirements on individual resources (CPU, memory, disk or network bandwidth) [24]. Alternatively, if tasks have unit-size requirements, simpler representations can be used, such as maximum weighted matching [1]. Bin packing approaches assume that machines' capacities are crisp and that, as long as machines are not overloaded, any allocation is equally good for tasks. In our model, machines' capacities are not crisp—instead, tasks' performance gradually decreases with increased load.

Statistical Approaches. Bobroff et al. [2] uses statistics of the past CPU load of tasks (CDF, autocorrelation, periodograms) to predict the load in the "next" time period; then they use bin packing to calculate a partition minimizing the number of used bins subject to a constraint on the probability of overloading servers. Di et al. [6] analyze resource sharing for streams of tasks to be processed by virtual machines. Sequential and parallel task streams are considered in two scenarios. When there are sufficient resources to run all tasks, optimality conditions are formulated. When the resources are insufficient, fair scheduling policies are proposed.

Analysis of Effects of Colocation. Studies showing performance degeneration when colocating data center tasks include [12,14,27]. [21] analyze the performance of colocated CPU-intensive benchmarks; and [13] measures performance of colocated HPC applications. Our $\alpha_{t,t'}$ coefficients are similar to their interference/affinity metrics. Additionally [13] shows a greedy allocation heuristics, but they don't study its worst-case performance nor the complexity of the problem.

8   Conclusion

We considered a problem of optimally allocating tasks to machines in the side-effects performance model. Performance of a task depends on the load of other tasks colocated on the same machine. We use a linear performance function: the influence of tasks of type t' is their total load times a coefficient $\alpha_{t',t}$, describing how compatible is t' with performance of t. We minimize the maximal cost. We prove that this NP-hard problem is hard to approximate if there are many types. However, handling a limited number of types is feasible: we show a PTAS and a fast approximation algorithm, as well as a series of heuristics (we prove their approximation ratios for two types in the accompanying technical report [19]). We simulate allocations resulting from algorithms on instances derived from one of Google clusters. Our simulations show that algorithms taking into account types lead to significantly lower costs than non-type algorithms.

Our results show a possible way to adapt to data centers the large body of work in scheduling, which development has been often inspired by advances in HPC platforms. We deliberately chose to study a fundamental problem, a minimal extension to $P||C_{\max}$. We envision that results for more realistic variants of data center resource management problem, taking into account release dates, non-clairvoyance or on-line, can be taken into account similarly as they are considered in classic scheduling.

We are also working on validating our model by a systems study. We are developing an extension for kubernetes that collects and correlates performance metrics reported by containers to derive the size/coefficient performance model.

Acknowledgements. We thank Paweł Janus for his help in processing the Google cluster data. This research has been partly supported by a Polish National Science Center grant Sonata (UMO-2012/07/D/ST6/02440), and a Polonium grant (joint programme of the French Ministry of Foreign Affairs, the Ministry of Science and Higher Education and the Polish Ministry of Science and Higher Education).

References

1. Beaumont, O., Eyraud-Dubois, L., Thraves Caro, C., Rejeb, H.: Heterogeneous resource allocation under degree constraints. IEEE TPDS **24**(5), 926–937 (2013)
2. Bobroff, N., Kochut, A., Beaty, K.: Dynamic placement of virtual machines for managing SLA violations. In: Proceedings of IM. IEEE (2007)
3. Bu, X., Rao, J., Xu, C.: Interference and locality-aware task scheduling for mapreduce applications in virtual clusters. In: Proceedings of HPDC. ACM (2013)
4. Chiang, R.C., Huang, H.H.: TRACON: interference-aware scheduling for data-intensive applications in virtualized environments. In: Proceedings of SC. ACM (2011)
5. Coffman Jr., E.G., Garey, M.R., Johnson, D.S.: Approximation algorithms for bin packing: a survey. In: Approximation Algorithms for NP-Hard Problems. PWS (1996)
6. Di, S., Kondo, D., Wang, C.: Optimization of composite cloud service processing with virtual machines. IEEE Trans. Comput. **64**(6), 1755–1768 (2015)
7. Garey, M.R., Johnson, D.S.: Computers and Intractability: A Guide to the Theory of NP-Completeness. W.H. Freeman & Co., New York (1979)
8. Graham, R.L.: Bounds on multiprocessing timing anomalies. SIAP **17**(2), 416–429 (1969)
9. Hochbaum, D.S., Shmoys, D.B.: Using dual approximation algorithms for scheduling problems theoretical and practical results. JACM **34**(1), 144–162 (1987)
10. Jersak, L.C., Ferreto, T.: Performance-aware server consolidation with adjustable interference levels. In: Proceedings of SAC (2016)
11. Jin, X., Zhang, F., Wang, L., Hu, S., Zhou, B., Liu, Z.: Joint optimization of operational cost and performance interference in cloud data centers. IEEE Trans. Cloud Comput. (2015). doi:10.1109/TCC.2015.2449839
12. Kambadur, M., Moseley, T., Hank, R., Kim, M.A.: Measuring interference between live datacenter applications. In: Proceedings of SC. IEEE (2012)

13. Kim, S., Hwang, E., Yoo, T.K., Kim, J.S., Hwang, S., Choi, Y.R.: Platform and co-runner affinities for many-task applications in distributed computing platforms. In: Proceedings of CCGrid. IEEE CS (2015)
14. Koh, Y., Knauerhase, R., Brett, P., Bowman, M., Wen, Z., Pu, C.: An analysis of performance interference effects in virtual environments. In: Proceedings of ISPASS. IEEE (2007)
15. Koutsoupias, E., Papadimitriou, C.: Worst-case equilibria. In: Meinel, C., Tison, S. (eds.) STACS 1999. LNCS, vol. 1563, pp. 404–413. Springer, Heidelberg (1999). doi:10.1007/3-540-49116-3_38
16. Kundu, S., Rangaswami, R., Dutta, K., Zhao, M.: Application performance modeling in a virtualized environment. In: HPCA. IEEE (2010)
17. Kundu, S., Rangaswami, R., Gulati, A., Zhao, M., Dutta, K.: Modeling virtualized applications using machine learning techniques. In: SIGPLAN Notices, vol. 47. ACM (2012)
18. Pascual, F., Rzadca, K.: Partition with side effects. In: Proceedings of HiPC 2015 (2015)
19. Pascual, F., Rzadca, K.: Optimizing egalitarian performance in the side-effects model of colocation for data center resource management. CoRR abs/1610.07339v3 (2017). http://arxiv.org/abs/1610.07339
20. Pietri, I., Sakellariou, R.: Mapping virtual machines onto physical machines in cloud computing: a survey. CSUR 49(3), Article No. 49 (2016)
21. Podzimek, A., Bulej, L., Chen, L.Y., Binder, W., Tuma, P.: Analyzing the impact of CPU pinning and partial CPU loads on performance and energy efficiency. In: Proceedings of CCGrid (2015)
22. Reiss, C., Tumanov, A., Ganger, G.R., Katz, R.H., Kozuch, M.A.: Heterogeneity and dynamicity of clouds at scale: Google trace analysis. In: Proceedings of SoCC. ACM (2012)
23. Song, W., Xiao, Z., Chen, Q., Luo, H.: Adaptive resource provisioning for the cloud using online bin packing. IEEE ToC 63(11), 2647–2660 (2014)
24. Stillwell, M., Vivien, F., Casanova, H.: Virtual machine resource allocation for service hosting on heterogeneous distributed platforms. In: Proceedings of IPDPS. IEEE (2012)
25. Tang, X., Li, Y., Ren, R., Cai, W.: On first fit bin packing for online cloud server allocation. In: Proceedings of IPDPS (2016)
26. Verma, A., Pedrosa, L., Korupolu, M., Oppenheimer, D., Tune, E., Wilkes, J.: Large-scale cluster management at Google with Borg. In: Proceedings of EuroSys. ACM (2015)
27. Xu, Y., Musgrave, Z., Noble, B., Bailey, M.: Bobtail: avoiding long tails in the cloud. In: Proceedings of NSDI (2013)

Generic Algorithms for Scheduling Applications on Hybrid Multi-core Machines

Marcos Amaris[1,2], Giorgio Lucarelli[1(✉)], Clément Mommessin[1],
and Denis Trystram[1]

[1] CNRS, Inria, LIG, Univ. Grenoble Alpes, 38000 Grenoble, France
{giorgio.lucarelli,clement.mommessin,denis.trystram}@imag.fr
[2] Institute of Mathematics and Statistics, University of São Paulo, São Paulo, Brazil
amaris@ime.usp.br

Abstract. We study the problem of executing an application represented by a precedence task graph on a multi-core machine composed
of standard computing cores and accelerators. Contrary to most existing approaches, we distinguish the allocation and the scheduling phases
and we mainly focus on the allocation part of the problem: choose the
most appropriate type of computing unit for each task. We address both
off-line and on-line settings. In the first case, we establish strong lower
bounds on the worst-case performance of a known approach based on
Linear Programming for solving the allocation problem. Then, we refine
the scheduling phase and we replace the greedy list scheduling policy used
in this approach by a better ordering of the tasks. Although this modification leads to the same approximability guarantees, it performs much
better in practice. In the on-line case, we assume that the tasks arrive in
any, not known in advance, order which respects the precedence relations
and the scheduler has to take irrevocable decisions about their allocation and execution. In this setting, we propose the first online scheduling
algorithm which takes into account precedences. Our algorithm is based
on adequate rules for selecting the type of processor where to allocate
the tasks and it achieves a constant factor approximation guarantee if
the ratio of the number of CPUs over the number of GPUs is bounded.
Finally, all the previous algorithms have been experimented on a large
number of simulations built on actual libraries. These simulations assess
the good practical behavior of the algorithms with respect to the state-
of-the-art solutions whenever these exist or baseline algorithms.

1 Introduction

The parallel and distributed platforms available today become more and more
heterogeneous. Such heterogeneous architectures have a growing impact on performance in high-performance computing. Hardware accelerators, such as General Purpose Graphical Processing Units (in short GPUs) [12], are often used in
conjunction with multiple Central Processing Units (CPUs) on the same chip
sharing the same common memory. As an instance of this, the number of platforms of the TOP500 equipped with accelerators has significantly increased during the last years [14]. In the future it is expected that the nodes of such platforms

© Springer International Publishing AG 2017
F.F. Rivera et al. (Eds.): Euro-Par 2017, LNCS 10417, pp. 220–231, 2017.
DOI: 10.1007/978-3-319-64203-1_16

will be even more diverse than today: they will be composed of fast computing nodes, hybrid computing nodes mixing general purpose units with accelerators, I/O nodes, nodes specialized in data analytics, etc. The interconnect of a huge number of such nodes will also lead to more heterogeneity. Using heterogeneous platforms would lead to better performances through the use of more appropriate resources depending on the computations to perform, but it has a cost in terms of code development and more complex resource management.

In this work, we present efficient algorithms for scheduling an application represented by a precedence task graph on hybrid computing resources. We are interested in designing generic approaches for efficiently implementing parallel applications where the scheduling is not explicitly part of the application. In this way, the code is portable and can be adapted to the next generation of machines.

Underlying Architecture. We consider an hybrid multi-core node composed of identical CPUs and GPUs. An application consists of tasks that are linked by precedence relations. Each task is characterized by two processing times depending on which type of processors it is assigned to. We assume that an exact estimation of both these processing times is available to the scheduler. This assumption can be justified by several existing models to estimate the execution times of tasks [2]. In several applications we always observe an acceleration of the tasks if they are executed on a GPU. However, we consider the more general case where the relation between the two processing times can differ for different tasks. This work focuses on the analysis of the qualitative behavior induced by heterogeneity since it may be assumed that the computations dominate local shared memory costs. Thus, no memory assignment or overhead for data management are considered, nor communication times between the shared memory and the CPUs or between CPUs and GPUs. As the application developers are mainly looking for performance, the objective of a scheduler is usually to minimize the completion time of the last finishing task.

Definition and Notations. We consider a parallel application which should be scheduled on m identical CPUs and k identical GPUs. Henceforth, we assume that $m \geq k$. The application is represented by a Directed Acyclic Graph $G = (V, E)$ whose nodes correspond to sequential tasks and arcs correspond to precedence relations among the tasks. We denote by $\mathcal{T}$ the set of all tasks. Let $\overline{p_j}$ (resp. p_j) be the processing time of a task T_j if it is executed on any CPU (resp. GPU). Given a schedule S, we denote by C_j the completion time of a task T_j in S. In any feasible schedule, for each arc $(i, j) \in E$, the task T_j cannot be executed before the completion of T_i. We say that T_i is a *predecessor* of T_j and we denote by $\Gamma^-(T_j)$ the set of all predecessors of T_j. Similarly, we say that T_j is a *successor* of T_i and we denote by $\Gamma^+(T_i)$ the set of all successors of T_i. We call *descendant* of T_j each task T_i for which there is a path from j to i in G.

The objective is to create a feasible non-preemptive schedule of minimum makespan. In other words, we seek a schedule that respects the precedence constraints among tasks, does not interrupt their execution and minimizes the completion time of the last task, i.e., $C_{\max} = \max_{T_j}\{C_j\}$. Extending the three-fields notation for scheduling problems introduced by Graham, this problem can be denoted as $(CPU, GPU) \mid prec \mid C_{\max}$.

Contributions and Outline. In this paper we study the above problem on both off-line and on-line settings. The goal is to design algorithms through a solid theoretical analysis that can be practically implemented in actual systems. Contrarily to most existing approaches (see for example [15]), we propose to address the problem by separately focusing on the following two phases:

– *allocation*: each task is assigned to a type of resources, either CPU or GPU,
– *scheduling*: each task is assigned to a specific pair of resource and time interval respecting the decided allocation as well as the precedence constraints.

We aim to study the two phases separately motivated by the fact that there are strong lower bounds on the approximability of known single-phase algorithms. For example, the approximation ratio of the well-known Heterogeneous Earliest Finish Time (HEFT) algorithm [15] cannot be better than $\Omega(\frac{m}{k^2})$ (Sect. 3), while it can be easily shown that List Scheduling policies have arbitrarily large approximation ratio, even if we consider some enhanced order of tasks, like prioritizing the task of the largest acceleration. The two-phases approach has been used by Kedad-Sidhoum et al. [11] where a linear program (which we call Heterogeneous Linear Program or simply HLP) in conjunction with a rounding have been proposed for the allocation phase, while the greedy Earliest Starting Time (EST) policy has been applied to schedule the tasks. This algorithm, henceforth called HLP-EST, achieves an approximation ratio of 6. Surprisingly, in Sect. 3, we show that the ratio of this algorithm is tight. In fact, our worst-case example does not depend on the scheduling policy applied in the second phase.

Based on this negative result, we propose to revisit both phases. In Sect. 4.1, we initially present three greedy rules which can be used to decide the allocation. Although these rules are of low complexity, a desired property in practice, they cannot guarantee any approximation ratio. However, a more enhanced set of rules that takes into account the actual schedule can lead to an algorithm of worst case ratio $O(\sqrt{\frac{m}{k}})$, even in an on-line context where the tasks arrive in any order that respects the precedence constraints, and the scheduler has to take irrevocable decisions for their execution at the time of their arrival. This is the first on-line upper-bound when precedence constraints are considered in the hybrid context. In Sect. 4.2, we propose to replace the EST policy in HLP-EST by a specific order of tasks which is based on both the allocation decisions taken in the first phase and the critical path. This refined algorithm preserves the approximation ratio of 6 and it also has a very good practical performance.

In Sect. 5, we describe the generation of the benchmark used in our experiments, which is freely available in Standard Workload Format (SWF). The experiments show that the new scheduling method based on HLP outperforms both HEFT and HLP-EST in most of the applications, while our proposed on-line algorithm has significantly better makespan than the baseline greedy algorithms.

Before continuing, we present in Sect. 2 the works related to our setting and, finally, we conclude in Sect. 6. Omitted proofs can be found in [3].

2   Related Works

Most papers of the huge existing literature about GPUs concern specific applications. There are only few papers dealing with generic scheduling in mixed CPU/GPU architectures, and very few of them consider precedence constraints.

From a theoretical perspective, the problem of scheduling tasks on two types of resources is more complex than the problem on parallel identical machines, $P \mid prec \mid C_{\max}$, but it is easier than the problem on unrelated machines, $R \mid prec \mid C_{\max}$. Moreover, if all tasks are accelerated by the same factor in the GPU side, then $(CPU, GPU) \mid prec \mid C_{\max}$ coincides with the problem of scheduling on uniformly-related parallel machines, $Q \mid prec \mid C_{\max}$. In this sense, we can say that the former is more general than the latter one; however, in our problem all tasks have only two different processing times, that makes it simpler. For $P \mid prec \mid C_{\max}$, Graham's List Scheduling algorithm [10] is a 2-approximation, while no algorithm can have a better approximation ratio assuming a particular variant of the Unique Games Conjecture [13]. Chudak and Shmoys [8] developed a polynomial-time $O(\log m)$-approximation algorithm for $Q \mid prec \mid C_{\max}$. For hybrid architectures, a 6-approximation algorithm has been proposed by Kedad-Sidhoum et al. [11]. In the case of independent tasks there is a $(\frac{4}{3} + \frac{1}{3k})$-approximation algorithm [5]. If the tasks arrive in an on-line order, a 4-competitive algorithm has been presented by Chen et al. [7] for hybrid architectures without precedence relations.

On a more practical side, there exist some work about off-line scheduling, such as the well-known algorithm HEFT introduced by Topcuoglu et al. [15], which has been implemented on the run-time system starPU [4]. Another work studied the systematic comparison of various heuristics [6]. Specifically, the authors examined 11 different heuristics. This study provided a good basis for comparison and insights on circumstances why a technique outperforms another. Finally, Bleuse et al. [5] compared their proposed $(\frac{4}{3} + \frac{1}{3k})$-approximation algorithm with HEFT. Note that the later two approaches considered only independent tasks.

3   Preliminaries and Lower Bounds

In this section we briefly present the two basic existing approaches for scheduling on heterogeneous/hybrid platforms and we discuss their theoretical efficiency by presenting lower bounds on their performance.

The first approach is the scheduling-oriented algorithm HEFT [15]. According to HEFT, the tasks are initially prioritized with respect to their precedence relations and their average processing times. Then, following this priority, tasks are scheduled with possible backfilling on the available pair of processor and time interval in which they feasibly complete as early as possible. Note that HEFT is a heuristic that works for platforms with several heterogeneous resources and also takes into account possible communication costs. However, even for the simpler setting which we study in this paper without communication costs, with only two types of resources and $k = 1$, HEFT cannot have a worst-case approximation guarantee better than $\frac{m}{2}$ [5]. This result depends only on the number of CPUs, since the example provided uses just one GPU. The following theorem, whose proof is omitted, slightly improves the above result for the case of a single GPU. More interestingly, it expresses the lower bound to the approximation ratio of HEFT using both the number of CPUs and of GPUs.

Theorem 1. *For any $k \leq \sqrt{m}$, the worst-case approximation ratio for HEFT is at least $\frac{m+k}{k^2}\left(1 - \frac{1}{e^k}\right)$, even in the hybrid model with independent tasks.*

The second approach is proposed by Kedad-Sidhoum et al. [11] and it distinguishes the allocation and the scheduling decisions. For the allocation phase, an integer linear program is proposed which decides the allocation of tasks to the CPU or GPU side by optimizing the standard lower bounds for the makespan of a schedule which are proposed by Graham [10], namely the critical path and the load. To present this integer linear program, let x_j be a binary variable which is equal to 1 if a task T_j is assigned to the CPU side, and zero otherwise. Let also C_j be a variable that indicates the completion time of T_j and λ the variable that corresponds to the maximum over all lower bounds used. Then, the Heterogeneous Linear Program (HLP) is as follows:

minimize λ

$$C_i + \overline{p_j}x_j + \underline{p_j}(1 - x_j) \leq C_j \qquad\qquad \forall T_j \in \mathcal{T}, T_i \in \Gamma^-(T_j) \qquad (1)$$

$$\overline{p_j}x_j + \underline{p_j}(1 - x_j) \leq C_j \qquad\qquad \forall T_j \in \mathcal{T} : \Gamma^-(T_j) = \emptyset \qquad (2)$$

$$C_j \leq \lambda \qquad\qquad \forall T_j \in \mathcal{T} \qquad (3)$$

$$\max\{\frac{1}{m}\sum_{T_j \in \mathcal{T}} \overline{p_j}x_j, \frac{1}{k}\sum_{T_j \in \mathcal{T}} \underline{p_j}(1 - x_j)\} \leq \lambda \qquad (4)$$

$$x_j \in \{0, 1\} \qquad\qquad \forall T_j \in \mathcal{T} \qquad (5)$$

$$C_j \geq 0 \qquad\qquad \forall T_j \in \mathcal{T}$$

Constraints (1), (2) and (3) describe the critical path, while Constraint (4) imposes that the makespan cannot be smaller than the load on CPU and GPU sides. Note that the particular problem of deciding the allocation to minimize the maximum over the three lower bounds is NP-hard, since it is a generalization of the PARTITION problem to which reduces if all tasks are independent, $m = k$, and $\overline{p_j} = \underline{p_j}$ for each T_j.

After relaxing the integrity Constraint (5), a fractional allocation can be found in polynomial time. To get an integral solution, the variables x_j are rounded as follows: If $x_j \geq \frac{1}{2}$ then T_j is assigned to the CPU side, otherwise to the GPU side. Finally, the Earliest Starting Time (EST) policy is applied for scheduling the tasks: At each step, the ready task with the earliest possible starting time is scheduled respecting the precedence relations and the decided allocation. We call this algorithm HLP-EST.

HLP-EST achieves an approximation ratio of 6 [11]. Surprisingly, the following theorem shows that this ratio is tight. In fact, the theorem implies an even stronger result since the worst case example does not depend on the scheduling policy which will be applied after the allocation step.

Theorem 2. *Any scheduling policy which is applied after the allocation decisions taken by the rounding of an optimal fractional solution of the relaxed HLP leads to an approximation algorithm of ratio at least $6 - O(\frac{1}{m})$.*

Proof (sketch). Consider an hybrid system with an equal number of CPUs and GPUs, i.e., $m = k$. The instance consists of $2m+3$ tasks that are partitioned into 3 sets as shown in Table 1. The only precedence relations exist between tasks of B_1 and B_2: for each task $T_j \in B_2$ we have that $\Gamma^-(T_j) = B_1$, that is no task in B_2 can be executed before the completion of all tasks in B_1. There are no precedences between tasks of the same set.

Any optimal solution of the relaxed HLP for the above instance will assign the task T_A on a CPU, i.e., $x_A = 1$. Hence, the objective value of any optimal solution will be at least $\frac{m(2m+1)}{m-1}$ due to Constraints (2) and (3).

On the other hand, we can show that the following assignment is optimal for the relaxed HLP: given a small constant $\epsilon > 0$, set $x_A = 1$, $x_j = \frac{1}{2}$ for each $T_j \in B_1$, $x_j = \frac{1}{2} - \epsilon$ for each $T_j \in B_i$, and $\lambda = \frac{m(2m+1)}{m-1}$. Given this optimal fractional assignment, the algorithm will round the fractional variables and allocate the tasks as follows: the task T_A is assigned to the CPU side, each task $T_j \subset B_1$ is assigned to the CPU side, and each task $T_j \in B_2$ is assigned to the GPU side. Then, assuming that $m \geq 3$, there is only one meaningful family of schedules for the tasks in $B_1 \cup B_2$. An illustration of such a schedule is given in Fig. 1.

The makespan of the created schedule is equal to $6(2m-1)$, while the optimal fractional solution for the relaxed HLP has objective value $\frac{m(2m+1)}{m-1}$. Hence, the approximation ratio achieved for this instance is $6 - O\left(\frac{1}{m}\right)$ and the theorem follows. □

Table 1. Tasks and their processing times for the input instance.

Sets of tasks	# tasks	$\overline{p_j}$	p_j
A	1	$\frac{m(2m+1)}{m-1}$	∞
B_1	$2m+1$	$2m-1$	1
B_2	$2m+1$	1	$2m-1$

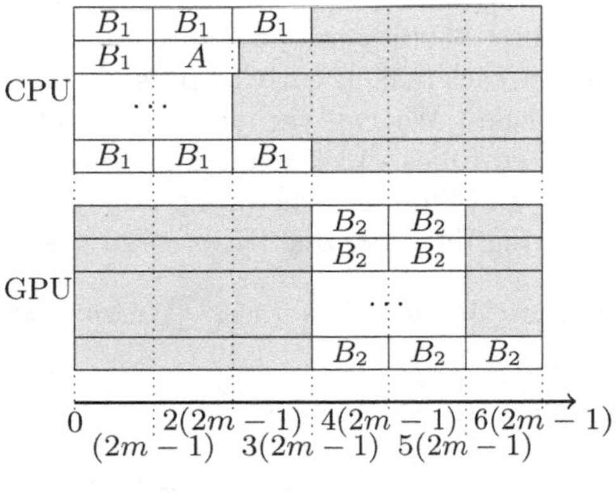

Fig. 1. The schedule created by the algorithm (the gray areas correspond to idle times).

4   Algorithms

In this section we focus separately on each of the two phases, allocation and scheduling, and we propose algorithms for them.

4.1   Allocation Phase

In the HLP-EST algorithm, an integer linear program was used to find an efficient allocation of each task to the CPU or GPU side. Although this program optimizes the classical lower bounds for the makespan, and hence informally optimizes the allocation, the resolution of its relaxation has a high complexity in practice. For this reason, we would like to explore some greedy, low complexity, policies. In this direction, we initially propose the following three simple greedy rules:

R1. If $\frac{\overline{p_j}}{m} \leq \frac{p_j}{k}$ then assign T_j to the CPU side, else assign it to the GPU side.
R2. If $\frac{\overline{p_j}}{\sqrt{m}} \leq \frac{p_j}{\sqrt{k}}$ then assign T_j to the CPU side, else assign it to the GPU side.
R3. If $\overline{p_j} \leq \underline{p_j}$ then assign T_j to the CPU side, else assign it to the GPU side.

However, these rules do not take into account neither the critical path nor the actual schedule and they cannot guarantee a bounded approximation ratio.

In what follows, we propose to use a more enhanced set of rules which combines R2 with a rule based on the structure of the actual schedule, in a similar way as in the 4-competitive algorithm proposed by Chen et al. [7] for the on-line problem with independent tasks. Our algorithm works also in the on-line setting.

To describe the new rule, we define τ^G to be the earliest time when at least one GPU is idle. Let also $R_j^G = \max\{\tau^G, \max_{i \in \Gamma^-(j)}\{C_i\}\}$ be the *ready time* of task T_j, i.e., the earliest time at which T_j can be executed on a GPU. Then, the new enhanced set of rules is defined as follows:

Step 1: If $\overline{p_j} \geq R_j^G + p_j$ then assign T_j to the GPU side.
Step 2: Otherwise apply R2.

This set of rules can be combined with a greedy List Scheduling policy that schedules each task as early as possible on the CPU or GPU side already decided by the rules. We call the algorithm obtained by this combination as ER-LS (Enhanced Rules - List Scheduling). Note that both the allocation policy based on rules and the List Scheduling policy can be applied in an on-line context, by considering the tasks one by one and taking irrevocable decisions for them.

Theorem 3. *ER-LS is a $(4\sqrt{\frac{m}{k}})$-competitive algorithm.*

4.2   Scheduling Phase

We propose here a new scheduling policy which prioritizes the tasks based on the solution obtained for HLP. The motivation of assigning priorities to the tasks is for taking into account the precedence relations between them. More specifically, we want to prioritize the scheduling of *critical tasks*, i.e., the tasks on the critical path, before the remaining (less critical) tasks.

To do this, we define for each task T_j a rank $Rank(T_j)$ in the same sense as in the HEFT algorithm. However, in our case, the rank of each task depends on HLP, while in HEFT it depends on the average processing time of the task. Specifically, the rank of each task T_j is computed after the rounding operation of the assignment variable x_j and corresponds to the length, in the sense of processing time, of the longest path between this task and its last descendant in the precedence graph. Thus, each task will have a larger rank than all its descendants. The rank of the task T_j is recursively defined as follows:

$$Rank(T_j) = \overline{p_j}x_j + \underline{p_j}(1 - x_j) + \max_{i \in \Gamma^+(T_j)} \{Rank(T_i)\}$$

After ordering the tasks in non-increasing order with respect to their ranks, we apply the standard List Scheduling algorithm adapted to two types of resources and taking into account the rounding of the assignment variables x_j. We call the above described policy Ordered List Scheduling (OLS), while the newly defined algorithm (including the allocation) is denoted by HLP-OLS.

Although this policy performs well in practice, as we will see in the experiments in the following section, its approximation ratio cannot be better than 6 due to the lower bound presented in Theorem 2. On the other hand, it is quite easy to see that HLP-EST and HLP-OLS have the same approximation ratio.

5   Experiments

In this section, we compare the performance of various scheduling algorithms by a simulation campaign using a benchmark composed of 6 parallel applications.

5.1   Benchmark

The benchmark is composed of five applications generated by *Chameleon*, a dense linear algebra software [1], and a more irregular application (*fork-join*) generated using *GGen*, a library for generating directed acyclic graphs [9].

The applications of *Chameleon*, named *getrf_nopiv*, *posv*, *potrs*, *potri* and *potrs*, are composed of multiple sequential basic tasks of linear algebra. Different number, denoted by *nb_blocks*, and sizes, denoted by *block_size*, of sub-matrices have been used for the applications; specifically, $nb\_blocks \in \{5, 10, 20\}$ and $block\_size \in \{64, 128, 320, 512, 768, 960\}$. The applications were executed with the runtime StarPU [4] on a Dual core Xeon E7 v2 machine with a total of 20 physical cores with hyper-threading of 3 GHz and 256 GB of RAM. This machine had 4 GPUs NVIDIA Tesla K20 with 4 GB of global memory, 200 GB/s of bandwidth and 2,496 cores divided in 13 multiprocessors.

The *fork-join* application corresponds to a real situation where the execution starts sequentially and then forks to *width* parallel tasks. The results are aggregated by performing a join operation, completing a phase. For our experiments, we used $p \in \{2, 5, 10\}$ phases and $width \in \{100, 200, 300, 400, 500\}$. The running time of each task on CPU was computed using a Gaussian distribution with center p and standard deviation $\frac{p}{4}$. We established various acceleration factors for the running time on GPU. In all configurations, there are five parallel tasks in each phase with an acceleration factor in $[0.1, 0.5]$ while the remaining tasks have an acceleration factor in $[0.5, 50]$. The data set and other information are available under Creative Commons Public License[1].

5.2 Environment and Algorithms

We compare the performance, in terms of makespan, of HLP-EST and HLP-OLS with HEFT. We also compare in on-line mode, where tasks arrive over a list, the algorithm ER-LS with two greedy algorithms: GreedyOn which allocates a task on the processor type which has the smallest processing time for that task, and RandomOn which randomly assigns a task to the CPU or GPU side.

The algorithms are implemented in Python (v. 2.7.6). The command-line *glpsol* (v. 4.52) solver of the GLPK package is used for the linear program. The number of tasks of the six applications range from 30 to 5011. Moreover, we test different machine configurations, combining 16, 32, 64 or 128 CPUs with 2, 4, 8 or 16 GPUs. Each combination of application and machine configuration is executed only once since all algorithms, except for the random greedy algorithm, are deterministic. For each run, we store the optimal objective solution of the linear program, denoted by LP^*, and the makespan of the six algorithms.

5.3 Analysis of Results

Off-Line Algorithms. To study the performance of the 3 off-line algorithms we computed the ratio between each makespan and LP^*, which corresponds to a good lower bound of the optimal makespan. Figure 2a shows the ratio of each instance of application and configuration. Notice that the red/bigger dot represents the mean value of the ratio for each application. We can see that HLP-EST is outperformed, on average, by the two other algorithms. The performances of HLP-OLS and HEFT are quite similar, on average, but we observe that HEFT does create more outlier makespans.

Figure 3 compares more specifically the two HLP-based algorithms and the algorithms HLP-OLS and HEFT, respectively, by showing the ratio between the makespans of the two algorithms. We can see that HLP-OLS clearly outperforms HLP-EST, except for a few instances with the application *potri*, with an improvement close to 10% on average. We also notice that, even if the two algorithms have similar performances, HEFT is on average outperformed by HLP-OLS by 5%. Moreover, HEFT has a significantly worse performance than HLP-OLS in strongly heterogeneous applications where there is a bigger perturbation in the (dis-)acceleration of the tasks on the GPU side, like *forkJoin*, since in these irregular cases the allocation problem becomes more critical.

---

[1] Hosted at: https://github.com/marcosamaris/heterogeneous-SWF.

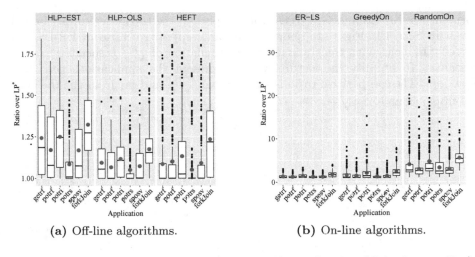

(a) Off-line algorithms.   (b) On-line algorithms.

Fig. 2. Ratios over LP^* for each instance, grouped by application. (Color figure online)

On-Line Algorithms. The ratios between the makespan of each of the 3 on-line algorithms and LP^* are compared in Fig. 2b which shows that, except for a few number of instances, RandomOn is significantly outperformed by ER-LS and GreedyOn. Figure 4a presents a more detailed comparison between GreedyOn and ER-LS, and shows that the ratio of their performance is on average greater than 1, meaning that GreedyOn is outperformed by ER-LS. The mean value of the ratio per application is between 1 and 1.5. For some instances, ER-LS can even perform up to 12.5 times better than GreedyOn. We also study the per-

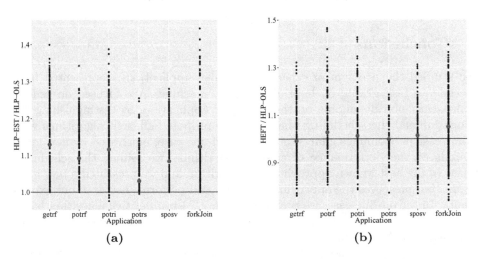

(a)   (b)

Fig. 3. Ratio between the makespans of HLP-EST and HLP-OLS (left) and HEFT and HLP-OLS (right) for each instance, grouped by application.

formance of ER-LS and GreedyOn with respect to the theoretical upper bound given in Sect. 4.1. Figure 4b shows the mean competitive ratio of ER-LS and GreedyOn along with the standard error in function of $\sqrt{\frac{m}{k}}$ associated to each instance. To simplify the lecture, we only present the applications *potri* and *fork-join*. The competitive ratio is smaller than $\sqrt{\frac{m}{k}}$ and far from the theoretical upper bound of $4\sqrt{\frac{m}{k}}$.

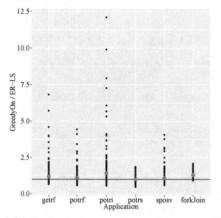

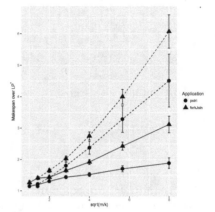

(a) Ratio between the makespans of GreedyOn and ER-LS.

(b) Competitive ratio of ER-LS (plain) and GreedyOn (dashed) in function of $\sqrt{\frac{m}{k}}$.

Fig. 4. Comparison of on-line algorithms.

6   Conclusions

We studied the problem of scheduling parallel applications, represented by a precedence task graph, on hybrid multi-core machines. We focused on generic approaches, non depending on the particular application, by distinguishing the allocation and the scheduling phases and we proposed efficient algorithms with worst-case performance guarantees. In the off-line case, motivated by new lower bounds on the performance of existing algorithms, we refined the scheduling phase of the best known approximation algorithm and we presented a new algorithm that preserves the approximation ratio and performs better in our experiments. In the on-line case, we presented a $O(\sqrt{\frac{m}{k}})$-competitive algorithm based on adequate rules, which can be considered as constant-factor since, practically, the ratio $\frac{m}{k}$ is bounded.

From the practical point of view, an extensive simulation campaign on representative benchmarks constructed by real applications showed that it is possible to outperform the classical HEFT algorithm keeping reasonable running times.

Moreover, the on-line algorithm based on rules is a good trade-off since it delivers a solution close to the optimal. We aim to implement it on a real run-time system (such as StarPU [4]) which currently uses HEFT on successive sets of independent tasks.

In this work we assumed that the communications between CPUs, GPUs and the shared memory are neglected. Our next step is to introduce communication costs in the algorithms, which should not be too hard in both integer program and greedy rules.

Acknowledgments. This work was partially supported by FAPESP (São Paulo Research Foundation, grant #2012/23300-7) and ANR Moebus Project.

References

1. Agullo, E., et al.: Poster: matrices over runtime systems at exascale. In: SC Companion, p. 1332 (2012)
2. Amaris, M., Cordeiro, D., Goldman, A., de Camargo, R.Y.: A simple BSP-based model to predict execution time in GPU applications. In: HiPC, pp. 285–294 (2015)
3. Amaris, M., Lucarelli, G., Mommessin, C., Trystram, D.: Generic algorithms for scheduling applications on hybrid multi-core machines. Technical report 01420798, HAL (2016). https://hal.inria.fr/hal-01420798
4. Augonnet, C., Thibault, S., Namyst, R., Wacrenier, P.A.: StarPU: a unified platform for task scheduling on heterogeneous multicore architectures. Concurr. Comput.: Pract. Exper. **23**(2), 187–198 (2011)
5. Bleuse, R., Kedad-Sidhoum, S., Monna, F., Mounié, G., Trystram, D.: Scheduling independent tasks on multi-cores with GPU accelerators. Concurr. Comput.: Pract. Exper. **27**(6), 1625–1638 (2015)
6. Braun, T.D., et al.: A comparison of eleven static heuristics for mapping a class of independent tasks onto heterogeneous distributed computing systems. J. Parallel Distrib. Comput. **61**(6), 810–837 (2001)
7. Chen, L., Ye, D., Zhang, G.: Online scheduling of mixed CPU-GPU jobs. Int. J. Found. Comput. Sci. **25**(06), 745–761 (2014)
8. Chudak, F.A., Shmoys, D.B.: Approximation algorithms for precedence-constrained scheduling problems on parallel machines that run at different speeds. J. Algorithms **30**(2), 323–343 (1999)
9. Cordeiro, D., Mounié, G., Perarnau, S., Trystram, D., Vincent, J.M., Wagner, F.: Random graph generation for scheduling simulations. In: SIMUTools, p. 60 (2010)
10. Graham, R.L.: Bounds on multiprocessing timing anomalies. SIAM J. Appl. Math. **17**(2), 416–429 (1969)
11. Kedad-Sidhoum, S., Monna, F., Trystram, D.: Scheduling tasks with precedence constraints on hybrid multi-core machines. In: HCW, pp. 27–33 (2015)
12. Lee, V.W., et al.: Debunking the 100x GPU vs. CPU myth: an evaluation of throughput computing on CPU and GPU. SIGARCH Comput. Archit. News **38**(3), 451–460 (2010)
13. Svensson, O.: Hardness of precedence constrained scheduling on identical machines. SIAM J. Comput. **40**(5), 1258–1274 (2011)
14. TOP-500-Supercomputer: http://www.top500.org
15. Topcuoglu, H., Hariri, S., Wu, M.Y.: Task scheduling algorithms for heterogeneous processors. In: HCW, pp. 3–14 (1999)

Low-Cost Approximation Algorithms
for Scheduling Independent Tasks
on Hybrid Platforms

Louis-Claude Canon[1,2]([⊠]), Loris Marchal[2], and Frédéric Vivien[2]

[1] FEMTO-ST Institute, Université de Bourgogne Franche-Comté, 16 route de Gray,
25 030 Besançon, France
louis-claude.canon@univ-fcomte.fr
[2] CNRS, Inria, ENS Lyon and University of Lyon, LIP Laboratory 46 allée d'Italie,
69 007 Lyon, France
loris.marchal@ens-lyon.fr, frederic.vivien@inria.fr

Abstract. Hybrid platforms embedding accelerators such as GPUs or
Xeon Phis are increasingly used in computing. When scheduling tasks
on such platforms, one has to take into account that a task execution
time depends on the type of core used to execute it. We focus on the
problem of minimizing the total completion time (or makespan) when
scheduling independent tasks on two processor types, also known as the
$(Pm, Pk)||C_{\max}$ problem. We propose BALANCEDESTIMATE and BAL-
ANCEDMAKESPAN, two novel 2-approximation algorithms with low complexity. Their approximation ratio is both on par with the best approximation algorithms using dual approximation techniques (which are, thus,
of high complexity) and significantly smaller than the approximation
ratio of existing low-cost approximation algorithms. We compared both
algorithms by simulations to existing strategies in different scenarios.
These simulations showed that their performance is among the best ones
in all cases.

1 Introduction

Modern computing platforms increasingly use specialized computation accelerators, such as GPUs or Xeon Phis: 86 of the supercomputers in the TOP500 list
include such accelerators, while 3 of them include several accelerator types [17].
One of the most basic but also most fundamental scheduling step to efficiently
use these hybrid platforms is to decide how to schedule independent tasks. The
problem of minimizing the total completion time (or makespan) is well-studied
in the case of homogeneous cores (problem $P||C_{\max}$ in Graham's notation [13]).
Approximation algorithms have been proposed for completely unrelated proces-
sors ($R||C_{\max}$), such as the 2-approximation algorithms by Lenstra et al. [14]
based on linear programming. Some specialized algorithms have been derived
for the problem of scheduling two machine types ($(Pm, Pk)||C_{\max}$, where m
and k are the number of machines of each type), which precisely corresponds
to hybrid machines including only two types of cores, such as CPUs and GPUs

© Springer International Publishing AG 2017
F.F. Rivera et al. (Eds.): Euro-Par 2017, LNCS 10417, pp. 232–244, 2017.
DOI: 10.1007/978-3-319-64203-1_17

(which corresponds to most hybrid platforms in the TOP500 list). Among the more recent results, we may cite the DADA [5] and DUALHP [3] algorithms which both use dual approximation to obtain 2-approximations. Bleuse et al. [6] also propose a more expensive $(\frac{4}{3} + \frac{1}{3k} + \epsilon)$-approximation relying on dynamic programming and dual approximation with a time complexity $O(n^2 m^2 k^3)$ (with n being the number of tasks). PTAS have even been proposed for this problem [7,12]. However, the complexity of all these algorithms is large, which makes them unsuitable for efficiently scheduling tasks on high-throughput computing systems.

Our objective is to design an efficient scheduling algorithm for $(Pm, Pk)||$ $C_{\max}$ whose complexity is as low as possible, so as to be included in modern runtime schedulers. Indeed with the widespread heterogeneity of computing platforms, many scientific applications now rely on runtime schedulers such OmpSs [16], XKaapi [5], or StarPU [2]. In this context, low complexity schedulers have recently been proposed. The closest approaches to our work in terms of cost, behavior, and guarantee are HETEROPRIO [4], a $(2 + \sqrt{2})$-approximation algorithm when spoliation is permitted, and CLB2C [10], a 2-approximation algorithm in the case where every task processing time, on any resource, is smaller than the optimal makespan. A more detailed and complete analysis of the related work can be found in the companion research report [9].

In this paper, we propose a 2-approximation algorithm, named BALANCEDESTIMATE, which makes no assumption on the task processing times. Moreover, we propose BALANCEDMAKESPAN which extends this algorithm with a more costly mechanism to select the final schedule, while keeping the same approximation ratio. We also present the simulations carried out to estimate in realistic scenarios the relative performance of the algorithms. Table 1 summarizes the comparison between our algorithms and existing solutions. Among many available high complexity solutions, we selected the ones whose running times were not prohibitive. The time complexity, when not available in the original articles, corresponds to our best guess, while performance are the range of the most frequent relative overheads of the obtained makespan with respect to a proposed lower bound that precisely estimates the minimum load on both processor types. In this table, BALANCEDESTIMATE and BALANCEDMAKESPAN achieve both the best approximation ratio and the best performance in simulation.

Therefore, the main contributions of this paper are:

1. Two new approximation algorithms, BALANCEDESTIMATE and BALANCEDMAKESPAN, which both achieve very good tradeoffs between runtime complexity, approximation ratios, and practical performance. The former has the smallest known complexity, improves the best known approximation ratio for low-complexity algorithms without constraints, and is on par with all competitors for practical performance, while the latter outperforms other strategies in most cases, at the cost of a small increase in the time complexity.
2. A new lower bound on the optimal makespan, a useful tool for assessing the actual performance of algorithms.

Table 1. Complexity and performance of the reference and new algorithms. The "performance" corresponds to the 2.5%–97.5% quantiles. The time complexity of HETERO-PRIO assumes an offline variant that needs to compute the earliest processor at each step. $A = \sum_i \max(c_i^1, c_i^2) - \max_i \min(c_i^1, c_i^2)$ is the range of possible horizon guesses for the dual approximations. (*: 3.42-approximation ratio for HETEROPRIO when spoliation is permitted; **: 2-approximation ratio for CLB2C restricted to the cases when $\max(c_i^1, c_i^2) \leq \text{OPT}$)

Name	Time complexity	Approx. ratio	Performance
BALANCEDESTIMATE	$n \log(nmk)$	2	0.2–15%
BALANCEDMAKESPAN	$n^2 \log(nmk)$	2	0.2–8%
HETEROPRIO [4]	$n \log(n) + (n + m + k) \log(m + k)$	3.42**	3.3–17%
CLB2C [10]	$n \log(nmk)$	2*	3.6–37%
DUALHP [4]	$n \log(nmkA)$	2	0.2–14%
DADA [5]	$n \log(mk) \log(A) + n \log(n)$	2	0.9–15%

3. A set of simulations including the state-of-the-art algorithms. They show that BALANCEDMAKESPAN achieves the best makespan in more than 96% of the cases. Moreover, its makespan is always within 0.6% of the best makespan achieved by any of the tested algorithms.

The rest of the paper is organized as follows. The problem is formalized in Sect. 2 and the proposed algorithms are described in Sect. 3. Section 4 is devoted to a sketch of the proof of the approximation ratio. Section 5 presents a new lower bound for the makespan. Finally, we report the simulation results in Sect. 6 and conclude in Sect. 7.

2   Problem Formulation

A set of n tasks must be scheduled on a set of processors of two types containing m processors of type 1 and k processors of type 2. Let c_i^1 (resp. c_i^2) be the integer time needed to process task i on processors of type 1 (resp. of type 2). We indifferently refer to the c_i's as *processing times* or *costs*. The completion time of a processor of type u to which a set S of tasks is allocated is simply given by $\sum_{i \in S} c_i^u$. The objective is to allocate tasks to processors such that the maximum completion time, or makespan, is minimized.

3   Algorithm Description

We now move to the description of the first proposed approximation algorithm: BALANCEDESTIMATE. We start by introducing some notations/definitions that are used in the algorithm and in its proof. In the following μ represents an allocation of the tasks to the two processor types: $\mu(i) = 1$ (resp. $\mu(i) = 2$) means that task i is allocated to some processor of type 1 (resp. 2) in the allocation μ.

The precise allocation of tasks to processors will be detailed later. Note that in the algorithms, allocation μ is stored as an array and thus referred to as $\mu[i]$, which corresponds to $\mu(i)$ in the text. For a given allocation μ, we define $W^1(\mu)$ (resp. $W^2(\mu)$) as the average work of processors of type 1 (resp. 2):

$$W^1(\mu) = \frac{1}{m} \sum_{i:\mu(i)=1} c_i^1 \quad \text{and} \quad W^2(\mu) = \frac{1}{k} \sum_{i:\mu(i)=2} c_i^2.$$

We also define the maximum processing time $M^1(\mu)$ (resp. $M^2(\mu)$) of tasks allocated to processors of type 1 (resp. 2):

$$M^1(\mu) = \max_{i:\mu(i)=1} c_i^1 \quad \text{and} \quad M^2(\mu) = \max_{i:\mu(i)=2} c_i^2.$$

The proposed algorithm relies on the maximum of these four quantities to estimate the makespan of an allocation, as defined by the following *allocation cost estimate*:

$$\lambda(\mu) = \max(W^1(\mu), W^2(\mu), M^1(\mu), M^2(\mu)).$$

Finally, we use $\text{imax}(\mu)$, which is the index of the largest task allocated to a processor of type 1 but that would be more efficient on a processor of type 2:

$$\text{imax}(\mu) = \underset{i:\mu(i)=1 \text{ and } c_i^1 > c_i^2}{\text{argmax}} c_i^1.$$

We can now define a *dominating* task j as a task such that $j = \text{imax}(\mu)$ and $\lambda(\mu) = c_{\text{imax}(\mu)}^1$.

The algorithm works in two passes: it first computes two allocations with good allocation cost estimates (Algorithm 1) and then builds a complete schedule using the Largest Processing Time first (LPT) rule from these allocations (Algorithm 2).

The allocation phase (Algorithm 1) starts by putting each task on their most favorable processor type to obtain an initial allocation μ. Without loss of generality, we assume that processors of type 2 have the largest average work, otherwise we simply switch processor types. Then, tasks are moved from processors of type 2 to processors of type 1 to get a better load balancing. During this process, we carefully avoid task processing times from becoming arbitrarily long: whenever some dominating task appears, it is moved back to processors of type 2. The allocation phase produces two schedules: the one with the smallest cost estimate (μ_{best}) and the one corresponding to the iteration when the relative order of the average works is inversed (μ_{inv}). We define μ_i (resp. μ_i') as the allocation before (resp. after) task i is allocated to processors of type 1 at iteration i on Line 10 ($\mu_{i_{\text{start}}} = \mu_{i_{\text{start}}-1}'$ is the initial allocation).

The scheduling phase (Algorithm 2) simply computes an LPT schedule for each processor type for the two previous allocations. The schedule with minimum makespan is selected as final result.

The time complexity of Algorithm 1 is $O(n \log(n))$ (computing the allocation cost estimate on Line 11 is the most costly operation). The time complexity of the subsequent scheduling phase (Algorithm 2) is $O(n \log(n) + n \log(m) + n \log(k))$.

Algorithm 1. Allocation Algorithm

    Input : number m of processors of type 1; number k of processors of type 2
    Input : number n of tasks; task durations c_i^l for $1 \le i \le n, 1 \le l \le 2$
    Output: a set of allocations
1 **for** $i = 1 \ldots n$ **do**
2   ⌊ **if** $c_i^1 < c_i^2$ **then** $\mu[i] \leftarrow 1$ **else** $\mu[i] \leftarrow 2$
3 **if** $W^1(\mu) > W^2(\mu)$ **then** switch processor types
4 $\mu_{best} \leftarrow \mu$
5 Sort tasks by non-decreasing c_i^1/c_i^2
6 $i_{start} = \min\{i : \mu[i] = 2\}$ /* first task on a processor of type 2 */
7 **for** $i = i_{start} \ldots n$ **do**
8   **if** $W^1(\mu) \le W^2(\mu)$ **and** $W^1(\mu) + c_i^1/m > W^2(\mu) - c_i^2/k$ **then**
9   ⌊ $\mu_{inv} \leftarrow \mu$ /* remember μ */
10    $\mu[i] \leftarrow 1$ /* move a task $(\mu_i \rightarrow \mu_i')$ */
11   **if** $\lambda(\mu) < \lambda(\mu_{best})$ **then**
12   ⌊ $\mu_{best} \leftarrow \mu$ /* update best allocation so far */
13   **if** $\lambda(\mu) = c_{imax(\mu)}^1$ **then**
14   ⌊ $\mu[imax(\mu)] \leftarrow 2$ /* move back a task $(\mu_i' \rightarrow \mu_{i+1})$ */

15 **if** μ_{inv} *is not defined* **then** $\mu_{inv} \leftarrow \mu$
16 **return** (μ_{best}, μ_{inv})

Theorem 1. BALANCEDESTIMATE *(Algorithm 2) is a 2-approximation for the makespan.*

We prove this result in the next section. Figure 1 provides an example showing that this 2-approximation ratio is tight. Both BALANCEDESTIMATE and BALANCEDMAKESPAN build the schedule on the left, which has a makespan of $2k-2$ (initially they assign all the tasks on processors of type 2 and then move all the small tasks on processors of type 1). The makespan of the optimal schedule (on the right) is equal to k. The ratio is thus $2 - \frac{2}{k}$.

BALANCEDESTIMATE balances the average works on both processor types during the allocation while ensuring that no single task will degrade the

---

Algorithm 2. BALANCEDESTIMATE

    Input : number m of processors of type 1; number k of processors of type 2
    Input : number n of tasks; task durations c_i^l for $1 \le i \le n, 1 \le l \le 2$
    Output: schedule of the tasks on the processors
1 Compute (μ_{best}, μ_{inv}) using Algorithm 1
2 **foreach** *Allocation* μ *in* (μ_{best}, μ_{inv}) **do**
3   Schedule tasks $\{i : \mu[i] = 1\}$ on processors of type 1 using LPT
4   Schedule tasks $\{i : \mu[i] = 2\}$ on processors of type 2 using LPT

5 **return** the schedule that minimizes the global makespan

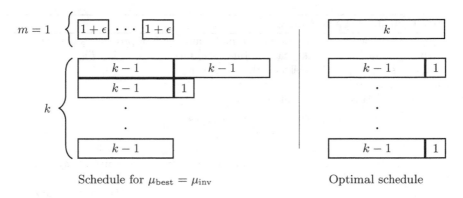

Schedule for $\mu_{\text{best}} = \mu_{\text{inv}}$ Optimal schedule

Fig. 1. Example with $m = 1$ processor of type 1, an arbitrary number $k > 1$ processors of type 2 and two types of tasks: k tasks with costs $c_i^1 = 1 + \epsilon$ (with $\epsilon < \frac{1}{k-1}$) and $c_i^2 = 1$, and $k + 1$ tasks with costs $c_i^1 = k$ and $c_i^2 = k - 1$.

makespan when scheduled. BALANCEDMAKESPAN (Algorithm 3) extends this approach by computing the LPT schedule of each allocation (μ_i and μ_i') considered by BALANCEDESTIMATE (including μ_{best} and μ_{inv}), and thus has the same approximation ratio. It uses the makespan instead of the allocation cost estimate to update μ_{best} and returns the schedule with the lowest makespan. Its time complexity is $O(n^2 \log(nmk))$ as it runs LPT $2n$ times. In Algorithm 3, $L(\mu)$ denotes the makespan of the schedule obtained using LPT on both processor types.

4 Approximation Ratio Proof

The proof that the previous scheduling algorithm produces a makespan at most twice the optimal one is quite long and technical (it includes seven lemmas, one corollary and the main proof requires the study of six different cases). For lack of space, we only present some of the key points of the proof in the present paper. The interested reader may find the whole detailed proof in the companion research report [9].

The proof starts by adding dummy tasks (with 0 cost on processors of type 2), to prove that μ_{inv} is always defined by Line 9: it corresponds to the last iteration where the relative order of the average works is inversed. We also prove that when Algorithm 1 completes, μ_{best} is the allocation with smallest cost estimate among all μ_i''s and μ_i's.

Then, our proof strongly relies on a new lower bound on the optimal makespan. Note that in the following property, μ is any allocation of the tasks to the processor types, not necessarily an allocation encountered by the algorithm.

Proposition 1. *Let μ be an allocation and $i_1 = \max\{i : \mu(i) = 1\}$ be the largest index of tasks that are on processors of type 1 (or 0 if there is none). Then,*

$$\min(W^1(\mu), W^2(\mu), \min_{\substack{1 \leq i < i_1, \\ \mu(i) = 2}} c_i^1) \leq \text{OPT}, \tag{1}$$

Algorithm 3. BALANCEDMAKESPAN

Input : number m of processors of type 1, number k of processors of type 2,
Input : number n of tasks, task durations c_i^l for $1 \leq i \leq n, 1 \leq l \leq 2$
Output: schedule of the tasks on the processors

1 **for** $i = 1 \ldots n$ **do**
2   if $c_i^1 < c_i^2$ **then** $\mu[i] \leftarrow 1$ **else** $\mu[i] \leftarrow 2$
3 **if** $W^1(\mu) > W^2(\mu)$ **then** switch processor types
4 $\mu_{best} \leftarrow \mu$
5 Sort tasks by non-decreasing c_i^1/c_i^2
6 $i_{start} = \min\{i : \mu[i] = 2\}$ /* first task on processors of type 2 */
7 **for** $i = i_{start} \ldots n$ **do**
8     $\mu[i] \leftarrow 1$ /* move a task */
9   **if** $L(\mu) < L(\mu_{best})$ **then**
10        $\mu_{best} \leftarrow \mu$ /* update best allocation so far */
11   **if** $\lambda(\mu) = c_{imax(\mu)}^1$ **then**
12        $\mu[imax(\mu)] \leftarrow 2$ /* move back a task $(\mu_i' \rightarrow \mu_{i+1})$ */
13   **if** $L(\mu) < L(\mu_{best})$ **then**
14        $\mu_{best} \leftarrow \mu$ /* update best allocation so far */

15 **return** the schedule of tasks using LPT on both types of processors from μ_{best}

---

where OPT *is the makespan of an optimal schedule.*

The proof of this property proceeds as follows: we look at where the set of tasks $S = \{1 \leq i < i_1 : \mu(i) = 2\}$ are processed in an optimal allocation.

(i) Either one of those tasks is allocated to a processor of type 1, and then $\min_{i \in S} c_i^1$ is a lower bound on OPT;

(ii) Or all tasks of S are on processors of type 2. We then transform μ into the optimal allocation by exchanging tasks and, thanks to the fact that tasks are sorted by non-decreasing c_i^1/c_i^2, we can prove that not both W^1 and W^2 can increase simultaneously. As $\max(W^1(\text{OPT}), W^2(\text{OPT})) \leq \text{OPT}$, then $\min(W^1(\mu), W^2(\mu)) \leq \text{OPT}$.

We also need a classical result for list scheduling algorithms, summarized in the following lemma.

Lemma 1. *For a given set of tasks, any list scheduling algorithm (such as LPT) builds a schedule on p identical processors with a makespan lower than or equal to $W + (1 - \frac{1}{p})M$ where W is the average work and M is the maximum cost of any task.*

Algorithm 1 produces two allocations: μ_{best} and μ_{inv}, and the final schedule comes from one of them. The extensive proof considers a large number of special cases, but here we restrict to two cases, which we find the most significant: one case considers μ_{best} while the other one considers μ_{inv}.

Case 1. Assume that the cost estimate of μ_{best} is achieved on M^1 or M^2 ($\lambda(\mu_{\text{best}}) = \max(M^1(\mu_{\text{best}}), M^2(\mu_{\text{best}}))$) and that there is no dominating task in μ_{best} ($\lambda(\mu_{\text{best}}) > c^1_{\text{imax}(\mu_{\text{best}})}$). Then, we prove that $\lambda(\mu_{\text{best}}) \leq \text{OPT}$ by considering the two possible cases:

- The maximum defining $\lambda(\mu_{\text{best}})$ is achieved by $M^1(\mu_{\text{best}}) = \max_{j:\mu_{\text{best}}(j)=1} c^1_j$. Let j be a task achieving this maximum. Note that $c^1_j \leq c^2_j$ because otherwise we would have $M^1(\mu_{\text{best}}) = c^1_{\text{imax}(\mu_{\text{best}})}$, which is not possible because $\lambda(\mu_{\text{best}}) > c^1_{\text{imax}(\mu_{\text{best}})}$. Consider an optimal schedule: $\text{OPT} \geq \min(c^1_j, c^2_j) = c^1_j = M^1(\mu_{\text{best}})$ and thus $\lambda(\mu_{\text{best}}) \leq \text{OPT}$.
- The maximum defining $\lambda(\mu_{\text{best}})$ is achieved by $M^2(\mu_{\text{best}}) = \max_{j:\mu_{\text{best}}(j)=2} c^2_j$. Let j be a task achieving this maximum. This case is analogous to the previous one by remarking that j was already allocated to processors of type 2 in the initial allocation, and thus $c^1_j \geq c^2_j$.

As $\lambda(\mu_{\text{best}}) \leq \text{OPT}$, we know by Lemma 1 that LPT on μ_{best} gives a schedule with makespan at most 2OPT.

Case 2. This case reasons on μ_{inv}. By an abuse of notation we call *inv* the iteration at which μ_{inv} was defined at Line 9. We recall that after adding the task with index inv on processors of type 1, μ'_{inv} has an average work larger on processors of type 1 while μ_{inv} had an average work larger on processors of type 2. We apply Proposition 1 on μ_{inv} and μ'_{inv} and forget the cases where the minimum is achieved on a c^1_i in Eq. (1). This gives $W^1(\mu_{\text{inv}}) \leq \text{OPT}$ and $W^2(\mu'_{\text{inv}}) \leq \text{OPT}$. We also forget the case where the cost estimate of either μ_{inv} or μ'_{inv} is given by M^1 or M^2 (which can be treated as in Case 1). We have

$$W^1(\mu'_{\text{inv}}) = W^1(\mu_{\text{inv}}) + \frac{c^1_{\text{inv}}}{m}.$$

and, since $W^1(\mu'_{\text{inv}}) \geq M^1(\mu'_{\text{inv}})$, $c^1_{\text{inv}} \leq W^1(\mu'_{\text{inv}})$. Those two relations bring

$$c^1_{\text{inv}} \leq \frac{W^1(\mu_{\text{inv}})}{1 - 1/m}.$$

Let M be the task with largest cost allocated on processors of type 1 in μ_{inv} ($c^1_M = M^1(\mu_{\text{inv}})$). We have

$$c^1_M \leq W^1(\mu'_{\text{inv}}) \leq W^1(\mu_{\text{inv}}) + \frac{c^1_{\text{inv}}}{m} \leq W^1(\mu_{\text{inv}}) + \frac{W^1(\mu_{\text{inv}})}{m-1} = \frac{m}{m-1} W^1(\mu_{\text{inv}}).$$

Consider the schedule built by Algorithm 2 on allocation μ_{inv}. On processors of type 1, we have $M^1(\mu_{\text{inv}}) = c^1_M$ bounded as above and the average work is $W^1(\mu_{\text{inv}}) \leq \text{OPT}$ (by assumption). Thanks to Lemma 1, we know that the makespan produced by LPT on this instance has a makespan bounded by:

$$C^1_{\max} \le W^1(\mu_{\text{inv}}) + \left(1 - \frac{1}{m}\right) M^1(\mu_{\text{inv}}) \le W^1(\mu_{\text{inv}}) + \left(1 - \frac{1}{m}\right) c^1_M$$

$$\le W^1(\mu_{\text{inv}}) + \left(1 - \frac{1}{m}\right) \frac{m}{m-1} W^1(\mu_{\text{inv}})$$

$$\le 2W^1(\mu_{\text{inv}}) \le 2\text{OPT}.$$

We now concentrate on processors of type 2. We know that

$$W^2(\mu_{\text{inv}}) = W^2(\mu'_{\text{inv}}) + \frac{c^2_{\text{inv}}}{k} \le W^2(\mu'_{\text{inv}}) + \frac{\text{OPT}}{k},$$

The above inequality comes from the fact that $\text{OPT} \ge \min(c^1_{\text{inv}}, c^2_{\text{inv}}) = c^2_{\text{inv}}$ as task inv was on processors of type 2 in the initial allocation. For the same reason, $M^2(\mu_{\text{inv}}) \le \text{OPT}$. Together with $W^2(\mu'_{\text{inv}}) \le \text{OPT}$, we finally get

$$W^2(\mu_{\text{inv}}) \le \left(1 + \frac{1}{k}\right) \text{OPT}.$$

Thanks to Lemma 1, we know that the makespan of Algorithm 2 on processors of type 2 of allocation μ_{inv} is bounded by

$$C^2_{\max} \le W^2(\mu_{\text{inv}}) + \left(1 - \frac{1}{k}\right) M^2(\mu_{\text{inv}})$$

$$\le \left(1 + \frac{1}{k}\right) \text{OPT} + \left(1 - \frac{1}{k}\right) \text{OPT} \le 2\text{OPT}.$$

Thus, $\max(C^1_{\max}, C^2_{\max}) \le 2\text{OPT}$ which yields the result for this case.

The whole proof with many other cases can be found in [9].

5   Lower Bound

We now present a new lower bound on the optimal makespan, which is then used as a reference in our simulations. Note that we could have used Proposition 1 to derive lower bounds, but this would require to first compute interesting allocations. On the contrary, we present here an analytical lower bound, which can be expressed using a simple formula, and which is finer than the previous one in the way it considers how the workload should be distributed.

The bound is obtained by considering the average work on all processors, as in the W/p bound for scheduling on identical machines. To obtain this bound, we consider the divisible load relaxation of the problem: we assume that all tasks can be split in an arbitrary number of subtasks which can be processed on different processors (possibly simultaneously). We are then able to show that the optimal load distribution is obtained when tasks with smaller c^1_i/c^2_i ratio are placed on processors of type 1, while the others are on processors of type 2, so that the load is well balanced. This may require to split one task, denoted by i in the theorem, among the two processor types.

Theorem 2. *Assume tasks are sorted so that $c_i^1/c_i^2 \leq c_j^1/c_j^2$ for $i < j$, and let i be the task such that*

$$\frac{1}{m}\sum_{j \leq i} c_j^1 \geq \frac{1}{k}\sum_{j > i} c_j^2 \quad \text{and} \quad \frac{1}{m}\sum_{j < i} c_j^1 \leq \frac{1}{k}\sum_{j \geq i} c_j^2.$$

Then, the following quantity is a lower bound on the optimal makespan:

$$\text{LB} = \frac{c_i^2 \sum_{j < i} c_j^1 + c_i^1 \sum_{j > i} c_j^2 + c_i^1 c_i^2}{k c_i^1 + m c_i^2}.$$

As this bound only considers average load, it may be improved by also considering the maximum processing time over all tasks: $\max_i \min(c_i^1, c_i^2)$ is the equivalent of the $\max c_i$ lower bound for scheduling independent tasks on identical machines.

6 Simulations

In the context of linear algebra computations, hardware is typically composed of several CPU cores and a few GPU units to compute hundreds of tasks. The following simulations consider 300 tasks, 20 CPU cores, and 4 GPU units. Task processing times are randomly generated and follow a gamma distribution with expected value 15 for the CPUs and 1 for the GPUs. These values are inspired from the measures in [1,3]. Moreover, the gamma distribution has been advocated for modeling job runtimes [11,15]. This distribution is positive and it is possible to specify its expected value and standard deviation by adjusting its parameters. The Coefficient of Variation (CV[1]) of both types of processing times is either 0.2 (low) or 1 (high). Each combination of CV for the CPUs and the GPUs leads to 100 instances. For each instance, the set of processing times is given as input to all six algorithms and the obtained makespans are then divided by the lower bound given by Theorem 2. The algorithms are implemented in R and the related code, data and analysis are available in [8].

The studied algorithms are the reference algorithms DUALHP, DADA, HETEROPRIO and CLB2C, and our two new algorithms, BALANCEDESTIMATE and BALANCEDMAKESPAN. HETEROPRIO and CLB2C both start by sorting the tasks by their acceleration ratios. In HETEROPRIO, each ready processor will then start the execution of the next best task. When all tasks are running, ready processors will steal a running task if this reduces its completion time. In CLB2C, at each iteration, the two tasks that are the best for each type of processors are considered and the one that can finish the soonest is scheduled.

Figure 2 depicts the ratios of the achieved makespans by the lower bound using boxplots in which the bold line is the median, the box shows the quartiles, the bars show the whiskers (1.5 times the interquartile range from the box) and additional points are outliers.

---

[1] The Coefficient of Variation is the ratio of the standard deviation to the mean.

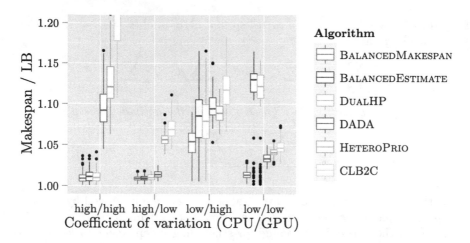

Fig. 2. Ratios of the makespan over a lower bound for 6 algorithms over 400 hundreds instances. For each instance, there are $n = 300$ tasks, $m = 20$ CPUs and $k = 4$ GPUs. The costs follow a gamma distribution with expected value 15 for the CPUs and 1 for the GPUs, while the coefficient of variation is either 0.2 (low) or 1 (high).

BALANCEDMAKESPAN has the best median in all cases and is often below 2% from the lower bound except when the CPU CV is low and the GPU CV is high, for which the lower bound seems to be the furthest. This case is also the most realistic [1,3]. BALANCEDESTIMATE and DUALHP have similar performance. It may be due to their similar mechanism: allocating the jobs to balance the average CPU and GPU works, and then scheduling the jobs in a second step. DADA, HETEROPRIO and CLB2C, which all schedule the jobs incrementally, perform similarly for most of the cases. There are classes of problems for which CLB2C has median performance that is more than 20% away from the lower bound. No other algorithms achieve so low performance.

When the CPU CV is high, BALANCEDESTIMATE is close to the lower bound (the median is around 1%). In the opposite case, however, CPU costs are more homogeneous and the performance degrades. The LPT scheduling step of BAL-ANCEDESTIMATE may schedule a last large task on a single CPU whereas it would have been better to allocate it to the GPUs. In comparison, BALANCED-MAKESPAN, HETEROPRIO, and CLB2C are not affected by this limitation because they build the schedule step by step and adjust the allocation depending on the actual finishing times.

Finally, we measured that BALANCEDMAKESPAN provides the best makespan among the six tested algorithms in more than 96% of the cases. Moreover, the makespan is always within 0.6% of the best makespan achieved by the different algorithms. By contrast, the next two best algorithms in this regard, BAL-ANCEDESTIMATE and DUALHP, both provide the best makespan in more than 36% of the cases and their makespan is always within 16% of the best makespan.

7   Conclusion

With the recent rise in the popularity of hybrid platforms, efficiently scheduling tasks on multiple types of processors such as CPUs and GPUs has become critical. This paper presents BALANCEDESTIMATE, a new algorithm for the $(Pm, Pk)||C_{max}$ problem. It balances the tasks from the most loaded processor type to the other type of processors. This algorithm is the first to achieve an approximation ratio of 2 in all cases with a low time complexity. We also propose BALANCEDMAKESPAN, a more costly variant with the same guarantee. Among these two algorithms, simulations showed the latter outperforms competing algorithms in more than 96% of the cases, while the former is on par with a more costly dual approximation. The performance of the algorithms was assessed using a new lower bound on the optimal makespan.

Future developments will consist in evaluating the robustness of the algorithm against incertainties in the processing time estimates and implementing this approach in a real runtime system to see its benefits in practical situations. Furthermore, the model could be extended to fit more closely to realistic environments by considering precedence constraints, more than 2 types of processors and taking into account startup times for launching tasks on GPUs.

Acknowledgments. This work was supported by the LABEX MILYON (ANR-10-LABX-0070) of Université de Lyon, within the program "Investissements d'Avenir" (ANR-11-IDEX-0007) operated by the French National Research Agency (ANR). This material is also based upon research supported by the SOLHAR project operated by the French National Research Agency (ANR).

References

1. Agullo, E., Beaumont, O., Eyraud-Dubois, L., Kumar, S.: Are static schedules so bad? A case study on Cholesky factorization. In: 2016 IEEE International Parallel and Distributed Processing Symposium, pp. 1021–1030. IEEE (2016)
2. Augonnet, C., Thibault, S., Namyst, R., Wacrenier, P.A.: StarPU: a unified platform for task scheduling on heterogeneous multicore architectures. Concurr. Comput.: Pract. Exp. **23**(2), 187–198 (2011)
3. Beaumont, O., Cojean, T., Eyraud-Dubois, L., Guermouche, A., Kumar, S.: Scheduling of linear algebra kernels on multiple heterogeneous resources. In: International Conference on High Performance Computing, Data, and Analytics (HiPC) (2016)
4. Beaumont, O., Eyraud-Dubois, L., Kumar, S.: Approximation proofs of a fast and efficient list scheduling algorithm for task-based runtime systems on multicores and GPUs (2016, to appear in IEEEIPDPS 2017). https://hal.inria.fr/hal-01386174
5. Bleuse, R., Gautier, T., Lima, J.V.F., Mounié, G., Trystram, D.: Scheduling data flow program in XKaapi: a new affinity based algorithm for heterogeneous architectures. In: Silva, F., Dutra, I., Santos Costa, V. (eds.) Euro-Par 2014. LNCS, vol. 8632, pp. 560–571. Springer, Cham (2014). doi:10.1007/978-3-319-09873-9_47
6. Bleuse, R., Kedad-Sidhoum, S., Monna, F., Mounié, G., Trystram, D.: Scheduling independent tasks on multi-cores with GPU accelerators. Concurr. Comput.: Pract. Exp. **27**(6), 1625–1638 (2015)

7. Bonifaci, V., Wiese, A.: Scheduling unrelated machines of few different types. arXiv preprint arXiv:1205.0974 (2012)
8. Canon, L.C.: Code for low-cost approximation algorithms for scheduling independent tasks on hybrid platforms. https://doi.org/10.6084/m9.figshare.4674841.v1
9. Canon, L.C., Marchal, L., Vivien, F.: Low-cost approximation algorithm for scheduling independent tasks on hybrid platforms. Research report 9029, INRIA, February 2017. https://hal.inria.fr/INRIA/hal-01475884v1
10. Cheriere, N., Saule, E.: Considerations on distributed load balancing for fully heterogeneous machines: two particular cases. In: Proceedings of IEEE International Parallel and Distributed Processing Symposium Workshop (IPDPSW), pp. 6–16. IEEE (2015)
11. Feitelson, D.G.: Workload Modeling for Computer Systems Performance Evaluation, 1st edn. Cambridge University Press, New York (2015)
12. Gehrke, J.C., Jansen, K., Kraft, S.E.J., Schikowski, J.: A PTAS for scheduling unrelated machines of few different types. In: Freivalds, R.M., Engels, G., Catania, B. (eds.) SOFSEM 2016. LNCS, vol. 9587, pp. 290–301. Springer, Heidelberg (2016). doi:10.1007/978-3-662-49192-8_24
13. Graham, R.L., Lawler, E.L., Lenstra, J.K., Kan, A.H.G.R.: Optimization and approximation in deterministic sequencing and scheduling: a survey. Ann. Discret. Math. **5**, 287–326 (1979)
14. Lenstra, J.K., Shmoys, D.B., Tardos, É.: Approximation algorithms for scheduling unrelated parallel machines. Math. Program. **46**(1–3), 259–271 (1990)
15. Lublin, U., Feitelson, D.G.: The workload on parallel supercomputers: modeling the characteristics of rigid jobs. J. Parallel Distrib. Comput. **63**(11), 1105–1122 (2003)
16. Sainz, F., Mateo, S., Beltran, V., Bosque, J.L., Martorell, X., Ayguadé, E.: Leveraging OmpSs to exploit hardware accelerators. In: IEEE International Symposium on Computer Architecture and High Performance Computing (SBAC-PAD), pp. 112–119 (2014)
17. TOP500 supercomputer site, list of November 2016. http://www.top500.org

High Performance Architectures and Compilers

Runtime-Assisted Shared Cache Insertion Policies Based on Re-reference Intervals

Vladimir Dimić[1,2]([⊠]), Miquel Moretó[1,2], Marc Casas[1,2], and Mateo Valero[1,2]

[1] Barcelona Supercomputing Center (BSC), Barcelona, Spain
{vladimir.dimic,miquel.moreto,marc.casas,mateo.valero}@bsc.es
[2] Universitat Politécnica de Catalunya, Barcelona, Spain

Abstract. Processor speed is improving at a faster rate than the speed of main memory, which makes memory accesses increasingly expensive. One way to solve this problem is to reduce miss ratio of the processor's last level cache by improving its replacement policy. We approach the problem by co-designing the runtime system and hardware and exploiting the semantics of the applications written in data-flow task-based programming models to provide hardware with information about the task types and task data-dependencies. We propose the Task-Type aware Insertion Policy, TTIP, which uses the runtime system to dynamically determine the best probability per task type for bimodal insertion in the recency stack and the static Dependency Type aware Insertion Policy, DTIP, that inserts cache lines in the optimal position taking into account the dependency types of the current task. TTIP and DTIP perform similarly or better than state-of-the-art replacement policies, while requiring less hardware.

Keywords: Shared cache · Replacement policy · Runtime system · Task-based programming model · Hardware-software co-design

1 Introduction

Throughout the last decades, main memory performance has been improving with a slower rate than the performance of CPUs, which has been described as the *Memory Wall* [28]. Misses happening in last level caches (LLC) result in memory accesses, which cause CPU to wait for the data. Non-blocking caches try to mitigate this problem by being able to serve several outstanding misses, but they cannot hide the memory latency in all cases. One way to approach this problem is to reduce the miss rate of the LLC. Optimizing the LLCs usage is a complex problem and requires identifying the important factors that impact its performance.

The access pattern of an application together with the memory hierarchy configuration (i.e. cache size, associativity, replacement policy, etc.) are some of these factors. Most commonly used applications can have several fundamental access patterns. Memory accesses with high spatial and temporal locality are

© Springer International Publishing AG 2017
F.F. Rivera et al. (Eds.): Euro-Par 2017, LNCS 10417, pp. 247–259, 2017.
DOI: 10.1007/978-3-319-64203-1_18

cache friendly and usually have good hit rates. Streaming access patterns are characterised by sequential or strided access of vectors in memory. In general, they have no reuse and, therefore, the choice of the cache placement policy has a low impact on the miss rate. Thrashing access patterns are the ones that have reuse distances bigger than the cache associativity. Repeated, circular, accesses to the same sequence of addresses cause the circular eviction of the cache lines, thus making all accesses resulting in misses. Many applications show more complex access patterns that are a combination of the simple ones. Choosing an appropriate replacement policy is important for achieving good performance when executing these applications.

The majority of modern CPUs are multi-core and have a multi-level cache hierarchy with shared LLC. The sequences of memory accesses coming from threads executing on different cores arrive into the LLC. If the LLC uses a replacement policy that does not take into account the priority of certain access patterns, such as LRU, accesses generated by a thread may trash the working set of another. Giving more priority to the lines of the trashed thread will improve its performance while not hurting the performance of the thrashing thread. There are several state-of-the-art replacement policies designed by taking access pattern priorities into account, such as DIP [19], DRRIP [9] and SHiP [27]. However, they do not consider application semantics, which can give useful information about access patterns for different memory regions and different code segments in the application. Using this information in designing a replacement policy for LLC can bring benefits in performance.

Applications written in a task-based programming model can provide more information about the semantics. Many programming models use the notion of task as a unit of work, such as OpenMP 4.0 [15], Cilk [5], Chapel [3], Intel TBB [21], Charm++ [11] and OmpSs [25]. In task-based data-flow programming models, task data-dependencies are used for synchronisation, meaning that tasks consuming a dependency cannot start executing before the task producing that dependency finishes. Special directives, inserted by programmers, instruct the compiler how to parallelise the code. The compiler translates these directives to calls to the runtime library, which manages the execution of the application.

Tasks perform different functions and access their dependencies in different ways. We argue that using information about task types and dependency types can help designing better replacement policies in the LLC. To approach the problem, we use a recently proposed idea [4, 26], where architectures and runtime systems collaborate in order to achieve better performance in modern and future computer systems. We exploit application semantics available in the runtime system and provide the processor with the necessary information to optimise the behaviour of the LLC. In this paper, we propose two insertion policies that utilise information about task types (TTIP) and task data-dependency types (DTIP), which are described in more detail in Sect. 3. TTIP dynamically determines the best probability per task-type for probabilistic insertion achieving 5.1% and 0.8% better execution time than LRU and DRRIP, respectively. DTIP statically assigns different insertion positions based on data-dependency type and is faster 4.8% and 0.3% than LRU and DRRIP, respectively.

2   Related Work

Cache replacement policies are a set of algorithms that maintain the logical order of cache lines inside a cache set. Insertion policies determine the position of the line in the logical queue on its insertion into the cache. Promotion policies update the line's position when it is accessed. Eviction policies decide which line to remove from the cache when a space for a new line is needed.

The optimal replacement policy, the Belady's MIN algorithm [1], evicts the line that is going to be referenced farthest in the future. It is unusable in real systems because it requires the knowledge of the future. Least-Recently Used (LRU) policy evicts the line that was used farthest in the past, while on insertion and promotion lines are moved to the top of the LRU stack. The cost of maintaining LRU states is increasing with set size, so it is not used in caches with high associativity (LLC). Pseudo LRU policies [7,14] sacrifice precision while simplifying the state management. On average, they perform similarly to LRU in caches with high associativity.

LRU performs poorly with scanning and thrashing workloads. Qureshi et al. [19] propose several insertion policies that try to reduce thrashing. Bimodal Insertion Policy (BIP) inserts a tunable percentage of lines in the LRU position, and the rest of the lines in the Most-Recently Used (MRU) position. LRU and BIP outperform each other in different cases, so Dynamic Insertion Policy (DIP) chooses the best of the two via sampling-based adaptive replacement [20].

Jaleel et al. [9] propose a cache replacement policy that uses Re-Reference Interval Prediction (RRIP) in order to prevent cache pollution by lines that are not going to be referenced for a long time. For managing the logical order of the lines, two bits per cache line are used to encode 4 different states: 00 (*immediate*), 01, 10 (*long*) and 11 (*distant*). Multiple lines can be in the same state. On a cache hit, the accessed line is promoted to *immediate* position. On eviction, a line with *distant* state is removed. If no such line exists, states of all lines are increased by one until at least one of the lines is in *distant* position. On insertion, a line is assigned a position that depends on the insertion policy.

Static RRIP (SRRIP) always assigns *long* re-reference interval to new lines, which protects lines with shorter re-reference interval from being evicted by scanning access patterns. In thrashing workloads, SRRIP performs poorly. Bimodal RRIP (BRRIP) solves this by inserting the majority of new lines with *distant*, and the rest with *long* re-reference interval. Both policies implement promotion and eviction similarly to NRU [14]. Dynamic RRIP (DRRIP) uses set dueling [18] to dynamically select the best performing policy. Finally, Wu et al. [27] propose Signature-based Hit Predictor (SHiP) that extends RRIP by predicting the re-reference interval of an incoming cache line based on its history. Cache line's PC-based signature is used for tracking the history of hits.

There have been several proposals that use the runtime system of task-based data-flow programming models to optimize the LLC performance. Papaefstathiou et al. [17] propose a prefetching scheme in which the runtime provides hardware with information about task data-dependencies. To minimize cache pollution, quotas are assigned to current and future tasks based on their footprint. The current task is given the highest priority, thus keeping its lines in cache. Manivannan and Stenstrom [13] propose cache coherence protocol, in which the runtime system exposes to the hardware which are the lines that will be reused. The coherence protocol can then reduce coherence traffic by invalidating or downgrading lines precisely. Pan and Pai [16] propose a runtime-assisted cache partitioning technique. Runtime knowledge about task inter-dependencies and future tasks is used in order to preserve useful data in the cache, while removing the data that will not be re-referenced in the future.

RADAR [12], a runtime-assisted scheme for dead-block management, consists of two independent algorithms for dead-block prediction, which are combined to give the better final algorithm. The first, *Look-ahead scheme*, uses information about task dependencies and current state of the task dependency graph to determine whether certain blocks of data will reused. The second, *Look-back scheme*, uses previous outcomes of cache accesses to estimate whether certain cache lines will be dead.

3   Runtime-Assisted Insertion Policies in the LLC

An important factor that affects the LLC performance is the memory access pattern. Runtime systems that support task-based data-flow programming models have information about task types and task data-dependencies of the application. We aim to utilise this information at the hardware level to improve the LLC performance by optimizing its insertion policy.

3.1   Task Type Aware Probabilistic Insertion

BRRIP is designed to overcome thrashing in access patterns with longer re-reference interval than the cache associativity. It achieves so by selecting the new line's insertion position in the recency stack based on a pre-determined static probability.

If multiple access patterns, including thrashing ones, meet in the LLC, it is beneficial to assign them different insertion probabilities. We assign probabilities per task type, thus giving them different priorities in the LLC. A higher probability means inserting more lines into the *long* position, so the lines have more chances to be preserved in cache. Tasks that show more locality in their accesses should get a higher insertion probability than the tasks having scanning access patterns. Moreover, using a larger set of probabilities instead of a fixed one gives more opportunities to tune the tasks' performance in complex scenarios where many different task types compete for the LLC resources. The optimal probability depends on the co-runners that share the LLC at the moment. In complex applications, instances of a given task type may execute with different co-runners in different phases of the application, which means that the optimal probability may change.

We develop a dynamic mechanism that aims to determine the best probability per task type during the execution of an application. The proposed mechanism alternates between two phases, training phase and stable phase, for each task type independently. The goal of the training phase is to find the optimal probability for the given task type which is then used during the stable phase.

At the beginning of the application, all task types are set to run in the training phase. When a task instance is scheduled on a given core, the algorithm selects a probability from the pool of preselected probabilities $\mathcal{P}$ and instructs the LLC to use that probability for all accesses issued by this task instance. Upon completion of each task instance, the algorithm records the number of misses generated by that task with the selected probability. The same probability is used for **K task instances**. Probabilities are selected sequentially from the pool until all probabilities are evaluated. In total, $K \times |\mathcal{P}|$ task instances are used for training during one training phase for one task type. This concludes the training phase and the stable phase begins. The algorithm then selects the probability that induced lowest average number of misses and uses it for the next **N instances** of the given task type. After that, the whole process repeats until the end of the application's execution.

Consequently, TTIP is able to select the best probability parameter for a given task type appropriate for the current conditions in the LLC.

3.2   Dependency Type Aware Insertion

We reason in Sect. 1 that task data-dependencies show different access patterns. Input dependencies are read-only data useful for the current task instance. Output dependencies are generated by a task in order to be consumed by its successors in the task dependency graph. Therefore, it may be beneficial to insert cache lines belonging to outputs in higher positions of the recency stack, thus giving them more chances to stay in the cache until the moment they are required by the consumer task. A similar reasoning applies to dependencies denoted as *inouts*, as they are also inputs of a future task. Non-dependencies are the local variables in the call stack and the global variables that are not specified as task dependencies. In some of our benchmarks, like CG, they are predominantly accesses to large global variables that have streaming-like access patterns. In other benchmarks, where this is not true, decisions that we make for non-dependencies do not harm the performance.

We develop an insertion policy that inserts lines in positions based on which dependency type they belong to. We call this policy Dependency Type aware Insertion Policy (DTIP). The policy configuration can be formally defined as a function $f : \mathcal{DT} \rightarrow \mathcal{IP}$, where $\mathcal{DT} = \{input, output, inout, non\text{-}dependency\}$ and $\mathcal{IP} = \{immediate, long, distant\}$. To determine the impact of mapping dependency types to specific positions in the recency stack, we perform an exhaustive design space exploration where we try all possible functions f. Number of different policy configurations per benchmark is $|\mathcal{IP}|^{|\mathcal{DT}|} = 3^4 = 81$. For all benchmarks, we run 405 simulations. On average, the best performing policy is the one that inserts *inputs* and *non-dependencies* on the *distant* position in the recency stack and *outputs* and *inouts* on *long* or *immediate* positions. This is consistent with the intuitive expectations described above.

3.3   Implementation

In this section, we describe the hardware and runtime extensions necessary for implementation of our policies. The cost of their implementation is discussed in detail in Sect. 4.5.

Hardware Extensions. To be able to use different insertion probabilities for different task types, TTIP requires a small and fast hardware structure in the LLC that maps a hardware thread ID to the appropriate probability. It is designed as a SRAM memory containing probabilities and is addressed by the hardware thread ID, which is already required to enforce coherence in the LLC. The mapping table is accessed on a new miss, in parallel with creation of a new MSHR entry. The read probability from the table is used to calculate the insertion position, which is cached in the newly created MSHR entry. The runtime modifies the structure via memory-mapped registers. To track the performance under each probability, we use one hardware counter per hardware thread for misses to LLC. The counters are exposed to the runtime as a set of registers.

To identify the dependency type of an access, which is necessary for DTIP, we add a special hardware structure that stores the mappings of dependency regions to the dependency type for all running tasks. We assume that only one task is executing concurrently on any given hardware thread. If tasks are switched, the runtime or the operating system updates the mapping table with dependency regions of the new task. There might be several tasks using the same region at the same time, but the runtime scheduler inherently guarantees that the region will have the same dependency type in all these tasks.

The mapping table is read on every occurrence of a miss in the LLC to determine the dependency type of the missing line. The missing line's address is fed to the table, which simultaneously compares all stored region boundaries and selects the entry containing the dependency type corresponding to the region of the missed address. This is done in parallel with creating a new MSHR entry, thus not introducing any additional latency. The dependency type of the line is stored in the newly created MSHR entry. Upon serving the request from main memory, the new line is inserted into the position in recency stack determined by the stored dependency type.

Hardware structures of both TTIP and DTIP are centralised and located in the LLC. They are accessed by the core via special requests through the memory hierarchy. The requests are propagated to the LLC and do not change the contents of the private caches.

Runtime System Extensions. To implement TTIP, several runtime modifications are required. The runtime system contains a per-task data structure that tracks the performance in terms of number of misses for each probability. When a task starts, before its user code starts executing, the runtime decides which probability to use for that task instance and writes it in the probability table on the position specified by the core ID on which the task is scheduled to run. At the end of execution of a task, the number of misses produced by that task in the LLC is read by the runtime and stored in the software data structure mentioned above.

DTIP requires several changes in the runtime system. When a new task starts executing on a core, the runtime system updates the mapping table with the information for the new task by issuing store instructions to the memory-mapped registers. This does not require changes to the ISA, since many modern processors have a support for memory-mapped registers. If there are several consecutive dependency regions of the same type, the runtime may perform two optimizations to reduce the storage requirements in the mapping table. The first optimization merges the consecutive dependency regions of the same dependency type into one. The second does not insert the region if it already exists in the table, which happens if two or more tasks are sharing the same region. Since the mapping table is not readable by the runtime to simplify the hardware design, the runtime keeps a software copy of the mapping information.

4 Evaluation

4.1 Simulation Infrastructure

We use TaskSim [23], a trace-driven [22] computer architecture simulator that simulates applications written in data-flow task-based programming models. The simulated system is a 4-core processor with a cache hierarchy consisting of 3 levels, two of which are private, L1 (4-way, 32 KB) and L2 (8-way, 256 KB), and the LLC is shared (16-way, 8 MB). All caches are write-back and write-allocate. Access latencies are 4, 10 and 24 cycles, respectively. Each cache can serve up to 16 outstanding misses and 4 write-back requests which are served when the bus is not in use. Private caches use LRU replacement policy. The size of a cache line in all caches is 64 B. Only memory instructions are simulated in detail while other instructions are simulated on a simple CPU model. Inter-dependencies of memory accesses are respected. The reorder buffer contains 128 entries. The main memory has a latency of 200 ns and a bandwidth of 2.4 GB/s per core.

4.2 Benchmarks

In order to evaluate our proposals in relevant scenarios, we use benchmarks that cover a wide range of modern applications and kernels used in HPC and show variability in task sizes and dependency types. PARSECSs [6] is a task-based implementation of widely-accepted benchmark suite of parallel applications, PARSEC [2]. Benchmarks that fulfil our requirements are facesim and ferret. We use *simlarge* input set, the largest input set suitable for simulation. Moreover, we use two HPC applications used in previous works [22,23], specfem3D and stap. The inputs are selected to balance between simulation time and LLC footprint. Finally, we use benchmark CG, a conjugate gradient method [24], implemented in OmpSs by Jaulmes et al. [10]. The input is the matrix *qa8fm* from The University of Florida Sparse Matrix Collection [8]. The algorithm is decomposed in 8 blocks and runs until convergence (97 iterations).

4.3   TTIP Parameters Space Exploration

TTIP's performance depends on two parameters K and N, which are described in Sect. 3.1. These parameters determine how many task instances per probability are used in training, and how many instances for running with the best probability in the stable phase. We explore the set of configurations (K, N) where $K \in \{1, 2, 4, 8, 16\}$ and $N \in \{10, 50, 100, 500, 1000, \infty\}$. Configurations where $N = \infty$ have only one training phase which is followed by one stable phase that lasts until the end of execution. Intuitively, choosing a larger K offers better precision by having more time to evaluate one probability. However, too large K can hurt the overall performance if certain probabilities perform badly. Configurations with larger N use the best probability for a longer period of time, but are less able to adapt to potential changes in application behaviour. Using a smaller N can be bad for the final performance because a larger percentage of the execution is spent in the training phase.

Figure 1 shows the performance of TTIP in terms of MPKI depending on the choice of parameters K and N. For most benchmarks except specfem3D we can observe a performance improvement as N increases. This is due to the fact that, in the majority of benchmarks, instances of the same task type have similar behaviour. For cg, we can notice the trend of performance degradation when increasing K for a constant N. Similar behaviour can be noticed for stap. Stap highly benefits from configurations where $N = \infty$ due to having a large number of task instances. Having many training phases in case of stap means repeatedly evaluating sub-optimal probabilities, thus hurting the overall performance. Ferret does not show significant sensitivity to K and N. Facesim obtains better performance with larger K due to having a lot of small task instances and, therefore, needing more instances per probability to properly evaluate the performance of each probability. The configuration that performs the best on average for all our benchmarks is $(N, K) = (\infty, 8)$, which we will use for further evaluation of TTIP in the remaining of the paper.

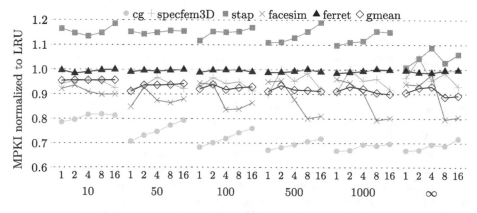

Fig. 1. TTIP sensitivity to $N \in \{10, 50, 100, 500, 1000, \infty\}$ and $K \in \{1, 2, 4, 8, 16\}$

4.4   Performance Results

Figure 2 compares TTIP and DTIP with LRU and state-of-the-art SRRIP, BRRIP and DRRIP in terms of MPKI and speedup normalised to LRU. For BRRIP we use the probability for inserting into the *long* position $\epsilon = 1/32$ and for DRRIP SDM with 32 sets.

TTIP upgrades BRRIP by supporting multiple probability values and being able optimize the probability per task type. It achieves up to 32.1% and on average 11.2% reduction in MPKI compared to LRU. The speedup over LRU is up to 12.3% and on average 5.1%. TTIP performs similarly as DRRIP, having 3.3% higher MPKI and being 0.8% faster than DRRIP. However, it does not need the hardware for Set Dueling, but instead uses a small mapping table described in Sect. 3.3 and whose cost is discussed in the Sect. 4.5.

DTIP improves MPKI over LRU for up to 33.3% and on average 16.8%. The largest contribution of improvement in MPKI comes from specfem3D, where misses to *output* dependencies of the largest task are reduced by inserting *outputs* in *immediate* position. This decision does not significantly impact the number of misses to *inputs* and *non-dependencies*. DTIP is faster than LRU for up to 12.1% and on average 4.8%. Compared to SRRIP, which is another static RRIP policy, DTIP achieves up to 29.1% (12.8% on average) lower MPKI and performs up to 10.5% (3.7% on average) faster. The improvement over SRRIP comes from the fact that DTIP differentiates the cache lines by their data-dependency types. DTIP is able to benefit from this information by inserting the new lines in a more optimal position in the recency stack so that different access patterns that

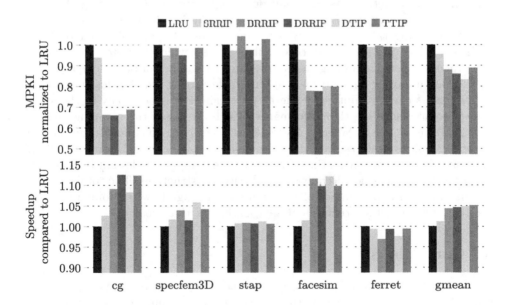

Fig. 2. Performance of TTIP and DTIP

collide in LLC have least possible negative effects on each other. DTIP reduces MPKI by 3.1% on average and is faster 0.3% than DRRIP.

Even though it shows higher MPKI than DTIP on average, TTIP achieves better execution time. The contributor to this effect is cg, where DTIP fails to achieve a speedup comparable to TTIP and DRRIP. The largest task type, which performs a matrix-vector multiplication, is the main source of MPKI improvement of DTIP over TTIP. However, three smaller, but still important tasks, show higher execution time with DTIP due to increased number of misses to *inputs* and *non-dependencies*. The improvement in execution time achieved in the largest task is not enough to compensate losses in three smaller tasks, because hits in the largest task are hidden by the unavoidable misses to the matrix.

4.5   Design Costs

To store the state of the recency stack, both TTIP and DTIP need $2n$ bits per cache set, the same as DRRIP, whereas LRU requires $n \log n$ bits per set, where n is the cache associativity. In the system evaluated in this work ($n = 16$), RRIP policies consume $2\times$ less space than LRU.

The mapping table required by TTIP has 4 entries, one for each core. Probabilities are stored with resolution of 6 bits, making the size of the structure 4×6 bit $= 3$ B. In addition, TTIP requires 4 hardware counter registers, each one being 32 bit long. The total additional hardware cost required by TTIP is 3 B $+ 4 \times 32$ bit $= 19$ B. After each task instance, the runtime reads the corresponding hardware counter and potentially sets the new probability for the new task instance, which incurs overhead of few instructions. Calculating the best probability after the training period takes less than hundred instructions.

The mapping table for DTIP technique contains 32 pairs of 48-bit physical addresses, thus providing each core with 8 entries, which is more than enough to cover the most demanding tasks in regards to number of data-dependencies. In the case of larger demand for mapping table entries, smaller, less important dependencies can be omitted or merged with another dependency of the same type without degrading the performance. The total size of the mapping table is $32 \times 2 \times 48$ bit $= 348$ B. When a new task instance is scheduled for execution, the mapping table is updated with data-dependencies of the task. Upon completion of a task, the runtime clears the entries from the mapping table that belong only to that task. Both actions require several tens of instructions. The total runtime overhead in terms of number of instructions is negligible when compared with the total number of instructions of any benchmark that we use.

5   Conclusions

Improving LLC performance is of great importance in modern and future systems. In multi-core processors, threads generating various access patterns are competing for LLC resources. To achieve best performance, it is necessary to protect certain access patterns from being thrashed by accesses coming from another thread. In this paper we aim to exploit semantic information about applications written in data-flow task-based programming model to better manage the LLC. The runtime system provides the information about task types and task data-dependencies to the LLC in order to improve the insertion policy. We propose two techniques:

TTIP - Task Type aware Insertion Policy tries to determine the best probability for inserting lines in the recency stack by using runtime-guided dynamic approach that evaluates the performance of several pre-set probabilities and chooses the best performing one.

DTIP - Dependency Type aware Insertion Policy is a static policy that inserts lines in the recency stack based on the type of data-dependency they belong to. Data that will be used by the next tasks is given more chance to stay in cache by inserting it in higher positions of the recency stack, while read-only data is given less priority.

Our policies use the runtime system for providing the hardware with the necessary information for determining appropriate insertion positions, which simplifies hardware design. The overheads of the runtime extensions are negligible. The performance benefits compared to LRU are significant for both policies. TTIP performs slightly worse than DRRIP, but uses simpler hardware. DTIP performs better than DRRIP on average, which proves the benefits of using runtime information about the application in designing LLC replacement policies. In comparison with DRRIP, our policies do not use set dueling monitors and do not require a decoder for determining *dedicated follower* sets.

Possible improvements for TTIP include discarding probabilities that perform badly from the training process. DTIP can be extended to distinguish between dependencies, since different dependencies of the same type may have slightly different access patterns that benefit from different insertion positions. Further benefits could be obtained by also taking into account task type.

Acknowledgments. This work has been supported by the RoMoL ERC Advanced Grant (GA 321253), by the European HiPEAC Network of Excellence, by the Spanish Ministry of Science and Innovation (contract TIN2015-65316-P), by Generalitat de Catalunya (contracts 2014-SGR-1051 and 2014-SGR-1272). V. Dimić has been partially supported by AGAUR of the Government of Catalonia (contract 2017 FLB 00855). M. Moretó has been partially supported by the Ministry of Economy and Competitiveness under Juan de la Cierva postdoctoral fellowship number JCI-2012-15047. M. Casas has been supported by the Secretary for Universities and Research of the Ministry of Economy and Knowledge of the Government of Catalonia and the Cofund programme of the Marie Curie Actions of the 7th R&D Framework Programme of the European Union (contract 2013 BP B 00243).

References

1. Belady, L.A.: A study of replacement algorithms for a virtual-storage computer. IBM Syst. J. **5**, 78–101 (1966)
2. Bienia, C.: Benchmarking modern multiprocessors. Ph.D. thesis, Princeton (2011)
3. Blumofe, R., Joerg, C., Kuszmaul, B., et al.: Cilk: an efficient multithreaded runtime system. J. Parallel Distrib. Comput. **37**, 55–69 (1995)
4. Casas, M., et al.: Runtime-aware architectures. In: Träff, J.L., Hunold, S., Versaci, F. (eds.) Euro-Par 2015. LNCS, vol. 9233, pp. 16–27. Springer, Heidelberg (2015). doi:10.1007/978-3-662-48096-0_2
5. Chamberlain, B., Callahan, D., Zima, H.: Parallel programmability and the Chapel language. Int. J. High Perform. Comput. Appl. **21**, 291–312 (2007–2008)
6. Chasapis, D., Casas, M., Moretó, M., Vidal, R., Ayguadé, E., Labarta, J., Valero, M.: PARSECSs: evaluating the impact of task parallelism in the PARSEC benchmark suite. In: TACO (2015)
7. Chen, W., Liu, P., Stelzer, K.: Implementation of a pseudo-LRU algorithm in a partitioned cache, US Patent 7,069,390 (2006)
8. Davis, T., Hu, Y.: The University of Florida sparse matrix collection. ACM Trans. Math. Softw. **38**(1), 1 (2011)
9. Jaleel, A., Theobald, K.B., Steely Jr., S.C., Emer, J.: High performance cache replacement using re-reference interval prediction (RRIP). SIGARCH Comput. Arch. News **38**, 60–71 (2010)
10. Jaulmes, L., Casas, M., Moretó, M., et al.: Exploiting asynchrony from exact forward recovery for due in iterative solvers. In: SC (2015)
11. Kale, L.V., Krishnan, S.: CHARM++: a portable concurrent object oriented system based on C++. In: OOPSLA (1993)
12. Manivannan, M., Papaefstathiou, V., Pericas, M., Stenstrom, P.: RADAR: runtime-assisted dead region management for last-level caches. In: HPCA (2016)
13. Manivannan, M., Stenstrom, P.: Runtime-guided cache coherence optimizations in multi-core architectures. In: IPDPS (2014)
14. Sun Microsystems: UltraSPARC T2 supplement to the UltraSPARC architecture 2007, draft D1.4.3 (2007)
15. OpenMP Arch. Rev. Board: OpenMP Application Program Interface, v4.0 (2013)
16. Pan, A., Pai, V.S.: Runtime-driven shared last-level cache management for task-parallel programs. In: SC (2015)
17. Papaefstathiou, V., Katevenis, M.G., Nikolopoulos, D.S., Pnevmatikatos, D.: Prefetching and cache management using task lifetimes. In: ICS (2013)
18. Qureshi, M., Jaleel, A., Patt, Y., Steely, S., Emer, J.: Set-dueling-controlled adaptive insertion for high-performance caching. In: Micro. IEEE (2008)
19. Qureshi, M.K., Jaleel, A., Patt, Y.N., Steely, S.C., Emer, J.: Adaptive insertion policies for high performance caching. In: ISCA (2007)
20. Qureshi, M.K., Lynch, D.N., Mutlu, O., Patt, Y.N.: A case for MLP-aware cache replacement. In: ISCA (2006)
21. Reinders, J.: Intel Threading Building Blocks. First edn. (2007)
22. Rico, A., Duran, A., Cabarcas, F., Etsion, Y., Ramirez, A., Valero, M.: Trace-driven simulation of multithreaded applications. In: ISPASS (2011)
23. Rico, A., Cabarcas, F., Villavieja, C., et al.: On the simulation of large-scale architectures using multiple application abstraction levels. In: TACO (2012)
24. Shewchuk, J.R.: An introduction to the conjugate gradient method without the agonizing pain. Technical report (1994)

25. Teruel, X.: OmpSs quick overview, a practical approach (2013)
26. Valero, M., Moreto, M., Casas, M., Ayguade, E., Labarta, J.: Runtime-aware architectures: a first approach. Supercomp. Front. Innov. **1**, 29–44 (2014)
27. Wu, C.J., Jaleel, A., Hasenplaugh, W., et al.: SHiP: signature-based hit predictor for high performance caching. In: MICRO (2011)
28. Wulf, W.A., McKee, S.A.: Hitting the memory wall: implications of the obvious. SIGARCH Comput. Arch. News **23**, 20–24 (1995)

Rewriting System for Profile-Guided Data Layout Transformations on Binaries

Christopher Haine[1]([✉]), Olivier Aumage[2], and Denis Barthou[3]

[1] LaBRI, University of Bordeaux, Bordeaux, France
christopher.haine@inria.fr
[2] Inria, Bordeaux, France
olivier.aumage@labri.fr
[3] Bordeaux INP, Bordeaux, France
denis.barthou@inria.fr

Abstract. Careful data layout design is crucial for achieving high performance. However exploring data layouts is time-consuming and error-prone, and assessing the impact of a layout transformation on performance is difficult without performing it. We propose to guide application programmers through data layout restructuring by providing a comprehensive multidimensional description of the initial layout, built from trace analysis, and then by giving a performance evaluation of the transformations tested and an expression of each transformed layout. The programmer can limit the exploration to layouts matching some patterns. We apply this method to two multithreaded applications. The performance prediction of multiple transformations matches within 5% the performance of hand-transformed layout code.

Keywords: Performance tuning · Data layout restructuring · Memory traces

1 Introduction

Adapting data allocations and structures to the way data is used is a key optimization for parallel architectures. Changing data layout can enhance spatial data locality and memory consumption, having a large impact on code performance. Associated with instruction rescheduling and loop nest transformations, layout restructuring has a strong impact on vectorization and may lead to a better use of cache hierarchy, through temporal and spatial locality. Data restructuring is a global optimization in general, requiring interprocedural analysis, and in languages such as C, possible aliases hamper the scope of transformations. When considering combined data layout and control-flow transformation, dependence analyse is further limits the applicability of the methods. Finally, due to the complexity of memory hierarchy, the impact on performance of a data structure change is difficult to assess. To illustrate this difficulty, the simple choice between an array of structures (AoS) or a structure of arrays (SoA)

© Springer International Publishing AG 2017
F.F. Rivera et al. (Eds.): Euro-Par 2017, LNCS 10417, pp. 260–272, 2017.
DOI: 10.1007/978-3-319-64203-1_19

is highly dependent on the use of the structure. Depending on the locality of data, it may be beneficial to use the SoA version if when using a single field at a time or the AoS version when using multiple fields (such as a complex number, for instance). For a parallel code, an Array of Structures of Vectors/Arrays may have to be considered, resulting in portability issues and unacceptable program complexity for the human programmer [18].

Several works have studied data layout restructuring for specific applications [13,22] and for stencils [10]. In a recent work [1] we proposed a framework to analyze binary codes, and to formulate user-targeted hints about SIMDization potentials and hindrances. These hints provide the user with possible strategies to remove SIMDization hurdles, such as code transformations or data restructuring. However, this preliminary work conducted a qualitative analysis only, thus lacking an estimation in the transformation gains. In [8], we proposed a more quantified approach, to detect simple arrays and structures from execution traces, and suggest promising data layout transformations.

This paper proposes a novel approach for data restructuring. A formalization of data structures and of their transformations is described, independently of any control-flow or rescheduling optimization. We show that this framework can be used from memory traces in order to provide a quick assessment of potential gains (or lack of) to be expected from some transformations. For this purpose, we show how to setup mock-up executions for an application, in order to evaluate the impact of the transformation without the need to actually change the whole data structures or re-execute the whole application. This approach is evaluated on two real applications parallelized with OpenMP, combining restructuring and vectorization. The contributions proposed in this paper are the following:

- Description of data structure layouts and their transformations, independently of control-flow optimizations;
- Generation of mock-up codes with restructured layouts;
- Performance evaluation of mock-ups, with and without SIMDization.

The paper is organized as follows: Sect. 2 presents two motivating examples with sub-optimal data layout. Section 3 describes a method for finding an initial multi-dimensional layout matching a trace, and the possible transformations. Section 4 presents the evaluation methodology. The experimental results are discussed in Sect. 5 and Sect. 6 presents related work.

2   Motivating Examples

From a user perspective, abstract data types correspond to algorithmic requirements, but choosing the actual data layout requires to take compiler, runtime support and architectural constraints into consideration. We illustrate this gap between the data layout chosen for the two following applications. In the cardiac wave simulation [23], the hot spot of the OpenMP version of the application uses a large 4D array to store the whole data structure, as shown in Fig. 1. The first 2 dimensions have starting index of 1, creating unnecessary gaps between

```
for (X=1; X<Nx+1; ++X){
  for (Y=1; Y<Ny+1; ++Y){
    datarr[X][Y][13][(step−1)%2] =
      datarr[X][Y][13][(step−1)%2]
      −(2*Dp[0][0]+2*Dp[1][1])
      *datarr[X][Y][0][step%2]
      −Dp[1][0]*datarr[X−1][Y+1][0][step%2]
      +Dp[1][1]*datarr[X][Y+1][0][step%2]
      +Dp[1][0]*datarr[X+1][Y+1][0][step%2]
      +Dp[0][0]*datarr[X+1][Y][0][step%2]
      −Dp[1][0]*datarr[X+1][Y−1][0][step%2]
      +Dp[1][1]*datarr[X][Y−1][0][step%2]
      +Dp[1][0]*datarr[X−1][Y−1][0][step%2]
      +Dp[0][0]*datarr[X−1][Y][0][step%2];
}}
```

(a) Cardiac wave simulation excerpt

```
for(iL=0 ; iL < L/2 ; iL+=1) {
  for (j=0;j<4;j++) {
    r0  = U[idn[4*iL]][0]*tmp[j];
    r0 += U[idn[4*iL]][1]*tmp[n2+j];
    r0 += U[idn[4*iL]][2]*tmp[2*n2+j];
    r1  = U[idn[4*iL]][3]*tmp[j];
    r1 += U[idn[4*iL]][4]*tmp[n2+j];
    r1 += U[idn[4*iL]][5]*tmp[2*n2+j];
    r2  = U[idn[4*iL]][6]*tmp[j];
    r2 += U[idn[4*iL]][7]*tmp[n2+j];
    r2 += U[idn[4*iL]][8]*tmp[2*n2+j];
    ID2[j]     += r0 ;
    ID2[n2+j]  += r1;
    ID2[2*n2+j] += r2;
  }
}
```

(b) Lattice QCD simulation excerpt

Fig. 1. Two examples of codes needing data layout restructuring. In the Cardiac wave simulation, the 4-D array `datarr` is used as an array of structures. For the QCD simulation, all elements are `complex double` values. The space iterated by the outer loop is a 4-D linearized space and the indirection used for U accesses the white elements of a 4-D checkerboard.

lines. The third dimension is used as a structure with numbered fields, and the fourth dimension has a spatial locality issue, since it is indexed with the parity of the computation step (to keep only the previous computation results). While reordering dimensions here is not very complex, the ordering and locality choices for the last dimension depend on the computation itself and on the architecture.

The second example considered is a Lattice QCD application, based on ETMC simulation [2]. The hotspot of the application performs several matrix-vector computations. Each matrix is described as an element of a large array, U. The space iterated by iL is a 4D linearized space. In this 4D space, only the white elements of a checkerboard are accessed, through an indirection array. Deciding how to restructure this array and whether it is worth to get rid of the indirection is important for the code performance. This example is difficult to analyze statically and would require some additional information from the user. An analysis based on traces on the contrary would capture the regularity of the accesses, in spite of the indirection.

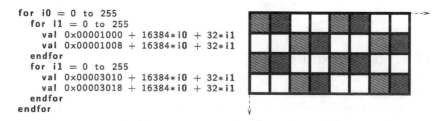

```
for i0 = 0 to 255
  for i1 = 0 to 255
    val 0x00001000 + 16384*i0 + 32*i1
    val 0x00001008 + 16384*i0 + 32*i1
  endfor
  for i1 = 0 to 255
    val 0x00003010 + 16384*i0 + 32*i1
    val 0x00003018 + 16384*i0 + 32*i1
  endfor
endfor
```

Fig. 2. Example trace for Qiral for array U accesses, simplified 2D version for conciseness. Each color in the map represents one line of the trace. (Color figure online)

3 Layout Description and Transformations

We give here a formal description for layouts and rules for transforming them.

3.1 Data Layout Description

Data structures are considered as any combination of arrays and structures, of any length. A layout is the description of this structure and of the elements that are accessed in it. A layout can be defined only for a limited code fragment. When considering a syntactic memory access expression in the code, it defines a set of memory address values. This set can be denoted as $base + I$ where $base$ is the base address and I is the set of positive integers, including 0. All addresses are within a range $[base, base + d - 1]$ where d is the diameter of I. The set of offsets I can be represented by a layout function $S_{I,d}$, characterizing I:

$$S_{I,d} : [0, d-1] \to \{0, 1\}$$
$$x \to 1 \text{ if } x \in I, 0 \text{ otherwise}$$

$S_{I,d}$ is called a *structure layout*. If $I = [0, d-1]$ (all elements are accessed), $S_{[0,d-1],d}$ is more specifically called an *array layout*, denoted A_d. Note that these terms of arrays and structures may not correspond to the structures really occurring in the source code. To build a multidimensional data structure, we define the product operator $\otimes$ and the sum $\oplus$ on layout functions L_1 and L_2:

$$L_1 \otimes L_2 : I_1 \times I_2 \to \{0, 1\} \qquad L_1 \oplus L_2 : I \to \{0, 1\}$$
$$x, y \to L_1(x) * L_2(y) \qquad\qquad x \to L_1(x) + L_2(x)$$

For the product, the two layout functions L_1 and L_2 may have two different domains, I_1 and I_2. For the sum, the domain of the two functions must be the same. The $+$ operation is a saturated addition between integers. With this notation, Array of Structures correspond to the combination of the two types of layout, described by $A_{d'} \otimes S_{I,d}$ for some values of d, d' and I. The formal description corresponds to the intuitive representation of the data. The same factorization identities exist with $\oplus$ and $\otimes$ as with integers. Some simplifications are possible between expressions involving both operators:

$$(S_{I,d} \otimes L) \oplus (S_{J,d} \otimes L) = S_{I \cup J, d} \otimes L, \quad (L \otimes S_{I,d}) \oplus (L \otimes S_{J,d}) = L \otimes S_{I \cup J, d}.$$

3.2 Finding the Initial Multidimensional Layout

In the general case, the memory accesses are given as flat, linearized addresses. The objective of this section is to find out the different multidimensional layouts used in the code fragment considered. On the source code, finding whether two memory accesses correspond to the same array region correspond to an alias analysis. Delinearization can be used in some simple cases to retrieve the multidimensional structure associated to the addresses. Because indirections or complex operations can be involved in the address computation, as shown in the two codes given as motivating examples, we propose in this paper to resort to memory traces. The code fragment is executed and all memory accesses generate a trace. This trace is compacted on-the-fly with the NLR method [12] in order to find possible recurring stride patterns. The following rewriting system transforms a flat layout into a multidimensional layout:

$$S_{I,m} \rightarrow S_{J,n} \otimes A_p \text{ if } I = \{j * p + k, j \in J, k \in [0, n]\} \tag{1}$$

$$S_{I,m} \rightarrow A_n \otimes S_{J,p} \text{ if } I = \{k * p + j, j \in J, k \in [0, n]\} \tag{2}$$

$$S_{n*I+p,m*n} \rightarrow S_{I,m} \otimes S_{\{p\},n} \text{ if } p < n \tag{3}$$

with $n * I + p = \{n * i + p, i \in I\}$. The first rule corresponds to the case where the initial layout is a structure of array, the second to an array of structure, and the third is the general case, where two structures layouts have been linearized. The initial multidimensional layout can be found by applying these rules iteratively until convergence. The rewriting system is confluent and convergent. Convergence comes from structures with diminishing sizes. We assume that array layouts are not rewritten. Confluence entails that the rules can be applied in any order and results from the fact that there is only one way to rewrite any given part of the addresses.

We apply the previous algorithm to restructure the trace given in Fig. 2. The trace, given as a `for..loop` enumerating addresses, is a simplified version for the memory access of matrix U (2D case, only first statement, no outer dimension). The following initial structure corresponds to the set of values accessed by the trace:

$$U + S_{\{2048*[0,255]+4*[0,255]\},d} \qquad U + A_{256} \otimes S_{\{0\},2} \otimes A_{256} \otimes S_{\{0,1\},4}$$

$$\oplus S_{\{2048*[0,255]+4*[0,255]+1\},d} \quad \Rightarrow \quad \oplus A_{256} \otimes S_{\{1\},2} \otimes A_{256} \otimes S_{\{2,3\},4}$$

$$\oplus S_{\{2048*[0,255]+4*[0,255]+1024+2\},d}$$

$$\oplus S_{\{2048*[0,255]+4*[0,255]+1024+3\},d}$$

Applying Rule 3, then merging the first two lines and the last two, and then applying Rule 2 and finally Rule 1 leads to the formulation on the right. This corresponds to an AoSoAoS: This is an array of 2 lines, even lines and odd lines. Even lines have 256 elements that are structures of 4 doubles, using only the first 2. Odd lines have 256 elements having 4 doubles, using only the last 2. This is represented in Fig. 2.

3.3   Transformations

We define layout transformations as rewriting rules that applies on the layouts described in previously defined formalism. For these rules, rules applying to structures S are assumed not to apply to arrays. If $S_{I,d}(x) = 1$, we will rather write it as: S_d. $\#I$ corresponds to the number of elements in I:

$$L \otimes L' \to L' \otimes L \quad (4) \qquad S_{I,n} \otimes S_{J,m} \to S_{I',n*m}, \; if \#I' = \#I \times \#J \quad (6)$$

$$A_{n*m} \to A_n \otimes A_m \quad (5) \qquad S_{I,d} \to S_{I',d'}, \; if \#I = \#I', d \le d' \quad (7)$$

Rule 4 permutes two layouts, Rule 5 cuts an array in two arrays. Rule 6 merges two structure layouts and the last one, Rule 7, removes unused elements in a structure. In a layout expression composed of different terms in a $\oplus$, all terms of the sum at the same position must be rewritten with the same rule, since it corresponds to the same sub-structure. All transformations preserve the number of elements in the layouts.

3.4 Exploring Layouts

The previous rewriting system generates a finite but potentially large number of layouts. We propose a strategy to limit the exploration. Rule 5 is only applied at most once to split an array for SIMDization purposes. One of the created array is then permuted in the rightmost position of the term in order to create a possible vector of elements. Rule 7 is applied whenever possible. Rule 6 simplifies code generation by fusing contiguous dimensions. This rule is only applied at the end of the rewriting. To further reduce exploration, we propose to guide the generation by proposing patterns of layouts. For instance, SIMDization requires that the layout ends with an array. Only terms in the form of the regular expression $* \otimes A$ are considered. For instance, on the two examples shown as motivating examples, we look for layouts of the form $* \otimes A$ or $* \otimes A \otimes S_c$ (with S_c the structure corresponding to complex numbers). This leads to the layouts presented in the following table:

Code	Initial Layout	Transformed Layouts [short name]	
Qiral excerpt	$A_L \otimes S_{\{1\},d} \otimes S_m \otimes S_c$	$A_{L/v} \otimes S_{m \times c} \otimes A_v$	[AoSoA-dbl]
Qiral precond. excerpt	$\bigoplus_{x,y,z,t \equiv 0[2]} (\bigotimes_{k=x,y,z,t} A_l \otimes S_{k,2})$ $\otimes S_{\{1\},d} \otimes S_m \otimes S_c$	$A_{L/v} \otimes S_m \otimes A_v \otimes S_c$	[AoSoA-cplx]
		$S_{m \times c} \otimes A_L$	[SoA-dbl]
		$S_m \otimes A_L \otimes S_c$	[SoA-cplx]
Qiral application	$A_L \otimes S_d \otimes S_m \otimes S_c$	$A_{L/v} \otimes S_d \otimes S_{m \times c} \otimes A_v$	[AoSoA]
		$S_d \otimes S_m \otimes A_L$	[SoA]
Cardiac Wave	$A_X \otimes A_X \otimes S_{\{0\},a} \otimes S_{\{0\},s}$	$A_X \otimes A_X$	

The preconditioned version for QIRAL has a detected 4D checkerboard pattern, here expressed in a concise form, and v has the size of a SIMD vector. Checkerboard compression leads to the same transformations, only with L half the size. The QIRAL excerpt corresponds to the code presented as the motivating example while the application includes a larger scope of code.

4 Transformation Evaluation

This section deals with the quantified part of the user feedback we provide. The idea is to estimate the potential speedup of transformations in order to help the user make a choice for data restructuring.

4.1   Principle of Mock-Up Evaluation

We propose an evaluation methodology that explores a set of different layout transformations. Because these transformations are based on the values collected by memory traces, the generated transformed codes are in general not semantically equivalent to the initial code, outside of the trace. However they can serve as performance mock-ups. The idea is to measure possible performance gains of the application by executing the mock-ups. To preserve the application execution conditions, the mock-up is executed in the context of the application. Checkpoint/restart technique is used for this objective: Assuming the user knows the hotspot of the application, the original binary code is patched with a checkpoint right before the hotspot and then run until the checkpoint is reached. This checkpoint generates an execution context, used for capturing the trace and running/evaluating the mock-ups. The binary code is instrumented in order to collect the memory trace and restarted from this context. Then several layout transformations are applied on the initial code, generating new versions of the code that are restarted from the same context. As the checkpoint/restart mechanism preserves the memory addresses in use, the addresses and sizes of layouts captured in the trace can be reused in the mock-up codes. We rely on this property for generating data layout copies and the transformed codes. Our approach does not preserve however the hotspot cache state. Cache warm-up may be a solution to this issue, but goes beyond the scope of this paper. Mock-ups are stopped when the control leaves the hotspot and the timing is deduced at this point. For checkpoint/restart, we resort to the BLCR library [9].

4.2   Automatic Mock-Up Generation Technique

Mock-ups are generated at compile time, as library functions. A mock-up corresponds to the initial hotspot, with different memory accesses and their address computation. The rest of the computation itself corresponds to the original code. Before executing the mock-up, the data layout has to be created and data copied. This copy-in operation is guided by the trace information. The objective is to optimize the hotspot performance, and to push away the copies from the kernel to minimize their impact, avoiding cache pollution due to the copy itself. We choose to move the copy up to the beginning of the function if applicable, the limit being the last write on the array we want to restructure. This is determined automatically by trace inspection. The sequence of transformation rules applied to the initial layout corresponds also to transformations on the iterators of these structures. The copy codes are simple loops changing one layout, with one iterator, into another. For the indexation of data in the computation code, the control is kept unchanged. New scalar iterators are created in order to map the previous index to the new index. For this, the trace provides for each individual assembly instruction the sequence of addresses accessed. This sequence of indices is transformed into a sequence of new indices, of the new layout. The binary code is parsed with the MAQAO tool [3], and the modified code of the mock-up is generated in a C file, using inline assembly. The advantage of this approach is to rely on the compiler for an optimized register allocation for all the new induction variables added for indexing, and for removing dead code. For instance, the loads corresponding to the indirection are removed when reindexing the data structure in a simpler way. The code generated is only valid within the scope of the values collected by the trace.

4.3   Combining Layout Restructuring with SIMDization

Data restructuring is a SIMDization-enabling transformation, as data can be placed contiguously to fill a vector. We perform SIMDization whenever dependences allows it, impacting the control (loops) of the hotspot. From the trace analysis, we build a dependence graph that determines whether some arrays can be vectorized. We rely on MAQAO for this analysis [1], as well as for the detection of loop structures and for loop counters. The generated vectorized loop has a shorter loop trip count by a factor equal to the architecture vector size. This loop trip count is retrieved from the memory traces. All instructions involving the initial data structure have to be replaced by their vectorized counterpart, including load and stores. Some compiler optimization can be untangled, such as partial loads that are replaced by a single packed load operation. Reductions are detected through dependence graph analysis, and are replaced using horizontal operations. We detect read-only arrays or constants and unpack them. However, our SIMDization step from binary code to assembly code (inline assembly) is still fragile and essentially only applies a straightforward vectorization scheme.

5   Experimental Results

The objective of the section is to show how relevant the speedup hints are, in the sense that they provide useful advice to the programmer. To do so, we compare our mock-up speedups with the actual performance observed by restructuring the C code by hand, using layouts defined in Sect. 3.4. All experiments are conducted on an Intel(R) Xeon(R) CPU E5-2650 2 GHz 2*8-core processor with SSE2 features, using icc 15.0.0 and gcc 5.3.1 compilers, both with -O3 flag.

Lattice QCD: Figure 3 shows performance of both mock-ups and hand-transformed codes for the loop nest in Fig. 1.(b). The hand-tuned code focuses only on restructuring layout and does not perform explicit SIMDization. It appears that gcc does not vectorize the code when handling `complex` data types and performs poorly even compared to the non-vectorized mock-ups. For the code without preconditioning (left graph), all mock-ups predict performance improvement for each of the four transformation presented, with an average relative error of 16% compared to the hand-tuned codes. For *AoSoA-cplx*, the mock-up under-estimate performance. The reasons comes from the fact that `icc` optimizes the complex multiply and the load/stores, outperforming the naive SIMDization of the mock-up. Similar conclusions hold for the code with even/odd preconditioning. For the whole multithreaded hotspot function, the manually

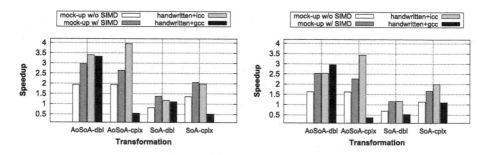

Fig. 3. Lattice QCD benchmark without preconditioning (left), with even/odd preconditioning (right) speedup, single thread.

restructured version resorts to intrinsics, as the compilers do not manage auto-vectorization. Predictions for *SoA* and *AoSoA* are reliable with an average relative error of 4%, as shown in Fig. 4, as mock-up SIMDization perform close to user restructured code. With a packed thread policy and hyper-threading disabled, the multithreaded context does not disrupt the mock-up prediction, since the code is parallel and compute-bound.

2D Cardiac Wave Propagation Simulation: The hotspot here is not initially vectorized, but it is successfully vectorized after data layout restructuring; Consequently no intrinsics are used in hand-tuned codes. We study layout restructuring impact on performance on two different datasets, corresponding to two different layout sizes. Speedups obtained after restructuring are shown in Fig. 5 for the Dataset-256. With only the restructuring, the mock-ups exhibit a speed-up of 2.4× on average. When considering mock-ups with SIMDization, the gain of SIMDization alone is around 2×. Mock-up prediction average relative error is 9% too optimistic in this experiment. This over-estimation is explained by the effect of cache warm-up. In the mock-ups, the data copy loads data in the cache right before the hotspot. In the application, such "prefetch" is not performed. The input size is multiplied by a factor 4 using Dataset-512. In

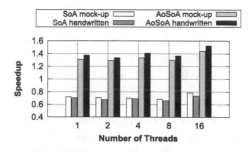

Fig. 4. Lattice QCD application restructuring+SIMD speedup with respect to thread number.

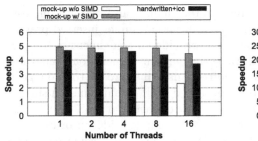
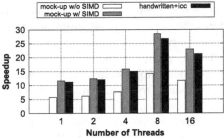

Fig. 5. 2D Wave propagation application restructuring+SIMDization speedup on dataset-256 (left) or on Dataset-512 (right)—with respect to reference using respectively equal number of threads—average relative error is $9\% \pm 8\%$ (left), $5\% \pm 2\%$ (right)

this new configuration, restructuring gain is dramatically higher than before, increasing with the number of threads and reaching roughly 14× with 8 threads, as application achieves to take full advantage of all private L2 caches. Moreover, prediction remains consistently slightly overoptimistic as memory cache may be warmer before kernel execution than actual real application cache, while still being accurate with an average relative error as low as 5%.

6   Related Work

Many modern languages, in particular object oriented languages, propose a layer of abstraction between data types and the data layout in memory (hierarchical arrays, C++ libraries). However, few works propose to restructure existing data, in codes written in C or Fortran. This abstraction layer is also provided by libraries, hiding in particular the complexity of AoSoA layouts with SIMDization to the user (Cyme [6], Boost:SIMD or Kokkos [5], to name a few). The StructSlim profiler [16] helps programmers into data restructuring through structure splitting. For GPU, copy is performed at transfer time and data layout change is also performed at this step [20]. Code analysis is performed statically, on OpenCL for instance. The same approach has been explored for heterogeneous architectures [15], assessing affinity between fields and clustering fields, and devising multi-phase AoS vs SoA data layouts and transforms. VP^3 [24] is a tool for pinpointing SIMDization related performance bottlenecks. It tries to predict performance gains by changing the memory access pattern or instructions. However, it does not propose high level restructuring. Similarly, ArrayTool [14] can be used to regroup arrays, to gain locality, but there is no deeper change in data layouts. Annotations and specific data layout optimizations with compiler support has been proposed by Sharma et al. [19]. The source-to-source transformation requires to describe in a separate file the desired array interleaving. Similarly, the array unification described by Kandemir [11] and Inter-Array Data regrouping [4] propose to merge different arrays at compile-time in order to gain locality.

The POLCA semantics-aware transformation toolchain is an Haskell framework offering numerous transformation operators using programmer inserted pragma annotations [21]. Neither of these approaches provide an assessment of the performance gains to guide the user restructuring or hint generation, and these compile-time approaches cannot handle indirections. An approach to find a good layout using profile information has been proposed by [17], but relies on simulation to test the layouts and does not address vectorization or AoS transformations. Delinearization is the first analysis on the compiler side, in order to be able to restructure the layout. Parametric delinearization, for some particular codes, has been proposed by Grosser *et al.* [7]. Specifically for stencil codes, using the polyhedral model, Henretty *et al.* [10] propose a complete restructuring of layout for SIMDization. This would not apply to the Lattice QCD code with the even/odd preconditioning (indirection) Compared to the authors previous work [8], the work presented in this paper gives a more general framework for the recognition of complex data layouts and systematic exploration of data layouts. The code generation and SIMDization are automatically achieved, for a given transformation.

7   Conclusion

We have presented in this paper an original contribution for assessing the impact on performance of data layout restructuring. The layout transformations, based on profile information and described by a rewriting system, can be shown and explained to the user, from the initial layout to the transformed one. These transformations can then be applied and explored directly on a binary code generating automatically a new binary code. A set of different restructuring has been combined with SIMDization and the evaluation has been conducted on two applications, with different parameters (size of input, preconditioning used) and using different number of threads. The results show that the performance prediction of mock-up restructuring is reliable compared to a hand-tuned transformation and SIMDization (below 5% in average of relative error).

References

1. Aumage, O., Barthou, D., Haine, C., Meunier, T.: Detecting SIMDization opportunities through static/dynamic dependence analysis. In: Workshop on Productivity and Performance (PROPER) (2013)
2. Barthou, D., Grosdidier, G., Kruse, M., Pene, O., Tadonki, C.: QIRAL: a high level language for lattice QCD code generation. In: PLACES Workshop, Tallinn, Estonia (2012). arXiv:1208.4035
3. Barthou, D., Rubial, A.C., Jalby, W., Koliai, S., Valensi, C.: Performance tuning of x86 OpenMP codes with MAQAO. In: Müller, M., Resch, M., Schulz, A., Nagel, W. (eds.) Tools for High Performance Computing. Springer, Berlin (2010). doi:10.1007/978-3-642-11261-4_7

4. Ding, C., Kennedy, K.: Inter-array data regrouping. In: Carter, L., Ferrante, J. (eds.) LCPC 1999. LNCS, vol. 1863, pp. 149–163. Springer, London (2000). doi:10. 1007/3-540-44905-1_10. http://dl.acm.org/citation.cfm?id=645677.663795
5. Edwards, H., Trott, C.: Kokkos: enabling performance portability across manycore architectures. In: Extreme Scaling Workshop, pp. 18–24, August 2013
6. Ewart, T., Delalondre, F., Schürmann, F.: Cyme: a library maximizing SIMD computation on user-defined containers. In: Kunkel, J.M., Ludwig, T., Meuer, H.W. (eds.) ISC 2014. LNCS, vol. 8488, pp. 440–449. Springer, Cham (2014). doi:10. 1007/978-3-319-07518-1_29
7. Grosser, T., Ramanujam, J., Pouchet, L.N., Sadayappan, P., Pop, S.: Optimistic delinearization of parametrically sized arrays. In: ACM on International Conference on Supercomputing, pp. 351–360. ACM, New York (2015)
8. Haine, C., Aumage, O., Petit, E., Barthou, D.: Exploring and evaluating array layout restructuring for SIMDization. In: Brodman, J., Tu, P. (eds.) LCPC 2014. LNCS, vol. 8967, pp. 351–366. Springer, Cham (2015). doi:10.1007/ 978-3-319-17473-0_23
9. Hargrove, P.H., Duell, J.C.: Berkeley lab checkpoint/restart (BLCR) for Linux clusters. J. Phys.: Conf. Ser. **46**(1), 494 (2006)
10. Henretty, T., Stock, K., Pouchet, L.-N., Franchetti, F., Ramanujam, J., Sadayappan, P.: Data layout transformation for stencil computations on short-vector SIMD architectures. In: Knoop, J. (ed.) CC 2011. LNCS, vol. 6601, pp. 225–245. Springer, Heidelberg (2011). doi:10.1007/978-3-642-19861-8_13
11. Kandemir, M.T.: Array unification: a locality optimization technique. In: Wilhelm, R. (ed.) CC 2001. LNCS, vol. 2027, pp. 259–273. Springer, Heidelberg (2001). doi:10.1007/3-540-45306-7_18
12. Ketterlin, A., Clauss, P.: Prediction and trace compression of data access addresses through nested loop recognition. In: ACM/IEEE International Conference on Code Generation and Optimization, pp. 94–103. ACM, New York (2008)
13. Kong, M., Veras, R., Stock, K., Franchetti, F., Pouchet, L.N., Sadayappan, P.: When polyhedral transformations meet SIMD code generation. In: ACM SIGPLAN Conference on Programming Language Design and Implementation (2013)
14. Liu, X., Sharma, K., Mellor-Crummey, J.: Arraytool: a lightweight profiler to guide array regrouping. In: Parallel Architecture and Compilation, pp. 405–416. ACM, New York (2014)
15. Majeti, D., Meel, K.S., Barik, R., Sarkar, V.: ADHA: automatic data layout framework for heterogeneous architectures. In: International Conference on Parallel Architectures and Compilation, pp. 479–480. ACM, New York (2014)
16. Roy, P., Liu, X.: StructSlim: a lightweight profiler to guide structure splitting. In: ACM/IEEE International Conference on Code Generation and Optimization (2016)
17. Rubin, S., Bodík, R., Chilimbi, T.: An efficient profile-analysis framework for data-layout optimizations. In: ACM SIGPLAN Notices, vol. 37, pp. 140–153. ACM (2002)
18. Satish, N., Kim, C., Chhugani, J., Saito, H., Krishnaiyer, R., Smelyanskiy, M., Girkar, M., Dubey, P.: Can traditional programming bridge the Ninja performance gap for parallel computing applications? In: International Symposium on Computer Architecture pp. 440–451. IEEE, Washington, DC (2012)
19. Sharma, K., Karlin, I., Keasler, J., McGraw, J.R., Sarkar, V.: Data layout optimization for portable performance. In: Träff, J.L., Hunold, S., Versaci, F. (eds.) Euro-Par 2015. LNCS, vol. 9233, pp. 250–262. Springer, Heidelberg (2015). doi:10. 1007/978-3-662-48096-0_20

20. Sung, I.J., Liu, G., Hwu, W.M.: DL: a data layout transformation system for heterogeneous computing. Innov. Parallel Comp. **2012**, 1–11 (2012)
21. Tamarit, S., Mario, J., Vigueras, G., Carro, M.: Towards a semantics-aware transformation toolchain for heterogeneous systems. In: Program Transformation for Programmability in Heterogeneous Architecture Workshop (2016)
22. Videau, B., Marangozova-Martin, V., Genovese, L., Deutsch, T.: Optimizing 3D convolutions for wavelet transforms on CPUs with SSE units and GPUs. In: Wolf, F., Mohr, B., Mey, D. (eds.) Euro-Par 2013. LNCS, vol. 8097, pp. 826–837. Springer, Heidelberg (2013). doi:10.1007/978-3-642-40047-6_82
23. Wang, W., Xu, L., Cavazos, J., Huang, H.H., Kay, M.: Fast acceleration of 2D wave propagation simulations using modern computational accelerators. PLoS ONE **9**(1), 1–10 (2014)
24. Wong, D.C., Kuck, D.J., Palomares, D., Bendifallah, Z., Tribalat, M., Oseret, E., Jalby, W.: Vp3: a vectorization potential performance prototype. In: Workshop on Programming Models for SIMD/Vector Processing, February 2015

Hardware Support for Scratchpad Memory Transactions on GPU Architectures

Alejandro Villegas[1]($\boxtimes$), Rafael Asenjo[1], Angeles Navarro[1], Oscar Plata[1], Rafael Ubal[2], and David Kaeli[2]

[1] Department of Computer Architecture, University of Málaga, Andalucía Tech, 29071 Málaga, Spain
{avillegas,asenjo,magonzalez,oplata}@uma.es
[2] Department of Electrical and Computer Engineering, Northeastern University, Boston, MA, USA
{ubal,kaeli}@ece.neu.edu

Abstract. Graphics Processing Units (GPUs) have become the accelerator of choice for data-parallel applications, enabling the execution of thousands of threads in a Single Instruction - Multiple Thread (SIMT) fashion. Using OpenCL terminology, GPUs offer a global memory space shared by all the threads in the GPU, as well as a low-latency local memory space shared by a subset of the threads. The latter is used as a scratchpad to improve the performance of the applications.

We propose GPU-LocalTM, a hardware transactional memory (TM), as an alternative to data locking mechanisms in local memory. GPU-LocalTM allocates transactional metadata in the existing memory resources, minimizing the storage requirements for TM support. In addition, it ensures forward progress through an automatic serialization mechanism. In our experiments, GPU-LocalTM provides up to 100X speedup over serialized execution.

Keywords: Transactional memory · Scratchpad memory · GPGPU

1 Introduction

Graphics Processing Units (GPUs) have been adopted as hardware accelerators given their ability to significantly improve the performance of data-parallel applications. Using OpenCL terminology, GPUs are organized as a set of highly multi-threaded Single Instruction - Multiple Thread (SIMT) cores called compute units (CUs) and feature two different memory spaces. The *global memory* space provides high capacity with high latency. In contrast, the *local memory* space (named *shared memory* in CUDA terminology) features a smaller capacity with lower latency. Programmers are encouraged to use local memory as a scratchpad to speedup their applications (in fact, 27 out of the 52 sample applications in the AMD APP SDK for OpenCL prove the benefit from using local memory).

© Springer International Publishing AG 2017
F.F. Rivera et al. (Eds.): Euro-Par 2017, LNCS 10417, pp. 273–286, 2017.
DOI: 10.1007/978-3-319-64203-1_20

Transactional Memory (TM) [6,7] has emerged as a promising alternative to locking mechanisms to coordinate concurrent threads. TM provides the concept of a transaction to determine the bounds of a critical section (usually providing TX_Begin and TX_Commit functions) enforcing atomicity and isolation. In contrast to traditional lock-based mechanisms, transactions are allowed to run in parallel. A conflict occurs if two transactions have to access to the same memory location and, at least, one of the accesses is a write. In such situations, one of the transactions aborts, discarding its updates to memory and restarting its execution. This is achieved by implementing appropriate conflict detection and version management mechanisms. Recently, TM solutions have been proposed for GPU global memory, both software [2,8,10,12] and hardware [3–5].

Motivating Example. The left side of Fig. 1 shows the traditional implementation of a spinlock. In the SIMT programming model, as threads execute in lockstep, only one of them is able to get the lock and leave the while-loop (line 1). As there is a divergence in the execution of the program, the SIMT programming model sets a convergence point at the end of the while-loop (line 2), creating an implicit barrier. This implicit barrier forces the thread who acquired the lock to wait for the rest to finish the execution of the while-loop. This will never happen, as the lock is held by the waiting thread and the remaining threads will not leave the while-loop until the lock is released. Thus, the classic spinlock creates a deadlock in the SIMT programming model. The central part of Fig. 1 shows the required transformation for this spinlock to work. In this case, all the active threads enter the while-loop (line 2). The convergence point (i.e., implicit barrier) for this loop is set in line 8, which will be eventually reached by all the threads. Then, only one of the threads acquires the lock (line 3) inside an if-statement. In this case, the convergence point is set at line 7. This way, the threads that did not acquire the lock perform the implicit barrier at line 7, while the thread that acquired the lock executes its critical section (line 4), sets itself to go to the convergence point of the while-loop (line 5), and releases the lock (line 6). With this code transformation we can safely implement coarse-grained locks in the SIMT programming model.

```
1 while (!getLock()){;}      1 bool done = false;
2                            2 while (!done){
3 //Critical Section         3    if (getLock()){         1 TX_Begin();
4 releaseLock();             4       //Critical Section   2    //Critical Section
                             5       done = true;          3 TX_Commit();
                             6       releaseLock();
                             7    }
                             8 }
```

Fig. 1. Coarse-grained lock implementation in CPUs (left), its required transformation to avoid deadlocks in the SIMT programming model (center), and the TM-based solution (right).

Using a coarse-grained lock creates an inefficient serialization of the execution of the critical sections. Fine-grained locks can help improving parallelism, but its use is complicated and error-prone. Furthermore, its implementation can be harder in the SIMT programming model, as transformations similar to the ones shown in Fig. 1 are required in order to avoid deadlocks and livelocks. In addition, the use fine-grained locks is application-specific and a generic template can not be provided. Thus, it is hard to implement automatic code transformations similar to the one explained above. Given these problems, TM has been proposed to both improve parallelism of the applications and ease programming. The right side of Fig. 1 shows how simple is the implementation of mutual exclusion using the TM interface. In order to discuss the performance of the TM implementation, the applications Hash Table (HT) and Genetic Algorithm (GA) (see Sect. 5 for a full description) were implemented on a GPU using fine-grained locks (FGL) as well as with TM to coordinate the execution of 256 threads (*work-items* in OpenCL terminology). The implementation of these applications were done taking advantage of the low-latency provided by the local memory. HT is a simple application and the 3 implementations require a similar programming effort. Both the FGL and TM versions outperform the serial execution (90X and 60X, respectively). To implement GA using a FGL approach, lock acquisition has to be serialized to avoid deadlocks, requiring more programming effort. Also, execution time increases by 30% due to lock management overhead. However, a TM-based solution halves the execution time and requires a similar programming effort as a serial implementation.

This paper introduces GPU-LocalTM, a lightweight hardware TM for local memory. The goal is to use TM as an efficient alternative to existing methods (i.e., locks). GPU-LocalTM is designed in a way that reuses existing memory resources (if active), and can be disabled (if not needed). The conflict detection and version management mechanisms are distributed per local memory bank, improving concurrency. Lastly, GPU-LocalTM implements an automatic serialization mechanism that ensures forward progress of the transactions without the need of any programmer action.

The rest of the paper is organized as follows. Section 2 provides the background and discusses the related work. Section 3 presents the design of GPU-LocalTM. Section 4 presents the simulation framework used for evaluation, and Sect. 5 discusses the experimental evaluation. Finally, Sect. 6 draws the conclusions.

2   Background and Related Work

Baseline GPU Architecture. We use OpenCL terminology to describe our baseline GPU architecture, which is the AMD's Southern Islands [1] (see Fig. 2). An *ultra-threaded dispatcher* assigns *work-groups* (work-groups are a set of computing threads called *work-items*) to the *Compute Units* (CUs). A work-group is assigned to a single CU, but a CU may contain several work-groups. This architecture supports a maximum of 256 work-items per work-group. This set of work-items are grouped in 4 *wavefronts* of 64 work-items executing in lockstep. Wavefronts are the schedulable unit within the CU. All work-groups share data through the physical *global memory* available on the GPU. Work-items within a work-group have access to the *local memory*, a low-latency memory used to speedup applications. Each CU contains a wavefront scheduler, 4 SIMD units (consisting of vector ALUs and general purpose vector registers), a scalar unit (with a scalar ALU and general purpose scalar registers), a local data share (LDS) unit and a L1 data cache.

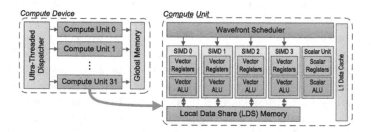

Fig. 2. Baseline GPU architecture: AMD's Southern Islands.

The LDS unit, which contains the *local memory*, deserves special attention as it is a key component in the GPU-LocalTM design. The LDS included in each CU features 64 KB distributed across 32 banks with interlaced addressing (consecutive memory addresses map to consecutive banks). Each work-group is allowed to use only 32 KB, leaving the other 32 KB reserved for concurrent work-group execution. The LDS unit is in charge of managing this local memory. The accesses to local memory issued by a wavefront are scheduled by the LDS unit, supporting up to 32 coalesced (i.e., without bank conflicts) accesses simultaneously. Uncoalesced memory accesses are serialized by the LDS unit.

Related Work. To the best of our knowledge, Kilo TM [3–5] is the only existing hardware TM for GPUs. Kilo TM [5] operates on global memory and implements conflict detection and version management at commit time (lazy) using a specific Commit Unit. Kilo TM was improved by considering read-only transactions and reducing bus communication [4], and to detect conflicts before sending transactions to the Commit Units and to stall transactions that are likely to conflict [3].

In our proposal, we target different applications: Kilo TM addresses applications that synchronize at global memory and our proposal supports synchronization at local memory. Both memory spaces have different purposes and very different characteristics. For instance, the difference in latency of both memory spaces affects application performance, even if they do not use any TM support. Once both TM approaches are integrated, applications can be developed taking full advantage of the complete GPU memory model. In addition, we explore eager (at memory access time) conflict detection and version management, in contrast to the lazy Kilo TM approach, by adding logic to the LDS unit instead of having a new dedicated unit for TM.

There are a number of software TM proposals for GPUs which only use the global memory space. Cederman *et al.* proposes two STM systems for graphics processors [2], operating at work-group granularity. Xu *et al.*, Holey *et al.*, and Shen *et al.* propose different STM approaches working at work-item granularity [8, 10, 12].

3   GPU-LocalTM Design

GPU-LocalTM is a hardware TM for GPU local memory. Transactional execution, conflict detection, and, version management are implemented with minor logic modifications in the wavefront scheduler, SIMD and LDS units. Required space is taken from the scalar register file and the local memory banks.

Transactional SIMT Execution. In our baseline architecture, control flow of the SIMT programming model is implemented with predication, using two 64-bit masks managed by the hardware and the compiler. The *execution mask* (EXEC) indicates, per wavefront, the work-items that are running or disabled (one bit per work-item). The *vector comparison mask* (VCC) stores, for each work-item within the wavefront, the resulting Z flag of arithmetic/logic operation. By combining EXEC and VCC, compilers implement loops and conditionals. The VCC and EXEC masks are mapped into two consecutive 32-bit scalar registers each one (four 32-bit registers in total) [1].

In order to define the bounds of a transactional block of code, we add two instructions to the ISA: TX_Begin and TX_Commit (see Fig. 1). These instructions work at a wavefront granularity as work-items within the wavefront execute in lockstep. Local memory operations performed between these instructions are *transactional* and are instrumented via hardware for conflict detection and version management. The TX_Begin sets the beginning of the transaction. When the TX_Commit instruction is reached, the transactional SIMT execution is responsible for restarting the execution of the conflicting work-items (if any).

To implement this, we introduce a new 64-bit *transaction conflict mask* (TCM) per wavefront (one bit per work-item). Similarly to EXEC and VCC masks, TCM is mapped to two consecutive scalar registers. TCM is used to mark conflicting work-items. The reason for not reusing EXEC is that it is explicitly managed by the compiler [1] and allowing implicit hardware modifications can lead to inconsistent situations. When the work-items within a wavefront execute the TX_Begin instruction, the TCM mask is reset (all bits to 0, meaning that no conflict occurred). If a work-item detects a conflict the corresponding bit in TCM is set to 1. When this bit is 1, it indicates the such work-item is disabled (i.e., the enabled work-items are those whose EXEC bit is 1 and whose TCM bit is 0). If all the TCM bits are 0 when the TX_Commit instruction is reached, then all transactions have finished with no conflicts. In other case, conflicting transactions must retry the execution by copying TCM to EXEC and returning to the TX_Begin instruction (and, again, TCM is reset).

Instruction	EXEC	TCM	Comments
TX_Begin	111...1	000...0	Wavefront starts transactions.
Mem Access	111...1	010...0	Conflict detected by WI 1, which is disabled.
TX_Commit	111...1	010...0	Transactions of all WIs but 1 end. Wavefront rollbacks and restarts WI 1 (TCM is copied to EXEC).
TX_Begin	010...0	000...0	Only WI 1 retries transaction
...	010...0	000...0	No new conflicts detected.
TX_Commit	010...0	000...0	Transaction of WI 1 ends. All transactions complete.

Fig. 3. Example of transactional SIMT execution. A work-item (WI) is enabled if EXEC[WI] & !TCM[WI]. Single lines separate transaction executions.

Figure 3 shows an example of transactional execution using TCM. In this example, during the execution of the transactions, work-item 1 detects a conflict, is marked by setting its bit in TCM, and is disabled immediately. At commit time, the rest of work-items successfully complete their transactions and wait while work-item 1 is restarted. This second time, work-item 1 is able to complete.

Forward Progress. A livelock situation can be detected if the TCM remains the same after two consecutive transaction re-executions. This means that two or more work-items were not able to progress, creating an infinite loop. To resolve this without requiring programmer action, GPU-LocalTM includes a two-level serialization mechanism: *wavefront serialization (WfS) mode* and *work-group serialization (WgS) mode*.

The basic WfS mode is enabled when a livelock situation is first detected. In this mode, the transaction is retried a third time but, instead of clearing TCM at the beginning of the transaction execution, only one of the active bits is reset. This action results in the execution of the only selected work-item within the wavefront during the next transaction retry (i.e., the rest are already marked as conflicting). If the execution ends with no new conflicts, the transaction is again retried but in normal mode (i.e., not using WfS). Otherwise, the conflict may come from a work-item that belongs to a different wavefront. In such situations, the basic WfS mode transfers to the basic WgS mode. In this mode, only the current wavefront re-executes transactionally. Transactions executing in other wavefronts are aborted, rolled back and stalled at the *TX_Begin* instruction until the selected work-item ends execution. Now that a single work-item within the work-group is accessing local memory, no conflicts can occur and forward progress is assured. After this execution, the transaction returns to normal mode and the stalled wavefronts are allowed to continue execution.

Version Management. GPU-LocalTM uses eager version management, where new local memory values are stored in place while old values are saved on the side. Specifically, old values are stored in a memory area called *shadow memory*, allocated in local memory. These values are used to restore the original state of the local memory in case of a transaction abort. As the local memory is multi-banked (32 banks in the case of our baseline GPU architecture), version

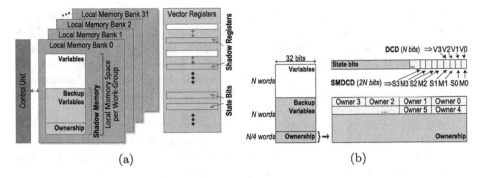

Fig. 4. Version management (LDS unit) and register checkpointing (SIMD units) (a) and shadow memory organization (b).

management and conflict detection can be carried out concurrently in different banks (i.e., there is a shadow memory per bank). The shadow memory area is organized in two spaces (see Fig. 4(a)): a backup space with enough room to store backups for all of the local memory variables declared within the kernel allocated in each bank, and an ownership space.

The shadow memory is organized as in Fig. 4(b): if there is a set of N words in local memory, a contiguous section of N words is allocated to backup the values, and after this section, $N/4$ additional words are reserved to store the owners. Each word in the ownership region stores 4 owners (1 byte each). Given this layout, when a memory access is issued to a location k, a backup value is stored at word position $N + k$, and the work-item ID (owner) is stored at word position $2N + k/4$, byte $k\%4$. By adopting this scheme, the hardware required to backup a memory value and store its owner is minimal, as it only performs integer addition and bit manipulation. In addition, capacity conflicts are avoided, as each memory location is ensured to have space for its backup. The shadow memory area is statically allocated by the compiler using the same mechanism used for regular local memory variables [1,11].

Register Checkpointing. When starting a transaction (TX_Begin instruction), the user-visible non-memory work-item state must be saved (and restored on transaction abort). This includes vector and scalar registers. Vector registers are checkpointed to a *shadow register* file. This is implemented by splitting the vector register file in each SIMD unit into two equally sized parts. Every two registers, one for each part, are paired together so as one of them acts as the backup (shadow) register of the other (see Fig. 4(a)). Scalar registers, on the other hand, are used to store scalar shared data for an entire wavefront, such as a for-loop index. As this information is shared by 64 work-items, if some of them commit their transactions while others abort, the value held by scalar registers become inconsistent. For this reason, scalar registers are not checkpointed at the beginning of a transaction. To allow for loops within a transaction, the compiler must promote the use of work-item-private vector registers.

Conflict Detection. GPU-LocalTM performs eager conflict detection at a work-item level. During the transactional execution of a wavefront, the LDS unit serializes all local memory accesses so that, at a given time, a memory bank is accessed by only one work-item. Parallel accesses to different banks do not present conflicts, as the banks have different address ranges. Assuming a multi-bank arrangement, conflict detection proceeds in two steps:

(1) *Intra-bank conflict detection:* conflicts are detected for memory accesses within a bank. The conflict detection mechanism works in parallel for all memory banks. This step is responsible of updating TCM, setting to 1 the bits for those work-items involved in a conflict.

(2) *Inter-bank conflict communication:* once a conflict is detected in a memory bank, it is communicated to the rest of banks in order to remove the shadow memory entries allocated for the conflicting work-item. This is accomplished through the TCM, avoiding the need of an expensive broadcast communication. TCM informs to each memory bank which work-items detected conflicts (bits set to 1). For each one of these work-items, all the backups are restored and the associated shadow memory is cleared.

We have designed two strategies for intra-bank conflict detection (inter-bank conflict communication is common for both approaches).

Directory-Based Conflict Detection (DCD). In order to detect conflicts, the DCD mechanism checks the ownership information associated to the memory location being accessed. Valid bit V, required to differentiate empty and non-empty entries, is stored in vector registers. The number of V bits required is equal to the number of words allocated in each bank (see Fig. 4(b)). Provided that N words are allocated, $N/32$ vector registers are needed to store the V bits. Depending on the result of the check, three actions may occur (see Table 1(a)):

(1) *First (new) access:* the shadow memory entry has no owner associated (valid bit V is 0). A copy of the current value of the memory location is stored in the corresponding shadow memory entry and its owner is set to the work-item that made the access (now V is set to 1).

(2) *Repeated access:* the owner of the shadow memory entry is the accessing work-item. If the access is a read, the value in memory is returned. If it is a write, the memory is updated.

(3) *Conflict:* the owner of the shadow memory entry is a different work-item than the one that made the access. TCM is updated to mark this conflict, setting to 1 the bit of the work-item accessing to memory. In addition, the backup values of the accessing work-item are restored and all ownership entries in the shadow memory for WI are deleted.

DCD is a simple and precise approach for detecting conflicts, but at the cost of an additional local memory access to check the ownership records. Note that this mechanism cannot filter out read-read conflicts.

Table 1. Conflict detection using DCD (a) and SMDCD (b). WI is the accessing work-item, o-WI is other work-item, "0/1" means 0 or 1. "Abort" means the following actions: restore backup for WI, delete WI ownership entries and set TCM[WI] = 1.

Current State		Mem.	Next State		Action
Owner	V	Operat.	Owner	V	
Not set	0	Read or Write	WI	1	back up value; read or write mem.
WI	1	Read or Write	WI	1	read or write memory
o-WI	1	Read or Write	o-WI	1	conflict; abort

(a)

Current State			Mem.	Next State			Action
Owner	S	M	Operat.	Owner	S	M	
Not set	1	1	Read	WI	0	0	read memory
			Write	WI	0	1	back up value; write memory
WI	0	0/1	Read	WI	0	0/1	read memory
			Write	WI	0	1	write memory
WI	1	0	Read	WI	1	0	read memory
			Write	WI	1	0	Conflict (R→W); abort
o-WI	0/1	0	Read	o-WI	1	0	read memory
			Write	o-WI	0/1	0	Conflict (R→W); abort
o-WI	0	1	Read	o-WI	0	1	Conflict (W→R); abort
			Write	o-WI	0	1	Conflict (W→W); abort

(b)

Shared-Modified DCD (SMDCD). The DCD mechanism can be improved by adding two state bits per memory location to the ownership records: the S bit, set to 1 if multiple work-items accessed the location, and the M bit, set to 1 if the location has been written. These bits replace the valid bit (V) (see Fig. 4(b)) and permit to filter out read-read conflicts. In this case, provided that N words are allocated per memory bank, $N/16$ 32-bit vector registers are used to store this information. The new mechanism is called *Shared-Modified Directory-based Conflict Detection* (SMDCD).

The case of both state bits set to 1 at the same time is used to encode the "not set" (i.e., $V = 0$) owner state. This way, when starting a transaction (TX_Begin), both S and M are set to 1. For each transactional access to local memory, the SMDCD mechanism carries out the actions specified in Table 1(b). Accessing a memory location for the first time sets the owner in shadow memory and performs a backup of the current memory value if the access is a write (bit M permits to distinguish between reads and writes). A read access to memory location owned by a different work-item is allowed as long as M is 0. These accesses set the S bit to 1. If M is, however, 1, a conflict is detected (read after write). A write access is allowed only if the owner is the accessing work-item and the memory location was not accessed by another work-item (bit S set to 0). These accesses set the M bit to 1. Otherwise, they are considered conflict (write after read, or write after write).

4   GPU-LocalTM Modeling

The implementation of GPU-LocalTM requires changes to the GPU microarchitecture. We have implemented these changes using the Multi2sim 4.2 simulation framework [11] which supports the AMD Southern Islands family of GPUs. These changes introduce memory and latency overheads in the microarchitecture.

Latency Overhead. The TX_Begin and TX_Commit instructions are modeled as scalar instructions with an extra cycle of latency to manage the EXEC and TCM masks. Accesses to shadow memory are modeled as local memory accesses, plus an extra cycle used to manage the state bits.

Storage Overhead. Storage resources required in GPU-LocalTM are taken from those available in the CU. The amount of local memory available per work-group depends on the size of the shadow memory. If the user requests N words to store local variables, the shadow memory allocates another N words for backups and $N/4$ words for the ownership records (see Fig. 4). As the physical amount of local memory is 64KB, the maximum value of N is 29126 bytes and $N/4$ is 7282 bytes. This represents and overhead of ~56% of the total local memory space. Vector registers are used to store the state bits. In the case of DCD, we need to store a V bit per word, requiring a maximum of 228 registers This supposes ~0.3% of 65536 available. In the case of SMDCD, the number of registers needed doubles. The 4 TCMs required for a work-group (one per wavefront) use 8 scalar registers (two 32-bit registers for a 64-bit TCM, ~0.4% of 2048 available). GPU-LocalTM may require to use the full amount of physical memory (64KB) for memory-demanding workloads, reducing potential concurrency. GPU-LocalTM is designed with the principle of not adding extra memory resources and to be fully configurable: no TM-dedicated memory needs to be added and the amount memory available is not affected if no TM support is needed. Furthermore, the programmer (or compiler) can opt for a lock implementation if no resources are available for TM support, and the runtime can assign new work-groups to a different CU to improve concurrency.

5   Evaluation

We have designed eight TM benchmarks to evaluate GPU-LocalTM in specific scenarios. All the experiments execute a single work-group with the maximum number of work-items allowed (i.e., 4 wavefronts of 64 work-items each, for a total of 256 work-items). The benchmarks are implemented in 3 different versions: a TM version, a fine-grained locks (FGL) or atomics version, and a third version serializing the critical section. In addition, each application uses two different inputs to test different levels of contention: high contention (HC) and low contention (LC). Table 2 summarizes the descriptions of these workloads.

Note that the HT, IT, DB and QU implementations using atomics are simple and the programming effort is comparable to the use of TM. However, GA, KM, GC and VA require extra lock management for FGL (17%, 10%, 42%, and 22% of the total code, respectively). The DB and QU applications are prone to conflicts and are designed to stress the TM to understand the possible sources of overhead (i.e., they test the TM beyond its expected capabilities). The serialization of the critical section is implemented by delegating the work of the whole work-group to a single work-item.

Table 2. Characteristics of the applications used for evaluation

Bench.	Description	Bench.	Description
HT	Inserts elements in a hash table, searching for the desired position. Features short and read-only transactions	IT	Similar to HT, but uses an index to point to the desired position. Features short and read-modify-write transactions
VA	The Vacation workload from the STAMP [9] suite, adapted and evaluated for inputs that modify from 2–4 elements. Features long transactions with a low probability of conflict	GA	Genetic algorithm used to solve an optimization problem searching for the best solution by combining a set of possible solutions. Features long and read-modify-write transactions
GC	Decentralized Graph Coloring algorithm. Features read-only transactions	KM	Implementation of the K-Means clustering algorithm. Features long transactions with multiple memory accesses
DB	Simulates an in-memory database composed of multiple IT tables. Features multiple memory accesses	QU	Simulates the queue and dequeue operations on a concurrent queue. Features short transactions with a high probability of conflict

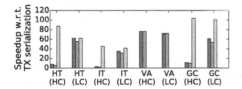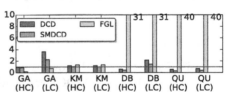

Fig. 5. Speedup w.r.t. TX. serialization (higher is better).

Speedup. Figure 5 presents the speedup achieved by the two different conflict detection strategies (DCD and SMDCD), fine-grained locks (FGL), and when serializing the critical sections. Performance is relative to serialized execution. In general, both DCD and SMDCD have similar performance. The exception are these applications with read-modify-write and read-only transactions that do not benefit from the SMDCD features. For the first set of applications (HT, IT, VA, and GC) both TM solutions and FGL outperform serial execution. The exception is VA when using FGL: the overhead of lock management is too high and such algorithm is not suitable for the use of fine-grained locks in a SIMT architecture. In the case of low contention scenarios, the performance of GPU-LocalTM is similar to FGL for applications such as HT and IT, and is in the same order of magnitude for GC. The second set of applications (GA, KM, DB, and QU) present a different scenario. As in VA, the extra lock management required for GA results in low performance when using FGL. For KM, GPU-LocalTM and FGL perform similar and close to the serial execution. The reason is that only 10% of the code of KM is able to take advantage of TM or FGL execution. DB and QU are challenging scenarios for GPU-LocalTM. The following metrics help to explain the reasons of their low performance.

Execution Breakdown. Figure 6 shows the execution breakdown using the two implementations of GPU-LocalTM. In all the scenarios, most of the overhead is introduced during the memory operations due to conflict detection and version management. As DCD aborts transactions on read-read conflicts while SMDCD waits until one of the memory operations is a write. Thus, in some cases, the overhead of SMDCD is larger as these conflicts are detected later. The overhead of TX_Begin and TX_Commit instructions is low and almost unnoticeable.

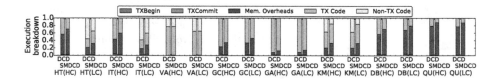

Fig. 6. Normalized execution breakdown.

Commit Ratio. Figure 7 shows the ratio of transactions committed over transactions started. In general, DCD and SMDCD conflict detection algorithms offer similar commit ratio. In the case of GA(LC), as transactions perform read-modify-write operations on the same memory location, DCD has some advantage over SMDCD as conflicts are detected during the read operation. GA, KM, DB, and QU suffer of a low commit ratio, harming performance (see Fig. 5). Future research will reduce the overhead of conflict detection in order to minimize the impact in performance of applications with a high probability of conflict.

Serialization Mechanism Evaluation. Figure 8 shows the percentage of transactions that proceed in transactional, WfS and WgS modes. Both DCD and SMDCD have similar results. We observe that many transactions (up to 90% in

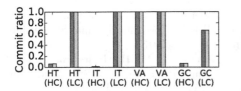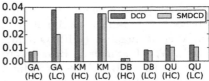

Fig. 7. Commit ratio (higher is better).

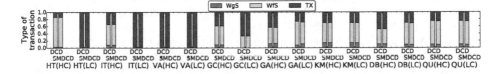

Fig. 8. Normalized transaction execution mode.

HT with high contention) need to make use of the serialization mechanism. The reason is that most of the conflicts continue to appear after a transaction retry due to lockstep execution.

6   Conclusions

In this paper we present GPU-LocalTM as a hardware TM for GPU architectures that focuses on the use of local memory. GPU-LocalTM is intended to limit the amount of additional GPU hardware needed to support TM. We propose two alternative conflict detection mechanisms targeting different types of applications. Conflict detection is performed per-bank, ensuring scalability of the solution. We find that for some applications the use of TM is not optimal and discuss how to improve our implementation for better performance. Furthermore, GPU-LocalTM introduces a serialization mechanism to ensure forward progress.

Acknowledgements. This work has been supported by projects TIN2013-42253-P and TIN2016-80920-R, from the Spanish Government, and P11-TIC8144 and P12-TIC1470, from Junta de Andalucia.

References

1. AMD: Southern Islands series instruction set architecture (2012)
2. Cederman, D., Tsigas, P., Chaudhry, M.T.: Towards a software transactional memory for graphics processors. In: 10th Eurographics Conference on Parallel Graphics and Visualization (EG PGV 2010), pp. 121–129 (2010)
3. Chen, S., Peng, L.: Efficient GPU hardware transactional memory through early conflict resolution. In: 22nd International Symposium on High Performance Computer Architecture (HPCA 2016) (2016)

4. Fung, W.W.L., Aamodt, T.M.: Energy efficient GPU transactional memory via space-time optimizations. In: 46th Annual IEEE/ACM International Symposium on Microarchitecture (MICRO 2013), pp. 408–420 (2013)
5. Fung, W.W.L., Singh, I., Brownsword, A., Aamodt, T.M.: Hardware transactional memory for GPU architectures. In: 44th Annual IEEE/ACM International Symposium on Microarchitecture (MICRO 2011), pp. 296–307 (2011)
6. Harris, T., Larus, J., Rajwar, R.: Transactional Memory, 2nd edn. Morgan & Claypool Publishers, San Rafael (2010)
7. Herlihy, M., Moss, J.E.B.: Transactional memory: architectural support for lock-free data structures. In: 20th Annual International Symposium on Computer Architecture (ISCA 1993), pp. 289–300 (1993)
8. Holey, A., Zhai, A.: Lightweight software transactions on GPUs. In: 43rd International Conference on Parallel Processing (ICPP 2014), pp. 461–470 (2014)
9. Minh, C.C., Chung, J., Kozyrakis, C., Olukotun, K.: STAMP: Stanford transactional applications for multi-processing. In: IEEE International Symposium on Workload Characterization (IISWC 2008), pp. 35–46 (Sept 2008)
10. Shen, Q., Sharp, C., Blewitt, W., Ushaw, G., Morgan, G.: PR-STM: priority rule based software transactions for the GPU. In: Träff, J.L., Hunold, S., Versaci, F. (eds.) Euro-Par 2015. LNCS, vol. 9233, pp. 361–372. Springer, Heidelberg (2015). doi:10.1007/978-3-662-48096-0_28
11. Ubal, R., Jang, B., Mistry, P., Schaa, D., Kaeli, D.: Multi2Sim: a simulation framework for CPU-GPU computing. In: 21st International Conference on Parallel Architectures and Compilation Techniques (PACT 2012) (2012)
12. Xu, Y., Wang, R., Goswami, N., Li, T., Gao, L., Qian, D.: Software transactional memory for GPU architectures. In: Annual IEEE/ACM International Symposium on Code Generation and Optimization (CGO 2014), pp. 1:1–1:10 (2014)

Parallel and Distributed Data Management and Analytics

Execution of Recursive Queries in Apache Spark

Pavlos Katsogridakis[1,2], Sofia Papagiannaki[1], and Polyvios Pratikakis[1(✉)]

[1] Institute of Computer Science,
Foundation for Research and Technology—Hellas, Heraklion, Greece
{katsogr,spapagian,polyvios}@ics.forth.gr
[2] Computer Science Department, University of Crete, Rethymno, Greece

Abstract. MapReduce environments offer great scalability by restricting the programming model to only map and reduce operators. This abstraction simplifies many difficult problems occuring in generic distributed computations like fault tolerance and synchronization, hiding them from the programmer. There are, however, algorithms that cannot be easily or efficiently expressed in MapReduce, such as recursive functions. In this paper we extend the Apache Spark runtime so that it can support recursive queries. We also introduce a new parallel and more lightweight scheduling mechanism, ideal for scheduling a very large set of tiny tasks. We implemented the aforementioned scheduler and found that it simplifies the code for recursive computation and can perform up to 2.1× faster than the default Spark scheduler.

1 Introduction

Modern analytics queries consist of complex computations operated on massive amounts of data. By restricting the programming model to only map and reduce, or equivalent operators, MapReduce [5] clusters scale out because they do not need to track task dependencies, have simpler communication patterns, and are tolerant to executor and even master node failures. However, this simplified programming model cannot easily express some applications, including applications with nested parallelism or hierarchical decomposition of the data. When faced with such algorithms, programmers often develop iterative versions that translate recursion into worklist algorithms. This may be inefficient as it introduces unnecessary barriers from one iteration to the next, and can be unintuitive and complicated to code.

The Barnes-Hut simulation [3] is an approximation algorithm for particle simulation with nested parallelism that cannot be easily expressed using flat map-reduce operators. In its simple two-dimensional version, the simulation first recursively splits the space into four quads and computes the center of mass for each, resulting in a tree structure that represents the whole space. In its second phase, it uses the tree of all the centers of mass to compute the forces applied to each body in the space. That reduces the N-Body problem complexity from $O(n^2)$ to $O(nlogn)$, by grouping all objects in distant quads into one force.

© Springer International Publishing AG 2017
F.F. Rivera et al. (Eds.): Euro-Par 2017, LNCS 10417, pp. 289–302, 2017.
DOI: 10.1007/978-3-319-64203-1_21

Figure 1 shows a simplified version of the recursive query that implements the second phase of the algorithm. Function `calcForces` traverses the tree computed during the first phase, to calculate all the forces applied to a single `particle`.

```
1  def calcForces(particle, tree) = {
2    if(isFar(particle, tree, THETA))
3      Array(force(particle, tree))
4    else
5      tree.map( child => {
6        calcForces(particle, child)
7      }).flatten
8  }
```

Fig. 1. N-Body recursive query

If the particle is far enough from all particles in the tree, then the total force can be computed using the center of mass of the whole space represented by the tree (lines 2–3). If the particle is near that space, then the function recurses to compute all forces applied to the input particle by each sub-tree (lines 5–7). This computation cannot be executed using the classic MapReduce abstraction, because it allows only flat map-reduce operations on the dataset. Assuming the `tree` argument is a distributed dataset, the map function would need to recursively apply a map-reduction to directly code the above algorithm.

In this paper we extend the Apache Spark MapReduce engine [18] to directly support such nested and recursive computations. Spark is an implementation of the MapReduce model that outperforms Hadoop [2] by packing multiple operations into single tasks, and by utilizing the RAM memory for caching intermediate data. We target Apache Spark because it is a widely used, efficient, state-of-the-art platform for data analytics, and currently the fastest-growing such open-source platform [4,13].

Spark expresses and executes in-memory fault-tolerant computations on large clusters using Resilient Distributed Datasets (RDD). RDD instances are immutable partitioned collections that can be either stored in an external storage system, such as a file in HDFS, or derived by applying operators to other RDDs. RDDs support two types of operations: (i) transformations, which create a new dataset from an existing one, and (ii) actions which return a value to the driver program after running a computation on the dataset. Examples of RDD transformations are *map* and *filter* operations, whereas *reduce* and *count* operations are typical actions. All transformations in Spark are lazy, which means that the result is not computed right away. Instead, Spark keeps track of all the transformations applied to the base dataset and they are only materialized when an action requires a result to be returned to the driver program.

Each RDD operator uses a User Defined Function (UDF) that manipulates the data. By default, this UDF is not itself allowed to operate on RDDs in Spark, as RDD objects and their dependency graph are allocated in the master node containing the Spark *scheduler* and *driver*, where the main program is executed, whereas UDFs are executed by the worker nodes containing the Spark *executors*. This restriction does not affect a large set of programs that do not use recursive computations. Moreover, even recursive computations can almost always be transformed to use a worklist and iteratively fixpoint, to bypass this restriction.

```
1  val file1 = sc.textFile("hdfs://file1")
2  val file2 = sc.textFile("hdfs://file2")
3  file1.map(word1 =>
4    file2.filter(word2 =>
5      (word1.length > word2.length))
6        .collect())
7    .collect()
```

Fig. 2. Example of nested RDD operations

That is, however, often ineffective in time and space, e.g., when not all recursive computations need to go to the same recursive depth, or when the created tasks are few and not load-balanced. Finally, refactoring a simple recursive computation into a worklist algorithm often introduces complexity and, with it, the possibility of errors. Barnes-Hut is an example of such a recursive application that cannot directly be expressed using the "vanilla" RDD abstraction, because it needs nested RDD operators to express the recursive function shown in Fig. 1.

This paper extends the Spark programming model and scheduler to support nested RDD operations, to facilitate expressing recursive and hierarchical computations. We implemented this by modifying the RDD scheduling mechanism in Spark and measured its performance. We found that recursive RDD operations can greatly simplify the code for algorithms of a recursive nature.

The current Spark driver does not optimally schedule such fine-grain tasks as it introduces comparatively large latency from the time one task finishes to the time another task is scheduled to execute on that executor node. As recursive and hierarchical decomposition of work tends to create small tasks, we designed and implemented an extension to the Spark scheduler that supports parallel, lightweight scheduling better suited for jobs with fine-grain tasks.

Overall, this paper makes the following contributions:

- We added support for nested RDD queries in the Spark scheduler and compare it against built-in operators implemented without nesting. To demonstrate the usability of the programming model extension we implement an N-Body particle simulation using the nested RDD mechanism.
- We modified the default Spark task-scheduling mechanism so that it can support many parallel light schedulers. We measured its performance against the default Spark scheduler, and found a speedup of up to 2.1× for computations using fine-grain tasks.

2 Spark Support for Nested Operations

Consider the example code shown in Fig. 2 that creates two RDDs from two HDFS files (lines 1–2) and performs a map operation on RDD `file1` (lines 3–7). The "mapper" function of the map operation performs a filter operation on RDD `file2` for every word in RDD `file1` to select all words of larger length. The calls to `collect()` are there to force the computation to take place and collect the results into an array, as otherwise RDDs would behave essentially like lazy futures. This is a simple example of nested operators.

By default, Spark does not support such nested RDD operations. This is mainly because the RDD metadata required to schedule new computations are stored only at the master node, with executor nodes simply running tasks assigned to them. This example could be easily encoded in SQL and resolved using a cartesian product. Our system, however, allows full recursion, where the map function could itself contain maps and be recursive. Moreover, using nesting we achieve better scheduling, and outperform standard Cartesian product by up to 7x, as shown in Sect. 4.

Handling nested RDD operators inside the user-defined functions of a map operation as shown in Fig. 2 (lines 4–6) requires the executor nodes that run the tasks of the outer RDD map operator (lines 3–7) to behave as the master node and schedule the "nested" filter job created in the mapper function (line 4). Adding such functionality to the executor nodes would greatly increase their complexity, as the RDD data would need to be replicated on executors, which would require maintaining RDD metadata consistent among all distributed copies of an RDD. Apart from being inefficient, this would undo the simplicity and efficiency of the MapReduce model. Thus, our design forwards the nested operators back to the master, to avoid a distributed scheduler setup.

In the example in Fig. 2, the outer collect method (line 7) will force the runtime to schedule the outer RDD computation. Since no shuffle operations are involved, the dependency DAG that Spark constructs to properly order consecutive RDD operations will consist of only one stage[1] that contains one transformation of the HadoopRDD `file1` to a MappedRDD returned by the `map` method. The Spark scheduler will try to submit this stage and since there are not waiting parent stages it will proceed with creating and submitting the missing tasks. Then the scheduler will create tasks that execute the mapper function (lines 4–6) for each word in the `file1` RDD. Specifically, the scheduler will serialize a closure of the mapper function and distribute it to the executors; then it will create a task for every partition of the `file1` RDD and send each task to an idle executor to run the mapper function on that partition and thus create the corresponding partition of the result RDD.

In the executor nodes, when the mapper function shown in Fig. 2 (lines 4–6) runs, it will try to invoke a filter operation on the `file2` RDD. We extended the executor functionality to capture this event and send a *CreateRDD* message to the scheduler node. The message contains an identifier of the RDD object referenced, the (reflective) name of the invoked operation, and a serialized version of the user-defined function that is applied.

We extended the Spark scheduler to receive such messages from the executors. Upon receiving such a forwarded RDD operation message, the scheduler looks

---

[1] In Spark, a stage is a set of consecutive operators that can be grouped and executed together, per partition.

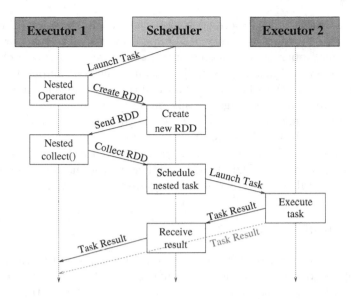

Fig. 3. Executor asks the scheduler to schedule a nested RDD operation (Color figure online)

up the RDD with the specified id and, using jvm reflection, invokes the specified operation. In the execution of the example code in Fig. 2 it will invoke the `map` method of the `file2` RDD, creating the desired RDD that describes the result. Note that, as RDDs are essentially futures in Spark, no computation will yet take place at this point. The scheduler then will simply send back to the executor an identifier of the created RDD. The executor, upon receiving that message, will create a proxy of that RDD object based on the identifier received, and use it to continue the computation of the mapper function for the task of the outer map operation on `file1`. When that mapper function calls `collect()` (line 6), the executor will send a *CollectRDD* message to ask the scheduler to collect the new RDD, using its identifier, and send back the result. Figure 3 shows the sequence of messages that will be sent for this example.

In the naïve master-executor protocol described above, the master schedules the nested job after receiving the CollectRDD message. When the nested job is done, it receives the result from all the executors where the job was scheduled, combines all partitions into a collected array, and sends the result to the executor that issued the nested operation. This would mean that there is an unnecessary transfer of data to the master node, and from there to the executor that issued the nested job. To avoid the transfer overhead that would also make the master node a centralized bottleneck for all nested computations, we modified the executor code to send the nested task result directly to the executor that issued the nested job (shown by the red dashed line) and also send an ack to the scheduler that the nested task finished, to free the executor resources. This way, the only transfer of data to the master is for `collect()` operations called at the master node in the top-level of the program.

Following the protocol described so far, the executor sends a CreateRDD message to the scheduler for every RDD operation that the mapper function of the `file1` map operation performs on `file2`. However, only the `collect()` operation requires the master to actually schedule a nested computation. This is because the Spark RDD abstraction is lazy and the operations are not computed immediately. We took advantage of this property by grouping all the nested operators into a single message. RDDs are both lazy and immutable, which permits us to pack all the RDD operator arguments in a per-executor global data structure. Then, at the end of a task or when a nested `collect()` is triggered, the executor sends all the RDD transformations to the master node, to create all the RDDs described and schedule any required computations.

3   Scheduling

Recursive decomposition of data tends to create many small tasks. Moreover, simple computations like summing or counting an RDD often result in many lightweight tasks where scheduling overhead is comparable to the actual task computation. Although computations rarely constitute the whole of a Spark program, they are often found within larger computations as, for instance, a stage in an analytics pipeline, or "inner" jobs in a Spark-nested program as described in the previous section. The default Spark scheduling algorithm underperforms for jobs like that, because:

1. The scheduling path is sequential, which means that if a job consists of many tiny tasks, scheduling itself will take a lot of time in the critical path of the computation, while the processing time will be negligible.
2. After a worker has finished a task, it sends a request message to the scheduler, so that the driver sends a new task to the worker. That increases the total time by at least one RTT for every task and every worker, since the scheduler receives and handles these messages sequentially.

These issues may be exacerbated when a large number of executors cannot be properly managed by a single, centralized Spark scheduler. To address this, we designed and implemented a parallel version of the Spark scheduler. We modified the Spark scheduler to send multiple tasks to each executor and amortize the idle time between tasks over many requests. This decreases the time between when a worker finishes a task and sends a message to the scheduler and when the scheduler answers with the next task to run. Specifically, we inserted a local task queue per executor, and modified the centralized scheduler to keep track of these coalesced task sets. Every time a worker core finishes a task, it first tries scheduling one of the tasks in the local task queue, and only generates network traffic and a request to the centralized scheduler if the local queue is empty.

Moreover, we modified the central Spark scheduler to schedule task-sets in parallel. Specifically, instead of using a single scheduler-master, we deploy a set of schedulers organized hierarchically as a set of *ProxyScheduler* actors under the standard Spark master node. The standard Spark scheduler creates a few large task-sets per job and sends them to the proxy schedulers; each proxy scheduler is then responsible for sending smaller task-sets or individual tasks to the executors. This reduces congestion at the master scheduler, occuring either because tasks are too small or because there is a large number of pending executor messages. We do not assign specific executor groups to the proxy schedulers, and instead allow all proxy schedulers to send work to all available executors. This works well in practice when the available work is much more than the executors, which is almost always the case in Spark analytics applications.

To schedule and track tasks to executors, each proxy scheduler keeps a copy of all the executor metadata that the standard Spark master normally maintains. This creates a consistency issue, as not all of these copies may be updated at the same time. We solve this by keeping all the "heartbeat" functionality Spark uses for tracking executor availability at the Spark master, and only forward information about executors from the master to the proxy schedulers. This means that at any given time the latest metadata about the state of one given executor's availability are at the master, and the metadata about all tasks in that executor's queue are distributed among all proxy schedulers that may have sent tasks to that executor.

To handle the case of executor state changes, the master scheduler sends a message to all proxy schedulers when the heartbeat process discovers that an executor has changed state. For example, when an executor is started, it sends a message to the master to inform that the executor is registered—as in the standard Spark scheduler. Then, the master broadcasts to all proxy schedulers the state of the newly registered worker. Eventually, all the schedulers will have the same view of the cluster state.

A similar problem of distributing copies of metadata occurs in tracking task completions. Specifically, the standard Spark scheduler uses *StatusUpdate* messages that contain information about whether a task has started, is executing, has finished, or has failed. In our distributed scheduler, these messages are sent from the workers to the proxy schedulers. The proxy schedulers eventually forward all *StatusUpdate* messages to the central Spark scheduler. We have not yet managed to recreate any cases where this creates a bottleneck; in that case we expect it would be straightforward to reduce the strain on the Spark scheduler by handling task completions and failures in the proxy schedulers without any forwarding of that information.

The standard Spark scheduler balances loads among executors by sending tasks only to the executors that have free cores. In avoiding the update messages by coalescing sets of tasks per executor and in allowing all proxy schedulers to send tasks to all executors, we have removed the load balancing guarantees of the standard Spark scheduler. However, we found that by tranferring some of the master functionality to the executors suffices in practice to give load-balanced executions.

Specifically, we use a best-effort approach for balancing task loads, where each executor locally schedules tasks from a queue to cores as they become available. The per executor local queue we inserted is visible by all executor threads. This means that in a case where an executor is loaded with some heavy and some light tasks, the threads executing the light tasks that will finish earlier, will dequeue and execute more tasks. Thus, when a job consists of some heavy tasks, even if they are scheduled on the same executor it is highly improbable that they will be executed by the same core.

Note however that this solution is best effort. In most cases given enough executor cpus the load will be equally balanced. In an extremely bad scenario where too many straggler tasks are scheduled into the same executor while the other executor takes all the lightweight tasks, the runtime will be highly affected. We tried to stress our best-effort solution by constructing benchmarks with highly-imbalanced tasks (Sect. 4, but were unable to create such a scenario in practice.)

4   Evaluation

We evaluated the performance of our scheduler using a set of micro-benchmarks and an operator from a real, large analytics application, that we were able to rewrite to use nested operators. The code for our scheduler and the micro-benchmarks is available at https://github.com/p01K/spark-nested.

We designed a set of micro-benchmarks to consist of non computationally demanding tasks, so that the scheduling overhead becomes a bottleneck. When such computations are used in analytics applications, it may not be feasible to create larger tasks, as the overhead of repartitioning is comparable to the scheduling overhead of fine-grain tasks.[2] The datasets contain integers or words, split into a defined number of partitions, and intentionally cached so that the tasks do not take extra time loading the data. We first invoke a count operation in all benchmarks, without counting it in the total run time, so that we ensure that the dataset is stored in memory. We ran each benchmark 15 times and measure the last 10 runs, so that the runtime is not affected by the JVM class loading, JIT compiling or other optimization techniques [6].

We used the following benchmarks:

- The filter benchmark generates a dataset of random numbers and returns those that are products of a defined number.
- The sum benchmark adds the dataset values using the reduce operator.
- The collect benchmark simply brings all the elements to the master node.
- The longtail benchmark simulates a taskset whose runtime follows a long tail distribution.
- The word count benchmark counts the references of each word.

We implemented our scheduler in Apache Spark 1.6.0. We ran all benchmarks on a cluster of 5 nodes, where each node has 4 Intel i5-3470 cores, 16 GB memory, and is running Debian Linux and OpenJDK7. The nodes are connected through

---

[2] We have encountered such small tasks in map and filter operations that operate on fine-grain partitions within larger workflows, in actual analytics applications.

1 GBs network. We measured the average round-trip time between any two nodes to be on the order of 0.1 ms.

We compare our scheduling algorithm with the default Spark scheduling. To have a valid comparison, we tried to use equal resources for scheduling and for task execution; the runs with default Spark use one node as a Spark master and 4 nodes as executors, while the runs with our distributed scheduler deploy all proxy schedulers together with the Spark master on one node, and use 4 nodes as executors. This way, both schedulers have exactly the same resources devoted to scheduling and to task execution.

We ran these benchmarks with a fixed number of elements (5M), and a variable number of partitions (64 to 8192) to measure how the number and granularity of tasks affects the runtime difference between the two schedulers. Figure 4(a) presents average running time of a simple filter operation on 5 million elements. The number of partitions of the input RDD is equal to the number of tasks. The y-axis shows the runtime in milliseconds. Our scheduler consistently outperforms the default Spark scheduler by at least 1.11× and up to 1.86×. Much of that difference seems to be a constant factor, which we believe is due to the reduction of worker idle time while waiting for the next task. As task granularity becomes smaller, both schedulers perform worse. The consistent performance "knee" observed for the default Spark scheduler at 512 tasks is not correlated with idle time in the worker cores nor network traffic measured, and could be due to partition migrations.

Figure 4(b) compares the default Spark scheduler to our distributed scheduler on a reduction that sums 5M random integers. The horizontal axis is the number of partitions that the dataset is distributed into. Reducing the number of messages and parallelization of scheduling gains a constant factor over the default Spark scheduler, resulting in 1.12× to 1.87× better performance. Figure 4(c) compares the two schedulers on simply collecting all the elements of a partitioned RDD to the master node. We observe the same behavior even when the task execution time is zero in this case, again due to the reduction in scheduling overhead and message latencies. To evaluate how well our best effort load balancing heuristic performs compared to the load balancing guarantees provided by the default Spark scheduler, we ran a microbenchmark that simulates tasks with highly different running times, following a long-tailed distribution. Figure 4(d) presents a comparison of the two schedulers on the long-tail benchmark. Again, the distributed scheduler achieves a speedup between 1.13× and 1.77× over the default Spark scheduler. This result is consistent accross executions with negligible variance; we expect that for executors with more than 4 cores it is highly unlikely that straggler tasks will cause imbalance and large latency in the total job execution time. Finally, Fig. 4(e) presents the comparison on a standard word count benchmark. Again, the distributed scheduler outperforms the default Spark scheduler by up to 2.15×.

We used the Cartesian product as a benchmark to compare the performance of nested queries versus flat queries. For the flat, non-nested version we used the cartesian RDD operator. Figure 4(f) compares the total running times between

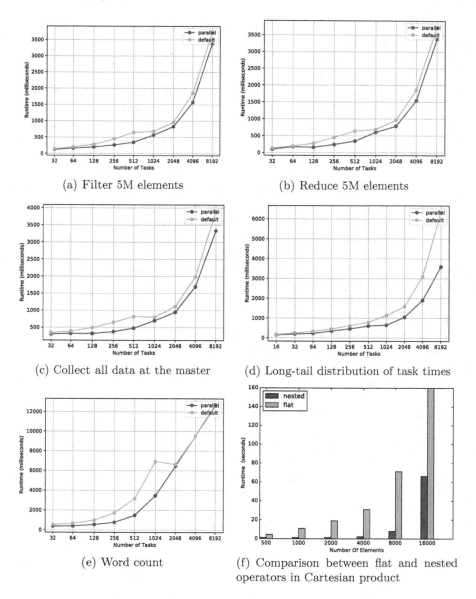

Fig. 4. Comparison with original Spark scheduler

the two versions. We found that writing a cartesian product as a two-level nested RDD operation parallelizes it into smaller but parallel jobs and achieves a total speedup of up to 8×, mainly due to the parallel scheduling of the work.

To demonstrate the programming expressiveness of using nested RDD operations we implemented the Barnes-Hut n-body gravity simulation algorithm using nested operators, and evaluated it for various numbers of data points, up to 8000

Dataset	Size	Nested	Flat
1 hour	46.45K	33s	39s
1 day	450MB	4m	4.4m
1 month	12.6G	57m	OOM
1 month	17.3G	1.5h	OOM
2 months	30G	3.8h	OOM

Fig. 5. Flat vs nested query

points	time (sec)
32k	3
64K	3.7
128K	7
256K	10
512K	20
1M	60

Fig. 6. N-Body

bodies. Note that there is no comparison against the default Spark scheduler as Barnes-Hut is recursive and thus not directly portable to flat MapReduce, without completely restructuring the algorithm to use explicit iterations and simulate a stack. Figure 6 presents the results.

To further evaluate the effect of nested queries, we used a (closed source, proprietary) analytics application used by a telecommunications provider to perform user characterization and classification from CDR data. We extracted a part of the full workflow that used nested loops to iteratively perform multiple map reductions, and rewrote it using nested map operators. Figure 5 presents a comparison on synthetic datasets of various sizes that closely match actual data[3]. The data sets used correspond to one hour, one day, one low-usage month and one high-usage month of data, while the last line uses a two-month dataset produced by concatenation of the two one-month datasets. We observed a large difference in scalability between the two versions. When the size of the dataset is relatively small, both versions execute in similar time, with the nested version having a small speedup. But for larger data sizes, the nested version executes successfully, while the flat terminates with OutOfMemory exception.

5 Related Work

Many analytics query execution engines use dataflow models and languages to express computations. Similar to Spark, Naiad [9] is a distributed data analytics engine for cyclic dataflow programs, Stratosphere [1] (now Flink), is a distributed data analytics engine aimed at stream analytics, and Hadoop is a map-reduce framework for large batch computations. Although all engines allow non-pure User Defined Functions in certain cases, none allow these computations to recursively include other queries(manually tried to use a MapFunction function inside a MapFunction function in Flink 1.1.2, which failed with a runtime error).

Spark supports the execution of SQL queries, which can be nested. Nesting of SQL statements, however, does not correspond to actual recursion in the

---

[3] Actual data was not available for analysis due to privacy constraints.

computed queries; nested SQL statements amount to simply sequenced computations. The same limitation applies to REX [8], which introduces a new programming model similar to SQL,, called RQL, that uses the notion of deltas (or small updates). Similarly, Datalog execution engines [14,15] can express queries on recursive relations in Spark. Although Datalog relations can be recursively defined and may correspond to fixpoint computations, they are closer to iterative fixpoints and do not amount to fully recursive computations; for instance it is not straightforward to express the Barnes-Hut n-body simulation in datalog, where the mapper and reducer functions apply themselves recursively in nested map-reductions.

The Spark default scheduler uses Delay scheduling [17] to send a task where its data are stored, before any available worker. Ousterhout et al. [11] propose Sparrow, a decentralized scheduling algorithm. The scheduling of a job is assigned to a random scheduler, that sends each task probe to 2 random workers. When the worker dequeues a task probe, it asks for the task binary from the scheduler and the corresponding scheduler sends the task to the worker that asks first. In comparison, our batching of small tasks simplifies the scheduling overhead and may have a probabilistically worse worst-case-scenario, although we did not observe this issue in practice. Moreover, solutions to straggler occurrence proposed by Ousterhout et al. [10] produce a lot of fine-grain tasks, decreasing that probability further.

Schwarzkopf et al. [12] present Omega, a distributed scheduling mechanism where each scheduler has full access to the cluster. Each scheduler is given a private, local, frequently-updated copy of the cluster state for making scheduling decisions. We chose not to replicate scheduling state between master and proxy schedulers, to avoid the complication of maintaining all copies coherent, thus introducing additional fail points in the scheduling algorithm. SkewTune [7] is a Hadoop extension that tries to eliminte skew in map reduce jobs. When SkewTune identifies a straggler it repartitions the remaining data, to increase parallelism. Yadwadkar et al. [16] describe a way to reduce straggler mitigation to multi-task learning. Their models can predict if a task will be a straggler, creating a separate model for each cluster node.

6   Conclusions

We present an extension of the default Spark scheduler that supports nested RDD operations and allows the programmer to express recursive computations intuitively. We demonstrate this by using it to implement the Barnes-Hut n-body simulation in Spark. We found that our extension of the RDD abstraction creates many small jobs, so we extended the default Spark scheduler with distributed scheduling to reduce scheduling overhead. We evaluated our system and found it outperforms the standard Spark scheduler by up to 2.15×.

Acknowledgements. This work was supported in part by the 7th Framework Programme of the European Community for Research, Technological Development and

Demonstration Activities (FP7) project ASAP (grant agreement 619706); and by the Horizon 2020 Framework Programme for Research and Innovation project ExaNeSt (grant agreement 671553).

References

1. Alexandrov, A., Bergmann, R., Ewen, S., Freytag, J.C., Hueske, F., Heise, A., Kao, O., Leich, M., Leser, U., Markl, V., Naumann, F., Peters, M., Rheinländer, A., Sax, M.J., Schelter, S., Höger, M., Tzoumas, K., Warneke, D.: The stratosphere platform for big data analytics. VLDB J. **23**(6), 939–964. http://dx.doi.org/10.1007/s00778-014-0357-y
2. Apache Software Foundation: Hadoop. https://hadoop.apache.org
3. Barnes, J., Hut, P.: A hierarchical O(N log N) force-calculation algorithm. Nature **324**, 446–449 (1986)
4. Databricks: Spark survey results (2015)
5. Dean, J., Ghemawat, S.: MapReduce: simplified data processing on large clusters. Commun. ACM **51**(1), 107–113. http://doi.acm.org/10.1145/1327452.1327492
6. Georges, A., Buytaert, D., Eeckhout, L.: Statistically rigorous Java performance evaluation. In: Object-oriented Programming, Systems, Languages, and Applications (2007). http://doi.acm.org/10.1145/1297027.1297033
7. Kwon, Y., Balazinska, M., Howe, B., Rolia, J.: SkewTune: mitigating skew in MapReduce applications. In: ACM SIGMOD International Conference on Management of Data (2012). http://doi.acm.org/10.1145/2213836.2213840
8. Mihaylov, S.R., Ives, Z.G., Guha, S.: Rex: recursive, delta-based data-centric computation. Proc. VLDB Endow. **5**(11), 1280–1291. http://dx.doi.org/10.14778/2350229.2350246
9. Murray, D.G., McSherry, F., Isaacs, R., Isard, M., Barham, P., Abadi, M.: Naiad: a timely dataflow system. In: Symposium on Operating Systems Principles (2013)
10. Ousterhout, K., Panda, A., Rosen, J., Venkataraman, S., Xin, R., Ratnasamy, S., Shenker, S., Stoica, I.: The case for tiny tasks in compute clusters. In: Hot Topics in Operating Systems, p. 14 (2013). http://dl.acm.org/citation.cfm?id=2490483.2490497
11. Ousterhout, K., Wendell, P., Zaharia, M., Stoica, I.: Sparrow: distributed, low latency scheduling. In: Symposium on Operating Systems Principles (2013). http://doi.acm.org/10.1145/2517349.2522716
12. Schwarzkopf, M., Konwinski, A., Abd-El-Malek, M., Wilkes, J.: Omega: flexible, scalable schedulers for large compute clusters. In: SIGOPS European Conference on Computer Systems (2013). http://eurosys2013.tudos.org/wp-content/uploads/2013/paper/Schwarzkopf.pdf
13. Shi, J., Qiu, Y., Minhas, U.F., Jiao, L., Wang, C., Reinwald, B., Özcan, F.: Clash of the titans: MapReduce vs. spark for large scale data analytics. Proc. VLDB Endow. **8**(13), 2110–2121. http://dx.doi.org/10.14778/2831360.2831365
14. Shkapsky, A., Yang, M., Interlandi, M., Chiu, H., Condie, T., Zaniolo, C.: Big data analytics with datalog queries on spark. In: ACM SIGMOD International Conference on Management of Data (2016). http://doi.acm.org/10.1145/2882903.2915229
15. Wang, J., Balazinska, M., Halperin, D.: Asynchronous and fault-tolerant recursive datalog evaluation in shared-nothing engines. PVLDB **8**(12), 1542–1553 (2015)
16. Yadwadkar, N.J., Hariharan, B., Gonzalez, J., Katz, R.H.: Faster jobs in distributed data processing using multi-task learning. In: SDM, pp. 532–540. SIAM (2015)

17. Zaharia, M., Borthakur, D., Sen Sarma, J., Elmeleegy, K., Shenker, S., Stoica, I.: Delay scheduling: a simple technique for achieving locality and fairness in cluster scheduling. In: European Conference on Computer Systems (2010). http://doi. acm.org/10.1145/1755913.1755940

18. Zaharia, M., Chowdhury, M., Franklin, M.J., Shenker, S., Stoica, I.: Spark: cluster computing with working sets. In: Hot Topics in Cloud Computing (2010). http:// dl.acm.org/citation.cfm?id=1863103.1863113

Replica-Aware Partitioning Design in Parallel Database Systems

Liming Dong[1,2(✉)], Weidong Liu[1], Renchuan Li[2], Tiejun Zhang[2], and Weiguo Zhao[3]

[1] Department of Computer Science and Technology, Tsinghua University, Beijing, China
dlm14@mails.tsinghua.edu.cn, liuwd@mail.tsinghua.edu.cn
[2] National Defense University of PLA, Beijing, China
hqxtgc@163.com, zhang_tj@126.com
[3] Army Logistics Information Center of PLA, Beijing, China
houjunzhaoweiguo@163.com

Abstract. In parallel database systems, data is partitioned and replicated across multiple independent nodes to improve system performance and increase robustness. In current practice of database partitioning design, all replicas are uniformly partitioned, however, different statements may prefer contradictory partitioning plans, so a single plan cannot achieve the overall optimal performance for the workload.

In this paper, we propose a novel approach of replica-aware data partitioning design to address the contradictions. According to the access graph of SQL statements, we use the k-medoids algorithm to classify workload into statement clusters, then we use the branch-and-bound algorithm to search for the optimal partitioning plan for each cluster. Finally, we organize replicas with these plans, and route statements to their preferred replicas. We use TPC-E, TPC-H and National College and University Enrollment System (NACUES) to evaluate our approach. The evaluation results demonstrate that our approach improves system performance by up to 4x over the current practice of partitioning design.

Keywords: Distributed database management system · Database design · Data partitioning · Workload clustering

1 Introduction

Partitioning design is an important topic to shared-nothing, parallel database systems. In such environments, data is partitioned across to multiple nodes, each of which is essentially an independent computer. In general, the communications and data movements between nodes are much more expensive than relational operations in one node. So a good partitioning plan should minimize them. The problem can be formally defined as [3]:

© Springer International Publishing AG 2017
F.F. Rivera et al. (Eds.): Euro-Par 2017, LNCS 10417, pp. 303–316, 2017.
DOI: 10.1007/978-3-319-64203-1_22

> Given a database **D**, a workload **W**, and a storage bound **S**, find a configuration **P** whose storage requirement does not exceed **S**, such that the $\sum_{Q \in W} f_Q \cdot \text{Cost}(\mathbf{Q}, \mathbf{P})$ is minimized.

Here, the Q is the statement in workload, and the f_Q is the weight of Q, it can be the multiplicity of Q in the workload, and $\text{Cost}(\mathbf{Q}, \mathbf{P})$ is the cost of statement Q if the database is partitioned by **P**. Many researchers have introduced a great deal of algorithms to search for the optimal partitioning plan [12–14], such as genetic algorithm, simulated annealing, hill climbing, branch and bound, etc. Even so, this problem is far from being resolved.

On one hand, different statements may prefer different partitioning plans, and those plans may mutually contradictory, so a one-size-fits-all partitioning plans cannot achieve the overall optimal performance for the workload.

On the other hand, in many real-world database systems, data is replicated to increase the robustness and availability, such as Microsoft SQL Azure [5] has 3 full database replicas, Amazon's Relational Database Service [4] has up to 5 read replicas of MySQL database, and Facebook's TAO also has 3 replicas of MySQL database [6]. In current practice of partitioning design, all replicas are uniformly organized. These two contradictory aspects motivate our research effort.

In this paper, we use multi-plan coexistence way to address this problem. In this fashion, replicas are organized by different partitioning plans heterogeneously, so different subsets of workload can be routed to different replicas for better performance.

The contributions of our work can be summarized as follows.

(1) We analyze the reasons for the contradiction of the statements. Our analysis reveals that the requirements for different attributes of the same table will result in contradictory partitioning plans.
(2) We propose an approach of replica-aware partitioning design. We leverage the access graph of SQL statement and database schema to measure the distance between statements, and use k-medoids to cluster the workload, and generate partitioning plan for each cluster, and organize replicas with these plans.
(3) We evaluate of our approach of Replica-Aware Partitioning Design (abbr. RAPD), and compare it with the Divergent Design [7], Schism [8], and the Current Practice of Partitioning Design (abbr. CPPD). The evaluation results demonstrate that our approach could increase system performance up to a factor of 4x compared with CPPD, and has a higher efficiency in the process of searching for partitioning plans.

2   Related Work

Many researchers have done a lot of outstanding work in replica-aware partitioning design, like the CliqueSquare [9], Divergent Design [7], and Trojan Data Layouts [11], etc.

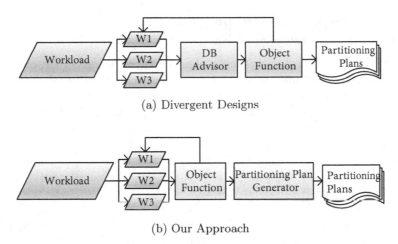

(a) Divergent Designs

(b) Our Approach

Fig. 1. Comparison of process flows for generating partitioning plans

Firstly, we have different process flow of generating partitioning plans (Fig. 1). They use the DB Advisor of DB2 [14] as a black box to generate partitioning plans, and iteratively evaluate the plans with an object function and repartition the workload until the plans satisfy some conditions. In contrast, we use data mining algorithms to classify the workload firstly, and use the branch-and-bound algorithm to search for the optimal partitioning plan for each subset of the workload. Secondly, we have different policy in dealing with the update statement, they assign the update statements in every cluster to generate partitioning plans while we use the *Query Completion* to address the update statements.

Jindal et al. proposed the Trojan Layout [11], we are different from them in 2 aspects: (i) they focus on improving the performance of Map phase of Map-Reduce jobs while we focus on data partitioning of distributed database systems, (ii) the Trojan Layout is designed for organizing data blocks of distributed file systems, and our approach is designed for organizing replications.

In addition to the works mentioned above, many researchers have done lots of works [8,12–15]. The biggest difference between us and them is that most of them treat the workload as a whole, and they did not take replicas into consideration to search for partitioning plans.

3   Motivation and Overview of Our Approach

In this section, we present the analysis of the contradictions which motivate our research effort, and provide an overview of our approach.

3.1   Analysis of Contradiction

Different SQL statements may prefer different partitioning plans. Assuming a table Table 1 has two attributes: *ID* and *Name*, and two query statements:

- SELECT * FROM table1 WHERE ID = '123456'
- SELECT * FROM table1 WHERE NAME = 'Michael'

Obviously, the optimal partitioning plans for these two query statements are contradictory. The first statement prefers Table 1 to be partitioned by *ID* while the second one prefers the table to be partitioned by *NAME*.

Although these contradictions can be partially addressed by creating more indices, but indices need extra storage and are very time consuming, so this limits the administrators from creating too many indices. Since we have full replications of tables already, then the contradictions can be addressed by organizing replications with different partitioning plans, more importantly, this will not increase the overall storage overhead.

In many real-world systems, many tables are connected by foreign keys, for example, TPC-E has 33 tables, 27 of which have a total of 50 foreign keys, that will lead to more prominent contradictions. In this paper, we make the assumption that two statements are contradictory if they access to different attributes of the same table.

3.2   Overview of Our Approach

Compared with [3], we take the replications into account, then the problem of replica-aware partitioning design can be define as:

Given a database $\mathbf{D}$, a workload $\mathbf{W}$, the number of replicas $\mathbf{N}$, and a storage bound $\mathbf{S}_i$ of each replica, find partitioning plans $\{\mathbf{P}_1 \ldots \mathbf{P}_n\}$ and workload clusters $\{\mathbf{W}_1 \ldots \mathbf{W}_n\}$, such that the $\sum_{W_i \in W} \text{Cost}(\mathbf{W}_i, \mathbf{P}_i)$ is minimized, and the storage requirement of $\mathbf{P}_i$ should not exceed $\mathbf{S}_i$.

The core idea of our approach is to cluster contradictory statements into different clusters ($\mathbf{W}_1 \ldots \mathbf{W}_n$), and generate partitioning plan ($\mathbf{P}_1 \ldots \mathbf{P}_n$) for each of them, then organize replicas with these plans. The $\text{Cost}(\mathbf{W}_i, \mathbf{P}_i)$ is the cost of cluster $\mathbf{W}_i$ when the replica is partitioned by $\mathbf{P}_i$.

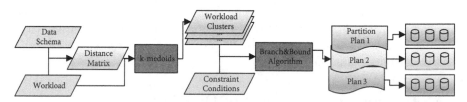

Fig. 2. Overview of our approach

Figure 2 shows the overview of our approach. Firstly, we traverse the workload and use data schema to get the distance matrix of statements. Secondly, we use *k*-medoids algorithm to cluster the workload. Thirdly, we use branch-and-bound algorithm to search the optimal partitioning plan for each statement cluster. Finally, we use these partitioning plans to organize replicas, and route each statement to the appropriate replica.

4   Clustering the Workload

The clustering algorithm we used is inspired by the well-known k-medoids, it has two important issues: the distance function and the number of clusters.

4.1   Distance Function

Many types of data can be used to measure the distance between statements [2,8,10,16]. Because the access graph can demonstrate the relationship between statements, so we use it to measure the distance of statements.

An access graph is derived from workload, it describes the relationship between a statement and the attributes (Example 1). If a statement Q accesses an attribute A, then the corresponding cell has a value of 1, otherwise it has a value of 0.

Example 1. A workload with 10 statements

	Q1	Q2	Q3	Q4	Q5	Q6	Q7	Q8	Q9	Q10
A1	1	1	1	1	0	0	0	0	0	0
A2	1	1	1	1	0	0	0	0	0	0
A3	0	0	0	0	1	1	1	1	1	1
A4	0	1	1	1	1	1	1	1	1	1

According to the analysis described in Sect. 3.1, we consider 2 types of access graphs.

Attributes Belong to Different Tables. In Example 1, attributes A1–A4 belong to different tables. For workload-driven algorithms which automatically generate partitioning plans [3,12–14], the smaller the difference in attributes that accessed by statements, the more likely they are to produce a better partitioning plan. So if the number of replicas is 3, then the cluster result is {{Q1}, {Q2, Q3, Q4}, {Q5, Q6, Q7, Q8, Q9, Q10}}, because in each cluster, all statements access the same attributes. Inspired by **CG-COST** [3], we use the co-accessed attributes to measure the distance.

Denote C_i is the number of attributes accessed by Q_i, and $C_{i,j}$ is the number of attributes that Q_i and Q_j co-accessed, then the distance is defined as:

$$dist1(Q_i, Q_j) = 1 - \frac{2 \cdot C_{i,j}}{C_i + C_j} \tag{1}$$

We can easily verify that the absolute-error criterion (Eq. 2) of the clustering result of Example 1 is minimal, where k is the number of clusters, and W is the workload.

$$E = \sum_{n=1}^{k} \sum_{Q_i, Q_j \in W_k} dist(Q_i, Q_j) \tag{2}$$

Attributes Belong to the Same Table. In the left table of Example 2, A2 and A3 belong to the same table, and other attributes belong to different tables respectively.

Example 2. A workload with 3 statements

	Q1	Q2	Q3		Q1 (500)	Q2 (200)	Q3 (700)
A1	1	0	0	A1	1	0	0
A2	1	0	1	**A2**	1	0	1
A3	0	1	0	**A3**	0	1	0
A4	0	1	1	A4	0	1	1
A5	0	1	1	A5	0	1	1

If the number of clusters is 2, then the cluster result is $\{\{Q1\}, \{Q2, Q3\}\}$. Because we can use Eq. 1 to calculate the distances of $Q1$–$Q3$ is 0.6, and $Q2$–$Q3$ is 0.33. However, $A2$, $A3$ are accessed by $Q2$, $Q3$ respectively, because $A2$, $A3$ belong to the same table, so this clustering result can lead to contradictory partitioning plans of the table which contains A2, A3. In this case, we introduce D_{ij}, it denotes the number of attributes belonging to the same table and accessed but not co-accessed by Qi, Qj. The distance is defined as:

$$dist2(Q_i, Q_j) = \frac{D_{ij}}{C_i + C_j} \tag{3}$$

If we add the *dist2* to *dist1*, then we can get the new distances of $Q1$–$Q3$ and $Q2$–$Q3$ is 0.6 and 0.67, so the attribute $Q3$ should be assigned with $Q1$.

Based on the above analysis, we can define the distance of Q_i, Q_j as:

$$dist(Q_i, Q_j) = dist1(Q_i, Q_j) + dist2(Q_i, Q_j). \tag{4}$$

Workload Compression. We can use Eq. 4 to compute the distance of any tow statements, then we get the distance matrix:

$$\mathcal{D} = \begin{bmatrix} 1 & & & \\ dist(Q_2, Q_1) & 1 & & \\ dist(Q_3, Q_1) & dist(Q_3, Q_2) & 1 & \\ \vdots & \vdots & \vdots & \ddots \\ dist(Q_n, Q_1) & dist(Q_n, Q_2) & \cdots\cdots & 1 \end{bmatrix} \tag{5}$$

However, in many cases, the workload is too large to fit into the memory. In these cases, we can compress all statements that access to the same attributes into one. For example, in Example 2, if there are 500 statements access to the same attributes as $Q1$, 200 statements access to the same attributes as $Q2$ and 700 statements access to the same attributes as $Q3$, then we can record this like the right table in Example 2. Similarly, in the computation of the distance matrix, the factors C_{ij} and D_{ij} also need to multiply the corresponding number.

4.2   The Number of Clusters

The most thorough way to resolve the contradictions is to generate partitioning plan for each statement of the workload [12], but this is infeasible and unnecessary, because there will be a great deal of problems under this circumstance, i.e. storage constraint, data consistency and hardware cost.

An appropriate value is the number of replicas, because we can use them without increasing the overall storage overhead and design complexity, and this is also consistent with our original idea. Therefore, we assume the number of clusters is equal to the number of replicas.

4.3   Clustering Algorithm

The input of the algorithm (Algorithm 1) is the attribute set A and the number of clusters k. Firstly, k statements are chosen randomly from the workload as the representative attributes (initial medoids) of k clusters ($o[k]$). Then the other statements are assigned to the cluster with the nearest distance. Afterwards, the algorithm iteratively replaces a representative statement c_i with a non-representative statement a and compute the $SwapCost$ until the representative statement set $o[k]$ does not change. In each iteration, if the $SwapCost < 0$, then a is the new representative statement of the cluster and reassign other statements, otherwise, the representative statement set is not changed. The $SwapCost$ is the difference between the new and the old absolute-error criterion (Eq. 2).

Algorithm 1. Statement Clustering

Input: W: Workload, k: the number of clusters
Output: k statement clusters
1: **function** ATTRIBUTECLUSTERING(W, k)
2:      $o[k]$← RandAttrib(W); Clusters[k] ← NULL
3:      **while** $o[k]$ is changed **do**
4:          **for all** $a \in (W - o[k])$ **do**
5:              Assign(a, Clusters[k])
6:          **end for**
7:          **for all** $c_i \in o[k]$, a $\in$(W$-o[k]$) **do**
8:              SwapCost=CalcCost(a,c_i)
9:              **if** SwapCost < 0 **then**
10:                  Swap(a,c_i)
11:              **end if**
12:          **end for**
13:      **end while**
14:      **return** Clusters[k]
15: **end function**

---

5 Generating Partitioning Plan

We use the branch and bound algorithm to search the optimal partitioning plan, which is designed for discrete and combinatorial optimization problems. The solution space is constructed to a tree structure, and the algorithm only expands the most promising node at each search stage.

The input of the algorithm (Algorithm 2) is the initial plan (RN) of a cluster, and the storage bound (B), and a cluster (W). We use DFS policy to choose the next tree node for expansion (NextNode). To improve the pruning efficiency and reduce the search time, we sort attributes and tables in descending order of the frequency of access. If the storage requirement of the new plan exceeds the constraint, then the new plan is pruned. Otherwise, we compute the cost of the new plan with the cost model [13], and if the cost of the temporary optimal plan (*OptimalPlan*) is greater than the cost of the new plan, then replace the temporary optimal plan with the new plan. The iteration ends when there is no partial plan can be partitioned, or a specified length of time has elapsed.

Algorithm 2. Branch and Bound Algorithm

Input: RN: Root node, B: Storage bound, W: Workload Cluster
Output: Partitioning Plan
 1: **function** BBSEARCH(RN, B)
 2:     $OptimalPlan \leftarrow null$; $CurrentPlan \leftarrow null$; $NewPlan \leftarrow null$
 3:     **while** (!$StopCondition()$) **do**
 4:         NewPlan= CreateChildPlans(NextNode(RN))
 5:         **if** storage requirement of NewPlan < B **then**
 6:             Cost=GetCost(NewPlan, W)
 7:             **if** NewPlan is a completed partitioning plan **then**
 8:                 **if** Cost < OptimalPlan.Cost **then**
 9:                     $OptimalPlan = NewPlan$; prune(NewPlan)
10:                 **end if**
11:             **else**
12:                 **if** OptimalPlan.Cost<Cost **then**
13:                     $prune(NewPlan)$
14:                 **end if**
15:             **end if**
16:         **else**
17:             $prune(NewPlan)$
18:         **end if**
19:     **end while**
20:     **return** $OptimalPlan$
21: **end function**

---

6 Routing Statements

In our approach, different replicas are organized with different plans, for a statement of workload, the response time may vary greatly when executed in different replicas. In order to forward each statement to its preferred replica, we use the triplet to maintain the mapping information of statement, workload cluster and replica.

$$< StatementID, ClusterID, ReplicaID >$$

On receiving a statement, the server can forward it directly by taking a lookup of the triplets, however, 2 types of statements need to be handled carefully.

6.1 New Statement

A *New Statement* is the statement that has never occurred in the process of clustering or generating partitioning plans. So the server cannot find the information of the statement in the triplets.

To forward this type of statement, we calculate the sum of the distances of this statement to each cluster firstly, that is $\sum_{s \in C_i} dist(n, s)$, where the n denotes the *New Statement*. Then, we can assign the *New Statement* to the cluster with the minimal value, and route it to the corresponding replica.

6.2 Update Statement

Different from query statement, the update statement has to be executed in all replicas. It can be time-consuming to execute the statement in the replica whose partitioning plan is generated without the statement. For example, three replicas are organized with *P1*, *P2*, and *P3*, and *P1*, *P2*, *P3* partition table *T* on attributes *C1*, *C2*, *C3* respectively. If the update statement only contains *C1*, then the replica which is organized by *P1* can complete the statement faster than the other replicas.

We present a method called *Query Completion* to address this issue. Figure 3 shows the process flow of an update statement. We update the replica which is partitioned by P1 (line 1) firstly, then construct a read-only query to retrieve corresponding tuples affected by former update query (line 2), and then complete the update query with C2 and C3, and send the completed statement to other replications finally (line 3).

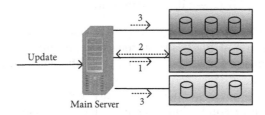

Fig. 3. Process flow of update statement

7 Experimental Evaluation

The main objective of our approach is to show that organizing replicas with different partitioning plans can improve system performance. So we carry out experiments to compare our approach (RAPD) with the current practice of single partitioning plan design (CPPD), Schism [8] and Divergent Design [7].

7.1 Data Sets and Experimental Platform

We choose TPC-E, TPC-H and a real-world system NACUES (National College and University Enrollment System) as the experimental datasets. The basic statistics are summarized in Table 1.

Table 1. Summary statistics of datasets

Data set	#Tables	#Attributes	#ForeignKeys	#Quereis	Size
TPC-E	33	188	50	12	40 GB
TPC-H	8	51	9	22	1 TB
NACUES	115	764	265	130	1 TB

TPC-E and TPC-H are widely used in many data management experiments. The real-world dataset NACUES is a system used by nearly 3000 colleges and universities in China to enroll students from all over the country. It contain scores, profiles, physical examinations, applications of students, basic information of colleges and universities and enrollment plans etc.

We use MyCat [1] as the distributed DBMS, which use MySQL as the underlying database. It supports distributed transaction, database partitioning, which can fully meet our experimental needs. We set up a cluster of 16 common commodity servers each with 32 GB RAM, 2 Intel Xeon-E5 processors and 2 TB hard disk, all servers are connected through 1000 Mbps LAN.

7.2 Proportion of Single-Site Statements

In general, single-site statement consumes less resources than multiple-site statement, so the proportion of single-site statement is an important measure of partitioning design. Figure 4 shows the proportion of different number of plans being deployed.

Obviously, the proportions increase rapidly with the number of partition plans, the underlying reason is that the contradictions in workload are gradually solved when more plans are deployed. The result means that our approach is effective to solve the contradictions in workload.

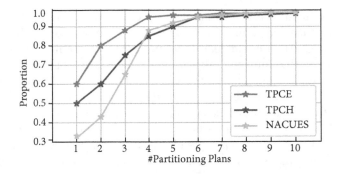

Fig. 4. Proportion of single-site statements

7.3   Performance of Our Approach

In order to evaluate the impact to system performance, we compare RAPD with the CPPD, Schism, and Divergent Design in different number of replications. We execute all of the statements (SQL) of different datasets and compare the execution times of these 4 approaches, the execution times is show in Fig. 5.

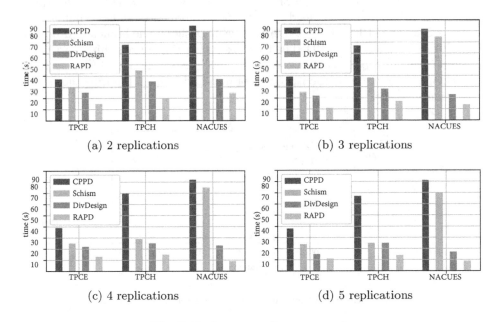

Fig. 5. Performance of our approach

On the whole, we can see that the execution time of all approaches except CPPD becomes shorter as the number of replications increases. The reason is that in CPPD, all replications have the same partitioning plan, so the executing time is not very sentitive to the number of replications. Also, we can see that the execution times are reduced substantially in our approach (RAPD). Take NACUES in Fig. 5(d) for example, it takes more than 80 s to finish the 130 queries of NACUES in CPPD, but only takes 9 s in our approach. The reason is that the more partition plans are deployed, the more contradictions of statements can be solved, and that will lead to the growth of the proportion of single-site statement, and result in the reduction of execution time of statements. Further more, we can see that RAPD is 1.5–2 times faster than Divergent Design under different number of replications, this means the clustering result of in RAPD can generate better partitioning plans, that is more efficient to resolve the contradictions of statements.

Also, we notice that the performance of Schism in NACUES is not as good as in TPC-E and TPC-H, the reason is that the access graph of NACUES created in Schism is more complicate than others, given the same number of vertices, the access graph of NACUES has far more edges than that of TPC-E and TPC-H, so the graph partition algorithm used in Schism cannot find a good way to partition the graph, leading to a limited improvement of system performance.

7.4   Comparison of Execution Time

To compare the execution time with Divergent Design, we carried out an experiment with TPC-E, the workload has 100–500 statements, and the number of replica is 3, and the Black-box used in Divergent Design is the branch-and-bound algorithm as we used in RAPD. The total execution time of searching partitioning plan of our approach is composed of the pre-processing and clustering time of workload, and the execution time of branch-and-bound. Figure 6 shows the experiment result.

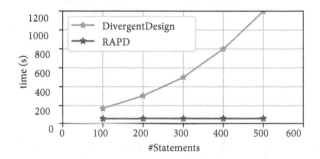

Fig. 6. Total execution time of searching partitioning plans

Compared with Divergent Design, the execution time of RAPD is much shorter, and is not affected by the number of statements. That is because RAPD cluster the workload first, and then search for the partitioning plans. Differently, in each of the iteration of workload clustering, Divergent Design needs to call the Branch and Bound algorithm, which is very time-consuming.

8   Future Work

Two of the most crucial issues of our approach are identifying contradictions and clustering the workload. There are only a slice of literatures on these two issues [12]. The analysis and assumption we made is only a tentative work, and the clustering algorithms of workload is quite straightforward. We would try other approaches in the future to make them more accurate, and formalized definitions and proofs are also our future work.

Another potential work is the algorithm of searching for the optimal partition plans. Although researchers have already conducted concrete work in this area, this problem is still far from being addressed. If the search algorithm cannot find a suitable partition plan, then different query clusters may conduct to similar partition plans, and we have encountered this phenomenon in our experiments of choosing algorithms.

9   Conclusion

In this paper, we present an approach of replica-aware partitioning design to resolve the contradictions in workload. Our approach uses access graph of statements to measure their distance and then cluster the workload and generate partitioning plans for each of them. By introducing the necessary modifications and data structures, replicas with different partitioning plans can work properly and more effectively. Through the experimental evaluation, we could see that our approach can improve system performance by up to 4x over the current practice of partitioning design.

References

1. Mycat (2017). http://www.mycat.org.cn/
2. Agrawal, S., Chaudhuri, S., Das, A., Narasayya, V.: Automating layout of relational databases. In: Proceedings 19th International Conference on Data Engineering, pp. 607–618. IEEE (2003)
3. Agrawal, S., Narasayya, V., Yang, B.: Integrating vertical and horizontal partitioning into automated physical database design. In: Proceedings of the 2004 ACM SIGMOD International Conference on Management of Data, pp. 359–370. ACM (2004)
4. Beach, B.: Relational database service. In: Beach, B. (ed.) Pro Powershell for Amazon Web Services, pp. 155–178. Springer, Heidelberg (2014)
5. Bernstein, P.A., Cseri, I., Dani, N., Ellis, N., Kalhan, A., Kakivaya, G., Lomet, D.B., Manne, R., Novik, L., Talius, T.: Adapting Microsoft SQL server for cloud computing. In: Proceedings of the 27th International Conference on Data Engineering (ICDE), pp. 1255–1263. IEEE (2011)
6. Bronson, N., Amsden, Z., Cabrera, G., Chakka, P., Dimov, P., Ding, H., Ferris, J., Giardullo, A., Kulkarni, S., Li, H.C., et al.: Tao: Facebook's distributed data store for the social graph. In: Proceedings of USENIX Annual Technical Conference, pp. 49–60 (2013)

7. Consens, M.P., Ioannidou, K., LeFevre, J., Polyzotis, N.: Divergent physical design tuning for replicated databases. In: Proceedings of the 2012 ACM SIGMOD International Conference on Management of Data, pp. 49–60. ACM (2012)
8. Curino, C., Jones, E., Zhang, Y., Madden, S.: Schism: a workload-driven approach to database replication and partitioning. Proc. VLDB Endow. **3**, 48–57 (2010)
9. Goasdoué, F., Kaoudi, Z., Manolescu, I., Quiané-Ruiz, J.A., Zampetakis, S.: CliqueSquare: flat plans for massively parallel RDF queries. In: Proceedings of the 31st International Conference on Data Engineering (ICDE), pp. 771–782. IEEE (2015)
10. Holmes, D.E., Jain, L.C.: Data Mining: Foundations and Intelligent Paradigms. Springer Publishing Company, Heidelberg (2012)
11. Jindal, A., Quiané-Ruiz, J.A., Dittrich, J.: Trojan data layouts: right shoes for a running elephant. In: Proceedings of the 2nd ACM Symposium on Cloud Computing, p. 21. ACM (2011)
12. Nehme, R., Bruno, N.: Automated partitioning design in parallel database systems. In: Proceedings of the 2011 ACM SIGMOD International Conference on Management of Data, pp. 1137–1148. ACM (2011)
13. Pavlo, A., Curino, C., Zdonik, S.: Skew-aware automatic database partitioning in shared-nothing, parallel OLTP systems. In: Proceedings of the 2012 ACM SIGMOD International Conference on Management of Data, pp. 61–72. ACM (2012)
14. Rao, J., Zhang, C., Megiddo, N., Lohman, G.: Automating physical database design in a parallel database. In: Proceedings of the 2002 ACM SIGMOD International Conference on Management of Data, pp. 558–569. ACM (2002)
15. Serafini, M., Mansour, E., Aboulnaga, A., Salem, K., Rafiq, T., Minhas, U.F.: Accordion: elastic scalability for database systems supporting distributed transactions. Proc. VLDB Endow. **7**, 1035–1046 (2014)
16. Zilio, D.C.: Physical database design decision algorithms and concurrent reorganization for parallel database systems. Ph.D. thesis. Citeseer (1998)

Cluster and Cloud Computing

A Simplified Model for Simulating the Execution of a Workflow in Cloud

Roland Mathá, Sasko Ristov$^{(\boxtimes)}$, and Radu Prodan

Institute for Computer Science, University of Innsbruck,
Technikerstr. 21a, 6020 Innsbruck, Austria
{roland,sashko,radu}@dps.uibk.ac.at

Abstract. Although simulators provide approximate, faster and easier simulation of an application execution in Clouds, still many researchers argue that these results cannot be always generalized for complex application types, which consist of many dependencies among tasks and various scheduling possibilities, such as workflows. DynamicCloudSim, the extension of the well known CloudSim simulator, offers users the capability to simulate the Cloud heterogeneity by introducing noisiness in dozens parameters. Still, it is difficult, or sometimes even impossible to determine appropriate values for all these parameters because they are usually Cloud or application-dependent. In this paper, we propose a new model that simplifies the simulation setup for a workflow and reduces the bias between the behavior of simulated and real Cloud environments based on one parameter only, the *Cloud noisiness*. It represents the noise produced by the Cloud's interference including the application's (in our case a workflow) noisiness too. Another novelty in our model is that it does not use a normal distribution naively to create noised values, but shifts the mean value of the task execution time by the cloud noisiness and uses its deviation as a standard deviation. Besides our model reduces the complexity of DynamicCloudSim's heterogeneity model, evaluation conducted in Amazon EC2 shows that it is also more accurate, with better *trueness* (closeness to the real mean values) of up to 9.2% and *precision* (closeness to the real deviation) of up to 8.39 times.

Keywords: Accuracy · Makespan · Modeling · Precision · Simulator · Trueness

1 Introduction

Sciences of various domains other than computer science use scientific workflows to model their complex computational pipelines, which brings them many benefits such as reusing the results of parts or entire workflows, failure management, or parallelisation. Managing the workflows' execution is a complex task, as each workflow requires different computing, memory or I/O capacity, making the designing of a common, but appropriate, distributed environment for all workflows types very difficult and sometimes almost impossible. Workflows can also be

© Springer International Publishing AG 2017
F.F. Rivera et al. (Eds.): Euro-Par 2017, LNCS 10417, pp. 319–331, 2017.
DOI: 10.1007/978-3-319-64203-1_23

executed in Cloud as similar as in traditional clusters, as many workflow management services that allow the effective utilisation of the Cloud's elastic resources already exist [23]. Still, Cloud produces many additional challenges compared with the traditional clusters [2] caused by its on-demand elastic resource provisioning, dynamic starting of instances [20], and variant performance of virtual machines (VMs) during a time period [22].

Instead of executing in a real Cloud environment to determine the behavior of an application, many researchers resort to simulators for their analysis [3], which allows them to reduce costs for purchasing and maintaining expensive hardware resources, and time for executing time-consuming algorithms [21] and later on to determine that its performance is over- or under estimated. Moreover, simulators can be used to experiment new prototype solutions and identify the "optimal" resource configurations before deployment of production platforms. Most common simulators allow users to create a virtual data center considering their latest computing, networking, energy, or cost requirements. However, although they can simulate an elastic Cloud data center, simulators usually neglect the Cloud performance fluctuation and uncertainty [10], which can lead to wrong estimation. This aspect is especially important for workflow executions, as they consist of a high number of data and control flow dependencies [15] that further affect their overall performance without any correlation [18]. A small disturbance in a task execution can dramatically affect the scheduling of the following workflow tasks, resulting in a completely inefficient schedule that increases the execution cost or execution time (the makespan), or sometimes even both [1].

Although some simulators, such as DynamicCloudSim [4], allow users to configure the simulation considering a certain heterogeneity and instability of Cloud, still, there are several deficiencies for a proper configuration. The configuration itself is a complex process, as users need to configure more than ten parameters, for which they do not know the exact values of parameters in order to configure a specific Cloud and application to be executed. For example, the default values that are intended for Amazon's EC2 are several years old, and cannot be used for other public or private Clouds. Additionally, public Clouds can be seen as a black-box whose internal parameters are unknown to regular users. Even by using results of previous research, some parameters still cannot be generalized as they are valid either for that specific Cloud, a specific application, or even a combination of both.

We therefore propose a simpler model that reduces the configuration of the noisiness to a single parameter the *Cloud noisiness*, instead of dozens. The injected noise causes an instability in *Task Execution Time* (TET), which improves the *accuracy*, represented through the *trueness* (i.e. closeness of the true mean value) and the *precision* (i.e. closeness of corresponding standard deviation) of the simulation, as defined in ISO-5725 standard [12]. We conduct a series of evaluation experiments in Amazon EC2 and the most common state-of-the-art simulator - DynamicCloudSim. The evaluation proves that our simpler model implemented in DynamicCloudSim shows up to 9.2% higher trueness and up to 8.39 times higher precision for workflow execution simulations compared to DynamicCloudSim. Not only that our proposed model shows better *accuracy* to the real execution, but its configuration is much simpler and easier.

The paper is structured in several sections as follows. Section 2 presents the related works in modeling the workflow execution instability and the features of cloud simulators in this domain. The models for workflow, Cloud, experiments and test cases that are used for our noisiness model are presented in Sect. 3. Our simplified, more accurate model of adding a noise in simulation is described in Sect. 4. Sections 5 and 6 present the testing methodology and results of the evaluation of our model and current state-of-the-art simulation model of DynamicCloudSim. Finally, we conclude the paper and present plans for future work in Sect. 7.

2   Related Work

Many Cloud features and parameters can cause the performance instability: heterogeneity of resources, instance types, number of instances, instance straggling, instance failures, multi-tenancy, networking bottlenecks, resource time-sharing, etc. As a consequence, an instance of the same type provides different performance for the same task over some time period. Dejun et al. [7] reported high performance deviations in Amazon EC2. Jackson et al. [13] determined that different underlying hardware for similar instances caused performance perturbation. Schad et al. [19] detected a long-term performance instability of Amazon EC2, which was correlated also to the CPU model of the same instance type, the hour of the day, and the day of the week. Iosup et al. [11] determined yearly and daily patterns of performance variability, but also periods of constant performance. All these behaviors depend also on the executed application.

CloudSim [5] simulates scheduling algorithms and resource provisioning in elastic Cloud environment, but Cloud performance instability remains unaddressed. Chen and Deelman [6] extended the Cloudsim into WorkflowSim, by introducing several parameters specific to workflows. Still, all these extensions do not introduce the Cloud performance instability. Other works developed scalable simulators covering up to hundreds of thousands of heterogeneous machines [8]. For example, GroudSim [16] is a scalable event-based simulator for Grid and Cloud environments. GloudSim [9] is a simulator that introduces some dynamics in execution by resizing the instances. Still, it does not offer a TET's instability, as the performance of specific VM is constant during a time period.

Bux and Leser [4] went further in this direction by developing the DynamicCloudSim simulator as an extension of CloudSim that introduces several additional characteristics to simulate the Cloud heterogeneity, such as heterogeneous underline hardware, VM stragglers, VM failures, long and short term fluctuations, etc. However, configuring dozens of parameters for heterogeneity is not an easy task, as users are usually not aware of the internal Cloud architecture. We therefore went a step further by treating the Cloud as a black-box and introduced much simpler approach that needs a configuration of the noise into one parameter only. It includes two instabilities in itself: *workflow noisiness* (e.g.

dependencies, structure, TET deviation) and *Cloud noisiness* (e.g. heterogeneity). Nevertheless, although it is a simple method, the results of the evaluation show that our model improves the accuracy compared to the related Dynamic-CloudSim's instability model. Schad et al. [19] reported that several performance parameters are unstable with a normal distribution. We also use the normal distribution to add a noise in TET, but instead of naively generating the variables distributed with a normal distribution, we inject the noisiness parameter by shifting the TET's mean value by the *Cloud noisiness* parameter.

3   Modeling the Workflow and Cloud

This section formally models the workflow and Cloud environment, which are used for our cloud noisiness model later on.

3.1   Workflow Application Model

We model a *workflow application* W as a precedence constraint graph (T, D) consisting of a set $T = \bigcup_{i=1}^{n} \{T_i\}$ of n tasks T_i, which are interconnected through a set of dependencies $D = \{(T_i, T_j, D_{ij}) \mid (T_i, T_j) \in T \times T\}$, where (T_i, T_j, D_{ij}) implies that T_i needs to be executed before T_j, and the file size to be transferred from T_i to T_j is D_{ij} bytes. The tasks are assumed to be non-preemptive, so it is not allowed to suspend one and resume it later on.

The function $pred : T \to \mathcal{P}(T)$, where $\mathcal{P}$ denotes the power set, returns the set of immediate *predecessors* of each task $T_i \in T$ (i.e. $T_j \in pred(T_i) \iff (T_j, T_i, D_{ji}) \in D$), while the function $succ : T \to \mathcal{P}(T)$ returns the set of immediate *successors* of the task T_i (i.e. $T_j \in succ(T_i) \iff (T_i, T_j, D_{ij}) \in D$). Each workflow has an *entry task* T_{entry} with no predecessors (i.e. $T_{entry} \in T : pred(T_{entry}) = \emptyset$) and an *exit task* T_{exit} with no successors (i.e. $T_{exit} \in T : succ(T_{exit}) = \emptyset$).

Each task T_i has a *requirement vector* R_i, which defines its hardware or software requirements such as the minimum value of memory or storage needed for execution. We express the *computational complexity* w_i (i.e. work) of each task T_i in million of instructions (MI).

Note that this is a simplified view of a workflow. Still, workflows with multiple entry/exit tasks are covered by adding a single "dummy" entry task with the computational complexity $w = 0$ (i.e. without any complexity) before all entry tasks or a single "dummy" exit task, also with the computational complexity $w = 0$, after all exit tasks, respectively.

3.2   Cloud Infrastructure Model

A Cloud offers a set of r *VM types* $IT = \bigcup_{k=1}^{r} \{IT_k\}$. Each instance type IT_k is characterized by two parameters: *computational speed* s_k in million instructions per second (MIPS) and *number of CPUs* c_k. We denote the set of available *VM instances* as: $I = \bigcup_{j=1}^{m} \{I_j\}$, whose number m is constant during the workflow execution. Each instance I_j has an associated instance type IT_k defined as a function: $type : I \rightarrow IT$.

We model the *expected TET* t_i^j of a task T_i as the ratio between its computational complexity and the speed of the instance I_j on which it is executed ($t_i^j = w_i/s_k$, $I_j \in I \wedge IT_k = type(I_j)$).

The *completion time* of a task T_i executed on an instance I_j is the latest completion time of all its predecessors plus its expected TET:

$$end(T_i, k) = \begin{cases} t_i^j, & T_i = T_{entry}, IT_k = type(I_j); \\ \max_{T_p \in pred(T_i)} \left\{ end(T_p, k) + t_i^j \right\}, & T_i \neq T_{entry}, IT_k = type(I_j). \end{cases}$$

In a single experiment, we are using a constant number of the same type VMs, which keep running. Thus, for an experiment that uses VM instances of type k, we define the workflow *makespan* $M = end(T_{exit}, k)$.

3.3 Experiment and Test Case Model

In order to model the environment-independent model, we define a set of *experiments* $EXP = \bigcup_{x=1}^{q} \{EXP_x\}$. Each element EXP_x is modeled as a triple $EXP_x(W, IT_k, v)$, which means that a workflow W is executed on a specific number of VMs v, all of the same type IT_k.

As we want to simulate Cloud's behavior, we repeat each experiment N times and we refer to each execution as a *test case*. Therefore, a *test case* $^x TC^c$ represents the c-th repetition of an experiment EXP_x. This means that an experiment can be considered as a matrix of N columns (workflow execution repetitions) and n rows (tasks within a workflow).

Let $^x t_i^c$ denotes the *measured TET* of a task T_i in a test case $^x TC^c$ of an experiment EXP_x. Analogue, the makespan of test case $^x TC^c$ will be denoted as $^x M^c$. As we want to analyze the distribution of makespans per experiment, we define the *TET's mean value* $^x \bar{t}_i = \frac{1}{N} \cdot \sum_{c=1}^{N} {}^x t_i^c$ of a task T_i and the *mean makespan* $^x \overline{M} = \frac{1}{N} \cdot \sum_{c=1}^{N} {}^x M^c$. Both mean values are defined for an experiment EXP_x.

4 Noise Simulation Model

In this section we present our new model of simulating a workflow execution in Cloud, which improves the accuracy through a much simpler approach that uses only one parameter for noising for all the tasks of a workflow - *Cloud noisiness*, instead of DynamicCloudSim's 13 parameters for heterogeneity and instability.

4.1 Workflow Noisiness

In order to define a model for the noisiness provided by the workflow, first we model the noisiness of a task $T_i \in T$ itself with the parameter *TET's deviation*

$^x\rho_i^{cd}$, which is defined in (1) as a relative TET difference of task T_i in two test cases $^xTC^c$ and $^xTC^d$ of an experiment EXP_x with $c, d \in [1, N] \wedge c \neq d$.

$$^x\rho_i^{cd} = \frac{|^xt_i^c - ^xt_i^d|}{max(^xt_i^c, ^xt_i^d)} \tag{1}$$

The TET's deviation $^x\rho_i^{cd}$ is used to introduce the *workflow noisiness* $^x\overline{\Delta}^{cd}$, which describes the total noisiness of all TETs within a workflow in two test cases $^xTC^c$ and $^xTC^d$ of an experiment EXP_x, as defined in (2). Formally, it represents a normalized mean TET's difference of all corresponding tasks T_i of the same workflow, in two test cases $^xTC^c$ and $^xTC^d$ of an experiment EXP_x.

$$^x\overline{\Delta}^{cd} = \frac{1}{n} \cdot \sum_{i=1}^{n} {}^x\rho_i^{cd} \tag{2}$$

The *workflow noisiness* $^x\overline{\Delta}^{cd}$ can be used to extract noisiness of Cloud environment and includes vertical average of TETs of all tasks within a workflow W. $^x\overline{\Delta}^{cd}$ is an intermediate metric and serves as input for the *Cloud noisiness*, which is explained in the following subsection.

4.2   Cloud Noisiness

The workflow noisiness shows the instability of a workflow in two executions only. As Cloud environment is unstable, we want to take some average of a set of test cases for a single experiment EXP_x. Therefore, we introduce the *Cloud noisiness* $^x\overline{\Delta}$ of an experiment EXP_x. As defined in (3), $^x\overline{\Delta}$ represents the average experiments' makespan instability of all N repetitions (test cases) of an experiment EXP_x.

$$^x\overline{\Delta} = \frac{1}{\frac{N \cdot (N-1)}{2}} \cdot \sum_{\forall c, d | 1 \leq c < d \leq N} {}^x\overline{\Delta}^{cd} \tag{3}$$

We measure the workflow noisiness $^x\overline{\Delta}^{cd}$ of each unique pair of test cases $^xTC^c$ and $^xTC^d$ for all N executions (test cases) of the same experiment EXP_x. Accordingly, the total number of unique pairs that can be generated from a set of N elements is $\binom{N}{2} = \frac{N \cdot (N-1)}{2}$. The *Cloud noisiness* $^x\overline{\Delta}$ includes horizontal average of all workflow executions (test cases) within a single experiment EXP_x.

4.3   Modeling the Noising

Now, after formally definition of cloud noisiness, we define how to model and add a noise in a simulation. The *noised TET* $^x\widetilde{\tau}_i$ of a task T_i is defined in (4), where $Gaussian(Mean, STDEV)$ represents a random function with Gaussian (normal) distribution.

$$^x\widetilde{\tau}_i = (1 + {}^x\overline{\Delta} + Gaussian(0, \sigma_{x\overline{\Delta}})) \cdot {}^x\overline{t}_i \tag{4}$$

Accordingly, the noise in (4) is modeled as a Gaussian distribution, where the mean value is the TET's mean value $^x\bar{t}_i$ of a task T_i, shifted with the Cloud noisiness $^x\overline{\Delta}$ in order to cover uncertain overheads, measured in the experiments. For noisiness, we use the standard deviation $\sigma_{x\overline{\Delta}}$ of all workflow noisiness of a single cloud noisiness, which is determined by each pair of test cases TC^c and TC^d $(\forall c,d \mid 1 \leq c < d \leq N)$ of a single experiment.

5 Testing Methodology

In this section we present the testing methodology in order to evaluate our noising model in Sect. 6.

5.1 Synthetic Workflow

The synthetic workflow that is used in our experiments consists of two parallel sections (Second and Fourth) of same size, with three synchronisation tasks (First, Third and Fifth) in between, as depicted in Fig. 1. The chosen workflow structure is the result of workflow characteristics analysis of several well known workflows, such as *EPIGENOMICS* and *SIPHT* [14]. The workflow size is related to the number of tasks in the parallel sections. In the experiments we use a parallel section size of 13 (SYNWF/13) and 44 (SYNWF/44). We use two different workflow sizes in order to cover balanced and unbalanced executions, such that one is a prime number and the other is dividable by the numbers 2 and 4, corresponding to the number of instances. Additionally, we used instance number of 3, which is not a divisor of neither workflow sizes. With this workflow structure and selected parameters, we also want to investigate if there is a correlation between the workflow parameters and the execution environment (chosen resources and the inefficient workflow execution).

As workflow makespan consists of computations and file transfers (including both the network and I/O), we have chosen different file transfer to computation

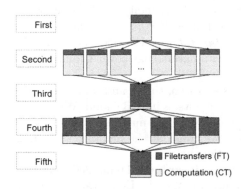

Fig. 1. The structure of the synthetic workflow with the file transfer to computation time ratios

Table 1. File transfer (FT) to computation time (CT) ratio in % for SYNWF/13 and SYNWF/44

Task type	SYNWF/13		SYNWF/44	
	FT[%]	CT[%]	FT[%]	CT[%]
First	30	70	30	70
Second	15	85	15	85
Third	90	10	95	5
Fourth	75	25	75	25
Fifth	90	10	95	5

time ratios for all five task types, as depicted in Fig. 1 and presented in Table 1. A file transfer describes the copying process of a set of files from one task to another and combines network bandwidth with I/O. The ratios of the First, Second and Fourth task types are assumed to be constant for different workflow sizes because the number and size of file inputs is not changing. This is different for the Third and Fifth task types, which are synchronization tasks and collect all the output files produced by the Second and Fourth tasks (parallel sections), correspondingly. Thus, in order to compensate this, we slightly increase the file transfer time for the workflow size 44. Moreover, the ratios of both parallel sections are inverse to each other.

5.2   Cloud Testing Environment

All Cloud experiments were executed in Amazon EC2 with the VM image *Amazon Linux AMI (ami-1ecae776)* in the availability zone *US East (N. Virginia)*. For the workflow execution and measurements of the TETs and makespan, we used the workflow execution engine Askalon [17]. We use two Amazon instance types $IT = \{t2.small, t2.medium\}$ as well as the number of instances $m = \{2, 3, 4\}$.

According the definition of experiments in Sect. 3.3, EXP_1 is defined as $EXP_1(SYNWF/13, t2.small, 2)$, which means that it executes the synthetic workflow with parallel section size 13, by using two small VMs. As we used two different workflows that are specified in the previous subsection, we define $q = 12$ experiments, and since we execute 20 repetitions (test cases) of each experiment, we execute a total of 240 test cases in Cloud. In order to cover different behavior of Amazon's EC2, we run all test cases of each experiments in the period of two weeks.

5.3   Simulation Testing Environment

In all our simulations, we used DynamicCloudSim, which extends CloudSim by adding features that allow a user to simulate the heterogeneity in Cloud described as the performance deviation of a resource, including *VM heterogeneity, host heterogeneity, File I/O heterogeneity,* and *Cloud instability, VM Stragglers* and *VM Failures*. DynamicCloudSim introduces 13 parameters that cover Cloud heterogeneity and instability, which are described in Table 2.

The same two workflows, two VM types and two, three, and four number of VMs are used to reproduce the same 12 experiments as in real Cloud. We execute $N = 20$ test cases per experiment in order to have equal number of experiments in real and simulated executions. Note that we consider the instance startup as warm up period and thus it is discarded in the experiments.

In order to evaluate our model, we compare it with the DynamicCloudSim's model (denoted as S_{sDCS}) with default values for Amazon EC2 (Table 2), which are based on other performance-based researches, experience, and assumptions.

Table 2. DynamicCloudSim heterogeneity parameter setup for S_{sDCS} and S_{noise}

Heterogeneity parameter	Description	S_{sDCS}	S_{noise}
cpuHeterogeneityCV	Randomize the power of the host	0.4	0
ioHeterogeneityCV	(CPU, I/O and bandwidth)	0.15	0
bwHeterogeneityCV		0.2	0
cpuNoiseCV	Randomize the performance characteristics	0.028	0
ioNoiseCV	of a VM (CPU, I/O and bandwidth)	0.007	0
bwNoiseCV		0.010	0
cpu/io/bw BaselineChangesPerHour	Randomize the dynamic changes of Cloud's performance	0	0
likelihoodOfStraggler	Probability of a VM being a straggler	0	0
stragglerPerformanceCoefficient	Diminished performance of a straggler	1	1
likelihoodOfFailure	Average rate of failure	0	0
runtimeFactorInCaseOfFailure	TET factor of a failed task	1	1

Our noisining model S_{noise}, adds noise to one parameter (TET) only. Thus, all other heterogeneity and noise related parameters are set to 0 in Dynamic-CloudSim. Note that also the *cpuNoiseCV* parameter is also set to 0, because we insert our noise through the Cloud noisiness parameter. Table 3 shows the measured Cloud noisiness ${}^x\overline{\Delta}$ and the corresponding standard deviations for S_{noise} in each experiment executed on Amazon EC2. It shows that EC2 provides computation instabilities from 8.9% up to 17.6% for various workflows and using different number of various instance types. The deviation of all test cases per a single experiment is in the range of 2.8% up to 11.2%.

Table 3. ${}^x\overline{\Delta}$ and $\sigma_{x\overline{\Delta}}$ values for S_{noise}

	W	2*S	3*S	4*S	2*M	3*M	4*M	W	2*S	3*S	4*S	2*M	3*M	4*M
${}^x\overline{\Delta}$	13	0.110	0.089	0.120	0.144	0.162	0.165	44	0.093	0.112	0.166	0.129	0.176	0.158
$\sigma_{x\overline{\Delta}}$		0.077	0.029	0.062	0.028	0.041	0.048		0.039	0.058	0.112	0.039	0.042	0.031

For a fair comparison, both simulations have equal base network, storage and computation speed. Moreover during the experiments in real Cloud, we did not detect any VM failures, and therefore the straggler, failure and cpu/io/bw BaselineChangesPerHour parameters are set to 0 for both simulations.

6   Evaluation

In this section we present the results of a series of experiments to evaluate our noising model. The summary of the evaluation shows not only that our model is simpler, but it is more accurate than DynamicCloudSim.

Figure 2 shows the mean makespans of both workflows SYNWF/13 and SYNWF/44. The experiments are denoted as the product of number of instances (m) and the abbreviation of VM type (M for t2.medium and S for t2.small VM type). For example, $2 * S$ denotes the experiment that uses two small instances, while $4 * M$ is used for the experiment with four medium instances.

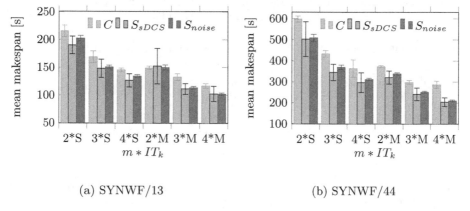

(a) SYNWF/13   (b) SYNWF/44

Fig. 2. Mean makespans with variations $\pm\sigma(mean\ makespan)$ of SYNWF/13 and SYNWF/44 using two, three or four instances of type t2.small (S) or t2.medium (M)

The mean values of makespans of all experiments with SYNWF/13 are depicted in Fig. 2a, along with the standard deviation. We observe that our S_{noise} model shows higher accuracy, that is, both higher trueness and precision, than S_{sDCS}. Increasing the number of small instances, S_{noise} improves its precision with 20.16% up to 71.61%, while S_{sDCS} has minimum 51.21% of precision offset compared to C. For all experiments, our noise model shows higher makespan trueness for real Cloud C, compared to S_{sDCS}. In detail, the trueness' offset of S_{noise} is between 6.0% and 10.7% for small instances, while S_{sDCS}'s is between 11.8% and 13.0%. Thus, S_{noise} is up to 7.0% better than S_{sDCS} for small instances. We observe a similar behavior with increasing number of medium instances, where the makespan trueness offset of S_{noise} is between 0.5% and 14.7%, while S_{sDCS}'s is between 2.3% and 16.3%. In the experiments with two medium instances, both simulations show higher makespan than C, but S_{noise} has still higher trueness with 0.5% offset.

Figure 2b shows the average makespan results for all experiments with the SYNWF/44 workflow. Similar to the experiments with the SYNWF/13 workflow, our model S_{noise} shows again higher accuracy than S_{sDCS}. The trueness of our model S_{noise} is better than S_{sDCS} for all experiments, while the precision is comparable, but slightly worse, only for experiments with 4 instances, and for all others our model S_{noise} is still better. In detail, S_{noise} shows between 15.29% and 20.59% higher standard deviation than C for 2 and 3 instances, while S_{sDCS} has up to 5 times higher offset. On experiments with 4 instances, S_{noise} shows between 76.94% and 86.21% precision offset, while S_{sDCS} has only up to 21.93%. Regarding the simulated makespans' trueness (closeness to the mean value), S_{noise} shows a better trueness than S_{sDCS} in all experiments. In detail, comparing the trueness offset of the simulated results and the real Cloud results, S_{noise} is still better with trueness offset between 9.4% and 26.6%, while S_{sDCS} has between 16.0% and 28.8%.

Comparing all experiments conducted with both workflows, S_{noise} shows higher and more closer precision than S_{sDCS} for all experiments with SYNWF/13. We observe similar behavior with SYNWF/44, except for experiments with 4 small and medium instances. Additionally, S_{noise} shows up to 9.2% higher makespans' trueness compared to S_{sDCS} for all experiments. We also observe that the precision of both models does not depend if the number of instances is a divisor or not of the workflow parallel section size, which can significantly reduce the number of experiments to determine the cloud noisiness.

7   Conclusion and Future Work

This paper presents a new simplified *Cloud noisiness* model for noising the workflow execution while it is simulated in order to behave as the real Cloud unstable environment. Instead of configuring dozens parameters in order to achieve a noised simulation, as it is required in DynamicCloudSim, our model configures only one - the Cloud noisiness. A series of experiments in Amazon EC2 that were reproduced in simulated environment show that our Cloud noisiness model simplifies the simulation configuration and improves the simulation trueness, and especially precision.

The main novelty in our model is the calculation of noisiness. Instead of using the normal distribution naively for the tasks' runtime, we shift the mean TET by the Cloud noisiness and then add a noise (deviation of the Cloud noisiness) of each task. The workflow noisiness smooths the impact of the workflow structure by calculating the average instability of all tasks in a workflow, while the Cloud noisiness estimates the environmental noise by calculating the horizontal average instability of the same task. With these two parameters, we inject not only the noise of a task itself, when being executed in Cloud, but we inject the impact of common tasks' noises within the workflow and environmental noise provided when a whole workflow is being repeatedly executed in that environment.

Although our Cloud noisiness approach requires several executions of a workflow in order to calculate the Cloud noisiness parameter, the results show that the instability is not correlated to the parallel section size, that is, if we execute a workflow efficiently or inefficiently. However, the experiments show that the instability is highly correlated with the instance type and the number of instances. We will try to extend our model with other parameters in order to reduce this dependency and therefore the cost of learning the Cloud noisiness. However, our analysis shows that the performance instability of up to 17% between two experiments is comparable with the standard deviation of up to 11% between test cases within a single experiment.

Our noisiness model improved the simulator's trueness for all and the precision for most instance types and number of instances. As the results show that the instability is instance type dependent, we will extend our model towards modeling network, as well as I/O, and including them in order to improve the trueness and precision even more.

Acknowledgments. This work is being accomplished as a part of project *ENTICE: "dEcentralised repositories for traNsparent and efficienT vIrtual maChine opErations"*, funded by the European Unions Horizon 2020 research and innovation programme under grant agreement No. 644179.

References

1. Alkhanak, E.N., Lee, S.P., Rezaei, R., Parizi, R.M.: Cost optimization approaches for scientific workflow scheduling in cloud and grid computing: A review, classifications, and open issues. J. Syst. Softw. **113**, 1–26 (2016)
2. Armbrust, M., Fox, A., Griffith, R., Joseph, A.D., Katz, R., Konwinski, A., Lee, G., Patterson, D., Rabkin, A., Stoica, I., Zaharia, M.: A view of cloud computing. Commun. ACM **53**(4), 50–58 (2010)
3. Basu, A., Fleming, S., Stanier, J., Naicken, S., Wakeman, I., Gurbani, V.K.: The state of peer-to-peer network simulators. ACM Comput. Surv. **45**(4), 46:1–46:25 (2013)
4. Bux, M., Leser, U.: DynamicCloudSim: Simulating heterogeneity in computational clouds. Future Gen. Comput. Syst. **46**, 85–99 (2015)
5. Calheiros, R.N., Ranjan, R., Beloglazov, A., De Rose, C.A., Buyya, R.: CloudSim: a toolkit for modeling and simulation of cloud computing environments and evaluation of resource provisioning algorithms. Softw.: Practice Exp. **41**(1), 23–50 (2011)
6. Chen, W., Deelman, E.: WorkflowSim: A toolkit for simulating scientific workflows in distributed environments. In: 2012 IEEE 8th International Conference on E-Science (e-Science), pp. 1–8, October 2012
7. Dejun, J., Pierre, G., Chi, C.-H.: EC2 performance analysis for resource provisioning of service-oriented applications. In: Dan, A., Gittler, F., Toumani, F. (eds.) ICSOC/ServiceWave -2009. LNCS, vol. 6275, pp. 197–207. Springer, Heidelberg (2010). doi:10.1007/978-3-642-16132-2_19
8. Depoorter, W., Moor, N., Vanmechelen, K., Broeckhove, J.: Scalability of grid simulators: an evaluation. In: Luque, E., Margalef, T., Benítez, D. (eds.) Euro-Par 2008. LNCS, vol. 5168, pp. 544–553. Springer, Heidelberg (2008). doi:10.1007/978-3-540-85451-7_58
9. Di, S., Cappello, F.: GloudSim: Google trace based cloud simulator with virtual machines. Softw. Pract. Exper. **45**(11), 1571–1590 (2015)

10. Fard, H.M., Ristov, S., Prodan, R.: Handling the uncertainty in resource performance for executing workflow applications in clouds. In: 9th IEEE/ACM International Conference on Utility and Cloud Computing, UCC 2016, pp. 89–98. ACM (2016). http://doi.acm.org/10.1145/2996890.2996902
11. Iosup, A., Yigitbasi, N., Epema, D.: On the performance variability of production cloud services. In: 2011 11th IEEE/ACM International Symposium on Cluster, Cloud and Grid Computing (CCGrid), pp. 104–113, May 2011
12. ISO: ISO 5725: 1994. http://www.iso.org/obp/ui/#iso:std:11833:en
13. Jackson, K.R., Ramakrishnan, L., Muriki, K., Canon, S., Cholia, S., Shalf, J., Wasserman, H.J., Wright, N.J.: Performance analysis of high performance computing applications on the Amazon web services cloud. In: 2010 IEEE Second International Conference on Cloud Computing Technology and Science (CloudCom), pp. 159–168, November 2010
14. Juve, G., Chervenak, A., Deelman, E., Bharathi, S., Mehta, G., Vahi, K.: Characterizing and profiling scientific workflows. Future Gen. Comput. Syst. **29**(3), 682–692 (2013). http://www.sciencedirect.com/science/article/pii/S0167739X12001732. Special Section: Recent Developments in High Performance Computing and Security
15. Malawski, M., Juve, G., Deelman, E., Nabrzyski, J.: Cost- and deadline-constrained provisioning for scientific workflow ensembles in IaaS clouds. In: Proceedings of the International Conference on HPC, Networking, Storage and Analysis, SC 2012, pp. 1–11 (2012)
16. Ostermann, S., Plankensteiner, K., Prodan, R., Fahringer, T.: GroudSim: An event-based simulation framework for computational grids and clouds. In: Guarracino, M.R., et al. (eds.) Euro-Par 2010. LNCS, vol. 6586, pp. 305–313. Springer, Heidelberg (2011). doi:10.1007/978-3-642-21878-1_38
17. Ostermann, S., Prodan, R., Fahringer, T.: Extending grids with cloud resource management for scientific computing. In: 2009 10th IEEE/ACM International Conference on Grid Computing, pp. 42–49. IEEE (2009)
18. Ristov, S., Mathá, R., Prodan, R.: Analysing the performance instability correlation with various workflow and cloud parameters. In: 2017 25th Euromicro International Conference on Parallel, Distributed and Network-based Processing (PDP), pp. 446–453, March 2017
19. Schad, J., Dittrich, J., Quiané-Ruiz, J.A.: Runtime measurements in the cloud: Observing, analyzing, and reducing variance. Proc. VLDB Endow. **3**(1–2), 460–471 (2010)
20. Tchernykh, A., Schwiegelsohn, U., Alexandrov, V., ghazali Talbi, E.: Towards understanding uncertainty in cloud computing resource provisioning. Procedia Comput. Sci. **51**, 1772–1781 (2015). International Conference on Computational Science (2015)
21. Tian, W., Xu, M., Chen, A., Li, G., Wang, X., Chen, Y.: Open-source simulators for cloud computing: comparative study and challenging issues. Simul. Modell. Practice Theory **58**(Part 2), 239–254 (2015). http://www.sciencedirect.com/science/article/pii/S1569190X15000970. Special issue on Cloud Simulation
22. Wu, F., Wu, Q., Tan, Y.: Workflow scheduling in cloud: A survey. J. Supercomput. **71**(9), 3373–3418. http://dx.doi.org/10.1007/s11227-015-1438-4
23. Zhao, Y., Li, Y., Raicu, I., Lu, S., Lin, C., Zhang, Y., Tian, W., Xue, R.: A service framework for scientific workflow management in the cloud. IEEE Trans. Serv. Comput. **8**(6), 930–944 (2015)

Dealing with Performance Unpredictability
in an Asymmetric Multicore Processor Cloud

Boris Teabe[(✉)], Patrick Lavoisier Wapet, Alain Tchana, and Daniel Hagimont

University of Toulouse, Toulouse, France
{boris.teabedjomgwe,patrick.wapet,alain.tchana,
daniel.hagimon}@enseeiht.fr

Abstract. In a Cloud computing data center and especially in a IaaS
(Infrastructure as a Service), performance predictability is one of the most
important challenges. For a given allocated virtual machine (VM) in one
IaaS, a client expects his application to perform identically whatever is
the hosting physical server or its resource management strategy. However, performance predictability is very difficult to enforce in a heterogeneous hardware environment where machines do not have identical performance characteristics, and even more difficult when machines are internally heterogeneous as for Asymmetric Multicore Processor machines.
In this paper, we introduce a VM scheduler extension which takes into
account hardware performance heterogeneity of Asymmetric Multicore
Processor machines in the cloud. Based on our analysis of the problem,
we designed and implemented two solutions: the first weights CPU allocations according to core performance, while the second adapts CPU allocations to reach a given instruction execution rate (Ips) regardless the
core types. We demonstrate that such scheduler extensions can enforce
predictability with a negligible overhead on application performance.

1 Introduction

Cloud Computing enables remote access to on-demand allocated resources. The
most popular cloud model is the so-called Infrastructure as a Service (IaaS)
model, since it offers a high flexibility to cloud users. In order to provide isolation,
IaaS clouds are often virtualized so that resources are allocated in terms of virtual
machines (VMs). The provider defines a VM catalog (e.g. t2.medium, t2.small
in Amazon EC2) presenting VM configurations which can be requested by cloud
users. A VM configuration defines a capacity for each resource types, that we
call virtual resource types as machines are virtual. Capacities are expressed as
follows:

- the capacity of the network is expressed in terms of a bandwidth value (e.g.
  100 MBps).
- the capacity of the hard disk is expressed in terms of both an IO bandwidth
  (e.g. 100 MBps) and a storage space (e.g. 1 TB).
- the capacity of the RAM is expressed in terms of a storage space (e.g. 10 GB).

© Springer International Publishing AG 2017
F.F. Rivera et al. (Eds.): Euro-Par 2017, LNCS 10417, pp. 332–344, 2017.
DOI: 10.1007/978-3-319-64203-1_24

– the capacity of the CPU is expressed in terms of a number of virtual CPU (noted vCPU, e.g. 4 vCPUs).

The analysis of the above capacity expressions raises one question: **from the user point of view, what is the real capacity of each virtual resource type, given that virtual resources are mapped to heterogeneous physical resources?** Concerning both the network and the hard disk, the answer is quite clear because they are expressed using absolute units (independent from the underlying hardware). This is not the case for the two other virtual resources. Both the RAM bandwidth (which is not presented to the user) and the vCPU computing capacity depend on the underlying hardware. Figure 1 left shows that the same VM type from Rackspace and Azure cloud delivers different performance levels according to the underlying processor. This results in the problem of performance unpredictability [16], which has been identified by Microsoft [2] as part of the five top significant challenges in the cloud.

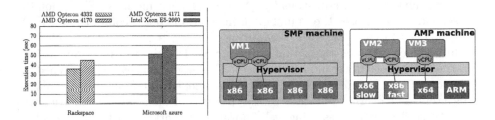

Fig. 1. Left figure: performance unpredictability illustration in Rackspace and Microsoft Azure clouds. The experimental application is π-app [6]. **Right figure:** SMP and AMP machines

The majority of research projects, if not all, have investigated this issue from the resource contention perspective [27, 30], seen as the only source of the problem. However, we have shown in a previous work [28] that heterogeneity (of memory and processor) is actively involved in performance unpredictability. In this previous work, we focused on heterogeneous Symmetric Multicores Processor machines (hereafter called SMP clouds) (Fig. 1 left). However, advances in semiconductor technologies have enabled processor manufacturers to integrate more and more cores on a chip. This will lead in the near future (for energy saving reasons [8,18]) to a new type of architecture called Asymmetric Multicores Processor (AMP) (Fig. 1 right). Such an architecture is composed of cores exporting the same Instruction Set Architecture (ISA) but delivering different performance [18]. This new architecture comes with new challenges which have begun to be studied [8,14]. This paper tackles the issue of performance unpredictability in AMP clouds in which three problematic situations can be identified:

1. A multi-vCPU VM whose vCPUs run atop different core types (e.g. in Fig. 1 right, a thread inside the $VM2$ can be scheduled either on "vCPU ×86 slow" or "vCPU ×86 fast");

2. the scheduling of one vCPU across different core types in the same machine (e.g. in Fig. 1 right, $VM3$'s vCPU can be scheduled either on "×86 slow", "×86 fast", "×64" or "ARM");
3. VM migration across different machine types.

The first two situations can only occur in an AMP cloud while the third situation can raise up in AMP and SMP clouds.

It is clear that providing the same vCPU computing capacity regardless the underlying core type allows addressing all of the above situations. Our analysis of this problem led us to the design of two solutions, which both include (1) an absolute metric to express a vCPU computing capacity, and (2) a scheduler which enforces the negotiated contract during the overall VM lifetime. The first solution consists in using a reference core (noted p_{ref}) as the basis of vCPU capacity expression. Relying on the proportionality coefficient between the actual core type and p_{ref}, the scheduler dynamically adjusts the allowable CPU time of the vCPU. This solution is an improvement of our previous work [28] (which was performing such an adjustment at VM migration time in an SMP cloud). The second solution uses the "number of instructions per second" (noted Ips) as the metric to express a vCPU computing capacity. It requires a new kind of scheduler which relies on the actual number of CPU retired instructions rather than the CPU time (the standard practice). Theses solutions were prototyped in the Xen 4.2.0 system, although their design is independent from any virtualization system. The overhead of these prototypes at runtime is almost nil. We have evaluated their effectiveness using well known benchmarks (SPEC CPU2006 [4], Blast [1], and wordpress [5]). The evaluation results show that our solutions almost cancel out the issue of performance unpredictability due to core heterogeneity.

The rest of the article is structured as follows. Section 2 presents the background. Section 3 presents our contributions. The evaluation results are reported in Sect. 4. The related work is presented in Sect. 5 and we present our conclusions in Sect. 6.

2   Background

Our work is based on the para-virtualized Xen system. Before going into the description of our contributions, we briefly present Xen and its CPU allocation mechanism.

2.1   The Xen Hypervisor

Xen [11] is a popular open-source Virtual Machine Monitor (VMM) system (also called *hypervisor*) which is widely espoused by several cloud providers such as Amazon EC2. Its implementation follows the para-virtualization [29] model. In this model, the hypervisor runs directly on the hardware, so taking the traditional place of the operating system (OS). Thus, the hypervisor has all privileges and rights to access the entire hardware. It provides the means to concurrently run several OS called virtual machines (VM). The host OS (seen as a special VM) is called *dom0* while the others are called *domU*. The former has more privileges than the latter since it is responsible for running Xen's management toolstack. The next section presents the Xen's CPU allocation mechanism.

2.2   CPU Allocation in Xen

Each VM is configured at start time with a number of vCPU and the hypervisor is responsible for scheduling vCPUs on cores. Roughly, each core runs a dedicated scheduler instance which manages a sub-group of vCPUs. The goal of each scheduler is to determine which vCPU will receive the core during the next quantum. Xen implements several scheduling policies including Simple Earliest Deadline First (SEDF) [11] and Credit [11]. SEDF is a scheduler which guarantees a minimum processing time to a VM. Concerning the Credit scheduler, it guarantees that a VM will strictly receive a portion (called *credit*) of the physical machine computing capacity. Credit is the default and the widely used scheduler. Therefore our work only considers this scheduler.

The Credit scheduler works as follows. Each VM (noted v) is configured at start time with a credit value (noted c) between 0 and 100 (full computing capacity). The scheduler defines *remainCredit*, a scheduling variable (associated with the VM) initialized to c. Each time a vCPU from v releases a core, (1) the scheduler translates into a credit value (let us say *burntCredit*) the time spent by v on the core. Subsequently, (2) the scheduler computes a new value of *remainCredit* by subtracting *burntCredit* from the previous *remainCredit*. When *remainCredit* reaches a lower threshold (configured in Xen), the VM enters a *"blocked"* state. In order to make blocked VMs schedulable in the future, the scheduler periodically increases their *remainCredit* according to their initial credit.

From the above presentation, we can see that the Credit scheduler is based on the notion of credit which depends on CPU time. The latter is a relative metric, as opposed to absolute metrics introduced in Sect. 1. Indeed, a vCPU capacity during a time period depends on the underlying core type. In other words, during the same time period, different core types result in different numbers of retired instructions for the same application. The next section presents our solutions which address this issue.

3   Performance Predictability Enforcement Systems

In public clouds, a vCPU is generally pinned to a dedicated core and is allowed to fully use this core. Our work is situated in this context[1]. In such a context, the provider presents to the user the vCPU capacity as a core capacity. This is ambiguous in AMP clouds since cores have different capacities. This

---

[1] Our solutions can also be easily applied to other contexts where several vCPUs share the same core.

paper addresses the issue of performance unpredictability which comes from this ambiguity. To do so, we adopt a two-step approach which is summarized by the following questions:

- Expressiveness: how to clearly express a vCPU computing capacity?
- Enforcement: how to enforce a booked vCPU computing capacity at runtime?

This section presents two ways to answer the above questions. Relying on the popular open source Xen hypervisor, we also present the implementation of each solution.

3.1   The First Solution

Expressiveness. In this solution, a vCPU computing capacity is presented to the user as the capacity of a specific core type (referred to as "reference core" and noted p_{ref}) available in the IaaS. p_{ref} is chosen once by the provider. It should be the core type with the lowest computing capacity, so that all other core types are able to provide this capacity.

Enforcement. Let us note *app* a single-thread CPU bound application (e.g. π-app [6]). $ExecutionTime(app, p)$ is the execution time of *app* when it exclusively runs on a core whose type is p. The enforcement system goal here is to ensure that given a vCPU v, $ExecutionTime(app, p) = ExecutionTime(app, p_{ref})$ regardless the actual core which runs v. We define the proportionality coefficient between p_{ref} and each core type p (noted $coef(p)$) as follows

$$coef(p) = \frac{ExecutionTime(app, p_{ref})}{ExecutionTime(app, p)} \tag{1}$$

The proportionality coefficient is computed once by the provider. Then, the enforcement system relies on an adaptation of the Xen Credit scheduler in order to dynamically scale each vCPU allowable CPU time according to the proportionality coefficient of its actual core. By doing so, the computing capacity associated with a vCPU is always that of p_{ref}. In the scheduler, the burnt CPU time (for a vCPU) is always translated as if it had been executed on p_{ref}. This translation is periodically performed after each scheduler intervention (typically every 30 ms in Xen). Unlike the native Credit scheduler (see the beginning of the section) which allows the vCPU to fully use its actual core (noted p), our modification enforces the use of only a fraction of p. The implementation of this solution is straightforward in the Xen Credit scheduler. It simply consists in modifying the $vCPUBurntCredit$ function (see Sect. 2) as follows

```
1 Unsigned int vCPUBurntCredit (...) {
2       ...
3       //burntCredit has been calculated above (in the ↖
             original Xen Credit scheduler)
4       burntCredit = burntCredit * coef(typeOf(core_id));
5       return burntCredit;
6 }
```

where $typeOf(core\_id)$ returns the current core type.

3.2   The Second Solution

Expressiveness. In this solution, a vCPU computing capacity is presented to the user as an instruction throughput (noted *Ips*): it is the maximum number of instructions the vCPU is allowed to performed per second. As well as the metric used to express a virtual network card capacity (Byte per second, *Bps*) is clear and absolute, *Ips* is also clear and absolute.

Enforcement. The enforcement system aims at ensuring that a vCPU's booked *Ips* is always satisfied regardless its actual core speed. Unlike the first solution which relies on the translation of a relative metric into an absolute metric, the second solution is directly based on an absolute metric. Therefore, the implementation of this solution cannot be implemented with a simple adaptation of the Xen Credit scheduler. It requires a monitoring system which is able to measure online the number of instructions performed by each vCPU. *Ips_Sched*, the new scheduler we have implemented, works as follows. *Ips_Sched* periodically collects the number of retired instructions (noted ri) related to each $vCPU$ during the sampling period (noted sp). In our prototype, ri is obtained using Perfctr-xen [24], a tool which allows accessing performance counters in a virtualized environment. Subsequently, *Ips_Sched* computes the actual instruction throughput (noted act_t) of each $vCPU$ using the following formula

$$act\_t = \frac{old\_t \times sp + ri}{2 \times sp} \tag{2}$$

where old_t is the throughput calculated during the previous sampling period. Note that old_t is zero if the vCPU was blocked during the previous sampling period. *Ips_Sched* keeps two queues namely $UNDER$ and $OVER$. If act_t is lower than the booked *Ips*, the vCPU is inserted into the $UNDER$ queue. Otherwise the vCPU is inserted into $OVER$. vCPUs which belong to the latter are not allowed to use the processor during the next sampling period (they are considered as blocked).

3.3   Comparison of the Two Solutions

This section presents both the advantages and the limitations of our two solutions. We have conducted a survey of cloud users (from two cloud provider partners) regarding the metrics used in the two solutions. The results of this survey show that the metric introduced in the first solution (the vCPU capacity is that of a reference core, p_{ref}) is more comprehensive than the metric used in the second solution (the vCPU capacity is an instruction throughput, *Ips*). The latter is suitable for HPC cloud users since they have the necessary expertise needed to deal with low level statistics such as *Ips*. Furthermore, *Ips* allows doing both fine grained and flexible CPU reservation. For instance, in the same way that physical AMP machines exist, the user can define AMP VMs[2] by expressing different

---

[2] Several research have highlighted the benefits of AMP VMs for energy saving improvements.

Ips per vCPU for the same VM. This is not possible using the first solution since all vCPUs should have the same capacity. Finally the implementation of the first solution requires more work (calibration of proportionality coefficients) from the provider than the second solution.

4   Evaluations

This section presents the evaluation results of our solutions. We evaluate the following aspects:

- Effectiveness: the capacity of the solutions to ensure a vCPU computing capacity.
- Overhead: the amount of resources consumed by both solutions.

Experimental Setup.

Hardware. The adopted experimental environment is similar to those used in prior work [15,26] in the domain of AMP. In those works, an AMP machine consists of two core types namely fast and slow cores. An AMP machine is simulated by an SMP machine whose cores work at different frequency levels: a fast core is emulated by running the core at the highest available frequency; a slow core is emulated by running the core at the lowest available frequency. Our testbed is composed of 2 DELL PowerEdge R420 machines. Each machine has 2 sockets, 6 cores per socket. The core's highest frequency is 2.2 GHz and the lowest frequency is 1.2 GHz. Each socket is organized into 3 fast cores and 3 slow cores. The operating system is Ubuntu 12.04 (Linux kernel version 3.8.0) virtualized with Xen 4.2.0. Our private IaaS is managed by OpenStack [3], a popular IaaS manager system.

Benchmarks. We evaluated our solutions using three reference benchmarks namely SPEC CPU2006 [4], Blast [1] and wordpress [5].

- SPEC CPU2006 [4] is a suite of single-threaded applications, stressing a system's processor, memory subsystem and compiler.
- Blast [1] is a multi-threaded application which simulates a typical workload from a health institute.
- Wordpress [5] is a web application commonly deployed in the cloud. Its performance metrics are the throughput (req/sec) and the response time.

4.1   The Effectiveness

Methodology. Performance predictability is guaranteed when the same workload execution results in the same performance regardless the core type. This contract is respected in an SMP machine because cores are identical (obviously) and we avoid other sources of problem (e.g. resource contention [30]) in order to only focus on the issue related to core heterogeneity. Therefore, we first execute applications on SMP machines managed with the native Xen system (representing the "baseline"). Afterwards, we run the same applications on AMP machines managed with the native Xen (def) and with our solutions (sol1 and sol2). Finally, we compare the obtained results: our solutions are effective if they provide the same results as the baseline. In addition, to highlight the criticality of the addressed issue, we evaluate the use of the native Xen system to manage AMP machines. Notice that each experiment is repeated several times. In the evaluation of the first solution (sol1), p_{ref} is set to the slow core type. Concerning the evaluation of the second solution, the booked Ips of any vCPU is set to 50 $Mega\ Ips$.

Results. The first experiment uses CPU bound applications (SPEC CPU2006 and Blast) to evaluate the effectiveness of our solutions. As well as SPEC CPU2006 and Blast are respectively single-threaded and multi-threaded applications, they were ran respectively in single-vCPU and four-vCPU VMs. Each application is the subject of several executions, so that all vCPU to core type mappings are experimented. Performance predictability is achieved if the execution time of an application is almost the same in all executions. Figure 2 contains box plots presenting the normalized execution time of each benchmark (normalized to the baseline). The height of the boxes corresponds to the performance variation between various executions of benchmarks. We can observe that our solutions (sol1 and sol2) lead to a unique execution time which is equal to the baseline execution time. This is not the case for the native Xen system (def). The latter results in up to five different execution times, which correspond to the various vCPU to core type mappings: SPEC CPU2006 and Blast applications have respectively two and five possible vCPU to core mappings.

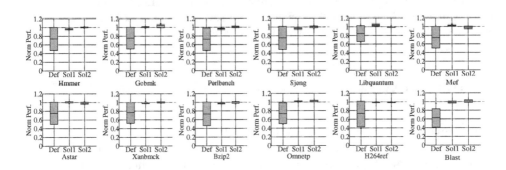

Fig. 2. Effectiveness evaluation of our solutions with SPEC CPU2006 and Blast.

The second experiment type is based on wordpress, an internet service application. We configure the benchmark as a two-tier application composed of a load balancer (Haproxy) which distributes requests among two Apache web servers (see Fig. 3 left). Each Apache server runs in a single-vCPU VM and a constant workload is submitted to wordpress. We experimented several vCPU to core type mappings (VM to core mappings). The results of this experiment are presented through a Cumulative Distribution Function (CDF) in Fig. 3 right. We can observe that our solutions (sol1 and sol2) provide almost the same response time values as the baseline regardless the vCPU to core type mappings. Conversely, the native Xen (def) system results in two response time values (691 and 44385 micro sec) corresponding to the scenario where the two Apache servers (the two VMs) run on different core types.

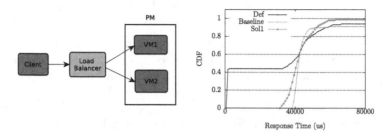

Fig. 3. Effectiveness evaluation of our solutions with wordpress. The right side figure presents the Cumulative Distribution Function (CDF) of the obtained response times.

4.2 The Overhead

The overhead of our solutions is almost nil. In reality, only the second solution could have introduced a possible overhead during performance counters collection. However, Perfctr-xen [24] authors and several other researches [10] have reported that this fear is unjustified. This also corresponds to what we have observed.

5 Related Work

The Heterogeneity Issue in SMP Clouds

Several researches have investigated the problem of hardware heterogeneity in today's clouds. [12] evaluates the impact of assuming a heterogeneous cloud as being homogeneous. It proposes a metric to express an application sensibility facing heterogeneity. [25] proposed to standardize the representation of the processing power of CPU by using Processing Units. [13] based on this Processing Units, presents the Execution and Resources Homogenization Architecture (ERHA). ERHA aims to provide mechanisms for submitting and executing batch applications in private IaaS clouds using homogeneous virtual environments created over heterogeneous physical infrastructure. Concerning public clouds, some (such as Amazon EC2) avoid the issue of hardware heterogeneity by dedicating the same hardware type to each VM type. For instance, EC2 announces to their customers that a m3.medium VM instance will always run atop an Intel Xeon

CPU E5-2650 2.00 GHz processor. This strategy is constraining for VM colocation. Indeed, a VM could not be deployed on a machine even if this machine
has enough resources to host the VM. Concerning other public clouds such as
Rackspace, the allocation unit is a vCPU and no more information is given
about the real computing capacity. The actual computing capacity of a VM on
this IaaS depends on the underlying core type, as illustrated in the introduction
(see Fig. 1).

The Heterogeneity Issue in AMP Clouds
Several research works on AMP systems have focused on the scheduling issue and
not on the predictability issue. Most of them have been conducted in the context
of native systems. [9,17,18,21–23,26] aim at determining the best thread to core
mapping in order to improve thread performance. [26] investigates applications
which are composed of both parallel and sequential phases. [26] improves the
scheduler by running sequential phase threads on fast cores. [7] tries to ensure
fair sharing of the fast cores while [20] proposes to assigned vCPUs to core
according to their speed. Therefore, fast core run-queues receive more vCPUs
than slow cores. [9] shows that in an AMP, dynamic thread migration policies
provide larger performance improvements than static policies. Their dynamic
thread migration policy executes the threads for a small time duration on each
core to measure their IPC (Instruction Per Cycle). Based on this, a thread that
achieves only modest performance improvements from running on a fast core is
executed on a slow core, and a thread that benefits significantly from running
on a fast core is executed on the fast core. Researches conducted in virtualized
systems [15,18,19,26] consist in translating native system solutions in virtualized
systems (vCPUs are seen as threads). For instance, [15] proposes to realize a fair
sharing of fast cores on AMP machines. They present a scheduling technique
for hypervisors implemented in Xen. To ensure that all virtual CPUs (vCPUs)
equally share the fast physical cores, the quota of a VM is decided depending
on the number of vCPUs in it.

Positioning of Our Work
From far of our knowledge, no research study has investigated the issue of performance unpredictability in AMP clouds. The majority of research projects,
if not all, have investigated this issue in SMP clouds. Also, they have mainly
focused on the resource contention perspective, seen as the only source of the
unpredictability problem. We have shown that heterogeneity (of memory and
processor) is significantly involved in performance unpredictability. This paper
is the only one to proposed solutions to the unpredictability in AMP clouds.

6   Conclusion

This paper addresses the issue of performance unpredictability due to the ambiguity of vCPU computing capacity expression in AMP clouds. We have presented
two solutions and their implementations within the Xen virtualized system. Each
solution includes both an absolute metric definition and an enforcement system.

The first solution relies on a reference core (p_{ref}) as the basis of vCPU capacity expression. Subsequently, relying on the proportionality coefficient between the actual core type and p_{ref}, the scheduler dynamically adjusts the allowable CPU time of the vCPU. The second solution directly introduces an absolute metric namely the "number of instructions per second" (noted Ips). We have demonstrated the effectiveness of each solution by experimenting several reference benchmarks.

References

1. Blast. http://fiehnlab.ucdavis.edu/staff/kind/Collector/Benchmark/Blast_Bench mark. Accessed 3 Feb 2015
2. Microsoft's top 10 business practices for environmentally sustainable data centers. http://www.microsoft.com/environment/news-and-resources/datacenter-best-practices.aspx. Accessed 10 Feb 2015
3. Open Stack. https://www.openstack.org/enterprise/virtualization-integration/. Accessed 3 Feb 2015
4. SPEC CPU2006. http://www.spec.org/cpu2006/. Accessed 3 Dec 2015
5. Wordpress. https://fr.wordpress.org/. Accessed 3 Feb 2015
6. y-cruncher - A multi-threaded Pi-program. http://www.numberworld.org/y-cruncher/#Benchmarks. Accessed 3 May 2014
7. Balakrishnan, S., Rajwar, R., Upton, M., Lai, K.: The impact of performance asymmetry in emerging multicore architectures. In: Proceedings of the 32Nd Annual International Symposium on Computer Architecture, ISCA 2005, pp. 506–517. IEEE Computer Society, Washington (2005). https://doi.org/10.1109/ISCA.2005.51
8. Baumann, A., Barham, P., Dagand, P.E., Harris, T., Isaacs, R., Peter, S., Roscoe, T., Schüpbach, A., Singhania, A.: The multikernel: a new OS architecture for scalable multicore systems. In: Proceedings of the ACM SIGOPS 22nd Symposium on Operating Systems Principles, SOSP 2009, pp. 29–44. ACM, New York (2009). http://doi.acm.org/10.1145/1629575.1629579
9. Becchi, M., Crowley, P.: Dynamic thread assignment on heterogeneous multiprocessor architectures. In: Proceedings of the 3rd Conference on Computing Frontiers, CF 2006, pp. 29–40. ACM, New York (2006). http://doi.acm.org/10.1145/1128022.1128029
10. Bui, V.Q.B., Teabe, B., Tchana, A., Hagimont, D.: Kyoto: applying the polluters pay principle to cache contention in an IaaS. In: Proceedings of the International Workshop on Virtualization Technologies, VT15, pp. 1–6. ACM, New York (2011). http://doi.acm.org/10.1145/2835075.2835077
11. Cherkasova, L., Gupta, D., Vahdat, A.: Comparison of the three CPU schedulers in Xen. SIGMETRICS Perform. Eval. Rev. **35**(2), 42–51. http://doi.acm.org/10.1145/1330555.1330556
12. Fedorova, A., Vengerov, D., Doucette, D.: Operating system scheduling on heterogeneous core systems. In: Proceedings of 2007 Operating System Support for Heterogeneous Multicore Architectures (2007)
13. Jin, X., Park, S., Sheng, T., Chen, R., Shan, Z., Zhou, Y.: ERHA: execution and resources homogenization architecture. In: The Third International Conference on Cloud Computing, GRIDs, and Virtualization, CLOUD COMPUTING (2015)

14. Jin, X., Park, S., Sheng, T., Chen, R., Shan, Z., Zhou, Y.: FTXen: making hypervisor resilient to hardware faults on relaxed cores. In: 21st IEEE International Symposium on High Performance Computer Architecture, HPCA 2015, Burlingame, CA, USA, 7–11 February 2015, pp. 451–462 (2015). https://doi.org/10.1109/HPCA.2015.7056054

15. Kazempour, V., Kamali, A., Fedorova, A.: AASH: an asymmetry-aware scheduler for hypervisors. SIGPLAN Not. **45**(7), 85–96. http://doi.acm.org/10.1145/1837854.1736011

16. Koh, Y., Knauerhase, R.C., Brett, P., Bowman, M., Wen, Z., Pu, C.: An analysis of performance interference effects in virtual environments. In: Proceedings of 2007 IEEE International Symposium on Performance Analysis of Systems and Software, San Jose, California, USA, 25–27 April 2007, pp. 200–209 (2007). https://doi.org/10.1109/ISPASS.2007.363750

17. Koufaty, D., Reddy, D., Hahn, S.: Bias scheduling in heterogeneous multi-core architectures. In: Proceedings of the 5th European Conference on Computer Systems, EuroSys 2010, pp. 125–138. ACM, New York (2010). http://doi.acm.org/10.1145/1755913.1755928

18. Kumar, R., Tullsen, D.M., Ranganathan, P., Jouppi, N.P., Farkas, K.I.: Single-ISA heterogeneous multi-core architectures for multithreaded workload performance. In: Proceedings of the 31st Annual International Symposium on Computer Architecture, ISCA 2004, pp. 64–77. IEEE Computer Society, Washington (2004). http://dl.acm.org/citation.cfm?id=998680.1006707

19. Kwon, Y., Kim, C., Maeng, S., Huh, J.: Virtualizing performance asymmetric multi-core systems. In: Proceedings of the 38th Annual International Symposium on Computer Architecture, ISCA 2011, pp. 45–56. ACM, New York (2011). http://doi.acm.org/10.1145/2000064.2000071

20. Li, T., Baumberger, D., Koufaty, D.A., Hahn, S.: Efficient operating system scheduling for performance-asymmetric multi-core architectures. In: Proceedings of the 2007 ACM/IEEE Conference on Supercomputing, SC 2007, pp. 1–11. ACM, New York (2007). http://doi.acm.org/10.1145/1362622.1362694

21. Liu, G., Park, J., Marculescu, D.: Dynamic thread mapping for high-performance, power-efficient heterogeneous many-core systems. In: 2013 IEEE 31st International Conference on Computer Design, ICCD 2013, Asheville, NC, USA, 6–9 October 2013, pp. 54–61 (2013). https://doi.org/10.1109/ICCD.2013.6657025

22. Luo, Y., Packirisamy, V., Hsu, W.C., Zhai, A.: Energy efficient speculative threads: Dynamic thread allocation in same-ISA heterogeneous multicore systems. In: Proceedings of the 19th International Conference on Parallel Architectures and Compilation Techniques, PACT 2010, pp. 453–464. ACM, New York (2010). http://doi.acm.org/10.1145/1854273.1854329

23. Morad, T.Y., Kolodny, A., Weiser, U.C.: Scheduling multiple multithreaded applications on asymmetric and symmetric chip multiprocessors. In: Third International Symposium on Parallel Architectures, Algorithms and Programming, PAAP 2010, Dalian, China, 18–20, pp. 65–72 (2010). https://doi.org/10.1109/PAAP.2010.50

24. Nikolaev, R., Back, G.: Perfctr-Xen: a framework for performance counter virtualization. In: Proceedings of the 7th ACM SIGPLAN/SIGOPS International Conference on Virtual Execution Environments, VEE 2011, pp. 15–26. ACM, New York (2011). http://doi.acm.org/10.1145/1952682.1952687

25. Rego, P.A.L., Coutinho, E.F., Gomes, D.G., de Souza, J.N.: FairCPU: architecture for allocation of virtual machines using processing features. In: Proceedings of the 2011 Fourth IEEE International Conference on Utility and Cloud Computing, UCC 2011, pp. 371–376. IEEE Computer Society, Washington (2011). http://dx.doi.org/10.1109/UCC.2011.62

26. Shelepov, D., Saez Alcaide, J.C., Jeffery, S., Fedorova, A., Perez, N., Huang, Z.F., Blagodurov, S., Kumar, V.: HASS: a scheduler for heterogeneous multicore systems. SIGOPS Oper. Syst. Rev. **43**(2), 66–75. http://doi.acm.org/10.1145/1531793.1531804

27. Tang, L., Mars, J., Soffa, M.L.: Contentiousness vs. sensitivity: improving contention aware runtime systems on multicore architectures. In: Proceedings of the 1st International Workshop on Adaptive Self-Tuning Computing Systems for the Exaflop Era, EXADAPT 2011, pp. 12–21. ACM, New York (2011). http://doi.acm.org/10.1145/2000417.2000419

28. Teabe, B., Tchana, A., Hagimont, D.: Enforcing CPU allocation in a heterogeneous IaaS. Future Gener. Comput. Syst. **53**(C), 1–12. http://dx.doi.org/10.1016/j.future.2015.05.013

29. Whitaker, A., Shaw, M., Gribble, S.D.: Scale and performance in the Denali isolation kernel. In: Proceedings of the 5th Symposium on Operating Systems Design and implementation Copyright Restrictions Prevent ACM from Being Able to Make the PDFs for This Conference Available for Downloading, OSDI 2002, pp. 195–209. USENIX Association, Berkeley (2002). http://dl.acm.org/citation.cfm?id=1060289.1060308

30. Zhuravlev, S., Blagodurov, S., Fedorova, A.: Addressing shared resource contention in multicore processors via scheduling. In: Proceedings of the Fifteenth Edition of ASPLOS on Architectural Support for Programming Languages and Operating Systems, ASPLOS XV, pp. 129–142. ACM, New York (2010). http://doi.acm.org/10.1145/1736020.1736036

Deadline-Aware Deployment for Time Critical Applications in Clouds

Yang Hu[1,2]([✉]), Junchao Wang[1], Huan Zhou[1,2], Paul Martin[1], Arie Taal[1],
Cees de Laat[1], and Zhiming Zhao[1]

[1] University of Amsterdam, Amsterdam, The Netherlands
{Y.Hu,j.wang2,H.Zhou,P.W.Martin,A.Taal,delaat,Z.Zhao}@uva.nl
[2] National University of Defense Technology, Changsha, China

Abstract. Time critical applications are appealing to deploy in clouds due to the elasticity of cloud resources and their on-demand nature. However, support for deploying application components with strict deadlines on their deployment is lacking in current cloud providers. This is particularly important for adaptive applications that must automatically and seamlessly scale, migrate, or recover swiftly from failures. A common deployment procedure is to transmit application packages from the application provider to the cloud, and install the application there. Thus, users need to manually deploy their applications into clouds step by step with no guarantee regarding deadlines. In this work, we propose a Deadline-aware Deployment System (DDS) for time critical applications in clouds. DDS enables users to automatically deploy applications into clouds. We design bandwidth-aware EDF scheduling algorithms in DDS that minimize the number of deployments that miss their deadlines and maximize the utilization of network bandwidth. In the evaluation, we show that DDS leverages network bandwidth sufficiently, and significantly reduces the number of missed deadlines during deployment.

1 Introduction

Cloud computing is the platform of choice for deploying and running many of today's businesses. When executing applications in clouds, deployment is an important step to make required software and data of an application available before execution. In cloud environments, Software as a Service (SaaS), e.g., Google Apps, or Platform as a Service (PaaS), e.g., Amazon EMR, aim at hiding the deployment complexity by automating deployment during resource provisioning [13]. However, these solutions are not sufficient for applications that require infrastructure-level optimization under the given platform services or application-level customized environments, which are not included in predefined virtual machines or container images.

Time critical applications, such as disaster early warning systems, often have very high performance requirements for data communication and processing [18]. To support time critical applications using cloud environments, developers often use Infrastructure as a Service (IaaS) to optimize overall system-level performance by selecting the most suitable virtual machines, customizing their network

© Springer International Publishing AG 2017
F.F. Rivera et al. (Eds.): Euro-Par 2017, LNCS 10417, pp. 345–357, 2017.
DOI: 10.1007/978-3-319-64203-1_25

topology and optimizing the scheduling of execution on the virtual infrastructure [6,16,20]. During the execution, the virtual infrastructure often has to be adapted, e.g., virtual machines scaling out/in or up/down to handle dynamically changing workloads [19]. A deployment service is thus needed not only before the application execution for making the environment available, but also at runtime. In particular, it is necessary to ensure that components can be deployed immediately whenever the application needs to re- scale to handle increased workloads, or migrate components to new VMs. Moving the repository of components closer to the application is necessary to ensure that such deployments can be handled as rapidly as possible for time critical applications. Furthermore, the deployment service also has to be aware of time constraints, e.g., deadlines, required for acceptable system performance. Deployments that fail to finish within certain deadlines harm user experience, affect application performance, and even incur penalties for application failure. However current cloud providers lack explicit support for deploying time critical applications where users need to manually deploy their applications step by step and have no guarantee regarding deployment deadlines.

In this paper, we propose a Deadline-aware Deployment System (DDS) for time critical applications in clouds. DDS enables users to automatically deploy time critical applications and provide scheduling mechanisms to guarantee deployment deadlines. First, DDS helps users to create a local repository for application components instead of using a remote repository, providing a guarantee of bandwidth for transmitting application packages where the transmission rate directly from the remote repository is widely varying. To be deadline-aware, DDS schedules deployment requests based on Earliest Deadline First (EDF) [8] which is a classical scheduling technique to minimize the number of deployments that miss deadlines. Furthermore, we design bandwidth-aware EDF to facilitate DDS to satisfy a greater number of deadline requirements and achieve sufficient utilization of bandwidth. In the evaluation, we demonstrate that DDS significantly reduces the number of deployments that miss deadlines, and leverages bandwidth sufficiently. We summarize our contributions as follows:

- We design and implement DDS, a deadline-aware deployment system which can support automatic deployments of time critical applications in clouds.
- We build on DDS to implement deployment scheduling algorithms that minimize the number of deployments that miss deadlines and maximize the utilization of bandwidth.
- We experimentally evaluate the benefits of DDS on the ExoGENI [2] test-bed and large-scale simulations by comparing it with three different scheduling techniques.

2   Problem Statement

A typical scenario for deploying distributed applications in clouds involves two basic steps: transmitting necessary application packages or software components from remote repositories to virtual machines (VMs) in the provisioned infrastructure; and installing the software once runnable. In this paper, we assume containers, e.g., Docker [9], are the default way to wrap application components.

For a distributed application, the deployment service has to know the location of application components, and the location to deploy (VMs) for each component. Those container images are often stored in a repository, e.g., Docker hub, which is not a part of the provisioned virtual infrastructure. The deployment service should schedule the sequence of each component based on the application description for transmitting and installing each individual component. The time for deploying a single container (T_d) typically contains time cost for transmitting the component from its repository (T_f) and installing (extracting files from the Docker image) the component (T_i). The total time of the deployment of the whole application starts from the first component transmission until the last component finishes its installation. When an application contains more components, careless scheduling of the deployment sequence might lead to a high time cost, which can eventually influence the execution of the application if key application components are delayed during deployment.

T_f depends on the size of the container and the network bandwidth between repository and target. T_i mainly depends on the performance of the VM and the complexity of the container itself. In many cases, T_f is much bigger than T_i. Table 1 shows some observations in a private cloud environment (ExoGENI [2]). We created VMs which are "xo.medium" configuration in three different locations: Boston, Washington and Houston. We found that T_f is widely varying because the internet connection between VMs and Docker hub is different between different locations, and T_i is stable for the same VM configurations. For meeting the deployment time constraints of time critical applications in provisioned virtual infrastructure, the key challenge is how to minimize the transmission time T_f and predict the installation time T_i. Installation time prediction is not the focus on this paper—we assume that existing predictors [11] can achieve good estimations of installation time. In this paper, we focus on the transmission process (T_f) of deployment.

Table 1. Comparison of transmission time and installation time in different locations

Docker image	Image size	Boston rack	Washington rack	Houston rack
ubuntu	400 Mb	$T_f : 40.8\,\mathrm{s}(\pm 2.2\,\mathrm{s})$	$T_f : 27.0\,\mathrm{s}(\pm 1.5\,\mathrm{s})$	$T_f : 20.3\,\mathrm{s}(\pm 1.5\,\mathrm{s})$
		$T_i : 6.3\,\mathrm{s}(\pm 0.5\,\mathrm{s})$	$T_i : 6.4\,\mathrm{s}(\pm 0.4\,\mathrm{s})$	$T_i : 6.3\,\mathrm{s}(\pm 0.6\,\mathrm{s})$
nginx	576 Mb	$T_f : 58.7\,\mathrm{s}(\pm 2.5\,\mathrm{s})$	$T_f : 38.9\,\mathrm{s}(\pm 2.6\,\mathrm{s})$	$T_f : 29.2\,\mathrm{s}(\pm 1.8\,\mathrm{s})$
		$T_i : 9.3\,\mathrm{s}(\pm 0.7\,\mathrm{s})$	$T_i : 9.1\,\mathrm{s}(\pm 0.5\,\mathrm{s})$	$T_i : 9.3\,\mathrm{s}(\pm 0.6\,\mathrm{s})$
mongodb	1200 Mb	$T_f : 122.4\,\mathrm{s}(\pm 3.0\,\mathrm{s})$	$T_f : 81.0\,\mathrm{s}(\pm 3.4\,\mathrm{s})$	$T_f : 60.9\,\mathrm{s}(\pm 1.9\,\mathrm{s})$
		$T_i : 15.4\,\mathrm{s}(\pm 0.5\,\mathrm{s})$	$T_i : 15.7\,\mathrm{s}(\pm 0.8\,\mathrm{s})$	$T_i : 15.5\,\mathrm{s}(\pm 0.8\,\mathrm{s})$
cassandra	1296 Mb	$T_f : 132.2\,\mathrm{s}(\pm 3.1\,\mathrm{s})$	$T_f : 87.5\,\mathrm{s}(\pm 3.4\,\mathrm{s})$	$T_f : 65.7\,\mathrm{s}(\pm 2.3\,\mathrm{s})$
		$T_i : 17.1\,\mathrm{s}(\pm 0.9\,\mathrm{s})$	$T_i : 17.3\,\mathrm{s}(\pm 0.7\,\mathrm{s})$	$T_i : 17.4\,\mathrm{s}(\pm 0.6\,\mathrm{s})$

The deployment model in this work is a set of deployment requests. The deployment service has to optimize the time cost by scheduling component transmissions carefully, and parallelize the data transfer based on the time constraint obtained from the application. We model the deployment request as a tuple $R_i = (v_i, s_i, d_i)$, where v_i is the target virtual machine to deploy request R_i, s_i is the application size (e.g., Mb), and d_i is its deadline. As we concentrate on transmission, we model bandwidth information for provisioned VMs as sets $B = \{b_1, b_2, b_3, \ldots, b_n\}$, where b_i denotes the bandwidth of virtual machine i. This means that the *throughput* of virtual machine i can not exceed b_i during the transmission process, and the bandwidth is stable based on the SLA provisioning mechanisms [3] in this context. We denote the bandwidth of the target machine v_i as b_j, so that the transmission time of request R_i can be represented as $T_f = \frac{s_i}{b_j}$. Similarly, the deployment time can be represented as $T_d = \frac{s_i}{b_j} + T_i$. The problem of this paper is thus to investigate the scheduling mechanisms needed to meet the deployment deadlines (i.e., ensure that $T_d \leq d_i$) of time critical applications in clouds.

3   Deadline-Aware Deployment System

This section highlights our approach in DDS. DDS aims to provide a deadline-aware, efficient and automatic deployment system that supports time critical applications on infrastructure as a service on cloud systems. As we mainly consider the transmission part of the deployment procedure in this paper, DDS focuses on the network of the underlying distributed system to provide the best guarantee for deployment within deadlines.

3.1   Design Principles

Repository Location. The repository for the application is a shared storage from which application packages can be fetched to be installed on another machine. The repository can be located in a remote server or in the cloud already. The location of the repository can directly impact the deployment time because the network bandwidth between cloud VMs and between a VM and a remote repository in a different location can be very different. Compared to a remote repository, a local repository within a cloud has some obvious advantages. First, the local repository has greater transmission capacity than the remote repository. Second, the bandwidth of the local repository inside a cloud is more stable, which provides a guarantee regarding the transmission time. Third, the local repository is more flexible due to the possibility of personalized configuration. Thus, DDS would help users to create a local repository first if there is only a remote repository from which to fetch application packages.

Deadline-Aware Mechanism. As the goal of DDS to meet the deadline of requests, whether the system is aware of the deadline is important for deployment. Consider a common time critical application scenario involving two deployment requests sent to the same application component provider simultaneously,

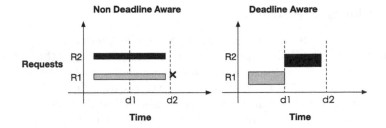

Fig. 1. Awareness of deadlines can be used to meet two deadlines

where one request has a tighter deadline than the other. The resulting requests share a bottleneck via which to transmit application packages. As shown in Fig. 1, with today's setup, the transport protocol (e.g., TCP) strives for fairness and the transmission finishes for both requests almost simultaneously. However, only one of the requests meets its deadline which makes the another request useless or degrades its value. Alternatively, given explicit information about deployment deadlines, the system can arrange the transmission order to better meet the deployment deadline.

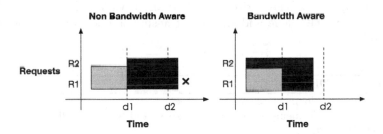

Fig. 2. Awareness of bandwidth can be used to meet two deadlines

Bandwidth-Aware Mechanism. In addition to deadline-aware scheduling, to be aware of bandwidth is another significant attribute for deployment. Consider another scenario with two deployment requests, where the second request pulls a larger application package. The resulting requests also share a link to transmit their respective packages. As shown in Fig. 2, the deployment system has information about the deadlines and schedules the transmission based on those deadlines. However only one request meets its deadline. Because the transmission bottleneck is the bandwidth of the target machine, there is some spare bandwidth on the server which is not used. Thus, given explicit information about the bandwidth capacity of each machine in the cloud, the system could schedule more deployment requests and leverage the bandwidth more efficiently.

3.2   Scheduling Algorithm

In this section, we zoom in on the design principles presented in Sect. 3.1 by providing an algorithmic description. The main goal of our algorithms is to minimize the deadline miss rate: the application packages should be transmitted to the target machine within the deadline wherever possible. In addition to minimizing miss rate, we should maximize the bandwidth utilization to reduce the total transmission time. To achieve both these goals, we employ EDF to prioritize requests and design bandwidth-aware EDF to support parallel transmission and realize dynamic rate control.

EDF Scheduling. The key insight guiding the design of deadline-aware scheduling is derived from the classic real-time scheduling algorithm Earliest Deadline First (EDF) [8], which prioritizes tasks based on their deadline. EDF is an optimal scheduling algorithm in that if a set of deadlines can be satisfied under some schedule, then EDF can satisfy them too.

We adopt EDF to schedule deployment requests. When a deployment request comes, DDS compares the deadline of new request with previous requests and then sets the corresponding priority relative to the other deadlines. DDS then puts the new request into the request queue where the requests are sorted by priority. The algorithm is described in Algorithm 1. Consequently, DDS obtains the request from the queue and starts to transmit application packages to the target machine.

Algorithm 1. EDF scheduling

Input: The new deployment request Ri
Output: The request queue RQ where requests sorted by the deadline
 1: **for** each $Rj \in RQ$ **do**
 2:     **if** $Ri.deadline < Rj.deadline$ **then**
 3:         $RQ.insert(Ri)$
 4:         **return** RQ
 5:     **end if**
 6: **end for**
 7: $RQ.append(Ri)$
 8: **return** RQ

Bandwidth-Aware EDF Scheduling. In addition to EDF scheduling, we design bandwidth-aware scheduling in cooperation with EDF scheduling. The key idea of bandwidth-aware scheduling is to make use of the spare bandwidth available between the local repository and the target as much as possible for parallelizing multiple requests. Thus, DDS needs the bandwidth information for each machine in the cloud. DDS would collect the bandwidth information before the whole deployment procedure begins.

Algorithm 2. Bandwidth-aware EDF scheduling

Input: *throughput* and *bandwidth* of the local repository
1: **while** *throughput* < *bandwidth* **do**
2:    **if** $RQ \notin \emptyset$ **then**
3:       $R_i = RQ.pop()$
4:       $b_j = $ **GetBandwidth**(v_i)
5:       **if** *throughput* $+ b_j < $ *bandwidth* **then**
6:          *throughput* = *throughput* $+ b_j$
7:       **else**
8:          **SetTransmissionRate**$(R_i, bandwidth - throughput)$
9:          *throughput* = bandwidth
10:      **end if**
11:      **StartTransmission**(R_i)
12:   **end if**
13: **end while**
14: **return**

EDF is optimal when the deadlines can be satisfied. However, without bandwidth information, EDF would schedule requests in a sequential way which leads to insufficient utilization of bandwidth or even missed deployment deadlines. However if we directly schedule requests in a parallel way, the bandwidth contention among different requests can also cause deployment deadlines to be missed. Therefore, the challenge of bandwidth-aware scheduling is how to dynamically allocate transmission rates for deployment requests in order to avoid unnecessary contention. For this purpose, we design bandwidth-aware EDF algorithm as described in Algorithm 2.

As per the description of bandwidth-aware EDF, if there is spare bandwidth in the local repository, DDS will continue to obtain requests from the request queue until the required bandwidth is equal or greater than the local repository bandwidth. DDS then sets the specific rate for the last deployment request to make sure the total required bandwidth is equal to the bandwidth of local repository. Consequently, it avoids bandwidth contention with previous deployment requests and makes full use of spare bandwidth to transmit. Once a new deployment request arrives, DDS performs bandwidth-aware EDF scheduling after putting the request in the request queue. When one deployment request finishes, DDS will allocate the released bandwidth for the running requests first, and then perform bandwidth-aware EDF scheduling again.

4   Evaluation

In this section, we describe experiments for quantitative evaluation of the deadline-aware deployment system. We perform three kinds of experiments. First, we evaluate the transmission time using a DDS local repository versus a remote repository. Second, we evaluate DDS in comparison with three typical scheduling algorithms by running experiments on our cloud test-bed. Third, we evaluate DDS in larger-scale simulations.

4.1   Repository Evaluation

In this section, we compare the transmission time to a target machine from a
DDS local repository and a remote repository based on Docker. In most common
cases, the application provider only has the repository outside cloud. Thus, DDS
would help users to create local repository within their cloud first. We provision
two virtual machines with 50Mbps bandwidth in the ExoGENI Boston rack and
create a local repository in one of them. Then, we use the other machine to
fetch the image from the local repository and also the original remote repository
(Docker Hub). The comparative results are shown in the Table 2. Note that the
transmission time (T_f) from the local repository is much less than from the
remote repository, the reason being that the bandwidth inside cloud is much
better than outside.

Table 2. Comparison of transmission time from different repository

Docker image	Image size	Local repository	Remote repository
ubuntu	400 Mb	T_f : 8.1 s($\pm$1.1 s)	T_f : 40.8 s($\pm$2.2 s)
nginx	576 Mb	T_f : 11.7 s($\pm$1.3 s)	T_f : 58.7 s($\pm$2.5 s)
mongodb	1200 Mb	T_f : 24.4 s($\pm$1.2)	T_f : 122.4 s($\pm$3.0 s)
cassandra	1296 Mb	T_f : 26.4 s($\pm$1.5)	T_f : 132.2 s($\pm$3.1 s)

4.2   Testbed Experiments

In this section, we evaluate DDS alongside three typical scheduling algorithms in ExoGENI [2] test-bed. ExoGENI is a networked infrastructure-as-
a-service (NIaaS) platform where researchers can define the network topology
and bandwidth of virtual infrastructures. In our experimental setup, we chose
the "xo.xlarge" type of machine as our local repository, and all other application
nodes we chose "xo.medium" type machines. The guest OS in VMs which are
provisioned for evaluation is Ubuntu 14.04. In the experiment, we use *iPerf* [12]
to simulate the application package transmission, therefore the size of application package can be customized via *iPerf* in the evaluation. For transmission rate
control, we leverage Linux Traffic Control (TC) to perform deployment request
rate limiting. We use two-level Hierarchical Token Bucket (HTB) in TC: the root
node classifies requests to their corresponding leaf nodes based on IP address
and the leaf nodes enforce each request rate.

Schemes to Compare: We compare the following schemes with DDS.

- **FIFO:** All the deployment requests are scheduled by the arrival time of the
  request in a sequential way.
- **EDF:** All the deployment requests are scheduled by the EDF algorithm in a
  sequential way.

- **PARALLEL:** All the deployment requests are scheduled immediately after arrival in a parallel way.

Through comparison with these three schemes, we can inspect the benefits from DDS for different aspects. FIFO is the most common scheduling algorithm in distribution. EDF is optimal in sequential scheduling when the deadline can be satisfied, but it is not bandwidth-aware. PARALLEL can make high utilization of the bandwidth, but it is not deadline-aware.

Metrics: In this section, we compare the number of schedulable requests (requests that meet the deadline) and the total deployment time among different schemes. The number of schedulable requests can indicate the satisfaction of deadline requirements. The total deployment time can indicate the utilization of network bandwidth.

In this experiment, we provision two kinds of bandwidth configuration to evaluate DDS as the Table 3 described. We instantiate four nodes to deploy time critical applications in ExoGENI. For these four nodes, we generate six deployment requests which include the target machine, application size, arrival time and the deadline as the Table 4 described. To understand the scheduling mechanisms in DDS better, we assume that the installation time T_i of each application is $1s$ in this experiment.

In Fig. 3, we inspect the number of schedulable requests on different schemes. We observe that DDS can schedule more requests in two different bandwidth configurations, because sequential scheduling (EDF, FIFO) can not meet all the deadlines when multiple requests emerge simultaneously, and direct parallel scheduling suffers from bandwidth contention. Figure 4 shows the total deployment time of various schemes. We note that the total deployment time of DDS is less than EDF & FIFO, and similar to PARALLEL. This indicates that DDS makes full use of network bandwidth.

4.3 Large-Scale Simulations

Our simulations evaluate DDS considering the common public cloud provider (EC2, Azure) in this section. We evaluate the deployment schedulable ratio which is the percentage of schedulable requests in different schemes.

Table 3. Bandwidth configuration

(a) Configuration A (Mbps)

Repository	Node1	Node2	Node3	Node4
100	20	50	70	100

(b) Configuration B (Mbps)

Repository	Node1	Node2	Node3	Node4
100	70	70	70	70

Table 4. Deployment request

Machine	Size	Deadline	Arrival time
Node1	200 Mb	14 s	0 s
Node1	160 Mb	20 s	10 s
Node2	320 Mb	9 s	11 s
Node2	560 Mb	15 s	30 s
Node3	960 Mb	20 s	30 s
Node4	640 Mb	25 s	30 s

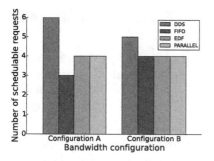

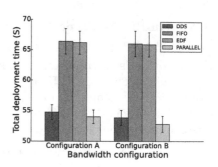

Fig. 3. Comparison of the number of schedulable requests in various schemes

Fig. 4. Comparison of the total deployment time in various schemes

VMs Configuration: We equip the deployment server with 10 Gbps bandwidth connection and application node with 1 Gbps bandwidth connection which are typical configuration in public cloud. In the simulation, the number of application nodes range over 10, 20, 40 and 80 nodes which are sufficient to account for most distributed cloud applications.

Deployment Requests: We simulate the deployment service running 10 days ($T_{running}$) in the experiment. During this period, we generate deployment requests in different densities to simulate deploying various applications on each node. We denote S^i_{total} as the total application size of all deployment requests on node i. The request density of node i is equal to $\frac{S^i_{total}}{T_{running}*10Gigabit}$, and the request density of whole system is the average for each node. The overall request density varies from 0.1 to 0.9. In the experiment, the deadline (d_i) of each request ranges from $10s$ to $100s$, and the application size is equal to $d_i * 1Gigabit$. We assume the installation time (T_i) is $1s$ in the simulation.

Figure 5 shows the deployment schedulable ratio in different scenarios. We observe that DDS can reduce from 24% to 83% of the deployment deadline miss ratio compared to EDF, from 26% to 89% compared to FIFO, and up to 86% compared to PARALLEL. Because EDF and FIFO schedule deployment requests in sequential way, DDS can take advantage of parallelized deployments. The PARALLEL scheme parallelizes deployments but suffers severe bandwidth contention as request density increases. In contrast, DDS is bandwidth-aware and provides dynamic transmission rate control to avoid bandwidth contention for different deployment requests. In summary, DDS significantly reduces the number of deadline missing requests for deploying cloud applications.

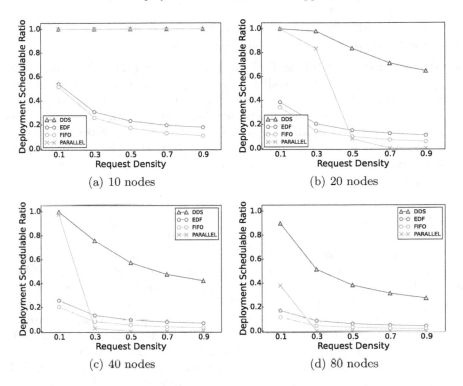

Fig. 5. Comparison of the deployment schedulable ratio in different scenarios

5 Related Work

In recent years, deployment has been an important topic in distributed environment, service-oriented systems and cloud computing. The techniques in DDS are related to the following areas of research:

Automatic Cloud Application Deployment. To enable automatic deployment has been the focus of several recent works. SO-MVDS [5] allows users to design and create virtual machines with specific services running in them and define a service deployment request to enhance the efficiency of service deployment. Li et al. [7] propose a general approach to application deployment. They adopt contextualization process which is to embed various scripts in VM images to initiate applications. DDS, on the other hand, is compatible with Docker containers, achieving automatic deployment more easily.

On-Demand Image Distribution. The idea of distributing images in clouds efficiently has been explored in recent works. Vaquero et al. [15] proposes a solution based on combining hierarchical and Peer to Peer (P2P) data distribution techniques. VDN [10], a new VM image distribution network on the top of chunk-level, enables collaborate sharing in cloud data centers. These approaches focus on fast transmission. In contrast, DDS is not only transmitting images efficiently but is also aware of deadlines via scheduling mechanisms.

Deadline-Aware Scheduling Techniques. D^3[17] and D^2TCP [14] are transport protocols designed for deadline-aware transmission inside data centers. These protocols add the deadline information to TCP and provide control mechanisms based on the deadline information. Techniques like Karuna [4] and pFabric [1] prioritize network flows to transmit. All these approaches schedule transmission at flow level. In contrast, DDS exploits the information of bandwidth to schedule transmission in application level which is more relevant to users requirements.

6   Conclusion

It is challenging to deploy time critical applications into clouds while meeting the time constraints of deployment. This is an important and practical problem, but has been neglected by prior work in this field. In this paper, we propose a Deadline-aware Deployment System (DDS) which helps users to create local repository and automatically deploy applications into clouds. We investigate the scheduling mechanisms in cloud deployment system and implement bandwidth-aware EDF scheduling algorithm in DDS. DDS schedules deployment requests based on deadline and bandwidth information to make better scheduling decision. In the evaluation, we showed that DDS leverages network resources sufficiently and significantly reduces the number of missed deployment deadlines. Furthermore, we plan to investigate multiple repositories deployment and inter-data center network for time critical cloud applications.

Acknowledgments. This research has received funding from the European Union's Horizon 2020 research and innovation program under grant agreements 643963 (SWITCH project), 654182 (ENVRIPLUS project) and 676247 (VRE4EIC project). The research is also partially funded by the COMMIT project.

References

1. Alizadeh, M., Yang, S., Sharif, M., Katti, S., McKeown, N., Prabhakar, B., Shenker, S.: pFabric: minimal near-optimal datacenter transport. In: ACM SIGCOMM Computer Communication Review, vol. 43, pp. 435–446. ACM (2013)
2. Baldin, I., Chase, J., Xin, Y., Mandal, A., Ruth, P., Castillo, C., Orlikowski, V., Heermann, C., Mills, J.: ExoGENI: a multi-domain infrastructure-as-a-service testbed. In: McGeer, R., Berman, M., Elliott, C., Ricci, R. (eds.) The GENI Book, pp. 279–315. Springer, Cham (2016). doi:10.1007/978-3-319-33769-2_13
3. Casalicchio, E., Silvestri, L.: Mechanisms for SLA provisioning in cloud-based service providers. Comput. Netw. **57**(3), 795–810 (2013)
4. Chen, L., Chen, K., Bai, W., Alizadeh, M.: Scheduling mix-flows in commodity datacenters with Karuna. In: Proceedings of the 2016 conference on ACM SIGCOMM 2016 Conference, pp. 174–187. ACM (2016)

5. Gao, W., Jin, H., Wu, S., Shi, X., Yuan, J.: Effectively deploying services on virtualization infrastructure. Front. Comput. Sci. **6**(4), 398–408 (2012)
6. Hu, Y., Li, H., Peng, Y.: NVLAN: a novel VLAN technology for scalable multi-tenant datacenter networks. In: 2014 Second International Conference on Advanced Cloud and Big Data (CBD), pp. 190–195. IEEE (2014)
7. Li, W., Svärd, P., Tordsson, J., Elmroth, E.: A general approach to service deployment in cloud environments. In: 2012 Second International Conference on Cloud and Green Computing (CGC), pp. 17–24. IEEE (2012)
8. Liu, C.L., Layland, J.W.: Scheduling algorithms for multiprogramming in a hard-real-time environment. J. ACM (JACM) **20**(1), 46–61 (1973)
9. Merkel, D.: Docker: lightweight Linux containers for consistent development and deployment. Linux J. **2014**(239), 2 (2014)
10. Peng, C., Kim, M., Zhang, Z., Lei, H.: VDN: virtual machine image distribution network for cloud data centers. In: 2012 Proceedings IEEE INFOCOM, pp. 181–189. IEEE (2012)
11. Smith, W., Foster, I., Taylor, V.: Predicting application run times using historical information. In: Feitelson, D.G., Rudolph, L. (eds.) JSSPP 1998. LNCS, vol. 1459, pp. 122–142. Springer, Heidelberg (1998). doi:10.1007/BFb0053984
12. Tirumala, A., Qin, F., Dugan, J., Ferguson, J., Gibbs, K.: Iperf: the TCP/UDP bandwidth measurement tool (2005). http://dast.nlanr.net/Projects
13. Tsai, W., Bai, X., Huang, Y.: Software-as-a-service (SaaS): perspectives and challenges. Sci. China Inf. Sci. **57**(5), 1–15 (2014)
14. Vamanan, B., Hasan, J., Vijaykumar, T.: Deadline-aware datacenter TCP (D2TCP). ACM SIGCOMM Comput. Commun. Rev. **42**(4), 115–126 (2012)
15. Vaquero, L.M., Celorio, A., Cuadrado, F., Cuevas, R.: Deploying large-scale datasets on-demand in the cloud: treats and tricks on data distribution. IEEE Trans. Cloud Comput. **3**(2), 132–144 (2015)
16. Wang, J., Taal, A., Martin, P., Hu, Y., Zhou, H., Pang, J., de Laat, C., Zhao, Z.: Planning virtual infrastructures for time critical applications with multiple deadline constraints. Future Gener. Comput. Syst. (2017)
17. Wilson, C., Ballani, H., Karagiannis, T., Rowtron, A.: Better never than late: meeting deadlines in datacenter networks. In: ACM SIGCOMM Computer Communication Review, vol. 41, pp. 50–61. ACM (2011)
18. Zhao, Z., Martin, P., De Laat, C., Jeffery, K., Jones, A., Taylor, I., Hardisty, A., Atkinson, M., Zuiderwijk, A., Yin, Y., Chen, Y.: Time critical requirements and technical considerations for advanced support environments for data-intensive research. In: 2nd International Workshop on Interoperable Infrastructures for Interdisciplinary Big Data Sciences (IT4RIs) in the Context of IEEE Real-Time System Symposium (RTSS) (2016)
19. Zhao, Z., Martin, P., Wang, J., Taal, A., Jones, A., Taylor, I., Stankovski, V., Vega, I.G., Suciu, G., Ulisses, A., et al.: Developing and operating time critical applications in clouds: the state of the art and the SWITCH approach. Procedia Comput. Sci. **68**, 17–28 (2015)
20. Zhou, H., Hu, Y., Wang, J., Martin, P., De Laat, C., Zhao, Z.: Fast and dynamic resource provisioning for quality critical cloud applications. In: 2016 IEEE 19th International Symposium on Real-Time Distributed Computing (ISORC), pp. 92–99. IEEE (2016)

More Sharing, More Benefits?
A Study of Library Sharing
in Container-Based Infrastructures

José Bravo Ferreira[1]([✉]), Marco Cello[2], and Jesús Omana Iglesias[2]

[1] Princeton University, Princeton, USA
josesf@princeton.edu
[2] Nokia Bell Labs, Dublin, Ireland
{marco.cello,jesus.omana_iglesias}@nokia-bell-labs.com

Abstract. Container-based infrastructures have surged in popularity, offering advantages in agility and scaling, while also presenting new challenges in resource utilization due to unnecessary library duplication. In this paper, we consider sharing libraries across containers, and study the impact of such a strategy on overall resource requirements, scheduling, and utilization. Our analysis and simulations suggest significant benefits arising from library sharing. Furthermore, a small fraction of libraries shared between any two containers, on average, is enough to reap most of the benefits, and even naïve schedulers, such as a First Fit scheduler, succeed at doing so. We also propose a score maximization, mixed-integer linear-programming scheduler for handling bulk request arrivals (such as large jobs composed of many smaller tasks), which compares favorably against state-of-the-art schedulers in these scenarios.

1 Introduction

Container-based infrastructures are gaining popularity both in Infrastructure-as-a-Service (IaaS) and Platform-as-a-Service (PaaS) models. In IaaS (e.g. Pantheon and Amazon ECS) abstracting away the host operating system allows providers to make system-wide changes quickly, to provision new containers with little delay, and to scale up without worrying about architecture. This is also the case for PaaS (e.g. Heroku and Google's App Engine), where providers must automatically manage and maintain necessary infrastructure behind the scenes.

Containers can be added and removed in seconds, allowing for greater flexibility in dynamically scaling applications and in running mostly idle services. Modern container hypervisors, such as LXD[1], or container managers, such as Docker[2] or Kubernetes[3], facilitate the management of containers, with automatic scheduling, scaling and storage orchestration. This is accomplished while running seamlessly on most infrastructures using open standard containers.

---

[1] https://linuxcontainers.org/lxd/.
[2] https://www.docker.com/.
[3] https://kubernetes.io.

© Springer International Publishing AG 2017
F.F. Rivera et al. (Eds.): Euro-Par 2017, LNCS 10417, pp. 358–371, 2017.
DOI: 10.1007/978-3-319-64203-1_26

The adoption of container-based infrastructures is bolstered by the increasing popularity of a microservices approach to software design, focused on scalability, agility, resilience, and developer efficiency [3]. However, breaking down an application into many smaller processes that need large-scale replication might also require loading the same set of libraries inside each container, resulting in memory duplication.

Existing schedulers, such as Tetris [5] or dominant resource fairness [4] can successfully schedule and pack tasks in an efficient way, but a large increase in the number of containers demands answers to new challenges related to volume, locality (runtime environments), and dependencies between containers [9].

As an extreme example of microservices design, recent efforts in *Serverless* solutions, such as AWS Lambda[4], incentivize the application developer to implement their services as a composition of stateless functions, often triggered by predefined events (e.g. a user request or a database change) and written in predefined programming languages. This leads the cloud provider to instantiate many containers loaded with similar runtime environments and the same language-specific libraries, so that library-sharing could be not just beneficial but an actual necessity. The analysis presented in [8, Figs. 3 and 13] shows that current Docker images contained in Docker Hub[5] already share some amount of libraries since they share common AUFS layers.

In this paper, we analyze the possible benefits of library-sharing across containers as a potential solution in current container-based infrastructures. Conceptually, we consider a scenario in which libraries are shared using a union file system across Linux containers (LXC), and study the impact on resource utilization through simulations and mathematical analysis. We:

1. Study library-sharing in single- and multi-resource scenarios analytically and through simulation, illustrating that even small levels of sharing yield significant savings in memory-bound scenarios (Sects. 4.1 and 4.2);
2. Propose a scheduling algorithm based on mixed-integer linear-programming (MILP) for handling bulk arrivals, which compares favorably against state-of-the-art schedulers and can be adapted to custom goals via a scoring function Sect. 4.2 providing improvements over naïve schedulers.

Section 2 lays down the motivation for this work in greater detail, Sect. 3 describes the methodology used in the paper, Sect. 4 presents the results of the analysis, and Sect. 5 summarizes the main conclusions.

2   Motivation

Current standard practice in container-based applications is to package all needed libraries in the container [7]. This approach has several advantages, such

---

[4] https://aws.amazon.com/lambda/.
[5] https://hub.docker.com/u/library/.

as ensuring that the application uses the intended version of the libraries. However, this solution suffers from redundantly loading libraries in memory that could otherwise be shared across containers.

Sharing libraries is a form of *memory deduplication* (MD), defined as a set of techniques to reduce the memory footprint of a running system by merging memory pages[6] with the same contents. A way to implement MD is through the use of union filesystem, such as AUFS[7]. AUFS takes a list of directories on a single Linux host and provides a single unified view. These directories are often referred to as *layers* and the technology used to layer them is known as a union mount. In AUFS, all the layers but the top one are read-only, and the unified view is exposed through its own directory called merged

In order to showcase the benefits of AUFS, we present results when 3 containers are running in the same host. Let us denote the three containers by c1, c2 and c3. c1 and c2's filesystem directories are AUFS union mount points, composed of 3 layers: *ubuntu base* (Ubuntu base OS), *gsl layer* (GNU scientific libraries), and *container layer* (writeable layer containing the binary test file). In contrast, c3's filesystem directory is a regular ext4 filesystem containing Ubuntu base OS, GNU scientific libraries and the binary test file. Figure 1 shows how the filesystem directories are created for the three containers. When the LXC containers are created, c1 and c2 share both Ubuntu base OS files and GSL scientific libraries on disk, while c3 does not share any file with the other two.

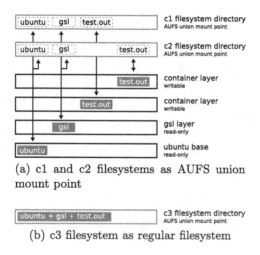

(a) c1 and c2 filesystems as AUFS union mount point

(b) c3 filesystem as regular filesystem

Fig. 1. Creation of testbed container filesystems.

---

[6] A fixed-length contiguous block of virtual memory, described by a single entry in the page table. It is the smallest unit of data for memory management in a virtual memory operating system.

[7] http://aufs.sourceforge.net/aufs.html.

A C executable, `test.out`, using GSL, is ran in all three containers. We considered different scenarios in which containers and the binary are running:

S1 Only `c1+test.out` is running on the host.
S2 Both `c1+test.out` and `c2+test.out` are running on the host.
S3 Both `c1+test.out` and `c3+test.out` are running on the host.

To show the amount of memory shared by GSL libraries (used internally by `test.out`) across containers we make use of the linux command `pmap`[8] which displays the process map of any process and its actual memory consumption.

Table 1 shows part of the output of the `pmap` command for scenarios **S1**, **S2**, and **S3**. The `Shrd` column shows the amount of memory which is shared with other processes and has not been modified, while the `Priv` column shows the amount of memory which is private to this process. Note that `libgsl` is not shared in **S1**. In **S2**, all libraries are now shared by the two containers, such that the total memory utilized is $\approx 2780 + 2 \cdot 156 = 3092$ kB. Finally, in scenario **S3**, we see the same numbers as in scenario **S1**, indicating no additional libraries are being shared. In this instance, $\approx 1288 + 2 \cdot 1472 = 4232$ kB are in use.

Table 1. Memory usage by c1 in scenarios S1, S2, and S3 [in kB].

S1		S2		S3		
Shrd	Priv	Shrd	Priv	Shrd	Priv	
0	4	0	4	0	4	`test.out`
0	56	64	0	0	56	`libgcc`
1156	0	1244	0	1156	0	`libc`
0	128	128	32	0	128	`libm`
0	752	748	28	0	752	`libstdc++`
0	44	44	0	0	44	`libgslcblas`
0	472	420	92	0	472	`libgsl`
128	0	128	0	128	0	`ld`
1288	1472	2780	156	1288	1472	**Total**

With this analysis, we verified that when two containers are sharing some of the libraries (in this case GSL libraries) on disk (using AUFS), they can actually share libraries in memory (**S2**). Moreover, from an operational point of view, AUFS is no more complex than other filesystems.

In this work, we analyze and quantify the improvements in resource utilization from sharing libraries. In particular, we highlight that even if two containers share, on average, only a small fraction of their libraries, the resulting memory deduplication is still substantial. Therefore, when memory is the limiting

---

[8] https://linux.die.net/man/1/pmap.

resource, as in today's data intensive applications, library sharing can result in improved server utilization. Meanwhile, resource isolation of containers is not affected, as it is handled by the linux control groups (cgroups) regardless of the union filesystem used (e.g. AUFS or OverlayFS).

3   Analysis Description

We begin by describing an abstracted model of a cloud environment for use in mathematical analysis and simulations (Subsect. 3.1). This is followed by a description of our methodology (Subsect. 3.2), and, finally, by a brief presentation of the simulator developed for this analysis (Subsect. 3.3).

3.1   Abstract Representation of a Cloud Environment

This work considers an arbitrary cloud environment, which could be a Platform-as-a-Service (PaaS) or a Serverless (Computation-as-a-Service, CaaS) platform in which the applications are designed following microservices or stateless functions principles. Users' requests for a specific application arrive at the scheduler[9] according to a well-defined distribution, and the scheduler schedules containers in an available server to complete each request. A request and a container are equivalent since container start-up and wind-down times are small relative to the duration of the container, and the containers' duration is randomly sampled, such that start-up and wind-down times can be absorbed into the distribution.

The cloud platform is composed of n_s servers, with normalized capacity of 1 in each resource (memory, cpu). Fixed, nonzero server boot-up and shut-down times are assumed throughout. The scheduler is assumed to have perfect knowledge of the state of the system (i.e. resource availability at each server). This is the case at different granularity levels in typical cloud environments [11].

3.2   Analysis Methodology

This work presents theoretical analysis and simulation results of single- and multi-resource scenarios. The two types of analysis are described in the following:

Mathematical analysis, Sect. 4.1. The memory requirements of containers are studied and parameterized by the average level of sharing across containers (f), the ratio of library to container memory requirements (r), and the memory requirements of the containers (v). The analysis considers a single-resource scenario (memory), where containers have similar memory requirements and their library sets are randomly sampled from a finite set of libraries.

Simulations, Sect. 4.2. Several simulation scenarios are considered in order to: (1) validate the mathematical analysis, (2) study the performance of the system under different scheduling algorithms and under realistic load traces. Details about the setting and traces are provided in the relevant sections.

---

[9] Or frontend. We refer here to the logical entity in the cloud infrastructure in charge of receiving requests and assigning them to the cloud's resources.

3.3 Simulator

In order to single-out the parameters of our abstracted cloud model in a large-scale context, we designed and implemented an event-driven simulator in Python 2.7, for arrival and scheduling across an arbitrary number of abstracted servers using four different scheduling algorithms, (First Fit, Greedy Fit, Tetris [5], and a mixed-integer linear-programming scheduler), in both single and multi-resource scenarios (memory, CPU, disk, I/O, and so on).

The simulator can generate requests on the fly according to predefined probability distributions, or use predefined container types (both described in Sect. 4) arriving according to Poisson distributions or uniformly on a time interval. Scheduling events periodically trigger the orchestrator, which queries the state of the servers and then runs the chosen algorithm to schedule containers in available servers. A hysteresis controller governs the boot-up and shut-down of servers by estimating resource utilization at future times assuming linear system dynamics [1]. The state of the simulation is logged periodically.

A pictorial representation of the inner workings of the simulator is presented in Fig. 2 below.

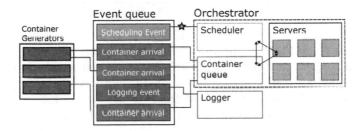

Fig. 2. Container generators (left) produce container arrival events, which contribute to form a container queue. Scheduling events trigger the orchestrator, which prompts the scheduler to query the queue and the servers and schedule containers appropriately. The status of the simulator is logged periodically. The controller (not shown) monitors the container queue and the servers, estimates resource utilization at future times assuming linear system dynamics, and triggers server boot-ups and shut-downs as needed to handle the load using a hysteresis-based approach [1].

4   Performance Evaluation

Terminology. Server capacities are normalized to 1 for each resource. The memory requirements of a container (excluding libraries) are denoted by v. The memory requirements of the library set for a container is given by $r \cdot v$, so that the total memory required by the container is $v \cdot (1 + r)$. A value of $r = 1$ thus indicates that 50% of the container's total required memory is due to the library set. If a container shares libraries with other containers on the same server, then the effective memory required by the libraries is smaller. We introduce the variable f to represent the fraction of libraries shared by any two containers, on average. Therefore, if two containers require a library set of 10 libraries, a value of $f = 0.1$ would indicate that the containers would share 1 library, on average.

The following section describes the mathematical analysis. This is followed by a discussion of the simulations.

4.1   Mathematical Analysis

The goal of this analysis is to study the relationship between memory utilization and the three variables: v, r, and f. Assume each container has the same resource requirements v, and utilizes a library set of m libraries, selected uniformly at random from a set of n libraries, such that, in expectation, $f = m/n$. The scheduler schedules each container in the first available server that can accommodate it (FirstFit).

Under the conditions defined above, the expected number of containers that fit in each server, N, is given by the following implicit equation:

$$N \approx \frac{\mathbb{E}[c_{\text{avail}}]}{v} = \frac{1 - \frac{v \cdot r}{f}(1 - (1 - f)^N)}{v}. \tag{1}$$

For a derivation of this result see Appendix A.

To quantify the impact of library sharing, we introduce the concept of **relative utilization**, u, which is the ratio of the total utilized resources to the total utilized resources when libraries are not shared (the worst-case scenario).

Figure 3 shows the value u obtained from solving Eq. (1) for various values of v and r, with f varying between 0 and 1. Several aspects are worthy of note:

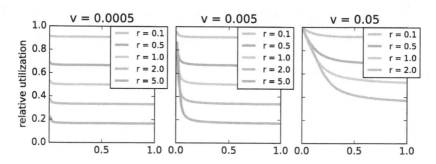

Fig. 3. Relative utilization as a function of f for various values of v and r, obtained from solving the implicit Eq. (1).

Observation 1: Higher values of f reduce the effective resource requirements of containers.

> **Observation 2:** r governs the "steady-state" of utilization in terms of f, determining the savings that can be obtained through library sharing by regulating the relative impact of libraries on the overall resource requirements of the tasks.

> **Observation 3:** A low f is sufficient to yield significant savings.

Observation 3 is less intuitive than the others, but of great importance, as it suggests that even small levels of library-sharing across containers suffice to achieve most of the memory savings that one could hope for. Note, for example, that for $v = 0.005$ there is little difference between $f = 0.1$ and $f = 1$.

> **Observation 4:** Larger v (the memory requirements of a container, excluding libraries) and r (the ratio of library memory requirements relative to v) both result in a delay of the "steady-state" in terms of f (the fraction of libraries shared by any two containers, on average).

Observation 4 implies that a larger f is required to produce the same savings when resource requirements of each container are larger, suggesting that container-based approaches have more to gain from library sharing, as container memory requirements are typically small relative to the server capacities.

4.2   Simulations

Three sets of simulations were conducted, exploring different scenarios.

The first set of simulations, **A1**, studies a single-resource scenario similar to the one assumed by the analysis in Sect. 4.1. **A2** considers a multi-resource scenario with multiple container types arriving in a Poisson fashion. Finally, **A3** studies a multi-resource scenario where requests arrive in bulk (100 s of containers at the same time).

A1. This is a single-resource simulation with 50 servers, representative of a small cluster [5], each with capacity $c = 1$. Four different container types and distributions are considered, with different v, r, and Poisson rate of arrival, λ. These are specified in Table 2 below. A FirstFit algorithm that places each container in the first available server that can accommodate it was used for

Table 2. Parameters for simulation set **A1**.

	S1.a	S1.b	S1.c	S1.d
v	$U(0, 0.01)$	$U(0, 0.01)$	$U(0, 0.003)$	$U(0, 0.1)$
r	1.0	0.1	5.0	1.0
λ	50	50	50	5

scheduling. The key difference between this simulation and the setting in Sect. 4.1 is that the container sizes, v, are sampled uniformly in some interval.

Figure 4 shows the results of simulation **S1**.a for different values of f (left), where we see that $f = 0.05$ reduces utilized memory by nearly 50%, confirming the previous finding that even a small level of overlap between container library sets suffices to yield significant savings. Figure 4 also shows the agreement in relative utilization between the simulations and the analysis in Sect. 4.1 (right), validating Eq. 1 even when v is randomly sampled.

The initial bump in the active server count is a result of the finite server boot-up times, as the controller initializes a large number of servers to accommodate the requests accumulated at the beginning of the simulation.

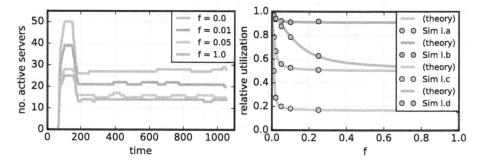

Fig. 4. Left: Number of active servers over time in a simulation with $v \sim U(0, 0.01)$, $r = 1$, and $f \in (0, 0.01, 0.05, 1.0)$. Each simulation runs until $5 \cdot 10^5$ containers are processed. Right: Comparison of relative total utilization in simulations **A1** versus theoretical results from Sect. 4.1, showing clear agreement.

A2. The second set of simulations considers a multi-resource scenario (memory and cpu) with 20 container types, each arriving according to a Poisson distribution where the arrival rate, $\lambda = 0.4$ (number of arrivals per unit of time). The container size, v, for both memory and cpu is sampled according to the cumulative distribution functions described in [10], falling in the range $(10^{-4}, 10^{-1})$. Each container type's library sets were chosen such that $r = 1$ and such that any two container types share 10% of their libraries (so that $f = 0.1$). Note that this inflates the memory requirement of the containers relative to [10], but it illustrates the point when memory is the dominant resource.

Figure 5 shows the result of the simulation when libraries are not shared (left) and when libraries are shared (right). We observe a drastic drop of about 40% in the required number of servers when libraries are being shared. We also note that by reducing the memory saturation, fewer inputs for server boot-ups and shut-downs are needed from the controller, resulting in a more stable number of active servers over time.

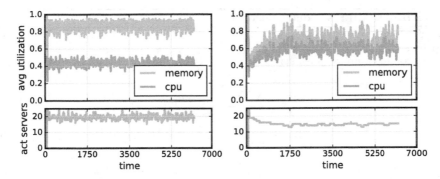

Fig. 5. Normalized memory and cpu utilization and number of active servers over time for simulation **A2**. The plots on the left show the result when libraries are not shared, while the plots on the right showcase the results when libraries are shared.

A3. This simulation set considers a multi-resource scenario where containers arrive in bulk, representing large *jobs* such as map-reduce tasks. Each job is randomly chosen as small (100 containers) or large (500 containers) with equal probability. Containers are chosen randomly from 20 container types, with randomly chosen libraries such that $f = 0.1$ across container types. Each container type is either high- or low-memory and high or low-cpu ($v = 0.10$ or $v = 0.025$, respectively). The size of the libraries is adjusted such that $r = 1.0$. Arrival times are sampled uniformly between $t = 0$ and $t = 3600$, and there are 200 jobs in total. This simulation setting is similar to the one in [5].

Having quantified the memory savings one can achieve through library sharing, this simulation considers how to best take advantage of library set overlaps between different containers, at the scheduler's level. To do this, we propose a mixed-integer linear-programming (MILP) scheduling algorithm that exploits the cost of libraries on each server, while attempting to minimize waiting time.

MILP scheduler: Let $X_{(i,j),k}$ be the number of containers of type i from job j scheduled on server k. Let $\mathsf{t}_{(i,j),k}$ be the total resource requirements of container of type i from job j on server k and $\mathbf{c}_k$ be the vector of resource capacities for server k. Let $A_{(i,j),k}$ be the corresponding score of scheduling a container of type i from job j on server k. Each entry $A_{(i,j),k}$ is a weighted combination of scores for waiting time $(t_{\max} - t_{(i,j),k})$, the shortest time remaining to finish (STRF) metric $(s_{\max} - s_{(i,j),k})$, and a fairness score (amount of resources below the job's fair-share). The algorithm is summarized below.

This is a score maximization program with linear constraints. Note that constraint 4 ensures that at most $n_{(i,j)}$ containers of type i from job j get scheduled, while constraint 5 prevents the servers' capacities from being exceeded, thereby avoiding overallocation. Gurobi [6] was used to obtain an approximate solution to the problem at each allocation interval ($<100\,$ms per scheduling event).

Algorithm 1. MILP scheduling algorithm

---
letN=Y

Require: containers, jobs, servers

  $A \leftarrow$ score(containers, jobs, servers)

  Solve:

$$\max_{X} \quad \sum_{(i,j)} \sum_{k} X_{(i,j),k} A_{(i,j),k} \tag{2}$$

$$\text{s.t.} \quad \sum_{k} X_{(i,j),k} \le n_{(i,j)}, \forall (i,j) \tag{3}$$

$$\sum_{(i,j)} X_{(i,j),k} \mathbf{t}_{(i,j),k} \le \mathbf{c}_k, \forall k \tag{4}$$

$$X_{(i,j),k} \in \mathbb{Z}_0^+, \forall (i,j), k \tag{5}$$

  for each $(i,j), k$ **do**

    schedule $X_{(i,j),k}$ containers of type i from job j on server k

---

Efficiency: The size of the problem is proportional to the number of servers and of distinct job/container type tuples. Scheduling separately on different sets of servers can help improve efficiency in scheduling at a small cost in the solution quality (provided that the server subsets are still large enough). Jobs and container types can also be classified into a smaller, perhaps fixed, number of job and container type classes, or divided into separate scheduling groups in order to minimize the scaling effects on the solver (approaches of this flavor have been adopted in scheduling literature before [2]). Note that this scheduler assigns many tasks to servers in a single scheduling event, such that such events can happen at less regular intervals.

Tetris. For comparison purposes, we also adapted the Tetris scheduler [5] to our problem, as it has been found to perform well in reducing job processing times. In this simulation we do not consider writes and reads over the network, which are explicitly accounted for in Tetris.

    Figure 6 shows the average waiting times for the 20 different container types for all three algorithms. Waiting times using the MILP scheduler were reduced by 22% and 41% compared with Tetris and FirstFit, respectively. Job processing times (arrival to end of processing of the job's last task) were reduced by 18% and 19%. This can be attributed to the fact that the algorithm schedules all available containers in a single-pass, thus taking explicit advantage of the overlap between the containers' library sets and those already loaded in the servers.

    Note that, unlike Tetris, the MILP scheduler accounts for packing in the constraints, so it does not require an alignment score in the cost function. This also contributes to the improved results. Overall, the results suggest that accounting for containers' libraries explicitly when allocating a large number of containers simultaneously is advantageous in a shared-library setting.

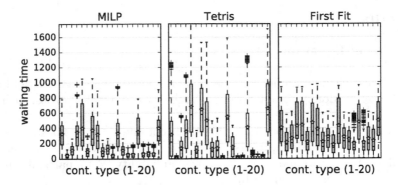

Fig. 6. Boxplot of waiting times for the 20 different container types in **A3** using three algorithms: MILP, Tetris, and First Fit.

4.3 Real Case Scenario

The analysis above covers a very large spectrum of real case scenarios. As an example, the analysis in [8] presents results about Docker images contained in Docker Hub and describes a situation in which different images share common AUFS layers. For the most downloaded docker container images, the authors show that the top layer of 90% of the images represents less than 10% of the size of the whole image [8, Fig. 13].

These scenarios fall within the parameterization in our analysis. Specifically, the results in [8] suggest a large value of $r > 5.0$ (since the topmost layer is typically a small fraction of the container), and a value of $v < 0.005$ for a server with 32 GB of RAM, in the majority of cases. The fraction of shared layers is not explicitly reported, but as the analysis in the above section has made clear, a small f of even 0.05 would drastically reduce the memory required by the containers. In particular, Fig. 3 and Eq. 1 suggest that if the images share 5% of their layers, then for $r = 5.0$ and $v = 0.005$ one could expect a relative utilization of 33.1% of that achieved when layer sharing is not used.

5 Conclusions and Future Work

Sharing libraries using filesystems such as AUFS offers a convenient yet effective solution to combat memory duplication in container-based cloud applications. Our mathematical analysis and simulations showed that the memory used by a container can be reduced by nearly 50% when the containers' library sets are as large as the container itself ($r = 1$), even if any two containers share just 10% of their libraries, on average. Our proposed MILP scheduler further improved on the results by considering the scheduling of hundreds of containers at once when requests arrive in bulk, reducing waiting times and processing times by about 22% and 18% respectively, relative to state-of-the-art schedulers. Its generality as a score-maximization algorithm also opens the door to many possible scoring functions that could include locality and architectural constraints [9].

Appendix A

Derivation of Equation 1

Recall that each container has the same resource requirements v, and a set of m libraries randomly sampled from a larger set of n total libraries, such that $f = m/n$.

The probability that a particular library is not one of the m libraries used by a particular container is simply $(n-m)/n = 1-f$. Letting N denote the number of containers in a particular server, then the probability that a particular library is loaded in that server is given by

$$p = 1 - (1-f)^N \tag{6}$$

The expected number of unique libraries in the server, n_L, is thus $\mathbb{E}[n_L] = n \cdot p$.

Using the chosen terminology, the memory required by each library is given by $s_L = v \cdot r/m$. We can therefore estimate the expected available capacity in a server after discounting all libraries loaded in memory:

$$\mathbb{E}[c_{\text{avail}}] = 1 - s_L \cdot \mathbb{E}[n_L] = 1 - \frac{v \cdot r}{m} \cdot n \cdot (1 - (1-f)^N) = 1 - \frac{v \cdot r}{f}(1 - (1-f)^N).$$

The remaining capacity is used for the containers themselves, each requiring v resources. As a result, we have

$$N \approx \frac{\mathbb{E}[c_{\text{avail}}]}{v} = \frac{1 - \frac{v \cdot r}{f}(1 - (1-f)^N)}{v} \tag{7}$$

which implicitly defines N in terms of v, r, and f.

References

1. Bodík, P., Griffith, R., Sutton, C., Fox, A., Jordan, M., Patterson, D.: Statistical machine learning makes automatic control practical for internet datacenters. In: Proceedings of the 2009 Conference on Hot Topics in Cloud Computing, Hot-Cloud 2009. USENIX Association, Berkeley (2009). http://dl.acm.org/citation. cfm?id=1855533.1855545
2. Delimitrou, C., Kozyrakis, C.: Paragon: QoS-aware scheduling for heterogeneous datacenters. SIGPLAN Not. **48**(4), 77–88 (2013)
3. Dragoni, N., Giallorenzo, S., Lluch-Lafuente, A., Mazzara, M., Montesi, F., Mustafin, R., Safina, L.: Microservices: yesterday, today, and tomorrow. CoRR abs/1606.04036 (2016). http://arxiv.org/abs/1606.04036
4. Ghodsi, A., Zaharia, M., Hindman, B., Konwinski, A., Shenker, S., Stoica, I.: Dominant resource fairness: fair allocation of multiple resource types. In: Proceedings of the 8th USENIX Conference on Networked Systems Design and Implementation, pp. 323–336. NSDI 2011. USENIX Association, Berkeley (2011). http://dl. acm.org/citation.cfm?id=1972457.1972490

5. Grandl, R., Ananthanarayanan, G., Kandula, S., Rao, S., Akella, A.: Multi-resource packing for cluster schedulers. SIGCOMM Computer Communication Review, vol. 44, no. 4, August 2014
6. Gurobi Optimization Inc.: Gurobi optimizer reference manual (2015). http://www.gurobi.com
7. Haas, F.: Containers: just because everyone else is doing them wrong, doesn't mean you have to. https://www.hastexo.com/blogs/florian/2016/02/21/containers-just-because-everyone-else/. Accessed 10 Feb 2017
8. Harter, T., Salmon, B., Liu, R., Arpaci-Dusseau, A.C., Arpaci-Dusseau, R.H.: Slacker: fast distribution with lazy Docker containers. In: 14th USENIX Conference on File and Storage Technologies (FAST 2016), pp. 181–195. USENIX Association (2016)
9. Hendrickson, S., Sturdevant, S., Harter, T., Venkataramani, V., Arpaci-Dusseau, A.C., Arpaci-Dusseau, R.H.: Serverless computation with OpenLambda. In: 8th USENIX Workshop on Hot Topics in Cloud Computing. USENIX Association, June 2016
10. Reiss, C., Tumanov, A., Ganger, G.R., Katz, R.H., Kozuch, M.A.: Heterogeneity and dynamicity of clouds at scale: Google trace analysis. In: Proceedings of the 3rd ACM Symposium on Cloud Computing, SoCC 2012, pp. 7:1–7:13. ACM, New York (2012). http://doi.acm.org/10.1145/2391229.2391236
11. Schwarzkopf, M., Konwinski, A., Abd-El-Malek, M., Wilkes, J.: Omega: flexible, scalable schedulers for large compute clusters. In: Proceedings of the 8th ACM European Conference on Computer Systems, EuroSys 2013, pp. 351–364. ACM, New York (2013). http://doi.acm.org/10.1145/2465351.2465386

An Efficient Communication Aware Heuristic for Multiple Cloud Application Placement

Pedro Silva[✉] and Christian Perez

University of Lyon, Inria, CNRS, ENS de Lyon, UCBL 1, LIP, Lyon, France
{pedro.silva,christian.perez}@inria.fr

Abstract. To deploy a distributed application on the cloud, cost, resource and communication constraints have to be considered to select the most suitable Virtual Machines (VMs), from private and public cloud providers. This process becomes very complex in large scale scenarios and, as this problem is NP-Hard, its automation must take scalability into consideration. In this work, we propose a heuristic able to calculate initial placements for distributed component-based applications on possibly multiple clouds with the objective of minimizing VM *renting costs* while satisfying applications' *resource* and *communication* constraints. We evaluate the heuristic performance and determine its limitations by comparing it to other placement approaches, namely exact algorithms and meta-heuristics. We show that the proposed heuristic is able to compute a good solution much faster than them.

1 Introduction

To *place* an application onto the Cloud, in the context of Infrastructure as a Service (IaaS), a designer must choose the best set of machines, generally virtual machines, from public and private *cloud providers*, which satisfies application performance constraints. When the placement aims at minimizing renting costs, the abundant number of available cloud providers and their offerings makes this task challenging. Although automation becomes crucial, the placement problem is *NP-hard*, and hence *scalability* must be taken in consideration, particularly in the cases where applications are large and *time constraints* are tight.

In spite of important contributions made by previous works, issues concerning, mainly, *scalability* and the *modeling of communication constraints* are still open, in particular in the case of multiple cloud deployment. Scalability issues are observed in works that propose time consuming solutions based on exact algorithms, meta-heuristics or solvers. Issues related to modeling communication constraints become apparent in works that either do not consider them at all or assume complete knowledge of cloud network and application topologies. In reality, users usually do not have access to the exact network topology of cloud provider data centers. Furthermore, due to hardware virtualization, the identity and location of physical machines where VM instances run may vary. Hence, placement algorithms that rely on those assumptions may not work correctly.

© Springer International Publishing AG 2017
F.F. Rivera et al. (Eds.): Euro-Par 2017, LNCS 10417, pp. 372–384, 2017.
DOI: 10.1007/978-3-319-64203-1_27

We tackle the problem of finding an *initial* placement for *distributed applications* modeled as *component-based* applications on *multiple clouds*. For brevity, we call this problem *CAPDAMP*, for *Communication Aware Placement of Distributed Applications on the Multi-cloud Problem*. The objective is to map each *application component* to an instance of a *virtual machine* (VM) minimizing renting *costs* and *satisfying* resource and communication constraints. Components can be any piece of code. They expose what they provide/require through interfaces, hiding their implementations to enhance reusability.

Each application component has *resource requirements* and *communication requirements* for its *connections* to other components. VM types have their *capacities, renting prices* and *communication capacities* to other VM types. This means that the resource capacities of a VM instance *must be larger than or equal to* the sum of resource requirements of the components it hosts. We call those resource capacities or requirements *dimensions*. Similarly, communication requirements between components must be inferior or equal to the communication capacities between the VM instances hosting them. We assume communication requirements and capacities can be expressed numerically.

Our hypothesis is that users describe communication constraints because they want a placement that respects their application *latency* requirements. Thus, to satisfy this constraint and to overcome the lack of available information about network topologies of public cloud providers, we introduce a flexible approach that allows an application designer to describe communication constraints using a less accurate view of the Cloud topology as well as a more accurate schema when in the context of private cloud providers.

Benefiting from this model, we propose an efficient and scalable heuristic that mixes graph clustering techniques and which is able to compute good quality placements very quickly for small to large scenarios. As this work considers *initial* placements, we do not assume *a priori* information concerning expected workload, renting times, or dynamic actors that would allow online modifications of the placement. This is left for future work. This paper extends our previous work [18], where we proposed bin packing based greedy heuristics to solve a *communication-oblivious* placement problem.

Section 2 deals with the state of the art. Section 3 presents our application and cloud models and details the proposed heuristic which is evaluated in Sect. 4. Finally, Sect. 5 concludes the paper and discusses future directions.

2 Related Work

We divide the related work into three groups based on the approach used to tackle the CAPDAMP and related *communication-aware* problems: exact approaches, meta-heuristic approaches, and heuristic based approaches. Then, we discuss them with respect to the CAPDAMP.

Exact Algorithms: In [19], a Mixed Integer Programming (MIP) is proposed for the placement of distributed applications on the Cloud. The objective is to maximize availability by modeling fault-tolerance measures. Similarly, [10] proposes a MIP to minimize application downtime. Both approaches neither consider renting cost minimizations nor allow for more than two dimensions of interest. In [13], a very expressive MIP to compute the placement of services on multiple clouds is presented. Despite allowing for cost optimization, heterogeneous VM types, and resource constraints, it does not allow for an explicit description of communication constraints. Finally, in [12], a hierarchical approach to the process placement in multi-core clusters is presented. However, only the *communication problem* is considered and both processes and hosting machines are homogeneous, contratry to our work.

Meta-heuristics: In [3,20], the authors propose two very similar approaches based on genetic algorithms to calculate the placement of services on the Cloud targeting cost minimization while satisfying CPU, memory, disk and latency constraints. In [9], a simulated annealing based approach to the VM consolidation problem is presented. In the same topic, an ant colony algorithm for a multi-objective VM consolidation problem aiming at minimizing energy consumption and resource waste is described in [7]. In [6] another ant colony based approach for the VM consolidation problem is proposed.

Heuristics: A communication-aware greedy heuristic for calculating the task mapping on supercomputer clusters is presented in [4]. Using a max-clique based approach, [2,14] describe algorithms for the consolidation of VM types. An analogous problem is addressed in [16], which adds the challenge of having to place a virtual network aiming at satisfying resource and network constraints. Using a min cut approach, a hierarchical representation of the network and a graph modeling of the application, [15] tackles the traffic aware virtual machine placement on data centers. A hierarchical approach for the deployment of distributed scientific applications on the Cloud is presented in [5]. In [21], a graph matching algorithm based on a *graph query* approach for the service placement on the cloud is proposed. [8] presents a heuristic based on a relaxed MILP to compute a solution for a VM consolidation problem. In [11], an approach for placing services onto clouds while minimizing *communication* costs is proposed. Despite presenting a hierarchical cloud topology description and clustering heuristics similar to ours, the only considered resources is CPU. Communication constraints are viewed as soft constraints.

2.1   Discussion

As the CAPDAMP is NP-hard, using *exact algorithms* to calculate optimal placements is feasible only for very small problem instances. To overcome this limitation there is a plethora of more scalable approaches based mainly on meta-heuristics and heuristics. *Meta-heuristics* have their solution qualities proportional to the time given to process a problem. Hence, depending on problem size, using a meta-heuristic may still be unfeasible. Furthermore, as they are generic tools, meta-heuristics tend to be very sensitive to parameter tuning specific for each scenario.

Other *heuristics* usually aim primarily at solving the graph partitioning (or communication constraint) problem letting the packing (or resource constraint problem) in second place. Graph-based modeling can efficiently describe communication constraints, however, describing at the same time resource constraints and renting costs tends to be more difficult. Thus, issues like VM heterogeneity, renting costs and multi-dimensionality are not addressed at the same time.

The main contribution of this paper is an efficient and scalable heuristic (cf. Sect. 3) which addresses the aforementioned problems. Using a graph clustering and multidimensional bin packing strategies, it manages to calculate good quality solutions very quickly, as described in Sect. 4.

3   The 2PCAP Heuristic

Before presenting the heuristic proposed in Sect. 3.1, we introduce the communication topology *models* for applications and multi-clouds upon which our heuristic strongly relies on.

Multi-cloud Network Topology: In this work, we model the *network* topology as a tree. It is a hierarchical approximation of intra cloud provider and long distance networks as well as an approximation of their inherent communication capacity *uncertainties*.

Figure 1(a) gives an example of this modeling. *Leaves* are sets of *rentable* resources, like VM types (or physical machines), that we call *machine groups*. An *inner node* m of the multi-cloud tree models a level of *connection* between all machine groups available in the sub-tree having m as root. The level of an inner node represents the *quality* of the machine group connection. In Fig. 1(a), machine groups $m1$ and $m2$ are connected at levels 0, 1, and 2. Thus, their *connection qualities* may be 0, 1 or 2. Machine groups $m1$ and $m3$ have a connection quality 1. Resources in the same machine group are always connected with a connection quality equals to the level of the leaves. In Fig. 1(a), all connections between VM types inside the same machine group have quality 3.

The concept of *connection quality* aims at characterizing the *latency* of a connection. The closest an internal node is to the leaves, the smallest the latency is. This is sufficiently general to describe detailed internal data center topologies as well as general Internet links. We suppose that this model is sufficient for describing VM localization (within the same data center, city, or country).

Application Communication Topology: In this work, we represent a component-based application as a *graph*. Components are nodes and connections between components are weighted edges. Weights are connection requirements, defined in terms of *connection quality* matching the multi-cloud topology. In Fig. 2, components $c1$ and $c2$ communicate and require a connection quality of *at least* 2, while $c2$ and $c3$ require at least 1.

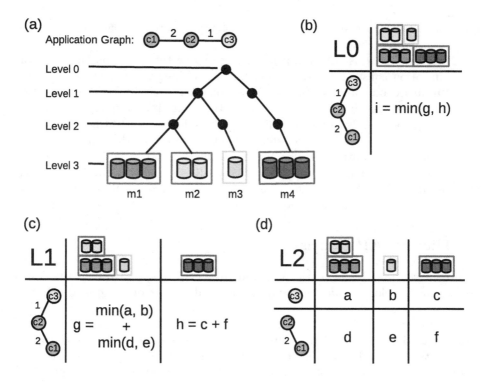

Fig. 1. Placement example.

3.1   Two Phase Communication Aware Placement Heuristic

We propose a divide-and-conquer heuristic called *Two Phase Communication Aware Placement Heuristic* (2PCAP) to calculate solutions for the CAPDAMP. 2PCAP, described in Algorithm 1, has two phases. (i) It recursively *decomposes* components and machine groups into *subsets*, creating communication-aware *sub-placements*, until sub-placements can be calculated with *communication-oblivious* heuristics. (ii) From the leaves to the root of the tree, sub-placements with best costs *compose* the solution for their parents.

Phase 1 – Decomposition: A *component subset* i_ℓ is a set of nodes from a connected subgraph from the application graph. Component subsets have the property that every connection between its components has a communication quality requirement superior or equal to ℓ, where $0 \leq \ell < H$ and H is the height of the multi-cloud tree. A *machine group subset* s_ℓ contains machine groups from sub-trees of the multi-cloud tree topology. All machine groups contained in the same subset are connected with connection quality superior or equal to ℓ.

The process that *generates* component and machine group subsets is called *decomposition*. Given a level ℓ, machine group subsets are generated through the gathering of leaves whose subtree roots are in level ℓ. Component subsets

---

Algorithm 1. Pseudo-code of 2PCAP.

Input: $level, comp\_subset, mg\_subset$
Output: min_cost_plac
1: $min\_cost\_plac \leftarrow \infty$
2: **if** $is\_calculated(comp\_subset \Rightarrow mg\_subset)$ **then**
3: $\quad$ **return** $plac(comp\_subset \Rightarrow mg\_subset)$
4: **else if** $level = l\_max$ **then**
5: $\quad$ $calculate(comp\_subset \Rightarrow mg\_subset)$
6: $\quad$ **return** $plac(comp\_subset \Rightarrow mg\_subset)$
7: **else if** $level < l\_max$ **then**
8: $\quad$ **if** $size(decompose(mg\_subset, level)) = 1$ **then**
9: $\quad\quad$ $plac \leftarrow null$
10: $\quad\quad$ **for** cs **in** $decompose(comp\_subset, level)$ **do**
11: $\quad\quad\quad$ $temp\_plac \leftarrow 2PCAP(level + 1, cs, mg\_subset)$
12: $\quad\quad\quad$ $plac \leftarrow compose(plac + temp\_plac)$
13: $\quad\quad$ $min\_cost\_plac \leftarrow plac$
14: $\quad$ **else if** $size(decompose(mg\_subset, level)) > 1$ **then**
15: $\quad\quad$ $plac \leftarrow null$
16: $\quad\quad$ **for** cs **in** $decompose(comp\_subset, level)$ **do**
17: $\quad\quad\quad$ $min\_plac \leftarrow null$
18: $\quad\quad\quad$ **for** ms **in** $decompose(mg\_subset, level)$ **do**
19: $\quad\quad\quad\quad$ $temp\_plac \leftarrow 2PCAP(level + 1, cs, ms)$
20: $\quad\quad\quad\quad$ **if** $cost(temp\_plac) < min\_plac$ **then**
21: $\quad\quad\quad\quad\quad$ $min\_plac \leftarrow temp\_plac$
22: $\quad\quad\quad$ $plac \leftarrow compose(plac + min\_plac)$
23: $\quad\quad$ $min\_cost\_plac \leftarrow plac$
24: $\quad$ **for** ms **in** $decompose(mg\_subset, l\_max)$ **do**
25: $\quad\quad$ $temp\_plac \leftarrow 2PCAP(l\_max, comp\_subset, ms)$
26: $\quad\quad$ **if** $cost(temp\_plac) < cost(min\_cost\_plac)$ **then**
27: $\quad\quad\quad$ $min\_cost\_plac \leftarrow plac$
28: **return** min_cost_plac

---

are connected sub-graphs resulting from the removal of all connections requiring connection qualities inferior to ℓ from the original application graph. $\mathcal{I}_\ell$ and $\mathcal{S}_\ell$ are the sets containing, respectively, all components and machine groups subsets *constructed on* level ℓ.

In Fig. 1(b), (c) and (d) there are examples of machine group and component decompositions. Table names (L0, L1 and L2) refer to the level of decomposition, component subsets ($\mathcal{I}_\ell$) are represented in the left and machine group subsets ($\mathcal{S}_\ell$), in the upper part.

A *sub-placement* is the placement of a subset of components on a subset of machine groups. It also aims at minimizing VM renting costs while satisfying resource and communication constraints. Given a level ℓ, $i_\ell \in \mathcal{I}_\ell$ and $s_\ell \in \mathcal{S}_\ell$, the sub-placement of i_ℓ on s_ℓ can only be computed if it is a *bottom sub-placement* or if the sub-placements generated by the decomposition of i_ℓ and s_ℓ were *computed*.

A *bottom sub-placement* is a sub-placement that can be computed by communication oblivious heuristics while satisfying communication quality requirements. Hence, any pair of VM types from machine groups contained in s_ℓ will satisfy the communication requirements from any pair of components from i_ℓ.

Let l^{max} be the highest connection quality requirement present in the component graph. Observe that every sub-placement of $i_\ell \in \mathcal{I}_\ell$ on $s_{\ell max} \in \mathcal{S}_{\ell max}$ is a valid bottom sub-placement. Hence, there is no reason to continue the decomposition process beyond l^{max}.

Phase 2 – Composition: Bottom sub-placements are calculated by efficient communication-oblivious heuristics for the multi-dimensional bin packing problem presented in a previous work [18]. Once all necessary bottom sub-placements are calculated, 2PCAP starts the process of *composition of sub-placements*. The objective is to choose, at each composition step, the less expensive sub-placements. Given the set $\mathcal{I}'_{\ell+1}$ containing all component groups decomposed from $i_\ell \in \mathcal{I}_\ell$ and the set $\mathcal{S}'_{\ell+1}$ decomposed from the machine group $s_\ell \in \mathcal{S}_\ell$, let $u^{is}_{\ell+1}$ be the sub-placement of $i_{\ell+1}$ on $s_{\ell+1}$. Thus, the solution for the sub-placement of i_ℓ on s_ℓ is one of the following:

Case 1: $u^{is}_{\ell+1}$, if $\mathcal{S}_{\ell+1} = \mathcal{S}_\ell$ and $\mathcal{I}_{\ell+1} = \mathcal{I}_\ell$.
Case 2: $\sum_{i \in \mathcal{I}_{\ell+1}} u^{is}_{\ell+1}$ for $s \in \mathcal{S}_{\ell+1}$, if $|\mathcal{S}_{\ell+1}| = |\mathcal{S}_\ell|$ and $|\mathcal{I}_{\ell+1}| > |\mathcal{I}_\ell|$;
Case 3: $\sum_{i \in \mathcal{I}_{\ell+1}} min(u^{is}_{\ell+1}, \forall s \in \mathcal{S}_{\ell+1})$, if $|\mathcal{S}_{\ell+1}| > |\mathcal{S}_\ell|$;

In Case 1, The decomposed subset of components and machine groups are identical to the original subsets. Hence, $u^{is}_\ell = u^{is}_{\ell+1}$. This is described in lines 2 and 3 from Algorithm 1. In Case 2, the decomposed subset of machine groups is identical to the original, but this is not true for the decomposed component subset. In this case, 2PCAP composes the $|\mathcal{I}_{\ell+1}|$ sub-placements on $s_{\ell+1}$. Sub-placements c and f (cf. Fig. 1(d)) compose sub-placement h (cf. Fig. 1(c)). This situation is described between lines 8 and 13 from Algorithm 1. In Case 3, when $|\mathcal{S}_{\ell+1}| > |\mathcal{S}_\ell|$ machine groups are decomposed in more than one subset. Thus, for each decomposed component subset there are $|\mathcal{S}_{\ell+1}|$ possible sub-placements, from which, only the less expensive one is used in the composition process. Sub-placement i (cf. Fig. 1(b)) is composed by sub-placements g and h (cf. Fig. 1(c)). Furthermore, sub-placement g (cf. Fig. 1(c)) is composed by sub-placements a, b, d and e (cf. Fig. 1(d)). This can be observed between lines 14 and 23 from Algorithm 1.

3.2   Discussion

The 2PCAP heuristic does not compute, during the decomposition phase, all possible sub-placements. Doing this would result in a factorial complexity which would lead to prohibitive execution times for large problems. To further explore the solution space without increasing too much the time complexity, 2PCAP computes the sub-placement of every generated subset which is not part of a bottom sub-placement on machine group subsets generated at level l^{max} (cf. Lines 24 to 27 of Algorithm 1).

The complexity of 2PCAP is dominated by decomposition operations (*decompose* function) and the computation of placements (*plac* function). Let $\mathcal{I}$, $\mathcal{S}$ and $\mathcal{T}$ be the sets of components, sites and VM types, respectively. Decomposition operations have a $O(|\mathcal{I}|^3 + |\mathcal{I}| \times |\mathcal{S}|^2 \times log|\mathcal{S}|)$ complexity while the computation of placements has $O(|\mathcal{S}| \times |\mathcal{T}|log|\mathcal{T} \times |\mathcal{I}|^2)$.

4 Evaluation

As the CAPDAMP is NP-Hard, we divide the evaluation process in two steps. First, using *small problem instances* and a MIP solver, we compare 2PCAP solutions to optimal ones. Then, we compare 2PCAP on *medium* and *large* problem instances using meta-heuristics and a relaxed version of the CAPDAMP as baseline algorithms.

4.1 Methodology

An *experiment* is the resolution of a set of placement *problem instances* by a set of algorithms within a given *time*. Each problem instance has seven parameters: the number n_d of considered resources or *dimensions*, the number n_c of components, the number n_v of VM types, the number n_s of sites, the height h_t of the multi-cloud tree, the topology t_c of the component-based application and the multi-cloud tree connection schema x_t.

Experiments are organized in three *experiment classes*, namely A, B, and C. Small, and thus easier to solve, problem instances compose Class A; medium-sized problem instances are present in Class B, and, finally, large problems form Class C. Table 1 details the range of problem instance parameters that define each class and the total of generated problem instances per class.

Table 1. Parameters of experiment classes. Column t_c indicates the application topologies: line (l), star (s), full connected (f), or random (r). Column x_s indicates the multi-cloud tree connection schemas: distant (d), agglomerate (a), or uniform (u).

Class	n_d	n_c	n_v	n_s	h_t	t_c	x_s	# exps
A	4	$3, 5, 7, 10$	$100, 250, 500, 700$	$25, 50, 100$	$3, 5$	l, s, f, r	u	384
B	5	$10, 20, 30, 40, 50$	$500, 1k, 1.5k, 2k$	$100, 300, 500$	5	l, s, f, r	d, a, u	720
C	6	$60, 80, 100, 120, 140$	$2.5k, 5k, 7.5k, 10k$	$500, 750, 1k$	7	l, s, f, r	d, a, u	720

Component requirements and VM capacities are pseudo-random values, picked uniformly from pre-defined intervals (Table 2). We consider that VM types are distributed equally among the sites. We generate three different component communication patterns: *distant*, *agglomerated*, and *uniform*. The difference between them is the probability of connecting two or more subtrees. The *distant* pattern has higher probability to connect subtrees near the root; *agglomerated*

Table 2. Intervals of dimension data generation.

Dimension	(i)	(ii)	(iii)	(iv)	(v)	(vi)
Requirements	800–k	1–16	1–32	50–3.5k	5–30	1–8
Capacities	1k–3.5k	2–32	2–40	150–4k	10–80	1–16

gives higher connection probabilities to subtrees near the leaves and the uniform schema gives the same connection probability $\left(\frac{1}{h_t}\right)$ to every subtree.

The four component-based application topologies we consider are *line, star, full connected* (cf. Fig. 2), and *random*. In the random schema, a pair of components is connected with a probability of 50%. Communication requirements from component connections are pseudo-random integers picked uniformly between 0 and $h_t - 1$.

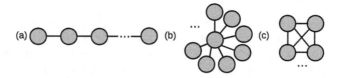

Fig. 2. Schemas of part of the generated application topologies. (a) *line*, (b) *star* and (c) *full connected*.

Renting prices depend on the resource dimensions of each VM. Let $c^*_{t,d}$ be the ratio $\frac{c_{t,d}}{max_d}$ between the capacity $c_{t,d}$ of dimension d from VM type t and max_d the maximum value for dimension d (cf. Table 2). Each dimension is multiplied by a coefficient to create scenarios where some dimensions are more expensive than others. Hence, the price of a VM type p_t is $\alpha + \beta + \gamma + \delta + \epsilon + \zeta$, where $\alpha = c^*_{t,1} \times random(1,3)$, $\beta = c^*_{t,2} \times random(8,20)$, $\gamma = c^*_{t,3} \times random(5,8)$, $\delta = c^*_{t,4} \times random(10,15)$, if $c^*_{t,4} \leq 500$, otherwise $\delta = c^*_{t,4} \times random(20,25)$, $\epsilon = c^*_{t,5} \times random(5,10)$, and $\zeta = c^*_{t,6} \times random(2,5)$.

The 2PCAP algorithm is implemented in Python. Experiments were conducted on Dell PowerEdge R630 2.4 GHz (2 CPUs, 8 cores) nodes from the *Parasilo* and *Paravance* clusters of the *Grid'5000* experimental platform[1].

4.2   2PCAP Performance on Small Problems

In this section we use the *SCIP* solver [1], a framework for constraint integer programming and branch-cut-and-price, together with an optimization formulation of the CAPDAMP to generate a set of optimal solutions which will be compared to solutions computed by 2PCAP. Problems from experiment Class A (Table 1) were used and SCIP was given 24 h to solve each one of them.

---

[1] cf. https://www.grid5000.fr.

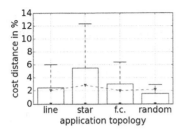
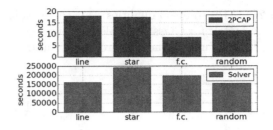

Fig. 3. (Left) Cost distances as percentage of 2PCAP solutions compared to optimal solutions aggregated by application topology type. The green solid line is the median and the brown dashed line is the average. (Right) Sum of execution times in seconds from 2PCAP and SCIP solver aggregated by application topology – SCIP: average 4180 s, median 1800s. 2PCAP: average 0.1 s, median: 0.08 s. (Color figure online)

SCIP solver was able to solve only around 48% of Class A problem instances in time, *i.e.*, 180 problem instances. Figure 3 illustrates the *cost distance* from solutions computed by 2PCAP to the optimal ones as a percentage of the latter for problem instances successfully solved by SCIP. Cost distances are grouped by application topology.

In Fig. 3 (Left) we can see that cost distances vary between 0% and at most 12.3%. The median is always 0% and the average between 2% and 3%. Figure 3 (Right) complements this data. It depicts the sum of the execution times in seconds that each approach used to calculate the 48% of Class A problem instances solved by SCIP, grouped by application topology schema. While 2PCAP takes some seconds to solve all problems, the solver's execution time is in the scale of days. Hence, in spite of being much faster than the solver, 2PCAP manages to produce a solution at most around 12% worse than the optimal and, in the median, the solutions are optimal.

4.3   2PCAP Performance on Large Problems

The evaluation of 2PCAP on large problems cannot rely on using a solver to generate optimal solutions. It is necessary to use scalable baseline algorithms.

Heuristics presented in Sect. 2 cannot handle the complexity of CAPDAMP. Hence, as a first approach, we implement a Simulated Annealing (SA) meta-heuristic for the CAPDAMP as a baseline algorithm. We used Python module *Simanneal* [17] and problem instances from Classes B and C. The meta-heuristic is initialized with a random – not necessarily valid – placement. Despite the timeout of 1 hour per problem instance, SA managed to calculate a solution for only around 10% of problem instances. As CAPDAMP's search space is very large, SA would need more time to be able to produce more solutions.

Running SA with an initial solution computed by 2PCAP shows how much SA can improve a 2PCAP solution in one hour. Figure 4 (Left) illustrates this metric for Class C problems. SA managed to improve the solutions by at most 9% and the median is always bellow 4%. This small improvement is a good indicator of 2PCAP's solution qualities. Due to space limitations, we do not illustrate the same metric for Class B problems, however the observed curves are very similar: the largest improvement is around 9% and the median is always bellow 2%.

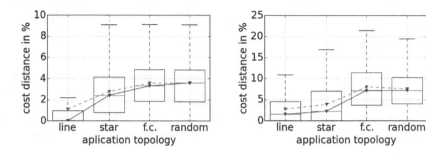

Fig. 4. (Left) Improvement of 2PCAP solutions by SA for Class C. (Right) Cost distances between 2PCAP and lower bound for Class C. The green solid line is the median and the brown dashed line is the average. (Color figure online)

In a second approach, we compute baseline solutions obtained through the relaxation of CAPDAMP's communication constraints and compare them to 2PCAP solutions. CAPDAMP is, thus, reduced to a cost-aware multi-dimensional bin packing placement problem which is calculated by an adapted SA meta-heuristic initialized with the less expensive placement among those calculated by 2PCAP and other efficient heuristics [18]. Figure 4 (Right) illustrates the evolution of cost distances between 2PCAP and SA solutions for Class C problems. Cost distances vary between 0% and around 22% and the median is always bellow 10%. Due to space constraints, we do not plot this metric for Class B problems, nevertheless, we observe a similar pattern: cost distances vary between 0% and 30% and the median is always bellow 10%. The consistent distance to baseline solution costs is a good indicator of the 2PCAP's solution quality. Concerning 2PCAP execution times for Classes B and C, the average was around 11 s and the median around 3 s for each problem instance. At most, 2PCAP took around 110 s to calculate a placement.

The results presented in this section indicate that, even on large scenarios, 2PCAP manages to quickly calculate compatible or better solutions than those calculated by SA.

5   Conclusion and Future Work

In this paper we presented an approach to calculate initial placements for component-based applications with the objective of minimizing costs while satisfying resource and communication constraints. This approach is based on a hierarchical model of the cloud topology which allows the introduction of latency requirements despite the uncertainties inherent to cloud networks, mainly due to virtualization. This model is used by 2PCAP, an efficient heuristic whose evaluation shows its capability of producing good quality solutions very quickly.

Future work aims to go beyond the initial placement by adding the notion of application reconfiguration and, consequently, modeling the migration of virtual machines. We also plan to extend the placement heuristics to support applications described with more abstract component models, including, for example, concepts such as cardinality, hierarchy, genericity, etc.

Acknowledgments. All experiments were carried out using the Grid'5000 testbed, supported by a group hosted by Inria and including CNRS, RENATER, and several Universities as well as other organizations (cf. https://www.grid5000.fr). This work was partially supported by the PaaSage (FP7-317715) EU project.

References

1. Achterberg, T.: SCIP: solving constraint integer programs. Math. Program. Comput. **1**, 1–41 (2009)
2. Biran, O., Corradi, A., Fanelli, M., Foschini, L., Nus, A., Raz, D., Silvera, E.: A stable network-aware VM placement for cloud systems. In: CCGrid (2012)
3. Chen, W., Qiao, X., Wei, J., Huang, T.: A profit-aware virtual machine deployment optimization framework for cloud platform providers. In: CLOUD (2012)
4. Deveci, M., Kaya, K., Uçar, B., Catalyurek, U.V.: Fast and high quality topology-aware task mapping. In: IPDPS (2015)
5. Fan, P., Chen, Z., Wang, J., Zheng, Z., Lyu, M.R.: Topology-aware deployment of scientific applications in cloud computing. In: CLOUD (2012)
6. Ferdaus, M.H., Murshed, M., Calheiros, R.N., Buyya, R.: Virtual machine consolidation in cloud data centers using ACO metaheuristic. In: Europar (2014)
7. Gao, Y., Guan, H., Qi, Z., Hou, Y., Liu, L.: A multi-objective ant colony system algorithm for virtual machine placement in cloud computing. J. Comput. Syst. Sci. **79**, 1230–1242 (2013)
8. Gu, L., Zeng, D., Guo, S., Xiang, Y., Hu, J.: A general communication cost optimization framework for big data stream processing in geo-distributed data centers. IEEE Trans. Comput. **65**, 19–29 (2016)
9. Hyser, C., Mckee, B., Gardner, R., Watson, B.J.: Autonomic virtual machine placement in the data center. Technical report HPL-2007-189, HP Laboratories (2007)
10. Jammal, M., Kanso, A., Shami, A.: High availability-aware optimization digest for applications deployment in cloud. In: ICC (2015)
11. Jayasinghe, D., Pu, C., Eilam, T., Steinder, M., Whally, I., Snible, E.: Improving performance and availability of services hosted on IaaS clouds with structural constraint-aware virtual machine placement. In: SCC (2011)
12. Jeannot, E., Mercier, G., Tessier, F.: Process placement in multicore clusters: algorithmic issues and practical techniques. IEEE Trans. Parallel Distrib. Syst. **25**, 993–1002 (2014)
13. Lucas-Simarro, J.L., Moreno-Vozmediano, R., Montero, R.S., Llorente, I.M.: Scheduling strategies for optimal service deployment across multiple clouds. Future Gener. Comput. Syst. **29**, 1431–1441 (2013)
14. Alicherry, M., Lakshman, T.V.: Network aware resource allocation in distributed clouds. In: INFOCOM (2012)

15. Meng, X., Pappas, V., Zhang, L.: Improving the scalability of data center networks with traffic-aware virtual machine placement. In: INFOCOM (2010)
16. Nonde, L., El-Gorashi, T.E.H., Elmirghani, J.M.H.: Energy efficient virtual network embedding for cloud networks. J. Lightwave Technol. **33**, 1828–1849 (2015)
17. Perry, M.: Simanneal: Python module for simulated annealing optimization. https://github.com/perrygeo/simanneal
18. Silva, P., Perez, C., Desprez, F.: Efficient heuristics for placing large-scale distributed applications on multiple clouds. In: CCGrid (2016)
19. Spinnewyn, B., Braem, B., Latre, S.: Fault-tolerant application placement in heterogeneous cloud environments. In: CNSM (2015)
20. Yusoh, Z.I.M., Tang, M.: Clustering composite SaaS components in cloud computing using a grouping genetic algorithm. In: CEC (2012)
21. Zong, B., Raghavendra, R., Srivatsa, M., Yan, X., Singh, A.K., Lee, K.W.: Cloud service placement via subgraph matching. In: ICDE (2014)

Energy-Driven Straggler Mitigation in MapReduce

Tien-Dat Phan[1], Shadi Ibrahim[2(✉)], Amelie Chi Zhou[2], Guillaume Aupy[3], and Gabriel Antoniu[2]

[1] ENS Rennes/IRISA, Rennes, France
tien-dat.phan@irisa.fr
[2] Inria Rennes - Bretagne Atlantique Research Center, Rennes, France
{shadi.ibrahim,chi.zhou,gabriel.antoniu}@inria.fr
[3] Inria Bordeaux - Sud-Ouest Research Center, Bordeaux, France
guillaume.aupy@inria.fr

Abstract. Energy consumption is an important concern for large-scale data-centers, which results in huge monetary cost for data-center operators. Due to the hardware heterogeneity and contentions between concurrent workloads, straggler mitigation is important to many Big Data applications running in large-scale data-centers and the speculative execution technique is widely-used to handle stragglers. Although a large number of studies have been proposed to improve the performance of Big Data applications using speculative execution, few of them have studied the energy efficiency of their solutions. In this paper, we propose two techniques to improve the energy efficiency of speculative executions while ensuring comparable performance. Specifically, we propose a hierarchical straggler detection mechanism which can greatly reduce the number of killed speculative copies and hence save the energy consumption. We also propose an energy-aware speculative copy allocation method which considers the trade-off between performance and energy when allocating speculative copies. We implement both techniques into Hadoop and evaluate them using representative MapReduce benchmarks. Results show that our solution can reduce the energy waste on killed speculative copies by up to 100% and improve the energy efficiency by 20% compared to state-of-the-art mechanisms.

Keywords: MapReduce · Energy efficiency · Straggler mitigation · Detection · Copy allocation

1 Introduction

Energy consumption has started to severely constrain the design and the way that data-centers are operated. Energy bill has become a substantial part of the monetary cost for data-center operators (e.g., the annual electricity usage and bill are over 1,120 GWh and \$67 M for Google, and over 600 GWh and \$36 M for Microsoft [13]). Moreover, as a result of the explosion of Big Data and

© Springer International Publishing AG 2017
F.F. Rivera et al. (Eds.): Euro-Par 2017, LNCS 10417, pp. 385–398, 2017.
DOI: 10.1007/978-3-319-64203-1_28

applications becoming more data-intensive, it is natural for data-center operators to extend their infrastructure with more machines, which are energy-hungry. This makes energy consumption a major concern for Big Data systems [7,11].

In parallel, the increasing scale of data-centers results in a noticeable performance variation in operations [21,22]. This is due to: (i) the hardware heterogeneity caused by the gradual scaling out of data-centers [10], and (ii) the dynamic resource allocation when adopting the virtualization technique to collocate different users [20]. The performance variation results in a large number of stragglers, i.e., tasks that take significantly longer time to finish than the normal execution time (e.g., 700–800% slower [1]). Since the job execution time is determined by the latest task, stragglers can severely prolong the job execution time. Speculative execution is a widely-used straggler mitigation technique to improve the performance of jobs. It launches a speculative copy for each straggler upon its detection. As soon as the straggler or the copy finishes, the other one is killed and the task is considered finished. Nonetheless, using speculative execution is not always beneficial. For example, Ren et al. [14] have shown that speculative execution can reduce the task execution time in *21%* of the time while the unsuccessful speculative copies consume more than *40%* extra resources. Thus, there exists a trade-off between performance gain and extra energy/resource consumption when using speculative execution [12].

Existing speculative execution mechanisms cannot achieve good trade-off between performance and energy efficiency. *First*, existing speculative execution mechanisms detect as many stragglers as possible in order to cut the jobs' heavy-tails. This policy is good for improving the performance, but can cause much extra energy consumption. *Second*, different speculative copy allocation decisions can result in different performance and energy consumption results [12]. For example, launching speculative copies on nodes with a small number of running tasks can result in short task execution time but leads to a high power consumption (refer to Sect. 3). Unfortunately, existing copy allocation methods do not consider this aspect. In this paper we make the following contributions.

- We introduce a novel straggler detection mechanism to improve the energy efficiency of speculative execution. The goal of this detection mechanism is to identify critical stragglers which strongly affect the job execution times and reduce the number of killed speculative copies which lead to energy waste. This hierarchical straggler detection mechanism can work as a secondary layer on top of any existing straggler detection mechanisms (Sect. 5).
- We propose an energy-aware copy allocation method to reduce the energy consumption of speculative execution. The core of this allocation method is a performance model and an energy model which expose the trade-off between performance and energy consumption when scheduling a copy (Sect. 6).
- We evaluate our hierarchical detection mechanism and energy-aware copy allocation method on the Grid'5000 [8] testbed using three representative MapReduce applications. Experimental results show a good reduction in the resource wasted on killed speculative copies and an improvement in the energy efficiency compared to state-of-the-art mechanisms (Sect. 7).

2   Related Work

There is a rich body of research on straggler mitigation in MapReduce [4,9]. **Straggler Detection in MapReduce.** Dean and Ghemawat [4] presented a straggler detection mechanism based on progress score, a 0-to-1 number represents the ratio of processed data over the total input data. A task, which has a progress score less than the average progress score minus 20%, is marked as a straggler. This mechanism has shown a reduction to the job execution times by 44%. Zaharia *et al.* [20] noticed that the progress score alone does not accurately reflect how fast a task runs as different tasks start at different times. Therefore, they present a new detection mechanism (i.e., *LATE*) which takes into consideration both the progress score and the elapsed time (i.e., the time each task takes from the moment it starts). These two parameters are used to calculate the progress rate of each task. In practice, this straggler detection mechanism can reduce the job execution times by a factor of 2. Recent studies [2,3,5,6,17,18] have shown that there still exist several reasons that lead to incorrect straggler detections, including data locality and task execution skew. Ananthanarayanan *et al.* [2] proposed a *cause-aware* straggler detection mechanism. It keeps monitoring the performance and resource consumption of tasks and uses this information to infer the causes of slow task executions (e.g., non-local task and data skew). *Our hierarchical straggler detection mechanism complements these mechanisms to enforce identifying the most critical stragglers and hence reduce the extra energy consumption imposed by speculating non-critical ones.*

Straggler Handling in MapReduce. Ren *et al.* [15] proposed a speculation-aware scheduler, named Hopper. Hopper reserves spare resources to run speculative copies whenever needed. Ananthanarayanan *et al.* [1] presented Dolly, a straggler handling approach which launches multiple copies (i.e., clones) for each task when starting MapReduce applications. *While previous studies mainly answer the question of **when** to allocate the resources to speculative copies, this paper tackles the problem of **where** to allocate speculative copies. In particular, it leverages the heterogeneity of resources (in terms of performance and energy) to reduce the energy consumption of MapReduce applications.*

3   On the Energy Inefficiency of Speculative Execution

In this section, we discuss the energy inefficiency of the default speculative execution mechanism in Hadoop.

3.1   Huge Energy Waste Due to Unsuccessful Speculative Copies

Speculative execution is initially designed to handle stragglers and improve job performance. The common wisdom applied in existing straggler detection mechanisms is to detect as many stragglers as possible in order to cut the heavy-tails in job execution. For example, *Default* [4] decides a task with progress less than 80% of the average progress as straggler. *LATE* [20] marks the tasks with speed

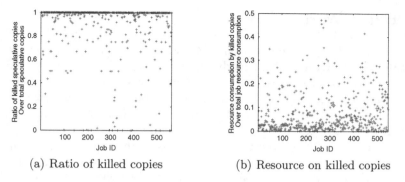

(a) Ratio of killed copies   (b) Resource on killed copies

Fig. 1. Production Hadoop cluster trace analysis: (a) More than 65% of the jobs have zero successful speculative copies; (b) The resource consumption caused by the unsuccessful copies can be substantial. In some cases, it can reach 40% of the total resource consumption.

less than the mean speed minus the standard deviation as stragglers. *Mantri* [2] considers tasks with 1.5x times longer execution time than average execution time as stragglers. To understand the energy efficiency of these straggler detection mechanisms, we have analyzed one month traces (October 2012) collected from a Hadoop production cluster in CMU [14]. Figure 1 shows the ratio of killed speculative copies, i.e., unsuccessful copies, over all copies for each Hadoop job, as well as the ratio of resources consumed by the killed copies over the total resource consumption of a job. We observe that many speculative copies are unsuccessful and are wasting a lot of resources. For example, among the total 568 jobs, there are 370 jobs which have speculative execution with no successful copy. For some jobs, the killed copies consumed more than 40% of the job's total resource consumption. The large number of unsuccessful speculative copies is mainly due to the late detection and the wrongly detected stragglers. To conclude, the philosophy of detecting as many stragglers as possible in speculative execution is no longer optimal from the energy perspective.

3.2 Speculative Copy Allocation Matters

We have observed that there is a trade-off between the performance and energy consumption for tasks executing on different nodes, according to the current status of the nodes. Figure 2 shows the average task execution time and the energy consumption of a node when executing different numbers of tasks concurrently. The application used is WordCount and the number of cores in the node is four. For example, we find that when the number of concurrent tasks is three, we can obtain the lowest energy consumption, without sacrificing too much the performance. Thus, allocating speculative copies to different locations, which may have different numbers of running tasks, can result in different performance and energy consumption results. Unfortunately, existing copy allocation methods have ignored such a trade-off. For example, *Default* [4] follows the simple

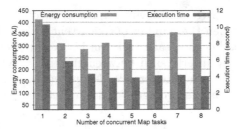

Fig. 2. Variability in execution times and energy consumptions with different numbers of concurrent map tasks for WordCount application.

FCFS policy to allocate copies to the first freed slot, without considering any of the performance and energy objectives. In *Mantri*, the task placement is mainly based on the performance objective which ensures that a copy is more likely to finish earlier than the original task. In order to improve the energy efficiency of speculative execution, it is important to take into consideration the impact of different copy allocation decisions to the overall energy consumption.

Based on the two observations, in the following sections, we present a novel straggler detection mechanism and a smart speculative copy allocation method, in order to improve the energy efficiency of speculative executions.

4 Architectural Model

Considering the straggler mitigation problem in a cluster, we provide the following models to describe the energy and performance behaviors of tasks running in the cluster.

Power and Energy Model. For any node in the cluster, we assume there are c cores which support t threads each. The power consumption of a running node is composed of two parts, namely the fixed static power consumption $\mathcal{P}_{\text{static}}$ and the dynamic power consumption proportionally related to the number of active cores. We use $\mathcal{P}_{\text{dyn}}$ to denote the power consumption resulted by activating one core and n to denote the number of tasks running on the node. Then the total power consumption $\mathcal{P}$ of a running node can be modeled as in Eq. 1.

$$\mathcal{P} = \begin{cases} \mathcal{P}_{\text{static}} + n \cdot \mathcal{P}_{\text{dyn}} & \text{for } 0 \leq n \leq c \\ \mathcal{P}_{\text{static}} + c \cdot \mathcal{P}_{\text{dyn}} & \text{for } c < n \leq ct \end{cases} \tag{1}$$

The energy consumption E of a node is its power integrated over time and thus can be modeled as $E = \int_0^T \mathcal{P}(t)dt$. We use T to denote the execution time of tasks running on the node. The energy efficiency EE is defined as the ratio of the throughput to the power consumption, namely $EE = 1/E$.

Average Slowdown Factor and Interference Model. We model the slowdown to a task caused by interference between concurrent tasks running on the same node using the average slowdown factor α defined for a node. We observe that α equals to one when the number of concurrent tasks is less than the number of cores c. This is because each task can be executed on a dedicated core and there is hardly any interference between the tasks. When the number of tasks increases beyond c, the interference also increases. Denote the number of running tasks as n, then the average slowdown factor α can be calculated as below.

$$\alpha = \begin{cases} 1 & \text{for } 1 \leq n \leq c \\ \frac{n}{c} & \text{for } c < n \leq ct \end{cases} \tag{2}$$

5   Hierarchical Straggler Detection Mechanism

In this section, we present the architecture of our hierarchical straggler detection mechanism. Our hierarchical mechanism works as a secondary layer on top of an existing straggler detection mechanism. The goal of this detection layer is to select the *critical stragglers*, i.e., the long-running stragglers which strongly affect the job execution time, from the list of stragglers detected by an existing detection mechanism. The secondary detection layer considers the stragglers at the node-level. That means, it detects only the stragglers on very slow nodes. The reason for this strategy is that most stragglers are caused by node-level problems, such as a node with worn-out hardware and node-level resource contentions which lead to slow tasks [2]. We identify all the nodes with performance less than β of the average node performance as slow nodes. In the evaluation, we discuss the impact of this parameter on the speculative execution results.

Figure 3 shows the design of the secondary straggler detection layer. Specifically, it takes the stragglers detected by the underlying straggler detection layer as input. Then, it calculates the performance of each node and filters out the stragglers that are not hosted on slow nodes. We calculate the performance of a node using the following equation.

$$Perf_{host} = \frac{1}{n} * \alpha * \sum_{i=1}^{n} Perf_{task}^{i} \tag{3}$$

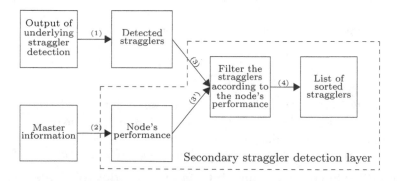

Fig. 3. Hierarchical straggler detection architecture.

where α is the slowdown factor and

$$Perf^i_{task} = \frac{progress * input}{duration} \tag{4}$$

Equation 4 evaluates the performance for a specific task, where *progress* represents the ratio of finished work over the task's total work, *input* is the size of the task's input data in bytes and *duration* is the time from the starting moment of the task. This information of each task is extracted from the Master node's database. Equation 3 means that the performance of a host is defined as the sum of the performances of all tasks running on the host. After the filtering, the rest stragglers are sorted according to their own performance and the most critical straggler (with the worst performance) is placed in the beginning of the list. We filter and sort the stragglers according to Eqs. 3 and 4 with the consideration of optimizing the energy efficiency of speculative execution. Apparently, a slow straggler running on a poor performance node is expected to be more critical straggler. Such stragglers are the main reason of causing heavy-tails in job executions and as a result wasting a lot of energy. Thus, handling those critical stragglers first can potentially lead to better energy efficiency. It is important to note that our secondary straggler detection layer is independent from the underlying detection layer, and therefore it can be easily integrated with any existing straggler detection mechanisms.

6 Energy-Aware Speculative Copy Allocation

After having the list of stragglers detected by the hierarchical straggler detection mechanism, we propose an energy-aware speculative copy allocation method to further optimize the energy efficiency of speculative execution.

6.1 Problem Definition

Given a list of suspected stragglers, the copy allocation method maps each straggler to a node with idle slots (denoted as an idle node) and start a copy of the straggler on that node, in order to optimize the overall energy efficiency of speculative execution. Assume there are S copies (s_i, $i \in [1, S]$) to be launched and N idle nodes (n_j, $j \in [1, N]$) to host the copies. We can easily formulate the copy allocation problem as a variant of the classic bin packing problem, where the size of each bin (i.e., a node) equals to the number of idle slots in the bin. Thus, the copy allocation problem is a NP-hard problem. In the next subsection, we propose a heuristic to obtain a good solution to this problem.

When the value of N is small, there are not many choices to make copy allocation decisions and the optimized energy efficiency results may not be good. Thus, we adopt the same methodology as Delay scheduling [19]. That is, we first check the value of N when making the copy allocation decision. If N is small, we wait a few seconds to have more idle nodes for potentially better results. In our experiments, we wait three seconds when N equals to one.

6.2   Copy Allocation Heuristic

There are many existing heuristics such as first-fit and best-fit algorithms to solve bin-packing problems. In this paper, we propose a heuristic similar to best-fit for our copy allocation problem. Following the order of stragglers sorted by the hierarchical straggler detection, we search for the node that can best fit each copy sequentially. We define the fitness of mapping a copy to a node according to the energy efficiency of the map. As the energy efficiency is affected by both the energy consumption and the performance of job, given any map from copy of straggler i to node j, we first provide two models to estimate the job execution time change and the energy consumption change caused by launching a copy of straggler i on node j.

Execution Time Change Estimation. As the list of stragglers returned by hierarchical straggler detection mechanism are sorted according to their performances, the head of the list is always the most critical straggler. Handling the critical straggler can directly contribute to the reduction of job execution time. Thus, we can estimate the job execution time change ΔT_{ij} caused by launching a copy of straggler i on node j using the difference between the task execution time of straggler i before and after launching the copy. Assume that straggler i is running on node k.

$$\Delta T_{ij} = \alpha_k * \frac{(1 - progress_i) * input_i}{Perf_{host}^k} - \alpha_j * \frac{input_i}{Perf_{host}^j} \qquad (5)$$

where the first term stands for the left over time for the straggler to finish if no copy is launched and the second term stands for the execution time of the copy on node j.

Energy Consumption Change Estimation. Executing a new copy consumes more energy while at the same time saves energy due to shortening the execution time of the straggler task. We can formulate the energy consumption change caused by launching a copy of straggler i on node j as follows.

$$\Delta E_{ij} = (\mathcal{P}_k + \mathcal{P}_j) \cdot T_s - (\mathcal{P}_k + \mathcal{P}_j') \cdot T_c$$
$$= \mathcal{P}_k \cdot \Delta T_{ij} + \mathcal{P}_j \cdot T_s - \mathcal{P}_j' \cdot T_c \qquad (6)$$

where T_s equals to the first term of Eq. 5 and T_c equals to the second term of Eq. 5. $\mathcal{P}_j$ and $\mathcal{P}_j'$ are the power consumption of node j before and after adding a copy of straggler i, which can be calculated using Eq. 1.

Given the above two models and the definition of energy efficiency, we can choose the map which gives the best ΔE_{ij} result as the best fit solution (i.e., the highest improvement to energy efficiency). Algorithm 1 presents the general flow of our copy allocation heuristic, where *stragglers_list* contains the list of ordered stragglers and *idle_nodes* contains the list of nodes with idle slots.

```
1  while stragglers_list is not empty do
2  |    straggler i is the head of stragglers_list;
3  |    best_fitness = 0;
4  |    for node j in idle_nodes do
5  |    |    calculate ΔE_ij using Equation 6;
6  |    |    if ΔE_ij > best_fitness then
7  |    |    |    best_map = j;
8  |    |    |    best_fitness = ΔE_ij;
9  |    |    end
10 |    end
11 |    remove straggler i from stragglers_list;
12 |    launch a copy of straggler i to node best_map;
13 end
```

Algorithm 1. Speculative copy allocation heuristic.

7   Evaluation

In this section, we evaluate our hierarchical straggler detection mechanism and copy allocation method in real Hadoop cluster and compare them with existing straggler detection mechanisms and copy allocation methods. We implemented our techniques in the Hadoop 1.2.1 stable version, with roughly 1500 lines of JAVA code. Both mechanisms are implemented as extra modules to the core of Hadoop to allow users to easily adopt our techniques using the Hadoop general configuration file.

7.1   Experimental Setup

Testbed. All of our experiments were conducted on a cluster of 21 nodes from the Nancy site of Grid'5000 testbed [8]. We configured the cluster with one master and 20 workers. Each node in the cluster is equipped with 4-core Intel 2.53 GHz CPU, 16 GB of RAM and 1 Gbps Ethernet network. The power consumption of the nodes are monitored by Power Distribution Units. Thus, we can acquire fine-grained and accurate power consumption values during the experiments. All experiments are run for 10 times and the average values are reported.

Applications. We adopt three widely-used MapReduce applications chosen from the well-known Puma MapReduce benchmark suite [16]. The three applications have different characteristics, where *Kmeans* is a compute-intensive application, *Sort* is an I/O-intensive application and *WordCount* has similar requirements on the computation and I/O resources. The input data size of the applications are all set to 10 GB. The number of Map and Reduce tasks are both set to 160 tasks.

Straggler Injection. In order to inject stragglers, we use the Dynamic Voltage-Frequency Scaling technique (DVFS) to tune the CPU frequencies (hence the capabilities) of nodes. According to the CMU Hadoop production cluster traces [14], the ratio of stragglers varies from 0 to 40% of the total number of tasks. We choose the straggler ratio of 20% in our experiments. Thus, we set four nodes out of the 20 workers in our cluster to lower CPU frequencies, which are 1.20 Ghz, 1.33 Ghz, 1.46 Ghz and 1.60 Ghz.

Comparisons. We conduct two sets of comparisons. In the first set, we compare the hierarchical straggler detection mechanism with the Default detection mechanism [4] and LATE [20] detection mechanism. Second, we compare our proposed copy allocation heuristic (denoted as Smart) with the following two methods:

Performance-Driven Allocation: This method differs from Smart in that it launches speculative copies on nodes which give the best execution time reduction as calculated by Eq. 5.

Power-driven allocation: This method differs from Smart in that it launches speculative copies on nodes which cause the lowest additional power consumption. The additional power consumption for a node j equals to $\mathcal{P}'_j - \mathcal{P}_j$ as in Eq. 6.

7.2   Evaluation

Comparison Results on Straggler Detection Mechanisms. Figure 4 shows the performance and energy results of a single WordCount job running with different straggler detection mechanisms. We use the default copy allocation method in this experiment. In the x-axis, "D" stands for the Default straggler detection mechanism, "L" stands for the LATE detection mechanism, "D+Hx" and "L+Hx"stand for using the hierarchical straggler detection mechanism on top of Default and LATE, respectively, where "x" stands for the value of the β parameter used for node filtering in the hierarchical layer.

We have the following observations. First, from Fig. 4(a), we find that the hierarchical straggler detection layer can greatly reduce the number of unsuccessful speculative copies, and the reduction increases with the increase of β. As a result, the amount of resources wasted on the killed copies is reduced (see Fig. 4(b)) by up to 94% compared to Default and 88% compared to LATE. The total energy consumption is also reduced (see Fig. 4(d)) by up to 9% compared to both Default and LATE. Second, adding the hierarchical layer does not sacrifice the performance too much (except when $\beta = 0.2$) as shown in Fig. 4(c) and (e). When $\beta = 0.2$, there is an obvious degradation in the performance. This is mainly because that when β is too small, some of the real stragglers are missed and can still cause a heavy-tail to the job. Specifically, we can see that when $\beta = 0.4$, almost all the stragglers filtered by hierarchical are successful stragglers. Thus, when we reduce β to be smaller than 0.4, some of the real stragglers will be filtered out. Third, the hierarchical straggler detection mechanism can obtain better energy efficiency compared to Default and LATE (except when $\beta = 0.2$), as shown in Fig. 4(f). When $\beta = 0.5$, we obtain the best energy efficiency, which

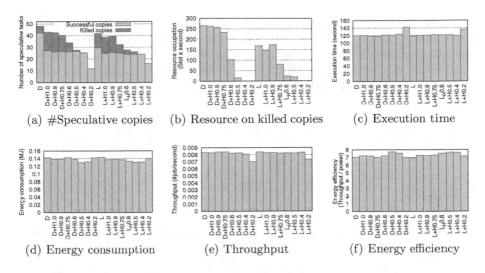

Fig. 4. WordCount application with different straggler detection mechanisms.

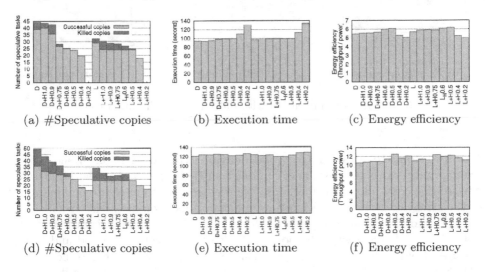

Fig. 5. Kmeans (a–c) and Sort (d–f) applications with different straggler detection mechanisms.

is 10% higher than both Default and LATE. Thus, we set β to 0.5 by default to have the best energy efficiency result while maintaining similar performance compared to existing mechanisms

Similar observations have also been found with the other two applications. Figure 5 shows the results obtained for the Kmeans and Sort applications. We can observe that, for the compute-intensive Kmeans application, we can obtain even higher reduction in the energy consumption while maintaining similar performance. When $\beta = 0.5$, we improve the energy efficiency by 13% and 10%

compared to Default and LATE, respectively. Thus, we can conclude that, the hierarchical straggler detection mechanism can greatly improve the energy efficiency of speculative executions with a comparable performance. In the following experiments, we focus on the WordCount application which shows the average improvement and use the default value of 0.5 for β.

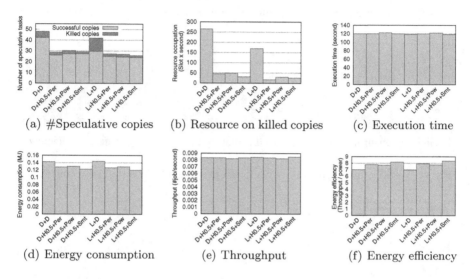

(a) #Speculative copies   (b) Resource on killed copies   (c) Execution time

(d) Energy consumption   (e) Throughput   (f) Energy efficiency

Fig. 6. WordCount application with different copy allocation methods.

Comparison Results on Copy Allocation Methods. Figure 6 shows the energy and performance results of running a single WordCount job with different speculative copy allocation methods. We evaluated in total eight combinations of the straggler detection mechanisms and copy allocation methods. Specifically, "D+D" and "L+D" are chosen as the baseline, which stand for using the Default detection mechanism with Hadoop's default copy allocation method and using the LATE straggler detection mechanism with default allocation, respectively. "D+H0.5+y" and "L+H0.5+y" refer to using hierarchical straggler detection mechanism on top of Default and LATE, respectively, where "y" stands for the copy allocation method used for allocating the copies.

We have the following observations. First, with our Smart copy allocation method, we can further reduce the energy consumption of speculative executions compared to existing mechanisms. For example, with the combination of Hierarchical and Smart, we can achieve 17% and 20% higher energy efficiency compared to Default and LATE using the default copy allocation method (see Fig. 6(f)). Second, considering only the performance or power during the copy allocation is not good enough. For example, from Fig. 6(a), we observe that Power-driven has the highest number of killed copies among the three compared allocation methods. This is because Power-driven tends to launch copies on nodes with low additional power consumption (i.e., highly utilized nodes) and thus can cause long execution time for the copies. As a result, some of the long running copies are killed and causing resource waste (see Fig. 6(b)) and thus extra energy consumption (see Fig. 6(d)). This suspicion can be verified with Fig. 6(c) and (e), which shows that Power-driven has the longest execution time (and the lowest throughput) compared to other allocation methods. Overall, Smart can improve the energy efficiency by 7% and 8% compared to Power-driven with the Default and LATE detection mechanisms, respectively. The improvement over Performance-driven are 5% and 6% using Default and LATE, respectively. The observations show that our Smart copy allocation method can further improve the energy efficiency of speculative execution.

8   Conclusion

Speculative execution is an important technique used for mitigating stragglers and improving performance of MapReduce jobs. However, few studies have looked at the energy efficiency of speculative executions. In this paper, we propose two techniques to trade-off the performance and energy efficiency for speculative executions. First, we propose a hierarchical straggler detection mechanism, which eliminates non-critical stragglers to reduce the energy waste on killed speculative copies. Second, we propose an energy aware speculative copy allocation method which consults the performance and energy models to allocate speculative copies to the most energy efficient locations. Experimental results using real implementation demonstrate that our solution can reduce the energy waste on killed speculative copies by up to 100% and improve the energy efficiency by up to 20% compared to state-of-the-art methods. For future work, we plan to study the impact of using reservation-based scheduling on the energy efficiency of speculative executions.

Acknowledgments. This work is supported in part by the ANR KerStream project (ANR-16-CE25-0014-01). The experiments presented in this paper were carried out using the Grid'5000 ALADDIN-G5K experimental testbed, an initiative from the French Ministry of Research through the ACI GRID incentive action, Inria, CNRS and RENATER and other contributing partners (see http://www.grid5000.fr/ for details).

References

1. Ananthanarayanan, G., Ghodsi, A., Shenker, S., Stoica, I.: Effective straggler mitigation: attack of the clones. In: USENIX NSDI 2013, pp. 185–198 (2013)
2. Ananthanarayanan, G., Kandula, S., Greenberg, A., Stoica, I., Lu, Y., Saha, B., Harris, E.: Reining in the outliers in MapReduce clusters using Mantri. In: USENIX OSDI 2010, pp. 1–16 (2010)
3. Chen, Q., Liu, C., Xiao, Z.: Improving MapReduce performance using smart speculative execution strategy. IEEE Trans. Comput. **63**(4), 29–42 (2014)
4. Dean, J., Ghemawat, S.: MapReduce: simplified data processing on large clusters. Commun. ACM **51**(1), 107–113 (2008)

5. Ibrahim, S., Jin, H., Lu, L., He, B., Antoniu, G., Wu, S.: Maestro: replica-aware map scheduling for MapReduce. In: IEEE/ACM CCGrid 2012, pp. 435–442 (2012)

6. Ibrahim, S., Jin, H., Lu, L., Wu, S., He, B., Qi, L.: LEEN: locality/fairness-aware key partitioning for MapReduce in the cloud. In: IEEE CloudCom 2010, pp. 17–24 (2010)

7. Ibrahim, S., Phan, T.D., Carpen-Amarie, A., Chihoub, H.E., Moise, D., Antoniu, G.: Governing energy consumption in Hadoop through CPU frequency scaling. Future Gener. Comput. Syst. 54(C), 219–232 (2016)

8. Jégou, Y., Lantéri, S., Leduc, J., Melab, N., Mornet, G., Namyst, R., Primet, P., Quetier, B., Richard, O., Talbi, E.G., Iréa, T.: Grid'5000: a large scale and highly reconfigurable experimental grid testbed. Int. J. High Perform. Comput. Appl. 20(4), 481–494 (2006)

9. Jin, H., Ibrahim, S., Qi, L., Cao, H., Wu, S., Shi, X.: The MapReduce programming model and implementations. In: Cloud Computing: Principles and Paradigms, pp. 373–390 (2011)

10. Lee, G., Chun, B.G., Katz, H.: Heterogeneity-aware resource allocation and scheduling in the cloud. In: USENIX HotCloud 2011, p. 4 (2011)

11. Leverich, J., Kozyrakis, C.: On the energy (in)efficiency of Hadoop clusters. SIGOPS Oper. Syst. Rev. 44(1), 61–65 (2010)

12. Phan, T.D., Ibrahim, S., Antoniu, G., Bouge, L.: On understanding the energy impact of speculative execution in Hadoop. In: IEEE DSDIS 2015, pp. 396–403 (2015)

13. Qureshi, A.: Power-demand routing in massive geo-distributed systems. Ph.D. dissertation. MIT (2010)

14. Ren, K., Kwon, Y., Balazinska, M., Howe, B.: Hadoop's adolescence: an analysis of hadoop usage in scientific workloads. VLDB Endow. 6(10), 853–864 (2013)

15. Ren, X., Ananthanarayanan, G., Wierman, A., Yu, M.: Hopper: decentralized speculation-aware cluster scheduling at scale. In: ACM SIGCOMM 2015, pp. 379–392 (2015)

16. Thottethodi, M., Ahmad, F., Lee, S., Vijaykumar, T.: Puma: Purdue MapReduce benchmarks suite. Technical report, Purdue University (2012)

17. Xu, H., Lau, W.C.: Resource optimization for speculative execution in a MapReduce cluster. In: IEEE ICNP 2013, pp. 1–3 (2013)

18. Xu, H., Lau, W.C.: Task-cloning algorithms in a MapReduce cluster with competitive performance bounds. IEEE ICDCS 2015, pp. 339–348 (2015)

19. Zaharia, M., Borthakur, D., Sen Sarma, J., Elmeleegy, K., Shenker, S., Stoica, I.: Delay scheduling: a simple technique for achieving locality and fairness in cluster scheduling. In: ACM EuroSys 2010, pp. 265–278 (2010)

20. Zaharia, M., Konwinski, A., Joseph, A.D., Katz, R., Stoica, I.: Improving MapReduce performance in heterogeneous environments. In: USENIX OSDI 2008, 29–42 (2008)

21. Zhou, A.C., He, B., Cheng, X., Lau, C.T.: A declarative optimization engine for resource provisioning of scientific workflows in geo-distributed clouds. In: ACM HPDC 2015, pp. 223–234 (2015)

22. Zhou, A.C., He, B., Liu, C.: Monetary cost optimizations for hosting workflow-as-a-service in IaaS clouds. IEEE Trans. Cloud Comput. 4(1), 34–48 (2016)

Leveraging Cloud Heterogeneity for Cost-Efficient Execution of Parallel Applications

Eduardo Roloff[(✉)], Matthias Diener, Emmanuell Diaz Carreño,
Luciano Paschoal Gaspary, and Philippe O.A. Navaux

Informatics Institute, Federal University of Rio Grande do Sul, Porto Alegre, Brazil
{eroloff,mdiener,edcarreno,paschoal,navaux}@inf.ufrgs.br

Abstract. Public cloud providers offer a wide range of instance types, with different processing and interconnection speeds, as well as varying prices. Furthermore, the tasks of many parallel applications show different computational demands due to load imbalance. These differences can be exploited for improving the cost efficiency of parallel applications in many cloud environments by matching application requirements to instance types. In this paper, we introduce the concept of heterogeneous cloud systems consisting of different instance types to leverage the different computational demands of large parallel applications for improved cost efficiency. We present a mechanism that automatically suggests a suitable combination of instances based on a characterization of the application and the instance types. With such a heterogeneous cloud, we are able to improve cost efficiency significantly for a variety of MPI-based applications, while maintaining a similar performance.

Keywords: Cloud computing · Cost efficiency · Heterogeneity · Performance

1 Introduction

Executing large parallel applications in the cloud has reached the mainstream and has become a major research topic in recent years. Compared to clusters, the cloud provides a higher flexibility and lower up-front costs for the hardware [14]. Public cloud providers such as Amazon's EC2 and Microsoft's Azure provide a large number of cloud instance types with different numbers of cores, processing speeds, and network interconnections [18]. Research in this area focuses mostly on porting applications to the cloud [12], evaluating their performance and cost efficiency [13,18], and improving communication performance [2–4].

An aspect that has received less attention is building a multi-instance cloud system out of different instance types. We refer to such a system as a *heterogeneous cloud* in this paper. Most multi-instance clouds currently use the same instance types, or use different instance types only in the context of accelerators (such as GPUs) [5]. A heterogeneous cloud is an interesting solution for the execution of large parallel applications, as these applications typically have

© Springer International Publishing AG 2017
F.F. Rivera et al. (Eds.): Euro-Par 2017, LNCS 10417, pp. 399–411, 2017.
DOI: 10.1007/978-3-319-64203-1_29

heterogeneous computational demands, with some tasks performing more work than others. In such a scenario, tasks that perform more work can be executed on faster but more expensive instances, while tasks that perform less work can be executed on slower and more cost-efficient instances.

In this paper, we investigate heterogeneous clouds, focusing on their potential for cost-efficient execution of parallel applications. Our main contributions are the following:

- We perform an in-depth evaluation of heterogeneous clouds with a variety of instance combinations and parallel application behaviors.
- We present a mechanism for determining instance combinations that is based on application behavior and instance characteristics.

Our proposal is compatible with a wide range of applications and requires no changes to the applications or runtime environments. In an evaluation with ten MPI-based benchmarks and scientific applications on several types of Microsoft Azure instances, we show that our proposal results in drastic cost reductions of executing parallel applications in heterogeneous clouds, while maintaining a similar performance, which leads to substantial improvements in cost efficiency of up to 18% (6.6% on average).

2   Performance and Cost Differences in the Cloud

Most public cloud providers offer a wide variety of instance types with different characteristics and prices. This section provides an analysis of homogeneous cloud clusters, that is, clusters that are composed of cloud instances of the same type, in terms of their computational performance and cost. We also measure the load imbalance of a set of parallel applications. Combining these two aspects leads us to motivate the introduction of heterogeneous clouds.

2.1   Methodology of the Analysis

Experiments in this section were performed with the following methodology. First, we selected a group of homogeneous clouds to run performance and cost tests, focusing on instance types that are similar to provide a better comparison. Based on these results, we selected instance types that will be used for the rest of this work. Second, we verified the computational load profile of several parallel applications by measuring the number of instructions per task.

All experiments were performed on the Microsoft Azure public cloud, which was selected since it has the largest number of instance types among the main cloud providers. We selected the A10, D4 v2, F8, G3, and H8 instances of Azure to verify their efficiency in terms of performance and cost. All chosen instance types consist of eight cores, which is the most common instance size in Azure. The multi-instance experiments use eight nodes, for a total number of 64 cores in all cases. The software environment consists of Ubuntu server 16.04, with Linux kernel 4.4. We use Open MPI [7] 1.10.2 as the parallel runtime environment. All

Table 1. Characteristics of the Azure instance types. Instance types that are evaluated in depth in this paper are marked in **bold**.

Instance name	Price/hour	Linpack perf. (GFlops)	Price/TFlop
A10	US$ 0.780	155.35	US$ 5.02
D4 v2	US$ 0.559	265.00	US$ 2.11
F8	US$ 0.513	246.10	US$ 2.08
G3	US$ 2.440	280.17	US$ 8.71
H8	US$ 0.971	324.34	US$ 2.99

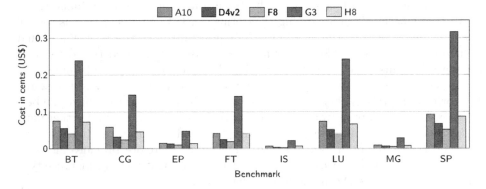

Fig. 1. Cost per execution (in US$ cents) of each NAS benchmark on homogeneous eight-instance cloud systems.

applications were compiled with gcc/gfortran 5.4.0, using the -O2 optimization level. We measured the raw computational performance of a single instance of each type with the High Performance Linpack (HPL) benchmark [11]. To evaluate the cost of the machines we calculate the price of a TFlop, based on performance results and the price for each instance, with the Linpack performance. Table 1 presents an overview of the characteristics of these instance types as well as the performance and cost results.

Experiments were performed with a variety of MPI-based parallel applications. We use the MPI implementation of the NAS Parallel Benchmarks (NPB) [1], version 3.3.1. Experiments were performed with input class *C*, which represents a medium-large input size. The *DT* application was not used because it needs at least 85 MPI processes to execute using input size *C*. *BRAMS* (Brazilian developments on the Regional Atmospheric Modeling System) [6] is the extended version of the RAMS (Regional Atmospheric Modeling System) weather prediction model. *Alya* [9] is a simulation code for multi-physics problems, based on a variational multi-scale finite element method for unstructured meshes.

The location used to allocate the machines on Microsoft Azure was "West USA". All experiments were executed 10 times. Applications were configured to run with 64 ranks (1 rank per core). In our experiments, we did not notice significant differences between executions at different times of day and between different allocations of instances.

2.2   Cost of Homogeneous Clouds

This section presents the cost results of executing the NAS benchmarks on homogeneous cloud instances. The instance types selected for the rest of this work are also discussed.

The cost per execution of the NAS benchmarks are shown in Fig. 1. The cost was calculated by multiplying the price per second of each instance with the execution time of the benchmark. The G3 instance presented the highest cost of all benchmarks. Despite its high performance, G3 has a cost that is several times bigger than the other instances. The other instance types show a similar behavior among them. The D4 v2 and F8 instances presented the lowest cost among all the instances tested, resembling thus the cost analysis of Linpack.

Based on these preliminary results, we selected two instance sizes, D4 v2 and F8, for our analysis in this paper. They were chosen because they have the best relation of cost and performance among all the types we evaluated. Furthermore, despite having differences in the price per hour and performance, their relation between cost and performance is very similar and therefore provides an interesting tradeoff between price and speed. For simplicity, the D4 v2 instance type will be referred to as D4 in the rest of the paper.

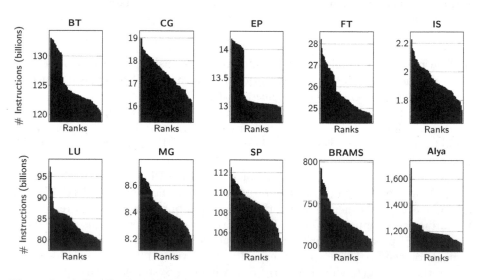

Fig. 2. Load distribution of the benchmarks, running with 64 ranks. Each bar corresponds to the number of instructions executed by a rank. Ranks are sorted according the numbers of instructions executed.

2.3   Load Imbalance

Another important aspect of our proposal is that parallel applications have different computational demands. Such a load imbalance can be caused for various reasons, such as an imperfect distribution of work, interference from other applications or users, or if an algorithm has different complexities for different regions of the input data. To evaluate the load imbalance of the parallel applications, we used the `perf` tool [10], measuring the number of instructions executed by each MPI rank. All applications were executed with 64 ranks.

Results of this experiment are shown in Fig. 2. In the figure, we show the numbers of instructions executed by each rank for each benchmark, sorted in descending order. The results show varying degrees of imbalance between the applications. In general, imbalance is considerable, with differences between the minimum and maximum numbers of instructions for each benchmark reaching up to 35% in the case of *Alya*. Some applications, such as *FT*, *SP*, and *Alya*, have considerable sequential parts that increase their imbalance. Others, such as *BT*, *EP*, and *FT*, show two distinct levels of numbers of instructions executed by the ranks. Executing the applications multiple times results in a very similar load profile, with similar loads for each rank.

3   A Mechanism to Improve Cost Efficiency in the Cloud

This section describes our proposed mechanism to automatically leverage the heterogeneity for an improved cost efficiency. The mechanism calculates for a given profile of an application and cloud instance types how many instances of each type should be used, and which MPI ranks should be executed on each instance. An overview of our proposal is shown in Algorithm 1.

Our mechanism receives as input the load profile of the application, the instance profile of the possible instance types. Currently, two different instance types are taken into account, which we refer to as HI (higher performance and cost) and LO (lower performance and cost), which correspond to the D4 and F8 instances in our experiments, respectively. We focus on two instance types since many of the applications show a two-level load distribution. The mechanism outputs the instance combination, that is, how many instances of each type should be used, and which ranks should be placed on each instance.

3.1   Mechanism Inputs

Our mechanism requires the following inputs. The first two, application profile and instance profile, are generated automatically.

Application Profile. The load profile of the application is generated via the `perf` tool [10]. We focus on the number of instructions per rank, as in Sect. 2. This could be extended to a more fine-grained differentiation for several types of instructions (for example, floating point or integer operations) and other types

---

Algorithm 1. Algorithm of our proposed mechanism

   Data: Application profile, Instances profiles
   Result: MPI rankfile (mapping of MPI ranks to instances)
1 calculate instance performance ratio;
2 **while** *ranksize/VMs count < rankgroup* **do**
3   calculate ratio (rankgroup[n], rankgroup[n+1]);
4   **if** *rankgroup ratio < instance performance ratio* **then**
5   assign rankgroup to a HI VM;
6   fetch next rankgroup;
7   **else**
8   assign rest of rankgroups to LO VMs;
9   **end**
10 **end**
11 output rankfile;

---

of resources (such as communication, memory, I/O). This application profile usually needs to be generated only once for a given set of input data and number of ranks. The result of this stage is the load vector of the application.

Instance Profile. The mechanism generates the instance profile of the instance types by measuring the execution time of the desired application on homogeneous instances. The result of this stage is the relative performance between the two instance types.

3.2   Mechanism Outputs

Our mechanism outputs the instance combination, as well as which ranks should run on which instance. For the discussion in this section, we first sort the load vector in descending order, as shown in the load distributions in Fig. 2.

Instance Combination. The first output step of our mechanism is to determine the instance combination. We group the sorted list of ranks into groups of the same size as the number of cores per instance and calculate the cumulative load of each group. The mechanism then iterates over the list of groups and calculates the load ratio between subsequent groups. Until the ratio reaches a threshold, groups will be executed on HI instances. When the ratio is above the threshold, all subsequent groups will be executed on LO instances. The threshold is determined by the performance ratio of the instance types.

Rank Placement. After determining the number of HI and LO instance types, our mechanism assigns ranks to the instances in the following way. It iterates over the sorted list of ranks, and assigns ranks to instances sequentially, starting with the ranks with the highest load, which are assigned to the HI instances.

As soon as one instance has the maximum number of ranks assigned to it, the mechanism continues the rank placement with the next instance, until all ranks are assigned. In the final step, our mechanism creates a rank file that specifies the task to instance assignment for Open MPI [15].

4   Results

This section presents the evaluation methodology used to validate our proposal, as well as the obtained results.

For our experiments, we use the same Azure instance types as before, D4 and F8. All experiments use eight instances for a total of 64 cores. We vary the mix of instances between:

- fully homogeneous: all eight instances are of the same type, D4 or F8.
- heterogeneous to varying degrees: 1–7 instances of each type, totaling eight instances.

We evaluate all possible combinations of the D4 and F8 instances.

Machines of all instance types were only allocated once and not reallocated between executions. Further experiments after deallocating and allocating new instances of the same types (not shown in the paper) resulted in quantitatively and qualitatively very similar behaviors. Results show the average values of 10 executions. We begin with a discussion of the NAS benchmarks, followed by the *BRAMS* and *Alya* applications.

4.1   The NAS Benchmarks

The cost efficiency results of the NAS benchmarks are shown in Fig. 3. In the figures, the line represents the cost efficiency when varying the mix of instance types. To calculate the cost efficiency metric, we use the following equation [13].

$$cost\ efficiency = execution\ time \times price\ of\ execution \qquad (1)$$

Lower values of the metric indicate a higher cost efficiency.

In the figures, the y axes show the values of the metric, while the x axes indicate the mix of instance types in the form a/b, where a represents the number of D4 instances and b represents the number of F8 instances. 0/8 and 8/0 are the homogeneous clouds, while $1/7 - 7/1$ are heterogeneous instances. The most cost efficient instance combination is marked with a dashed circle (⟡). The results of the instance combination determined by our mechanism are marked with an unbroken circle (O).

Several interesting results can be pointed out. First of all, heterogeneous clouds are the most cost efficient environments for the majority of the benchmarks. Heterogeneous environments are beneficial for five out of the eight benchmarks (*BT*, *EP*, *FT*, *MG*, and *SP*), while homogeneous environments are more appropriate for *CG*, *IS*, and *LU*. The five benchmarks have an increased cost

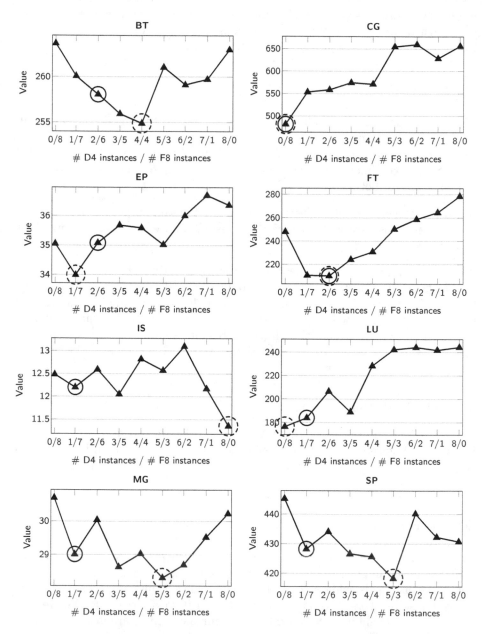

Fig. 3. Cost efficiency results for the NAS benchmarks on the D4 and F8 instances for different combinations of instances. Lower values indicate a higher cost efficiency. The highest cost efficiency is marked with a dashed circle ⦾. The results of our mechanism are marked with an unbroken circle ○.

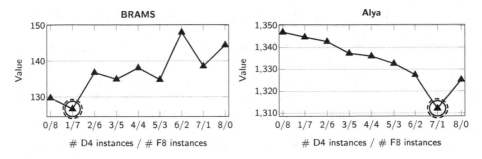

Fig. 4. Cost efficiency results for *BRAMS* and *Alya* on the D4 and F8 instances. Lower values indicate a higher cost efficiency. The highest cost efficiency is marked with a dashed circle ⊙. The results of our mechanism are marked with an unbroken circle ○.

efficiency between 3.0% (*SP*) and 18.0% (*FT*) compared to the best cost efficiency of a homogeneous environment. Over all NAS benchmarks, cost efficiency was improved on average by 6.6%. These results show that cost efficiency can be improved substantially via heterogeneous clouds.

Although not achieving the optimal gains for all applications, our mechanism is able to result in substantial cost efficiency improvements close to the optimum in most scenarios, with an average improvement of 4.7%. This shows that profiling all possible instance combinations is not required in order to reduce costs. Another important result is that almost the whole spectrum of heterogeneous and homogeneous instances is the most cost efficient environment at least in one experiment. This indicates that simple policies that do not take the specific characteristics of the environment and application behavior into account can not result in optimal cost efficiency.

The performance analysis of the heterogeneous allocations is also an important aspect for the user. There are four benchmarks that presented performance losses (*BT*, *EP*, *MG*, and *SP*), between 0.2% (*SP*) to 5.5% (*MG*). It is important to remark that when comparing the performance loss with the cost efficiency gain, the heterogeneous allocations present better ratios for all the cases. This means that the performance decrease is less than the cost efficiency gain. The best ratios were obtained with *SP* (0.2% performance loss, 3.0% cost efficiency gain) and *EP* (0.7% performance loss, 3.1% cost efficiency gain). On average, performance was reduced by 0.4% in the optimal case, and 1.2% with our mechanism.

4.2 *BRAMS* and *Alya*

The cost efficiency results for the two scientific applications, *BRAMS* and *Alya*, are shown in Fig. 4. The results echo our analysis of the NAS benchmarks. Both applications can benefit significantly from a heterogeneous environment and show significant cost efficiency improvements in almost all cases. When comparing the results of *BRAMS*, we observed that *BRAMS* presented a cost efficiency gain of 4.6%.

When analyzing the results of *Alya*, we observed a performance loss of 0.4%, while presenting a cost efficiency gain of 1.8% for the cloud tenant. Observing the load distribution of *Alya* in Fig. 2, we note that the imbalance of Alya is high, with a few processes executing much more operations than the average. The instances used in our experiments, D4 and F8, present a close performance. Due to the *Alya* load distribution, we can conclude that it could benefit from instances with higher differences between them, and from mixing more instances types.

5 Related Work

Yeo and Lee [17] analyzed how periodically upgrading hardware in datacenters introduced heterogeneity and how the service provider could mitigate its impact on performance for the end user. However, this work does not allow the cloud tenants to exploit the information about the underlying infrastructure to improve the cost/efficiency of their applications.

Zhang et al. [19] present a dynamic capacity provisioning manager that allows workload division using a heterogeneity-aware algorithm. Their work considers heterogeneity in machine hardware from production datacenters and from the workload in them. They evaluate their algorithm simulating a heterogeneous cluster. They were able to improve the utilization of the cluster and scheduling without compromising the workload. Their work takes the heterogeneity of VMs into account, but their focus is on improvements from the provider perspective.

Gupta et al. [8] propose a technique to improve the performance of parallel applications in the cloud with task placement. The authors place the tasks according to the interference between different applications by analyzing their cache memory usage, and from a description provided by the user. They do not take different types of instances into account.

Zhang et al. [20] exploited cloud heterogeneity in several MapReduce clusters to select the best cost/performance deployment. They simulate their configurations of 3 instance sizes looking to obtain the same application performance but with different provisioning costs. The validation was done on Amazon using MapReduce jobs with no data dependencies between them. Their results showed a difference in cost when using homogeneous or heterogeneous deployments. For some of the applications evaluated they obtained significant cost savings. Our work include MPI applications, and benchmarks with communication between instances.

Carreño et al. [4] created a communication-aware task mapping for cloud environments with multiple instances. Their work analyzes heterogeneity in communication between the tasks and in the network interconnections between cloud instances. They use this information to map tasks that communicate a lot to faster instances, improving inter-instance communication performance. However, their work uses the same type of VMs for each execution and they do not take computational performance into account. In our work, we compare the performance when mixing different types of VMs.

Wang and Shi [16] developed a task-level scheduling algorithm to comply with budget and deadline constrains. They analyze heterogeneity as the variety of options of virtual machines from a provider and the underlying variations in hardware that exists for each instance. They developed a parallel greedy algorithm that improves deployment to comply with the constrains. Their work is different because it does not try to optimize the cost/efficiency of the solution but tries to respect the user constrains. Also their work was not validated using an actual public cloud infrastructure.

6   Conclusions

The cloud has become an interesting environment for the execution of parallel applications due to the easy and flexible availability of different instance types that vary in performance and price. Most current cloud deployments for parallel applications are homogeneous, that is, they are composed of a number of instances of the same type. In this paper, we motivated and analyzed a new type of deployment that is based on heterogeneous instances of different types. Since the computational demands of parallel applications are not uniform in most cases, such a heterogeneous cloud can better match the requirements of the application, improving the price and cost efficiency of the execution.

Our evaluation with MPI-based applications on an Azure cloud shows that the cost efficiency can be improved significantly, by up to 18%, depending on the load imbalance of the application, while maintaining a similar performance. Gains achieved by our mechanism were close to the optimum in most cases, showing that improvements from heterogeneous execution do not require a time-consuming evaluation of all possible instance combinations.

For the future, we plan to take communication within the parallel application into account when making placement decisions, and we will extend our analysis to consider more than two different types of instances with different numbers of cores on each type.

Acknowledgments. This research received funding from the EU H2020 Programme and from MCTI/RNP-Brazil under the HPC4E project, grant agreement no. 689772. Additional funding was provided by FAPERGS in the context of the GreenCloud Project.

References

1. Bailey, D.H., Barszcz, E., Barton, J.T., Browning, D.S., Carter, R.L., Dagum, L., Fatoohi, R.A., Frederickson, P.O., Lasinski, T.A., Schreiber, R.S., Simon, H.D., Venkatakrishnan, V., Weeratunga, S.K.: The NAS parallel benchmarks. Int. J. Supercomput. Appl. 5(3), 66–73 (1991)
2. Bassem, C., Bestavros, A.: Network-constrained packing of brokered workloads in virtualized environments. In: 15th IEEE/ACM International Symposium on Cluster, Cloud and Grid Computing (2015)
3. Bhatele, A., Titus, A.R., Thiagarajan, J.J., Jain, N., Gamblin, T., Bremer, P.T., Schulz, M., Kale, L.V.: Identifying the culprits behind network congestion. In: IEEE International Parallel and Distributed Processing Symposium (IPDPS), pp. 113–122 (2015)
4. Carreño, E.D., Diener, M., Cruz, E.H.M., Navaux, P.O.A.: Communication optimization of parallel applications in the Cloud. In: IEEE/ACM International Symposium on Cluster, Cloud, and Grid Computing (CCGrid), pp. 1–10 (2016)
5. Crago, S.P., Walters, J.P.: Heterogeneous cloud computing: the way forward. Computer 48(1), 59–61 (2015)
6. Freitas, S.R., Longo, K.M., Silva Dias, M.A.F., Chatfield, R., Silva Dias, P., Artaxo, P., Andreae, M.O., Grell, G., Rodrigues, L.F., Fazenda, A., Panetta, J.: The coupled aerosol and tracer transport model to the Brazilian developments on the regional atmospheric modeling system (CATT-BRAMS) - Part 1: model description and evaluation. Atmos. Chem. Phys. 9(8), 2843–2861 (2009)
7. Gabriel, E., et al.: Open MPI: goals, concept, and design of a next generation MPI implementation. In: Kranzlmüller, D., Kacsuk, P., Dongarra, J. (eds.) EuroPVM/MPI 2004. LNCS, vol. 3241, pp. 97–104. Springer, Heidelberg (2004). doi:10.1007/978-3-540-30218-6_19
8. Gupta, A., Kalé, L.V., Milojicic, D., Faraboschi, P., Balle, S.M.: HPC-aware VM placement in infrastructure clouds. In: IEEE International Conference on Cloud Engineering (IC2E), pp. 11–20 (2013)
9. Houzeaux, G., Vázquez, M., Aubry, R., Cela, J.M.: A massively parallel fractional step solver for incompressible flows. J. Comput. Phys. 228(17), 6316–6332 (2009). http://dx.doi.org/10.1016/j.jcp.2009.05.019
10. de Melo, A.C.: The new Linux 'perf' tools. In: Linux Kongress (2010)
11. Petitet, A., Whaley, R.C., Dongarra, J., Cleary, A.: HPL - a portable implementation of the high-performance linpack benchmark for distributed-memory computers (2012). http://www.netlib.org/benchmark/hpl/
12. Roloff, E., Birck, F., Diener, M., Carissimi, A., Navaux, P.O.A.: Evaluating high performance computing on the Windows Azure platform. In: IEEE International Conference on Cloud Computing (CLOUD), pp. 803–810 (2012)
13. Roloff, E., Diener, M., Carissimi, A., Navaux, P.O.A.: High performance computing in the Cloud: deployment, performance and cost efficiency. In: IEEE International Conference on Cloud Computing Technology and Science (CloudCom), pp. 371–378 (2012)
14. Saad, A., El-Mahdy, A.: Network topology identification for Cloud instances. In: International Conference on Cloud and Green Computing, pp. 92–98 (2013)
15. The Open MPI project: mpirun man page (2013). http://www.open-mpi.de/doc/v1.6/man1/mpirun.1.php#sect9
16. Wang, Y., Shi, W.: Budget-driven scheduling algorithms for batches of MapReduce jobs in heterogeneous clouds. IEEE Trans. Cloud Comput. 2(3), 306–319 (2014)

17. Yeo, S., Lee, H.H.: Using mathematical modeling in provisioning a heterogeneous Cloud computing environment. Computer **44**(8), 55–62 (2011)
18. Zant, B.E., Gagnaire, M.: Performance and price analysis for Cloud service providers. In: Science and Information Conference (SAI), pp. 816–822 (2015)
19. Zhang, Q., Zhani, M.F., Boutaba, R., Hellerstein, J.L.: Harmony: dynamic heterogeneity-aware resource provisioning in the Cloud. In: Proceedings of the 2013 IEEE 33rd International Conference on Distributed Computing Systems, ICDCS 2013, pp. 510–519. IEEE Computer Society, Washington, DC (2013)
20. Zhang, Z., Cherkasova, L., Loo, B.T.: Exploiting Cloud heterogeneity for optimized cost/performance MapReduce processing. In: Proceedings of the Fourth International Workshop on Cloud Data and Platforms, CloudDP 2014, pp. 1:1–1:6 (2014)

Distributed Systems and Algorithms

A Consensus-Based Fault-Tolerant Event Logger for High Performance Applications

Edson Tavares de Camargo[1,2]([✉]), Elias P. Duarte Jr.[2], and Fernando Pedone[3]

[1] Department of Informatics, Federal University of Paraná (UFPR), Curitiba, Brazil
[2] Federal Technology University of Paraná (UTFPR), Toledo, Brazil
edson@utfpr.edu.br, elias@inf.ufpr.br
[3] University of Lugano (USI), Lugano, Switzerland
fernando.pedone@usi.ch

Abstract. Most message logging protocols rely on a centralized event logger to store information (i.e., the determinants) to allow the recovery of an application process. This centralized approach, besides suffering from the single point of failure problem, represents a bottleneck for the efficiency of message logging protocols. In this work, we present a fault-tolerant distributed event logger based on consensus that outperforms the centralized approach. We implemented the event logger of MPI determinants using the Paxos algorithm. Our event logger inherits the Paxos properties: safety is guaranteed even if the system is asynchronous and liveness is guaranteed despite processes failures. Experimental results are reported for the performance of the distributed event logger based both on classic Paxos and parallel Paxos applied to AMG (Algebraic Multi-Grid) and NAS Parallel Benchmark applications.

1 Introduction

Most traditional strategies to deal with failures in HPC systems are based on rollback-recovery mechanisms [3,6,16]. These strategies allow applications to recover from failures without losing previously computed results. Message logging is a class of rollback-recovery technique that unlike coordinated checkpoint strategies does not require all processes to coordinate to save their state during normal execution and to restart after a single process failure.

Message logging relies on the piecewise deterministic assumption. This assumption states that all nondeterministic events that a process executes can be identified and the information necessary to replay each event during recovery can be logged in tuples called *determinants* [7]. By replaying the determinants in their exact original order, a process can deterministically recreate its pre-failure state. Most message logging protocols suppose that reception events (i.e., message receiving events) are the only possible nondeterministic events in the execution [3]. Consequently, a crucial task in message logging is to reliably save and restore the determinants without penalizing the performance.

© Springer International Publishing AG 2017
F.F. Rivera et al. (Eds.): Euro-Par 2017, LNCS 10417, pp. 415–427, 2017.
DOI: 10.1007/978-3-319-64203-1_30

The component responsible for reliably logging determinants is the *event logger*. The event logger receives the determinants from the application processes, stores them locally, and notifies the application processes. Previous works based on message logging typically assume that the event logger is a centralized entity (e.g., [1,4,17]), and thus it cannot tolerate failures. Indeed, the failure of the event logger would bring the execution to a halt as application processes would no longer be able to save the determinants.

The main goal of this paper is to propose a fault-tolerant event logger that has performance comparable to or better than a centralized event logger. In particular, our replicated event logger does not require extra system resources (i.e., physical nodes) in comparison with a centralized event logger and can tolerate a configurable number of failures. When configured to tolerate a single failure, our consensus-based event logger needs the same number of messages and communication steps (i.e., network delays) to log a determinant as a centralized event logger. We also show in the paper that the myth that fault tolerance introduces overheads is not completely unfounded since the indiscriminate use of existing fault-tolerance techniques can indeed lead to expensive solutions.

We implemented two fault-tolerant event loggers based on the Paxos algorithm [11]. One is based on classic Paxos and the other on a configuration we call parallel Paxos. We conducted a number of experiments comparing them to a centralized event logger. We evaluated the performance of our event logger implementations using the LU and MG kernels from the NAS Parallel Benchmarck (NAS-PB) and the Algebric MultiGrid (AMG) application. Our results show that the replicated event logger based on parallel Paxos consistently outperforms a centralized event logger while providing configurable fault tolerance.

The rest of the paper is organized as follows. Section 2 briefly overviews rollback-recovery, including message logging, and the event logger. Section 3 reviews the Paxos algorithm and presents our consensus-based event loggers. Section 4 presents our implementations of the event logger and experimental results and Sect. 5 concludes the paper.

2   Log-Based Rollback Recovery

Rollback-recovery techniques are often used to provide fault tolerance to HPC applications so that they can restart from a previously saved state [3,6]. Rollback-recovery assumes a distributed system that is a collection of application processes that communicate through a network and have access to stable storage that survives failures [7]. Processes save recovery information periodically on stable storage during their failure-free execution. After the occurrence of a failure, the process that failed uses the recovery information to restart its computation from a past state. The recovery information includes at least the state of the participating processes, called *checkpoints*. Some protocols may also include the logging of nondeterministic events, encoded in tuples called *determinants*.

Log-based approaches, or simply "message logging", use both checkpoints and logging of nondeterministic events to avoid the drawbacks of both uncoordinated and coordinated checkpointing [14]. Message logging protocols assume the application is piece-wise deterministic [10]. This assumption asserts that all nondeterministic events executed by a process can be identified and the information necessary to replay each event during recovery can be logged in determinants. An *event* corresponds to a computational or communication step of a process. Most message logging protocols assume that message reception is the only nondeterministic event.

Depending on how determinants are logged, message logging protocols can be pessimistic, optimistic or causal [7]. In pessimistic logging, a process first stores the determinant of a nondeterministic event (e.g., in remote storage) before delivering the message. Despite the fact that pessimistic logging simplifies recovery and garbage collection, it presents an overhead on failure-free scenarios: the application has to wait for the determinant to be stored in order to proceed. In optimistic logging, processes log determinants asynchronously, thereby reducing the overhead. However, optimistic protocols allow orphan processes to be created due to failures and lead to more expensive recovery.

Usually, in message logging approaches the determinant of every received message is logged. However, it is possible to reduce the overall number of logged messages by identifying which events are deterministic and which are nondeterministic [2]. An event is deterministic when from the current state there is only one possible outcome state for the event. If an event can result in several different states, then it is nondeterministic. Message receptions with an explicitly identified sender are deterministic events and do not need to be logged; if the source is left unspecified then message receptions are nondeterministic. Message receptions with an explicitly identified sender are deterministic events and do not need to be logged; if the source is left unspecified then message receptions are nondeterministic. For example, a nondeterministic event occurs in MPI when the receiving process uses the tag MPI_ANY_SOURCE in MPI_Recv. As stated in [5], several MPI applications contain only deterministic communication events. However, many important MPI applications are nondeterministic, including all master-slave applications. Furthermore, programmers usually include nondeterministic communication events in the code to improve performance.

2.1   The Event Logger

The event logger plays an important role in message-logging protocols [1]. It receives the determinants from the application processes, stores them locally, and notifies the application processes after determinants are stored. The performance of the event logger has a major impact on the efficiency of message-logging protocols as showed in [1,17,18], and many protocols implement the event logger as a centralized (i.e., non-replicated) component [1,3].

To the best of our knowledge, the only existing distributed event logger is proposed in [18] for O2P [17]. That protocol offers a distributed way to save determinants. Despite being related to our work, the entire solution fails if an acknowledgement is not received by the sender; i.e., the fault tolerance of the solution is not guaranteed. Our proposed event logger based on consensus is both distributed and fault-tolerant. The Paxos protocol ensures progress with a majority of non-faulty processes and safety even if the system is asynchronous.

3 · Consensus and Message Logging

Consensus is a fundamental abstraction in fault-tolerant distributed computing. In this section, we review the consensus problem, present Paxos, one of the most prominent consensus algorithms, and discuss how to efficiently implement a fault-tolerant event logger with Paxos.

3.1   Consensus and State Machine Replication

Consensus can be used to build a highly available event logging service using the state machine replication approach [19]. State machine replication regulates how commands must be propagated to and executed by the replicas in order for the service to be consistent. In our particular case, the commands are requests to save a determinant, propagated to and executed by replicas of the event logger. Command propagation has two requirements: (i) every non-faulty replica must receive every command and (ii) no two replicas can disagree on the order of received and executed commands. If command execution is deterministic, then replicas will reach the same state and produce the same output upon executing the same sequence of commands.

Intuitively, consensus captures the command propagation requirements of state machine replication. More precisely, consensus is defined by three abstract properties: (a) If a replica decides on a value, then the value was proposed by some process (*validity*). (b) No two replicas decide differently (*agreement*). (c) If a non-faulty process proposes a value, then eventually all non-faulty replicas decide some value (*termination*). From the requirements of state machine replication and the guarantees provided by consensus, it should be clear that state machine replication can be implemented as a series of consensus instances, where the i-th consensus instance decides on the i-th command (or batch of commands) to be executed by the replicas [11].

State machine replication and consensus provide a principled approach to ensuring that replicas are consistent despite failures. This approach should not be overlooked since ad hoc solutions to replication must face subtle impossibilities in the design of distributed systems subject to process failures [8].

3.2   The Paxos Protocol

Paxos is a fault-tolerant consensus algorithm designed for state machine replication [12]. Paxos has important characteristics: it is safe under asynchronous assumptions, live under weak synchronous assumptions, ensures progress with a majority of non-faulty processes, and assumes a crash-recovery failure model.

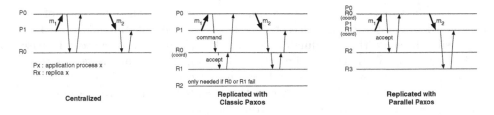

Fig. 1. Three implementations of an event logger. The centralized approach has a single event logger (R_0) and thus cannot tolerate any failures. The Paxos-based approaches can tolerate one failure (i.e., $f = 1$). Paxos coordinators already executed the first phase of the protocol and can proceed with the second phase upon receiving a command.

Paxos distinguishes the following roles that a process can play: *proposers*, *acceptors* and *learners*. Proposers propose a value, acceptors choose a value, and learners learn the decided value. A single process can assume any of those roles, and multiple roles simultaneously. Paxos is resilience-optimum [13]: to tolerate f failures it requires $2f + 1$ acceptors—that is, to ensure progress, a quorum of $f + 1$ acceptors must be non-faulty.

An instance of Paxos proceeds in two phases: during the first phase, a proposer selects a unique round number and sends a *prepare* request to a quorum of acceptors. Upon receiving a prepare request with a round number bigger than any round the acceptor previously received, the acceptor responds to the proposer promising that it will reject any future requests with smaller round numbers. If the acceptor already accepted a command for the current instance (explained next), it will return this command to the proposer, together with the round number received when the command was accepted. When the proposer receives answers from a quorum of acceptors, it proceeds to the second phase.

In the second phase, the proposer selects a command according to the following rule. If no acceptor in the quorum of responses accepted a command, the proposer can select a new command for the instance; however, if any of the acceptors returned a command in the first phase, the proposer chooses the command with the highest round number. The proposer then sends an *accept* request with the round number used in the first phase and the command chosen to a quorum of acceptors. When receiving such a request, the acceptors acknowledge it by sending a message to the coordinator and learners, unless the acceptors have already acknowledged another request with a higher round number. When a quorum of acceptors accepts a command consensus is reached.

If multiple proposers simultaneously execute the procedure above for the same instance, then no proposer may be able to execute the two phases of the protocol and reach consensus. To avoid scenarios in which proposers compete indefinitely, a *coordinator* process can be chosen. In this case, proposers submit commands to the coordinator, which executes the first and second phases of the protocol. If the coordinator fails, another process takes over its role. Paxos ensures consistency despite concurrent coordinators and termination in the presence of a single coordinator.

A coordinator can optimize performance by executing the first phase of the protocol for a batch of instances before it receives any commands [11]. This is possible because the coordinator only sends commands in the second phase of the protocol. With this optimization, a command can be chosen in three communication steps: the message from the proposer to the coordinator, the accept request from the coordinator to the acceptors, and the response to this request from the acceptors to the coordinator and learners.

3.3   Consensus-Based Message Logging

We now propose two protocols based on Paxos to render the event logger fault-tolerant: Classic Paxos and Parallel Paxos. Similarly to a centralized event logger, our protocols log nondeterministic events only; the message payload is saved by the sender- [9]. A determinant contains the sender of a message, the message identifier, and the message receiving order. Periodically, each process performs a checkpoint in order to save its state.

Our first protocol, Classic Paxos, is based on classic state machine replication. Application processes are proposers and the event logger replicas are acceptors and learners. Every application process submits commands to the coordinator, a process among the acceptors, to log determinants. The coordinator receives commands, executes Paxos to log the commands in a quorum of replicas, and sends replies to the application process (see Fig. 1). In "good executions" (i.e., in the absence of process failures) a determinant is logged after four communication steps and $2f + 2$ point-to-point message exchanges. By contrast, a centralized event logger can log events after two communication steps and two message exchanges.

In our second protocol, Parallel Paxos, we assign a separate sequence of Paxos executions to each application process. This means that each process has its set of replicas, which allows important optimizations. First, since each process has its own sequence of Paxos executions, the process does not compete with other processes in executions of Paxos and therefore, there is no need for a coordinator; in good executions, the process is the only proposer in its sequence of Paxos. Second, by using different sets of replicas, performance is no longer capped by what the coordinator and the acceptors can handle. Third, we can now co-locate the application process and the acceptor-coordinator in the same process. In good runs, this scheme can log a determinant after two communication steps and $2f$ messages.

An event logger implemented with Parallel Paxos presents the same number of communication steps as a centralized event logger, while tolerating a configurable number of failures and scaling performance. When configured to tolerate one failure ($f = 1$), it exchanges the same number of messages per logging operation as the centralized logger. Moreover, to save resources, "free acceptors" (i.e., acceptors not collocated with application processes) can be placed in the same physical node. For example, a single node can host all free acceptors, i.e. Parallel Paxos can use the same amount of nodes required by a centralized strategy.

Upon recovering from a failure, an application process must retrieve all its logged determinants. With the centralized approach, the application process contacts the event logger. With the replicated approaches, this is done by contacting a quorum of acceptors.

4 Evaluation

In this section we describe an implementation of the proposed consensus-based event logger and present experimental results, including a comparison with the traditional centralized alternative. Results are presented for the execution of three MPI applications: AMG 2013 (Algebraic Multigrid Solver) of the Lawrence Livermore National Laboratory, LU (Lower-Upper Gauss-Seidel solver) and MG (Multi-Grid on a sequence of meshes). Both LU and MG are on the NAS parallel benchmarks version 3.2. The applications were executed through Open MPI version 1.10. The experiments were conducted on a dedicated cluster that consists of 40 nodes each with two Intel(R) Quad-Core Xeon L5420 2.5 GHz processors and 8 Gbytes of RAM interconnected on a Gigabit Ethernet network.

We intercept MPI primitives using the MPI standard profiling interface (PMPI) [15]. If the interceptor detects a nondeterministic event, as defined in [2], it builds a determinant related to the event and makes a submission to the event logger. We implemented three event loggers: a traditional centralized logger, a distributed replicated logger based on Classic Paxos, and the distributed replicated logger based on Parallel Paxos (all described in Sect. 3.3). The Parallel Paxos event logger can be configured to log messages synchronously or asynchronously. In the synchronous mode, after submitting a determinant, an application process waits for an acknowledgement from the event logger before submitting the next determinant; in asynchronous mode the application process can submit multiple determinants before it receives acknowledgments from the event logger. Unless stated otherwise, our experiments use the synchronous mode. The interceptor and event loggers were implemented in C using the libevent version 2.022. We used the Paxos library libpaxos version 3.

The centralized event logger is hosted on a dedicated node. In Classic Paxos, a coordinator was deployed on a dedicated node while three acceptors (i.e., $f = 1$) were deployed each on a single node. There were also three learners, each one colocated with an acceptor. The learners are responsible for replying to the MPI processes as soon as a determinant is stored. In Parallel Paxos, each sequence of Paxos executions uses three acceptors (i.e., $f = 1$), each one deployed on a dedicated node. In Parallel Paxos each MPI process is both a proposer and a learner. Acceptors can be configured to store commands (i.e., determinants) on disk or in memory. In all experiments, the centralized event logger and the acceptors log values in main memory. We justify this choice by the fact that persistent memory technologies such as non-volatile RAM (NVRAM) and battery-backed memory are increasingly popular.

4.1 The Event Logger

To evaluate the performance of the event logger alone, we built a simple MPI application where a process only submits a new determinant to the logger after it receives a response acknowledging that the previously submitted determinant has been logged. Since application processes do not communicate among themselves in these experiments, determinants are fixed-content 50-byte messages.

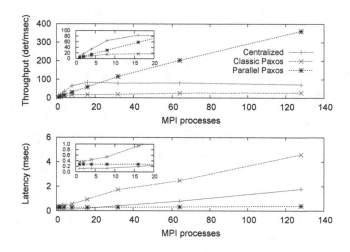

Fig. 2. Throughput and latency for the three event logger approaches.

Figure 2 shows the throughput in logged determinants per millisecond (det/msec) and latency (in msec) when we increased the number of MPI processes up to 128. The centralized event logger reaches the maximum throughput of about 83 det/msec with 16 processes. Classic Paxos reaches a maximum throughput of 28 det/msec with a latency of 4.6 msec with 128 MPI processes. Parallel Paxos never saturates in these experiments: throughput increases proportionally to the number of processes and the latency remains approximately constant, below 4 msec. With 128 processes, Parallel Paxos has 5 times the throughput of the centralized scheme and 13 times the throughput of Classic Paxos, with much lower latency.

4.2 AMG

AMG is a parallel algebraic multigrid solver for linear systems which can be classified as a nondeterministic application that employs "any-source" receptions and nondeterministic deliveries. All calls to Iprobe use the any_source tag and only one call to Recv, among many, uses the any_source tag. AMG also has calls to the Test and Testall primitives. Although during the execution there was a large number of Iprobe, Test and Testall invocations, a determinant for an

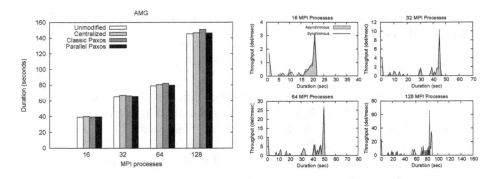

Fig. 3. AMG performance and throughput.

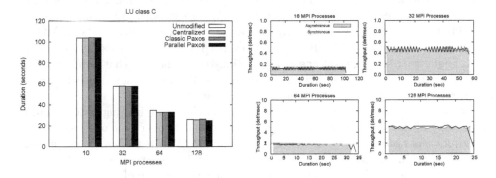

Fig. 4. LU class C performance and throughput.

`Iprobe` with the `any_source` tag is only created when the message is ready to be received. Similarly, for `Test` and `Testall` invocations, we count the number of invocations but only submit the determinant to the event logger when the MPI message related to `Test` or `Testall` is ready to be delivered.

Figure 3 (left) presents results for the AMG application, including the replicated event loggers. The "Unmodified" label refers to executions without any event logging. Although all strategies introduce an overhead, with 64 and 128 processes Classic Paxos increased the duration of the original application by approximately 3.8%, the worst-performing technique. The centralized scheme presented an overhead of approximately 2% for 16, 32 and 64 processes. Parallel Paxos presented the lowest overhead, below 1.3% for all configurations.

Figure 3 (right) shows the number of determinants logged per milliseconds considering both the synchronous and asynchronous Parallel Paxos modes, for 16, 32, 64 and 128 MPI processes. In the asynchronous mode, application processes never wait for the logger; thus, this case provides an upper bound for the performance of the event logger. As it can be seen, log requests are not uniformly distributed over time. For the case with 128 processes, between time instants 80 s and 90 s a peak can be distinguished, that reaches approximately 34 det/msec in the synchronous mode and 66 det/msec in the asynchronous mode. These results help understand how the overhead of Parallel Paxos is distributed over time.

4.3   LU and MG

LU and MG are kernels of the NAS parallel benchmarks. As pointed out in [2], only MG and LU among the NAS-PB kernels generate nondeterministic events. We assess classes C and D of the kernels in deployments with 16, 32, 64 and 128 MPI processes. LU contains both `Recv` and `Irecv` primitives. The last one is used with the `any_source` tag. MG receives all its messages through `MPI_Irecv` with the `any_source` tag.

The total number of events logged in LU is less than 1% of the total of all its receptions in class C. The MG kernel however has almost 100% of nondeterministic events among its receptions. Although both AMG e MG solve similar problems, the reason for much more nondeterministic events in MG is its implementation. Unlike MG, AMG does not receive all its messages through `MPI_Irecv` with the `any_source` tag. This illustrates the fact that nondeterminism is often a programmer's choice (e.g., to boost performance), rather than a requirement coming from the problem being solved.

From our experimental evaluation, we concluded that logging determinants using any of the three event logging strategies presents nearly no overhead when logging events of classes C and D of the LU kernel. This is somewhat surprising since logging introduces some overhead in the AMG application and both classes C and D of the LU benchmark contain a higher percentage of nondeterministic events than AMG contains. Figure 4 (left) shows the results for class C of the LU kernel. By inspecting the number of determinants logged during the execution in Fig. 4 (right), we notice that determinants are more uniformly distributed in LU class C than in AMG and they happen at a rate that is within the limits the event logger can sustain (see Sect. 4.1). The difference between class C and D of the LU is that the last one has longer duration and lower throughput. As a consequence, the event logger never becomes an execution bottleneck in LU.

On the contrary, the logging of determinants introduces a considerable overhead to MG classes C and D (Figs. 5 and 6, respectively). In class C, while Classic Paxos presents an overhead of more than 125% and 200% for 64 and 128 processes, the overhead of the centralized event logger is below 31% and 55% for 64 and 128 processes, respectively. Parallel Paxos sports even lower overheads: 17,71% and 24,26% for 64 and 128 processes, respectively. The results for MG class D show a similar trend, with Parallel Paxos outperforming both the two other techniques. The MG kernel is highly communication-bound and all its receive events use the `any_source` tag. As the number of application processes increases, the event logger reaches its limits with the centralized and the Classic Paxos strategies. Parallel Paxos is able to scale performance by distributing the load among the various series of Paxos.

Figures 5 and 6 also show the rate of logged determinants per milliseconds for the synchronous and asynchronous Parallel Paxos-based event logger. The throughput of the synchronous mode is close to the asynchronous mode for MG

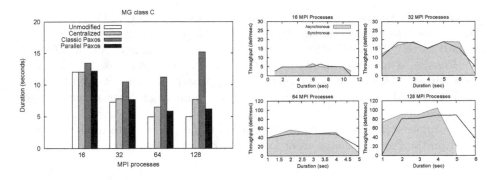

Fig. 5. MG class C performance and throughput.

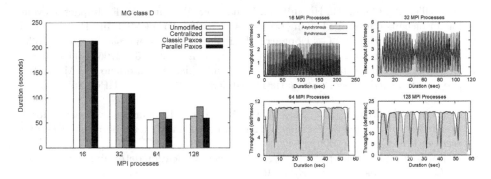

Fig. 6. MG class D performance and throughput.

class C with 16, 32 and 64 processes. For 128 processes, the asynchronous mode presents a throughput that is higher than that of the synchronous mode and finishes approximately 1 s earlier. MG class D has lower throughput than MG class C. The throughputs of both synchronous and asynchronous Parallel Paxos are very similar. In all configurations, both the synchronous and the asynchronous modes display a uniform rate over time.

5   Conclusion

In this work we presented a fault-tolerant and distributed event logger based on consensus for HPC applications. The event logger is the component responsible for reliably logging determinants and its performance can represent a significant impact on the efficiency of message logging protocols. We implemented two fault-tolerant event loggers based on the Paxos algorithm. By using Paxos, our event loggers guarantee safety even if the system is asynchronous and liveness despite processes failures. Our first protocol is based on classic state machine replication. In our second protocol, which we call Parallel Paxos, we assign a separate sequence of Paxos executions to each application process. We assessed experimentally the performance of a centralized event logger and our two event loggers based on consensus. Besides evaluating the event loggers by themselves, we used three MPI applications to evaluate their performance: AMG, MG and LU. Results of all experiments show that the event logger based on Parallel Paxos always outperformed the centralized approach in terms of both the execution time and the throughput in terms of the number of determinants logged per millisecond.

The implementation of a recovery protocol using the nondeterministic events stored on the Parallel Paxos event logger is left as future work.

References

1. Bouteiller, A., Collin, B., Herault, T., Lemarinier, P., Cappello, F.: Impact of event logger on causal message logging protocols for fault tolerant MPI. In: IPDPS (2005)
2. Bouteiller, A., Bosilca, G., Dongarra, J.: Redesigning the message logging model for high performance. Concurr. Comput.: Pract. Exp. **22**(16), 2196–2211 (2010)
3. Bouteiller, A., Hérault, T., Krawezik, G., Lemarinier, P., Cappello, F.: MPICH-V project: a multiprotocol automatic fault-tolerant MPI. Int. J. HPC Appl. **20**(3), 319–333 (2006)
4. Bouteiller, A., Ropars, T., Bosilca, G., Morin, C., Dongarra, J.: Reasons for a pessimistic or optimistic message logging protocol in MPI uncoordinated failure, recovery. In: Cluster (2009)
5. Cappello, F., Guermouche, A., Snir, M.: On communication determinism in parallel HPC applications. In: ICCCN (2010)
6. Egwutuoha, I.P., Levy, D., Selic, B., Chen, S.: A survey of fault tolerance mechanisms and checkpoint/restart implementations for HPC systems. J. Supercomput. **65**(3), 1302–1326 (2013)
7. Elnozahy, A., Wang, J.: A survey of rollback-recovery protocols in message-passing systems. CSURV Comput. Surv. **34**, 375–408 (2002)
8. Fischer, M.J., Lynch, N.A., Paterson, M.S.: Impossibility of distributed consensus with one faulty processor. J. ACM **32**(2), 374–382 (1985)
9. Johnson, D.B., Zwaenepoel, W.: Sender-based message logging. In: FTCS (1987)
10. Kshemkalyani, A.D., Singhal, M.: Distributed Computing: Principles, Algorithms, and Systems. Cambridge University Press, Cambridge (2011)
11. Lamport, L.: Paxos made simple. SIGACTN: SIGACT News (ACM Spec. Interest Group Automata Comput. Theory) **32**, 51–58 (2001)
12. Lamport, L.: The part-time parliament. ACM Trans. Comput. Syst. **16**(2), 133–169 (1998)
13. Lamport, L.: Lower bounds for asynchronous consensus. Distrib. Comput. **19**(2), 104–125 (2006)
14. Lemarinier, P., Bouteiller, A., Krawezik, G., Cappello, F.: Coordinated checkpoint versus message log for fault tolerant MPI. Int. J. High Perform. Comput. Netw. **2**, 146–155 (2006)
15. MPI Forum: document for a standard message-passing interface 3.1. Technical report, University of Tennessee (2015). http://www.mpi-forum.org/docs/mpi-3.1
16. Riesen, R., Ferreira, K., Silva, D.D., Lemarinier, P., Arnold, D., Bridges, P.G.: Alleviating scalability issues of checkpointing protocols. In: SC (2012)

17. Ropars, T., Morin, C.: Active optimistic message logging for reliable execution of MPI applications. In: Sips, H., Epema, D., Lin, H.-X. (eds.) Euro-Par 2009. LNCS, vol. 5704, pp. 615–626. Springer, Heidelberg (2009). doi:10.1007/978-3-642-03869-3_58

18. Ropars, T., Morin, C.: Improving message logging protocols scalability through distributed event logging. In: D'Ambra, P., Guarracino, M., Talia, D. (eds.) Euro-Par 2010. LNCS, vol. 6271, pp. 511–522. Springer, Heidelberg (2010). doi:10.1007/978-3-642-15277-1_49

19. Schneider, F.B.: Implementing fault-tolerant services using the state machine approach: a tutorial. ACM Comput. Surv. **22**(3), 299 (1990)

Families of Graph Algorithms: SSSP Case Study

Thejaka Amila Kanewala[1,2(✉)], Marcin Zalewski[2], and Andrew Lumsdaine[2,3]

[1] School of Informatics and Computing, Indiana University, Bloomington, IN, USA
thejkane@indiana.edu
[2] Pacific Northwest National Laboratory, Seattle, WA, USA
{marcin.zalewski,andrew.lumsdaine}@pnnl.gov
[3] University of Washington, Seattle, WA, USA

Abstract. Single-Source Shortest Paths (SSSP) is a well-studied graph problem. Examples of SSSP algorithms include the original Dijkstra's algorithm and the parallel Δ-stepping and KLA-SSSP algorithms. In this paper, we use a novel Abstract Graph Machine (AGM) model to show that all these algorithms share a common logic and differ from one another by the order in which they perform work. We use the AGM model to thoroughly analyze the family of algorithms that arises from the common logic. We start with the basic algorithm without any ordering (Chaotic), and then we derive the existing and new algorithms by methodically exploring semantic and spatial ordering of work. Our experimental results show that new derived algorithms show better performance than the existing distributed memory parallel algorithms, especially at higher scales.

Keywords: Single-source shortest paths (SSSP) · Distributed-memory graph algorithms

1 Introduction

Given a graph problem, how many ways can it be solved in? In this paper, we consider the seemingly simple problem of *single-source shortest paths* (SSSP), where the task is to find the shortest path from a source vertex s to every other vertex in the graph. A number of sequential algorithms exist. The well-known Dijkstra's algorithm [3] is "work optimal", where vertices are ordered in a priority queue based on their distance from the source s, and every edge is traversed only once. Work optimality, however, comes at a cost of limited parallelism and extensive synchronization. Subsequent development concentrated on relaxing the strict ordering of the Dijkstra algorithm to make more work available in parallel at the cost of some "wasted work" that has to be invalidated and repeated. For example, the Δ-stepping [9] algorithm groups vertices into Δ-sized *buckets*, based on their distances from the source s, giving an approximation of Dijkstra ordering. Vertices in a bucket are processed in parallel, and picking an appropriate Δ ensures the right balance between parallelism and wasted work.

© Springer International Publishing AG 2017
F.F. Rivera et al. (Eds.): Euro-Par 2017, LNCS 10417, pp. 428–441, 2017.
DOI: 10.1007/978-3-319-64203-1_31

The *KLA-SSSP* [6] algorithm is similar, but it uses topological distances instead of shortest path distances from the source s to order work into buckets[1].

Table 1. Orderings in SSSP algorithms.

Algorithm	Ordering
Dijkstra's	Global priority queue
Δ-stepping	Global distance equivalence classes defined by Δ
KLA	Global topological distance equivalence classes defined by k
Chaotic	None

Algorithm 1. The SSSP relax function

1: **Input:** Task (v, d), distances D
2: **if** $d < D(v)$ **then**
3:    $D(v) \leftarrow d$
4:    $\forall v_n \in$ neighbors(G, v) :
5:       Task$(v_n, d_v + $ weight$(v, v_n))$

In both Δ-stepping and KLA-SSSP, processing of the buckets inserts implicit synchronization points, since processing of a bucket cannot begin until all previous buckets are finished. The *Chaotic SSSP* does away with synchronization altogether by processing all the vertices in parallel in an arbitrary order, resulting in maximum available parallelism at the cost of more wasted work.

Despite the variety of algorithms, analysis reveals that they are all based on the same core logic of *relaxation*, as shown in Algorithm 1. Relaxation takes as the input a vertex-distance pair and a distance map (D), and produces more vertex-distance pairs if the distance was improved. These newly produced pairs are further relaxed, and the algorithms differ by how these relaxations are ordered (Table 1). In this paper, we methodically investigate this similarity between the seemingly different SSSP algorithms. To do that, we model the algorithms using the *Abstract Graph Machine* (AGM) [7]. An AGM represents a graph algorithm as two distinct components: the *processing function* that models the core functionality of the algorithm and an ordering of the work tasks that define the characteristics of the algorithm (as in Table 1, for example). The work ordering relation of an AGM is defined based on one or more attributes of work tasks. For the SSSP algorithms, it can be the distance in vertex-distance pair, or it can be an additional attribute introduced specifically for a given algorithm (see the next section for details). The work ordering relation is a *strict weak ordering*. It divides work into ordered *equivalence classes*, where work within an equivalence class is unordered and can be executed in parallel, but work within separate equivalence classes is executed according to an ordering induced by the strict weak ordering relation.

We present AGM models for all the algorithms listed in Table 1, and we show that they change by the way in which they order work. Then we show that new algorithms can be developed by methodically discovering new orderings. We introduce *extended AGM* (EAGM) that incorporates information about spatial distribution into algorithms modeled in AGM. With EAGM, we develop

---

[1] KLA-SSSP with single-hop buckets is equivalent to the Bellman-Ford algorithm [1].

variations of algorithms presented in Table 1 with additional ordering at different spatial levels of architecture such as node (process), numa (non-uniform memory access) region, and thread, resulting in *nine* different SSSP algorithms. We compare the weak scaling performance of the new algorithms with existing distributed memory parallel algorithms and also with the SSSP algorithm in PowerGraph [5] and in Parallel Boost Graph Library (PBGL) [4] for a performance base line. Our results show that some of the new variations of SSSP algorithms perform better than the well-known algorithms, especially at large scales.

In summary, our main contributions are generalizing SSSP algorithms using the AGM formulation, an approach to generate variations of primary distributed SSSP algorithms listed in Table 1 using EAGM, and experimental evaluation showing that algorithm variations generated by EAGM specification perform better compared to the well-known algorithms listed in Table 1.

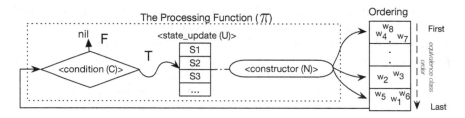

Fig. 1. An overview of the Abstract Graph Machine execution.

2   Abstract Graph Machine (AGM)

The *Abstract Graph Machine* (AGM) approach captures the core logic of an algorithm and the semantic work ordering that impacts the performance of the algorithm. Such principled approach allows discovery of families of algorithms by varying work ordering where it affects the performance but not semantics of an algorithm. In this section, we introduce AGM framework, and in Sect. 3 we apply it to the SSSP algorithms.

At the heart of AGM is the *processing function* that captures the logic of an algorithm. A processing function takes a single *workitem*, the smallest unit of work performed in the algorithm, and it generates zero or more new *workitems* from the input *workitem*. The processing function can access the graph and per-vertex and per-edge state when computing new *workitems*. The set of all the *workitems* generated by an algorithm is denoted using *WorkItem*. In other words, the *WorkItem* represent all the *workitems* generate during the whole lifetime of the algorithm's execution. The order of execution of *workitems* generated by processing functions is dictated by a strict weak ordering relation defined on the *WorkItem*. Figure 1, shows an overview of the AGM. An AGM consists of a definition of a *Graph*, a definition of a *WorkItem* set, a set of *states*, a *processing function*, a *strict weak ordering* relation, and of an *initial workitem set*.

Graph Definition. The graph definition takes the form, $G = (V, E, vmaps, emaps)$, where V is the set of vertices and $E \subseteq V \times V$ is the set of edges. *vmaps* is a set of functions each of the form $f : V \longrightarrow X$, and *emaps* is another set of functions each of the form $f : E \longrightarrow X$. For example, a weighted graph is represented as $G = (V, E, \{\}, \{weight : E \longrightarrow \mathbb{R}\})$.

The Set, *WorkItem*. A *workitem*($\in WorkItem$) is a *tuple*. The first element of the tuple is a vertex, and the remainder are the state and the ordering attribute values. For example, the Chaotic SSSP algorithm stores a vertex and a distance in a *workitem*. The size of the tuple is determined by the states and the ordering attributes used in the AGM formulation of a given algorithm. The *workitem* tuple elements are accessed using the *bracket operator*; e.g., if $w \in WorkItem$ and $w = \langle v, p_0, p_1 \ldots, p_n \rangle$, then $w[0] = v$, $w[1] = p_0$, $w[2] = p_1$, and so on. The *workitem* data (i.e., the tuple elements) are used by the processing function to generate new work items and update state.

States. An AGM maintains state values as *mappings*. The domain of the state mappings is the set V. The co-domain depends on the possible values that can be held in states. For example, in Dijksta's SSSP algorithm the state mapping is *distance* : $V \longrightarrow \mathbb{R}$. In AGM terminology, accessing a state value associated with a vertex (or edge) "v" is denoted as "mapping[v]" (e.g., distance[v]).

Processing Function. A processing function $\pi : WorkItem \longrightarrow \mathbb{P}(WorkItem)^2$ takes a *workitem* as an argument and produces zero or more *workitems*. The body of the processing function consists of a set of *statements (Sts)*. A statement contains a *condition* $C : WorkItem \longrightarrow Bool$ based on input *workitem*, an *update to states* $U : WorkItem \longrightarrow Bool$, and a *constructor* $N : WorkItem \longrightarrow \mathbb{P}(WorkItem)$ describing how new *output workitems* should be constructed. The condition C is evaluated first. If it evaluates to *True*, state update U is evaluated. If both are *True*, the constructor N is invoked. The C indicates whether a St is applicable to a *workitem*, and the U evaluates to *True* if states are changed when processing the input *workitem*. The N of a statement is evaluated only if its C and U both evaluate to *True*. States are not explicit parameters to the processing function, and changes to state are treated as *side effects*. An implementation of an AGM must ensure that state updates happen atomically. To define a processing function statement, the condition (C), state update (U), and the *workitem* constructor (N) must be provided.

We use notation loosely based on set-comprehension notation to represent processing functions. The format of a processing function $\pi : WorkItem \longrightarrow \mathbb{P}(WorkItem)$ takes the form $\pi(w) = \{\{w_n | \langle N(w) \rangle, \langle U(w) \rangle, \langle C(w) \rangle\}, \ldots\}$. In this notation, w_n is the new *workitem* generated by N from the input *workitem* w. U and C represent the state update and the condition. This notation describes one statement. For processing functions where there are more than one statements, the notation can be duplicated for each statement and separate each

---

[2] We denote a powerset of a set A as $\mathbb{P}(A)$.

statement using a comma. Note that we use angle brackets ($\langle \ldots \rangle$) to deliminate parts of processing function. This is not a standard notation in set comprehension, but it makes parts of the processing function clear. Furthermore, we will provide the U part of AGM as a side effect, but we will treat it as a boolean (*True* when the side effect occurs, *False* if it does not).

Strict Weak Ordering Relation. The *workitems* generated by a processing function are ordered according to a strict weak ordering relation (represented using $<_{wis}$) defined on *WorkItem*, which induces equivalence classes on *workitems*. The *workitems* in an equivalence class are not comparable to each other, but any two *workitems* in different equivalence classes are. In the AGM, the *workitems* belonging to the same equivalence class can be processed by the processing function in parallel, but *workitems* belong to different equivalence classes are ordered according to the ordering on equivalence classes.

Initial Work Item Set. The initial *workitem* set contains *workitems* that represent the input to the algorithm. For example, for SSSP, the initial set of *workitems* will contain the *workitem* corresponding to the source vertex s.

The AGM. Having defined all supporting concepts we now give the definition of an AGM in Definition 1.

Definition 1. *An* Abstract Graph Machine *(AGM) is a 6-tuple (G, WorkItem, Q, π, $<_{wis}$, S), where*

1. $G = (V, E, vmaps, emaps)$ *is the input graph,*
2. $WorkItemSet \subseteq (V \times P_0 \times P_1 \cdots \times P_n)$ *where each P_i represents a state value or an ordering attribute,*
3. Q - *Set of states represented as mappings,*
4. $\pi : WorkItem \longrightarrow \mathbb{P}(WorkItem)$ *is the processing function,*
5. $<_{wis} : WorkItem \times WorkItem$ - *Strict weak ordering relation on workitems,*
6. $S \subseteq WorkItem$ - *Initial workitem set.*

3   SSSP Algorithms in AGM

In this section, we present AGM models for algorithms discussed in Table 1. To specify these models, we need to provide AGM elements from Definition 1. First, we provide the input graph, the *WorkItem*, the set of states, the processing function, and the initial *workitem* set. Then, we show that adding different orderings to the AGM models, we get existing distributed SSSP algorithms.

The input graph for the SSSP problem is a weighted graph: $G = (V, E, vmaps = \{\}, emaps = \{weight\})$. The basic *workitem* includes a vertex and its distance and *WorkItem* for SSSP is defined as $WorkItem^{sssp} \subseteq (V \times Distance)$. The basic *workitem* is extended by additional ordering attributes when necessary (e.g., in KLA-SSSP). The set of states includes a single mapping *distance* for storing the distance from the source vertex. The *distance* mapping is defined as $distance : V \longrightarrow \mathbb{R}_+^*$. The processing function for SSSP changes the distance state if the input *workitem*'s distance for a given vertex is less than what is already stored for that vertex in the distance map. The list of adjacent vertices of a given vertex are accessed through the *neighbors* $: V \longrightarrow \mathbb{P}(V)$ function. The basic (it will be extended with additonal functionality for some algorithms) processing function for the SSSP graph problem is defined in Definition 2.

Definition 2. $\pi^{sssp} : WorkItem^{sssp} \rightarrow \mathbb{P}(WorkItem^{sssp})$

$$\pi^{SSSP}(w) = \begin{cases} \{w_n | \langle w_n[0] \in neighbors(w[0]) \\ \quad \text{and } w_n[1] = w[1] + weight(w[0], w_n[0]) \rangle, \\ \langle distance(w[0]) \longleftarrow w[1] \rangle, \\ \langle if \ w[1] < distance(w[0]) \rangle \} \end{cases}$$

The SSSP processing function (π^{sssp}) has a single statement. The statement is executed only if the input *workitem*, *ws*' distance is less than the value stored in the *distance* map for the vertex in the *workitem* ($w[0]$, the first element of the *workitem* tuple). Constructor of the statement specifies how to construct the new *workitem* w_n. The processing function defines the core logic that needs to be achieved by any SSSP algorithm. Some of the algorithms discussed in Table 1 extend this definition because of the way they order *workitems*.

Chaotic SSSP. The Chaotic SSSP algorithm does not order *workitems*. Therefore, the strict weak ordering relation is defined in such a way that no two *workitems* are related (defined in Definition 3).

Definition 3. $<_{ch} : WorkItem^{sssp} \times WorkItem^{sssp}$ *is a binary relation where* $\forall w_1, w_2 \in WorkItem^{sssp} : w_1 \not<_{ch} w_2$.

This relation induces only one equivalence class, and all the *workitems* in this class can be executed in parallel. The AGM model for Chaotic SSSP algorithm is given in Proposition 1. The presented AGM uses the strict weak ordering defined in Definition 3.

Proposition 1. *Chaotic Algorithm is an instance of an AGM where*

1. $G = (V, E, vmaps = \{\}, emaps = \{weight\})$ *is the input graph,*
2. $WorkItem = WorkItem^{sssp}$,
3. $Q = \{distance\}$ *is the state (initially* $\forall v \in V, distance(v) = \infty$*)*,
4. $\pi = \pi^{sssp}$,
5. *Strict weak ordering relation* $<_{wis} = <_{ch}$,
6. $S = \{<v_s, 0>\}$ *where* $v_s \in V$ *and* v_s *is the source vertex.*

Dijkstra's SSSP. The Dijkstra's SSSP algorithm globally orders *workitems* by their associated distances (Definition 4).

Definition 4. $<_{dj}$: $WorkItem^{sssp} \times WorkItem^{sssp}$ is a relation where $\forall w_1$, $w_2 \in WorkItem^{sssp}$: $w_1<_{dj}w_2$ iff $w_1[1]<w_2[1]$.

The AGM formulation for Dijkstra's SSSP is same as the AGM formulation in Proposition 1 except for the strict weak ordering. In $<_{dj}$, two *workitems* belong to the same equivalence class if they have the same distance. In general, the equivalence classes generated by $<_{dj}$ are small, hence the parallelism available in Dijkstra's SSSP algorithm is limited.

Δ-Stepping Algorithm. Δ-Stepping [9] SSSP algorithm arranges vertex-distance pairs into distance *buckets*) of size $\Delta \in \mathbb{N}$ and executes buckets in order. Within a bucket, vertex-distance pairs can be executed in any order. Processing a bucket may produce extra work for the same bucket or for successive buckets. The strict weak ordering relation for Δ-stepping algorithm is given in Definition 5. As for Dijkstra's algorithm, Δ-stepping AGM is as in Proposition 1 with ordering replaced by $<_{\Delta}$.

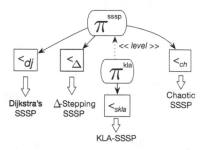

Fig. 2. Summary of AGMs for SSSP algorithms.

Definition 5. $<_{\Delta}$: $WorkItem^{sssp} \times WorkItem^{sssp}$ is a relation where $\forall w_1, w_2 \in WorkItem^{sssp}$: $w_1<_{\Delta}w_2$ iff $\lfloor w_1[1]/\Delta \rfloor<\lfloor w_2[1]/\Delta \rfloor$.

KLA-SSSP Algorithm. The *K-Level Asynchronous* (KLA) paradigm [6] processes vertices up to k topological levels asynchronously (k can be varied). Correspondingly, the KLA-SSSP AGM orders *workitems* by their *level*. To do this, *workitems* include an additional *ordering attribute*. The KLA-SSSP *WorkItem* is defined as $WorkItem^{kla} \subseteq V \times Distance \times Level$ where $Level \subseteq \mathbb{N}$. The processing function also is extended to populate the level attribute (Definition 6).

Definition 6. π^{kla} : $WorkItem^{kla} \longrightarrow \mathbb{P}(WorkItem^{kla})$

$$\pi^{kla}(w) = \begin{cases} \{w_n | \langle w_n[0] \in neighbors(w[0]) \\ \quad \text{and } w_n[1] = w[1] + weight(w[0], w_k[0]) \\ \quad \text{and } w_n[2] = w[2] + 1 \rangle, \\ \langle distance(w[0]) \longleftarrow w[1] \rangle, \\ \langle if \ w[1]<distance(w[0]) \rangle \} \end{cases}$$

The *workitems* within consecutive k levels can be executed in parallel. The strict weak ordering relation for KLA-SSSP is given in Definition 7. The AGM for KLA-SSSP algorithm is as AGM in Proposition 1 except for the processing function, which is replaced with π^{kla}, and for the strict weak ordering, which is replaced with $<_{skla}$ defined in Definition 7.

Definition 7. $<_{skla}$: $WorkItem^{kla} \times WorkItem^{kla}$ is a relation where $\forall w_1, w_2 \in WorkItem^{kla}$: $w_1<_{skla}w_2$ iff $\lfloor w_1[2]/K \rfloor<\lfloor w_2[2]/K \rfloor$.

Family of SSSP Algorithms. The SSSP AGMs are summarized in Fig. 2. Dijkstra's, Δ-stepping, and Chaotic algorithms share the same processing function but with different orderings. Both Dijkstra's algorithm and Δ-stepping algorithm use distance to define their strict weak orderings. KLA-SSSP uses levels to order *workitems*. The only difference between π^{sssp} and π^{kla} is that π^{kla} has logic to update level attribute in newly generated *workitems*. In Fig. 2, we represent this with a dashed arrow to indicate that π^{kla} is an *extended* version of π^{sssp}. Because all the algorithms use the same processing function (with ordering extension for KLA-SSSP), they form an *algorithm family*.

4   Extended Abstract Graph Machine

AGMs are abstract and independent of implementation details. However, distributed graph algorithms are strongly impacted by properties of the distributed architecture they run on. To capture that impact, we introduce *extended* AGM (EAGM) that represents *spacial distribution* on a distributed memory platform. Currently, we recognize 4 hierarchical levels of distribution that roughly match modern distributed systems (arrows indicate inclusion):

Table 2. Thread ordered, numa ordered and process ordered EAGMs for Δ-stepping, KLA and Chaotic AGMs.

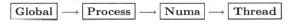

	buffer	threadq	numaq	nodeq
Δ-stepping	$<_\Delta$	$<_\Delta$	$<_\Delta$	$<_\Delta$
	$<_{ch}$	$<_{ch}$	$<_{ch}$	$<_{dj}$
	$<_{ch}$	$<_{ch}$	$<_{dj}$	$<_{ch}$
	$<_{ch}$	$<_{dj}$	$<_{ch}$	$<_{ch}$
KLA-SSSP	$<_{kla}$	$<_{kla}$	$<_{kla}$	$<_{kla}$
	$<_{ch}$	$<_{ch}$	$<_{ch}$	$<_{dj}$
	$<_{ch}$	$<_{ch}$	$<_{dj}$	$<_{ch}$
	$<_{ch}$	$<_{dj}$	$<_{ch}$	$<_{ch}$
Chaotic	$<_{ch}$	$<_{ch}$	$<_{ch}$	$<_{ch}$
	$<_{ch}$	$<_{ch}$	$<_{ch}$	$<_{dj}$
	$<_{ch}$	$<_{ch}$	$<_{dj}$	$<_{ch}$
	$<_{ch}$	$<_{dj}$	$<_{ch}$	$<_{ch}$

Given the spatial hierarchy, we use EAGMs to specify *spatial orderings* for AGM graph algorithms. Spatial orderings apply non-semantic ordering on *workitems* throughout the spatial hierarchy of a distributed machine. The ordering at the **Global** level is the same as in the underlying AGM, keeping the semantics of an AGM intact. Since the global ordering maintains the equivalence classes of AGM, *workitems* can be further ordered at the lower levels of the hierarchy. For example, two different EAGM spatial orderings for Δ-stepping are $<_\Delta \rightarrow <_{ch} \rightarrow <_{ch} \rightarrow <_{ch}$ and $<_\Delta \rightarrow <_{ch} \rightarrow <_{ch} \rightarrow <_{dj}$ where each ordering corresponds to the EAGM level (the orderings are as defined in the previous section). The first spatial ordering enforces $<_\Delta$ at the global level, but leaves execution in buckets unordered ($<_{ch}$). The second spatial ordering applies Dijkstra's ordering at the **Thread** level ($<_{dj}$), which means that *workitems* at every thread are ordered in a priority queue as they reach the thread in the spatial distribution. In summary, an EAGM consists of an AGM and a spatial architecture hierarchy annotated by spatial orderings.

In Table 2, we apply Dijkstra's strict weak ordering relation (Definition 4) to spatial hierarchy levels of Process (`nodeq`), Numa (`numaq`), and of Thread (`threadq`) to derive EAGMs for algorithms in Table 1. The *buffer* represents the original algorithm without spatial level orderings. The table shows orderings for each combination of ordering and AGM, where the ordering chain corresponds to the archtectural hierarchy given at the beginning of this section. Each EAGM generates a variation of the main algorithm defined by its corresponding AGM. By methodical application of spatial ordering, we derive a family of SSSP algorithms. In the next section, we evaluate the performance of different EAGMs.

5   Experiments and Results

In this section, we implement and compare the weak scaling performance of each derived EAGM in Table 2. In addition, we also compare the performance of the EAGMs to the performance of SSSP algorithms available in two well-known graph processing frameworks PowerGraph [5] and PBGL [4].

Weak scaling performance is measured on two types of synthetic *R-MAT* [2] graphs: RMAT1 graphs with R-MAT parameters $A = 0.57, B = C = 0.19, D = 0.05$ and with edge weights ranging 0–100, and RMAT2 graphs with R-MAT parameters $A = 0.5, B = C = 0.1, D = 0.3$ and with edge weights 0–255. All experiments were carried out on Cray XE6/XK7 nodes, each with 2 AMD Opteron Abu Dhabi CPUs (for total of 32 cores), and 64 GB of memory per node (4 numa domains, 2 per CPU).

The algorithms are implemented in AM++ [14], a light-weight active messaging framework. Graph vertices are equally distributed among distributed processes and in-node graph structure is stored in *compressed sparse row* format. Disjktra's orderings is implemented using concurrent priority queues at the process and the numa levels, and using standard priority queue at the thread level.

5.1   Scaling Results

The weak scaling results are presented in Figs. 3, 4 and 5. Experiment results for basic AGMs are represented using the `buffer` designator. As in Table 2, EAGMs with thread-level, node-level and numa-level Dijkstra orderings are represented using `threadq`, `nodeq` and, `numaq` designators. We tested the performance of Δ-stepping EAGMs for three delta values ($\Delta = 3, 5, 7$) and KLA-SSSP EAGMs with three k values ($k = 1, 2, 3$). In the following, we discuss results in detail.

Δ-**Stepping Variations.** The basic Δ-stepping (`buffer`) algorithm performs the best in-node (up to 32 cores). Since no communication is involved, the additional ordering provided by the other implementations does not provide a sufficient benefit for its overhead. In general, the `threadq` variation is the fastest in the distributed setting for both RMAT1 and RMAT2 graph inputs. The `nodeq` and the `numaq` variations perform better with increasing deltas, but they are not competitive with the `buffer` implementation.

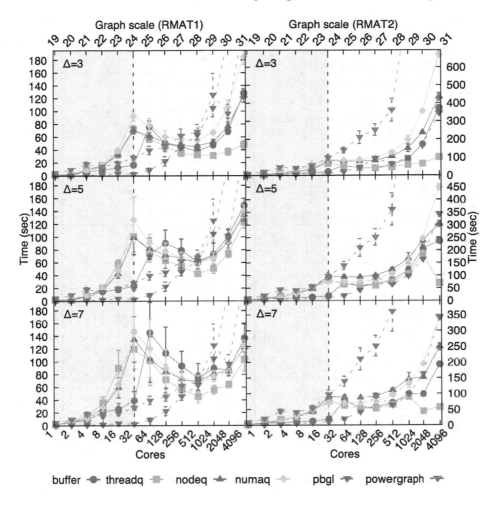

Fig. 3. Timing results of Δ-stepping. Shaded region indicates single node runs.

For RMAT1 graph inputs, PoweGraph shows better distributed performance for small scale graphs. However, for larger graph inputs, PowerGraph does not scale well. All the Δ-stepping EAGMs outperform PowerGraph at higher scales, especially for RMAT2. The `threadq` EAGM shows better performance than PBGL on RMAT2 graphs, and for RMAT1 graphs, all EAGMs outperform PBGL.

In summary, while in-node performance is dominated by the basic Δ-stepping algorithm (excluding PowerGraph and PBGL results), the distributed execution shows significant improvement with the `threadq` EAGM. Although the `numaq` and `nodeq` variations provide more ordering than the `threadq` variation, the overhead of the concurrent ordering reduces the performance of `numaq` and `nodeq`.

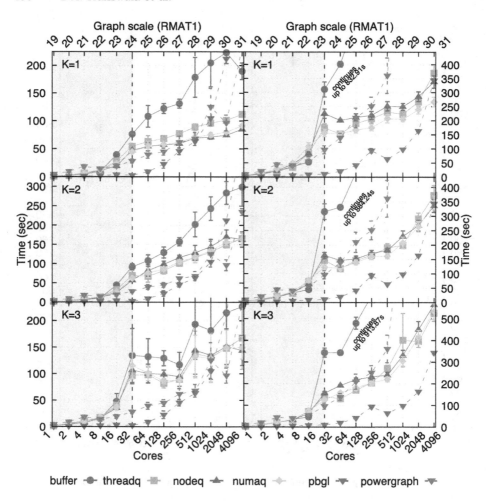

Fig. 4. Timing results of KLA. Shaded region indicates single node runs.

KLA Variations. KLA variations show different performance characteristics than Δ-stepping. For KLA, the `nodeq` and the `numaq` variations perform the best at scale, with $K = 1$. At greater K values, the performance of `threadq` is comparable to `nodeq` and `numaq`, but, in absolute terms, the performance at higher K values is worse than at $K = 1$. The `numaq` and `nodeq` provide the best potential ordering by ordering the most items. The overheads are kept at bay because at $K = 1$ all the writes to the next level's queue occur before all the reads. For higher K values, writes and reads get more mixed, and the advantage of `numaq` and `nodeq` becomes less pronounced. In KLA, for both RMAT1 and RMAT2 inputs, all EAGM variations (`threadq`, `nodeq` and `numaq`) perform better compared to the basic `buffer` variation.

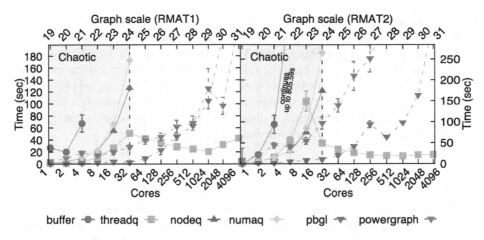

Fig. 5. Timing results of the Chaotic EAGM. Shaded region indicates single node runs.

For RMAT1 graph inputs, PowerGraph outperforms almost all the KLA EAGMs. However, PowerGraph execution time tends to increase with the scale, but KLA-SSSP EAGM variations tend to scale well with the increasing scale. For RMAT2 graph inputs, all the KLA SSSP EAGM variations, except for `buffer`, outperform PowerGraph in distributed execution. However, for RMAT2, PBGL outperforms almost all EAGMs, and `numaq` and `nodeq` tend to perform better at higher scales with $K = 1$. All the EAGMs show better performance than PBGL for RMAT1 graphs.

Chaotic Variations. For chaotic EAGMs, the thread-level ordering shows good performance, specially in distributed execution. For RMAT2, `threadq` weak scales almost perfectly in distributed execution. In addition, the `threadq` variation outperforms GraphLab and PBGL for both RMAT1 and RMAT2 graphs in distributed execution. Furthermore, the `threadq` Chaotic EAGM is faster than all other EAGMs in terms of absolute performance, demonstrating how the structured (E)AGM approach may result in new, highly performant algorithms.

6   Related Work

Abstract Models–For shared memory systems ordering in graph algorithms is studied as schedulers. Nguyen and Pingali synthesized concurrent schedulers in [11]. Pingali et al. ([12] and [13]) discussed a data-centric formulation, that treats graphs as abstract data types, called *operator formulation*. Ordering is achieved using an operator called "ordered set iterator". The AGM formulations' processing function works at the *workitem* level while operator formulation is applied on the graph. In addition, their ordering formulation is different from the AGM ordering formulation.

Spatial Ordering–Though, parallel processing in SSSP is well studied, spatial level orderings for SSSP problem are not common. Pingali et al.has done research on shared memory systems with Galois [10] scheduler, OBIM [8] that include spatial characteristics of the machine. In summary, shared memory models may not extend to distributed memory immediately due to cost factors that are significant in distributed memory than in shared memory (e.g., low compute/communication ratios, overhead of barriers, overhead of subgraph computations etc.,). The AGM model is designed to minimize such overheads.

7   Conclusions

Using the AGM abstraction, we showed that existing distributed graph algorithms; Dijkstra's SSSP, Δ-stepping SSSP and KLA-SSSP has the same processing logic but with different orderings. These orderings generate different equivalence class either based on distance or based on the level. We also showed, proposed EAGM model generates more fine-grained orderings at less synchronized spatial levels. Results of our experiments showed that some of the generated algorithms perform better compared to standard distributed memory, parallel SSSP algorithms under different graph inputs.

Acknowledgments. This research is based upon work supported by the National Science Foundation under grant 1319520. Access to computational resources was supported in part by Lilly Endowment, Inc., through its support for the Indiana University Pervasive Technology Institute, and in part by the Indiana METACyt Initiative. The Indiana METACyt Initiative at IU was also supported in part by Lilly Endowment, Inc. Significant part of this work was performed while the authors were affiliated with Indiana University.

References

1. Bellman, R.: On a routing problem. Technical report, DTIC Document (1956)
2. Chakrabarti, D., Zhan, Y., Faloutsos, C.: R-MAT: a recursive model for graph mining. In: SDM, vol. 4, pp. 442–446. SIAM (2004)
3. Dijkstra, E.W.: A note on two problems in connexion with graphs. Numer. Math. 1(1), 269–271 (1959)
4. Edmonds, N., Breuer, A., Gregor, D., Lumsdaine, A.: Single-source shortest paths with the parallel boost graph library. In: The Ninth DIMACS Implementation Challenge: The Shortest Path Problem, Piscataway, NJ, pp. 219–248 (2006)
5. Gonzalez, J.E., Low, Y., Gu, H., Bickson, D., Guestrin, C.: PowerGraph: distributed graph-parallel computation on natural graphs. In: OSDI, vol. 12, p. 2 (2012)
6. Harshvardhan, Fidel, A., Amato, N.M., Rauchwerger, L.: KLA: a new algorithmic paradigm for parallel graph computations. In: Proceedings of 23rd International Conference on Parallel Architectures and Compilation, pp. 27–38. ACM (2014)
7. Kanewala, T.A., Zalewski, M., Lumsdaine, A.: Abstract graph machine. arXiv preprint arXiv:1604.04772 (2016)

8. Lenharth, A., Nguyen, D., Pingali, K.: Priority queues are not good concurrent priority schedulers. The University of Texas at Austin, Department of Computer Sciences. Technical report TR-11-39 (2011)
9. Meyer, U., Sanders, P.: δ-stepping: a parallelizable shortest path algorithm. J. Algorithms **49**(1), 114–152 (2003)
10. Nguyen, D., Lenharth, A., Pingali, K.: A lightweight infrastructure for graph analytics. In: Proceedings of 24th ACM Symposium on Operating Systems Principles, pp. 456–471. ACM (2013)
11. Nguyen, D., Pingali, K.: Synthesizing concurrent schedulers for irregular algorithms. In: ACM SIGPLAN Notices, vol. 46, pp. 333–344. ACM (2011)
12. Pingali, K., Nguyen, D., Kulkarni, M., Burtscher, M., Hassaan, M.A., Kaleem, R., Lee, T.H., Lenharth, A., Manevich, R., Méndez-Lojo, M., et al.: The tao of parallelism in algorithms. ACM SIGPLAN Not. **46**(6), 12–25 (2011)
13. Prountzos, D., Manevich, R., Pingali, K.: Elixir: a system for synthesizing concurrent graph programs. ACM SIGPLAN Not. **47**(10), 375–394 (2012)
14. Willcock, J.J., Hoefler, T., Edmonds, N.G., Lumsdaine, A.: AM++: a generalized active message framework. In: Proceedings of 19th Internatational Conference on Parallel Architectures and Compilation Techniques, pp. 401–410. ACM (2010)

SEMem: Deployment of MPI-Based In-Memory Storage for Hadoop on Supercomputers

Thanh-Chung Dao$^{(\boxtimes)}$ and Shigeru Chiba

Graduate School of Information Science and Technology,
The University of Tokyo, Tokyo, Japan
chung@csg.ci.i.u-tokyo.ac.jp, chiba@acm.org

Abstract. This paper reports our experiments to compare various deployment strategies of memcached-like in-memory storage for Hadoop on supercomputers, where each node often does not have a local disk but shares a slow central disk. For the experiments, we developed our own memcached-like file system, named *SEMem*, for Hadoop. Since SEMem was designed for supercomputers, it uses MPI for communication. SEMem is configurable to adopt various deployment strategies and our experiments revealed that a good deployment strategy was allocating some nodes that work only for in-memory storage but do not directly perform map-reduce computation.

1 Introduction

This research is motivated by the challenges of running data-intensive frameworks, such as Hadoop [15], Spark [16], and Flink [5] on supercomputers to meet their design. A supercomputer is a big machine consisting of thousands of high-performance nodes that are connected to each other through high-speed network. Not only running efficiently compute-intensive but also data-intensive workloads, for example, clustering and classification in machine learning and graph processing, are challenges on supercomputers.

In today's top supercomputers, each compute node does not have a local disk or is equipped only with a small size solid state drive (SSD) due to its relative costs and high failure rate. It makes writing and reading intermediate data during job execution (Hadoop/Spark) become a bottleneck since those data must be stored on the distributed central disk whose access time is considered slower five orders of magnitude than one of main memory [9]. To solve that problem, a natural approach is using in-memory intermediate data storage in order to avoid spilling to disk. We call that approach as *memcached-like* style [7] since in-memory storage could be at either a local or remote node.

How to deploy memcached-like file systems on supercomputers is not an easily answerable question and combination of memcached-like in-memory storage and Hadoop is not studied well as far as we know. A feature of supercomputers is that the number of compute nodes is often huge and supercomputer users submit a job to a job queue in order to request a number of nodes they need. When

© Springer International Publishing AG 2017
F.F. Rivera et al. (Eds.): Euro-Par 2017, LNCS 10417, pp. 442–454, 2017.
DOI: 10.1007/978-3-319-64203-1_32

compute nodes are given to users, should we deploy in-memory storage on every node? should we allocate dedicated nodes from the given nodes for in-memory usage only? or should we allow using memory of remote nodes?

In this paper, we answer that research question by designing experiments of different in-memory storage deployment strategies for figuring out which one achieves a good performance when running data-intensive MapReduce applications on supercomputers. For experiments, we have designed our own memcached-like file system, named *SEMem*. Since Hadoop and Spark are good choices to run data-intensive applications even on supercomputers in aspects of productivity and maturity, we integrated our SEMem with the implementation of Hadoop. The deployment of SEMem is easily configurable and the intra-communication is through MPI, which is the de facto networking protocol on supercomputers. We examined the following deployment strategies:

1. SEMem is deployed as RAM disks where data is stored only in local memory.
2. SEMem is deployed on every node and data can be stored in remote memory.
3. SEMem is deployed only on dedicated nodes that are used only for storage.

Note that the original memcached software [11] is not a file system, does not support Hadoop directly, and uses TCP socket for data exchange. That is the reason why we developed SEMem from scratch.

Our experimental results reveal that allocating a group of nodes used only to store data in memory shows a good result in data-intensive applications with 7–10% improvement in comparison with deploying the memcached-like file system on every computation node. The benefit has been achieved in the context in which the ratio of the dedicated nodes to the total nodes is small (less than 12%). Note that there is no computation task running on those dedicated nodes. No computation task on the dedicated nodes might give a chance of allocating bigger memory space to in-memory storage and makes those nodes less busy.

Moreover, our experiments reveal that supercomputer centers can consider in-memory storage (e.g. SEMem) instead of installing SSD storage for flexible hardware resource configuration and supercomputer users can choose in-memory storage as an alternative of SSD. Compared to the central disk and SSD storage on TSUBAME supercomputer [13], our experimental results show that SEMem reduces execution time by 25% and 5%, respectively, on average when data size is bigger than 128 GB. In this experiment, SEMem runs on dedicated nodes and for fairness of this experiment, all three configurations use the same total number of nodes. In case of SEMem, some nodes are assigned to only storing data, whereas they are used for computation in the central-disk and SSD configurations. That means SEMem uses a smaller number of computation nodes.

In the context in which the ratio of the dedicated nodes to the total nodes is small, better performance from using fewer compute nodes demonstrates that Hadoop aims for data organization rather than computation.

2   Motivation

2.1   Running Hadoop MapReduce on Supercomputers

In today's top supercomputers, it is typical that there is no local disk on each compute node, but SSD is sometimes equipped [13]. Local disk on each node can be a point of failure and when it happens, it is difficult to fix. Instead of local disk, there is a shared storage called *central disk*. Disk I/O from and to the central disk is slow. SSD can be integrated in each compute node. Note that SSD might be a temporary storage where data will be deleted after job execution.

When running Hadoop MapReduce on supercomputers, writing/reading intermediate data is a performance bottleneck since it must be stored on the central disk. There are two main phases in Hadoop MapReduce workflow: mapping and reducing. Mapping tasks generate intermediate data that is written to a node's local disk and deleted after being sent to reducers. On supercomputers, the central disk is used to store that intermediate data instead of local disks. Reducing tasks fetch data from nodes where intermediate data is available and execute the reducing function. Figure 1 shows execution timeline of tera-sort application on TSUBAME supercomputer consisting of 256 mapping tasks and 128 reducing tasks. It reveals that in mapping tasks, writing time of intermediate data to the central disk (red color) is relatively long in comparison with the total execution time. In the figure, mapping tasks have shorter execution time than reducing ones. Using a local SSD helps improve writing/reading performance, but it is not always available.

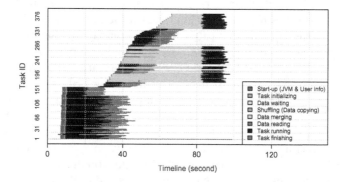

Fig. 1. Tera-sort running on TSUBAME supercomputer using its central disk: shorter running tasks are mappers, the longer ones are reducers.

2.2   In-Memory Approach and Deployment

In-memory storage is a natural approach that helps avoid disk spilling by keeping intermediate data in memory [4,12,16]. We call that approach as memcached-like style [7] since in-memory storage could be at either a local or remote node.

Memcached [11] is a distributed memory cache software that is used widely in web applications to speed up database accessing. A typical deployment of Memcached is installing its daemon on dedicated nodes used only for in-memory storage.

How to deploy memcached-like file systems on supercomputers is not an easily answerable question, even on commodity or off-the-shelf clusters, such as laboratory clusters and Amazon EC2. In this paper, we focus only on the supercomputer environment since the modern (or future) cloud systems [3] look like supercomputers. A feature of supercomputers is that the number of compute nodes are often huge and supercomputer users submit a job to a job queue in order to request a number of nodes they need. When compute nodes are given to users, should we deploy in-memory storage on every node? should we allocate dedicated nodes from the given nodes for in-memory usage only? or should we allow using memory of remote nodes? Moreover, combination of memcached-like storage and Hadoop is not studied well as far as we know.

3   Experiment Design

We answer the above research question by designing experiments of different in-memory storage deployment strategies for figuring out which one achieves a good performance when running data-intensive MapReduce applications on supercomputers. For experiments, we have designed our own memcached-like file system named SEMem. We examined the following deployment strategies:

RamDisk: SEMem is deployed as RAM disks where data is stored only in local memory. Memory size on each node is limited, data might not fit into memory. When out of memory happens, the task must be stopped or restarted on other nodes. For large-scale datasets, this approach is not feasible. Our expectation is this deployment strategy is fast in small-scale datasets.

Every Node: SEMem is deployed on every computation node and data can be stored in remote memory. We call nodes that are responsible for running applications *computation nodes*. Computation nodes are used to run a job's tasks, e.g. Mapping or Reducing tasks in Hadoop MapReduce. The SEMem daemon is run on all computation nodes and helps share a node's in-memory storage with other nodes. This strategy solves the problem of out of memory when data size is bigger than a node's in-memory storage size.

Dedicated Nodes: SEMem is deployed only on dedicated nodes that are used only for storage. We allocate a group of nodes that is only used to store data in their memory. There is no computation task running on that group of nodes. We call those nodes *memory nodes* and their memory *external memory*. The SEMem daemon is run only on each memory nodes. In this deployment strategy, we trade computation resource for data storage by using memory nodes only for keeping data. A question is that whether this approach is a complete waste of resources or not. No computation task on memory nodes gives a chance of allocating bigger memory space to SEMem and makes the memory nodes less busy.

SEMem Architecture: In this section, we describe our own in-memory storage called SEMem. SEMem is easy to be configured to change the deployment strategy of in-memory storage. SEMem is designed to tightly integrate with Hadoop MapReduce framework.

In original Hadoop MapReduce workflow (Fig. 2a), intermediate data generated by mapping tasks is written to a node's local disk. In case of supercomputer, instead of local disks, the central disk or SSD is used to store that data. Figure 2a shows how map output is copied from mappers to reducers. At the mapping side, map output is buffered in memory, and then when its size reaches buffer size, it is spilled to the local disk. The spilled files are merged into a final map output at the end of the mapping phase. There is a *shuffle server* (thread) running on each computation node waiting for fetching requests from reducers. When a request comes, the shuffle server will look up map output metadata, read again those data from the local disk, and send back to the reducer.

In the RamDisk deployment (Fig. 2b), map output is stored totally in memory to avoid writing to and reading from the local disk. Map output is kept in memory instead of spilling to the local disk when the buffer is full. After merging, map output is sent to the shuffle server. A memory space is created on each shuffle server to keep map output in memory. When a fetching request comes, the shuffle server looks up the memory space and is able to send back immediately to the reducer. The size of the memory space on each shuffle server is limited, so out

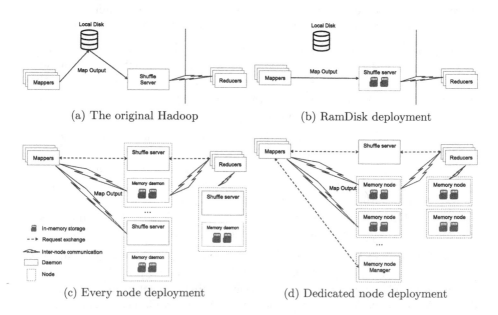

(a) The original Hadoop

(b) RamDisk deployment

(c) Every node deployment

(d) Dedicated node deployment

Fig. 2. SEMem configuration for each deployment strategy: a shuffle server is integrated into NodeManager of Hadoop framework. Memory daemon (or node) is a separate process running on each node of the every-node and dedicated-node strategies and responsible for in-memory storage. In the every-node strategy, the memory daemon and shuffle server are available on the same node.

of memory might happen during data fetching. For example, suppose that the memory space size is 8 GB and there are 20 map tasks running on the node. If each input data is 512 MB and running tera-sort application, the total size of map output is 10 GB. Those data cannot fit into the memory space. Although the map output can be deleted right after it is sent to the corresponding reducer, that out of memory error can happen at any time.

In Every-node deployment (Fig. 2c), SEMem daemon (called memory daemon) is run on the same node with the shuffle server. In contrast to RamDisk where data is stored at a shuffle server, data can be kept at any node's in-memory storage (memory daemon). Round-robin data affinity is used to store in-memory data since it makes data more distributed and helps speed up data fetching later. This kind of data affinity does not use the local memory for storage as long as possible since unbalanced intermediate data might be a performance bottleneck.

Dedicated-node deployment (Fig. 2d) is to create a group of nodes (called *memory nodes*) used only for storing map output and there is no map or reduce task running on those nodes. On supercomputer environment, those nodes are requested on the same job as the nodes used to run Hadoop applications. In Fig. 2d, the group of memory nodes consists of one node manager (master) and slave nodes (just called memory nodes). Node manager is responsible for data placement and monitoring memory left on each memory node. Since there is no task running on memory nodes, the amount of memory allocated can be bigger.

In comparison with RamDisk design, data exchange among nodes of SEMem in Every-node and Dedicated-node is more complex. First, the mapper requests its shuffle server to send map output. If the shuffle server still has empty space, data is sent then. If the shuffle server's memory space is full, the mapper requests the memory node manager to send map output. The node manager will find a relevant place and send back to the mapper. Then, the mapper starts sending map output to the specified memory node. When finishing sending map output, the mapper also informs the shuffle server about the location of map output on memory nodes.

What is the best strategy for storing map output in external memory? Should we distribute map output to as many memory nodes as possible or just store on a memory node and when it is full, the next memory node will be used? The former helps increase fetching throughput since reducers can request to more memory nodes. The latter is useful if map output is packaged and sent once to a reducer. In the current design, we have implemented a round robin scheduler on the memory node manager. Data will be distributed on all memory nodes.

Communication Protocol: SEMem uses MPI as communication protocol, which is the de facto protocol on supercomputers and exploits underlaying hardware such as remote DMA. This is a reason why we developed SEMem from scratch since Memcahced uses TCP/IP. SEMem uses the direct buffer memory of Java and MPI binding for Java [14] included in OpenMPI 1.7.5. It also uses our HPC-Reuse framework [6] to avoid MPI-Spawn or other methods to keep MPI connections available when a new process starts. To multiplex non-blocking communication, SEMem runs a dedicated thread on every node to handle it. Note that our supercomputers do not support *MPI_THREAD_MULTIPLE* mode.

Storage Size: Storage size of SEMem depends on the number of memory nodes. To waste less CPU resources on memory node, it is necessary to minimize the number of memory nodes, although out of memory must not happen. In our current design, the number of memory nodes is estimated roughly based on the size of input data. Our assumption is that total size of map output is equal to one of input data. Therefore, the number of memory nodes chosen satisfies the condition that the total size of memory space on shuffle servers and the memory nodes must be bigger than the size of input data. It might not achieve the best performance of data fetching, but it helps prevent out of memory error. That error is more serious if it happens since the whole task will be restarted.

Minimizing Changes in Hadoop: Keeping the original source code (e.g. Hadoop or Spark) unchanged as much as possible is important to increase SEMem's capability in order to be integrated easily to other different data-intensive frameworks. In our implementation of Hadoop integration, Hadoop source code is changed with the below ratio:

- Line of code/total of Hadoop: 443/1,851,473
- Number of classes/total of Hadoop: 8/35,142

4   Experimental Results

In this section, first we compare three in-memory deployment strategies including *RamDisk*, *Every-node*, and *Dedicated-node* that are described in Sect. 3. We use three workloads in Puma benchmark suit [1]: WordCount, InvertedIndex, and SequenceCount. Second, we evaluate how fast SEMem (using the dedicated-node deployment strategy) is in comparison with the central-disk-based and SSD-based storage. There are three test configurations in this experiment: *Central-disk*, *SSD*, and *SEMem* storages. Tera-sort application is chosen for comparison since the size of intermediate data is big enough to show the bottleneck of the central disk.

Our experiments are conducted on Fujitsu FX10 supercomputer at The University of Tokyo [8] and TSUBAME supercomputer at Tokyo Institute of Technology [13]. A FX10 node is equipped with SPARC64 IXfx 1.848 GHz (16 cores) and 32 GB memory. FX10 nodes are connected with each other through Tofu interconnection [2]. The maximum throughput of that interconnection is 80 Gbps. A TSUBAME node has less cores (Intel Xeon X5670 2.93 GHz - 12 cores) and 54 GB memory. Each node is connected with Infiniband device Grid Director 4700. Another feature of TSUBAME is that 120 GB of SSD storage is available on each node.

SEMem has been implemented using Java since it helps integrate more easily with Hadoop, Spark, or Flink frameworks. We use Hadoop v2.2.0 for experiments, but any Hadoop version *2.x* can be integrated with SEMem. Spark can also use SEMem as an intermediate storage. Our Hadoop cluster consists of one resource manager (master) and 31 slave nodes. Each slave node can run at most four MapTasks or ReduceTasks simultaneously and maximum heap size of a JVM is 4096 MB of memory. Block size of Hadoop Distributed File System (HDFS) is 256 MB. In our experiments, all input data is stored in HDFS running on the central disk.

4.1 Deployment Strategies

This experiment is aimed to show which deployment strategy of in-memory storage shows a better performance in data-intensive applications. We compare three configurations on Fujitsu FX10 supercomputer: RamDisk, Every-node, and Dedicated-node. Moreover, for comparison of in-memory storage and spilling data to the central disk, we compare three strategies with another configuration called *Central-disk*. The largest size of input data is 120 GB. The number of reducers is set to 128 for all datasets. Note that running time is 0 (zero) denoting that out of memory happens and the corresponding job is stopped.

Regarding fairness of this experiment, all three configurations use the same total number of nodes. In case of dedicated-node, some nodes are assigned to only storing data, but they are used for computation as well in Ramdisk and Every-node. In this experiment, while we use 32 nodes for computation and 4 nodes for SEMem storage, 36 nodes are allocated for computation in Ramdisk and every-node configurations.

Figure 3 reveals that RamDisk is the fastest strategy, but out of memory happens when data size is bigger than 120 GB. Dedicated-node shows a better performance (10% on average) than Every-node when data size is bigger than 40 GB. Compared with central-disk configuration, Dedicated-node is always faster, especially 32% improvement in SequenceCount workload, whereas Every-node is slower in WordCount and InvertedIndex, but faster in SequenceCount 26% on average.

RamDisk is the fastest deployment strategy since data is stored at local memory and no inter-node communication. However, due to uneven distribution of input data, intermediate data is not fit into memory at some nodes. That is why out of memory happens. In WordCount and InvertedIndex workloads, Every-node is slower than central-disk configuration since more communication is required and computation nodes might be busier when SEMem daemon is run. By contrast, central-disk is the slowest configuration in SequenceCount because size of intermediate data is larger.

4.2 SEMem (Dedicated-Node) vs. Central-Disk (HDD) and SSD

This experiment is aimed to show how fast SEMem is in comparison with the central-disk-based and SSD-based approaches. We compare three test configu-

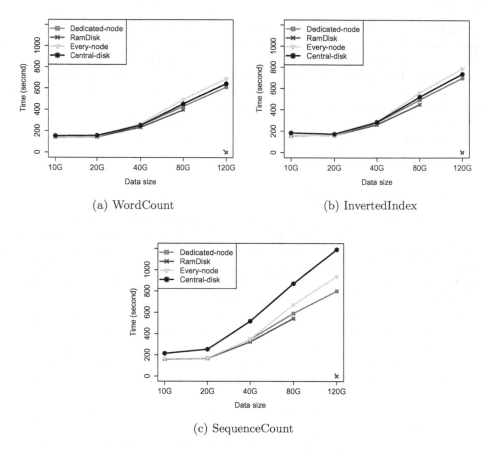

(a) WordCount

(b) InvertedIndex

(c) SequenceCount

Fig. 3. Running time on different deployment strategies: zero at 120 GB at RamDisk denotes that out of memory happens and the corresponding job is stopped.

rations on TSUBAME: the central-disk-based Hadoop, SSD-based Hadoop, and our approach (SEMem). Tera-sort is used for comparison and input data is generated by tera-gen. The largest size of input data is 1 Terabyte. We run each experiment of a data size twice and calculate the average execution time. The number of reducers is fixed to 128 for all data sizes. The number of nodes (#) is denoted in the figure.

In this experiment, SEMem runs on dedicated nodes and for fairness of this experiment, all three configurations use the same total number of nodes. In case of SEMem, some nodes are assigned to only storing data, whereas those nodes are used for computation in the central-disk and SSD configurations. That means SEMem uses a smaller number of computation nodes.

Figure 4a shows that as the size of input data increases, SEMem is faster than central-disk-based storage, and close to SSD-based storage. Compared to central disk and SSD storage, SEMem reduces execution time by 20% and 5%, respectively, on average when data size is bigger than 512 GB. SSD storage has better performance when data size is less than 256 GB.

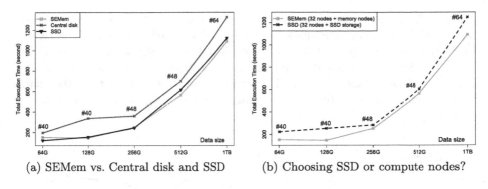

(a) SEMem vs. Central disk and SSD   (b) Choosing SSD or compute nodes?

Fig. 4. SEMem vs. central disk and SSD

Choosing SSD or SEMem storage? at the supercomputer centers, when they design a new supercomputer, a question is that whether each node should be equipped with a SSD storage or not. SSD storage is considered difficult for maintenance and it can be a point of failure. For example, data on SSD storage of TSUBAME must be deleted manually after each job. If they do not want to install SSD, a question is whether SEMem can be an alternative. Moreover, if SSD is available and also become a paid resource on supercomputers, whether supercomputer users should buy SSD storage or choose to increase number of computation nodes in order to create SEMem. We design an experiment to answer those questions. This experiment is conducted on TSUBAME.

We keep the same number of computation nodes for both SEMem and SSD test configurations. We assume that SEMem and SSD is two types of resources that users can choose. SEMem has a defined number of nodes used for storage. Tera-sort is used for comparison and maximum input data is 1 Terabyte.

Figure 4b reveals that SEMem is always faster than SSD storage, especially 41% improvement at 128 GB of input data. When input size is 1 Terabyte, the improvement is 13% in comparison with SSD storage, but SEMem helps decrease the total execution time (1249 s) by 159 s. The figure shows that SEMem is feasible to become an alternative of SSD storage.

4.3   Communication Protocol

This experiment is aimed to check how fast our MPI implementation on SEMem is in comparison with TCP communication and whether the improvement achieved by using SEMem comes mainly from in-memory storing or fast MPI communication. We run the original Hadoop in memory and compare it with SEMem-based Hadoop. The original Hadoop uses TCP communication for data exchange between reducers and shuffle servers. This comparison is fair because SEMem is an in-memory storage, but uses MPI for data exchange. Tera-sort workload is used for comparison and the number of nodes (#) is denoted in the figure.

Figure 5a shows there is no difference when the size of input data is smaller than 128 GB. However, MPI-based Hadoop is faster 10% and 5%, respectively, when input size is 256 and 512 GB. Compared with Fig. 4a at the data size of 256 GB, MPI communication contributes less than 20% to the performance improvement by using SEMem. This experiment has proved that the main source of improvement (80%) comes from in-memory storing on memory nodes of SEMem.

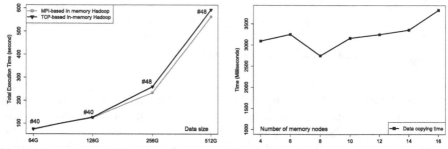

(a) MPI-based vs. TCP-based in-memory Hadoop MapReduce

(b) Average data copying time when changing the number of memory nodes

Fig. 5. Evaluation of implementation issues

4.4   Storage Size of SEMem

This experiment is designed to measure performance impacts of storage size. SEMem's memory capacity can be configured based on number of memory nodes. We have conducted an experiment by keeping the same number of computation nodes and changing number of memory nodes. The purpose of this experiment is to check whether our current approach of finding the number of memory nodes is effective or not. We always run tera-sort application on 32 computation nodes. The number of memory nodes ranges from 4 to 16. The size of input data is 64 GB generated using tera-gen application. According to our estimation, required number of memory nodes should be 4–8 nodes. We measure data copying time (between shuffle servers and memory nodes and reducers) rather than total execution time. Figure 5b shows that when number of memory nodes is 8, data is copied fastest. However, if increasing number of memory nodes from 8 to 16, copying time is slower due to complexity in node management.

5   Related Work

There are several proposals of using in-memory storage in Hadoop, but they did not clearly describe and evaluate deployment strategies including location of in-memory instances and storage size. M3R [12] is an in-memory Hadoop engine implemented using X10 programming language and M3R instances running on each node is responsible for in-memory storage by providing a shared heap-state. Although X10 supports where data is stored through *places* and *activities* operators, but the paper did not mention it explicitly and also have any evaluation. HaLoop [4] provides caching preferences, such as reducer input and output cache and mapper input cache, but intermediate data is only shared on the same node between jobs and deployment strategies are not relevant in this context. Spark [16] is a data-intensive framework and uses in-memory storage to improve performance compared with Hadoop. It proposed a programming model based on Resilient Distributed Dataset (RDD) and intermediate data is built and generated from RDDs. It is possible to choose a location for a RDD through *preferredLocations()* operator, but there was no evaluation of RDD deployment in the paper. Moreover, the supercomputer context makes our contribution unique.

Memcached software [11] is close to our implementation of SEMem since it is a distributed caching system. The combination of Hadoop and Memcached is a study topic. However, to the best our knowledge, there is no study on using Memcached to store intermediate data implicitly in Hadoop MapReduce workflow. We also evaluated advantages of that combination SEMem and Hadoop. Memcached uses TCP-based communication and RDMA-based Memcached [10] is an extension that speeds up internode communication by using RDMA. In our SEMem, we use MPI for communication among memory nodes. RDMA could be also enabled automatically in MPI communication on supercomputers.

6 Conclusion

In this paper, we have examined in-memory storage deployment strategies including RamDisk, Every-node, and Dedicated-node. For experiments, we have designed our own memcached-like file system called SEMem. Dedicated-node shows a good result in data-intensive applications with 10% improvement in comparison with Every-node strategy. Dedicated-node is motivated by a feature of supercomputers that the number of compute nodes is often huge and supercomputer users can request a number of nodes they need. There is no computation task running on that group of nodes.

SEMem is an easily configurable in-memory storage for different deployment strategies. It is tightly integrated with Hadoop, but Spark can use SEMem as preferred servers in the *preferredLocations()*. The performance of Hadoop MapReduce with SEMem should be the same as Spark since both of them are supporting in-memory storage. In our SEMem, however, users can choose the best in-memory storage deployment strategy for their applications. MPI communication on SEMem is an advantage in comparison with other Memcached-like software.

When we have only a fixed number of nodes, increasing the number of dedicated nodes according to the dataset size should affect the performance. Finding the best ratio of the dedicated nodes to the total nodes is our future work. Moreover, when the dataset does not fit into memory, SEMem needs to be adapted to use the central disk or SSD storage if available.

References

1. Ahmad, F., Lee, S., Thottethodi, M., Vijaykumar, T.: Puma: Purdue MapReduce benchmarks suite (2012)
2. Ajima, Y., Sumimoto, S., Shimizu, T.: Tofu: a 6D mesh/torus interconnect for exascale computers. Computer **11**(42), 36–40 (2009)
3. Amazon Web Services: High Performance Computing (2017). https://aws.amazon.com/hpc/
4. Bu, Y., Howe, B., Balazinska, M., Ernst, M.D.: Haloop: efficient iterative data processing on large clusters. Proc. VLDB Endow. **3**(1–2), 285–296 (2010)
5. Carbone, P., Katsifodimos, A., Ewen, S., Markl, V., Haridi, S., Tzoumas, K.: Apache flink: stream and batch processing in a single engine. Bull. IEEE Comput. Soc. Tech. Committee Data Eng. **36**(4), 28 (2015)
6. Dao, T.C., Chiba, S.: HPC-Reuse: efficient process creation for running MPI and Hadoop MapReduce on supercomputers. In: 2016 16th IEEE/ACM International Symposium on Cluster, Cloud and Grid Computing (CCGrid), pp. 342–345. IEEE (2016)
7. Fitzpatrick, B.: Distributed caching with memcached. Linux J. **2004**(124), 5 (2004)
8. FX10: User's Guide (2015). http://www.cc.u-tokyo.ac.jp/system/fx10/index-e.html
9. He, J., Jagatheesan, A., Gupta, S., Bennett, J., Snavely, A.: Dash: a recipe for a flash-based data intensive supercomputer. In: Proceedings of the 2010 ACM/IEEE International Conference for High Performance Computing, Networking, Storage and Analysis, pp. 1–11. IEEE Computer Society (2010)
10. Jose, J., Subramoni, H., Luo, M., Zhang, M., Huang, J., Wasi-ur Rahman, M., Islam, N.S., Ouyang, X., Wang, H., Sur, S., et al.: Memcached design on high performance RDMA capable interconnects. In: 2011 International Conference on Parallel Processing, pp. 743–752. IEEE (2011)
11. Memcached: A caching system (2017). https://memcached.org
12. Shinnar, A., Cunningham, D., Saraswat, V., Herta, B.: M3R: increased performance for in-memory Hadoop jobs. Proc. VLDB Endow. **5**(12), 1736–1747 (2012)
13. TSUBAME: User'sGuide (2016). http://tsubame.gsic.titech.ac.jp/en/top
14. Vega-Gisbert, O., Roman, J.E., Squyres, J.M.: Design and implementation of Java bindings in Open MPI (2014)
15. White, T.: Hadoop: The Definitive Guide. O'Reilly Media Inc., Sebastopol (2012)
16. Zaharia, M., Chowdhury, M., Das, T., Dave, A., Ma, J., McCauley, M., Franklin, M.J., Shenker, S., Stoica, I.: Resilient distributed datasets: a fault-tolerant abstraction for in-memory cluster computing. In: Proceedings of the 9th USENIX conference on Networked Systems Design and Implementation, p. 2. USENIX Association (2012)

Parallel and Distributed Programming, Interfaces, and Languages

Supporting the Xeon Phi Coprocessor in a Heterogeneous Programming Model

Ana Moreton-Fernandez$^{(\boxtimes)}$, Eduardo Rodriguez-Gutiez,
Arturo Gonzalez-Escribano, and Diego R. Llanos

Departamento de Informática, Edif. Tecn. de la Información,
Universidad de Valladolid, Campus Miguel Delibes, 47011 Valladolid, Spain
{ana,eduardo,arturo,diego}@infor.uva.es

Abstract. Supercomputers are becoming more heterogeneous. They are composed by several machines with different computation capabilities and different kinds and families of accelerators, such as GPUs or Intel Xeon Phi coprocessors. Programming these machines is a hard task, that requires a deep study of the architectural details, in order to exploit efficiently each computational unit.

In this paper, we present an extension of a GPU-CPU heterogeneous programming model, to include support for Intel Xeon Phi coprocessors. This contribution extends the previous model and its implementation, by taking advantage of both the GPU communication model and the CPU execution model of the original approach, to derive a new approach for the Xeon Phi. Our experimental results show that using our approach, the programming effort needed for changing the kind of target devices is highly reduced for several study cases. For example, using our model to program a Mandelbrot benchmark, the 97% of the application code is reused between a GPU implementation and a Xeon Phi implementation.

1 Introduction

Supporting computational accelerators such as GPUs or Xeon Phi coprocessors in current programming models is vital to exploit modern parallel platforms. Different kinds and families of accelerators are used in modern high-performance platforms, as we observe in the configuration of the TOP500 supercomputers [17]. However, programming solutions for an efficient deployment in accelerator devices in general is a very complex task [12], that relies on the manual management of memory transfers and execution configuration parameters. For each different computing device, the programmer has to carry out a deep study of the particular data needed to be computed at each moment, considering architectural details to exploit efficiently the specific execution system [1].

Many works address the problem of heterogeneous systems management (e.g. [3,4,15]) following two alternatives: automatically generating specific codes from sequential or higher-level programming abstractions, or using runtime libraries that make transparent the use of different device types. Using current heterogeneous code generators or compilers, the code should be recompiled

© Springer International Publishing AG 2017
F.F. Rivera et al. (Eds.): Euro-Par 2017, LNCS 10417, pp. 457–469, 2017.
DOI: 10.1007/978-3-319-64203-1_33

for each different execution platform in order to better exploit the performance capabilities of the system. One example is OpenAcc [19]. It provides a simple and abstract programming framework for accelerators. However, the code should be recompiled with their specific compilers for each different execution architecture in order to achieve a good performance.

As for libraries, some works focused on specific kind of applications, address the portability problem internally using several native programming models. For example, MAGMA library [5] provides a unified programming environment for heterogeneous systems using both CPUs and accelerators, such as GPUs or Intel Xeon Phi, for dense linear algebra algorithms. However, most heterogeneous libraries rely on the OpenCL abstraction. OpenCL [16] is a widespread programming framework to deal with heterogeneous devices. The OpenCL *context* abstraction allows the memory management of multiple devices of the same nature (using the same *platform* in OpenCL notation). The abstractions introduced by OpenCL have been proved to prevent the obtaining of the same efficiency as when using directly the vendor programming models, for several common situations [9]. Many state-of-the-art heterogeneous frameworks and libraries with a high level of abstraction [2,7,8,14,18,20], that rely on OpenCL as execution layer, typically inherit some of these problems. Additionally, during the last decade several high-performance libraries targeting specific accelerator devices or CPU architectures, have been developed using the vendor specific programming models, such as cuBLAS [13] or MKL. For making the most of such works, it is advisable the use of such native or vendor programming models and compilers, for each different kind of device.

In this paper, we extend a programming model for heterogeneous platforms that is not based on the use of OpenCL. The original proposal, named *Controller* [11], is presented as a library that internally exploits vendor-specific programming models available on the platform. It introduces an abstract entity to allow the transparent launching of series of tasks on a GPU or on a CPU. It exploits their native or vendor specific programming models, thus enabling the potential performance obtained by them. In this work we present an extension of this Controller heterogeneous programming model that includes the support for Intel Xeon Phi coprocessors, also known as Many Integrated Cores (MICs). The model is based on the mix of the communication model originally designed for GPUs in the Controller library with the execution model originally designed for groups of CPU cores. We develop a complete runtime execution system that includes methods for task launching, transparent data transfers between the MIC accelerator and the host, and a queue system to manage the kernel executions with a customized grain choice. It perfectly fits with the previous Controller library, thus standardizing and abstracting to the programmer the issues related to the programming of different kinds of accelerators. It provides a MIC runtime support for a heterogeneous programming model, that unifies the programming for heterogeneous systems composed by MIC coprocessors, GPUS, or CPUs, also obtaining the same performance than using their native programming models.

We also present an experimental study with four study cases. We show that our approach is highly flexible, with minimum programming effort for changing the kind of target devices. Moreover, the performance results show that our implementation does not introduce significant performance penalties compared with reference codes which use the native/vendor programming models directly.

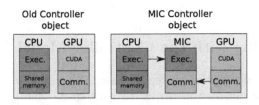

Fig. 1. Left: previous Controller model, only supporting CPU and GPU. Right: the MIC Controller proposed model, mixing features from the GPU-CPU submodels.

2   Approach to Support MIC Accelerators

The work presented in [11] proposed the Controller, a simple heterogeneous programming model to deal with the issues of hybrid computation in an abstract way to the programmer. This model defines an object able to transparently manage either a group of CPU cores or a GPU accelerator using internally native programming techniques (OpenMP and CUDA respectively).

For our new proposal, we distinguish two internal parts in the Controller, which provide support for each kind of computational device: Execution and communication management models (see left of Fig. 1). The abstract device formed by CPU-cores shares the memory space with the host. Thus, the controller object only has to provide an execution model that manages a task queue and that adapts the fine-grain computations used in the Controller model to a coarser granularity, more appropriate for CPU threads. On the other hand, for GPUs, the CUDA programming model already provides an execution system to enqueue and launch kernels with the same granularity level used in the Controller model. However, the communication operations across different memory spaces on host and GPUs required the implementation of a more sophisticated mechanism to integrate different policies and techniques in the Controller model.

In this work we understand as independent parts in the Controller abstraction both, the execution and the communication management models from different kind of devices. Thus, we propose their mixture to support a new type of accelerator such as the MIC coprocessors. In order to do that, we use: (1) In terms of execution, the Controller model for groups of CPU cores, that blends blocks of fine grained kernels into coarse CPU tasks, is appropriated for MIC coprocessors. (2) In terms of memory management, the abstract model for data communications needed for the MIC coprocessors is equivalent to the GPU communication model in the old Controller approach.

The application of this idea leads to a homogeneous programming model for heterogeneous systems including MIC coprocessors, where the issues related to the programming of different types of accelerators are transparent for the programmer. In this work we show the implementation of this idea in the Controller library, to support computational devices such as MIC coprocessors, GPUs, and groups of CPU-cores, without redesigning or changing the high-level programming model and interface.

3 Programming with the Controller Model

In this section we describe the concepts related to programming using the Controller model. It introduces the reader to Hitmap [6], the library used for the managing of data-structures, and the properties of the Controller model [11] abstract interface and its programming methodology.

Hitmap Library. Hitmap is the library used in the Controllers to provide a common interface for the data management inside the generic portable kernels. Hitmap defines the *HitTile* structure, an abstract entity for n-dimensional arrays and array tiles of arbitrary size. A *HitTile* structure is a handler to store array meta-data, along with the pointer to the actual memory space. There are only three functions of Hitmap needed to work with the Controller library. The function *hit_tileDomainAlloc* is used to declare the index domains of a tile array and allocate the data memory. The function *hit_tileFree* is used to free the data memory and clean the handler. The function *hit_tileElem* is used in the host or kernel codes to access the elements of a tile. It receives a tile name, a number of dimensions, and the indexes values of the desired element. The data are accessed in row major order in all cases, independently of the device implementation.

Controller Features. The Controller model provides a systematic programming methodology together with several important features: (1) A mechanism to define from common kernels reusable across different types of devices, to specialized kernels for specific device kinds; (2) A transparent mechanism of memory management, including optimized communications of the data structures between the host and the corresponding images in the accelerators; (3) An optimization system to select proper values for kernel-launching configuration parameters (such as the threadblock geometry), guided by simple qualitative code characterization provided by the programmer. These features makes the use of our proposal adaptable to the programmer knowledge. Thus, for non-experts users, it is possible to program a generic approach achieving good performance. On the other hand, a user with programming experience in the execution platform can take advantage of this knowledge and achieve better results.

Kernel Definitions. In the Controller library, a kernel is declared by using the primitive KERNEL_<type>. Where type may be empty to indicate a kernel usable on any kind of device, or may be a specific value for a given type of device indicating a specialized code. The original library supported declarations KERNEL_GPU for CUDA code targeting NVIDIA's GPUs, KERNEL_CPU for host machine code targeting sets of CPU cores, and KERNEL_GPU_WRAPPER, KERNEL_CPU_WRAPPER, for code to execute in the host which includes calls to specialized GPU or CPU libraries, such as cuBLAS or MKL routines.

```
1   /* Matrix addition: Generic kernel code for any type of device */
2   KERNEL(MatAdd, 3,
3           OUT, HitTile_float, C,  IN,  HitTile_float, A,  IN,  HitTile_float, B ){
4     int x = thread.x; int y = thread.y;
5     hit_tileElem( C, 2, x, y ) = hit_tileElem( A, 2, x, y ) +
6                                  hit_tileElem( B, 2, x, y );
7   }
8   /* Host program using the Controller library */
9   int main(){
10    int SIZE = 10000;
11    /* Stage 1: Controller creation */
12    Cntrl comm;
13    CntrlCreate(&comm, CNTRL_GPU, 0);
14    /* Stage 2: Data structures creation and initialization */
15    HitTile_float A; HitTile_float B; HitTile_float C;
16    hit_tileDomainAlloc( &A, float, 2, SIZE, SIZE );
17    hit_tileDomainAlloc( &B, float, 2, SIZE, SIZE );
18    hit_tileDomainAlloc( &C, float, 2, SIZE, SIZE );
19    initMatrices(&A, &B, &C);
20    /* Stage 3: Data structures attachment */
21    CntrlAttach(&comm, &A); CntrlAttach(&comm, &B); CntrlAttach(&comm, &C);
22    /* Stage 4: Kernel launching */
23    Thread threadsSpace;
24    ThreadInit( threads, 2, SIZE, SIZE );
25    CntrlLaunch(comm, MatAdd, threadsSpace, 3, &A, &B, &C);
26    /* Stage 5: Data structures detachment */
27    CntrlDetach(&comm, &C);
28  }
```

Fig. 2. Kernel definition and configuration, and host program of a matrix addition using the Controller library.

We can see a kernel definition in lines 2–7 of Fig. 2. The kernel-definition primitive specifies in brackets the number of parameters of the kernel, with a tuple of information for each parameter. The parameter information includes its type, name, and input/output role.

Programming Methodology. Building a Controller host program follows simple development guidelines: (1) The Controller entity creation, associating to this object the computational device to be managed. A Controller entity should be created for each computational device that will be used for computation. (2) The attachment of the data structures to the Controller object. Data structures that will be accessed by a kernel should be previously attached to the Controller entity. (3) The launching of the computational kernels on the Controller object. (4) The detachment of the data structures.

Figure 2 shows a matrix addition implementation that performs the computation on a GPU using the Controller model. In the main program, first, a

Controller object is created, assigning a GPU to the object (lines 12 to 13). Data structures are created and initialized on the host (lines 15 to 19). After that, these data structures are attached to the previously created Controller (line 21). In the step 4, the program launches the kernel *MatAdd*. It uses a *Thread* object to specify the number and index space of the threads to be launched. In this example a thread is launched for each element of the matrix C (lines 23 to 25). Finally, the program detaches the matrix with the results (line 27).

In this paper, we propose a method to integrate the support of MIC coprocessors in this model, that allows the efficient execution of this program on the Xeon Phi, only by changing the `CNTRL_GPU` parameter by a new `CNTRL_XPHI` parameter on the line 13 of the code.

4   Integrating MIC coprocessors in the Controller library

The original version of the Controller library supports the deployment of kernels on GPUs or virtual computational devices formed by groups of CPU-cores. In this section we present the support of the MIC devices in the Controller library. We implement the **MIC controller object** containing several functionalities, such as the identification, initialization and management of MIC devices, an adapted internal queue to manage the asynchronous kernel executions, and a method to lock accesses to the HitTile data structures on the host while they are managed in the device memory.

```
1   /* Internal attach function */
2   void attachToXPHI(CntrlXPHI* cntrl,
3                     HitTile *tile){
4     Lock(tile, cntrl);
5     int MIC= cntrl->MIC;
6     char *data = (char *)(*tile).data;
7     int numBytes = hit_tileSize(tile);
8     #pragma offload target(mic:MIC)      \
9                 in( data:length(numBytes) \
10                    alloc_if(1) free_if(0) )
11  }
```

```
1   /* Internal detach function */
2   void detachToXPHI(CntrlXPHI* cntrl,
3                     HitTile *tile){
4     int MIC= cntrl->MIC;
5     char *data = (char *)(*tile).data;
6     int numBytes = hit_tileSize(tile);
7     #pragma offload target(mic:MIC)      \
8         in( data:length(0)               \
9             alloc_if(0) free_if(0) )     \
10        out( data:length(numBytes)       \
11            alloc_if(0) free_if(1) )
12    Unlock(tile, cntrl);
13  }
```

Fig. 3. Excerpts of the Controller internal code that perform data transfers of a HitTile object. Left: from the host to a MIC coprocessor. Right: from a MIC coprocessor to the host.

4.1   Attaching and Detaching Data Structures on the MIC

In computational devices such as GPUs or MIC coprocessors, where their memory spaces are separated from the host memory space, the attachment/detachment operation also implies a data transfer.

We have implemented two internal functions to perform the data transfers to/from the MIC coprocessor, using the Intel Language Extensions for Offload (LEO). These functions are executed internally when the program invokes an attachment or a detachment operation respectively. Figure 3 shows a summarized version of the code of both functions.

On the left, we see the code used to attach a tile to a MIC controller object (represented in the figure by the CntrlXPHI type). In this function, first the attached tile is locked on the host. Second, the code extracts: (1) The MIC identifier assigned to the controller object (line 5); (2) The pointer to the actual data (line 6); and (3) The number of bytes to be transferred (line 7); After that, the function performs the actual data transfer from the host to the MIC, ensuring that there is allocated memory space in the target device (using alloc_if(1)), and that after this offloading the actual data will be maintained (using free_if(0)).

On the right, we show the code used to detach a tile whose data have been modified from a MIC controller object. As in the attachment, first the code extracts the information about the data transfer (lines 4 to 6). Second, the actual data transfer from the coprocessor to the host is specified using a pragma. For determining the pointer of the data previously transferred, the program uses the *in* modifier to make the data pointer available in the Xeon Phi, and sets the *length* to 0 to prevent any data from being copied (lines 8 to 9). Once the pointer is available on the MIC, the pragma also specifies the data transfer and the freeing of the MIC space memory (lines 10 to 11). Finally, the data structure is unlocked on the host.

```
1   /* Auxiliar macros for kernels with one parameter */
2   #define STRINGIFY(a) #a
3   #define XPHI_WRAPPER_PARAMS1(io1, type1, value1)                    \
4           type1 value1
5   #define XPHI_WRAPPER_VALUES1(io1, type1, value1)                    \
6           value1
7   #define XPHI_WRAPPER_CAST1(io1, type1, value1)                      \
8           type1 value1_p = (type1)args[2];                            \
9           HitTile value1_t = *(HitTile*)value1_p;                     \
10          char *data_tile1= (char *) (value1_t).data;
11  #define XPHI_OFFLOAD_PARAMS1(MIC, io1, type1, value1)               \
12          offload target(mic:MIC) in(threads:length(3)) in(value1_t)  \
13                          in(data_tile1:length(0) alloc_if(0) free_if(0))
14  #define XPHI_POINTERS1(io1, type1, value1)                          \
15          HitTile value1 = value1_t;                                  \
16          value1.data = data_tile1;
```

Fig. 4. Auxiliary macros defined for a one parameter kernel.

4.2 New Kernel Definitions

A kernel definition specifies the device that fits with the contained code by declaring it using the primitive KERNEL_<type>. We extent the Controller framework to support also MIC kernel definitions. A MIC kernel definition is rewritten

```
1    /* Macro of the kernel definition */
2    #define KERNEL_XPHI(name, nparams, params...)                              \
3      /* Single-element function declaration */                              \
4      static void __attribute__((target(mic)))                               \
5        kernel_xphi_##name(Thread threadId, XPHI_WRAPPER_PARAMS##nparams(params)); \
6                                                                             \
7    /* Parallel coarse-grained function */                                   \
8      static inline void wrapper_xphi_##name(void** args){                   \
9        int MIC=cntrl->MIC;                                                  \
10       CntrlXPHI* cntrl = (CntrlXPHI*) args[0];                             \
11       Thread* threads = (Thread*)args[1];                                  \
12       XPHI_WRAPPER_CAST##nparams(params);                                  \
13       _Pragma( STRINGIFY(XPHI_OFFLOAD_PARAMS##nparams(MIC, params)) )       \
14       {                                                                   \
15       XPHI_POINTERS##nparams(params);                                      \
16       _Pragma("omp parallel"){                                             \
17       int i,j,k;                                                           \
18       Thread threadId;                                                     \
19         _Pragma("omp for private(i,j,k)")                                  \
20       for(i=0; i<=threads->x; i++){                                        \
21         for(j=0; j<=threads->y; j++){                                      \
22           for(k=0; k<=threads->z; k++){                                    \
23             threadId.x = i;                                                \
24             threadId.y = j;                                                \
25             threadId.z = k;                                                \
26             kernel_xphi_##name(threadId, XPHI_WRAPPER_VALUES##nparams(params)); \
27       } } }                                                                \
28       }}                                                                   \
29                                                                             \
30   /* Task addition function */                                             \
31   void name##_xphi(CntrlXPHI* cntrl, Thread thread,                         \
32                    XPHI_WRAPPER_PARAMS##nparams(params)){                   \
33     CntrlXPHIAddTask(cntrl, wrapper_xphi_##name, thread, nparams,           \
34                    XPHI_WRAPPER_VALUES##nparams(params));                   \
35   }                                                                        \
36   /* Single-element function definition */                                 \
37   static void __attribute__((target(mic)))                                 \
38     kernel_xphi_##name(Thread threadId, XPHI_WRAPPER_PARAMS##nparams(params)) \
```

Fig. 5. Functions internally generated by the MIC kernel definition: (1) Function
to be executed by each fine-grain virtual thread: kernel_xphi_##name; (2) Function
that executes a dequeued kernel, grouping virtual threads in coarse-grained OpenMP
threads: wrapper_xphi_##name; (3) Function to enqueue a kernel-launching request:
name##_xphi.

as three functions using macro functions. We show examples of the code of the
three resulting functions in Fig. 5.

Fine-Grain Virtual Thread Function: The first function implements the
kernel code that the programmer defined to execute for one index element of the
fine-grain virtual threads space. In most array operations, it is used to compute
one data element. The function is named kernel_xphi_##name, where ##name
is the kernel name, taken from the first parameter of the kernel definition primitive. It is defined as a MIC function using the attribute target(mic). The
parameters are a multi-dimensional index represented by a Thread object, that
represents a point in the execution domain, and the actual kernel parameters. In
Fig. 5, lines 4 to 5 show the function declaration and lines 37 to 38 the function
definition.

Parallel Coarse-Grained Function: The second one (`wrapper_xphi_##name`) performs the offloaded coarse-grained parallel computation in the MIC device. It receives a variable number of parameters. The first one is the controller object, the second one the domain of fine-grain thread indexes to compute and the rest are the data structures corresponding to the real parameters. Lines 10 to 12 of Fig. 5 show how the information is extracted from the parameters (auxiliary macros for the transformations were defined in Fig. 4). The rest of the body of the function defines the offload region. The offload pragma transfers the data-structure handlers, the domain represented by a `Thread` object, and the pointer to the actual data for each HitTile. As in the detachment operation, in order to determine the data previously transferred, the offload pragma uses the `in` modifier to make the data pointer available in the Xeon Phi, and sets the *length* to 0 to prevent any data from being copied (see line 13 of Fig. 4). Inside the offload region, the HitTile handlers update their data pointer to the actual offloaded data (line 15). After that, the parallel computation is performed on the specified domain (lines 16 to 28), grouping virtual thread indexes in actual coarse-grained threads, by using an OpenMP parallel loop.

Kernel Launch Request: The third one is named `name##_xphi`. It is the internal implementation of a kernel launch for a MIC. In its body, the function implements the enqueuing of the kernel execution request in the Controller object. The information needed is: The controller object, the pointer to the coarse-grained parallel computation function, and its real parameters (the index space where the application will be executed, the number of kernel parameters, and the actual kernel parameters). See lines 31 to 35 of Fig. 5.

4.3   Queue Management and Kernel Launching

As opposite as the CUDA programming model, the offloading MIC coprocessor programming model does not provide a queue system to manage asynchronous kernel launchings. We have developed a queue system for the asynchronous execution of several kernel launches on the MIC coprocessor, currently using a FIFO policy in our prototype. When a MIC controller object is created, an asynchronous `OpenMP task` is launched. This task uses OpenMP locks to block until there are kernel-launching requests in the queue. Then, it dequeues the request and dispatches/executes it. The execution of a task on the MIC is carried out by simply executing the already offloaded parallel `wrapper_xphi_##name` generated function, specified in the request structure, that contains pointers to the function and parameters. The Controller destructor enqueues a special request that notifies to the OpenMP queue-controlling task that it should release the Controller resources and finish.

5   Experimental Study

We perform an experimental study to evaluate the potential advantages and constraints of the integration of the MIC coprocessor in the original Controller library. The section includes: (1) A description of the considered study cases, (2) a performance study of our proposal, and (3) a development effort comparison between programming using the new Controller extension and using device vendor programming models.

5.1 Study Cases

We select four benchmarks to test our approach and implementation.

Matrix Addition. It implements a sum of two matrices, storing the result in a third one: $C = A + B$. For the Controller version, we use the same generic kernel implementation tested in previous works for CPU-cores and GPUs, without any modification.

Black-Scholes. The Black-Scholes formula is based on a mathematical model of a financial market. The result estimates the price of European-style options. The original program, obtained from the CUDA Toolkit Samples, independently applies the formula to the input values of an array, calculating and storing their results. Again, the Controller version uses the same generic kernel definition for both GPUs, and MICs accelerators.

Matrix Multiplication. It computes the product of two matrices, storing the result in a third one: $C = A * B$. The read patterns on A and B matrices should be adapted to exploit coalescence and shared memory in GPUs, and to properly exploit caches and vectorization on MICs. These features lead to different optimizations in both types of accelerators. Thus, the Controller version declares different specialized and optimized kernels for each kind of device.

Mandelbrot Algorithm. The Mandelbrot algorithm is used to compute fractal geometric images. The Controller version uses a single generic kernel definition for both GPUs and MICs accelerators.

Table 1. Performance results (seconds) comparing LEO reference codes with Controller codes for different input sizes (left/right). Experiments executed on a Intel Xeon E5-2620 v2 @2.1 GHz, 32 Gb DDR3 main memory, and with the Xeon Phi Knights Corner 3120A coprocessor. Compiler used: ICC 17.0.0 version with the flags -*O3*, and -*openmp*.

Code	Mat. Add.	Black-Scholes	Mat. Mult.	Mandel-brot	Code	Mat. Add.	Black-Scholes	Mat. Mult.	Mandel-brot
Size	5000^2	10^6	4096^2	4000^2	**Size**	20000^2	$5 * 10^7$	8192^2	20000^2
LEO Code	1.67	0.60	2.59	6.49	LEO Code	24.99	5.49	19.87	148.47
Ctrl. Code	1.43	0.74	2.88	6.86	Ctrl. Code	24.65	5.01	19.27	147.36

Table 2. Measurements of development effort metrics for the codes of the study cases. Left: comparison of number of code lines, code tokens, and cyclomatic complexity between the Controller version and the version using native programming models. Right: comparison in terms of the percentage of words that are common and can be reused, should be deleted, or should be changed, when porting codes between GPU and MIC versions using the native models, or the Controller library.

Case study	Version	Lines of Code	#Tokens	Cyclomatic Complexity
Matrix addition	LEO	26	210	3
	Ctrl.MIC	35	317	1
Black Scholes	LEO	80	525	6
	Ctrl.MIC	89	693	5
Matrix mult.	LEO	23	217	4
	Ctrl.MIC	37	337	3
Mandelbrot	LEO	32	319	5
	Ctrl.MIC	46	488	4

Case study	CUDA → LEO	Ctrl.GPUs → Ctrl.MICs
Matrix Addition	Common 13% Delete 30% Change 57%	Common 92% Delete 0% Change 8%
Black-Scholes	Common 53% Delete 25% Change 22%	Common 69% Delete 21% Change 10%
Matrix multiplication	Common 8% Delete 43% Change 48%	Common 49% Delete 3% Change 47%
Mandelbrot	Common 32% Delete 61% Change 7%	Common 97% Delete 0% Change 3%

5.2   Performance Study

In this section we show how low is the performance overhead produced by the implementation of our proposed MIC library extension. Table 1 shows the total times spent (including computation and data transfers) by the four benchmarks with two different problem sizes. Codes have been implemented with our proposal, and directly with the Intel Language Extensions for Offload (LEO) and OpenMP. A similar comparison for groups of CPU-cores and GPUs were presented in [11]. Both studies indicate only a small constant penalty performance due to the management of the queue system, that is only noticeable in the results for the smaller problem sizes presented on the left of Table 1. For bigger problem sizes, some performance gain is obtained due to Hitmap optimizations in the internal management of the data structures. In general terms, the performance obtained by using our approach is similar to the native programming models.

5.3   Development Effort Measures

This section includes two development effort comparisons. First, between the proposed Controller implementation and the reference codes (using LEO and OpenMP for MIC, and CUDA for GPUs). Secondly, comparing measures of the code changes needed to port a GPU implementation to a MIC implementation, using the Controller or the native programming models.

The results of the first comparison are presented on the left of Table 2. We measure three classical development effort metrics: Number of lines of code; Number of tokens, and McCabe's cyclomatic complexity [10]. The measured codes include kernel definitions, kernel characterizations, the coordination host code, and data structures management. We observe that the use of the Controller library implies less cyclomatic complexity, but more number of lines and tokens.

However, the goal of the library is to provide an homogeneous interface to deal with any kind of accelerator. For this reason, we also compare the effort needed for transforming GPU codes in order to port them to a MIC device. See results on the right of Table 2. We analyze the percentage of words of each implementation that are common and can be reused, should be deleted, or should be changed. The largest changes are on the matrix multiplication benchmark, because of the implementation of different optimized kernels for each device. For the other benchmarks, we see that using our proposal the programming effort needed to change the target computational device is extremely low. These measures show the level of abstraction and standardization achieved by our proposal.

6   Conclusions

In this paper we propose an extension to support the Intel Xeon Phi (MIC) coprocessors in a CPU-GPU homogeneous programming model for heterogeneous systems, that is implemented as a compiler agnostic library. To provide support for MIC coprocessors, our approach reuses and mixes the internal execution features for CPU-cores, and the internal memory and communication management features of the original GPU model. We have completely integrated the support for a MIC coprocessor in the library, without adding any constraint to the programming model. The experimental study shows the high flexibility of our approach, that implies a minimum programming effort for changing the execution target devices, without significatively penalizing the performance. Future work includes the integration of scientific libraries, such as MKL, as kernels in the Controller implementation, and an evaluation with applications of other domains.

Acknowledgments. This research has been partially supported by MICINN (Spain) and ERDF program of the European Union: HomProg-HetSys project (TIN2014-58876-P), CAPAP-H6 (TIN2016-81840-REDT), and COST Program Action IC1305: Network for Sustainable Ultrascale Computing (NESUS).

References

1. Contassot-Vivier, S., Vialle, S.: Algorithmic scheme for hybrid computing with CPU, Xeon-Phi/MIC and GPU devices on a single machine. Parallel Comput.: Road Exascale **27**, 25–34 (2016)
2. Deepika, H., Mangala, N., Babu, S.C.: Automatic program generation for heterogeneous architectures. In: 2016 International Conference on Advances in Computing, Communications and Informatics (ICACCI), pp. 102–109. IEEE (2016)
3. Diogo, M., Grelck, C.: Towards heterogeneous computing without heterogeneous programming. In: Loidl, H.-W., Peña, R. (eds.) TFP 2012. LNCS, vol. 7829, pp. 279–294. Springer, Heidelberg (2013). doi:10.1007/978-3-642-40447-4_18
4. Dolbeau, R., Bihan, S., Bodin, F.: HMPP: a hybrid multi-core parallel programming environment. In: Workshop on General Purpose Processing on Graphics Processing Units (GPGPU 2007), vol. 28 (2007)

5. Dongarra, J., Gates, M., Haidar, A., Jia, Y., Kabir, K., Luszczek, P., Tomov, S.: HPC programming on Intel many-integrated-core hardware with Magma port to Xeon Phi. Sci. Program. **2015**(9), 1–11 (2015)
6. Gonzalez-Escribano, A., Torres, Y., Fresno, J., Llanos, D.R.: An extensible system for multilevel automatic data partition and mapping. IEEE Trans. Parallel Distrib. Syst. **25**(5), 1145–1154 (2014)
7. Grasso, I., Pellegrini, S., Cosenza, B., Fahringer, T.: A uniform approach for programming distributed heterogeneous computing systems. J. Parallel Distrib. Comput. **74**(12), 3228–3239 (2014)
8. Hijma, P., Jacobs, C.J., van Nieuwpoort, R.V., Bal, H.E.: Cashmere: heterogeneous many-core computing. In: 2015 IEEE International Parallel and Distributed Processing Symposium (IPDPS), pp. 135–145. IEEE (2015)
9. Karimi, K., Dickson, N.G., Hamze, F.: A performance comparison of CUDA and OpenCL. arXiv preprint (2010). arXiv:1005.2581
10. McCabe, T.J.: A complexity measure. IEEE Trans. Softw. Eng. **4**, 308–320 (1976)
11. Moreton-Fernandez, A., Ortega-Arranz, H., Gonzalez-Escribano, A.: Controllers: an abstraction to ease the use of hardware accelerators. Int. J. High Perform. Comput. Appl. (2017). http://dx.doi.org/10.1177/1094342017702962
12. NESUS, Network for Sustainable Ultrascale Computing (Cost Action IC1305): A roadmap for research in sustainable ultrascale systems, October 2016
13. NVIDIA Corporation: Cublas library. NVIDIA Corporation, Santa Clara, California, vol. 15, no. 27 (2008)
14. Pérez, B., Bosque, J.L., Beivide, R.: Simplifying programming and load balancing of data parallel applications on heterogeneous systems. In: Proceedings of the 9th Annual Workshop on General Purpose Processing using Graphics Processing Unit, pp. 42–51. ACM (2016)
15. Riebler, H., Vaz, G., Plessl, C., Trainiti, E.M., Durelli, G.C., Del Sozzo, F., Santambrogio, M.D., Bolchini, C.: Using just-in-time code generation for transparent resource management in heterogeneous systems. In: 2016 IEEE 2nd International Forum on Research and Technologies for Society and Industry Leveraging a Better Tomorrow (RTSI), pp. 1–5. IEEE (2016)
16. Stone, J.E., Gohara, D., Shi, G.: OpenCL: a parallel programming standard for heterogeneous computing systems. Comput. Sci. Eng. **12**(1–3), 66–73 (2010)
17. TOP500.org: Top500 supercomputing sites, January 2017. http://www.top500.org/
18. Viñas, M., Fraguela, B.B., Andrade, D., Doallo, R.: Towards a high level approach for the programming of heterogeneous clusters. In: 2016 45th International Conference on Parallel Processing Workshops (ICPPW), pp. 106–114. IEEE (2016)
19. Wienke, S., Springer, P., Terboven, C., Mey, D.: OpenACC—first experiences with real-world applications. In: Kaklamanis, C., Papatheodorou, T., Spirakis, P.G. (eds.) Euro-Par 2012. LNCS, vol. 7484, pp. 859–870. Springer, Heidelberg (2012). doi:10.1007/978-3-642-32820-6_85
20. Wu, S., Dong, X., Chen, H., Dang, B.: OCLS: a simplified high-level abstraction based framework for heterogeneous systems. In: Park, J., Yi, G., Jeong, Y.S., Shen, H. (eds.) Advances in Parallel and Distributed Computing and Ubiquitous Services. LNEE, vol. 368, pp. 57–65. Springer, Singapore (2016). doi:10.1007/978-981-10-0068-3_7

GLT: A Unified API for Lightweight Thread Libraries

Adrián Castelló[1]([✉]), Sangmin Seo[2], Rafael Mayo[1], Pavan Balaji[2],
Enrique S. Quintana-Ortí[1], and Antonio J. Peña[3]

[1] Universitat Jaume I de Castelló, Castellón de la Plana, Spain
{adcastel,mayo,quintana}@uji.es
[2] Argonne National Laboratory, Lemont, IL, USA
{sseo,balaji}@anl.gov
[3] Barcelona Supercomputing Center (BSC), Barcelona, Spain
antonio.pena@bsc.es

Abstract. In recent years, several lightweight thread (LWT) libraries
have emerged to tackle exascale challenges. These offer programming
models (PMs) based on user-level threads and incorporate their own
lightweight mechanisms. However, each library proposes its own PM,
exposing different semantics and hindering portability.

To address this drawback, we have designed Generic Lightweight
Thread (GLT), an application programming interface that frames the
functionality of the most popular LWT libraries for high-performance
computing under a single PM. We implement GLT on top of Argobots,
MassiveThreads, and Qthreads. We provide GLT as a dynamic library,
as well as in the form of a static version based on macro preprocessing
resolution to reduce overhead. This paper discusses the GLT PM and
demonstrates its minimal performance impact.

1 Introduction

The number of processors in high-performance computing (HPC) systems has
been continuously increasing, as reflected in the supercomputers of the June
Top500 lists [5]. Following this trend, exascale systems are expected to leverage
hundreds of millions of cores. Hence, future applications will have to accommodate massive concurrency.

Leveraging this massive intranode parallelism efficiently with traditional
threading approaches may be difficult because of their relatively expensive context switching and synchronization mechanisms. In response, dynamic scheduling
and lightweight thread (LWT) and tasklet models are designed to deal with the
required levels of parallelism.

Different user-level thread (ULT) and tasklet libraries have been implemented in the past, such as Windows Fibers [14], Solaris Threads [2], Conver-
seThreads [13], Nanos++ [8], MassiveThreads [15], Qthreads [20], and Argobots [16] were the last three LWT solutions are compared. These solutions demonstrate semantic and performance benefits over the classic POSIX threads [3].

© Springer International Publishing AG 2017
F.F. Rivera et al. (Eds.): Euro-Par 2017, LNCS 10417, pp. 470–481, 2017.
DOI: 10.1007/978-3-319-64203-1_34

The variety of LWT libraries, however, hinders portability. Their programming models (PMs) and internal strategies differ among implementations, and hence developing and maintaining applications and runtime systems for different LWT approaches require considerable effort. In this scenario, a unified standard interface can be highly beneficial, as long as it supports most of the functionalities offered by the LWT libraries while maintaining their performance.

In this paper we introduce the design of a unified LWT application programming interface (API), named Generic Lightweight Thread (GLT), that groups the functionality of popular LWT solutions for HPC under the same PM. To the best of our knowledge, this is the first paper proposing a unified API for LWT solutions oriented to HPC. GLT is presented as a proof of concept in order to spark a joint effort from the community to design a standard LWT API.

We implement GLT on top of Argobots, MassiveThreads, and Qthreads. The library choices are based on the work presented in [9], where a set of LWT implementations was reviewed, from the semantic point of view, using a set of OpenMP microbenchmarks.

In addition to a dynamic GLT library that enables switching the underlying LWT implementation, we provide a static version to minimize the overhead. Using the GLT API, application programmers can develop a single code for different LWT approaches. The design of a single API to take advantage of the functionality of different LWT libraries, along with an efficient implementation composed primarily of wrappers resolved at compile time, provides a semantically powerful, efficient framework for LWT programming.

Our experiments demonstrate the feasibility of a GLT implementation, which does not exert any perceivable negative performance impact on applications. In our experiments, the average performance overhead when using static and dynamic GLT approaches, instead of the original LWT libraries, is 0.08% and 0.6%, respectively.

In summary, the contributions of this paper are as follows: (1) analysis of the semantics/PMs of the three major LWT solutions for HPC; (2) design of a generic LWT API capable of offering the functionality of its underlying libraries efficiently; (3) practical demonstration of the GLT portability; and (4) experimental performance evaluation of the GLT API on top of three reference LWT libraries for HPC.

The rest of the paper is organized as follows. Section 2 reviews related work. Section 3 offers background on our reference LWT libraries. Section 4 justifies the need for a unified LWT API. Section 5 discusses the GLT PM. Section 6 introduces the GLT unified API. Section 7 provides an in-depth performance analysis. Section 8 contains conclusions and future work proposals.

2   Related Work

In computer science, libraries commonly offer similar functionality. This situation may be caused by several circumstances, for example, a topic that is being developed by different institutions at the same time (e.g., MPICH [4] and Open

MPI [12]) or new implementations that aim to improve legacy or commercial codes (e.g., BLIS [19]).

In the past, some efforts have been made to join several solutions under a unique API. These common APIs aim to gather significant common features of the original libraries and offer them to users, who benefit from having to learn only a single API. One of these efforts in peer-to-peer overlay is [10], in which all the common functionality of the underlying libraries is joined as Tier-0 capabilities and offered under a unified API. Part of the community in cloud computing also proposed a common API in [17]. There have been also efforts in the unified runtime systems with the aim to unify heterogeneous multi-core architectures [6] and task scheduling [7].

No unified API has been available, however, for the diverse LWT libraries that exist today.

3   Background

In this section we provide an overview of the most widely adopted stand-alone LWT solutions for HPC.

Qthreads presents a PM with three hierarchical levels composed of shepherds, workers, and work units. In Qthreads, a large number of user-level threads may access any word in memory. Associated full/empty bits are used for synchronizing between ULTs as well as leveraging *mutex* mechanisms. As a drawback, allowing all threads to access any word in memory requires hidden synchronization, which may severely impair performance.

MassiveThreads exposes a recursive-oriented PM. It follows a work-first policy by default, which implies that upon creation, a ULT is immediately executed, pushing the ULT in execution into a *ready queue*. This policy may be configured at library compile time. MassiveThreads exploits the concept of worker as a hardware resource (generally a core), which is created at initialization time. This library does not allow creating ULTs in other threads' queues. Instead, it relies on a work-stealing mechanism.

Argobots is a flexible, mechanism-oriented LWT library. It supports two types of work units: ULTs and tasklets. While the former are the base for all the aforenamed libraries, the latter provides a lighter stackless work unit. Argobots provides the programmer with absolute control of all library resources. Programmers may dynamically create as many execution streams (abstraction of hardware resources) as desired during runtime instead of at initialization. Users can also decide the number of required work unit pools. Although there are default schedulers for each pool, programmers may create their own instances.

4   Benefits of a Unified LWT API

A unified threading API implemented on top of several underlying libraries avoids having to modify the application code in order to execute it on top of different threading solutions. Different hardware platforms may leverage distinct native LWT libraries for technical or strategic reasons. If more than one is available, users may want to select the library delivering the best performance for their particular case.

To support this assertation experimentally, we have designed two simple microbenchmarks that create fine-grained ULTs. These microbenchmarks are merely created in order to demonstrate how a programmer could benefit from the common API, selecting the desired underlying solution and achieving the best performance possible without modifying the application code.

In the first microbenchmark, each *thread* creates and executes a range of ULTs. In the second microbenchmark, a single *thread* creates all the ULTs, which are executed by all the *threads*. These microbenchmarks have been implemented on top of each native LWT library (Argobots, Qthreads, and MassiveThreads), as well as using the GLT API. Each test has been executed using 72 *threads* with 72, 720, and 1,440 ULTs. The results are the average of 1,000 executions on a 36-core (72-hardware thread) machine equipped with two 18-core Intel Xeon E5-2699 v3 (2.30 GHz) CPUs and 128 GB of RAM. The LWT libraries are Argobots 03-2016, Qthreads version 1.10, and MassiveThreads version 0.95.

Figure 1 shows the microbenchmarks' performance results. Although the GLT implementations are executed on top of the three libraries, only that offering the highest performance is shown. In Fig. 1a this corresponds to GLT over Argobots for 72 and 720 ULTs and to GLT over MassiveThreads for the largest size. In Fig. 1b, on the other hand, GLT over Argobots is the best option for the smallest dataset size, while GLT over the Qthreads library offers the highest performance for the other two problem sizes.

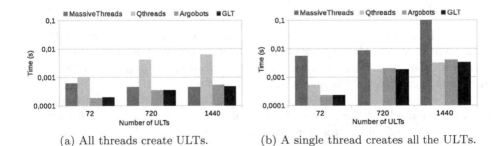

(a) All threads create ULTs.   (b) A single thread creates all the ULTs.

Fig. 1. Performance of the underlying LWT libraries and the best GLT implementation choice when a set of ULTs are created and executed.

These experiments demonstrate the benefits of using a unified LWT API on top of different underlying native implementations. Within the same platform, different LWT libraries may yield distinct performance for different applications. Even the same application may benefit from different LWT implementations depending on the dataset sizes. Therefore, a unified LWT API such as GLT enables users to select the most appropriate underlying native LWT implementation while avoiding the additional work of implementing the same application using several LWT APIs. Determining the best underlying implementation for a particular case is left out of the scope of this paper.

5   GLT Programming Model

As introduced in Sect. 3, each LWT library offers its own PM. Therefore, choosing a correct default PM for GLT is critical.

Figure 2 depicts the set of elements that compose the GLT PM. A *GLT_thread* is composed of the operating system (OS) thread, a queue of ULTs/tasklets, and a scheduler that sets the order of the execution of these work units. The different functionality exposed by their PMs is explained in this section.

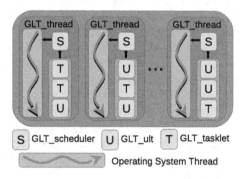

Fig. 2. GLT PM elements abstraction.

A GLT thread executes ULTs in an OS thread. GLT threads are conceptually equivalent to *shepherds* in Qthreads, *execution streams* in Argobots, and *workers* in MassiveThreads. ULTs are conceptually equivalent to *qthreads* in Qthreads and to *threads* in Argobots and MassiveThreads.

GLT sets the environment during the initialization function. By default, one thread is created per CPU core. This number, however, can be defined by the user by means of an environment variable. Each thread is bound to a specific CPU core in the system.

Furthermore, nothing prevents users from changing the default initial resources for the underlying LWT library (e.g., number of pools in Argobots or number of workers per thread in Qthreads) by means of its own environment variables, which is honored by the GLT implementation. Affinity is always enabled mapping one GLT_thread to each CPU system. No other bindings are allowed due to the GLT PM.

While all our reference libraries provide ULTs, Argobots additionally supports tasklets. Tasklets are lighter than ULTs, but they cannot migrate or yield because a tasklet does not own a stack. These work units are suitable for computation codes that do not include blocking calls. All codes that can be executed by a tasklet can also be executed by a ULT. If GLT is used on top of a library with no native support for tasklets, ULTs are transparently used underneath instead, yielding the expected functionality but no performance benefits.

GLT scheduling relies on the underlying library. This may be specified during the configuration step prior to building those libraries or, as in the case of Argobots, can be changed at execution time.

6   GLT Design and Implementation Details

This section discusses the GLT design choices and describes several implementation details.

6.1   API

GLT objects start with the upper-case prefix "GLT_". Table 1 shows the equivalences between the main GLT object types and those of the reference libraries.

Table 1. GLT object equivalences (prefix shown next to each library name).

GLT (GLT_)	Argobots (ABT_)	Qthreads	MassiveThreads (myth_)
ult	thread	aligned_t	thread_t
tasklet	task	aligned_t	thread_t
thread	xstream	qthread_shepherd_id_t	thread_t
mutex	mutex	aligned_t	mutex_t
barrier	barrier	qt_barrier_t	barrier_t
cond	cond	aligned_t	cond_t

GLT functions are organized into modules depending on their functionality. Many GLT functions are simple wrappers to those in the underlying LWT libraries, hence yielding low performance overhead. Some other GLT functions require more elaborate implementations because no direct mapping to the underlying library functionality exists.

GLT is divided into modules that enclose the main necessary semantics. The functionality supported by a complete unified LWT PM is distributed into the following 7 API modules:

- **Setup.** This module initializes and finalizes the library.
- **Work Unit.** It is composed of 18 functions that are used for work unit management. It supports two types of work units: ULTs and tasklets. In case the underlying library does not support tasklets, ULTs are leveraged to deliver analogous functionality.
- **Mutex.** This module includes 5 basic functions to create, destroy, lock, unlock, and try to lock mutexes. Qthreads supports only locking and unlocking natively because of the full/empty-bit mechanism; the remaining functions have been implemented on top of these semantics.
- **Barrier.** Three functions are provided for barrier management.
- **Condition.** Five condition management functions are supported natively by Argobots and MassiveThreads and developed for Qthreads.
- **Util.** It consists of 6 functions to measure elapsed times or to obtain a timestamp and 2 functions that return the number of threads and the rank of the current thread.
- **Key.** This module hosts 4 work-unit data management functions. Natively supported by Argobots and MassiveThreads and implemented for Qthreads.

Although some LWT libraries offer a more complete set of functions, we have included only those that are relevant for the PM we propose. However, we plan to study the addition of the extra functionality if any PM benefits from them.

6.2   Implementations

Our GLT implementation can be used in two ways. On the one hand, a set of *dynamic* libraries compiled on top of the different reference libraries may be generated. This eases the switch among the underlying LWT implementations by linking the application to a different library at load time. On the other hand, we have devised our GLT implementation as a *header-only* library. This second approach offers higher performance than the former because all the functions are labeled as `static inline`. Most compilers will honor these modifiers and prevent the additional function call. The performance result in most cases is analogous to that obtained if the user employs the original library directly, yielding no performance impact for those functions with a direct mapping to the underlying library.

6.3   Semantic Mapping

GLT is largely composed of wrappers to the underlying LWT library functions. The mapping between the most important functions of the GLT API and the reference libraries is shown in Table 2.

The lack of tasklet support in Qthreads and MassiveThreads is compensated with the use of the ULT functions. Moreover, since MassiveThreads does not allow creating ULTs in other workers' ready queue, when a `glt_tasklet/ult_creation_to` is called, the library just creates a ULT in the current worker's queue. Despite the fact that the different implementation approaches over different underlying native LWT libraries may have performance implications, these

Table 2. Mapping between some GLT functions and their equivalent in the underlying libraries (prefix shown next to each library name).

GLT (glt_)	Argobots (ABT_)	Qthreads (qthread_)	MassiveThreads (myth_)
tasklet_creation	task_create	fork	create
ult_creation	thread_create	fork	create
ult_creation_to	thread_create	fork_to	create
yield	thread_yield	yield	yield
ult_join	thread_free	readFF	join

all conform to the exposed GLT semantics (offering the same functionality to GLT users) while transparently leveraging the most efficient mechanism underneath.

7 Performance Evaluation

We next compare the performance of our test cases implemented directly on top of the low-level libraries with the codes that use the GLT API. The results correspond to the average of 1,000 executions. The software and hardware configuration employed was introduced in Sect. 4.

7.1 Microbenchmarks

We leverage the Callgrind profiling tool [18] to measure the overhead in terms of instructions per call of the most frequently used functions of the GLT code for our three reference LWT libraries. These functions are initialization (`Init`), work unit allocation (`Malloc`), work unit creation (`Creation`), yield (`Yield`), join (`Join`), and number of threads query (`Num_thr`).

Figure 3 shows our results for the Qthreads, MassiveThreads, and Argobots GLT implementations, comparing the results with the native approaches. The plots expose a common pattern: `Init`, `Malloc`, and `Creation` show a small increment in the number of instructions in both GLT variants (*dynamic* vs *static*); but `Yield`, `Join`, and `num_threads` experience this increment only in the stand-alone version of GLT. These results reflect that the second group of functions contains pure wrappers to the original functions and that the additional function call overhead is added only in case of leveraging a separate GLT library. The library initialization function adds a relatively high number of instructions because of the GLT environment set up. Nevertheless, this is a one-time overhead introducing merely 10–15% additional instructions compared with the native LWT solutions. The `Malloc` overhead (up to 4 instructions per call) is caused by the type casting of the value returned by the allocation function to the appropriate work unit pointer. The instructions added in `Creation` are due to the function pointer casting and the return of the work unit handler. These results confirm that the use of the GLT library as a high-level LWT API introduces fairly low overhead.

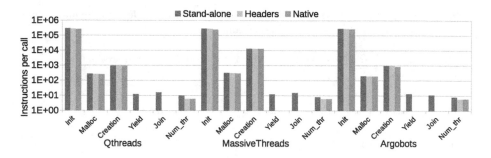

Fig. 3. Overhead (%) GLT approaches compared with overhead (%) native libraries.

7.2 N-Queens

We evaluated the overhead of the GLT API using a translation from an OpenMP version of N-Queens [11]. The number of lines of code needed in the translation are 185 for Argobots code compared with 158 for Qthreads, MassiveThreads, and GLT. Our unified API does not add more lines to the code; indeed, it even reduces the number compared with Argobots. The reason is the automatic environment setup described in Sect. 6.

In the base OpenMP implementation, a single thread creates the first set of tasks (to place a queen in a cell) and executes a `taskwait`. Each task creates more tasks and waits for their termination. Our implementation of this algorithm using LWTs follows the same philosophy. The main thread creates the first work units, and each of these is placed into other threads' queue until each thread has at least one work unit to be executed. Once that is completed, each thread creates its own work. The threads wait for the finalization using the *join* function.

Table 3 summarizes the average overhead of several thread configurations (from 1 to 72 threads), for three problem sizes—10, 11, and 12 queens—and the reference LWT libraries. While the average overhead for the stand-alone version varies from 0.28% to 0.56%, for the header-only GLT deployment this overhead is less than 0.1%.

These results showcase the low overhead introduced by the use of the GLT API. The results also show a constant behavior that indicates that the overhead is not caused by the size problem. The largest cost with respect to the native implementations is under 0.6%.

7.3 UTS Benchmark

UTS Benchmark is a parallel code that measures the performance attained when executing an exhaustive search on an unbalanced tree. The tree is built at execution time by using a divisible random number generator that splits the structure, making possible the parallel processing while still generating a deterministic tree. We translated the original code written in Pthreads to our GLT API using 71 code lines for the Argobots implementation and 38 for MassiveThreads, Qthreads, and GLT.

Table 3. Average overhead (%) executing the N-Queens application using *headers* (H) and *stand-alone* (S) GLT implementations over the three libraries.

GLT underlying library (mode)	Number of Queens		
	10	11	12
Argobots (H)	0.01	0.06	0.04
Argobots (S)	0.28	0.36	0.32
MassiveThreads (H)	0.02	0.01	0.00
MassiveThreads (S)	0.48	0.33	0.49
Qthreads (H)	0.08	0.08	0.09
Qthreads (S)	0.43	0.51	0.56

In the original Pthreads implementation, the main thread initializes the tree and places the first (tree) node into its own queue. Then all threads execute the same function. First, the next node in the queue is executed, and this node creates more nodes that are pushed into the local queue. If its local queue is empty, a thread tries to steal a certain number of nodes from other queues.

In our implementation, a work unit is created for each thread, and work-stealing is performed as in the original code. Accessing other threads' queues requires synchronization among threads and is done via *GLT_mutex*.

In this scenario, GLT can leverage the lighter tasklet work unit because the code does not include any blocking or system call. As discussed in Sect. 6, GLT implementations over MassiveThreads and Qthreads employ ULTs instead of tasklets. For reference, we also include the results for native Argobots based on ULTs.

Table 4. GLT average overhead executing the UTS benchmark using headers (H) and stand-alone (S) GLT implementations over the three underlying libraries.

GLT underlying library (mode)	Problem size			
	T1	T1L	T1XL	T1XXL
Argobots task (H)	0.06	0.00	0.01	0.00
Argobots task (S)	0.08	0.36	0.39	0.28
Argobots ULT (H)	0.03	0.01	0.01	0.00
Argobots ULT (S)	0.24	0.55	0.22	0.53
MassiveThreads (H)	0.11	0.00	0.08	0.05
MassiveThreads (S)	0.45	0.50	0.45	0.18
Qthreads (H)	0.00	0.01	0.02	0.06
Qthreads (S)	0.30	0.55	0.58	0.29

We calculated the average overhead for all the executions of different problem sizes in order to obtain a global vision of the overhead introduced by the

GLT API. Table 4 shows the average overhead when executing the UTS benchmark with problems T1, T1L, T1XL, and T1XXL (of 4 million, 102 million, 1.6 billion, and 4.2 billion nodes, respectively), on top of the three underlying libraries, modifying the number of threads from 1 to 72. As in the N-Queens case, the difference using the stand-alone (S) and header-only (H) GLT versions is perceivable, being under 0.6% for the former and just slightly above 0.1% for the latter. The results also show a trend that does not correspond with the problem size, so it indicates that the overhead is not caused by the size problem.

8   Conclusions

In this work we have introduced the GLT API [1]. This library proposes a unified API for LWT solutions that is the first attempt to standardize those PMs. Moreover, we have implemented GLT on top of the major general-purpose LWT solutions for HPC: Argobots, MassiveThreads, and Qthreads.

In addition, we have discussed the GLT PM and decomposed the API's modules. Furthermore, we have presented an example of the semantic mapping between the GLT API with the LWT solutions. Using two microbenchmarks we have also justified the need for a unified LWT API from the point of view of portability.

Our performance evaluation, based on stand-alone and header-only implementations of the GLT API, demonstrates the low performance overhead of this approach. We have demonstrated this overhead with a set of microbenchmarks that measure the instructions per call added with GLT. Moreover, we have assessed the overhead by comparing the execution time of two applications where, the stand-alone implementation produced an average overhead under 0.6%, while the header-only version showed an average overhead below 0.1%.

In conclusion, we have demonstrated the portability benefits that a unified API for LWT libraries can offer to programmers translating their applications from OpenMP and Pthreads to GLT API. As part of future work, we plan to implement several high-level PMs on top of the GLT API, such as OpenMP or OmpSs. Moreover, we plan to augment the API with additional functionality that some PMs/applications can benefit from.

Acknowledgements. Researchers from the Universitat Jaume I de Castelló were supported by project TIN2014-53495-R of the MINECO, the Generalitat Valenciana fellowship programme Vali+d 2015, and FEDER. Antonio J. Peña is cofinancied by the Spanish Ministry of Economy and Competitiveness under Juan de la Cierva fellowship number IJCI-2015-23266. This work was partially supported by the U.S. Dept. of Energy, Office of Science, Office of Advanced Scientific Computing Research (SC-21), under contract DE-AC02-06CH11357.

References

1. Generic Lightweight Thread. http://github.com/adcastel/GLT
2. Programming with Solaris Threads. http://docs.oracle.com/cd/E19455-01/806-5257/

3. Pthreads API. https://computing.llnl.gov/tutorials/pthreads/
4. MPICH, High-Performance Portable MPI (2016). http://www.mpich.org/
5. TOP500 Supercomputer Sites (June 2016). www.top.500.org/
6. Augonnet, C., Namyst, R.: A unified runtime system for heterogeneous multi-core architectures. In: César, E., Alexander, M., Streit, A., Träff, J.L., Cérin, C., Knüpfer, A., Kranzlmüller, D., Jha, S. (eds.) Euro-Par 2008. LNCS, vol. 5415, pp. 174–183. Springer, Heidelberg (2009). doi:10.1007/978-3-642-00955-6_22
7. Augonnet, C., Thibault, S., Namyst, R., Wacrenier, P.A.: Starpu: a unified platform for task scheduling on heterogeneous multicore architectures. Concurr. Comput.: Pract. Exp. **23**(2), 187–198 (2011)
8. BSC: Nanos++. http://pm.bsc.es/projects/nanox/
9. Castelló, A., Peña, A.J., Seo, S., Mayo, R., Balaji, P., Quintana-Ortí, E.S.: A review of lightweight thread approaches for high performance computing. In: IEEE International Conference on Cluster Computing, Taiwan, September 2016
10. Dabek, F., Zhao, B., Druschel, P., Kubiatowicz, J., Stoica, I.: Towards a common API for structured peer-to-peer overlays. In: Kaashoek, M.F., Stoica, I. (eds.) IPTPS 2003. LNCS, vol. 2735, pp. 33–44. Springer, Heidelberg (2003). doi:10.1007/978-3-540-45172-3_3
11. Duran González, A., Teruel, X., Ferrer, R., Martorell Bofill, X., Ayguadé Parra, E.: Barcelona OpenMP tasks suite: a set of benchmarks targeting the exploitation of task parallelism in OpenMP. In: 38th International Conference on Parallel Processing, pp. 124–131 (2009)
12. Gabriel, E., Fagg, G.E., Bosilca, G., Angskun, T., Dongarra, J.J., Squyres, J.M., Sahay, V., Kambadur, P., et al.: Open MPI: goals, concept, and design of a next generation MPI implementation. In: Kranzlmüller, D., Kacsuk, P., Dongarra, J. (eds.) EuroPVM/MPI 2004. LNCS, vol. 3241, pp. 97–104. Springer, Heidelberg (2004). doi:10.1007/978-3-540-30218-6_19
13. Kalé, L.V., Bhandarkar, M.A., Jagathesan, N., Krishnan, S., Yelon, J.: Converse: an interoperable framework for parallel programming. In: Proceedings of the 10th International Parallel Processing Symposium (IPPS), pp. 212–217, April 1996
14. Microsoft MSDN Library: Fibers. http://msdn.microsoft.com/en-us/library/ms682661.aspx
15. Nakashima, J., Taura, K.: MassiveThreads: a thread library for high productivity languages. In: Agha, G., Igarashi, A., Kobayashi, N., Masuhara, H., Matsuoka, S., Shibayama, E., Taura, K. (eds.) Concurrent Objects and Beyond. LNCS, vol. 8665, pp. 222–238. Springer, Heidelberg (2014). doi:10.1007/978-3-662-44471-9_10
16. Seo, S., Amer, A., Balaji, P., Bordage, C., Bosilca, G., Brooks, A., Carns, P., Castelló, A., Genet, D., Herault, T., Jindal, P., Kalé, L.V., Krishnamoorthy, S., Lif-flander, J., Lu, H., Meneses, E., Snir, M., Sun, Y., Beckman, P.: Argobots: a light-weight threading/tasking framework (2017). https://collab.cels.anl.gov/display/ARGOBOTS/
17. Silva, L.A.B., Costa, C., Oliveira, J.L.: A common API for delivering services over multi-vendor cloud resources. J. Syst. Softw. **86**(9), 2309–2317 (2013)
18. Developers, V.: Callgrind: a call-graph generating cache and branch prediction profiler (2010)
19. Van Zee, F.G., van de Geijn, R.A.: BLIS: a framework for rapidly instantiating BLAS functionality. ACM Trans. Math. Softw. **41**(3), 14 (2015)
20. Wheeler, K.B., Murphy, R.C., Thain, D.: Qthreads: An API for programming with millions of lightweight threads. In: Proceedings of the 2008 Workshop on Multithreaded Architectures and Applications (MTAAP), April 2008

PASCAL: A Parallel Algorithmic SCALable Framework for N-body Problems

Laleh Aghababaie Beni$^{(\boxtimes)}$ and Aparna Chandramowlishwaran

University of California Irvine, Irvine, USA
{laghabab,amowli}@uci.edu

Abstract. We propose PASCAL, a *parallel unified algorithmic framework* for generalized N-body problems. PASCAL utilizes tree data structures and user-controlled pruning or approximations to reduce the asymptotic runtime complexity from being linear in the number of data points to be logarithmic. In PASCAL, the domain scientists express their N-body problem in terms of application-specific operations, and PASCAL generates the pruning and approximation conditions automatically from this high-level specification. In order to evaluate PASCAL, we generate solutions for six problems: k-nearest neighbors, range search, Euclidean minimum spanning tree, kernel density estimation, expectation maximization (EM), and Hausdorff distance chosen from various domains.

We show that applying domain-specific optimizations and parallelizations to the algorithms generated by PASCAL achieves 10× to 230× speedup compared to state-of-the-art libraries on a dual-socket Intel Xeon processor with 16 cores on real world datasets. We also obtain a novel out-of-the-box asymptotically optimal algorithm for Hausdorff distance calculation and an improved algorithm for EM. This shows the impact and potential of PASCAL in rapidly extending to a larger class of problems that are yet to be explored.

Keywords: N-body problems · kd-trees · Multi-core parallelization

1 Introduction and Motivation

N-body problems are those in which an update to a single element in the system depends on every other element. The general form applies a set of operators $\{op_1, ..., op_m\}$ to m datasets using a kernel function, $\mathcal{K}$, as follows.

$$op_1, ..., op_m \text{ Compute } \mathcal{K}(x_1, ..., x_m) \tag{1}$$

where $x_1 \in \mathcal{D}_1,..., x_m \in \mathcal{D}_m$ and $\mathcal{D}_1...\mathcal{D}_m$ are the m datasets. The naive computation of these problems is asymptotically $O(N^m)$ which is expensive.

N-body problems are ubiquitous, with applications in various domains ranging from scientific computing simulations to machine learning [8,9,16]. N-body methods were identified as one of the original seven dwarfs or motifs [2] and

© Springer International Publishing AG 2017
F.F. Rivera et al. (Eds.): Euro-Par 2017, LNCS 10417, pp. 482–496, 2017.
DOI: 10.1007/978-3-319-64203-1_35

are believed to be important in the next decade. In fact, the well-known Fast Multipole Method (FMM) made the list for the top 10 algorithms having the greatest influence on the development of science and engineering in the 20th century [7]. According to data mining researchers, EM is one of the top ten algorithms having the most impact on data mining research [17].

However, a big gap exists between the algorithm one designs on paper and the code that runs efficiently on a billion-core system. It is time-consuming to write fast, parallel, and scalable code for an N-body problem on any architecture. On the other hand, the sheer scale and growth of modern scientific datasets necessitate exploiting the power of both *asymptotically fast parallel algorithms* and *approximation algorithms* where we can potentially trade-off accuracy for performance [11]. The goal of PASCAL is to automate the generation of asymptotically optimal N-body algorithms using the definition of the problem provided by domain scientists. This is especially useful in rapidly growing fields such as machine learning and data mining where new models are created at a much faster rate than optimal algorithms and implementations for the models.

Contributions and Findings. First, this paper strives to combine two areas that traditionally have not combined forces, namely high-performance computing and machine learning. We apply the knowledge and expertise gained from optimizing and tuning scientific N-body computations to N-body problems from other domains. We make the following contributions.

1. We design an algorithmic framework for N-body problems called PASCAL to automatically generate prune and approximate conditions from a high-level user specification. PASCAL can generate $\mathcal{O}(N \log N)$ and $\mathcal{O}(N)$ algorithms if the operators, and kernel function in Eq. 1 satisfy the decomposability property over subsets, and monotonically decrease with distance respectively. PASCAL is also the first to generalize beyond two operators by the design of a *Nested Prune* generator (Sect. 4).
2. We apply domain-specific optimizations and parallelize the algorithms generated by PASCAL. An asymptotically optimal algorithm generated by PASCAL combined with optimizations and parallelization results in 10–230× speedup compared to state-of-the-art libraries and software such as Weka, Scikit-learn, MLPACK, and MATLAB (Sects. 5 and 7).
3. PASCAL is able to generate an approximation condition for the log-likelihood step of EM which results in an improved EM algorithm for Gaussian Mixture Models. This algorithm is 7–16× faster compared to the best competing implementation. PASCAL also generates a nested prune condition for Hausdorff distance resulting in a new $\mathcal{O}(N)$ algorithm. To the best of our knowledge, this is the first dual-tree algorithm for Hausdorff distance (Sect. 4).

As a result, this paper lays a solid foundation for future scalable implementations of N-body problems on emerging systems. PASCAL enables us to rapidly obtain both an optimal algorithm and its parallel implementation for new and existing N-body problems.

2   Related Work

N-body Algorithms in Physical Simulations. The most popular and widely used fast algorithms for classical N-body problems are the Barnes-Hut [3] and the Fast Multipole Method (FMM) [9]. They use trees to approximate distance computations and achieve sub $\mathcal{O}(N^2)$ asymptotic runtime. There has been significant work on parallelizing tree codes [12].

PASCAL differs from the preceding work in many ways. First, PASCAL supports algorithms and operations beyond what is usually considered in classical physics. This makes PASCAL more general. Second, we consider high-dimensional trees (e.g. kd-trees, ball-trees, cover trees) which are required to handle high-dimensional datasets. Third, our approach is more portable and easily extensible compared to previous approaches which focus on optimizing a specific algorithm for a specific architecture.

N-body Algorithms in Machine Learning. While parallel N-body algorithms in physics have received significant attention, the same is not true for machine learning (ML). There are a number of freely accessible ML libraries, however, each of them lacks in one or both of the two ways, (a) efficient optimal algorithms and (b) parallelism and scalability on modern machines. For instance, MLPACK [6] which is a state-of-the-art C++ ML library offers a limited set of fast algorithms but is not parallel, or distributed. Other popular libraries emphasize ease of use but scale poorly such as Weka toolkit [10]. Even others implement fast algorithms but in languages such as Python resulting in poor performance such as Scitkit-learn [15].

Luckily, there is a theory on *generalized N-body* algorithms [5,8] which is similar in spirit to long studied physics algorithms such as FMM that run in linear time. This theory is a stepping stone to our work but it is limited in two ways – (a) the pruning and approximation conditions are designed manually for every problem, and (b) the theory is limited to problems with only 2 operators. Although this is a useful first step, this approach is not scalable. In this paper, we address the above limitations by proposing an algorithm to automate the design of pruning and approximation conditions for two or more operators.

3 N-body Problems

This section provides an overview of N-body problems, and their main structure. Later, in Sect. 4, we will see how they fit in the PASCAL framework.

Given a system of N *reference* points (N_r) and N *query* points (N_q), an update to a single element depends on every other element in the system. The most familiar example arises in physical simulations and has the following form.

$$\forall_q, \sum_r K(x_q, x_r) \cdot s(x_r),   \tag{2}$$

where $s(x_r)$ is the density of the reference point and $K(x_q, x_r)$ is an interaction kernel that specifies *the physics* of the problem. For instance, Laplace kernel is defined as, $K(x_q, x_r) = \frac{1}{||x_q - x_r||}$ which models gravitational interactions.

This style of N-body problem arises in other significant domains and the common theme that brings these problems under a single umbrella is the insight that their inner-loop computations are analogous and naively require $\mathcal{O}(N^2)$ operations for the all-pairs computation. Below, we present six examples.

(a) **k-Nearest Neighbor (k-NN) Search.** One of the most ubiquitous N-body problems in ML is k-NN search which is defined as, $\forall q$, $\arg\min_r^k ||x_q - x_r||$ where, for each query point x_q we want to find its k nearest neighbors, *i.e.* the k reference points x_r whose distance to x_q is minimal. Comparing this to our familiar physical summation (Eq. 2), we see that the *kernel function* in this case is the Euclidean distance function and the operator sum has been replaced by another operator, arg min. The inputs for PASCAL in this case are the operators set, $\{\forall, \text{arg min}\}$ and the kernel function, $||x_q - x_r||$.

(b) **Range Search (RS).** A related problem is range search, where the kernel function is a *delta* function. We want to find all the reference points that fall within a range $(h_{\min}, h_{\max})$ of a query point, x_q defined as $\forall q$, $\bigcup \arg_r I(h_{\min} \leq ||x_q - x_r|| \leq h_{\max})$ where $I(h_{min} \leq ||x_q - x_r|| \leq h_{max})$ is a delta function.

(c) **Kernel Density Estimation (KDE).** Another example of sum-based accumulations from statistics is KDE, which is a widely used method for non-parametric density estimation. The goal is to estimate the probability density at each x_q, using a kernel function K_σ. It is defined as $\forall q$, $\frac{1}{|N_r|} \sum_r K_\sigma \left(\frac{||x_q - x_r||}{\sigma} \right)$ where K_σ is a zero-centered probability density function (*e.g.* Gaussian) and σ is the bandwidth of the kernel. When the distance between two points $||x_q - x_r||$ is very large, the contribution of the kernel function to the probability density at x_q is small. Therefore, we can approximate the kernel sum at the expense of reduced precision to achieve a faster algorithm similar to Barnes-Hut and FMM.

(d) **Minimum Spanning Tree (MST).** This is one of the oldest problems in computational geometry. Given a set of points $S \in \mathbb{R}^d$, the goal is to find the lowest weight spanning tree in the complete graph G, where the edge weights are given by the Euclidean distance between two points. We consider the iterative Boruvka's algorithm for MST [14]. Borukva's MST is an iterative algorithm that connects each component to its nearest vertex until only one component, the MST, remains. The computational bottleneck in MST is finding the nearest neighbor component which is identical to example (a). Computing all neighbor pairs efficiently will result in an efficient Boruvka's algorithm.

(e) **Expectation Maximization (EM).** EM is a popular algorithm used in mixture models. Here, we consider problems where EM is used to learn the parameters of a multivariate Gaussian Mixture Model (GMM). Consider a dataset $D = \{x_1, x_2, .., x_N\}$, where $x_i \in \mathbb{R}^d$ generated independently from an underlying distribution $p(x)$. If $p(x)$ is a Gaussian distribution, we can define a GMM as,

$$p(x|\theta) = \sum_{k=1}^{K} \pi_k f(x|\mu_k, \Sigma_k), \quad f(x_i|\theta_k) = \frac{1}{\sqrt{2\pi|\Sigma_k|}} e^{-\frac{1}{2}(x_i-\mu_k)^T \Sigma_k^{-1}(x_i-\mu_k)}$$

where K is the number of Gaussian mixture components, and $\theta_k = \{\mu_k, \Sigma_k\}$ are the parameters of Gaussian component, k, with mean vector μ_k and covariance matrix Σ_k. π_k are the mixing weights ($\sum_{k=1}^{K} \pi_k = 1$). EM starts with an initial estimate of θ (generated randomly, or using k-means), and iteratively updates θ until convergence (i.e. log-likelihood change is less than a threshold) as follows.

1. **E-step**: Compute the *responsibility*, $r_{nk} = \frac{\pi_k f(x_n|\mu_k, \Sigma_k)}{\sum_{j=1}^{K} \pi_j f(x_n|\mu_j, \Sigma_j)}$ (weight factor of data point n for cluster k).
2. **M-step**: Re-estimate θ using the responsibilities measured in the E-step.
3. Compute the **log-likelihood**, $l(\theta) = \sum_{n=1}^{N} \log \sum_{k=1}^{K} \pi_k f(x_n|\mu_k, \Sigma_k)$ for convergence check.

E-step and log-likelihood computation are the two N-body problems in EM.

(f) Hausdorff Distance. The last example is Hausdorff distance calculation which has applications in computer vision. The Hausdorff distance between two subsets is computed as, $\max_q, \min_r \|x_q - x_r\|$ where $\|x_q - x_r\|$ is the Euclidean distance which is the kernel function and the set of operators is $\{\texttt{max}, \texttt{min}\}$.

4   PASCAL Framework

Leveraging the commonalities between N-body problems gives rise to the PASCAL framework shown in Fig. 1, which consists of space partitioning trees, a prune/approximate condition generator, and a tree-traversal scheme. We then apply domain specific transformations and parallelize the algorithms generated by PASCAL to produce an efficient code for comparison against other state-of-the-art libraries and software. The blue shaded boxes in the figure represent the contributions which we will discuss in detail in the rest of this paper.

Space-Partitioning Trees. A powerful class of space-partitioning tree-based algorithms exist that can reduce the complexity of N-body problems from $\mathcal{O}(N^2)$ to $\mathcal{O}(N \log N)$ or even $\mathcal{O}(N)$ [3,9]. These algorithms use techniques such as approximation and pruning to estimate or discard regions of the space.

An example we consider is kd-trees which are used in data analytics and mining [4]. These are high-dimensional binary trees which maintain a bounding

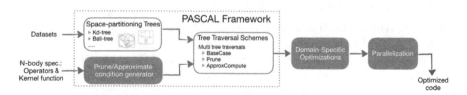

Fig. 1. Block diagram outlining the overall approach. The dotted box represents the PASCAL framework and the blue shaded boxes are the contributions. (Color figure online)

box for all the points in each node. Children are formed by recursively sub-dividing the parent's bounding box along the median of its largest dimension. We stop partitioning when each node contains no more than l points ($l > 0$). The bounding box information allows us to efficiently compute the minimum and maximum node-to-point or node-to-node distances during evaluation without accessing the actual points in each node, which is critical for performance.

Tree Traversals. Algorithm 1 describes multi-tree traversal given two inputs, a set of nodes and a rule set. The rule set consists of the following 3 functions.

BaseCase implements the direct point-to-point computation. For instance, for k-NN, this is equivalent to computing the distance between all the points in the reference node to every point in the query node.

Prune or Approximate checks to see if the computation for that set of nodes can be *approximated* or *pruned* based on the condition generated by Algorithm 2. In some cases, the

---

Algorithm 1. MultiTreeTraversal

Input: Nodes set $\{\mathcal{N}_1, \mathcal{N}_2, ..., \mathcal{N}_m\} \approx \mathcal{N}^{all}$, rule set $\mathcal{R}$.
1: **if** $\mathcal{R}$.Prune/Approximate($\mathcal{N}_1, \mathcal{N}_2, ..., \mathcal{N}_m$) **then**
2:    **return** $\mathcal{R}$.ComputeApprox($\mathcal{N}_1, \mathcal{N}_2, ..., \mathcal{N}_m$)
3: **if** ($\forall \mathcal{N}_i \in \mathcal{N}^{all}$ is leaf) **then**
4:    $\mathcal{R}$.BaseCase($\mathcal{N}_1, \mathcal{N}_2, ..., \mathcal{N}_m$)
5: **else**
6:    **for all** $\mathcal{N}_i \in \mathcal{N}^{all}$ **do**
7:       **if** $\mathcal{N}_i$ is leaf **then** $\mathcal{N}_i^{split} = \mathcal{N}_i$
8:       **else** $\mathcal{N}_i^{split} = \{\mathcal{N}_i.right, \mathcal{N}_i.left\}$
9:    PowerSet-Tuples = $\{(\mathcal{N}'_1, ..., \mathcal{N}'_m) | \mathcal{N}'_i \in \mathcal{N}_i^{split}\}$
10:   **for all** $(\mathcal{N}''_1, ..., \mathcal{N}''_m) \in$ PowerSet-Tuples **do**
11:      MultiTreeTraversal($(\mathcal{N}''_1, ..., \mathcal{N}''_m)$)

---

algorithm prunes entire sub-trees, so the nodes and their descendants will not be visited.

ComputeApprox replaces the computation with the center contribution of each node multiplied by the density of that node which is equivalent to the number of data points in that node. This is only for approximation problems.

While the operations above are not completely orthogonal, they are convenient and powerful to express the range of N-body algorithms. Not only does this representation abstract the actual computation from the traversal, it also abstracts the tree type which gives us the freedom to plug and play with different trees. Moreover, we are able to express both *pruning* and *approximation* algorithms in the same framework which enables us to translate our optimizations and parallelization to a much larger class of algorithms.

Prune/Approximate Condition Generator. In order to generate a prune or approximate condition, we first classify N-body problems into 3 categories namely, (a) approximation, (b) single pruning, and (c) nested pruning. Approximation problems are those in which the contribution by a subset of the data to the solution can be approximated by a smaller subset. Two examples are KDE and EM. Pruning problems are those in which a part of the data and associated computation are discarded. The main distinction between single and nested pruning is that former has only one pruning opportunity (*e.g.* k-NN) while the latter has more than one opportunity for pruning (*e.g.* Hausdorff distance).

Algorithm 2 generates one of three conditions and distinguishes the category of problems by maintaining a queue of possible prune opportunities called `PrunePipeline` (Line 1). We iterate through the operators' set, OP and kernel function, $\mathcal{K}$ and check if there is any pruning opportunity. If so, we push the `reverse` of OP and/or $\mathcal{K}$ into the `PrunePipeline` (Lines 2–6). The `reverse` function is defined for operators and kernel function, and defines the reverse of their functionality. For example, the `reverse` of $||x_q - x_r|| < h$ is $||x_q - x_r|| > h$, and the `reverse` of `min` operator is the relational operator *greater than* ($>$).

Algorithm 2. Prune/Approximate Condition Generator

Input: Node set $\{\mathcal{N}_1, \mathcal{N}_2, ..., \mathcal{N}_m\} \approx \mathcal{N}^{all}$, kernel function $\mathcal{K}$, operators set OP, threshold σ.

Output: The prune/approximate condition

1: queue<Function> PrunePipeline
2: **for all** $(op_i \in OP)$ **do**
3:    **if** $(op_i.\text{isComparative}())$ **then**
4:       PrunePipeline.push(reverse(op_i))
5: **if** $\mathcal{K}.\text{isComparative}()$ **then**
6:    PrunePipeline.push(reverse($\mathcal{K}$))
7: // Approximation category[a]
8: **if** (PrunePipline.size == 0) **then**
9:    $\mathcal{K}_{\min} \leftarrow \min\{\mathcal{K}(\mathcal{N}_1, \mathcal{N}_2, ..., \mathcal{N}_m)\}$
10:   $\mathcal{K}_{\max} \leftarrow \max\{\mathcal{K}(\mathcal{N}_1, \mathcal{N}_2, ..., \mathcal{N}_m)\}$
11:   $(\mathcal{N}_1^c, \mathcal{N}_2^c, ..., \mathcal{N}_m^c) \leftarrow$ tuple of node centers
12:   $\mathcal{K}_{\text{center}} \leftarrow \mathcal{K}(\mathcal{N}_1^c, \mathcal{N}_2^c, ..., \mathcal{N}_m^c)$
13:   **return** $\mathcal{K}_{\max} - \mathcal{K}_{\min} < \sigma \times \mathcal{K}_{\text{center}}$
14: // Single prune category
15: **if** (PrunePipline.size == 1) **then**
16:   $\tau \leftarrow$ threshold by $\mathcal{K}$ or a boundary default
17:   $\mathcal{N}_m^{\text{border}} \leftarrow \{(b_1, .., b_d), b_i \in \{b_{i,\min}, b_{i,\max}\}_{i=1}^d\}$
18:   $op_\oplus \leftarrow$ PrunePipeline.pop()
19:   **return** $op_\oplus(\tau, \mathcal{K}(x_1, ..., x_m))$
20:   $\{\forall x_i \in \mathcal{N}_i (i = 1, ..., m-1), \forall x_m \in \mathcal{N}_m^{\text{border}}\}$
21: // Nested Prune category
22: **if** (PrunePipline.size > 1) **then**
23:   **return** NestedPrune(PrunePipeline)

---

[a] min, max, and center computations are meta-data generated during tree construction.

The problem falls under *approximation* if the size of `PrunePipeline` is zero (Lines 8–13). For approximating the contribution of a node, we check if the minimum and maximum contribution of that node are very close (*i.e.* less than a threshold). If so, we know that all the data points in that node have a similar contribution and therefore, PASCAL uses the center to approximate the computation of that node. Note that $(\mathcal{N}_1^c, \mathcal{N}_2^c, ..., \mathcal{N}_m^c)$ defined in line 11, represents the centers of nodes $\mathcal{N}_i \in (\mathcal{N}_1, \mathcal{N}_2, ..., \mathcal{N}_m)$ and this is pre-computed as metadata information during tree construction.

The problem falls under the *single prune* category if the size of `Prune Pipeline` is one (Lines 15–19). First, we define a threshold for pruning. To do so, we randomly choose points in each set and compute a temporary value using the kernel function. We define $\mathcal{N}_r^{border}$ as the set of border data points which have either maximum or minimum values in each dimension. Line 18 pops the prune operator and Line 19 generates the prune condition by applying the operator on the tuple of points from the nodes in $\mathcal{N}_1, ..., \mathcal{N}_{m_1}$, and border points of $\mathcal{N}_m$.

Note that in Algorithm 2, the notation $op_\oplus$ is similar to non-member function operators in C++ language. For instance, $op_\le(x_r, x_q)$ is equal to $x_r \le x_q$.

When the size of the `PrunePipeline` is greater than one, the problem belongs to the *nested prune* category and the nested prune Algorithm 3 is called in line 22. In Line 2, for each node, we calculate the border data points using the maximum and minimum values of data points in each dimension as defined in $\{b_{\min}, b_{\max}\}_{i=1}^{d}$. Line 3 pops the prune operator from the `PrunePipeline`. Initially, a temporary threshold τ is defined for each prune operator. Subsequently, τ is refined as the computation progresses. Line 5 returns the nested prune condition that we generate. For generating this condition, first, we apply the innermost operator to the border points in the innermost dataset. The result of this is used to call the next innermost operator, and so on. We will continue this process from the innermost operator to the outermost operator in the `PrunePipeline` and apply each operator on the corresponding node borders with the computed thresholds. Each prune operator corresponds to one level in the multi-tree. Note that single prune can be considered as a special case of nested prune with a nesting level of one.

Case Studies. In this section, we show how N-body algorithms are generated using PASCAL. Specifically, we consider the six N-body problems discussed in Sect. 3 as case studies. The choice of these six problems is because they cover (a) approximation, single pruning, and nested pruning problems, (b) both direct and iterative algorithms, and (c) problems from multiple domains.

Algorithm 3. NestedPrune(PrunePipeline)

Input: Node set $\mathcal{N}_1...\mathcal{N}_m$, kernel function $\mathcal{K}$.

Output: The nested pruning condition

1: **for all** $\mathcal{N}_j \in \mathcal{N}_1...\mathcal{N}_m$ **do**
2:     $\mathcal{N}_j^{\text{border}} \leftarrow \{(b_1, b_2, ..., b_d),$
        $b_i \in \{b_{i,\min}, b_{i,\max}\}_{i=1}^{d}\}$ for $\mathcal{N}_j$
3:     $op_{\oplus j} \leftarrow$ PrunePipeline.pop()
4:     $\tau_j \leftarrow \mathcal{K}(x_1', ..., x_m')$ or defined by $\mathcal{K}$
5: **return** $op_{\oplus 1}(\tau_1, \mathcal{K}(x_1, ..., x_m) | op_{\oplus 2}(\tau_2, ...$
        $| op_{\oplus m}(\tau_m, \mathcal{K}(x_1, ..., x_m)...)$
s.t.$\{\forall x_1 \in \mathcal{N}_1^{\text{border}}, ..., \forall x_m \in \mathcal{N}_m^{\text{border}}\}$

In all the problems, the `BaseCase` is the direct point-to-point computation at the leaf nodes. So, we will focus specifically on how the prune/approximate condition is generated since this is the most challenging step.

(a) k-NN Search. k-NN has only one pruning opportunity, `arg min`, so it is classified as a single prune problem by PASCAL. PASCAL generates the prune condition using Algorithm 2. The prune operator that is pushed into `PrunePipeline` is `arg min` and the `reverse` is $\ge$. The `reverse` of `arg min` is similar to the `reverse` of `min` since they both compute the minimum. The difference is the return value, the latter returns the value of minimum while the former returns the argument of it. The threshold τ is initialized at the beginning with a temporary computation of the kernel (or a default value such as the maximum value of double precision) and is updated through the algorithm.

PASCAL evaluates $\mathcal{K}$ for each reference point in $\mathcal{N}_r^{\text{border}}$ with respect to the query point x_q. Then, it checks to see if it is greater than or equal to τ. So, the prune condition is $op_\oplus(\tau, \mathcal{K}(x_q, x_r)) \implies \mathcal{K}(x_q, x_r) \ge \tau, \quad \forall x_r \in \mathcal{N}_r^{\text{border}}$.

(b) Range Search (RS). Range search has only one pruning opportunity via its kernel function, $I(h_{\min} \leq ||x_q - x_r|| \leq h_{\max})$. The **reverse** of this kernel function that is saved in `PrunePipeline` is $h_{\min} > ||x_q - x_r||$ or $||x_q - x_r|| > h_{\max}$) which is used as $op_\oplus$ to generate the prune condition ($op_{\oplus_1}$ is $>$, $op_{\oplus_2}$ is $<$). The two thresholds, τ_1 and τ_2 are defined by the kernel function as $h_{\max}$ and $h_{\min}$. We evaluate the kernel function on the points in $\mathcal{N}_r^{\text{border}}$ for each x_q as δ, $\mathcal{K}(x_q, x_r) = \delta$. Then, the prune condition is defined as follows.

$$op_{\oplus_1}(\tau_1, \mathcal{K}(x_q, x_r)) \quad \text{or} \quad op_{\oplus_2}(\tau_2, \mathcal{K}(x_q, x_r)) \implies \delta > \tau_1 | \delta < \tau_2, \forall x_r \in \mathcal{N}_r^{\text{border}}$$

(c) Kernel Density Estimation (KDE). This is an approximation problem since there is no pruning opportunity by the definition of the problem, and the `PrunePipeline` queue is empty. `ComputeApprox` will return the probability density at the center of the node, K_{center}, multiplied by the number of data points in that node. In this problem, τ is a default constant that can be overridden by the user to adjust the overall accuracy. PASCAL uses Algorithm 2 to generate the approximation condition, $(K_{\max} - K_{\min}) < \tau \times K_{\text{center}}$.

(d) Minimum Spanning Tree (MST). MST is an iterative algorithm and in each iteration, it uses the same operations as k-NN search. So PASCAL generates exactly the same prune condition and rule set as k-NN.

(e) Expectation Maximization (EM). EM is an approximation problem. EM has three steps namely, E-step, M-step, and Log-likelihood where 99% of the time is spent in E-step and Log-likelihood. Moore [13] proposed a powerful space-partitioning tree-based algorithm to reduce the complexity of E-step from $\mathcal{O}(KN)$ to $\mathcal{O}(K \log N)$, where N is the number of data points and K is the number of clusters. We extend Moore's idea and propose a fast algorithm for estimating both the E-step and log-likelihood computation in $\mathcal{O}(K \log N)$.

The *first* N-body computation in EM is the E-step. In the E-step, if the difference between the maximum and the minimum responsibility of the points i from cluster j, r_{ij}, is less than a threshold, we can approximate the influence of these data points. This is because all the data points in that node will approximately have a similar responsibility to the cluster. PASCAL generates the approximation condition $(r_{ij}^{\max} - r_{ij}^{\min}) < \sigma \times r_{ij}^{\text{center}}$, $i = 1, .., K$ where, σ is the threshold parameter, r_i^{center} is the responsibility of the center data points in the node from cluster i, $r_i^{\min}$ and $r_i^{\max}$ are the minimum and maximum responsibilities between all the data point from cluster i.

`ComputeApprox` will return the value of responsibility at the center of the node multiplied by the number of data points in that node. Note that in this algorithm, the distance we compute is the Mahalanobis distance which is defined as $(x - \mu)^T \Sigma^{-1} (x - \mu)$ for a Gaussian with $\theta = (\mu, \Sigma)$.

The *second* N-body computation in EM is the log-likelihood computation. In order to calculate the log-likelihood, we traverse the same tree as in the E-step. The computation pattern is similar in style to E-step albeit with a different approximation condition generated by PASCAL presented below. To the best of our knowledge, this is the first $\mathcal{O}(K \log N)$ algorithm for computing log-likelihood.

$$\log \sum_{i=1}^{K} \pi_i f(x_{\max}|\theta_i) - \log \sum_{i=1}^{K} \pi_i f(x_{\min}|\theta_i) < \sigma |\log(\sum_{i=1}^{K} \pi_i f(x_{\text{center}}|\theta_i))|$$

(f) Hausdorff Distance. One of the N-body problems with more than one pruning opportunity is Hausdorff distance. In this problem, the *kernel function* is the Euclidean distance with the operators set {max, min} both of which provide pruning opportunities. PASCAL generates the prune condition using the nested prune algorithm, Algorithm 3.

First, PASCAL constructs dual-trees and applies each of its operators on one of the levels of the tree. The PrunePipeline queue consists of the **reverse** of max and min which are $\leq$ and $\geq$. Therefore, $op_{\oplus_1}$ is $<$ and $op_{\oplus_2}$ is $\geq$. To form the prune condition, PASCAL creates two nested loops. The inner loop runs over the borders of the inner tree (for example, reference dataset) applying the inner operator which is $\geq$. The outer loop covers the borders of the second tree (for example, the query dataset), applying the $\leq$ operator.

Note that by the definition of the N-body problem, each operator that is applied to a dataset is regarded as the operator that is applied to the tree built for that dataset. We define two thresholds, τ_1 and τ_2 and the nested prune condition generated is shown below.

$$op_{\oplus_1}(\tau_1, \mathcal{K}(x_q, x_r)|op_{\oplus_2}(\tau_2, \mathcal{K}(x_q, x_r))) \implies \tau_1 \geq (\mathcal{K}(x_q, x_r)|\tau_2 \leq \mathcal{K}(x_q, x_r)),$$
$$s.t. \quad \forall x_q \in \mathcal{N}_q^{\text{border}}, \forall x_r \in \mathcal{N}_r^{\text{border}}$$

5   Domain-Specific Optimizations and Parallelization

In order to achieve an optimized code, we first apply numerous optimizations to both the tree construction and the computational core of the evaluation. Then, we parallelize the tree traversal defined by Algorithm 1, and finally tune empirically for the associated tuning parameters (*e.g.* leaf size).

Incremental Bounding Box Calculation. During tree construction described in Sect. 4, we associate each node with its bounding box data. This is critical for efficient evaluation during traversal. For instance, during range search, we check if the reference node is within a specified range of the query node and if not, the entire node is pruned. This check requires computing the minimum and maximum node-to-point and node-to-node distances. Pre-computing the bounding box information significantly reduces the time to compute these distances since we do not have to access the actual data points each time.

For kd-trees, this is essentially computing the hyper-rectangle boundary information in each dimension. At the start of the computation, the root bounding box is computed from all the N points. During partitioning, we only incrementally update the bounding box of the dimension that is being split at each node based on the splitting value. This results in a complexity of $\mathcal{O}(Nd)$.

Optimal Metric Calculation. The evaluation can be performed using a variety of distance metrics. We consider Euclidean: $\sqrt{\sum_{i=1}^{d}(x_i - y_i)^2}$, Manhattan: $\sum_{i=1}^{d}|x_i - y_i|$, Chebyshev: $\max_{i=1}^{d}|x_i - y_i|$, and Mahalanobis: $(\overrightarrow{x} - \overrightarrow{\mu})^T \Sigma^{-1}(\overrightarrow{x} - \overrightarrow{\mu})$ (μ and Σ are distribution's parameters) metrics for real-valued vector spaces.

Outlined below are two techniques to efficiently compute these metrics which are repeatedly used in all phases of the algorithm. Additionally, we ensure that the compiler generates vectorized code for the metric calculation.

1. Each metric defines both a distance and a **reduced distance**, which is often faster to compute and is used whenever possible. For example, in the case of Euclidean distance, the reduced distance is squared Euclidean distance. This eliminates the expensive `sqrt` instruction which has long latencies.
2. **Partial** distance between two d-dimensional points x and y is defined as the distance computed on a subset of the d dimensions. For example, when searching for k-nearest neighbors, we compute the distance between two points and insert the reference point into our neighbor list only if the computed distance is smaller than the kth largest distance in our sorted list. When d is large as in the case for some of our datasets, this optimization offers additional savings in processing time where we can terminate the computation earlier if the computed partial distance exceeds our threshold.

Incremental Distance Calculation. This idea was introduced by Arya and Mount [1] where the node-to-point distance at each node during single-tree traversal is incrementally computed from the parent's distance in constant time independent of dimension. For datasets with large d, this has the potential for significant savings in computation at the cost of minimal additional storage of distance information. We support this optimization and note that it is possible to extend this idea for computing node-to-node distances as well in multi-trees.

Parallelization and Tuning. After applying serial optimizations, we parallelize the multi-tree traversal using Cilk. Since there are dependencies across the recursion, we exploit a combination of data and task parallelism. At first, we spawn Cilk tasks recursively until all the threads are saturated, at which point we switch to data parallelism. Since the tree traversal is abstracted from the actual computation, parallelizing the tree traversal leads to parallel implementations of all six algorithms. Moreover, for any new algorithm expressed in PASCAL, we can obtain parallel multi-tree implementations at no additional cost. This greatly accelerates the ability to scale new problems in rapidly growing domains.

Algorithmically, the tree is parameterized by the maximum number of points per leaf node, l. As l increases, the cost of tree construction decreases at the expense of increased cost in performing the `BaseCase`. On the other hand, small l results in a large number of nodes and an increase in the cost of tree traversal. We exhaustively tune l for all implementations.

6   Experimental Setup

Libraries. We compare PASCAL's performance against state-of-the-art software namely, WEKA [10], Scitkit-learn [15], MLPACK [6], and MATLAB.

Architecture and Compilers. We evaluate our implementations on a dual-socket Intel Xeon E5-2630 v3 processor (Haswell-EP). Each socket has 8 cores, for a total of 16 cores (32 threads with hyper-threading) and a theoretical double precision peak performance of 614.4 GFlop/s. We use Intel C++ compiler (icpc version 15.0.2) with C++11 feature support. We use Python v2.7.6 for scikit-learn and Java v1.8.0 for Weka.

Benchmarks. We present results on five real-world datasets characterized in Table 1. These include Yahoo! front page module user click log dataset, v1.0 (Yahoo!), Higgs boson's signals and background process dataset

Table 1. Description of the datasets. N: number of points, d: dimensionality.

Dataset	N	d
Yahoo!	41904293	11
IHEPC	2075259	9
HIGGS	11000000	28
Census	2458285	68
KDD	4898431	42

(HIGGS), Individual Household Electric Power Consumption dataset (IHEPC), US Census data from 1990 (Census), and KDD Cup 1999 dataset (KDD) from the UCI ML repository.

7   Results and Discussion

The combined benefits of asymptotically optimal algorithms, optimizations, and parallelization are substantial. In this section, we first compare our performance against state-of-the-art ML libraries and software. Then, we break down the performance gain step by step and finally, evaluate the scalability of our algorithms.

Performance Summary. Figure 2 presents the performance of k-NN and EM. The choice of these two algorithms is because they are the only ones supported by all competing libraries and therefore make good candidates for a comprehensive comparison. Moreover, the choice of these two algorithms albeit space constraints is because k-NN is a direct pruning algorithm while EM is an iterative approximation algorithm that represents two ends of the spectrum.

Across the board, our implementation shows significantly better performance compared to Scikit-learn, MLPACK, MATLAB, and Weka.

Performance Breakdown. To gain a better understanding of the factors contributing to the performance improvement, we break down the speedups in Table 2. Specifically, it helps distinguish the improvements that are purely algorithmic (tree algorithm) from improvements via optimization and parallelization. For example, for the Yahoo! dataset, we observe a 3.1× speedup from an asymptotically faster algorithm, 12.1× due to optimizations on top of the tree algorithm, and 173.1× with parallelization for k-NN. The breakdown for EM are 1.6×, 3.2×, and 53.7× respectively for the same dataset.

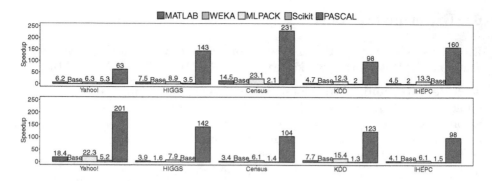

Fig. 2. Speedup summary of single-tree EM (top) and dual-tree k-NN for $k = 3$ (bottom). The slowest library is used as the baseline for comparison.

Table 2. Speedup breakdown. Alg stands for algorithmic improvement, +Opt refers to optimization on top of Alg, and +Par is parallelization on top of Opt.

	KNN			EM			KDE			HD			RS			EMST		
	Alg	+Opt	+Par	Alg	+Opt	+Par	Alg	+Opt	+Par	Alg	+Opt	+Par	Alg	+Opt	+Par	Alg	+Opt	+Par
Yahoo!	3.1	12.1	173.1	1.6	3.2	53.7	2.1	9.1	92.1	2.5	11.5	161.1	2.2	9.1	126.8	2.9	11.9	166.7
HIGGS	2.1	7.3	108.1	1.5	6.8	117.6	1.7	4.7	50.1	1.9	6.1	89.6	1.9	6.3	86.5	2.0	6.9	102.8
Census	1.4	6.5	90.8	1.3	11.2	190.0	1.4	8.1	75.6	1.3	10.2	141.8	1.3	10.4	144.9	1.4	10.9	151.6
KDD	1.6	6.8	100.7	1.4	4.1	70.9	1.5	3.1	33.5	1.4	3.8	54.4	1.4	5.1	70.5	1.5	3.8	55.5
IHEPC	3.0	4.3	61.5	1.5	7.6	127.6	2.0	5.4	53.6	2.5	6.8	101.3	2.1	6.3	94.1	2.9	7.1	107.1

We observe that each dataset benefits differently from algorithmic changes, optimizations, and parallelization based on the number of data points, dimensionality, and distribution of the points.

Scalability. Figure 3 shows the scalability of the six algorithms namely, (i) k-NN with $k = 3$, (ii) RS with range between 0 and 2, (iii) KDE for Gaussian kernel, K with bandwidth, $\sigma = 0.1$ and relative error tolerance set to 0.1, (iv) EM with error tolerance of 0.1, (v) MST, and (vi) Hausdorff distance.

We observe good scaling on all six algorithms. Note that 32 threads is with hyper-threading enabled where we assign 2 threads per core. In all cases, hyper-threading further improves the performance resulting in 14×, 16×, 13×, 14×, 10×, and 14× speedup for Yahoo! over the serial optimized code for k-NN, EM, RS, MST, KDE, and Hausdorff distance respectively.

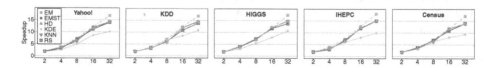

Fig. 3. Multicore scalability using Cilk. X-axis is the number of threads.

Scalability Difference in Multi-trees. Tree algorithms are irregular. The dynamic nature of pruning/approximation of sub-trees during tree-traversal makes these problems challenging to parallelize. This load-balancing problem is further exacerbated in dual-tree traversal. As a result, we observe that EM which uses single-tree traversal with one tree (we use a single-tree over a dual-tree traversal for EM because of the small number of clusters) shows better scalability compared to the other five algorithms which use dual-tree traversals.

We currently defer to Cilk to manage scheduling of tasks using its work-stealing scheduler. In future work, we will explore a locality aware work-stealing scheduler for better load balance which is critical especially on NUMA machines.

In summary, these results show the potential of our approach to achieve orders of magnitude improvement in performance through the use of tree data structures, optimizations, and parallelization.

8   Conclusions

In this paper, we proposed PASCAL, a parallel unified algorithmic framework for N-body problems. PASCAL generates prune and approximation conditions automatically from the high-level specification of the problem, which is one the most challenging components in the design of these algorithms. We evaluated PASCAL with six N-body problems from different domains and observe 10–230× speedup compared to state-of-the-art libraries/software. The broader impact is to enable scientific discovery not only for N-body problems in scientific computing and machine learning but also to a number of related problems in other unexplored domains that can be expressed in the same style of execution to obtain an out-of-the-box parallel optimized implementation.

Acknowledgments. This work was supported in part by the National Science Foundation (NSF) under award number 1533917.

References

1. Arya, S., Mount, D.M.: Algorithms for fast vector quantization. In: Proceeding of DCC 1993: Data Compression Conference, pp. 381–390. IEEE Press (1993)
2. Asanovic, K., Bodik, R., Catanzaro, B.C., Gebis, J.J., Husbands, P., Keutzer, K., Patterson, D.A., Plishker, W.L., Shalf, J., Williams, S.W., Yelick, K.A.: The landscape of parallel computing research: a view from Berkeley. Technical report, UCB/EECS-2006-183, University of California, Berkeley (2006)
3. Barnes, J., Hut, P.: A hierarchical $\mathcal{O}(n \log n)$ force-calculation algorithm. Nature **324**, 446–449 (1986)
4. Bentley, J.L.: Multidimensional binary search trees used for associative searching. Commun. ACM (CACM) **18**(9), 509–517 (1975)
5. Curtin, R., March, W., Ram, P., Anderson, D., Gray, A., Isbell, C.: Tree-independent dual-tree algorithms. In: Proceedings of the 30th International Conference on Machine Learning (ICML 2013), vol. 28, pp. 1435–1443, May 2013
6. Curtin, R.R., Cline, J.R., Slagle, N.P., March, W.B., Ram, P., Mehta, N.A., Gray, A.G.: MLPACK: a scalable C++ machine learning library. J. Mach. Learn. Res. **14**, 801–805 (2013)

7. Dongarra, J., Sullivan, F.: Guest editors introduction to the top 10 algorithms. Comput. Sci. Eng. **2**(1), 22–23 (2000)

8. Gray, A.G., Moore, A.W.: N-body problems in statistical learning. In: Proceeding of NIPS, vol. 4, pp. 521–527 (2000)

9. Greengard, L., Rokhlin, V.: A fast algorithm for particle simulations. J. Comput. Phys. **73**, 325–348 (1987)

10. Hall, M., Frank, E., Holmes, G., Pfahringer, B., Reutemann, P., Witten, I.H.: The WEKA data mining software: an update. ACM SIGKDD Explor. Newsl. **11**(1), 10–18 (2009)

11. Kambatla, K., Kollias, G., Kumar, V., Grama, A.: Trends in big data analytics. J. Parallel Distrib. Comput. **74**(7), 2561–2573 (2014)

12. Lashuk, I., Chandramowlishwaran, A., Langston, H., Nguyen, T.A., Sampath, R., Shringarpure, A., Vuduc, R., Ying, L., Zorin, D., Biros, G.: A massively parallel adaptive fast multipole method on heterogeneous architectures. Commun. ACM (CACM) **55**(5), 101–109 (2012)

13. Moore, A.W.: Very fast EM-based mixture model clustering using multiresolution KD-trees. In: Advances in Neural Information Processing Systems, pp. 543–549 (1999)

14. Nešetřil, J., Nešetřilová, H.: The origins of minimal spanning tree algorithms-Boruvka and Jarník. In: Documenta Mathematica, pp. 127–141 (2012)

15. Pedregosa, F., Varoquaux, G., Gramfort, A., Michel, V., Thirion, B., Grisel, O., Blondel, M., Prettenhofer, P., Weiss, R., Dubourg, V., Vanderplas, J., Passos, A., Cournapeau, D., Brucher, M., Perrot, M., Duchesnay, E.: Scikit-learn: machine learning in python. J. Mach. Learn. Res. **12**, 2825–2830 (2011)

16. Salmon, J.K., Warren, M.S.: Fast parallel tree codes for gravitational and fluid dynamical n-body problems. Int. J. High Perform. Comput. Appl. **8**(2), 129–142 (1994)

17. Wu, X., Kumar, V., Quinlan, J.R., Ghosh, J., Yang, Q., Motoda, H., McLachlan, G.J., Ng, A., Liu, B., Philip, S.Y., Zhou, Z.H., Steinbach, M., Hand, D.J., Steinberg, D.: Top 10 algorithms in data mining. Knowl. Inf. Syst. **14**(1), 1–37 (2008)

GASPI/GPI In-memory Checkpointing Library

Valeria Bartsch[(✉)], Rui Machado, Dirk Merten, Mirko Rahn,
and Franz-Josef Pfreundt

Competence Center for High Performance Computing,
Fraunhofer ITWM, Kaiserslautern, Germany
{bartsch,machado,dirk.merten,mirko.rahn,
franz-josef.pfreundt}@itwm.fhg.de

Abstract. Fault tolerance becomes an important feature at large computer systems where the mean time between failure decreases. Checkpointing is a method often used to provide resilience. We present an in-memory checkpointing library based on a PGAS API implemented with GASPI/GPI. It offers a substantial benefit when recovering from failure and leverages existing fault tolerance features of GASPI/GPI. The overhead of the library is negligible when testing it with a simple stencil code and a real life seismic imaging method.

Keywords: Checkpointing · Resilience · Partitioned global address space

1 Introduction

With decreasing mean time between faults at large computer systems resilience to hardware faults and failures become a more and more important issue. In this paper we describe a light-weight checkpointing library supporting the application developer. Checkpointing is a classical and probably the most often used technique to minimize the effect of failures when running a parallel program. It simply consists of saving a snapshot of a program's state or produced data. An application can use such a snapshot to recover from a failure by continuing the execution from the saved point.

The novelty of our approach is that the data transfer is asynchronous using RDMA principles. So the communication cost of the data transfers for the checkpointing methods are hidden. Our approach allows to run applications which are scalable and fault tolerant at the same time. To avoid the large overhead of I/O when writing to persistent storage, an often pointed drawback of checkpointing, we opted for an in-memory checkpointing where the snapshot of a process is saved in the memory of a neighboring node. In case of failure, a spare node can fetch the checkpoint from the neighbor of the failing process (mirror) and continue the work from that point. Using a PGAS approach allows to design the library in such a way that instead of bulk synchronous communication, one-sided and asynchronous communication mechanisms can be used

© Springer International Publishing AG 2017
F.F. Rivera et al. (Eds.): Euro-Par 2017, LNCS 10417, pp. 497–508, 2017.
DOI: 10.1007/978-3-319-64203-1_36

with which communication and computation times may be overlapped. Thus we choose GASPI/GPI [12] as communication layer of the checkpointing library. A consequence of the GASPI/GPI architecture is that when non-volatile memory like NVRAM becomes widely available such an approach includes persistence automatically. The drawback of any in-memory checkpointing method is that it uses additional memory to save the data from the checkpoint. Because we are using asynchronous methods the data from the previous checkpoint still needs to be available in case of a failure while writing the checkpoint, duplicating the size of the checkpointing memory.

To be able to detect faults and provide resilience the underlying communication library and runtime infrastructure needs to allow the application to react on hardware failures. Currently some communication models lack such a support in a generic way as described in [16]. GASPI/GPI supports tolerant mechanisms concerning hardware faults. The checkpointing library keeps the GASPI/GPI core lean and checkpointing as a separate option. The library can be called from any parallel program, i.e. the interface to the checkpointing library is independent of GASPI/GPI. E.g. we have tested that an application based on Berkeley UPC [5] is able to call the checkpointing library and exploit the resilience features. Even though MPI code can call the checkpointing library [14] it is difficult to achieve resilience within the current MPI standard (see [8] for a POSIX-compliant strategy) due to a lack of support for node failures [16].

After briefly summarizing related work in Sect. 2 the design of the checkpointing library is described in Sect. 3. Performance results using the implementation under GPI-2 are shown in Sect. 4. In Sect. 5 we draw some conclusions and point to future work.

2   Related Work

Checkpointing and roll-back is probably the most often used technique for recovering from single node failures in parallel programs. The run-time overhead from IO when writing checkpoints to file easily becomes signficant. It can be reduced by optimizing data layout and access patterns to the underlying file system [3]. Avoiding IO by using the main memory and additional communication for checkpointing seems natural for a parallel application. A framework for supporting the user in doing this under an implementation of MPI is described in [9]. In the context of PGAS programming models, detailed control about the partitioning of data within the address space can be utilised for checkpointing, as done for Fortran Global Arrays in [1] and for specialized distributed arrays in [6]. Current checkpointing strategies have to be re-evaluated in the presence of virtualization as common in cloud computing facilities. Corresponding benefits and restrictions of are discussed in [2].

3   In-memory Checkpointing

3.1   Short Description of GASPI/GPI

GPI-2 (Global address space Programming Interface), an implementation of the GASPI standard [10], is a PGAS API designed to maximize scalability and performance. GPI employs the RDMA model: it relies on one-sided and asynchronous communication that allows communication hiding. The PGAS API of GASPI/GPI is semantically very similar to the (asynchronous) MPI communication commands. GASPI/GPI allows for efficient thread-safe implementations. The global memory can be accessed by other nodes using the GASPI/GPI API and is divided into so-called segments. A segment is a continuous space of globally accessible memory which can be addressed in terms of offset of the data. Thus any data can be stored on the segments independent of the data structure which needs to be handled fully by the application developers. GASPI/GPI memory segments were conceived to represent any sort of available memory. NVRAM is one such sort.

GASPI/GPI supports fault-tolerance mechanisms which go beyond mechanisms provided by most PGAS languages. (A comparison with other PGAS approaches like UPC [7] and CAF [13] can be found at [4].) GASPI/GPI currently supports fault tolerance of applications by providing local timeout mechanisms. All operations that involve the remote side feature a timeout with a defined exit status. GASPI/GPI maintains a local vector with the state of all ranks. A rank can get that state vector to check for any detected problems with other ranks. Both mechanisms can be used by applications to detect a fault. Together with the proposed library, the application can recover and continue its execution. The checkpointing interface consists of different calls to initialize and finalize the checkpointing infrastructure and perform and restore a checkpoint.

3.2   Application View

The presented library is not a full fledged fault tolerant solution from an application point of view. To take advantage of checkpoints and fault tolerance, the application must be extended to use the proposed checkpoint interface and take advantage of the GASPI/GPI timeout and error state vector mechanisms in order to detect timeouts and possibly related faults.

The application decides when it is more reasonable to perform a checkpoint. In case of the pseudocode in Fig. 1 e.g. at a given iteration number. It is recommended to use in a realistic application adaptive checkpointing which starts to write a new checkpoint after checking that the previous one has been finished. The application must also detect a fault and enter a recovery process. The application can use one or more spare nodes which are not part of the **active_group** in the pseudo code. The number of spare nodes is small compared to the number of active nodes, otherwise the job has to be considered as failed, because the compute system is not stable enough. The spare node(s) take the place of the failed node(s). In case of more than one error, the checkpointing approach

```
int main()
{
    gaspi_proc_init (...);
    gaspi_size_t const size = ...;
    gaspi_segment_create (segment_id_checkpoint, size, ...);

    gaspi_cp_description_t checkpoint_description =
                            GASPI_CP_DESCRIPTION_INITIALIZER();
    gpi_cp_init (segment_id_checkpoint,
                    gaspi_offset_t (0), size,
                    gaspi_queue_id_t (4), cp_policy,
                    active_group, &checkpoint_description,
                    timeout);
    for (iteration)
    {
        if (checkpoint_this_iteration)
        {
            gpi_cp_commit (&checkpoint_description, timeout);
            // setup segment with id segment_id_checkpoint
            // -> application specific
            // store to be checkpointed data in
            // segment_id_checkpoint, e.g.
            // memcpy (ptr (segment_id_checkpoint),
            //                 ptr (segment_id_work), size  8);
            // memcpy (ptr (segment_id_checkpoint) + size - 8,
            //                 &state, 8);
            gpi_cp_start (&checkpoint_description, timeout);
        }
        ...
    }
    gpi_cp_finalize (&checkpoint_description, timeout);
}
```

Fig. 1. Pseudocode for an application with checkpointing library calls

still works with at least k spare nodes unless k errors happen at the same time and affect both copies of the same data. If k errors happen at the same time without affecting both copies of the same data, this approach can still recover all data. If the probability of two simultaneous errors that might affect both copies of the data is high in comparison to the cost for the recomputation, one could easily use three or more copies if enough memory is available. One can use an approach without spare nodes and redistribute the tasks and data of the failed node to the remaining nodes. Such an approach without spare nodes would have the advantage of decreasing the CPU power needed and the disadvantage of a more complex process in case of a node failure. In the recovery process presented in this paper, a spare node takes the place of the failed one, the last

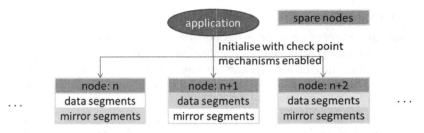

Fig. 2. Sketch of the initialization with application-driven in-memory checkpointing enabled

checkpoint is read and the application can continue its execution. The code of the checkpointing library can be found at [11].

3.3 Initialization Phase

As sketched in Fig. 2 the initialization of the checkpoint infrastructure is done by invoking **gpi_cp_init**. Currently and following the GASPI/GPI semantic, the application must provide a segment, offset and size where the data to be saved will be placed by the application. This is application specific. Moreover, a checkpoint policy and group must be given. The group is a GASPI/GPI construct and corresponds to the group of ranks that will be active and will perform checkpoints. The checkpoint policy corresponds to the selection of the neighbor where the mirrored data will be placed (e.g. ring topology). Other topologies are also possible and the checkpoint topology object can be chosen by the application.

After initialization, a checkpoint description is returned. This checkpoint description is then used to invoke other routines. One important consequence of this initialization design is that several snapshots are possible by simply invoking the initialization multiple times. This way, an application can have different checkpoints with different policies, different priorities and redundancy or persistence levels.

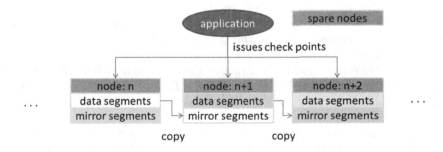

Fig. 3. Sketch of the data segment mirrors used during checkpointing

3.4   Checkpointing

Our in-memory checkpoint approach follows what we call an asynchronous, coordinated checkpointing approach. It is coordinated because at some point in time we ensure consistency of a snapshot. In the easiest case this would be global consistency of a snapshot specifying a certain point by means of a collective operation (**gaspi_barrier**). In other words, all active processes ensure that they have one particular snapshot that is consistent on all processes. To make this approach scalable for large computer systems, it makes sense to build checkpointing groups which need to be in a consistent state only amongst themselves but not globally to run the checkpoints. This can be done by initializing the checkpoint **gpi_cp_init** several times with a different sets of **active_group**. It is up to the application developer to check if the application can handle such a loosened consistency definition. The approach is asynchronous because we take advantage of GASPI/GPI communication. When a checkpoint is started, the data is transferred asynchronously to the mirror as depicted in Fig. 3. In the meantime the computation of the application resumes overlapping computation and communication.

Performing a checkpoint is a two step procedure: the application must start a checkpoint and commit the checkpoint. Again, this split-phase semantic matches that of GASPI communication and aims at hiding the costs of communication required by mirroring. Starting a checkpoint (**gpi_cp_start**) initiates the copy of checkpoint data to the neighboring mirror. All the details required to post that communication are included in the checkpoint description object. Committing the checkpoint (**gpi_cp_commit**) is a global operation and ensures the completion of a previously started checkpoint operation on all nodes. At this point, a valid snapshot exists to which the application can return to. Being a global operation and following the GASPI semantic, the commit operation has a timeout to avoid blocking.

3.5   Fault Detection

The detection of faults is orthogonal to checkpoints and currently has to be programmed by the application. GASPI already provides mechanisms for that: timeouts and the error state vector. In the current GPI implementation, the hardware fault of a node can be detected locally by a process running on a node requesting communication to the faulty node. If a communication request is erroneous or returned a timeout, the process can check the error state vector which is set after every non-local operation. Each rank can either have a state of **GASPI_STATE_HEALTHY** or **_CORRUPT**. This error state vector can be queried by the application (using **gaspi_state_vec_get**) to determine the state of a remote partner in case of timeout or error.

If a problem is detected, the fault needs to be acknowledged by all other running processes. After that all of the remaining and healthy processes can enter consistently the recovery process. An example of how to build fault tolerant applications with GASPI/GPI can be found in [15]. The reliable way to propagate the fault detection information is beyond the scope of this paper.

```
    ...
// create a new_group exchanging the faulted process with the spare process

    gpi_cp_restore (segment_id_checkpoint,
                    gaspi_offset_t (0), size,
                    gaspi_queue_id_t (4), cp_policy,
                    new_group, &checkpoint_description,
                    timeout);
// copy the checkpointed data into the execution buffer
// make new_group the new active_group
    ...
```

Fig. 4. Pseudocode for an application restoring the data from a checkpoint

3.6 Recovery

Once a fault is detected, the remaining processes must enter a recovery step. Such recovery step will generally involve 3 actions as sketched in the pseudo code in Fig. 4: add spare node(s) to the group of active nodes to replace the failed node(s), create the new group of active processes, restore the data from consistent checkpoint. The first 2 actions must be programmed in the application although in principle it should be possible to perform this in a more automatic way. The third action corresponds to the **gpi_cp_restore** call of our in-memory checkpointing interface. The gpi_cp_restore call is symmetric to the **gpi_cp_init**. The differences are that a new group of active processes is provided and the checkpoint description object is updated on the set of survivor nodes and created anew for the new joining (spare) nodes. Moreover, a valid snapshot will be retrieved from the corresponding mirrors and when the procedure returns successfully the data will be available in the provided memory segment. After this the application can continue from that point on.

4 Results

4.1 Performance Metrics

The use of the in-memory checkpoint interface incurs in some extra overhead to the normal application execution in terms of memory, CPU time incurred mainly by the additional communication which adds to the inflight communication of the application. The memory usage, i.e. the data size of the checkpoint needs to be optimized by the application, the CPU time overhead must be kept minimal. Particularly in the case of failure-free execution, the modified application should run with minimal performance impact. The total overhead is composed of several parts (writing a checkpoint, rebuilding the active group, reading the checkpoint, etc.) that should be analyzed separately, identifying possible bottlenecks. In an ideal world the frequency of the checkpointing should be self-adapting by using the method **gpi_cp_commit** to check that the data of the checkpoint have been written. The ideal time of the start of a new checkpoint depends on the size of the data communicated by the application plus the size of data written to a checkpoint and the computation time of the application between checkpoints and therefore the overlap between communication and computation heavily depends on the application itself.

To assess the effectiveness of this approach we have evaluated the performance with a small demonstrator application as a proof of principle and in a real-life application with a slightly different checkpointing scenario compared to the demonstrator application. This mechanism should be integrated and used with a real application.

The performance tests were executed on a local cluster on up to 50 nodes consisting of Dell PowerEdge M620, dual Intel Xeon E5-2670 (Sandy Bridge), i.e. 16 CPU cores per node. One process per node has been run. The nodes are connected via QDR Infiniband.

4.2   Performance Measurement with a Simple Stencil Code Example

As example to test the functionality of the code a simple stencil code has been used. In general stencil codes are wide-spread in HPC. The checkpointing library provides an important additional tool.

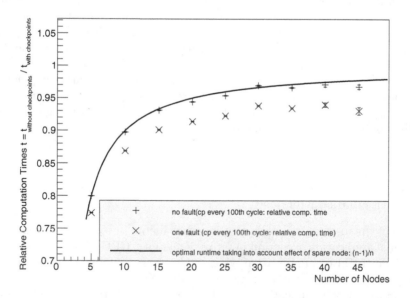

Fig. 5. Relative computation times with in-memory checkpointing versus number of nodes

Figure 5 shows the relative computation times with in-memory checkpointing versus the number of nodes. The computation times are the execution times of the application excluding the initialization and the finalization of the program and only measuring the part where the application runs through its computation and communication cycle. The computation times range from (283.87 ± 0.04) sec on 5 nodes to (29.14 ± 0.12) sec on 50 nodes without any checkpoint overhead. The exchange between the different processes is done within a loop with a maximum iteration number of 1000 with a checkpoint cycle of 100. Thus 10 checkpoints have been written during the execution of the application. The size of the checkpoints has been 59 MBytes. The process with the maximum computation times of an application without checkpointing has been divided by the computation time of an application with checkpointing to get a relative computation time. The error of the relative computation time is calculated by calculating the error of the three independent executions of the distributed application using error propagation. In the current setup one spare node is reserved when computing with checkpoints. Thus it is expected that the ideal curve follows $(n-1)/n$ where n is the number of nodes. Figure 5 shows that the additional cost of writing checkpoints during the execution of the program is less than 1%. One can also see that the relative computation times in a scenario with checkpointing and one simulated failure are a 4% lower compared to the execution time without failure. However the overhead is still small.

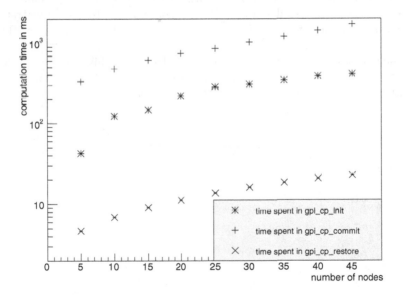

Fig. 6. Checkpointing overhead when writing a checkpoint in every 100th cycle: accumulated time spent in **gpi_cp_init**, **gpi_cp_commit** and **gpi_cp_restore** in ms

Figure 6 shows the details of the time spent in methods of the in-memory checkpointing library. The process of the distributed application with the maximum time in **gpi_cp_init**, **gpi_cp_commit** and **gpi_cp_restore** respectively in each execution of the program has been selected. The time spent in **gpi_cp_init** is quite small. The time spent in **gpi_cp_start** (not shown) is negligible. This is due to the fact that in this method the transfer is only started. The **gpi_cp_commit** method checks if the checkpoint has already been completely transferred. It is independent of the number of nodes as long as the checkpointing frequency is chosen in such a way that enough time is available for the asynchronous operation to be run. Also the time spent in the **gpi_cp_restore** method is quite small. One has to keep in mind that the time for a restore after a fault consists of several components since the time spent to make sure that a common state is observed in a distributed application and to get back to the computational state where the error occurred have to be added.

4.3   Performance Measurement with a Real-Life Application: GRT Angle Migration

GRT Angle Migration is a ray-based method in seismic imaging, that does not only recreate a structural image of the sub-surface from reflected acoustic signals but also provides direct access to the angle dependency of the reflection coefficient at the sub-surface scatterer. In migration algorithms, amplitudes picked from seismic traces according to travel-times are summed up for each output point. In GRT, this integration is performed within the angle domain of incident and reflected ray, resulting in a quasi-random access to the input traces. In modern surveys, these traces cover areas of a few $1000 \, km^2$, leading to TBytes of data.

In the current implementation of the GRT algorithm, this input data is loaded into GASPI memory during the initialization phase and can be accessed on demand by each worker node during the calculation phase. The calculation is

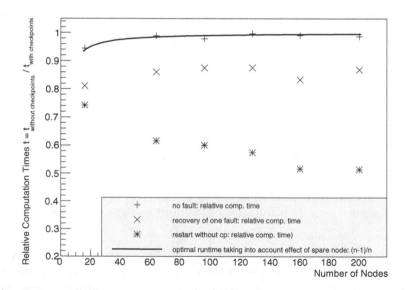

Fig. 7. Relative computation time of the GRT angle migration example with in-memory checkpointing, recovery and manual restart.

parallelized in the output domain, each partial result is written to disk. Thus, a restart of this application in case of a failure is possible without recalculating these partial results, but the initialization phase has to be redone. And this phase includes some expensive pre-processing, data analysis and arrangement steps, including a parallel sorting of the full data set and a distribution of corresponding meta data. Redoing this after a failure should be avoided by creating one checkpoint of this meta data as soon as possible.

The execution time has been measured for a medium sized seismic data set of 264 GB and a target oriented output-area of one line. Figure 7 shows calculation times with checkpointing and with checkpointing, restoring and recovering relative to the calculation times without any checkpoint. The overhead for creating the checkpoint during a successful run can be neglected against the optimal run time including the effect of one spare process (solid line). In case of one failure, the overhead is about 15%. This overhead contains the synchronization after the simulated failure, recovering the meta data from the checkpoint and reloading the seismic data according to this meta data on the spare node. But it avoids a re-initialization of the entire data set an all nodes, as discussed above. In order to stress this point, Fig. 7 also shows the computation time for running with simulated fault and manual restart without checkpointing for comparison. In this mode, the overhead is much larger. More important, it increases with the number of processes, caused by some global operations during initialization. Avoiding this gives a clear benefit for this application.

5   Conclusions

The in-memory checkpointing library offers a number of benefits to the application developer. It provides a light-weight interface independent of GASPI/GPI which can be called from any parallel program. Measurements of a simple stencil code and a real-life seismic imaging method GRT show that the low latency and asynchrony cause negligible overheads. The library allows the user to specify the data to be replicated and to select the frequency writing the checkpoints to maximize the benefits of the method. As future work we intend to evaluate our approach on larger systems and experiment with persistency as provided by NVRAM. We will continue to improve our library with particular focus on turning some fault tolerance aspects (e.g. fault detection) more automatic.

Acknowledgments. The work was funded by the European Commission through the EXA2CT project (grant agreement no. 610741).

References

1. Ali, N., Krishnamoorthy, S., Govind, N., Palmer, B.: A redundant communication approach to scalable fault tolerance in PGAS programming models. In: 2011 19th International Euromicro Conference on Parallel, Distributed and Network-Based Processing, pp. 24–31, February 2011

2. Amoon, M.: A framework for providing a hybrid fault tolerance in cloud computing. In: 2015 Science and Information Conference (SAI), pp. 844–849, July 2015
3. Bent, J., Gibson, G., Grider, G., McClelland, B., Nowoczynski, P., Nunez, J., Polte, M., Wingate, M.: PLFS: a checkpoint filesystem for parallel applications. In: Proceedings of the Conference on High Performance Computing Networking, Storage and Analysis, SC 2009, pp. 21:1–21:12. ACM, New York (2009). http://doi.acm.org/10.1145/1654059.1654081
4. Breitbart, J., Schmidtobreick, M., Heuveline, V.: Evaluation of the global address space programming interface (GASPI). In: 2014 IEEE International Parallel Distributed Processing Symposium Workshops (IPDPSW), pp. 717–726, May 2014
5. Chen, W.Y., et al.: A Performance Analysis of the Berkeley UPC Compiler (2003)
6. Dun, N., Fujita, H., Fang, A., Liu, Y., Chien, A.A., Balaj, P., Iskra, K., Bland, W., Siegel, A.: Flexible error recovery using versions in global view resilience. In: 2015 IEEE International Conference on Cluster Computing, pp. 512–513, September 2015
7. El-Ghazawi, T., et al.: UPC: Distributed Shared-Memory Programming. Wiley, Hoboken (2005)
8. Fajerski, J., et al.: Fast in-memory checkpointing with POSIX API for legacy exascale-applications. In: SPPEXA Symposium 2016 (2016, accepted for publication)
9. Gamell, M., Katz, D.S., Kolla, H., Chen, J., Klasky, S., Parashar, M.: Exploring automatic, online failure recovery for scientific applications at extreme scales. In: International Conference for High Performance Computing, Networking, Storage and Analysis, SC 2014, pp. 895–906, November 2014
10. GASPI Forum: GASPI: Global Address Space Programming Interface version 16.1 (2016)
11. Machado, R.: (2016). https://github.com/cc-hpc-itwm/gpi_cp
12. Machado, R., Lojewski, C.: The fraunhofer virtual machine: a communication library and runtime system based on the RDMA model. Comput. Sci. Res. Dev. **23**, 125–132 (2009)
13. Numrich, R.W., Reid, J.: Co-array fortran for parallel programming. SIGPLAN Fortran Forum **17**(2), 1–31 (1998). http://doi.acm.org/10.1145/289918.289920
14. Rotaru, T.: Best Practice Guide for Writing GASPI-MPI Interoperable Programs (2016)
15. Shahzad, F., et al.: Building a fault tolerant application using the GASPI communication layer. In: 2015 IEEE International Conference on Cluster Computing, pp. 580–587 (2015)
16. Vishnu, A., et al.: Fault-tolerant communication runtime support for data-centric programming models. In: 2010 International Conference on High Performance Computing, pp. 1–9, December 2010

Multicore and Manycore Parallelism

Optimized Batched Linear Algebra
for Modern Architectures

Jack Dongarra[1,2,3], Sven Hammarling[3], Nicholas J. Higham[3],
Samuel D. Relton[3(✉)], and Mawussi Zounon[3(✉)]

[1] University of Tennessee, Knoxville, TN, USA
dongarra@icl.utk.edu
[2] Oak Ridge National Laboratory, Oak Ridge, TN, USA
[3] School of Mathematics, The University of Manchester, Manchester, UK
sven.hammarling@btinternet.com,
{nick.higham,samuel.relton,mawussi.zounon}@manchester.ac.uk

Abstract. Solving large numbers of small linear algebra problems simultaneously is becoming increasingly important in many application areas. Whilst many researchers have investigated the design of efficient batch linear algebra kernels for GPU architectures, the common approach for many/multi-core CPUs is to use one core per subproblem in the batch. When solving batches of very small matrices, 2×2 for example, this design exhibits two main issues: it fails to fully utilize the vector units and the cache of modern architectures, since the matrices are too small. Our approach to resolve this is as follows: given a batch of small matrices spread throughout the primary memory, we first reorganize the elements of the matrices into a contiguous array, using a block interleaved memory format, which allows us to process the small independent problems as a single large matrix problem and enables cross-matrix vectorization. The large problem is solved using blocking strategies that attempt to optimize the use of the cache. The solution is then converted back to the original storage format. To explain our approach we focus on two BLAS routines: general matrix-matrix multiplication (GEMM) and the triangular solve (TRSM). We extend this idea to LAPACK routines using the Cholesky factorization and solve (POSV). Our focus is primarily on very small matrices ranging in size from 2×2 to 32×32. Compared to both MKL and OpenMP implementations, our approach can be up to 4 times faster for GEMM, up to 14 times faster for TRSM, and up to 40 times faster for POSV on the new Intel Xeon Phi processor, code-named Knights Landing (KNL). Furthermore, we discuss strategies to avoid data movement between sockets when using our interleaved approach on a NUMA node.

1   Introduction

Over the last decade, the high-performance computing (HPC) community has made significant strides in solving large-scale matrix problems efficiently. Another major challenge is to achieve good performance when computing a large batch of small matrix problems: this situation occurs commonly in applications including deep learning libraries [1,3], multifrontal solvers for sparse linear

© Springer International Publishing AG 2017
F.F. Rivera et al. (Eds.): Euro-Par 2017, LNCS 10417, pp. 511–522, 2017.
DOI: 10.1007/978-3-319-64203-1_37

systems [5], and radar signal processing [4] etc. In deep learning applications, for example, many applications require the solution of thousands of independent (and very small) general matrix-matrix multiplication (GEMM) in Eq. (1), where *batch_count* is number of independent problems in the batch.

$$C^{(i)} \leftarrow \alpha^{(i)} A^{(i)} B^{(i)} + \beta^{(i)} C^{(i)}, \qquad i = 1 : batch\_count. \tag{1}$$

The challenge is to make more efficient use of computational cores than a simple `for loop` around a single call to a vendor optimized GEMM kernel, where there may not be enough work to keep the cores running at full efficiency. Note that, depending on the application, the batch can contain matrices of different sizes and $\alpha^{(i)}$ and $\beta^{(i)}$ can have different values. But in this work, we focus on the "fixed batch" case, which is more common in applications. In a fixed batch the values of α and β are the same for all the problems in the batch and the matrices have a constant size, i.e. the dimensions of $A^{(i)}$ are the same for all i in $[1, batch\_count]$ and similarly for the matrices $B^{(i)}$ and $C^{(i)}$.

To address the need for efficient libraries to perform batches of small linear algebra operations in parallel, new APIs have been investigated and a comparative study of these APIs is given in [11]. While most research focuses on providing high-performance batch linear algebra implementation for GPU architectures, there is—at the time of writing—no better solution than using one core per problem when it comes to many/multi-core architectures. When solving batches of very small matrices, 2×2 for example, this design exhibits two main problems. Due to the small size of the matrices we fail to fully utilize the vector units and the cache of modern architectures.

In this work, we focus on level 3 BLAS routines because they are the critical building blocks of many high-performance software. Our motivation to focus on GEMM and triangular solve (TRSM) is that all of level 3 BLAS routines except TRSM can be viewed as a specialized GEMM [8]. However, regardless of these considerations, our proposed solutions are easily extended to all BLAS kernels including the level 1 and 2 algorithms.

The key aspect of our approach is as follows: given a batch of small matrices spread throughout RAM we first reorganize the elements of the matrices into a contiguous array, using a block interleaved memory format, which allows us to process the small independent problems as a single large matrix problem. The large problem is solved using blocking strategies that attempt to optimize the use of the cache. The solution is then converted back to the original storage format.

Compared to the MKL batched BLAS implementation and an OpenMP `for loop` around MKL BLAS kernels, our implementation is up to 4 times faster for DGEMM and up to 14 times faster for DTRSM on the new self-hosted Intel Xeon Phi processors, code named Knights Landing (KNL). By extending this idea to LAPACK routines, specifically the Cholesky factorization and solve (POSV), we can see that our approach can be extremely efficient and performs up to 40 times faster than using an OpenMP `for loop` on the Intel KNL architecture.

The paper is organized as follows. In Sect. 2 we present the current state of the art in batch BLAS algorithms and their limitations. Section 3 describes our approach, the block interleaved batch BLAS, followed by some performance analyses. In Sect. 4, we discuss how to extend batch operations to include LAPACK routines, with a focus on Cholesky factorization and solve. We then discuss the main performance issues raised when using NUMA nodes in Sect. 5 before giving some concluding remarks in Sect. 6.

2   Related Work

Motivated by the efficiency of vendor supplied libraries for small problems on many/multi-core CPU architectures, the currently accepted method for solving batches of small problems is to have a single core per problem in the batch [6]. Therefore, most of the effort in recent years has been devoted to developing efficient batch kernels for GPUs. Our aim is to challenge the conventional wisdom in many/multi-core CPU architectures, however a reader interested in efficient CUDA kernels for batch BLAS operations may look at [2,7,9,10].

2.1   Multicore CPUs and Xeon Phi Implementations

At first glance, batched BLAS operations on multicore CPUs seemed to be reduced to the choice between: (i) solving one problem at the time using all the available cores or (ii) solving many independent problems in parallel using a single core per problem. Whenever small matrices are used the second approach is preferred can be implemented simply: merely an OpenMP for loop around vendor supplied BLAS kernels is required.

When processing thousands of very small matrices, the error checking procedure implemented by most of optimized vendor kernels can be significantly time-consuming. To alleviate this overhead, Intel MKL allows us to skip the error checking thanks to the MKL_DIRECT_CALL or MKL_DIRECT_CALL_SEQ macros. Hence, the common wisdom for a fixed batched BLAS implementation con sists in checking the arguments once, as all the problems in the batch share the same error prone arguments, then perform an OpenMP for loop over optimized BLAS kernels.

While these solutions are acceptable for batches of matrices of medium size, they may fail to exploit efficiently wide vector units on modern architectures. For example, the AVX-512 vector units available in the Intel KNL, enable the completion of 8 double precision vector operations within each cycle, while a 2×2 matrix can fill only half of such a vector unit.

Furthermore, some BLAS routines don't offer enough parallelism. For example in the case of batched TRSM, the computation of each entry of each right-hand side requires a single division before the updates. When one right-hand side is required, regardless of the matrix size, the common approach will perform only one double precision division in one clock cycle on a core capable of 8 double precision divisions. However, by using the interleaved memory layout described in Sect. 3 one can saturate the vector units at all steps of the algorithm thanks to cross-matrix vectorization.

3 Data Layout Optimization

Dealing with thousands of independent, small matrices requires a careful choice of memory layout, and a good memory layout should be user-friendly without penalizing performance. There are currently 3 competing data layouts advocated by the linear algebra community for batched BLAS operations. In this section, we illustrate the underlying idea of each data layout using the example of solving three independent 2×2 matrix problems ($A^{(1)}$,$A^{(2)}$, $A^{(2)}$).

3.1 Pointer-to-pointer Layout

Most of the existing interfaces for both CPU and GPU architectures use an array of pointers, where each pointer leads to a matrix in memory. We call this the pointer-to-pointers (P2P) layout. As depicted in Fig. 1, it allows us to allocate matrices independently. This is the solution currently used in *cblas_dgemm_batch* and *cublasDgemmBatched*, the batch DGEMM kernels available in Intel MKL 11.3 beta and NVIDIA cuBLAS version 4.1, respectively. This approach is very flexible but has two main issues as reported in [7,11]. First, the allocation and deallocation of thousands of small matrices can be excessively time-consuming. Second, processing very small matrices stored separately can increase the number of memory accesses required and induces sub-optimal cache use. In addition, the array of pointers approach suffers from high data movement costs when data is offloaded to hardware accelerators.

$A^{(1)}$
$a_{0,0}$ $a_{1,0}$ $a_{0,1}$ $a_{1,1}$
$A^{(2)}$
$a_{0,0}$ $a_{1,0}$ $a_{0,1}$ $a_{1,1}$
$A^{(3)}$
$a_{0,0}$ $a_{1,0}$ $a_{0,1}$ $a_{1,1}$

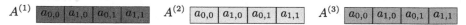

Fig. 1. Pointer to pointer (P2P) memory layout. The three matrices are stored in different memory locations in column major order.

3.2 Strided Layout

To alleviate the design issues intrinsic to the pointer to pointers memory layout, NVIDIA cuBLAS advocated another interface called the strided layout [12]. It consists of storing a collection of matrices in one contiguous block of memory. As illustrated in Fig. 2, this involves allocating a large chunk of memory to store all the A^i matrices.

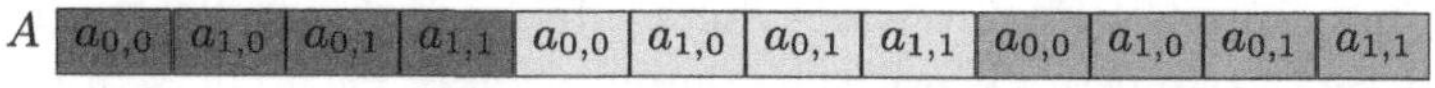

A
$a_{0,0}$ $a_{1,0}$ $a_{0,1}$ $a_{1,1}$ $a_{0,0}$ $a_{1,0}$ $a_{0,1}$ $a_{1,1}$ $a_{0,0}$ $a_{1,0}$ $a_{0,1}$ $a_{1,1}$

Fig. 2. Strided memory layout. The three matrices are stored in one contiguous chunk of memory.

3.3   Interleaved Memory Layout

Solving batches of small size matrix problems on modern architectures is challenging because these architectures are primarily designed to address large-scale problems. The main objective of the interleaved memory layout approach is to reformulate the thousands of independent small BLAS operations as a single large-scale problem. This involves providing a relevant way to store the independent matrices. Interleaving the entries of different matrices enables cross-matrix vectorization to fill the vector units on modern architectures. As illustrated in Fig. 3, the interleaved layout is a permutation of the strided memory layout.

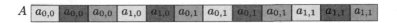

Fig. 3. Interleaved memory layout. The three matrices are stored in one contiguous chunk of memory, but their elements are mixed together.

3.4   Design of Interleaved Batch BLAS

While the interleaved layout has the potential for better vectorization and data locality, it requires redesigning the BLAS algorithms. This is achieved by adding inner $\texttt{for}$ $\texttt{loops}$ to the original algorithms in order to create batches of floating point operations. We illustrate this in a simplified version of an interleaved TRSM displayed in Algorithm 1. For the sake of simplicity and readability, A and B denote the interleaved layout containing $m \times m$ lower triangular matrices $A^{(i)}$ and the $m \times n$ right hand side matrices $B^{(i)}$, respectively; and the notation $A[i][j][idx]$ is used to refer to the entry $a_{i,j}$ of the matrix $A^{(idx)}$ in the batch.

Compared to the original TRSM algorithm, our interleaved version has an additional $\texttt{for}$ $\texttt{loop}$ (Algorithm 1, line 5) that accesses each matrix in the batch. Some operations have also been moved to the innermost loop (Algorithm 1, line 7 and 10), for the sake of better vectorization without affecting the numerical stability. The innermost loop contains thousands of floating point operations parallelized among cores thanks to the $\texttt{\#pragma}$ $\texttt{openmp}$ $\texttt{parallel}$ $\texttt{for}$ directive whilst the $\texttt{simd}$ directive makes use of vector pipelines within each core.

3.5   Block Interleaved Layout

While the interleave layout increases the vectorization within the floating point units, it may lead to a high cache miss rate: since the first entries of the matrices are stored followed by the second entries etc., the next entries required by the algorithm are unlikely to be in the cache at any given time. To alleviate this problem, we divide the initial batch into small sub-batches (blocks), then apply the interleaved strategy within each block. The block size is selected such that each sub-batch could be solved efficiently by a single core. The optimal block size

---

Algorithm 1. Interleaved TRSM algorithm:$B^{(i)} \leftarrow \alpha(A^{(i)})^{-1}B^{(i)}$

1: **for** $j \leftarrow 1$ to n **do**   ▷ Iterate over n right hand sides
2:     **for** $k \leftarrow 1$ to m **do**   ▷ Iterate over rows of A
3:         **for** $i \leftarrow k$ to m **do**   ▷ Iterate over columns of A
4:             `#pragma omp parallel for simd`
5:             **for** $idx \leftarrow 1$ to $batch\_count$ **do**   ▷ Iterate over problems in the batch
6:                 **if** $k == 0$ **then**
7:                     $B[i][j][idx] \leftarrow \beta \times B[i][[j][idx]$ ▷ Apply α
8:                 **end if**
9:                 **if** $i == k$ **then**
10:                    $B[k][j][idx] \leftarrow B[k][j][idx]/A[k][k][idx]$ ▷ Division by $a_{k,k}$
11:                    continue
12:                 **end if**
13:                 $B[i][j][idx] \leftarrow B[i][j][idx] - B[k][j][idx] \times A[i][k][idx]$ ▷ Update
14:             **end for**
15:         **end for**
16:     **end for**
17: **end for**

---

is a tunable parameter and depends on the number of cores and the memory hierarchy of the target machine. In our experiments we let InterleaveTRSM denote Algorithm 1. For the block interleaved TRSM (BlockInterleaveTRSM) we replace `#pragma omp parallel for simd` by `#pragma simd` in Algorithm 1 and use an OpenMP for loop over the blocks defined above.

3.6 Interleaved Batch BLAS User Interfaces

We note that data layout utilized by the user and that used internally to the computation need not be the same. Indeed our code has two interfaces: a simple P2P interface for user convenience (which performs all the memory layout conversion internally) and, for expert users, we expose the interleaved layout kernels and the associated conversion functions directly. For the simpler functions with P2P-based interfaces, the design is as follows:

1. Convert from user layout to block interleaved layout.
2. Call block interleaved kernels.
3. Convert back to the user layout.

The conversion routines are designed for better data locality, and exploit both thread and vector level parallelism. For safety, the user is required to provide the extra memory intended for conversion. More details on the API and the codes can be found on our Github repository[1].

---

[1] https://github.com/sdrelton/bblas_interleaved.

3.7   Experimental Results

The aim of this subsection is to evaluate how the block interleaved (`Blkintl`) batch kernels compare to both the optimized Intel MKL batch BLAS kernels (`MKL`) and OpenMP `for loop` over Intel MKL BLAS kernels (`OpenMP`). The experiments are performed on a 68-core Intel KNL[2] configured in flat mode with all data allocated in the high bandwidth memory. To obtain more reliable results, we take the average time over ten runs and carefully flush the cache between each run.

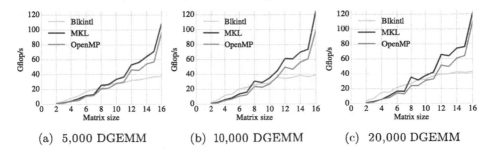

(a) 5,000 DGEMM   (b) 10,000 DGEMM   (c) 20,000 DGEMM

Fig. 4. Performance comparison of different implementations of batch DGEMM using 68 threads on the Intel KNL with different batch sizes on square matrices ranging in size from 2×2 to 16×16.

The first experiment displayed in Fig. 4, compares the performance in GFlop/s (the higher the better) of three batch DGEMM implementations. A batch containing a few thousand matrices is enough to saturate the KNL, and the performance doesn't increase significantly when doubling the batch size. It is important to notice that we also consider layout conversion time in the performance of `Blkintl`. The conversion overhead is significant for GEMM because it involves three batches of matrices ($A^{(i)}$, $B^{(i)}$ and $C^{(i)}$). Despite this overhead, `Blkintl` outperforms `MKL` for very small matrices ranging from 2×2 to 7×7, and `OpenMP` for matrices up to 11×11. In the particular case of a batch of 20,000 2×2, `Blkintl` is four times faster than `MKL`. As the matrix sizes increase, both `MKL` and `OpenMP` outperform `Blkintl` for two main reasons: (i) the increasing cost of data layout conversion, and, (ii) the current `Blkintl` implementation is not taking advantage of advanced memory prefetching strategies. Since the three kernels are performing the same floating point operations in a different order, we can view this as a race to fill the vector units within the cores.

Furthermore, on average, `MKL` is 15% better than `OpenMP`. This suggests that the `MKL` approach to batch BLAS is more sophisticated than a simple OpenMP `for loop` over optimized BLAS kernels.

---

[2] https://ark.intel.com/products/94035/Intel-Xeon-Phi-Processor-7250-16GB-1_ 40-GHz-68-core.

As MKL provides only batch kernels for DGEMM, in Fig. 5 we can only compare the performance of Blkintl and OpenMP for a batch of 10,000 DTRSM. Compared to GEMM, TRSM has a lower numerical intensity, but the performance can be increased by operating on multiple right-hand sides. In Fig. 5a and b, for example, the performance almost doubled for both OpenMP and Blkintl from one right-hand side to two. The superiority of Blkintl over OpenMP is significant even with matrix sizes up to 32×32, which is consistent with our analysis in Subsect. 2.1. Interleaving multiple triangular solves alleviates the synchronization penalty of performing only one division per right-hand side before parallel updates. Another factor is a lower conversion overhead: since the TRSM algorithm operates on triangular matrices and a few right-hand sides, the conversion overhead is reasonably low when compared to GEMM.

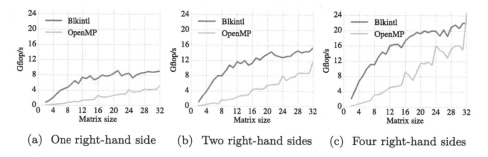

(a) One right-hand side   (b) Two right-hand sides   (c) Four right-hand sides

Fig. 5. Performance of a batch of $10,000$ DTRSM operations using 68 threads on the Intel KNL with different numbers of right hand sides (rhs), on matrices ranging in size from 2×2 to 32×32. Blkintl is 14 times better than OpenMP in (a) for 2×2 matrices.

4   Application to Batched Cholesky Factorization and Solve

Efficient LAPACK kernel implementations are commonly achieved by dividing the matrices in blocks or tiles, and taking advantage of Level 3 BLAS routines as much as possible to process the blocks or tiles. However, very small matrices cannot easily be divided into blocks. To solve batches of very small LAPACK problems we can extend the interleaved approach to LAPACK routines. This allows us to optimize the use of wide vector units and also take advantage of interleaved BLAS kernels whenever possible. In particular we will focus on the Cholesky solve (POSV) algorithm which solves $Ax = b$, where A is a symmetric definite positive matrix. It starts with a Cholesky factorization (POTRF) $A = LL^T$, then performs a forward substitution (TRSM kernel, $Ly = b$) before finally performing a backward substitution (TRSM kernel, $L^T x = y$). In this example, the implementation effort involves mainly developing the Blkintl POTRF kernel, as Blkintl TRSM has already been discussed above.

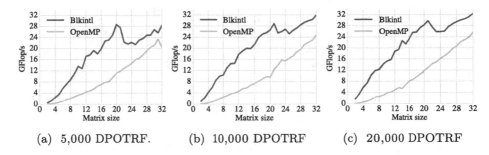

(a) 5,000 DPOTRF.   (b) 10,000 DPOTRF   (c) 20,000 DPOTRF

Fig. 6. Performance of batch Cholesky factorization (DPOTRF) using 68 threads on the Intel KNL, with different batch sizes, on matrices ranging in size from 2×2 to 32×32. `Blkintl` is 18 times better than `OpenMP` in (c) for 2×2 matrices.

As illustrated in Fig. 6, `Blkintl` POTRF outperforms the `OpenMP` version for the same reasons discussed for the `Blkintl` TRSM kernel: better use of the vector units and low memory conversion overhead, and the conversion cost is even lower than the TRSM case since it involves only one triangular matrix per problem in the batch. An overview of the `Blkintl` POSV algorithm is provided in Algorithm 2.

Algorithm 2. `Blkintl` POSV algorithm: $B^{(i)} \leftarrow (A^{(i)})^{-1} B^{(i)}$

1: Conversion of $A^{(i)}$ and $B^{(i)}$ into `Blkintl` format
2: Call `Blkintl` POTRF
3: Call `Blkintl` TRSM (forward substitution)
4: Call `Blkintl` TRSM (backward substitution)
5: Convert $A^{(i)}$ and $B^{(i)}$ back to the user's format

The two main features of Algorithm 2 are: (i) conversions are performed once before using the three `Blkintl` kernels, (ii) reuse of `Blkintl` BLAS kernels. In particular, performing the conversion only once allows us to obtain very good performance with this approach. The results shown in Fig. 7, for example, show that the gap in performance between `Blkintl` and `OpenMP` is larger than the one observed for TRSM in Fig. 5.

The same strategy is applicable to other batched LAPACK kernels, with lots of potential for large speedups over an OpenMP `for` loop.

5   Efficient Batch Linear Algebra on NUMA Nodes

As explained in Subsect. 3.7, obtaining good performance is a race to fill the vector units of the cores as quickly as possible. In addition, data layout conversions required by `Blkintl` make our algorithms sensitive to data locality and data movement. These two factors are potential limitations for achieving good

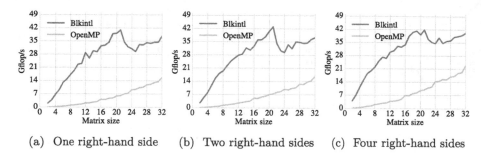

(a) One right-hand side   (b) Two right-hand sides   (c) Four right-hand sides

Fig. 7. Performance on a batch of $10,000$ Cholesky solve (DPOSV) using 68 threads on the Intel KNL with different numbers of right-hand sides, on matrices ranging in size from 2×2 to 32×32. `Blkintl` is 40 times better than `OpenMP` in (a) for 2×2 matrices.

performance on non-uniform memory access (NUMA) nodes. In fact, when running a batch of very small matrices on a 2-socket NUMA node for example, the matrices are more likely to be allocated on a single socket, and the second socket will have only a remote access to data. This induces a high communication cost and performance drop due to the cost of remote memory access. This issue is commonly addressed by interleaving the data allocation thanks to the `numactl -interleave=all` option available on Linux systems. Memory will then be allocated using a round robin procedure between the nodes. As depicted in Fig. 8, there is a slight performance improvement for both `Blkintl` and `OpenMP` when changing the standard memory allocation (Fig. 8a) into the interleaved allocation configuration (Fig. 8b). In general spreading the memory allocation improves the performance but, in the case of batch operations, there is no guarantee that we will allocate all data required for each independent problem on the same node. For example $A^{(i)}$ may be allocated on the first socket while the corresponding $B^{(i)}$ allocated on the second socket.

One way to significantly improve the performance is to split the batch into two independent batches and use one socket per batch. Unfortunately current OpenMP runtimes are not NUMA aware, however the user can manage the memory allocation themselves to enforce optimal data placement, using the `libnuma` API for example. The user can then call our batch BLAS kernel on each socket in parallel. This strategy should improve the performance significantly as observed in Fig. 8c, but requires a lot of user effort.

On the particular machine we used, the NUMA node vector units are half the size of the Intel KNL vector units. This explains the decrease of the performance gap between `Blkintl` and `OpenMP` when compared to those observed for Intel KNL. We believe that further studies can help in designing new efficient batch kernels which are specially optimized for NUMA nodes.

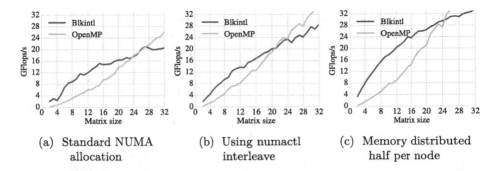

(a) Standard NUMA   (b) Using numactl   (c) Memory distributed
    allocation   interleave   half per node

Fig. 8. Performance of a batch of 10,000 Cholesky solve (DPOSV) operations using 20 threads on a NUMA node of two 10-core sockets, Intel Xeon E5-2650 v3 (Haswell), with different numbers of right-hand sides, on matrices ranging in size from 2×2 to 32×32.

6   Concluding Remarks

In this research we have explained, and demonstrated the large potential of, the block interleaved strategy for batched BLAS operations. We have shown that our approach can offer significant performance improvements over an OpenMP `for loop` around vendor optimized BLAS kernels, with speedups of up to 40× for a batched Cholesky solve.

While generally satisfactory speedups are achieved on the Intel KNL architecture, we noted that further prefetching techniques may help to further improve the performance of the `Blkintl` DGEMM kernel. We have also shown that advanced memory placement configurations are necessary to increase the performance of batched kernels on NUMA nodes.

Finally, this study has focused only on an element-wise interleaving strategy. However, we believe that other data interleaving approaches such as row interleaving, column interleaving, and mixtures of the above could also provide similar (or even better) performance. It is clear that there is a large amount of further investigation to be done in this area.

Acknowledgements. The authors would like to thank The University of Tennessee for the use of their computational resources. This research was funded in part from the European Union's Horizon 2020 research and innovation programme under the NLAFET grant agreement No. 671633.

References

1. Abadi, M., Agarwal, A., Barham, P., Brevdo, E., et al.: TensorFlow: large-scale machine learning on heterogeneous systems (2015). tensorflow.org
2. Abdelfattah, A., Haidar, A., Tomov, S., Dongarra, J.J.: Performance, design, and autotuning of batched GEMM for GPUs. In: Proceedings of High Performance Computing - 31st International Conference, ISC High Performance 2016, Frankfurt, Germany, 19–23 June 2016, pp. 21–38 (2016)

3. Al-Rfou, R., Alain, G., Almahairi, A., Angermueller, C., Bahdanau, D., et al.: Theano: a python framework for fast computation of mathematical expressions. arXiv e-prints, http://arxiv.org/abs/1605.02688, May 2016
4. Anderson, M.J., Sheffield, D., Keutzer, K.: A predictive model for solving small linear algebra problems in GPU registers. In: 2012 IEEE 26th International Parallel and Distributed Processing Symposium (IPDPS), pp. 2–13. IEEE (2012)
5. Duff, I., Reid, J.K.: The multifrontal solution of indefinite sparse symmetric linear equations. ACM Trans. Math. Softw. **9**(3), 302–325 (1983)
6. Haidar, A., Dong, T.T., Tomov, S., Luszczek, P., Dongarra, J.: A framework for batched and GPU-resident factorization algorithms applied to block householder transformations. In: Kunkel, J.M., Ludwig, T. (eds.) ISC High Performance 2015. LNCS, vol. 9137, pp. 31–47. Springer, Cham (2015). doi:10.1007/978-3-319-20119-1_3
7. Jhurani, C., Mullowney, P.: A gemm interface and implementation on NVIDIA GPUs for multiple small matrices. J. Parallel Distrib. Comput. **75**, 133–140 (2015)
8. Kågström, B., Ling, P., van Loan, C.: GEMM-based level 3 BLAS: high-performance model implementations and performance evaluation benchmark. ACM Trans. Math. Softw. **24**(3), 268–302 (1998)
9. Lopez, M.G., Horton, M.D.: Batch matrix exponentiation. In: Kindratenko, V. (ed.) Numerical Computations with GPUs, pp. 45–67. Springer, Cham (2014). doi:10.1007/978-3-319-06548-9_3
10. Masliah, I., Abdelfattah, A., Haidar, A., Tomov, S., Baboulin, M., Falcou, J., Dongarra, J.: High-performance matrix-matrix multiplications of very small matrices. In: Dutot, P.-F., Trystram, D. (eds.) Euro-Par 2016. LNCS, vol. 9833, pp. 659–671. Springer, Cham (2016). doi:10.1007/978-3-319-43659-3_48
11. Relton, S.D., Valero-Lara, P., Zounon, M.: A comparison of potential interfaces for batched BLAS computations. MIMS EPrint 2016.42, Manchester Institute for Mathematical Sciences, The University of Manchester, UK (2016)
12. Shi, Y., Niranjan, U.N., Anandkumar, A., Cecka, C.: Tensor contractions with extended BLAS kernels on CPU and GPU. arXiv preprint arXiv:1606.05696 (2016)

New Efficient General Sparse Matrix Formats for Parallel SpMV Operations

Jan Philipp Ecker[1], Rudolf Berrendorf[1(✉)], and Florian Mannuss[2]

[1] Computer Science Department, Bonn-Rhein-Sieg University of Applied Sciences, Sankt Augustin, Germany
{jan.ecker,rudolf.berrendorf}@h-brs.de
[2] EXPEC Advanced Research Center, Saudi Arabian Oil Company, Dhahran, Saudi Arabia
florian.mannuss@aramco.com

Abstract. The Sparse Matrix-Vector Multiplication (SpMV) is an important building block in High Performance Computing. Performance improvements for the SpMV are often gained by the development of new optimized sparse matrix formats either by utilizing special sparsity patterns of a matrix or by taking bottlenecks of a hardware architecture into account. In this work a requirements analysis is done for sparse matrix formats with an emphasis on the parallel SpMV for large general sparse matrices. Based on these requirements, three new sparse matrix formats were developed, each combining several optimization techniques and addressing different optimization goals/hardware architectures. The CSR5 Bit Compressed (CSR5BC) format is an extension to the existing CSR5 format and optimized for GPUs. The other two formats, Hybrid Compressed Slice Storage (HCSS) and Local Group Compressed Sparse Row (LGCSR), are new formats optimized for multi-core/-processor architectures including the Xeon Phi Knights Landing. Results show that all three storage formats deliver good parallel SpMV performance on their target architectures over a large set of test matrices compared to other well performing formats in vendor and research libraries.

Keywords: SpMV · Sparse matrix format · Requirements analysis · CPU · GPU · Xeon Phi knights landing · CSR5BC · HCSS · LGCSR

1 Introduction

The Sparse Matrix-Vector Multiplication (SpMV) $\vec{y} \leftarrow A * \vec{x}$ is an important building block for many scientific and engineering applications. Much effort has been spent in the past to optimize this operation. To do so, many development parameters have to be considered simultaneously, among them the storage format for the sparse matrix, the data access pattern in an SpMV operation, the sparsity structure of the matrix, performance characteristics of the target processor architecture, and for a parallel execution the balance of load. This work subsumes requirements for sparse matrix storage formats with an emphasis on an

© Springer International Publishing AG 2017
F.F. Rivera et al. (Eds.): Euro-Par 2017, LNCS 10417, pp. 523–537, 2017.
DOI: 10.1007/978-3-319-64203-1_38

efficient parallel execution of SpMV operations and summarizes important existing optimization techniques for such operations on different target platforms.

The main contribution of this work is the description of three new storage formats targeted for different parallel processor architectures that address most of the raised requirements. The relevant hardware platforms are the building blocks in current HPC systems: single- and multi-processor CPU systems, Intel Xeon Phi Knights Landing and Nvidia GPUs. Each of the newly developed formats has different optimization goals, which resulted in fundamentally different matrix formats with different performance properties. Two of the three new formats do not assume (and do not take advantage of) any special matrix structure. The third format is optimized for matrices with many 1D blocks.

The rest of this paper is structured as follows. Section 2 presents the requirements analysis of the SpMV operation, a discussion of known optimization techniques and related work. Section 3 introduces the three newly developed matrix formats. In Sect. 4 the performance of the formats is evaluated on a large set of test matrices. Section 5 summarizes the findings of the work.

2   Requirements Analysis, Existing Optimization Techniques and Related Work

In our effort to optimize the parallel SpMV operation, we found several bottlenecks in existing formats and implementations that could not easily be eliminated. The development of the new formats presented in this work is based on an extensive requirements analysis of the parallel SpMV operation. The identified requirements are divided into strong and weak requirements as shown in Table 1. Strong requirements are essential in the development process for every sparse matrix format, while weak requirements are more important in the implementation step. But there is no sharp distinction between the two requirement types. In the following, we briefly explain the requirements and discuss important existing optimization techniques that can be used to tackle them. The related work is in so far included in the following discussion.

The SpMV is due to its low computational complexity for large matrices a memory bound operation. Therefore the focus of the sparse matrix formats should be on the reduction of the required memory transfer demand. All sparse storage formats require much less memory compared to storing a dense matrix, but even *further* memory savings (R1) can be reached by using additional optimizations. One approach is the use of blocked formats like Blocked Compressed Sparse Row (BCSR) [4], blocked row-column (BRC) [3] or Dynamic Blocking (DynB) [16]). Another widely used optimization is index compression. This reaches from approaches where smaller data types are used for storing the index data [19] to complex bit compression strategies [9,21]. These techniques can also be combined to reach an even higher compression.

Further memory bandwidth savings can be reached by reusing data. For the SpMV operation, this is only possible for the $\vec{x}$ vector (R2), since the data of the matrix is read only once. Blocking or pattern based formats can be used for

Table 1. List of the strong requirements (left) and weak requirements (right).

#	Short Description	#	Short Description
R1	Reduce amount of moved data	C1	Prevent interleaved writes on $\vec{y}$
R2	Improve data reuse of $\vec{x}$	C2	NUMA-awareness
R3	Improve access latency on $\vec{x}$	C3	prevent synchronized writes on $\vec{y}$
R4	Allow consecutive memory accesses	C4	Ensure proper memory alignment
R5	Allow utilization of vector units	C5	Prevent branching / low complexity
R6	Improve load balancing of the SpMV	C6	Efficient format creation
		C7	Efficient matrix element updates
		C8	Prevent tuning parameters

Table 2. Selection of existing and new formats and their fulfilled requirements.

Format	R1	R2	R3	R4	R5	R6	C1	C2	C3	C4	C5	C6	C7	C8
CSR				✓	(~)		✓	✓	✓		✓	✓	✓	✓
BCSR	✓	✓		✓	(~)		✓	✓	✓	(~)	✓	✓	✓	
ELL				✓	✓		✓	✓	✓	✓	✓	✓	✓	✓
CSR5				✓	✓	✓	✓	✓	(~)	✓		✓	✓	✓
ELL-BRO	✓			✓	✓		✓	✓	✓	✓		✓	✓	✓
SELL-C-σ				✓	✓		✓	✓	✓	✓	✓	✓	✓	
DynB	✓	(~)		✓	(~)	✓	✓	✓	✓		(~)			
CSR5BC	✓			✓	✓	✓	✓	✓	(~)	✓		✓	✓	✓
HCSS	✓			✓	✓	✓	✓	✓	✓	✓	✓	✓	✓	✓
LGCSR	✓	✓		✓	(~)	✓	✓	✓	✓			✓	✓	✓

increasing the data reuse. By storing dense blocks of the matrix, elements with the same column index are processed as a group. Another technique for data reuse is a partitioning of the matrix into vertical tiles. When the size of the tiles is selected appropriately and the slices are processed one after each other, the data reuse of the $\vec{x}$ vector can be improved, since the number of possible column indices is reduced. This technique has been proposed by Yang et al. [24] and was also used in other matrix formats [20,23]. Matrix reordering techniques can also be used to improve locality/data reuse [14].

The accesses on the $\vec{x}$ vector depend on the structure of the sparse matrix. Typically these accesses are not consecutive and they can not be prefetched by a hardware prefetcher. This can lead to a high memory access latency (R3), since many elements have to be loaded from the main memory. Reordering techniques [15] can help to provide more consecutive memory accesses to the x vector. This could allow a more efficient prefetching of the required elements and thus lead to a lower memory access latency. In general this technique is not very applicable, since it introduces a significant overhead for the reordering itself.

Efficient sparse matrix formats should furthermore ensure consecutive memory accesses (R4). This is important especially on GPU-based systems but also other platforms with vector units can benefit from consecutive accesses [8]. Since all current hardware platforms have vector units or could be described as vector processors, the utilization of vector units is very important. Whether consecutive memory accesses are possible or not strongly depends on the data layout of the matrix format. Nevertheless different techniques can be used to increase consecutive memory accesses and the utilization of vector units (R5). Using the already mentioned blocking or pattern based approaches can be advantageous. Another rather new approach in this context is the use of a segmented sum algorithm, which has been proposed with the Block Compressed Common Coordinate (BCCOO) format [23] and the CSR5 format [13]. The segmented sum algorithms work independent of the row boundaries, which can improve the memory access pattern and simplify the efficient utilization of vector units.

On modern hardware the available parallelism is steadily increasing, which increases the need for a proper load balancing (R6). This is especially problematic for matrices with a highly irregular structure. Multiple techniques have been proposed to handle such imbalances. Examples are row-splitting and row-merging approaches [7,22], which try to reduce/increase the length of rows to allow a more balanced calculation. Furthermore, the already mentioned segmented sum algorithms can be used to improve the load balancing. By ignoring the row boundaries, the calculation of the SpMV is independent of the matrix structure which in theory should improve the load balance.

Additionally to our requirements analysis, we have evaluated a large number of matrix formats. Table 2 presents a small selection of formats and the fulfilled requirements. It furthermore presents the same analysis for the three newly developed formats which will be described in the following section. It can be seen that most of the existing formats fulfill 10 requirements at the most, with the only exception being the BCSR format. Additionally none of the formats fulfill the requirement R3, which is the improvement of the access latency, where no general optimization technique could be found. As mentioned, reordering techniques could solve this problem, but these methods introduce significant overhead to the format conversion and can introduce other, unwanted, changes to the matrix structure. Furthermore, it can be seen that only about half of the formats directly tackle the primary performance bottleneck of the SpMV operation, which is the limited memory bandwidth (requirement R1 and R2). All our newly developed formats focus on saving memory bandwidth, while not neglecting the other important requirements. Overall, the developed formats fulfill a slightly larger number of the identified requirements.

No existing publication could be found, which has done a comprehensive requirements analysis of the SpMV operation. The work of Langr Tvrdík [11] discusses important criteria when comparing different sparse matrix formats, which partially imply some of the requirements identified in this work.

3   New Formats for Efficient Parallel SpMV Operations

Based on the systematic requirements analysis and gathering of known optimization techniques, we structurally improved (CSR5 Bit Compressed (CSR5BC)) and developed completely new formats (Hybrid Compressed Slice Storage (HCSS), Local Group Compressed Sparse Row (LGCSR)) that address most requirements and perform well on their target hardware architectures. In the following sections, the three new sparse matrix formats are motivated and described.

3.1   CSR5 Bit Compressed—CSR5BC

The CSR5BC format has been developed especially for the use on GPUs and it is based on the existing CSR5 format of Liu [13]. The original CSR5 format utilizes a segmented sum algorithm to allow efficient parallel SpMV calculations that are mostly independent of the matrix structure. The matrix can be partitioned independently of the row boundaries, which allows an even distribution of the work on the available hardware units. This is especially important on GPU processors. The new format CSR5BC now introduces an additional index compression technique, which furthermore reduces the memory consumption of the CSR5BC format compared to Compressed Sparse Row (CSR) and CSR5. It requires less valuable memory bandwidth by using a little bit more meta information and some extra computation suitable to a GPU.

We start with a brief description of the original CSR5 format. The CSR5 format organizes the non-zero elements in blocks, which are also called tiles. The size of these tiles is optimized for the specific hardware platform. The width ω of the blocks is defined through the size of the available vector units, while the height σ depends on the hardware platform and matrix structure. For every block additional meta information has to be stored to allow an efficient calculation of the SpMV. Further details can be found in the original publication [13].

To further reduce memory bandwidth demands, the additional compression technique of the CSR5BC format is illustrated in Fig. 1. The compression works on a tile level and in a first step the index number space is reduced using two different techniques. First, the smallest column index of the tile, also called global offset, is identified and subtracted from all column indices of the tile (400 in the example). Afterwards a column-wise delta encoding is calculated. The delta encoding respects the row boundaries of the elements, which means when a new row begins, the delta encoding is reset.

In the next step, for each row of the tile the largest column index and the required number of bits for storing it is determined. The actual number of bits used for storing all column indices is identical for all elements of the same row. Since the SpMV calculations of the elements in the same row is done in parallel, this compression allows coalesced memory access which is an important requirement for all GPUs. In addition to the existing data structures of the CSR5 format, new arrays are required because of the compression. The CSR5BC format introduces a new array called compressionPointer that holds all required meta information in one place. This includes the offset in the compressed columnIndex array and the global offset that has been used to reduce the number space. Furthermore, the number of required bits for every row of the tile is stored, which

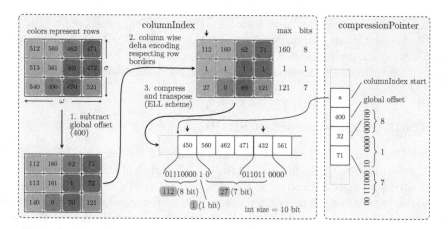

Fig. 1. Simplified part of the data structure of the CSR5BC format. One 3×4 tile is shown.

is again bit compressed into 6 bit per tile row. This in total results in a significant memory reduction and even more important memory bandwidth reduction compared to the existing CSR5 format.

3.2   Hybrid Compressed Slice Storage—HCSS

The HCSS format is a new hybrid format for CPU-based systems and Xeon Phi with the focus on a high utilization of the available vector units. The HCSS format partitions the matrix into slices of a fixed size, equal to the size of the available vector units and each slice is then stored in an individual most suitable format. Currently three different slice formats are used: ELLpack (ELL) [17], compressed ELL and a modified CSR. The ELL format is very well suited for the use of vector units, since it is inherently aligned. Furthermore, it allows the processing of multiple rows in parallel, which is advantageous compared to a row-based approach, because it avoids the use of an additional reduction operation. For this reason HCSS tries to store as many slices of the matrix using ELL.

The compressed ELL format utilizes the same data organization as the traditional ELL format, but it introduces a very simple bit compression technique. To reduce the number space of the column indices, first a delta encoding is done. Since the delta encoding has no effect on the first column index of every row and some type of diagonal structure is very often present, the first index of every row is not compressed and stored using a full integer value (32 bit). All following elements are stored in groups of two, where an integer value (32 bit) is split into two (16 bit) parts which are used for storing the index information. Whenever a row can not be stored evenly using pairs of two (excluding the first element), one additional padding element is introduced at the end of the row. The compressed ELL format can only be used for slices with a proper structure, without large gaps between multiple non-zero values.

The biggest drawback of the ELL format is the inherently required padding, that can result in a very large memory footprint. For this reason the CSR format is used for slices of the matrix, that would require the introduction of large amount of padding. To allow a proper memory alignment throughout the complete HCSS format and to simplify the calculation of the CSR slice, a small amount of padding is introduced to the modified CSR format, that is used in HCSS. Every row of the CSR format is padded to a number of elements that is a multiple of the size of the available vector units. Overall, these techniques ensure that each slice of the matrix is properly aligned.

The proper format for every slice is selected based on the non-zero structure of the rows in the slice. This is done by a very simple but effective heuristic that is based on empirical findings. As previously described the heuristic prefers the use of ELL (and compressed ELL) over CSR. The heuristic compares the number of non-zero elements of the row with the least and most entries in every slice and decides on two simple parameters whether the slice should be stored using ELL or CSR. Elements are only stored using CSR, when the row with the least entries has at least 16 elements and the row with the highest number of non-zeros has at least 20% more elements. The compressed ELL format is used, whenever the row contains at least 3 elements and the slice structure allows a compression of the elements into values of 16 bits.

Figure 2 shows the simplified data structure of the HCSS format. The HCSS format overall requires 5 arrays. The `rowPtr` is identical to the same array in the CSR format and is only required for the calculation of the CSR slices. The `slicePtr` array is similar to the CSR `rowPtr` and allows the addressing of the slices in the HCSS format. Because of the used index compression, it stores two index information per slice, the offset in the `values` and `columnIndex` array. The first 2 bits of every entry, 4 bit per slice, are used for storing the type of every slice. This allows the use of up to 16 different matrix formats. For systems with a vector size of at least 4, this step does not reduce the maximal possible

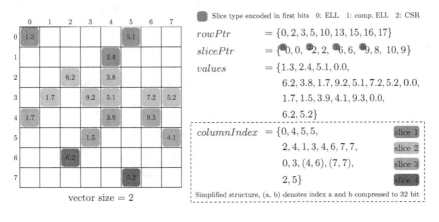

Fig. 2. Simplified data structure of the HCSS format.

matrix size compared to CSR. Since the number of non-zero elements in every slice is dividable by the vector unit size, the number space can be reduced by the same factor. Therefore, the first bits can be used to encode the type of the slices. By using an additional array, called `blockStart` (not presented in the figure), the load balance of the format is improved. The array stores the first and last slice that should be processed by every thread. The distribution is based on the number of non-zero elements in the relevant rows, but an implementation could use any block based distribution that is more adequate.

3.3   Local Group Compressed Sparse Row—LGCSR

The LGCSR format is a new matrix format for CPU-based systems that utilizes row-wise 1D blocks of non-zero values of variable size. This format assumes therefore more structural properties of a sparse matrix, but in such cases can deliver an even better performance than general formats. We have found out that many sparse matrices from different application fields often have many small variable sized block structures all over the whole matrix that can be efficiently utilized in one or the other way [16]. The LGCSR format is based on 1D row blocks and stores the index information of these row blocks or local groups highly bit compressed. For each group the column index of the first entry and the number of elements in the group has to be stored. The column index is stored as delta to the previous group to reduce the number space. To further reduce the memory consumption, these two information are highly bit-compressed in so called *packages*. The structure of these packages is depicted in Fig. 4. Each

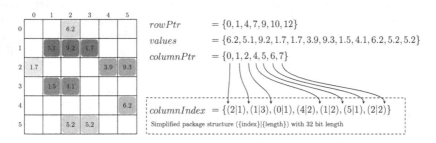

Fig. 3. Simplified data structure of the LGCSR format.

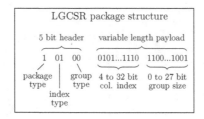

Fig. 4. Detailed description of the package structure of the LGCSR format.

package consists of a 5 bit header and the group's index information itself. The header encodes the amount of bits necessary for storing each part of the index information. One bit is used to store whether it is a group or a single element to handle non-blocks (i.e., single non-zero values) efficiently, too. Two bits encode the length of the column index and the last two bits encode the length of the number of elements in the group. Since only two bits are used for encoding the length information, only one of 4 sizes can be selected. These range from 4 to 32 bits for the column index information and from 4 to 27 bits for the group length. When the single element is stored, no group size information are stored. The maximum overall package size is 64 bit.

Figure 3 presents the simplified data structure of the LGCSR format. Overall 5 arrays are necessary for storing the required meta information and non-zero values. The LGCSR format reuses the `rowPtr` and `values` vectors of the classic CSR format. Because of the index compression, additional addressing is required for the `columnIndex`, which is stored in the `columnPtr` array. It works similar to the `rowPtr` and points to the first element of every row in the `columnIndex` array. The described, bit compressed, *packages* are stored in the `columnIndex` array. Identical to the HCSS format, an additional `blockStart` array is used for load balancing which stores the first and last row every thread should process.

4   Evaluation

In this section the performance of all three presented formats is evaluated. First the evaluation methodology is explained. Afterwards the performance on the three relevant hardware platforms is discussed.

4.1   Evaluation Methodology

The performance of the different formats is evaluated by comparing the runtime of the parallel SpMV operation for a large set of matrices. The set consists of 78 larger square sparse matrices with different sizes and structural properties from the University of Florida Sparse Matrix Collection [6] and the Comparative Solution Project [18]. The CSR memory footprint of the matrices ranges from 62 MB to 9.4 GB using 32 bit indices. The bare SpMV calculation time is measured, so no memory transfer times are considered (e.g., no transfer times to the GPU). Each measurement is repeated 100 times and the median runtime is used in the evaluation.

The CPU measurements have been done on a system with two Intel Xeon E5-2680 v3 processors (Haswell) with 128 GB of main memory. One GPU of a Nvidia Tesla K80 has been used for the GPU benchmarks. The system for the Xeon Phi Knights Landing (KNL) measurements consists of a Xeon 7250 processor with 96 GB of additional main memory. This system is configured in the quadrant cluster mode using the flat configuration, which requires manual allocations to utilize the available MCDRAM. The code was compiled using the Intel compiler version 17.0.0 and CUDA version 8.0.

In our test framework we have implemented many different matrix formats ourselves and integrated some formats using third party research libraries (clSPARSE [1], GHOST [2], CSB library [5], bhSPARSE [12]). In total we used the formats BCSR, CMRS, COO, CSB, CSC, CSR, CSR5, CSR5BC, DynB, ELL, ELL-BRO, ESB, HCSS, LGCSR, SELL-C-σ, VBL in our own and/or vendor/research library implementation. The performance of every format implementation has been measured for varying thread numbers. The final performance numbers are measured with one fixed number of threads per matrix format, the best performing one for this format. For all formats shown in the results, on the CPU the use of the full parallelism or 48 threads delivered the best performance. On the Xeon Phi there were differences between the formats on the optimal thread count. The MKL implementation of the CSR format and our HCSS implementation delivered the best performance using 128 threads. Our own CSR implementation performed optimally using the full parallelism with 272 threads. On the KNL we used 512 bit vector instruction and manually allocated all important data structures in the MCDRAM.

Rather than giving some absolute performance values for the new formats that might be hard to interpret, we relate the numbers to widely accepted base performance numbers of vendor library functions. First, we looked for the best performing matrix format in the vendor library on a system, taking all matrices into account. On the CPU and the Xeon Phi system that was the CSR format in the Intel MKL library V2017. On the GPU, this was the HYB format of Nvidia cuSPARSE. The performance value of this vendor library call for a specific matrix was used as a base value. For all other matrix formats evaluated, we measured the SpMV time for every matrix and calculated a speedup value for that call in relation to the base value.

4.2   Overhead and Memory Footprint Analysis

Figure 5a presents the memory savings compared to the traditional CSR format for the used matrix set. It can be seen, that the HCSS format achieves only moderate memory savings for most matrices, with a median of about 8% and even requires more memory than CSR for a few matrices. This can be explained by the very simple compression technique used in HCSS. The median memory savings of the CSR5BC format are much higher with 19%. Furthermore, the compression factor is much more consistent over the full matrix set, which is related to the more sophisticated compression approach and no additional padding of CSR5BC. The utilization of the blocked structure of matrices in the LGCSR format results in significant memory savings of about 26% in median for our matrix set. For matrices without 1D blocks the compression of the LGCSR format does not work and only small or no memory savings can be reached.

Figure 5b presents the sequential conversion times from CSR to the formats measured in the number of sequential iterations that can be done in the same time using the CSR format. It can be seen, that the conversion overhead is quite small (8/13/33 SpMV iterations for HCSS/LGCSR/CSR5BC,

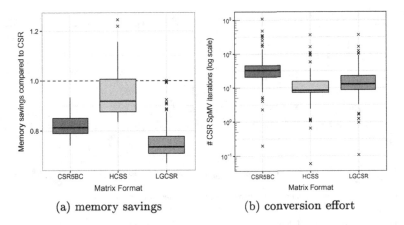

(a) memory savings   (b) conversion effort

Fig. 5. Comparison of the memory savings and conversion effort of the three developed formats.

respectively). Overall all the conversion times are very low, compared to the achieved performance improvements of the formats, which will be presented in the rest of this section.

4.3   Performance Evaluation

Gathering the speedup values compared to the vendor implementation over all matrices, the overall results for all three architectures are summarized in Fig. 6 using boxplots which allows a more compact presentation of the data. A small number of very high outliers has been cut off in the plot for presentation reasons. In addition to the performance of our new formats, the performance of all best performing matrix formats is presented in the plots. Formats not shown in the plots had a worse performance. See Sect. 4.1 for a list of all used formats.

On the CPU-based system, the best performing formats were DynB [16], HCSS, LGCSR, CSR (our own implementation), CSR5 [13] and CSR5BC. It can be seen that the performance of the blocked formats, LGCSR and DynB, varies much more compared to the non blocked formats CSR and HCSS. This is not surprising, since these formats are more sensitive to matrix structures and perform well for matrices with related block structures, but often very poor for matrices without such structures. Overall the formats HCSS and LGCSR show (additionally to DynB) the best median performance, with a corresponding median speedup of about 15 to 16% compared to MKL CSR. The boxplot furthermore shows that while the rather general formats CSR and HCSS deliver very decent performance for most matrices, they are outperformed for a large number of matrices by the blocked formats that are optimized for such structures. Overall, the HCSS format shows a significant performance increase over the MKL CSR implementation without any matrices with performance degradation (i.e., is always better). The blocked LGCSR format has advantages to all other formats on those matrices that have 1D blocks of non-zeros. Overall both

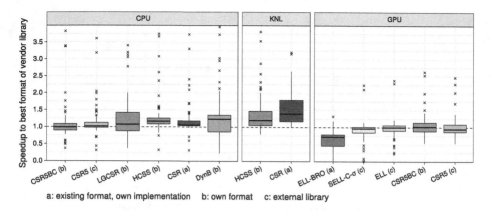

Fig. 6. Performance of all best performing formats on the three hardware platforms. ELL is for some matrices not possible. See the text for additional remarks.

newly developed formats, HCSS and LGCSR, show good performance numbers compared to the other existing matrix formats. HCSS is a rather general format, LGCSR should preferably be used when suitable block structures can be assumed in the matrix. Both the formats CSR5 and CSR5BC show no significant improvement over the MKL CSR implementation. Speedups could only be reached for a small number of matrices.

On the Xeon Phi KNL, the best performing formats were CSR (our own implementation) and HCSS. It can be seen that out CSR implementation outperforms the library implementation for all matrices and reaches a median speedup of about 40%. The newly developed HCSS format also outperforms the MKL for most matrices with a median speedup of about 20%. HCSS delivers a very similar relative performance compared to the CPU, while the CSR format delivers a much better relative performance on the KNL. This can be explained by multiple reasons: The CSR format works on a row basis and HCSS works on slices of rows, which allows the CSR format a finer grained load balance. Furthermore, the CSR format requires no padding at all and has an even lower code complexity compared to HCSS. The LGCSR format does not perform well on the KNL, which can be explained by its very high code complexity. The microarchitecture of the KNL performs less well on complex code than CPUs.

On the GPU, the best performing formats were CSR5BC, CSR5 [13], ELL, Sell-C-σ [10] and ELL-BRO [21]. It can be seen that all performance values are much closer to the vendor library values. The newly developed CSR5BC format outperforms the existing CSR5 format slightly due to the reduced memory bandwidth demand. The median performance improvement of CSR5BC over CSR5 is about 3.5% without relevant performance losses. The CSR5BC format furthermore outperforms all ELL-based matrix formats for most matrices. The median speedup of CSR5BC to cuSPARSE HYB is about 3.2%. Furthermore, the performance of CSR5BC is much more consistent and achieves good performance for most matrices, while the performance of the ELL-based formats varies much more. All ELL-based formats suffer high performance losses for matrices with a disadvantageous matrix structure. Some matrices could even not be processed using the ELL-based formats, because too much padding was required. This is different for CSR5BC (and CSR5), which was able to handle all matrices. Overall, CSR5BC as an extension to CSR5 is well suited for the use on the GPU.

5 Summary

In this paper we proposed three new matrix formats for the three currently most popular hardware architectures. The CSR5BC format is based on the existing CSR5 format and it delivers much more consistent performance results compared to most ELL-based matrix formats on a GPU. Therefore, it is more universally applicable and much less dependent on the matrix properties. The same is also true for the original CSR5 format. Due to the additional index compression and therefore reduced memory bandwidth demand, CSR5BC has shown small but regular performance improvements compared to the original CSR5 format on the GPU. Furthermore it performed reasonable well on the CPU.

The newly developed HCSS and LGCSR formats performed well on the CPU for almost all matrices. For matrices with many 1D blocks, higher speedups can be reached when the LGCSR format is used. On the Xeon Phi, only the HCSS format delivered good performance, because it is better suited for the simpler microarchitecture. The higher code complexity of the LGCSR format prevented a similar relative performance gain on the Xeon Phi compared to the CPU.

Acknowledgements. We would like to thank the CMT team at Saudi Aramco EXPEC ARC for their support and input. Especially we want to thank Ali H. Dogru for making this research project possible. Additionally we thank Weifeng Liu for giving us access to his CSR5 code and for discussions. We used the following libraries in our evaluation where we thank the original authors for access to the code: bhSPARSE, clSPARSE, GHOST, CSB library.

References

1. clSPARSE. https://github.com/clMathLibraries/clSPARSE. Accessed Feb 2017
2. GHOST. https://bitbucket.org/essex/ghost. Accessed Feb 2017
3. Ashari, A., Sedaghati, N., Eisenlohr, J., Sadayappan, P.: An efficient two-dimensional blocking strategy for sparse matrix-vector multiplication on GPUs. In: Proceedings of 28th ACM International Conference on Supercomputing (ICS 2014), pp. 273–282. ACM (2014)
4. Barrett, R., Berry, M., Chan, T.F., Demmel, J., Donato, J., Dongarra, J., Eijkhout, V., Pozo, R., Romine, C., der Vorst, H.V.: Templates for the Solution of Linear Systems: Building Blocks for Iterative Methods, 2nd edn. SIAM, Philadelphia (1994)
5. Buluç, A.: Compressed Sparse Blocks (CSB) Library. http://gauss.cs.ucsb.edu/~aydin/csb/html/index.html. Accessed Feb 2017
6. Davis, T.A., Hu, Y.: The University of Florida sparse matrix collection. ACM Trans. Math. Softw. **38**(1), 1:1–1:25 (2010)

7. Feng, X., Jin, H., Hu, K., Zeng, J., Schao, Z.: Optimization of sparse matrix-vector multiplication with variant CSR on GPUs. In: Proceedings of 2011 IEEE 17th International Conference on Parallel and Distributed Systems, pp. 165–172. IEEE (2011)
8. Intel: Intel® 64 and IA-32 Architectures Optimization Reference Manual, June 2016. http://www.intel.com/content/dam/www/public/us/en/documents/manuals/64-ia-32-architectures-optimization-manual.pdf. Accessed Feb 2017
9. Kourtis, K., Goumas, G., Koziris, N.: Optimizing sparse matrix-vector multiplication using index and value compression. In: Proceedings of 5th Conference on Computing Frontiers (CF 2008), pp. 87–96. ACM (2008)
10. Kreutzer, M., Hager, G., Wellein, G., Fehske, H., Bishop, A.R.: A unified sparse matrix data format for efficient general sparse matrix-vector multiply on modern processors with wide SIMD units. SIAM J. Sci. Comput. 26(5), C401–C423 (2014)
11. Langr, D., Tvrdík, P.: Evaluation criteria for sparse matrix storage formats. IEEE Trans. Parallel Distrib. Syst. 27(2), 428–440 (2016)
12. Liu, W.: bhSPARSE. https://github.com/bhSPARSE. Accessed Feb 2017
13. Liu, W., Vinter, B.: CSR5: an efficient storage format for cross-platform sparse matrix-vector multiplication. In: Proceedings 29th International Conference on Supercomputing (ICS 2015), pp. 339–350. ACM (2015)
14. Pichel, J.C., Heras, D.B., Cabaleiro, J.C., Rivera, F.F.: Improving the locality of the sparse matrix-vector product on shared memory multiprocessors. In: Proceedings of 12th Euromicro Conference on Parallel, Distributed and Network-Based Processing, pp. 66–71. IEEE (2004)
15. Pinar, A., Aykanat, C.: Sparse matrix decomposition with optimal load balancing. In: Proceedings of Fourth International Conference on High-Performance Computing, pp. 224–229. IEEE (1997)
16. Razzaq, J., Berrendorf, R., Hack, S., Weierstall, M., Mannuss, F.: Fixed and variable sized block techniques for sparse matrix vector multiplication with general matrix structures. In: Proceedings of Tenth International Conference on Advanced Engineering Computing and Applications in Sciences (ADVCOMP 2016), pp. 84–90 (2016)
17. Saad, Y.: Iterative Methods for Sparse Linear Systems, 2nd edn. SIAM, Philadelphia (2003)
18. Society of Petroleum Engineers: SPE Comparative Solution Project. http://www.spe.org/web/csp/. Accessed Feb 2017
19. Stathis, P., Vassiliadis, S., Cotofana, S.: A hierarchical sparse matrix storage format for vector processors. In: Proceedings of International Parallel and Distributed Processing Symposium, p. 8–pp (2003)
20. Tang, W.T., Zhao, R., Lu, M., Liang, Y., Huyng, H.P., Li, X., Goh, R.S.M.: Optimizing and auto-tuning scale-free sparse matrix-vector multiplication on Intel Xeon Phi. In: 2015 IEEE/ACM International Symposium on Code Generation and Optimization (CGO), pp. 136–145 (2015)
21. Tang, W., Tan, W., Ray, R., Wong, Y., Chen, W., Kuo, S., Goh, R., Turner, S., Wong, W.: Accelerating sparse matrix-vector multiplication on GPUs using bit-representation-optimized schemes. In: Proceedings of International Conference on High Performance Computing, Networking, Storage and Analysis (SC 2013). ACM (2013). Article No. 26
22. Wong, J., Kuhl, E., Darve, E.: A new sparse matrix vector multiplication GPU algorithm designed for finite element problems. Int. J. Numer. Methods Eng. 102(12), 1784–1814 (2015)

23. Yan, S., Li, C., Zhang, Y., Zhou, H.: yaSpMV: yet another SpMV framework on GPUs. In: Proceedings of 19th ACM SIGPLAN Symposium on Principles and Practice of Parallel Programming (PPoPP 2014), pp. 107–118 (2014)
24. Yang, X., Parthasarathy, S., Sadayappan, P.: Fast sparse matrix-vector multiplication on GPUs: implications for graph mining. Proc. VLDB Endowment (PVLDB) **4**, 231–242 (2011)

Lazy Parallel Kronecker Algebra-Operations on Heterogeneous Multicores

Wasuwee Sodsong[1](✉), Robert Mittermayr[2], Yoojin Park[1],
Bernd Burgstaller[1](✉), and Johann Blieberger[2]

[1] Yonsei University, Seoul, Korea
wasuwee.s@yonsei.ac.kr, {yoojin1.park,bburg}@cs.yonsei.ac.kr
[2] Vienna University of Technology, Vienna, Austria
{robert,blieb}@auto.tuwien.ac.at

Abstract. Kronecker algebra is a matrix calculus which allows the generation of thread interleavings from the source-code of a program. Thread interleavings have been shown effective for proving the absence of deadlocks. Because the number of interleavings grows exponentially in the number of threads, deadlock analysis is still a challenging problem.

To make the computation of thread interleavings tractable, we propose a lazy, parallel evaluation method for Kronecker algebra. Our method incorporates the constraints induced by synchronization constructs. To reduce problem size, only interleavings legal under the locking behavior of a program are considered. We leverage the data-parallelism of Kronecker sum- and product-operations for multicores and GPUs. Proposed algebraic transformations further improve performance. For one synthetic and two real-world benchmarks, our GPU implementation is up to 5453× faster than our multi-threaded version. Lazy evaluation significantly reduces memory consumption compared to both the sequential and the multicore versions of the SPIN model-checker.

Keywords: Kronecker algebra · Lazy evaluation · Deadlock detection · Heterogeneous multicores · GPUs

1 Introduction

The complexity of software-development for multicore processors has raised the interest in verification techniques for multi-threaded applications. To prove a property of a multi-threaded program, e.g., deadlock freedom, all possible thread interleavings must be considered. The number of interleavings increases exponentially in the number of threads. This combinatorial explosion is referred as the state explosion problem. All state-of-the-art methods suffer from the state explosion problem, including model checking (see, e.g., [4]).

Kronecker algebra is a matrix calculus that has been applied to model multi-threaded shared-memory systems [2,10,11,16]. Kronecker algebra encodes the

© Springer International Publishing AG 2017
F.F. Rivera et al. (Eds.): Euro-Par 2017, LNCS 10417, pp. 538–552, 2017.
DOI: 10.1007/978-3-319-64203-1_39

control-flow graphs (CFGs) of threads and synchronization primitives as adjacency matrices. In applying combinations of Kronecker sum and product operations, all interleavings of the underlying threads can be generated (see Sect. 2).

Related to the state explosion problem, the order of adjacency matrices grows exponentially in the number of threads. It has been observed in prior, unpublished work [10] that it is not necessary to compute adjacency matrices in their entirety: the use of synchronization constructs in a multi-threaded program induces constraints that can be exploited to greatly limit the number of thread interleavings that must be considered by static program analysis.

Kronecker algebra operations have been devised that are able to capture the constraints on possible thread interleavings resulting from semaphore-based producer-consumer synchronization and from mutual exclusion using mutexes and semaphores. Kronecker algebra can be applied with higher-level, monitor-like synchronization constructs such as Ada's protected objects, and with barriers [3, 9, 10, 12].

We propose a lazy evaluation method for Kronecker algebra operations, which computes only thread interleavings which are legal under the synchronization behavior of a given program. This lazy evaluation scheme greatly reduces problem sizes by considering only those distinctive portions of each adjacency matrix, which represent the legal thread interleavings of the program at hand.

We found the Kronecker matrix calculus to contain a vast amount of data-parallelism. Our lazy evaluation method is able to harness this parallelism on multicore CPUs and GPUs. Algebra transformations for particular matrix instances further enhance the performance of our matrix operations.

This paper thus makes the following contributions:

1. We devise a two-step lazy evaluation scheme for Kronecker sum- and product-operations: expression trees are constructed and then evaluated lazily.
2. We provide Kronecker algebra operations optimized for multicore CPUs.
3. We devise an execution scheme that utilizes both the multicore CPU and the GPU. This scheme conducts lazy evaluation of Kronecker algebra operations on the GPU. CPU cores are used to maintain the computed thread interleavings, and for coordinating the GPU-based evaluation process.
4. We perform an extensive evaluation, showing that the GPU implementation is up to 5453× faster than our multi-threaded CPU implementation.

This paper is organized as follows. The relevant background on Kronecker algebra is discussed in Sect. 2. We provide an overview of our execution scheme in Sect. 3. Our multicore CPU and GPU implementations are discussed in Sect. 4. Experimental results are provided in Sect. 5. We review the related work in Sect. 6 and draw our conclusions in Sect. 7.

2   Background

For the verification of concurrent systems using Kronecker algebra, threads and semaphores are represented by CFGs. The usual CFG representation consists

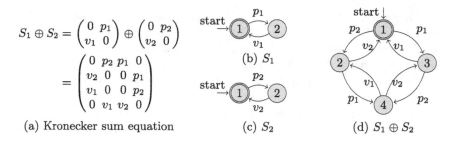

$$S_1 \oplus S_2 = \begin{pmatrix} 0 & p_1 \\ v_1 & 0 \end{pmatrix} \oplus \begin{pmatrix} 0 & p_2 \\ v_2 & 0 \end{pmatrix}$$

$$= \begin{pmatrix} 0 & p_2 & p_1 & 0 \\ v_2 & 0 & 0 & p_1 \\ v_1 & 0 & 0 & p_2 \\ 0 & v_1 & v_2 & 0 \end{pmatrix}$$

(a) Kronecker sum equation   (b) S_1 (c) S_2 (d) $S_1 \oplus S_2$

Fig. 1. (a) A Kronecker sum $S_1 \oplus S_2$ of two binary semaphores S_1 (b) and S_2 (c) generates all possible interleavings (d).

of nodes representing basic blocks and edges representing transfer of control. Because our matrix calculus manipulates CFG edges, we move basic blocks onto the incoming edges of a node. Each CFG is encoded as an adjacency matrix, and CFG edges are labeled by the elements of a semiring [7,10].

Example CFGs of binary semaphores and their adjacency matrix representations are depicted in Fig. 1. Each matrix row-index corresponds to the node ID of the tail of a CFG edge, and the matrix column-index corresponds to the node ID of the head of a CFG edge. For example, the first row of the result adjacency matrix, $0\, p_2\, p_1\, 0$, specifies that there is an edge labelled "p_2" from Node 1 to Node 2 and another edge labelled "p_1" from Node 1 to Node 3. Multiple outgoing edges represent branches in a program. The Kronecker matrix calculus interprets the CFG of a thread as a deterministic finite automaton (DFA). Nodes of the CFG represent DFA states, and edges represent the transitions of the DFA. The DFA's start-state corresponds to the entry-node of the CFG, and the accepting state to the CFG's exit node. In the remainder of this section we provide an overview of Kronecker algebra operations. Details and proofs of the stated properties can be found in [3,9,10,12].

Kronecker Product. Given an m-by-n matrix A and a p-by-q matrix B, their Kronecker product of size mp-by-nq is defined by

$$A \otimes B = \begin{pmatrix} a_{1,1} \cdot B & \cdots & a_{1,n} \cdot B \\ \vdots & \ddots & \vdots \\ a_{m,1} \cdot B & \cdots & a_{m,n} \cdot B \end{pmatrix}. \tag{1}$$

The Kronecker product $A \otimes B$ represents a DFA where A and B execute in lock-step (i.e., A and B perform each transition simultaneously).

Kronecker Sum. Given a square matrix A of order m and B of order n, their Kronecker sum denoted by $A \oplus B$ is a matrix of order $m \times n$ defined by

$$A \oplus B = A \otimes I_n + I_m \otimes B, \tag{2}$$

where I_m and I_n are identity matrices of order m and n respectively. The Kronecker sum generates all possible interleavings of DFAs A and B. Figure 1 demonstrates a Kronecker sum of two binary semaphores S_1 and S_2. The semaphore

DFAs are depicted in Fig. 1(b) and (c). Their sum $S_1 \oplus S_2$ is defined in Fig. 1(a). Figure 1(d) depicts all possible interleavings of S_1 and S_2.

A concurrent system is defined by a tuple $\langle \mathcal{T}, \mathcal{S}, \mathcal{L} \rangle$, where $\mathcal{T}$ is a set of threads, $\mathcal{S}$ is a set of synchronization primitives, and $\mathcal{L}$ are labels. For the ensemble of k threads $T^{(i)} \in \mathcal{T}$, we obtain a matrix T representing the thread interleavings. Similarly, for all synchronization primitives $S^{(j)} \in \mathcal{S}$, we obtain a matrix S representing the r interleaving semaphores.

Selective Kronecker Product. Given an m-by-n matrix A and a p-by-q matrix B, we call $A \oslash_L B$ their selective Kronecker product. For all $l \in L \subseteq \mathcal{L}$ let $A \oslash_L B = (a_{i,j}) \oslash_L (b_{r,s}) = (c_{t,u})$, where

$$c_{(i-1) \cdot p + r, (j-1) \cdot q + s} = \begin{cases} l \text{ if } a_{i,j} = b_{r,s} = l, \ l \in L, \\ 0 \text{ otherwise.} \end{cases}$$

The selective Kronecker product synchronizes identical labels $l \in \mathcal{L}_s$ of the left and right matrices. It ensures that a semaphore operation in the left operand is paired with the operation in the right operand.

An adjacency matrix representing a program P can be computed by

$$P = T \oslash_{\mathcal{L}_S} S + T_{\mathcal{L}_V} \otimes I_{o(S)}. \tag{3}$$

Therein, $\mathcal{L} = \mathcal{L}_V \cup \mathcal{L}_S$ describes the set of CFG edge labels $\mathcal{L}$ which is composed from the label-set $\mathcal{L}_S$ representing calls to synchronization primitives (e.g., p, v), and the label-set $\mathcal{L}_V$ that represents the remaining, non-synchronizing computations of a program (sets $\mathcal{L}_V$ and $\mathcal{L}_S$ are disjoint). Intuitively, given a concurrent system $\langle \mathcal{T}, \mathcal{S}, \mathcal{L} \rangle$, matrix P describes all possible interleavings of the thread ensemble $\mathcal{T}$ under the constraints imposed from synchronizing with the synchronization primitives $\mathcal{S}$ [10].

3 Kronecker Algebra Evaluation

A deadlock manifests through unreachable components in a program's adjacency matrix [10]. Figure 2(a) depicts a CFG with an invalid use of a binary semaphore: the p()-operations on the right path constitute a self-deadlock. With the second p()-operation, the semaphore is unobtainable, which results in self-deadlock at Node 6; Nodes 5 and 8 are unreachable from the starting node.

Considering two CFGs of m and n nodes, both the space- and time-complexity of a Kronecker sum or product operation that produces an adjacency matrix of m-by-n nodes is $\mathcal{O}(m^2 n^2)$. An additional operation to a CFG of k nodes increases the complexities to $\mathcal{O}(k^2 m^2 n^2)$. Hence, the space- and time-complexities grow exponentially in the number of Kronecker operations.

Lazy evaluation of Kronecker operations delays all computations until proven to be required. (Only reachable nodes are analyzed.) In our example in Fig. 2(b), the reachable nodes (i.e., successors) from the starting node, Node 1, are represented by the non-zero entries in Row 1 of the 8×8 result-matrix, i.e., Node 4 and Node 6. Node 4 has one successor, Node 7. Nodes 6 and 7 have no successors

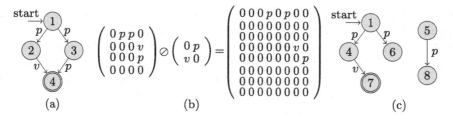

Fig. 2. Kronecker analysis of a CFG (a) with a self-deadlock (right path) on a binary semaphore; Kronecker algebra operation (b), and the resulting graph (c) showing an unreachable path (Node 5 and Node 8) from the starting node, Node 1. The self-deadlock manifests through the non-reachability of the exit-node (Node 7) from Node 6.

and all reachable nodes have been visited, thus the analysis terminates. Because we only require non-zero elements of the result matrix, we restrict the evaluation of a Kronecker operation to the non-zero elements of its operands.

Lazy evaluation consists of two steps: a Kronecker expression is converted to an expression tree, followed by the lazy evaluation of the tree's operations. We employ sparse matrices for the adjacency matrix representation of CFGs and semaphores. They are operands of the algebra computation and constitute the leaf nodes of a tree. Successors of a node are retrievable by reading a sparse matrix. Kronecker operations constitute internal nodes. The intermediate results are stored as lazy matrices, which are represented by the algebra operator and pointers to the operands (i.e., children) in the tree. No actual computation happens until the result matrix is required, which allows us to optimize expression trees as they are constructed.

Lazy evaluation starts once the result matrix is required. Algorithm 1 computes all successors of a node. Node IDs and successor IDs of parent operations are constructable from IDs of child nodes and vice versa. Hence, from the starting node, we recursively find corresponding IDs of child nodes (Line 6–7) until the leaves are encountered. Successor IDs of leaf nodes are retrievable as they are presented as sparse matrices. Consequently, the successor IDs of parent nodes, then, are constructed in a bottom-up fashion. Newly found successors will later be evaluated. When no more successors are found, evaluation terminates. To keep track of processed nodes, we hash node IDs in a hash-table.

Kronecker Sum Optimizations: We can compute a Kronecker sum in a single step, to improve the formulation from Eq. (2). An example sum of order two is stated in Eq. (4). We observe three properties of the result matrix:

- The elements along the diagonal are the summations of the diagonal elements of the operands A and B.
- The first Kronecker product term in Eq. (2) produces a dot product of elements from matrix A and I_n. The elements of matrix A are spread along the

Algorithm 1. Successor search

```
1 list  succ (Matrix M, T node ):
2 if M. getOperation != +:
3   sizeR= M. getRightMatSize
4   lid =((node−1)/sizeR)+1
5   rid =((node−1)%sizeR)+1
6   lsu=succ (M. leftMat , lid )
7   rsu=succ (M. rightMat , rid )
8 switch (M. getOperation ):
9   case +:
10    su=succ (M. leftMat , node)
11    + succ (M. rightMat , node)
12  case ⊗: for l in lsu :
13    for r in rsu :
14      su . push (( l−1)∗sizeR+r )
15  case ⊘: for l in lsu :
16    for r in rsu :
17      if ( label ( l )=label ( r )):
18        su . push (( l−1)∗sizeR+r )
19  case ⊕: for l in lsu :
20    su . push (( l−1)∗sizeR+rid )
21    for r in rsu :
22      su . push (( lid −1)∗sizeR+r )
23  case leafNodes :
24    su=readSparseMat (M, node )
25 return su
```

Algorithm 2. Successor search for Kronecker sums of same-sized operands

```
1 list KSumSuccs (SparseMat M,
2                 T node ,
3                 int totalSize ,
4                 int nrKSums ):
5 offset =0
6 size=M. size
7 for i in (0 : nrKSums +1):
8   stripe=totalSize / size
9   leaf=succ (M, ⌊ node/stripe ⌋% M. size )
10  for su in leaf :
11    T sid=offset
12      +(su ∗ stripe )
13      +(node% stripe )
14    su . push ( sid )
15  offset +=⌊ node/(offset+stripe) ⌋∗stripe
16  size ∗= size
17 return su
```

diagonal of sub-matrices of size n. Successors of a given node ID, x, must be n elements apart with an initial offset of $(x − 1)\%n$.

- The second Kronecker product term in Eq. (2) duplicates matrix B along the diagonal of the result matrix. Given a node x, the successors must be located between 0 to n from $\lfloor \frac{(x−1)}{n} \rfloor * n$.

$$A \oplus B = \left(\begin{array}{cc|cc} a_1 + b_1 & b_2 & a_2 & 0 \\ b_3 & a_1 + b_4 & 0 & a_2 \\ \hline a_3 & 0 & a_4 + b_1 & b_2 \\ 0 & a_3 & b_3 & a_4 + b_4 \end{array} \right) = \left(\begin{array}{c|c} (a_1 \cdot I) + B & a_2 \cdot I \\ \hline a_3 \cdot I & (a_4 \cdot I) + B \end{array} \right) \quad (4)$$

From these properties, the successors of a Kronecker sum operand can be computed in one operation (see Algorithm 1). We further optimize sum operations for multiple adjacency matrices of the same order with non-zero values located at the same locations. This case mainly applies to sums of semaphores. Figure 3 depicts the results of such Kronecker sums of two and three binary

$$
\begin{pmatrix}
0 & p_2 & p_1 & 0 \\
v_2 & 0 & 0 & p_1 \\
v_1 & 0 & 0 & p_2 \\
0 & v_1 & v_2 & 0
\end{pmatrix}
$$

(a) $S_1 \oplus S_2$

$$
\begin{pmatrix}
0 & p_3 & p_2 & 0 & p_1 & 0 & 0 & 0 \\
v_3 & 0 & 0 & p_2 & 0 & p_1 & 0 & 0 \\
v_2 & 0 & 0 & p_3 & 0 & 0 & p_1 & 0 \\
0 & v_2 & v_3 & 0 & 0 & 0 & 0 & p_1 \\
v_1 & 0 & 0 & 0 & 0 & p_3 & p_2 & 0 \\
0 & v_1 & 0 & 0 & v_3 & 0 & 0 & p_2 \\
0 & 0 & v_1 & 0 & v_2 & 0 & 0 & p_3 \\
0 & 0 & 0 & v_1 & 0 & v_2 & v_3 & 0
\end{pmatrix}
$$

(b) $S_1 \oplus S_2 \oplus S_3$

Fig. 3. Kronecker sum of (a) two and (b) three binary semaphores.

semaphores. These sums create a pattern that separates the p and v operations of different semaphores. Binary semaphore p and v are located at the upper-right and lower-left entry of a 2×2 adjacency matrix respectively. In Fig. 3(b), p_1 and v_1 of $S1$, the left most operand, appear along the diagonal of 4×4 sub-matrices at the upper-right and lower-left quadrants of the result matrix. Similarly, p_2 and v_2 of $S2$ appear along the diagonal of 2×2 sub-matrices of the upper-left and lower-right 4×4 matrices. The pattern repeats for the remaining Kronecker sum operations, where the size of sub-matrices is reduced by half after each operation. Hence, given a node ID, the total number of Kronecker sums and the shape of the operands' sparse matrices, we can compute successors of Kronecker sums of same-sized matrices using Algorithm 2.

The lazy evaluation scheme only evaluates nonzero entries of reachable nodes in adjacency matrices. Hence, the time complexity is reduced to successor search. Considering a Kronecker operation produces a result matrix of size m-by-n nodes, a successor search takes up to $\mathcal{O}(pq)$, where the left child's matrix has p $\leq$ m successors and the right child's matrix has q $\leq$ n successors. The overall complexity is $\mathcal{O}(rpq)$, with r $\leq$ mn reachable nodes. In practice, the memory requirement is reduced to the number of reachable nodes, and memory occupied by nodes queued in unprocessed node queues.

4   Parallel Kronecker Algebra

The computation of finding successor nodes has a dependency between a node and its successors. Therefore, lazy evaluation is well-suited for parallelization where a worker thread processes per node instead of per successor. We employ hash-tables to record nodes that have already been processed, to avoid duplication of work. For example, with the CFG from Fig. 1(d), Node 2 will be encountered twice: as a successor of Node 1 and Node 4.

4.1   Multi-threaded CPU Implementation

With our lazy evaluation scheme, each worker thread maintains a local work-queue to store to-be-processed nodes. A new set of successors will be discovered during the evaluation of a node. We employ a hash-function which hashes the node IDs of the newly-discovered successors onto the work-queues of the worker threads. With the help of this hash-function, a worker thread will distribute the newly-discovered successors among the work-queues of all worker threads. We have implemented each work-queue as a lock-free queue, employing the `boost::lockfree::queue` template of the boost C++ library (version 1.61). We use the row-index of a node in the adjacency matrix as the node ID (key) with this hashing operation. The hash-function guarantees that a node is assigned to exactly one worker.

Note that a worker thread will use the hash-tables of processed nodes to avoid duplication of work (i.e., re-processing of nodes). Because each worker thread processes a unique set of node IDs, it maintains a local hash-table of processed nodes. Only if a node is not already contained in the hash-table, it will be assigned for processing. If the table already contains a given node, it implies that this node has already been processed or is currently in a work-queue. Contrary, successful hashing (i.e., entering a new node into the hash-table) indicates that this node has not been encountered yet and must be assigned to a worker thread for processing.

4.2 GPU Implementation

As shown in Algorithm 1, the CPU implementation contains complex control-flow constructs including a switch-case statement and recursion. Because of potential branch divergence, such control-flow constructs are prone to low performance on a GPU. However, because all GPU threads will work on the same matrix algebra operation, they will branch to the same arm in the switch-case statement. Therefore, we found that the switch-case statement incurred very low branch divergence with our GPU kernel.

Similarly to the multicore CPU computations, we designed our GPU kernel such that one thread processes one node. A GPU has a considerably smaller memory than a CPU. As problem sizes grow, GPU memory is insufficient to keep track of all processed nodes. Hence, we maintain all computed thread interleavings on the CPU, using multiple threads. The list of processed nodes obtained from the GPU is unsorted. Thus, we utilize one hash-table of processed nodes in this implementation. Because the hash-table is highly contended, we employ lock-free synchronization to keep synchronization overhead low. We use libcuckoo, which is a lock-free hash-table of competitive performance [8]. In analogy to the multicore CPU implementation, if the table already contains a given node, it implies that this node has been processed or is currently in a work-queue. Contrary, successful hashing indicates a newly discovered node which must be assigned to a worker thread for processing.

Preprocessing: In the initial stage of the parallel execution, we prepare an expression tree and adjacency matrices for the GPU. Problem sizes vary in the number of input CFGs and CFG sizes. Each of these CFGs can be relatively small. A binary semaphore is represented as an adjacency matrix of size 2×2.

Algorithm 3. Successor search on a GPU

```
1 void  succ (T *BigSucc ,T node ,
2              optTree *opt ,T *su ):
3   nid [0]= node
4   for i in  (1:NumOpts):
5     pid=nid [ opt [ i ]. parent ]
6     nid [ i]=getID ( opt [ i ] , pid )
7   for i in  (NumOpts:0: −1):
8     su=succ ( opt , nid [ i ] , BigSucc )
```

Algorithm 4. Estimation of the maximum number of successors

```
1 T maxSucc (LazyMat M, T node ):
2   lsu=maxSucc (M. leftMat , node )
3   rsu=maxSucc (M. rightMat , node )
4   switch (M. getOperation ):
5     case +: n=lsu+rsu
6     case ⊗: n=lsu∗rsu
7     case ⊘: n=min ( lsu , rsu )
8     case ⊕: n=lsu∗rsu
9   return n
```

Merging all matrices into a large buffer further decreases the data transfer overhead between CPU and GPU.

CFG edges are associated with labels in the form of strings. The length of such strings depends on the input-problem and hence cannot be determined at compile-time. Performing string operations such as label comparisons with selective Kronecker products or string concatenation with matrix addition can be highly difficult and inefficient on a GPU. Thus, we re-code all string labels to a numeric representation. All labels are known at the time of constructing a problem's basic matrices. We implemented a lookup table which converts between string labels and numbers during the initial execution stage.

Eliminating Recursion: Because of the limited maximum recursion depth of GPUs, we replaced the recursive calls of our CPU implementation (Algorithm 1) by two loops as depicted in Lines 4 and 7 in Algorithm 3. All intermediate data, passed between recursive calls, is kept on stacks. The first loop pre-calculates node IDs at all levels of an expression tree in a top-down fashion. The node IDs of all intermediate and leaf matrices of the expression tree are stored in a fixed-length array. Based on the node ID information of the first loop and the known successors of the leaves, the second loop determines a list of successors in a bottom-up fashion. Function succ() in Line 8 is similar to Algorithm 1, without the recursive calls in Lines 6–7, and the successor of the plus operation being a combination of successors of previously calculated successors of a left- and right-hand child. The number of successors can vary between nodes. We preserve the maximum number of slots for each operation. The maximum number of successors can be estimated beforehand by Algorithm 4. Notably, the selective Kronecker product finds an exact label match of successors of the left and right child nodes. Thus, the number of matches cannot exceed the minimum number of labels of the two children.

Pipelined Execution Scheme: For further performance improvements, we exploit pipeline-parallelism between the CPU and the GPU. The GPU computation is split into iterations, where each iteration computes a fixed number of nodes. We choose heuristically optimal sizes according to GPU performance and memory usage. Depending on the expression tree, the stacks that store intermediate data on the GPU occupied most GPU memory.

Hashing on CPU cores happens in parallel to the GPU kernel computations. Because hashing requires a list of newly discovered successors from the GPU, it is not guaranteed to retrieve data in time from the current iteration. Hence, we delayed the CPU computation by one iteration. CPU threads always hash nodes from the previous iteration.

5   Experimental Results

We have evaluated our method on one multicore system and three desktop/embedded GPU systems (platform specifications are stated in Table 1). With performance measurements, we have omitted file I/O and GPU context creation times, because they do not reflect the actual computation times. For measurement consistency, we do not stop our analysis when a deadlock is detected. Rather, we have the analysis compute all possible, legal thread interleavings (the entire problem size). Our rationale was that with parallel execution, where multiple nodes are being analyzed concurrently, the node processing order may vary, and a deadlock may be detected earlier or later.

We perform deadlock analysis on one synthetic and two real-world examples: (1) Dijkstra's Dining Philosopher's, (2) Linux kernel threads, and a (3) railway system. We verify the correctness of our optimizations to the unoptimized implementation proposed in [10]. With the first problem, we employed n philosophers with n forks placed between them. Each philosopher constitutes an individual thread; each fork is represented by a binary semaphore. This set-up will result in the well-known deadlock if all n philosophers pick up their left fork simultaneously. For the remainder of this section, we refer to the multi-threaded implementation as KA-N for N threads, and to the GPU implementation as KA-G.

We use the sequential implementation as our yardstick. Figure 4 shows the obtained execution times on the GPU systems. Note that the y-axis is in log-scale: as the number of philosophers (threads) increases, the number of nodes to be processed grows exponentially. Five philosophers generate 392 nodes reachable

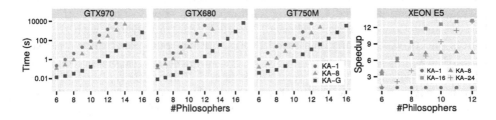

Fig. 4. Execution times on the GPU systems and speedup over KA-1 on the multicore system for the Dining Philosophers problem

Table 1. Evaluation Platform Specifications.

		GTX680	GT750M	GTX970	Xeon E5
CPU	Model	i7-3770k	i7-4850HQ	i7-6700	Xeon E5-2697
	# cores	4 (8 threads)	4 (8 threads)	4 (8 threads)	28 (56 threads)
	Memory	32 GB	16 GB	16 GB	256 GB
	Clock freq.	3.5 GHz	2.3 GHz	3.4 GHz	1.8 GHz
	Bandwidth	15.9 GB/s	11.4 GB/s	20.4 GB/s	12.0 GB/s
GPU	Model	GeForce GTX 680	GeForce GT 750M	GeForce GTX 970	N/A
	# cores	1536	384	1664	
	Memory	2048 MB	1971 MB	4029 MB	
	Clock freq.	1006 MHz	926 MHz	1329 MHz	
	Bandwidth	12.1 GB/s	6.3 GB/s	12.7 GB/s	

from the starting node, while 17 philosophers result in more than 662 million reachable nodes. Once a problem becomes sufficiently large to fully utilize the GPU, the GPU implementation shows the best performance. Due to the long execution time of the single-threaded CPU version, we were unable to measure our yardstick up to as many philosophers as with the parallel versions. The GPU implementation is 140×, 176× and 51× faster than the multi-threaded implementation on the GTX 970, GTX 680 and GT 750M systems. Scalability of the multi-threaded version is depicted for the XEON E5 platform. The speedups of KA-8 and KA-16 over single-threaded execution saturate at 7.5× and 13.1×, respectively. For 12 philosophers, KA-24 is on par with KA-16, but on an upward trend (whereas KA-16's scalability is already saturated).

We applied Kronecker algebra to detect deadlocks in Linux kernel threads (for Linux kernel version 3.10). We analyze two ensembles of three and five kernel threads that share eight and ten locks. LLVM was used to inline called functions into kernel threads and to obtain CFGs. Computations unrelated to synchronization were pruned from CFGs, because they are irrelevant for deadlock analysis. The details of this automated conversion are outside the scope of this paper and explained in [15].

Kronecker-based deadlock analysis of railway systems has been introduced in [14]. Train routes and track sections can be viewed as thread CFGs and semaphores. At most one train can use a section at any time. During the occupation, a section is locked as if using a semaphore p()-operation. Once the train leaves the section, the lock is released. We analyze a train system with six train routes and twelve sections illustrated in Fig. 5. Each route constitutes a thread. E.g., Route 1 is defined as $L_1 = p_5, v_2, p_6, p_9, v_5, v_6, p_{11}, v_9, p_{12}, v_{11}, v_{12}$. The double-slip switch, located between Sections 4, 6, 7 and 9, is replaced with two switches connected by Section 6 of zero-length. If a train is too long to fit in a section, a sufficient number of sections ahead must be reserved. E.g., in Route L1, because Section 6 has zero-length, Section 9 is reserved ahead of time.

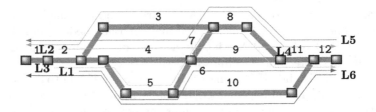

Fig. 5. A train system with six train routes and twelve track sections.

Table 2. Performance of multi-threaded SPIN (SPIN-8) and our multi-threaded (KA-8) and GPU (KA-G) implementations on three practical problems (times in seconds).

		Linux (3 threads)	Linux (5 threads)	Railway
GTX970	SPIN-8	N/A	N/A	1.64
	KA-8	154	68024	4.15
	KA-G	0.30	14.64	0.050
GTX680	SPIN-8	N/A	N/A	1.68
	KA-8	181	77107	4.89
	KA-G	0.29	14.14	0.049
GT750M	SPIN-8	N/A	N/A	2.05
	KA-8	316	144321	5.86
	KA-G	0.52	69.10	0.066

The analysis times obtained for Linux kernel threads and the railway system are depicted in Table 2. Sequential execution was intractable and has been excluded. The speedups of the GPU implementation of up to 5453× are proportional to the problem sizes and memory requirements. The GPU kernel computes in parallel with the hashing of processed nodes on the CPU. Hence, the GPU computation is *"hidden"* behind the CPU computation.

We compared our GPU implementation, KA-G, to SPIN, the state-of-the-art model checker [5] (version 6.4.5), in Fig. 6 and Table 2. We conducted experiments using one (SPIN-1) and eight threads (SPIN-8). For Dining Philosophers, KA-G is up to 1.9× faster than SPIN-1. However, it is struggling to outperform the multi-threaded version of SPIN. In the analysis of railway systems, however, KA-G is 33× faster than multi-threaded SPIN.

We have observed that the Kronecker algebra approach consumes considerably less memory than SPIN. SPIN reports its total memory usage, and we use the PAPI library and the CUDA API to observe the memory consumption of our approach. The smaller CPU memory footprint allows our approach to analyze larger problem sizes. E.g., the performance comparison reported in Fig. 6 had to be limited to a maximum of 15 philosophers; With 16 philosophers, SPIN-1's memory consumption exceeded the 32 GB RAM of our test-platform, and performance trashed as a result of excessive swapping. (We stopped SPIN on this test-run after 48 h.) In comparison, KA-G stores some intermediate buffers in the GPU memory space; consequently, our approach handled 17 philosophers in less than 24 GB of RAM. SPIN-8 has higher memory requirements and is thus unable to handle more than 14 philosophers.

The relative CPU and GPU memory consumption of KA-G to SPIN is shown in Fig. 7. Up to 12 philosophers, the GPU computation of KA-G consumes more memory than SPIN-1, because memory must be reserved for each GPU thread. The GPU kernel operates in iterations, where all buffers are reused. Thus, the GPU memory requirement does not grow with the problem size. In fact, the GPU memory consumption grows linearly in proportion to the number of Kronecker algebra operations while the CPU memory consumption grows in the number of reachable nodes. Because the CPU and GPU memory spaces are disjoint and the memory consumption on the GPU does not constrain the problem size, we only compare our CPU memory consumption to SPIN. Our implementation consumes up to 4.8× and 8.1× less memory than SPIN-1 and SPIN-8, respectively.

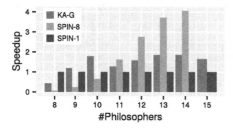

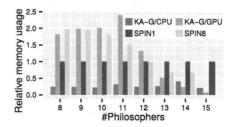

Fig. 6. Speedup comparison of our GPU implementation to SPIN.

Fig. 7. Relative memory consumption comparison of KA-G and SPIN-8 with respect to SPIN-1

6   Related Work

Kronecker algebra-based concurrent program verification has been introduced in [10] and subsequently extended to support worst-case execution time analysis [11,13], and the analysis of protected objects, semaphores and barriers [3,9,10,12]. Unlike prior work, this paper addresses performance improvements of Kronecker algebra operations, to cope with real-world static analysis problem sizes. The SPIN model checker [5,6] is a verification tool for concurrent programs. Spin employs state-transition graphs and depth-first search to check a program's safety and liveness properties. Bartocci [1] has parallelized SPIN on a GPU, such that computed thread interleavings are located in the GPU's memory. The limited memory space of GPUs constrains the solvable problem size to 15 philosophers. Kronecker algebra allows us to store thread interleavings on the CPU and thereby analyze larger problem sizes.

7   Conclusions

We have optimized Kronecker algebra operations for heterogeneous multicores. Our two-step lazy-evaluation approach constructs expression trees, followed by parallel, lazy evaluation. Lazy evaluation substantially speeds up analysis by omitting all unreachable nodes. Our pipelined execution scheme performs lazy Kronecker algebra operation evaluation on the GPU and uses the CPU to maintain the computed thread interleavings. Our experiments show speedups of up to $5453\times$ over the multicore CPU implementation. Our implementation consumes up to $8.1\times$ less memory than SPIN and can therefore analyze larger problem sizes.

Acknowledgments. This research was supported by the Austrian Science Fund (FWF) project I 1035N23, and by the Next-Generation Information Computing Development Program through the National Research Foundation of Korea (NRF), funded by the Ministry of Science, ICT & Future Planning under grant NRF2015M3C4A-7065522.

References

1. Bartocci, E., DeFrancisco, R., Smolka, S.A.: Towards a GPGPU-parallel SPIN model checker. In: 2014 International SPIN Symposium on Model Checking of Software, pp. 87–96. ACM (2014)
2. Buchholz, P., Kemper, P.: Efficient computation and representation of large reachability sets for composed automata. Discrete Event Dyn. Syst. **12**(3), 265–286 (2002)
3. Burgstaller, B., Blieberger, J.: Kronecker algebra for static analysis of Ada programs with protected objects. In: Ada-Europe International Conference on Reliable Software Technologies, vol. 8454, pp. 27–42 (2014)
4. Clarke, E., Grumberg, O., Jha, S., Lu, Y., Veith, H.: Progress on the state explosion problem in model checking. In: Wilhelm, R. (ed.) Informatics. LNCS, vol. 2000, pp. 176–194. Springer, Heidelberg (2001). doi:10.1007/3-540-44577-3_12
5. Holzmann, G.J.: The model checker SPIN. IEEE Trans. Softw. Eng. **23**, 279 295 (1997). IEEE Computer Society
6. Holzmann, G.J., Bosnacki, D.: The design of a multicore extension of the SPIN model checker. IEEE Trans. Softw. Eng. **33**, 659–674 (2007)
7. Kuich, W., Salomaa, A.: Semirings, Automata, Languages. Springer, Heidelberg (1986)
8. Li, X., Andersen, D.G., Kaminsky, M., Freedman, M.J.: Algorithmic improvements for fast concurrent cuckoo hashing. In: Proceedings of the Ninth European Conference on Computer Systems, EuroSys 2014. ACM (2014)
9. Mittermayr, R., Blieberger, J.: Static partial-order reduction of concurrent systems in polynomial time. In: Margaria, T., Steffen, B. (eds.) ISoLA 2008. CCIS, vol. 17, pp. 619–633. Springer, Heidelberg (2008). doi:10.1007/978-3-540-88479-8_44
10. Mittermayr, R., Blieberger, J.: Shared memory concurrent system verification using Kronecker algebra. Technical report 183/1-155, TU Vienna. http://arxiv.org/abs/1109.5522 (Sept 2011)

11. Mittermayr, R., Blieberger, J.: Timing analysis of concurrent programs. In: 12th International Workshop on Worst-Case Execution Time Analysis, pp. 59–68 (2012)
12. Mittermayr, R., Blieberger, J.: Kronecker algebra for static analysis of barriers in Ada. In: Bertogna, M., Pinho, L.M., Quiñones, E. (eds.) Ada-Europe 2016. LNCS, vol. 9695, pp. 145–159. Springer, Cham (2016). doi:10.1007/978-3-319-39083-3_10
13. Mittermayr, R., Blieberger, J.: Deadlock and WCET analysis of barrier-synchronized concurrent programs. Computing pp. 1–22 (2017)
14. Mittermayr, R., Blieberger, J., Schöbel, A.: Kronecker algebra-based deadlock analysis for railway systems. PROMET-Traffic Transp. **24**(5), 359–369 (2012)
15. Park, Y.: Kronecker algebra-based deadlock analysis in the Linux kernel. Technical report, Yonsei University. http://elc.yonsei.ac.kr/publications/KernelDeadlockAnalysis.pdf
16. Plateau, B.: On the stochastic structure of parallelism and synchronization models for distributed algorithms. In: ACM SIGMETRICS, vol. 13, pp. 147–154 (1985)

Performance Evaluation of Computation and Communication Kernels of the Fast Multipole Method on Intel Manycore Architecture

Mustafa Abduljabbar[1]([✉]), Mohammed Al Farhan[1]([✉]), Rio Yokota[2], and David Keyes[1]

[1] King Abdullah University of Science and Technology, Thuwal, Saudi Arabia
{Mustafa.AbdulJabbar,mohammed.farhan,david.keyes}@kaust.edu.sa
[2] Tokyo Institute of Technology, Tokyo, Japan
rioyokota@gsic.titech.ac.jp

Abstract. Manycore optimizations are essential for achieving performance worthy of anticipated exascale systems. Utilization of manycore chips is inevitable to attain the desired floating point performance of these energy-austere systems. In this work, we revisit ExaFMM, the open source Fast Multiple Method (FMM) library, in light of highly tuned shared-memory parallelization and detailed performance analysis on the new highly parallel Intel manycore architecture, Knights Landing (KNL). We assess scalability and performance gain using task-based parallelism of the FMM tree traversal. We also provide an in-depth analysis of the most computationally intensive part of the traversal kernel (i.e., the particle-to-particle (P2P) kernel), by comparing its performance across KNL and Broadwell architectures. We quantify different configurations that exploit the on-chip 512-bit vector units within different task-based threading paradigms. MPI communication-reducing and NUMA-aware approaches for the FMM's global tree data exchange are examined with different cluster modes of KNL. By applying several algorithm- and architecture-aware optimizations for FMM, we show that the N-Body kernel on 256 threads of KNL achieves on average 2.8× speedup compared to the non-vectorized version, whereas on 56 threads of Broadwell, it achieves on average 2.9× speedup. In addition, the tree traversal kernel on KNL scales monotonically up to 256 threads with task-based programming models. The MPI-based communication-reducing algorithms show expected improvements of the data locality across the KNL on-chip network.

Keywords: AVX-512 · Fast multipole method · Intel knights landing

1 Preliminaries and Outline

Contemporary High-Performance Computing (HPC) systems are assembled from thousands of shared-memory compute nodes, which are progressively metamorphosing from multicore to manycore architecture with a hybrid layered memory

© Springer International Publishing AG 2017
F.F. Rivera et al. (Eds.): Euro-Par 2017, LNCS 10417, pp. 553–564, 2017.
DOI: 10.1007/978-3-319-64203-1_40

hierarchy. Emerging manycore processors feature energy efficient, low frequency compute cores that support lightweight processing thread(s). For example, the second generation Intel Xeon Phi "Knights Landing" (KNL) can accommodate, in a single chip, up to 72 cores and 4 threads per core, which access an on-die high bandwidth memory. This immense computational power can be exploited by compute-intensive scientific algorithms.

The N-Body problem is used to sum up mutual interactions of discrete entities in $O(N^2)$ steps, which is a practical example of a compute-intensive kernel that can utilize the emerging manycore hardware. Its importance stems from the fact that it appears in many scientific applications such as electromagnetics, electrostatics, fluid mechanics, and astrophysics. In the form of the Fast Multipole Method (FMM), it is used either as a direct solver, or as an accelerator within an iterative solver for particular matrix-vector multiplications arising from the solution of Laplace or Helmholtz Partial Differential Equations (PDEs). N-Body methods can be considered as "matrix-free" methods, where a matrix is dynamically built before being multiplied by the source-point vector. This makes them favorable when the geometry of a problem changes rapidly such as particle-based methods where particles evolve every time step [15]. Tree codes like Barnes-Hut [3] build a geometric quad/oct tree to bring the quadratic complexity of N-body problem down to $O(N \log N)$. This is done by introducing a cutoff distance beyond which particles interact as cells located at the center of mass. FMM is an example of a tree code that uses hierarchical multipole expansions to approximate the far-field interactions up to specific error bound (ϵ) derived from the Multipole Acceptance Criteria (MAC) [7]. It solves the N-Body problem in asymptotically linear time complexity ($O(N)$). FMM is a highly computationally intensive algorithm that is favorable to manycore architectures.

1.1 Main Components of Parallel FMM

The general scheme of any parallel Fast Multipole solver consists of the several modules specified below. These typically execute in a fork-join sequence, with some exceptions mentioned in [2,17].

- Partitioning stage: Domain-decomposes the input while maximizing locality across processes. Foundations can be found in [12].
- Oct/Quad tree construction.
- Upward pass: A bottom-up sweep of the tree to execute the Particle-to-Multipole (P2M) and Multipole-to-Multipole (M2M) kernels. FMM kernels are explained in [7].
- Traversal: A depth-first local and global tree traversal to calculate near-field interaction by calling the Particle-to-Particle (P2P) or aggregate multipoles to local expansions for the far-field (i.e., Multipole-to-Local (M2L)).
- Communication: The far-field cells are propagated to other processes in a sender-initiated fashion.
- Downward pass: A top-down traversal that reduces local expansions using Local-to-Local (L2L) and Local-to-Particle (L2P).

Sections 2 through 4 briefly explain the P2P, traversal and communication modules, which contribute to the bulk of the total execution time, in the context of manycore parallelism.

Major fundamental and incremental contributions describe parallel FMM algorithms and implementations on shared and distributed memory [6]. Among these contributions are parallel FMM libraries that include PVFMM [13], pfa-clON, PEPC and ExaFMM [16]. Our choice for this paper is ExaFMM due to its reported efficient shared-memory optimizations, which range from adaptability to different task-based threading models to low-level Advanced Vector eXtension (AVX) vectorization. On a single socket Intel Xeon X560, ExaFMM outperforms the traditional FMM libraries [14]. Furthermore, Bédorf et al. provide an implementation and analysis of a gravitational N-Body tree code, that has been redesigned to run on top of the GPU architecture [4]. This results in a processing rate of 2.8 million particles/second.

1.2   Paper Contributions

The main contributions of this paper are:

- Exploit aggressive Single Instruction Multiple Data (SIMD) optimizations to vectorize the N-Body kernel, and also optimize the outer and the inner loop via certain loop tiling techniques with a specific stride size.
- Perform performance comparisons and analysis of the N-Body kernel between: (1) handwritten vectorization code using Intel Intrinsics and the compiler's auto-vectorization, and (2) inner and the outer loop tiling, on the state-of-the-art manycore and multicore Intel architectures.
- Carry out in-depth performance analysis and benchmarking of different task-based programming paradigms to parallelize the Tree Traversal kernel of FMM on KNL architecture.
- Analyze the performance of various MPI-based NUMA-aware communication algorithms of FMM within a single node to overcome the hurdles of cache line transfer inside the on-chip network of KNL, and study multiple cluster modes of KNL.

2   Direct N-Body Kernel on Modern Intel Architectures

The direct N-Body Kernel is manifested as the P2P near-field interactions within FMM. Along with the M2L kernel, P2P contributes to the bulk of execution time by performing the largest share of FMM computations [9]. The number of Floating Point Operations (FLOPs) per each P2P call is $20 \times n_i \times n_j$, where n_i is the size of the target cell (outer loop), n_j is the size of the source cell (inner loop), and 20 is the number of operations needed to calculate: (1) the smoothed Laplace potential ($\phi_i = \sum_{j=1}^{N} \frac{m_j}{r_{ij}}$), (2) the accelerations ($a_i = \nabla \phi_i = -\sum_{j=1}^{N} \frac{m_j r_{ij}}{r_{ij}^3}$), and (3) the distance between bodies located at x_i and x_j, given ϵ as the smoothing factor ($r_{ij} = \sqrt{(x_i - x_j)^2 + (y_i - y_j)^2 + (z_i - z_j)^2 + \epsilon^2}$). We store source and target fields in separate vectors to avoid loop conflict dependencies. This facilitates automatic and handwritten SIMD optimizations to exploit each core's two Vector Processing Units (VPUs) [10]. The outer loop is parallelized using OpenMP and the effect of hyperthreading is explored with two and four threads per a KNL core. A classical question that arises in the situation of nested for loops is at which level the loop should be vectorized. Along with the SIMD optimization techniques, this question is addressed thoroughly in the subsequent results section.

3   Task-Based Traversal of ExaFMM

As mentioned in Sect. 1.1, the traversal stage calculates near-field or self interactions (P2P); whereas far-field potentials are aggregated to well-separated cells through M2L kernel calls. The essential difference between pure tree codes and FMM is that the former usually constructs the tree using a linked-list data structure; the tree is traversed in a recursive top-down manner, and well-separated cells are identified by applying the MAC. In contrast, adaptive FMM does not traverse the tree, nor does it construct a linked-list between parent and child cells. It, however, constructs a Hilbert/Morton key by interleaving bits of $X - Y - Z$ cell coordinates. Typically the parent's neighbor's child cell is considered well-separated. Nonetheless, there are several downsides of this technique, which are highlighted in [14].

Due to potential task-based parallelism, we configure ExaFMM to use Dual-Tree-Traversal (DTT), which traverses the source and target cells at the same time. Classical OpenMP threading is not applicable for the lack of an outer-loop over target cells. DTT takes a source and a target cell, and expands the larger until either MAC is satisfied or both are leaf cells. Algorithms 1 and 2 demonstrate the general structure of DTT code. Nested task-parallelism can be effectively incorporated by passing an integer *nspawn* that indicates the size of cells that can spawn a task as shown in Line 8 of Algorithm 2.

Algorithm 1. DualTreeTraversal(C_i, C_j)

---

1 if $C_i > C_j$ then
2   foreach c_i in $C_j.Children$ do
3   Interact (c_i, C_j)
4 else
5   foreach c_j in $C_i.Children$ do
6   Interact (C_i, c_j)

Algorithm 2. Interact(C_i, C_j)

---

1 **if** C_i and C_j are leafs **then**
2 | P2P(C_i,C_j)
3 **else**
4 | **if** C_i and C_j satisfy MAC **then**
5 | | M2L(C_i,C_j)
6 | **else**
7 | | **if** SizeOf $(C_i,C_j)>$ nspawn **then**
8 | | | Spawn (DualTreeTraversal (C_i,C_j))
9 | | **else**
10 | | | DualTreeTraversal (C_i,C_j)

---

4 NUMA-Aware Communication Reducing Algorithms

The local essential tree (LET) is the union of trees representing the entire domain as perceived by the local process. LET communication is known to be the major factor that hinders FMM's perfect scaling. References [1, 8] describe specific communication protocols named $\mathcal{HSDX}$ and $\mathcal{NBX}$ respectively. They provide optimizations that are specific to distributed sparse data exchange, which generally suits the communication structure of FMM's global tree. We explore the effect of different communication strategies within the KNL chip. Note that we implemented all of these strategies on an ExaFMM branch [16]. Table 1 briefly highlights various techniques that we benchmark. Note that "Hierarchical" protocol means that the data is aggregated along a structured hierarchy such as graphs and trees, whereas "sparse-aware" protocol avoids direct communication with partitions without or with very little data to exchange (almost negligible). In the context of NUMA systems, hierarchical protocols tend to maximize locality of the data within each local caches, and in the case of data exchange, each process requires the data only from its neighboring MPI ranks. Hence, the communication is mostly localized inside the NUMA socket. However, if the required data happens to be in different NUMA socket, then MPI would communicate the cache line from the socket's memory, which is very negligible in proportion to locality maximizing communication protocols.

5 Results and Discussions

5.1 Experimental Setup

For KNL experiments, we used two Linux servers that run CentOS Linux 7.3.1611 Operating System. Both servers are powered by Intel Xeon Phi CPU 7210, which is equipped with 64 hardware cores that execute at 1.30 GHz clock frequency, and both have access to 116 GB of DRAM. The typical specifications of the KNL chip that we used here can be found in [10]. For Broadwell experiments, we used a Linux server that runs Ubuntu 14.04.5 LTS Operating System.

Table 1. MPI-based communication paradigms

Name	MPI calls	Complexity	Hierarchical	Sparse-aware
Alltoallv	MPI_Alltoallv	MPI specific	Yes	No
Hierarchical Alltoallv	MPI_Comm_Split MPI_Alltoallv	MPI specific	Yes	No
Point-to-Point	MPI_Isend MPI_Irecv MPI_Wait	$O(P)$	No	No
Hypercube	MPI_Comm_Split MPI_Isend MPI_Irecv	$O(\log P)$	Yes	Yes
$\mathcal{NBX}$	MPI_Ssend MPI_Srecv MPI_Ibarrier	$O(\log P)$	No	Yes
$\mathcal{HSDX}$	MPI_Distgraph_create MPI_Neighbor_alltoallv	$\Omega(\log P)\ O(\log^2 P)$	Yes	Yes
One-sided	MPI_Win_create MPI_Get	$O(P)$	No	No

The server is powered by dual sockets of Intel Xeon CPU E5-2680 v4, each of which is equipped with 14 hardware cores that execute at 2.40 GHz clock frequency. Each socket has access to a single address space of size 64 GB of DRAM. Therefore, the server has a NUMA node of in total 28 hardware cores and 128 GB of DRAM. For KNC experiments, we used a Linux server that runs Scientific Linux release 6.4 (Carbon) Operating System. The server is powered by two Intel Xeon Phi 7120P coprocessors, each of which is equipped with 61 hardware cores that run at 1.238 GHz clock frequency, and each has access to 16 GB of DRAM. The typical specifications of the KNC chip that we used here can be found in [5]. The two KNC chips are hosted by a dual socket Intel Sandy Bridge E5-2670 CPU. Each socket consists of 8 hardware cores (in total 16 cores). The CPU clock speed is 2.6 GHz. Both sockets share a 64 GB DRAM (32 GB per socket). All of the experiments here were run with Intel Parallel Studio XE 2017 as the main software stack that comes with Intel ICC, MPI, TBB, OpenMP, and Cilk. The data sets are based on a single precision Laplace kernel with Cartesian coordinates, and the FMM order of expansion is set to 4. For the KNL results, all of the experiments are ran with `-xMIC-AVX512`, and for KNC, we use `-mmic` compiler option. For Broadwell, on the other hand, we use `-xHost` compiler flag. All of the experiments are compiled with `-O3` compiler optimization flag. All of the experiments here are summarized using the arithmetic mean of the CPU wall clock time across 10 independent runs, which forms the sample space, and an error bar is drawn to show the $+/-$ standard deviation of the mean for each experimental sample.

5.2   SIMD Optimizations of the N-Body Kernel

The N-Body kernel is constructed with two nested `for loops`. The outer loop is the target loop and the inner loop is the source loop. We explore loop

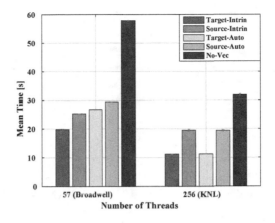

Fig. 1. Direct N-Body kernel running on two Intel architectures, KNL (quadrant cluster and flat memory modes) and Broadwell [Problem Size: 1 million Particles]

tiling on each loop, with 16 stride size for KNL. Therefore, in a single CPU cycle, each OpenMP thread fetches 16 bytes of data into the vector unit. In the case of two threads per core, each thread processes 16 bytes simultaneously utilizing the two vector units per core of KNL. However, if one thread per core is running, the next 16 bytes are pipelined in the second vector unit, and the thread scheduler alternates between them in a serialized manner, which keeps the core busy as much as possible. Furthermore, when the full number of threads per core are running, the threads are pipelined to process the data of both vector units. Therefore, with four threads per core, KNL utilizes both vector units and the pipelining potentials available in the out-of-core execution of the core's instruction pipeline. We observe that tiling targets' as opposed to sources' wins consistently in KNL; in each outer loop iteration, cache lines pertaining to elements in the target vector are loaded only once to AVX512 register using `_mm512_load_ps` intrinsic. This in turn does not require calling `_mm512_reduce_add_ps` after iterating over sources, which must be done otherwise because vectorizing effects of source fields must eventually be reduced to one value at target. Note that this kernel is run independent of FMM to explore the effect of the used techniques in detail, hence the chosen problem sizes are relatively small due to the quadratic compute and memory complexities. Figure 1 presents the performance of the N-Body kernel running on KNL comparing five different optimization techniques: (1) Target-Intrin: N-Body outer-loop tiling. (2) Source-Intrin: N-Body inner-loop tiling. (3) Target-Auto: outer-loop wrapping with `#pragma simd`. (4) Source-Auto: inner-loop wrapping with `#pragma simd`. (5) No-vec: scaler code.

We note that the handwritten vectorization does not improve much over auto-vectorization in KNL. It even appears that the ICC compiler was able to detect the event of reciprocal square root known as `_mm512_rsqrt28_ps`. Overall, vectorization benefits the kernel and shows significant improvements compared to

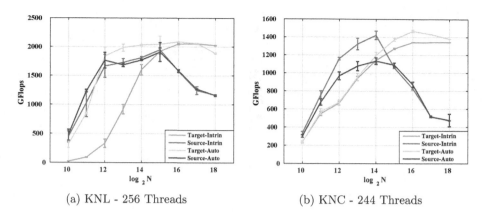

(a) KNL - 256 Threads   (b) KNC - 244 Threads

Fig. 2. FLOP/s performance across the 2 Intel manycore generations, KNL (quadrant cluster and flat memory modes) and KNC

the non-vectorized version of the code. This is not entirely the case in Broadwell; the variations are not proportional to their rivals in KNL, which suggests that outer-loop manual tiling cannot be avoided in Broadwell. We infer that KNL's AVX512 has a more sophisticated mechanism of matching correct vectorization than AVX2.

Figure 2 draws a comparison between floating point applicabilities of the 2 manycore generations by Intel, namely KNC and KNL, in terms of the aforementioned vectorization techniques. Error bars suggest reasonable stability in clocking frequency in both generations. Auto-vectorization in KNL reaches maximum FLOPs rate in an at least four times smaller problem, which strongly suggest that it utilizes local caches in a much more efficient manner. The drop in performance for slow versions happens exactly at the time when the performance of manual target vectorization saturates. This also suggests that the drop happens when prefetching and cache reuse could no more hide the overhead caused by source vectorization [5], which is 2^{15} in KNL (Fig. 2a) and 2^{14} in KNC (Fig. 2b).

5.3   Dual Tree Traversal with Task-Based Threading

Figure 3 shows traversal scalability using several threading libraries. The purpose of this test is to assess the DTT (Algorithm 1) performance using task-based/lightweight threading libraries on manycore architectures. Error bars are hardly observable, because frequency scaling has been disabled on KNL to stabilize performance. As expected, there is a general loss of scalability aspect when hyperthreading is enabled. Intel TBB perfectly scales up to 64 threads (1 thread/core). Scaling to the full chip, i.e., 256 threads, its relative speedup is 14, 94, with an efficiency of 0.469, compared to 0.4249 in Intel Cilk and 0.1912 in OpenMP tasks. It is observed that there is a weak separation between user-level and OS-level threads in OpenMP tasks. This is due to the very marginal performance gain from enabling hyperthreading in OpenMP tasks [5] (1.1× speedup

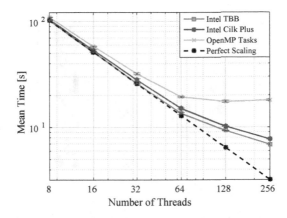

Fig. 3. Dual tree traversal using different task threading models. [Problem Size: 100 million Particles]

between 64 and 128 threads). Intel TBB, therefore, has the lowest task creation overhead, due to its efficient performance for heavily recursive tasks. However, Cilk does not seem to pose significant degradation in performance although it has minimal development time since it is integrated as a C++ language extension in modern Intel compilers.

5.4   Communication Reducing on KNL

As compute nodes are packaged with more low frequency cores, it is essential that MPI communication scales within main memory or across the NUMA sockets. Therefore, we apply various MPI communication reducing algorithms from Table 1 to FMM's tree communication. Results that are shown in Fig. 4 are executed with 64 MPI ranks, and a single thread per each rank, so that the effect of locality-maximizing behavior can be clearly observed.

$\mathcal{HSDX}$ (Distgraph) performs better that the others, and this is due to restricting exchanges to neighbors only, which makes it potentially NUMA-aware and yields acceptable on-chip performance. In other words, in $\mathcal{HSDX}$ algorithm, we tend to maintain a load balance between the KNL tiles, so that each tile acts like a sender and receiver of the cache lines. Thus, this model of communication prevents any long distance cache line transfer inside the chip, and maintains load balance of the cache line distributions across the tiles. To further prove this, we investigate this phenomena when we change the cluster mode of KNL. As you can see in Fig. 5, the $\mathcal{HSDX}$ the cluster modes of KNL do not have significant performance impact on the algorithm, and the performance differences between different modes are very negligible. Note that SNC-2 and SNC-4 modes are still experimental modes [11].

One-sided communication has a large overhead for shared window creation using MPI_Win_create, which requires soft locking prior to data access. This latency cannot be hidden when fetching sparse data either from the memory or

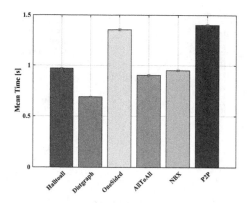

Fig. 4. Comparison of different MPI communication algorithms of LET communication kernel running on KNL (quadrant cluster/flat memory modes) [Problem Size: 80 million Particles]

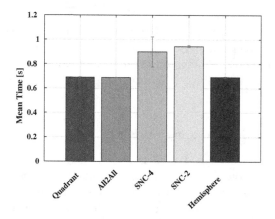

Fig. 5. Comparison of different cluster modes of KNL running Distgraph communication algorithm with 64 MPI ranks and 1 TBB Thread per MPI rank [problem size is 80 million particles]

from the other L2 caches. Even though, KNL has a great support for AVX512 prefetching instructions, locking the window before accessing the data imposes an implicit synchronization barrier on every data read. This creates a significant overhead on a cache-coherent systems.

6   Conclusion and Future Work

Facing manycore processors with high degree of fine-grained thread parallelism within a single shared-memory compute node, practitioners are now compelled to investigate strong thread scaling. In this paper, we present optimizations and thorough analysis of an FMM code on a modern high performance Intel manycore architecture, KNL. We extract the potential SIMD and thread-level parallelisms of three different computationally intensive kernels, namely P2P, tree traversal, and LET communication kernels. We demonstrate several shared-memory optimizations on these kernels, including different task-based threading paradigms, vectorization, loop tiling, and NUMA-aware communication-reducing. Our shared-memory optimizations present significant improvements that are reflected on the N-Body kernel compare to the out-of-the-box compilation of the non-optimized version. These feature in excess of 2.8x speedup on two Intel multi and many architectures, KNL and Broadwell. Furthermore, the task-based parallelism of the tree traversal kernel shows almost linear scaling, within a massively parallel single compute node, up to 64 thread contexts of KNL. With hyperthreading the performance gain becomes slightly monotonic. The NUMA-aware communication algorithm based on optimizing MPI alltoall communication protocol to maintain load balancing and shorter cache line transfers within a chip are explored. It is found that $\mathcal{HSDX}$ performs considerably faster than any other communication models; even across different cluster modes of KNL it still maintains marginally the same performance.

In the future, we plan to carry out a comprehensive comparison study across other FMM codes optimized for multi and manycore architectures. We are extending the study to include other x86 architectures, including IBM POWER8, and the bleeding edge release of Intel Xeon (i.e., Skylake). In addition, we are exploring multiple problem sizes to study the performance effects of workload variations on KNL. We are applying certain algorithmic optimizations to improve the performance of FMM on KNL, especially to overcome the stagnation and saturation of performance with hyperthreading enabled. To exploit the MCDRAM, we are working on optimizing the tree traversal kernels, which include the N-Body kernel. This is achieved by issuing simultaneous memory accesses throughout the kernel execution and utilizing the AVX512 prefetching instructions. Finally, we are building an extensive performance model to analyze the behavior of hybrid programming paradigms (MPI+TBB) on KNL. Multiple strategies are being developed to extract the best combinations of different programming models within a chip. These include thread/task pinning to a thread, core, tile, quadrant, and node, through low-level programming interfaces.

References

1. Abduljabbar, M., Markomanolis, G.S., Ibeid, H., Yokota, R., Keyes, D.: Communication reducing algorithms for distributed hierarchical N-body problems with boundary distributions. In: Kunkel, J.M., Yokota, R., Balaji, P., Keyes, D. (eds.) ISC 2017. LNCS, vol. 10266, pp. 79–96. Springer, Cham (2017). doi:10.1007/978-3-319-58667-0_5
2. AbdulJabbar, M., Yokota, R., Keyes, D.: Asynchronous execution of the fast multipole method using CHARM++. arXiv preprint arXiv:1405.7487 (2014)
3. Barnes, J., Hut, P.: A hierarchical $o(n \log n)$ force-calculation algorithm. Nature 324(6096), 446–449 (1986)

4. Bédorf, J., Gaburov, E., Zwart, S.P.: A sparse octree gravitational N-body code that runs entirely on the GPU processor. J. Comput. Phys. **231**(7), 2825–2839 (2012)

5. Farhan, M.A.A., Kaushik, D.K., Keyes, D.E.: Unstructured computational aerodynamics on many integrated core architecture. Parallel Comput. **59**, 97–118 (2016). Theory and Practice of Irregular Applications

6. Greengard, L., Gropp, W.D.: A parallel version of the fast multipole method. Comput. Math. Appl. **20**(7), 63–71 (1990)

7. Greengard, L., Rokhlin, V.: A fast algorithm for particle simulations. J. Comput. Phys. **73**(2), 325–348 (1987)

8. Hoefler, T., Siebert, C., Lumsdaine, A.: Scalable communication protocols for dynamic sparse data exchange. In: Proceedings of the 15th ACM SIGPLAN Symposium on Principles and Practice of Parallel Programming, PPoPP 2010, pp. 159–168. ACM, New York (2010). http://doi.acm.org/10.1145/1693453.1693476

9. Ibeid, H., Yokota, R., Keyes, D.: A performance model for the communication in fast multipole methods on high-performance computing platforms. Int. J. High Perform. Comput. Appl. **30**, 423–437 (2016)

10. Jeffers, J., Reinders, J., Sodani, A.: Intel Xeon Phi Processor High Performance Programming (Knights Landing Edition), 2nd edn. Morgan Kaufmann, Boston (2016)

11. Ramos, S., Hoefler, T.: Capability models for manycore memory systems: a casestudy with xeon phi KNL. In: Proceedings of the 31st IEEE International Parallel & Distributed Processing Symposium (IPDPS 2017). IEEE, May 2017

12. Warren, M.S., Salmon, J.K.: A fast tree code for many-body problems. Los Alamos Sci. **22**(10), 88–97 (1994)

13. Ying, L., Biros, G., Zorin, D., Langston, H.: A new parallel kernel-independent fast multipole method. In: 2003 ACM/IEEE Conference Supercomputing, p. 14. IEEE (2003)

14. Yokota, R.: An FMM based on dual tree traversal for many-core architectures. J. Algorithms Comput. Technol. **7**(3), 301–324 (2013)

15. Yokota, R., Abduljabbar, M.: N-body methods. In: Reinder, J., Jeffers, J. (eds.) High Performance Parallelism Pearls - Multicore and Many-Core Programming Approaches, Chap. 10, pp. 175–183. Elsevier, Amsterdam (2014). 1 edn

16. Yokota, R., et al.: ExaFMM (2016). https://github.com/exafmm/exafmm

17. Zandifar, M., Abdul Jabbar, M., Majidi, A., Keyes, D., Amato, N.M., Rauchwerger, L.: Composing algorithmic skeletons to express high-performance scientific applications. In: Proceedings of the 29th ACM on International Conference on Supercomputing, ICS 2015, pp. 415–424. ACM (2015)

Efficient Non-blocking Radix Trees

Varun Velamuri[(✉)]

Siemens Corporate Research, Bangalore, India
varun.velamuri@siemens.com

Abstract. Radix trees belong to the class of trie data structures, used for storing both sets and dictionaries in a way optimized for space and lookup. In this work, we present an efficient non-blocking implementation of radix tree data structure that can be configured for arbitrary alphabet sizes. Our algorithm implements a linearizable set with contains, insert and remove operations and uses single word compare-and-swap (CAS) instruction for synchronization. We extend the idea of marking the child edges instead of nodes to improve the parallel performance of the data structure. Experimental evaluation indicates that our implementation out-performs other known lock-free implementations of trie and binary search tree data structures using CAS by more than 100% under heavy contention.

Keywords: Concurrent · Non-blocking · Lock-free · Radix tree · Trie · Performance

1 Introduction

A trie is an efficient information retrieval data structure which stores keys with a common prefix under the same sequence of edges, eliminating the need for storing the same prefix each time for each key. Radix trees are space optimized tries in which any node that is the only child is merged with its parent. They are widely used in practical applications like IP address lookup in routing systems [6], memory management in Linux kernel [3] etc.

The search complexity of a radix tree is $O(k)$ where k is the key length. For fixed length key sets like integers, this becomes $O(\log U)$ where U is the size of integer universe. In a sequential setting, other balanced tree data structures like AVL or red-black trees offer a better search complexity of $O(\log n)$ (where n is the number of keys in the set) as $n < U$. These data structures re-balance the tree after updates to guarantee logarithmic search complexity. In a concurrent scenario, re-balancing the data structure requires complex synchronization as nodes move higher up the tree which can significantly impact the parallel performance of these data structures.

Radix trees do not require re-balancing and still guarantee logarithmic search complexity for integer key sets. For variable length key sets like strings, radix trees have a better search complexity of $O(k)$ compared to AVL and red-black

© Springer International Publishing AG 2017
F.F. Rivera et al. (Eds.): Euro-Par 2017, LNCS 10417, pp. 565–579, 2017.
DOI: 10.1007/978-3-319-64203-1_41

trees whose complexity is $O(k \log n)$. The simplicity of the structure and better search complexity makes radix trees good candidates for concurrent applications.

Various constructions for concurrent non-blocking tries exist in the literature. Non-blocking implementations ensure that system-wide progress is guaranteed even in presence of multiple thread failures making them desirable for concurrent applications. Shafiei [10] proposed a non-blocking implementation of Patricia trie data structure using compare-and-swap (CAS) instruction. A Patricia trie is a binary radix tree or a radix tree with radix value equal to 2. They extend the node level marking scheme from Ellen et al. [4] to tries. Each node in their algorithm has a structure linked to it which will be updated with the necessary information required to complete an operation. Any thread that is blocked by an on-going operation reads this structure to help finish the operation thereby achieving non-blocking progress. Even though this approach guarantees non-blocking progress, not more than one thread can simultaneously update a node limiting the parallelism of the structure. This can significantly influence the parallel performance of the structure especially with large number of operating threads.

Prokopec et al. [9] proposed a non-blocking hash trie data structure using CAS instruction. Hash tries are space efficient tries which combine the features of hash tables and tries. Each node in the hash trie maintains an invariant that the length of array containing the child pointers is always equivalent to the number of non-null children in the node. This eliminates sparse child arrays with null values, making them space efficient. The index of the child that needs to be traversed is calculated using a hash function. Non-blocking progress is achieved using the node level marking scheme from Ellen et al. [4] because of which the algorithm does not support simultaneous updates at a node limiting the amount of parallelism in the structure. Repetti et al. [11] proposed a non-blocking radix tree data structure using restricted transactional memory (RTM) extensions. The limited availability of transactional memory extensions in commercial processor architectures restricts the applicability of their algorithm.

In this work, we propose a concurrent non-blocking implementation of a radix tree data structure using single word compare-and-swap (CAS) instruction. Our algorithm can be configured to support arbitrary alphabet sizes and implements a linearizable set with **Contains**, **Insert**, and **Remove** operations. We extend the idea of marking the individual child pointers from Natarajan and Mittal [7] to radix trees. This allows threads to simultaneously update a node which can significantly improve the parallel performance of the structure. To the best of our knowledge, this is the first non-blocking implementation of a radix tree data structure using single word CAS that can be configured for arbitrary alphabet sizes and supports simultaneous updates on a node.

We implemented our algorithm in C++ and compared its performance with other non-blocking tries, binary search tree (BST) and k-ary tree data structures. Experimental results indicate that our algorithm performs better and scales best among other known lock-free algorithms. Due to space constrains, only a brief outline of the correctness proof is presented in this paper and the complete proof is provided elsewhere [12]. In the next few sections, we discuss our algorithm in detail and later present the experimental evaluation of our implementation.

2   Overview

We assume an asynchronous shared memory multiprocessor system that supports atomic compare-and-swap (CAS) instruction along with atomic read and write instructions. A `CAS(ptr, old, new)` instruction compares the value in memory referenced by `ptr` to `old` value and if they are same, then updates the memory referenced by `ptr` with `new` value atomically. Duplicate keys are not considered in our model. The size of an alphabet that is used to represent the key (e.g. binary, hexadecimal or ASCII) can be configured at the beginning of algorithm and it remains constant throughout.

Each node in our tree stores the prefix of a key, the size of the prefix in number of symbols and a boolean value to distinguish between leaf and internal nodes. Additionally, internal nodes have an array of child pointers. Leaf nodes store the key with all its symbols i.e. the actual or full key. This means that a key is considered to be present in the tree only if it matches the key in a leaf node.

The `Contains(k)` validates the presence of key `k` in the tree and returns *true* if `k` is found to be present in a leaf node. Otherwise, it returns *false*. An `Insert(k)` operation updates the data structure with a leaf node containing key `k` only if `k` is not already present in the tree. It returns *false* if the target key is found in the tree at the time of traversal. A suitable location for insertion is identified by traversing the tree and a leaf node containing the target key is updated into the tree using a CAS instruction. On a successful CAS, insert operation returns *true*.

A `Remove(k)` operation removes key `k` from the tree only if a leaf node containing `k` is found to be present in the tree at the time of traversal. Otherwise, remove operation returns *false*. The leaf node containing `k` is removed from the tree by updating the memory referenced by the parent pointer to `NULL` value using CAS instruction. After removing the leaf node, the number of non-null child pointers of the parent node is counted and if it is found to have '0' or '1' non-null child pointers, then the parent node is removed from the tree and remove operation returns *true*. This ensures that any internal node with zero or one child will always be removed thereby maintaining the space efficiency of radix trees.

If `Insert` or `Remove` operations are blocked by an on-going update operation, they will first help finish the on-going update to complete and then restart their operation. Also, if the CAS instruction that is used to update the tree fails because of simultaneous updates by other threads, the corresponding operation is restarted. For simplicity, we assume that the memory allocated to nodes that are not a part of the tree is not reclaimed. This allows us to assume that all the new nodes have unique addresses and ignore the ABA problem.

3   Algorithm

In this section, we present the structures used in our algorithm and the implementation details of `Contains`, `Insert` and `Remove` operations.

3.1   Data Structures

The declarations of various structures used are presented as pseudo-code in Algorithm 1. Our data structure is built using leaf (*lNode*) and internal (*iNode*) node objects which are subtypes of *Node* object. Each node in our data structure contains three fields: *label* of type *KEY* to store the prefix, *size* of type integer to store the size of *label* in number of symbols and *isLeaf* of type boolean to distinguish between leaf nodes and internal nodes. The value of *isLeaf* is set to *true* for leaf nodes and *false* for internal nodes. For fixed length key sets like integers, *KEY* refers to an integer and for variable length key sets like strings, *KEY* refers to an array of characters. The fields *label*, *isLeaf*, and *size* of a node are immutable i.e. their value will not change after initialization. Each internal node additionally has an array of child pointers with the size of array equivalent to the size of the alphabet (`ALPHABET_SIZE`) i.e. 16 for a hexadecimal alphabet and 2 for a binary alphabet.

Two bits from each of the child pointers are used to represent the state of an on-going remove operation. On most modern machines, memory is aligned on a 4/8-byte boundary leaving the lower 2/3 bits of the address unused. These bits can be used to store auxiliary information like the state of an operation which can be used by other threads to help complete the operation in case of contention. Two of these bits represented by boolean values *flag* and *freeze* are used from each of the child pointers to represent the state of an remove operation.

For a pointer, if the value of *freeze* bit is set to '1', it means that the node containing the pointer is undergoing removal from the tree and the pointer is considered frozen. Similarly for a pointer, if the value of *flag* bit is set to '1', it means that the node referred by the pointer is being removed from the tree and the pointer is considered flagged. For the tree shown in Fig. 1c, node B is undergoing removal and therefore, node A's child pointer has the flag bit set to '1' and all the child pointers of B has the freeze bit set to '1'. In the pseudo-code presented, we use the notation $<ptr, flag, freeze>$ to represent the value of *pointer*, *flag* and *freeze* bits. E.g., $<ptr, 1, *>$ implies that the value of *pointer* is ptr, the value of *flag* bit is '1' and the value of *freeze* bit can either be '0' or '1'.

The *SeekRecord* structure is used to store the result of tree traversal. It contains 5 members: (i) `curr`: Last traversed node in the tree (ii) `par`: Parent node of `curr` (iii) `currIndex`: Index of the `curr` node in the child pointer array of *par* node (iv) `gPar`: Grandparent of *curr* node or parent of *par* node (v) `parIndex`: Index of the `par` node in the child pointer array of `gPar` node.

The `root` node always points to the head of the tree. It is initialized as an internal node with an empty *label* (ϵ) and zero label *size*. Two leaf nodes `lMin` and `lMax` are always assumed to be present in the tree and are never deleted.

```
1  struct lNode : Node { // Leaf node structure. Subtype of Node structure
2      KEY label;        // Stores the key's prefix
3      Int size;         // Size of 'label' in number of alphabets
4      Bool isLeaf;      // Value is true for leaf nodes
5  };
6  struct iNode : Node { // Internal node structure. Subtype of Node structure
7      KEY label;        // Stores the key's prefix
8      Int size;         // Size of 'label' in number of alphabets
9      Bool isLeaf;      // Value is false for internal nodes
       // Array of child pointers initialized to NULL
10     {NodePtr ref, Bool flag, Bool freeze} child[ALPHABET_SIZE];
11 };
12 struct SeekRecord {
       // Grand parent of curr node, parent of curr node and curr node
13     NodePtr gPar, par, curr;
       // Index of 'curr' node in 'par' child array, 'par' node in 'gPar' child array
14     Int currIndex, parIndex;
15 };
   // root will always point to the head of tree
16 NodePtr root = new Node(ε, 0, false);
17 NodePtr lMin = new Node(KEY_MIN, Sizeof(KEY_MIN), true);
18 NodePtr lMax = new Node(KEY_MAX, Sizeof(KEY_MAX), true);
19 root→ child[0] = lMin;
20 root→ child[ALPHABET_SIZE - 1] = lMax;
```

Algorithm 1. Structure declarations and initializations

This ensures that the root node has at least two leaf nodes always present and is never removed from the tree. We use the SizeOf(k) method to count the number of symbols present in key k.

3.2 Search

Search is a helper method used by Contains, Insert and Remove operations to locate the position of a node containing the target key (*key*) or a target node (*node*) in the tree. The pseudo-code is presented in Algorithm 2. Starting from the root node, Search method traverses the tree one node at a time by comparing the node's label with first '*size*' number of symbols from target key's prefix. The MatchPrefix method (Line 27) performs this comparison and returns *true* if there is a match. Otherwise, MatchPrefix method returns *false* and Search terminates the traversal.

On a successful prefix match, the search proceeds further by traversing through a child pointer located at the index corresponding to the '*size+1*' symbol in the target key. The GetIndex method (Line 29) computes the index of child pointer that needs to be traversed. It takes the target key and the size of current node's label as inputs and returns the index corresponding to the symbol at prefix location '*size+1*' in the target key.

Search method continues with the traversal until a NULL child pointer or a leaf node is encountered i.e. the nodes after which the tree does not exist. Also, if the location of the target node is found, Search method will terminate the traversal. The results of traversal are updated in the *record* object (Line 31).

```
21  void Search(KEY key, NodePtr targetNode, SeekRecordPtr record)
22  begin
        // Initialize the search parameters
23      NodePtr <gPar, *, *> = root, <par, *, *> = root, <curr, *, *> = root;
24      Int parIndex = -1, currIndex = -1;
25      Bool flagged = false, frozen = false;

        // Traverse the tree until a NULL node is encounterd
26      while (curr != NULL) do
            /* Stop the traversal if 'curr' is leaf node or target node of interest or the
               node's label doesnot match the key's prefix                             */
27          if (curr→isLeaf or (curr == targetNode) or (MatchPrefix(key, curr)) == false)
            then break;

28          gPar = par, par = curr, parIndex = currIndex;
            // Get the index of the child pointer that needs to be traversed
29          currIndex = GetIndex(key, curr→size);
30          <curr, flaged, frozen> = curr→child[currIndex];

        // Update the recod structure with the results of traversal
31      *record = {gPar, par, <curr, flagged, frozen>, parIndex, currIndex};

32  Bool Contains(KEY key, SeekRecord *record)
33  begin
34      Search(key, NULL, record);  // Locate the poistion of 'key' using Search
35      NodePtr <curr, *, *> = record→curr;
36      return (curr == NULL ? false : ((curr→label == key) and curr→isLeaf));
```

Algorithm 2. Search and Contains methods

3.3   Contains

The pseudo-code for Contains method is presented in Algorithm 2. It uses the results of traversal by Search method to validate the presence of a key in the tree. If the last traversed node (i.e. curr) is either NULL or an internal node, then Contains method returns *false* as all valid keys are stored in the leaf nodes of the tree. Otherwise, it returns the result of comparison between curr node's label and target key (Line 36).

3.4   Remove

The pseudo-code for Remove operation is presented in Algorithm 3. It first validates the presence of a key using the Contains method (Line 39) and returns *false* if the key is not found to be present in the tree. Otherwise, it tries to remove the leaf node containing the target key from the tree using CAS (Line 46) by updating memory referenced by the parent pointer to NULL value. If this CAS fails due to simultaneous updates on the node, Remove operation is restarted to locate the new position of the node containing target key.

On a successful CAS, the MakeConsistent method is called to count the number of non-null child pointers of par node and remove it from the tree if it has less than two non-null child pointers. This ensures that any internal node with zero or one child will always be removed thereby maintaining the space efficiency of radix trees. The pseudo-code for MakeConsistent method is presented in Algorithm 4.

Removal of an internal node begins by updating the *flag* bit of the parent pointer to '1' using CAS (Line 70). Note that, the *flag* bit is set to '1' only

```
37  Bool Remove(KEY key, SeekRecordPtr record)
38  begin
        // Validate the presence of target key
39      if (Contains(key, record) == false) then return false;

40      NodePtr <gPar, *, *> = record→gPar, <par, *, *> = record→par;
41      NodePtr <curr, *, frozen> = record→curr;
42      Int currIndex = record→currIndex, parIndex = record→parIndex;

43      if frozen then // 'par' node is undergoing removal. Help remove the 'par' node
44          HelpFreeze(par); RemoveNode(gPar, par, parIndex);
45          return Remove(key, record);

        // Remove the leaf node with target key from the tree
46      else if CAS(par→child[currIndex], <curr, 0, 0>, NULL) then
            /* Check the number of non-null children of 'par' node and remove it if the
               count is less than 2                                                    */
47          MakeConsistent(gPar, par, parIndex, record);
48          return true;

49      else return Remove(key, record);// Restart as CAS failed due to contention
```

Algorithm 3. Remove method

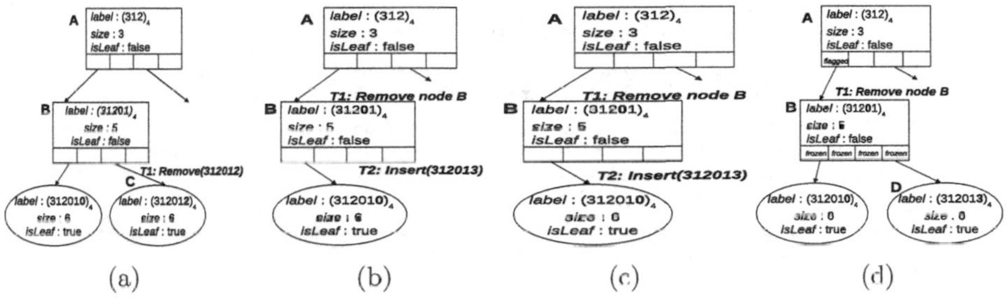

Fig. 1. Removal of internal node and simultaneous insertion

for pointers referring to internal nodes and pointers referring to leaf nodes will never be flagged. Also, we maintain an invariant that both the *flag* and *freeze* bits of a pointer can not have the value '1' at the same time. This means that, if the parent pointer of curr node is flagged, the node containing parent pointer i.e. par node can not be removed from the tree until the *flag* bit is cleared which can happen only during the successful removal of curr node from the tree.

After successfully flagging the parent pointer, the HelpFreeze method is called (Line 71) to set the *freeze* bit of all the child pointers to '1' using CAS. Once the *freeze* bit of a pointer is set to '1', it can not be undone. This prevents any further insertions at the internal node and therefore the node can safely be removed from the tree. HelpFreeze returns only after all the child pointers have the *freeze* bit set to '1'. This means that once a thread decides to freeze the node, by calling HelpFreeze method it can not be undone. When freezing the child pointers, if any of the pointer is observed to have the *flag* bit set to '1', then HelpFreeze helps the removal of the node referred by child pointer and then attempts to set the *freeze* bit again. Freezing the child pointers begins only after flagging the parent. This means that if a child pointer has *freeze* bit set to '1', then it's parent is already flagged.

```
50  Void MakeConsistent(NodePtr par, NodePtr curr, SIZE currIndex, SeekRecordPtr record)
51  begin
          // Count the number of non-null children and return if count is greater than 1
52        Int childCount = CheckChild(curr); if (childCount > 1) then return;
53        NodePtr gPar = NULL; Int parIndex = -1;
          // Parent information not known. Search in the tree for the location of 'curr' node
54        if par == NULL then
55            Search(curr→label, curr, record);
56            NodePtr <newCurr, *, *> = record→curr;
57            if newCurr == curr then
58                gPar = record→gPar, par = record→par;
59                currIndex = record→currIndex, parIndex = record→parIndex;
60                NodePtr <*, flagged, frozen>=record→curr;
61            else return; // 'curr' node is removed from the tree. Therefore, return
62        if frozen then // 'par' node is being removed from the tree. Help remove 'par' node
63            HelpFreeze(par); Search(par→label, par, record);
64            NodePtr <newPar, *, *> = record→curr;
65            if newPar == par then
66                gPar = record→par, parIndex = record→currIndex;
67                RemoveNode(gPar, par, parIndex);
68                MakeConsistent(record→gPar, gPar, record→parIndex, record);
              // Check the consistency of 'curr' node after 'par' node removal
69            return MakeConsistent(NULL, curr, currIndex, record);
          // Flag parent pointer in-order to remove 'curr' node from the tree
70        else if (flagged or CAS(par→child[currIndex], curr, <curr, 1, 0>)) then
71            HelpFreeze(curr); RemoveNode(par, curr, currIndex);
72            return MakeConsistent(gPar, par, currIndex, record);
          // Another thread inserted new node at par. Check consistency with new parent
73        else if <par→child[currIndex], *, *> != curr then
74            return MakeConsistent(NULL, curr, currIndex, record);
```

Algorithm 4. MakeConsistent method

```
75  Void HelpFreeze(NodePtr node)
76  begin
77        Int index = 0;
78        while (index < ALPHABET_SIZE) do // For each child pointer of the node
79            NodePtr <child, flagged, frozen> = node→child[index];
80            if flagged then // Help the removal of node referred by 'child' before freezing
81                HelpFreeze(child), RemoveNode(node, child, index);
              // Freeze the child pointer using CAS instruction
82            else if (frozen or CAS(node→child[index], <child, 0, 0>, <child, 0, 1>)) then
83                index++;

84  Int CheckChild(NodePtr node)
85  begin
86        Int childCount = 0, index = 0;
87        while (index <ALPHABET_SIZE) do // Count the number of non-null child
          pointers in node
88            NodePtr <ptr, *, *> = node→child[index];
89            if ptr != NULL then childCount++;
90            index++;
91        return childCount;
```

Algorithm 5. Helper methods for remove

The `RemoveNode` method presented in Algorithm 6 removes an internal node from the tree. It updates the parent pointer to point to the new child or to a `NULL` value if all the child pointers are `NULL`. A particularly tricky case can arise when removing an internal node from the tree which is illustrated in Fig. 1. Thread T1 finds the leaf node of interest i.e. node C and removes it from the tree. As node B has only one non-null child, $T1$ decides to freeze the child pointers of node B. Simultaneously, thread $T2$ successfully inserts new leaf node D as child of B. After freezing all the child pointers, node B contains more than one non-null child pointer and therefore should not be removed from the tree.

```
92  Bool RemoveNode(NodePtr par, NodePtr curr, Int currIndex)
93  begin
        // Count the number of non-null child pointers
94      Int childCount = CheckChild(curr), index = 0;
95      NodePtr ptr = NULL;

96      if childCount == 1 then // Update 'ptr' to point to the only valid child node
97          while (index < ALPHABET_SIZE) do
98              NodePtr <childPtr, *, *> = node→child[index];
99              if childPtr != NULL then ptr = childPtr, break;
100             index++;

        /* More than one non-null child pointers. Create a new internal node and copy the
           non-null child pointers to child array of new internal node            */
101     else if childCount > 1 then
102         ptr = new Node(node→label, node→size, false);// Create new internal node
            while (index < ALPHABET_SIZE) do
103             NodePtr <childPtr, *, *> = node→child[index];
104             if childPtr != NULL then ptr→child[index] = childPtr;
105             index++;

        // Remove 'curr' node from the tree using CAS and update parent to point to 'ptr'
106     CAS(par→child[currIndex], <curr, 1, 0>, <ptr, 0, 0>);
```

Algorithm 6. RemoveNode method

This scenario is taken care by checking the non-null pointer values after freezing the child array. If more than one non-null pointer value exists, then a new internal node is created and all the child pointer values are copied to the new internal node (Lines 102–105). Otherwise, the parent pointer is updated to point to the only leaf node or to a `NULL` value (if all the pointer values in child array are `NULL`) using CAS (Line 106). The `MakeConsistent` method repeats this process recursively until an internal node with more than one non-null child pointer is encountered and only then the `Remove` operation returns *true*.

When flagging the parent pointer, the CAS (Line 70) can succeed only if the parent pointer is not frozen for deletion and it refers to the node of interest (i.e. `curr` node). If the parent pointer is frozen, `MakeConsistent` will first remove the parent node from the tree (Lines 61–69) and then tries to remove the node of interest. If the information about parent node is not available, then its location is identified by traversing down the tree using `Search` method. Similarly, when removing the leaf node from the tree, if the parent pointer is frozen for deletion, the remove operation will first help removal of the parent node from the tree before trying to remove the leaf node of interest.

3.5   Insert

The pseudo code for `Insert` method is presented in Algorithm 7. An `Insert(k)` operation updates the tree with a node containing key `k` only if it is not already present in the tree. The presence of a key is validated using the `Contains` method (Line 109) and `Insert` operation returns *false* if target key is found to be present in the tree. Otherwise, it creates a new node(s) and adds them to the tree using CAS (Line 128). The location for insertion is obtained from the `record` structure which is updated with the result of traversal during `Contains` operation.

```
107  Bool Insert(KEY key, SeekRecord* record)
108  begin
109      if Contains(key, record) then return false;// Validate the presence of target key
110      NodePtr <gPar, *, *> = record→gPar, <par, *, *> = record→par;
         // Read the last traversed node from 'record' along with the pointer status
111      NodePtr <curr, flagged, frozen> = record→curr; NodePtr ptr = NULL;
112      Int currIndex = record→currIndex, parIndex = record→parIndex;

         // Search terminated at null node. Therefore, create a leaf node
113      if curr == NULL then  ptr = new Node(key, Sizeof(key), true) ;
114      else // Create new internal and leaf nodes

             // Find common prefix between target key and label of last traversed node
115          KEY commonPrefix = GetCommonPrefix(key, curr);
116          Int commonSize = SizeOf(commonPrefix);

             // Create internal node with common prefix and leaf node with target key
117          ptr = new Node(commonPrefix, commonSize, false);
118          NodePtr leaf = new Node(key, SizeOf(key), true);
119          Int leafIndex = GetIndex(key, commonSize);
120          Int newCurrIndex = GetIndex(curr→label, commonSize);
121          ptr→child[newCurrIndex] = curr; ptr→child[leafIndex] = leaf;

122      if flagged then // 'curr' node undergoing removal. Help remove 'curr' node
123          HelpFreeze(curr), RemoveNode(par, curr, record);
124          return Insert(key, record);

125      else if frozen then // 'par' node undergoing removal. Help remove 'par' node
126          HelpFreeze(par), RemoveNode(gPar, par, record);
127          return Insert(key, record);

         // Insert node with target key into the tree using CAS
128      else if CAS(par→child[currIndex], <curr, 0, 0>, <ptr, 0, 0>) then  return true;
         // CAS failed. Retry insert operation
129      else return Insert(key, record);
```

Algorithm 7. Insert method

If the traversal has terminated at a null child, a new leaf node is created with the label as target key (Line 113). If the traversal has terminated at a non-null child, then it implies that there exists a prefix mismatch between the label of last traversed node and the target key. In this case, two nodes are created: an internal node containing the largest common prefix between the target key and the last traversed node, a leaf node containing the target key (Lines 117–121). The `GetCommonPrefix` method (Line 115) computes the largest common prefix between the node's label and target key. The child pointers of the newly created internal node are updated to point to the `curr` node and new leaf node (Line 121).

CAS at line 128 adds the newly created node(s) into the tree. A successful CAS implies that the node with target key is now reachable from the **root** node and therefore **Insert** method returns *true*. CAS (Line 128) can succeed only if the parent pointer is not flagged or frozen for deletion. If the parent pointer is already flagged or frozen, then **Insert** will help the corresponding remove operation before trying to update the node(s). The status of the parent pointer is retrieved from the result of traversal (Line 111).

The status *flagged* implies that the **curr** node is undergoing removal and status *frozen* implies that the **par** node undergoing removal. In both the cases, **Insert** method will help the removal of the corresponding node by freezing all its child pointers and later removing it from the tree. After the removal, **Insert** restarts its operation to locate the new position for insertion. If the CAS at line 128 fails due to a simultaneous insertion at the same location by another thread, **Insert** will restart the operation to locate the new position of target key in the tree.

4   Correctness

In this section, we define the linearization points for each of **Contains**, **Insert** and **Remove** operations and prove the non-blocking nature of our implementation. Due to space constraints, we only provide a brief sketch of proof and the complete proof is presented in [12].

4.1   Linearizability

The **Contains** operation has two possible outcomes, either the key is present in tree or not. For a successful **Contains**, if the leaf node returned by the **Search** method is still a part of the tree, then its linearization point is defined to be the point at which the **Search** method terminates the traversal. Otherwise, its linearization point is defined to be the point just before the leaf node is removed from the tree. For an unsuccessful **Contains**, the linearization point is the point at which the **Search** method terminates the traversal.

The linearization point of an successful **Insert** operation is defined to be the point at which it performs CAS instruction (Line 128) successfully. For an unsuccessful **Insert**, the linearization point is same as that of a successful **Contains** where the target key is already found to be present in the tree. The linearization point of **Remove** operation is defined to be the point at which the CAS instruction successfully removes the leaf node containing target key from the tree (Line 46). For an unsuccessful **Remove**, the linearization point is same as that of an unsuccessful **Contains**, where the target key is not found in the tree. It can be proved that, when the operations are ordered according to their linearization points, then the resulting sequence of operations is legal.

4.2 Non-blocking Progress

The non-blocking property of our algorithm is proved by describing various interactions between reading and writing threads. If the system reaches a state in which no update operation completes, then a non-faulty thread performing `Contains` will always return as the tree does not undergo any structural changes.

A non-faulty thread trying to modify the tree can remain blocked in two scenarios: (i) An infinite number of insert operations succeed adding new nodes to the tree. This means that other threads are able to make progress by adding new nodes (i.e. achieving system-wide progress) making the implementation non-blocking (ii) The state of the pointer is not normal i.e. either the *flag* or *freeze* bit is set to '1'. It is easy to observe from the `Insert` and `Remove` methods that, during update if a thread encounters a pointer whose *flag* or *freeze* bit is set to '1', it first helps the removal of the corresponding node and then restarts its operation only after the node is removed from the tree. This ensures that next time the thread is traversing the tree, the node containing the pointer is no longer present in the tree.

If all the pointers in the thread's path have then *flag* or *freeze* bits set to '1', then `Insert` or `Remove` methods will help the removal of all the corresponding nodes. As `root` node is never removed from the tree, the operation will eventually complete unless other threads update the tree. In either cases, at least one thread makes a progress with its operation making the implementation non-blocking.

5 Experimental Evaluation

For our experiments, we considered four different alphabet sizes: binary (2-RT), quaternary (4-RT), octal (8-RT) and hexadecimal (16-RT). The source code of our implementation is available at [12]. We compared the results of our implementation with three other implementations: (i) `PatTrie`: Patricia trie from Shafiei [10] (ii) `NBBST`: Non-blocking binary search tree from Natarajan and Mittal [7] (iii) `K4AryTree`: Non-blocking k-ary free from Brown and Helga [2] with k = 4. The source code for `NBBST` is taken from syncrobench [5] test suite, for `PatTrie` the Java version of the source code is taken from the author and ported to C++. For `K4AryTree`, the Java version of the source code is taken from [1] and was ported to C++.

The experiments were conducted on a machine equipped with Ubuntu 14.04 OS, 64 GB RAM and two Intel Xeon E5-2680 v2 processors each clocked at 2.80 GHz with 32 KB L1D cache per core and 2.5 MB LLC. Each processor has 10 physical cores with hyperthreading enabled yielding 40 logical cores in total. Hyperthreading is enabled prior to a simulation run and thread binding to cores is disabled to facilitate context switching. All our implementations are written in C/C++ and compiled using g++ 4.8.4 with optimization level set to O3. Random integers were considered for keys which were generated using a Mersenne twister generator from the C++11 random library on 32-bit word length.

Each experiment was run for fifty seconds, and the total number of operations completed by end of the run were calculated to determine the system throughput.

The results were averaged over five runs. To capture the steady state behavior, the tree is pre-populated with 50% of its maximum size prior to starting a simulation run. The cache performance of the data structure is analyzed using cachegrind from Valgrind [8] toolchain. To compare the performance of different implementations, we considered four different key ranges from one thousand to one million and the number of threads was varied from 1 to 256. Three different workloads i.e. write-dominated (0% contains, 50% inserts and 50% removes), mixed (70% contains, 20% inserts and 10% removes) and read-dominated (90% contains, 5% inserts and 5% removes) were considered.

The results of our experiments are presented in Fig. 2. Table 1 presents the comparison of cache performance for a mixed workload with 32 threads. From

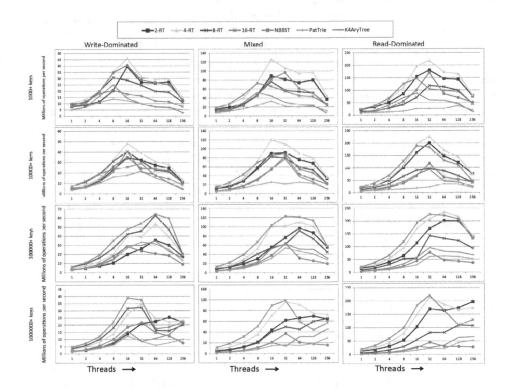

Fig. 2. Experimental results for different workloads

Table 1. Comparison of D1 cache miss percentage

Key range	2-RT	4-RT	8-RT	16-RT	PatTrie	NBBST	K4AryTree
1000+ keys	1.3%	0.9%	1.6%	1.3%	3%	2.1%	2%
10000+ keys	2.3%	2.1%	3.3%	2.7%	6%	4.1%	3.5%
100000+ keys	4.8%	4.3%	5.2%	3.1%	10.1%	8.7%	6.3%
1000000+ keys	8.6%	3.9%	6%	3.7%	13.4%	7.9%	7.6%

the graphs, it is clear that our algorithm has better throughput (by more than 100% in some scenarios) compared to other implementations. This is because our algorithm supports simultaneous updates on a node and has better cache performance compared to other implementations (Table 1). For smaller key ranges in all the workloads, the performance of 4-RT is better compared to 8-RT and 16-RT as nodes in 8-RT and 16-RT were spread across multiple cache lines resulting in higher cache miss percentage. For the 2-RT implementation, the number of pointer accesses were relatively high which contributed to higher cache miss percentage and slowdown in performance. For larger key ranges, 16-RT performed better as the impact of contention is reduced which resulted in less cache miss percentage and the number of pointer accesses required to traverse the leaf node are also reduced because of high branching factor.

In write dominated workload, for smaller key ranges, it can be see than NBBST performs slightly better compared to the 2-RT implementation as they use fewer atomic CAS instructions (Table 2) for synchronization compared to our implementation. However, for larger key ranges, the maximum height of

Table 2. CAS instructions

	Insert	Remove
2-RT	1	5
PatTrie	3	4
NBBST	1	3

the tree was observed to be twice more than $logN$ (N being the maximum key range) which resulted in more pointer accesses and slowed down the implementation. High synchronization cost and serialization of update operations in PatTrie and K4AryTree resulted in slowness of their implementation. Also, the cache miss percentage of K4AryTree was observed to be relatively high. This is because, in their algorithm, during insert operations each k-ary node is replaced with a new k-ary node. Similar behavior is also observed in remove operations in some cases. Therefore, even though the nodes individually support good cache locality, updating the nodes resulted in higher cache miss percentage. This is not the case in our implementation as we update only the child pointers in most of the scenarios.

6   Conclusion

We presented a concurrent, non-blocking and linearizable design for radix tree data structure. We implemented it using C++ and measured its performance against Shafiei [10] Patricia trie, BST from Natarajan and Mittal [7] and k-ary search tree from Brown and Helga [2]. Experimental results indicated that our implementation performs better and scales best for small and large key ranges under all types of workloads. The cache performance of our implementation was also analyzed and the D1 cache miss percentage is observed to be less compared to other implementations which contributed to the better performance of our algorithm.

References

1. Brown, T., Helga, J.: Source code for non-blocking k-ary search trees. http://www.cs.toronto.edu/~tabrown/ksts/

2. Brown, T., Helga, J.: Non-blocking k-ary search trees. In: Fernàndez Anta, A., Lipari, G., Roy, M. (eds.) OPODIS 2011. LNCS, vol. 7109, pp. 207–221. Springer, Heidelberg (2011). doi:10.1007/978-3-642-25873-2_15
3. Corbet, J.: Trees I: Radix trees. Linux kernel data structures. Linux Weekly News (2006). http://lwn.net/Articles/175432
4. Ellen, F., Fatourou, P., Ruppert, E., van Breugel, F.: Non-blocking binary search trees. In: Proceedings of ACM PODC, pp. 131–140 (2010)
5. Gramoli, V.: More than you ever wanted to know about synchronization: synchrobench. In: Proceedings of ACM PPoPP, pp. 1–10 (2015)
6. Guthaus, M.R., Ringenberg, J.S., Ernst, D., Austin, T.M., Mudge, T., Brown, R.B.: Mibench: a free, commercially representative embedded benchmark suite. In: Proceedings of the Workload Characterization, WWC 2001, pp. 3–14 (2001)
7. Natarajan, A., Mittal, N.: Fast concurrent lock-free binary search trees. In: Proceedings of ACM PPoPP, pp. 317–328 (2014)
8. Nethercote, N., Seward, J.: Valgrind: a framework for heavyweight dynamic binary instrumentation. SIGPLAN Not. 42(6), 89–100 (2007)
9. Prokopec, A., Bronson, N.G., Bagwell, P., Odersky, M.: Concurrent tries with efficient non-blocking snapshots. In: Proceedings of ACM PPoPP, pp. 151–160 (2012)
10. Shafiei, N.: Non-blocking patricia tries with replace operations. In: Proceedings of IEEE ICDCS, pp. 216–225 (2013)
11. Repetti, T.J., Herlihy, M.P.: A Case Study in Optimizing HTM-Enabled Dynamic Data Structures: Patricia Tries (2015). https://cs.brown.edu/research/pubs/theses/masters/
12. Velamuri, V.: Appendix and source code for efficient non-blocking radix trees (2017). https://github.com/varun1312/RadixTrees

A Concurrency-Optimal Binary Search Tree

Vitaly Aksenov[1,2], Vincent Gramoli[3], Petr Kuznetsov[4], Anna Malova[5], and Srivatsan Ravi[6(✉)]

[1] Inria Paris, Paris, France
aksenov.vitaly@gmail.com
[2] ITMO University, Sankt-peterburg, Russia
[3] University of Sydney, Sydney, Australia
vincent.gramoli@sydney.edu.au
[4] LTCI, Télécom ParisTech, Université Paris-Saclay, Paris, France
petr.kuznetsov@telecom-paristech.fr
[5] Washington University in St. Louis, St. Louis, USA
an.forgotenn@gmail.com
[6] Information Sciences Institute, University of Southern California, Los Angeles, USA
srivatsan@srivatsan.in

Abstract. The paper presents the first *concurrency-optimal* implementation of a binary search tree (BST). The implementation, based on a standard sequential implementation of a partially-external tree, ensures that every *schedule*, i.e., interleaving of steps of the sequential code, is accepted unless linearizability is violated. To ensure this property, we use a novel read-write locking protocol that protects tree *edges* in addition to its nodes.

Our implementation performs comparably to the state-of-the-art BSTs and even outperforms them on few workloads, which suggests that optimizing the set of accepted schedules of the sequential code can be an adequate design principle for efficient concurrent data structures.

Keywords: Concurrency optimality · Binary search tree · Linearizability

1 Introduction

To meet modern computational demands and to overcome the fundamental limitations of computing hardware, the traditional single-CPU architecture is being replaced by a concurrent system based on multi-cores or even many-cores. Therefore, at least until the next technological revolution, the only way to respond to the growing computing demand is to invest in smarter concurrent algorithms.

Synchronization, one of the principal challenges in concurrent programming, consists in arbitrating concurrent accesses to shared *data structures*: lists, hash tables, trees, etc. Intuitively, an efficient data structure must be *highly concurrent*: it should allow multiple processes to "make progress" on it in parallel. Indeed, every new implementation of a concurrent data structure is usually claimed to enable such a parallelism. But what does "making progress" mean precisely?

© Springer International Publishing AG 2017
F.F. Rivera et al. (Eds.): Euro-Par 2017, LNCS 10417, pp. 580–593, 2017.
DOI: 10.1007/978-3-319-64203-1_42

Optimal Concurrency. If we zoom in the code of an operation on a typical concurrent data structure, we can distinguish *data accesses*, i.e., reads and updates to the data structure itself, performed as though the operation works on the data in the absence of concurrency. To ensure that concurrent operations do not violate correctness of the implemented high-level data type (e.g., *linearizability* [1] of the implemented set abstraction), data accesses are "protected" with *synchronization primitives*, e.g., acquisitions and releases of locks or atomic read-modify-write instructions like compare-and-swap. Intuitively, a process makes progress by performing "sequential" data accesses to the shared data, e.g., traversing the data structure and modifying its content. In contrast, synchronization tasks, though necessary for correctness, do not contribute to the progress of an operation.

Hence, "making progress in parallel" can be seen as allowing concurrent execution of pieces of locally sequential fragments of code. The more synchronization we use to protect "critical" pieces of the sequential code, the less *schedules*, i.e., interleavings of data accesses, we accept. Intuitively, we would like to use exactly as little synchronization as sufficient for ensuring linearizability of the high-level implemented abstraction. This expectation brings up the notion of a *concurrency-optimal* implementation [2] that only rejects a schedule if it does violate linearizability.

To be able to reason about how concurrent two different implementations of the same data structure employing different synchronization techniques are, we consider the recently introduced metric of the "amount of concurrency" defined via sets of accepted (*correct*) schedules [2]. A correct schedule, intuitively, requires the sequence of sequential steps locally observed by every given process to be consistent with *some* execution of the sequential algorithm. Note that these sequential executions can be different for different processes, i.e., the execution may not be *serializable* [3]. Combined with the standard correctness criterion of linearizability, the concurrency properties of two correct data structure implementations can be compared on the same level: implementation A is "more concurrent" than implementation B if the set of schedules accepted by A is a strict superset of the set of schedules accepted by B. Thus, a *concurrency-optimal* implementation accepts *all* correct schedules.

A Concurrency-Optimal Binary Search Tree. It is interesting to consider binary search trees (BSTs) from the optimal concurrency perspective, as they are believed, as a representative of *search* data structures [4], to be "concurrency-friendly" [5]: updates concerning different keys are likely to operate on disjoint sets of tree nodes (in contrast with, e.g., operations on queues or stacks).

We present a novel linearizable concurrent BST-based set implementation. We prove that the implementation is concurrency-optimal with respect to a standard *partially-external* sequential tree [2]. The proposed implementation employs the optimistic "lazy" locking approach [6] that distinguishes *logical* and *physical* deletion of a node and makes sure that read-only operations are *wait-free* [1], i.e., cannot be delayed by concurrent processes.

The algorithm also offers a few algorithmic novelties. Unlike most implementations of concurrent trees, the algorithm uses multiple locks per node: one lock for the *state* of the node, and one lock for each of its descendants. To ensure that only conflicting operations can delay each other, we use *conditional* read-write locks, where the lock can be acquired only under a certain condition. Intuitively, only changes in the relevant part of the tree structure may prevent a thread from acquiring the lock. The fine-grained conditional read-write locking of nodes and edges allows us to ensure that an implementation rejects a schedule only if it violates linearizability.

Concurrency-Optimality and Performance. Of course, optimal concurrency does not necessarily imply performance nor maximum progress (à la *wait-freedom* [7]). An extreme example is the transactional memory (TM) data structure. TMs typically require restrictions of serializability as a correctness criterion. And it is known that rejecting a schedule only if it is not serializable (the property known as *permissiveness*), requires very heavy local computations [8,9]. But the intuition is that looking for concurrency-optimal search data structures like trees pays off. And this work answers this question in the affirmative by demonstrating empirically that the Java implementation of our concurrency-optimal BST is either out-performing or is competitive against state-of-the-art BST implementations [10–13] on all basic workloads. Apart from the obvious benefit of producing a highly efficient BST, this work suggests that optimizing the set of accepted schedules of the sequential code can be an adequate design principle for building efficient concurrent data structures.

Roadmap. The rest of the paper is organized as follows. Section 2 describes the details of our BST implementation, including the sequential implementation of *partially-external* binary search tree and our novel conditional read-write lock abstraction. Section 3 formalizes the notion of concurrency-optimality and sketches the relevant proofs; detailed proofs are given in the technical report [14]. Section 4 provides details of our experimental methodology and extensive evaluation of our Java implementation. Section 5 articulates the differences with related BST implementations and presents concluding remarks.

2   Binary Search Tree Implementation

This section consists of two parts. At first, we describe our *sequential* implementation of the set type using partially-external binary search tree. Then, we present our concurrent implementation (Algorithm 2), constructed from the sequential one by adding synchronization primitives.

We begin with a formal specification of the set type. A set object stores a set of integer values, initially empty, and exports operations insert(v), remove(v), contains(v). The update operations, insert(v) and remove(v), return a boolean

---

Algorithm 1. Concurrent implementation: node structure and traversal function.

```
 1: Shared Variables:                        15: traversal(v):     ▷ wait-free traversal from
 2:   node is a record with fields:              vertex start
 3:     val, its value                        16:   gprev ← null; prev ← null
 4:     slock = Lock⟨state⟩, a lock that guards  17:   curr ← root        ▷ starting traversal from
        its state,                                root
 5:       where state ∈ {DATA, ROUTING}      18:   while curr ≠ null do
 6:     llock = Lock⟨left⟩, a lock that guards  19:     if curr.val = v then
        a pointer left to the left child     20:       break
 7:     rlock = Lock⟨right⟩, a lock that guards  21:     else
        a pointer right to the right child   22:       gprev ← prev
 8:     deleted, a boolean flag indicating   23:       prev ← curr
        the node is logically deleted or not 24:       if curr.val < v then
 9:   Initially the tree contains one node root, 25:         curr ← curr.left      ▷ go to the left
10:     root.val ← +∞                            subtree
11:     root.slock.init(DATA)                26:       else
12:     root.llock.init(null)                27:         curr ← curr.right  ▷ go to the right
13:     root.rlock.init(null)                   subtree
14:     deleted ← false                      28:   return ⟨gprev, prev, curr⟩
```

---

response, *true* if and only if v is absent (for insert(v)) or present (for remove(v)) in the *set*. After insert(v) is complete, v is present in the set, and after remove(v) is complete, v is absent. The contains(v) returns a boolean response, *true* if and only if v is present.

A *binary search tree* (BST) is a rooted ordered tree in which each node v has a left child and a right child, either or both of which can be null. A node without children is called a *leaf*. The order is carried by a *value property*: the value of each node is strictly greater than the values in its left subtree and strictly smaller than the values in its right subtree.

2.1 Sequential Implementation

As for a sequential implementation, we chose the well-known *partially-external* binary search tree. Such a tree combines the idea of an *internal* binary search tree, where the values from all nodes constitute the implemented set, and an *external* binary search tree, where the set is represented by the values in the leaves, and the internal nodes are used for "routing" from the root to the leaves. A partially-external tree supports two types of nodes: *routing* and *data*. To bound the number of routing vertices by the number of data nodes, the tree should satisfy an additional condition that all routing nodes must have exactly two children.

The **traversal** function takes a value v, traverses the tree down from the root respecting the value property, as long as the current node is not null or its value is not v. The function returns the last three visited nodes. The **contains** function takes a value v, checks the last node visited by the traversal and returns whether it is null. The **insert** function takes a value v and uses the traversal function to find the place to insert the value. If the node with value v is found, the algorithm checks whether the node is data or routing: in the former case, the function returns *false* (v is already in the set); in the latter case, the algorithm simply changes the state of the node from routing to data. If the node with value v is not found, then the algorithm assumes that v is not in the set and inserts a new node with value v as the child of the latest non-null node visited by the traversal function call. The **delete** function takes a value v and uses the traversal function to find the node to delete. If the node with value v is not found or its state is routing, the algorithm assumes that v is not in the set and finishes. Otherwise, there are three cases depending on the number of children that the found node has: (i) if the node has two children, then the algorithm changes its state from data to routing; (ii) if the node has one child, then the algorithm unlinks the node; (iii) finally, if the node is a leaf then the algorithm unlinks the node, in addition if the parent is a routing node then it also unlinks the parent.

2.2   Concurrent Implementation

Our concurrency-optimal BST is built on top of the described above sequential implementation using the *optimistic* approach. Traversals are *wait-free* (no synchronization is employed), the locations to be modified are locked and then the reads performed during the traversal are *validated*. If validation fails, the operation is restarted.

Read Fields. Since our algorithm is optimistic, we do not want to read the same field twice. To overcome this problem when the algorithm reads the field it stores it in the "cache" and further accesses return the "cached" value. For example, the reads of the *left* field in Lines 53 and 54 of Algorithm 2 return the same (cached) value.

Deletion Mark. As usual in concurrent algorithms with wait-free traversals, the deletion of the node happens in two stages. At first, the delete operation logically removes a node from the tree by setting the boolean flag to **deleted**. Secondly, the delete operation updates the links to physically remove the node. By that, any traversal that suddenly reaches the "under-deletion" node, sees the deletion node and could restart the operation.

Locks. At the beginning of the section we noted that we have locks separately for each field of a node and the algorithm takes only the necessary type of lock: read or write. For that, we implemented read-write lock simply as one *lock* variable. The smallest bit of *lock* indicates whether the write lock is taken or not, the rest part of the variable indicates the number of readers that have taken a lock. In other words, *lock* is zero if the lock is not taken, *lock* is one if the write lock is taken, otherwise, *lock* divided by two represents the number of times the read lock is taken. The locking and unlocking are done using the atomic compare-and-set primitive. Along, with standard tryWriteLock, tryReadLock, unlockWrite and unlockRead we provide additional six functions on a node: tryLockLeftEdge(Ref|Val)(exp), lockRightEdge(Ref|Val)(exp) and try(Read|Write)LockState(exp) (from there on, we use the notation of bar | to not duplicate the similar names; such notation should be read as either we choose the first option or the second option.).

Function tryLock(Left|Right)EdgeRef(exp) ensures that the lock is taken only if the field (*left* or *right*) guarded by that lock is equal to *exp*, i.e., the child node has not changed, and the current node is not deleted, i.e., its deleted mark is not set. Function tryLock(Left|Right)EdgeVal(exp) ensures that the lock is taken only if the value of the node in the field (*left* or *right*) guarded by that lock is equal to *exp*, i.e., the node could have changed but the value inside did not, and the current node is not deleted, i.e., its deletion mark is not set. Function try(Read|Write)LockState(exp) ensures that the lock is taken only if the value of the *state* is equal to *exp* and the node is not deleted, i.e., its deletion mark is not set.

These six functions are implemented in the same manner: the function reads necessary fields and a *lock* variable, checks the conditions, if successful it takes a corresponding lock, then checks the conditions again, if unsuccessful it releases the lock. In most cases in the pseudocode we used a substitution tryLockEdge(Ref|Val)(node) instead of tryLock(Left|Right)Edge(Ref|Val)(exp). This substitution, given not-null value, decides whether the *node* is the left or right child of the current node and calls the corresponding function providing *node* or *node.value*.

Concurrency-Optimal BST. Above we already described everything needed to write the algorithm. Each node is represented as a union of records (see Algorithm 1): *val*, the value in the node of arbitrary comparable type, *slock*, the lock that guards the state, *llock* and *rlock*, the locks that guard the pointers to left and right children, correspondingly, and *deleted*, the flag of logical deletion. The pseudocode of the concurrent algorithm is provided in Algorithms 1 and 2. To shrink the pseudocode in size we have not put a restart instruction explicitly for all failed "try lock" operations, but it should be read so. The traversal function is identical to the sequential algorithm (see Algorithm 1). The contains has an additional check, whether the node's deleted mark is set or not. In the former case, the function returns *false*. The insert and delete functions largely follow the structure of the sequential code, but take locks on the *modification* part of the tree using the above described read-write conditional lock. Due to space constraints, we refer the reader to the pseudocode of Algorithm 2 for the specifics of the implementation.

Algorithm 2. Concurrent implementation.

1: contains(v):
2:    ⟨gprev, prev, curr⟩ ← traversal(v)
3:    return curr ≠ null ∧ curr.state = DATA

4: insert(v):
5:    ⟨gprev, prev, curr⟩ ← traversal(v)
6:    if curr ≠ null then
7:       go to Line 12
8:    else
9:       go to Line 16
10:   Release all locks
11:   return true

   Update existing node
12:   if curr.state = DATA then
13:      return false
14:   curr.tryWriteLockState(ROUTING)
15:   curr.state ← DATA

   Insert new node
16:   newNode.val ← v
17:   if v < prev.val then
18:      prev.tryLockLeftEdgeRef(null)
19:      prev.slock.tryReadLock()
20:      if prev.deleted then
21:         Restart operation
22:      prev.left ← newNode
23:   else
24:      prev.tryLockRightEdgeRef(null)
25:      prev.slock.tryReadLock()
26:      if prev.deleted then
27:         Restart operation
28:      prev.right ← newNode

29: delete(v):
30:   ⟨gprev, prev, curr⟩ ← traversal(v)
                    ▷ All restarts are from this Line
31:   if curr = null ∨ curr.state ≠ DATA then
32:      return false
33:   if curr has exactly 2 children then
34:      go to Line 44
35:   if curr has exactly 1 child then
36:      go to Line 53
37:   if curr is a leaf then
38:      if prev.state = DATA then
39:         go to Line 73
40:      else
41:         go to Line 83
42:   Release all locks
43:   return true

   Delete node with two children
44:   curr.tryWriteLockState(DATA)
45:   if curr does not have 2 children then
46:      Restart operation
47:   curr.state ← ROUTING

   Lock acquisition routine for vertex with one child
48:   curr.tryLockEdgeRef(child)
49:   prev.tryLockEdgeRef(curr)
50:   curr.tryWriteLockState(DATA)
51:   if curr has 0 or 2 children then
52:      Restart operation

   Delete node with one child
53:   if curr.left ≠ null then
54:      child ← curr.left
55:   else
56:      child ← curr.right
57:   if curr.val < prev.val then
58:      perform lock acquisition at Line 48
59:      curr.deleted ← true
60:      prev.left ← child
61:   else
62:      perform lock acquisition at Line 48
63:      curr.deleted ← true
64:      prev.right ← child

   Lock acquisition routine for leaf
65:   prev.tryLockEdgeVal(v)
66:   if v < prev.key then   ▷ get current child
67:      curr ← prev.left
68:   else
69:      curr ← prev.right
70:   curr.tryWriteLockState(DATA)
71:   if curr is not a leaf then
72:      Restart operation

   Delete leaf with DATA parent
73:   if curr.val < prev.val then
74:      perform lock acquisition at Line 65
75:      prev.tryReadLockState(DATA)
76:      curr.deleted ← true
77:      prev.left ← null
78:   else
79:      perform lock acquisition at Line 65
80:      prev.tryReadLockState(DATA)
81:      curr.deleted ← true
82:      prev.right ← null

   Delete leaf with ROUTING parent
83:   if curr.val < prev.val then
84:      child ← prev.right
85:   else
86:      child ← prev.left
87:   if prev is left child of gprev then
88:      perform lock acquisition at Line 65
89:      prev.tryEdgeLockRef(child)
90:      gprev.tryEdgeLockRef(prev)
91:      prev.tryWriteLockState(ROUTING)
92:      prev.deleted ← true
93:      curr.deleted ← true
94:      gprev.left ← child
95:   else
96:      perform lock acquisition at Line 65
97:      prev.tryEdgeLockRef(child)
98:      gprev.tryEdgeLockRef(prev)
99:      prev.tryWriteLockState(ROUTING)
100:     prev.deleted ← true
101:     curr.deleted ← true
102:     gprev.right ← child

3 Concurrency Optimality and Correctness

In this section, we show that our implementation is *concurrency-optimal* [2]. Intuitively, a concurrency-optimal implementation employs as much synchronization as necessary for ensuring correctness of the implemented high-level abstraction—in our case, the linearizable set object [1].

Recall our *sequential* BST implementation and imagine that we run it in a *concurrent* environment. We refer to an execution of this concurrent algorithm as a *schedule*. A schedule thus consists of reads, writes, node creation events, and invocation and responses of high-level operations.

Notice that in every such schedule, any operation witnesses a *consistent* tree state locally, i.e., it cannot distinguish the execution from a sequential one. It is easy to see that the local views *across operations* may not be mutually consistent, and this simplistic concurrent algorithm is not linearizable. For example, two insert operations that concurrently traverse the tree may update the same node so that one of the operations "overwrites" the other (so called the "lost update" problem). To guarantee linearizability, one needs to ensure that only correct (linearizable) schedules are accepted. We show first that this is indeed the case with our algorithm: all the schedules it *accepts* are correct. More precisely, a schedule σ is accepted by an algorithm if it has an execution in which the sequence of high-level invocations and responses, reads, writes, and node creation events (modulo the restarted fragments) is σ [2].

Theorem 1 (Correctness). *The schedule corresponding to any execution of our BST implementation is observably correct.*

A complete proof of Theorem 1 is given in the technical report [14].

Further, we show that, in a strict sense, our algorithm accepts *all* correct schedules. In our definition of correctness, we demand that at all times the algorithm maintains a *BST* that does not contain nodes that were previously *physically* deleted. Formally, a set of nodes reachable from the *root* is a *BST* if: (i) they form a tree rooted at node *root*; (ii) this tree satisfies the *value property*: for each node with value v all the values in the left subtree are less than v and all the values in the right subtree are bigger than v; (iii) each routing node in this tree has two children.

Now we say that a schedule is *observably correct* if each of its prefixes σ satisfies the following conditions: (i) subsequence of high-level invocations and responses in σ is linearizable with respect to the set type; (ii) the data structure after performing σ is a BST; (iii) the BST after σ does not contain a node x such that there exist σ' and σ'', such that σ' is a prefix of σ'', σ'' is a prefix of σ, x is in the BST after σ', and x is not in the BST after σ''.

We say that an implementation is *concurrency-optimal* if it accepts *all* observably correct schedules.

Theorem 2 (Optimality). *Our BST implementation is concurrency-optimal.*

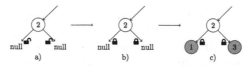

(a) Scenario depicting a concurrent execution of insert(1) and insert(3); rejected by popular BSTs like [10–13], it is accepted by a concurrency-optimal BST

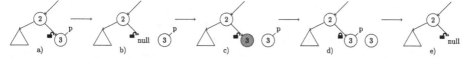

(b) Scenario depicting an execution of two concurrent delete(3) operations, followed by a successful insert(3); rejected by all the popular BSTs [10–13, 15], it is accepted by a concurrency-optimal BST

Fig. 1. Examples schedules rejected by concurrent BSTs not concurrency-optimal

A proof of Theorem 2 is given in the technical report [14]. The intuition behind the proof is the following. We show that for each observably correct schedule there exists a matching execution of our implementation. Therefore, only schedules not observably correct can be rejected by our algorithm. The construction of an execution that matches an observably correct schedule is possible, in particular, due to the fact that every critical section in our algorithm contains exactly one event of the schedule. Thus, the only reason to reject a schedule is that some condition on a critical section does not hold and, as a result, the operation must be restarted. By accounting for all the conditions under which an operation restarts, we show that this may only happen if, otherwise, the schedule violates observable correctness.

Suboptimality of Related BST Algorithms. To understand the hardness of building linearizable concurrency optimal BSTs, we explain how some typical correct schedules are rejected by current state-of-the-art BST algorithms against which we evaluate the performance of our algorithm. Consider the concurrency scenario depicted in Fig. 1a. There are two concurrent operations insert(1) and insert(3) performed on a tree. They traverse to the corresponding links (part a)) and lock them concurrently (part b)). Then they insert new nodes (part c)). Note that this is a correct schedule of events; however, most BSTs including the ones we compare our implementation against [10–13] reject this schedule or similar. However, using multiple locks per node allows our concurrency-optimal implementation to accept this schedule.

The second schedule is shown in the Fig. 1b. There is one operation $p =$ delete(3) performed on a tree shown in part a). It traverses to a node v with value 3. Then, some concurrent operation delete(3) unlinks node v (part b)). Later, another concurrent operation inserts a new node with value 3 (part c)).

Operation p wakes up and locks a link since the value 3 is the same (part d)). Finally, p unlinks the node with value 3 (part e)). Note that this is a correct schedule since both the delete operations can be successful; however, all the BSTs we are aware of reject this schedule or similar [10–13, 15]. While, there is an execution of our concurrency-optimal BST that accepts this schedule.

4 Implementation and Evaluation

Experimental Setup. For our experiments, we used two machines to evaluate our concurrency-optimal binary search tree. The first is a 4-processor Intel Xeon E7-4870 2.4 GHz server (Intel) with 20 threads per processor (yielding 80 hardware threads in total), 512 Gb of RAM, running Fedora 25. The second machine is a 4-processor AMD Opteron 6378 2.4 GHz server (AMD) with 16 threads per processor (yielding 64 threads in total), 512 Gb of RAM, running Ubuntu 14.04.5. Both machines have Java 1.8.0_111-b14 and HotSpot JVM 25.111-b14.

Binary Search Tree Implementations. We compare our algorithm, denoted as Concurrency Optimal or CO, against four other implementations of concurrent BST. They are: (1) the lock-based Concurrency Friendly (or CF) tree by Crain et al. [10], (2) the lock-based Logical Ordering (or LO) AVL-tree by Drachsler et al. [11], (3) the lock based BCCO tree by Bronson et al. [12], and (4) the lock-free EFRB tree by Ellen et al. [13]. All these implementations are written in Java and taken from the synchrobench repository [16]. In order to make a fair comparison, we remove rotation routines from the CF-, LO- and CO- trees implementations. We are aware of efficient lock-free tree by Natarajan and Mittal [15], but, unfortunately, we are unaware of any implementation in Java.

Experimental Methodology. For our experiments, we use the environment provided by the Synchrobench library. To compare the performance we considered the following parameters: (i) **Workloads.** Each workload distribution is characterized by the percent $x\%$ of update operations. This means that the tree will be requested to make $100 - x\%$ of contains calls, $x/2\%$ of insert calls and $x/2\%$ of delete calls. We considered three different workload distributions: 0%, 20% and 100%. (ii) **Tree size.** On the above workloads, the tree size depends on the size of the key space (the size is approximately half of the range). We consider three different key ranges: 2^{15}, 2^{19} and 2^{21}. To ensure consistent results, rather than starting with an empty tree, we pre-populated the tree before execution. (iii) **Degree of contention.** This depends on the number of hardware threads, but we take enough points to reason about the behavior of curves.

In fact, we made experiments on a larger number of settings but we shortened our presentation due to lack of space. We chose the settings such that we had two extremes and one middle point. We chose 20% of attempted updates as a middle point, because it corresponds to real life situation in database management where the percentage of successful updates is 10%. (In our testing environment we expect only half of update calls to succeed.)

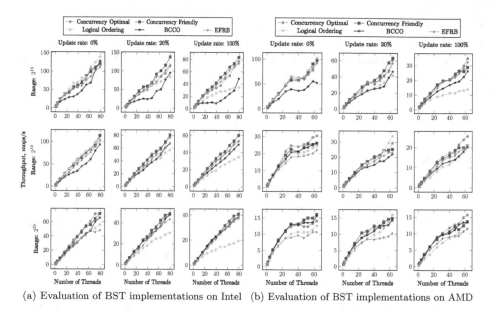

(a) Evaluation of BST implementations on Intel   (b) Evaluation of BST implementations on AMD

Fig. 2. Performance evaluation of concurrent BSTs

Results. To get meaningful results we average through 25 runs. Each run is carried out for 10 seconds with a warmup of 5 seconds. Figure 2a (and resp. Fig. 2b) contains the results of executions on Intel (and resp. AMD) machine. It can be seen that with the increase of the size the performance of our algorithm becomes better relatively to CF-tree. This is due to the fact that with the bigger size the cleanup-thread in CF-tree implementation spends more time to clean the tree out of logically deleted vertices, thus, the traversals have more chances to pass over deleted vertices, leading to longer traversals. By this fact and the shown trend, we could assume that CO-tree outperforms CF-tree on bigger sizes. On the other hand, BCCO-tree was much worse on 2^{15} and became similar to CO-tree on 2^{21}. This happened because the races for the locks become more unlikely. This helped the BCCO-tree, because its locking is coarse-grained. Since, our algorithm is "exactly" the same without the order of locking, on bigger sizes we could expect that CO- and BCCO-trees will perform similarly. We could conclude that our algorithm works well regardless of the size. As the percentage of contains operations increases, the difference between our algorithm and CF-tree becomes smaller and in most workloads, we perform better than other BSTs.

5   Related Work and Discussion

Measuring Concurrency. Measuring concurrency via comparing a concurrent data structure to its sequential counterpart was originally proposed [17]. The metric was later applied to construct a concurrency-optimal linked list [18], and to compare synchronization techniques used for concurrent *search* data structures, organizing nodes in a directed acyclic graph [2]. Although lots of efforts have been devoted to improve the performance of BSTs as under growing concurrency, to our knowledge, the existence of a concurrency-optimal BST has not been earlier addressed.

Concurrent BSTs. The transactional red-black tree [19] uses software transactional memory without sentinel nodes to limit conflicts between concurrent transactions, but restarts the update operation after its rotation aborts. Optimistic synchronization, as seen in transactional memory, was used to implement a practical lock-based BST [12]. The speculation-friendly tree [20] is a partially-external binary search tree that marks internal nodes as logically deleted to reduce conflicts between software transactions. It decouples a structural operation from abstract operations to rebalance when contention disappears. Some red-black trees were optimized for hardware transactional memory and compared with bottom-up and top-down fine-grained locking techniques [21]. The contention-friendly tree [10] is a lock-based partially-external binary search tree that provides lock-free lookups and rebalances when contention disappears. The logical ordering tree [11] combines the lock-free lookup with on-time removal during deletes. The first lock-free tree proposal [13] uses a single-word CAS and does not rebalance. Howley and Jones [22] proposed an internal lock-free binary search tree where each node keeps track of the operation currently modifying it. Chatterjee et al. [23] proposed a lock-free BST, but we are not aware of any implementation. Natarajan and Mittal [15] proposed an efficient lock-free binary search tree implementation that uses edge markers. It outperforms both the lock-free BSTs from Howley and Jones [22] and Ellen et al. [13]. Since it is not implemented in Java, we could not compare it against ours; however, we know that neither this nor any of the above mentioned BSTs are concurrency-optimal (cf. Fig. 1).

Search for Concurrency-Optimal Data Structures. Concurrent BSTs have been studied extensively in literature; yet by choosing to focus on minimizing the amount of synchronization, we identified an extremely high-performing concurrent BST implementation. We proved our implementation to be formally correct and established the concurrency-optimality of our algorithm. Apart from the intellectual merit of understanding what it means for an implementation to be highly concurrent, our findings suggest a relation between concurrency-optimality and efficiency. We hope this work will inspire the design of other concurrency-optimal data structures that currently lack efficient implementations.

Acknowledgements. Vincent Gramoli was financially supported by the Australian Research Council (Discovery Projects funding scheme, project number 160104801 entitled "Data Structures for Multi-Core"). Vitaly Aksenov was financially supported by the Government of Russian Federation (Grant 074-U01) and by the European Research Council (Grant ERC-2012-StG-308246).

References

1. Herlihy, M.: Wait-free synchronization. ACM Trans. Program. Lang. Syst. **13**(1), 123–149 (1991)
2. Gramoli, V., Kuznetsov, P., Ravi, S.: In the search for optimal concurrency. In: Suomela, J. (ed.) SIROCCO 2016. LNCS, vol. 9988, pp. 143–158. Springer, Cham (2016). doi:10.1007/978-3-319-48314-6_10
3. Papadimitriou, C.H.: The serializability of concurrent database updates. J. ACM **26**, 631–653 (1979)
4. Chaudhri, V.K., Hadzilacos, V.: Safe locking policies for dynamic databases. J. Comput. Syst. Sci. **57**(3), 260–271 (1998)
5. Sutter, H.: Choose concurrency-friendly data structures. Dr. Dobb's J. (2008)
6. Heller, S., Herlihy, M., Luchangco, V., Moir, M., Scherer, W.N., Shavit, N.: A lazy concurrent list-based set algorithm. In: OPODIS, pp. 3–16 (2006)
7. Herlihy, M., Shavit, N.: On the nature of progress. In: OPODIS, pp. 313–328 (2011)
8. Guerraoui, R., Henzinger, T.A., Singh, V.: Permissiveness in transactional memories. In: DISC, pp. 305–319 (2008)
9. Kuznetsov, P., Ravi, S.: On the cost of concurrency in transactional memory. In: International Conference on Principles of Distributed Systems (OPODIS), pp. 112–127 (2011)
10. Crain, T., Gramoli, V., Raynal, M.: A contention-friendly binary search tree. In: Wolf, F., Mohr, B., Mey, D. (eds.) Euro-Par 2013. LNCS, vol. 8097, pp. 229–240. Springer, Heidelberg (2013). doi:10.1007/978-3-642-40047-6_25
11. Drachsler, D., Vechev, M., Yahav, E.: Practical concurrent binary search trees via logical ordering. In: Proceedings of 19th ACM SIGPLAN Symposium on Principles and Practice of Parallel Programming, PPoPP 2014, pp. 343–356 (2014)
12. Bronson, N.G., Casper, J., Chafi, H., Olukotun, K.: A practical concurrent binary search tree. In: PPoPP (2010)
13. Ellen, F., Fatourou, P., Ruppert, E., van Breugel, F.: Non-blocking binary search trees. In: PODC, pp. 131–140 (2010)
14. Aksenov, V., Gramoli, V., Kuznetsov, P., Malova, A., Ravi, S.: A concurrency-optimal binary search tree. CoRR abs/1702.04441 (2017)
15. Natarajan, A., Mittal, N.: Fast concurrent lock-free binary search trees. In: PPoPP, pp. 317–328 (2014)
16. Gramoli, V.: More than you ever wanted to know about synchronization: Synchrobench, measuring the impact of the synchronization on concurrent algorithms. In: PPoPP, pp. 1–10 (2015)
17. Gramoli, V., Kuznetsov, P., Ravi, S.: From sequential to concurrent: correctness and relative efficiency (brief announcement). In: Principles of Distributed Computing (PODC), pp. 241–242 (2012)
18. Gramoli, V., Kuznetsov, P., Ravi, S., Shang, D.: A concurrency-optimal list-based set (brief announcement). In: Distributed Computing - 29th International Symposium, DISC 2015, Tokyo, Japan, 7–9 October 2015
19. Cao Minh, C., Chung, J., Kozyrakis, C., Olukotun, K.: STAMP: Stanford transactional applications for multi-processing. In: IISWC (2008)
20. Crain, T., Gramoli, V., Raynal, M.: A speculation-friendly binary search tree. In: PPoPP, pp. 161–170 (2012)
21. Siakavaras, D., Nikas, K., Goumas, G., Koziris, N.: Performance analysis of concurrent red-black trees on HTM platforms. In: 10th ACM SIGPLAN Workshop on Transactional Computing (Transact) (2015)

22. Howley, S.V., Jones, J.: A non-blocking internal binary search tree. In: SPAA, pp. 161–171 (2012)
23. Chatterjee, B., Nguyen, N., Tsigas, P.: Efficient lock-free binary search trees. In: PODC (2014)

Scalable Fine-Grained Metric-Based Remeshing Algorithm for Manycore/NUMA Architectures

Hoby Rakotoarivelo[1,2]([⊠]), Franck Ledoux[1], Franck Pommereau[2], and Nicolas Le-Goff[1]

[1] CEA, DAM, DIF, 91297 Arpajon, France
{franck.ledoux,nicolas.le-goff}@cea.fr
[2] IBISC, Université d'Évry Val d'Essonne, Évry, France
{hoby.rakotoarivelo,franck.pommereau}@ibisc.fr

Abstract. In this paper, we present a fine-grained multi-stage metric-based triangular remeshing algorithm on manycore and NUMA architectures. It is motivated by the dynamically evolving data dependencies and workload of such irregular algorithms, often resulting in poor performance and data locality at high number of cores. In this context, we devise a multi-stage algorithm in which a task graph is built for each kernel. Parallelism is then extracted through fine-grained independent set, maximal cardinality matching and graph coloring heuristics. In addition to index ranges precalculation, a dual-step atomic-based synchronization scheme is used for nodal data updates. Despite its intractable latency-boundness, a good overall scalability is achieved on a NUMA dual-socket Intel Haswell and a dual-memory Intel KNL computing nodes (64 cores). The relevance of our synchronization scheme is highlighted through a comparison with the state-of-the-art.

Keywords: Irregular parallelism · Manycore · Anisotropic remeshing

1 Introduction

In computational fluid dynamics, large-scale direct numerical simulations require a high discretization (mesh) resolution to achieve a good accuracy. Moreover, the computational domain needs to be periodically re-discretized to avoid degenerated or mixed cells in case of lagrangian-based or multi-materials simulations [4]. In this context, triangular mesh adaptation aims at reducing the computational effort of these simulations while preserving the required accuracy. However, its parallelization remains challenging due to dynamically evolving data dependencies and workload, resulting in a poor locality and efficiency at high number of cores. On the other hand, manycore architectures have been emerged in HPC landscape, with an increasing number of cores but a decreasing memory and frequency per core, and an asymmetric memory latency in case of NUMA multi-socket machines. To take advantage of these architectures, the challenge is to expose a high concurrency and data locality for such an irregular algorithm.

© Springer International Publishing AG 2017
F.F. Rivera et al. (Eds.): Euro-Par 2017, LNCS 10417, pp. 594–606, 2017.
DOI: 10.1007/978-3-319-64203-1_43

RELATED WORKS. Most of existing parallel remeshing schemes are coarse-grained, and not suitable to manycore machines. They rely on domain parti-tioning and dynamic cell migration for load balancing. They focus on reducing the unavoidable synchronization for domain interface consistency, and on find-ing reliable heuristics for cell migration [7]. Fine-grained schemes have emerged but most of them rely on a speculative execution model [2,5]. In 2015, Rokos *et al.* devised a clean lock-free scheme in [11,12], based on an initial idea of Freitag *et al.* [6]. Task conflicts are expressed by a graph, and non-conflictual tasks are then explicitly extracted. To avoid data races, mesh data updates are stacked locally and committed later. Their solution scaled well on a dual-socket Sandy-Bridge machine, but worse on a quad-socket Opteron one due to NUMA effects. Indeed, data placement is not taken into account on tasklists reduction. Furthermore, their deferred updates scheme involves a lot of data moves, increas-ing NUMA effects while reducing the arithmetic intensity. In [10], we extended their work by using kernel-specific graphs to increase parallelism, and a combi-natorial map [3] data structure to avoid synchronization for mesh data updates. We attempted a theoretical characterization of performance metrics, based on machine parameters (e.g. bandwidth). Our solution scaled well on a dual-socket Haswell machine, but the contraction kernel suffers from memory indirections on stencil data retrieval.

CONTRIBUTIONS. This paper is an extension of our preliminary work in [10]. It differs from [10–12] in many points:

1. We use a dual-step atomic-based synchronization scheme for topological updates, with a node-centered data structure. We show that it is a good trade-off between data locality and synchronization cost (overhead, data moves). This way, we improve the efficiency of the contraction kernel which was the main drawback in [10]. We also show that taking into account the graph num-ber of connected components would increase the parallelism for this kernel.
2. We use a fine-grained maximal graph matching heuristic for task extraction in the swapping kernel. We are the first to apply such a scheme in parallel meshing and we show that it is efficient in practice.
3. Evaluations are made on both a NUMA dual-socket and a dual-memory machines. Our results show that the latency-boundness of such an algorithm is intractable due to its high irregularity, but may be eased by the use of hyperthreading. Such an evaluation was not yet done on Intel Xeon-Phi KNL in parallel meshing context.

2   Problem Overview

The purpose is to rebuild a discretization (mesh) of a domain Ω, such that the interpolation error of a given solution field u is bounded and equi-distributed on Ω. It is done by an iterative procedure, and involves a numerical solver and a metric-based remesher. It ends when a given error treshold is achieved (Algo-rithm 1). In our context, a node refers to a mesh point and a cell refers to a mesh triangle.

REMESHING. To control the interpolation error of u, cells size and density must fit the variation of the physical solution field over the domain. Basically, it may be achieved by three ways:

- *variational:* node sampling is obtained by minimizing an energy function, and resulting nodes are then triangulated using a Delaunay kernel.
- *hyperspace embedding:* nodal coordinates, solution field and related gradient are embedded in $\mathbb{R}^6$. The domain is then remeshed in this hyperspace, using local or global kernels.
- *metric-based:* a tensor field is associated to each node v_i, and encodes cell size and stretching (anisotropy) prescription in the vicinity of v_i. An uniform mesh is then built in the riemannian metric space induced by the tensor field.

We opt for a metric-based scheme since it is local and preserve well anisotropy compared to the two others. A standard sequence of operations is used for that purpose. First, we compute a nodewise tensor field from nodal discrete second derivatives. A gradation is then performed to smooth out sudden changes in size requirements. Afterwards, we apply the geometric and topological operations on mesh, using 4 local kernels:

- the *refinement* which aims at splitting long edges by recursive cell dissection.
- the *contraction* which aims at collapsing short edges by vertex merging.
- the *swapping* which improves cell pair qualities by edge flips.
- the *smoothing* which improves stencil qualities by relocating nodes using an anisotropic laplacian operator.

Algorithm 1. Adaptive loop	**Algorithm 2.** Kernel parallel stages
input: mesh, error and quality tresholds.	**repeat**
output: optimal couple mesh-solution.	1. filter active nodes/cells.
repeat	2. build a task graph $G = (V, E)$
solve the solution field (u_p) on mesh.	3. extract non-conflictual tasks
derive a tensor field from (u_p).	4. apply operations
apply gradation on tensor field.	5. repair topology
while min. quality not optimal **do**	**until** no marked cells
refinement	
contraction	
swapping	
smoothing	
end while	
until error threshold is reached	
return couple mesh-solution	

PARALLELIZATION. Remeshing is a data-driven algorithm. Tasks (gradation, refinement, contraction, swapping, smoothing) are related to a dynamically evolving subset of nodes or cells. In fact, processing a task may generate some others, and need to be propagated. In our case, the required number of rounds is data-dependent. Finally, tasks within a same round may be conflictual [9].

Here, data dependencies are related to mesh topology, and evolves accordingly:

- gradation, contraction and smoothing involve the vicinity of each active node;
- refinement involves a subset of the vicinity of each active cell;
- swapping involves the vicinity of each active cell pair.

In fact, two issues must be addressed: topological inconsistency and data races. Indeed, conflictual tasks may invalid the mesh (crosses, holes or boundary loss) whereas nodal or incidence data may be corrupted if updates are not synchronized. The former is solved by an explicit parallelism extraction (Sect. 3), whereas the later is solved by an explicit synchronization scheme (Sect. 4).

Kernels are parallelized independently using a fork-join model. Each of them iteratively performs 5 stages (Algorithm 2). Here, any data updated in a given stage cannot be used within the same stage.

3   Extracting Fine-Grained Parallelism

For each kernel, we extract a task graph $G = (V, E)$. Their descriptions are given in Fig. 1. However, no graph is required for refinement since cells may be processed asynchronously. V is a set of active tasks, and E represents task conflicts. Parallelism is then extracted through fine-grained graph heuristics (Table 1).

Table 1. Task graphs per kernel and related heuristics

Kernel	Graph extracted from	Heuristic
Gradation	Mesh primal graph	Coloring
Refinement	None	–
Contraction	Mesh primal graph	Indep. set
Swapping	Mesh dual graph	Matching
Smoothing	Mesh primal graph	Coloring

CONTRACTION. For each topological update, mesh conformity must be preserved such that holes and edge crosses are avoided. However, collapsing two neighboring nodes may result in a hole, so they cannot be processed concurrently. Thus, the idea is to extract independent nodes such that they can be processed in a safe way. For it, we derived a heuristic from a graph coloring scheme in [1]. Here, the number of connected components σ_G of G increase through iterations. In our case, we always pick the lowest available color according to neighbors values, then the ratio of independent tasks increases according to σ_G. We resolve conflicts only for the first color to accelerate the procedure. Also, tie breaks are based on vertex degree (Algorithm 3). A comparison with a monte-carlo based heuristic [8] shows that taking the variation of σ is relevant in our context. Indeed, the ratio of independent nodes on $|V|$ is greater in this case (Fig. 2).

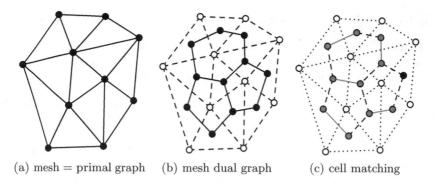

(a) mesh = primal graph   (b) mesh dual graph   (c) cell matching

Fig. 1. Graph descriptions and cell pair matching in swapping kernel

SWAPPING. Flipping more than one edge per cell may result in an edge cross. For each cell K_i, the unique edge e to be flipped, and thus the neighboring cell K_j sharing e, must be identified. Therefore, we aim at extracting a subset of cell pairs to be flipped. For it, the idea is to extract a maximal cardinality matching from the dual graph (Fig. 1). To do that, we adapt the Karp-Sipser's heuristic. It is based on vertex-disjoint augmenting path retrievals using depth first searches in G (Algorithm 4). Here, it is irrelevant to maintain different tasklist according to cell degrees, since we know that they are whether 2 or 3. The ratio of matched cells shows that this greedy scheme is convenient for our purposes (Fig. 2).

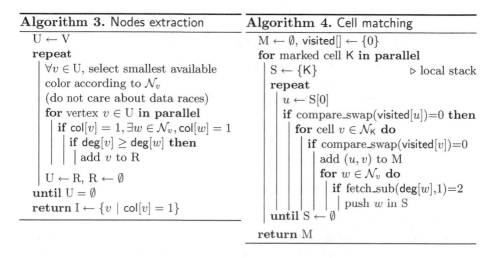

Algorithm 3. Nodes extraction	**Algorithm 4.** Cell matching

U ← V
repeat
  $\forall v \in$ U, select smallest available
  color according to $\mathcal{N}_v$
  (do not care about data races)
  for vertex $v \in$ U **in parallel**
    if col$[v] = 1, \exists w \in \mathcal{N}_v$, col$[w] = 1$
      if deg$[v] \geq$ deg$[w]$ **then**
        add v to R
  U ← R, R ← $\emptyset$
until U = $\emptyset$
return I ← $\{v \mid$ col$[v] = 1\}$
	M ← $\emptyset$, visited$[] ← \{0\}$
	for marked cell K **in parallel**
	  S ← $\{$K$\}$ ▷ local stack
	  repeat
	    u ← S[0]
	    if compare_swap(visited$[u]$)=0 **then**
	      for cell $v \in \mathcal{N}_K$ **do**
	        if compare_swap(visited$[v]$)=0
	          add (u, v) to M
	          for $w \in \mathcal{N}_v$ **do**
	            if fetch_sub(deg$[w]$,1)=2
	              push w in S
	  until S ← $\emptyset$
	return M

GRADATION *and* SMOOTHING. In these kernels, the computed value of a given node v_i is interpolated from its neighbors $\mathcal{N}[v_i]$. However, processing v_i and any $v_j \in \mathcal{N}[v_i]$ may result in data races. Thus, we aim at extracting a nodal partition such that no two neighboring nodes will be scheduled concurrently. For that, we use a fine-grained graph coloring in [1]. In our case, kernels convergence rate decreases linearly on the number of colors. Thanks to the planarity of the graph, the practical number of colors remains low (between 5 and 7).

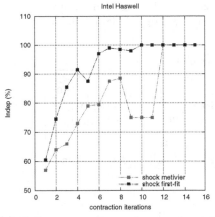
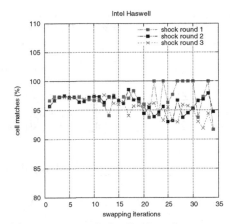

(a) Ratio comparison of our heuristic (First-fit) and a Monte-Carlo based scheme (Metivier) on independent nodes extraction.

(b) Ratio of matched cells throughout swapping rounds while |V| is decreasing linearly

Fig. 2. Heuristics performance on tasks extraction for contraction and swapping kernels (Color figure online)

4 Synchronizing for Topological Updates

In our case, mesh topology is explicitly stored by maintaining incidence lists. Here, extracting non-conflictual tasks does not avoid data races on topological data updates. To resolve it, we define an explicit thread synchronization scheme.

CELL INSERTIONS. For the sake of spatial data locality, we store mesh data in shared flat arrays. Since we don't use the same pattern for refinement, then the number of nodes and cells to be inserted cannot be predicted. They can be stacked locally before being globally copied like in [11,12], but it would result in a high amount of data moves. Instead we infer the number of new cells in order to find the right index range per thread. First, we store the pattern to be applied for each cell in an array `pattern` during the filtering step. Then, each thread t_i performs a reduction on `pattern` within its iteration space $(n/p) \cdot [i, i+1]$, with n the number of tasks and p the number of threads. The result is then stored in an array `offset[i]`. Finally a prefix-sum is done on `offset` to retrieve the right index ranges per thread for cell insertions.

INCIDENCE DATA UPDATES. We use a node-centered data structure: each node stores the index of cells connected to it. Here, updates may be stacked locally using the deferred mechanism in [11,12] (Table 2). Due the huge amount of data moves, it would increase significantly the overhead of this step (Fig. 8). We use a dual-step synchronization scheme instead. First, cells indices are added asynchronously in nodal incidence lists (Algorithm 5). For that, threads increment atomically a nodal offset array `deg`. Each node is then atomically marked as to be fixed, since its incidence list may contain obsolete references. Finally, incidence lists of each marked node are fixed in a separate step (Algorithm 6).

Table 2. Deferred updates mechanism in [11,12]. Thread t_i stores data of node v_k in def_op[i][j] list, with j=hash(k)%p. Finally, each thread t_i copy all data in def_op[k][i]$_{k=1,p}$ in mesh

		updates processed by				
		t_0	t_1	t_2	$\cdots$	t_{n-1}
committed by	t_0	def_op[0][0]	def_op[1][0]	def_op[2][0]	$\cdots$	def_op[n-1][0]
	t_1	def_op[0][1]	def_op[1][1]	def_op[2][1]	$\cdots$	def_op[n-1][1]
	t_2	def_op[0][2]	def_op[1][2]	def_op[2][2]	$\cdots$	def_op[n-1][2]
	$\vdots$	$\vdots$	$\vdots$	$\vdots$	$\vdots$	$\vdots$
	t_{n-1}	def_op[0][n-1]	def_op[1][n-1]	def_op[2][n-1]	$\cdots$	def_op[n-1][n-1]

Algorithm 5. step 1: asynch. adds

input: data, n
  atomic_compare_swap(fix[i], 1)
  $k \leftarrow$ atomic_fetch_add(deg[i], n)
  if $n + k$ exceeds incid[i] capacity **then**
    #pragma omp critical
    /* double check pattern */
    if not yet reallocated **then**
      realloc incid[i] to twice its capacity
  end if
  copy data to incid[i][k]

Algorithm 6. step 2: repair sweep

  $R \leftarrow \emptyset$ ▷ local to thread
  for node v_i in mesh **in parallel**
    if fix[i] **then**
      for cell K in incid[i] **do**
        if $v_i \in$ K **then**
          add K in R
      incid[i] $\leftarrow \emptyset$, deg[i] $\leftarrow$ |R|
      sort R and swap with incid[i].
    end if

---

5   Evaluation

Our algorithm is implemented in C++ using OpenMP4 and C++11 capabilities.

BENCHMARK PARAMETERS. Our code is compiled with the Intel compiler suite (version 15) with -O3 flag enabled. Thread-core affinity is done by setting the environment variable KMP_AFFINITY to scatter on normal mode and compact on hyperthreading. Benchmarks are run on a NUMA dual-socket Intel Xeon Haswell E5-2698 v3 machine (2×16 cores at 2.3 Ghz, 3 cache levels), and an Intel Xeon-Phi KNL machine (72 cores at 1.5 Ghz, 2 cache levels, 4 HT/core). KNL has two memory: an on-chip MCDRAM at 320 GB/s and a DDR4 at 60 GB/s. We use the quadrant clustering mode to ease cache misses worst case penalties (Fig. 3).

We use 3 solution fields with different anisotropy levels for our tests (Fig. 4). For each testcase, an input grid of 1 005 362 cells and 504 100 nodes is used. It is initially renumbered by a Hilbert space-filling curve scheme, but no reordering is done during the execution. For each run, a single adaptation is performed with 3 rounds. Mesh density factor is set to 0.9, and no metric gradation is performed.

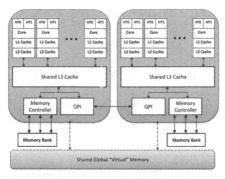
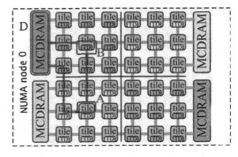

(a) Cache/memory hierarchy in Haswell. L2/L3 cache latencies ≈ 4.7 ns and 6.4 ns. Local and remote memory ≈ 18 ns, 40 ns.

(b) KNL quadrant clustering mode. Each tile consists of a dual-core and a shared L2 cache. Physical addresses are mapped to tag directories such that memory requests do not need to go across quadrants.

Fig. 3. Cache and memory organization in Intel Haswell and KNL computing nodes.

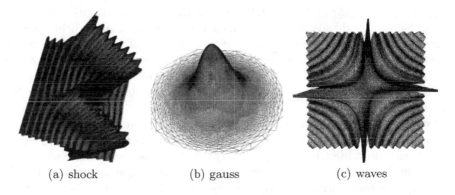

(a) shock   (b) gauss   (c) waves

Fig. 4. Solution fields used in our benchmarks

STRONG SCALING. The mean makespan and scaling efficiency $E_p = t_1/(p \cdot t_p)$ are given in Fig. 5, with t_n the makespan on n threads. Hyperthreading is systematically used on KNL (4 per core) to hide memory access latency (30 and 28 ns for MCDRAM and DDR4 respectively). We use both MCDRAM and DDR4 by binding memory through `numactl`. All testcases behaves similarly and a good scaling is achieved on both architectures. Surprisingly, there was no significant improvement in the use of the high bandwidth MCDRAM. Indeed, the algorithm is not bandwidth-sensitive. The efficiency falls to 30% on KNL on 256 threads due to high contentions, but scales better than on Haswell on lower number of cores. Makespan is still improved when using hyperthreading on Haswell, and NUMA effects are significantly eased, thanks to a locality-aware data updates scheme.

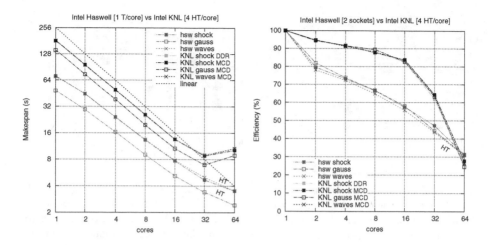

Fig. 5. Mean makespan and scaling efficiency on 3 rounds.

OVERHEADS PER KERNEL. For each kernel, the time spent distribution per step is given in Fig. 6. Overheads related to parallelism extraction and synchronization are depicted in red. These steps do not exceed 15% of the makespan for all kernels. Furthermore, they are negligible in case of contraction and smoothing. Also, these ratios remain constant despite the number of threads, and scale at the same rate as other steps. For the refinement, operations are structured such that no parallelism extraction is required. Moreover, the filtering step does not require a full consistent mesh topology for adjacency requests, in the sense that stored incidence lists may contain obsolete references, but each new cell $\mathsf{K} : (v_0, v_1, v_2)$ must be referenced in incidence lists of $(v_i) \in \mathsf{K}$. For this kernel, the repair sweep involved in the synchronization scheme is performed once at the very end of the procedure. For the contraction, the vicinity $\mathcal{N}[v_i]$ of each node v_i is required by the filtering step in order to find the right $v_j \in \mathcal{N}[v_i]$ where v_i should collapse to (even in sequential). Hence, the primal graph is recovered at the beginning of each round. This step mainly consist of data accesses but represents roughly 22% of the overall makespan. It involved a high amount of cache misses in [10] due to memory indirections when requesting the combinatorial map data structure. In our case, stencil retrieval involves only one level of indirection (instead of two), leading to a better scalability (Algorithms 7 and 8). For swapping, the main overhead is related to graph matching stage with a mean ratio of 15%. Its convergence is linear to the search depth δ_G on augmenting paths retrievals. This step is highly irregular and is asymptotically in $\mathcal{O}(\log n)$ with n the number of vertices of the dual graph. In practice, $\delta_G \approx 4$ with static scheduling, and nearly 12 rounds is required for step convergence. For smoothing, the primal graph is recovered at the beginning of the procedure, but no synchronization sweep is required since mesh topology remains unchanged. For this kernel, the unique overhead is related to the graph coloring step. In practice, a low number of rounds is required for convergence (roughly 3).

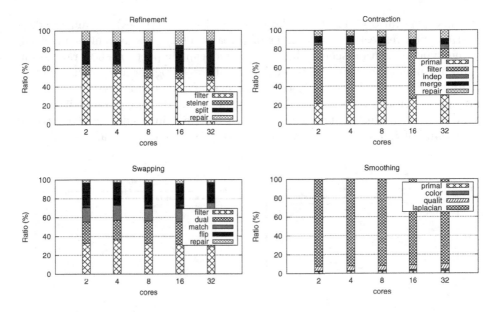

Fig. 6. Time ratio distribution per step for each kernel on Haswell.

Algorithm 7. stencil retrieval of v_i	**Algorithm 8.** stencil retrieval in [10]
for each K : $(p_0, p_1, p_2) \in$ incid$[v_i]$ **do**	init $\leftarrow v_i$.edge; cur $\leftarrow$ init
if $p_i = v_i$ **then**	**repeat**
$(j, k) : (i+1 \mod 3, i+2 \mod 3)$	add cur.v2 to $\mathcal{N}[v_i]$
add p_j, p_k in $\mathcal{N}[v_i]$	inv $\leftarrow$ opp[cur], cur $\leftarrow$ next[inv]
sort $\mathcal{N}[v_i]$ and remove duplicates	**until** cur = init

PERFORMANCE PER KERNEL. Task and floating-point operations (FLOP) rates per kernel on Haswell are given in Fig. 7. Refinement and swapping have higher task rates since they are both much local and less compute-intensive than the two others. Refinement involves the vicinity $\mathcal{N}[K]$ of each cell K, because when an edge is split then the two surrounding cells are dissected. However, the dissection step is purely local because the index of the node to be inserted is already resolved in the steiner point computation step. Therefore, cells may be dissected individually. Swapping steps involve the shell of each edge[1] to be flipped which size is constant, whereas contraction and smoothing steps involve the stencil $\mathcal{N}[v_i]$ of each node v_i, whose size is variable and related to anisotropy.

All kernels scale well in terms of FLOP rate. Most of floating-point operations occur during the filtering step, except for smoothing. This step involves geodesic distance calculation for refinement and contraction, and cell quality computation sweep for swapping and smoothing. In our case, the arithmetic

---

[1] The two cells (K_1, K_2) sharing this edge, and the stencil $\mathcal{N}[v_k]$ of each $v_k \in K_i$.

intensity (the ratio of FLOP on the amount of data accesses) remain roughly constant with respect to the number of threads. Thus data-movement involved by the synchronization scheme has not a significant impact on FLOP rate, even on higher number of threads. Smoothing scales even better since it has higher arithmetic intensity. In the anisotropic laplacian computation step, coordinates and metric tensor of a given node v_i are interpolated from those of its vicinity $\mathcal{N}[v_i]$, and reajusted iteratively such that v_i remain inside the geometrical convex hull of $\mathcal{N}[v_i]$. Thus, it involves a better reuse of cached data.

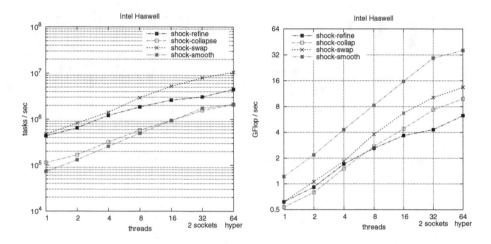

Fig. 7. Task rate and floating-point operations per second of each kernel on Haswell

SYNCHRONIZATION COST. We faithfully implemented the deferred mechanism used in [11,12] (Table 2) in order to compare it with our dual-step atomic-based synchronization scheme for nodal data updates. To reduce NUMA effects, first-touch policy is applied and no memory reallocation is performed on both cases. Makespan and related overheads are given in Fig. 8 on Haswell and KNL. Both schemes scale well, but makespan has doubled in case of the deferred update scheme. In this case, data movement overhead has a significant impact on total execution time of the algorithm. Indeed, deferred mechanism overheads are 5 times the overhead of our synchronization scheme for contraction and swapping kernels.

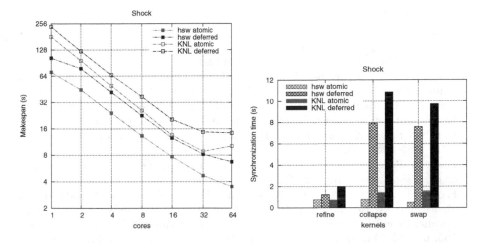

Fig. 8. Cost comparison of atomic-based and deferred synchronization schemes

6   Conclusion

A fine-grained multi-stage algorithm for anisotropic triangular mesh adaptation on manycore and NUMA architectures is proposed. It is based on explicit parallelism extraction using fine-grained graph heuristics, and a dual-step synchronization scheme for topological data updates. It follows a fork-join model and is implemented in C++ using OpenMP4 and auto-vectorization capabilities. Its scalability is evaluated on both a NUMA dual-socket Intel Haswell and dual-memory Intel KNL computing nodes. A good overall scalability is achieved since a mean efficiency of 48% and 65% is reached on Haswell and KNL on 32 cores. Due to higher contentions, a lower efficiency (roughly 30%) is achieved on KNL on 64 cores with 256 threads. Task rate and floating-point operations per second scale in a nearly linear way for all kernels. Overheads related to parallelism extraction as well as synchronization do not exceed 15% of overall makespan. They remain negligible for contraction and smoothing (5–7%), and scale linearly on other stages makespan. Further efforts have to be done to reduce the latency-sensitiveness of the algorithm, and to take advantage of the high bandwidth on-chip MCDRAM in KNL. Also, a comparison with a task-based version with work-stealing capabilities would be interesting. It would highlight performance sensitiveness if whether data locality is privileged at expense of load imbalance and vice-versa. An extension to a distributed-memory scheme is expected, with a constraint that the bulk-synchronous property of the algorithm should be preserved. In this case, a multi-bulk synchronous parallel bridging model [13] may be used to theoretically characterize its performance, given bandwidth and latency at each level of the memory hierarchy.

References

1. Çatalyurek, U., et al.: Graph colouring algorithms for multicore and massively multithreaded architectures. JPC, 576–594 (2012)
2. Chrisochoides, N.P., et al.: A multigrain Delaunay mesh generation method for multicore SMT-based architectures. JPDC, 589–600 (2009)
3. Damiand, G., Lienhardt, P.: Combinatorial Maps: Efficient Data Structures for Computer Graphics and Image Processing. A.K.Peters, Natick (2014)
4. Del Pino, S.: Metric-based mesh adaptation for 2D Lagrangian compressible flows. JCP, 1793–1821 (2011)
5. Foteinos, P.A., et al.: High quality real-time image-to-mesh conversion for finite element simulations. In: ICS 27, pp. 233–242 (2013)
6. Freitag, L.A., Jones, M.T., Plassmann, P.E.: The scalability of mesh improvement algorithms. In: Heath, M.T., Ranade, A., Schreiber, R.S. (eds.) Algorithms for Parallel Processing. The IMA Volumes in Mathematics and its Applications, vol. 105, pp. 185–211. Springer, New York (1998). doi:10.1007/978-1-4612-1516-5_9
7. Loseille, A., et al.: Parallel generation of large-size adapted meshes. In: IMR 24, pp. 57–69 (2015)
8. Métivier, Y., et al.: An optimal bit complexity randomized distributed MIS algorithm. JDC **23**, 331–340 (2011)
9. Pingali, K., et al.: Amorphous data-parallelism in irregular algorithms. Technical report 09–05, University of Texas (2009)
10. Rakotoarivelo, H., et al.: Fine-grained locality-aware parallel scheme for anisotropic mesh adaptation. In: IMR 25, pp. 123–135 (2016)
11. Rokos, G.: Scalable multithreaded algorithms for mutable irregular data with application to anisotropic mesh adaptivity. Ph.D. thesis, Imperial College London (2014)
12. Rokos, G., et al.: Thread parallelism for highly irregular computation in anisotropic mesh adaptation. In: EASC, pp. 103–108 (2015)
13. Valiant, L.: A bridging-model for multicore computing. JCSS, 154–166 (2011)

Performance Evaluation of Thread-Level Speculation in Off-the-Shelf Hardware Transactional Memories

Juan Salamanca[1]($\boxtimes$), José Nelson Amaral[2], and Guido Araujo[1]

[1] Institute of Computing, UNICAMP, Campinas, SP, Brazil
{juan,guido}@ic.unicamp.br
[2] Computing Science Department, University of Alberta, Edmonton, AB, Canada
amaral@cs.ualberta.ca

Abstract. Thread-Level Speculation (TLS) is a hardware/software technique that enables the execution of multiple loop iterations in parallel, even in the presence of some loop-carried dependences. TLS requires hardware mechanisms to support conflict detection, speculative storage, in-order commit of transactions, and transaction roll-back. There is no off-the-shelf processor that provides direct support for TLS. Speculative execution is supported, however, in the form of Hardware Transactional Memory (HTM)—available in recent processors such as the Intel Core and the IBM POWER8. Earlier work has demonstrated that, in the absence of specific TLS support in commodity processors, HTM support can be used to implement TLS. This paper presents a careful evaluation of the implementation of TLS on the HTM extensions available in such machines. This evaluation provides evidence to support several important claims about the performance of TLS over HTM in the Intel Core and the IBM POWER8 architectures. Experimental results reveal that by implementing TLS on top of HTM, speed-ups of up to 3.8× can be obtained for some loops.

Keywords: Thread-Level Speculation · Transactional memory

1 Introduction

Loops account for most of the execution time in programs and thus extensive research has been dedicated to parallelize loop iterations [2]. Unfortunately, in many cases these efforts are hindered when the compiler cannot prove that a loop is free of *loop-carried* dependences. However, sometimes when static analysis concludes that a loop has a *may* dependence—for example when the analysis cannot resolve a potential alias relation—the dependence may actually not exist or it may occur in very few executions of the program [12]. *Thread-Level Speculation* (TLS) is a promising technique that can be used to enable the parallel execution of loop iterations in the presence of *may* loop-carried dependences. TLS assumes that the iterations of a loop can be executed in parallel—even in

© Springer International Publishing AG 2017
F.F. Rivera et al. (Eds.): Euro-Par 2017, LNCS 10417, pp. 607–621, 2017.
DOI: 10.1007/978-3-319-64203-1_44

the presence of potential dependences—and then relies on a mechanism to detect dependence violations and correct them. The main distinction between TLS and HTM is that in TLS speculative transactions must commit in order.

Recently hardware support for speculation has been implemented in commodity off-the-shelf microprocessors [3,4]. However, the speculation support in these architectures was designed with *Hardware Transactional Memory* (HTM) in mind and not TLS. The only implementation of hardware support for TLS to date is in the IBM Blue Gene/Q (BG/Q), a machine that is not readily available for experimentation or usage. HTM extensions, available in the Intel Core and in the IBM POWER8 architectures, allow for the speculative execution of atomic program regions [3–5]. Such HTM extensions enable the implementation of three key features required by TLS: (a) conflict detection; (b) speculative storage; and (c) transaction roll-back.

Until now, the majority of the attempts to estimate the performance benefits of TLS were based on simulation studies [10,11]. Unfortunately, studies of TLS execution based on simulation have serious limitations. The availability of speculation support in commodity processors allowed for the first study of TLS on actual hardware and led to some interesting research questions: (1) can the existing speculation support in commodity processors, originally designed for HTM, be used to support TLS? and (2) if it can, what performance effects would be observed from such implementations? Earlier work has provided a cautiously positive answer to the first question, i.e. supporting TLS on top of HTM hardware is possible, but it requires several careful software adaptations [9]. To address the second question, this paper presents a careful evaluation of the implementation of TLS on top of the HTM extensions available in the Intel Core and in the IBM POWER8. This evaluation uses the same loops from an earlier study by Murphy *et al.* [6] and led to some interesting discoveries about the relevance of loop characterization to predict the potential performance of TLS. The experimental results indicate that: (1) small loops are not amenable to be parallelized with TLS on the existing HTM hardware because of the expensive overhead of: (a) starting and finishing transactions, (b) aborting a transaction, and (c) setting up loop for TLS execution; (2) loops with potential to be successfully parallelized in both Intel Core and IBM POWER8 architectures have better performance on the POWER8 because TLS can take advantage of the ability of this architecture to suspend and resume transactions to implement *ordered transactions*; (3) the larger storage capacity for speculative state in Intel TSX can be crucial for loops that execute many read and write operations; (4) the ability to suspend/resume a transaction is important for loops that execute for a longer time because their transactions may abort due to OS context switching; and (5) the selected size of the strip can be critical for the increase of aborts due to order inversion.

The remainder of this paper is organized as follows. Section 2 describes the relevant aspects of the implementation of HTM in both Intel Core and IBM POWER8 architectures. Section 3 details the related work. Benchmarks, methodology and settings are described in Sect. 4. Finally, Sect. 5 shows experimental results and a detailed analysis.

2   How to Support TLS over HTM

This section reviews HTM extensions and discusses how they can be effectively used to support the TLS execution of hard-to-parallelize loops containing (*may*) loop-carried dependences.

2.1   Intel Core and IBM POWER8

Transactional memory systems must provide transaction *atomicity* and *isolation*, which require the implementation of the following mechanisms: *data versioning management*, *conflict detection*, and *conflict resolution* [9].

Both Intel and IBM architectures provide instructions to begin and end a transaction, and to force a transaction to abort. To perform such operations Intel Core's *Transactional Synchronization Extensions* (TSX) implements the *Restricted Transactional Memory* (RTM), an instruction set that includes xbegin, xend, and xabort. The corresponding instructions in the POWER8 are tbegin, tend, and tabort.

All data conflicts are detected at the granularity of the cache line size because both processors use cache mechanisms—based on physical addresses—and the cache coherence protocol to track transactional states. Aborts may be caused by: memory access conflicts, capacity issues due to excessively large transactional read/write sets or overflow, conflicts due to false sharing, and OS and microarchitecture events that cause aborts (*e.g.* system calls, interrupts or traps) [4,7].

The main differences between POWER8 and the Intel Core HTMs, summarized in Table 1, are: (1) transaction capacity; (2) conflict granularity; and (3)

Table 1. HTM implementations of Intel Core and IBM POWER [7].

Processor type	Intel i7-4770	POWER8
Conflict-detection granularity (cache line)	64 B	128 B
Tx load capacity	4 MB	8 KB
Tx store capacity	22 KB	8 KB
L1 data cache	32 KB, 8-way	64 KB
L2 data cache	256 KB	512 KB, 8-way
SMT level	2	8

Table 2. HTM Architectural Features.

Features	TLS	Intel	P8
Eager conflict detection	✓	✓	✓
Resolution conflict policy	✓		
Ordered transactions	✓		
Multi-versioned caches	✓		
Suspend/resume			✓
Lazy conflict detection			
Data forwarding	✓		
Word conflict detection	✓		

```
1   for(count = 0; count < WEIGHT; count++){
2     /* Start sequential segment 1 */
3     if (cond) glob++; /* Global scalar*/
4     /* End sequential segment 1 */
5
6     /* Start sequential segment 2 */
7     for(i = 0; i < factor; i++){
8       /* Global array, A */
9       int tmp = A[factor*(count%4) + i];
10      tmp += count*5;
11      if(tmp%2 == 0){
12        A[factor*(count%4) + i] = tmp;
13      }
14    }
15    /* End sequential segment 2 */
16  }
```

```
1   d= STRIP_SIZE;
2   inc=(NUM_THREADS-1)*STRIP_SIZE;
3   count=param->count;
4
5   for(; count < WEIGHT; count += inc){
6     prev_count=count;
7   Retry:
8     if (!BEGIN()){
9       for (; count-prev_count < d &&
                count < WEIGHT; count++){
10        if(cond) glob++;
11      }
12      END();
13    }
14    else goto Retry;
15  }
```

Fig. 1. A loop with two *may* loop-carried dependences. Adapted from [6].

Fig. 2. Code of each thread to parallelize Fig. 1's loop with TLS on ideal HTM system.

ability to suspend/resume a transaction. The maximum amount of data that can be accessed by a transaction in the Intel Core is much larger than in the POWER8. This speculative storage capacity is limited by the resources needed both to store read and write sets, and to buffer transactional stores.

In POWER8 the execution of a transaction can be paused through the use of suspended regions—implemented with two new instructions: `tsuspend` and `tresume`. As described in [9], this mechanism enables the implementation of an *ordered-transaction* feature in TLS [5].

2.2 Thread-Level Speculation

Thread-Level Speculation (TLS) has been widely studied [10,11]. Proposed TLS hardware systems must support four primary features: (a) data conflict detection; (b) speculative storage; (c) ordered transactions; and (d) rollback when a conflict is detected. Some of these features are also supported by the HTM systems found in the Intel Core and the POWER8, and thus these architectures have the potential to be used to implement TLS. Table 2 shows the necessary features required to enable TLS on top of an HTM-supporting mechanism, and its availability in some modern architectures. Neither Intel TSX nor the IBM POWER8 provide all the features necessary to carry out TLS effectively [9].

Lets examine how TLS can be applied to a simplified version of the loop example of Fig. 1 (the inner loop is omitted) when it runs on top of an ideal HTM system containing: (a) ordered transactions in hardware; (b) multi-versioning cache; (c) eager-conflict detection; and (d) conflict-resolution policy. Figure 2 shows the loop after it was strip-mined and parallelized for TLS on four cores. Assume that the END instruction implements: (a) ordered transactions, i.e., a transaction executing an iteration of the loop has to wait until all transactions executing previous iterations have committed, and (b) a conflict-resolution policy that gives preference to the transaction that is executing the earliest iteration of the loop while rolling back later iterations. Multi-versioning allows for the removal of Write-After-Write (WAW) and Write-After-Read (WAR) loop-carried dependences on the `glob` variable. As shown in Fig. 3, in the first four iterations `cond` evaluates false and the iterations finish without aborts. Then, at iteration 4, the eager-conflict detection mechanism detects the RAW loop-carried dependence violation on variable `glob` between iterations 4 and 5, thus rolling back iteration 5 because it should occur after iteration 4. Subsequent iterations wait for the previous iterations to commit.

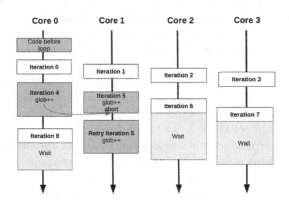

Fig. 3. Execution flow of Fig. 2's code with `STRIP_SIZE` = 1 and `NUM_THREADS` = 4.

3   Previous Research on TLS

Murphy *et al.* [6] propose a technique to speculatively parallelize loops that exhibit transient loop-carried dependences—a loop where only a small subset of loop iterations have actual loop-carried dependences. The code produced by their technique uses a TM hardware (TCC hardware) and software (Tiny STM) model running on top of the HELIX time emulator. They developed three approaches to predict the performance of implementing TLS on the HELIX time emulator: coarse-grained, fine-grained, and judicious. The *coarse-grained approach* speculates a whole iteration while the *fine-grained approach* speculates sequential segments and executes parallel segments without speculation. The *judicious approach* uses profile data at compile time to choose which sequential segment to speculate or synchronize so as to satisfy (may) loop-carried dependences. They conclude that TLS is not only advantageous to overcome limitations of the compiler static data-dependence analysis, but that performance might also be improved by focusing on the transient nature of dependences.

Murphy *et al.* evaluated TLS on emulated HTM hardware using `cBench` programs [1] and, surprisingly, predicted up to 15 times performance improvements with 16 cores [6]. They arose at these predictions even though they did not use strip mining to decrease the overhead of starting and finishing transactions as previous work suggested [8,9]. Particularly, fine-grained speculation without strip mining can result in large overheads due to multiple transactions (sequential segments) per iteration, even larger than coarse-grained speculation. They parallelized loops in a round-robin fashion which can result in small transactions, large number of transactions, high abort ratio, bad use of memory locality, and false sharing. Their over-optimistic predictions are explained by the fact that their emulation study does not take into account the overhead of setting TLS up—which is specially high without strip mining. For instance, their emulation study predicted speed-ups even for small loops. However, when executing such loops in real hardware, the TLS overhead—setup, begin/end transactions, and aborts—would nullify any gain from parallel execution.

Odaira and Nakaike, Murphy *et al.* and Salamanca *et al.* use coarse-grained TLS to speculate a (strip-mined) whole iteration and perform conflict detection and resolution at the end of the iteration to detect RAW dependence violations [6,8,9]. The advantages of coarse-grained TLS are: (a) it is simple to implement because it does not need an accurate data dependence analyzer. (b) the number of transactions is smaller than or equal to the fine-grained or judicious approaches; and (c) there is no synchronization in the middle of an iteration. The downside is that even a single frequent actual loop-carried dependence will cause transactions to abort and serialize the execution. To illustrate this, assume an execution of the example of Fig. 1 where `cond` always evaluates true, and thus the `glob` variable is increased at each iteration of the outer loop. With coarse-grained TLS the execution of this outer loop would be serialized.

Salamanca *et al.* describe how speculation support designed for HTM can also be used to implement TLS [9]. They focused their work on the impact of false sharing and the importance of judicious strip mining and privatization to achieve performance. They provide a detailed description of the additional software support that is necessary in both the Intel Core and the IBM POWER8 architectures to support TLS. This paper uses that method to carefully evaluate the performance of TLS on Intel Core and POWER8 using 22 loops from `cBench` focusing on the characterization of the loops. This loop characterization could be used in the future to decide if TLS should be used for a given loop.

4   Benchmarks, Methodology and Experimental Setup

The performance assessment reports speed-ups and abort/commit ratios (Transaction Outcome) for the coarse-grained TLS parallelization of loops from the Collective Benchmark (`cBench`) benchmark suite [1] running on Intel Core and IBM POWER8. For all experiments the default input is used for the `cBench` benchmarks. The baseline for speed-up comparisons is the serial execution of the same benchmark program compiled at the same optimization level. Loop times are compared to calculate speed-ups. Each software thread is bound to one hardware thread (core) and executes a determined number of pre-assigned iterations. Each benchmark was run twenty times and the average time is used. Runtime variations were negligible and are not presented.

Table 3. Loops extracted from cBench applications.

Class	Loop	Previous ID	Benchmark	Location	Function	%Cov	Invocations
I	A	14	automotive_bitcount	bitcnts.c,65	main1	100%	560
	B	18	automotive_susan_c	susan.c,1458	susan_corners	83%	344080
	C	22	automotive_susan_e	susan.c,1118	susan_edges	18%	165308
	D	24	automotive_susan_e	susan.c,1057	susan_edges	56%	166056
	E	28	automotive_susan_s	susan.c,725	susan_smoothing	100%	22050
	F	15	automotive_bitcount	bitcnts.c,59	main1	100%	80
II	G	19	automotive_susan_c	susan.c,1457	susan_corners	83%	782
	H	23	automotive_susan_e	susan.c,1117	susan_edges	18%	374
	I	25	automotive_susan_e	susan.c,1056	susan_edges	56%	374
	J	29	automotive_susan_s	susan.c,723	susan_smoothing	100%	49
III	K	1	consumer_jpeg_c	jfdcint.c,154	jpeg_fdct_islow	5%	1758848
	L	2	consumer_jpeg_c	jfdcint.c,219	jpeg_fdct_islow	5%	1758848
	M	4	consumer_jpeg_c	jcphuff.c,488	encode_mcu_AC_first	10%	5826184
	N	6	consumer_jpeg_d	jidcint.c,171	jpeg_idct_islow	14%	7280000
	O	7	consumer_jpeg_d	jidcint.c,276	jpeg_idct_islow	15%	7280000
	P	13	automotive_bitcount	bitcnts.c,96	bit_shifter	35%	80000000
	Q	16	automotive_susan_c	susan.c,1615	susan_corners	7%	344080
	R	26	automotive_susan_s	susan.c,735	susan_smoothing	96%	198450000
	S	34	security_rijndael_d	aesxam.c,209	decfile	7%	31864729
	T	3	consumer_jpeg_c	jccolor.c,148	rgb_ycc_convert	10%	439712
	U	5	consumer_jpeg_c	jcphuff.c,662	encode_mcu_AC_refine	17%	5826184
Others	V	17	automotive_susan_c	susan.c,1614	susan_corners	7%	782

Loops from **cBench** were instrumented with the necessary code to implement TLS, following the techniques described by Salamanca *et al.* [9]. They were then executed using an Intel Core i7-4770 and the IBM POWER8 machines, and their speed-ups measured with respect to sequential execution. Based on the experimental results, the loops studied are placed in four classes that will be explained later. Table 3 lists the twenty two loops from **cBench** used in the study. The table shows (1) the loop class (explained later); (2) the ID of the loop in this study; (3) the ID of the loop in the previous study [6]; (4) the benchmark of the loop; (5) the file/line of the target loop in the source code; (6) the function where the loop is located; (7) %Cov, the fraction of the total execution time spent in this loop; and (8) the number of invocations of the loop in the whole program.

This study uses an Intel Core i7-4770 processor with 4 cores with 2-way SMT, running at 3.4 GHz, with 16 GB of memory on Ubuntu 14.04.3 LTS (GNU/Linux 3.8.0-29-generic x86_64). The cache-line prefetcher is enabled (by default). Each core has a 32 KB L1 data cache and a 256 KB L2 unified cache. The four cores share an 8 MB L3 cache. The benchmarks are compiled with GCC 4.9.2 at optimization level −O3 and with the set of flags specified in each benchmark program.

The IBM processor used is a 4-core POWER8 with 8-way SMT running at 3 GHz, with 16 GB of memory on Ubuntu 14.04.5 (GNU/Linux 3.16.0-77-generic ppc64le). Each core has a 64 KB L1 data cache, a 32 KB L1 instruction cache, a 512 KB L2 unified cache, and a 8192 KB L3 unified cache. The benchmarks are compiled with the XL 13.1.1 compiler at optimization level −O2.

5 Classification of Loops Based on TLS Performance

The cbench loops were separated into four classes according to their performance when executing TLS on top of HTM. The following features, shown in Table 4, characterize the loops: (1) N, the average number of loop iterations; (2) $Tbody$, the average time in nanoseconds of a single iteration of the loop on Intel Core; (3) $Tloop$, $Tbody \times N$; (4) $\%lc$, the percentage of iterations that have loop-carried dependences for the default input; (5) the average (and maximum) size in bytes read/written by an iteration. The right side of Table 4 describes TLS execution: (1) the type of privatization within the transaction used in TLS implementation;[1] (2) ss, the *strip size* used for the experimental evaluation in Intel Core; (3) Transaction Duration in the Intel Core, which is the product $ss \times Tbody$; (4) the average speed-ups with four threads for Intel Core after applying TLS; (5) the ss for POWER8; (6) the speed-ups for POWER8; and (7) the predicted speed-up from TLS emulation reported in [6] for coarse-grained (C), fine-grained (F), and judicious (J) speculation using 16 cores.

For all the loops included in this study $N > 4$, thus they all have enough iterations to be distributed to the four cores in each architecture. When the duration of a loop, $Tloop$, is too short there is not enough work to parallelize and the performance of TLS is low—in the worst case, LoopS, TLS can be 100 times slower than the sequential version. Even a small percentage of loop-carried dependences, $\%lc$, materializing at runtime may have a significant effect on performance depending on the distribution of the loop-carried dependences throughout loop iterations at runtime; thus TLS performance for those loops is difficult to predict. The size of the read/write set in each transaction can also lead to performance degradation because of capacity aborts. For the Intel Core the duration of each transaction is important: rapidly executing many small transactions leads to an increase of order-inversion aborts[2]. The number of such

Table 4. Characterization and TLS Execution of Classes.

Class	Loop ID	Loop Characterization				Read Size		Write Size		Privatization	TLS Execution					Speed-ups in [6]		
		N Intel's	Tbody Intel's (ns)	Tloop (ns)	%lc	avg	max	avg	max		Intel Core ss	Duration (ns)	Speed-up	IBM POWER8 ss	Speed-up	C	F	J
I	A	1125000	5.0	5680000	0%	12 B	24 B	0 B	20 B	Reduction	502	2600.0	2.20	502	3.80	14.0	14.3	14.3
	B	590	12.7	7500	0%	48 B	176 B	0 B	36 B	No	59	749.0	1.20	59	1.59	10.2	12.0	12.0
	C	592	8.1	4810	0%	14 B	192 B	0 B	32 B	Array	72	584.0	1.20	68	1.21	7.5	8.0	8.0
	D	594	14.1	8420	0%	76 B	176 B	0 B	28 B	Array	88	1240.0	1.28	72	2.22	13.0	15.0	15.0
	E	600	198.0	118000	0%	14 B	192 B	0 B	32 B	Array	15	2970.0	1.60	15	3.18	14.0	15.0	15.0
	F	7	5840000.0	40800000	0%	48 B	268 B	155 B	604 B	Array	1	5840000.0	0.98	2	2.40	1.0	2.5	2.5
II	G	440	7710.0	3390000	0%	2 KB	3 KB	29 B	328 B	No	1	7710.0	1.23	1	1.15	13.0	15.0	15.0
	H	442	4790.0	2120000	0%	3 KB	8 KB	37 B	260 B	Array	1	4790.0	2.09	2	0.84	12.0	13.8	13.8
	I	444	8680.0	3850000	0%	4 KB	4 KB	206 B	1 KB	Array	2	17300.0	1.76	1	1.05	13.0	15.0	15.0
	J	450	117000.0	52900000	0%	3 KB	8 KB	37 B	260 B	Array	1	117000.0	1.89	1	0.73	1.0	1.0	1.0
III	K	8	8.7	69	0%	16 B	32 B	16 B	32 B	Array	1	8.7	0.07	1	0.03	5.5	6.0	6.0
	L	8	8.5	68	0%	16 B	32 B	16 B	32 B	Array	1	8.5	0.06	1	0.03	5.5	6.0	6.0
	M	38	5.4	205	100%	12 B	68 B	4 B	36 B	Scalar	1	5.4	0.07	1	0.02	0.5	1.0	0.5
	N	8	8.1	65	0%	23 B	64 B	16 B	32 B	Array	1	8.1	0.05	1	0.05	4.0	4.2	4.2
	O	8	9.4	75	0%	24 B	68 B	5 B	16 B	Array	1	9.4	0.07	1	0.05	5.8	6.0	6.0
	P	23	1.1	26	0%	4 B	12 B	4 B	16 B	Reduction	3	3.4	0.02	3	0.02	1.0	2.3	2.3
	Q	590	1.0	567	0.14%	4 B	212 B	0 B	36 B	Scalar	118	113.0	0.46	95	0.49	9.0	8.5	8.5
	R	15	1.8	27	0%	12 B	68 B	4 B	56 B	Reduction	10	18.2	0.05	10	0.04	4.0	4.0	4.0
	S	16	1.3	21	0%	7 B	8 B	4 B	16 B	Array	2	2.6	0.02	2	0.01	1.0	3.0	3.0
	T	162	2.5	404	0%	40 B	44 B	12 B	24 B	Array & Scalar	8	19.9	0.15	30	0.33	11.0	11.0	2.0
	U	63	4.6	289	30%	7 B	8 B	4 B	20 B	Scalar	9	41.4	0.20	10	0.16	10.0	11.0	11.0
Others	V	440	511.0	225000	34%	1 KB	4 KB	20 B	196 B	Scalar	1	511.0	1.25	1	1.34	2.5	2.5	1.0

---

[1] A Reduction privatization is a scalar privatization of a reduction operation.

[2] A order-inversion abort rolls back a transaction that completes execution out of order using an explicit abort instruction (`xabort`).

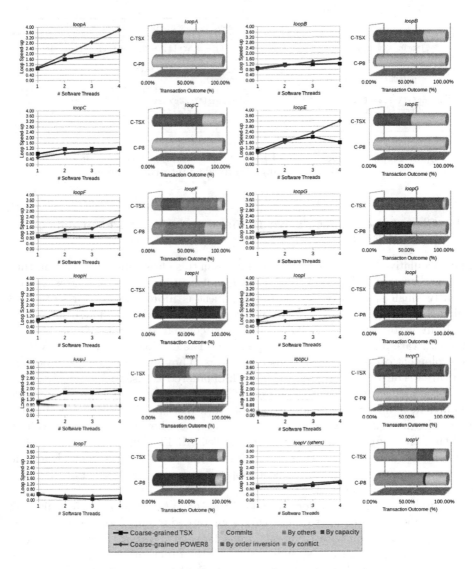

Fig. 4. Speed-ups and abort ratios for TLS execution on TSX and POWER8.

aborts is lowest for medium-sized transactions that have balanced iterations—
when the duration of different iterations of the loop varies the number of order-
inversion aborts also increases. Finally, long transactions in both architectures
may cause aborts due to traps caused by the end of the OS quantum.

```
1  for (i=0; i < FUNCS; i++){//loopF
2    for (j=n=0, seed=1;
          j<iterations; j++, seed+=
          13)//loopA
3      n += pBitCntFunc[i](seed);
4    if (print)
5      printf("%-38s> Bits: %ld\n",
          text[i], n);
6  }
```

Fig. 5. loopA and loopF

```
1  for (is=0; is<FUNCS; is+=STRIP_SIZE){//loopF
2    for (i=is; i-is < STRIP_SIZE && i<FUNCS; i++)
3      for (j = n_arr[i] = 0, seed=1; j<iterations;
            j++,seed+=13)//loopA
4        n_arr[i] += pBitCntFunc[i](seed);
5    if (print)
6      for (i=is; i-is < STRIP_SIZE && i< FUNCS; i++)
7        printf("%-38s> Bits: %ld\n", text[i],
            n_arr[i]);
8  }
```

Fig. 6. loopF after applying strip mining and dividing into two components.

5.1 Class I: Low Speculative Demand and Better Performance in POWER8

The speculative storage requirement of loops in this class is below 2 KB and thus they are amenable for TLS, and see speed-ups, in both architectures. A sufficiently small speculative-storage requirement is more relevant for POWER8 which has smaller speculative-storage capacity (see Table 1). These loops also result in better scaling in POWER8, when compared to Intel Core, because they can take advantage of the **suspend** and **resume** instructions of POWER8 to implement ordered transactions in software. They do not scale much beyond two threads on Intel Core due to the lack of ordered transactions support.

Table 4 shows the characterization of Class I. These loops typically provide a sufficient number of iterations to enable their distribution among the threads. They also have a relatively moderate duration, as shown by the *Tloop* values, and thus they have enough work to be parallelized. TLS makes most sense when the compiler cannot prove that iterations are independent, but dependences do not occur at runtime, therefore most loops that are amenable for TLS (loops in Class I and II) have %lc of zero.

A typical example of a loop in Class I is loopA, shown in Fig. 5. This loop achieves speed-ups of up to 3.8× with four threads. This loop calls the same bit-counting function with different inputs for each iteration. Even though this loop has *may* loop-carried dependences inside the functions called, none of these dependences materialize at runtime. A successful technique to parallelize this loop relies on the privatization of variable n and partial accumulation of results to a global variable after each transaction commits. The successful parallelization of loopA stems from a moderate duration (*Tloop*), no actual runtime dependences, and a read/write set size that is supported by the HTM speculative-storage capacity. The large number of iterations of this loop allows increasing the strip size (*ss*), and thus the new *Tbody* (after strip mining)—*ss* × *Tbody*— is longer; after that, order-inversion aborts decrease (loopB has more order-inversion aborts than loopA, although its *Tbody* is longer).

For most of the loops in this class the performance is directly related to the effective work to be parallelized, represented by *Tloop*. In the Intel Core the proportion of order-inversion aborts is inversely related to the transaction

```
1  for(j=mask_size;j<x_size-mask_size;j++){//loopE
2    area = 0;
3    total = 0;
4    centre = in[i*x_size+j];
5    ...// calulating area and total
6    tmp = area-10000;
7    if (tmp==0)
8      *out++=median(in,i,j,x_size);
9    else
10     *out++=((total-(centre*10000))/tmp);
11 }
```

```
1  n=0;
2  for(i=5;i<y_size-5;i++)//loopV
3    for(j=5;j<x_size-5;j++){//loopQ
4      x = r[i][j];
5      if (x>0 &&(/*compare x*/)){
6        corner_list[n].info=0;
7        corner_list[n].x=j;
8        corner_list[n].y=i;
9        ...
10       n++;
11     }
12  }
```

Fig. 7. loopE

Fig. 8. loopQ and loopV

duration because very short transactions may reach the commit point even before previous iterations could commit. Another issue is that very long transactions may abort due to traps caused by the end of OS quantum. loopF has the longest $ss \times Tbody$ among all loops evaluated and thus many transactions abort due to traps caused by the end of the OS quantum, which explains this loop showing a high abort ratio by *other causes* in Fig. 4. Whole Coarse-grained TLS parallelization of loopF is not possible because each iteration has a printf statement that is not allowed within a transaction in either architecture. Therefore, each iteration of loopF must be divided into two components: loopA and the printf (as shown in Fig. 6), before applying TLS only to the first component. The second component is always executed non-speculatively.

The performance of loopC from one to three threads is higher on Intel Core than on POWER8 because the larger speculative store capacity in the Intel Core allows for the use of a larger strip size. With four threads, there is a small improvement in POWER8 due to the reduction of order-inversion aborts. The increment in the number of threads intensifies the effect of order inversion in performance. Therefore, for machines with a higher number of cores, better speed-ups should be achieved in POWER8 than in Intel Core.

In loopC, loopD, and loopE consecutive iterations write to consecutive memory positions leading to false sharing when these iterations are executed in parallel in a round-robin fashion. For instance, loopE, shown in Fig. 7, writes to *out++ (consecutive memory positions) in consecutive iterations generating false sharing in a round-robin parallelization. The solution is privatization: write instead into local arrays during all the transaction and copy the values back to the original arrays after commit [9] (Fig. 8).

5.2 Class II: High Speculative Demand and Better Performance in Intel Core

These loops can scale better in the Intel Core compared to the POWER8 because of the larger transaction capacity of the Intel Core: the read/write sizes of these loops overflow the transaction capacity of the POWER8 (see Table 1) leading to a high number of capacity aborts.

Table 4 shows the characterization of loops in Class II. With more than 400 iterations and a loop execution time *Tloop* larger than 2 ms these loops have enough work to be parallelized. Also, no dependences materialize at runtime for the default inputs ($\%lc = 0$).

The smaller write size in loopG means that 50% of its transactions do not overflow the POWER8 speculative-storage capacity resulting in this loop showing speed-ups of up to 15% with four threads on POWER8. In the Intel Core this loop has a large number of order-inversion aborts because it has significant imbalance between its iterations [6]. A contrast is loopH that has better performance in the Intel Core even though its transactions are shorter. loopH results in much fewer order-inversion aborts because the durations of its transactions are balanced. loopJ has long transaction duration and suffer aborts due to OS traps.

5.3 Class III: Not Enough Work to Be Parallelized with TLS

These are loops where TLS implementation does not have enough work to be distributed among the available threads resulting in poor performance in any architecture. The overhead of setting up TLS for these loops is too high in comparison to the benefits of parallelization. Murphy *et al.* [6] reported speed-ups in these loops because their emulation of TLS hardware did not take into consideration these costs. The experiments in this section reveal that their emulated numbers overestimate the potential benefit of TLS for these loops. As shown in Table 4 the available work to be parallelized, *Tloop* in all the loops in this class is below 0.6 μs, which is too small to benefit from parallelization. For instance, loopO (and other loops as loopP) has no aborts in POWER8, but their performance is poor because of the overhead of setting TLS up.

Most of the loops in this category have many order-inversion aborts in Intel Core because their transaction duration is below 120 ns leading to a fast end of the transactions/iterations probably even before previous iterations could commit. loopT presents a high order-inversion abort rate in Intel Core because its transactions last less than 20 ns. In POWER8, the strip size needed to increase the loop body and the privatization of three arrays lead to aborts because the speculative capacity of the HTM is exceeded.

5.4 Others

They are a special case because of they are loops that have sufficient work to be parallelized but whose dependences materialize at runtime. For instance, loopV has 34% of probability of loop-carried dependences, but TLS can still deliver some performance improvement. As explained in [6], this loop finds local maxima in a sliding window, with each maximum being added to a list of corners, each iteration of loopQ processes a single pixel whereas a complete row is processed by each iteration of loopV. The input of this loop is a sparse image with most of the pixels set to zero, and the suspected corners (iterations with loop-carried dependences) are processed close to each other.

Table 5. Characterization of 6 loops from SPEC CPU 2006.

Loop ID	Benchmark	Location	%Cov	N	Tbody (ns)	Tloop (ns)	%lc	Iteration Size	Class
mcf	429.mcf	pbeampp.c,165	40%	300	20	6000	3%	300 B	Others
milc	433.milc	quark_stuff.c,1523	20%	160000	94	15000000	0%	1 KB	I
h264ref	464.h264ref	mv-search.c,394	36%	1089	156	170000	0%	6 KB	II
sphinx3	482.sphinx3	vector.c,513	37%	2048	29	60000	0%	1 KB	I
astar	473.astar	Way2_.cpp,100	60%	1234	41	50000	20%	1 KB	Others
lbm	470.lbm	lbm.c,186	99%	1300000	55	71000000	0%	500 B	I

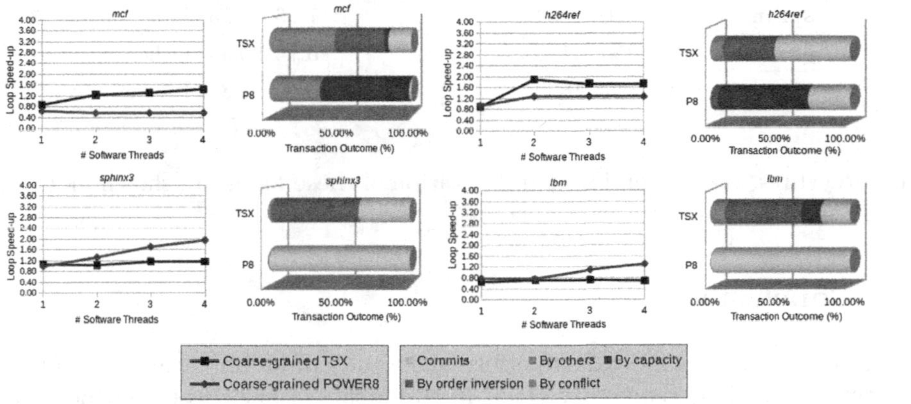

Fig. 9. Four SPEC2006 Loops. Speed-ups and abort ratios for coarse-grained TLS execution on TSX and POWER8.

5.5 Predicting the TLS Performance for Other Loops

The characterization of the loops given in Table 4 and the performance evaluation presented could also be used to predict the potential benefit of applying TLS for new loops that were not included in this study. For loops with short *Tloop*, such as those in class III, TLS is very unlikely to result in performance improvements in either architecture. For loops with small read/write sets and no dependences materializing at runtime, such as those in class I, TLS is likely to result in modest improvement for the Intel Core and more significant improvements for the POWER8. Loops that have sufficient work to be parallelized and no actual dependences but have larger read/write sets, such as those in Class II, are likely to deliver speed improvements in the Intel Core but will result in little or no performance gains in the POWER8 because of the more limited speculative capacity in this architecture. Finally, loops that have sufficient work to be parallelized but whose dependences materialize at runtime are difficult to predict—such as loopV. The distribution of loop-carried dependences among the iterations of such loops must be studied.

Six loops from the SPEC CPU 2006 suite are characterized (Table 5) to predict to which class they belong according to the classification described in Sect. 5. Loops milc, sphinx3, and lbm are classified as Class I; h264ref as Class II; and mcf and astar as Others. Based on this classification a prediction can be made about the relative performance of the loops on TLS over HTM for both

Table 6. TLS Execution for 6 loops from SPEC CPU 2006.

Loop ID	ss		Intel Tx Duration (ns)	Speed-up		Loop Class
	Intel	P8		Intel	P8	
mcf	20	48	400	1.45	0.60	Others
milc	4	4	375	1.44	1.50	I
h264ref	16	6	2490	1.74	1.27	II
sphinx3	8	16	234	1.16	1.95	I
astar	128	256	5180	0.74	0.49	Others
lbm	33	17	1800	0.69	1.30	I

architectures. Results of TLS parallelization of these loops are shown in Table 6 and Fig. 9 and confirm the predictions.

6   Conclusions

This paper presents a detailed performance study of an implementation of TLS on top of existing commodity HTM in two architectures. Based on the performance results it classifies the loops studied and doing so provides guidance to developers as to what loop characteristics make them amenable to the use of TLS on the Intel Core or on the IBM POWER8 architectures. Future design of hardware support for TLS may also benefit from the observations derived from this performance study.

Acknowledgments. The authors would like to thank FAPESP (grants 15/04285-5, 15/12077-3, and 13/08293-7) and the NSERC for supporting this work.

References

1. cTuning Foundation: cBench: Collective benchmarks (2016). http://ctuning.org/cbench
2. Hurson, A.R., Lim, J.T., Kavi, K.M., Lee, B.: Parallelization of doall and doacross loops-a survey. Adv. Comput. **45**, 53–103 (1997)
3. IBM: Power ISA Transactional Memory (2012). www.power.org/wp-content/uploads/2012/07/PowerISA_V2.06B_V2_PUBLIC.pdf
4. Intel Corporation: Intel architecture instruction set extensions programming reference. Intel transactional synchronization extensions, Chap. 8 (2012)
5. Le, H., Guthrie, G., Williams, D., Michael, M., Frey, B., Starke, W., May, C., Odaira, R., Nakaike, T.: Transactional memory support in the IBM POWER8 processor. IBM J. Res. Dev. **59**(1), 8:1–8:14 (2015)
6. Murphy, N., Jones, T., Mullins, R., Campanoni, S.: Performance implications of transient loop-carried data dependences in automatically parallelized loops. In: International Conference on Compiler Construction (CC), pp. 23–33, Barcelona, Spain (2016)

7. Nakaike, T., Odaira, R., Gaudet, M., Michael, M.M., Tomari, H.: Quantitative comparison of hardware transactional memory for Blue Gene/Q, zEnterprise EC12, Intel Core, and POWER8. In: International Conference on Computer Architecture (ISCA), pp. 144–157, Portland, OR (2015)
8. Odaira, R., Nakaike, T.: Thread-level speculation on off-the-shelf hardware transactional memory. In: International Symposium on Workload Characterization (IISWC), pp. 212–221, Atlanta, Georgia, USA, October 2014
9. Salamanca, J., Amaral, J.N., Araujo, G.: Evaluating and improving thread-level speculation in hardware transactional memories. In: IEEE International Parallel and Distributed Processing Symposium (IPDPS), pp. 586–595, Chicago, USA (2016)
10. Steffan, J., Mowry, T.: The potential for using thread-level data speculation to facilitate automatic parallelization. In: High Performance Computer Architecture (HPCA), p. 2, Washington, DC, USA (1998)
11. Steffan, J.G., Colohan, C.B., Zhai, A., Mowry, T.C.: A scalable approach to thread-level speculation. In: International Conference on Computer Architecture (ISCA), pp. 1–12, Vancouver, BC, Canada (2000)
12. Tournavitis, G., Wang, Z., Franke, B., O'Boyle, M.F.: Towards a holistic approach to auto-parallelization: integrating profile-driven parallelism detection and machine-learning based mapping. In: Programming Language Design and Implementation (PLDI), pp. 177–187, PLDI 2009, ACM, Dublin, Ireland (2009)

Theory and Algorithms for Parallel Computation and Networking

Addressing Volume and Latency Overheads in 1D-parallel Sparse Matrix-Vector Multiplication

Seher Acer, Oguz Selvitopi, and Cevdet Aykanat$^{(\boxtimes)}$

Bilkent University, 06800 Ankara, Turkey
{acer,reha,aykanat}@cs.bilkent.edu.tr

Abstract. The scalability of sparse matrix-vector multiplication (SpMV) on distributed memory systems depends on multiple factors that involve different communication cost metrics. The irregular sparsity pattern of the coefficient matrix manifests itself as high bandwidth (total and/or maximum volume) and/or high latency (total and/or maximum message count) overhead. In this work, we propose a hypergraph partitioning model which combines two earlier models for one-dimensional partitioning, one addressing total and maximum volume, and the other one addressing total volume and total message count. Our model relies on the recursive bipartitioning paradigm and simultaneously addresses three cost metrics in a single partitioning phase in order to reduce volume and latency overheads. We demonstrate the validity of our model on a large dataset that contains more than 300 matrices. The results indicate that compared to the earlier models, our model significantly improves the scalability of SpMV.

Keywords: Communication cost · Sparse matrix-vector multiplication · Hypergraph partitioning · One-dimensional partitioning

1 Introduction

A key building block found in many applications is the ubiquitous sparse matrix-vector multiplication (SpMV) operation. The scalability of this kernel operation on distributed memory systems heavily depends on the communication overheads. The irregular sparsity pattern of the coefficient matrix may cause high volume and/or latency overhead and necessitate addressing multiple communication cost metrics for efficient parallel performance.

There are several communication cost metrics that determine the volume overhead such as total volume and maximum volume of data communicated by a processor. Similarly, the latency overhead is determined by cost metrics such as total message count and maximum message count. As the communication cost of SpMV generally depends on more than one of these metrics, solely minimizing a single one of them may not always lead to a scalable performance.

In this work, we propose a hypergraph partitioning model for one-dimensional-parallel (1D-parallel) SpMV, which reduces three important communication cost metrics simultaneously: total volume, maximum volume, and

© Springer International Publishing AG 2017
F.F. Rivera et al. (Eds.): Euro-Par 2017, LNCS 10417, pp. 625–637, 2017.
DOI: 10.1007/978-3-319-64203-1_45

total message count. Our model utilizes two earlier models [1,9], where [1] addresses multiple volume-based cost metrics, whereas [9] addresses total volume and message count. The proposed model achieves partitioning in a single phase and exploits the recursive bipartitioning (RB) paradigm in order to target the cost metrics other than total volume. In our model, the maximum volume is addressed by representing the amount of communicated data with vertex weights while the total message count is addressed by encapsulating the communicated messages as message nets. We present our model for rowwise partitioning with conformal partitions on input and output vectors, however, it can easily be adapted to columnwise partitioning.

There are a few early works [2,5,12] as well as some recent works [1,3,7,9,10] that focus on reducing multiple communication cost metrics. Among these, the works in [2,3,12] are two-phase methods, where different cost metrics are handled in distinct phases. The disadvantage of these two-phase methods is that each phase is oblivious to the metrics handled in the other phase. Our model is able to address all cost metrics in a single phase. In [5], the checkerboard hypergraph model is proposed for reducing total volume and bounding message count. This work differs from ours in the sense that it achieves a nonconformal partition on vectors. UMPa [7] is a single-phase hypergraph partitioning tool that can handle multiple metrics. Despite this, it imposes a prioritization on the metrics in which the secondary metrics are considered only in the tie-breaking cases in the refinement algorithm. This may lead to poor optimization of the secondary metrics. There are very recent works [1,9] that are both single-phase and based on the RB paradigm. Our work builds upon these two works.

The rest of the paper is organized as follows. Section 2 provides the background material. We present the proposed hypergraph partitioning model in Sect. 3. Section 4 gives the experimental results and Sect. 5 concludes.

2   Background

2.1   Hypergraph Partitioning

A hypergraph $\mathcal{H} = (\mathcal{V}, \mathcal{N})$ is a general type of graph that consists of vertices and nets where edges/nets can connect more than two vertices. $\mathcal{V}$ and $\mathcal{N}$ respectively denote the sets of vertices and nets. The set of vertices connected by net $n \in \mathcal{N}$ is denoted with $Pins(n)$. Each vertex $v \in \mathcal{V}$ is assigned a weight denoted with $w(v)$. Similarly, each net $n \in \mathcal{N}$ is assigned a cost denoted with $c(n)$.

$\Pi(\mathcal{H}) = \{\mathcal{V}_1, \ldots, \mathcal{V}_K\}$ is a K-way vertex partition of $\mathcal{H}$, if each vertex part $\mathcal{V}_k$ is nonempty, parts are pairwise disjoint, and the union of the parts gives $\mathcal{V}$. In $\Pi(\mathcal{H})$, $\lambda(n)$ denotes the number of parts in which net n connects vertices, i.e., the number of parts connected by n. A net $n \in \mathcal{N}$ is a cut net if it connects at least two parts, i.e., $\lambda(n) > 1$. The cutsize of a partition $\Pi(\mathcal{H})$ is defined as

$$cut(\Pi(\mathcal{H})) = \sum_{n \in \mathcal{N}} (\lambda(n) - 1)c(n).$$

The weight $W(\mathcal{V}_k)$ of part $\mathcal{V}_k$ is the sum of the weights of the vertices in $\mathcal{V}_k$. $\Pi(\mathcal{H})$ is said to be balanced if $W(\mathcal{V}_k) \leq W_{avg}(1 + \epsilon)$ for all $k = 1,\ldots,K$, where W_{avg} and ϵ respectively denote the average part weight and a maximum allowed imbalance ratio. Then, the hypergraph partitioning problem is defined as obtaining a K-way partition of a given hypergraph with the objective of minimizing cutsize and the constraint of maintaining balance on the part weights.

2.2   Reducing Total Volume via Hypergraph Partitioning

There are two hypergraph models [4] (column-net and row-net) for obtaining one-dimensional (1D) partitioning of a given SpMV of the form $y = Ax$. The column-net and row-net models are used for obtaining rowwise and columnwise partitions, respectively. We only discuss the column-net model since they are dual of each other.

In the column-net hypergraph $\mathcal{H} = (\mathcal{V},\mathcal{N})$, $\mathcal{V}$ contains a vertex v_i for each row i of A, whereas $\mathcal{N}$ contains a net n_j for each column j. n_j connects v_i if and only if $a_{ij} \neq 0$. In a conformal partition, x_i and y_i are assigned to the same processor for each i. To achieve a conformal partition, v_i represents row i, x_i, y_i, and the inner product associated with row i, i.e., $y_i = \langle a_{i*} \cdot x \rangle$, where a_{i*} denotes row i. n_j represents the dependency of the inner products on x_j. Note that an inner product $\langle a_{i*} \cdot x \rangle$ depends on x_j if and only if $a_{ij} \neq 0$. The weight $w(v_i)$ of $v_i \in \mathcal{V}$ is the number of nonzeros in row i, which is the number multiply-and-add operations in $\langle a_{i*} \cdot x \rangle$. Each $n_j \in \mathcal{N}$ is assigned a unit cost. A K-way partition $\Pi(\mathcal{H})$ is decoded as assigning row i, x_i, and y_i to processor P_k, for each $v_i \in \mathcal{V}_k$. This is often visualized as block-partitioned matrix

$$A^{\pi} = QAQ^{T} = \begin{bmatrix} R_1 \\ \vdots \\ R_K \end{bmatrix} = \begin{bmatrix} A_{11} & \cdots & A_{1K} \\ \vdots & \ddots & \vdots \\ A_{K1} & \cdots & A_{K1} \end{bmatrix},$$

where Q is the permutation matrix. Here, row stripe R_k and the corresponding y- and x-vector elements are assigned to processor P_k. The processor that owns a row performs the computations regarding its nonzeros due to the owner-computes rule [8]. In A^{π}, each nonzero segment of column j in off-diagonal block $A_{\ell k}$ incurs a unit communication as P_k sends x_j to P_ℓ. Then, the volume of communication incurred by sending x_j is equal to the number of nonzero segments of column j in off-diagonal blocks of A^{π}. The segment of column j in block $A_{\ell k}$ is a nonzero segment if and only if net n_j connects part $\mathcal{V}_\ell$. Assuming all the diagonal entries are nonzero in A, the total volume then amounts to the cutsize of $\Pi(\mathcal{H})$. Hence, the objective of minimizing cutsize corresponds to minimizing total volume. Since each processor P_k performs multiply-and-add operations proportional to the number of nonzeros in R_k, maintaining balance on the part weights corresponds to maintaining balance on the computational loads of the processors.

3   Simultaneous Reduction of Maximum Volume, Total Volume and Total Message Count

The proposed model relies on the recursive bipartitioning (RB) paradigm to address the cost metrics other than total volume. In RB, a given hypergraph $\mathcal{H}$ is recursively bipartitioned until the desired number of parts is reached. This process induces a full binary tree in which nodes represent hypergraphs. The rth level of the RB tree contains 2^r hypergraphs: $\mathcal{H}_0^r, \ldots, \mathcal{H}_{2^r-1}^r$. Note that the level that a hypergraph belongs to is indicated in the superscript. Bipartitioning $\mathcal{H}_k^r = (\mathcal{V}_k^r, \mathcal{N}_k^r)$ generates hypergraphs $\mathcal{H}_{2k}^{r+1}$ and $\mathcal{H}_{2k+1}^{r+1}$. At the end of the RB process, vertex sets of the hypergraphs in the $\lg_2 K$th level induce the resulting K-way partition of the given hypergraph $\mathcal{H}$ as $\Pi(\mathcal{H}) = \{\mathcal{V}_0^{\lg K}, \ldots, \mathcal{V}_{K-1}^{\lg K}\}$.

Our model is summarized in Algorithm 1. As inputs, it takes the column-net hypergraph $\mathcal{H} = (\mathcal{V}, \mathcal{N})$ of a given $y = Ax$, the number of processors K, the maximum allowable imbalance ratio ϵ, and coefficients α and β. We first compute the imbalance ratio ϵ' used in each bipartitioning in order to result in an imbalance ratio not exceeding ϵ in the final K-way partition (line 1). We start the RB process with the given column-net hypergraph $\mathcal{H}$ as $\mathcal{H}_0^0 = \mathcal{H}$ (line 2). The nets in $\mathcal{H}$ are referred to as volume nets as they capture the total communication volume of the corresponding parallel SpMV. The bipartitionings in the RB process are carried out in breadth-first order, as seen in lines 3–4 of Algorithm 1. At each RB step, after obtaining bipartition $\Pi(\mathcal{H}_k^r) = \{\mathcal{V}_{2k}^{r+1}, \mathcal{V}_{2k+1}^{r+1}\}$ (line 8), hypergraphs $\mathcal{H}_{2k}^{r+1}$ and $\mathcal{H}_{2k+1}^{r+1}$ belonging to the next level of the RB tree are immediately formed with volume nets via cut-net splitting technique (lines 9–12). The function calls in lines 6–7 enable the simultaneous reduction of cost metrics. These function calls introduce an additional cost of $O(V \lg_2 K)$ to the overall partitioning.

In our model, the matrix rows and x- and y-vector elements corresponding to the vertices in $\mathcal{H}_k^r$ are assumed to be assigned to processor group $\mathcal{P}_k^r$, for each hypergraph $\mathcal{H}_k^r$ in the RB tree. We also assume that the RB process is currently at the beginning of the for-loop iteration in which hypergraph $\mathcal{H}_k^r$ is bipartitioned. In the current RB tree, the leaf hypergraphs are listed from left to right as $\mathcal{H}_0^{r+1}, \ldots, \mathcal{H}_{2k-1}^{r+1}, \mathcal{H}_k^r, \ldots, \mathcal{H}_{2^r-1}^r$.

3.1   Reducing Maximum Volume

We formulate the objective of minimizing the maximum volume of processors as additional constraints [1]. These constraints are satisfied by maintaining balance on the communication loads of processor groups $\mathcal{P}_{2k}^{r+1}$ and $\mathcal{P}_{2k}^{r+1}$ for each bipartition $\Pi(\mathcal{H}_k^r)$. To do so, in addition to the standard vertex weights that capture the computational loads of processors, we utilize vertex weights that capture the communication loads.

ADD-COMMUNICATION-WEIGHTS function assigns the communication loads to the vertices in $\mathcal{H}_k^r$ (line 6 of Algorithm 1). The details of this function are given in Algorithm 2. Here, we consider the maximum volume as the maximum

---

Algorithm 1. The Proposed Hypergraph Partitioning Model

Input : Column-net hypergraph $\mathcal{H} = (\mathcal{V}, \mathcal{N})$, number of processors K,
imbalance ratio ϵ, coefficients α and β.

Output: K-way partition of $\mathcal{H}$.

1 $\epsilon' \leftarrow (1 + \epsilon)^{\frac{1}{\lg K}} - 1$

2 $\mathcal{H}_0^0 \leftarrow \mathcal{H}$ ▷ $\mathcal{N}$ contains only volume nets

3 **for** $r \leftarrow 0$ **to** $\lg K - 1$ **do**

4   **for** $k \leftarrow 0$ **to** $2^r - 1$ **do**

5   **if** $r > 0$ **then**

         ▷ Addressing maximum volume

6   ADD-COMMUNICATION-WEIGHTS($\mathcal{H}$, $\mathcal{V}_k^r$, α)

         ▷ Addressing total message count

7   ADD-MESSAGE-NETS($\mathcal{H}$, $\mathcal{H}_k^r$, β)

8        $\Pi(\mathcal{H}_k^r) = \{\mathcal{V}_{2k}^{r+1}, \mathcal{V}_{2k+1}^{r+1}\} \leftarrow$ HypergraphPartitioning($\mathcal{H}_k^r$, 2, ϵ')

       ▷ Form $\mathcal{H}_{2k}^{r+1}$ and $\mathcal{H}_{2k+1}^{r+1}$ with volume nets by net splitting

9        $\mathcal{N}_{2k}^{r+1} \leftarrow$ Split volume nets of $\mathcal{H}_k^r$ in $\mathcal{V}_{2k}^{r+1}$

10       $\mathcal{N}_{2k+1}^{r+1} \leftarrow$ Split volume nets of $\mathcal{H}_k^r$ in $\mathcal{V}_{2k+1}^{r+1}$

11       $\mathcal{H}_{2k}^{r+1} \leftarrow (\mathcal{V}_{2k}^{r+1}, \mathcal{N}_{2k}^{r+1})$

12       $\mathcal{H}_{2k+1}^{r+1} \leftarrow (\mathcal{V}_{2k+1}^{r+1}, \mathcal{N}_{2k+1}^{r+1})$

13 **return** $\Pi(\mathcal{H}) = \{\mathcal{V}_0^{\lg K}, \ldots, \mathcal{V}_{K-1}^{\lg K}\}$

---

send volume of the processors. Recall that processor group $\mathcal{P}_k^r$ owns x_i for each $v_i \in \mathcal{V}_k^r$. Hence, $\mathcal{P}_k^r$ sends x_i to each processors group $\mathcal{P}_\ell^q$ that needs x_i, where $q \in \{r, r+1\}$. Note that $\mathcal{P}_\ell^q$ needs x_i if it is assigned a row j with $a_{ji} \neq 0$. This situation is captured by net n_i connecting vertex v_j where $v_j \in \mathcal{V}_\ell^q$ (lines 3–4). Here, we utilize the global view of net n_i of the initial column-net hypergraph $\mathcal{H}$ to determine the communications between $\mathcal{P}_k^r$ and the other processor groups.

The communication volume incurred by sending x_i amounts to the number of parts connected by n_i different than $\mathcal{V}_k^r$. This value is denoted with $|Con(n_i)|$ in Algorithm 2 and computed in lines 2–5.

The communication weight $|Con(n_i)|$ associated with vertex v_i is unified to its computational weight (line 6). This unification scheme is proven to be more successful than assigning the communication weights as separate second weights [1]. The unification scheme scales the communication weight by a coefficient α which denotes the ratio of the per-word transfer time to the per-word multiply-and-add time in the parallel system. As a result, the unified weight gives the time required to send x_i and to compute inner product of row i with x in terms of the time of an individual multiply-and-add operation.

With the unified communication and computation vertex weights, maintaining balance on the part weights while bipartitioning $\mathcal{H}_k^r$ corresponds to maintaining a unified balance on the computational and communication loads of processor groups $\mathcal{P}_{2k}^{r+1}$ and $\mathcal{P}_{2k+1}^{r+1}$. Balancing the communication volumes of processors corresponds to minimizing the maximum volume of processors under the condition that the total communication volume is minimized.

Algorithm 2. ADD-COMMUNICATION-WEIGHTS

    Input : Original hypergraph $\mathcal{H} = (\mathcal{V}, \mathcal{N})$, vertex set $\mathcal{V}_k^r$, coefficient α

1 **foreach** $v_i \in \mathcal{V}_k^r$ **do**

2 | $Con(n_i) \leftarrow \emptyset$

3 | **foreach** $v_j \in Pins(n_i)$ in $\mathcal{H}$ **do**

4 | | **if** $v_j \notin \mathcal{V}_k^r$ **then**

      | | | ▷ Let $v_j \in \mathcal{V}_\ell^q$

5 | | | $Con(n_i) \leftarrow Con(n_i) \cup \{\mathcal{V}_\ell^q\}$

      | ▷ $|Con(n_i)|$ is the communication load due to sending x_i

6 | $w(v_i) \leftarrow w(v_i) + \alpha|Con(n_i)|$

Algorithm 3. ADD-MESSAGE-NETS

    Input : Original hypergraph $\mathcal{H} = (\mathcal{V}, \mathcal{N})$, hypergraph $\mathcal{H}_k^r$ to be bipartitioned, message net cost β

1 **foreach** $v_i \in \mathcal{V}_k^r$ **do**

2 | **foreach** $v_j \in Pins(n_i)$ in $\mathcal{H}$ **do**

3 | | **if** $v_j \notin \mathcal{V}_k^r$ **then**

      | | | ▷ Let $v_j \in \mathcal{V}_\ell^q$

4 | | | **if** message net $s_\ell^q \in \mathcal{N}_k^r$ **then**

5 | | | | $Pins(s_\ell^q) \leftarrow Pins(s_\ell^q) \cup \{v_i\}$

6 | | | **else**

7 | | | | $c(s_\ell^q) \leftarrow \beta$

8 | | | | $Pins(s_\ell^q) \leftarrow \{v_i\}$ and $\mathcal{N}_k^r \leftarrow \mathcal{N}_k^r \cup \{s_\ell^q\}$

9 | **foreach** n_j in $\mathcal{H}$ with $v_i \in Pins(n_j)$ **do**

10 | | **if** $v_j \notin \mathcal{V}_k^r$ **then**

      | | | ▷ Let $v_j \in \mathcal{V}_\ell^q$

11 | | | **if** message net $r_\ell^q \in \mathcal{N}_k^r$ **then**

12 | | | | $Pins(r_\ell^q) \leftarrow Pins(r_\ell^q) \cup \{v_i\}$

13 | | | **else**

14 | | | | $c(r_\ell^q) \leftarrow \beta$

15 | | | | $Pins(r_\ell^q) \leftarrow \{v_i\}$ and $\mathcal{N}_k^r \leftarrow \mathcal{N}_k^r \cup \{r_\ell^q\}$

3.2 Reducing Total Message Count

We use message nets in order to encapsulate the messages sent and received [9]. A message net connects the vertices that represent the rows or vector elements that require a message together. To encapsulate the up-to-date messages among processor groups in the RB process, the message nets are formed and added to the hypergraphs just prior to their bipartitioning (line 7 in Algorithm 1). Note that on the contrary, since volume nets do not depend on the state of the other parts, we form them as soon as their vertex set is formed (lines 9–10).

ADD-MESSAGE-NETS function adds message nets to hypergraph $\mathcal{H}_k^r$, which contains only volume nets before the respective function call. The details of this function are given in Algorithm 3. There are two types of message nets: send nets and receive nets. For each processor group $\mathcal{P}_\ell^q$ that $\mathcal{P}_k^r$ sends a message to, we add a send net s_ℓ^q to $\mathcal{H}_k^r$. Net s_ℓ^q connects vertices that represent the x-vector elements to be sent to $\mathcal{P}_\ell^q$. $\mathcal{P}_k^r$ sends x_i to $\mathcal{P}_\ell^q$ if a row j with $a_{ji} \neq 0$ is assigned to $\mathcal{P}_\ell^q$. Then, the set of vertices connected by net s_ℓ^q is formulated as

$$Pins(s_\ell^q) = \{v_i : n_i \text{ of } \mathcal{H} \text{ connects } \mathcal{V}_\ell^q\},$$

as computed in lines 2–8. As in Sect. 3.1, we make use of the global view of n_i of the initial column-net hypergraph $\mathcal{H}$ to determine the communications $\mathcal{P}_k^r$ performs. Similarly, for each processor group $\mathcal{P}_\ell^q$ that $\mathcal{P}_k^r$ receives a message from, we add a receive net r_ℓ^q to $\mathcal{H}_k^r$. Net r_ℓ^q connects vertices that represent the A-matrix rows whose multiplications need x-vector elements to be received from $\mathcal{P}_\ell^q$. $\mathcal{P}_k^r$ receives x_j from $\mathcal{P}_\ell^q$ if row i and x_j are respectively assigned to $\mathcal{P}_k^r$ and $\mathcal{P}_\ell^q$, where $a_{ij} \neq 0$. Then, the set of vertices connected by net r_ℓ^q (computed in lines 9–15) is formulated as

$$Pins(r_\ell^q) = \{v_i : n_j \text{ of } \mathcal{H} \text{ connects } \mathcal{V}_k^r \text{ due to } v_i \text{ and } v_j \in \mathcal{V}_\ell^q\}.$$

The message nets are assigned a cost of β whereas the volume nets are assigned unit cost. Here, coefficient β denotes the ratio of per-message startup time to per-word transfer time in the parallel system. With both volume and message nets having the mentioned costs, minimizing the cutsize in each bipartitioning throughout the RB process corresponds to minimizing total volume and total message count in 1D-parallel SpMV.

4 Experiments

4.1 Setting

We consider a total of four schemes for comparison. The total volume metric is common to all schemes and it is addressed by default in all schemes. One scheme addresses a single metric, two schemes address two metrics and the proposed scheme addresses three metrics simultaneously. These schemes are listed as follows:

- BL: Proposed in [4], this scheme solely addresses total volume (Sect. 2.2).
- MV: Proposed recently in [1], this scheme considers two metrics related to volume: total volume and maximum send volume. α is set to 10.
- TM: Proposed in another recent work [9], this scheme considers one metric related to volume and one metric related to latency: total volume and total message count. β is set to 50.
- MVTM: This scheme is the one proposed in this work (Sect. 3) and considers all three metrics: total volume, maximum volume and total message count.

The values of α and β are respectively picked in the light of the experiments of [1] and [9]. For a more detailed discussion on these parameters, we refer the reader to these two studies. Note that MV and TM are special cases of MVTM, with $\alpha = 10$ and $\beta = 0$ for MV, and $\alpha = 0$ and $\beta = 50$ for TM.

We test for five different number of processors: $K \in \{64, 128, 256, 512, 1024\}$. The partitioning experiments are conducted on an extensive set of matrices from the SuiteSparse Matrix Collection [6]. We selected the square matrices that have more than 5,000 rows/columns and nonzeros between 50,000 and 50,000,000, resulting in 964 matrices. Among these, in order to select the matrices that have high volume and/or latency overhead, we used the following two criteria considering the partitioning statistics of BL for any tested K: (i) the partitions whose maximum volume is greater than or equal to 1.5 times the average volume and (ii) the partitions whose average message count is greater than or equal to $1.3 \lg_2 K$. The first criterion aims to include the matrices that are volume bound, i.e., the matrices with more than 50% imbalance in volume when partitioned with BL. The second criterion aims to include the matrices that are latency bound. We empirically found out that the matrices having around $\lg_2 K$ number of messages per processor exhibit insignificant latency overhead. By multiplying this value with a coefficient of 1.3 we were able to filter out such matrices. Note that our aim in this work is not to show the proposed scheme is better than the other tested three schemes for *any* matrix, but for the matrices that are bound by both volume and latency, hence the motivation to the selection criteria. After filtering, there exist respectively 317, 335, 363, 374 and 373 matrices for 64, 128, 256, 512 and 1024 processors. Partitionings regarding the four schemes are performed on these sets of matrices. Parallel runtime experiments with the SpMV operation are performed on a set of 15 matrices for 64, 128, 256, and 512 processors.

The schemes are realized using the hypergraph partitioner PaToH [4] (line 8 of Algorithm 1). The parallel SpMV is realized in C using the message passing paradigm [11]. The parallel experiments are performed on a Lenovo NeXtScale supercomputer[1] that consists of 1512 nodes. A node on this system has two 18-core Intel Xeon E5-2697 Broadwell processors clocked at 2.30 GHz each with 64 GB of RAM. The network topology of this system is a fat tree.

4.2   Partitioning and Parallel Runtime Results

Table 1 presents the average values obtained by the compared schemes in terms of three different communication cost metrics for 64, 128, 256, 512 and 1024 processors. These metrics are total volume, maximum volume and total message count, which are respectively denoted in the table as "tot vol.", "max vol." and "tot msg.". Total and maximum volume are in terms of number of words. The table consists of two column groups. In the first group, the actual values obtained by the schemes are given. In the second group, the values obtained by MV, TM and MVTM are normalized with respect to those obtained by BL. Each value is the geometric mean of the values obtained for the matrices in the respective dataset.

Considering maximum volume and total message count metrics, the best values obtained in these metrics belong to MV and TM, respectively, as expected. For example for 512 processors, MV obtains an improvement of 26% in maximum volume compared to BL, while TM obtains an improvement of 24% in message

---

[1] https://www.cineca.it/en/content/marconi.

Table 1. Partition statistics of four schemes.

K	Scheme	Actual values			Normalized w.r.t. BL		
		Tot vol.	Max vol.	Tot msg.	Tot vol.	Max vol.	Tot msg.
64 (317 matrices)	BL	52331	1757	1316	–	–	–
	MV	51250	1454	1344	0.98	0.83	1.02
	TM	64242	2279	887	1.23	1.30	0.67
	MVTM	62788	1855	911	1.20	1.06	0.69
128 (335 matrices)	BL	67310	1253	3298	–	–	–
	MV	65940	991	3419	0.98	0.79	1.04
	TM	87462	1732	2219	1.30	1.38	0.67
	MVTM	85248	1342	2296	1.27	1.07	0.70
256 (363 matrices)	BL	92008	944	7556	–	–	–
	MV	90013	728	7846	0.98	0.77	1.04
	TM	122337	1379	5306	1.33	1.46	0.70
	MVTM	118801	967	5546	1.29	1.02	0.73
512 (374 matrices)	BL	129345	792	17174	–	–	–
	MV	125915	589	17869	0.97	0.74	1.04
	TM	171887	1145	13030	1.33	1.45	0.76
	MVTM	165680	733	13712	1.28	0.93	0.80
1024 (373 matrices)	BL	176058	735	35768	–	–	–
	MV	170016	518	37364	0.97	0.71	1.04
	TM	228866	1036	29073	1.30	1.41	0.81
	MVTM	217871	613	30996	1.24	0.83	0.87

count compared to BL. Since these two schemes address solely one of these metrics along with total volume, they are clear winners in those metrics. MVTM reveals itself as a tradeoff between MV and TM by ranking second among these three schemes in both metrics. In other words, its maximum volume is worse than MV but better than TM, while its total message count is worse than TM but better than MV.

Another important aspect of MVTM is that, when we compare MV, TM and MVTM in maximum volume and total message count metrics in Table 1, MVTM always appears to be the second best scheme and the difference between MVTM and the best scheme is generally smaller than the difference between MVTM and the third best scheme. For example for 256 processors, MVTM's maximum volume is 33% worse than MV's while TM's maximum volume is 89% worse than MV's, and MVTM's message count is 5% worse than TM's while MV's message count is 48% worse than TM's. For these reasons, MVTM is expected to be a better remedy compared to MV and TM for the matrices with high volume and latency overhead, which is validated by the parallel experiments given in the rest of the section.

The performances of four schemes are compared in terms of parallel SpMV runtimes for 15 matrices on 64, 128, 256 and 512 processors. These matrices and the obtained parallel runtimes are presented in Table 2. The times are in microseconds and correspond to a single SpMV operation. We only give the detailed results for 128 and 512 processors, as similar improvements are observed for 64 and 256 processors. On 128 processors, MVTM obtains the best runtimes in 11 of 15 matrices, while MV obtains the best runtimes in three matrices and TM obtains in only one. On 512 processors, MVTM obtains the best runtimes in all matrices. These results indicate that MVTM is more successful than the other three schemes in addressing volume and latency overheads.

In Table 3, we present the parallel SpMV runtime averages (geometric means) for four schemes for these 15 matrices on 64, 128, 256 and 512 processors. The first column group of the table gives the actual values obtained by the schemes while the second column group gives the normalized values of MV, TM and MVTM with respect to those of BL. In any number of processors, the best scheme is

Table 2. Detailed parallel SpMV runtimes (microseconds).

matrix	#rows/ #columns	#nonzeros	128 processors				512 processors			
			BL	MV	TM	MVTM	BL	MV	TM	MVTM
144	144,649	2,148,786	139.5	135.1	153.9	**116.8**	91.8	83.5	91.7	**79.5**
598a	110,971	1,483,868	93.8	92.6	93.7	**77.4**	77.8	67.6	58.4	**54.9**
ASIC_680ks	682,712	2,329,176	184.1	165.9	154.1	**131.8**	128.6	127.2	153.2	**106.3**
cage13	445,315	7,479,343	453.0	**413.0**	445.0	416.5	336.4	332.2	288.9	**284.7**
cfd1	70,656	1,828,364	97.1	94.0	88.8	**86.7**	65.5	60.2	60.9	**54.2**
crystk03	24,696	1,751,178	87.3	88.6	83.9	**82.6**	67.8	67.6	52.3	**50.5**
Ga19As19H42	133,123	8,884,839	484.3	437.2	**427.1**	440.8	417.4	281.0	281.4	**256.0**
gas_sensor	66,917	1,703,365	90.6	90.8	84.5	**78.5**	64.4	67.9	46.7	**44.3**
kkt_power	2,063,494	14,612,663	604.0	**582.5**	610.7	586.9	261.8	234.7	244.2	**198.9**
m14b	214,765	3,358,036	162.5	169.4	165.2	**146.0**	105.8	95.5	95.7	**74.5**
offshore	259,789	4,242,673	202.1	182.5	202.7	**178.4**	113.1	114.1	116.1	**97.4**
pre2	659,033	5,959,282	246.3	**240.3**	245.2	243.3	120.2	117.5	109.7	**91.5**
raefsky4	19,779	1,328,611	69.3	65.8	67.4	**62.8**	63.9	63.9	46.8	**44.4**
Si34H36	97,569	5,156,379	315.2	300.1	303.2	**289.2**	348.1	258.9	243.7	**212.6**
webbase-1M	1,000,005	3,105,536	248.4	271.3	210.5	**192.0**	274.0	301.1	243.1	**173.7**

Table 3. Average parallel SpMV runtimes (microseconds).

K	Actual values				Normalized w.r.t. BL		
	BL	MV	TM	MVTM	MV	TM	MVTM
64	280.1	277.2	275.7	268.8	0.99	0.98	0.96
128	185.7	179.7	178.1	163.5	0.97	0.96	0.88
256	144.9	136.6	134.8	115.9	0.94	0.93	0.80
512	134.4	124.8	115.0	99.2	0.93	0.86	0.74

MVTM, followed by TM, MV and BL. For example on 512 processors, MVTM obtains a 26% improvement over BL, while MV and TM respectively obtain 7% and 14% improvement over BL. Observe that with increasing number of processors, the improvements obtained by all schemes over BL become more pronounced. This can be attributed to the increased importance of different communication cost metrics with increasing number of processors, which implies that addressing more cost metrics leads to better parallel runtime performance.

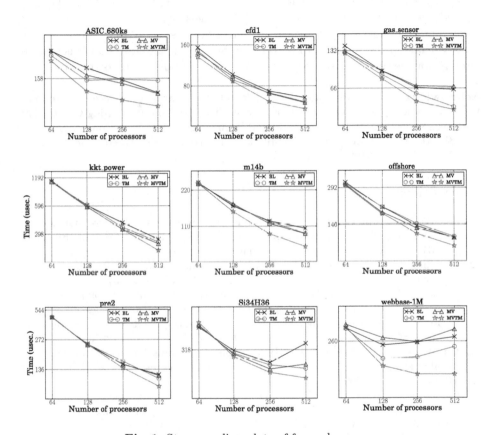

Fig. 1. Strong scaling plots of four schemes.

In Fig. 1, we plot the parallel SpMV runtimes obtained by the schemes for nine matrices. These nine matrices are a subset of the matrices given in Table 2. The x and y axes in the plots are both log-scale and respectively denote the number of processors and SpMV runtime (microseconds). As seen from these plots, MVTM scales significantly better than the other three schemes. These plots validate the claim that MVTM handles the tradeoff between volume and latency overheads better than TM and MV.

5   Conclusion

This work focused on the aspects of reducing communication bottlenecks of a key kernel, sparse matrix-vector multiplication. We argued that there exist several communication cost metrics that affect the parallel performance and proposed a model to reduce three such metrics simultaneously: total volume, maximum volume and total message count. With extensive experiments, it is shown that the proposed model strikes a better tradeoff between these volume- and latency-related cost metrics compared to the other models that address only one or two cost metrics. Realistic experiments up to 512 processors on a large-scale system showed that our model leads to better scalability and validated that it is a better remedy for the SpMV instances that are bound by both volume and latency.

Acknowledgments. We acknowledge PRACE for awarding us access to resource Marconi (Lenovo NextScale) based in Italy at CINECA Supercomputing Centre. This work was supported by The Scientific and Technological Research Council of Turkey (TUBITAK) under Grant EEEAG-114E545. This article is also based upon work from COST Action CA 15109 (COSTNET).

References

1. Acer, S., Selvitopi, O., Aykanat, C.: Improving performance of sparse matrix dense matrix multiplication on large-scale parallel systems. Parallel Comput. **59**, 71–96 (2016). Theory and Practice of Irregular Applications
2. Bisseling, R.H., Meesen, W.: Communication balancing in parallel sparse matrix-vector multiply. Electron. Trans. Numer. Anal. **21**, 47–65 (2005)
3. Boman, E.G., Devine, K.D., Rajamanickam, S.: Scalable matrix computations on large scale-free graphs using 2D graph partitioning. In: Proceedings of the International Conference on High Performance Computing, Networking, Storage and Analysis SC 2013, NY, USA, pp. 50:1–50:12. ACM, New York (2013)
4. Çatalyürek, U.V., Aykanat, C.: Hypergraph-partitioning-based decomposition for parallel sparse-matrix vector multiplication. IEEE Trans. Parallel Distrib. Syst. **10**(7), 673–693 (1999)
5. Çatalyürek, U., Aykanat, C.: A hypergraph-partitioning approach for coarse-grain decomposition. In: Proceedings of the 2001 ACM/IEEE Conference on Supercomputing SC 2001, NY, USA, pp. 28–28. ACM, New York (2001)
6. Davis, T.A., Hu, Y.: The University of Florida sparse matrix collection. ACM Trans. Math. Softw. **38**(1), 1:1–1:25 (2011)
7. Deveci, M., Kaya, K., Uçar, B., Çatalyürek, U.: Hypergraph partitioning for multiple communication cost metrics: model and methods. J. Parallel Distrib. Comput. **77**, 69–83 (2015)
8. Kumar, V.: Introduction to Parallel Computing, 2nd edn. Addison-Wesley Longman Publishing Co., Inc., Boston (2002)
9. Selvitopi, O., Acer, S., Aykanat, C.: A recursive hypergraph bipartitioning framework for reducing bandwidth and latency costs simultaneously. IEEE Trans. Parallel Distrib. Syst. **28**(2), 345–358 (2017)
10. Slota, G.M., Madduri, K., Rajamanickam, S.: PuLP: Scalable multi-objective multi-constraint partitioning for small-world networks. In: 2014 IEEE International Conference on Big Data (Big Data), pp. 481–490, October 2014

11. Uçar, B., Aykanat, C.: A library for parallel sparse matrix vector multiplies. Technical report BU-CE-0506, Bilkent University (2005)
12. Uçar, B., Aykanat, C.: Encapsulating multiple communication-cost metrics in partitioning sparse rectangular matrices for parallel matrix-vector multiplies. SIAM J. Sci. Comput. **25**(6), 1837–1859 (2004)

Improving the Network of Search Engine Services Through Application-Driven Routing

Joe Carrión[1]([⊠]), Daniel Franco[1], Veronica Gil-Costa[2], Mauricio Marin[3], and Emilio Luque[1]

[1] Computer Architecture and Operative Systems Department,
Universitat Autònoma de Barcelona, 08193 Bellaterra, Spain
`joe.carrion@caos.uab.es`, {`daniel.franco,emilio.luque`}`@uab.es`
[2] Universidad Nacional de San Luis, San Luis, Argentina
`gvcosta@unsl.edu.ar`
[3] Universidad de Santiago de Chile, Santiago, Chile
`mauricio.marin@usach.cl`

Abstract. We studied a search engine service in order to evaluate the impact of the traffic pattern on network performance. This paper focuses on how the routing algorithm can improve the query latency of a search engine. The architecture of the service includes three main components: Front Service, Cache Service and Index Service. This service receives queries from users, and after a process of seeking in a cluster, a set of results are returned to users. This workload produces unbalanced traffic throughout the network. As a result, this behavior impacts the network performance in terms of latency and throughput and increases the user timeout. This paper proposes an application-driven routing policy based on the application architecture which merges a set of criteria and prioritizes the Cache Service messages. We evaluated the performance using real traces and simulation techniques. The experiment results show a reduction of network latency and throughput when we apply the application-driven routing policy.

Keywords: Routing · Application-driven network · Search engine services

1 Introduction

Large-scale search engines can be seen as multicomponent systems whose individual design, implementation, deployment, and operation are always in constant evolution. A search engine is usually built as a collection of services deployed on a large cluster of processors, wherein each service is distributed onto a set of processors. Such services include the computation of the top-k documents, advertisement, snippet computation, etc. The processors and the communication network are expected to be constructed from commodity hardware. Message passing is performed among processors through a high speed communication network such as the Fat-tree [1].

© Springer International Publishing AG 2017
F.F. Rivera et al. (Eds.): Euro-Par 2017, LNCS 10417, pp. 638–650, 2017.
DOI: 10.1007/978-3-319-64203-1_46

In this work, we studied a Search Engine Service (SES) with a typical configuration based on three components: Front Service (FS), Cache Service (CS) and Index Service (IS). These components are deployed on a cluster of processors designed to support the query processing. To achieve an efficient SES, the deployment of the services on the cluster of processors has to consider user demand which is reflected in query traffic and the popularity of queries. The scope of this proposal improves current configurations of the network for the search engine by tuning the routing mechanism on the network devices based on the communication pattern generated by the SES.

The SES demands three basic requirements, the first one is to keep the time to solve a user query under a peak; the second one is holding a distributed workload on nodes, and finally, a balance between incoming and outgoing requests (throughput). These requirements are addressed by two approaches: application design and topology design. Application design focuses on three system components: FS, CS and IS. The components divide the workload and use algorithms to distribute the queries among the nodes. On the other hand, the network is designed taking into account the topology and the network size. The network size is computed based on the network latency and the network throughput.

In this context, we have evaluated the traffic behaviour and concluded that we can apply the same approach as CS. We know that traffic generated by FS to CS introduces new workload into the network fabric, traffic from FS to IS produces a large workload, but on the other hand traffic from CS to FS is lightweight and could potentially provide queries solved for the final user. However, the CS traffic competes with heavy traffic (FS and IS), causing CS traffic to spend time on queues among channel buffers.

We propose a routing algorithm based on the application (Application-driven routing). We analysed the software components, the traffic pattern and how this traffic impacts network performance in terms of network latency and throughput. Experiment results outperform current default settings and routing mechanisms from literature.

2   Problem Statement

The SES process users query through a FS. The user query (Q) is solved by the support of a CS or IS [8]. The FS sends the queries to the CS to check if they have been previously processed. If not, the queries are sent to the IS. The output of the system is a list of relevant documents (K) for Q. The main requirement of the SES is processing a Q in a defined period of time, time is related to the Throughput (T) of the service. T is defined by the relation between the number of K divided by number of Q.

SES is supported by a large number of resources in terms of nodes, links and network devices. The number of users submitting queries can be of thousands of Q per second. There are two main scenarios by which this problem can be addressed; first, the application design based on the architecture provided by FS, CS and IS components; and second, the network infrastructure.

We focus on the latter, but started our research with an analysis of the software architecture, after which, we studied the network infrastructure, and then analyzed in detail the communication pattern generated for a specific configuration of the system, in terms of network size, topology and mapping. We analyzed the impact of the traffic on network performance in order to propose a better network configuration with an alternative routing algorithm.

3   Search Engine Service Architecture

The workload is distributed among the FS, CS and IS. The FS that handles submitted user queries by routing them to the appropriate service, it also manages the delivery of final results (K) to the user. The CS implements a partitioned distributed cache storing previously computed results for the most popular queries. And the IS, holds an index of the document collection and it is responsible of delivering partial results to FS. To reduce query response times and increase throughput of Q, most services are implemented as arrays of P × D processing nodes, where P is the level of partitioning and D is the level of replication of each service partition. These services are deployed on clusters of computers and its processing nodes are allocated in racks connected via network switches.

Each query is received by the FS, which redirects it towards the CS (as status *new*). The CS then checks whether the same query has already been solved and if its results (document IDs) are stored in the service. The CS answers to FS with either a cache hit or a cache failure (query status *hit* or *no_hit*). In the latter, the FS sends the query to the IS (as *new for IS*), which proceeds to compute the top-K results of the query and sends them back to the FS (as status *done*). The IS performs a ranking operation with the documents to retrieve the most relevant document for the query. We show a basic overview in Fig. 1(a)

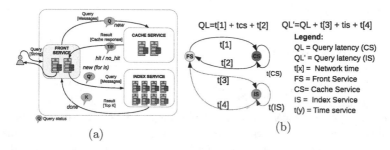

Fig. 1. (a) Overview of query flows through SES. (b) Scenarios to compute the QL

The architecture is described in detail in [6,7,9]. It uses partitioning and redundancy schemes to improve the performance of the SES in terms of Q response time. The sets of nodes are created based on the network addressing, and they are installed on different racks, we call them Point of Delivery (POD).

FS, CS and IS instances are mapped among POD using a technique based on performance. Figure 2(a) shows a scheme of the mapping, each POD includes instances of FS, CS and IS. Figure 2(b) depicts a sample of the interconnection scheme using the Fat-tree topology with 16 nodes. This scheme causes some Q be solved by nodes located in the same rack or nodes located in different racks.

The nodes are grouped in different segments of a network addressing and a set of racks. The nodes support instances of the FS, CS and IS according to the number of nodes and topology capacity.

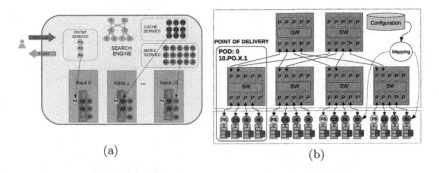

(a)   (b)

Fig. 2. Overview of SES infrastructure and mapping.

3.1 SES Network Architecture

The architecture and the network addressing are based on [1]. The network configuration used is a Fat-tree topology, with $k \times n$. The switches are arranged in n levels (Level 0 to $n-1$). FS, CS and IS are deployed over the nodes according with a defined configuration. The configuration has been computed based on benchmarks and experiments with real workload in order to compute the number of FS, CS and IS nodes. For instance in Fig. 2(b) we show a sample of a topology and configuration with sixteen nodes, four POD, four FS, four CS and eight IS.

4 Performance Evaluation of SES

This section focuses on evaluation of the current system in order to identify the main challenges in terms of network performance. A performance evaluation in terms of software architecture is out of the scope of this paper.

First, we describe the configuration used for this research. Table 1 summarizes the traces used to analyze the network performance. This analysis uses a two real trace files for two networks. We use simulation techniques and a modified version of Booksim simulator published in [8].

Table 1. Summary of settings for a SES using two set of parameters

Parameter	Trace A	Trace B
Front service (nodes)	12	40
Cache service (nodes)	3	20
Index service (nodes)	100	180
Network topology	3-level Fat-tree	3-level Fat-tree
Qty of core switches	16	25
Qty of aggregation switches	32	50
Qty of edge switches	32	50
Qty of pods	8	10
Qty of nodes per pod	16	25
Max. nodes capacity	128	250
Qty (current) hosts	115	240

4.1   Traffic Pattern

Each node contacts a delimited set of the services. For instance, a CS node submits messages to FS nodes, and a IS node submits messages only to FS nodes. Using the Flow-traffic conditions of the SES described in Fig. 1(a), the set of couples is deterministic. The tendency reduces the set of couples and creates an unbalanced traffic. On the one hand, if there are unused resources the network could be reduced. On the other hand, there are buffers overloaded producing bottlenecks.

4.2   Performance SES

This section describes the performance of the SES based on the query latency (QL). The QL is defined by the time needed to solve Q. The are two main scenarios; the first one is a Q solved by the CS (which we call Cached queries); and the second one, Q is solved by the IS (which we call Indexed queries). QL is defined by the arriving time to the CS plus the time to be processed by the CS and the time to return to the FS. In the second scenario, the QL is increased by time required to reach to the IS plus the processing time in the IS and the time required to return to FS. Figure 1(b) summarizes both scenarios.

The mapping used to deploy the instances of services on each nodes impacts upon network latency, because some queries are solved by nodes located in the same network device (switch), or some queries are solved by nodes located in different switches in the same rack. Additionally, some queries are solved by a node connected to another rack. Figure 3(a) depicts how the queries are solved based on the location of the instances of FS, CS and IS. This context allow us to classify the queries by the number of switches the queries need to pass through. The trace produces three kind of queries. Queries solved by 1, 2 or 5 switches.

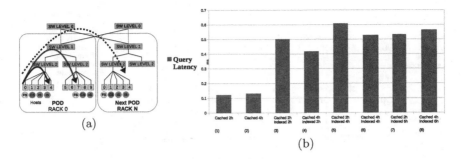

Fig. 3. QL comparison by hops (h)

It is possible that Indexed queries have passed by the three Cached queries scenarios. In this case we have twelve scenarios in total.

The configuration we are evaluating produces eight scenarios. Figure 3(b) shows the QL on axis Y and on axis X the eight scenarios in brackets. We see that scenario (1) and (2) reach the lowest QL and they are Cached Queries, then we conclude that the number of hops (2h and 4h) does not impact the QL. However, scenarios (3) to (8) show that QL increases considerably for Indexed Queries. Also, the best QL for Indexed Queries is achieved with two hops (scenarios 3 and 4). Finally, the worst QL are scenarios (5) and (8).

5 Previous Work

Interconnection networks studies related to adapting the resources on demand go back until Active Network Research proposed in [10]. Studies like [4] describe how application traffic pattern has an impact on network status. Adaptive routing algorithms aim to make decisions based on network status. For instance, [5] introduced Distributed Routing Balancing (DRB), which adapt the resources by creating new paths between nodes and reducing the path-length. The output is a balanced message distribution. In [3], PR-DRB (Predictive DRB) extends DRB to real applications by monitoring the best paths and storing them to make routing decisions based on alternative paths.

The authors in [2] described an application pattern analysis of SES and the behaviour on buffer channels was depicted. In addition, the traffic was compared with synthetic traffic based on mathematical models to highlight the importance of conducting a research based on the application traffic pattern.

6 Application-Driven Routing Policy

Based on the analysis presented in previous sections, we present a routing policy called Application-Driven Routing (ADR), which allocates network resources based on application profile. This routing algorithm has been designed and tuned

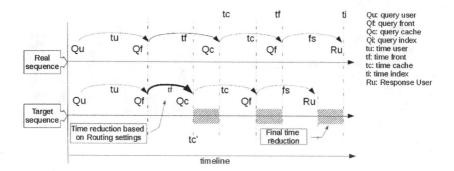

Fig. 4. Query processing sequence scheme. Real sequence with default settings and target sequence with network settings based on application

to process a specific application, i.e. SES, then we call it Search Engine - Application Driven Routing (SE-ADR). However, the QL depends on the time to process the query on nodes plus the network performance. This paper focuses on the network, and we show in Fig. 4 a scheme of this approach. There is a real sequence of query processing. We propose to improve the network performance in order to reduce the QL.

6.1   Criteria Based on Application

The architecture of SES defines two main flows. We call traffic between FS and CS workload of CS (W_{cs}). The traffic between FS and IS is Workload W_{is}. Cached queries need less time than Indexed queries, thereby while IS processes the queries, there is time to process Cached queries. We propose a fair policy to balance network resources by prioritizing the W_{cs}.

We propose to distinguish the traffic between Primary traffic (W_{cs}) and Secondary traffic (W_{is}) based on the software architecture and we introduce this criteria on network settings. Next criterion is to balance the traffic among channels and the path length that queries need for being solved. This idea is based on network topology. Figure 5(a) summarizes the idea to introduce a model of routing algorithm based on application traffic.

The workload generated by IS is very high compared to CS workload. However, traffic generated by CS is potentially output for users. If we process more CS traffic we improve the throughput of the SES. The time needed to solve an Indexed query is higher compared to Cached query. Then we allocate network resources with high priority for Cached queries; and we penalize the Indexed queries without impacting the time to process them. With this context, we analyze the buffer occupancy in order to balance the traffic and we submit the Primary traffic to less used buffers. Default network settings produce CS spends time waiting for a channel while it is used by IS traffic. The initial scenario shows that traffic FS only competes with itself, later CS competes with high workload produced by FS. Figure 5(b) shows this idea. This paper proposes a policy to

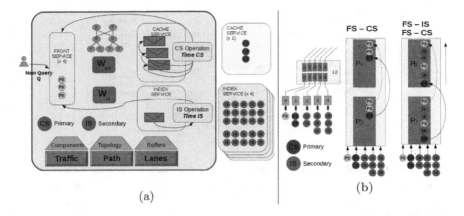

(a)

(b)

Fig. 5. (a) Model to define an application-driven routing algorithm. Primary traffic is based on application and network architecture. Balancing approach is based on fair network allocation. (b) Default buffer occupancy scheme.

move CS traffic with priority to the less used buffer. As you can see in Fig. 5, in a period of time, messages from nodes go inside the switch (L2) through ports 0 to 4. However, as new traffic arrives, the buffers are shared by traffic from FS, CS and IS. In this case CS has to wait for messages from FS or IS, then it is necessary too distinguish the traffic based on SES requirements and to move the CS toward buffers with lower occupancy.

6.2 Criteria Based on Network Architecture

Currently the routing algorithm applied in real system is based on a Two-Level Routing Table proposed by [1]. This algorithm scales when network size increases, and it avoids the network cost increasing. The current technology allows increase the number of channels and bandwidth. The links provided by the current network are misused and they allow us to use alternative paths. We take advantage of them to balance the workload among different channels.

6.3 Criteria Based on Traffic

We propose a routing policy based on prioritizing the Primary traffic by monitoring the buffer occupancy. Figure 6 shows the routing policy model. Three main components are introduced into the routing policy. The first one is a Buffer occupancy monitor (BOM), the second one is a Deep Packet Inspection (DPI) mechanism and finally a Decision Maker (DM). BOM monitors the buffer occupancy. DPI checks if a packet belongs to a specific service. The DM based on information of BOM and DPI redirects the traffic by allocating output channels. Packets belonging to Primary traffic are redirected to output ports with less BO. This approach allows us to allocate network resources proportionally to service demand. The workload is distributed toward less-used network areas.

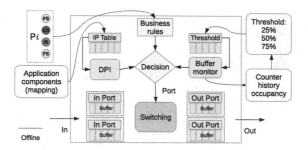

Fig. 6. Routing policy components based on application for SES.

7   Evaluation

This research uses trace log files generated by a SES and a mapping file. The data for the experimentation corresponds to trace files used by authors of [6] and it was obtained by Yahoo Search Engine in 2005. The mapping file defines the topology, network size and the host distribution among the racks. The trace file is the workload generated by the users and the messages between the nodes. We analyze the latency and throughput of the network.

7.1   Experimental Environment

We use simulation techniques to process as entry the *trace file* (tf) and *mapping file* (mf). We compute the QL and the throughput based on the trace. The *mf* includes one line per host, the POD where the host is located, the instance (FS, CS, IS) installed in the host and a flag R for replica or NR for none-replica and finally the IP of the replica. The *tf* includes a query identifier, timestamp of the host, the operation executed by the host, a flag to recognize the processing time, sender, receiver, switch, message size and processing time on host.

We parsed *tf* and *mp* to generate the topology to be loaded into the simulator. This simulator has been modified to process the *tf* and simulate the query injection into the network. The simulator processes the trace without the real time (timestamp) column, because we are simulating the query processing instead of the real time; after, real time is replaced by simulation time. The simulator generates a *Trace File Simulated* (tfs) for future review.

7.2   Results

Based on literature, the topology supports different routing approaches; currently a routing policy is used based on tables (deterministic routing). However, the network supports channel redundancy, therefore it is possible to use different paths to reach the destination (adaptive routing). Finally, we can distribute the traffic among channels to balance the workload.

We compared SE-ADR with three routing modeles compared on scheme on Fig. 7. A deterministic routing algorithm which provides the shortest path (minimum path: min), an adaptive algorithm which chooses different paths with a round robin criteria (diversity path: div), and finally we balance the workload monitoring the buffer occupancy (balanced routing bal). SE-ADR adds a new tier to this stack by dividing the workload based on the application.

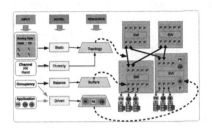

Fig. 7. Current routing models to manage the traffic.

On Fig. 8(a) we show the network latency obtained by the four routing algorithms. On axis X we show the traffic injected to the network. The current settings provided by static routing (min) are outperformed by others. The best latency reached by DIV, BAL and SE-ADR methods belongs to the interval from 15% to 35% of the network capacity. And from 20% to 30% we can see that SE-ADR slightly outperforms other mechanisms in a light way, for this interval, on average, SE-ADR outperforms BAL by 7%.

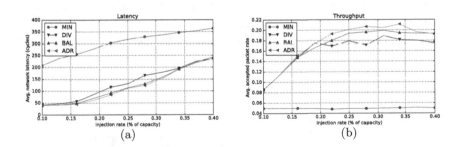

Fig. 8. Latency and throughput comparison with 115 nodes.

The network throughput is shown in Fig. 8(b). The injection rate does not have impact using routing static (min) because it always uses the same path and the workload is not distributed uniformly to the channels. When the network works at less than 17% of its capacity, methods DIV, BAL and SE-ADR do not impact the throughput because they produce the same accepted traffic. But when the network workload is over 18% of its capacity, the accepted traffic decreases, and then it is necessary to apply a different routing algorithm. When the network works from 20% to 38% of its capacity, SE-ADR provides the best performance. The increase reaches 15% over other methods.

In order to evaluate the performance when the size of the network increases, we applied the routing algorithm with Trace B from Table 1. The results for network with 240 host show that, the network latency grow up as injection rate increases, as you can see in Fig. 9(a). Therefore we concentrate on throughput to define an interval with the best throughput. Figure 9(b) shows that from 20% to 30%, the proposed method SE-ADR provides the higher value. On average the gain provided by SE-ADR is around 5% against BAL. However regarding the latency, the SE-ADR outperforms BAL on an average 15%.

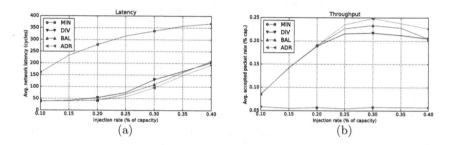

Fig. 9. Latency and throughput comparison with 240 nodes.

Figure 10 shows the real QL and the simulated QL. We achieve in the simulation a QL of 35.8 ms. against 34.8 ms. in the real trace, which indicates a 97.1% of accuracy. Now we get almost the same QL using different routing algorithms, however we plan to explore different configurations of the SES properties, such as mapping, topology or network size in order to take advantage of the better latency and throughput of the network.

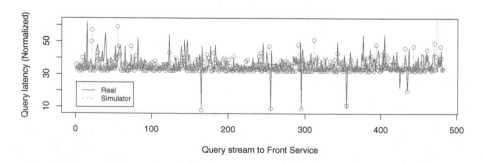

Fig. 10. Sequence of input using a sample of 480 queries.

8   Conclusions

In this paper we presented a routing algorithm to improve the network performance of a datacenter supporting a Search Engine Service. We based our method around an analysis of the service architecture, the topology and mapping and the application pattern; we balance the workload based on traffic generated by CS. Experiments using real traces show that our method outperforms the current configuration of the system and we improve methods based on literature. Our method reaches a reduction of latency for an interval of network capacity. Finally, we increase the throughput for an interval of network capacity. Future work will be focused on balancing the network capacity and the cost while the network reaches its best performance in terms of users query.

Acknowledgments. This research has been supported by the MINECO Spain under contract TIN2014-53172-P. SENESCYT (Secretaría Nacional de Educación Superior, Ciencia, Tecnología e Innovación) under contract 2013-AR7L335. The authors would like to thank to Centro de Biotecnología y Bioinformática under Basal Project.

References

1. Al-Fares, M., Loukissas, A., Vahdat, A.: A scalable, commodity data center network architecture. In: ACM SIGCOMM Computer Communication Review, vol. 38, pp. 63–74. ACM (2008)
2. Carrión, J., Franco, D., Luque, E.: Application aware routing policy based on application pattern traffic. In: Proceedings of the International Conference on Parallel and Distributed Processing Techniques and Applications (PDPTA), p. 142. The Steering Committee of The World Congress in Computer Science, Computer Engineering and Applied Computing (WorldComp) (2015)
3. Castillo, C.N., Lugones, D., Franco, D., Luque, E., Collier, M.: Predictive and distributed routing balancing, an application-aware approach. Procedia Comput. Sci. **18**, 179–188 (2013)
4. Dally, W.J., Towles, B.P.: Principles and practices of interconnection networks. Elsevier, Amsterdam (2004)
5. Franco, D., Garces, I., Luque, E.: A new method to make communication latency uniform: distributed routing balancing. In: Proceedings of the 13th international conference on Supercomputing, pp. 210–219. ACM (1999)
6. Gil-Costa, V., Lobos, J., Inostrosa-Psijas, A., Marin, M.: Capacity planning for vertical search engines: an approach based on coloured petri nets. In: Haddad, S., Pomello, L. (eds.) PETRI NETS 2012. LNCS, vol. 7347, pp. 288–307. Springer, Heidelberg (2012). doi:10.1007/978-3-642-31131-4_16
7. Inostrosa-Psijas, A., Wainer, G., Gil-Costa, V., Marin, M.: DEVS modeling of large scale web search engines. In: 2014 Winter Simulation Conference (WSC), pp. 3060–3071. IEEE (2014)
8. Jiang, N., Balfour, J., Becker, D.U., Towles, B., Dally, W.J., Michelogiannakis, G., Kim, J.: A detailed and flexible cycle-accurate network-on-chip simulator. In: 2013 IEEE International Symposium on Performance Analysis of Systems and Software (ISPASS), pp. 86–96. IEEE (2013)

9. Marin, M., Gil-Costa, V.: Simulating search engines. Comput. Sci. Eng. **1**, 1–1 (2017)
10. Tennenhouse, D.L., Smith, J.M., Sincoskie, W.D., Wetherall, D.J., Minden, G.J.: A survey of active network research. IEEE Commun. Mag. **35**(1), 80–86 (1997)

Parallel Numerical Methods and Applications

Accelerating the Tucker Decomposition with Compressed Sparse Tensors

Shaden Smith[(✉)] and George Karypis

University of Minnesota, Minneapolis, USA
{shaden,karypis}@cs.umn.edu

Abstract. The Tucker decomposition is a higher-order analogue of the singular value decomposition and is a popular method of performing analysis on multi-way data (*tensors*). Computing the Tucker decomposition of a sparse tensor is demanding in terms of both memory and computational resources. The primary kernel of the factorization is a chain of tensor-matrix multiplications (TTMc). State-of-the-art algorithms accelerate the underlying computations by trading off memory to memoize the intermediate results of TTMc in order to reuse them across iterations. We present an algorithm based on a compressed data structure for sparse tensors and show that many computational redundancies during TTMc can be identified and pruned without the memory overheads of memoization. In addition, our algorithm can further reduce the number of operations by exploiting an additional amount of user-specified memory. We evaluate our algorithm on a collection of real-world and synthetic datasets and demonstrate up to 20.7× speedup while using 28.5× less memory than the state-of-the-art parallel algorithm.

1 Introduction

Tensors, which are the generalization of matrices to higher orders, are a natural way of representing multi-way data (i.e., data which features variables interacting in more than two dimensions). Tensors occupy three or more dimensions (called *modes*) which can represent multi-way interactions between variables. *Tensor factorization* is a technique for enabling structure discovery on multi-way data. The objective of tensor factorization is to model the potentially high-dimensional data in a low rank form that captures the key multi-way interactions found in the data. Tensor factorization is used extensively in areas such as anomaly detection [9], healthcare [29], recommender systems [20], and web search [28]. Common traits among all of these applications are the high dimensionality and extreme level of sparsity of the data.

Tensor factorization takes several forms, with the two most popular being the canonical polyadic decomposition (CPD) and the Tucker decomposition [14]. The CPD has been extensively studied by the HPC community in recent years [12,13,26]. However, the Tucker decomposition, which is computationally more challenging than the CPD, has received relatively less attention. Computing the Tucker decomposition of a sparse tensor is challenging in terms of

© Springer International Publishing AG 2017
F.F. Rivera et al. (Eds.): Euro-Par 2017, LNCS 10417, pp. 653–668, 2017.
DOI: 10.1007/978-3-319-64203-1_47

both time and space. At its core is a tensor-times-matrix chain (TTMc), which multiplies a sparse tensor by dense matrices aligned to all but one of its modes.

Existing strategies for performing TTMc either rely on memoizing intermediate results to save computation [2,11] or operating in a memory-efficient manner at the expense of additional floating-point operations (FLOPs) [15]. The memory overhead of memoization is closely tied to the dimensionality and the sparsity pattern of the tensor, and can result in significant memory overhead. Meanwhile, the memory-efficient strategies require orders of magnitude more computation and are often impractical for large and sparse tensors.

We restructure the underlying computations in order to remove two forms of redundant computations that occur during TTMc. We present an algorithm for performing TTMc with a sparse tensor that is often as computationally efficient as memoized algorithms, while requiring a negligible amount of additional intermediate memory. Our algorithm relies on the recently-developed data structure for tensors called compressed sparse fiber (CSF) [22]. The CSF data structure provides a view of the tensor's sparsity structure that makes these redundancies possible to exploit. Furthermore, we show that an additional, user-specified amount of memory can be used to further reduce computational costs by constructing additional views of the tensor. Our contributions include:

1. A parallel algorithm for TTMc which is memory-efficient while being computationally competitive to the state-of-the-art.
2. An analysis of the TTMc algorithm and demonstration of its potential for asymptotic improvement.
3. A strategy for leveraging multiple compressed tensor representations to further reduce the number of required operations.
4. An experimental evaluation against the state-of-the-art parallel algorithms across a variety of real-world datasets.
5. Integration of our source code into SPLATT [23], an open source library for sparse tensor factorization.

The rest of the paper is organized as follows. Section 2 provides an overview of tensors and tensor factorization. Section 3 reviews related work on TTMc. Section 4 presents and analyzes our algorithm for performing TTMc operations that leverage the sparse tensor representation. Section 5 discusses the benefits of using multiple views of the tensor data and provides a heuristic algorithm for selecting advantageous views. Section 6 presents experimental results. Lastly, Sect. 7 offers concluding remarks.

2   Preliminaries

2.1   Notation

Matrices are denoted using bold letters ($\mathbf{A}$) and tensors using bold calligraphic letters ($\boldsymbol{\mathcal{X}}$). Tensors have N modes with lengths $I_1, \ldots, I_N$, respectively. We denote the number of non-zeros in a tensor as nnz($\boldsymbol{\mathcal{X}}$). Entries in matrices and

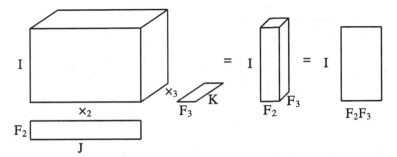

Fig. 1. TTMc with an $I \times J \times K$ tensor. The result is a dense tensor $\mathcal{Y} \in \mathbb{R}^{I \times F_2 \times F_3}$, which can conceptually be unfolded to $\mathbf{Y}_{(1)} \in \mathbb{R}^{I \times F_2 F_3}$.

tensors are denoted $\mathbf{A}(i, j)$ and $\mathcal{X}(i_1, \ldots, i_N)$, respectively. A colon in the place of an index takes the place of all non-zero entries. For example, $\mathcal{X}(i, j, :, \ldots, :)$ is the set of all non-zeros in $\mathcal{X}$ whose first two indices are (i, j). Similarly, $\mathbf{A}(i, :)$ is the ith row of $\mathbf{A}$. A *fiber* is the generalization of a row or column and is the result of holding all but one index constant (e.g., $\mathcal{X}(i_1, \ldots, i_{N-1}, :)$ or $\mathcal{X}(:, i_2, \ldots, i_N)$).

2.2 Tensor and Matrix Operators

Unfolding. Tensors can be "unfolded" along a mode to form a matrix. Unfolding is accomplished by forming columns from the fibers that run along the desired mode. For example, a mode-1 unfolding is denoted $\mathbf{X}_{(1)}$ and has dimension $I_1 \times \prod_{j=2}^{N} I_j$.

Kronecker Product. The Kronecker product (KP) of $\mathbf{A} \in \mathbb{R}^{m \times n}$ and $\mathbf{B} \in \mathbb{R}^{p \times q}$, denoted $\mathbf{A} \otimes \mathbf{B}$, is an $mp \times nq$ matrix and defined as

$$\mathbf{A} \otimes \mathbf{B} = \begin{bmatrix} \mathbf{A}(1,1)\mathbf{B} & \ldots & \mathbf{A}(1,n)\mathbf{B} \\ \vdots & \ddots & \vdots \\ \mathbf{A}(m,1)\mathbf{B} & \ldots & \mathbf{A}(m,n)\mathbf{B} \end{bmatrix}.$$

The KP is a generalization of the vector outer product. Throughout our discussion, we will work in terms of KPs but refer to visualizations of outer products. They are the same operations, but outer products better visualize growth in dimensionality.

Tensor-Matrix Product. The tensor-matrix product, or *n-mode product* [14], multiplies a tensor by a matrix along the nth mode. Suppose $\mathbf{B}$ is an $F \times I_n$ matrix. The tensor-matrix product for the nth mode, denoted $\mathcal{X} \times_n \mathbf{B}$, emits a tensor with dimensions $I_1 \times \ldots \times I_{n-1} \times F \times I_{n+1} \times \ldots \times I_N$. Elementwise,

$$(\mathcal{X} \times_n \mathbf{B})(i_1, \ldots, i_{n-1}, f, i_{n+1}, \ldots, i_N) = \sum_{i_n=1}^{I_n} \mathcal{X}(i_1, \ldots, i_N)\mathbf{B}(f, i_n).$$

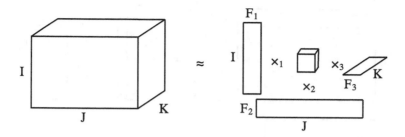

Fig. 2. A rank-$\{F_1, F_2, F_3\}$ Tucker factorization of an $I \times J \times K$ tensor.

Note that the resulting mode-n fibers are generally dense regardless of the sparsity pattern of $\mathcal{X}$.

A common task is to multiply a tensor by a set of matrices. This operation is called the tensor-times-matrix chain (TTMc). When multiplication is performed with all N modes, we write $\mathcal{X} \times \{\mathbf{A}\}$, where $\{\mathbf{A}\}$ is the set of N matrices. More commonly, one wishes to multiply with all modes but one. We write this operation as $\mathcal{X} \times_{-n} \{\mathbf{B}\}$, where n is the mode left unmultiplied:

$$\mathcal{X} \times_{-n} \{\mathbf{B}\} = \mathcal{X} \times_1 \mathbf{B}^{(1)} \times_2 \cdots \times_{n-1} \mathbf{B}^{(n-1)} \times_{n+1} \mathbf{B}^{(n+1)} \times_{n+2} \cdots \times_N \mathbf{B}^{(N)}.$$

This case is the focus of this work, and we will refer to solely it as TTMc for the remaining discussions. TTMc for $n = 1$ is illustrated in Fig. 1. Due to the increasingly dense output of each n-mode product, the size of the intermediate results during TTMc can greatly exceed the size of the inputs or output. This is referred to as the *intermediate blowup problem* [15].

2.3   Tucker Decomposition

Illustrated in Fig. 2, the objective of the Tucker decomposition is to model a tensor $\mathcal{X}$ with a set of orthonormal matrices $\mathbf{A}^{(1)} \in \mathbb{R}^{I_1 \times F_1}, \ldots, \mathbf{A}^{(N)} \in \mathbb{R}^{I_N \times F_N}$ and a core tensor, $\mathcal{G} \in \mathbb{R}^{F_1 \times \cdots \times F_N}$. The orthonormal matrices are referred to as *factor matrices*. The resulting optimization problem is non-convex:

$$\begin{aligned} \underset{\{\mathbf{A}\}, \mathcal{G}}{\text{minimize}} \quad & \tfrac{1}{2} \|\mathcal{X} - \mathcal{G} \times \{\mathbf{A}\}\|_F^2 \\ \text{subject to} \quad & \mathbf{A}^{(n)T} \mathbf{A}^{(n)} = \mathbf{I} \qquad n = 1, \ldots, N. \end{aligned}$$

Several optimization algorithms have been developed to compute the Tucker decomposition, including the higher-order SVD (HOSVD) [7] and higher-order orthogonal iterations (HOOI) [8]. HOSVD is popular for decomposing dense tensors and efficient parallel algorithms have been developed [1,5]. However, the computation becomes progressively more dense during HOSVD and it is not often applied to sparse computations. Thus, HOOI is the most popular algorithm for sparse tensors and is the focus of this work. HOOI is an iterative

Algorithm 1. Tucker Decomposition with HOOI

```
1: while 𝒢 not converged do
2:     for n = 1, . . . , N do
3:         𝒴 ← 𝒳 ×_{-n} {A^T}
4:         A^{(n)} ← F_n leading left singular vectors of Y_{(n)}
5:     end for
6:     𝒢 ← 𝒴 ×_N A^{(N)T}
7: end while
```

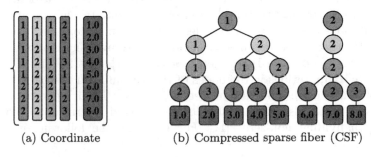

(a) Coordinate   (b) Compressed sparse fiber (CSF)

Fig. 3. Two encodings of a $2 \times 2 \times 2 \times 3$ tensor with 5 non-zeros.

algorithm which cyclically updates each factor matrix until convergence. Algorithm 1 details the steps in computing the factor matrices and core tensor using HOOI. TTMc (Line 3) is the dominant computation during each update.

Most applications involving sparse tensors are not interested in an exact model of a tensor, but instead a low-rank factorization. Therefore, in this work we focus on the case when $\max(F_1, \ldots, F_N) \ll \max(I_1, \ldots, I_N)$.

2.4 Data Structures for Sparse Tensors

The most prevalent data structure for representing sparse tensors is *coordinate format*. Each non-zero is encoded as a tuple of indices and a non-zero value (Fig. 3a). *Dimension trees* are flexible data structures which partition the modes of a tensor in a hierarchical fashion [10]. An important configuration arranges the tensor modes into a binary tree with N leaves [11]. A special case of the dimension tree is the linear arrangement of modes equivalent to coordinate format.

In previous work, we proposed a compressed data structure for sparse tensors called *compressed sparse fiber* (CSF) [22,26]. CSF can be viewed as a generalization of compressed sparse row, a popular storage format for sparse matrices. Shown in Fig. 3b, CSF stores the sparsity pattern as a forest of I_1 trees, each with N levels. Each path from a root to a leaf node encodes a non-zero. The nnz($\mathcal{X}$) leaf nodes store the final index in the non-zero's coordinate and are also accompanied by the non-zero value.

3 Related Work

Li et al. developed parallel algorithms for performing a single TTM kernel for both dense [16] and sparse [17] tensors.

Memory-Efficient Tucker [15] avoids memory blowup by selectively computing columns or elements of $\mathbf{Y}_{(n)}$ at a time. Intermediate memory costs are minimized at the expense of additional FLOPs and passes over the tensor structure.

Baskaran et al. [2] observed that partial computations can be reused across
TTMc kernels. Consider updating the first two factors of a four-mode tensor.
Each TTMc kernel constructs the partial computation $\boldsymbol{\mathcal{X}} \times_3 \mathbf{A}^{(3)T} \times_4 \mathbf{A}^{(4)T}$,
despite its value not changing between kernels. Baskaran et al. introduced mem-
oization to TTMc by partitioning the tensor modes into two halves, and reusing
the computations from one half to accelerate the computations in the other half.
Kaya and Uçar extended this memoization strategy by using binary dimension
trees to accelerate both the Tucker decomposition [11] and CPD [13]. They store
intermediate computations in the nodes of the tree and can effectively limit the
number of individual n-mode products to $\log(N)$ per TTMc operation.

Kaya and Uçar also showed that one can avoid intermediate blowup by
processing individual non-zeros [11]. For example, the following is used for
mode-1:

$$\mathbf{Y}_{(1)}(i_1,:) \leftarrow \mathbf{Y}_{(1)}(i_1,:) + \boldsymbol{\mathcal{X}}(i_1,\ldots,i_N) \left[\mathbf{A}^{(2)}(i_2,:) \otimes \cdots \otimes \mathbf{A}^{(N)}(i_N,:) \right]. \quad (1)$$

A row of $\mathbf{Y}_{(1)}$ is the only memory required to process a non-zero. The computational complexity of using (1) to perform one TTMc kernel via streaming
through each non-zero is

$$\mathrm{nnz}(\boldsymbol{\mathcal{X}}) \underbrace{\sum_{i=2}^{N} \prod_{j=2}^{i} F_j}_{\text{KP construction}} + \mathrm{nnz}(\boldsymbol{\mathcal{X}}) \underbrace{2 \prod_{j=2}^{N} F_j}_{\text{accumulation}} = \mathcal{O}\left(\mathrm{nnz}(\boldsymbol{\mathcal{X}}) \prod_{j=2}^{N} F_j \right). \quad (2)$$

4   TTMc with a Compressed Sparse Tensor

We now detail our operation- and memory-efficient parallel algorithm for TTMc.
We first perform a reformulation of the underlying computations in order to
remove redundancies and then describe a parallel algorithm which uses CSF to
exploit these redundancies. We then analyze the computational complexity of
our algorithm.

4.1   Formulation

We work from (1) which processes individual non-zeros. There are two forms of
arithmetic redundancies that we eliminate during TTMc:

Distributive Kronecker Products. Consider two adjacent non-zeros in a three-
mode tensor. Performing a TTMc operation for the first mode results in the
following computations:

$$\mathbf{Y}_{(1)}(i,:) \leftarrow \mathbf{Y}_{(1)}(i,:) + \boldsymbol{\mathcal{X}}(i,j,k_1) \left[\mathbf{A}^{(2)}(j,:) \otimes \mathbf{A}^{(3)}(k_1,:) \right], \quad (3a)$$

$$\mathbf{Y}_{(1)}(i,:) \leftarrow \mathbf{Y}_{(1)}(i,:) + \boldsymbol{\mathcal{X}}(i,j,k_2) \left[\mathbf{A}^{(2)}(j,:) \otimes \mathbf{A}^{(3)}(k_2,:) \right]. \quad (3b)$$

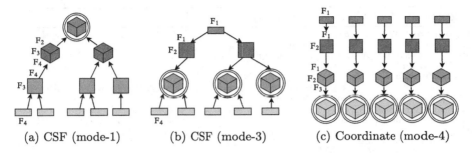

(a) CSF (mode-1)   (b) CSF (mode-3)   (c) Coordinate (mode-4)

Fig. 4. TTMc with CSF and coordinate data structures. The number of FLOPs performed on a node is equal to its volume. Circled nodes produce updates to the output.

The KP is a distributive operation, and so we combine (3a) and (3b) to eliminate a KP and reach a more efficient update:

$$\mathbf{Y}_{(1)}(i,:) \leftarrow \mathbf{Y}_{(1)}(i,:) + \mathbf{A}^{(2)}(j,:) \otimes \left[\boldsymbol{\mathcal{X}}(i,j,k_1)\mathbf{A}^{(3)}(k_1,:) + \boldsymbol{\mathcal{X}}(i,j,k_2)\mathbf{A}^{(3)}(k_2,:) \right].$$

This can be exploited for any set of non-zeros that reside in the same fiber. For each fiber, we accumulate all of the linear combinations of rows of $\mathbf{A}^{(3)}$ into a row vector, followed by a single KP. This eliminates the construction and accumulation of $\mathrm{nnz}(\boldsymbol{\mathcal{X}}(i,j,:))-1$ KPs, resulting in a reduction of $2F_2F_3(\mathrm{nnz}(\boldsymbol{\mathcal{X}}(i,j,:))-1)$ FLOPs. This strategy generalizes to any number of modes:

$$\mathbf{Y}_{(1)} \leftarrow \sum_{\boldsymbol{\mathcal{X}}(i_1,:,\ldots,:)} \mathbf{A}^{(2)}(i_2,:) \otimes \left(\sum_{\boldsymbol{\mathcal{X}}(i_1,i_2,:,\ldots,:)} \mathbf{A}^{(3)}(i_3,:) \otimes \ldots \left(\sum_{\boldsymbol{\mathcal{X}}(i_1,\ldots,i_{N-1},:)} \boldsymbol{\mathcal{X}}(i_1,\ldots,i_N)\mathbf{A}^{(N)}(i_N,:) \right) \right).$$

Redundant Kronecker Products. Consider the case of performing mode-3 TTMc:

$$\mathbf{Y}_{(3)}(k_1,:) \leftarrow \mathbf{Y}_{(3)}(k_1,:) + \boldsymbol{\mathcal{X}}(i,j,k_1)\left[\mathbf{A}^{(1)}(i,:) \otimes \mathbf{A}^{(2)}(j,:) \right],$$
$$\mathbf{Y}_{(3)}(k_2,:) \leftarrow \mathbf{Y}_{(3)}(k_2,:) + \boldsymbol{\mathcal{X}}(i,j,k_2)\left[\mathbf{A}^{(1)}(i,:) \otimes \mathbf{A}^{(2)}(j,:) \right].$$

Note that $[\mathbf{A}^{(1)}(i,:) \otimes \mathbf{A}^{(2)}(j,:)]$ appears in the processing of both non-zeros. We eliminate operations by reusing the KP for both non-zeros. Reusing the shared KP for an entire fiber saves $F_1F_2(\mathrm{nnz}(\boldsymbol{\mathcal{X}}(i,j,:))-1)$ FLOPs. As before, this process can be generalized to any number of tensor modes.

Operation-Efficient Algorithm. Using the two previous optimizations, we can devise an algorithm which uses the CSF data structure to eliminate redundant operations. A branch in the tree structure at the ith level represents a set of non-zeros which overlap in the previous $i-1$ indices, which is precisely the scenario that the previous optimizations target. Our TTMc algorithm is described in Algorithm 2 and illustrated in Fig. 4. Intuitively, partial computations begin at

Algorithm 2. TTMc with a CSF Tensor (Fig. 4).

```
 1: function TTMC(𝒳, mode)
 2:     for i₁ = 1, …, I_N in parallel do
 3:         CONSTRUCT(𝒳(i₁, :, …, :), mode, 1)
 4:     end for
 5: end function
 6:                                    ▷ Construct Kronecker products and push them down to level mode−1.
 7: function CONSTRUCT(node, mode, above)
 8:     d ← level(node)                        ▷ The level in the tree (i.e., distance from the root).
 9:     i_d ← node_id(node)                    ▷ The partial coordinate of a non-zero (Fig. 3).
10:
11:     if d < mode then
12:         above ← above ⊗ A^(d)(i_d, :)
13:         for c ∈ children(node) do
14:             CONSTRUCT(c, mode, above)
15:         end for
16:
17:     else if d = mode then
18:         below ← ∑_{c∈children(node)} ACCUMULATE(c)
19:         Lock mutex i_d.
20:         Y_(d)(i_d, :) ← Y_(d)(i_d, :) + (above ⊗ below)                    ▷ Update Y_(d).
21:         Unlock mutex i_d.
22:     end if
23: end function
24:                                    ▷ Pull Kronecker products up from the leaf nodes.
25: function ACCUMULATE(node)
26:     i_d ← node_id(node)
27:     if level(node) = N then
28:         return 𝒳(i₁, …, i_d) · A^(N)(i_d, :)
29:     else
30:         return A^(d)(i_d, :) ⊗ ∑_{c∈children(node)} ACCUMULATE(c)
31:     end if
32: end function
```

the root and leaf levels of the tree and grow inward towards the level representing the mode of computation. Algorithm 2 avoids intermediate memory blowup by processing the tree depth-first, which limits the intermediate memory to a single row of $\mathbf{Y}_{(n)}$.

Parallelism. Algorithm 2 is parallelized by distributing the I_1 trees to threads. Each thread performs a depth-first traversal, and thus the thread-local storage overhead is asymptotically limited to a single row of $\mathbf{Y}_{(n)}$. A consequence of this distribution is the potential for write conflicts when updating any modes other than the first. This can be observed in Fig. 3, in which node IDs are only unique within the root-level nodes. The same synchronization challenges are present while computing the CPD, which was the first application of the CSF data structure. We present synchronization using mutexes for simplicity, but note that the algorithm can benefit from other mechanisms such as tiling [22] or transactional memory [25].

4.2 Complexity Analysis

We now analyze the computational complexity of Algorithm 2. Let nodes(i) be the number of nodes present in the ith level of a CSF structure (by convention, the 1st level is the root level). The number of FLOPs required to perform TTMc for the nth mode is $\sum_{i=1}^{N} \text{nodes}(i) \times \text{cost}(i, n)$, where "cost" is defined as

$$\text{cost}(i, n) = \begin{cases} \prod_{j=1}^{i-1} F_j & \text{if } i < n, \\ 2 \prod_{j=i}^{N} F_j & \text{if } i > n, \\ 2 \prod_{\substack{j=1 \\ j \neq i}}^{N} F_j & \text{if } i = n. \end{cases} \tag{4}$$

Intuitively, the cost of a node above level-n is the cost of constructing a KP, and the cost at or below level-n is the cost of constructing *and* accumulating a KP.

When computing for the leaf mode of the tensor, Algorithm 2 assembles KPs and pushes them down the tree from root to leaves. The complexity grows with each level of the tree, with the final level having the same asymptotic complexity as (2). At the other extreme, when $n = 1$, the computation moves upwards from leaves to root. Interestingly, the dimensionality of the KPs is non-decreasing, and at the same time the number of nodes in each level is non-increasing. In the worst case, non-zeros have no overlapping indices and the algorithm is equivalent to operating with a tensor stored in coordinate format. However, lower complexities are possible under some assumptions on the CSF structure and the ranks of the factorization. To see, compare the costs of levels i and $i-1$:

$$\frac{\text{nodes}(i) \times 2 \prod_{j=i}^{N} F_j}{\text{nodes}(i-1) \times 2 \prod_{j=i-1}^{N} F_j} = \frac{\text{nodes}(i)}{\text{nodes}(i-1) F_{i-1}}.$$

Suppose that the cost of the ith mode always exceeds mode $i-1$:

$$\text{nodes}(i) > \text{nodes}(i-1) F_{i-1}, \qquad i = 2, \ldots, N$$

then the Nth mode dominates the computation, arriving at a reduced complexity of $\mathcal{O}(\text{nodes}(N) F_N) = \mathcal{O}(\text{nnz}(\boldsymbol{\mathcal{X}}) F_N)$.

5   Utilizing Additional CSF Representations

Section 4.2 showed that Algorithm 2 has the potential for an asymptotic speedup over the competing memory-efficient approaches. This depends on the costs of the lower levels of the tree dominating those at the top, which is possible if: (i) the branching factor at each level is larger than the corresponding rank; and (ii) the mode on which we are operating is found at or near the top of the tree. Fortunately, CSF places no restriction on the ordering of modes. Indeed, constructing a unique CSF representation for each mode of the tensor was used in other kernels to expose parallelism [26] and to reduce communication costs [24].

Table 1. Summary of datasets.

Dataset	Modes	Non-zeros	Dimensions
NELL-2 [4]	3	77M	12K, 9K, 29K
Netflix [3]	3	100M	480K, 18K, 2K
Enron [19]	4	54M	6K, 6K, 244K, 1K
Alzheimer [27]	5	6.27M	5, 1K, 156, 1K, 396
Poisson3D, Poisson4D [6]	3,4	100M	3K, ..., 3K

K and **M** stand for thousand and million, respectively.

We construct multiple CSF representations in order to minimize the required number of operations. Utilizing multiple CSF representations allows computations to occur near the roots of the tree structures while also favoring mode orderings which result in large branching factors.

There are $N!$ possible orderings of the tensor modes. To evaluate the cost of a representation, we must sort the non-zeros in order to inspect the tree structure and count the number of nodes. Thus, an exhaustive search is impractical for even small values of N. We begin from an existing heuristic: sort the modes by their lengths, with the shortest mode placed at the top level [26]. The intuition behind this heuristic is that ordering shorter modes prior to longer ones discovers indices with high levels of overlap, resulting in a large branching factor.

Suppose there is memory available for up to K representations of the tensor data, denoted $\mathcal{X}_1, \ldots, \mathcal{X}_K$. We select $\mathcal{X}_1$ by sorting the modes as previously discussed. The remaining $K-1$ representations are selected in a greedy fashion: at step k, use (4) to examine the costs associated with TTMc for each mode when provided with $\mathcal{X}_1, \ldots, \mathcal{X}_{k-1}$. The mode with the highest cost is placed at the top level of $\mathcal{X}_k$, and the remaining modes are sorted by increasing length. At the end of this procedure, each mode has the choice of K representations to use for TTMc computation. We assign each mode to the representation with the lowest cost, and use that representation for TTMc. Importantly, if ties are broken in a consistent manner, then it happens in practice that several modes can be assigned to the same $\mathcal{X}_k$, meaning that fewer than K representations need be kept in memory for computation. This is later demonstrated in Sect. 6.2.

6 Experimental Methodology and Results

6.1 Experimental Setup

Experiments are conducted on the Mesabi supercomputer at the Minnesota Supercomputing Institute. Compute nodes have two twelve-core Intel Haswell E5-2680v3 processors and 256 GB of RAM. Our source code is written in C and parallelized with OpenMP. All source code is configured to use double-precision floating point numbers and 32-bit integers. We compile with the Intel compiler version 16.0.3 and Intel MKL for BLAS/LAPACK routines. We bind threads to cores via KMP_AFFINITY=granularity=fine,compact,1.

Reported runtimes are the arithmetic mean of twenty iterations. We measure only the time spent on TTMc, as that is the focus of this study and the remaining computational steps do not differ between the implementations. Reported times and speedups are based on performing all of the required computations for TTMc over a full HOOI iteration. Measuring a full HOOI iteration instead of individual kernels allows us to compare memoized and non-memoized algorithms.

We compare against two algorithms implemented in the C++ library Hyper-Tensor [11], the state-of-the-art parallel software for the Tucker decomposition. HyperTensor uses MPI for distributed-memory parallelism and OpenMP for shared-memory parallelism. The efficient distributed-memory algorithm used by HyperTensor combines the communication steps associated with the TTMc and the following truncated SVD, preventing us from measuring the runtime corresponding to only TTMc. Thus, we run HyperTensor with one MPI rank and twenty-four OpenMP threads. We denote the two algorithms as HT-FLAT, which is a direct implementation of (1), and HT-BTREE, which uses memoization via binary dimension trees.

Datasets. Table 1 provides an overview of the datasets used in our evaluation. NELL-2 is from the Never Ending Language Learning project [4] and its modes represent *entities*, *relations*, and *entities*. Netflix [3] is constructed from movie ratings and has modes representing *users*, *movies*, and *dates*. Enron [19] is parsed from an email corpus spanning three years. Its non-zero values are word frequency and its modes represent *senders*, *receivers*, *words*, and *dates*. Alzheimer is constructed from public gene expression data related to Alzheimer's disease, provided by MSigDB [27]. Its values are binary and its five modes represent cell type, drug, binned dosage, gene, and binned amplitudes. Poisson is a set of synthetically-generated tensors whose values follow a Poisson distribution. We generated tensors following the method of Chi and Kolda [6] with three and four modes of length 3000 and 100-million non-zeros. All tensors except Netflix and Alzheimer are freely available as part of the FROSTT collection [21].

6.2   Results

Operation Efficiency. Figure 5 shows the number of FLOPs required to perform TTMc. HT-FLAT (coordinate format) is used as a baseline because a CSF tensor will match its complexity if it achieves no compression.

A single CSF representation (CSF-1) reduces computational costs by 59% − 83% compared to the baseline. Interestingly, CSF-1 is nearly identical in cost to the memoized HT-BTREE algorithm on the three-mode datasets. This is due to the limited amount of memoization possible for a three-mode tensor: one TTMc is computed at full cost and is used to optimize the remaining two operations. This matches the limitation of CSF-1, in which the leaf-level mode must still be computed at full cost. Optimizing for the leaf mode by using CSF-2 is sufficient to achieve the best-possible FLOP performance on all three-mode tensors.

Both HT-BTREE and the CSF variants improve over HT-FLAT as the number of modes increase, because additional tensor modes bring additional TTMc

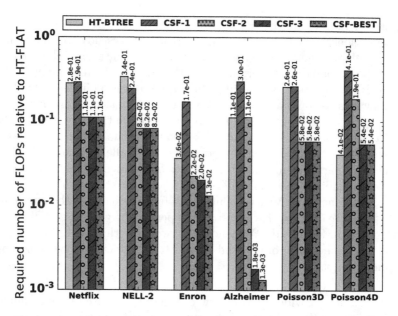

Fig. 5. The number of required FLOPs for rank-20 TTMc on all modes, relative to HT-FLAT (i.e., coordinate form). **CSF-X** is the solution found using X CSF representations. No dataset utilized more than three CSF representations. **CSF-BEST** is the optimal configuration using multiple CSF representations, found by exhaustive search.

operations which can be optimized. The benefits of CSF are most apparent on the five-mode `Alzheimer` tensor, in which the greedily-selected CSF-A requires $555\times$ fewer FLOPs than HT-FLAT and $61\times$ fewer FLOPs than HT-BTREE.

Observe that HT-BTREE is more operation-efficient than CSF-based methods on the synthetic `Poisson4D` tensor. The number of $\mathcal{X}(i_1, i_2, :, \ldots, :)$ sub-tensors is 88% of the total number of non-zeros, meaning that the redundancies that CSF exploits do not exist in the lower levels of the tree.

Parallel Scalability. Figure 6 shows speedup as we scale from 1 to 24 cores. We include results for CSF-A which dedicates a CSF representation for each mode of the tensor, despite fewer representations being sufficient in terms of FLOP efficiency. CSF-A allows us to measure performance without fine-grained synchronization overheads because there are no race conditions to consider when the output mode is located at the root level of the tree.

Synchronization overheads prevent CSF-1 from scaling beyond one CPU socket, whereas additional CSF representations achieve near-linear scaling. The cost of synchronization dominates when computing for the bottom levels of the CSF structure: there are more nodes present in the tree (i.e., more synchronizations) and also the amount of work performed during synchronizations exponentially increases.

All methods exhibit poor scalability on the `Alzheimer` tensor. This is attributed to its unusually short dimensions; the presented methods parallelize

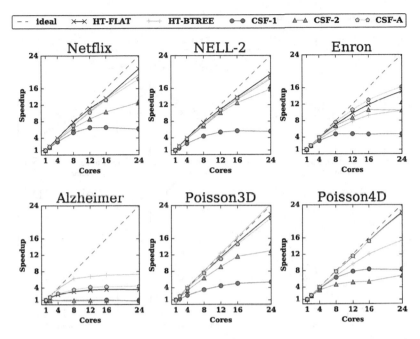

Fig. 6. Parallel speedup for rank-20 TTMc. **CSF-A** denotes dedicating one CSF representation for each mode of the tensor.

over the outer dimensions of the tensor and thus have idle threads when the outer dimension is small. This limitation has also been observed in other tensor kernels [18], and has been remedied via alternative parallel decompositions [2,25]. Exploring these alternative decompositions is left to future work.

Runtime and Memory Trade-Offs. Figure 7 shows the memory costs and average runtime for TTMc. We measure memory consumption via instrumented source code which tracks the storage used for the tensor structure, thread-local storage, and memoization. We omit the storage dedicated to the factor matrices and output because they are the same between methods.

Despite CSF-A not providing additional computational savings, we can see that it always achieves the best runtime across all datasets and algorithms. This is expected due to its lack of synchronization overheads and structured writes to memory. CSF-A ranges from 1.5× − 20.7× faster than HT-BTREE, and also uses less memory for four of the six datasets. We note that while `Poisson4D` is the only tensor for which memoization achieves a better operation reduction than the CSF variants, but CSF-A is 1.5× faster in runtime.

We can see the benefit of supporting a flexible number of CSF representations. CSF-1 is always the most space-efficient, while CSF-A is always the fastest algorithm. CSF-2 provides a reasonable trade-off when time and space are both limited by dedicating a special CSF representation to the most expensive mode which will also exhibit the highest synchronization costs.

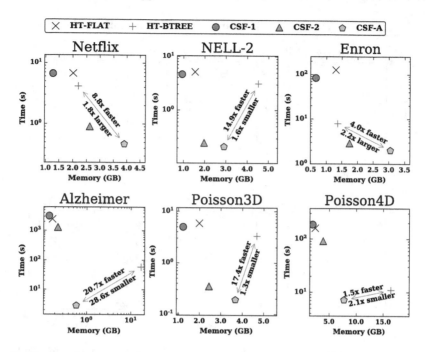

Fig. 7. Time and space trade-offs for rank-20 TTMc on 24 cores. **Time** is the mean number of seconds spent on TTMc during a full iteration of HOOI. **Memory** is the storage required for the tensor memoization, and structures for parallelism.

7   Conclusions and Future Work

A sparse tensor-times-matrix chain (TTMc) is the key computational kernel when computing the Tucker decomposition, which is an important technique for analyzing sparse tensors. We presented a formulation, complexity analysis, and performance evaluation for performing sparse TTMc with a compressed data structure (CSF). We showed that our formulation is both memory-efficient and can be asymptotically faster than competing methods. Our performance evaluation demonstrated up to 20× speedup over the state-of-the-art while at the same time using 28× less memory on a real-world dataset. This effectively reduces the time-to-solution from several hours to a few minutes on a workstation.

Furthermore, we presented a method of tuning the trade-off between the time and memory footprint of the computation. Users can have either the fastest execution, the smallest memory footprint, or in-between the two extremes.

There are several topics of future work. One major advantage of multiple CSF representations is the enhanced scalability via eliminated mutexes. Other CSF algorithms have had success with techniques such as tiling [22,25] or transactional memory [25], and we will investigate their benefits on TTMc. Alternative parallel decompositions (such as tiling) are also expected to improve parallel scalability on tensors such as `Alzheimer`, which presented difficulties for all methods. Lastly, our cost model could be improved by considering synchronization costs.

Acknowledgments. The authors would like to thank Oguz Kaya for sharing the HyperTensor source code, Muthu Baskaran for providing the `Alzheimer` tensor, Jee W. Choi for providing the synthetic tensor generator, and anonymous reviewers for their valuable feedback. This work was supported in part by NSF (IIS-0905220, OCI-1048018, CNS-1162405, IIS-1247632, IIP-1414153, IIS-1447788), Army Research Office (W911NF-14-1-0316), a University of Minnesota Doctoral Dissertation Fellowship, Intel Software and Services Group, and the Digital Technology Center at the University of Minnesota. Access to research and computing facilities was provided by the Digital Technology Center and the Minnesota Supercomputing Institute.

References

1. Austin, W., Ballard, G., Kolda, T.G.: Parallel tensor compression for large-scale scientific data. In: International Parallel and Distributed Processing Symposium (IPDPS'17), pp. 912–922. IEEE (2016)
2. Baskaran, M., Meister, B., Vasilache, N., Lethin, R.: Efficient and scalable computations with sparse tensors. In: 2012 IEEE Conference on High Performance Extreme Computing (HPEC), pp. 1–6. IEEE (2012)
3. Bennett, J., Lanning, S.: The netflix prize. In: Proceedings of KDD cup and workshop, vol. 2007, p. 35 (2007)
4. Carlson, A., Betteridge, J., Kisiel, B., Settles, B., Hruschka, E.R., Mitchell, T.M.: Toward an architecture for never-ending language learning. In: In AAAI (2010)
5. Chakaravarthy, V.T., Choi, J.W., Joseph, D.J., Liu, X., Murali, P., Sabharwal, Y., Sreedhar, D.: On optimizing distributed tucker decomposition for dense tensors. In: 31st IEEE International Parallel and Distributed Processing Symposium (IPDPS 2017) (2017)
6. Chi, E.C., Kolda, T.G.: On tensors, sparsity, and nonnegative factorizations. SIAM J. Matrix Anal. Appl. **33**(4), 1272–1299 (2012)
7. De Lathauwer, L., De Moor, B., Vandewalle, J.: A multilinear singular value decomposition. SIAM J. Matrix Anal. Appl. **21**(4), 1253–1278 (2000a)
8. De Lathauwer, L., De Moor, B., Vandewalle, J.: On the best rank-1 and rank-(r 1, r 2,., rn) approximation of higher-order tensors. SIAM J. Matrix Anal. Appl. **21**(4), 1324–1342 (2000b)
9. Fanaee-T, H., Gama, J.: Tensor-based anomaly detection: an interdisciplinary survey. Knowl.-Based Syst. **98**, 130–147 (2016)
10. Grasedyck, L.: Hierarchical singular value decomposition of tensors. SIAM J. Matrix Anal. Appl. **31**(4), 2029–2054 (2010)
11. Kaya, O., Uçar, B.: High-performance parallel algorithms for the tucker decomposition of higher order sparse tensors. Technical report (2015a)
12. Kaya, O., Uçar, B.: Scalable sparse tensor decompositions in distributed memory systems. In: Proceedings of the International Conference for High Performance Computing, Networking, Storage and Analysis, p. 77. ACM (2015b)
13. Kaya, O., Uçar, B.: Parallel CP decomposition of sparse tensors using dimension trees. Research report RR-8976, Inria - Research Centre Grenoble - Rhône-Alpes, November 2016

14. Kolda, T.G., Bader, B.W.: Tensor decompositions and applications. SIAM Rev. **51**(3), 455–500 (2009)
15. Kolda, T.G., Sun, J.: Scalable tensor decompositions for multi-aspect data mining. In: 2008 Eighth IEEE International Conference on Data Mining, ICDM 2008, pp. 363–372. IEEE (2008)
16. Li, J., Battaglino, C., Perros, I., Sun, J., Vuduc, R.: An input-adaptive and in-place approach to dense tensor-times-matrix multiply. In: Proceedings of the International Conference for High Performance Computing, Networking, Storage and Analysis, p. 76. ACM (2015)
17. Li, J., Ma, Y., Yan, C., Vuduc, R.: Optimizing sparse tensor times matrix on multi-core and many-core architectures. In: Proceedings of the Sixth Workshop on Irregular Applications: Architectures and Algorithms, pp. 26–33. IEEE Press (2016)
18. Rolinger, T.B., Simon, T.A., Krieger, C.D.: Performance evaluation of parallel sparse tensor decomposition implementations. In: Proceedings of the 6th Workshop on Irregular Applications: Architectures and Algorithms. IEEE (2016)
19. Shetty, J., Adibi, J.: The enron email dataset database schema and brief statistical report. Information Sciences Institute Technical report 4, University of Southern California (2004)
20. Shi, Y., Karatzoglou, A., Baltrunas, L., Larson, M., Hanjalic, A., Oliver, N.: TFMAP: optimizing MAP for top-n context-aware recommendation. In: Proceedings of the 35th international ACM SIGIR Conference on Research and Development in Information Retrieval, pp. 155–164. ACM (2012)
21. Smith, S., Choi, J.W., Li, J., Vuduc, R., Park, J., Liu, X., Karypis, G.: FROSTT: the formidable repository of open sparse tensors and tools (2017a). http://frostt.io/
22. Smith, S., Karypis, G.: Tensor-matrix products with a compressed sparse tensor. In: 5th Workshop on Irregular Applications: Architectures and Algorithms (2015)
23. Smith, S., Karypis, G.: SPLATT: The Surprisingly ParalleL spArse Tensor Toolkit (2016). http://cs.umn.edu/splatt/
24. Smith, S., Park, J., Karypis, G.: An exploration of optimization algorithms for high performance tensor completion. In: Proceedings of the 2016 ACM/IEEE conference on Supercomputing (2016)
25. Smith, S., Park, J., Karypis, G.: Sparse tensor factorization on many-core processors with high-bandwidth memory. In: 31st IEEE International Parallel & Distributed Processing Symposium (IPDPS 2017) (2017b)
26. Smith, S., Ravindran, N., Sidiropoulos, N.D., Karypis, G.: SPLATT: efficient and parallel sparse tensor-matrix multiplication. In: International Parallel and Distributed Processing Symposium (IPDPS 2015) (2015)
27. Subramanian, A., Tamayo, P., Mootha, V.K., Mukherjee, S., Ebert, B.L., Gillette, M.A., Paulovich, A., Pomeroy, S.L., Golub, T.R., Lander, E.S., et al.: Gene set enrichment analysis: a knowledge-based approach for interpreting genome-wide expression profiles. Proc. Nat. Acad. Sci. **102**(43), 15545–15550 (2005)
28. Sun, J.T., Zeng, H.J., Liu, H., Lu, Y., Chen, Z.: Cubesvd: a novel approach to personalized web search. In: Proceedings of the 14th International Conference on World Wide Web, pp. 382–390. ACM (2005)
29. Wang, Y., Chen, R., Ghosh, J., Denny, J.C., Kho, A., Chen, Y., Malin, B.A., Sun, J.: Rubik: knowledge guided tensor factorization and completion for health data analytics. In: Proceedings of the 21th ACM SIGKDD International Conference on Knowledge Discovery and Data Mining, pp. 1265–1274. ACM (2015)

Shared Memory Pipelined Parareal

Daniel Ruprecht[1,2(✉)]

[1] School of Mechanical Engineering, Leeds LS2 9JT, UK
d.ruprecht@leeds.ac.uk
[2] Institute of Computational Science, Università della Svizzera italiana,
Via Giuseppe Buffi 13, 6900 Lugano, Switzerland

Abstract. For the parallel-in-time integration method Parareal, pipelining can be used to hide some of the cost of the serial correction step and improve its efficiency. The paper introduces a basic OpenMP implementation of pipelined Parareal and compares it to a standard MPI-based variant. Both versions yield almost identical runtimes, but, depending on the compiler, the OpenMP variant consumes about 7% less energy and has a significantly smaller memory footprint. However, its higher implementation complexity might make it difficult to use in legacy codes and in combination with spatial parallelisation.

Keywords: Parareal · Parallel-in-time integration · Pipelining · OpenMP

1 Introduction

Computational science faces a variety of challenges stemming from the massive increase in parallelism in state-of-the-art high-performance computing systems. One important requirement is the development of new and inherently parallel numerical methods. Parallel-in-time integration has been identified as a promising direction of research for the parallelisation of the solution of initial value problems [6].

Probably the most widely studied and used parallel-in-time method is Parareal [13], but see Gander's overview for a discussion of a variety of other methods [7]. Parareal iterates between an expensive fine integrator run in parallel and a cheap coarse method which runs in serial and propagates corrections forward in time. While the unavoidable serial part limits parallel efficiency according to Amdahl's law, some of its cost can be hidden by using a so-called *pipelined* implementation [2,14]. Pipelining reduces the effective cost of the serial correction step in Parareal and therefore improves speedup. Even more optimisation is possible by using an event-based approach [5], but this requires a suitable execution framework that is not available on all machines.

Pipelining happens automatically when implementing Parareal in MPI but it is not straightforward in OpenMP and so far no shared memory version of Parareal with pipelining has been described. Previous studies almost exclusively

© Springer International Publishing AG 2017
F.F. Rivera et al. (Eds.): Euro-Par 2017, LNCS 10417, pp. 669–681, 2017.
DOI: 10.1007/978-3-319-64203-1_48

used MPI to implement Parareal and the very few using OpenMP considered only the non-pipelined version [11]. However, using shared memory can have advantages, since it avoids e.g. the need to allocate buffers for message passing. The disadvantage is that naturally OpenMP is limited to a shared memory unit. Since convergence of Parareal tends to deteriorate if too many parallel time slices are computed [8] and given the trend to "fat" compute nodes with large numbers of cores, shared memory Parareal might nevertheless be an attractive choice. It could be useful, e.g., for simulations of power grids and other applications where comparatively small systems of differential(-algebraic) equations have to be solved faster than real-time [12]. This paper introduces an OpenMP-based version of pipelined Parareal and compares it to a standard MPI-based implementation. It relies on standard features like parallelised loops, following a fork-join paradigm, while leaving the investigation of more recent OpenMP features providing task-base parallelism [3] for future work.

2   The Parareal Parallel-in-Time Integration Method

The starting point for Parareal is an initial value problem

$$\dot{\mathbf{q}} = \mathbf{f}(\mathbf{q}(t), t), \ \mathbf{q}(0) = \mathbf{q}_0, \ t \in [0, T], \tag{1}$$

which, in the numerical example below, arises from the spatial discretisation of a PDE ("method-of-lines") with $\mathbf{q} \in \mathbb{R}^{N_{\text{dof}}}$ being a vector containing all degrees-of-freedom. Let $\mathcal{F}_{\delta t}$ denote a numerical procedure for the approximate solution of (1), for example a Runge-Kutta method. Denote further by $\mathbf{q} = \mathcal{F}_{\delta t}(\tilde{\mathbf{q}}, t_2, t_1)$ the result of approximately integrating (1) forward in time from some starting value $\tilde{\mathbf{q}}$ at a time t_1 to a time $t_2 > t_1$ using $\mathcal{F}_{\delta t}$.

To parallelise the numerical integration of (1), decompose $[0, T]$ into time-slices $[t_p, t_{p+1}]$, $p = 0, \ldots, P - 1$ where P is the number of cores, equal to the number of processes (MPI) or threads (OpenMP). For simplicity, assume here that all time slices have the same length and that the whole interval $[0, T]$ is covered with a single set of time slices so that no restarting or "sliding window" is required [17].

Parareal needs a second time integrator denoted $\mathcal{G}_{\Delta t}$, which has to be cheap to compute but can be much less accurate (commonly referred to as the "coarse propagator"). It begins with a prediction step, computing rough guesses of the starting value $\mathbf{q}_p^0$ for each time slice by running the coarse method once. Here, subscript p indicates an approximation of the solution at time t_p. It then computes the iteration

$$\mathbf{q}_{p+1}^k = \mathcal{G}_{\Delta t}(\mathbf{q}_p^k, t_{p+1}, t_p) + \mathcal{F}_{\delta t}(\mathbf{q}_p^{k-1}, t_{p+1}, t_p) - \mathcal{G}_{\Delta t}(\mathbf{q}_p^{k-1}, t_{p+1}, t_p) \tag{2}$$

concurrently on each time slice for $p = 0, \ldots, P - 1$, $k = 1, \ldots, K$. Because the computationally expensive evaluation of the fine propagator can be parallelised across time slices, iteration (2) can run in less wall clock time than running $\mathcal{F}_{\delta t}$ serially – provided the coarse method is cheap enough and the number of required iterations K is small.

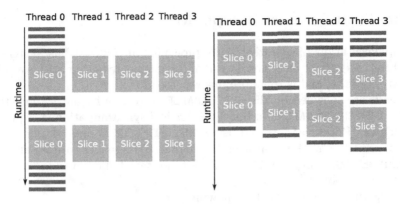

Fig. 1. Execution diagram for Parareal without (left) and with (right) pipelining. Red blocks correspond to c_f, the time needed to run the fine integrator $\mathcal{F}_{\delta t}$ over one time slice $[t_p, t_{p+1}]$ while blue blocks correspond to c_c, the time required by the coarse method $\mathcal{G}_{\Delta t}$. Pipelining allows to hide some of the cost of the coarse method. While it comes naturally when using MPI to implement Parareal (there, Thread would refer to a Process), using simple loop-based parallelism with OpenMP results in the non-pipelined version shown on the left. (Color figure online)

The expected performance of Parareal can be described by a simple theoretical model [14]. Denote by c_c the cost of integrating over one time slice using $\mathcal{G}_{\Delta t}$ and by c_f the cost when using $\mathcal{F}_{\delta t}$. Because all time slices are assumed to consist of the same number of steps and an explicit method is used here, it can be assumed that c_f and c_c are identical for all time slices. Neglecting overhead, speedup of Parareal using K iterations against running the fine method in serial is approximately

$$s_{np}(P) = \frac{Pc_f}{(1+K)Pc_c + Kc_f} = \frac{1}{(1+K)\frac{c_c}{c_f} + \frac{K}{P}}. \tag{3}$$

It is possible to hide some of the cost of the coarse propagator and the name *pipelining* has been coined for this approach [14]. Figure 1 sketches the execution diagrams of both a non-pipelined (left) and pipelined (right) implementation for four time slices. As can be seen, pipelining reduces the effective cost of the coarse correction step in each iteration from $P \times c_c$ to c_c – but note that the initial prediction step still has cost $P \times c_c$ as before. For pipelined Parareal, estimate (3) changes to

$$s_p(P) = \frac{Pc_f}{Pc_c + Kc_c + Kc_f} = \frac{1}{\left(1 + \frac{K}{P}\right)\frac{c_c}{c_f} + \frac{K}{P}}. \tag{4}$$

Because $K/P \ll K$, the pipelined version allows for better speedup, that is $s_{np}(P) \leq s_p(P)$. However, because pipelining only hides cost from the coarse integrator, the effect is smaller when the coarse method is very cheap and $c_c/c_s \ll 1$. In that case, the term K/P dominates the estimate which is not affected by pipelining.

3   Pipelined Parareal in OpenMP

The implementation of Parareal with pipelining in OpenMP is sketched in
Algorithm 1. A description of how Parareal is implemented using MPI is available
in the literature [1] and is therefore not repeated here.

Threads are spawned by the OMP PARALLEL directive in line 1.2 and terminated by OMP END PARALLEL in line 1.37. Manual synchronisation is required so
that P OpenMP locks are created using OMP_INIT_LOCK in line 1.4, one for each
thread. During the fine integrator and update step, these locks are set and unset
using OMP_SET_LOCK and OMP_UNSET_LOCK to protect buffers during writes and
avoid race conditions.

The algorithm consists of the following parts:

- **Prediction step:** lines 1.5–1.13. Each thread is computing its own coarse
  prediction of its starting value $\mathbf{q}_p^0$ in a parallelised loop. The coarse value
  $\mathcal{G}_{\Delta t}(\mathbf{q}_p^0, t_{p+1}, t_p)$ is also computed and stored for use in the first iteration.
  The later the time slice (indicated by a higher thread number p), the more
  steps the thread must compute and thus the larger its workload (cf. Fig. 1).
  Therefore, at the end of the coarse prediction loop, the NOWAIT clause is
  required to avoid implicit synchronisation and enable pipelining.
- **Parareal iteration:** lines 1.14–1.36. Here, both the fine integrator and
  update step are performed inside a single loop over all time slices, parallelised by OMP DO directives. Because parts of the loop (the update step) have
  to be executed in serialised order, the ORDERERD directive has to be used in
  line 1.15. Again, to avoid implicit synchronisation at the end of the loop, the
  NOWAIT clause is required in line 1.35.
  - **Fine integrator:** lines 1.17–1.20. Before the fine integrator is executed,
    an OMP_LOCK is set to indicate that the thread will start writing into buffer
    $q(p)$. Because thread $p-1$ accesses this buffer in its update step, locks
    are necessary to prevent race conditions and incorrect solutions. After the
    lock is set, the thread proceeds with the computation of $\mathcal{F}_{\delta t}(\mathbf{q}_p^k, t_{p+1}, t_p)$
    and computation of the difference δq between coarse and fine value. Then,
    since $q(p)$ is now up to date and δq ready, the lock can be released.
  - **Update step:** lines 1.21–1.33. The update step has to be performed in
    proper order, from first to last time slice. Therefore, it is enclosed in
    ORDERED directives, indicating that this part of the loop is to be executed
    in serial order. Then, as in the two other versions, the update step is
    initialised with $\mathbf{q}_0^{k+1} = \mathbf{q}_0$. For every time slice, the coarse value of the
    updated initial guess is computed and the update performed. The updated
    end value is written into buffer $q(p+1)$ to serve as the new starting value
    for the following time slice. However, to prevent thread p from writing
    into $q(p+1)$ while thread $p+1$ is still running the fine integrator, thread
    p sets OMP_LOCK number $p+1$ while performing the update.

Algorithm 1: Parareal with pipelining using OpenMP

---

    input: Initial value q_0; number of iterations K

1.1 $q(0) \leftarrow q_0$

1.2 OMP PARALLEL

1.3 $P = \text{OMP\_GET\_MAX\_THREADS}()$

1.4 OMP_INIT_LOCK(P)

1.5 OMP DO

1.6 **for** $p = 0, P - 1$ **do**

1.7 $q(p) \leftarrow q(0)$

1.8   **if** *Thread not first* **then**

1.9 $q(p) \leftarrow \mathcal{G}(q(p), t_p, 0)$

1.10   **end**

1.11 $g_c(p) \leftarrow \mathcal{G}(q(p), t_{p+1}, t_p)$

1.12 **end**

1.13 OMP END DO NOWAIT

1.14 **for** $k = 1, K$ **do**

1.15   OMP DO ORDERED

1.16   **for** $p = 0, P - 1$ **do**

1.17   OMP_SET_LOCK(p)

1.18 $q(p) \leftarrow \mathcal{F}_{\delta t}(q(p), t_{p+1}, t_p)$

1.19 $\delta q(p) \leftarrow q(p) - q_c(p)$

1.20   OMP_UNSET_LOCK(p)

1.21   OMP ORDERED

1.22   **if** *Thread is first* **then**

1.23   OMP_SET_LOCK(0)

1.24 $q(0) \leftarrow q_0$

1.25   OMP_UNSET_LOCK(0)

1.26   **end**

1.27 $q_c(p) \leftarrow \mathcal{G}_{\Delta t}(q(p), t_{p+1}, t_p)$

1.28   **if** *Thread not last* **then**

1.29   OMP_SET_LOCK(p+1)

1.30 $q(p + 1) \leftarrow q_c(p) + \delta q(p)$

1.31   OMP UNSET LOCK(p+1)

1.32   **end**

1.33   OMP END ORDERED

1.34   **end**

1.35   OMP END DO NOWAIT

1.36 **end**

1.37 OMP END PARALLEL

The implementation described here computes a fixed number of iterations K. While useful for testing, this is not necessarily optimal since it will perform iterations even on time slices that have already converged. A simple optimisation would be to leave threads idle for time slices that have converged. For larger problems where not the whole time interval can be covered with time slices, either restarting or some form of "sliding window" should be employed. Both cases require to replace the outer FOR loop by some form of adaptive control of iterations and are not considered here.

4   Numerical Results

This section compares the pipelined OpenMP implementation to a straightforward MPI variant with respect to runtime, memory footprint and energy consumption. The code used here for benchmarking is written in Fortran 90 and available for download [16]. It is special-purpose and solves the nonlinear 3D Burgers' equation

$$u_t + u \cdot \nabla u = \nu \Delta u \tag{5}$$

on $[0, 1]^3 \subset \mathbb{R}^3$ with periodic boundary conditions using finite differences. Both implementations of Parareal use the same modules to provide the coarse and fine integrator and spatial discretisation. Tests guarantee that the two implementations of Parareal produce results that are identical up to a tolerance of $\varepsilon = 10^{-14}$ and thus essentially to round-off error. To detect possible race conditions, the comparison is run multiple times. Up to 100 instances of the test were passed on both used architectures. Furthermore, both implementations of Parareal use three auxiliary buffers per time-slice: q to store the fine value and for communication, δq to store the difference $\mathcal{F}_{\delta t}(q) - \mathcal{G}_{\Delta t}(q)$ needed in the correction step and q_c to store the coarse value from the previous iteration.

A strong stability preserving Runge-Kutta method (RK3-SSP) [18] with a fifth order WENO finite difference discretisation [18] for the advection term and a fourth order centred difference for the diffusion term is used for $\mathcal{F}_{\delta t}$. For $\mathcal{G}_{\Delta t}$, a first order forward Euler with a simple first order upwind stencil for the advection term and a second order centred stencil for the diffusive term is used. Being a simplified version of the Navier-Stokes equations, (5) is a popular benchmark and finite difference stencils are a widely used motif in computational science, so that the results can be expected to hold for more general scenarios, at least qualitatively.

Parameters for the simulation are a viscosity parameter of $\nu = 0.02$ and a spatial discretisation on both levels with $N_x = N_y = N_z = 40$ grid points in every direction. The simulation is run until $T = 1.0$ with a coarse time step of $\Delta t = 1/192$ and a fine step of $\delta t = 1/240$. Because of the high computational cost of the WENO-5 method in comparison to a cheap first order upwind scheme and the fact that RK3SSP needs three evaluations of the right hand side per step while the Euler method needs only one, the coarse propagator is about a factor of forty faster, despite the fact that the coarse step is only a factor of 1.25 larger than the fine. Using a coarse time step $\Delta t \approx \delta t$ prevents stability issues in the coarse propagator and improves convergence of Parareal.

To fix the number of iterations to a meaningful value which guarantees comparable accuracy from Parareal and serial fine integrator, we estimate the discretisation error of $\mathcal{F}_{\delta t}$ by comparing against a reference solution with time step $\delta t/10$. This gives estimates for the fine relative error at $T = 1$ of about $e_{\text{fine}} \approx 5.9 \times 10^{-5}$ and for the coarse error of about $e_{\text{coarse}} \approx 7.3 \times 10^{-2}$. For $P = 24$ time slices, after three iterations, the defect between Parareal and the fine solution is approximately 1.4×10^{-4}, after four iterations 1.5×10^{-5}. We therefore fix the number of iterations to $K = 4$ so that for all values of P Parareal produces a solution with the same accuracy as the fine integrator.

Benchmarks are run on two systems. The first is a commodity work station with an 8-core Intel Xeon(R) E5-1660 CPU and 32 GB of memory running CentOS Linux 7. Flags -O3 and -fopenmp were used when compiling the code for maximum optimisation and to enable OpenMP. As the code is stand alone no external libraries have to be linked. The used MPI implementation is mpich-3.0.4, compiled with GCC-4.8.5.

The second system is one node of PIZ DORA at the Swiss National Supercomputing Centre CSCS.[1] DORA is a Cray XC40 with a total of $1,256$ compute nodes. Each node contains two 12-core Intel Broadwell CPUs and has 64 or 128 GB of RAM and nodes are connected through a Cray Aries interconnect, using a dragonfly network topology. Two compilers are tested, the GCC-4.9.2 and the Cray Fortran compiler version 8.3.12. Both use the MPICH MPI library version 7.2.2. Compiler flags -O3 and -fopenmp (GCC) or omp (Cray compiler) are used for compilation. Performance data for each completed job is generated using the Cray *Resource Utilisation Reporting* tool RUR [4]. RUR collects compute node statistics for each job and provides data on user and system time, maximum memory used, amount of I/O operations, consumed energy and other metrics. However, it only collects data for a full node and not for individual CPUs or cores.

4.1 Wall Clock Time and Speedup

At first, runtime and speedup compared to the serial execution of the fine integrator are assessed. On both the Linux work station and DORA, five runs are performed for each variant of Parareal and each value of P and the average runtime is reported. Measured runtimes are quite stable across different runs: the largest relative standard deviation of all performed five-run ensembles is smaller than 0.05 on Linux and smaller than 0.01 on DORA. Therefore, plots show only the average values without error bars, because those are hardly recognisable and clutter the figure.

Figure 2 shows runtimes in seconds depending on the number of cores on DORA using the Cray compiler (left) and Linux (right). The Cray compiler generates faster code than GCC in the case studied here, but for comparison results using GCC on DORA are shown in Fig. 4. The runtime of the serial fine integrator is indicated by a horizontal black line. The CPU in the Linux system has a slightly higher clock speed so that runtimes are a bit faster than on DORA. For $P = 8$ cores, for example, OpenMP-Parareal runs in slightly less than 5 s there while taking about 5.7 s on DORA. Differences between the OpenMP and MPI version are small on both systems, but for $P = 8$ OpenMP-Parareal is marginally faster than the MPI version on the work station.

In addition, Fig. 3 shows the speedup relative to the fine integrator run serially. The black line indicates projected speedup according to (4). Both versions fall short of the theoretically possible speedup. Because of overheads, running P instances of $\mathcal{F}_{\delta t}$ on P cores does take longer than running a single instance.

---

[1] http://www.cscs.ch/.

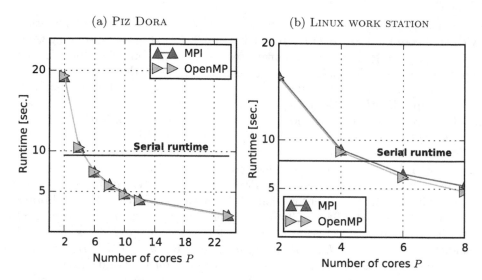

Fig. 2. Five run averages of runtime with relative standard deviation below 0.01 on DORA (2a) and 0.05 on a Linux work station (2b).

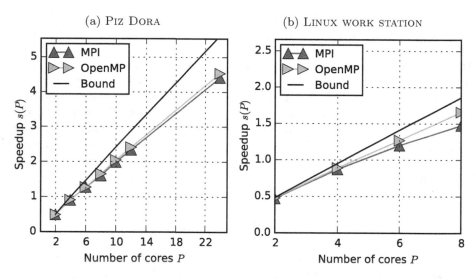

Fig. 3. Speedup computed from average runtimes shown in Fig. 2 on DORA (3a) and a Linux work station (3b).

However, differences between MPI and OpenMP are small. As far as runtimes and speedup are concerned, there is no indication that using the more complex OpenMP version provides significant benefits.

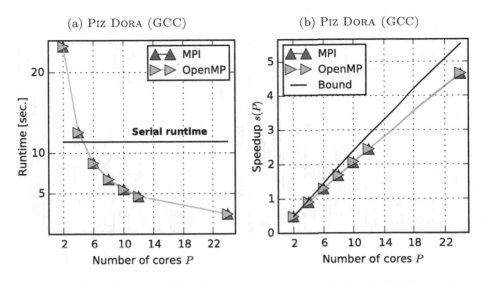

Fig. 4. Runtime (4a) and speedup (4b) on Piz Dora using GCC.

4.2 Memory Footprint

The memory footprint of the code is measured only on DORA where RUR is available. In contrast to runtime and energy, the memory footprint, as expected, does not vary between runs. Therefore Fig. 5 shows a visualisation of the data from a single run with no averaging. The bars indicate the maximum required memory in MegaByte (MB) while the black line indicates the expected memory consumption using P cores computed as

$$m(P) = P \times m_{\mathrm{serial}} \tag{6}$$

where m_{serial} is the value measured for a reference run of the fine integrator. Because copies of the solution have to be stored for every time slice, the total memory required for Parareal can be expected to increase linearly with the number of cores in time. Note, however, that memory required *per core* stays constant if it follows (6).

For the OpenMP variant compiled with GCC, the memory footprint shown in Fig. 5a exactly matches the expected values. The Cray compiler, shown in Fig. 5b, leads to a smaller than expected memory footprint, but memory requirements still increase linearly with the number of time slices. For both compilers, the MPI version causes a noticeable overhead in terms of memory footprint, most likely because of internal allocation of additional buffers for sending and receiving [15]. For both OpenMP and MPI, the total memory footprint is *larger* for the Cray than for the GCC compiler, but the effect is much more pronounced for the MPI implementation (329 MB versus 261 MB) than for the OpenMP variant (200 MB versus 193 MB).

It is important to note that both implementations allocate three auxiliary buffers per core. The overhead in terms of memory in MPI does thus not simply

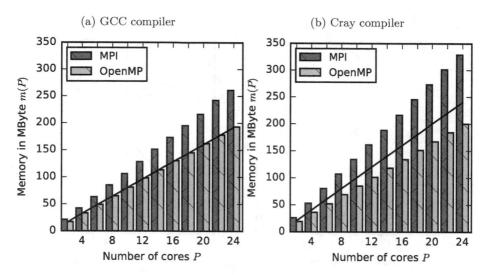

Fig. 5. Maximum memory allocated in MegaByte for GCC (5a) and Cray compiler (5b) for the three different versions of Parareal depending on the number of used cores P. The black line indicates expected memory consumption computed as number of cores time memory footprint of serial fine integrator.

stem from allocating an additional buffer for communication but comes from within the MPI library. The OpenMP implementation avoids this overhead.

It should be pointed out that the MPI baseline relies on two-sided `MPI_RECV` and `MPI_SEND` directives for communications. Exploring whether an implementation based on one-sided remote memory access in MPI [9] retains the advantages of OpenMP would be an interesting continuation of the presented work.

4.3   Energy-to-Solution

The RUR tool reports the energy-to-solution for every completed job. Because RUR can only measure energy usage for a full node, results are reported here for runs using the full number of $P = 24$ cores available on a DORA node. Unfortunately, this makes measuring the energy consumption of the fine propagator largely meaningless since it can use only a single core of the node. Therefore, no corresponding measurements were taken to quantify the overhead of Parareal in terms of energy.

In contrast to runtimes and memory footprint, energy measurements show significant variations between runs due to random fluctuations. Thus, the presented values are averages over ensembles of 50 runs for each version of Parareal. This number of runs has been sufficient to reduce the relative standard deviation to below 0.09 in both configurations and therefore gives a robust indication of actual energy requirements. Table 1 shows the results including 95% confidence intervals, assuming energy-to-solution is normally distributed. For comparison, energy-to-solution is also shown for a simple non-pipelined

OpenMP implementation where only the loop around $\mathcal{F}_{\delta t}$ is parallelised using OMP PARALLEL DO.

Table 1. Average energy-to-solution for the three different variants run on $P = 24$ cores. Since RUR only measures energy consumption of a full node, it was not possible to meaningfully measure energy-to-solution of the serial propagator and quantify the energy overhead.

GCC compiler			
	∅energy (Joule)	confidence (Joule)	∅runtime (s)
MPI	844.04	±15.89	2.455
OpenMP	801.14	±13.18	2.930
OpenMP (pipelined)	783.72	±11.53	2.448
Cray compiler			
	∅energy (Joule)	confidence (Joule)	∅runtime (s)
MPI	784.24	±11.93	2.146
OpenMP	833.12	±20.99	2.400
OpenMP (pipelined)	784.72	±12.18	2.088

When using the GCC compiler, MPI-Parareal consumes more energy than both the pipelined and non-pipelined OpenMP versions. The averages are well outside the confidence interval for the MPI version, so this is very unlikely just a chance result. Moreover, because runtimes are almost identical for MPI and pipelined OpenMP, the differences in energy-to-solution cannot solely be attributed to differences in time-to-solution. This is supported by the fact that non-pipelined OpenMP, despite being significantly slower, still consumes less energy than the MPI variant. Tracking down the precise reason for the differences in energy-to-solution and power requirement will require detailed tracing of power uptake which is only possible on specially prepared machines [10] and thus left for future work.

For code generated with the Cray compiler, both OpenMP and MPI lead to almost identical energy requirements. Confidence intervals are 784.24 ± 11.93 J for MPI and 784.24 ± 12.18 J for OpenMP. It seems likely that the compiler optimises the message passing to take advantage of the shared memory on the single node. Supposedly, the MPI version handles communication in a way that is similar to what is explicitly coded in the OpenMP version. However, as shown in Subsect. 4.2, this automatic optimisation comes at the expense of a significantly larger memory footprint.

Note that the energy consumption of Parareal has previously been studied [1]. By comparing against a simple theoretical model, it has been shown that the energy overhead of Parareal (defined as energy-to-solution of Parareal divided by energy-to-solution of the fine serial integrator), is mostly due to Parareal's intrinsic suboptimal parallel efficiency. While improving parallel efficiency of parallel-in-time integration clearly remains the main avenue for improving energy efficiency, the results here suggest that in some cases a shared memory approach can provide non-trivial additional savings.

5 Summary

The paper introduces and analyses an OpenMP implementation of the parallel-in-time method Parareal with pipelining. Pipelining allows to hide some of the cost of the serial coarse correction step in Parareal and is important to optimise its efficiency (even though it cannot relax the inherent limit on parallel efficiency given by the inverse of the number of required iterations). Pipelining comes naturally in a distributed memory MPI implementation, but is not straightforward when using OpenMP. The new OpenMP implementation is compared to the standard MPI variant in terms of runtime, memory footprint and energy consumption for both a Cray compiler and the GCC. Both versions produce essentially identical runtimes. For both compilers, using OpenMP leads to reductions in memory footprint, but the effect is more pronounced for the Cray compiler. In terms of energy-to-solution, the results strongly depend on the compiler: while for GCC the OpenMP version is more energy efficient than the MPI version, there is no difference for the Cray compiler.

The results show that contemplating a shared memory strategy to implement "parallel-across-the-steps" methods like Parareal can be worthwhile. Even though it is more complicated, it can reduce memory requirements. However, more advanced features like task-based parallelism in OpenMP, remote memory access for MPI or a more advanced iteration control to prevent superfluous computation on converged time slices are not explored here. Another potential caveat is whether the benefits carry over to the full space-time parallel case, where a parallel-in-time method is combined with spatial decomposition. For Parareal without pipelining the potential of such a hybrid space-time parallel approach has been illustrated [11] but whether this applies to the pipelined version introduced here remains to be seen.

References

1. Arteaga, A., Ruprecht, D., Krause, R.: A stencil-based implementation of parareal in the C++ domain specific embedded language STELLA. Appl. Math. Comput. **267**, 727–741 (2015). http://dx.doi.org/10.1016/j.amc.2014.12.055
2. Aubanel, E.: Scheduling of tasks in the parareal algorithm. Parallel Comput. **37**, 172–182 (2011). http://dx.doi.org/10.1016/j.parco.2010.10.004
3. Ayguade, E., Copty, N., Duran, A., Hoeflinger, J., Lin, Y., Massaioli, F., Teruel, X., Unnikrishnan, P., Zhang, G.: The design of OpenMP tasks. IEEE Trans. Parallel Distrib. Syst. **20**(3), 404–418 (2009)
4. Barry, A.: Resource utilization reporting: gathering and evaluating HPC system usage. In: CUG 2013 Proceedings (2013). https://cug.org/proceedings/cug2013_proceedings/includes/files/pap103.pdf

5. Berry, L.A., Elwasif, W.R., Reynolds-Barredo, J.M., Samaddar, D., Sánchez, R.S., Newman, D.E.: Event-based parareal: a data-flow based implementation of parareal. J. Comput. Phys. **231**(17), 5945–5954 (2012). http://dx.doi.org/10.1016/j.jcp.2012.05.016
6. Dongarra, J., et al.: Applied mathematics research for exascale computing. Technical report, LLNL-TR-651000, Lawrence Livermore National Laboratory (2014). http://science.energy.gov/%7E/media/ascr/pdf/research/am/docs/EMWGreport.pdf
7. Gander, M.J.: 50 years of time parallel time integration. In: Carraro, T., Geiger, M., Körkel, S., Rannacher, R. (eds.) Multiple Shooting and Time Domain Decomposition Methods. CMCS, vol. 9, pp. 69–113. Springer, Cham (2015). doi:10.1007/978-3-319-23321-5_3
8. Gander, M.J., Vandewalle, S.: Analysis of the parareal time-parallel time-integration method. SIAM J. Sci. Comput. **29**(2), 556–578 (2007). http://dx.doi.org/10.1137/05064607X
9. Gerstenberger, R., Besta, M., Hoefler, T.: Enabling highly-scalable remote memory access programming with MPI-3 one sided. Sci. Program. **22**(2), 75–91 (2014)
10. Isci, C., Martonosi, M.: Runtime power monitoring in high-end processors: methodology and empirical data. In: Proceedings of 36th Annual IEEE/ACM International Symposium on Microarchitecture, MICRO 36, p. 93 (2003). http://dl.acm.org/citation.cfm?id=956417.956567
11. Krause, R., Ruprecht, D.: Hybrid space–time parallel solution of Burgers' equation. In: Erhel, J., Gander, M.J., Halpern, L., Pichot, G., Sassi, T., Widlund, O. (eds.) Domain Decomposition Methods in Science and Engineering XXI. LNCSE, vol. 98, pp. 647–655. Springer, Cham (2014). doi:10.1007/978-3-319-05789-7_62
12. Lecouvez, M., Falgout, R., Woodward, C., Top, P.: A parallel multigrid reduction in time method for power systems (2016). http://www.osti.gov/scitech/biblio/1281664
13. Lions, J.L., Maday, Y., Turinici, G.: A "parareal" in time discretization of PDE's. Comptes Rendus de l'Académie des Sciences - Series I - Mathematics **332**, 661–668 (2001). http://dx.doi.org/10.1016/S0764-4442(00)01793-6
14. Minion, M.L.: A hybrid parareal spectral deferred corrections method. Commun. Appl. Math. Comput. Sci. **5**(2), 265–301 (2010). http://dx.doi.org/10.2140/camcos.2010.5.265
15. Rabenseifner, R., Hager, G., Jost, G.: Hybrid MPI/OpenMP parallel programming on clusters of multi-core SMP nodes. In: 17th Euromicro International Conference on Parallel, Distributed and Network-based processing, pp. 427–436 (2009)
16. Ruprecht, D.: PararealF90: shared memory pipelined Parareal (2017). http://doi.org/10.5281/zenodo.260095
17. Schreiber, M., Peddle, A., Haut, T., Wingate, B.: A decentralized parallelization-in-time approach with Parareal (2015). http://arxiv.org/abs/1506.05157
18. Shu, C.W., Osher, S.: Efficient implementation of essentially non-oscillatory shock-capturing schemes II. J. Comput. Phys. **83**, 32–78 (1989)

Nonintrusive AMR Asynchrony
for Communication Optimization

Muhammad Nufail Farooqi[1]([⊠]), Didem Unat[1]([⊠]), Tan Nguyen[2],
Weiqun Zhang[2], Ann Almgren[2], and John Shalf[2]

[1] Koç University, Istanbul, Turkey
{mfarooqi14,dunat}@ku.edu.tr
[2] Lawrence Berkeley National Laboratory, Berkeley, CA, USA
{tannguyen,weiqunzhang,asalmgren,jshalf}@lbl.gov

Abstract. Adaptive Mesh Refinement (AMR) is a well known method
for efficiently solving partial differential equations. A straightforward
AMR algorithm typically exhibits many synchronization points even
during a single time step, where costly communication often degrades
the performance. This problem will be even more pronounced on future
supercomputers containing billion way parallelism, which will raise the
communication cost further. Re-designing AMR algorithms to avoid synchronization is not a viable solution due to the large code size and complex control structures. We present a nonintrusive asynchronous approach to hiding the effects of communication in an AMR application.
Specifically, our approach reasons about data dependencies automatically using domain knowledge about AMR applications, allowing asynchrony to be discovered with only a modest amount of code modification.
Using this approach, we optimize the synchronous AMR algorithm in the
BoxLib software framework without severely affecting the productivity
of the application programmer. We observe around 27–31% performance
improvement for an advection solver on the Hazel Hen supercomputer
using 12288 cores.

Keywords: Asynchronous execution · Adaptive mesh refinement ·
AMR algorithm · Communication hiding

1 Introduction

Many computational science and engineering problems are modelled in the form
of partial differential equations (PDEs). Although a high resolution mesh is
required for improved accuracy of PDE solvers, usually some mesh regions are of
more interest, where additional accuracy is desired. Adaptive mesh refinement
(AMR) provides the mechanism to locally refine areas of interest [8]. Block-
structured AMR (SAMR) is a type of AMR method that uses structured grids
organized into a grid hierarchy. Areas of interest are refined gradually in a nested
manner from the coarsest level, which covers the whole domain to the finest.

© Springer International Publishing AG 2017
F.F. Rivera et al. (Eds.): Euro-Par 2017, LNCS 10417, pp. 682–694, 2017.
DOI: 10.1007/978-3-319-64203-1_49

One of the scalability challenges for AMR applications is that they consist of many synchronization points. These costly synchronization points appear in the nearest-neighbor communication including boundary exchange, in the global reduction, and in the inter-AMR level update. The former has become increasingly costly due to the system design trend focusing on fewer but more powerful compute nodes [6]. Asynchronous execution can reduce synchronization cost with the help of description of dependencies between AMR subgrids and the partial ordering among them. Given the partial ordering information, a scheduler can assign ready subgrids on available resources while other subgrids are waiting on their inputs.

In this paper we propose an asynchronous AMR algorithm that reduces the most of the synchronization costs without bringing too much programming overhead. In our asynchronous algorithm, each subgrid at different AMR levels is considered as a task. A task within a specific level can perform computation independent of other tasks at the same level as soon as its boundary data is available. Even though there is more opportunity for overlap in an AMR algorithm, for example, a subgrid located at *any* level can perform computation independent of other subgrids, we enforce the completion of computation of subgrids in a single level before moving onto the computation at other levels for the sake of programming simplicity. Our method enables legacy application implemented using the synchronous AMR algorithm to get the benefits of the communication and computation overlap. We discuss the implementation of our asynchronous algorithm in the context of the BoxLib AMR framework and present results on the advection solver, which contains all the communication scenarios present in a typical AMR application. We compared our results with the existing BoxLib execution model, where communication at each level is completed before starting computation. The performance improvement is about 27% for both strong and weak scaling on 12288 cores.

Rest of the paper is organized as follows. Next section discusses related work. In Sect. 3 we provide some background on Block-Structured AMR. Section 4 explains the AMR algorithm in general and Sect. 5 proposes a methodology to asynchronously execute the AMR algorithm. Implementation is discussed in Sect. 6. Results are shown in Sect. 7. Finally, Sect. 8 concludes the paper.

2 Related Work

A plethora of work can be found in literature that focuses on speeding up of AMR computations using diverse techniques while targeting specific problems or architectures. Some of the high level AMR frameworks are BoxLib [1], Cactus [12], Chombo [10], Enzo [2], FLASH [11], and Paramesh [15]. Wahib et al. [20] presented a compiler-based framework named *Daino* that generates parallel AMR code optimized for GPUs from an annotated uniform grid code. In [19], authors introduced an asynchronous integration scheme with local time stepping for multi-scale gas discharge simulations.

Chan et al. [9] classified AMR execution models into four modes ranging from *fully synchronous* to *fully asynchronous*. The trade-off between the modes is the amount of synchronization and the programmability. The more asynchronous the execution becomes, the harder it is to program and debug. *Full synchronous* is the most restricted one, which will be discussed in Algorithms 1 and 3 in Sect. 4. *Rank synchronous* reduces the global synchronization down to rank level and runs synchronously within a rank. *Rank synchronous* model avoids global synchronization but enforces local restrictions on task processing order. BoxLib currently implements a *rank synchronous* model. In *phase asynchronous*, a subgrid within a specific level can perform computation independent of other subgrids at the same level as soon as dependencies are met and communication for a subgrid is overlapped within a single time step. Each rank will finish its communication for all the subgrids before starting computation on any subgrid. In a *fully asynchronous* model, a subgrid located at any level can perform computation independent of other subgrids as soon as its own dependencies are met. Here we present an asynchronous AMR algorithm that is analogous to the *phase asynchronous* execution model.

To the best of our knowledge, the literature that explains the asynchronous AMR algorithm and its corresponding implementation is rare. A few notable contributions are as follows. Langer et al. [14] proposed a distributed regridding algorithm to enable *fully asynchronous* AMR execution for oct-tree based AMR implementations. They used Charm++ [13] for implementation where each subgrid is represented by a *chare* that can run independently and communication of one *chare* is overlapped with computation of another. Our proposed asynchronous algorithm can work with traditional regridding algorithms and can be implemented using any threading library. Uintah [16] is a software framework that implements a runtime to execute AMR applications asynchronously. They also use subgrid level asynchronous task execution to overlap communication and computation. They mostly discussed the runtime optimization details but do not explain the asynchronous AMR algorithm.

3   Block-Structured Adaptive Mesh Refinement (SAMR)

AMR provides a computationally efficient approach for solving PDEs by using finer meshes only at regions of interest. SAMR [8], one of the many AMR methods, is established on a chain of nested and logically rectangular grids. Starting from a coarse grid that covers the entire domain at level 0, grids are refined to finer grids at the higher levels with the finest grid at the top level. Figures 1a and b show sample SAMR grids having two levels of refinements. Each level is composed of non-overlapping rectangular grids nested from grids on the lower level in the hierarchy. The nested grid at a finer level is extended from a single grid or multiple adjacent grids at the coarser level. All grids at a level are of the same resolution. Given maximum number of levels at start, the number of refinement levels can vary dynamically during the simulation.

Generally, two types of communication are involved in the parallel AMR implementations: (1) intra-level communication is only between neighboring/adjacent grids, and (2) inter-level communication is only between consecutive levels. Two basic operations, *restriction* and *prolongation*, are needed for

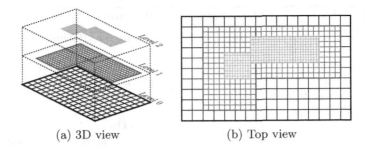

| (a) 3D view   (b) Top view |

Fig. 1. Block-structured AMR in 2 dimensions with two levels of refinement

inter-level communication. In prolongation, data is interpolated when communicated from a coarser grid to a finer one. In restriction, data is averaged when copied from a finer to coarser grid.

4   Synchronous AMR Algorithm

Algorithms 1 and 2 show the basic AMR algorithm described in [18]. Algorithm 1 contains a time step loop, which runs a specified number of times. In each iteration it first finds the time step dt for the current time step. Computing dt generally involves a global reduction operation to find a minimum value. Next a recursive procedure *AMRTimeStep* is called that starts from the coarsest level and iterates over all levels to compute a single time step.

Algorithm 2 shows the recursive procedure that computes a single time step of the AMR algorithm. The procedure first checks whether regridding the finer level is needed. If needed, it estimates the error at finer level $(l+1)$ and regrids the finer level. When a regrid operation is performed on a finer level, it will subsequently be carried out for all the upper levels up to the finest level. Boundary data is filled from current refinement level l if available otherwise data is filled from physical boundary conditions or interpolated from the coarser level $l-1$. Upon receiving of all the boundary data, all the grids at the current level l are integrated in time. Next, the *AMRTimeStep* procedure is called r times recursively to compute the finer level at smaller time steps. This is known as subcycling in time where r specifies the desired number of cycles that is normally set to the refinement ratio. The value of r can be set to 1 if no-subcycling is desired. Data between the current level and the finer level is synchronized after the finer level reaches the same time t as the current level. All the levels are integrated independent of each other. Lastly, data is synchronized between two successive levels to resolve the inconsistencies at coarse and fine level boundaries.

In the synchronous execution of an AMR algorithm there are multiple synchronization points. First synchronization point is in the computation of time step value dt where a global reduction operation occurs. Next synchronization point is when boundary data is filled and this synchronization happens every time

Algorithm 1 Basic AMR algorithm	**Algorithm 2** Single Time Step

Procedure AMRTimeLoop(time t, num of steps s)
for $i \leftarrow 1$ to s **do**
    dt $\leftarrow$ compute_dt()
    AMRTimeStep(0, t, dt)
    $t \leftarrow t + dt$
end for
Procedure AMRTimeLoop
	Procedure AMRTimeStep(level l, time t, dt)
	if isRegrid($l + 1$) **then**
	    estimateError($l + 1$)
	    generateGrids($l + 1$)
	end if
	if $l = 0$ **then**
	    fillBoundary(level $0 \leftarrow$ level 0)
	else
	    fillBoundary($l \leftarrow l$ and $l - 1$)
	end if
	for each grid g in grids at level l **do**
	    integrate(l, $t + dt$, g)
	end for
	if $l < l_{max}$ **then**
	    repeat $j \leftarrow 1$ **to** r **times:**
	        AMRTimeStep ($l + 1$, t, $\frac{j \times dt}{r}$)
	end if
	synchronizeData($l \leftarrow l + 1$)
	End Procedure AMRTimeStep

the *AMRTimeStep* procedure is called. Last synchronization is when data is synchronized between two adjacent levels to correct coarse and fine level boundaries. Next, we discuss our proposed asynchronous algorithm that overcomes some of these synchronization overheads.

5   Asynchronous AMR Algorithm

In the AMR algorithm listed in Algorithm 2 data needed for all grids at a level is communicated before starting computation on that level. Thus all the grids at the same level are computed when all of their dependencies are fulfilled. In the synchronous algorithm, all grids at the same level are considered as one big task that is carried out as a whole. For an asynchronous execution, we reduce the task granularity to subgrid size where each subgrid is considered as a task. A task can start computing as soon as its dependencies are fulfilled. Here, dependencies for a task are the data at boundaries that are copied from other tasks.

The asynchronous version of Algorithm 1 is the same as the synchronous except the reduction operation is performed asynchronously. Algorithm 3 shows the asynchronous AMR algorithm for a single time step. Before executing Algorithm 1, a task graph is created that contains information about tasks at all levels and their dependencies. Dependencies in the task graph are based on the grid structure therefore the task graph remains valid until there is a change in the grid structure. Asynchronous task graph is updated when a regridding occurs to reflect the changes in the grids and their dependencies. In Algorithm 3 all the *fillboundary_send* calls are non-blocking while the receives are blocking.

Algorithm 3 Asynchronous AMR Algorithm - Single Time Step

Procedure AMRTimeStep(level l, time t, dt, iteration $iter$)

if isRegrid $(l + 1)$ **then**

    estimateError$(l + 1)$

    generateGrids$(l + 1)$

    updateTaskGraph$(l + 1)$

end if

if $FirstTimeStep$ and $iter = 1$ and $l < l_{max}$ **then**

    if $l = 0$ **then** fillBoundary_send_allGrids (level $0 \leftarrow$ level 0) //*non-blocking*

    fillBoundary_send_allGrids $(l + 1 \leftarrow l + 1)$ //*non-blocking*

end if

for each grid g in grids at level l **do** //*Out-of-order loop iterator*

    if $l = 0$ **then**

        fillBoundary_receive(level $0 \leftarrow$ level 0, g) //*blocking*

    else

        fillBoundary_receive($l \leftarrow l$ and l - 1, g) //*blocking*

    end if

    integrate(l, $t + dt$, g)

    if $l < l_{max}$ **then**

        fillBoundary_send $(l+1 \leftarrow l, g)$ //*non-blocking*

    else

        fillBoundary_send $(l \leftarrow l, g)$ //*non-blocking*

    end if

end for

if $l < l_{max}$ **then**

    repeat $j \leftarrow 1$ **to** r **time:** AMRTimeStep $(l + 1, t, \frac{j \times dt}{r}, j)$

end if

if $l < l_{max}$ **then** synchronizeData_receive_allGrids $(l \leftarrow l + 1)$ //*blocking*

if $l > 0$ **then** synchronizeData_send_allGrids $(l - 1 \leftarrow l)$ //*non-blocking*

if $l < l_{max}$ **then** fillBoundary_send_allGrids $(l \leftarrow l)$ //*non-blocking*

End Procedure AMRTimeStep

In the first time step, to overlap the intra-level communication at the finer level $(l+1)$ for timestep (t) with computation of the current level (l) for timestep (t), we can start sending the boundary data for the finer level because data at that level is already initialized during the initialization of the application. After initiating the intra-level communication at the finer level, a loop iterates over all grids at the current level. The loop iterator is designed to iterate over the grids for which dependencies are met and it uses the dependency graph to identify the task dependencies. This out-of-order execution enables ready grids to start computing while allowing more time for grids which are still waiting for their boundary data. Receive calls although blocking do not wait idle for communication because the loop iterator ensures that the dependencies for the

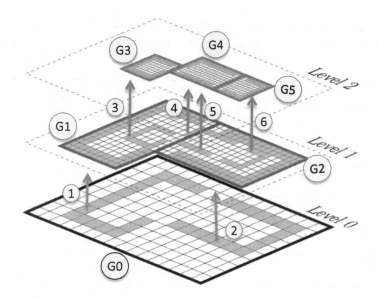

Fig. 2. Asynchronous computation and communication overlap

subgrid are already met. As the dependencies for the task are met, the grid fills the boundaries with the received data from current and coarser level $(l-1)$. After performing the computation (integrate) on the grid, the boundary data is sent to the dependent grids at finer level$(l+1)$ when current level is not the finest level. If the current level is the finest level $(l = l_{max})$ then it sends the boundary data to dependent grids at the same level for next time step $(t + dt)$ or next iteration if subcycling is enabled. Thus boundary data communication between adjacent levels or within the finest level for next subcycling iteration is overlapped with computation of the current level (l) or current subcycling iteration. Next, data at current level is synchronized with the received data from the finer level for all grids and the synchronized data is then sent to the coarser level. Lastly, for levels below the finest level we can initiate its intra-level communication for the next time step $(t + dt)$ or the next subcycling iteration. This enables to overlap intra-level boundary data communication for finer levels with the computation at next time step of their coarser levels. However, for iterations within a time step when subcycling is enabled the overlap will only be with the computation of grids at the same level. For the coarsest level (0), this can be possibly overlapped with the global reduction operation required for the next time step value.

Figure 2 shows an example how we enable overlap of computation and communication for Algorithm 3. After computation of grid $G0$ at level 0, communication for boundary data takes place as shown by arrows 1 and 2. For example, if the communication represented by arrow 1 completes first the grid $G1$ at level 1 will start computation. After $G1$ finishes computation it can start sending the boundary data (shown with arrows 3 and 4) to the grids $G3$ and $G4$ at level 2. Communication represented with arrows 3 and 4 will be overlapped with computation of the grid $G2$ at level 1. After completion of the grid $G2$ and initiating the boundary data communication (shown with arrows 5 and 6), any grid at level 2 that receives its boundary data can start computation. That is if 3 finishes first then $G3$ can start its computation or if both 4 and 5 finish first then $G4$ can start its computation. Similarly $G5$ can start computation when 6 is finished.

6 Implementation

We implemented the asynchronous AMR algorithm in BoxLib [1], which is a publicly available software framework used for implementing Block Structured AMR applications. Some of the large BoxLib applications are for astrophysics (CASTRO [3] and MAESTRO [7]), cosmology (Nyx [5]) and low Mach number combustion (LMC [4]) simulations. BoxLib contains two notable classes, *Amr* and *AmrLevel*, that are related to the AMR algorithm implementation. The *Amr* class implements the AMR algorithm described in Algorithms 1 and 2. *AmrLevel* manages data and operations required on them for a single level. *AmrLevel* contains some virtual functions that the application programmers override to implement their solver. These virtual functions are called for each level inside the *Amr* class's function that implements the AMR algorithm. Two of these virtual functions are *advance* and *post_timestep*. The *advance* subroutine should implement the fill boundary data and integration part of the AMR algorithm. Data management and MPI communication is handled by BoxLib as it provides *fillPatch* subroutine that manages the fill boundary data and the programmer can use it in the *advance* subroutine to fill the boundary data. Programmer overrides the *post_timestep* subroutine to synchronize data between the levels. Data synchronization between the levels also known as restriction can be performed using the *average_down* subroutine provided by BoxLib.

To implement the asynchronous execution of the AMR algorithm, we extended some of the BoxLib functionalities. We added two more virtual functions *initAsynchronousExec* and *finalizeAsynchronousExec* to the *AmrLevel* class so that applications can override them to initialize and destroy asynchronous task graphs for a level. Task graphs from all levels are combined together inside BoxLib to construct dependencies for the entire AMR grid hierarchy. *FillPatch* and *average_down* previously implement synchronous MPI communication for all grids at a level. To enable communication for a single grid without waiting for the other grids, we divided the execution of *FillPatch* and *average_down* into two parts; *push* and *pull*. *FillPatch_push* starts sending boundary data from a single grid to all dependent grids whether at current level or at the finer level. *FillPatch_pull* receives the boundary data for a single grid from all the relevant grids. To pick the ready tasks, we implemented an iterator that iterates over all the tasks in the asynchronous task graph. Our scheduler similar to the runtime scheduler in [17], backs the iterator to support out-of-order execution. The scheduler keeps track of the ready tasks and handles all the communications generated by the asynchronous *fillPatch* and *average_down* subroutines.

Both new applications and legacy applications developed using BoxLib can be easily adapted to the new asynchronous framework with reasonable programming effort. Application programmers need to implement the *initAsynchronousExec* and *finalizeAsynchronousExec* virtual functions to initialize the task graphs for the corresponding level. To ease this process, we implemented a class named *RegionGraph* that can create a task graph for a level automatically using the metadata from BoxLib. A programmer can create a task graph simply by passing an object of the *MultiFab* class to the *RegionGraph* class constructor. A *MultiFab* contains all grids for a single level. A programmer has to replace the function calls to *fillPatch* and *average_down* with their asynchronous *push* and *pull* versions. Inside the newly developed task graph iterator, programmers can first pull, then compute, and then push the tasks using these asynchronous function calls. End users are insulated from the rest of the complexity involved in the asynchronous execution, which is handled inside the asynchronous BoxLib framework.

Currently, our implementation of the asynchronous AMR algorithm is restricted to a single time step. The asynchronous execution starts before computation of the coarsest level and continues all the way up to the finest. We synchronize all the processes after data is synchronized for the coarsest level. We currently compute the time step using a synchronous global reduction and our implementation does not support asynchronous regridding yet. In the future we will further increase asynchrony, which would support asynchronous task graph update when grid structure changes, asynchronous global reduction to compute time step, and asynchronous communication across time steps.

7   Results

We carried out performance study on the Hazel Hen supercomputer located at the HPC Centre, Stuttgart Germany. Compute node specifications on Hazel Hen are provided in Table 1. For performance measurement we use an explicit advection code based on BoxLib. The advection solver advects a scalar field with a prescribed time-dependent velocity on adaptive meshes. A finite-volume method with explicit time stepping is employed to solve the PDE. Although this is a simple system, the code contains all the AMR algorithmic components and communication patterns for building an explicit solver for a more complicated system of conservation law equations such as gas dynamics. For example, inter- and intra-AMR-level communication are needed for filling ghost cells. The mismatch of finite-volume flux at the coarse/fine interface needs to be corrected so that the conservation law is preserved. For comparison we use the existing Boxlib execution model as our baseline which implements Algorithm 2 with rank synchronous execution model discussed in the related work section. BoxLib reduces the global synchronization down to rank level and runs synchronously within a rank. All the experiments were performed using three levels of refinement, two subcycling iterations and a refinement ratio of 2.

Figure 3 shows strong scaling up to 12K cores where each bar is labeled with percent improvement obtained by the proposed asynchronous algorithm over

Table 1. Machine specifications for Hazel Hen

CPUs	Intel E5-2680 v3 (Haswell)	**Shared L3 (MB)**	30
Sockets/cores per socket	2/12	**Main memory (GB)**	128
Threads per core	2	**Memory bandwidth**	68 (GB/s)
Clock rate (GHz)	2.5	**Network bandwidth**	11.7 (GB/s)

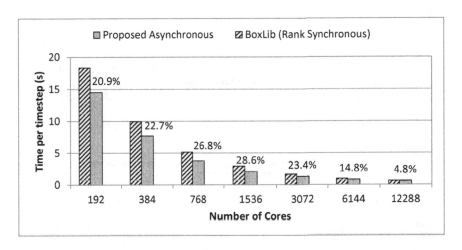

Fig. 3. Strong scaling for advection code on Hazel Hen

BoxLib. We used 1024^3 grid size as input for strong scaling studies. The y-axis shows the time spent in a single step of Algorithms 2 and 3. It does not include the time spent in timestep dt computation and global reduction. Proposed asynchronous algorithm achieves up to 28.6% performance improvement over BoxLib on 1536 cores. Performance improvement declines as we further increase the number of cores because the number of subgrids per process becomes too small to overlap any computation. There are a total of 6041 subgrids with size ranging from 128^3 to 8^3. For the maximum performance improvement case there are about 95 subgrids/rank while it reduces to less than 12 subgrids/rank in 12K cores. Although not shown here, we observe the same strong scaling behavior when two levels of refinements with subcycling and three levels of refinements without subcycling are used.

Figure 4 compares weak scaling for BoxLib's rank synchronous and proposed asynchronous algorithms. Grid size starts from 1024^3 for 768 cores and then doubled in x, y and z directions respectively. The proposed asynchronous algorithm achieves the same weak scaling behavior as BoxLib but with sustained performance improvement of more than 27%. This is possible because there are always sufficient number of subgrids per process to hide communication.

A breakdown (for strong scaling) of the time spent during computation (integration), restriction and prolongation for rank synchronous algorithm compared

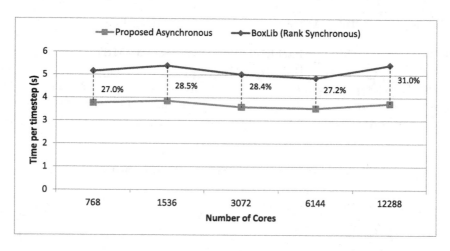

Fig. 4. Weak scaling for advection code on Hazel Hen

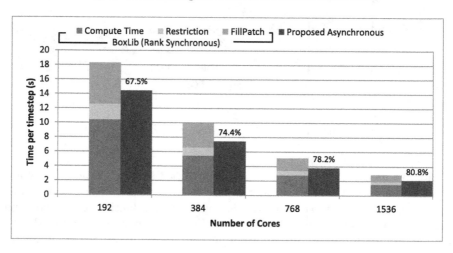

Fig. 5. Breakdown of performance for strong scaling achieved on Hazel Hen

to the proposed asynchronous algorithm is shown in Fig. 5. Both restriction and prolongation introduce communication. We can overlap only prolongation with computation because while performing restriction there is no computation to overlap with. The proposed asynchronous algorithm hides about 80% of the communication overhead due to prolongation behind the computation as shown in Fig. 5.

8 Conclusions

In this paper, we presented an asynchronous execution model for the AMR algorithm. Our asynchronous execution model allows a subgrid within a level to perform computation independent of other subgrids at the same level to provide scalability but also maintains the programming simplicity for both AMR framework developers and the end users. We also discussed how our asynchronous algorithm can be integrated into an AMR framework. The results show that with affordable programming effort our asynchronous AMR algorithm can be adapted into AMR software frameworks to achieve decent speedup and scalability.

Acknowledgments. Authors from Koç University are supported by the Turkish Science and Technology Research Centre Grant No: 215E185. Dr. Unat is supported by the Marie Sklodowska Curie Reintegration Grant 655965 by the European Commission. We acknowledge PRACE for awarding us access to the Hazel Hen supercomputer in Germany. Authors from Lawrence Berkeley National Laboratory were supported by the Office of Advanced Scientific Computing Research in the Department of Energy Office of Science under contract number DE-AC02-05CH11231.

References

1. Boxlib: An AMR software framework. https://ccse.lbl.gov/BoxLib/
2. Enzo: AMR project. http://enzo-project.org/
3. Almgren, A.S., Beckner, V.E., Bell, J.B., Day, M.S., Howell, L.H., Joggerst, C.C., Lijewski, M.J., Nonaka, A., Singer, M., Zingale, M.: CASTRO: a new compressible astrophysical solver. I. Hydrodynamics and self-gravity. Astrophys. J. **715**(2), 1221–1238 (2010)
4. Almgren, A.S., Bell, J.B., Rendleman, C.A., Zingale, M.: Low Mach Number Modeling of Type Ia Supernovae. I. Hydrodynamics. Astrophys. J. **637**(2), 922–936 (2006)
5. Almgren, A., Bell, J., Lijewski, M., Lukić, Z., Van Andel, E.: Nyx: a massively parallel AMR code for computational cosmology. Astrophys. J. **765**, 39 (2013)
6. Ang, J., Barrett, R., Benner, R., Burke, D., Chan, C., Cook, J., Donofrio, D., Hammond, S., Hemmert, K., Kelly, S., Le, H., Leung, V., Resnick, D., Rodrigues, A., Shalf, J., Stark, D., Unat, D., Wright, N.: Abstract machine models and proxy architectures for exascale computing. In: 2014 Hardware-Software Co-Design for High Performance Computing, pp. 25–32. IEEE, November 2014
7. Bell, J.B., Day, M.S., Lijewski, M.J.: Simulation of nitrogen emissions in a premixed hydrogen flame stabilized on a low swirl burner. Proc. Combust. Inst. **34**(1), 1173–1182 (2013)
8. Berger, M.J., Oliger, J.: Adaptive mesh refinement for hyperbolic partial differential equations. J. Comput. Phys. **53**(3), 484–512 (1984)
9. Chan, C.P., Bachan, J.D., Kenny, J.P., Wilke, J.J., Beckner, V.E., Almgren, A.S., Bell, J.B.: Topology-aware performance optimization and modeling of adaptive mesh refinement codes for exascale. In: Proceedings of 1st Workshop on Optimization of Communication in HPC, COM-HPC 2016, pp. 17–28. IEEE Press, Piscataway (2016)
10. Colella, P., Graves, D.T., Johnson, J.N., Johansen, H.S., Keen, N.D., Ligocki, T.J., Martin, D.F., Mccorquodale, P.W., Modiano, D., Schwartz, P.O., Sternberg, T.D., Straalen, B.V.: Chombo software package for AMR applications design document. Technical report (2003)

11. Fryxell, B., Olson, K., Ricker, P., Timmes, F.X., Zingale, M., Lamb, D.Q., MacNeice, P., Rosner, R., Truran, J.W., Tufo, H.: Flash: an adaptive mesh hydrodynamics code for modeling astrophysical thermonuclear flashes. Astrophys. J. Suppl. Ser. **131**(1), 273 (2000)

12. Goodale, T., Allen, G., Lanfermann, G., Massó, J., Radke, T., Seidel, E., Shalf, J.: The cactus framework and toolkit: design and applications. In: Palma, J.M.L.M., Sousa, A.A., Dongarra, J., Hernández, V. (eds.) VECPAR 2002. LNCS, vol. 2565, pp. 197–227. Springer, Heidelberg (2003). doi:10.1007/3-540-36569-9_13

13. Kale, L.V., Krishnan, S.: Charm++: a portable concurrent object oriented system based on C++. In: Proceedings of Conference on Object Oriented Programming Systems, Languages and Applications, pp. 91–108 (1993)

14. Langer, A., Lifflander, J., Miller, P., Pan, K.C., Kalé, L.V., Ricker, P.: Scalable algorithms for distributed-memory adaptive mesh refinement. In: 2012 IEEE 24th International Symposium on Computer Architecture and High Performance Computing, pp. 100–107, October 2012

15. MacNeice, P., Olson, K.M., Mobarry, C., de Fainchtein, R., Packer, C.: PARAMESH: a parallel adaptive mesh refinement community toolkit. Comput. Phys. Commun. **126**(3), 330–354 (2000)

16. Meng, Q., Luitjens, J., Berzins, M.: Dynamic task scheduling for the Uintah framework. In: 2010 IEEE Workshop on Many-Task Computing on Grids and Supercomputers (MTAGS), pp. 1–10. IEEE (2010)

17. Nguyen, T., Unat, D., Zhang, W., Almgren, A., Farooqi, N., Shalf, J.: Perilla: Metadata-based optimizations of an asynchronous runtime for adaptive mesh refinement. In: Proceedings of International Conference for High Performance Computing, Networking, Storage and Analysis, SC 2016, pp. 81:1–81:12. IEEE Press, Piscataway (2016)

18. Rendleman, C.A., Beckner, V.E., Lijewski, M., Crutchfield, W., Bell, J.B.: Parallelization of structured, hierarchical adaptive mesh refinement algorithms. Comput. Vis. Sci. **3**(3), 147–157 (2000)

19. Unfer, T., Boeuf, J.P., Rogier, F., Thivet, F.: Multi-scale gas discharge simulations using asynchronous adaptive mesh refinement. Comput. Phys. Commun. **181**(2), 247–258 (2010)

20. Wahib, M., Maruyama, N., Aoki, T.: Daino: a high-level framework for parallel and efficient AMR on GPUs. In: Proceedings of International Conference for High Performance Computing, Networking, Storage and Analysis, SC 2016, pp. 53:1–53:12. IEEE Press, Piscataway (2016)

Accelerator Computing

Balanced CSR Sparse Matrix-Vector Product on Graphics Processors

Goran Flegar$^{(\boxtimes)}$ and Enrique S. Quintana-Ortí

Departamento de Ingeniería y Ciencia de Computadores,
Universidad Jaume I, 12071 Castellón, Spain
{flegar,quintana}@uji.es

Abstract. We propose a novel parallel approach to compute the sparse matrix-vector product (SpMV) on graphics processing units (GPUs), optimized for matrices with an irregular row distribution of the non-zero entries. Our algorithm relies on the standard CSR format to store the sparse matrix, requires an inexpensive pre-processing step, and consumes only a minor amount of additional memory compared with significantly more expensive GPU-specific sparse matrix layouts. In addition, we propose a simple heuristic to determine whether our method or the standard CSR SpMV algorithm should be used for a specific matrix. As a result, our proposal, combined with the standard CSR SpMV, can be adopted as the default choice for the implementation of SpMV in general-purpose sparse linear algebra libraries for GPUs.

Keywords: Sparse matrix-vector product · Sparse matrix data layouts · Sparse linear algebra · Performance · GPUs

1 Introduction

The sparse matrix-vector product (SpMV) is a classical yet pivotal kernel for the solution of numerical linear algebra problems via iterative methods [10]. In the last years, this operation has also gained relevance for big data analytics [3] and web search [6]. It is thus natural that, over the past decades, a considerable research effort has been applied to design specialized data structures that offer a compact representation of the problem data to reduce the storage requirements, facilitate its manipulation, and diminish the volume of data movements for sparse computational kernels such as SpMV.

Among the variety of storage layouts for sparse matrices, the CSR (Compressed Sparse Row) format [10] conforms the current standard layout because of its storage efficiency which, in general, results in faster serial algorithms [2]. For this reason, CSR has become ubiquitous in sparse matrix computations [2,4,10].

For graphics processing units (GPUs), CSR can be outperformed by specialized sparse matrix layouts that sacrifice storage efficiency for fast (coalesced) memory access. Among these GPU-oriented formats, ELLPACK, ELLR-T [11] and SELL-C-σ [1,5] have shown notable performance. Unfortunately, none of

© Springer International Publishing AG 2017
F.F. Rivera et al. (Eds.): Euro-Par 2017, LNCS 10417, pp. 697–709, 2017.
DOI: 10.1007/978-3-319-64203-1_50

these formats is truly general. Some suffer from increased memory consumption, which can grow significantly for irregular sparsity patterns, while others (like NVIDIA's HYB [9]) are only suitable for a few types of matrix operations (computational kernels) and/or require expensive format conversions. Another common issue arising in SpMV computations on GPUs is load imbalance. This has been a topic of some recent research, resulting in new matrix formats like CSR5 [7] and BCCOO [12], which enable well-balanced SpMV algorithms.

In this paper, we re-visit the CSR format, proposing a CSR-based SpMV variant that provides increased efficiency on GPUs and offers the following properties compared with standard CSR algorithm and GPU-specific solutions:

- Our balanced CSR algorithm for irregular matrices (CSR-I) ensures an even distribution of the workload among the CUDA threads participating in the SpMV, at the cost of using atomic updates to avoid race conditions.
- CSR-I maintains the same data structure as CSR, and augments this with an additional vector of a dimension that is linear in the amount of available parallelism. For moderate to large-scale problems this introduces a negligible storage overhead, in general much lower than that incurred by ELLPACK-type formats and sliced versions (SELL-∗).
- The additional data structure leveraged by CSR-I can be built at execution time, e.g. the first time an SpMV is invoked, for a very small computational cost, similar to that of reading once the solution vector for the SpMV.
- Our experiments with a subset of a sparse matrix benchmark show that CSR-I outperforms CSR for about 40–50% of the cases on NVIDIA architectures providing hardware support for atomic updates. Furthermore, it is easy to detect *a priori* when CSR-I should be the preferred option. This property leads to an optimal hybrid kernel that employs either CSR-I or CSR, depending on the target problem.

2   CSR-Based Formats and Algorithms for SpMV

CSR represents a sparse matrix $A \in \mathbb{R}^{m \times n}$ in compact form using three arrays: vector `val` stores the n_z non-zero values by rows; `colidx` keeps the column index for each value in the same order; and `rowptr` contains $m + 1$ row pointers that mark the initial and final position of each row within the other two arrays; see Fig. 1. Storing the sparse matrix A in CSR format thus requires $\mathcal{S}_{CSR} = n_z(s_v + s_i) + (m + 1)s_i$ bytes, where s_v and s_i respectively denote the number of bytes occupied by each value and integer index.

In [8], Bell and Garland (BG) explored the performance of different sparse formats and implementations of SpMV for throughput-oriented GPUs from NVIDIA. BG's SpMV kernels based on CSR parallelize the product across the matrix rows, with one CUDA thread assigned to each row in the *scalar* kernel (CSR-s) or, alternatively, one warp per row in the *vector* kernel (CSR-v). CSR-s has two major issues though: first, for sparse matrices with an irregular row distribution of their non-zero entries, many threads within a warp will likely remain idle. Second, since each thread of a warp works on a different row, the memory

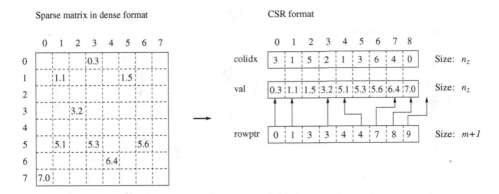

Fig. 1. Data layouts for an 8×8 sparse matrix with $n_z = 9$ nonzero entries.

accesses are noncoalesced. CSR-v aims to amend the second issue, though it requires that the rows contain a number of nonzeros greater than the warp size in order to deliver high performance [8].

A couple of examples illustrate the advantages/deficiencies of CSR-s and CSR-v. Consider first an arrowhead matrix, with all its nonzero entries lying on the main diagonal and the last column/row of the matrix. (This problem type appears in domain decomposition methods, when discretizing partial differential equations.) This matrix structure poses an ill-case scenario for both BG kernels, as it produces a highly unbalanced mapping of the workload to the threads. In contrast, a tridiagonal matrix (often encountered in computational physics), results in an almost perfectly balanced distribution of the workload for both BG CSR kernels, but yields a significant waste of resources for CSR-v.

Figure 2 provides a motivating example for our work. The left-hand side plot there shows the sparsity pattern for matrix FREESCALE/TRANSIENT from the SuiteSparse Matrix Collection.[1] The distribution of the nonzeros for this problem, arising in circuit simulation, shows quite an unbalanced pattern, with most of the elements concentrated in a few rows of the matrix. Concretely, more than 95% of the rows contain 10 or less nonzeros; 99.95% comprise 100 or less nonzeros; only 5 rows contain more than 10^3 nonzeros; and only 2 more than 10^4, with the densest row comprising 60,423 nonzero entries.

The right-hand side plot in Fig. 2 reports the execution time on an NVIDIA GTX1080 GPU for double-precision SPMV kernels based on CSR and HYB (implemented in cuSPARSE [9]), SELL-P (from MAGMA-sparse[2]), and our balanced version of CSR (CSR-I). ELL and ELLR-T are not included because, for this problem instance, they both need to store an $m \times 60,423$ matrix just for the array `val` (i.e., more than 79.5 Gbytes in double precision), which exceeds the memory of the target GPU. For this particular matrix both CSR and SELL-P

---

[1] Formerly known as the University of Florida Matrix Collection: http://www.cise.ufl. edu/research/sparse/matrices/.
[2] http://icl.cs.utk.edu/magma/.

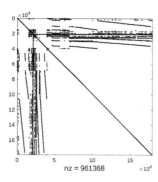
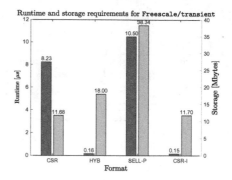

Fig. 2. Left: sparsity pattern for FREESCALE/TRANSIENT. Right: execution time (blue) and memory consumption (red) on a GTX1080 using different SpMV kernels. (Color figure online)

exhibit poor performance compared with HYB and CSR-I. SELL-P also suffers from considerably higher memory consumption than other implementations. CSR-I is the best performing algorithm in this case, achieving slightly better performance than HYB, while maintaining the storage efficiency of CSR.

3   Balanced SpMV Kernel

The culprit for the unbalance in the SpMV implementations discussed in Sect. 2 is the irregular distribution of arrays `val` and `colidx` (and therefore workload) among the threads. This irregularity can result in significant performance loss, since the two vectors comprise the majority of CSR's data structure. Hence, the key objective of our kernel is to attain a balanced distribution of these arrays among the threads. The trade-off for this comes in the form of an increased number of integer operations and the introduction of potential race conditions, which may result in slightly lower performance on regular sparsity patterns.

General Idea. In order to distribute the arrays `val` and `colidx`, both of size n_z, evenly among T threads, thread $k \in \{0, 1, \ldots, T-1\}$ is given a segment of the arrays starting at $\lfloor kn_z/T \rfloor$ (inclusive) and ending at $\lfloor (k+1)n_z/T \rfloor$ (exclusive). During the execution of the SpMV $y := Ax + y$, with an $m \times n$ matrix A, each thread multiplies the elements in its segment of `val` with those of the input vector x determined by the corresponding indices in `colidx` (dot product). The result has to be accumulated into the correct position of the output vector y. Thus, the thread has to keep track of the current row it is operating on, as well as the last entry of the row, in order to detect a change to the next row once this entry is reached. The sequential C routine in Fig. 3 illustrates this idea. Since there can be multiple threads operating on the same row, the updates on the solution vector y have to be implemented as atomic transactions, resulting in one transaction per matrix element which rapidly becomes a performance bottleneck. However, this problem can be amended by accumulating the result

```
1  const int T = thread_count;  // degree of thread concurrency
2  void SpMVI(int m, int *rowptr, int *colidx, float *val, float *x, float *y) {
3    int row = -1, next_row = 0, nnz = rowptr[m];
4    for (int k = 0; k < T; ++k) {  // this loop should be parallelized
5      for (int i = k*nnz / T; i < (k+1)*nnz / T; ++i) {
6        while (i >= next_row) next_row = rowptr[ ++row+1 ];
7        y[row] += val[i] * x[ colidx[i] ];
8  }}}
```

Fig. 3. A (sequential) C implementation of the CSR-I algorithm. In a parallel implementation each thread needs to efficiently determine its starting value of the row variable. This is discussed in Sect. 3, "Determining the first row of each segment".

to a thread-local variable, and updating the output vector only after the thread has finished processing the row. With this option, the upper limit on the number of atomic transactions is reduced to $m + T$.

Achieving Good Performance on GPUs. Although the approach underlying CSR-I does result in a balanced distribution of the data among the threads, it is not suitable for GPUs in such form. Concretely, since each thread operates on a different matrix segment, with that formulation the memory accesses of the threads within a warp will be noncoalesced. In a memory-bounded kernel like SpMV, this severely reduces performance. To tackle the issue, the segments can be distributed at the warp-level, so that each segment is assigned to one warp (instead of to one thread). The warp then reads its segment in chunks of 32 elements, with each thread within the warp reading one value of the chunk and accumulating the result into its local registers. After reaching the end of a row, all threads need to write their results to the output vector. If this was realized using atomic instructions, it would cause significant overhead, as the threads inside one warp are synchronized and all of them would then try to update the result at exactly the same time. Instead, the results are first accumulated by a single thread, using reduction via warp shuffles, and then a single atomic addition updates the result in global memory.

A second question arising from the warp-level segment distribution is how to handle rows that end in the middle of a chunk. Waiting for the entire warp to complete the processing of a row before moving to the next one would cause a partial serialization in case the rows consisted of a few elements only. To address this, the threads are allowed to work on different rows at the same time, and the information about the current and the next rows becomes thread-specific. As a consequence, the algorithm to accumulate the results before writing to main memory needs to be changed. Each time at least one of the threads moves to a different row, the entire warp executes a segmented scan (instead of a reduction) which accumulates the result for each row in the register of the first thread working on that particular row. At this point the local results of the remaining threads are reset to zero, while the first threads will update the global output vector once they are finished with their row. This eliminates all race conditions inside a warp, since each thread updates a different location of the output vector. Determining whether at least one thread moved to the next row can be realized in only one instruction per chunk by using warp vote functions.

Warp-level segment distribution also causes additional reads from `rowptr`, since each thread may need to move multiple rows after each chunk. However, as the last thread in a warp always has the most up-to-date information about the starting row of the next chunk, the number of reads can be reduced by broadcasting this information to the other threads within the warp using a single warp shuffle. Finally, in order to ensure aligned accesses to arrays `val` and `colidx`, and fully utilize each fetched cache line, the segment sizes can be restricted to an integer multiple of the chunk size. Since the chunk size is a multiple of the cache-line size, if `val` and `colidx` arrays are aligned, the start of each segment will also be aligned.

Determining the First Row of Each Segment. At the beginning of the CSR-I algorithm each warp has to determine the first row of its segment. This can be done by first constructing a histogram of `rowptr` with T bins associated with the segments of `val` and `colidx`. The number of elements n_i in each bin corresponds to the number of rows which end in the segment associated with this particular bin. Since the first row of segment k is equal to the number of rows ending in previous segments (i.e., $\mathtt{srow}_k = n_1 + n_2 + \ldots + n_{k-1}$), the indices of these first rows can be determined by computing the exclusive scan of the histogram.

In order to avoid repeating this computation at each SpMV invocation, the array `srow` can be saved and "attached" to the CSR matrix structure. We note that the optimal number of warps T does not depend on the matrix A, but only on the hardware-specific degree of thread-concurrency, adding a constant amount of storage overhead. Even though the procedure can be realized on the GPU in parallel, this is generally not needed, as its computational cost is very low compared with that of SpMV: the entire computation requires only one pass over `rowptr` and one over the resulting histogram, comprising a total of $m + T$ data accesses and integer operations. Instead, it can be performed sequentially on the CPU and overlapped with the (initial) memory transfer of matrix A to the GPU.

4 Experimental Evaluation

Setup and Metrics. The GPUs used in the experiments cover a fair subset of recent compute capabilities from NVIDIA: 3.5 ("Kepler" K40) and 6.1 ("Pascal" GTX1080). Since the experiments run only on the GPU, the details of the host CPU are not relevant. Experiments on even older architectures (Fermi and earlier) are not possible since these GPUs do not support warp shuffle instructions required by the CSR-I algorithm. We use NVIDIA's compilers in the CUDA toolkit 8.0, and report numbers for single precision (SP) and double precision (DP) arithmetic. All kernels are implemented using the CUDA programming model and are designed to be integrated into the MAGMA-sparse library, which is also leveraged as a testing environment. In addition, the CSR-I algorithm will be publicly available in a future version of MAGMA.

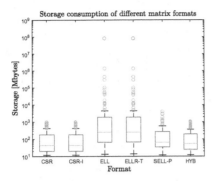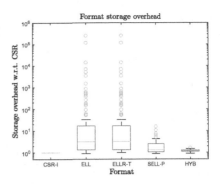

Fig. 4. Storage consumption of different sparse matrix formats (left) and overhead compared to CSR for these formats (right). The data is shown for 100 selected matrices from SMC, assuming $s_v = 8$ (double precision) and $s_i = 4$.

Among the implementations of SPMV based on CSR we compare the two variants from BG: CSR-s, which is implemented in MAGMA-sparse and an implementation of CSR-v taken from BG's article, as well as the CSR algorithm from NVIDIA's cuSPARSE library. Among the specialized formats, we include the implementations of SPMV for ELLPACK, ELLR-T and SELL-P from MAGMA-sparse, and that for the HYB format from cuSPARSE.

In order to obtain a comprehensive evaluation we compare the storage formats and SPMV implementations from the perspectives of performance and storage cost. For the performance, we report either the speed-up/slow-down relative to the CSR kernel from cuSPARSE or the absolute performance in terms of GFLOPS rate (billions of floating-point arithmetic operations, or flops, per second). The flop count for SPMV used for all examples is $2n_z$, even though some of the implementations of SPMV may actually perform a larger number of flops (because they operate with zero entries). All experiments are repeated 1,000 times and the average time of these runs is used in the calculations.

The CSR-I algorithm has one tunable parameter: the number of warps T launched to compute the SPMV. The optimal value for T is proportional to the degree of hardware concurrency, i.e. $T = l \cdot n_C/32$, where n_C is the number of CUDA cores available on the GPU and l is the desired load per core. Our experiments reveal that the optimal load is $l = 64$ for both the K40 and GTX1080 architectures and this setting is used for all experiments in this section.

We determine the storage requirements for the CSR, ELLPACK and ELLR-T formats from the basic properties of the matrix A as:

$$\mathcal{S}_{CSR}, \quad \mathcal{S}_{ELL} = m \cdot l_M(s_v + s_i), \quad \text{and} \quad \mathcal{S}_{ELLR-T} = \mathcal{S}_{ELL} + m \cdot s_i,$$

where l_M is the number of nonzero elements in the densest matrix row. Determining the storage requirements for the remaining two formats is more involved. For SELL-P we use a conversion routine from CSR to SELL-P implemented in MAGMA-sparse and modify each memory allocation to instead increase a

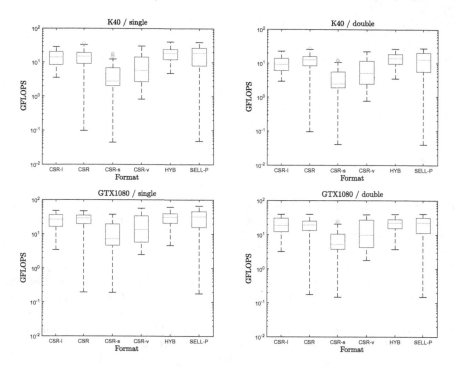

Fig. 5. GFLOPS distribution of SpMV implementations on K40 (top) and GTX1080 (bottom), using SP and DP arithmetic (left and right, respectively).

counter by the amount that it was supposed to allocate. This is not possible for HYB, as the source code is not available. For this case, we use the `cudaMemGetInfo` routine from the CUDA Runtime API to get the total amount of free device memory before and after allocating the matrix in HYB format. The difference between the two values is the actual storage required by HYB. This strategy allows us to measure the storage consumption without actually allocating the required data for all formats except HYB. Thus, we are able to evaluate the cost even if the problem does not fit into the GPU memory.

The experiments are carried out using a subset of the SuiteSparse Matrix Collection (SMC). Concretely, we first filtered the complete collection (2,757 problem instances) keeping only real-valued instances with $10^6 \leq n_z < 10^8$ (491 problems), and then randomly selected 100 cases[3] among these (about 20% of the filtered problems and 3.6% of the complete collection). The limits for n_z were chosen to allow the utilization of the full processing potential of GPUs, while keeping the storage requirements low enough to fit the matrix into the GPU memory. We believe this is a representative subset of the problems for which a GPU accelerator can be beneficial, not being biassed to any particular format.

---

[3] The list of cases employed in the experiments can be downloaded from http://www3.uji.es/~flegar/2017_csri/matrices.txt.

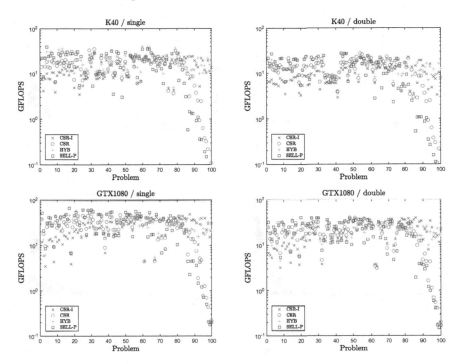

Fig. 6. Comparison of SpMV implementations on K40 (top) and GTX1080 (bottom), using SP and DP arithmetic (left and right, respectively).

Memory Consumption. We commence our evaluation with an analysis of storage consumption of different matrix formats for the 100 selected matrices from SMC. Figure 4 shows that, for most cases, CSR is the format that requires the lowest amount of memory, and the additional storage required to save the `srow` array in CSR-I is negligible. HYB requires some additional memory, but this is still within a limit of 2× compared with CSR. SELL-P performs quite poorly for some cases, consuming up to 11× more memory than CSR; while ELLPACK and ELLR-T consume even up to 5 orders of magnitude more storage space in some cases. As a result, even though the storage required by CSR and HYB is under 1 Gbyte for all selected problems, the storage requirements can grow to 3 Gbytes for SELL-P and even to 100 Tbytes for ELLPACK and ELLR-T. This shows that the last two layouts cannot be considered as general formats. Since the focus of this work is on SpMV algorithms for general matrices, possibly with an irregular nonzero distribution, we omit ELLPACK and ELLR-T from the following experiments.

Global Comparison. The results in Fig. 5 show the distribution of the GFLOPS rates by means of "box-and-whisker" plots. This experiment reveals that the median GFLOPS rate for our CSR-I format (red line inside the blue boxes) is similar to those of the specialized kernel for CSR in cuSPARSE, HYB and SELL-P; and all four present considerably higher GFLOPS medians than

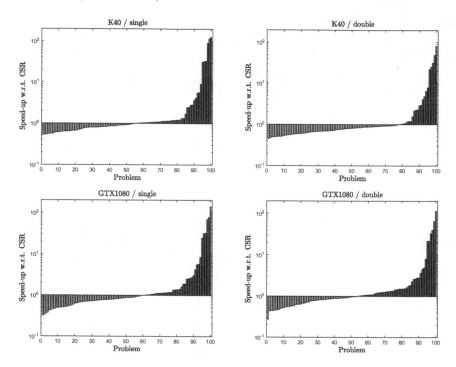

Fig. 7. Comparison between CSR and CSR-I implementations of SpMV on K40 (top) and GTX1080 (bottom), using SP and DP arithmetic (left and right, respectively).

those observed for CSR-s and CSR-v. For this reason, we omit CSR-s and CSR-v from further discussion. Furthermore, the lower "whisker" attached to the boxes in Fig. 5, which comprises the first quartile (i.e. 25%) of the cases, show that both CSR and SELL-P encounter a considerable number of "ill-conditioned" cases from the point of view of performance, delivering notably lower GFLOPS rates for those. In contrast, CSR-I and HYB feature a more consistent performance rate. This behaviour can also be observed in Fig. 6. (The problem instances in this figure are ordered by speed-up/slow-down of CSR-I over cuSPARSE CSR.) For regular cases, appearing in the left-hand side of the plots, CSR-I is outperformed by all implementations due to its higher arithmetic intensity and use of atomic operations. In contrast, for irregular problems, in the right-hand side of the plots, the only implementation that matches its performance is HYB, which, in addition to higher storage consumption, is not suitable for other types of operations. We do not evaluate the cost of transformation from CSR to the other formats included in our experiments. For CSR-I, as discussed in the previous section, this cost is small, or even negligible if this transformation is overlapped with the first transfer of the matrix data to the GPU memory.

Detailed Comparison of CSR and CSR-I. As argued at the beginning of this paper, the specific goal for our CSR-I variant is to ensure an efficient execution of SpMV when the matrix exhibits an irregular row distribution of its

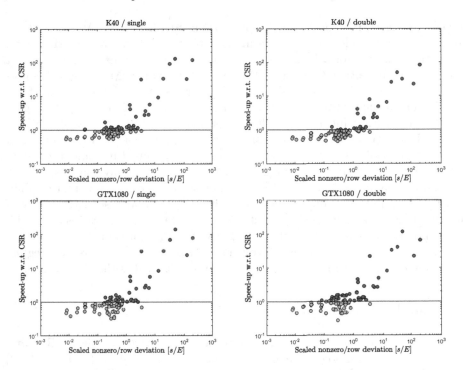

Fig. 8. Relationship between $s[n_{zr}]/E[n_{zr}]$ (x-axis) and speed-up/slow-down of CSR-I over CSR (y-axis) on K40 (top) and GTX1080 (bottom) using SP and DP arithmetic (left and right, respectively).

nonzero entries, while maintaining the data layout of the regular version of CSR (and roughly its memory requirements). To close the experiments, we evaluate the performance of these two formats in more detail. Figure 7 illustrates the throughput of the CSR-I variant with respect to that of CSR from cuSPARSE for each problem instance. In these plots, we employ a logarithmic scale for the y-axis, and the problems instances are sequenced in the x-axis in increasing order of difference in favour of CSR-I. For three of the configurations: K40-SP and GTX 1080-SP/DP, CSR-I outperforms CSR in about 40–50% of the problems, and the difference in favour of the former comes in a factor that can raise more than 100×. Compared with this, the highest loss of CSR-I shows a factor that is at most 0.3×. For K40-DP CSR-I is superior for 24% of the problem instances. This is explained by the lack of hardware support for DP atomic updates in this architecture.

Even though CSR-I shows notable acceleration over CSR for a fair fraction of the problem instances, an optimal hybrid strategy is obtained if CSR-I is applied to compute SPMV for matrices in this subset only, while the operation relies on CSR for the remaining cases. Note that this is possible because CSR-I maintains the same structure as CSR, with just an additional vector to store the starting rows of each segment. In contrast, an attempt to combine CSR with any of the other GPU-specialized formats (HYB, SELL-P, ELLPACK, ELLR-T) would incur a considerable increase in the amount of stored information (even a complete duplication). Still, a relevant question is whether we can choose *a priori* to rely on either CSR or CSR-I for a particular SpMV. Figure 8 shows that this is indeed the case if we have a rough statistical estimation of the distribution of the number of nonzero entries per row n_{zr}. Concretely, the figure depicts the relationship between the performance of CSR-I over CSR and the standard deviation-to-mean ratio: $s[n_{zr}]/E[n_{zr}]$. The plots in the figure show a clear separation at $s[n_{zr}]/E[n_{zr}] = 1$ for both architectures and precisions. For ratios grater than one, CSR-I is slightly slower for only one test matrix and shows a significant acceleration for the rest of the cases on GTX1080. The K40 GPU exhibits a similar behaviour, with only several cases slightly slower and the majority achieving significantly higher performance for ratios above this threshold. For ratios between 0.1 and 1, the faster algorithm depends on the matrix, but the majority of cases favour cuSPARSE CSR. For extremely regular sparsity patterns, with ratios below 0.1, cuSPARSE CSR is the clear winner.

5   Conclusions

We have re-formulated the parallelization of SpMV based on the CSR sparse matrix format to enforce a balanced partitioning of the data (and workload) on GPUs, optimized for matrices with an irregular row distribution of the non-zero entries. Our approach departs from the conventional parallelization across matrix rows advocated by standard implementations of CSR SpMV and other GPU-specific formats, instead facing potential race conditions via atomic trans-actions (supported by hardware in recent GPU architectures). Furthermore, our algorithm preserves the standard CSR format to store the sparse matrix, aug-mented with a vector which holds the row indexes of some key matrix elements. This additional array can be built inexpensively and consumes only a minor amount of additional memory.

Our experiments on two recent GPU architectures from NVIDIA, using both single and double precision arithmetic, show that our algorithm can be composed with the standard CSR SpMV to yield a GPU kernel that becomes a strong candidate for the implementation of SpMV in general-purpose sparse linear algebra libraries for this type of accelerators.

Acknowledgements. This work was supported by the CICYT project TIN2014-53495-R of the MINECO and FEDER and the EU H2020 project 732631 "OPRE-COMP. Open Transprecision Computing".

References

1. Anzt, H., Tomov, S., Dongarra, J.: Implementing a sparse matrix vector product for the SELL-C/SELL-C-σ formats on NVIDIA GPUs. Technical report, ut-eecs-14-727, University of Tennessee (2014)

2. Buluç, A., Fineman, J.T., Frigo, M., Gilbert, J.R., Leiserson, C.E.: Parallel sparse matrix-vector and matrix-transpose-vector multiplication using compressed sparse blocks. In: Proceedings of the 21st Annual Symposium on Parallelism in Algorithms and Architectures, SPAA 2009, pp. 233–244. ACM (2009)
3. Buono, D., Gunnels, J.A., Que, X., Checconi, F., Petrini, F., Tuan, T.C., Long, C.: Optimizing sparse linear algebra for large-scale graph analytics. Computer **48**(8), 26–34 (2015)
4. Davis, T.A.: Direct Methods for Sparse Linear Systems. SIAM, Philadelphia (2006)
5. Kreutzer, M., Hager, G., Wellein, G., Fehske, H., Bishop, A.R.: A unified sparse matrix data format for efficient general sparse matrix-vector multiplication on modern processors with wide SIMD units. SIAM J. Sci. Comput. **36**(5), C401–C423 (2014)
6. Langville, A.N., Meyer, C.D.: Google's PageRank and Beyond: The Science of Search Engine Rankings. Princeton University Press, Princeton (2011)
7. Liu, W., Vinter, B.: CSR5: an efficient storage format for cross-platform sparse matrix-vector multiplication. In: Proceedings of the 29th ACM on International Conference on Supercomputing, pp. 339–350. ACM (2015)
8. Nathan, B., Michael, G.: Efficient sparse matrix-vector multiplication on CUDA. Technical report, NVIDIA Technical Report NVR-2008-004 (2008)
9. NVIDIA. cuSPARSE library (2017). http://docs.nvidia.com/cuda/cusparse/
10. Saad, Y.: Iterative Methods for Sparse Linear Systems. SIAM, Philadelphia (2003)
11. Vázquez, F., Fernández, J.J., Garzón, E.M.: A new approach for sparse matrix vector product on NVIDIA GPUs. Concur. Comput.: Pract. Exp. **23**(8), 815–826 (2011)
12. Yan, S., Li, C., Zhang, Y., Zhou, H.: yaSpMV: yet another SPMV framework on GPUs. In: ACM SIGPLAN Notices, vol. 49, pp. 107–118. ACM (2014)

To Distribute or Not to Distribute:
The Question of Load Balancing
for Performance or Energy

Esteban Stafford[1]([⊠]), Borja Pérez[1]([⊠]), Jose Luis Bosque[1]([⊠]), Ramón Beivide[1],
and Mateo Valero[2]

[1] Universidad de Cantabria, Santander, Spain
{esteban.stafford,borja.perez,joseluis.bosque,ramon.beivide}@unican.es
[2] Barcelona Supercomputing Center, Barcelona, Spain
mateo@ac.upc.edu

Abstract. Heterogeneous systems are nowadays a common choice in
the path to Exascale. Through the use of accelerators they offer outstanding energy efficiency. The programming of these devices employs
the host-device model, which is suboptimal as CPU remains idle during
kernel executions, but still consumes energy. Making the CPU contribute
computing effort might improve the performance and energy consumption of the system. This paper analyses the advantages of this approach
and sets the limits of when its beneficial. The claims are supported by
a set of models that determine how to share a single data-parallel task
between the CPU and the accelerator for optimum performance, energy
consumption or efficiency. Interestingly, the models show that optimising performance does not always mean optimum energy or efficiency as
well. The paper experimentally validates the models, which represent an
invaluable tool for programmers when faced with the dilemma of whether
to distribute their workload in these systems.

1 Introduction

There is an ever growing interest on heterogeneous systems in the HPC community, by integrating GPUs, as they increase the computing power and improve
the energy efficiency of these large systems [10]. The programming of these is
based mainly in frameworks or APIs like CUDA and OpenCL, designed around
the *Host-Device programming model*. Which relies on offloading data-parallel sections to the accelerator while the CPU remains idle. During the latter, despite
not contributing computational effort to the system, the devices still draw a
significant amount of power, known as static power consumption [5]. This leads
to think that a load-balanced co-execution might be necessary to improve the
efficiency of the system. However, with the above frameworks, co-execution is
possible but far from trivial, and neither is determining the optimal load balance.

Despite the difficulties, co-execution can give benefits in terms of performance
and energy efficiency. If the task is successfully balanced among the devices, the

F.F. Rivera et al. (Eds.): Euro-Par 2017, LNCS 10417, pp. 710–722, 2017.
DOI: 10.1007/978-3-319-64203-1_51

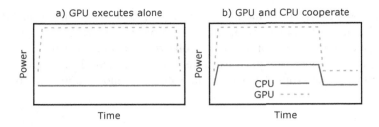

Fig. 1. Power using a host device model versus device cooperation.

computing power of the heterogeneous system is the sum of that of the devices, consequently improving the performance. Regarding energy consumption, without co-execution idle devices still require energy to operate, called *static energy*, consequently reducing the energy efficiency of the heterogeneous system as a whole. Given the execution of a data-parallel task, Fig. 1.a shows the power consumed by the system when only the GPU is used. The CPU consumes power even though it is only waiting for the GPU. Figure 1.b shows that the collaboration of the CPU improves performance, as the computation is finished faster, but might also improve the total energy consumption.

This paper studies, from an analytical point of view, whether co-execution of a single massively data-parallel kernel in a heterogeneous system with two devices is beneficial. And how load balancing affects each of the proposed metrics: the performance, the energy consumption or the energy efficiency, and if they can be optimised simultaneously. This allows programmers decide beforehand on the suitability of co-execution in their applications, thus reducing the programming effort.

The main contributions of this paper are:

- To aid the programmer to take an early decision on whether it is worth dividing the workload of a single kernel among the devices of a heterogeneous system.
- Obtaining a series of models that allow determining the workload sharing proportion that optimises the performance, energy consumption or efficiency.
- Conducting an experimental study that proves the validity of the proposed models. The values given by the models match those of the experiments.

Some proposals can be found in the literature, that allow the CPU and the accelerator to share the execution of data-parallel sections [2,3,6–9,12,15]. These focus on sharing the workload among the devices to maximise performance. Some of these include both static [7,8] and dynamic [2,3,6,9,15] load balancing algorithms. In general, these allow optimising only the performance of the systems, ignoring their energy consumption, which is one of the most important challenges of computers nowadays. There are other approaches to the problem of optimising the performance of single kernels co-executed on several devices [16]. But, to the extent of the authors' knowledge, this paper is the first that proposes an analytical model that can be used to take an a priori decision on the suitability of co-execution, taking energy into account.

The rest of this paper is organized as follows. Section 2 describes the proposed load balancing models. Section 3 explains the experimental methodology, while Sect. 4 evaluates the proposals. Finally in Sect. 5, the most important conclusions are presented.

2   Load Balancing Model

To sustain the claims of this paper, it is necessary to obtain a series of models and algorithms that allow determining an optimal share of the load among the computing devices. A definition of a set of concepts and parameters is necessary, as they characterize both the parallel application and the devices of the system.

- **Work-item**: in OpenCL is the unit of concurrent execution. This paper assumes that each one represents the same amount of compute load.
- **Total Workload** (W): is the number of work-items needed to solve a problem. It is determined by some input parameters of the application.
- **Device Workload** (W_C, W_G): is the number of work-items assigned to each device: W_C for the CPU and W_G for the GPU.
- **Processing speeds of devices** (S_C, S_G): are the number of work-items that each device can execute per time unit, taking into account the communication times.
- **Processing speed of the system** (S_T): is the sum of the speeds of all the devices in the system.

$$S_T = S_C + S_G$$

- **Device execution time** (T_C, T_G): is the time required by a device to complete its assigned workload.

$$T_C = \frac{W_C}{S_C} \qquad T_G = \frac{W_G}{S_G}$$

- **Total execution time** (T): is the time required by the whole system to execute the application, determined by the last device to finish its task.

$$T = max\{T_C, T_G\}$$

- **Workload partition** (α): dictates the proportion of the total workload that is given to the CPU. Then, the proportion for the GPU is $1 - \alpha$.

$$W_C = \alpha W \qquad W_G = (1 - \alpha)W$$

Based on the above, the total execution time (T) is obtained from the workload of each device and their processing speed:

$$T = max\left\{\alpha\frac{W}{S_C}, (1 - \alpha)\frac{W}{S_G}\right\} \tag{1}$$

It is also necessary to model the energetic behaviour of the system, by considering the specifications of the devices.

- **Static power** (P_C^S, P_G^S): is consumed by each device while idle. This is unavoidable and will be consumed throughout the execution of the application.
- **Dynamic power** (P_C^D, P_G^D): is consumed when the devices are computing.
- **Device energy** (E_C, E_G): is consumed by each device during the execution.
- **Total energy** (E): is the drawn by the heterogeneous system while executing the application. And it is the sum of the energy of each device.

The total consumed energy is the addition of the static (first term in Eq. 2) and dynamic (second term in Eq. 2) energies. The static energy is consumed by both devices throughout the execution of the task. Thus is obtained by multiplying the static power of the devices P_C^S, P_G^S by the total execution time T (Eq. 1). The dynamic energy is consumed only when the device is computing. The dynamic energy of the CPU is $P_C^D T_C$ and $P_G^D T_G$ for the GPU.

$$E = \left[(P_C^S + P_G^S)\, max\left\{\alpha \frac{W}{S_C}, (1-\alpha)\frac{W}{S_G}\right\}\right] + \left[\alpha P_C^D \frac{W}{S_C} + (1-\alpha)P_G^D \frac{W}{S_G}\right] \quad (2)$$

2.1 Optimal Performance Load Balancing

Attending strictly to performance, an ideal load balancing algorithm causes both devices to take the same time T_{opt} to conclude their assigned workload. Because none of them incur in idle time waiting for the other to finish.

$$T_{opt} = T_C = T_G = \frac{W}{S_T}$$

The question remains as to which that work distribution is, or what α satisfies the above equation. Intuitively, it will depend on the speeds of the devices. In Expression 1, it was shown that the execution times of each device are determined by the workload assigned to them, as well as their processing speed.

$$T_C = \alpha \frac{W}{S_C} \qquad T_G = (1-\alpha)\frac{W}{S_G}$$

Both times are linear with α, so they each define a segment in the range $(0 \leq \alpha \leq 1)$. T_C has positive slope and its maximum value is reached at $\alpha = 1$. While T_G has its maximum value at $\alpha = 0$ and negative slope. Then, where both segments cross, both devices are taking the same time to execute, and therefore the optimal α_{opt} share is found.

$$\alpha_{opt}\frac{W}{S_C} = (1 - \alpha_{opt})\frac{W}{S_G} \Rightarrow \alpha_{opt}(\frac{W}{S_C} + \frac{W}{S_G}) = \frac{W}{S_G} \Rightarrow \alpha_{opt} = \frac{S_C}{S_C + S_G} \quad (3)$$

Finally, it is also possible to determine the gain (or speedup) of the optimal execution compared to running on each of the devices alone.

$$G_C = \frac{1}{\alpha_{opt}} \qquad G_G = \frac{1}{1 - \alpha_{opt}}$$

2.2   Optimal Energy Load Balancing

The value of α_{opt} determined by Expression 3 tells how to share the workload between both devices to obtain the best performance. Now it is interesting to know if this sharing also gives the best energy consumption.

Regarding the total energy of the system (Expression 2), note that it uses the *maximum* function. To analyse this, also note that α_{opt} is the turning point where the CPU finishes earlier than the GPU, and where the *maximum* is going to change its result. Then the total energy of the system can be expressed in a piece-wise manner with two linear segments joined at α_{opt}. This expression is not differentiable but it is continuous. In order to determine local minima, three cases have to be analysed.

1. Both segments have positive slope, so $\alpha = 0$ will give the minimum energy.
2. Both segments have negative slope. Then the minimum is found at $\alpha = 1$.
3. The slope of the left segment is negative and the right is positive. Then the minimum occurs at $\alpha_{opt} = \frac{S_C}{S_C + S_G}$.

The problem is now finding when each of the cases occur. For this, each segment has to be analysed separately.

Left Side. In the range of $(0 < \alpha < \alpha_{opt})$ the CPU is being underused. Its workload is not enough to keep it busy and has to wait for the overworked GPU to finish. Therefore the execution time is dictated by the GPU, and the energy of the whole system is:

$$E = (P_C^S + P_G^S + P_G^D)(1 - \alpha)\frac{W}{S_G} + P_C^D \alpha \frac{W}{S_C}$$

To find when the segment has a negative slope, it is differentiated with respect to α and compared to 0:

$$\frac{dE}{d\alpha} = -(P_C^S + P_G^S)\frac{W}{S_G} + P_C^D \frac{W}{S_C} - P_G^D \frac{W}{S_G} < 0 \Rightarrow \frac{S_G}{S_C} < \frac{P_C^S + P_G^S + P_G^D}{P_C^D} \quad (4)$$

Right Side. In the range $(\alpha_{opt} < \alpha < 1)$ the opposite situation occurs. The CPU is overloaded, taking longer to complete its workload than the GPU. Then the execution time is determined by the CPU, and the system energy is:

$$E = (P_C^S + P_G^S + P_C^D)\alpha \frac{W}{S_C} + P_G^D(1 - \alpha)\frac{W}{S_G}$$

As before the slope of the segment is found differentiating, only this time it is desired to find when the slope is positive.

$$\frac{dE}{d\alpha} = (P_C^S + P_G^S)\frac{W}{S_C} + P_C^D \frac{W}{S_C} - P_G^D \frac{W}{S_G} > 0 \Rightarrow \frac{S_G}{S_C} > \frac{P_G^D}{P_C^S + P_G^S + P_C^D} \quad (5)$$

Satisfying both Expressions (4 and 5) means that the third case occurs, where the minimum energy is found at $\alpha_{opt} = \frac{S_G}{S_C + S_G}$. Combining these leads to:

$$\frac{P_G^D}{P_C^S + P_G^S + P_C^D} < \frac{S_G}{S_C} < \frac{P_C^S + P_G^S + P_G^D}{P_C^D} \tag{6}$$

This indicates that the ratio between the speeds of the devices must lie within a given range in order for the sharing to make sense from an energy perspective. The energy consumed in this case can be expressed as:

$$E = \frac{W}{S_T}(P_C^S + P_G^S + P_C^D + P_G^D) \tag{7}$$

Should the above condition not be satisfied, then it is advisable to use only one of the devices. If $\frac{S_G}{S_C} < \frac{P_G^D}{P_C^S + P_G^S + P_C^D}$, then the minimum appears at $\alpha = 0$. Meaning that using the CPU is pointless, as no matter how small the portion of work, it is going to waste energy. The consumption in this case is:

$$E = \frac{W}{S_G}(P_C^S + P_G^S + P_G^D) \tag{8}$$

When the condition is not satisfied on the other side: $\frac{S_G}{S_C} > \frac{P_C^S + P_G^S + P_G^D}{P_C^D}$, the minimum is found at $\alpha = 1$. Then it is the CPU that must be used exclusively. As assigning the smallest workload to the GPU is going to be detrimental to the energy consumption of the system.

$$E = \frac{W}{S_C} \cdot (P_C^S + P_G^S + P_C^D) \tag{9}$$

2.3   Optimal Energy Efficiency Load Balancing

Finally, this section analyses the advantage of co-execution when considering the *energy efficiency*. The metric used to evaluate the efficiency is the Energy-Delay Product (EDP), of the product of the consumed energy and the execution time of the application. The starting point is then combining the expressions of time and energy (1 and 2) of the system.

Again, since both expressions include the *maximum* function they have to be analysed in pieces. This time, both pieces will be quadratic functions of α, that may have local extrema at any point in the curve. Therefore it is necessary to equate the differential to 0 and solve for α.

Left Side. If $(0 < \alpha < \frac{S_C}{S_T})$ the expressions for time and energy are multiplied obtaining the EDP. Differentiating on α and solving the differential equated to 0 leads to an extreme point at α_{left}.

$$\alpha_{left} = \frac{2S_C(P_C^S + P_G^S + P_G^D) - S_G P_C^D}{2S_C(P_C^S + P_G^S + P_G^D) - 2S_G P_C^D}$$

Right Side. Now the range ($\frac{S_C}{S_T} < \alpha < 1$) is considered. Again, combining the time and energy expressions for this interval gives the EDP, which is differentiated and equated to 0 to locate the extremum at α_{right}.

$$\alpha_{right} = \frac{S_C P_G^D}{2\left[S_C P_G^D - S_G(P_C^S + P_G^S + P_C^D)\right]}$$

The analysis of both sides shows that determining the minimum EDP is less obvious than in previous analysis. There are five possible α values. The first three are, $\alpha = 0$, α_{opt} and $\alpha = 1$. But due to the quadratic nature of both parts of the EDP expression, it is possible to find a local minimum in each of them. As was shown above, these can occur in α_{left} and α_{right}. However, these minima are only relevant if they lie within the appropriate ranges $0 < \alpha_{left} < \frac{S_C}{S_T}$ and $\frac{S_C}{S_T} < \alpha_{right} < 1$. To find the optimum workload share, the energy efficiency is evaluated at the relevant points, and the best is chosen. Again, if the optimal α is not 0 or 1, it means that it is advisable to use co-execution.

3   Methodology

To validate the above models, a set of experiments has been carried out on two different machines. The first machine used for experimentation is composed of two 2.0 GHz Intel Xeon E5-2620 CPUs with six cores each and a Kepler GPU. Thanks to the QPI connection the CPUs are treated as a single device. Therefore, throughout the remainder of this document, any reference to the CPU of this system includes both processors. The GPU is a NVIDIA K20m with 13 stream multiprocessors, 2496 cores. The experiments for this system have been performed with the maximum and minimum frequencies supported by the GPU: 324 and 758 MHz. Henceforth referenced as *Kepler 324* and *Kepler 758*. Increasing the frequency naturally escalates the power consumption and reduces the execution times, all having an impact in the energy efficiency of the system. At the lowest frequency, the computing speed of GPU is comparable to that of the CPU, thus making the system less heterogeneous.

The second system includes one 3.60 GHz Intel i3-4160 CPU with two cores and a NVIDIA GTX950 with 6 Stream Multiprocessors and 768 cores. Any reference to this system will be labeled as *GTX950*.

The experiments have been carried out with a static algorithm. This means that the work assigned to each device is determined at the beginning of the execution, allowing full control of how the workload is assigned to each device. Six benchmarks have been used, four of which are part of the AMD APP SDK [1] (MatMul, NBody, Binomial, Mandelbrot) and two are in-house developments. One performs a bidimensional Taylor approximation for a set of points and the other calculates the Gaussian blur of an image. Each application has been run using a problem size big enough to justify its distribution among the available devices. For MatMul 12800 by 12800 matrices were used. For NBody 51200 elements were considered for simulation. Binomial uses 20480000 options. Mandelbrot generates a 20480 by 20480 pixel image. Taylor calculates the approximation for a mesh of 1000 by 1000 points. Finally, Gaussian performs the blur on a 8000 by 8000 pixel image using an 81 by 81 pixel filter.

The performance has been measured as the time required to complete the kernel execution, including data distribution, kernel launch overhead and result collection. From these times the values for the computational speeds S_C and S_G were calculated. Additionally, the consumed energy must be measured. A measurement application, named *Sauna* was developed to, periodically monitor the different compute devices and gather their power consumption [13]. This takes advantage of the *Running Average Power Limit (RAPL)* registers [14] in Intel CPUS and the *NVIDIA Management Library (NVML)* [11] for the GPUs. The sampling rate used for the measurements was 33 Hz. To obtain the energy efficiency of the system, the time and energy measurements must be multiplied, giving the EDP [4].

4   Experimental Evaluation

This section presents the results of the experiments performed to validate the models proposed in Sect. 2. Due to the similar behaviour of MatMul and Gaussian to that of NBody and Binomial, only the results of the latter are presented. The four applications executed on the three systems lead to twelve different scenarios. Table 1 shows the parameters of the models, extracted from test executions, where the performance is shown normalised to S_C. Figures 2, 3 and 4 all have a similar structure, they show the execution time, consumed energy and EDP of the different benchmarks and the three systems: Kepler 324, Kepler 758 and GTX950. Note that this last system is referred to the right axis. The horizontal axis sweeps α from 0, where all the work is done by the GPU, through 1, where only the CPU is used.

Regarding execution time, the first observation that can be made is that all benchmarks present a minimum time value that depends on the ratio of the computing speeds of the devices (See Fig. 2). The exact values of α where the execution time is minimum are listed in Table 1, together with the measured optimal α. It is noteworhty that the model accurately predicts the results. The small discrepancies between the model and experiments are due to the interval with which α was swept.

In the case of the GTX950, with Taylor and Mandelbrot, a larger error is observed. The explanation is a combination of two factors. For these benchmarks, the device speed ratio $\frac{S_G}{S_C}$ is less than 1, meaning that the CPU is more productive than the GPU. On the other hand, when the GPU concludes its workload, it rises an interrupt that the CPU must handle immediately. And taking into account that this machine has only two cores, one of them will be devoted entirely to attending the GPU interruption. The observed error is then explained because the CPU suffers an overhead that was not included in the model. This lowers the effective speed of the CPU and the observed value of α_{opt}, as the GPU has more time to do extra work. This has been experimentally confirmed, running the benchmarks in one core, leaving the other free to attend the GPU.

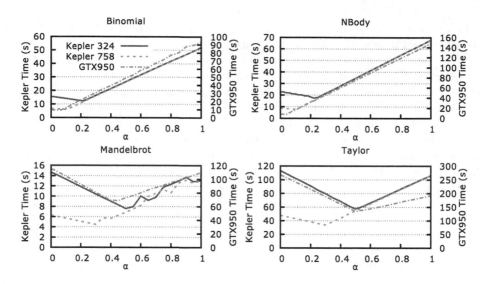

Fig. 2. Execution time for each benchmark and system.

Table 1. Model parameters, theoretical and experimental α values

Machine	Benchmark	$\frac{S_G}{S_C}$	P_C^S	P_G^S	P_C^D	P_G^D	α_{opt}	Exp. α_{opt}	Rel. Error
Kepler 324	Binomial	3.3559	50	16.5	70	27.5	0.23	0.22	4.5%
	Nbody	3.1370	50	16.5	50	27.5	0.24	0.22	9%
	Mandelbrot	0.8916	50	16.5	70	44	0.53	0.50	6%
	Taylor	0.9375	50	16.5	50	29.5	0.52	0.50	4%
Kepler 758	Binomial	7.9220	50	48	70	98.5	0.11	0.10	10%
	Nbody	7.9012	50	48	50	105.5	0.11	0.10	10%
	Mandelbrot	2.0711	50	48	70	115	0.33	0.30	10%
	Taylor	2.2083	50	48	50	103.5	0.31	0.30	3.3%
GTX950	Binomial	9.7893	41	12.5	18	54	0.09	0.06	50%
	Nbody	17.7458	33	12	9	76	0.05	0.04	25%
	Mandelbrot	0.9730	40	10	7	48	0.51	0.45	13%
	Taylor	0.7175	32	12	10.55	46	0.58	0.50	16%

Regarding the energy, the model gives three possibilities for the optimum α depending on whether the device speed ratio $\frac{S_G}{S_C}$ falls within a particular range or not (Expression 6). Figure 3 shows examples of the three behaviours and confirm the predictions of the model.

With Binomial and NBody, the minimum energy is consumed with $\alpha = 0$. This is because the speed ratio falls on the left side of the range, and consequently both segments in the energy graph have positive slope. In practical terms this means that although from a pure performance point of view the CPU contributes, from an energy perspective using it becomes wasteful. On the Mandelbrot and

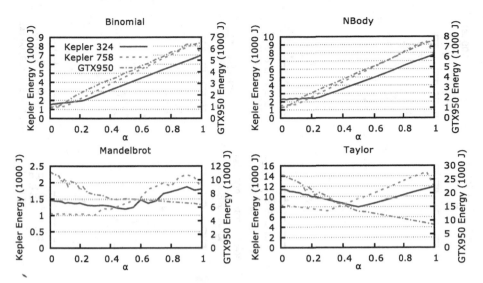

Fig. 3. Total energy consumption for each benchmark and system.

Table 2. Theoretical and experimental α_{opt} for energy-efficiency

Machine	α_{opt}	Binomial	Nbody	Mandelbrot	Taylor
Kepler 324	α_{opt}	0	0.242	0.529	0.516
	Exp. α_{opt}	0	0.22	0.5	0.5
	Rel. Error	0%	10%	5.8%	3.2%
Kepler 758	α_{opt}	0	0	0.326	0.312
	Exp. α_{opt}	0	0	0.3	0.3
	Rel. Error	0%	0%	8.6%	4%
GTX950	α_{opt}	0	0.053	0.507	1
	Exp. α_{opt}	0	0.06	1	1
	Rel. Error	0%	13%	97%	0%

Taylor benchmarks, and both Kepler 324 and Kepler 758, the ratio lies within the range. Meaning that the points of optimum energy consumption and maximum performance coincide in the same α_{opt}. However, on the GTX950, the ratio falls to the right, indicating that both segments will have negative slope and the minimum energy will be found at $\alpha = 1$. That is, the GPU is wasting energy. These results show that co-execution is only worth pursuing in four of the twelve analysed cases, two of them benefit of using the CPU alone, while in the rest using only the GPU is the most advisable solution.

Finally, regarding the energy efficiency of the system, the model presented in Sect. 2 declares five points susceptible of being the optimal workload share. Namely $\alpha = 0$, α_{opt}, $\alpha = 1$, α_{left} and α_{right}. For the tested benchmarks and systems, α_{left} and α_{right} always lie outside their valid ranges, except for α_{left} for

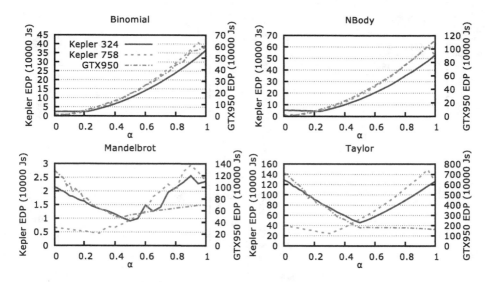

Fig. 4. EDP for each benchmark and system.

Binomial on Kepler 324. Studying these points, it was determined that the minimum EDP would occur at the α values specified in Table 2. This also presents the corresponding experimental α, extracted from the results shown in Fig. 4.

It can be said that the model for energy efficiency always predicted the correct α value that minimises the EDP. A second observation reveals that these points coincide with either the α that maximises performance or the one that minimises energy. However, the model states that this might not always be the case as local minimums could be found. In fact, there are many cases, those with $\alpha = 0$ or $\alpha = 1$ in Table 2, where it is better using only one device to optimise EDP, even when this does not give the optimum performance.

5   Conclusion

This paper analyses the advantages of co-execution and load balancing in heterogeneous systems when considering three different metrics: performance, energy consumption and energy efficiency. Through the proposal of a set of analytical models, it allows determining if co-execution is beneficial in terms of the three metrics. Since co-execution represents a large programming effort, the use of these models allow the programmer to predict if such an approach is worth.

From a performance perspective, the model shows that there is always an advantage in co-execution. It also predicts the gain of this solution. In practical terms, if the gain is very small it might not be noticeable due to diverse overheads in the load balancing algorithm. On contrast, when considering energy consumption or efficiency, the model clearly shows that there are cases in which it is not advisable to use co-execution. Through experimental evaluation, the paper shows that the models accurately predict the observed results. The proposed models consider an ideal load balancing algorithm, this means that provided that the used algorithm is good enough, the predictions of the models will be met, regardless of it being static or dynamic.

In the future, it is intended to extend the models to systems with more than two devices, and consider irregular applications. Also, the experimentation will be extended to cover other kinds of accelerator devices.

Acknowledgments. This work has been supported by the University of Cantabria (CVE-2014-18166), the Spanish Science and Technology Commission (TIN2016-76635-C2-2-R), the European Research Council (G.A. No 321253) and the European HiPEAC Network of Excellence. The Mont-Blanc project has received funding from the European Unions Horizon 2020 research and innovation programme under grant agreement No 671697.

References

1. AMD Accelerated Parallel Processing (APP) Software Development Kit (SDK) V3. http://developer.amd.com/tools-and-sdks/opencl-zone/amd-accelerated-parallel-processing-app-sdk/. Accessed November 2016
2. Binotto, A., Pereira, C., Fellner, D.: Towards dynamic reconfigurable load-balancing for hybrid desktop platforms. In: Proceedings of IPDPS, pp. 1 4. IEEE Computer Society, April 2010
3. Boyer, M., Skadron, K., Che, S., Jayasena, N.: Load balancing in a changing world: dealing with heterogeneity and performance variability. In: Proceedings of the ACM International Conference on Computing Frontiers, pp. 21:1–21:10 (2013)
4. Castillo, E., Camarero, C., Borrego, A., Bosque, J.L.: Financial applications on multi-CPU and multi-GPU architectures. J. Supercomput. **71**(2), 729–739 (2015)
5. Hong, S., Kim, H.: An integrated GPU power and performance model. SIGARCH Comput. Archit. News **38**(3), 280–289 (2010)
6. Kaleem, R., Barik, R., Shpeisman, T., Lewis, B.T., Hu, C., Pingali, K.: Adaptive heterogeneous scheduling for integrated GPUs. In: Proceedings of PACT. ACM (2014)
7. de la Lama, C.S., Toharia, P., Bosque, J.L., Robles, O.D.: Static multi-device load balancing for OpenCL. In: Proceedings of ISPA, pp. 675–682. IEEE Computer Society (2012)
8. Lee, J., Samadi, M., Park, Y., Mahlke, S.: Transparent CPU-GPU collaboration for data-parallel kernels on heterogeneous systems. In: Proceedings of PACT, pp. 245–256. IEEE Press, Piscataway (2013)
9. Ma, K., Li, X., Chen, W., Zhang, C., Wang, X.: GreenGPU: a holistic approach to energy efficiency in GPU-CPU heterogeneous architectures. In: 41st International Conference on Parallel Processing, ICPP (2012)
10. Mittal, S., Vetter, J.S.: A survey of methods for analyzing and improving GPU energy efficiency. ACM Comput. Surv. **47**(2), 19:1–19:23 (2014)
11. NVIDIA: NVIDIA Management Library (NVML). https://developer.nvidia.com/nvidia-management-library-nvml. Accessed April 2016
12. Pérez, B., Bosque, J.L., Beivide, R.: Simplifying programming and load balancing of data parallel applications on heterogeneous systems. In: Proceedings of the 9th Workshop on General Purpose Processing using GPU, pp. 42–51 (2016)

13. Pérez, B., Stafford, E., Bosque, J.L., Beivide, R.: Energy efficiency of load balancing for data-parallel applications in heterogeneous systems. J. Supercomput. **73**(1), 330–342 (2017)
14. Rotem, E., Naveh, A., Rajwan, D., Ananthakrishnan, A., Weissmann, E.: Power management architecture of the 2nd generation Intel Core microarchitecture, formerly codenamed Sandy Bridge. In: IEEE International Symposium on High-Performance Chips (2011)
15. Wang, G., Ren, X.: Power-efficient work distribution method for CPU-GPU heterogeneous system. In: International Symposium on Parallel and Distributed Processing with Applications, pp. 122–129, September 2010
16. Zhang, F., Zhai, J., He, B., Zhang, S., Chen, W.: Understanding co-running behaviors on integrated CPU/GPU architectures. IEEE Trans. Parallel Distrib. Syst. **28**(3), 905–918 (2017)

Author Index

Printed in the United States
By Bookmasters